UNDERSTANDING ABNORMAL CHILD PSYCHOLOGY

UNDERSTANDING ABNORMAL CHILD PSYCHOLOGY

VICKY PHARES, PH.D.
University of South Florida

JOHN WILEY & SONS, INC.

Acquisitions Editor   *Timothy Vertovec*
Marketing Manager   *Kevin Molloy*
Senior Production Editor   *Valerie A. Vargas*
Senior Designer   *Harry Nolan*
Cover Image   *Mike Regnier/The Image Bank/Getty Images*
Photo Editor   *Sara Wight*
Photo Researcher   *Teri Stratford*

This book was set in *Times Roman* by *Argosy* and printed and bound by *R. R. Donnelley–Willard*.
This cover was printed by *Phoenix Color.*
The book is printed on acid-free paper.

ISBN: 0-471-38874-2

Printed in the United States of America

10 9 8 7 6 5 4 3 2 1

To Nikki and Kelly—
For showing me the perfect outcome of childhood
And to Carson—
For showing me the perfect beginning

CONTENTS

OTHER PROBLEMS

APPLYING WHAT YOU'VE LEARNED

PREFACE

If you are reading this book, you probably have at least some interest in children. You may have grown up with the idea of seeking a career in which you can help children because they are the future of humanity. You may have already found ways to learn from and about children throughout your educational and personal life.

Well, okay, maybe you are just trying to fulfill a requirement and the class for which this book is assigned happens to meet at a time convenient to your schedule. Maybe you have no interest in children because you find them to be loud and obnoxious. Maybe you cannot stand to sit near a crying infant on an airplane. Maybe you think that children, especially infants, should be banned from public places.

In either case—this book is for you. In *Understanding Abnormal Child Psychology*, you will learn about both normative and abnormal development throughout children's lives. If you already love children, this book should provide you with a glimpse into what makes them tick and how their behavior can give us clues about their individual functioning. After reading this book, you may grow to love children even more. If you are not that fond of children at this point, my hope is that this book will help you learn to appreciate them for who they are. Instead of groaning the next time you hear a child screaming in the video store, pay attention to what happens when the child screams and how the parents or caretakers handle the child's request. Does the eight-year-old get to rent the violent and sexually explicit video that he or she wants, or does the parent set limits and give the child more appropriate choices? Although no book can make everyone love children, I am hopeful that this book will give everyone a greater appreciation of them.

As you read each chapter, you will notice that there are certain themes that run throughout this book.

Developmental psychopathology. The first concept that you will learn about in Chapter 1 is developmental psychopathology. I will not spoil the surprise and define the concept for you here, but suffice it to say that this book is not just about listing disorders that children and adolescents experience. Rather, this book will help you see that children's and adolescents' behaviors are on a continuum from very adaptive to very maladaptive, with only the latter being conceptualized as pathological. A cornerstone in the philosophy of this book is the importance of knowing the range of normal behavior before trying to identify and treat abnormal behavior. One way of understanding children's and adolescents' behavior that helps take the focus away from labeling children with a specific disorder is to understand that many factors relate to the development of troubled behavior in children. Specifically, factors that put children at greater risk for problems (e.g., physical abuse, sexual abuse, interparental conflict, poverty) and factors that protect children from the development of problems (e.g., secure attachment to a stable primary caretaker, family strength and support, role models outside of the family) will be discussed in individual chapters as well as throughout the discussion of specific disorders. After reading this book, you should feel that you have some knowledge of specific disorders as well as of the factors that are related consistently to the development and prevention of these problems.

Strengths and healthy outcomes. Inherent in the developmental psychopathology perspective is a focus on strengths and adaptive functioning in children's and adolescents' behavior rather than a sole focus on children's deficits and problems. Problematic behavior is discussed with an eye toward how it might have served an adaptive function at some time. In addition, since focusing on a child's strengths is a cornerstone of working to decrease problematic behavior through therapy, strengths and healthy outcomes are discussed in relation to effective therapies that help children and families. Prevention of emotional/behavioral problems is also a goal in creating psychologically healthy children. For this reason, preventive efforts are highlighted throughout the book.

Making abnormal child psychology come to life. You can read all of the research that you want, but until you meet a child with problems or at least read a story about a child with problems, you might not be able to understand the magnitude of these problems. For this reason, case studies and stories about children, adolescents, and families will be presented throughout the book in order to make the scholarly literature more real. In addition, readings and films will be suggested at the end of each chapter for those who want more firsthand accounts of abnormal child psychology. Reading an in-depth memoir by someone who was touched by abnormal child psychology is an excellent way to gain a better understanding of the personal side of these issues. Finally, there are numerous opportunities for you to become involved with child and adolescent cases actively by creating treatment plans, considering therapeutic options, imagining progress in therapy, and learning how to document treatment effectiveness. To understand abnormal child psychology, you need to know not only the professional research literature but also the personal side of the field. Hopefully, this book will provide a good balance between the two.

Diversity, inclusion, and understanding. A critique of early work in psychology and education was its focus on middle- and upper-class Caucasian boys and men. The scholarly field has changed greatly since those early days, with greater awareness of the differences and commonalities across diverse groups. Throughout this book, special attention will be given to issues of race/ethnicity, gender, family constellation, religious orientation, primary language, socioeconomic status, and physical differences. In addition, there are highlighted sections that help you to see the commonalities and differences of abnormal child behavior within a cross-cultural and international context.

Fathers as well as mothers. Nearly every book I have seen on abnormal child psychology, abnormal psychology, developmental psychology, and even introductory psychology has all but ignored the father–child relationship as it relates to children's and men's well-being. Although this book continues to explore the knowledge base regarding mothers and their children, it also emphasizes fathers and their children. In addition to this focus on fathers, other primary figures within families (i.e., siblings, stepparents, care-taking grandparents, foster parents) will be discussed in relation to abnormal child psychology as well as healthy outcomes of children.

Abnormal child psychology in everyday life. As should be evident from the examples provided at the beginning of this preface (e.g., the screaming child in the video store, the unhappy baby on the airplane), child behavior is everywhere. Even if you do not have children in your life right now, you are bound to run into them eventually. From Bart Simpson to the latest installment of the Harry Potter series, popular culture is filled with examples of child behavior. This book will illustrate how understanding abnormal child behavior can help you understand events that are specific to your life, as well as specific to the local, national, and international communities. When you read the newspaper and see stories of child abuse or of children and teenagers hurting themselves and others, you probably wonder why such horrific things happen. This book will try to help you understand events that occur in your everyday life and in everyday society. Although I cannot promise an answer to why such troubling events occur, I will attempt to explain the factors that are related to disturbing events that affect children and adolescents in society today.

Settings that relate to abnormal child psychology. Not only is child behavior everywhere you look in your life and in popular culture, but it is also evident in a number of settings where you might want to work eventually (e.g., schools, medical hospitals, mental health facilities, day care facilities). This book will cover abnormal child psychology within the fields of psychology, education, social work, and psychiatry. Given that children are influenced by so many environments, and in turn have an influence on so many environments, this book will provide a full overview of the many areas in which abnormal child psychology is evident. For example, children and adolescents spend a great deal of their time in school. Not only are schools a setting for education, but they are also a setting for socialization, for developing friendships, and for modeling others' behavior (both good and bad).

Thus, the school environment will be mentioned throughout this book in order to understand one of the locations where children might develop maladaptive behavior and one of the locations where children might be treated for abnormal behavior.

How to make a difference. One chapter relatively unique to this book is the final one, on how to help children and families who experience problems. In many universities, students might find it hard to access information about career paths that are open to them. The last chapter of this book focuses on the many ways that nonprofessionals and professionals can make a difference in children's lives. Whether you plan a career in the helping field or not, this chapter should illustrate the diverse ways in which children and families can be helped.

As you may have gathered from this overview, this book is intended as a textbook that will be used in departments of psychology, education, and social work. Its presumed audience is advanced undergraduate students (i.e., juniors and seniors), as well as beginning graduate students who are just starting to learn about abnormal child behavior.

I am hopeful that both the scholarly and personal side of abnormal child psychology will intrigue you throughout this book. As for myself, I have been intrigued with children for as long as I can remember. In fact, I first began volunteering at an inpatient mental health facility when I was in high school. Throughout my undergraduate and graduate training, I remained intrigued with children and adolescents in all of their complexities. As a professor and licensed psychologist, I remain intrigued with what we can learn from youth and what we can teach them in return. I hope that you enjoy the sometimes painful, sometimes uplifting adventure of learning about abnormal child psychology.

Vicky Phares

ACKNOWLEDGMENTS

I began the acknowledgments section of my dissertation by stating that I would keep it short and sweet (kind of like some children I know). I'll try to follow the same sentiments here.

To begin with, Karyn Drews and Tim Vertovec at John Wiley and Sons, Inc., have been instrumental in getting this book published. The reviewers for the project have been exceedingly helpful at various stages of this project. They include Catherine L. Bagwell, University of Richmond; Myra Beth Bundy, Eastern Kentucky University; Mari L. Clements, Pennsylvania State University; David Crystal, Georgetown University; Deidre Beebe Fitzgerald, Eastern Connecticut State University; Laura Freberg, California Polytechnic State University; Gerald P. Koocher, Harvard Medical School; Kristin Lindahl, University of Miami; C. H. Madsen, Jr., Florida State University; Erin McClure, Emory University; Jill Norvilitis, Buffalo State College; Nina Parker-Cohen, University of Utah; and Charles Schaefer, Fairleigh Dickinson University.

There are too many people to thank in my own professional realm, but suffice it to say that I've learned from some of the best. My graduate students have also taught me a lot, especially about having fun and getting work done (usually in that order). There are also too many people to thank in the personal realm, where there, too, I've learned from some of the best. I continue to appreciate my friends from graduate school and from my academic jobs who have allowed a seamless integration of work and fun. My nonwork friends, and especially my women's group, have taught me about life beyond work.

There are also too many people in my family to thank, but here again, they are the best. On both sides of the aisle, the Phares/Brandt families and the Owen families have made me appreciate family ties more each day.

Of special note are the people who suffered the most while I was working on this textbook. My ever-tolerant husband, Chuck, is supportive beyond belief. Ironically, both of us had deadlines for big writing projects at the same time (he with musical notes and me with words), so neither of us really noticed that the other was completely bonkers for a while. Further thanks go to Nikki and Kelly, who also lost out during this writing project. Admittedly, they mainly lost out on computer time to instant message their friends, but I appreciate their tolerance nonetheless. It is my sincere hope that Carson didn't lose out on anything due to this textbook. If writing is only done when the baby is sleeping, then the baby doesn't miss out on anything—right? Anyway, Carson, people tell me that I began this textbook before you existed. But frankly, I don't recall a time when you didn't exist. Amazing, simply amazing.

CHAPTER 1

CONCEPTUALIZATIONS OF NORMALITY AND ABNORMALITY IN CHILDREN AND ADOLESCENTS

CHAPTER SUMMARY

When they said "sit down," I stood up. Ooh . . . growin' up.
—Bruce Springsteen "Growin' Up" (1973)

NORMALITY AND ABNORMALITY IN CHILDREN AND ADOLESCENTS

Let's put your life on fast-forward for a moment. Imagine that you are a well-established clinical psychologist working in a community mental health center. You get a call from a father who is extremely upset about his daughter's behavior. The father states that his daughter recently began seeing things that no one else can see and she talks to the visions that she sees. In addition, the daughter

seems to think that she has special powers, such as the ability to read her puppy's mind. The father goes further to state that he's very worried about her behavior and he thinks she needs therapy or medication.

Once you have listened to this father's concerns, what is the first question you would ask him? Before reading further, you may want to take a minute to jot down the questions you think are necessary to help this father.

Lots of questions might come to mind. Has the daughter had any recent traumas in her life, such as her parents' divorce, the death of a loved one, or some type of abuse? Is there a history of schizophrenia or other psychotic disorders in the family? What type of attention does the girl receive from her parents and teachers, both when she is not seeing things and when she reports that she sees things? What type of friends does she have, if any? Does the family hold any religious beliefs that include seeing visions? What type of television shows and movies has the girl been allowed to watch? A few business-minded students might even want to ask first about whether or not the family has insurance that covers assessment and therapy services.

All of these questions are good ones, and you probably thought of other good questions yourself, but the one question that is screaming out to be asked is: How old is the girl? Read the first paragraph again with a $2\frac{1}{2}$-year-old in mind and then read it once more with a 17-year-old in mind. Obviously, the behaviors reported by the father deserve a lot more concern if the daughter is a teenager rather than a toddler. In fact, many of the behaviors are considered developmentally appropriate for a young child (e.g., having imaginary playmates, feeling special powers). In contrast, these same behaviors in an adolescent might be related to serious problems, such as schizophrenia or use of hallucinogenic substances. The main point is that we need to know a child's age and developmental level in order to understand her or his behavior. Behavior that is developmentally appropriate in one age group may be inappropriate and maladaptive in another.

This is where I get to say: Welcome to the study of developmental psychopathology. The term **developmental psychopathology** is the combination of two important areas of study: The word *developmental* relates to the course and causes of changes (i.e., developmental) over a person's life span, and the word *psychopathology* refers to patterns of behaviors, cognitions, and emotions that are abnormal, disruptive, or distressing either to the person or others around the person. Thus, developmental psychopathology is a developmental approach to the study of psychopathology "to help us understand troublesome behavior in light of the developmental tasks and processes that characterize human growth" (Achenbach, 1982, p. 9). Developmental psychopathology takes into consideration maturational and developmental processes when conceptualizing abnormal behavior (Kazdin, 1989; Luthar, Burack, Cicchetti, & Weisz, 1997). In other words, we need to know what is normal for girls and boys in a given age range before we can define what is abnormal. This concept applies to people of all ages, but it is especially relevant for children and adolescents. Think of the changes and growth that occur in the first 12 months of life, and then consider the changes that the average person goes through during the 12 months from the age of 22 to 23. Many 22-year-olds grow and change a lot in those 12 months, but the amount of developmental changes and challenges in the younger years are more immense than the changes at any other time of life.

Developmental psychopathology is concerned with children from diverse ages and backgrounds.

Also central to the study of developmental psychopathology is the understanding of risk and protective factors. **Risk factors** are characteristics, events, or processes that put the individual at risk for the development of psychological problems. Thus, risk factors increase the likelihood that a problem may occur in the future. Risk factors can be centered in the individual (e.g., difficult child temperament); in the family (e.g., parental psychopathology, interparental conflict, large number of siblings); or in the school and community (e.g., overcrowded schools, poverty, violence; Dierker, Merikangas, & Szatmari, 1999; Luthar et al., 1997;

Werner & Smith, 2001). The study of risk factors leads naturally to the question of protective factors. **Protective factors** are characteristics, events, or processes that seem to protect an individual from the development of psychological problems even when that individual faces adverse circumstances (Luthar, Cicchetti, & Becker, 2000). Thus, protective factors serve to decrease the likelihood that a problem will occur in the future. Like risk factors, protective factors can be centered in the individual (e.g., at least average intelligence, good coping skills); in the family (e.g., warm and supportive parents, stable role models); or in the school and community (e.g., competent and caring

Case Study: Al, The Boy with the Unique Behaviors

Al was the first-born child of parents who would remain married throughout his childhood. He had a younger sister who was two and a half years his junior. From all accounts, Al's parents got along well together and were caring parents. In general, Al was well behaved, but there were a number of odd behaviors that were noted during his early years. For example, when Al was a little over two years old, his maternal grandmother, who referred to him as "dear" and "good," also mentioned that he had "droll ideas," which were apparently communicated in a non-verbal fashion. Al's parents consulted a doctor because Al was still not talking by the age of three. Once when Al was ill in bed at the age of four or five, his father gave him a magnetic compass to play with. Al became obsessed with the compass and discussed it as though it had changed his life. There were other, similar obsessions later in his childhood. For example, at the age of 12, Al became obsessed with a book on Euclidean geometry and referred to it as "the holy geometry booklet." Al had a number of other peculiar behaviors. He was a loner and did not play games with other children. Instead, he would spend hour upon hour building houses of cards that sometimes reached 14 stories high. In older childhood, Al admitted that he had the "peculiarity" of repeating his own words softly. In addition, he often refused to eat certain foods, such as pork.

Al's schooling also showed signs of trouble. Although he did quite well, he seemed to hate school (especially the rote instruction). His preference was to study what interested him, such as mathematics and physics, rather than what the teachers wanted him to study. Al acknowledged that he had a poor memory for words and that he had trouble concentrating on subjects that did not interest him. One teacher pointedly told him, "You will never amount to anything." In seventh grade, this teacher asked Al to transfer to another school because of his attitude toward school and the teachers. When Al was 15, his family moved to another country but left Al behind to complete his schooling. He was so miserable and lonely that he dropped out of school and joined his family. In the new country, he did not enroll in school.

Given what you know about this case and the ages at which the behaviors occurred, what types of diagnoses might come to

mind? You might want to pursue an assessment of one of the pervasive developmental disorders, given the delayed speech, the difficulty in social connections, and the perseveration (i.e., repeated focus) on specific objects and activities. This perseveration on specific objects and activities, along with the obsessive nature of Al's interests, might lead you to assess for obsessive-compulsive disorder. You might also want to consider a learning disorder, given Al's difficulty with certain subjects in school and his failure to remain in school during his adolescence.

Although all of these behaviors might be indicators of a clinical disorder, you might be interested to know that Al (better known as Albert Einstein) went on to change the world with the theory of relativity and other advances in physics and the sciences. If you re-read those symptoms and behaviors with the knowledge that they were exhibited by someone who was obviously brilliant and a revolutionary thinker, it might allow you to gain an appreciation that unusual behavior in children is not necessarily a bad thing. Albert Einstein's fascination with the compass and with building houses of cards was probably reflective of a very active and intelligent mind. His refusal to eat pork as a child was related to his strong beliefs in the Jewish faith. His difficulty in school was probably related to his intrinsic interest in certain subjects, which is sometimes difficult for school personnel to handle.

Overall, this case should highlight the importance of not pathologizing unusual behaviors in children. Throughout this book, you will read about cases of children with unusual and unique behaviors. You will learn the diagnostic criteria for clinical disorders, and you will learn about the treatment methods used to decrease or even eliminate these unusual behaviors. But keep in mind that unique and unusual behaviors sometimes signify creativity or even brilliance and thus should not always be viewed as problematic. One of the challenges for any professional working with children is trying to determine which unique behaviors are harmful and which are reflective of the strong diversity that exists in human beings. Hopefully, this book will help you grapple with this issue, which is partially an empirical question and partly a philosophical question.

SOURCE: Hoffmann (1972).

teachers, stable role models outside the family, involvement in prosocial organizations; Luthar et al., 1997; Werner & Smith, 2001). Overall, the concepts of risk and protective factors are central to understanding psychopathology from a developmental perspective. These concepts will be addressed in separate chapters as well as throughout each chapter individually.

One other concept central to developmental psychopathology is the continuity/discontinuity continuum. Specifically, developmental psychopathologists are interested in how behavior stays the same (i.e., continuity) or changes (i.e., discontinuity) over time. It is important to note that the same behaviors may have very different meaning at various ages (Caspi & Moffitt, 1995; Cicchetti, Rogosch, & Toth, 1997; Maughan & Rutter, 1998). A toddler's crying may mean something very different from what a teenager's crying means. Conversely, different behaviors may have the same essential meaning at various points in time. Social isolation might be shown by a 6-year-old who sits alone in the corner of the playground and by a 17-year-old who drives around aimlessly in a car. Overall, researchers interested in developmental psychopathology examine changes and similarities in behavior over the life span.

The field of developmental psychopathology is relatively new. Approximately 50 years ago, theorists such as Piaget, Vygotsky, and Werner used developmental theories to understand intellectual and emotional disabilities in children (Hodapp, 1997). In the 1960s, Zigler applied developmental theories to the understanding of intellectual limitations (Hodapp, 1997; Hodapp & Zigler, 1995; Zigler & Phillips, 1961). In 1974, Dr. Tom Achenbach began the first edition of his book *Developmental Psychopathology* by noting, "This is a book about a field that hardly exists yet." Since that time, there has been a wealth of information on developmental psychopathology. Notably, a professional journal entitled *Development and Psychopathology* was first published in 1989, with Dr. Dante Cicchetti as the first editor. These facts are not meant to suggest, however, that children's abnormal behavior was investigated from a developmental perspective beginning only in 1974. Although the study of children's behavior has lagged behind the study of abnormal behavior in adults, there is a long history of trying to understand children's and adolescents' abnormal behavior.

One of the most obvious facts about grown-ups, to a child, is that they have forgotten what it is like to be a child.

—Randall Jarrell

HOW ABNORMAL CHILD BEHAVIOR WAS UNDERSTOOD IN THE PAST

Unfortunately, the history of dealing with troubled children is riddled with stories of painful and sometimes abhorrent treatment. The account given here focuses on Western cultures, since these are the ones in which most of the history has been documented (Reagan, 2000). Troubled children in all cultures have been dealt with in ways influenced by the prevailing **Zeitgeist** (the spirit or outlook characteristic of a period of time). In ancient Greece, boys and girls with either mental or physical disabilities were often scorned in public or abandoned by their families (Donohue, Hersen, & Ammerman, 2000). The Greeks also practiced **infanticide**, the intentional murder of an infant or child. Public scorn, abandonment, and infanticide were also thought to have occurred in the Roman Empire (Donohue et al., 2000).

In Europe during the Middle Ages (500–1300), children were often neglected and treated as laborers and slaves regardless of whether or not they were well-functioning (Donohue, Hersen, & Ammerman, 1995). Severe beatings of children were not uncommon, and child mortality rates were high. Mental differences and "insanity" in children and adults were thought to be the work of the devil or other evil spirits (Achenbach, 1982). These beliefs were largely espoused by the Catholic Church and by Calvin and Luther (Donohue et al., 1995). Attempts to rid disturbed children of evil spirits included imprisonment, public humiliation, and sometimes torture or burning at the stake. Although there is some evidence of humane and compassionate treatment of troubled children during this time in history (Neugebauer, 1979), it is clear that many suffered greatly.

The European belief in demonic possession continued into the Renaissance (1300–1600). Punishment for what we now consider to be psychological symptoms was routine for children in both wealthy and poor families (Donohue et al., 1995). Yet over the course of the Renaissance, infanticide was eventually stopped and troubled children were often placed in orphanages rather than being put to death. Unfortunately, mortality rates in European orphanages were high; most children in such institutions did not survive into adolescence (Rie, 1971).

The same harsh circumstances existed for children in colonial America in the 1600s (Donohue et al., 1995). Children were often thought of as cheap labor, and many were abused, regardless of their level of mental health. In fact, the Stubborn Child Law of 1654 allowed parents in American colonies to put "stubborn" children to death if the children were not following orders or were not otherwise compliant with adults.

Children in Europe and colonial America, and especially children in wealthy families, began to receive better treatment toward the end of the 1600s and into the 1700s (Rie, 1971). Mental health problems came to be thought of as an organic disease, so there was a focus on treatment rather than punishment. Benjamin Rush (1745–1813), the first psychiatrist in the United States, began to study mental problems in children around this time. There was also an increased interest in the study of children in general.

In the late 1700s and early 1800s, a well-publicized case caught the attention of many individuals who were interested in the psychological and intellectual functioning of children. A young boy, later named Victor but most commonly known as the Wild Boy of Aveyron, was found in a forest near Aveyron, France, in 1798. Victor had apparently grown up in the forest without any caretaking by humans. His verbal ability consisted of only limited guttural sounds, and he did not behave in a civilized manner. French physician Jean Itard tried to train Victor with a technique known as sensory-motor instruction, which he had used successfully with deaf children (Achenbach, 1982). Although Victor made some progress, Itard eventually concluded that Victor was retarded and would not develop adequate behavior. The publicity surrounding Victor's treatment highlighted the need for humane treatment of troubled children.

In the mid-1800s, a former schoolteacher, Dorothea Dix (1802–1887), observed that many troubled children in the United States were put in cages and in cellars with deplorable living conditions. She advocated for more humane treatment of troubled children and was instrumental in developing federal funding for treatment centers. Her tireless efforts led to the development of 30 new mental hospitals that offered humane and ethical treatment of troubled children (Achenbach, 1982).

In 1874, the American Society for the Prevention of Cruelty to Animals brought attention to a case of child abuse, with the suggestion that human children should have the same rights and protections as animals (see "The Case of Mary Ellen"). The following years, the New York Society for the Prevention of Cruelty to Children was founded to try to prevent child abuse. Even with all of these movements, however, there were still limits to the humane treatment of children. For example, the mental health hospitals that Dorothea Dix helped to develop often became overcrowded and underfunded. Thus, even when humane treatment was begun, it was not always continued (Donohue et al., 1995).

During the late 1800s, there continued to be an interest in studying children to understand the factors that might lead to problems. In fact, the field of experimental psychology was in the process of being developed. In Leipzig, Germany, in 1879, Wilhelm Wundt (1832–1920) founded the first psychological laboratory. Attention was

---

Case Study: Mary Ellen, The Tragic Case That Started a Movement

"My mother and father are both dead. I don't know how old I am. I have no recollection of a time when I did not live with the Connollys. I call Mrs. Connolly mamma . . . I have had no shoes or stockings on this Winter. I have never been allowed to go out of the room where the Connollys were, except in the night time, and then only in the yard . . . My bed at night has been only a piece of carpet stretched on the floor underneath a window, and I sleep in my little undergarments, with a quilt over me. I am never allowed to play with any children, or to have any company whatever. Mamma (Mrs. Connolly) has been in the habit of whipping and beating me almost every day. She used to whip me with a twisted whip—a raw-hide. The whip always left a black and blue mark on my body. I have now the black and blue marks on my head which were made by mamma and also a cut on the left side of my forehead which was made by a pair of scissors. She struck me with the scissors and cut me. I have no recollection of ever having been kissed by any one . . . Whenever mamma went out I was locked up in the bedroom. I do not know for what I was whipped—mamma never said anything to me when she whipped me. I do not want to go back to live with mamma, because she beats me so . . ." (*New York Times,* April 10, 1874).

This heart-wrenching account was given by a 10-year-old child named Mary Ellen McCormack in a statement to the court that was investigating this case of abuse. At the time, there were, ironically, statutes intended to prevent of cruelty to animals, but none that dealt with cruelty to children. This case served as a catalyst to begin the New York Society for the Prevention of Cruelty to Children. The account of how Mary Ellen was identified clearly shows that many of the Connolly's neighbors knew about the abuse but did nothing to report it. Many people still felt that the treatment of children by parents (or, as in this case, foster parents) was a family matter and not an issue in which neighbors should get involved. Unfortunately, it took another hundred years for the U.S. legal system to require that abuse be reported by teachers, psychologists, physicians, and other professionals.

also given to children's functioning specifically. Toward the end of the 1800s, G. Stanley Hall (1844–1924), who had studied with Wundt and founded the first psychology laboratory in the United States (in 1887) and who was the first president of the American Psychological Association (in 1892), began to systematically study children's development (Achenbach, 1982). In what was referred to as a "baby biography," Hall sent out questionnaires to parents, teachers, mental health professionals, and children themselves in order to document normative developmental changes in children and adolescents. In 1904, he published a two-volume book that summarized these data and helped identify adolescence as a period of development distinctly different from earlier childhood.

Meanwhile, there was also an attempt to categorize disturbing behavior in adults as well as in children. In 1883, German psychiatrist Emil Kraepelin (1856–1926) published his first edition of a taxonomy of mental disorders. Kraepelin, who focused on adult disorders, assumed that mental disorders were evidence of brain pathology. His books set the stage for the development of taxonomies of childhood disorders. By the end of the 1800s, some attempts had been made to codify abnormal behavior in children. There was a great deal of attention to the classification of different levels of mental retardation in children, but there were also efforts to define and categorize problems such as hyperactivity, psychosis, aggression, and "masturbatory insanity" (Rie, 1971).

There was increased attention in the late 1800s and early 1900s to helping disturbed children without hospitalizing them. In 1896, American psychologist Lightner Witmer (1867–1956) founded the world's first psychological clinic. Notably, it served as a child guidance clinic, and its first client was a boy who showed both learning and behavior problems. As a professor of psychology at the University of Pennsylvania, Witmer coined the term *clinical psychology* with the idea that psychological knowledge and therapeutic skills would lead to improved lives for both children and adults (Trull & Phares, 2001). Witmer's clinic focused on addressing observable behavior in children, and the emphasis was clearly on rehabilitation rather than punishment of emotional, behavioral, learning, and intellectual problems.

Continuing with this humane modality of helping children, psychiatrist William Healy and psychologist Grace Fernald established the Juvenile Psychopathic Institute in Chicago in 1909 in order to help delinquent children. This clinic was used as a model for the development of many other child guidance clinics (Rie, 1971). In 1917, Healy and his wife, psychologist Augusta Bronner, founded the Judge Baker Guidance Center in Boston. In the early

1920s, psychiatrists began working in the U.S. school system, with the idea that they could help prevent problems related to learning difficulties (Rie, 1971). Also in the early 1920s, the National Committee on Mental Hygiene and the Commonwealth Fund began programs to establish additional child guidance clinics (Rie, 1971). There were 200 child guidance clinics in the United States by 1932 (Donohue et al., 2000).

Before World War II there tended to be a focus on helping children, sometimes even to the detriment of helping adults. However, given the heavy mental health needs of veterans returning from the war, the fields of psychology and psychiatry turned to helping adults, often to the detriment of programs that helped children (Trull & Phares, 2001). This focus on adults, to the exclusion of children and adolescents, was reflected in the early categorizations of mental disorders.

Not until we have fallen do we know how to rearrange our burden.
—Proverb of Africa

MORE RECENT DIAGNOSTIC CLASSIFICATION SYSTEMS

In 1952, the American Psychiatric Association published the first edition of the *Diagnostic and Statistical Manual of Mental Disorders*, known as the *DSM-I*. As the following sections show, the *DSM* series has been and continues to be very influential in the categorization of mental disorders that occur in people of all ages. *DSM-I* referred to disorders as "reactions of the psychobiologic unit" (Achenbach, 1982). This definition implies that psychiatrists considered disorders to be evident when an individual had difficulty adjusting (both physically and mentally) to some type of life situation. In some respects, the *DSM* system is counter to developmental psychopathology because it categorizes behavior into diagnoses rather than exploring behavior on a continuum. As I will discuss later in this chapter and throughout the book, behavior exists on a continuum and can be understood more thoroughly from a dimensional perspective than from a categorical perspective. (These two perspectives are defined later in this chapter.)

DSM-I paid only limited attention to children and adolescents. Possibly because of the postwar focus on adults to the exclusion of children, very few disorders were specified for children and adolescents in that 1952 publication. The limited specifications also could have been due to the fact that children at that time were seen as miniature adults (Achenbach, 1982), a conceptualization known as **adultomorphism**. Because children were thought to fall into the categories that applied to adults, the developers of *DSM-I* saw no need to create specific diagnoses for children.

The few disorders that *DSM-I* identified for children and adolescents were somewhat vague and diffuse (Donohue et al., 2000). For example, the section titled "Transient Situational Personality Disturbance" included the diagnosis of adjustment reactions of infancy, childhood, and adolescence, which was further broken down into habit disturbances (such as thumb sucking, masturbation, tantrums, and enuresis); conduct disturbances (such as stealing, destructiveness, cruelty, truancy, sexual offenses, and use of alcohol); and neurotic traits (such as tics, stammering, overactivity, and somnambulism). Within the psychotic disorders domain, there was a disorder known as "schizophrenic reaction—childhood type," which by current standards would be similar to autistic disorder. There was also a diagnosis known as "chronic brain syndrome associated with birth trauma," which was often diagnosed in infancy and childhood. Although children and adolescents could be diagnosed with disorders listed for adults when appropriate, the majority of children and adolescents received either a diagnosis of adjustment reaction or no diagnosis at all (Achenbach, 1982).

Although the first *DSM* was relatively well received within the United States, in 1965 the World Health Organization published an international diagnostic system that (by the time of its sixth edition) included both medical and mental disorders. Known as the *International Classification of Diseases* (*ICD*), this system is currently in its 10th edition (World Health Organization, 1992). The *ICD-10* is especially helpful for allowing comparable diagnostic processes in cross-cultural and international research.

In 1968, the American Psychiatric Association published the second edition of the *DSM*. Known as *DSM-II*, this revision was more inclusive of disorders related specifically to childhood and adolescence. There was a section entitled "Behavior Disorders of Childhood and Adolescence," with 11 diagnoses specific to childhood: hyperkinetic reaction, withdrawing reaction, overanxious reaction, runaway reaction, undersocialized aggressive reaction, group delinquency reaction, adjustment reactions, learning disturbances, enuresis, feeding disturbances, and other reactions of childhood. The section entitled "Transient Situational Disturbances" remained from the first edition. As in the first edition, *DSM-II* gave few operational definitions for any of these disorders, so the process of diagnosis remained subjective. *DSM-II*

has also been criticized for having a psychodynamic theoretical orientation in the conceptualization of mental disorders. Specifically, the psychodynamic theoretical orientation argues that past events and the underlying meanings of behaviors are more important than observable behavior. Despite the addition of diagnoses relevant to children and adolescents, the majority of youth continued to be diagnosed with adjustment reaction (Achenbach, 1982).

The American Psychiatric Association published the third revision of the *DSM* in 1980. *DSM-III* proved to be a great departure from, and most would say improvement over, *DSM-II*. *DSM-III* provided operational definitions that were observable and behavioral. Thus, the diagnostic categories were thought to be well defined, objective, and well articulated. *DSM-III* was also considered to be **atheoretical** (i.e., without any theoretical orientation). Although some might argue that a psychodynamic orientation was replaced by a behavioral orientation, the behavioral descriptions in *DSM-III* were intended to make the diagnostic criteria more objective but not to imply the etiology, or causation, of disorders. A strength of *DSM-III* was the addition of decision trees to aid with **differential diagnosis** (the attempt to distinguish one disorder from another in an individual client). Clinicians must perform differential diagnosis when a client exhibits symptoms that are common across two or more disorders, or when there is not a clear-cut diagnosis.

In addition to these improvements, *DSM-III* also introduced a method of **multiaxial evaluation**, which means that individuals were rated on multiple axes, or dimensions, of functioning. The rationale behind multiaxial evaluation is that there is more to an individual than his or her clinical problems. Thus, individuals were diagnosed not only on their clinical problem but also on long-standing problems, physical functioning, life stressors, and global functioning.

Another major improvement in *DSM-III* was its categorization of disorders experienced by children and adolescents. It listed nine major categories of disorders related to infants, children, and adolescents. It also contained a section for other conditions that were not considered mental disorders but that were the focus of attention or treatment; the labels for these conditions are known as **V-Codes**. In addition to the disorders listed in the section titled, "Disorders Usually First Evident in Infancy, Childhood, or Adolescence," a number of other disorders—such as major depression, alcohol abuse, and adjustment disorder—listed in other sections of *DSM-III* could be applied to children and adolescents. Overall, *DSM-III* was comparable to the diagnostic system that is

TABLE 1.1   Clinical Disorders in *DSM-IV* That Can Be Diagnosed in Children and Adolescents*

Disorders Usually First Diagnosed in Infancy, Childhood, or Adolescence	Other Clinical Disorders That Can Be Diagnosed in Childhood or Adolescence
Mental Retardation (Coded on Axis II) 5 levels of diagnoses (based on functioning) **Learning Disorders** Reading disorder Mathematics disorder Disorder of written expression **Motor Skills Disorder** Developmental coordination disorder **Communication Disorders** Expressive language disorder Mixed receptive-expressive language disorder Phonological disorder Stuttering **Pervasive Developmental Disorders** Autistic disorder Rett's disorder Childhood disintegrative disorder Asperger's disorder **Attention-Deficit and Disruptive Behavior Disorders** Attention-deficit/hyperactivity disorder (3 types) Conduct disorder (2 types) Oppositional defiant disorder **Feeding and Eating Disorders of Infancy or Early Childhood** Pica Rumination disorder Feeding disorder of infancy or early childhood **Tic Disorders** Tourette's disorder Chronic motor or vocal tic disorder Transient tic disorder (2 types) **Elimination Disorders** Encopresis Enuresis (3 types) **Other Disorders of Infancy, Childhood, or Adolescence** Separation anxiety disorder Selective mutism Reactive attachment disorder of infancy or early childhood (2 types) Stereotypic movement disorder	**Substance-Related Disorders** Alcohol use disorders (2 types) Alcohol-induced disorders (12 types) Specific substance-related disorders (97 types) **Schizophrenia and Other Psychotic Disorders** Schizophrenia (5 types) Schizophreniform disorder Schizoaffective disorder **Mood Disorders** Major depressive disorder (2 types) Dysthymic disorder (2 types) Bipolar I disorder Bipolar II disorder Cyclothymic disorder **Anxiety Disorders** Panic disorder (3 types) Specific phobia Social phobia Obsessive-compulsive disorder Posttraumatic stress disorder Acute stress disorder Generalized anxiety disorder **Somatoform Disorders** Somatization disorder (2 types) Conversion disorder Pain disorder (2 types) Hypochondriasis Body dysmorphic disorder **Eating Disorders** Anorexia nervosa Bulimia nervosa **Impulse-Control Disorders Not Elsewhere Classified** Intermittent explosive disorder Kleptomania Pyromania Pathological gambling Trichotillomania **Adjustment Disorders (6 types)**

*Unless otherwise noted, all disorders are coded on Axis I. This list is not exhaustive. There are other categories of disorders (such as Delirium, Amnestic, and Other Cognitive Disorders; Factitious Disorders; Dissociative Disorders; Sexual and Gender Identity Disorders; Sleep Disorders; and Personality Disorders) that can be diagnosed in children and adolescents, but are quite rare in youngsters. Also note that diagnoses referred to as not otherwise specified (NOS) are not listed in this table.

SOURCE: American Psychiatric Association (2000). Reprinted with permission from the *Diagnostic and Statistical Manual of Mental Disorders, Fourth Edition, Text Revision.* Copyright 2000 American Psychiatric Association.

in current use. The thoroughness of this diagnostic system helped allow an explosion of research into child and adolescent disorders.

Partially in reaction to a large part of this research, *DSM-III-Revised (DSM-III-R)* was published in 1987. Like its predecessor, *DSM-III-R* continued to add specific diagnoses related to child and adolescent disorders: There were 11 major categories of disorders specific to infancy, childhood, and adolescence, and there were a number of other diagnoses that could be used for individuals of any age.

Further research and refining of the diagnostic system led to the publication of *DSM-IV* in 1994. In 2000, the American Psychiatric Association published *DSM-IV-TR (Text Revision)*, with revisions in the written information but no revisions in the majority of diagnostic categories (American Psychiatric Association, 2000). Given that *DSM-IV* is the current diagnostic system used in the United States as well as in many other countries, a thorough description of it is warranted. Table 1.1 lists the 10 major categories of disorders that fall into the section entitled "Disorders Usually First Diagnosed in Infancy, Childhood, and Adolescence." Within these categories, there are a total of 38 specific disorders (not including disorders listed as "not otherwise specified"). In addition, there are over 200 other disorders that can apply to people of all ages. Specifics of many disorders will be covered in later chapters, but the overview of diagnoses in Table 1.1 indicates the range of disorders covered by *DSM-IV*. Interested students should consider reading the *DSM-IV Training Guide for Diagnosis of Childhood Disorders* (Rapoport & Ismond, 1996), which provides a clear and comprehensive overview of the diagnostic process with children and adolescents.

DSM-IV continues *DSM-III*'s use of a multiaxial evaluation system to help professional diagnose and understand children and adolescents (American Psychiatric Association, 2000). Each axis includes information about different domains in a child's or adolescent's life in order to help clinicians plan and evaluate appropriate treatments for the client. The five axes are listed in Table 1.2. The inclusion of all five axes is meant to allow a broad view of the child's or adolescent's overall functioning, rather than simply focusing on the presenting clinical symptoms (American Psychiatric Association, 2000). Because it is important to understand all five axes, I will describe each one separately.

In some respects, Axis I contains what most people think about when they think about a clinical diagnosis. On Axis I, the clinician lists a child's or adolescent's primary clinical disorder or mental disorder, along with any other

TABLE 1.2 Multiaxial Evaluation in *DSM-IV*

Axis I	Clinical Disorders
	Other Conditions That May Be a Focus of Clinical Attention
Axis II	Personality Disorders
	Mental Retardation
Axis III	General Medical Conditions
Axis IV	Psychosocial and Environmental Problems
Axis V	Global Assessment of Functioning

SOURCE: American Psychiatric Association (2000). Reprinted with permission from the *Diagnostic and Statistical Manual of Mental Disorders, Fourth Edition, Text Revision.* Copyright 2000 American Psychiatric Association.

conditions that may be a focus of clinical attention. According to *DSM-IV*, a **mental disorder** "is conceptualized as a clinically significant behavioral or psychological syndrome or pattern that occurs in an individual and that is associated with present distress (e.g., a painful symptom) or disability (i.e., impairment in one or more important areas of functioning) or with a significantly increased risk of suffering death, pain, disability, or an important loss of freedom" (American Psychiatric Association, 2000, p. xxxi). Inherent in this definition is that:

- The behavior is not what is expected for the individual of that age, gender, culture, and background.

- The behavior is either distressing or is related to impairments in daily life.

- The behavior can put the individual at risk for further harm or distress.

The terms *clinical disorder* and *mental disorder* are used interchangeably in *DSM-IV*. In either case, these problems are noted on Axis I.

If a child or adolescent meets criteria for more than one clinical disorder, multiple disorders can be listed on Axis I. If a client does not meet criteria for any clinical disorder or V-Code, a clinician would note that there was no diagnosis or condition on Axis I. All of the clinical disorders and other conditions listed in Table 1.1 would be noted on Axis I, except mental retardation and personality disorders (which are listed on Axis II). Table 1.3 lists other conditions that may be a focus of clinical attention (i.e., V-Codes); *DSM-IV*'s inclusion of the V-Codes is a laudable effort to acknowledge subthreshold diagnoses. V-Codes, however, remain controversial in both child and adult diagnoses.

V-Codes can be listed on Axis I (or on Axis II in the case of borderline intellectual functioning) with or

TABLE 1.3 Selected Other Conditions That May Be a Focus of Clinical Attention (V-Codes)

Relational Problems
Relational problem related to a mental disorder or general medical condition
Parent–child relations problem
Partner relational problem
Sibling relational problem

Problems Related to Abuse or Neglect
Physical abuse of child
Sexual abuse of child
Neglect of child

Additional Conditions That May Be a Focus of Clinical Attention
Noncompliance with treatment
Malingering
Child or adolescent antisocial behavior
Borderline intellectual functioning (coded on Axis II)
Bereavement
Academic problem
Identity problem
Religious or spiritual problem
Acculturation problem
Phase of life problem

SOURCE: American Psychiatric Association (2000). Reprinted with permission from the *Diagnostic and Statistical Manual of Mental Disorders, Fourth Edition, Text Revision.* Copyright 2000 American Psychiatric Association.

without other disorders. Unfortunately, very little research has been completed on the V-Codes. For those who wish to help children access mental health services, it is also unfortunate to note that most insurance companies and other third-party payers (such as health maintenance organizations and preferred provider organizations) do not cover mental health services for V-Codes (Patterson & Lusterman, 1996). One possibility is that these "conditions" may not be perceived as serious as clinical disorders. In fact V-Codes and other relationship problems have often been considered second-class diagnoses in the diagnostic system (Borduin, Schaeffer, & Heiblum, 1999). Another possibility for the lack of insurance coverage for V-Codes is that they are not considered to be illnesses like clinical disorders and physical illnesses (Simola, Parker, & Froese, 1999). Ironically, when children and adolescents diagnosed with V-Codes were studied, they were found to have clinically significant problems that may lead to impairment (Simola et al., 1999). Thus, a number of writers have argued that V-Codes should be covered by insurance companies (Patterson & Lusterman, 1996; Simola et al., 1999). Many therapists consider V-Codes to be less stigmatizing for children than other diagnoses, and many also believe

them to be more reflective of children's and adolescents' problems. The *DSM-IV Training Guide for Diagnosis of Childhood Disorders* notes that V-Codes are especially useful when the real focus of the problem is the parent or family rather than the child him- or herself (Rapoport & Ismond, 1996). Thus, it appears that additional research should be done to explore whether or not V-Codes capture children's and adolescents' experience of problems in a meaningful way and to try to establish whether or not these categorizations should be given the same coverage that other clinical disorders receive.

Axis II was developed to provide individual attention to mental retardation and personality disorders (American Psychiatric Association, 2000). For children and adolescents, the majority of Axis II diagnoses are related to mental retardation rather than personality disorders (Rapoport & Ismond, 1996). Although most of the long-standing personality disorders can be diagnosed in childhood and adolescence, these disorders tend to be diagnosed more consistently in adults than in youngsters. There is some interest in diagnosing personality disorders in children and adolescents (Bernstein et al., 1993), but there is also resistance to making such diagnoses given that the disorders are considered to be long-standing and maladaptive for long-term functioning (Rapoport & Ismond, 1996). Thus, personality disorders in children and adolescents will not be addressed in any depth in this book.

Axis III allows the clinician to note any general medical conditions that are relevant for the child or adolescent. Specifically, any medical conditions that might be relevant to the understanding or treatment of the child's or adolescent's clinical disorders should be listed on Axis III. Diseases of the nervous system (such as Tay-Sachs disease), diseases of the respiratory system (such as cystic fibrosis), neoplasms (such as leukemia), endocrine diseases (such as childhood diabetes), nutritional diseases (such as obesity), and hematological diseases (such as sickle-cell anemia) are among the different types of medical conditions that would be listed. The inclusion of Axis III is meant to highlight the need for a thorough evaluation of the client and to facilitate communication among professionals working with the client (American Psychiatric Association, 2000).

Axis IV gives attention to psychosocial and environmental problems. These problems are relevant to the diagnosis, treatment, and prognosis of clinical disorders in children and adolescents. Psychosocial and environmental problems include, but are not limited to:

- Problems with the primary support group (such as sexual abuse, physical abuse, parental overprotection;

inadequate discipline; and disruption of family by separation, divorce or estrangement).

- Problems related to the social environment (such as difficulty with acculturation, death or loss of a significant friend, and inadequate social support system).
- Educational problems (such as discord with classmates or teachers, inadequate school environment, and academic problems).
- Occupational problems (such as stressful work schedule and discord with boss or co-workers).
- Housing problems (such as homelessness, inadequate housing, and living in an unsafe neighborhood).
- Economic problems (such as living in extreme poverty).
- Problems with access to health care services (such as inadequate care).
- Problems related to interaction with the legal system/crime (such as being arrested or incarcerated, and being the victim of a crime).
- Other psychosocial and environmental problems (such as exposure to war, and discord with nonfamily caregivers such as a counselor or social worker).

As this list suggests, a large number of psychosocial and environmental problems can be noted on Axis IV. The inclusion of Axis IV in *DSM-IV* was meant to encourage clinicians to consider the relevant contexts in which clients' clinical disorders develop and are maintained.

The final axis, Axis V, lists the clinician's global assessment of functioning (GAF) score. Specifically, the clinician rates the client on a scale of 1 to 100 (with higher numbers reflecting better functioning). This rating system can be used for adults as well as for youth. Clinicians consider information on the child's or adolescent's psychological, social, and academic functioning in order to determine the GAF score. Most often, clinicians rate the child's or adolescent's current GAF, but sometimes clinicians rate an intake and a discharge GAF (i.e., to note how children or adolescents were functioning when they were first brought to the mental health facility and then to note how they were functioning when they were discharged from the mental health facility) or note children's and adolescents' highest functioning within the past year. The following categories, chosen from the total of 10, should give you a good understanding of the range and meaning of GAF scores (American Psychiatric Association, 2000):

- **1–10**: Persistent danger of severely hurting self or others (e.g., recurrent violence) OR persistent inability to maintain minimal personal hygiene OR serious suicidal act with clear expectation of death.

- **41–50**: Serious symptoms (e.g., suicidal ideation, severe obsessional rituals, frequent shoplifting) OR any serious impairment in social, occupational, or school functioning (e.g., no friends, unable to keep a job).
- **91–100**: Superior functioning in a wide range of activities; life's problems never seem to get out of hand; client is sought out by others because of his or her many positive qualities. No symptoms.

RELIABILITY AND VALIDITY OF DIAGNOSTIC CATEGORIES

Now that you understand the current *DSM-IV* system, you might be wondering about its reliability and validity. **Reliability** refers to the consistency of the diagnostic system; in a reliable system, the same diagnosis would be reached across time and across clinicians. **Validity** refers to the degree to which the diagnostic system is accurate for diagnoses as they actually exist. The combination of reliability and validity is known as the **psychometric property** of a diagnostic system. It is interesting to note that psychometric properties were not included in the *DSM-IV* itself. Four years after the publication of *DSM-IV*, the fourth volume of the *DSM-IV Sourcebook* was published with reliability and validity data on some, but not all, of the disorders of childhood and adolescence (American Psychiatric Association, 1998).

As you might imagine, it is difficult to establish meaningful ways to measure reliability and validity for a diagnostic system. One way of exploring the reliability of a diagnostic system is to study **test–retest reliability**. To check for reliability, a clinician conducts diagnostic interviews at two points in time, usually one or two weeks apart. In general, the test–retest reliabilities for disorders in childhood and adolescence are not as strong as for disorders in adulthood (American Psychiatric Association, 1998). For example, disorders such as attention-deficit/hyperactivity disorder, oppositional defiant disorder, and conduct disorder all have test–retest reliabilities that are considered to be in the fair range (.51 to .64 for kappas; American Psychiatric Association, 1998) but not in the strong or excellent range.

Another way of exploring reliability is to assess the correspondence between two clinicians' ratings, which is known as **inter-rater reliability**. In studies that involved experienced clinicians' diagnoses of childhood disorders, clinician-to-clinician agreement was stronger for some disorders, such as autism (with a kappa of .85), than for others, such as oppositional defiant disorder (with a kappa of .55; American Psychiatric Press, 1998). Note that the

Case Study: Eric, An Example of Multiaxial Evaluation Using *DSM-IV*

Eric is 9 years old and lives with his two brothers, his mother, and his father. For the past three months, he has been afraid of attending the three-hour religious classes at his church after school. He had been performing quite well in these classes but said that he was afraid of failing them. His progress in regular school classes had begun to deteriorate, partially due to frequent absences and difficulty with concentrating in class. In addition to having trouble sleeping, Eric also had many somatic complaints, such as headaches and stomachaches. He often felt sad and did not seem to enjoy activities that used to be enjoyable. Eric often cried for what seemed to be no apparent reason. He had always been shy, but he did have some friends with whom he would occasionally spend the night.

Eric's parents had been married for more than 20 years, but they fought frequently and had many marital problems. Eric and his brothers were often the topic of their parents' arguments. In addition, Eric's mother had received treatment for major depressive disorder on three separate occasions.

When interviewed, Eric reported that he was distressed about causing his parents to worry about him. He quickly began to sob and stated that he felt awful nearly all the time. He said that he and his family would be better off if he were dead, but he did not seem to have a specific plan to attempt suicide.

Diagnosis

Axis I	Major depressive disorder, single episode
Axis II	No diagnosis
Axis III	None
Axis IV	Problems with primary support group Parent–child problems Psychiatric disorder in mother Family discord
Axis V	GAF = 70 (current) GAF = 85 (highest level in the past year)

Eric met criteria for major depressive disorder, which is coded as a clinical disorder on Axis I. Although he reported symptoms of anxiety, these symptoms were not enough to warrant diagnosis of an anxiety disorder. There was no evidence of a personality disorder or mental retardation, so no diagnosis was warranted on Axis II. The somatic complaints were thought to be due to his depression and symptoms of anxiety, rather than an actual physical problem. If he had experienced a physical problem, it would have been coded on Axis III. Axis IV was used to note that Eric had experienced many psychosocial and environmental problems. Axis V was used to note two global assessment of functioning (GAF) scores for Eric, one currently and one for the highest level within the past year.

SOURCE: Rapoport & Ismond (1996).

kappa statistic for inter-rater reliability is the percentage of agreement between two raters, while controlling for chance agreement. Overall, inter-rater and other types of reliability tend to be stronger for disorders that are relatively objective and observable. For example, the average correspondence between parents' and adolescents' reports of adolescents' psychopathology was .30. This average, however, hides a wide range of correspondence for different disorders. Parent–adolescent correspondence was stronger for observable disorders such as conduct disorder (.79) and anorexia nervosa (.75) than for other, less observable disorders such as major depressive disorder (.31) and alcohol abuse (.19; Cantwell, Lewinsohn, Rohde, & Seeley, 1997). Overall, reliabilities of disorders in childhood and adolescence have lagged behind reliabilities of disorders in adulthood. Validity has also been difficult to establish, though there are indications that certain observable disorders (such as autism and anorexia nervosa) have shown evidence of strong validity (American Psychiatric Association, 1998).

Education, in short, cannot be better described than by calling it the organization of acquired habits of conduct and tendencies to behavior.

—William James

CHILDREN IN THE SCHOOL SYSTEM

Because children are in school for so much of their time, schools have become a central setting for diagnosing and treating mental health problems (R. L. Taylor, 1997). A number of laws have been established to ensure that children receive appropriate services in school systems nationwide:

- **Public Law 94-142: Education for All Handicapped Children Act.** This national law, established in 1975, has a number of crucial components. To begin with, all children with special needs should be provided with free, appropriate public education. Special-needs children must be evaluated in a nondiscriminatory manner, which means that they should be assessed in their native language with tests that have been validated

The school environment can be an important part of children's lives.

appropriately for that specific purpose. Each child should have an individualized education program (IEP), which should include documentation of the child's current level of functioning, yearly goals, short-term objectives, and evaluation procedures to verify accomplishment of the short-term goals. All children should be educated and treated in the most appropriate and least restrictive environment possible (e.g., a mainstreamed classroom with special pull-out services is considered less restrictive than a special education classroom, which is in turn considered less restrictive than a residential setting). Finally, the law established the legal right for parents to be informed about decisions regarding their children and to encourage parental participation in the child's educational and therapeutic process.

- **Public Law 99-457: Education of the Handicapped Act, Amendments of 1986.** This law was used to amend PL 94-142 to include children from birth to three years old (see also Box 1.1). The focus of this law was to mandate the availability of free, appropriate assessment and intervention services for infants and toddlers. In addition, it clarified the fact that PL 94-142 funds were to be used to establish diagnostic and treatment services for children ages three to five.

- **Public Law 101-476: Education of the Handicapped Act, Amendments of 1990.** This law served to change the name of the act to Individuals with Disabilities Education Act (IDEA). All instances of the word handicap in PL 94-142 and its subsequent revisions were changed to disability; for example, the phrase "infants and toddlers with disabilities" replaced "handicapped infants and toddlers." The IDEA was established to serve individuals from birth to the age of 21.

- **Public Law 101-336: Americans with Disabilities Act (ADA).** In 1990, the ADA served as civil rights legislation for all individuals with any type of disability (including certain clinical disorders). The law was established to maintain the accessibility of education and other publicly funded activities for people with disabilities. The ADA is a far-reaching law, covering everything from making buildings accessible (by use of wheelchair ramps) to granting students with documented learning disorders special provisions for taking tests. The ADA served as sweeping legislation to protect the rights of the disabled from infancy into elderly adulthood.

Overall, these public laws have had a drastic effect on the educational and therapeutic services provided to special-needs children in the school system (R. L. Taylor, 1997). Children who do not meet criteria for services under the IDEA can still access services through Section 504 of the Rehabilitation Act of 1973, which mandates that services be provided to children identified by professionals outside the school system (such as physicians or private psychologists; Witt, Elliott, Daly, Gresham, & Kramer, 1998).

The IDEA requires that assessment and classification be performed by a multidisciplinary team that includes at least one professional (such as a special education teacher) who has expertise in the area of the suspected disability. Decisions regarding placement of the child must be made by professionals who know the child, who know the placement options, and who can understand and interpret the assessment results (Witt et al., 1998). Classification in educational settings is most often consistent with the IDEA, but school psychologists and other professionals within the school system can also use *DSM-IV*

BOX 1.1

DIAGNOSTIC CLASSIFICATION OF MENTAL HEALTH AND DEVELOPMENTAL DISORDERS OF INFANCY AND EARLY CHILDHOOD

Many people do not realize that even infants and toddlers can experience mental health problems. Although *DSM-IV* lists some disorders relevant to infants and toddlers, the publication *Diagnostic Classification: 0–3* (Zero to Three/National Center for Clinical Infant Programs, 1994) is meant to classify a breadth of disorders and problems that occur in the first three years of life. As the table shows, both primary disorders (within the youngster) and relationship disorders (between the youngster and the caretaker) can be classified.

Primary Diagnosis

Traumatic stress disorder
Anxiety disorders of infancy and early childhood
Mood disorder: prolonged bereavement/grief reaction
Mood disorder: depression of infancy and early childhood
Mixed disorder of emotional expressiveness
Childhood gender identity disorder
Reactive attachment deprivation/maltreatment disorder of infancy and early childhood
Adjustment disorder
Regulatory disorder: hypersensitive
Regulatory disorder: under-reactive
Regulatory disorder: motor processing— impulsive, motorically disorganized
Sleep behavior disorder
Eating behavior disorder
Disorders of relating and communicating:
Multisystem developmental disorder
Pervasive developmental disorder

Relationship Disorder Classification

Overinvolved
Underinvolved
Anxious/tense
Angry/hostile
Mixed
Abusive
Verbally abusive
Physically abusive
Sexually abusive

Like *DSM-IV, Diagnostic Classification: 0–3* proposed the use of a multiaxial evaluation system. Also like *DSM-IV,* there are five axes on which to code infants' and toddlers' functioning:

Axis I	Primary Classification
Axis II	Relationship Classification
Axis III	Physical, Neurological, Developmental and Mental Health Disorders or Conditions
Axis IV	Psychosocial Stressors
Axis V	Functional Emotional Developmental Level

Overall, this system is still quite new. Further research is needed to establish its reliability and validity, but this diagnostic system provided a good start to classifying problems in infants, toddlers, and their primary caretakers. Students interested in mental health issues of infancy and toddlerhood should also consider reading the *Handbook of Infant Mental Health,* second edition (Zeanah, 1999), which is a compendium of research on mental health issues in infants and their caretakers.

criteria for diagnosis of clinical disorders in children (Witt et al., 1998).

In addition to the identification and remediation of learning and emotional/behavioral disorders that disrupt the educational experience, there are a number of other factors related to children's functioning that are salient in the school environment. Problem-solving abilities, achievement-related beliefs, social competence, and self-efficacy are all important in the school setting (Hintze & Shapiro, 1999). In addition, language, communication, and adaptive functioning are all crucial components to children's success in the school setting (Witt et al., 1998). Box 1.2 discusses two school programs meant to help prevent the development of problems in children.

All kids need is a little help, a little hope, and somebody who believes in them.

—Earvin "Magic" Johnson

DISORDERS IN THE FUTURE OF *DSM*

In an effort to help encourage research on possible new diagnoses, there is an appendix in *DSM-IV* that describes disorders that are being considered for inclusion in *DSM-V*, expected to be published by 2005 (Compas & Gotlib, 2002). Although none of the disorders is specific to children or adolescents, two will be highlighted here to show some possible diagnoses of the future. If included in

DSM-V, these disorders could be used for children and adolescents as well as adults.

- Mixed anxiety-depressive disorder is reflective of symptoms of both anxiety and depression that are not severe enough to warrant a diagnosis of major depressive disorder or an anxiety disorder.

- Factitious disorder by proxy is when a parent or other caretaker intentionally inflicts physical or psychological harm on a child (or pretends that such harm or psychological symptoms exist in the child) so that the parent or caretaker can receive the social and emotional benefits of the child's illness. That is, the parent or caretaker hopes to gain attention and sympathy. This problem has often been referred to as Munchausen by proxy.

It is unclear whether these two disorders will be listed in the final edition of *DSM-V*. These examples illustrate the attempt to develop more specific diagnoses that might help classify abnormal behavior across the life span. In addition, the task force for *DSM-V* plans to pay more attention to dimensional conceptualizations of psychopathology (Widiger & Clark, 2000).

ADVANTAGES AND DISADVANTAGES OF *DSM-IV*

With any system of classification like *DSM-IV*, there are bound to be strengths and weaknesses. Among the many strengths of *DSM-IV*, probably the most salient is the wide acceptance and use of the system. It has been estimated that more than 500,000 mental health professionals in the United States utilize *DSM-IV* in their work (Nathan, 1997). Thus, a client diagnosed in California would have probably received the same diagnosis had she or he been diagnosed in New York. Similarly, researchers across the nation can use the same terminology to compare and contrast their research samples. Having such a widely followed system also allows professionals from many different disciplines and many different countries to share a common diagnostic language. Thus, even though the *DSM* system was developed by psychiatrists, it is used by school psychologists, social workers, clinical psychologists, counselors, and so on. The system's commonality reaches to many other countries as well, so cross-cultural research is possible (e.g., Fergusson, Horwood, & Lynskey, 1993).

In keeping with the benefit of a common diagnostic language, another advantage of *DSM-IV* is that many insurance companies have adopted its use to establish coverage for certain clinical disorders. Although not all insurance companies cover treatment of mental health problems, most of those that do provide coverage use *DSM-IV*.

As mentioned previously, *DSM-IV* represents an improvement on earlier versions, with the inclusion of multiaxial evaluation, adequate conceptualizations of psychosocial and environmental problems, greater attention to some disorders of childhood and adolescence, an attempt to be atheoretical, and increased attention to details in diagnostic criteria (American Psychiatric Association, 2000). In addition, the *DSM-IV* classification system is thought to be as good as or better than the previous versions regarding reliability and validity, even though only limited psychometric data have been published to date (Nathan & Langenbucher, 1999). Overall, *DSM-IV* has been helpful in allowing researchers and clinicians to have a common language with which to discuss clients.

The limitations of the *DSM-IV* system are reflected in the terminology related to diagnosis itself. Achenbach (1998) distinguished between diagnosis solely for

---

Case Study: Carl, The Boy with Problems in School

On the suggestion of a school psychologist, seven-year-old Carl was given a full battery of assessment measures to find out why he might be struggling in school. Although Carl's parents did not report any problems at home, Carl's teachers reported that he had difficulty with his schoolwork, that he did not pay attention to them, that he seemed immature, and that he had poor coordination.

Upon examination, Carl seemed like a sweet, friendly, and cooperative child. His speech was clear, but his vocabulary and syntax were not as developed as would be expected for a child of his age. He was found to meet criteria for an expressive language disorder (coded on Axis I). A full evaluation of his learning abilities showed that there was a possibility of a reading disorder, so the diagnosis was noted as reading disorder/provisional (coded on Axis I). Finally, there was also some evidence that Carl had heightened problems with attention, so a provisional diagnosis of attention-deficit/hyperactivity disorder, predominantly inattentive type, was made (coded on Axis I). Note that the provisional diagnoses are meant to highlight the need to monitor Carl in these areas and to reevaluate for these problems at a later date. It was thought that the expressive language disorder, which falls into the category of communication disorders, played the central role in Carl's difficulties.

SOURCE: Rapoport & Ismond (1996).

BOX 1.2

PREVENTION AND THE SCHOOLS: TWO SCHOOL-BASED PREVENTION PROGRAMS THAT WORK

The prevention of mental health problems, along with the concomitant promotion of competence in children, is a central theme in developmental psychopathology. A large number of prevention programs have been instituted in school systems nationwide. The following examples highlight two excellent programs designed to prevent children from experiencing distress and psychological problems.

- **Primary Mental Health Project (PMHP).** Developed by Dr. Emory Cowen and his colleagues, the PMHP has been in existence for more than 40 years and is now located in several thousand schools nationally and internationally. The PMHP is considered a secondary prevention program, which means that the program identifies children at risk for the development of problems. Although the project began with a focus on preventing school failure, it soon began to focus on other characteristics related to school functioning, such as problem solving, social competence, and personal empowerment. Children identified as at risk for school failure are given extra help and guidance by a volunteer in the program. Often, these volunteers serve as mentors and role models for children. The PMHP has been extraordinarily successful in preventing school failure and in preventing the development of emotional/behavioral problems (Cowen, Work, & Wyman, 1997).

- **The Improving Social Awareness–Social Problem Solving (ISA-SPS) Project.** The ISA-SPS Project, in existence for more than 20 years, is aimed at helping children progress from elementary to middle school without developing emotional/behavioral problems. The project

centers on teaching children skills for solving social problems. This program is considered a primary prevention program because it allows all children, not just those at risk, to be exposed to the prevention program. Through classes conducted at school, children are taught eight steps that encompass social decision making and problem solving:

1. *Look for signs of different feelings.*
2. *Tell yourself what the problem is.*
3. *Decide on a goal.*
4. *Stop and think of as many solutions to the problem as you can.*
5. *For each solution, think of all the things that might happen.*
6. *Choose your best solution.*
7. *Plan it and make a final check.*
8. *Try it and rethink it. (Battistich, Elias, & Branden-Muller, 1992; p. 220)*

These steps are consistent with a number of other cognitive-behavioral programs designed to help children learn impulse control and social skills. In the ISA-SPS Project, children not only learn these strategies but are offered many opportunities to role-play their new skills and try out their newly acquired solutions to social problem solving. The program has been successful at teaching children new skills and in decreasing the social and emotional difficulties that often accompany transition from elementary to middle school. The program now is instituted in a number of schools, from elementary through high schools (Battistich et al., 1992).

---

classification purposes and diagnostic formulations, which explore the nature, etiology, and conclusions about a particular problem. Unfortunately, *DSM-IV* is usually used solely for classification. Children and adolescents are classified into diagnostic categories, and little attention is given to what led to the problems or what would help alleviate the problems. Diagnostic formulations, in contrast, not only would evaluate the appropriateness of an actual diagnosis but also would consider the child's functioning in other areas (such as developmental history, genetic predisposition, physical functioning, educational functioning, cognitions, family issues, social networks, strengths, and interests). Although the *DSM-IV* system does not prevent more thorough diagnostic formulations from occurring, it may

inadvertently allow clinicians to think that the evaluation process is concluded when a diagnosis is reached.

Another significant criticism of *DSM-IV* (and of *ICD-10*) is that it was formulated within the medical model. **Medical model** is a term that refers to the application of the medical system to mental health issues. The medical model is evident when behaviors are referred to as symptoms, when mental health problems are referred to as diseases or disorders, and when the individual's problem is located within the individual her- or himself rather than in the individual's environment or some other context (Trull & Phares, 2001). The medical model has been criticized for a number of reasons, including encouraging biological rather than social, psychological, familial, or environmental views of mental health problems; focusing attention on deficits rather than strengths of individuals; and conceptualizing clients as passive in the therapeutic process (Korchin, 1976). In fact, even the terminology that clinicians use is sometimes reflective of the medical model. In many settings, individuals receiving services are referred to as patients rather than clients or consumers. The terms client and consumer imply an active role on the part of the individual and should convey the message that professionals are not the only ones who have expertise in healthy functioning (Trull & Phares, 2001).

Most of the limitations of *DSM-IV* listed so far are related to the diagnostic system in general. There are, however, specific limitations to *DSM-IV* that concern the diagnostic classification of children and adolescents rather than adults. First, the reliability of diagnoses of children and adolescents lags far behind the reliability of diagnoses of adults (American Psychiatric Association, 1998). The process of diagnosing children and adolescents, which is newer to the field than that of diagnosing adults, may eventually catch up, but it is possible that the current diagnoses just do not capture the actual behaviors of children and adolescents in a meaningful and distinct manner. Second, in light of the fact that so many disorders can be diagnosed in the same child or adolescent, some researchers have raised questions about the utility of the *DSM-IV* altogether (Caplan, 1995; Kutchins & Kirk, 1997).

The poor reliability of diagnoses in childhood and adolescence may merely be a reflection of the complexity of youth. Even in very reliable assessment systems, different informants—such as mothers, fathers, and teachers—often have very different perspectives on children's behavior (Achenbach, McConaughy, & Howell, 1987). Thus, the difficulty of establishing reliable diagnoses may be related to the complexity of children's behavior and the possibility of children behaving differently in different environments.

A related issue is the lack of developmental sensitivity and specificity in the diagnostic criteria for child and adolescent disorders. As noted at the beginning of this chapter, age and developmental level are extremely important factors to consider when evaluating children's and adolescents' behavior. Although *DSM-IV* contains a specific section on disorders first evident in infancy, childhood, and adolescence the diagnostic criteria throughout the entire system lack developmental sensitivity. Clinicians are left to use their own judgment about what is expected for a child of a particular age, developmental level, gender, racial or ethnic background, and culture. Most of the diagnostic criteria for childhood disorders do continue to note the importance of diagnosing only behavior that is maladaptive and inconsistent with developmental level, but without empirically validated assessment measures, clinicians are left to make this judgment themselves.

Finally, but probably most important, a diagnostic system such as *DSM-IV* allows children and adolescents to be labeled for behavior that may or may not be an important part of their character. **Labeling** occurs when information about a child's diagnostic classification is communicated in a negative manner that leads to stigma for the child (Hobbs, 1975; Sternberg & Grigorenko, 2000). There is concern that labeling and diagnoses might lead to **self-fulfilling prophecies**, whereby children and adolescents act in a manner that confirms the diagnosis simply because they know about the diagnosis (Hobbs, 1975). For example, if a boy is diagnosed with attention-deficit/hyperactivity disorder, combined type, he may inadvertently act even more overactive, impulsive, and inattentive than he did before the diagnosis simply because he has been told of the diagnosis. Sometimes parents and professionals unwittingly reinforce self-fulfilling prophecies by acting as though the diagnosis is a central characteristic of that child.

For this, and numerous other reasons, many mental health professionals have advocated for more careful usage of terminology related to diagnoses. Think about the different implications in the following two sentences: *She's an autistic child* versus *She's a child with autism*. The first sentence might lead you to think that there is nothing else important to know about this child other than her autism. The second sentence might convey that, although the child has been diagnosed with autism, there are many other important characteristics to know about her. Although labeling can occur no matter what terminology is used, these issues of language were noted in *DSM-IV* (American Psychiatric Association, 2000) to encourage professionals to be conscientious when discussing their clients.

Youth is the turning point of life, the most sensitive and volatile period, the state that registers most vividly the impressions and experience of life.

—Richard Wright

DIFFERENCES BETWEEN CATEGORICAL AND DIMENSIONAL UNDERSTANDING OF BEHAVIOR

To counteract many of the limitations in the diagnostic process, and especially to address the somewhat subjective process of decision making that led to the inclusion or exclusion of diagnoses in systems such as *DSM-IV* or *ICD-10*, a number of researchers and clinicians have opted for a more empirically based (i.e., research-based) understanding of children's and adolescents' emotional/behavioral problems. To understand these contrasting approaches, we need to step back and think about the essence of the diagnostic process in its current form. Both *DSM-IV* and *ICD-10* represent a **categorical approach** to the description of children's mental health problems. As the name implies, a categorical approach attempts to *categorize* mental health problems into distinct diagnoses. This approach allows a clinician to make a dichotomous decision (i.e., "Yes, the child meets the criteria for that disorder" or "No, the child does not meet the criteria").

Categorical approaches are thought to be most appropriate when there is great homogeneity within each category (i.e., a lot of similarity among children diagnosed with the same disorder); when there are clear boundaries and differences between categories (i.e., the disorders do not overlap in descriptions); and when categories are mutually exclusive (i.e., if you meet criteria for one disorder, then you cannot meet criteria for another disorder; American Psychiatric Association, 2000). Although some of these assumptions are accurate for certain disorders in the *DSM-IV* diagnostic system, many professionals have expressed hesitation about a categorical system of classifying mental health problems (e.g., Achenbach, 1982; Clark, Watson, & Reynolds, 1995). Many professionals think that the categorical approach is inappropriate for understanding child psychopathology and that it limits research advances in this area (Sonuga-Barke, 1998). For these reasons, many professionals have tried to identify appropriate alternatives to the categorical approach of diagnostic classification.

The **dimensional approach** is an alternative way of conceptualizing children's mental health problems. As its name implies, this approach focuses on different *dimensions* or levels of a child's behavior. Rather than determine whether or not a child meets criteria for a particular disorder, a clinician using the dimensional system would look at the varying levels of different behaviors that a child exhibits. The range of behaviors would be evaluated on a continuum, without an artificial limit that puts the child into a diagnostic category or keeps the child from meeting a diagnosis. Dimensional conceptualizations are advantageous (1) because they reduce large numbers of diagnoses into smaller numbers of dimensions of behaviors and (2) because they highlight the level of severity for remediation and treatment of behaviors that are considered problematic (Clark et al., 1995). They are also advantageous because behavior exists on a continuum rather than distinct units. In other words, different individuals show varying levels of behaviors, and it is unlikely that certain individuals show lots of a particular behavior while other individuals show almost none of that particular behavior. Thus, the dimensional approach is consistent with behavior as it actually exists (Clark et al., 1995). In a comprehensive review of mental health by the U. S. surgeon general, psychological problems were noted to be on a continuum (Satchel, 2000, 2001).

Dimensional approaches to children's and adolescents' emotional/behavioral problems are consistent with **empirically based taxonomies**. Given that the word *empirical* means "measurable" or "verifiable," an empirically based taxonomy is a system in which "assessment of behavioral and emotional functioning is viewed as a measurement process that identifies quantitative gradations in the target phenomena" (Achenbach & McConaughy, 1997; p. 3). In other words, empirically based taxonomies rely on actual data to understand and interpret children's and adolescents' behavior. Most other diagnostic systems (such as the *DSM* system and the *ICD* system) use data as only one part of the process to inform committees and professionals who establish the diagnostic criteria.

In contrast, an empirically based taxonomy originates from research data and is modified solely on research data. Achenbach and McConaughy (1997) developed an empirically based taxonomy guided by the following principles:

- Collect information in a standardized manner from a large, representative sample of children and adolescents by asking different informants (such as parents, teachers, and children themselves) about the competencies and problems of the members of the sample.

- Analyze the assessment data through empirical and quantitative methods in order to explore connections and associations among the behaviors reported for the children and adolescents.

- After associations are identified among children's and adolescents' problem behaviors, syndromes are identified to show higher-order groupings of the behavior problems.

- Scales (such as anxious/depressed or aggressive) are developed based on the behavioral items. In order to score individual youngsters on these scales, professionals use normative data to compare an individual child's behavior with what would be expected from children of that age range and gender.

Case Study: Julie, An Example of the Dimensional Conceptualization of Behavior

At the age of 14, Julie was arrested for shoplifting a sweater from a local clothing store. Although this was her first arrest, Julie had experienced a troubled childhood. Her biological parents had a conflicted and violent marriage that ended when Julie was 5. From the age of 5 to 10, Julie was transferred back and forth between her mother's and father's homes. She was often left unsupervised in both homes, and she was physically abused by her father and by her mother's boyfriend. Her parents both experienced alcohol and drug abuse problems. In addition, her mother was diagnosed with bipolar disorder (often known as manic depression). When Julie was 10 years old, the state protective agency intervened and took her away from her parents. Eventually, parental rights were terminated.

Julie was placed with foster parents who eventually adopted her. Initially, she appeared sad, sullen, moody, and irritable. Moreover, she had few friends. Her adoptive parents tried to talk with her and attempted to provide her a stable, nurturing environment. By the age of 13, Julie seemed to have become happier and more outgoing. Her adoptive parents became concerned, however, when Julie began associating with "troublemakers" in the community and staying out past her curfew. Julie became more involved in illicit activities with her friends and also became involved in sexual activities with three different boys.

The profile shown below illustrates Julie's adoptive parents' reports of her behavior at the age of 10 and at the age of 14 (after the arrest for shoplifting). Higher scores represent more problems. Scores above the highest dotted line are considered to be in the clinical range. At the age of 10, Julie's greatest problems, according to her parents, were related to being withdrawn, having social problems, and having attention problems. At the age of 14, Julie's most salient problem was in the area of delinquency, with some continuing problems in being withdrawn.

After the arrest, Julie received counseling services and was encouraged to become involved in prosocial activities at school, such as band, drama, and after-school clubs. She also volunteered in a hospital to honor the community service hours that were required after her shoplifting arrest. By the time she turned 15, there had been dramatic reductions in Julie's delinquent behavior, and she appeared to be happy and well-adjusted. She continued in counseling in order to deal with her feelings of anger and abandonment from her biological parents.

This case illustrates a way of conceptualizing a child's behavior from a dimensional, rather than a categorical, framework. The assessment showed higher and lower levels of problems, without categorizing Julie's behavior into a specific diagnostic category.

SOURCE: Achenbach & McConaughy (1997).

CBCL/4–18 Profile for Girls—Problem Scales

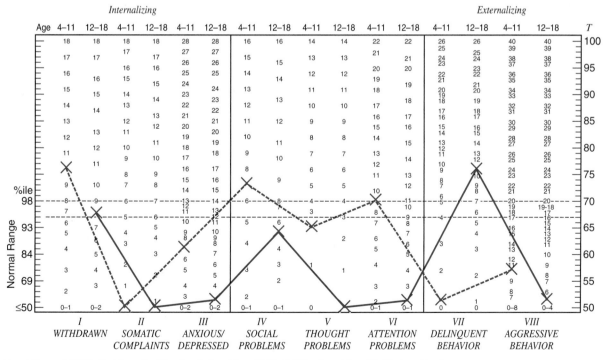

Hand-Scored CBCL Problem Profiles for Julie at Age 14 (Solid Line) and Age 10 (Broken Line)

- An individual child or adolescent can be assessed with the same standard instruments that were used in the original development of the empirically based taxonomy.

Because they tend to be conceptualized within empirically based taxonomies, dimensional systems also tend to be oriented toward empirical data. One of the primary reasons a dimensional approach is advantageous over a diagnostic system such as *DSM-IV* is that it is based on research data that reflect children's and adolescents' behavior.

Note that, although there is a history of polarizing the categorical and dimensional approaches, there has been some attention to the mutual strengths of both approaches. Both the categorical and dimensional approaches have strengths that are necessary for thorough evaluations of children and adolescents (Jensen & Watanabe, 1999). In a study that compared a categorical evaluation process with a dimensional evaluation process, children who showed problems through one approach but not the other were still thought to have problems that were in need of attention (Jensen & Watanabe, 1999). In other words, children who met diagnostic criteria but did not score high on a dimensional evaluation and, conversely, children who did not meet diagnostic criteria but did score high on a dimensional evaluation were still likely to need help regardless of what pattern they showed. Thus, both categorical and dimensional approaches were necessary for understanding children's and adolescents' emotional/behavioral problems (Jensen & Watanabe, 1999). The two systems could be used in a complementary rather than an adversarial manner to help professionals comprehensively understand children's and adolescents' functioning. Some recent empirically based dimensional scales also provide information on how each child's scores correspond to *DSM* criteria (Achenbach & Rescorla, 2001).

Regardless of whether you use a categorical or a dimensional approach to understand children's and adolescents' functioning, it is crucial to remember that behavior can change over time. If a child shows elevated levels of a problem at a particular point, it does not necessarily mean that she or he will always show high levels of that problem. Figure 1.1 shows that, even in adolescence, there are many possible pathways of developmental adaptation.

PREVALENCE OF CHILDREN'S AND ADOLESCENTS' PROBLEM BEHAVIOR

After understanding the different conceptualizations of children's and adolescents' emotional/behavioral problems, the next logical issue is the extent to which youth experience these problems. The term **epidemiology** refers to the study of the prevalence, incidence, and distribution of mental disorders or emotional/behavioral problems within a particular population. **Prevalence** refers to the total number of cases (e.g., number of youth with a clinical disorder, or number of youth who score in the clinical range on a particular measure) at a particular time. **Incidence** refers to the number of new cases in a given period of time (such as how many youth developed a particular problem within the past year). Prevalence rates are usually cited when describing the commonality or rarity of specific clinical disorders (e.g., this disorder is more common than that disorder). Incidence rates are usually discussed when looking at changes over time in rates of clinical disorders (e.g., has there been an increase in children experiencing a particular clinical disorder over the past 10 years). The epidemiology of different disorders and emotional/behavioral problems will be discussed in each chapter separately, but a few comments on overall prevalence rates are in order to put abnormal child behavior in context.

EPIDEMIOLOGICAL RATES BASED ON THE CATEGORICAL APPROACH

Although there have been a number of epidemiological studies over the years, the largest and most comprehensive epidemiological study of children and adolescents in the United States has been the Methods for the Epidemiology of Child and Adolescent Mental Disorders (MECA) study (Lahey et al., 1996). Funded by the National Institute of Mental Health (NIMH), the MECA study was conducted by more than 30 psychologists, psychiatrists, public health researchers, and other professionals, as well as their research staffs. The MECA study was meant to parallel NIMH's Epidemiologic Catchment Area (ECA) study of clinical disorders in adults (Robins & Regier, 1991). Based on the ECA study, it was estimated that 29.5% of adults experienced a clinical disorder at some point in the past year.

All of the results are not yet published, but the important MECA study has yielded a number of interesting and enlightening papers (Flisher, Kramer, Grosser et al.,

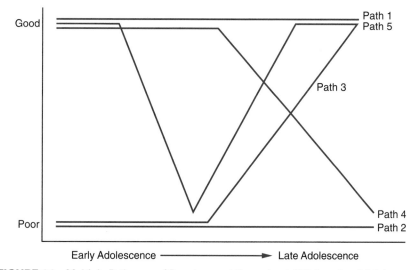

FIGURE 1.1 Multiple Pathways of Development throughout Childhood and Adolescence

Path 1   Stable adaptation (few problems, good self-worth, low risk exposure).

Path 2   Stable maladaptation (chronic adversities, little parental protection).

Path 3   Reversal of maladaptation (important life change creates new opportunity, such as transfer to new school with caring teachers and a prosocial peer group).

Path 4   Decline of adaptation (environmental or biological shifts bring adversity, such as parental divorce that contributes to problems).

Path 5   Temporal maladaptation (can reflect transient experimental risk taking, such as use of illegal drugs).

Source: Compas, Hinden, & Gerhardt (1995). Reprinted with permission from the *Annual Review of Psychology* 46, © 1995 by Annual Reviews (www.AnnualReviews.org).

1997; Flisher, Kramer, Hoven et al., 1997; Goodman et al., 1998; Kandel et al., 1999; Lahey et al., 1996; Leaf et al., 1996; Schwab-Stone et al., 1996; Shaffer et al., 1996). The sample was comprised of nearly 1,300 children and adolescents (ages 9–17) and their parents, who were recruited from four primary sites: Connecticut; Georgia; New York; and San Juan, Puerto Rico. Parents and youth were interviewed with the Diagnostic Interview Schedule for Children (DISC; Shaffer et al., 1996), which is a structured interview that can be completed by parents and youth separately. In the sample, there were approximately equal numbers of boys and girls (53% and 47%, respectively). There was an attempt to recruit youth and their parents from ethnically diverse and socioeconomically diverse areas; however, the final distribution of race/ethnicity in the MECA study showed an overrepresentation of Hispanic/Latino/Latina participants and a slight underrepresentation of African American participants (Lahey et al., 1996). The median family income was somewhat higher than what would be expected from families in those target areas. Overall, the sample in the MECA study was somewhat more representative than

previous epidemiological studies, but the sample was still not truly representative of children and adolescents in the United States.

Given this caveat, it is still worthwhile to explore the information gained from the MECA study. Overall, when parents were interviewed, 19.2% of children and adolescents met criteria for a clinical disorder and showed the level of impairment that was necessary for being diagnosed with that disorder (Shaffer et al., 1996). When children and adolescents were interviewed, the prevalence rate was shown to be 19.6%. When parents and youth were combined, a total of 32.8% of the sample met criteria for a clinical disorder (Shaffer et al., 1996). In a refined analysis of these data, it appeared that only 6.6% of children and adolescents met criteria for a diagnosis (with impairment) when both the youth and the parent reported the same types of problems (Leaf et al., 1996). Thus, when trying to summarize the prevalence data from the MECA study, the answers depend on who took part in the interviews. This issue is relevant in any type of research with children and adolescents, so it is not unique to the MECA study.

Given the range of prevalence rates from 6.6% to 32.8%, it should be noted that the most consistent reports of prevalence rates of child and adolescent disorders usually fall between 14% and 20% (Brandenburg, Friedman, & Silver, 1990; Costello, Burns, Angold, & Leaf, 1993; Offord, Boyle, & Racine, 1989). It is also important to consider lifetime prevalence rates, which explore whether or not the child has ever experienced a psychiatric disorder in his or her lifetime. Parent reports of lifetime prevalence for children and adolescents have been estimated at 23.5%, and adolescent self-reports have been estimated at 37.7% (Cantwell et al., 1997). Overall, these prevalence data suggest that a significant number of children and adolescents experience some type of psychopathology at some point during their childhood. Table 1.4 shows the prevalence rates that were listed in *DSM-IV* for specific disorders.

Epidemiological rates vary by country. One review found wide differences in prevalence rates of childhood psychopathology, including 12.4% in France, 17.6% in New Zealand, 25.4% in Ireland, 26.0% in the Netherlands, and 51.3% in Germany (Bird, 1996). It is important, however, not to diagnose children in one culture with the definitions of psychopathology from another culture (Lopez & Guarnaccia, 2000).

As you might expect, the rates of different disorders vary according to a number of factors, such as gender and age. In this book, epidemiological data on specific disorders will be presented in separate chapters, but there are some patterns of prevalence rates that might be helpful to keep in mind when considering psychopathology in childhood. Girls, and especially adolescent girls, tend to experience major depressive disorder, some types of anxiety disorders, eating disorders, and adjustment disorders to a greater extent than do adolescent boys (American Psychiatric Association, 2000; Eme, 1979). Before adolescence, boys show higher rates of oppositional defiant disorder than do girls. Both before and during adolescence, boys show higher rates of other disruptive disorders (such as attention-deficit/hyperactivity disorder and conduct disorder) than do girls (American Psychiatric Association, 2000; Eme & Kavanaugh, 1995). As you might already have noticed, girls show higher rates of nondisruptive problems and boys show higher rates of disruptive problems. These patterns of gender differences will be explored for specific disorders in later chapters, but suffice it to say here that there are a wide range of explanations for these gender differences, including biological, genetic, socialization, and cognitive differences (Eme & Kavanaugh, 1995).

Different chapters of this book will also address patterns of the co-occurrence of disorders within children

and adolescents of both genders. **Comorbidity** is the term used to describe the co-occurrence of two or more diagnosed disorders in one individual. Within the study of child and adolescent psychopathology, comorbidity is the rule rather than the exception (Angold, Costello, & Erkanli, 1999). There are high rates of comorbidity between attention-deficit/hyperactivity disorder and conduct disorder, major depressive disorder and anxiety disorders, major depressive disorder and conduct disorder, and major depression and substance use disorders (Angold et al., 1999; Joiner & Lonigan, 2000; Swendsen & Merikangas, 2000). In addition, high rates of comorbidity are evident between learning disorders and other psychological disorders (Willcutt & Pennington, 2000). These high rates of comorbidity have been interpreted in a number of different ways, from establishing the fact that distressed children are often distressed in many different ways, to suggesting that the categorical approach is inadequate due to the overlap between categories that were meant to be separate and distinct. Specifically, high rates of comorbidity call into question a categorical system such as *DSM-IV* (Achenbach, 1990/1991; Caron & Rutter, 1991; Meehl, 2001; Waldman & Lilienfeld, 2001). Comorbidity rates have, however, been used to support genetic influences for multiple disorders (Simonoff, 2000). The issue of comorbidity is relevant to the understanding of psychopathology from a dimensional perspective, given that the dimensional perspective, by definition, allows children and adolescents to

TABLE 1.4 **Prevalence Estimates of Selected Clinical Disorders in Children and Adolescents**

Clinical Disorder	Estimated Prevalence*
Mental retardation	1%
Learning disorders	2%–10%
Autistic disorder	< 1% (.02%–.05%)
Attention-deficit/hyperactivity disorder (in school-age children)	3%–7%
Conduct disorder	1%–10%
Oppositional defiant disorder	2%–16%
Separation anxiety disorder	4%

*Note that prevalence rates vary according to a number of factors, including the methodology, the sample characteristics, and the assessment measures. These prevalence rates are the estimates presented in *DSM-IV* for children and adolescents (American Psychiatric Association, 2000). Prevalence rates for children and adolescents were not listed in *DSM-IV* for a number of disorders (such as major depressive disorder and a number of the anxiety disorders). Epidemiological information will be discussed at greater length throughout this book.

SOURCE: American Psychiatric Association (2000).

show lower and higher levels of problems in different areas of functioning.

EPIDEMIOLOGICAL RATES BASED ON THE DIMENSIONAL APPROACH

Dr. Tom Achenbach and colleagues (Achenbach, Howell, McConaughy, & Stanger, 1995a, 1995b, 1995c; Achenbach, Howell, Quay, & Conners, 1991; Achenbach & Rescorla, 2001) have conducted some of the most well-designed and comprehensive studies exploring children's and adolescents' functioning from a dimensional approach. Using measures such as the Child Behavior Checklist (CBCL; Achenbach & Rescorla, 2001), which is completed by parents, Achenbach and his colleagues have conducted large-scale national and international investigations into the occurrence of children's and adolescents' emotional/behavioral problems.

In order to understand children's and adolescents' functioning from a dimensional perspective, it is important to understand the distinction between internalizing and externalizing emotional/behavioral problems. **Internalizing problems** are feelings or behaviors that are overcontrolled and primarily experienced internally by the child (such as anxiety, depression, and withdrawal). **Externalizing problems** are behaviors that are undercontrolled and primarily experienced externally to the child (such as rule breaking and aggression). These two broad dimensions of children's and adolescents' emotional/behavioral functioning have been well established within the United States (Achenbach & Rescorla, 2001) as well as in many other countries (Heubeck, 2000).

A study of more than 3,200 parents' reports of matched clinical and nonclinical children revealed a number of items with clear distinctions between youth who were receiving mental health services and those who were not. Table 1.5 indicates that behaviors ranging from inattention to sadness were helpful in distinguishing troubled children from well-functioning children. As will be discussed in Chapter 5, on assessment, the use of a measure like the CBCL allows children's and adolescents' behavior to be compared with a normative sample and to be evaluated on a continuum. Although there are clinical cutoffs to help in the identification of troubled children and adolescents, this type of dimensional system allows children's and adolescents' behavior to be considered on a continuum rather than in a dichotomous or categorical fashion. It is interesting to note that the referral status of children (i.e., whether or not they were referred for therapy) was the most salient characteristic that showed dif-

TABLE 1.5 Gender, Age, and Race: Items on the Child Behavior Checklist That Showed More Than 20 Percent Difference in the Variance Between Children in Different Groups

Referred for Treatment vs. Not Referred

Can't concentrate, can't pay attention for long
Cruelty, bullying, or meanness to others
Disobedient at home
Disobedient at school
Doesn't get along with other kids
Breaks rules at home, school, or elsewhere
Impulsive or acts without thinking
Lying or cheating
Poor schoolwork
Sudden changes in mood or feelings
Temper or hot temper
Unhappy, sad, or depressed
Total problems

Note: When items were compared for boys and girls, no item showed a difference of more than 20% of the variance and, in fact, no item showed more than 6% of the variance on the Child Behavior Checklist. When younger children were compared with adolescents, no items showed a difference of greater than 20% and no item showed more than 10% variance. When items were compared for race/ethnicity and socioeconomic status, very few differences emerged.

Source: Achenbach & Rescorla, 2001.

ferences between the items. Differences between boys and girls were very limited, as were differences between younger and older children, youth from different racial and ethnic groups, and youth from higher versus lower socioeconomic brackets (Achenbach & Rescorla, 2001).

Table 1.6 presents the broadband and narrowband factors that have been established through empirically based assessments in national surveys of children and youth, ages 6 to 18. In a three-year follow-up study, there were strong correlations from adolescence to adulthood for most of these types of syndromes (Achenbach, Howell, McConaughy, & Stanger, 1995a, 1995b, 1995c).

Another way of exploring children's and adolescents' emotional/behavioral functioning is to conduct large-scale studies through a national sample, without attempting to recruit youth from clinical facilities. One such study collected information on 1,400 youth, ages 5–17, in a national sample in the United States (McDermott & Weiss, 1995). The researchers wanted to focus on the variability of children's and adolescents' behavior, with an eye toward all levels of functioning—not just the maladjusted end of the continuum. Based on teachers' ratings, 15.3% of the group showed good adjustment, where the youth were considered well functioning. A total of 28.9% showed adequate adjustment with some level of either inhibition, disruptiveness, apprehension, or

TABLE 1.6 Broadband and Narrowband Emotional/Behavioral Problem Factors from the Child Behavior Checklist, Youth Self-Report, and Teacher's Report Form

Internalizing Problems		Externalizing Problems
Anxious/depressed	Social problems	Rule-breaking behavior
Withdrawn/depressed	Thought problems	Aggressive behavior
Somatic complaints	Attention problems	

Note: In addition to these emotional/behavioral problem factors, there is also a measure of competence on each of these measures.
SOURCE: Achenbach & Rescorla, 2001.

indifference. There were an additional 34.4% who showed marginal adjustment with either withdrawal, motivation deficit, avoidance, attention-seeking behavior, moodiness, nonparticipation, or dependency. A total of 16.2% were shown to be at risk, with evidence of undersocialized aggression, oppositional behavior, provocative attention seeking, provocative manipulative behavior, impulsive aggressive behavior, or attention-deficit/hyperactivity behavior. The final 5.2% were considered to be maladjusted, with either instrumental aggressive behavior, defiant aggressive behavior, avoidant problems, or schizoid problems with depressed mood. Overall, there were 22 different levels of children's and adolescents' emotional/behavioral functioning, with a great deal of variation shown at all levels of the continuum of behavior. The 21.4% of children and adolescents who showed at-risk or maladjusted behavior were thought to be in need of mental health services (McDermott & Weiss, 1995). In addition, this study showed the immense variability of children's and adolescents' behavior and highlighted the importance of exploring behavior at all ends of the spectrum.

HOW CHILDREN'S ENVIRONMENTS INFLUENCE THEIR BEHAVIOR

Within the study of developmental psychopathology, there has been increasing interest in understanding the social context in which children's problematic behaviors occur (Adelman, 1995; Boyce et al., 1998; Steinberg & Avenevoli, 2000). Researchers recently began exploring children's and adolescents' behavior within a specific context in order to identify young people by environmental interactions such as different settings like home and school. In an intensive observational study of troubled children's social interactions at a therapeutic summer

camp, researchers found that children high in internalizing problems tended to withdraw in aversive situations with peers and adults, children with high externalizing problems tended to show higher rates of aggression toward peers but not adults, and children high in both internalizing and externalizing problems tended to show both withdrawal and aggression in reaction to their peers' talking and showed surprisingly little withdrawal when they were teased or threatened by their peers (Wright, Zakriski, & Drinkwater, 1999). This research highlights the reciprocal nature of children's behavior, and it allows an important investigation into the interactions between children and their environment (Adelman & Taylor, 1993; Keiley, Bates, Dodge, & Pettit, 2000; Wright & Zakriski, 2001). (Box 1.3 discusses a cross-cultural study that also relates to environmental context.)

A crucial aspect of children's and adolescents' environment is their **socioeconomic status (SES)**, which refers to a combination of factors, including the family's income, the parents' educational level, and the parents' occupational level (Luthar, 1999). SES and race/ethnicity are highly related within the United States. A total of 21.8% of children under 18 live at or below the poverty line within the United States. This figure varies according to race/ethnicity (Baugher & Lamison-White, 1996), where:

- 16.8% of Caucasian youth live in poverty.
- 45.9% of African American youth live in poverty.
- 40.4% of Hispanic/Latino/Latina youth live in poverty.

Throughout this book, whenever differences related to race and ethnicity are discussed, it will be important to keep in mind the confounding factor of family socioeconomic status. For example, rates of many types of psychopathology are higher in children from lower SES families, but it appears that the effects of poverty are even more severe for the mental health of African American children than children of other races and ethnicities (Luthar, 1999). In addition, the connection between children's mental health problems and lower SES may be mediated by harsh, inconsistent parenting and more severe stressors in the children's lives (McLoyd, 1998). As can be seen in Figure 1.2, children in the most severe poverty groups who live with a singe parent are exposed to more parental psychological symptoms than children in other groups (Urban Institute, 1999a). Thus, the issues of socioeconomic status, racial/ethnic identity, and mental health are very complex.

BOX *1.3*

CROSS-CULTURAL ISSUES: HOW DO PARENTS FROM DIFFERENT NATIONS FEEL ABOUT THEIR CHILDREN'S BEHAVIOR?

In an extraordinary series of investigations, Dr. John Weisz and his colleagues have investigated the similarities and differences between the behaviors of children in the United States and children in Thailand (Weisz & Weiss, 1991; Weis, Suwanlert, Chaiyasit, Weiss, Achenbach, & Trevatham, 1988; Reviewed in Weisz, McCarty, Eastman, Chaiyasit, & Suwanlert, 1997). One of the interesting findings to emerge from this project was the way in which parents perceive their children's behavior. Overall, parents from both countries felt that externalizing behaviors were more worrisome, more serious, and less likely to improve than internalizing problems. The accompanying figure shows interesting differences between parents in both countries. Specifically, parents in the United States rated children's behavior problems as more worrisome, more serious, less likely to improve, and more unusual than parents in Thailand. These findings were parallel to the findings from teachers in the United States and in Thailand. Overall, this research highlights the fact that there are both similarities and differences between parents and teachers in different nations and in different cultures. These similarities and differences are important to explore in order to gain a more complete understanding of children's and adolescents' problems and competencies.

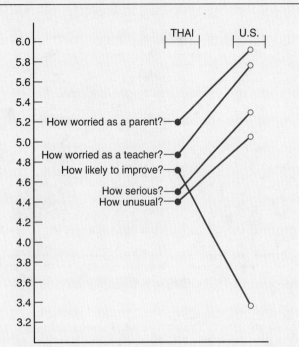

Parents' Perceptions of Child Behavior in Thailand and the U.S.

Source: Weisz, Suwanlert, Chaiyasit, Weiss, Walter & Anderson (1988).

Nothing that grieves us can be called little: by the eternal laws of proportion a child's loss of a doll and a king's loss of a crown are events of the same size.

—Mark Twain

DIFFERENT PERSPECTIVES ON PROBLEMS

Any discussion of children's and adolescents' emotional/behavioral functioning is not complete without considering the issue of who is distressed by the behavior. In a classic study, children receiving mental health services were compared with children not receiving mental services (Shepherd, Oppenheim, & Mitchell, 1971). The children were comparable on the severity of behavior problems, but the study sought to identify the factor that distinguished those who had been referred for services from those who had not been referred. As it turned out, mothers' perceptions of the severity of the problem, along with maternal competence, family dysfunction, and maternal depression were the primary factors that distinguished the two groups. This study suggests that the definition of problem behavior can be related to more than just the actual behavior.

Not surprisingly, youth, parents, and teachers differ on which behaviors are bothersome. In a school-based sample of young adolescents, adolescents thought that their parents would be much more distressed about adolescents' externalizing problems versus internalizing problems (Phares & Compas, 1990). Conversely, adolescents reported greater distress over their own internalizing problems than over their externalizing emotional/behavioral problems. In a special education clinical sample of adolescents with elevated emotional/behavioral problems, both parents and teachers reported more distress over externalizing behavior problems than did adolescents (Phares & Danforth, 1994). Parents reported greater distress than either teachers or adolescents about

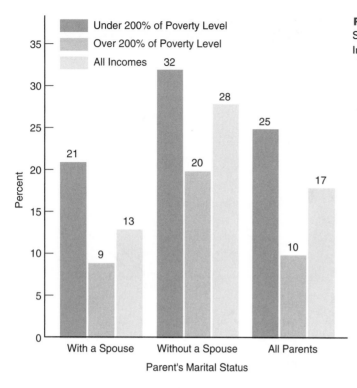

FIGURE 1.2 Children Living with a Parent Whose Symptoms Suggested Poor Mental Health, by Family Income and Parent's Marital Status, 1997

adolescents' internalizing problems. These studies suggest that a part of the evaluation process should include information about how different individuals feel about the child's or adolescent's behavior. Because children and adolescents rarely refer themselves for therapy, it is likely that most clinicians will hear more from parents who are distressed by their children's behavior regardless of how the children and adolescents feel about the behavior themselves.

If you really want to hear about it, the first thing you'll probably want to know is where I was born, and what my lousy childhood was like, and how my parents were occupied and all before they had me, and all that David Copperfield kind of crap, but I don't feel like going into it.

—J.D. Salinger

TROUBLED FAMILIES RATHER THAN TROUBLED CHILDREN

There is some evidence that exploring family issues can be at least as useful as exploring issues related to the individual child. In the 1950s and 1960s, when *DSM-I* was still being used, a number of researchers and therapists were trying to identify issues within the family that might be related to children's maladaptive behavior (Bateson, Jackson, Haley, & Weakland, 1956; Laing & Esterson, 1965). Emotional and behavioral problems were thought to be due to problems in the family's structure, rather than in the child her- or himself (Minuchin, Montalvo, Guerney, Rosman, & Schumer, 1967). In fact, family theorists argue that children's problems are primarily a reflection of actual problems that exist in the family (Cox & Paley, 1997; Dadds, 1995; Kaslow, 2001; L'Abate, 1994, 1998). Characteristics in families of troubled youth include:

- Parental psychopathology.
- Verbal and physical fighting between parents.
- Dysfunctional family structure.
- Troubled expression of emotions within the family.

These issues (reviewed in Kaslow, 2001; L'Abate, 1994, 1998) will be discussed in greater detail in Chapter 2 on theories and mechanisms, as well as throughout the book. As can be seen in the case study of Peta, cases that appear to be related to troubled behavior in the child can actually be due to troubled behavior patterns within the family.

Case Study: Is It Obsessive-Compulsive Disorder or a Troubled Family (or Both)?

Peta is an eight-year-old girl who meets diagnostic criteria for obsessive-compulsive disorder (OCD). Peta worries extensively about the loss of her belongings and about the death of family and friends close to her. Before leaving home in the morning, she checks the garbage to make sure that none of her belongings have been thrown out. Before leaving school in the afternoon, she checks and verifies that her pencils, papers, and books are located in the correct places. Her checking behaviors take at least an hour a day to complete, and they interfere with Peta's schoolwork and social relationships. Peta has shown this checking behavior for more than six months. Peta experiences a high level of anxiety until she conducts these checking rituals. Although she gains some relief from the anxiety when she checks her belongings, the anxiety soon returns and she needs to begin the rituals over again in order to get temporary relief from the anxiety.

If this information was presented with the focus on Peta (as it just was), the diagnosis of OCD would be given without question. There are a number of other factors, however, that might call the diagnosis into question.

Peta's parents, David and Liza, have had an unstable marriage in which David used to be physically violent toward Liza. Liza reported that she had been physically and sexually abused by her own father. In order to overcome her own difficult childhood, Liza has dedicated her life to caring for Peta and has become extremely involved in every aspect of Peta's life. David, however, makes all of the decisions for the family and is overtly disrespectful to Liza and her feelings. David thinks that Peta's problems are due to Liza's lack of discipline. Liza worries that Peta's problems are due to the history of schizophrenia, depression, alcohol abuse, and OCD in David's family. There have also been a number of significant losses in Peta's young life, including the death of her grandfather, with whom she was close; the severe illness of a favorite teacher; and the loss of three cats in car accidents. Peta's grandmother apparently teases her by saying that someone else in the family will die soon.

Overall, there are a number of factors that could be related to the development and maintenance of Peta's OCD behavior. She may have a genetic predisposition to psychopathology given the family history of psychopathology. There are a number of risk factors, such as spousal abuse, teasing, loss, and parental instability that could relate to her behavior. A family therapist would argue that Peta's problems are rooted in the dysfunction within the family rather than in Peta herself. This case should highlight the complex and multifaceted factors that can relate to children's and families' problems. When learning about each disorder in this book, it is essential to take the family context and social context into consideration in addition to understanding the individual's symptoms of psychopathology.

Source: Schwartz (1992).

Often the family environment can be harmful to children.

SUMMARY AND KEY CONCEPTS

Normality and Abnormality in Children and Adolescents

A central theme in this book, and in **developmental psychopathology** in general, is that you need to know what is normal before you can determine what is abnormal. Also central to the understanding of developmental psychopathology are the concepts of **risk factors** and **protective factors**, which can put the child at increased and decreased risk for the development of problems, respectively.

How Abnormal Child Behavior Was Understood in the Past

There is a long and troubled history of the treatment of children with psychological problems, which was often influenced by the **Zeitgeist**. From levying public scorn, to practicing **infanticide**, to abandoning troubled children in orphanages, the treatment of troubled children was less than humane throughout much of the history of Western civilization.

More Recent Diagnostic Classification Systems

The primary classification system in the United States is the *Diagnostic and Statistical Manual of Mental Disorders,* whose fourth edition is currently in use. Nationally and internationally, the *International Classification of Diseases (ICD-10)* is also used frequently. Early versions of the *DSM* system were biased by the belief that children were just miniature adults (a concept known as **adultomorphism**). More recently, there has been an attempt to be cognizant of the developmental processes that might influence disorders of childhood and adolescence. *DSM-IV*, intended to be **atheoretical**, allows the use of **differential diagnosis** in order to distinguish between two or more disorders in a child or adolescent. A strength of *DSM-IV* is that it allows the clinician to complete a **multiaxial evaluation**, which includes an evaluation of a possible **mental disorder** (or other conditions that are the focus of attention or treatment, known as **V-Codes**); personality disorder; mental retardation; general medical condition; psychosocial and environmental problem; and global functioning.

Reliability and Validity of Diagnostic Categories

Reliability (such as **test–retest reliability, inter-rater reliability**, and use of the **kappa statistic**) and **validity** refer to the **psychometric property** of a diagnostic system.

Children in the School System

Increasingly, professionals in the school system have had to deal with troubled children. Federal guidelines (such as PL 94-142, PL 99-457, PL 101-476, and PL 101-336) have protected the rights of special-needs children in the school system as well as in other settings.

Disorders in the Future of *DSM*

Research that will help inform the next revision of the *DSM* is being conducted continuously. Disorders such as mixed anxiety-depressive disorder and factitious disorder by proxy are all under consideration for inclusion in *DSM-V.*

Advantages and Disadvantages of *DSM-IV*

There are a great many strengths to the *DSM* system. The overarching strength of *DSM-IV* is the wide acceptance and use of the diagnostic language. The weaknesses of *DSM-IV* include the use of the **medical model**, the possible harm of **labeling** children's and adolescents' divergent behaviors, and the possibilities of children developing **self-fulfilling prophecies** due to receiving a diagnosis.

Differences Between Categorical and Dimensional Understandings of Behavior

DSM-IV is based on a **categorical approach** to classification of children's and adolescents' emotional/behavioral problems, in which behavior is classified into distinct diagnoses. In contrast, the **dimensional approach** views behavior in a continuous manner, where children and adolescents can show higher levels of some problems and lower levels of other problems and the problems are not classified into a distinct category. Dimensional approaches are largely influenced by **empirically based taxonomies**, which are conceptualizations of behavior based on research data.

Prevalence of Children's and Adolescents' Problem Behavior

The study of **epidemiology** includes the investigation of **prevalence** rates and **incidence** rates. Rates vary somewhat depending on whether you are exploring epidemiology from a categorical or a dimensional approach.

Epidemiological Rates Based on the Categorical Approach

The largest and most comprehensive study of epidemiology to date is the Methods for the Epidemiology of Child and Adolescent Mental Disorders (MECA) study. In many studies of epidemiology, high rates of **comorbidity** are found.

Epidemiological Rates Based on the Dimensional Approach

In the investigation of children's and adolescents' emotional/behavioral problems from a dimensional approach, it is crucial to understand that youngsters' problems fall into two primary areas: **internalizing problems** and **externalizing problems**.

How Children's Environments Influence Their Behavior

Another central theme in understanding children's behavior from a developmental psychopathology perspective is to understand the influence of environment and context. Individual characteristics, such as gender, age, race/ethnicity, and **socioeconomic status** are all crucial in understanding children's and adolescents' functioning.

Different Perspectives on Problems

Even with all of the sophisticated classification systems and dimensional conceptualizations of children's and adolescents' behavior, it is still important to reflect on different perspectives about children's and adolescents' behavior. It is imperative to determine the different perspectives of various individuals involved in the child's life.

Troubled Families Rather Than Troubled Children

In many cases, the child's problems are merely a reflection of a troubled family system. Factors such as parental psychopathology, interparental conflict and violence, dysfunctional family structure, and troubled expression of emotions within families are related to emotional/behavioral problems in children and adolescents.

KEY TERMS

developmental
   psychopathology
risk factors
protective factors
Zeitgeist
infanticide
adultomorphism
atheoretical

differential
   diagnosis
multiaxial
   evaluation
V-Codes
mental disorder
reliability
validity

psychometric
   property
test–retest reliability
inter-rater reliability
kappa statistic
medical model
labeling
self-fulfilling
   prophecies

categorical approach
dimensional
   approach
empirically based
   taxonomies
epidemiology
prevalence
incidence
comorbidity

internalizing
   problems
externalizing
   problems
socioeconomic
   status (SES)

SUGGESTED READINGS

Hayden, Torey, L. *One Child*. New York: Avon Books, 1980. Written by a compassionate special education teacher, this book chronicles the life of a severely emotionally disturbed girl who suffered extreme interfamilial abuse.

Shakur, Sanyika. *Monster: The Autobiography of an L.A. Gang Member*. New York: Penguin, 1993. This eloquent memoir illustrates both risk factors (such as living in poverty, racism, exposure to violence from an early age, and paternal absence) as well as protective factors later in life (such as faith and social support).

SUGGESTED VIEWINGS

Ordinary People (1980). Robert Redford (director), Alvin Sargent (screenwriter) based on novel by Judith Guest. VHS/DVD. This classic film illustrates the connections between family dysfunction and the well-being of an adolescent.

Down in the Delta (1998). Maya Angelou (director), Myron Goble (writer). VHS/DVD. This film highlights both risk factors (such as maternal substance abuse, poverty, and racism) and protective factors (such as strong family ties, role models, and faith).

CHAPTER 2

THEORIES OF NORMALITY AND ABNORMALITY IN CHILDREN AND ADOLESCENTS

CHAPTER SUMMARY

In violence, we forget who we are.

—Mary McCarthy

On April 20, 1999, 12 adolescents and one teacher were shot to death at Columbine High School in Littleton, Colorado, and 23 others were injured. The two gunmen, who killed themselves at the school, were students who reportedly felt that they had been teased too much.

During the same week as the Columbine massacre, a 14-year-old eighth grader, Dajuan Owens, was asleep in his bed in St. Louis, Missouri. Dajuan, his mother, and his siblings had become homeless recently, so they were staying with friends who took them in. At approximately 2:00 A.M., a 21-year-old man entered the house to pick up money that was owed to him by the homeowner's son. Although the son paid him the debt, an argument ensued and both individuals pulled out handguns and began firing. Dajuan was shot in the cross fire; he staggered to the front door and died on the sidewalk. It was not clear whose gun fired the bullet that hit him.

On September 11, 2001, three commercial U.S. airliners were hijacked and used as missiles to attack the World Trade Center's twin towers in New York and the Pentagon in Washington, D.C. A fourth hijacked plane may have been headed toward another target but crashed in a field in Pennsylvania. It is estimated that more than 3,000 people lost their lives in the September 11 attacks. Victims represented more than 80 countries. An estimated 2,000 infants, children, and adolescents lost at least one parent in the attacks, in many cases losing the only parent they had ever known. For example, 14-year-old Amy Vazquez, already a mother herself, lost her own mother (her baby's grandmother) that day (Jones, 2001).

Two months later, five Palestinian boys, ages 7 to 14, were playing peacefully in a refugee camp in the Gaza strip when a bomb exploded. The bomb killed them

Thousands of children were affected by the attacks on the twin towers of the World Trade Center.

instantly. The boys were all part of the same extended family (Associated Press, 2001).

In response to tragedies like the ones just described, most people have only one question: Why? The nation and much of the rest of the world asked this question after the massacre at Columbine High School in 1999 and the massacre of the plane crashes on September 11, 2001. A much smaller group of family and friends asked this question after Dajuan Owens got caught in the crossfire while he slept and after the five Palestinian boys were killed by the bomb as they played. That essential question—why—relates directly to the theories of abnormal or deviant behavior. (Box 2.1 discusses children and gun-related violence.)

Do not confuse the issue of violence, however, with that of emotional/behavioral difficulties in children and adolescents. Only a small percentage of children and adolescents with psychological problems show the type of violent behavior that results in another person's death

(Group for the Advancement of Psychiatry, 1999; Wiener, 1999). Similarly, only a small percentage of adults with psychological disorders show extremely violent behavior (Wiener, 1999). Conversely, a great number of adults without any diagnosable clinical disorder commit acts of violence (Wiener, 1999). Because of the way they process the information that is available to them, many people come to the erroneous conclusion that mental problems and violence are connected. After a tragedy that receives media attention, there is most often an investigation into whether or not the person or persons responsible for it had a history of psychological problems. If psychological problems were apparent, then the news stories highlight them. If psychological problems were not evident, then the stories highlight something else—without mentioning the fact that no psychological problems were evident. In addition, the vast majority of nonviolent children, adolescents, and adults who experience psychological problems remain unnoticed. Given the confidential nature of assessment and treatment of psychological problems, clinicians (or news reporters, for that matter) cannot highlight all of the accomplishments of people who have experienced psychological problems. Thus, many people are left with hearing only about horrific occurrences and not the quiet and productive lives of those who cope with their problems every day.

Because of importance of understanding why abnormal behavior occurs, this chapter covers the primary theories that relate to the development of problems in children and adolescents. Note, however, that no one theory predominates the field and that no one theory has been developed to explain all types of child and adolescent psychopathology. The chapter therefore covers theories related to specific disorders separately for those disorders. This discussion that follows is meant to give you a brief overview of the overarching theories of the development of psychopathology.

THE IMPORTANCE OF THEORY

A **theory** is a systematic set of statements designed to help analyze, explain, predict, and even suggest ways of controlling certain phenomena of interest. In the study of childhood disorders, the phenomena of interest are the different types of disorders. Even the most basic theory should serve a number of purposes, including:

- To understand the phenomena of interest.
- To predict future associations in relation to the phenomena of interest.

BOX 2.1

PREVENTION AND CULTURE

"Nearly Thirteen Children Die from Gunfire Every Day in America" was the subtitle of an article in the *CDF Reports* (a publication of the Children's Defense Fund) just a few months after the 1999 tragedy in Littleton, Colorado. Thirteen children die every day due to firearms, and an additional 50 are injured—and that is just in the United States. Homicide is the third leading cause of death among children ages 5 to 14, and the second leading cause of death among adolescents and young adults ages 15 to 24. These figures reach every race and ethnicity. Between 1968 and 1996, half of all gun homicides and 92% of the gun suicides in the United States were of Caucasian Americans. Homicide is the leading cause of death among African American males 14 to 24 years old.

There is a prevalent myth that gun homicides are committed by people who are strangers to the victim. The truth is that the majority of gun homicides are committed by family members, neighbors, or acquaintances. Children are much more likely to be killed by an adult than by another juvenile. They are also more likely to be killed in their own home or in the home of a friend than in school or in a public setting. In a recent survey, 59% of parents who acknowledged having a firearm in their house admitted that they did not keep the gun locked up and safely away from their children. Interestingly, in states that have enacted laws that make adults responsible for guns that are left accessible to children, there was an average of 23% fewer accidental shooting deaths of children under the age of 15 between 1990 and 1994.

Marian Wright Edelman, the president of the Children's Defense Fund, said:

Escalating violence against and by our children and youths is no coincidence. What we're witnessing is the cumulative, convergent, and heightened manifestation of a range of serious and too-long neglected problems. Factors such as poverty, economic inequality, racial intolerance, drug and alcohol abuse, domestic violence, violence in popular culture, births to unmarried mothers, and divorce all have contributed to the disintegration of the family, community, and spiritual values. If you add to these crises easy access to deadlier firearms, lonely and neglected children and youths left to fend for themselves by absentee parents of all races and income groups, gangs of inner-city and suburban young people relegated to the margins of American life without education, jobs, or hope, and political leadership that pays more attention to foreign than domestic enemies, and to the rich than to the poor, then you can understand the social and spiritual disintegration of American society that confronts us today.

After discussing the need for better education, support for families, and stricter control of access to guns, Edelman went on to encourage each person to make a difference: "It takes just one person to change a child's life. Those of us who care about children and the future of our country need to keep on working until we change the odds for all American children by making the violence of guns, poverty, preventable disease, and family neglect un-American."

SOURCE: *CDF Reports* (1999).

- To organize and interpret the research data that are collected in relation to the phenomena of interest.
- To generate future research into the phenomena of interest.

In evaluating the quality of a theory, there are a number of important characteristics to consider (summarized in Bordens & Abbott, 1988). A good theory:

- Accounts for the majority of the existing research information and data related to the phenomena of interest.
- Gives a relevant explanation that shows logical reasons for believing that the phenomena of interest would exist under the specified conditions.

- Can be tested for accuracy.
- Predicts new events and can incorporate new relevant phenomena.
- Provides parsimony, with the most direct and simple explanation possible (and the fewest assumptions and deductions) for the phenomena of interest.
- Provides logical consistency, where the theory does not contradict itself and where the theory shows internal consistency.

Theories are crucial for helping guide and evaluate research on developmental psychopathology (Rapport, 2001). Without theories, research data would be left open to the subjective interpretations of the researchers and of the consumers of the research. In a sense, theories are meant to keep researchers honest so that they will evaluate their findings in light of the other research done on that topic.

As Dr. Tom Achenbach (1982) has pointed out, "There is not now (and probably never will be) a *single* developmental theory of *all* psychopathology. Instead, the role of a developmental approach is to help us understand troublesome behavior in light of the developmental tasks, sequences, and processes that characterize human growth" (p. 1). Because of the wide range of children's problem behaviors (e.g., anxiety, abuse, distress, hyperactivity) and the wide range of domains in children's lives that require explanation (e.g., familial, educational, psychosocial, cognitive), it is likely that a matching number of theories will be required to explain the many types of developmental psychopathology (Rapport, 2001; Simeonsson & Rosenthal, 1992). In addition, there is a need to remain somewhat flexible with developmental theories of psychopathology, given that the best explanation of a particular disorder may be an integration of different facets from individual theories. It is possible that "mini-theories" will be needed for different components of each separate psychopathology (Kazdin, 1989).

Note that the theories presented in this chapter are meant to explain the **etiology**, or cause, of emotional/behavioral problems in children and adolescents. The reason that the word *cause* is rarely used in professional writing about developmental psychopathology is that the research methods necessary to suggest or prove causation are often unethical. As you will see in Chapter 4 on research methods, in order to argue causality, the researcher must conduct a study with an experimental design that assigns participants randomly to two or more groups. If differences are found between the groups after researchers manipulate the research variables, then researchers can say that their manipulation caused those differences. Without random assignment, some other factor besides the one being studied can influence the results.

If researchers wanted to argue, say, that physical abuse by parents causes emotional/behavioral difficulties in children, they would have to recruit healthy children into the study, assign them either to be abused by their parents or to not be abused by their parents, and then measure their emotional/behavioral difficulties at the end of the study. Such a study would not only be unethical for obvious reasons but also ridiculous to even contemplate. Given these constraints, researchers are left with having to rely on studies that show *connections* between physical abuse and emotional/behavioral difficulties as they occur naturally (Wolfe, 1999). These studies can refer only to the *relations* between physical abuse and emotional/

behavioral difficulties in children, but can not be used to argue that the abuse *caused* the children's emotional/behavioral difficulties. It could be that both the abuse and the emotional/behavioral difficulties are related to another factor, such as overall family distress, or dysfunctional parenting, or genetic loading that put the parent at risk for being abusive and put the child at risk for the development of emotional/behavioral problems.

This point about causation is crucial when discussing theories. Although theories attempt to explore the etiology of psychopathology within children and adolescents, most studies that test theories can do so only through correlational methods that prevent assumptions of causation. With this point in mind, the next sections explore the following etiological theories of developmental psychopathology: psychodynamic, biological and genetic, behavioral genetics, behavioral, cognitive-behavioral, family systems, social context and peer relationships, and developmental psychopathology.

PSYCHODYNAMIC THEORY

Psychodynamic theory was developed originally by Sigmund Freud (1894). Although the theory has, historically, influenced the field of developmental psychopathology, it has not been maintained as an active or effective theory in understanding the development of psychopathology in children and adolescents.

Freud proposed that children advance through a series of psychosexual stages and that if a child were to become stuck or fixated at one of these stages, then certain psychological problems would likely develop. The following are the psychosexual stages and related problems that Freud proposed would develop if a child became fixated at that stage:

- The **oral stage**, thought to occur within the first year of life, was defined as a time when infants focus on the world and get pleasure from food and objects through their mouth. Freud proposed that fixation at this stage could result from weaning the infant either too early or too late. Problems associated with oral fixation included overindulgence in food, alcohol, or cigarettes; childlike dependence; or the tendency to level severe sarcasm at others.

- The **anal stage**, thought to occur during toilet training in the second year of life, was characterized by the pleasure that develops from the anal region. Freud proposed that fixation at the anal stage could occur if toilet training was completed too early, too late, or in too harsh a manner. Fixation behaviors related to this stage were considered symbolic of withholding feces (such as being stingy, obsessive-compulsive, or too neat) or of expelling feces (such as being impulsive or explosive).

• The **phallic stage**, which Freud believed would occur between the ages of three and five, was characterized by children experiencing pleasure with their genitals. (The word *phallic* was used because Freud focused primarily on the development of boys rather than girls.) Freud argued that during this stage, a child would sexually desire the opposite sex parent and would want to literally or symbolically kill the parent of the same sex. This desire was known as the **Oedipus complex** in boys and the **Electra complex** in girls. According to Freud, because these murderous impulses were disturbing to the child, he or she would

begin to identify with the parent of the same sex and would repress the incestuous impulses toward the parent of the opposite sex. Note that these complexes were based on the development of heterosexual children and did not deal with the feelings of homosexual children. Fixation at the phallic stage was thought to be the result of unresolved issues that arose that during this stage and could result in long-standing problems with romantic relationships in adulthood or in difficulties with authority figures.

• The **latency period**, which was thought to occur between the age of five and sometime in adolescence, was characterized by the lack of attention to sexual pleasures or other sexual matters. Freud did not expand greatly on this stage, nor did he discuss in detail the problems that would occur from becoming fixated at the latency period.

BOX 2.2

PARENTAL GENDER: BLAMING MOTHERS AND IGNORING FATHERS

Inherent in a number of theories of developmental psychopathology is the idea that mothers are either directly or indirectly to blame for their children's troubled behavior (summarized in Phares, 1996, 1999). In the late 1940s, the term *schizophrenogenic mother* was used to describe a mother who "caused" schizophrenia in her child (Fromm-Reichmann, 1948). This type of mother was thought to be alternatively overinvolved and distant from her child. Another term, *refrigerator mother,* was also popularly used in the 1940s to describe a mother who "caused" autism in her child by being aloof and cold to the child (Kanner, 1943). Although these ideas have been shown to be completely inaccurate, remnants of blaming mothers and ignoring fathers remain in clinical research and clinical work even today.

In clinical research, mothers are studied to a much greater extent than fathers (Caplan & Hall-McCorquodale, 1985; Phares & Compas, 1992). A review of research published in well-respected empirical journals showed that 48% of clinical child research included mothers only, 26% included both mothers and fathers but analyzed them separately, 25% included "parents" without specifying mothers or fathers, and just 1% of the articles included fathers only (Phares & Compas, 1992). In dissertation research, 59% of the studies included mothers only, 30% included both parents, and 11% included fathers only (Silverstein & Phares, 1996). Interestingly, male researchers were more likely to include fathers in their research than were female researchers. No other characteristics (such as type of doctoral degree, gender of

adviser, or area of research) were related to the likelihood of including fathers in dissertation research (Silverstein & Phares, 1996).

Therapists also tend to ignore fathers and inadvertently blame mothers in clinical practice. A number of therapists even neglect to invite fathers into therapy sessions that are meant to help deal with the child's emotional/behavioral problems (Hecker, 1991). Unfortunately, mothers and fathers have also taken on some of these beliefs about mothers' responsibility for children's emotional/behavioral problems. Two studies that investigated parents' perceptions of blame for their children's emotional/behavioral problems found that mothers blamed themselves and fathers blamed mothers (Penfold, 1985; J. Watson, 1986).

Overall, there has been a long history of blaming mothers and ignoring fathers for children's and adolescents' emotional/behavioral difficulties. Because it is rarely advantageous to place blame, however, many professionals have moved toward trying to understand the systems in which children's problems have developed (e.g., the family system, the school system, the community). In addition, many problems in childhood cannot be "blamed" on any one factor. The multitude of theories related to the development of psychopathology in children and adolescents suggest that it is rare for only one factor to be identified as the sole etiology of any type of psychopathology. As a result, it is important not to blame mothers (or fathers) but instead to look for ways in which children can be helped.

- The **genital stage**, Freud said, would occur during adolescence at the onset of sexual desires and impulses. Again, the genitals would become the focus of pleasurable activities. Given that this stage was thought to remain into adulthood and was thought to be the healthy outcome of development, fixation at this stage was not considered problematic.

Overall, Freud's psychodynamic theory and resultant psychodynamic therapies helped establish the field of psychology. In addition, Freud's focus on childhood in relation to adult development was helpful in focusing attention on the importance of a healthy childhood (see also Box 2.2).

More recent psychodynamic theorists have focused on **object relations theory**, which highlights the importance of the infant's relationship with the parent or caregiver (Fonagy, 1998). Object relations theorists such as Margaret Mahler (1968) and Melanie Klein (1957) argued that individuals' perceptions of themselves and of the world are formulated from their first relationship with their primary caregiver. If this relationship was healthy (i.e., the primary caregiver was stable, nurturing, accepting of the infant, and encouraging of the infant's and child's growing independence), then the infant would grow into a psychologically healthy individual. If this relationship was troubled (i.e., the primary caregiver was inconsistent, too demanding, or not involved enough), then the infant would grow into an individual with troubled emotions and behaviors. Currently, the object relations segment of the psychodynamic theory is followed to

some extent, but is not as prevalent as other theories related to the development of psychopathology in children and adolescents.

Attachment theory, which is related to the theory of object relations, focuses on attachments between the infant and primary caregiver. The original theory of attachment was developed by such theorists as Bowlby (1969) and Ainsworth (Ainsworth, Blehar, Waters, & Wall, 1978). The basic premise was that infants are attached to their primary caretaker(s) in a manner that impacts children's emotional well-being throughout their lives. Both this early work and more recent research have identified two basic types of infant–caretaker attachment. The first, **secure attachment**, is shown when the infant uses the parent as a base from which to explore a new environment. After being separated from the parent, a securely attached infant will welcome the parent's return with happiness and joy. Parents with securely attached infants are usually stable, sensitive to the infant's needs, and responsive (Cassidy & Shaver, 1999; Karen, 1994). The second type, **anxious insecure attachment**, is itself split into three primary types: avoidant attachment (where the infant ignores or avoids the parent after a separation); ambivalent attachment (where the infant shows distress when the parent leaves, but shows anger or rejection when the parent returns); and **disorganized attachment** (where the infant shows an inconsistent pattern of attachment, sometimes reaching out for the returning parent without looking at him or her and sometimes rejecting the parent altogether).

Infants can show equally strong attachment to their father as well as their mother.

The attachment relationship is thought to serve as a template for relationships in later childhood and adulthood (Karen, 1994; Sroufe, Carlson, Levy, & Egeland, 1999; Waters, Hamilton, & Weinfield, 2000). Intervening factors, however—such as parental divorce, loss of a parent, parental or child illness, and parental psychopathology—can change the course of attachment (Hamilton, 2000; Waters, Merrick, Treboux, Crowell, & Albersheim, 2000). Aside from these intervening factors, attachment during infancy is related to later outcomes. For example, anxious insecure attachment styles are associated with the development of psychopathology (Cicchetti, Rogosch, & Toth, 1997; Greenberg, DeKlyen, Speltz, & Endriga, 1997). Insecure attachment puts children at risk for further complications throughout their lives (Solomon & George, 1999; Sroufe et al., 1999). Disordered attachment has been linked to conduct disorder, hyperactivity, and physical abuse (Cicchetti et al., 1997). In addition, parental psychopathology is linked to the type of attachments parents have with their infants (Cicchetti et al., 1997). Overall, attachment theory has been helpful in exploring the early parent–child relationship in relation to later functioning in the child and adolescent. Note, however, that secure attachment is defined differently in various cultures, so cultural sensitivity is necessary when conducting research on attachment (Rothbaum, Weisz, Pott, Miyake, & Morelli, 2000).

If you know his father and grandfather, don't worry about his son.

—Proverb of Africa

GENETIC AND BIOLOGICAL THEORIES OF DEVELOPMENTAL PSYCHOPATHOLOGY

Later chapters address specific genetic and biological theories related to various disorders. This section considers the general principles used in research on genetic and biological theories.

The rationale behind most genetic theories is that genes inherited from biological parents play a central role in the development of emotional/behavioral problems in children and adolescents (Goldsmith & Gottesman, 1996; Hewitt, Silberg, et al., 1997; Plomin & Crabbe, 2000; State, Lombroso, Pauls, & Leckman, 2000). Before discussing types of genetic research, let us define some common terms. The word **genotype** refers to a child's genetic makeup. **Phenotype** refers to the set of observable characteristics in a child that are created from the interaction of heredity and environment. **Heritability** is the proportion of variation is a given trait (such as intelligence) that is genetic, or inherited, rather than environmental. It is calculated by dividing the variance due to genotype by the variance due to phenotype. Thus, heritability estimates are usually given in the form of a proportion that ranges from 0 (no genetic influence) to 1.0 (perfect genetic correspondence). Of course, most psychological and behavioral characteristics are between 0 and 1 rather than at either extreme.

One of the primary methods used to investigate genetic contribution to the development of psychopathology is to study **monozygotic (MZ) twins** (known as identical twins) and **dizygotic (DZ) twins** (known as fraternal twins) who were raised either in the same or different environments. Monozygotic twins develop from the same fertilized egg, so they both have the same genotype. Dizygotic twins, who develop from separate eggs, have 50 percent of shared genetic material on average. Every human, twin or not, has a different phenotype, given that one's phenotype is a combination of both genes and the environment. Thus, studying twins reared together and apart can help clarify the genetic contributions and the environmental contributions to the development of psychopathology in children and adolescents. In essence, the correspondence rates between identical twins are compared with the correspondence rates between fraternal twins, nontwin siblings, biological parents, adoptive parents, and other relatives.

In research with twins, one of the basic formulas used to estimate of the heritability of a particular characteristic is as follows:

$$
\begin{array}{ll}
\text{Difference between} & = \text{Genetic effects} + \\
\quad \text{DZ twins' scores} & \quad \text{Environmental effects} \\
- \text{Difference between} & = \text{Environmental effects} \\
\quad \text{MZ twins' scores} & \\
\hline
& = \text{Genetic effects}
\end{array}
$$

The idea is that DZ twins differ in both genetic and environmental effects, whereas MZ twins differ only in environmental effects (Achenbach, 1982). Thus, with regard to a given characteristic or disorder, the differences between the sets of DZ twins and MZ twins helps identify the genetic contributions to that characteristic or disorder. There are caveats to this research design, however. Because MZ twins appear to spend more time together, to engage in similar activities, and to be treated by others in similar ways, their environmental experience is more similar than that of DZ twins or nontwin siblings (Lombroso, Pauls, & Leckman, 1994; State et al., 2000).

Adoption studies compare both DZ and MZ twins who are raised apart and those who are raised together. Environmental effects can be controlled somewhat with this method, assuming that twins raised in different households would not necessarily share any common environmental effects. Note, however, that a complicating factor in adoption studies is that children who are adopted tend to be overrepresented in outpatient mental health centers when compared to their nonadopted peers (B. C. Miller, Fan, Christensen, Grotevant, & vanDulmen, 2000; B. C. Miller, Fan, Grotevant, Christensen, Coyl, & vanDulmen, 2000).

Twin studies have found certain disorders (such as schizophrenia and bipolar disorder), and many temperamental and personality characteristics (such as anger proneness, positive emotionality, emotional regulation) to be highly genetically related (Comings, 1997; Depue, Collins, & Luciana, 1996; Goldsmith & Gottesman, 1996; State et al., 2000; Zahn-Waxler, Schmitz, Fulker, Robinson, & Emde, 1996). In adoption studies of many personality and behavioral characteristics (e.g., adjustment scores, extroversion, neuroticism, aggression, behavioral inhibition), MZ twins reared apart continue to show higher correspondence than DZ twins reared together (Achenbach, 1982; Goldsmith & Gottesman, 1996; State et al., 2000).

A number of studies have suggested genetic loading for a variety of disorders in childhood and adolescence.

The following specific findings highlight the diversity of studies that support genetic influences in developmental psychopathology:

- Some studies suggest that genetic contributions to certain disorders (schizophrenia, bipolar affective disorder, and autism) are higher than 75% (Rutter, Silberg, O'Connor, & Simonoff, 1999b).
- Attention-deficit/hyperactivity disorder is highly influenced by genetic factors, even in adolescence (Eaves et al., 1997).
- Conduct disorder is linked genetically, as well as environmentally, to parental substance abuse and antisocial personality disorder (Merikangas, Dierker, & Szatmari, 1998).
- Anxiety disorders and fears may be more heavily genetically loaded for girls than for boys (Lichtenstein & Annas, 2000).
- Rates of comorbidity suggest some genetic loading (Simonoff, 2000).
- Genetics may influence the level of socioeconomic status that people attain (Lichtenstein & Pedersen, 1997).
- Children's adjustment to parental divorce is influenced by genetics to some extent (O'Connor, Caspi, DeFries, & Plomin, 2000).

Case Study: D.S., A Child with Down's Syndrome

One example of a problem that develops from chromosomal abnormalities is Down's syndrome, which is caused by an extra chromosome. Specifically, children born with a trio rather than a pair of chromosome 21 will be born with Down's syndrome. Intellectual functioning of individuals with Down syndrome usually ranges between 40 and 50 (based on an intelligence quotient [IQ] where 100 is average), although functioning can be much higher or much lower. As will be seen in Chapter 14, mental retardation is diagnosed when the IQ is below 70 and when there are deficits in adaptive functioning, all of which are present before the age of 18. Children with Down's syndrome also share several distinctive physical traits: thick facial features, thick folds in the eyelids, a tongue that protrudes slightly, and a noticeable large crease in the palms of the hands. Quite often, unrelated children with Down's syndrome look more like each other than they look like their own family members.

D.S. is a 15-year-old boy who displays all of the physical and intellectual signs of Down's syndrome. His IQ is 45. He is a large boy, at about five feet nine inches tall and almost 200 pounds. From the time he was 8, D.S. has attended special schools and has lived away from home. Each time his parents would visit, he would beg to be taken home. "Mommy, take me

home" was D.S.'s most common response when he saw his mother on visiting days. Racked with guilt, his mother would take him home about once a year with the idea of raising him there. Soon, however, D.S. would become unmanageable, and his mother would have to admit him into yet another special school.

When D. S. was 11 years old, his parents divorced and his father moved to another state. D.S. does not have any brothers or sisters.

About six months ago, D.S.'s mother again tried to take care of him at home. She recently took him to an emergency room and pleaded, "You've got to admit him; I just can't take it anymore." Over those six months at home, D.S. had shown more and more behavioral problems. He began to lose his temper quite often, and he had angry outbursts and tantrums that his mother could not control. On more than one occasion, D.S. hit his mother when she tried to stop him from acting out. For example, D.S. recently was banging a broom on the apartment floor; when his mother tried to stop him, he hit her on the shoulders and arms. D.S.'s mother felt that she had no other alternative than to place him in a special setting again.

SOURCE: Spitzer, Gibbon, Skodol, Williams, & First (1994).

Overall, these studies suggest a high amount of heritability in some characteristics but limited amounts of heritability in other characteristics.

The other influence that is often linked with genetic contributions in the development of psychopathology relates to biological contributions to the development of disorders (Birbaumer & Flor, 1998; Mash & Dozois, 1996; Rutter, Silberg, O'Connor, & Simonoff, 1999a; Skuse, 2000). The study of biological influences includes, but is not limited to, the study of the connection between psychological and behavioral processes in relation to:

- Physiological mechanisms.
- Brain structure and functioning.
- Central nervous system functioning.
- Neuroendocrinology (including hormones and the immune system).
- Neuropharmacological mechanisms.
- Maturational rates (especially, the onset of puberty).

It is rare to find a clinical disorder that is considered to be due solely to biological influences. For example, although there have been extensive studies that utilize neuroimaging (such as magnetic resonance imaging) on children with developmental disorders like autism, reading disorders, and attention-deficit/hyperactivity disorder, none of these disorders has been linked to clear-cut, discrete focal lesions or other structural differences in the brain (Filipek, 1999). There are, however, a number of biological factors that have been linked to different facets of clinical disorders. For example, impaired attention is thought to be due to biological factors in relation to the development of schizophrenia (Cornblatt, Dworkin, Wolf, & Erlenmeyer-Kimling, 1996) and in relation to attention-deficit/hyperactivity disorder (Barkley, 1997b; Klorman, 1995). In addition, the differential gender rates of depression before and after puberty have been linked to biological factors to some extent (Emslie, Weinberg, Kennard, & Kowatch, 1994). Also note that there is some evidence of influences related to evolutionary biology in some disorders, such as dyslexia (i.e., reading disorders), autism, and attention-deficit/hyperactivity disorder (Leckman & Mayes, 1998).

Parents are like shuttles on a loom. They join the threads of the past with threads of the future and leave their own bright patterns as they go.

—Fred Rogers (Mr. Rogers)

BEHAVIORAL GENETICS

Closely linked to the study of genetics is the study of **behavioral genetics**. Although many researchers use the terms *genetics* and *behavioral genetics* synonymously (Lenzenweger & Haugaard, 1996), this chapter looks at them separately in order to highlight the distinct contributions of the study of behavioral genetics. Behavioral genetics focuses on the connections between inherited genetic influences and environmental influences in relation to the development of psychopathology. Thus, behavioral genetics is the study of the interaction of genetics and the environment. Currently, it is rare to find any researchers who argue solely for the role of genetic factors or solely for the role of environmental factors in the development of psychopathology (Maccoby, 2000). Given the wealth of knowledge about both genetic and environmental factors, it is more common for researchers to try to understand the different contributions of both genetic heritability (i.e., nature) and the environment (i.e., nurture). Rather than asking if a certain disorder is related to nature or nurture, the more logical question is, "To what extent are given behaviors due to variations in genetic endowment, variations within the environment, or the interaction between these two factors?" (Mash & Dozois, 1996, p. 46).

Behavioral geneticists have made exciting contributions to the understanding of environmental influences. Not only do researchers in behavioral genetics explore genetic influences, but they explore environmental influences in a number of ways. Specifically, researchers acknowledge that children raised in the same household do not always experience the same environment (Feinberg & Hetherington, 2000; Feinberg, Neiderhiser, Simmens, Reiss, & Hetherington, 2000). Think about your brothers or sisters, if you have any. Chances are that, although there were similarities in the family environment in which you all grew up, there were also differences. Maybe you were the oldest child and your parents were more strict with you than they were with your younger siblings. Or maybe your sibling was born at a time when your parents were particularly distressed with each other but you were born at a time when your parents were getting along well. These examples highlight the different family environments that siblings can experience. The term **shared environment** refers to the common experiences in siblings' environments, such as living in the same house, living in the same neighborhood, and having the same family traditions. The term **nonshared environment** refers to the unique aspects of the family that each sibling experiences differently, such as being a favored child by one or both parents, or having higher or lower amounts of attention and financial resources at a particular developmental point.

In a book entitled *Separate Lives: Why Are Siblings So Different,* Judy Dunn and Robert Plomin (1990) summarized a number of interesting findings from the behavioral genetics research literature. For example, although the development of schizophrenia is thought to be due largely to genetic factors, there is more to it than that. Twin and adoption studies have suggested that the percentage of variance that accounts for the development of schizophrenia is 45% nonshared environment, 40% genetic, 5% shared environment, and 10% unknown (or measurement error). This distribution is presented graphically in the pie chart in Figure 2.1. Thus, even a disorder that is thought to be highly genetically related is also highly environmentally related in terms of the nonshared environment.

More recently, a number of disorders have been studied within a behavioral genetic theoretical framework, including delinquency (Slomkowski, Rende, Conger, Simons, & Conger, 2001); conduct disorder (Lytton, 2000), attention-deficit/hyperactivity disorder (Faraone & Biederman, 2000); and anxiety disorders (Lichtenstein & Annas, 2000). Overall, there is evidence of combined influences between genetics, shared environment, and nonshared environment in the development of psychopathology. Note, however, that behavioral genetics research has been criticized for focusing too much on the genetics side of the equation and not enough on the environmental (and especially, parenting) side of the equation (Collins, Maccoby, Steinberg, Hetherington, & Bornstein, 2000; Maccoby, 2000).

The thing that impresses me most about America is the way parents obey their children.

—King Edward VIII (Duke of Windsor)

BEHAVIORAL THEORIES AND DEVELOPMENTAL PSYCHOPATHOLOGY

Behavioral theories of developmental psychopathology began primarily with John B. Watson's (1913) suggestion that most human behavior was governed by the consequences that followed the behavior. Thus, according to Watson, behavioral tendencies were learned and not inherited. In addition, Watson highlighted the importance of exploring observable behaviors rather than internal, subjective processes. With regard to the development of psychopathology, Watson demonstrated that a child, known as Little Albert, could be conditioned to fear a previously neutral stimulus (a fluffy white rat) by pairing it with an aversive experience (a loud bang). Over time, Little Albert showed a fear response not only to white rats but also to rabbits and even to a Santa Claus beard (Watson & Rayner, 1920). This work led to the idea that most, if not all, psychopathologies were the result of behavioral conditioning.

Since the time of Watson's studies, there has been growing awareness that some disorders are more linked to behavioral contingencies than others (reviewed in Achenbach, 1982). Phobias (March, 1995); enuresis (Caddy & Bollard, 1988); and certain oppositional problems in children (Barkley, 1997d) continue to be linked strongly to behavioral contingencies. Imagine the following scenario in your local grocery store:

- James, a cute four-year-old, and his father are in the cookie aisle.

- James says, "I want lots of chocolate Koala Yummie Bears."

FIGURE 2.1   The Different Sources of Variance That Account for the Development of Schizophrenia

Source: Dunn & Plomin (1990).

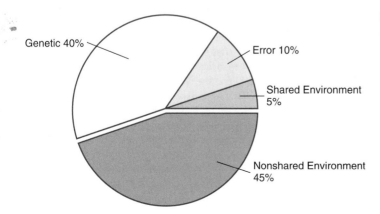

Genetic 40%

Error 10%

Shared Environment 5%

Nonshared Environment 45%

- James's father says, "No, we already have fruit for dessert at home."

- James grabs a package of Koala Yummie Bears and replies loudly, "I want Yummie Bears!"

- James's father again firmly says, "No, you cannot get the Yummie Bears," as he returns the cookies to the shelf.

- James grabs for the Yummie Bears and knocks down a number of other boxes of cookies off the shelf, yelling, "Give me my Yummie Bears!"

- James's father says loudly, "James put those Yummie Bears back."

- James then starts stomping on the boxes on the floor and begins yelling, "Yummie Bears! Yummie Bears! Yummie Bears!"

- Exasperated, James's father says, "Okay, you can have your Koala Yummie Bears," as he quickly tries to put the smashed boxes back on the shelves while avoiding the stares of onlooking shoppers.

James's father has inadvertently rewarded James's bad behavior (yelling and throwing a tantrum) by giving him what he wanted in the form of a tangible reinforcement (delicious chocolate Koala Yummie Bears). Behavioral principles would suggest that this scenario will create a likelihood for James's bad behavior to occur again in the future. A number of oppositional and defiant behaviors are inadvertently created in children by adults who do not realize what they are doing (Barkley, 1997d). As we will see in the chapter on therapies and interventions, many behavioral therapies are effective for disorders that seem to be linked to behavioral contingencies.

COGNITIVE-BEHAVIORAL THEORIES AND DEVELOPMENTAL PSYCHOPATHOLOGY

Although many disorders have been linked to behavioral contingencies, many other disorders have been linked to the combination of behavioral and cognitive processes. The idea behind cognitive-behavioral theories is that observable behavior can be influenced by mental processes. In other words, how an individual acts and feels may be related to how the individual thinks about the situation. Much of the work on cognitive-behavioral theories started with Dr. Aaron Beck's (1976) development of the cognitive theory of depression in adults. Beck argued that clients often have distorted negative cognitions (i.e., thoughts) about themselves, the world, and the future. The more the clients focus on these negative thoughts, the more depressed they will become. Cognitive-behavioral theorists have added a behavioral component to these cognitive theories, with regard to conceptualizing depression as well as many other disorders (e.g., Kaslow, Brown, & Mee, 1994; Kendall & Braswell, 1993; Lochman & Dodge, 1994). Not only might a depressed child experience distorted cognitions and an attributional style that is likely to exacerbate the depression, but he or she might also have discontinued previously enjoyable activities and thereby further

---

Case Study: Regina, Who Has the "Terrible Twos" as a Six-Year-Old

Regina was six years old when her parents brought her to a psychology clinic for help. Her parents reported that she was "ruining their marriage" due to her outbursts and poor behavioral control. Both parents were personally dedicated to Regina, but they both appeared to be overwhelmed by her behavior. The father thought that the mother spoiled Regina and did not provide consistent discipline. The mother reported that she tried to do her best with Regina.

Regina had always been considered a difficult child. Her parents seemed to think that she had never outgrown the "terrible twos." They reported that she was extremely difficult and demanding. Regina often ruined family activities due to her misbehavior. In addition, when playing with friends at home, Regina would often throw a tantrum and the children would be sent home. Her teachers had her play by herself at school because she seemed to annoy the other students. Both at home and at school, Regina would throw things or slap people when she did not get her way. Many times she was given what she wanted after her outbursts.

During the first interview at the clinic, Regina seemed to enjoy the individual attention of the clinician, but she showed herself to be very demanding. In addition, she refused to help clean up the toys after the session was over and she demanded that she be allowed to take a number of toys home with her even after she was told that she could not do so.

From a behavioral perspective, Regina had inadvertently been rewarded for her problematic behaviors. It could have been that the parents gave in to her demands when she was younger and then felt it necessary to continue giving in to her demands when she was older. Behavioral parent training (Barkley, 1997d) would probably be the most beneficial treatment to alleviate Regina's acting-out behaviors.

SOURCE: Rapoport & Ismond (1996).

increased feelings of depression (Kaslow et al., 1994). Imagine the following scenario:

- Rosa, a beautiful and intelligent 14-year-old girl, is somewhat sad because her parents have not been getting along very well lately.
- At school, a boy she likes does not say hello to her in the hallway, even though she smiles at him.
- Rosa automatically thinks that the boy does not like her, and she further reasons that she is not worthy of being liked (because, she thinks, she is dumb, unattractive, and chubby).
- A few minutes later, a group of her friends invite Rosa to go to the mall after school to watch a movie.
- Even though she used to enjoy hanging out with her friends, Rosa declines their offer because she does not feel like she will be good company for them.
- Instead, Rosa stays alone in her room after school and thinks about how she'll never have a boyfriend and wonders if she'll have any friends when she gets older.

This scenario illustrates a number of salient components of cognitive-behavioral theories, especially related to the development and maintenance of depression. Rosa shows negative **automatic thoughts**, which are immediate, unquestioned thoughts that individuals experience when faced with a new or recurrent situation or event. In this situation, Rosa immediately thought that the boy did not like her because he did not say hello. That explanation may have been accurate, but it is also possible that the boy did not see Rosa or that the boy likes her but is too shy to speak with her. As will be discussed in Chapter 6, on therapies and interventions, a therapist would try to help Rosa develop other plausible alternative thoughts that might counteract her negative automatic thoughts.

Rosa also showed **cognitive distortions**, which are thoughts that are distorted or otherwise changed from reality. Given that Rosa is actually beautiful and intelligent, Rosa's thinking that she is dumb, unattractive, and chubby is probably a distortion of reality. In addition, given that she has friends who invited her to the mall, she probably has little reason to be concerned about not having friends in the future. Cognitive distortions appear to help develop and maintain depressive symptomatology (Leitenberg, Yost, & Carroll-Wilson, 1986). Finally, the behavioral part of cognitive-behavioral theory was evidenced by Rosa's decision not to go to the mall with her friends. Although Rosa used to enjoy going to the mall, she declined the offer, which limits the possibility of her experiencing pleasant events (Hollon & Beck, 1994). When children withdraw from activities that used to be pleasurable, they limit their opportunity to experience joy

---

BOX 2.3

TROUBLED CHILDREN IN THE SCHOOL SETTING

Increasingly, teachers and other school professionals are being called upon to identify and treat troubled children. In a book on school-based cognitive-behavioral interventions for childhood depression, Kevin Stark (1990) gives the following examples:

- An English teacher becomes concerned about a student whose journal entries focus solely on death and self-hatred.
- A beautiful sixth-grade girl, who is active in volleyball, cheerleading, and academic excellence, reports to everyone who will listen that she is fat, ugly, stupid, and not worthy of friends.
- A fourth-grade boy is taken to the nurse's office because he falls asleep in class, complains of headaches, and looks tired constantly.
- The grades of a fifth-grade girl drop suddenly, and she is known to alienate herself from peers and to run away from home occasionally.

- A third-grader hides under his desk frequently and cries.
- An art teacher becomes alarmed when a student draws a picture of himself on top of a tall building, looking down at the sidewalk far below him.

Teachers not only deal frequently with attention-deficit/hyperactivity disorder and learning disorders but are also exposed to all types of psychopathology in children and adolescents (as well as in parents). Many children and adolescents can be helped in the school setting via group cognitive-behavioral therapies that focus on their thoughts, feelings, and actions. Although these techniques are usually conducted by school psychologists, teachers are a crucial piece of the puzzle because they are often the ones to notice troubled children before anyone else does. Many school psychologists have tried to help train teachers to identify children and adolescents at risk for the development of psychopathology (Stark, 1990).

Families can provide both strengths and weaknesses in children's development.

and happiness. In cognitive-behavioral therapy, the therapist would not only work on helping Rosa to change her cognitions but also help her increase her opportunities for pleasurable experiences (Kaslow, Brown, & Mee, et al., 1994). Note that cognitive-behavioral theories have also been applied to emotional/behavioral problems that are evident in the classroom (Wahlberg, 1998). (Box 2.3 discusses the school setting in particular.) Because of the limited cognitive development in young children, however, cognitive-behavioral theories have not been used extensively with very young children (Kendall & Braswell, 1993).

Sticks in a bundle are unbreakable.

—Proverb of Africa

THEORIES OF FAMILY FUNCTIONING AND ABNORMAL BEHAVIOR IN CHILDREN AND ADOLESCENTS

The previous section's cognitive-behavioral description of Rosa's experience focused almost solely on Rosa (i.e., her cognitions, her interpretation of events, the behavior in which she engaged). You might have wondered about the issue that was making her sad, namely, that her parents were not getting along very well. From a family theory perspective, Rosa is the **identified problem**, or identified patient, who is showing problems that are reflective of troubles within the family system (Cox & Paley, 1997).

Most family theorists argue that the majority of problems shown in children and adolescents are due to problems within the family structure and that the child or adolescent is expressing problems (usually unintentionally) so that the family can get the help it needs. Note that the concept of "family" is defined broadly by most family theorists to include a diversity of family constellations, such as families in which the parents are divorced or were never married, single-parent families, stepfamilies, families where the children are being raised by a grandparent or other relative, or families headed by lesbian or gay male couples (L'Abate, 1998).

Family theories have existed in the mainstream of psychology and education for more than 40 years (Lebow & Gurman, 1998; Wamboldt & Wamboldt, 2000). Although there are a number of different theories of family functioning (e.g., N. W. Ackerman, 1958; Bateson et al., 1956; Bowen, 1978; Haley, 1976; Minuchin, 1974; Satir, 1983; Selvini-Palazzoli, Boscolo, Cecchin, & Prata, 1978), there are certain central themes (summarized in Cox & Paley, 1997; L'Abate, 1998) that apply to nearly all family theories of the development of psychopathology:

- Children's problems are a reflection of problems within the family or within the parents' relationship.

- Families have a tendency to want to maintain **homeostasis** (i.e., to stay the same) even when distressing patterns have emerged.

- Structures within the family (e.g., children having more power and control than parents) or alliances within the family (e.g., a son and a noncustodial father being allied against a caretaking mother and a daughter) are often disrupted in troubled families.

- Communication styles are often disrupted in families with problems, such as sharing too much or not enough information with each other, or expressing too many or too few emotions when communicating with each other.

- Issues related to personal distance and closeness are often problematic in troubled families. **Enmeshed families** show too much closeness, **disengaged families** show too much distance.

Cultural and ethnic/racial differences and similarities in families are also of central importance (Hall & Barongan, 2002; McGoldrick, Giordano, & Pearce, 1996; Rothbaum, Morelli, Pott, & Liu-Constant, 2000). This point is relevant both within and outside of the United States (Rey et al., 2000). Historically, a "healthy" family system was based on the model of a middle-class white family of Western European descent, with the idea that a fair amount of emotional distance was appropriate (McGoldrick & Giordano, 1996). Many families from other cultural backgrounds were labeled as enmeshed and troubled when compared with this biased ideal. More recently, researchers and writers have highlighted the importance of understanding and respecting the cultural and ethnic/racial heritage of families (Hall & Barongan, 2002; L'Abate, 1998; McGoldrick et al., 1996). With this concept in mind, many family therapists now try to understand both the family system and the cultural and contextual system from which the family developed (see Box 2.4).

BOX 2.4

ETHNICITY, FAMILIES, AND CULTURE

In order to think more personally about ethnicity, culture, and families, you might want to consider answering some of the following questions for yourself:

- How would you describe yourself ethnically?
- Who in your family experience most influenced your sense of ethnic identity?
- Which ethnic group, other than your own, do you think you understand the best?
- Which general characteristics of your ethnic group do you like the most, and which do you like the least?
- How do you think that your own family would react when asked to attend family therapy?

These are questions that are often used to train family therapists in ethnic and cultural sensitivity and awareness. One of the issues in working with families is to balance respect for their ethnic and cultural background with their clinical issues about which they are seeking help. Some families' difficulties may be very tied to their ethnic and cultural identity. Other families' difficulties may have little to do with their ethnic and cultural identity. Family therapists must try to assess the family's perceptions of the connection between their ethnic identity and their presenting problem.

It is also important for family therapists to acknowledge that the style of therapy may need to differ for families. Perceptions about the usefulness of therapy and talking itself may differ among families from various ethnic and cultural backgrounds. The following are some of the general differences that family therapists need to consider:

- Families with a strong Irish heritage may use words as a way of buffering their experience, either to cover up their painful experiences or to embellish their experiences.
- Within families of Italian descent, words are often used for dramatic purposes and to share emotional experiences with each other.
- In the Chinese culture, food is often used as a way of communicating in lieu of words. The dominant idea in America of speaking openly is often not accepted.
- Within the Jewish culture, words are often used to articulate, understand, analyze, and acknowledge one's experience.
- Within the Anglo culture, words are often used to achieve particular goals, but not to share any high degree of emotions.
- Within the Sioux culture, the way in which family members talk is often prescribed by the roles in which they find themselves. For example, a woman may never utter a word to her father-in-law and yet may feel great closeness with him.

Although there are differences for individuals in each ethnic and cultural group, some of these generalities may help therapists to think about a way of approaching families in therapy.

SOURCE: McGoldrick et al. (1996).

Without human companions, paradise itself would be an undesirable place.

—Proverb of Africa

THE INFLUENCE OF SOCIAL CONTEXT ON THE DEVELOPMENT AND MAINTENANCE OF PROBLEM BEHAVIOR

Another system that is crucial to understand when considering the development of psychopathology is the social context of behavior, including the peer network. Overall, there are a number of important aspects to consider in understanding the social context of the development of psychopathology:

- Contexts are multidimensional and nested within each other (e.g., the school system is nested within the community, and the family system is nested within both the larger community and a subset of communities, such as the neighborhood or religious community).

- As children grow older, contexts become broader and more differentiated, more specific, or deeper.

- Contexts and children's development are determined mutually, with a reciprocal nature of influences.

- The meaning of a context to a child influences the effects of the context on the child. These effects are ultimately based on the ability of the context to provide for the child's fundamental needs.

- When assessing the social contexts that are relevant to the child, it is important to acknowledge specific questions or outcomes that are of interest regarding the child (e.g., assessing parents', peers', and community members' attitudes about substance use would be appropriate in relation to an adolescent who was abusing marijuana; Boyce et al., 1998; Steinberg & Avenevoli, 2000).

Dr. Urie Bronfenbrenner (1979), who developed the ecological system theory, provided a necessarily complex diagram of the various contexts in which children and adolescents exist. There are a multitude of settings and systems that must be considered when trying to understand the etiology of psychopathology in children and adolescents. The **macrosystem**, which is most distant from the child, contains the beliefs and values of the cultures. These values might be related to beliefs about violence and war, the acceptance or nonacceptance of maltreatment of others, and values of family and community functioning. The **exosystem**, which is a bit closer to the child, includes a number of social structures such as the family, the neighborhood, socioeconomic status, support systems, and other aspects of the community in which the child and family live. The **mesosystem** consists of the interconnections between the various community systems, such as peer groups, schools, and religious organizations. The **microsystem** is even closer to the child, with a focus on the immediate environment in which the child lives, including the immediate family, the school, and any work setting. Finally, the **ontogenic development** of the child, which has been added since Bronfenbrenner's original model, is the child's internal development and adaptation, such as biological factors, affect regulation, and intellectual level (Cicchetti et al., 1997). This comprehensive conceptualization of ecological factors is good to keep in mind when considering individual facets of children's and adolescents' development.

Social contexts are multidimensional and become more intense and more meaningful as children age (Boyce et al., 1998). With regard to the peer network, peers and friends are usually linked to children through the school system and through children's extracurricular activities (e.g., sports activities; religious organizations; and, for older children and adolescents, employment). Peers within the school setting are thought to exert a great deal of influence on children's development of academic-related beliefs, prosocial behaviors, and the development of emotional/behavioral problems (Hintze & Shapiro, 1999). Peers can be so influential that programs have been developed in which well-functioning children help children who are troubled or otherwise in need of assistance (Foot, Morgan, & Shute, 1990). Interestingly, peer relationships appear to be influenced by whether children have same-sexed or opposite-sexed siblings (Updegraff, McHale, & Crouter, 2000).

There is growing interest in the peer network related to the socialization of children. Box 2.5 discusses national interest in the importance of peers. Although the national debate has become extreme at times (e.g., suggesting that parents have no influence and that peers are the only ones who influence children; Harris, 1995), it is important to acknowledge the extensiveness of peers' influence on the development of psychopathology. As early as first grade, bullying and reactive aggression are associated with high peer status (i.e., popularity) in African American boys from lower- and lower-middle-income families (Coie, Dodge, Terry, & Wright, 1991). In later years, both antisocial and prosocial behaviors are associated with high peer status, depending on the peer group (Luthar, 1999). Peer victimization (e.g., being teased, bullied, picked on) is associated with depression, social maladjustment, and

BOX 2.5

CONTEXT AND CHILDREN'S FRIENDSHIPS

Do parents have any important long-term effects on the development of their child's personality? This is a provocative question, and an even more provocative answer is no. According to Judith Rich Harris (1995), the group socialization theory of development argues that children are most influenced by their peer group and by their friends: "Children learn how to behave outside the home by becoming members of, and identifying with, a social group" (p. 482). Although these conclusions contradict years of research, Harris's ideas have received a great deal of attention. Harris's first major article on this issue appeared in 1995 in *Psychological Review,* which is a highly respected journal published by the American Psychological Association. Harris (1998a) went on to publish a book on the topic, *The Nurture Assump-*

tion: Why Children Turn Out the Way They Do. Since then, a number of publications, including *The New Yorker,* have covered this issue (Gladwell, 1998) and a debate has ensued in the professional literature (Collins et al., 2000; Eisenberg, Spinrad, & Cumberland, 1998; Harris, 1998b; Hartup, 1999). The work by Harris has raised interesting questions about the extent to which peer influence has been integrated into the professional literature. It is unlikely that any extreme, unidimensional view would be supported by the data (e.g., only peers can influence children or only parents can influence children), but the questions may lead researchers to look closer at the many ways children and adolescents are influenced.

psychological maladjustment (Hawker & Boulton, 2000; Keltner, Capps, Kring, Young, & Heerey, 2001).

There is a great deal of research interest in the differential influence of peers versus parents. Overall, a number of studies suggest that parental influence far outweighs peer influence (e.g., Gerrard, Gibbons, Zhao, Russell, & Reis-Bergan, 1999). A study of inner-city Latino/Hispanic adolescents showed that deviant peer modeling was associated with use of tobacco, alcohol, and marijuana, as well as gang involvement (Frauenglass, Routh, Pantin, & Mason, 1997). Family support, however, seemed to decrease the impact of deviant peers. Thus, adolescents with higher social support from their parents tended to be less influenced by their peers, especially regarding use of tobacco and marijuana (Frauenglass et al., 1997). In a cross-cultural study of African American and Caucasian American adolescents in the United States and Chinese adolescents in Beijing, there was a great deal of consistency found across cultural and ethnic groups (Pilgrim, Luo, Urberg, & Fang, 1999). Specifically, adolescents who had parents with an authoritative parenting style (i.e., parents who set firm, age-appropriate limits in addition to showing high levels of warmth toward the adolescents) and adolescents who showed low sensation-seeking behavior reported lower rates of illicit substance use. The substance use of a close friend also had some influence on adolescents' substance use, but this finding was true only for the Caucasian American and the Chinese adolescents (Pilgrim et al., 1999).

There is also compelling evidence that adolescents in a deviant peer group do not suddenly find themselves there;

rather, it is more of an intentional process (Gerrard et al., 1999). In a process known as **niche-picking**, children and adolescents are thought to choose their peer group and friends based on their own level of deviant behavior (Maughan & Rutter, 1998). Parents' monitoring of their adolescents' behavior and of their friendship networks is related to the types of peers with whom adolescents get involved. In a two-year longitudinal study of adolescents' problem behavior (i.e., antisocial behavior, high-risk sexual behavior, academic failure, and substance use), high rates of family conflict, low levels of parent-child involvement, poor parental monitoring, and association with deviant peers were all associated with adolescents' problem behavior (Ary, Duncan, Duncan, & Hops, 1999). The pattern appeared to be directional, with high family conflict being linked to low parent–child involvement, which then was linked to poor parental monitoring and association with deviant peers one year later. Parental monitoring (e.g., parents who know the whereabouts of their adolescent most of the time, parents who make it a point to know their adolescent's friends, parents who provide age-appropriate control and guidance over their adolescent's activities) is associated strongly with better behavioral outcomes in adolescents (Ary, Duncan, Duncan, & Hops, 1999). Overall, it seems pointless to argue that parents have no influence on their children, just as it seems pointless to argue that peers have no influence on children. There are complex associations in the links between parents, peers, and the behavior of children and adolescents.

The peer network is just one example of a social context. Another salient example has to do with the cultural context of behavior. Increasing attention has been given to the cultural context of behavior, both in the development of prosocial behaviors and in the development of psychopathology (Hall & Barongan, 2002; Kazarian & Evans, 1998). The word culture refers not only to the country in which the child lives but also to the child's and family's ethnic/racial background, religious affiliation, social network, community, and neighborhood (Hall & Barongan, 2002; Luthar, 1999).

The predominant culture can be conveyed to children through a number of media, from print media (e.g., newspapers, magazines, and books) to computer games to the Internet to television and movies. Within the area of eating disorders and body image disturbance, for example, a number of studies have pointed to the unrealistic and unhealthy portrayal of female bodies (i.e., bodies that are significantly underweight) within various media (Jasper, 1993). Higher rates of viewing magazines, for example,

are associated with body image disturbance in adolescent and college-age girls and women (Turner, Hamilton, Jacobs, Angood, & Dwyer, 1997). This relationship appears to be stronger for Caucasian American females than for African American females, given that the former appear to have more body image concerns than the latter (C. M. Lawrence & Thelen, 1995).

A specific area of concern in the study of cultural context has been the predominant culture's attitude toward violence. There have been thousands of studies of the influence of violence in the media (Bushman & Anderson, 2001; Peterson & Newman, 2000; Villani, 2001). That children and adolescents (as well as adults) are exposed to excessive amounts of violence on television should not be news to you. By the time they graduate from elementary school, children will, on average, have viewed at least 100,000 acts of violence and more than 8,000 murders on television (Donnerstein, Slaby, & Eron, 1994; Huston et al., 1992; Kunkel et al., 1996; reviewed in Swan, Meskill, & DeMaio, 1998). Many music videos, such as those shown on MTV, are known to be violent and further, to be explicit in relation to sexual violence (J. L. Peterson & Newman, 2000; Villani, 2001). In the United States, cartoons average 20 acts of violence per hour and prime-time programs average 5 acts of violence per hour (Radecki, 1990). Box 2.6 focuses on violence in computer and video games.

Overall, research has shown links between viewing violence and behaving aggressively (Bushman & Anderson, 2001; Danish & Donohue, 1996; J. L. Peterson & Newman, 2000; Van Evra, 1998; Villani, 2001). Although this research finding might lead you to assume that violence in the media "causes" aggression in children, the issue is not that simple. There are factors related to both the depiction of violence and the individuals viewing the media violence that are related to the potential impact of the violence.

With regard to media violence, certain types of violence are more heavily associated with higher rates of aggression and aggressive fantasies in children. Depictions of violence and aggression on television and in other media are more harmful when:

- There is a lack of punishment, or when there is some type of reward for the violence that is depicted.

- The violence is depicted in a realistic and graphic manner.

- The violence is presented in a way that implies it is justified.

- The violence is seen through the perpetrator's viewpoint and identification with the perpetrator is encouraged.

Violence on television can be associated with aggression in children.

BOX *2.6*

COMPUTER GAMES, VIDEO GAMES, AND VIOLENCE

BOY (nine years old): When I've finished playing on my own, I sometimes turn it on to two players and then just leave the other player there so I can just kick and punch them.

RESEARCHER: What's the point if there's no one playing with you who can move the other joystick?

BOY: Well, I like to be able to work out the death moves—I can do torso removal and it rips the other body in half. (He laughs loudly.) (This dialogue apeared in Sanger, Wilson, Davies, & Whitakker, 1997, p. 1: Reprinted with permission from Taylor and Francis, *Young Children, Videos, and Computer Games.*)

Computer games and video games are an integral part of many children's lives these days. What concerns adults is that games are often rife with violence and sexism. In a recent study of the most popular video games, nearly 80% showed high levels of aggression and violence (Dietz, 1998). Although over half of the games (59%) did not include any female characters, those that did include female characters tended to show them as sex objects.

A number of professionals argue that children's use of video games should be monitored by parents and teachers. It appears, however, that such monitoring is the exception rather than the rule. One study of children's use of computer games and video games at home and at school showed that parents and teachers often did not closely monitor children's use of video games and computer games (Sanger et al., 1997). Although there is still limited research into the connections between violent video games and children's aggression, the parallels between television and video game violence appear warranted. In general, certain vulnerable or impressionable children are put at greater risk for behaving aggressively when exposed to massive amounts of violent video games (Sanger et al., 1997). It is unlikely, however, that playing a violent video game would make an otherwise well-functioning, nonviolent child express violence (Sanger et al., 1997). Overall, this is a complicated issue. Its exploration must be similarly complex and thorough.

- Sexually explicit violence is strongly related to attitudes that are conducive to sexual assault (Swan et al., 1998; Van Evra, 1998).

There are also characteristics of the child or adolescent that are related to the impact of viewing violence. Harmful effects of exposure to media violence are associated with:

- Children who already have tendencies toward aggression, such as those with oppositional defiant disorder or conduct disorder.

- Less parental monitoring, which is associated with more emotional/behavioral problems in children and adolescents, and is associated with greater exposure to peers with maladjusted behavior.

- Conflict and aggression within the child's or adolescent's family situation (Swan et al., 1998; Van Evra, 1998).

Overall, there is no easy answer to the whether viewing violent material causes violent or aggressive behavior. Although violence in the media is associated with higher levels of aggression with some impressionable and vulnerable children, not every child is affected adversely by media violence (Lande, 1993; Villani, 2001). In fact, the majority of children and adolescents who watch television and movies never show any overt violent behavior. Obviously, the media are not the only means by which children and adolescents are exposed to violence and aggression. Given the complexity of this issue, it is important to keep in mind all of the personal, familial, social, and cultural factors that are associated with problematic behavior in youth. Note also that television programs designed to prevent violent behavior and aggression have been used with good results (Sanders, Montgomery, & Brechman-Toussaint, 2000).

It is better to support schools than jails.

—Mark Twain

THE OVERARCHING THEORY OF DEVELOPMENTAL PSYCHOPATHOLOGY

The theory of developmental psychopathology attempts to integrate divergent theories (Achenbach, 1982; Luthar, Burack, Cicchetti, & Weisz, 1997; Mash & Dozois, 1996). These theories encompass the impact of neurobiological and physiological factors, behavioral and emotional factors, family and genetic factors, and sociocultural factors within both the school and the community

(Costello & Angold, 1996). The multiple influences in the development of psychopathology are intertwined and influenced by the context (Cicchetti & Toth, 1997; R. M. Lerner, Walsh, & Howard, 1998; Willis & Cleary, 2000). One of the major theorists and writers on developmental psychopathology, Dante Cicchetti (1990), has noted: "Developmental psychopathology . . . should bridge fields of study, span the life cycle, and aid in the discovery of important new truths about the processes underlying adaptation and maladaptation, as well as the best means of preventing or ameliorating psychopathology" (p. 20). With this perspective in mind, there are a number of central questions that the theory of developmental psychopathology should explore (Sroufe, 1988, 1997):

- Which pathways will lead to similar outcomes?
- What are the variations in outcome associated with a given pathway?
- What factors determine the choice of a given pathway?
- What factors determine whether a child continues on the path initially chosen or is deflected off that path?
- When do pathways become fixed, in the sense that deviation from the existing path becomes significantly less likely?

A central component to developmental psychopathology is understanding **developmental trajectories** (i.e., how behavior changes over time). For example, increasing numbers of studies are looking at changes that occur from infancy to young adulthood (Arnett, 2000). Inherent in the exploration of developmental trajectories are the concepts of **multifinality** and **equifinality**. Multifinality suggests that one particular experience may lead to a number of different outcomes in various children (Cicchetti et al., 1997). For example, having a depressed parent is associated with a variety of outcomes in children such as depression, withdrawal, aggression, and oppositional behavior (Downey & Coyne, 1990). Equifinality, in contrast, suggests that a particular outcome can have many different sources (Cicchetti et al., 1997). For example, oppositional behavior in children may be due to genetic predisposition, poor disciplinary practices, or a poor fit between child temperament and family environment (Frick, 1998b). Overall, developmental psychopathology researchers are focused on trying to understand variabilities in functioning over the life span.

A primary goal of developmental psychopathology is to understand the normative developmental process in order to understand the development of emotional/behavioral problems (Achenbach, 1982; Costello & Angold,

1996; Kazdin, 1989). Another central goal is to explore continuities and discontinuities in development (i.e., to explore which behaviors stay the same over time and which behaviors change over time; Rutter, 1996). Table 2.1 lists some of the many normal developmental tasks that must be mastered throughout infancy, childhood, and adolescence. Although these tasks are not necessarily completed in one specific sequence for everyone, it appears that the majority of people do master these tasks at some time during childhood (Masten & Coatsworth, 1998).

In addition to exploring normative developmental tasks, it is also important to consider the development of problems at different ages. Consistent with the exploration of problems from a developmental level, the types of problems that are investigated by developmental psychopathologists include the following (Campbell, 1998):

- Difficult temperament in infants.
- Troubled attachment patterns between infants and caretakers.
- Defiance or overly independent strivings in toddlers and preschoolers.
- Aggressive behavior.

TABLE 2.1 Examples of Developmental Tasks

Age Period	Task
Infancy to preschool	Attachment to caregiver(s) Language Differentiation of self from environment Self-control and compliance
Middle Childhood	School adjustment (attendance, appropriate conduct) Academic achievement (e.g., learning to read, do arithmetic) Getting along with peers (acceptance, making friends) Rule-governed conduct (following rules of society for moral behavior and prosocial conduct)
Adolescence	Successful transition to secondary schooling Academic achievement (learning skills needed for higher education or work) Involvement in extracurricular activities (e.g., athletics, clubs) Forming close friendships within and across gender Forming a cohesive sense of self: identity

SOURCE: Masten & Coatsworth (1998).

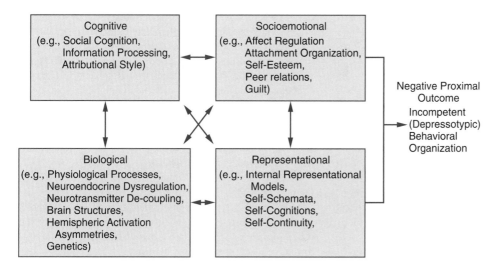

FIGURE 2.2 Emerging Competence as the Organization of Biological and Behavioral Systems

Source: Cicchetti & Toth (1995).

- Social withdrawal.
- School problems.
- Peer problems.

Developmental psychopathology also focuses on **resilience**, which is the ability of a child to overcome adverse environments and achieve healthy developmental outcomes (Luthar, Cicchetti, & Becker, 2000; Masten & Coatsworth, 1998). Resilient children show a number of advantageous characteristics at the level of the individual, the family, and the extrafamilial context. On the individual level, resilient children show good intellectual functioning, self-confidence, faith, and a disposition that is easygoing, sociable, and appealing (Masten & Coatsworth, 1998; Werner & Smith, 2001). On the level of the family, resilient children tend to have at least one close and stable relationship with a caring parental figure, have connections with an extended family network, and have parents who show an authoritative parenting style in which they show high levels of warmth and structure

along with providing high expectations of success (Masten & Coatsworth, 1998; Werner & Smith, 2001). At the larger level of the extrafamilial context, resilient children have strong bonds to prosocial adults outside the family (e.g., a caring teacher, a stable coach); show connections with prosocial organizations; and attend effective schools (Masten & Coatsworth, 1998; Werner & Smith, 2001). Note that all of these levels of influence are reciprocal and can influence each other individually and collectively. Overall, a central theme in the theory of developmental psychopathology deals with how children in adverse environments are able to avoid developing psychological problems. In addition, there is a strong focus on the malleability of children's behavior, given that a child who is diagnosed with a clinical disorder can still develop into a well-functioning child (Sroufe, 1997).

Figure 2.2 provides an example of a model of the development of psychopathology (in this case, depression). This model shows the complexity of the many variables that are associated with adverse outcomes.

SUMMARY AND KEY CONCEPTS

The Importance of Theory

Nearly all well-respected research into the development of psychopathology is based on a **theory**, which is a systematic set of statements designed to help analyze, explain, predict, and even suggest ways of controlling certain phenomena of interest. The theories discussed in this chapter focus primarily on **etiology**, which is the exploration of what leads to, or "causes," the development of a particular type of psychopathology.

Psychodynamic Theory

Based on Freud's work, psychodynamic theory suggests that children and adolescents usually go through five psychosexual stages, the **oral stage**, the **anal stage**, the **phallic stage** (which includes the **Oedipus complex** or the **Electra complex**), the **latency period**, and the **genital stage**. A more recent psychodynamic theory is referred to as **object relations theory**. In addition, **attachment theory**, which presupposes the importance of the parent-infant pattern of attachment, focuses on early childhood in relation to later development. Attachment styles fall into two primary categories, **secure attachment** and **anxious insecure attachment**, the latter of which is further broken down into avoidant, ambivalent, and disorganized attachment.

Genetic and Biological Theories of Developmental Psychopathology

Most genetic theories focus on the characteristics that are inherited from one's parents. **Genotype** refers to a child's inherited characteristics, and **phenotype** refers to a child's observable characteristics. **Heritability** is a term used to refer to the proportion of genetic influence regarding a particular characteristic. In order to assess the genetic versus environmental influences of different characteristics, **monozygotic (MZ) twins** and **dizygotic (DZ) twins** are often studied in what are known as **adoption studies**.

Behavioral Genetics

The study of **behavioral genetics** focuses on the combined influences of genetic and environmental factors in the development of psychopathology. In addition to the focus on inherited genetic factors, environment is explored at two levels: **shared environment** and **nonshared environment**.

Behavioral Theories and Developmental Psychopathology

Behavioral theories argue that observable behaviors are the most important aspect of a child's or adolescent's functioning (although there is some acknowledgment of the importance of cognitions). Behavioral disorders are thought to be developed due to the antecedents and consequences related to the behavior.

Cognitive-Behavioral Theories and Developmental Psychopathology

Closely linked to behavioral theories, cognitive-behavioral theories add a child's or adolescent's cognitions to the understanding of the development of psychopathology. Not only can clinical disorders develop in the context of adverse behavioral conditions, but adverse cognitions (such as **automatic thoughts** and **cognitive distortions**) can also be linked to the development of certain types of psychopathology.

Theories of Family Functioning and Abnormal Behavior in Children and Adolescents

Within family theories, a main hypothesis is that the problem rarely resides in the child or adolescent him- or herself. Rather, the child is referred to as the **identified problem** or **identified patient** who is expressing the problems that are actually present in the family system. Quite often when families seek help for their child's behavior, they unknowingly might try to maintain **homeostasis** so that nothing in the family changes. Problems within the family are often thought to be related to troubled structures within the family, disrupted communication styles, and difficulty with personal closeness and distance (**enmeshed families** are consider too close, and **disengaged families** too distant).

The Influence of Social Context in the Development and Maintenance of Problem Behavior

Children are embedded within a number of contexts, including peer networks, the school system, religious affiliations, the neighborhood, the community, and the culture as a whole. According to Urie Bronfenbrenner's conceptualizations of the ecology of childhood, children are nested within all of the following contexts: the **macrosystem** (represented by the beliefs and values of the child's culture); the **exosystem** (represented by the social structures closer to the child, such as the family, the neighborhood, socioeconomic status, support systems, and other aspects of the community); the **mesosystem** (represented by the interconnections between many different social systems, such as peer groups, schools, and religious organizations); the **microsystem** (reflective of the child's immediate environment including the family, the school, and any work setting); and the **ontogenic development** (the internal state of the child). A process known as **niche-picking** suggests that children and adolescents choose their own peer groups consistent with their own level of deviant behavior.

The Overarching Theory of Developmental Psychopathology

The study of developmental psychopathology has focused extensively on **developmental trajectories**, **multifinality**, **equifinality**, and **resilience**. Developmental trajectories, multifinality, and equifinality are all related to the ways in which children's behavior changes over time. Resilient children develop into well-functioning and exceptional young people in the face of often terrible adverse circumstances. Overall, the theory of developmental psychopathology tries to bridge the gaps between many other theories and tries to help identify the most crucial aspects of the individual or the environment that can help children achieve healthy outcomes.

KEY TERMS

theory	object relations	monozygotic (MZ)	cognitive distortions	microsystem
etiology	theory	twins	identified problem	ontogenic
oral stage	attachment theory	dizygotic (DZ) twins	identified patient	development
anal stage	secure attachment	adoption studies	homeostasis	niche-picking
phallic stage	anxious insecure	behavioral genetics	enmeshed families	developmental
Oedipus complex	attachment	shared environment	disengaged families	trajectories
Electra complex	genotype	nonshared	macrosystem	multifinality
latency period	phenotype	environment	exosystem	equifinality
genital stage	heritability	automatic thoughts	mesosystem	resilience

SUGGESTED READINGS

Bragg, Rick. *All Over But the Shouting*. New York: Random House, 1998. A number of stressors and risk factors are illustrated in this autobiography, including parental alcoholism, abuse, and rural poverty.

Mah, Adeline Yen. *Falling Leaves: The Memoir of an Unwanted Chinese Daughter*. New York: Broadway Books, 1997. Within this autobiography, which documents verbal and physical abuse, there is an overriding theme of resilience and protective factors.

SUGGESTED VIEWINGS

American History X (1998). Tony Kaye (director), David McKenna (writer). VHS/DVD. This powerful film illustrates the connections between violence, racism, and other risk factors in relation to functioning within the family, the school system, and the community.

The Sweet Hereafter (1997). Atom Egoyan (director and screenwriter), based on novel by Russell Banks. VHS/DVD. This film provides a look at the complexity of events that can be intertwined when a traumatic event occurs to children and families.

CHAPTER 3

ETHICS IN WORKING WITH CHILDREN AND FAMILIES

CHAPTER SUMMARY

ETHICAL RESPONSIBILITIES OF PROFESSIONALS WORKING WITH CHILDREN AND FAMILIES

   COMPETENCE

   MULTIPLE RELATIONSHIPS

INFORMED CONSENT AND ASSENT IN ASSESSMENT AND THERAPY WITH CHILDREN AND FAMILIES

CONFIDENTIALITY AND LIMITS TO CONFIDENTIALITY

CHILDREN'S LEGAL RIGHTS IN TREATMENT DECISIONS

ETHICS OF CONDUCTING RESEARCH

SUMMARY AND KEY CONCEPTS

KEY TERMS

SUGGESTED READINGS

SUGGESTED VIEWINGS

Leave a good name behind in case you return.

—Proverb of Africa

Although in many fields different professional organizations each have their own ethical and professional guidelines, the majority of such organizations within the field of mental health and education provide similar guidelines for professionals (C. B. Fisher, Hatashita-Wong, & Greene, 1999). For example, school psychologists and clinical psychologists follow strikingly similar ethical codes of conduct and legal statutes (Paul, 1997; Reschly & Bersoff, 1999). In 1992, the American Psychological Association (APA) published a comprehensive set of ethical and professional principles for psychologists and other mental health professionals; the ones that relate to mental health professionals who work with children are excerpted in Table 3.1. (You may need to refer back to this table throughout the chapter as various ethical standards are discussed.) Readers interested in seeing the full text of the code should refer to the *American Psychologist*, a premier journal published by the APA. There are also additional ethical guidelines (American Psychological Association, 1994) and concerns (Bow & Quinnell, 2001; Hagan & Castagna, 2001; Kirkland & Kirkland, 2001) that are specific to evaluating children for custody arrangements during divorce proceedings. Interested readers should also consider locating a copy of *Ethics for Psychologists: A Commentary on the APA Ethics Code* (Canter, Bennett, Jones, & Nagy, 1994); *Ethics in Psychology: Professional Standards and Cases*, second edition (Koocher & Keith-Spiegel, 1998); or *Children, Ethics, and the Law: Professional Issues and Cases* (Koocher & Keith-Spiegel, 1990).

Note that the APA code is, as of this writing, under review by a task force and new ethical guidelines are expected to appear by the year 2004. A draft of the new guidelines first appeared in the *APA Monitor on Psychology* (the national newspaper for APA members), and comments were requested from readers (S. E. Jones, 2001). After these comments are received and the revised ethical guidelines obtain approval from the ethics board of APA, the new ethical guidelines will be published in *American Psychologist*. The working draft of the new ethics code can be found at www.apa.org/ethics.

Psychologists and other professionals are trained extensively in ethical and legal issues.

Morals are an acquirement—like music, like a foreign language, like piety, poker, paralysis—no one is born with them.

—Mark Twain

ETHICAL RESPONSIBILITIES OF PROFESSIONALS WORKING WITH CHILDREN AND FAMILIES

Competence

As noted in Table 3.1, there is both a general principle (Principle A) and an ethical standard (Ethical Standard 1.04) related to **competence**. The principles and the standard suggest that professionals get involved only in those activities for which they have been trained or otherwise gained knowledge or experience. These activities include, but are not limited to, conducting therapy, conducting assessments, implementing prevention programs, teaching classes, and conducting research (Snow, Grady, & Goyette-Ewing, 2000). Note that the competence must have been obtained through either formal education, formal training, organized supervised experience, or other appropriate professional experiences (Yanagida, 1998). Psychologists cannot deem themselves competent in an area without some documentation of formalized professional training.

The issue of competence has important ramifications for working with children, adolescents, and families. Professionals who have been trained only in working with individual adults would need to receive additional training before establishing competence in working with children, adolescents, and families. As discussed throughout this book, working with children is very different from working with adults. Although certain skills (e.g., good listening skills, strong interviewing skills, good therapeutic skills, knowledge of the empirical process) are required with both adults and children, the ways in which services are delivered can be very different. In addition, a number of issues are relevant in working with children that usually are not as relevant in working with adults, such as dealing effectively with parents, coordinating services with the school, and dealing with confidentiality issues when the parents are the legal holders of confidentiality yet the child is the individual client. (Also, see Box 3.1 for a discussion of competence with regard to gender, race/ethnicity, and culture.) For all of these reasons, it is imperative that professionals working with children, adolescents, and families receive specialized training. As will be discussed in Chapter 17, most general programs in clinical psychology, counseling psychology, social work, and psychiatry train professionals in both child and adult work.

Professionals can gain additional training in a number of ways. Most states require some type of continuing education even after professionals are licensed. These continuing education programs must be formal educational experiences that meet the requirements of the licensing board for that state and for that profession (e.g., clinical psychology, school psychology, social work, and psychiatry). Continuing education programs can range from a one-hour colloquium presentation to a week-long seminar involving intensive training experiences. These continuing education programs are often offered in the professional's local region, although professionals may have to

TABLE 3.1   Selected Ethical Principles of Psychologists and Code of Conduct

GENERAL PRINCIPLES

Principle A:	Competence
Principle B:	Integrity
Principle C:	Professional and Scientific Responsibility
Principle D:	Respect for People's Rights and Dignity
Principle E:	Concern for Others' Welfare
Principle F:	Social Responsibility

ETHICAL STANDARDS

1.   GENERAL STANDARDS

1.04   *Boundaries of Competence:* (a) Psychologists provide services, teach, and conduct research only within the boundaries of their competence, based on their education, training, supervised experience, or appropriate professional experience . . .

1.13   *Personal Problems and Conflicts:* (a) Psychologists recognize that their personal problems and conflicts may interfere with their effectiveness. Accordingly, they refrain from undertaking an activity when they know or should know that their personal problems are likely to lead to harm to a patient, client, colleague, student, research participant, or other person to whom they may owe a professional or scientific obligation . . .

1.17   *Multiple Relationships:* (a) . . . Psychologists must always be sensitive to the potential harmful effects of other contacts on their work and on those persons with whom they deal. A psychologist refrains from entering into or promising another personal, scientific, professional, financial, or other relationship with such persons if it appears likely that such a relationship reasonably might impair the psychologist's objectivity or otherwise interfere with the psychologist effectively performing his or her functions as a psychologist, or might harm or exploit the other party. (b) Likewise, whenever feasible, a psychologist refrains from taking on professional or scientific obligations when pre-existing relationships would create a risk of such harm . . .

2.   EVALUATION, ASSESSMENT, OR INTERVENTION

2.01   *Evaluation, Diagnosis, and Interventions in Professional Context:* (a) Psychologists perform evaluations, diagnostic services, or interventions only within the context of a defined professional relationship.

2.02   *Competence and Appropriate Use of Assessments and Interventions:* Psychologists who develop, administer, score, interpret, or use psychological assessment techniques, interviews, tests, or instruments do so in a manner and for purposes that are appropriate in light of the research on or evidence of the usefulness and proper application of the techniques . . .

2.04   *Use of Assessment in General and with Special Populations:* (a) Psychologists who perform interventions or administer, score, interpret, or use assessment techniques are familiar with the reliability, validation, and related standardization or outcome studies of, and proper applications and uses of, the techniques they use . . .

2.09   *Explaining Assessment Results:* . . . Psychologists ensure that an explanation of the results is provided using language that is reasonably understandable to the person assessed or to another legally authorized person on behalf of the client.

2.10   *Maintaining Test Security:* Psychologists make reasonable efforts to maintain the integrity and security of tests and other assessment techniques consistent with law, contractual obligations, and in a manner that permits compliance with the requirements of this Ethics Code . . .

3.   ADVERTISING AND OTHER PUBLIC STATEMENTS

3.03   *Avoidance of False or Deceptive Statements:* (a) Psychologists do not make public statements that are false, deceptive, misleading, or fraudulent, either because of what they state, convey, or suggest or because of what they omit, concerning their research, practice, or other work activities or those of persons or organizations with which they are affiliated . . .

4.   THERAPY

4.02   *Informed Consent to Therapy:* (a) Psychologists obtain appropriate informed consent to therapy or related procedures, using language that is reasonably understandable to participants.

4.03   *Couple and Family Relationships:* (a) When a psychologist agrees to provide services to several persons who have a relationship (such as husband and wife or parents and children), the psychologist attempts to clarify at the outset (1) which of the individuals are patients or clients and (2) the relationship the psychologist will have with each person.

4.05   *Sexual Intimacies with Current Patients or Clients:* Psychologists do not engage in sexual intimacies with current patients or clients.

4.06   *Therapy with Former Sexual Partners:* Psychologists do not accept as therapy patients or clients persons with whom they have engaged in sexual intimacies.

4.07   *Sexual Intimacies with Former Therapy Patients:* (a) Psychologists do not engage in sexual intimacies with a former therapy patient or client for at least two years after cessation or termination of professional services. (b) Because sexual intimacies with a former therapy patient or client are so frequently harmful to the patient or client, and because such intimacies undermine public confidence in the psychology profession and thereby deter the public's use of needed services, psychologists do not engage in sexual intimacies with former therapy patients and clients even after a two-year interval except in the most unusual circumstances . . .

(continued)

TABLE 3.1 *(continued)*

4.09 *Terminating the Professional Relationship:* (a) Psychologists do not abandon patients or clients. (b) Psychologists terminate a professional relationship when it becomes reasonably clear that the patient or client no longer needs the service, is not benefitting, or is being harmed by continued service.

5. *PRIVACY AND CONFIDENTIALITY*

5.01 *Discussing the Limits of Confidentiality:* (a) Psychologists discuss with persons and organizations with whom they establish a scientific or professional relationship (including, to the extent feasible, minors and their legal representatives) (1) the relevant limitations on confidentiality, including limitations where applicable in group, marital, and family therapy or in organizational consulting, and (2) the foreseeable uses of the information generated through their services.

5.02 *Maintaining Confidentiality:* Psychologists have a primary obligation and take reasonable precautions to respect the confidentiality rights of those with whom they work or consult . . .

6. *TEACHING, TRAINING, SUPERVISION, RESEARCH, AND PUBLISHING*

6.03 *Accuracy and Objectivity in Teaching:* (a) When engaged in teaching or training, psychologists present psychological information accurately and with a reasonable degree of objectivity.

6.06 *Planning Research:* (a) Psychologists design, conduct, and report research in accordance with recognized standards of scientific competence and ethical research . . .

6.10 *Institutional Approval:* Psychologists obtain from host institutions or organizations appropriate approval prior to conducting research, and they provide accurate information about their research proposals. They conduct the research in accordance with the approved research protocol.

6.11 *Informed Consent to Research:* (a) Psychologists use language that is reasonably understandable to research participants in obtaining their appropriate informed con-

sent . . . Such informed consent is appropriately documented . . .

6.18 *Providing Participants with Information About the Study:* (a) Psychologists provide a prompt opportunity for participants to obtain appropriate information about the nature, results, and conclusions of the research, and psychologists attempt to correct any misconceptions that participants may have.

7. *FORENSIC ACTIVITIES*

7.01 *Forensic Assessments:* (a) Psychologists' forensic assessments, recommendations, and reports are based on information and techniques (including personal interviews of the individual, when appropriate) sufficient to provide appropriate substantiation of their findings . . .

7.06 *Compliance with Law and Rules:* In performing forensic roles, psychologists are reasonably familiar with the rules governing their roles. Psychologists are aware of the occasionally competing demands placed upon them by these principles and the requirements of the court system, and attempt to resolve these conflicts by making known their commitment to this Ethics Code and taking steps to resolve the conflict in a responsible manner . . .

8. *RESOLVING ETHICAL ISSUES*

8.02 *Confronting Ethical Issues:* When a psychologist is uncertain whether a particular situation or course of action would violate this Ethics Code, the psychologist ordinarily consults with other psychologists knowledgeable about ethical issues, with state or national psychology ethics committees, or with other appropriate authorities in order to choose a proper response . . .

8.04 *Informal Resolution of Ethical Violations:* When psychologists believe that there may have been an ethical violation by another psychologist, they attempt to resolve the issue by bringing it to the attention of that individual if an informal resolution appears appropriate and the intervention does not violate any confidentiality rights that may be involved.

Note that state licensing boards sometimes have more strict rules than the American Psychological Association. In those cases, the stricter of the two rules must be followed in order to ensure compliance with all relevant legislation and ethical codes.

SOURCE: American Psychiatric Association (1992).

travel to the nearest city to participate in continuing education programs. Continuing education opportunities also exist at local and national conventions that are held by professional organizations. Increasingly, there are continuing education programs offered through the mail (e.g., study-at-home programs) or through the Internet (see www.apa.org for online continuing education offerings from the APA). Regardless of the modality through which professionals receive continuing education, it is imperative that they receive specialized training that leads to

competence in working with children, adolescents, and families if they wish to conduct professional duties with these populations (Corey, Corey, & Callanan, 1988).

Note that in addition to the general guidelines regarding competence, there are also specific guidelines regarding competence in assessment and intervention techniques (Ethical standards 2.02 and 2.04). Professionals who conduct assessments and interventions must know the correct usage of these techniques based on available empirical research (Ingram, Hayes, & Scott,

BOX 3.1

ETHICS AND COMPETENCE RELATED TO GENDER, RACE/ETHNICITY, AND CULTURE

Within the assessment and therapeutic process, issues often arise that relate to gender, race/ethnicity, and culture. Although these issues are not always present, ethical clinicians must at all times be aware of the potential for them to arise. Recommendations for ethical behavior in regard to gender, race/ethnicity, and culture include the following:

- Clinicians should recognize that gender, race/ethnicity, and culture are fundamental issues in all relationships. They should be able to understand clients' individual differences within this broader context.

- In the same way that mental health professionals should refrain from providing services when they are psychologically impaired, they should also refrain from providing services when their personal beliefs (e.g., sexism, racism, homophobia) prevent them from providing services in an objective and productive manner.

- Clinicians must remain abreast of the latest empirical and theoretical information regarding gender, race/ethnicity, and culture. If they are not able to maintain continued competence in these areas, they should refer clients to other practitioners who have shown competence in these areas.

- Clinicians should address issues of gender, race/ethnicity, and culture not only when working with clients but also when providing supervision, conducting research, and teaching in a scholarly setting.

- When clinicians are faced with ethical dilemmas regarding gender, race/ethnicity, or culture, they should seek consultation (in an anonymous fashion so as not to break confidentiality) with experts in the field or with their ethics board.

Overall, good ethical practice in the areas of gender, race/ethnicity, and culture is consistent with good ethical practice in all areas of concern. The same can be said for the issue of sexual orientation (Crawford, McLeod, Zamboni, & Jordan, 1999). Clinicians must remain vigilant about maintaining competence and proficiency in all areas within their practice and their research. As an example, Table 3.2 highlights information about traditional Korean values and mainstream American values that would be important to know when working with a Korean American who had difficulty integrating the two cultures.

SOURCES: American Psychological Association (1995); Goodwin (1997); G. C. N. Hall & Barongan (2002); Hampton & Gottlieb (1997).

TABLE 3.2   Korean Versus American Values

Traditional Korean Values	Mainstream American Values
Family Values	
Family-orientation	Individual orientation
Interdependency	Autonomy and independence
Vertical, authoritarian structure	Horizontal, democratic structure
Life Philosophy	
Collectivism	Individualism
Sense of stoicism and fatalism	Sense of optimism and opportunism
Reciprocity and obligation	Avoidance of obligation
Communication Style	
Emphasis on subtle nonverbal body language	Emphasis on overt verbal language
Control of feelings	Free expression of feelings
Little eye contact	Much eye contact

SOURCE: Adapted from W. J. Kim, Kim, & Rue (1997).

2000). With regard to assessments, professionals must be aware of the reliability, validity, and standardization issues of the measures that they administer. To conduct assessments in an ethical manner, it is not enough to know how to administer a particular assessment measure; professionals must also know how the measure was developed, what its strengths and weaknesses are, and what its appropriate uses are (C. B. Fisher et al., 1999; Turner, DeMers, Fox, & Reed, 2001). The same issue pertains to conducting therapy. Increasingly, there is a call for accountability in the selection of therapeutic techniques that is consistent with the use of empirically supported treatments (Ingram et al., 2000). There are also ethical consideration in the use of medication—see Box 3.2.

Character counts for a great deal more than either intellect or body in winning success in life.

—Theodore Roosevelt

Multiple Relationships

Ethical Standard 1.17 states that psychologists must refrain from becoming involved in **multiple relation-**

ships with their clients, research participants, and students. Formerly known as *dual relationships*, multiple relationships exist when psychologists have more than one role in relation to individuals with whom they work professionally (Yanagida, 1998). For example, a multiple relationship would exist if a psychologist were providing therapy to one of his or her students; the psychologist would be in the role of a therapist and also in the role of an instructor. Multiple relationships are forbidden because the dual roles may create a conflict of interest that may, in turn, result in harm to the client. To stay with the example of a psychologist who is both a therapist and an instructor with the same client/student, imagine that one of the primary themes in therapy is the client's concern about academic excellence. As a therapist, the psychologist could explore the meaning and importance of academic progress and empathetically help the client come to terms with his or her academic difficulties. As an instructor, however, the psychologist would need to maintain objective grading criteria and academic rigor. Imagine the impact on the therapeutic alliance should the warm, caring therapist have to flunk the client for inade-

quate academic functioning. Imagine the strain in the therapy session after grades are posted.

There are an unlimited number of potential multiple relationships that could be problematic (Koocher & Keith-Spiegel, 1998). In fact, more than half of the formal complaints made each year to the APA's ethics board concern inappropriate multiple relationships and other boundary problems that occur between clinicians and their clients (Sonne, 1994). Psychologists should not use the professional services of their clients. A therapist whose client is the best real estate agent in town must use another real estate agent for buying or selling his house. Similarly, a therapist whose personal physician asks her to evaluate his child for attention-deficit/hyperactivity disorder must decline the request— though she may refer her physician to another professional who could provide those services.

Although listed under the ethical standards related to therapy, the issue of sexual intimacies with clients has relevance to the topic of multiple relationships. Sexual intimacies with current clients are categorically forbidden (Ethical Standard 4.05), as is therapeutic involvement

---

BOX 3.2

ETHICAL CONSIDERATIONS IN THE USE OF MEDICATION

As will be discussed in Chapter 6, on therapy, there are pros and cons to treating children's and adolescents' emotional/behavioral problems with psychotropic medications. Only trained physicians (such as psychiatrists, pediatricians, and developmental pediatricians) can prescribe medication, but it is still necessary for other mental health professionals to remain aware of ethical issues regarding the proper use of medication. The following questions and considerations have been raised when dealing with medication for children's and adolescents' emotional/behavioral problems:

- To what extent should parents, rather than children, be the focus of treatment? Since parents and other adults are usually the ones who request services, maybe their issues should be explored before medicating children or adolescents.

- Are children and adolescents being overmedicated? There is evidence that psychotropic medications are being administered more quickly and more frequently than might be appropriate.

- Can the use of psychotropic medication inadvertently suggest biological causes for emotional/behavioral problems? In their rush to medicate children and adolescents, professionals may be sending the message that these

problems are based on a biological problem when there is no clear evidence of the etiological factors.

- How do psychotropic medications influence children's and adolescents' self-efficacy, locus of control, and motivation? There is evidence that children and adolescents, as well as their parents, attribute behavioral improvements to psychotropic medications, even when the actual "medication" was in the form of a placebo (such as an inert sugar pill).

- Can the use of psychotropic medications discourage the use of other interventions, such as special educational programs and therapeutic interventions? It is possible that the ease of medication may be the deciding factor, rather than choosing the most effective treatment, for children's and adolescents' emotional/behavioral problems.

- Is there enough empirical evidence to support the widespread use of psychotropic medications with children and adolescents? As will be discussed further in Chapter 6, many psychotropic medications have limited or equivocal support for use with children and adolescents and do not appear to be justified by the empirical evidence.

SOURCES: Barkley et al. (1990); Barnett & Neel (2000); Brown & Sawyer (1998).

with former sexual partners (Ethical Standard 4.06). In both instances, sexual involvement could be detrimental to the client. These restrictions also apply to the parents and other family members of child or adolescent clients, since treatment most often involves family members to some extent (S. E. Jones, 2001; Yanagida, 1998).

In general, the majority of research on therapist–client sexual involvement has been conducted with adult therapy clients. Interestingly, sexual misconduct by therapists working with adult clients has been associated with a history of sexual abuse and a current level of high psychological distress on the part of the therapist (Jackson & Nuttall, 2001). Sexual involvement between an adult therapist and a child or adolescent client would be forbidden due to regulations against sexual abuse with minors, so the issue of therapist–client sexual involvement in such a case would tend to be overshadowed by the issue of child sexual abuse. Overall, because harm can come to clients (even adult parents of child clients) when there are romantic or sexual intimacies between therapists and clients, it is in the best interest of both clients and therapists for these intimacies to not occur (Yanagida, 1998).

An interesting principle with regard to sexual intimacy appears in Ethical Standard 4.07, which allows sexual intimacies with former therapy clients if the therapy terminated at least two years before any romantic or sexual involvement and if the romantic or sexual involvement is not harmful to the former client. Prior to 1992, the APA code disallowed sexual intimacies with former therapy clients in perpetuity (i.e., forever), so the current code represents a change from previous thinking. In many states, however, the therapist–client relationship is still considered to exist in perpetuity, so in these states sexual involvement with former clients would still be considered unethical no matter how long ago the therapy was terminated. This discrepancy between the national ethical code and some state codes represents an interesting dilemma for psychologists in those states. Whenever two ethical codes are in conflict, it is wise to follow the more stringent of the two in order to maintain the highest level of ethical standards.

Case Study: Questions of Competence and Thorough Informed Consent

Dr. A had specialized in clinical work with older adolescents and adults, but she decided that she wanted to start working with younger children in order to increase the size of her practice. She had worked with a few children when she was on internship many years ago, but she did not have any additional formal training in working with youngsters.

Dr. A was referred a two-and-a-half-year-old girl, Alana, who showed oppositional behavior. Alana's parents were separated, and the child's behavior began to deteriorate significantly. Alana's mother reported that she had full legal and physical custody of Alana and that she would be paying for the therapy sessions. She requested that Dr. A not contact Alana's father because he was not supportive of Alana's therapy. Dr. A agreed to this request.

After three sessions, Alana's mother called Dr. A to report that Alana had said, "Daddy stuck his penis in my hole," after a weekend visit with her father. Dr. A requested to see Alana the next day, and in that session Alana confirmed what she had told her mother. Dr. A immediately made a sexual abuse report to the child protective services agency in that area. When Alana's father learned of the allegations and investigation, he contacted Dr. A. He provided documentation to show that he had joint legal and physical custody of Alana, and he informed Dr. A that he and Alana's mother were involved in a bitter custody dispute over Alana. He vehemently denied any sexual contact with his

daughter and noted that Alana's mother was making these charges in order to discredit his petition for custody. He informed Dr. A that he would be hiring an attorney for this matter and that he wanted Dr. A to terminate any contact with Alana.

Two primary issues are raised by this case study. First, Dr. A lacked sufficient training to deal with young children. Most clinicians trained to work with young children realize that children at the age of two and a half rarely use terminology as sophisticated as that Alana had used. A trained clinician might have at least wondered if Alana's mother had coached Alana prior to her session with Dr. A. In addition, trained clinical child therapists are usually very wary of parents' possible ulterior motives when they are separated or when they are going through a divorce.

Second, Dr. A failed to obtain informed consent from both parents. Too often, fathers are assumed to be inconsequential in treatment decisions and single mothers are not even asked to include fathers in treatment. In this case, Dr. A should not have agreed to see Alana without at least contacting Alana's father. Even if the father was not supportive of therapy, Dr. A could have consulted with him about his perspective on Alana's behavior and could have addressed his concerns about Alana's involvement in therapy. By contacting Alana's father at the outset, Dr. A would have been forewarned about the bitter custody battle and could have been more professional in dealing with the allegations of abuse.

SOURCE: Yanagida (1998).

Good name and honor are worth more than all the gold and jewels ever mined.

—Harry S. Truman

INFORMED CONSENT AND ASSENT IN ASSESSMENT AND THERAPY WITH CHILDREN AND FAMILIES

As discussed in Ethical Standard 4.02, **informed consent** is the process through which clients are told about therapy or assessment services that will take place (i.e., they are informed of these services in language that they understand) and through which they willingly agree to these services (i.e., they give their uncoerced consent to take part). **Informed assent** is the term that applies to the same process with child or adolescent clients. Formally, only competent adults age 18 and above can give their legal informed consent to therapy or assessment services. Thus, whereas parents need to provide informed consent for a child's therapy or assessment services (Pryzwansky & Wendt, 1999), the child can provide his or her informed assent. In fact, it is beneficial to involve the child in this process.

As part of the informed consent/assent process, it is important for therapists to inform clients about the kind of therapy or assessment services that will take place; the fees associated with the services; the possibility of other, more effective services that could be provided elsewhere; the approximate length of time in which to expect the services to be completed; and the potential outcomes of the services. For example, a formal assessment report might be the logical culmination of assessment services, whereas a decrease in emotional/behavioral problems might be a logical and reasonable goal of therapeutic services (Koocher & Keith-Spiegel, 1998).

As noted in Ethical Standard 4.03, whenever children and families are involved in assessments or therapy, it is incumbent upon the clinician to clarify who is and is not considered a client and what relationship the clinician will have with each client. As Figure 3.1 shows, family relationships, especially within stepfamilies, can be complex and can provide a challenge for clinicians trying to clarify their roles with different family members.

Most often, the issue of clarifying whether a person is a client arises when clinicians decide who will be involved in treatment and how the boundaries of that involvement are structured (Canter et al., 1994). For example, a clinician might begin family therapy with a single mother and her two sons. Initially, the clinician clarifies that all three family members (the mother and her two sons) are considered the clients. After three sessions, however, it becomes clear that the mother's difficulties are with her ex-husband (the boys' father). Based on what is in the best interests of this family, the clinician may begin therapy that focuses on co-parenting with the mother and father, without including the boys in therapy sessions. If that change were to happen, the clinician would need to reestablish the boundaries of his or her relationship with the mother and would also need to clarify that the father was now considered a client.

In general, it is good and ethical practice to clarify these relationships at the outset of therapy or at the beginning of any changed configuration of therapy. There are, however, some circumstances where changing a role with

Therapists must obtain informed consent from parents and informed assent from children before working with them.

clients is not in the best interest of the clients. Imagine that a clinician is working with a father in individual therapy. After two years of individual therapy, the father asks the therapist to also include his adolescent daughter in the sessions because she is having trouble in school. In this case, it would probably be most ethical for the clinician to refer the adolescent to another therapist rather than trying to treat her. If the daughter were to join the father's therapy for her own difficulties, she may never feel that the clinician could be objective, given the lengthy therapeutic relationship between the clinician and the father. Rarely are the rules set in stone about these decisions; rather, clinicians are left to apply the ethical guidelines to each situation individually as it arises. As noted in Ethical Standard 8.02, psychologists can consult with other professionals (if the confidentiality of their clients is maintained) in order to help resolve an ethical dilemma.

Always do right. This will gratify some people, and astonish the rest.

—Mark Twain

CONFIDENTIALITY AND LIMITS TO CONFIDENTIALITY

As noted in Ethical Standard 5.02, clinicians and therapists must maintain the confidentiality rights of their clients. **Confidentiality** means that, to the extent of the law, therapists must protect identifying information and personal clinical material about clients—including even the fact that a client is a client. This type of information is considered private and under the purview of only the therapist and the client. Unless clinicians have the written permission of the clients (or the parents of the client in the case of children), they cannot disclose any information regarding the therapy or assessment services to anyone other than the client. Legal and ethical limits to confidentiality will be discussed later in this section.

Imagine that a therapist is working with a family in which the 16-year-old son is having severe mood swings and is having difficulty in school. The therapist might feel that the best interventions could be made by conducting individual therapy with the boy, promising him confidentiality so that he will open up to the therapist without fear that his parents will learn about his personal difficulties. In this situation, the therapist would of course need to clarify the ground rules for confidentiality. One such rule might be nothing the boy says to the therapist will be disclosed to the parents unless it is life-threatening. (This limitation will be discussed later in this section.) Issues of substance abuse or sexual involvement (assuming these activities were not imminently life threatening) would be held in confidence. The parents and the adolescent would need to agree to these ground rules about confidentiality before the therapist could begin any individual sessions with the boy. The therapist would also have to honor these rules of confidentiality for the duration of therapy, unless he received the boy's permission to share information with the parents.

In some ways, the concept of confidentiality seems simple—everything between therapists and clients is private. Putting confidentiality into practice, however, is more of a challenge than might be evident at first glance (Koocher & Keith-Spiegel, 1998). Suppose, for example, that a teacher knows that a student is in treatment with a therapist. If the teacher calls the therapist, the therapist is not allowed to even acknowledge that he knows the stu-

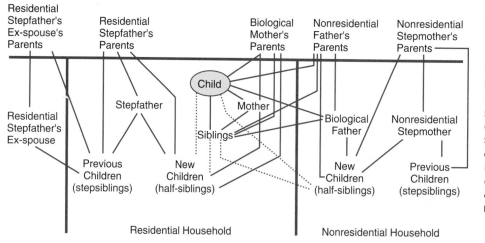

FIGURE 3.1 Potential complexity in stepfamilies. Solid lines represent biological relationships; dashed lines indicate stepsibling or half-sibling relationships.

Source: E. R. Anderson & Greene (1999). In Wendy K. Silverman & Thomas H. Ollendick, *Developmental issues in the clinical treatment of children,* Copyright © 1999 by Allyn & Bacon. Reprinted by permission.

Case Study: When the Roles in Therapy Change

Katie is an eight-year-old who attends a rigorous private school. Although she was born with congenital deformities that make her look different from her peers, she has been accepted by teachers and students alike. She has always had academic difficulties, but these difficulties have been becoming more intense. Katie's parents requested psychoeducational testing so that they could determine whether or not Katie had a learning disorder.

Dr. K evaluated Katie and found that she had average intelligence and average academic functioning. Although no learning disorders were identified, Dr. K suggested that Katie's parents consider transferring Katie to a less rigorous school. With average abilities, Katie was sure to fall behind in her current private-school placement.

During the feedback session, Katie's mother seemed relieved by the results and stated that she would support Katie's transfer to another, less rigorous school. Katie's father, however, was upset by the results and insisted that Katie should stay in her current school and that she would just have to receive additional tutoring and extra help. Dr. K contracted with the parents to

meet with them for a brief number of therapy sessions in order to resolve this issue. She clarified her changing role with the parents and met with them while Katie stayed with a babysitter.

During the therapy sessions, it became clear that Katie's father felt tremendous guilt about his daughter's physical deformities. He felt that her difficulties in school were yet another sign of his inability to be a good father. Through work with Dr. K, both parents were able to identify their own wishes for Katie and were able to separate those wishes from what was in Katie's best interest.

This case study provides an example of a therapist who was able to change the focus of clinical work with a family throughout the testing and therapy. Although sometimes different clients have conflicting needs, Dr. K was able to work with the family to come to a reasonable solution that suited the best interests of all of the family members (i.e., transferring Katie to a more appropriate school while also dealing with the father's feelings of being a failure).

SOURCE: Yanagida (1998).

---

dent unless he has written permission from the child and the child's parent. In another situation, imagine that a family therapist is at the movies with her romantic partner and she runs into a family she is treating. The therapist cannot initiate an acknowledgement of the family's presence but rather must wait for one of the family members to acknowledge her. In addition, the therapist cannot explain to her partner how or why she knows this family, because it would break the family's confidentiality. There are myriad difficult ethical situations that arise and test therapists' ability to maintain confidentiality (see, e.g., Box 3.3). Most of these situations can be dealt with through training and supervision, but even experienced clinicians are sometimes presented with dilemmas regarding confidentiality. In general, the most conservative choice (i.e., maintain confidentiality at all costs) is the most ethical choice.

Given the sacred nature of confidentiality, it is important to realize that confidentiality has its limits. As noted in Ethical Standard 5.01, therapists must discuss these limits with clients at the outset of therapy or assessment services. Confidentiality may be especially limited in family therapy. Therapists who work with children, adolescence, and families may decide who will have access to what information. A therapist might set up the rules so that all information shared by each family member may be shared with the other family members. That is, all information would still be kept within the family, but no individual confidentiality would be promised. Thus, if the father calls the therapist to acknowledge that he is having

an affair, the therapist would have to remind him that this information might be shared with his wife. Overall, there are few set rules to follow regarding confidentiality within the family other than the ethical guideline to make the rules known at the outset of the treatment or assessment process (Koocher & Keith-Spiegel, 1998). The case study of Donna illustrates what may happen if this guideline is not followed.

The ultimate measure of [people] is not where [they stand] in moments of comfort and convenience, but where [they stand] at times of challenge and controversy.

—Dr. Martin Luther King

The therapist working with families must also acknowledge at the outset that some limits to confidentiality are firmly established in state law. Most states do not allow the following topics to be kept confidential:

- Imminent suicide for clients of any age.
- Imminent homicide for clients of any age.
- Physical abuse of children under the age of 18.
- Sexual abuse of children under the age of 18 (or in some states a younger age, such as 16).
- Psychological or emotional abuse of children under the age of 18.
- Neglect of children under the age of 18.
- Abuse of an elderly or incapacitated adult.

BOX 3.3

THE ETHICS OF VIDEOTAPING THERAPY SESSIONS WITH CHILDREN

One wrinkle in the issue of confidentiality and consent to treatment is the use of video cameras (or other recording devices) during assessment and therapy sessions with children and adolescents. Most often, videotaping is conducted when the clinician is still in training. The videotapes are viewed by the clinician's supervisor so that the supervisor can suggest new and more effective therapeutic techniques in the assessment or therapy sessions.

Based on the ethics regarding informed consent and confidentiality, child clients and their parents must be informed of the wish to videotape, of who will have access to the videotapes, and of whether or not the videotapes will be saved. In most cases, videotapes are viewed only by the supervisor and the supervision group and are usually destroyed (or taped over) once the supervisor has viewed them. Like confidential written records, videotapes must be stored in a secure manner so that no one other than the therapist and supervisor has access to them. If any videotapes were chosen to be used for training and educational purposes outside the therapist's own supervision group, child clients and parents would need to provide their explicit agreement for the tapes to be used in this manner. Child clients and parents cannot be forced into agreeing to be videotaped regardless of the purpose of the videotaping.

SOURCE: Dodds (1985).

These limits to confidentiality are based on the idea that clinicians are in a unique position to prevent harm from coming to their clients, especially if those clients are children and adolescents (Pryzwansky & Wendt, 1999).

How a clinician should react to the issues listed above will depend somewhat on the situation. In the case of a child or adolescent who talks of committing suicide, clinicians would need to assess the severity of the suicidal wishes. This assessment usually includes discussion of whether the client has a plan for suicide, the lethality of the planned suicide, the accessibility to the planned suicide, and the history of suicidal behavior in the client. Clients are considered more at risk for imminent suicide if they have a specific plan (as opposed to general feelings of wanting to be dead); if the plan is lethal (e.g., guns and hanging are more lethal than taking a handful of aspirin); if they have access to the plan (e.g., if there is a gun in the house); and if they have a history of suicide attempts. Beyond conducting an assessment interview for suicidality, the therapist may use a standardized measure to assess the suicidal intent of children and adolescents.

Should the assessment indicate that a child or adolescent is imminently suicidal, the therapist can take any of a number of actions, but all actions should be geared toward preventing the suicide attempt (Pryzwansky & Wendt, 1999). The ultimate way of protecting children and adolescents from harming themselves is to admit them to a psychiatric hospital or a crisis unit where they can be monitored 24 hours a day. Parents can be involved in hospitalizing their children, but there are also involuntary commitment procedures that clinicians can initiate in order to get their clients immediate help in a safe environment. Involuntary commitment can range from 2 to 15 days (depending on the state) but must be reviewed by a judge in order to determine that the commitment is warranted (Pryzwansky & Wendt, 1999). Most states have strict limitations on involuntary commitment (with the goal of not hampering the civil liberties of individuals), and the therapist must understand the procedure thoroughly. Sometimes, children or adolescents report suicidal wishes to their therapist, only to recant these wishes when asked by the professionals conducting the involuntary commitment procedures. In these cases, the commitment procedures may still continue, given that the professionals may believe that the child's or adolescent's recantation is not veridical (i.e., genuine). In situations where the child or adolescent is not considered imminently suicidal but is still thought to be at some risk for suicide, clinicians may inform the parents of the child's or adolescent's wishes and may provide the parents with the local crisis number in case the child or adolescent becomes more serious about suicide. Parents are also informed that most local police departments can deal with suicidal clients in an emergency and that, in most jurisdictions, police officers can transport a suicidal client to a crisis center for the client's own protection.

In the case of homicidality, clinicians must take steps to prevent their client from harming someone else. Often, prevention takes the form of involuntary commitment for the client. If the intended victim is identifiable (e.g., if an adolescent boy says that he wants to kill his girlfriend because she cheated on him), then many states also mandate clinicians to warn the intended victim. Based on a California incident known as the **Tarasoff case**, these

Case Study: Parents of an Adolescent Who Feels Betrayed

Donna is a sexually active 15-year-old who feels alienated from her parents. In her therapy with Dr. C, she acknowledged that she had contracted genital herpes. At some point, Donna's parents discovered that she had genital herpes; when they challenged her on her sexual activity, she retorted that they were not as "understanding as Dr. C." Donna's parents were furious. They felt that, by not informing them, Dr. C had implicitly condoned Donna's sexual activity. The parents threatened to terminate Donna's treatment if Dr. C would not quickly set up a meeting with them. They also threatened to file an ethics complaint against Dr. C.

The primary problem in this case is that the rules of confidentiality were not established at the beginning of therapy. Dr. C should have met with the parents and Donna in the first session and described the ground rules of confidentiality within the therapy sessions. If the parents had been unwilling to abide by Dr. C's practice of keeping all but life threatening information confidential between herself and Donna, then they could have sought therapy services elsewhere. Conversely, if Donna's parents had agreed to this type of arrangement at the outset of therapy, they probably would not have been upset by Dr. C's knowledge of Donna's sexual activity. The parents may have still felt jealous or envious of Donna's trust and respect for the therapist, and they would undoubtedly have felt distress over Donna's sexual activity and sexually transmitted disease, but at least they would not have felt betrayed by Dr. C.

SOURCE: Koocher & Keith-Spiegel (1998).

---

laws suggest that clinicians must take steps not only to prevent the homicide from occurring but also must warn the intended victim so that he or she can take the necessary precautionary steps if the client is released from the crisis center or hospital. If the client has not broken the law, legal charges cannot be filed and he or she cannot be incarcerated in a jail or prison. For this reason, cases of homicidality are often dealt with through the involuntary hospitalization statutes in the client's jurisdiction. The rules vary somewhat in different states, and case law has established different standards of care in different states, so it is incumbent upon clinicians to know the relevant legal and ethical statutes in their area of practice. (Box 3.4 discusses a specialized area of duty-to-warn statues.)

In the case of physical abuse, sexual abuse, psychological or emotional abuse, or neglect of a child under the age of 18, clinicians are mandated to report their suspicions to the child protective agency in their area (Pryzwansky & Wendt, 1999). Clinicians are usually allowed to inform the family that they will file a report, but they are usually mandated to make the report even if the family tries to talk them out of doing so. Each state has its own system of reporting suspected abuse, but most follow a similar process. In most states, other professionals (such as teachers, physicians, social workers, and day care workers) are also mandated to report their suspicions of child abuse (Pryzwansky & Wendt, 1999; Reppucci & Aber, 1992). Most often, after the clinician (or teacher, or physician, or other professional, or caring citizen) makes the report to child protective services, that agency must investigate the report within a brief time frame (usually within 24 hours). After an investigation (which usually involves interviewing children or adolescents away from their parents, and also includes interviews with teachers, day care workers,

and family members), the child protective services agency must determine whether or not the abuse allegations are substantiated. From that point, many different scenarios may take place: Children may be removed from the home for their own safety; parents may be mandated to attend parenting classes or substance abuse programs; parents may be arrested and charged formally for child abuse and then dealt with through the criminal system; or the child protective agency, after determining that there are no grounds for the complaints, may close the case without any additional action. Figure 3.2 shows a flowchart of events that might follow a report of suspected child abuse from a clinician or other professional who was mandated to report the abuse.

Unfortunately, psychologists and other professionals continue to need a great deal of education in order to maintain compliance with child abuse reporting regulations (Haas, Malouf, & Mayerson, 1995). As long as clinicians make child abuse reports in good faith, they are not usually legally liable for filing complaints that are later found to be unsubstantiated. Note that finding a report to be unsubstantiated does not necessarily mean that no abuse occurred. Unfortunately, sometimes actual abuse cannot be substantiated easily, so the case has to be closed without immediate follow-up. In those cases, additional reports to the child protective agency might allow a reinvestigation that would enable a substantiation of the reports at the time.

The same process can occur for allegations of abuse of an elderly person or of an incapacitated adult (e.g., an adult who is severely developmentally delayed, or an adult who is physically ill and unable to protect him- or herself, or an adult who is in a coma). Most states have different agencies that handle reports of abuse of adults

BOX *3.4*

DUTY TO WARN AND THE POSSIBLE TRANSMISSION OF HUMAN IMMUNODEFICIENCY VIRUS (HIV)

An intriguing issue has arisen regarding clinicians' duty to warn when they know that their clients are HIV-positive and when they know that their clients are engaging in unprotected sex. Given the increasing numbers of adolescents who are HIV-positive or who have developed acquired immunodeficiency syndrome (AIDS), the question arises as to whether or not having unprotected sex or sharing tainted needles falls under the ethical guidelines regarding potential homicidality and the duty to warn intended victims, as delineated by the Tarasoff case. This area is relatively new within the discussion of ethics, and case laws are still being formulated in different U.S. states and in different countries.

Clinicians must consider these issues carefully before breaking confidentiality to warn a possible victim or to disclose a client's HIV status to the client's parents. The transmission of HIV through unprotected sex or needle sharing would almost never meet the same criteria as homicidality. The transmission of HIV is rarely intentional and is not a certainty even with repeated unprotected sexual encounters or sharing of tainted needles. Thus, this issue has yet to be clarified within either the courts or the ethics boards.

Professionals who work toward the prevention of HIV and AIDS argue that safer-sex methods are a two-way proposition. Specifically, any unprotected sex is potentially lethal, and therefore all partners should take responsibility for their own behavior and demand safer-sex methods (or abstinence) in order to protect themselves from HIV and AIDS. Some preventionists have argued that sexually active adolescents and adults should assume that any sexual partner is HIV-positive and therefore should take the appropriate precautions.

Although there are no clear-cut ethical guidelines to follow when these issues arise, there are some guidelines that clinicians can follow in order to protect their clients and in order to protect the public:

- First and foremost, clinicians should be familiar with state laws and cases regarding disclosure of HIV/AIDS status.
- Once clinicians know a client is HIV-positive, they should offer him or her appropriate resources (e.g., medical referrals, referrals to the local AIDS organization that can provide education, support, and medical services).
- Clinicians should work with their clients to protect further transmission of HIV, by discussing appropriate mechanisms through which to either abstain from sexual contact or to engage in safer-sex methods.
- Clinicians should discuss the advantages of clients' disclosure of their HIV status to their parents and their potential sexual partners.
- If clients refuse or are unable to take appropriate precautions against further transmission of HIV, clinicians must weigh the likelihood of transmission of HIV to a potential victim with the harm that could come from breaking confidentiality to report the client's HIV status (if allowed by state law).

Overall, this is an area that is still under consideration in nearly all countries and in nearly all mental health professions. Mental health professionals must pay attention to state statutes, the best interests of the client, and current case law. When in doubt, clinicians can (keeping the client's anonymity) consult with colleagues or state ethical boards to discuss the best and most ethical course of action.

SOURCES: C. B. Fisher et al. (1999); Knapp & Vande Creek (1990); McGuire, Nieri, Abbott, & Sheridan (1995); Stanard & Hazler (1995); Totten, Lamb, & Reeder (1990).

(e.g., an adult protective agency rather than a child protective agency).

Interestingly, nowhere on the list of limits to confidentiality is a rule involving the abuse of an able-bodied and cognitively competent adult, as in the case of domestic violence. In most states, clinicians who work with adults who are being abused within domestic relationships (e.g., an abused woman) cannot break confidentiality to report this abuse unless the abuse falls under the category of potential homicide. These rules tend to be based on the idea that able-bodied and cognitively competent adults can protect themselves from such abuse and should be

allowed to disclose its occurrence within the therapy or assessment process without fear of the therapist breaking confidentiality. Although clinicians can, of course, work with domestically abused adult clients and try to help them gain the courage and strength to report the abuse of their own free will, they cannot report the abuse without the client's formal written permission. Note, however, that some states are beginning to consider allowing the breach of confidentiality to report severe cases of domestic violence (Reaves & Ogloff, 1996).

Overall, there are strict guidelines for clinicians to follow regarding confidentiality within the assessment and therapy process. Although some states differ regarding the specific ways in which these guidelines are legislated, nearly all states have some formal manner through which to protect clients' confidentiality in the assessment and therapy process. Note also that children and adolescents have legal rights within the school system (Box 3.5).

Honesty: the best of all the lost arts.

—Mark Twain

CHILDREN'S LEGAL RIGHTS IN TREATMENT DECISIONS

In the most formal and legal sense of the word, parents are ultimately responsible for making treatment decisions for children and adolescents (Koocher & Keith-Spiegel, 1998; Pryzwansky & Wendt, 1999). There are some limitations to parental rights, such as with emancipated minors, but parents for the most part have control over treatment decisions for their children and adolescents (Melton & Ehrenreich, 1992). Not only do parents or

legal guardians have the legal right to request or deny assessment and treatment services, but they most often can provide or deny logistical access to assessment and treatment services for their offspring. A clinician in independent practice can prepare the most elegant treatment plan imaginable, and can have the cooperation of the child or adolescent client, but unless the parents are willing to provide transportation and payment (or insurance documentation) for these services, then the child or adolescent client will probably not receive them.

Conversely, it is not unheard of for parents to request assessment and treatment services for children and adolescents who do not desire those services. One study suggested that 79% of children and adolescents showed significant reluctance and dissatisfaction toward therapy (L. Taylor, Adelman, & Kaser-Boyd, 1985). Unless the assessment or treatment is court-mandated, children and adolescents cannot formally be required to participate. They can, however, be placed against their will in a clinician's office for a specified amount of time each week. Most clinicians will work with resistant children and adolescents in order to find a mutually agreed-upon area for

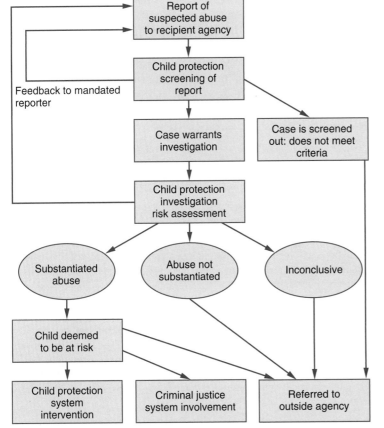

FIGURE 3.2 Flow of Events Following a Report of Suspected Child Maltreatment

Source: Kalichman (1993).

the intervention (Melton & Ehrenreich, 1992). For example, parents may want the therapist to work on the child's stubbornness, but the child may want to work on negotiating more flexibility in the parent–child relationship. Clinicians can work cooperatively with parents and children to find the treatment goals that are most appropriate and that serve the needs of all family members.

With regard to services within a hospitalized setting, parents in most states can hospitalize a child against the child's will. Ethical and honorable psychiatric hospitals and residential treatment facilities would accept admissions only for those children and adolescents who require their services. Most often, these services are reserved for children and adolescents who are in need of extensive treatment (e.g., due to suicidality, homicidality, severe conduct problems, or severe substance abuse). As with adults, children and adolescents can also be hospitalized against their will (and even against the parents' will) through legal involuntary commitment proceedings. Usually these proceedings are instituted only when children or adolescents are imminently suicidal or homicidal.

Overall, children and adolescents have fewer rights than do adults regarding involuntary treatment. There are a great number of safeguards to prevent unnecessary treatment of children and adolescents, especially if the source of the problem is located somewhere other than in the child or adolescent. There are, however, horror stories that are uncovered occasionally about children or adolescents who are hospitalized against their will for problems that have little to do with them. There has also been recent debate about the ethics of using electroconvulsive therapy (ECT) for young children against their will (P. Knapp, 2001; Rudnick, 2001). Mental health advocates frequently try to prevent any of these abuses from occurring.

ETHICS OF CONDUCTING RESEARCH

Specific ethical guidelines for conducting research in the field of mental health cover the areas of planning research (Ethical Standard 6.06), gaining institutional approval (Ethical Standard 6.10), obtaining informed consent for research participation (Ethical Standard 6.11), and providing participants with information about the study (Ethical Standard 6.18). All of these ethical standards are relevant to research with children as well as adults. These ethical standards are consistent with the ethical standards followed within other disciplines, such as school psychology (Phillips, 1999).

In essence, these guidelines suggest that research must be conducted with competence and in an objective manner that is consistent with scientific practice in that area. It is incumbent upon researchers to know the current standard practices within their area of research (Bersoff & Bersoff, 1999). Any research with children and adolescents must be approved by the **institutional review board** that monitors the researchers' work. Usually this type of board exists at the college or university in which the researcher works, but many schools and mental health facilities also have their own review board for any research that is requested at that facility. In these cases, researchers must acquire permission from all relevant review boards before beginning the research process. Many professors of psychology, education, social work, and psychiatry must gain approval from the scientific review committee in their department, from the research review board at the site where they wish to collect data (e.g., the school or mental health facility), and from the university's institutional review board (Bersoff & Bersoff, 1999). Although these multiple levels of review some-

---

Case Study: A Young Adolescent Who Wanted Help

Jackie is a 13-year-old boy who walked into a community mental health center and asked to speak to someone. He met with Dr. G and proceeded to tell him of the many difficulties and troubles in his life. He also reported to Dr. G that his parents severely abused him. He asked Dr. G not to talk with anyone about these issues, especially not his parents. Dr. G then informed Jackie that he could not provide therapy to anyone under with age of 18 without parental consent and went further to tell Jackie that he was mandated to report the physical abuse. Jackie felt betrayed by Dr. G.

There are two issues that arise in this case study. Dr. G should have mentioned the issue of parental consent immediately upon

meeting Jackie. This policy is not consistent across states, and some states allow a limited number of therapy sessions without parental consent if the therapist deems that parental consent would hamper the initial therapeutic process. Dr. G should also have discussed the issue of limits to confidentiality before Jackie began his self-disclosure. Dr. G's failure on these two issues not only led to Jackie's feeling of betrayal but may also have fostered a mistrust of mental health professionals in general that would prevent Jackie from seeking help in the future. This case illustrates the importance of covering these ground rules at the outset of therapy rather than waiting until a sensitive issue arises.

SOURCE: Koocher & Keith-Spiegel (1998).

times slow down the research process, they have been established in order to protect the rights of research participants and to ensure that the research has scientific merit.

As in therapy, informed consent and assent must be obtained from parents and children, respectively, who are involved in research. Parents must provide their written informed consent before researchers can ever contact individual children for data collection. Depending on the age of the children, informed assent from the children is usually warranted. Obviously, different research projects will have to follow different procedures depending on the child's age and level of functioning. No one in their right mind would suggest that infants should provide written informed assent to participate in research. Likewise, if children or adolescents are severely cognitively or psychiatrically impaired (due to developmental disabilities or psychosis), it may not be appropriate to request their

---

BOX 3.5

THE LEGAL RIGHTS OF STUDENTS

Beyond concerns about the rights of children and adolescents in therapy are those about the legal rights of children and adolescents within the school system. School psychologists and other professionals within the school system are often faced with the difficult task of trying to follow legal statutes that may or may not be in the best interests of children and adolescents. Some of these legal rights are different depending on the state and the country, but the following is a list of considerations regarding the legal rights of students:

- *Access to education:* Within the United States and many other countries, children and adolescents are mandated to have access to free public education. Both upper and lower age limits vary somewhat in different jurisdictions.
- *Compulsory attendance:* Most educational systems require attendance but also provide stipulations for nonattendance (e.g., due to a student's employment, hardship in traveling to the school, or religious restrictions).
- *Classifications:* Students can be classified for different services within the educational system, but these classification systems must follow appropriate state and federal guidelines (e.g., placing the student in the least restrictive environment; having the student and parents involved in the decision-making process; ensuring that the classification system is not prejudicial based on race, ethnicity, culture, or language abilities).
- *Health regulations:* Nearly all school systems have some regulations regarding immunization and health standards for students. These regulations are usually put in place to protect the welfare of students themselves as well as the other students and school staff.
- *Behavior outside of school:* Most school systems cannot regulate students' behavior outside of school, unless that behavior affects students' behavior during the school day.
- *Behavior during school:* Most school systems have some type of code of conduct for students during the school day. These codes of conduct can refer to everything from

clothing and hairstyles to behavior. Some court cases have disallowed certain dress codes within some schools (e.g., regulating hairstyle is often found to be unconstitutional, since there is no link between hairstyle and maladaptive behavior). Private schools have more leeway in mandating codes of clothing and hairstyle than do public schools.

- *Search and seizure:* State and federal statutes must be maintained in the possible search for and seizure of illegal drugs or weapons in the school setting. Although regulations vary in different jurisdictions, most school personnel have to rely on a "reasonable suspicion" in order to justify the search of students' lockers, students' cars, or students themselves. Some schools have instituted zero-tolerance policies on drugs and weapons, so even if the search was not conducted in such a way that criminal charges can be applied, the student may still be expelled or punished within the school system. Note that there have been some difficulties in the overenforcement of zero-tolerance policies, examples of which seem ridiculous (e.g., a girl being suspended for bringing an over-the-counter medication to school to help her deal with her painful menstrual cramps).
- *Freedom of speech:* Students must be allowed all of their constitutional rights within the school system, including free speech, as long as these rights do not hamper school discipline and crowd control.

Overall, the rights of students within the school system are consistent with their rights as citizens. Occasionally, the rights of students will conflict with the rights of school personnel to maintain a safe and orderly environment for all students. In most cases, reasonable compromises can be achieved through mediation between students and school personnel. In some cases, however, these issues must be brought in front of local, state, and sometimes federal judges in order to establish case laws and precedents regarding these specific issues.

SOURCE: Sales, Krauss, Sacken, & Overcast (1999).

informed assent for participation in research. Children, adolescents, and individuals who are involved in clinical services are considered to be "at risk" when it comes to research involvement. For this reason, professionals on institutional review boards are especially careful about reviewing research with these individuals. Care must be taken to ensure that these at-risk groups are protected from coercion to participate in research and from inappropriate research that is not in their best interest. A number of researchers have raised concerns about children's ability to assent to research, and they have suggested that clinical child researchers investigate children's understanding of the research process (Oesterheld, Fogas, & Rutten, 1998).

In rare instances, informed consent and informed assent are not required, such as when behavioral observations are conducted in a naturalistic setting and the identities of the children and parents are never known. For the overwhelming majority of studies in developmental psychopathology, however, strong adherence to the informed consent and informed assent process is required.

Participation in research should be educational to some degree (Bersoff & Bersoff, 1999). Most often, children and families are provided with a summary of the research findings after the study is completed. This summary should be written in language that is understandable to the participants. Sometimes researchers also share their overall findings with teachers or professionals in mental health facilities in which the research was conducted. The idea is that researchers should not just take information from the research participants and the research site, but should also give something back. In this way, researchers not only can add to the scholarly literature but also can use the research findings to better the lives of the participants in the research.

Regarding confidentiality, suffice it to say that confidentiality is protected within research as it is within assessment and therapy services. Limits to confidentiality in research are comparable to those in assessment and therapy. Research can also be conducted anonymously, so that participants' identities are never linked to any identifying information. Both confidential and anonymous research are allowed with children. In either case, parents and children must be informed as to which type of research is being conducted.

A cornerstone of the ethical guidelines from the American Psychological Association is that research participants must be treated with dignity and respect. There are too many horror stories of unethical research in the past. Currently, there is an attempt to maintain the highest ethical standards when it comes to research with children and adolescents. One of the subtle changes to encourage

---

Case Study: An Overzealous Researcher

Dr. S worked with disadvantaged children in an elementary school setting. Dr. S wanted to try to help these youngsters improve their self-esteem. The children lived in severe poverty. They tended to be teased and taunted by their classmates, and their academic work was substandard because of generations of educational disadvantages. Dr. S decided that she would conduct a study in which she taught the children the correct answers to the Wechsler Intelligence Scale for Children (WISC) and then administered the test. She reasoned that the children's IQs would show improvements and these improvements would help the children feel better about themselves. After receiving written permission from the parents, Dr. S conducted the study. She trained 25 students on the answers to the WISC, administered the test, and found that the student's IQ scores had been raised. Afterward, a colleague in the school system who learned of this research reported Dr. S to the ethics committee, claiming that Dr. S had violated Ethical Standard 2.10, which deals with maintaining the security of standardized tests.

Dr. S informed the ethics committee that her goals in the study were laudable. She felt that it was necessary to improve the self-esteem of the children she had worked with if they were going to have a chance at success in school and in larger society.

Dr. S also stated that there were other intelligence tests, so these children could be tested with alternative tests if needed.

The ethics board reprimanded Dr. S on a number of ethical violations. First, she did not receive approval from the school or from any institutional review board to conduct this study. It is likely that her colleagues would have denied approval for the study she had designed. Second, Dr. S destroyed the possibility of using the WISC with these children if they required standardized testing in the future. Although there are other standardized intelligence tests, the ethics board reasoned that the WISC was the primary intelligence test used at this school and with this population. In addition, the ethics board noted that there was no empirical basis for attempting to raise self-esteem by falsely inflating IQ scores. They reasoned that this tactic could have done more harm than good.

This case illustrates the need for well-formulated, well-reviewed research protocols. Review by an institutional review board is meant to ensure that researchers' ideas are consistent with standard research practices and that participants will not be harmed by their involvement in research. In addition, the detrimental effects of breaking test security were highlighted in this case.

SOURCE: American Psychological Association (1987).

BOX 3.6

ETHICS IN INTERPRETING DATA—IS CHILD SEXUAL ABUSE OKAY?

Although not discussed at length in this chapter, part of the APA's ethical code also suggests that researchers must be careful with how they interpret and present their research findings. A controversial example of this issue occurred in an unlikely source. In 1998, a leading journal in the field of psychology, *Psychological Bulletin*, published a review article entitled "A Meta-analytic Examination of Assumed Properties of Child Sexual Abuse Using College Samples" (Rind, Tromovitch, & Bauserman, 1998). The article summarized studies of college students who had experienced sexual abuse during childhood. The authors concluded: "Self-reported reactions to and effects from child sexual abuse indicated that negative effects were neither pervasive nor typically intense" (p. 22). In plain English, it appeared that the authors were stating that there were few, if any, problems associated with child sexual abuse.

This article led to a firestorm of controversy. A number of pedophile websites used the article as evidence that sex with children was not harmful; the popular radio talk-show host Dr. Laura Schlesinger announced her displeasure with the article and with the APA for publishing it; and the U.S. Congress even got into the act by condemning the idea that sex with "willing" children was acceptable (Ondersma et al., 2001). The APA defended the research as within the bounds of academic freedom, but it also provided significant space in *Psychological Bulletin* for published commentaries that disputed the conclusions in the original article (e.g., Dallam et al., 2001; Ondersma et al., 2001).

From an ethical standpoint, research findings should be presented in a careful and accurate manner in order to prevent misinterpretation or inflammatory responses by others. From a research standpoint, the title of one of the commentaries can best sum up the issue: "Sex with Children Is Abuse" (Ondersma et al., 2001).

respect for individuals involved in research is the use of the word *participants* rather than *subjects*. The word *subjects* implies that someone (i.e., the researcher) is doing something to the passive individual (i.e., the subject). The term *participants*, in contrast, implies the individual is an active member of a team trying to answer interesting research questions. Although the terminology differences are subtle, this change is part of the attempt to be more conscientious about the rights and dignity of individuals involved in research. There is currently a strong spirit of maintaining the dignity of research participants.

The basic premises of ethical research are, first, to be respectful of research participants and clients and, second, to do no harm to research participants and clients (Bersoff & Bersoff, 1999). Although ethical behavior cannot be monitored every second of professionals' lives, and although there are still sometimes examples of unethical research that are brought to light, the overwhelming majority of researchers and clinicians in the field of developmental psychopathology are highly ethical scholars who are greatly concerned about the welfare of children, adolescents, and their families. Box 3.6 provides an example of questionable interpretation and presentation of research results.

SUMMARY AND KEY CONCEPTS

Ethical Responsibilities of Professionals Working with Children and Families

Mental health professionals must show **competence** in their work with children and families. Mental health professionals must guard against **multiple relationships**, which means that they should guard against having different roles with their clients.

Informed Consent and Assent in Assessment and Therapy with Children and Families

Before the therapy or assessment process begins, parents of child clients must provide their written **informed consent** and child clients must provide their **informed assent** to take part in the services. In both cases, parents and children should be informed about what to expect from the professional services and should agree to these services of their own free will.

Confidentiality and Limits to Confidentiality

Confidentiality is one of the most strictly held principles within the mental health field. Clinicians should assure clients that the information that is shared with the clinician will not be disclosed to anyone other than the client. Limits to confidentiality include suicidality, homicidality, child physical abuse, child sexual abuse, child psychological abuse, child neglect, or abuse of an incapacitated or elderly adult. In many states, the **Tarasoff case** is also relevant, which means that clinicians not only should try to prevent homicide from occurring but also must warn an intended victim of their client's wishes to harm the potential victim.

Children's Legal Rights in Treatment Decisions

In most jurisdictions, parents or legal guardians have the ultimate legal rights when it comes to making treatment decisions for children and adolescents.

Ethics of Conducting Research

Ethical principles within research are similar to ethical principles within other domains of professional work with children, adolescents, and families. Before conducting any study, researchers must first have their studies reviewed by an **institutional review board** to verify that the research is ethical and meaningful.

KEY TERMS

competence	multiple relationships	informed consent informed assent	confidentiality Tarasoff case	institutional review board

SUGGESTED READINGS

Rhodes, Ginger, & Rhodes, Richard. *Trying to Get Some Dignity*. New York: William Morrow and Company, 1996. This book provides extraordinary first-person accounts of childhood abuse. These survivors' accounts of childhood abuse should make the ethics of reporting suspected abuse all the more salient.

Neugeboren, Jay. *Imagining Robert: My brother, madness, and survival*. New York: Henry Holt and Company, 1997. This memoir by the brother of a schizophrenic explore in depth the issues surrounding access to treatment, medication, and follow-up care.

SUGGESTED VIEWINGS

Prince of Tides (1991). Barbara Streisand (director), Pat Conroy and Becky Johnston (screenwriters), based on novel by Pat Conroy. VHS/DVD. In this painful film, a therapist helps a young woman and her brother cope with childhood trauma. Although there are many examples of unethical behavior (e.g., the therapist becomes romantically involved with her client's brother), the film illustrates some of the important features of a caring therapist.

Mrs. Doubtfire (1993). Chris Columbus (director), Randi Mayem Singer and Leslie Dixon (screenwriters), based on novel by Anne Fine. VHS/DVD. Although not a film about ethics per se, this comedy/drama addresses the issue of parental rights after divorce. Imagine being a therapist with this family and having to work with the battling parents in the children's best interests.

RESEARCH METHODS IN THE STUDY OF DEVELOPMENTAL PSYCHOPATHOLOGY

Facts are stubborn things; and whatever may be our wishes, our inclinations, or the dictates of our passions, they cannot alter the state of facts and evidence.

—John Adams

How do you know what you know? That is, how do you know that what you believe to be true is really true? From an existential standpoint, you might just say that you know what you know because of what you've experienced. Or, possibly, you just have a gut feeling about certain topics. From a more objective standpoint, one way of finding out accurate information is to conduct research. Consider these fictious headlines that you might read in your local newspaper:

- "Children from Single-Parent Homes More Likely to Be Arrested"
- "Music by Mozart Makes Children Smarter"
- "Mothers' Love Is Crucial to Development"

Such statements should be made only if there are empirical studies to back up the findings. Not only should social scientists conduct experimental research before making a summary statement, but they should use a specific type of experimental research design. Results from research must also be conveyed in a fair and objective manner.

Research methods are important in any field of study, but they are especially important in developmental psychopathology. What we think we know about children and their problems should be verified and clarified in rigorous studies. Before acting on clinical hunches simply because they seem to make sense, it is imperative to examine the issue at hand within a sound study. An illustration can be used to make this point.

In 1990, a technique called **facilitated communication (FC)** was popularized in the United States as a means of communicating with autistic children (Biklen, 1990; Biklen, Morton, Saha, & Duncan, 1991). In FC, a facilitator holds a letter board, keyboard, or a typing machine for the autistic child, and often holds the child's hand, while the child types out his or her thoughts and feelings. The idea behind FC was that autistic children had the cognitive capacities to communicate, but their disorder hampered their physical ability to do so. With this difficulty in mind, FC was meant to unlock the child's thoughts and feelings in a way that looked to be promising and powerful. Autistic children, who were previously thought to be developmentally delayed and incapable of sophisticated thoughts, were now doing algebra and writing poetry. The words that came from these children were amazing (Frontline documentary, 1993):

- "Autism held me hostage for 17 years but not anymore because now I can talk."
- "I cry a lot about my disability . . . It makes me feel bad when I can't do my work by myself."

The testimonials from teachers and parents were likewise amazing.

- "I thought it was wonderful. At last we were going to help these people communicate."
- "We find that once we open this world for the kids, they are social now, they are appropriate, they do have language, they do understand."

Thousands of facilitators throughout the United States and other countries were trained to use FC. Thousands, if not millions, of dollars were spent to purchase facilitating machines, to train facilitators, and to hire trained facilitators in special education schools. And why not? Look again at those testimonials. The people closest to these children knew that FC was a technique that worked. If you had been in one of those classrooms and seen FC in action, you probably would have been a believer. Why would anyone question the power of this exciting new technique?

Well, as it turns out, FC had not been tested in a rigorous manner to establish that it really worked. The belief in it was founded on anecdotes. It was only after FC was used to charge a number of parents and caretakers with sexual abuse that many professionals and families started wondering about who was actually typing those facilitated communications (e.g., Hudson, Melita, & Arnold, 1993). For this reason, a number of empirical studies were instituted to test out the FC process to ensure that it really was the autistic individual, and not the facilitator, who was authoring the words on the facilitation board.

These studies included a series of **double blind studies** in which the facilitator was placed next to the autistic child and both looked at pictures at the end of a long table. There was a partition between the facilitator and the autistic child so that neither participant could see what the other was seeing. Sometimes the facilitator and the autistic child were shown the same stimulus; at other times they were shown different stimuli. The test of FC came when the facilitator and child were shown different stimuli. If the child was shown a picture of a cat and the facilitator was shown a picture of a shoe, what would be typed? If FC worked, then the word *cat* should be typed because that is what the child saw. If the word *shoe* were typed, then the facilitator might actually be authoring the words that were supposed to be the child's words.

Study after study showed that it was really the facilitator who was authoring the words (Moore, Donovan, Hudson, & Dykstra, 1993; Myles & Simpson, 1994). For example, when an autistic child was shown a picture of a key and the facilitator was shown a picture of a dog, the word *dog* was typed. When the child was shown a picture of a box and the facilitator was shown a picture of an apple, the word *apple* was typed. Many studies found comparable results (Prior & Cummins, 1992). Even in the best of circumstances—when the facilitators were highly trained, and working with the most capable autistic children—the results still suggested that the words were the facilitator's and not the child's.

These findings are not meant to suggest that most facilitators were typing the words consciously. The overwhelming majority of facilitators were concerned individuals who thought that they were unlocking the inner thoughts of children who had been shut out from the world previously. Unfortunately, these beliefs were so unquestioned that even thoughtful, caring individuals were swept up in the hype. Even more unfortunate is that the autistic children were not being helped by this technique; still worse, some may have been harmed by the ramifications of this technique (e.g., false reports of sexual abuse that tore up otherwise stable family environments).

In most cases, as more information about the bogus nature of FC was established, the technique was dropped as quickly as it had been adopted. Although there are still some true believers (Biklen & Cardinal, 1997), academicians and educators have dismissed FC as a useless technique.

The FC debacle illustrates the extraordinary need for empirical research. Even when you "know" something to be true because you have seen it with your own eyes, you should question whether or not the knowledge has also been established through empirical research. (See Box 4.1 for a description of a classic empirical study.) The following description of research methods is meant to make you a better consumer of research and also to highlight ways that you can become involved in research. The research process is an exciting and powerful enterprise with the potential to help more children and families than can be helped by any individual therapy session.

If you are interested in a Ph.D. in clinical child psychology, school psychology, education, or a related field, it makes sense for you to get some experience as a research assistant in order to be competitive for those doctoral programs. In addition, serving as a research assistant will help you learn whether or not research is part of what you want to do, and it might help you make decisions about what type of graduate program to pursue. I got involved in research as an undergraduate because I knew I needed the experience to be a competitive applicant to doctoral programs. Until then, I had only heard about research that seemed uninteresting. When I joined a research project that explored mother–child interactions with hyperactive children, I found that research was not just a means to get into graduate school but also a fascinating and fulfilling pursuit. It can be viewed as a puzzle that challenges the researcher to understand why certain behaviors occur in different situations. Hopefully, you will find that the research process is yet another way to help children and families. This chapter is meant to provide the basics to help get you started.

RESEARCH METHODS USED IN THE STUDY OF DEVELOPMENTAL PSYCHOPATHOLOGY

Research methods used to study developmental psychopathology are comparable to research methods in other areas of inquiry (Drotar, 2000). Thus, if you are familiar with research methods in any area, the ones described in this section should sound familiar. There are, of course, specific issues within developmental psychopathology that are not addressed in other areas of research. Issues related to developmental changes, risk factors, and protective factors permeate the study of developmental psychopathology and are often ignored in other fields of study. Thus, although the methods are comparable to those used in other areas, their focus and application are often unique to the study of developmental psychopathology. In addition to the current discussion of these topics, interested readers are referred to the *Handbook of Research in Pediatric and Clinical Child Psychology: Practical Strategies and Methods* (Drotar, 2000), an excellent book that should help with the practical issues of conducting research.

As with so many other aspects of research methods, there is no single research design that is superior to all other designs (Proctor & Capaldi, 2001). The choice of a research design depends on the goals of the study and on the research questions and hypotheses that are to be tested. A well-designed study might use multiple methods of data collection (e.g., interviews, questionnaires, and direct observation) and different facets of many research designs (e.g., within an experimental design, there might also be a component of questionnaires that represent the survey method). Although research studies are often specific in the research questions and hypotheses, greater breadth of methodology usually adds strength to the

BOX *4.1*

A CLASSIC STUDY OF AGGRESSION IN CHILDHOOD

A study of aggression in childhood conducted by Dr. Albert Bandura, Dr. Dorothea Ross, and Dr. Sheila Ross (1961) was highlighted in a book entitled, *Forty Studies That Changed Psychology* (R. R. Hock, 1999). Dr. Bandura and his colleagues wanted to understand why some children showed aggression and others did not. They proposed to explore the social learning theory of the development of aggression.

The research was conducted at the Stanford University Nursery School, with 36 boys and 36 girls, ranging in age from three to five years old. The study utilized an experimental design whereby the children were randomly assigned to one of three conditions: the control group (which was not exposed to any model), the nonaggressive model group (which was exposed to a model who did not show aggression), and the aggressive model group (which was exposed to a model who showed aggression). Half of the participants in each group were boys, and half were girls. For children in the modeling groups, half were exposed to a model of the same sex and half viewed a model of the other sex. Thus, there were eight experimental groups and one control group. At the beginning of the study, children in different groups did not differ on levels of aggression.

Children in the control group were left in a playroom for 10 minutes without any other adult present. The playroom was the same for all of the children. It contained two different tables, one with craft activities and stickers, and the other with a Tinkertoy set and a mallet. This second table was near an inflated Bobo doll that was approximately five feet tall. Children in the nonaggressive model group were left in the playroom for 10 minutes with an adult who was playing with the Tinkertoys. Children in the aggressive model group were left in the playroom with the model who played with Tinkertoys for one minute and then interacted aggressively with the Bobo doll for the remaining nine minutes. The aggressive interactions included punching the Bobo doll, hitting it with the mallet, throwing it in the air, while making statements such as "Sock him in the nose," "Hit him down," and "Pow." These aggressive interactions were standardized so that all children in the aggressive model group witnessed the same amount and the same type of aggression.

After this 10-minute session, each child was taken individually to another room by the experimenter (not the model) and allowed to begin playing with a number of attractive toys (such as fire engines and doll sets). The child was soon told that those toys were reserved for other children, so he or she was escorted to yet another room. This intervention was meant to be a somewhat frustrating situation for the children, in order to allow aggression to be expressed later.

This final room was filled with lots of toys classified as either aggressive or nonaggressive. Toys such as mallets, dart guns, a tether ball with a face painted on it, a Bobo doll, tea sets, balls, dolls, cars, trucks, plastic farm animals, crayons, and paper were all presented to each child for his or her enjoyment. The experimenter then left the child alone in the room and the child was observed through one-way mirrors. Trained observers recorded children's aggressive behavior for 20 minutes.

Results of the study showed that children exposed to the aggressive model showed significantly more aggression during the 20-minute period. Boys showed 38.2 episodes of physical aggression on average, and girls showed 12.7 episodes of physical aggression on average. With regard to verbal aggression, boys showed an average of 17.0 verbal acts of aggression and girls showed an average of 15.7 verbal acts of aggression. Boys and girls in the control group and in the nonaggressive model group showed virtually no evidence of physical or verbal aggression.

This study was used as compelling evidence that children observe and imitate adult models, even when they themselves are not rewarded for their behavior. This study has been replicated and refined extensively (R. R. Hock, 1999). Overall, the conclusions still hold up today as one way of understanding children's and adolescents' tendencies to become aggressive merely by observing aggression in others around them.

research findings (Gliner et al., 2000; G. A. Morgan et al., 2000).

Experimental Designs

Experimental designs are the cornerstone of the scientific study of psychology. The basic premise of the **experimental design** is that the researcher recruits participants into the study; conducts **random assignment**, in which participants are put randomly into one of two or more groups; administers an **independent variable** that is the experimental manipulation provided by the researcher (often a type of treatment intervention or different situation that the child or family has to deal with); and then measures the **dependent variable** in order to determine the impact of the independent variable. An example from work on the prevention of psychopathology is highlighted by a study conducted in Minneapolis, Minnesota. Dr. Lauren Braswell and her colleagues (Braswell, August, Bloomquist, & Realmuto, 1997) identified children at risk for the development of disruptive disorders, randomly assigned children to receive either a multicomponent competence enhancement intervention (MCEI) or some basic information and attention (control group). The researchers then measured the outcome of psychological functioning two years later. In this example, the preventive intervention (MCEI versus control group) is the independent variable and the outcome (psychological functioning) is the dependent variable. This study found that, after two years, children in both the MCEI group and the control group showed increases in adaptive skills, increases in problem-solving skills, decreases in school problems, and decreases in internalizing symptoms. These results highlight the importance of a control group, given that the positive changes were not specific to the intervention (Braswell et al., 1997).

The strength of the experimental design is that researchers can argue for or against **causality** regarding the impact of the independent variable on the dependent variable. That is, the researcher can claim legitimately that the manipulation of the independent variable "caused" or "did not cause" the changes that were found in the dependent variable. This point is crucial in understanding research results. Because most other research designs do not allow researchers to claim causality, use of the experimental design provides researchers with unique confidence in their conclusions.

You may be wondering why not every researcher uses the experimental design. Given the strength of the design and the conclusions that can be drawn, why would a researcher use any other design? As you might have already guessed, there are a huge number of topics that cannot be addressed with the experimental design. Imagine that you wanted to assess the real impact of psychological abuse of children. In order to argue causality with an experimental design, you would need to recruit young, nonabused children into your study and then randomly assign them to either an abused group (where their parents are required to psychologically abuse them) or to a nonabused group (where their parents are encouraged not to psychologically abuse them). Obviously, this type of research is unthinkable. Thus, the experimental design does not work for many topics within the purview of developmental psychopathology. Sometimes a prospective longitudinal design can help researchers to argue causality (e.g., following children from infancy and then measuring the functioning later in childhood of those children who were or were not abused). In its truest form, however, the experimental design is the best design to enable conclusions related to causality.

Luckily, there are a number of clinical child issues that have been explored through the experimental design and through laboratory-based procedures, including anxiety (Vasey & Lonigan, 2000); depression (Garber & Kaminski, 2000); conduct problems (Frick & Loney, 2000); and attention-deficit/hyperactivity disorder (Rapport, Chung, Shore, Denney, & Isaacs, 2000).

A torn jacket is soon mended, but hard words bruise the heart of a child.

—Henry Wadsworth Longfellow

Quasi-Experimental Designs

For researchers who want to explore group differences where random assignment is impossible or unethical, the **quasi-experimental design** provides a useful option (Morgan, Gliner, & Harmon, 2000). The quasi-experimental design allows researchers to compare groups that already exist. The primary differences between the experimental method and the quasi-experimental method are the lack of random assignment and the lack of manipulation of the independent variable in the quasi-experimental method. Although the quasi-experimental method can help researchers infer the causal differences between groups, true conclusions of causality can be obtained only with the experimental design.

When researchers find differences between two already-existing groups through the quasi-experimental method, why not claim causality based on the characteristic that differs between the two groups? The answer is that there may be factors other than the independent variable that allow the two groups to differ. Imagine conducting a study of the health and responsiveness of neonates born to smoking mothers and fathers versus those born to nonsmoking mothers and fathers. The researcher could recruit smoking and nonsmoking couples who were expecting a baby and then measure the baby's health and responsiveness at birth. Even if differences are found—say, babies of nonsmoking parents are found to be healthier and more responsive at birth than babies of smoking parents—the researchers still cannot claim that smoking was the sole cause of the differences between the infants. Given what we already know about the negative ramifications of smoking during pregnancy, it could be that parents who continue to smoke during pregnancy may also have other characteristics that would make them different from parents who do not smoke during pregnancy. It could be that nonsmoking parents also eat healthier meals, ingest less liquor, and exercise more appropriately

Quasi-experimental research designs have been used to study the functioning of children who are homeless.

during pregnancy than do smoking parents. Thus, any differences found in the health and responsiveness of the neonates could be due to the smoking or to other health-related behaviors of the parents (or to some combination of these factors). (Box 4.2 provides another example of a quasi-experimental design.) Even with a quasi-experimental research design, researchers must be cautious about interpreting results from a causative perspective because the results may be due to other factors that were not controlled in the study (Morgan et al., 2000).

BOX 4.2

A CASE EXAMPLE OF A QUASI-EXPERIMENTAL DESIGN

A number of researchers have explored the psychological ramifications of homelessness. Obviously, researchers cannot conduct an experiment in which children and their families are assigned randomly either to be homeless or to have a home. Yet researchers can use a quasi-experimental design in which known groups of children (homeless versus not homeless) can be compared. The design does not allow formal conclusions of causality, but it does allow a detailed exploration of the differences between children and adolescents who either do or do not have a place to live.

One study explored homeless adolescents (McCaskill, Toro, & Wolfe, 1998). The researchers identified homeless adolescents and compared their functioning with matched adolescents who were housed. Many of the homeless adolescents were recruited from runaway shelters and through advocates for the homeless in an urban community. Housed adolescents were recruited from the neighborhoods in which the homeless adolescents used to reside.

Differences between the two groups emerged for some but not all of the variables in the study. Homeless adolescents showed higher rates of disruptive behavior, more alcohol abuse, more alcohol dependence, and greater overall emotional/behavioral problems than housed adolescents. There were no significant differences between the groups for rates of drug abuse or depression.

This study highlights the type of important questions that can be addressed with the quasi-experimental design. Although causality might be inferred from the study (e.g., homelessness leads to greater disruptive problems, alcohol problems, and overall emotional/behavioral problems), it could be that another factor was responsible for these findings. For example, it could be that adolescents with higher rates of disruptive behavior and alcohol problems are more likely to run away from homes or to be kicked out of their homes than are adolescents without those problems. For this reason, the quasi-experimental design can point researchers in a direction that is likely to explain the group differences but cannot provide causative conclusions with assurance.

Correlational Designs

In contrast to the experimental and quasi-experimental designs, **correlational designs** can be conducted for almost any topic. The term *correlational design* is actually used to represent a combination of many different types of research designed to study the correlation (the simultaneous, related existence) of two or more factors. In correlational designs, researchers do not manipulate any variables and cannot argue causality. The **survey method** is a common correlational design within the field of developmental psychopathology. As the name implies, the survey method uses surveys and questionnaires to assess variables that are later analyzed for connections. This type of research can include questionnaire reports from children, parents, teachers, guidance counselors, clinicians, or physicians. Overall, the survey method is a versatile means of collecting data.

Case Studies and Single-Subject Designs

Both **case studies** and **single-subject designs** (also known as **within-subject designs**) allow thorough investigation of one child or a small number of children (Gliner, Morgan, & Harmon, 2000). Case studies tend to be used at the very beginning of a research venture (when almost nothing is known about a particular constellation of behaviors) or in cases of very rare disorders (Linscheid, 2000). Examples of topics investigated with case studies include selective mutism, where a child talks in some situations but does not talk in other situations such as school (Masten, Stacks, Caldwell-Colbert, & Jackson, 1996), and autoerotic suicide, where adolescents try to intensify their masturbatory orgasm by limiting blood flow to the brain through some type of constricting rope

around their neck and inadvertently end up killing themselves (Sheehan & Garfinkel, 1988). These behaviors are not frequent enough for large-scale survey studies to be conducted, so researchers must piece together a lot of information about the rare cases that come to the attention of clinicians and researchers. Case studies offer a wealth of information about rare or little-understood phenomena, but they can be misleading if the individual children or adolescents are not representative of others who experience those phenomena.

The single-subject, or within-subject, design is well grounded in the behavioral tradition. Most often the single-subject design is used to assess changes in behavior related to a behavioral intervention. These types of studies are often done in special education classrooms and in institutionalized settings for children and adolescents. Recently, psychologists have used single-subject designs to assess the effectiveness of therapy in order be accountable to managed care companies that are paying some portion of the psychologists' fees (D. L. Morgan & R. K. Morgan, 2001).

One example of the single-subject design is the **A-B-A-B design**, also known as the **reversal design**. As illustrated in Figure 4.1 for a child who receives parental attention for appropriate peer interactions, the A-B-A-B design usually allows for baseline data to be collected in the first phase. Then a treatment or intervention is administered in the next phase, the intervention is withdrawn in the third phase, and the intervention is reinstated in the fourth phase. If the intervention works, the desired behavior should be evident in the second and fourth phases (the two B phases) but should be less evident in the first and third phases (the two A phases). This type of single-subject design is usually used with behaviors that can be modified through situational or environmental changes (e.g., attention, rewards, ignoring maladaptive behavior).

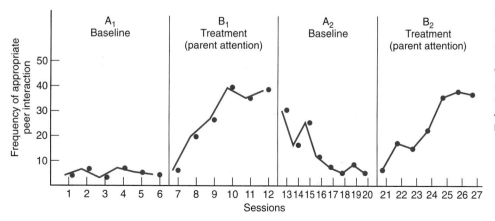

FIGURE 4.1 Example of an A-B-A-B Design

Source: Clifford J. Drew, Michael L. Hardman, & Ann Weaver Hart, *Designing and conducting research (2nd ed.),* Copyright © 1996 by Allyn & Bacon. Reprinted by permission.

The limitation to this design is that changes in behavior may be due to a factor other than the intervention that had not been controlled. For this reason, researchers who use single-subject designs must control the contingencies related to the behavior of interest carefully (Gliner et al., 2000).

High-Risk Designs

A number of studies within developmental psychopathology utilize a **high-risk design,** in which children in a disadvantaged situation are studied and compared with children who are not exposed to that disadvantaged situation. Children at high risk for the development of psychopathology include children living in the lowest socioeconomic status groups (Luthar, 1999; McLoyd, 1998); children from families with high levels of discord or where separation and divorce have occurred (Hetherington, Bridges, & Insabella, 1998); children who have a parent with some type of psychopathology (Kaslow, Deering, & Racusin, 1994; Phares, 1996); and children who have experienced some type of maltreatment (Emery & Laumann-Billings, 1998). Most of this research has the ultimate goal of reducing the children's risk of developing problems (Cicchetti & Rogosch, 1999).

Behavior-Genetic Designs

As mentioned in Chapter 2, a great deal of effort has been put into trying to disentangle genetic and environmental factors that might be related to the development of psychopathology. Even the exploration of neighborhood derivation (Caspi, Taylor, Moffitt, & Plomin, 2000) and parental divorce (O'Connor, Caspi, DeFries, & Plomin, 2000) have been explored within a **behavioral-genetics design**.

Behavioral-genetics studies typically use either a twin design (where monozygotic and dizygotic twins are compared on a series of characteristics) or an adoption design (where twins or siblings are adopted and raised in different households). Both types of studies can assess the differential contribution of genetic, nonshared environmental, and shared environmental characteristics that are associated with the development of psychopathology in children and adolescents (Cicchetti & Rogosch, 1999a; Deater-Deckard, 2000). Although social and biological approaches to understanding behavior have often been investigated separately, behavioral-genetics research and other techniques within social neuroscience can lead to a more comprehensive understanding of the development of behavior (Cacioppo, Berntson, Sheridan, & McClintock, 2000).

TIME FRAME OF THE STUDY

There are a number of different time frames during which research can be conducted. There is no one correct way to conduct research from the standpoint of time involvement. Rather, researchers must carefully consider the strengths and weaknesses of each strategy before deciding which to use.

Studies on twins can help behavioral geneticists clarify the different influences of nature and nurture.

Reason has no age.

—Proverb of Africa

Cross-Sectional Research

Cross-sectional research involves gathering data at a single point in a child's or adolescent's life (Cicchetti & Rogosch, 1999). The majority of research is cross-sectional largely because this type of study is cheaper and easier to complete than other types. For example, imagine that we wanted to explore the relationship between depressive symptoms and hyperactivity. We could recruit a group of 10-year-olds, some of whom have problems with depression, some of whom have problems with hyperactivity, and some of whom have no known emotional/behavioral problems. We would then assess this group's current symptoms of depression and hyperactivity, and we would not reassess the symptoms at any other point.

The cross-sectional research design provides a wealth of information about children at a particular time in their lives, but it does not allow researchers to look at changes over time. This limitation is especially problematic in the area of developmental psychopathology, where a great deal of emphasis is placed on the stability and changes in children's emotional/behavioral functioning over time. For those researchers who can afford it (both in terms of time and money), a stronger research design would involve the prospective longitudinal approach.

Life would be infinitely happier if we could only be born at the age of eighty and gradually approach eighteen.

—Mark Twain

Prospective Longitudinal Research

In contrast to the cross-sectional approach, the **prospective longitudinal research** design allows researchers to follow groups of children and adolescents over time. The time frame is often somewhat brief (e.g., six months), but it can be much longer—projects have, for example, ranged over 14 years (Hofstra, VanderEnde, & Verhulst, 2000) and more than 30 years (Werner, 1995; Werner & Smith, 2001). The advantage of prospective longitudinal research is that researchers can capture the developmental changes that are inevitable in children and adolescents. The drawback, however, is that the fact of being in the study might actually alter the behavior that is exhibited by the child or family (a process known as reactivity). Thus, even long-term prospective longitudinal research has limitations. A series of prospective longitudinal studies has been conducted by Caspi and his colleagues, who have explored long-term associations between toddlers' tem-

perament and young adults' psychopathology (Caspi, 2000); young adolescents' conduct problems and young adults' mental health difficulties (Arseneault, Moffitt, Caspi, Taylor, & Silva, 2000); and adolescents' school attendance and criminal behavior in adulthood (Henry, Caspi, Moffitt, Harrington, & Silva, 1999). Overall, this type of research is time-consuming and expensive but also helpful in identifying the life courses of problems found in early childhood. (See Box 4.3 for an example.)

Accelerated Longitudinal Research

Accelerated longitudinal research is also known as cohort-sequential or cross-sequential research. This design allows researchers to follow groups of children over time, with some attention given to overlap in their ages at the start of the study (Cicchetti & Rogosch, 1999). For example, rather than trying to conduct a five-year prospective longitudinal research study with five-year-old children, researchers might begin with a group of five-year-olds, six-year-olds, seven-year-olds, eight-year-olds, and nine-year-olds and then follow them for one year. In this manner, information can be gained about the developmental changes that occur between the ages of 5 and 10, but the researchers have spent only one year rather than five years to conduct the study. The accelerated longitudinal research design combines the strengths of both the cross-sectional and prospective longitudinal research designs.

Overall, there is no single time frame that is ideal for conducting research in the field of developmental psychopathology. In order to remain true to the developmental aspects of the field, it makes sense to follow children, adolescents, and families over time. It is also useful, however, to get a thorough understanding of functioning at a single point, especially at the beginning of a research endeavor.

Science is built up with facts, as a house is with stones. But a collection of facts is no more a science than a heap of stones is a house.

—Jules Henri Poincare

THE ACTUAL PROCESS OF RESEARCH

Most professional researchers develop a line of research from which they create a number of different but related projects. **Programmatic research**, during which researchers set out to build on their own previous research, is most commonly done by professors and researchers who

BOX *4.3*

A CASE EXAMPLE OF THE PROSPECTIVE LONGITUDINAL DESIGN

An excellent example of a prospective longitudinal design was conducted in New Zealand. More than 1,200 infants born in 1977 were followed for over 18 years (Woodward & Fergusson, 1999). The results of the investigation of peer relationships and later psychosocial functioning are highlighted here to show the advantages of prospective longitudinal designs.

Peer relationship problems that were reported by teachers when the children were 9 years old were related to externalizing behavior problems (such as criminal involvement and substance abuse) when the children were 18 years old. Early peer relationship problems were not related to later problems with anxiety disorders or depression. You might be inclined to think that early peer relationships caused the later exter-

nalizing problems, but the analyses of these data suggest otherwise. Further investigation showed that the externalizing behavior problems at the age of 18 seemed to be most related to conduct problems and poor parent–child relationships in early childhood. Thus, the functioning of children at the age of 18 seemed to be closely related to the functioning of the children at the age of 9 (i.e., they both stemmed from the same early-childhood events).

This type of prospective longitudinal design allows the exploration of a wealth of causative and associative relationships between variables. Although this type of research is difficult to conduct, it is well worth the effort given the comprehensiveness of the findings.

---

develop an expertise in a particular area. Most often, this research is driven by a theoretical framework that researchers are investigating (L. Peterson & Tremblay, 1999). The boxes throughout this chapter highlight programmatic research that has been conducted all over the world (see, for example, Box 4.4). Once a researcher identifies an area of investigation, it is often relatively easy the next study (and sometimes the next 20 studies). But what about the researcher who is just beginning the empirical process? How are research ideas identified, and how are samples chosen?

A good father is a little bit of a mother.

—Lee Salk

Choosing a Research Topic and Identifying Hypotheses

By the time graduate students in the social sciences begin the research process formally, they probably have already had at least some experience with research. Most often, especially in doctoral graduate programs, students choose a graduate program and a mentor that are consistent with their research interests. Sometimes research projects develop from a personal interest in a particular topic (e.g., Uncle Fred devastated his family with his alcoholism, so the student becomes interested in the family ramifications of alcoholism). Projects can also develop out of the sheer fascination with a research topic (e.g., a student wants to be part of identifying the etiologies of the perplexing disorder of autism). Sometimes students become interested in the research topic that their undergraduate or graduate

mentor is studying, so they continue on in that research area with their own unique additions to the empirical process.

One of the most common problems that students face in identifying a research topic is their desire to address a research question that is too large. I have heard undergraduate honors students say, "I want to find out which therapy is most effective" and "I want to show what causes attention-deficit/hyperactivity disorder." Although these are extraordinarily important questions, even researchers with millions of dollars of grant money and unlimited time continue to struggle with them. It is important for researchers to choose a topic that is feasible within their constraints of time, money, and expertise. No single study can answer an overarching issue. Individual studies can, however, be pieced together to make comprehensive statements about a particular area.

Once a feasible topic has been identified, students or professional researchers conduct a literature review to find out what else is known about that topic. Sometimes, the very study that the researcher would like to conduct has already been completed numerous times. Other times, the literature review reveals that similar studies have been conducted, but the exact study of interest has not yet been completed. Overall, researchers need to build their own new research on work that has been completed previously. Different sampling issues, measurement issues, and design issues can be highlighted when reviewing the research literature. Through the literature review, researchers develop their own hypotheses about what they expect to find in their study. It is much better to conduct

The father–child relationship can have both positive and negative ramifications, just like the mother–child relationship.

research that is driven by hypotheses than to simply go fishing for results. Once the literature has been reviewed thoroughly and the specific study has been identified and the hypotheses have been formulated, it is time to identify the sample of participants who will be part of the study.

Choosing a Sample

In an article titled "Most of the Subjects Were White and Middle Class," Dr. Sandra Graham (1992) reviewed the distressing pattern that empirical research is based largely on samples of middle-class Caucasian American individuals. Although she was discussing research in general, this pattern holds true in research on developmental psychopathology. It is imperative that research samples provide a representative, and therefore generalizable, sample of participants. The issues of representativeness include, but are not limited to, age and developmental level; gender; race and ethnicity; socioeconomic status; cultural diversity (including religion, native language, and acculturation); geographical region (e.g., rural, urban, suburban); and family constellation. A number of researchers have discussed the importance of inclusion of representative samples (e.g., Canino, Bird, & Canino, 1997; Hall & Maramba, 2001; Sue, Kurasaki, & Srinivasan, 1999). Notably, a special issue of *Journal of Family Psychology* is dedicated to the issue of cultural variation in families (Parke, 2000). Interested readers should also consider finding a copy of *Studying Minority Adolescents: Conceptual, Methodological, and Theoretical Issues* (McLoyd & Steinberg, 1998) and *Multicultural Psychology* (Hall & Barongan, 2002), both of which provide comprehensive reviews of research findings of diverse groups of youth and families.

BOX 4.4

A CASE EXAMPLE OF THE RESEARCH ODYSSEY

In a book entitled *The Developmental Psychologists: Research Adventures across the Life Span* (Merrens & Brannigan, 1996), 18 developmental psychologists explain why they investigate their chosen topics and how their research programs have changed over the years. Dr. Ross Parke (1996) provides an interesting explanation of how he came to study fathers. He became intrigued with the father–infant relationship for a number of reasons, including the theoretical importance of the topic, the social and scientific relevance of the topic, and the dearth of knowledge in this area. When Parke began much of his classic work in the late 1960s and early 1970s, nearly all of the research completed with infants and their parents focused on the mother–infant relationship. Parke's line of research on the father–infant relationship proved to be very important and productive. Parke has continued this line of inquiry for more than 30 years, and he continues to investigate the father–child relationship with regard to play, emotions, and social development.

In addition to these issues, it is also important for the researcher to consider which individuals of a family or school system will be invited to participate in the research. Historically, mothers have been overrepresented in clinical child research and fathers have been ignored (Phares, 1992). More recently, there has been attention to the need to include fathers in research related to developmental psychopathology, but the majority of studies continue to include mothers and not fathers (Phares, 1996, 1997b).

The school system is also a place where careful considerations about sampling must be made (Phillips, 1999). Depending on the research question, researchers may only be interested in children involved in regular education classrooms, or they may be interested in special education programs.

There is no one right way to identify a sample of children and adolescents for research on the development of psychopathology, but there are some guiding rules to follow:

- Make sure to consult previous research before identifying a research sample. It may be that the research question has already been answered with one population but not with another.
- Try to recruit a diverse sample.
- When a diverse sample cannot be gathered, explain why a diverse sample was not recruited and highlight the homogeneity of the sample as a possible limitation of the results.
- Do not generalize the data beyond the characteristics of the sample that was collected (e.g., if only boys were studied, then do not try to suggest the research results also apply to girls).

Overall, these guiding rules should increase representative and generalizable samples of children and adolescents in studies of developmental psychopathology (Hall & Barongan, 2002; McLoyd & Steinberg, 1998). No single study can address all of the issues within a research topic, so it is also important to acknowledge that other researchers can address the issues that your study was not able to address (Drotar, 2000). (Box 4.5 describes a study that involved a difficult sample.)

Choosing Psychometrically Sound Measures

Questionnaires and other assessment measures are discussed in more detail in Chapter 5. For the purposes of understanding the research process, it is important to consider what type of measurements will be used in the study. Measures with strong psychometric properties (i.e., reliability and validity) are imperative so that the data collected can be trusted. In addition, there are a number of methods of measurement that can be considered, including direct observation, interviews, questionnaires, educational measures, family measures, neuropsychological measures, physiological assessments, and medical/health measures. Regardless of which method is chosen, it is important to use well-established measures that have been shown to be reliable and valid. It is also helpful to use multiple methods of measurement, such as interviews and direct observation, to increase confidence in the findings.

I pass with relief from the tossing sea of Cause and Theory to the firm ground of Result and Fact.

—Sir Winston Spencer Churchill

Collecting Data

Once the measures and sample have been identified, the data collection process can begin. In most cases, parental

THE FAR SIDE By GARY LARSON

Late at night, and without permission, Reuben would often enter the nursery and conduct experiments in static electricity.

consent and child assent are required. (These issues were discussed in Chapter 3.) After consent and assent have been established, researchers and their assistants collect data. Sometimes the data collection process is relatively easy (e.g., hand out questionnaires to a group of well-behaved 10-year-olds in the school cafeteria), but at other times it is quite arduous (e.g., doing home visits and interviews with troubled families who have chaotic schedules and who are often not available for the interviews when the research assistants show up at the family's place of residence). Depending on the time frame of the research, the data collection process can take years (e.g., in prospective studies where children are followed from birth to seven years old).

Every experienced researcher has lots of horror stories, as well as lots of poignant anecdotes, about the data collection process. My own favorite horror story is from the beginning stages of data collection for my dissertation. It had taken about six weeks for me to get permission to collect data in a particular school district. The week that I was finally allowed to begin recruiting adolescents for the study was the week that the teachers chose to go on strike. Luckily for everyone concerned (especially the teachers), the strike was resolved quickly and I was allowed to get into the school about a month later, after the school system and classrooms had gotten back to normal.

One of my favorite positive anecdotes is from a family who recently came to the university for a research project that involved interviews and behavioral observation. The behavior observation required that the mother and the father talk with the adolescent separately for five minutes each while being videotaped. The videotapes were later transcribed and coded to explore parent–adolescent interactions. Both parents had a particularly difficult time finding five minutes' worth of conversation to have with their adolescent. They reported to me later that the behavioral observation had been a wake-up call for them. They had previously felt that they had an open and honest relationship with their adolescent, but when they found that it was a struggle to have a sustained conversation for five

---

BOX 4.5

A CASE EXAMPLE OF A DIFFICULT SAMPLE TO STUDY

A difficult topic to study is the death of a parent. Not only is this issue potentially painful for the children and guardians who might be recruited into the study, but it is difficult to identify enough children in this group to allow an adequate sample. For example, a researcher could not just go to a public school and expect to recruit enough children who had lost their parent to death.

One group of researchers dealt with this topic by recruiting children from a variety of sources (Thompson, Kaslow, et al., 1998). The researchers were able to recruit 80 children and adolescents who had experienced parental death within the last 4–24 months. Youth were identified through medical records at an inner-city hospital that serves primarily low-income and ethnic minority individuals and families, records from a victim and witness assistance program, referrals from a local hospice (which cares for individuals who are close to death), obituaries, an HIV clinic, and the medical examiner's office. Nonbereaved children and adolescents were recruited from a general medical clinic, a hospital newsletter, and through referrals from bereaved children and adolescents. The researchers recruited the control group of nonbereaved youth so that they were comparable to the bereaved group on their demographic characteristics, such as socioeconomic status, race/ethnicity, gender, and percentage receiving federal financial assistance.

Youngsters and their parent or guardian completed measures of emotional/behavioral functioning for the child. When children's and adolescents' reports were compared, there were no significant differences between the bereaved and nonbereaved groups. When parents' and guardians' reports were compared, children and adolescents in the bereaved group showed significantly more internalizing and externalizing problems than children and adolescents in the nonbereaved group. Interestingly, this finding was significant only for Caucasian American children and adolescents. Thus, when parents and guardians reported on children and adolescents from ethnic minority groups, the bereaved and nonbereaved children and adolescents did not differ between groups.

This study shows the complexity of research findings and the difficulty of interpreting results in group comparisons. It could be that youth do not experience significant emotional/behavioral problems after the death of a parent (as would be suggested by the youngsters' self-reports). It could also be that some children (notably Caucasian American children, according to this study) do experience difficulties that are noticeable to their surviving parent or guardian. More research is needed on this difficult and potentially painful topic in order to understand the factors that lead to adaptive versus maladaptive outcomes after the loss of a parent due to death.

minutes, they realized that they wanted to spend more quality time with their adolescent (rather than always running from one activity to another). Overall, the data collection process can be as fascinating as the actual data that are collected. It is a wise researcher who stays closely involved with the process of data collection so that she or he can learn from the research participants.

Data Analyses

Once the data are collected, they must be entered into a computer and analyzed. The many types of data analysis include the following:

- Frequencies, means, and standard deviations, which are statistics used to describe the characteristics of the sample.
- T-tests, analyses of variance (ANOVAs), and multivariate analyses of variance (MANOVAs), which are used to look at either group differences or differences between variables.
- Correlations and regressions, which are used to look at the correspondence between variables and to assess how the variables are related.
- Path analyses and structural equation modeling (SEM), which are used to explore the connections between variables and can be used to look at the directionality of the relationships between the variables.

Other, more sophisticated data analysis methods are available, but this list includes the main ones used in research on the development of psychopathology. Note that it is standard to use a **p-value** (probability value) of $p < .05$ in most research on developmental psychopathology. Although researchers can make arguments about using a stronger or a more lenient p-value, the standard is usually to use $p < .05$ unless otherwise noted. This standard means that, as researchers, we acknowledge that there may be significant findings by chance in fewer than 5 out of 100 analyses. If researchers wish to have more trust in their results, they might use a p-value of $p < .01$ or $p < .001$, either of which would allow more assurance of few chance findings.

Note that, even when a result is *statistically* significant, it is still incumbent upon the researcher to address whether or not the result is *clinically* significant (i.e., clinically meaningful; Beutler & Moleiro, 2001; Jensen, 2001; Kazdin, 2001). Sometimes results can be statistically significant, but the actual differences between groups, for example, are so small that they are clinically meaningless. Thus, clinical researchers are encouraged to remain cognizant of both statistical significance and clinical significance.

Writing Up, Presenting, and Publishing the Results

Once the data have been analyzed, it is time to write up the results. Specific writing tips can be found in the fifth edition of the *Publication Manual of the American Psychological Association* (2001). Most often, researchers try to present their findings at a professional conference while at the same time getting the findings published. There is usually a quicker turnaround time for decisions from professional conferences, and it is legitimate to first present research data at a conference and then publish the data in a journal. It is not, however, appropriate to publish data and then present it at a conference. Professional conferences are meant for the presentation of cutting-edge research, so presenting data that have already been published would defeat that purpose.

There are a number of conferences and journals appropriate for presenting and publishing research on developmental psychopathology. In addition to the following lists, interested students can look at the reference section of this book to get a sense of other outlets for research on developmental psychopathology. The following organizations usually have annual or biannual conferences at which empirical research on developmental psychopathology is presented:

- *American Psychological Association (APA).* APA is the largest professional organization of psychologists in the world. (Division 15 on educational psychology, Division 16 on school psychology, Division 37 on child, youth, and family services, Division 43 on family psychology, Division 53 on clinical child psychology, and Division 54 on pediatric psychology are especially likely to present research related to developmental psychopathology.)
- *American Psychological Society (APS).* APS is smaller than APA and more focused on research.
- *Society for Research on Child Development (SRCD).* SRCD focuses on developmental psychology but has many presentations on developmental psychopathology.
- *International Society for Research on Child and Adolescent Psychopathology (ISRCAP).* ISRCAP is a small but distinguished group of researchers who focus on the development of psychopathology.

- *National Association of School Psychologists (NASP)*. NASP is the largest organization of school psychologists in the United States.
- *American Association for Marital and Family Therapy (AAMFT)*. AAMFT focuses on the treatment of marital and family problems.

Groups that specialize in certain disorders (e.g., alcohol and substance abuse, anxiety disorders) are also possible outlets for research on developmental psychopathology. In addition, each region and state within the United States has separate conferences for that geographical area (e.g., the Western Psychological Association, the Florida Psychological Association). There is no shortage of conferences at which research on developmental psychopathology can be presented. If you cannot identify an appropriate outlet for your research, your research mentor or other colleagues may be able to help you identify appropriate outlets. Even if you are not a researcher yet, you may want to attend one or more academic conferences to get a glimpse of the research and scholarly process that takes place there. I attended my first APA conference when I was between my sophomore and junior years of undergraduate work. It was fascinating and overwhelming all at the same time—and it was definitely something that I would recommend to interested students.

When considering publishing research results, there are a number of viable venues for research in developmental psychopathology. Primary journals include the following:

- *Journal of Consulting and Clinical Psychology*
- *Journal of Abnormal Psychology*
- *Journal of Family Psychology*
- *Child Development*
- *Developmental Psychology*
- *Journal of Clinical Child Psychology*
- *Journal of Abnormal Child Psychology*
- *Development and Psychopathology*
- *Journal of the American Academy of Child and Adolescent Psychiatry*
- *Journal of Child Psychology and Psychiatry*
- *American Journal of Community Psychology*
- *Journal of School Psychology*
- *Journal of Educational Psychology*

In addition to these journals, interested researchers are also encouraged to find a copy of *Journals in Psychology*, fifth edition, which is published by the American Psychological Association (1997b). There are a number of specialty journals in which articles on developmental psychopathology might be published (e.g., *Journal of Affective Disorders*, *International Journal of Eating Disorders*, *Cultural Diversity and Ethnic Minority Psychology*). Many journals now also have Web sites that post information on topic coverage, acceptance rates, and length of time for an editorial decision. The publication process can be arduous, often with the manuscript having many rejections and revisions before finding a place for publication. But publication is a crucial link in helping disseminate research findings. When meaningful results are found, it is incumbent on the researcher to try to share those results with the scholarly public through presentations and publications.

The scientist values research by the size of its contribution to that huge, logically articulated structure of ideas which is already, though not yet half built, the most glorious accomplishment of [human]kind.

—Sir Peter Brian Medawar

Continuing the Research Process

Once a study is completed, many researchers are left with even more questions than they had before the study began. For this reason, the results of one study usually lead nicely into the hypotheses of another study. When good programmatic research is conducted, researchers can use previous research results to formulate the questions for research in the future. It is an exciting process that can lead to better ways of understanding and helping children, adolescents, their families, their schools, and their communities (R. M. Lerner, Fisher, & Weinberg, 2000). (Box 4.6 presents an example of research in the community.)

CHOOSING APPROPRIATE SAMPLES OF PARTICIPANTS

The issue of representativeness of samples has already been mentioned, but the topic warrants additional attention. In order for researchers to conduct studies whose results can be generalized to the larger population of children, they must include representative samples of children and adolescents. Representativeness includes considerations of age/developmental level; gender; race/ethnicity; socioeconomic status; geographic region (such as urban, rural, suburban); cultural diversity (including religion, native language, and acculturation); family constellation; and clinical versus nonclinical status.

BOX *4.6*

A CASE EXAMPLE OF RESEARCH IN THE COMMUNITY

In order to understand the connections between witnessing violence and experiencing antisocial behavior, one research group explored adolescents who were at risk for the development of antisocial behavior (L. S. Miller, Wasserman, Neugebauer, Gorman-Smith, & Kamboukos, 1999). Boys between the ages of 6 and 10 who lived in an urban setting and who had at least one sibling with a juvenile court conviction were recruited into the study. Slightly more than half of the participants were African American, and slightly less than half were Hispanic/Latino. The boys were interviewed at two different times, separated by 15 months.

Results of the study showed that boys' exposure to violence in the community was related to the later development of antisocial behavior (e.g., delinquency, fighting). This relation, however, was moderated by the family environment.

For boys with low levels of parent–child conflict, the witnessing of violence was a significant predictor of increased antisocial behavior more than one year later. For boys who experienced high levels of parent–child conflict, the additional witnessing of violence in the community did not predict any greater antisocial behavior a year later. Thus, it appeared that both high parent–child conflict and high exposure to community violence were associated with greater levels of antisocial behavior in the future.

This study combined the prospective longitudinal design with the high-risk design. Such forms of comprehensive and thoughtful research need to be conducted in order to establish the many factors that lead to the development of psychopathology in children.

Throughout the history of psychological and educational research, there are egregious examples of biased samples that were used to generalize to the broader population. In her book *In a Different Voice: Psychological Theory and Women's Development*, Dr. Carol Gilligan (1993) described the early research on moral development that was conducted with only boys and men and then was applied to girls and women. Once research on moral development was conducted with girls and women, it became clear that males and females differ in the process of moral development. In his book *Even the Rat Was White: A Historical View of Psychology*, second edition, Dr. Robert Guthrie (1998) illustrated a number of studies that were conducted with Caucasian Americans, the results of which were then applied to individuals of all races and ethnicities, often to the detriment of those individuals. These examples illustrate the importance of trying to identify representative samples of children and adolescents for all research topics. If researchers are not able to recruit a representative sample, then they must be extremely careful to apply the results to that specific type of sample only. Thus, if research is conducted with impoverished children from a rural community, the results should not be applied to impoverished children from the inner city. Similarly, if the process of developing a learning disorder is studied with a sample of children whose native language is English, then the results should not be applied to children who have learned English as their second (or third) language.

Another important consideration in the recruitment of participants is the adequate description of those partici-

pants. In a review of published clinical child research, Dr. Joyce Lum and I found that 36.7% of the studies did not include information about the socioeconomic status or the racial and ethnic distribution of their sample. Further, 80.4% of the studies did not include any information about parental marital status or family constellation (Phares & Lum, 1996). Given that research results should not be generalized beyond the characteristics of the sample, the results of this review are of concern. It is imperative that researchers describe their samples adequately.

LOCATIONS OF RESEARCH ON DEVELOPMENTAL PSYCHOPATHOLOGY

To some extent, research on developmental psychopathology can be completed wherever children and adolescents are found. This section highlights a number of specific research sites, but keep in mind that research can be conducted in almost any setting.

School-Based Research

Because children and adolescents spend so much of their week in school, it is not surprising to find that much of the research on developmental psychopathology is conducted within the school setting (Drotar, Timmons-Mitchell et al., 2000). Researchers can choose to conduct research within regular education classrooms to access a broad range of children (most of whom would be expected to

Researchers of developmental psychopathology try to include representative samples of children in their studies.

fall into the nonclinical range), or they can choose from a number of specialized programs within public schools (such as classrooms for children who are severely emotionally disturbed, children with severe intellectual limitations, and children who have both physical and intellectual limitations).

Obviously, school-related issues (such as learning disorders, behavioral disorders, peer interaction, issues related to intellectual functioning, and teacher–child interactions) can be studied within the school setting. Many other areas of research have also been conducted within the school setting (e.g., children's emotional/ behavioral functioning, eating disorders and body image problems within children and adolescents, gender differences, children's perceptions of family functioning, children's understanding of health issues). Often, researchers introduce the topic of study to a child in the classroom and then pull that child out of the classroom for the brief period of data collection once the child has received permission to participate in the study. Researchers are often asked to convey their overall results to school officials and teachers in order to show the value of the research and to educate school personnel about the research process. Overall, the school system is a wonderful place to collect data about children and adolescents. Especially in schools with a diverse student population, researchers have a chance of recruiting representative samples that can be generalized to other children and adolescents in that type of school setting. (Box 4.7 presents an example of research in the schools.)

Hospital-Based and Clinic-Based Research

Researchers often conduct studies of health and illness issues in medical hospitals (Drotar, Overholsen et al., 2000). For example, studies of children's emotional/ behavioral functioning regarding their sickle cell anemia (Barbarin, Whitten, Bond, & Conner-Warren, 1999; Noll, McKellop, Vannatta, & Kalinyak, 1998) or cystic fibrosis (R. J. Thompson, Gustafson, Gil, Godfrey, & Murphy, 1998) have been conducted in hospital settings and outpatient medical settings. Similarly, children are sometimes recruited into studies concerning a parent's medical illness, such as cancer (Compas et al., 1994) or AIDS (Rotheram-Borus & Stein, 1999). The hospital emergency room is a site for research on adolescent suicide, given that the emergency room is often the first contact that adolescents have with mental health professionals (Gothelf et al., 1998). In addition, a great wealth of research on developmental psychopathology has been conducted in inpatient psychiatric settings where children and adolescents are being treated for severe psychopathologies (e.g., Joiner, 1999).

Clinic-based research most often involves children and adolescents who are being seen by a therapist on an outpatient basis. These studies often explore specific types of psychopathology (Marks, Himelstein, Newcorn, & Halperin, 1999), but they can also deal with other topics such as parent–child interactions (Sheeber & Sorensen, 1998) and treatment outcome research (M. C. Roberts, Vernberg, & Jackson, 2000; Weisz, Donenberg, Han, & Weiss, 1995). Because the census of inpatient hospitals

---

BOX 4.7

A CASE EXAMPLE OF RESEARCH IN THE SCHOOLS

One research program in the schools attempted to decrease the stressors associated with the transition from elementary school to middle school (Elias & Clabby, 1989, 1991). The Improving Social Awareness–Social Problem Solving (ISA-SPS) program focused on two central themes during this difficult transitional time: initial transition difficulties (such as getting used to new routines and having to change classes for each subject) and longitudinal problems (such as peer pressure and acculturation into the social system of the new school). In addition to these central themes, the researchers identified more than 20 specific stressors, such as not remembering the combination to your locker and getting lost in the new school. The preventive intervention included three primary components:

- Development of self-control skills, group participation skills, and social awareness.

- Development of social-decision-making skills and problem-solving skills.

- Promoting skill acquisition and application in the school and home environment.

Evaluations of this program have shown that, when compared with children who did not receive the preventive intervention, children who participated in the program showed better adjustment and fewer conflicts with peers and authorities (Elias & Clabby, 1989, 1991). These studies illustrate the excellent research that can be conducted within the school setting, with the support of teachers and school administrators. In programs such as the ISA-SPS, teachers are often taught strategies for helping their students with psychosocial difficulties. Such strategies represent a direct benefit of these programs for teachers in addition to the benefits the programs offer to students.

---

has been decreasing over the years (due to deinstitutionalization and limits in funding; Scholle & Kelleher, 1998), research in clinics and in the community has increased while research with inpatient populations has declined (Rappaport & Seidman, 2000).

Community-Based Research

Research can be conducted within the community setting as well. Often, community-based research deals with issues relevant to the community (e.g., violence, overcrowding, racism) and can be used to inform social policy (R. M. Lerner et al., 2000; R. B. McCall & Groark, 2000). Recall from Box 4.2 that studies have explored the similarities and differences of homeless children and children who have homes (Masten, Miliotis, Graham-Bermann, Ramirez, & Neemann, 1993; McCaskill et al., 1998). Interestingly, these studies have found conflicting evidence, with some studies showing greater psychopathology in homeless adolescents (McCaskill et al., 1998) and other studies finding no differences between homeless children and those with homes (Masten et al., 1993). Much of the work on risk and protective factors (such as the Kauai studies; Werner, 1995; Werner & Smith, 2001) has been conducted within the community in which children and families live.

Laboratory-Based Research

When researchers want more of a structured setting in the data collection process, they may choose to do laboratory-based research. Imagine the difference between trying to interview a single mother in her home as opposed to in the laboratory. In the home, the phone might be ringing, the baby might be crying, and the television might be blaring. The information from the interview might be compromised by any or all of these distractions. Imagine, instead, interviewing a single mother in a laboratory setting, where the researchers have provided free child care during the interview, the room is quiet and comfortable, and the mother can focus her attention on the questions at hand. Laboratory-based research has some clear advantages, but its generalizability may have some limits, given that the setting is probably foreign to the research participants. Especially when conducting behavioral observations in the laboratory, researchers must be aware that research participants might be acting quite differently in the laboratory than they would act in their own home. Thus, there are both strengths and weaknesses to conducting research within a laboratory setting.

I've never seen a computer.

—Rosa, eight years old, Mexico

Research Sites in the Future

Although all of the data collection sites discussed above are expected to remain viable, one new method is looming large in the future. A number of studies (especially in the adult research literature) have begun using the Internet as a way of recruiting participants into studies and as a mechanism for collecting data. Researchers might contact potential participants by e-mail through Web-based advertisements and announcements. Participants can then complete questionnaires or interviews via the Web. Although this method is still new and has not been well established in the area of developmental psychopathology, it is worth considering. As with any site of data collection, the researcher must consider representativeness of the sample. Internet data collection would include only those individuals who have access to a computer and who are comfortable with Internet technology. As the Web becomes more a part of our culture, however, it is possible that a great deal of research will be conducted over the Internet.

Overall, there is no single site of research that is always better than another (Armstrong & Drotar, 2000; Drotar, Timmons-Mitchell et al., 2000). The appropriateness of the research site, just like that of the participant population, depends on the research questions and the goals of the research. As with selecting representative samples, researchers must take care to select sites that do not inadvertently bias their sample (e.g., collecting data at a public school would probably yield a more diverse sample than collecting data at an expensive private school). Further, they must be aware of the strengths and weaknesses of all possible research sites, as they should be in most decisions they make regarding their research.

QUANTITATIVE RESEARCH AND QUALITATIVE RESEARCH

Up to this point, the majority of research in this book has been **quantitative research**. Quantitative research uses the empirical process to collect data, analyze data, and draw conclusions based on objective and numerical data. Data are quantified into numbers and patterns that allow interpretation (e.g., Deater-Deckard, 2000). In contrast, **qualitative research** is less empirically driven and focuses more on the experience of the participants (Krahn & Eisert, 2000). Qualitative research is often conducted

through interviews and diaries of research participants. Patterns in the information are ascertained from reviewing the information rather than trying to quantify the information. Both types of research are meaningful in the area of developmental psychopathology.

The bulk of research on developmental psychopathology has been quantitative (Drotar, 2000). There are instances, however, when qualitative research can be helpful. For example, qualitative research can be enlightening at the beginning of a research venture in order to identify the important and salient issues in need of investigation. Qualitative research can also be helpful in understanding the experience of research participants and in getting a deeper look at the information collected through quantitative research. Thus, both quantitative and qualitative research can be helpful in the process to understand the development, prevention, and treatment of psychopathology in children and adolescents.

AREAS IN NEED OF FURTHER STUDY IN DEVELOPMENTAL PSYCHOPATHOLOGY

Throughout this book, areas in need of further research will be highlighted. Compared with other areas within psychology and education, developmental psychopathology is still a young field. For this reason, there are still wide areas of interest that have not received sufficient attention. For example, research is needed on the differences and similarities between the dimensional and categorical conceptualizations of children's and adolescents' functioning. More research is needed with sophisticated imaging techniques, such as function MRIs, so that brain functioning can be explored in relation to behavioral functioning (Hendren, DeBacker, & Pandina, 2000). A greater degree of sophisticated research on the connections between genes and behavior is needed (Compas & Gotlib, 2002). More work is needed to explore the impact of managed care companies and the accessibility and quality of therapeutic services that are available to children and families (D. L. Morgan & R. K. Morgan, 2001).

Research is needed to understand children and adolescents in multiple contexts, such as family, school, and community. More attention is needed to the bidirectionality of parent–child interactions and teacher–child interactions, in order to understand fully the interactions between children and the adults in their lives. Although most developmental psychopathologists are sensitive to diversity issues in their research, there is still a great need to explore underrepresented populations of children, such as children from ethnic minority backgrounds, children from other countries, and children from unique family constellations (e.g., children raised by a grandmother or children in families headed by lesbians or gay men).

Although no single study can address all of these issues, more cultural diversity in individual samples will lead to more research within developmental psychopathology that is consistent with the lives and experiences of children and adolescents. Findings from these representative samples can then be used to try to improve the lives of children and adolescents (R. M. Lerner et al., 2000; McCall & Groark, 2000).

SUMMARY AND KEY CONCEPTS

The research process is an integral part of understanding the development of psychopathology. One example that illustrates the need for empirical research is that of **facilitated communication (FC)**, which after empirical study was found to be bogus in the treatment of children with autism. In the **double blind** technique used to study FC, the facilitator and the autistic individual were presented with different stimulus material.

Research Methods Used in the Study of Developmental Psychopathology

There are a number of research methods used to study the development of psychopathology. In an **experimental design**, the researcher recruits participants into the study, conducts **random assignment** to separate the participants into groups, administers an **independent variable** (the experimenter's manipulation), and then measures the **dependent variable** that is thought to be influenced by the independent variable. The experimental design allows for researchers to argue **causality**, which means they can argue that the independent variable caused the changes that were seen in the dependent variable.

Another common design in the study of developmental psychopathology is the **quasi-experimental design**, which allows for known groups to be tested. The premise behind the **correlational design** is to explore how different variables relate to one another. Often, correlational designs are conducted through the **survey method**, which allows researchers to administer questionnaires to large numbers of participants and then the researcher assesses how the variables on the measures correlate with each other.

Case studies can be used to investigate thoroughly one or a few individuals who show a rare type of behavior. **Single-subject designs** (also known as **within-subject designs**) are often used with one participant or a small group of participants in order to assess their change in behavior after a behavioral intervention. A common single-subject design is the **A-B-A-B design** (also known as the **reversal design**).

Another research design within developmental psychopathology is the **high-risk design**, in which children who are thought to be at high risk for the development of psychopathology are studied to assess risk and protective factors that are related to the eventual development of psychopathology. The **behavioral-genetics design** allows the development of psychopathology to be explored through twin studies and through adoption studies.

Time Frame of the Research Study

There are a number of ways to conceptualize research when the time frame is taken into account. **Cross-sectional research** is conducted when data are collected at a single time. **Prospective longitudinal research** is conducted when children are followed over a period of time and data are collected at two or more points in time. **Accelerated longitudinal research** combines cross-sectional and prospective longitudinal research by collecting data from different groups of children at one point in time and then following all of those children over a period of time.

The Actual Process of Research

The majority of researchers conduct **programmatic research**, which means that they have a research program that attempts to answer related research questions (e.g., the study of child abuse could be studied in a variety of different ways by the same research group).

Choosing Appropriate Samples of Participants

It is imperative that researchers attempt to recruit representative samples of participants that can be generalized to the broader population. Researchers must be cognizant of issues related to age/developmental level, gender, race/ethnicity, socioeconomic status, geographic region, cultural diversity, family constellation, and clinical versus nonclinical status of the participants.

Locations of Research on Developmental Psychopathology

There are a number of common sites of research on developmental psychopathology, including schools, hospitals, clinics, communities, and laboratories.

Quantitative Research and Qualitative Research

Quantitative research uses the empirical process in order to address issues within developmental psychopathology. The majority of studies described in this chapter and in this book as a whole are quantitative. **Qualitative research** uses a less numeric approach to understanding developmental psychopathology.

Areas in Need of Further Study in Developmental Psychopathology

There are a great number of areas that are in need of further research in the study of developmental psychopathology. Dimensional versus categorical approaches to understanding developmental psychopathology and the study of bidirectional influences between children and their parents and teachers are just two of the topics that could use more exploration.

KEY TERMS

facilitated
  communication
  (FC)
double blind studies
experimental design
random assignment
independent variable

dependent variable
causality
quasi-experimental
  design
correlational design
survey method
case studies

single-subject (or
  within-subject)
  designs
A-B-A-B design
reversal design
high-risk design
behavioral-genetics
  design

cross-sectional
  research
prospective
  longitudinal
  research
accelerated
  longitudinal
  research

programmatic
  research
probability value
  (p-value)
quantitative research
qualitative research

SUGGESTED READINGS

Kozol, Jonathan. *Rachel's Children*. New York: Fawcett Columbine, 1988. This powerful book could be considered a case study of the effects of poverty and homelessness on children.

Williams, Donna. *Nobody Nowhere*. New York: Harper Trade, 1994. This intriguing autobiography is written by a woman who as a child was diagnosed with autism.

SUGGESTED VIEWINGS

Mad Love (1995). Antonia Bird (director), Paula Milne (writer). VHS/DVD. Similar to an in-depth case study, this fictional film shows the difficulties and triumphs of an adolescent who experiences depression and suicidality.

Welcome to the Dollhouse (1995). Todd Solondz (director and writer). VHS/DVD. This powerful film takes an in-depth look at an adolescent's troubled and troubling life, with a focus on the effects of teasing, peer pressure, and acquaintance rape.

CHAPTER 5

ASSESSMENT OF EMOTIONAL/ BEHAVIORAL PROBLEMS IN CHILDREN AND ADOLESCENTS

CHAPTER SUMMARY

Measurement began our might.

—W. B. Yeats

Assessment of emotional/behavioral problems involves testing and evaluation to ascertain a child's or adolescent's level of functioning and level of problems. As you may recall from the Chapter 1, the most important characteristic to know about children or adolescents is their age. But once you know their age, how can you tell if children's or adolescents' behaviors are within the normal range of behavior? This type of question can be answered with the use of developmentally appropriate assessment techniques (Geisinger, 2000; Sparrow, Carter, Racusin, & Morris, 1995). In fact, the assessment process has many purposes:

- To determine the level of problematic emotions and behaviors (e.g., How high or low are the levels of problems in the child or adolescent?).

- To determine the range of problematic emotions and behaviors (e.g., How many different types of problems are being experienced by the child or adolescent?).

- To help identify the appropriate diagnosis for a child or adolescent, if any.

- To identify strengths and competencies of a child or adolescent.

- To evaluate the effectiveness of treatment by assessing behaviors before, during, and after treatment.

- To determine the etiological factors of the child's or adolescent's problems.

- To identify children at risk for developing problems in the future.

Figure 5.1 shows a flowchart of effective assessment. Even before children are referred for assessments, parents and teachers can intervene to prevent the need for a formal assessment. When assessments occur, they should take into account the ecology or environmental aspects of the child's functioning and the legal and ethical guidelines for assessment (such as the Individuals with Disabilities Education Act, which will be discussed more in depth in Chapter 15, on learning disorders). In addition, assessment measures should have strong psychometric properties (e.g., reliability and validity) and should provide recommendations that are focused (Prevatt, 1999b).

Overall, assessment techniques are almost always used when working therapeutically with children and adolescents. Assessments can also calm the fears of worried parents. Imagine the following scenario: A worried mother calls a mental health clinic for an evaluation and treatment

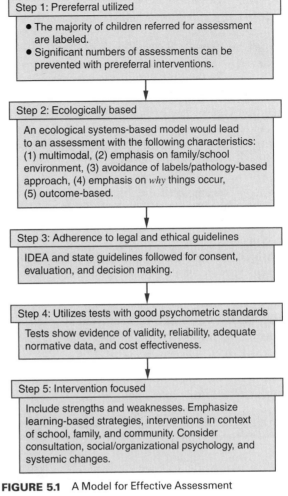

FIGURE 5.1 A Model for Effective Assessment
Source: Prevatt (1999b).

of her 11-year-old daughter. She states that her daughter has only three good friends and that, although her daughter talks with the friends on the phone and sees her friends on weekends, she is worried that her daughter is socially isolated and socially anxious. The mother recalls having lots more friends during childhood, and she is worried that her daughter is missing out on social opportunities. The mother and daughter come to the clinic for an evaluation, and the results all point to a happy and healthy preadolescent. In addition, the clinician evaluates the mother's functioning, and the mother is found to be competent and concerned. Rather than progressing with unnecessary treatment, the clinician can allay the mother's fears and suggest ways for her to be reassured of her daughter's status as a well-functioning child. Given that the daughter is happy with her friendships and her social support network, no intervention is necessary for the daughter. This example illustrates that assessments do not necessarily end in the identification of problems in children and adolescents.

Assessors must choose between depth versus breadth in assessing the functioning of children and adolescents. That is, if a child is referred for problems of hyperactivity, should the clinician assess only the hyperactivity in depth or a broader range of emotional/behavioral problems in addition to hyperactivity? Although there is no right or wrong answer to this question, many clinicians choose to assess for depth as well as for breadth. There are a number of specific measures for different emotional/behavioral problems, and there are a number of broad-based measures of emotional/behavioral problems. Both types of measures can be used in comprehensive assessments of children and adolescents.

In the following sections, you will read about the many different types of measures that are available for assessing children's and adolescents' emotional/behavioral functioning. The most comprehensive and conclusive assessment would include many different types of assessment techniques (a process known as **multimethod assess-**

ment) and would include many different types of individuals to report on the child's or adolescent's behavior (a strategy known as **multiple informants**). Thus, a multimethod assessment might start with an interview of the child and the parent and then proceed to the completion of behavior checklists from the child, parent, and teacher; academic achievement testing and intellectual testing; and finally behavioral observation of the child in multiple settings. Depending on the age of the child and the referral problem, additional measures for personality functioning and family functioning might also be completed. As for the inclusion of multiple informants, that process most often includes the child, the parent or parents, and the teacher or teachers. Although the use of multiple informants depends on the age of the child and the referral problem, children, parents, and teachers are most often the best informants on children's behavior. The use of multiple informants is an integral part of comprehensive assessments of children and adolescents. Often one informant knows something about the child that other informants do not know (G. J. Meyer et al., 2001).

TABLE 5.1 Multiaxial Assessment Procedures

Age Range	Axis I Parent Reports	Axis II Teacher Reports	Axis III Cognitive Assessment	Axis IV Physical Assessment	Axis V Direct Assessment of Child
2 to 5	CBCL/2–3 CBCL/4–18 Developmental history Parent interview Vineland Social Maturity Scale (Sparrow et al., 1984)	TCRF/2–5 Preschool record Teacher interview	Ability tests, e.g., McCarthy (1972) Perceptual-motor tests Language tests	Height, weight Medical exam Neurological exam	Observation during testing and play interview
6 to 11	CBCL/4–18 Developmental history Parent interview	TRF School records Teacher interview	Ability tests, e.g., Kaufman & Kaufman (1983) Achievement tests Perceptual-motor tests Language tests	Height, weight Medical exam Neurological exam	SCICA DOF
12 to 18	CBCL/4–18 Developmental history Parent interview	TRF School records Teacher interview	Ability tests, e.g., WAIS-R; WISC-III (Wechsler, 1981, 1991) Achievement tests	Height, weight Medical exam Neurological exam	SCICA DOF YSR Self-concept measures Personality tests

Note: CBCL=Child Behavior Checklist, TCRF=Teacher/Caregiver Report Form, TRF=Teacher's Report Form, WAIS-R=Wechsler Adult Intelligence Scale-Revised, WISC-III=Wechsler Intelligence Scale for Children–Third Edition, SCICA=Semistructured Clinical Interview for Children and Adolescents, DOF=Direct Observation Form, YSR=Youth Self-Report.

Source: (Achenbach & McConaughy (1997).

Case Study: Michael, An Example of Multiaxial Assessment

When Michael was two years old, his parents divorced and he was raised by his mother with his five older brothers and sisters. As he grew up in this impoverished household, Michael fantasized increasingly about violence and aggression; he dreamed of being a martial arts expert. Although he was Caucasian, Michael was convinced that his father and grandfather were ninja warriors. He spent countless hours watching violent television shows and playing with guns, knives, and other weapons. At the age of nine, Michael attacked his mother with a kitchen knife. After the police and a social worker intervened, Michael was taken to a residential treatment facility where professionals could monitor his behavior closely. Michael was in the residential treatment facility for three years, during which time he took part in behavior management programs and received individual therapy, medication, and special education services.

By the time he was 12, there had been significant improvements, so Michael was moved to a therapeutic foster home more comparable to a family environment than the treatment facility was. Although Michael continued to see his mother and siblings once a month, his mother still had difficulty dealing with his behavior, so Michael remained in structured therapeutic living facilities. Michael's mother agreed with this living arrangement.

Below are some of the results from Child Behavior Checklists that were completed when Michael was 9 and again when he was 12. Although there were obviously improvements in his behavior, Michael continued to experience social problems and elevated aggression at the age of 12, according to his foster parent. These profiles illustrate how empirically validated assessment tools, such as the Child Behavior Checklist (discussed later in this chapter), can be used to compare different informants' perspectives on children's behavior and how they can be used to show change over time in children's behavior.

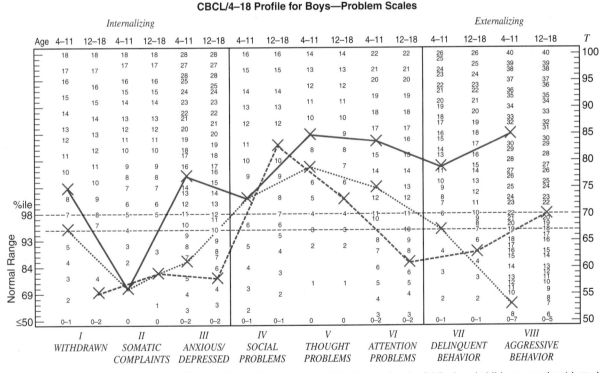

Child Behavior Checklist problem profiles for Michael scored at age 9 by his mother (solid line) and child care worker (dotted line), and at age 12 by his foster parent (broken line).

SOURCE: Achenbach & McConaughy (1997).

The average child is an almost non-existent myth. To be normal one must be peculiar in some way or another.

—Heywood C. Broun

MULTIAXIAL ASSESSMENT OF CHILDREN AND ADOLESCENTS

Recall from Chapter 1 that *DSM-IV* uses a multiaxial evaluation system for rating children and adolescents. Note that the word *multiaxial* means simply that there are different axes, or dimensions, to consider. Within the realm of assessment of children and adolescents, the term *multiaxial assessment* is used commonly. **Multiaxial assessment** requires that different aspects of children be assessed with different informants (Achenbach & McConaughy, 1997). Although the word *informant* is used on television shows about police officers to refer to a "snitch," in multiaxial assessment it refers to individuals who can inform the clinician about the child's functioning. As shown in Table 5.1, multiaxial assessment includes reports by parents (Axis I) and teachers (Axis II) in addition to evaluation of cognitive functioning (Axis III); physical functioning (Axis IV); and behavioral, self-concept, and personality functioning (Axis V). Specific measures in Table 5.1 are described later in this chapter.

The point of this multiaxial assessment system is to gain a comprehensive and thorough understanding of the child's or adolescent's functioning, regardless of the specific referral question. Obviously, different referral questions will lead to somewhat different assessment protocols. But with the multiaxial assessment system, the clinician can provide a comprehensive assessment of the child or adolescent. In order to conduct multiaxial assessments, clinicians must know many different assessment techniques and modalities, including interviews, behavioral assessment, behavior checklists and rating scales, personality measures, family methodology, intellectual and achievement testing, educational assessment, and neuropsychological assessment.

No one is without knowledge except he who asks no questions.

—Proverb of Africa

INTERVIEWS WITH CHILDREN AND THEIR PARENTS

To determine whether or not a child or family has a problem, clinicians usually first conduct an interview. Usually, the interview process begins at the point of the **intake phone call**, which is when the clinician first talks with a family member about the problems the child and family are experiencing. The main goal of any interview (whether it is in the intake phone call or at the time of the first appointment) is to gather information about the child and the family.

When clinicians interview children, they must be cognizant of the child's developmental level. With younger children, clinicians may need to ask questions that are more concrete and objective than those they would ask with older children and adolescents (Compas & Gotlib, 2002).

Interviews can be broken down into three categories: unstructured interviews, semistructured interviews, and structured interviews. **Unstructured interviews** consist of interviews that do not follow a specific, rigid format. That does not mean, however, that clinicians ask questions in a random order. With unstructured interviews, clinicians usually follow their own format for collecting

Interviews are almost always the first step in a thorough assessment.

information. If an important topic arises, however, they can deviate from their regular format and pursue questioning related to that new topic. **Semistructured interviews** suggest a specific format that the clinician follows but also allow the clinician some flexibility to follow up on important topics. In contrast, **structured interviews** do not allow much deviation from the original format. Structured interviews are most often used to determine a diagnosis, so there are specific questions that must be asked in a specific order. Although clinicians have the option to return to important topics after the formal structured interview is completed, they should follow the format of the structured interview closely in order to retain its psychometric properties. Since each type of interview has its own characteristics and issues, they are discussed separately below.

Unstructured Interviews

Even when clinicians plan to use a structured interview in the assessment process, they usually begin the very first session with an unstructured interview. Both parents and children can be involved in unstructured interviews, but often different information is gathered when children and parents are interviewed together versus separately (McConaughy, 2000). At the outset of an unstructured interview, clinicians need to build rapport with the child and the parents. **Rapport**, which consists of the feelings of trust and openness that a client develops toward a therapist, is at the foundation of the professional therapeutic relationship. Although rapport is most crucial for clinicians who conduct therapy, it remains an essential part of conducting accurate and thorough clinical assessments. Think for a minute about how rapport affects the type of information clinicians receive. Imagine a surly 15-year-old boy who has been brought in by his parents against his will. Without rapport, the clinician might get yes-and-no answers from the teen—and then only if he or she is lucky. With rapport, the teen may feel comfortable disclosing his concerns about the problems that he is experiencing. He might blame all of the problems on his parents and teachers, but at least he would be expressing his feelings rather than refusing to share any information.

Rapport can be facilitated when the clinician feels acceptance, respect, and mutual confidence toward the client (Sattler, 1998). With children and adolescents, the mere fact that the clinician wants to hear their side of the story, rather than relying on their parents' version, should bode well for establishing rapport. In addition, asking about children's or adolescents' interests, and having some working knowledge of those interests, is helpful in building rapport with children (Bostic & Pataki, 2000). For example, if as of this writing you worked with children and you did not know anything about Harry Potter, then the 10-year-old you were interviewing would probably think that you were pretty dumb. Popular crazes change rapidly, so clinicians who work with children and adolescents are well advised to keep track of what youth of a given age, gender, and so on are involved in. Even before you ask, you may notice clients wearing clothes or carrying items that broadcast their interests. Whether it's the local baseball team, or the hot new music star, youth often express their interests in the clothes they wear or the items they buy. Observant clinicians let their clients know that they pay attention to such details.

Among the other strategies that a clinician can use in an unstructured interview to help develop rapport with both youth and their parents are the following (Sattler, 1998):

- Give the child or parent your undivided attention. Do not focus on the next question without listening to their answer about the previous question.
- Give the child or parent reassurance and support by using a warm and expressive tone, maintaining appropriate eye contact, and listening in an open and non-judgmental manner.
- Ask tactful questions that do not convey harsh, biased, or judgmental opinions.
- Show good listening skills and convey to the child or parent that you want to understand his or her situation and that you can be trusted.
- Time your questions appropriately. Do not interrupt the child or parent unless it is necessary.
- Focus on the child's or parent's experience rather than imposing your own hypotheses or interests onto that experience.

Overall, the same clinical skills that are used to build rapport are also used to conduct good interviews. These skills are usually learned in graduate training programs where clinical psychologists, school psychologists, social workers, counseling psychologists, psychiatrists, and other mental health professionals are taught through readings, lectures, and feedback on practical experience.

Once rapport is established, the other crucial goal of the unstructured interview is to gather information. Table 5.2 shows an example of the information that might be gathered in an unstructured interview. For interested readers, two excellent resources on conducting interviews with children and families are Dr. Jerome Sattler's *Clinical and Forensic Interviewing of Children and*

Families (1998) and Dr. Annette La Greca's, *Through the Eyes of the Child: Obtaining Self-Reports From Children and Adolescents* (1990). These books provide both scholarly and practical clinical knowledge that could help improve the interviewing skills of even the most seasoned clinician.

TABLE 5.2 Information That Can Be Collected in an Unstructured or a Semistructured Interview

Information from Both Parents and Children/Adolescents

History of current difficulties (e.g., onset of difficulties, precipitating factors, consequences to the difficulties, how the child and parents feel about the problems)

Child's educational history (e.g., grades and academic performance, favorite and least favorite subjects, favorite and least favorite teachers)

Home environment (e.g., family activities, family rituals and beliefs, strengths and difficulties within the home)

Expectations for child (e.g., how parents and child feel about the likelihood of improvement for the child, what parents and child expect from therapy)

Child's strengths, competencies, and accomplishments (e.g., what the child and parents are most proud of in the child, in which domains the child excels)

Information from Parents (Usually without Child Present)

Details of pregnancy and birth (e.g., smoking or substance use during pregnancy, delivery complications at birth)

Child's developmental history (e.g., age of sitting, standing, walking, talking; development of self-help skills and personal-social relationships)

Child's medical history (e.g., dates and types of injuries, major illnesses, hospitalizations)

Family characteristics and family history (e.g., parents' marital status, family constellation, siblings' and parents' mental health history)

Child's interpersonal skills (e.g., child's ability to form friendships, child's social activities, child's relationships with children and adults)

Information from Children/Adolescents (Usually without Parents Present)

Child's or adolescent's occupational history, if any (e.g., jobs held, job training, career aspirations)

Child's or adolescent's friendships (e.g., how many friends, what age and gender, activities that are done with friends)

Child's or adolescent's sexual involvements, if any (e.g., romantic and sexual relationships with others of the same or opposite sex, current involvements and past involvements)

Child's or adolescent's involvement with illicit substances (e.g., drug use, drinking alcohol, smoking cigarettes)

Source: Sattler (1998).

Special consideration should be taken in conducting interviews when sexual abuse, physical abuse, or child neglect is suspected. Table 5.3 provides a list of suggestions when interviewing a child in such a case. While crucial in cases of suspected abuse, these suggestions are also relevant to any type of interviewing with children and adolescents. (See also Box 5.1 for an example of an unstructured interview in a case of suspected abuse.)

Overall, unstructured interviews are usually used as a foundation on which the rest of the assessment process will be built. Strengths of unstructured interviews include their usefulness in establishing rapport, the wealth of information that is usually generated, and the flexibility of the interviews. There are drawbacks, however, to unstructured interviews. Multiple clinicians may get varied information from the same clients because they chose to follow up on different issues. For this reason, the reliability of unstructured interviews has been questioned repeatedly (La Greca, 1990). Semistructured

TABLE 5.3 Suggestions for Interviewing Children Who Are Suspected of Being Abused

The interviewer should not:
- Ask leading questions.
- Provide answers for the child.
- Add to the child's sense of guilt.
- Make the child discuss topics with which he or she is extremely uncomfortable.
- Allow the child to be interviewed by a "team" of professionals.
- Be critical of the way in which the child expresses her or himself.
- Make the child think that the interviewer is shocked or disgusted by the events that the child reports.

The interviewer should:
- Develop the child's trust through legitimate means.
- Be supportive and warm with the child and make sure that the child does not feel that the abuse was her or his fault.
- Interview the child in a private setting that feels comfortable to the child.
- Sit near the child, without a desk or table in between.
- Be as honest as possible about future actions and litigation, without frightening the child or making promises that cannot be kept.
- Clarify any misunderstandings with the child (e.g., the meanings of words that the child uses, fears that the child expresses about getting in trouble).

Note: Readers interested in further suggestions for interviewing children who are suspected of being abused are referred to *Recognizing Child Abuse: A Guide for the Concerned* (Besharov, 1990).

BOX *5.1*

UNSTRUCTURED INTERVIEW WITH A CHILD IN A CASE OF SUSPECTED ABUSE

The interviewer has provided the six-year-old child with a number of anatomically correct dolls (i.e., dolls with genitalia that are proportioned appropriately for the size of the doll's body). In this interview, the interviewer is trying not to use leading questions and is also trying not to identify body parts for the child. Rather, an attempt is made to allow the child to use her own language to explain the abuse.

The child chooses the adult male doll and the child female doll and positions the adult male doll on top of the child doll.

INTERVIEWER: What is happening?

CHILD: They are sleeping.

INTERVIEWER: Is anything else happening?

CHILD: He is humping her.

INTERVIEWER: It is hard for me to see this. Can you show me what humping means?

CHILD (using the dolls to demonstrate): This thing goes in that thing.

INTERVIEWER: It looks like you are putting the man's thing in the girl's thing. Is that correct?

CHILD: Yes.

INTERVIEWER: Remind me what you call these parts. A man's thing is . . .

CHILD: Penis.

INTERVIEWER: Okay, and a girl's thing is . . .

CHILD: Private.

INTERVIEWER: Okay, so the man's penis went in the girl's private?

CHILD: Yes.

INTERVIEWER: How do you know this happened?

CHILD: Because that is what he did to me.

INTERVIEWER: The man's penis went into your private?

CHILD: Yes.

INTERVIEWER: How do you know his penis went into your private?

CHILD: I could feel it and it hurt!

INTERVIEWER: Who was the man?

CHILD: My dad.

SOURCE: M. Morgan (1995).

---

and structured interviews have been developed as a means to ensure reliability.

Semistructured Interviews

This section highlights one semistructured interview to illustrate the characteristics common to all such interviews. The Semistructured Clinical Interview for Children and Adolescents (SCICA; McConaughy & Achenbach, 2001) is a comprehensive interview that allows the clinician not only to follow a set format but also to follow up on relevant questions and themes. The interview is appropriate for children and adolescents from 6 to 18 years old. As Table 5.4 shows, the SCICA covers a broad range of topics and concerns. After asking the prescribed questions, the interviewer then presents the child with three to six behavioral items of concern to the parents and teachers. The child is asked for his or her perception of these behaviors. A standardized achievement test is considered optional during the SCICA but can be given by a clinician who wants to do a thorough assessment. In addition, children can be screened for fine motor and gross motor and language difficulties (McConaughy

& Achenbach, 2001). Following the interview, the clinician completes a standardized observation form about the child's behavior and a standardized questionnaire about the child's self-reported concerns. The clinician analyzes these forms and calculates standardized scores from the normative data base on these measures. Overall, the SCICA represents an empirical interview system that still allows clinicians flexibility in the interview process.

Structured Interviews

Although semistructured interviews provide more consistent information than unstructured interviews, there is still concern that variable information might be collected from different interviewers. In addition, a semistructured interview might not lead to diagnostic information unless the clinician specifically targets that type of information. For these reasons, structured interviews have received a great deal of interest. Most structured interviews are focused on the diagnostic process. That is, at the end of the interview, the clinician makes a diagnosis or confirms the lack of a clinical disorder. Examples of structured diagnostic interviews include the Diagnostic Interview

TABLE 5.4 Topics and Sample Questions from the Semi-structured Clinical Interview for Children and Adolescents (SCICA)

Topic/Domain	Sample Questions
Activities	What do you like to do in your spare time, like when you're not in school?
	What is your favorite TV show?
School	What do you like best in school?
	If you could change something about school, what would it be?
Job (ages 12–18)	Do you have a job?
	How do you feel about your job/boss?
Friends	How many friends do you have?
	Tell me about someone you like.
	Tell me about someone you don't like.
Family relations	Who are the people in your family?
	How do your parents get along?
Fantasies	If you had three wishes, what would you wish?
	What would you like to be when you're older?
Self-perception, feelings	What makes you happy?
	What makes you sad?
	What do you worry about?
Somatic complaints, alcohol and drugs, trouble with the law (ages 12–18)	Have you had headaches?
	Have you drunk beer, wine, or liquor?
	Have you used tobacco?
	Have you been in trouble with the police or law?

SOURCE: McConaughy & Achenbach (2001).

TABLE 5.5 Sample Questions from the Diagnostic Interview Schedule for Children (DISC)

Attention-Deficit/Hyperactivity Disorder (AD/HD Module)

Children and adolescents are asked to think about the past 12 months, and they are asked to answer these questions in a yes/no format. If a child answers yes to one of these questions, then follow-up questions are completed to obtain more details and to ascertain whether the symptoms have been present for at least four weeks. There is also a parent interview with parallel questions.

• In the last year, have you often made a lot of mistakes because it's hard for you to do things carefully?
• In the last year, did you often have trouble keeping your mind on what you were doing for more than a short time?
• In the last year, did you often not listen when people were speaking to you?
• In the last year, have you often left your seat when you weren't supposed to?
• In the last year, were you often "on the go" or did you move around as if you were "driven by a motor"?

SOURCE: Shaffer et al. (2000). Reprinted with permission.

for Children and Adolescents–Revised (DICA-R; Reich, 1996); the Child Adolescent Schedule (CAS; K. Hodges, 1997); the Schedule for Affective Disorders and Schizophrenia for School-Age Children (known as the Kiddie-SADS-IVR; Ambrosini & Dixon, 1996); the Interview Schedule for Children (Kovacs, 1985); and the Diagnostic Interview Schedule for Children–IV (DISC; Shaffer, Fisher, Lucas, Dulcan, & Schwab-Stone, 2000). There are also a number of structured interviews that assess one particular problem in depth, such as the Anxiety Disorders Interview Schedule for Children (ADIS-C/P; Silverman & Nelles, 1988). Since the DISC is the most widely used structured diagnostic interview, it is described in detail in the remainder of this section.

As mentioned in Chapter 1, the DISC interview was used in the Methods for the Epidemiology of Child and Adolescent Mental Disorders (MECA) study. In fact, some critics have wondered if the MECA study actually served as a large-scale psychometric study of the DISC rather than as an epidemiological study. The DISC is highly structured, with little to no room for variations in questions. Because of this rigorous structure, the DISC can be given by trained individuals with only a bachelor's degree. (Both unstructured interviews and semistructured interviews are usually valid only if well-trained graduate-level clinicians administer them.)

Table 5.5 illustrates the types of questions that are asked within the DISC. The questions cover nearly every clinical disorder that can be experienced by children or adolescents, including attention-deficit/hyperactivity disorder, conduct disorder, and depression. Note that there is a child-report and a parent-report version of the DISC. The primary purpose of the DISC is to establish present and lifetime diagnoses in the child or adolescent. It is appropriate for children ages 6 to 18. Based on extensive psychometric studies, the DISC appears to be very reliable (Shaffer et al., 2000). Although there are still concerns about getting different answers from parents and children, this issue appears to be due to the way in which children and their parents recall information rather than a weakness in the DISC itself. In addition, when only the child or only the parent reports psychopathology, the disorder is usually a legitimate concern (Jensen et al., 1999).

Overall, there are no right or wrong answers when choosing between unstructured, semistructured, and structured interviews. The strengths of a structured interview (e.g., reliable information, clinical diagnoses) may be supplemented by those of an unstructured or semi-structured interview (e.g., breadth of information, well-established rapport, strengths and weaknesses of the child in a number of domains). Thus, the choice between interview formats depends largely on the goals of the assessment and the specific referral question. As with most other types of assessment, the clinician uses his or her skill and knowledge to determine the best and most comprehensive assessment techniques for a particular child or adolescent.

BEHAVIORAL ASSESSMENT

There are three primary types of behavioral assessment: behavioral observation, functional assessment, and self-monitoring.

Behavioral Observation

Behavioral observation consists of the clinician's observing the child at school, at home, in a research laboratory, or in the clinician's office. Having just read about unstructured and structured interviews, you will probably not be surprised to learn that there are also unstructured and structured behavioral observation techniques. Nearly any clinician who meets with a child will observe the child's behavior. With the permission of the parents and teacher, clinicians can also visit the school in order to observe the child in the school setting. These unstructured observations provide a wealth of information about the

child's behavioral functioning. Often, clinicians observe the child's behavior in relation to its **antecedents** (what occurs before the behavior) and its **consequences** (what occurs after the behavior). Imagine that a child has been referred for disruptive behavior in the classroom. When observing the child in the classroom, the clinician notices that the child receives no attention (good or bad) when she is staring quietly into space while sitting at her desk. As soon as she starts throwing her pencils around, she receives a great deal of attention: negative attention from the teacher in the form of a reprimand, and positive attention from the other children in the form of laughter. These observations might lead the clinician to hypothesize that the disruptive behavior was at least partially reinforced by its consequences.

Like unstructured interviews, unstructured behavioral observations can collect a wealth of information but can also be biased by the clinician's own way of viewing the situation. For this reason, structured behavioral observation systems have been developed. One example is the Direct Observation Form (DOF; Achenbach, 1991a), for which the child is observed in a standardized manner and, in addition, another child of the same age and gender is observed as a comparison child. The DOF allows clinicians to report on a series of behaviors that may have gone unnoticed without the prompt of the DOF stimulus material. Overall, the DOF's psychometric properties make it a strong addition to the available tools for observation of children's and adolescents' behaviors. There are also myriad other ways to observe children's behavior in a structured manner, many of which occur either in a research laboratory (see the special issue of *Journal of Clinical Child Psychology* edited by Frick, 2000) or at the child's

Observations of children in their natural environments, such as school, can help clinicians understand a great deal about children's behavior.

home (Power, Costigan, Leff, Eiraldi, & Landau, 2001).

A great advantage of behavioral observation is that the clinician can see the child's environment. A clinician can learn a lot more about a child's being teased at school by observing the child at school than by merely listening to the child's report of the teasing while in the clinician's office. Similarly, seeing a child interact with teachers and parents is often more compelling than listening to the child describe such interactions. These benefits of behavioral observation are also present in functional assessment.

Functional Assessment

Functional assessment consists of the evaluation of actual behaviors and the child's ability to perform those behaviors. Imagine that you were asked to work with a seven-year-old boy who reportedly had poor social skills. In addition to getting information from the boy's parents, teachers, and day care workers, you might also want to observe the child interacting with others. Functional assessment allows you to observe the child while he exhibits the behaviors of interest. Not only would functional assessment help you determine whether or not there was a problem, but you would also be able to identify what specific behavioral strengths and weaknesses the boy exhibited (Witt et al., 1998). In observing the boy, for example, you might find that he stands far too close when speaking with other children and that he tries to continue conversations even after the other child is ready to leave. With this information, the functional assessment would identify specific target behaviors for treatment. Treatment effectiveness could then be assessed more accurately through functional outcome measures, which would evaluate the changes in the specific target behaviors (Quittner, 2000).

Self-Monitoring

Self-monitoring is an assessment technique that allows the child to keep track of a specific behavior by recording the occurrence of the behavior (Kratochwill, Sheridan, Carlson, & Lasecki, 1999). For example, imagine a 10-year-old girl who reportedly has a learning disorder. Before administering a formal test, the school psychologist asks the girl to self-monitor her completion of homework assignments using a prepared grid. Figure 5.2 shows the grid, which lists each day of the week for the next two weeks along the top of the page. Along the left side of the page are three aspects of her homework that she is asked to record: total number of homework assignments, total of assignments completed, and percentage of assignments

completed. The school psychologist would use the information from this grid to begin to understand why the girl might be having difficulties in school. If, on the one hand, she never does her homework, then an intervention could be developed to address that problem (whether it stemmed from lack of motivation or lack of ability). If, on the other hand, the girl was completing her assignments but still not doing well on tests at school, then more formal testing for a learning disorder might be appropriate.

Overall, behavioral assessment techniques provide a wealth of information about the child in different environments, but they do have potential problems. The primary concern is related to **reactivity**, which occurs if children behave differently solely because they are being observed (Kratochwill et al., 1999). It is not unusual for a child to try to act more appropriately (or sometimes less appropriately) when being observed. Similarly, children who self-monitor their own behavior may actually behave better when they are paying attention to their actions. For this reason, clinicians often try to observe behavior either unobtrusively (e.g., before they have met the child so the child does not know their identity) or for a long enough period of time that reactivity decreases.

Silence is also speech.

—Proverb of Africa

CHECKLISTS AND RATING SCALES

Among the least expensive and most commonly used assessment techniques with children and adolescents are checklists and rating scales. Both are usually easy to administer, and they provide a wealth of information about children's functioning without being time-consuming. Most of the measures discussed in this section take between 5 and 15 minutes to complete. Checklists and rating scales can be broken down into roughly two cate-

	M	T	W	T	F	M	T	W	T	F
Total number assigned										
Total completed										
Percentage completed										

FIGURE 5.2 Example of a Self-Monitoring Worksheet
Source: Kratochwill et al. (1999).

gories: broad measures and specific measures. Broad measures cover a variety of emotional/behavioral problems, whereas specific measures focus on one or two areas of concern. Both types of measures can be used in a comprehensive assessment. For example, if a 14-year-old girl is referred for depression, the clinician would certainly want to administer a specific measure that assessed depression and suicide, but he or she might also want to administer a broad measure that would assess other possible problems such as anxiety, attentional problems, and somatic complaints. By using both broad and specific measures, the clinician can assess the referral problem in depth while also screening for other problems that were not mentioned in the intake phone call.

Broad Measures

This section highlights two well-known systems of broad measures. Both systems provide checklists to be completed by youth, parents, and teachers; assess competencies as well as emotional/behavioral problems in children; and are empirically based and well established in the research literature. Finally, both systems have immeasurably furthered our understanding of children's and adolescents' emotional/behavioral functioning.

The most widely used and well-established broad measure of children's emotional/behavioral functioning was originally developed by Dr. Tom Achenbach and Dr. Craig Edelbrock (1983). The system was later revised and renormed by Dr. Tom Achenbach and his research group in 1991 (Achenbach, 1991a, 1991b, 1991c, 1992) and revised and renormed again more recently by Dr. Tom Achenbach and Dr. Leslie Rescorla (Achenbach & Rescorla, 2000, 2001). The system is now referred to as the Achenbach System of Empirically Based Assessment (ASEBA). For school-age children, the Child Behavior Checklist (CBCL/6–18) is the parent report version within this system, the Teacher's Report Form (TRF) is

---

Case Study: B, The Boy Who Set Fires

During his first three years, B had a relatively stable home life with his mother, father, and four siblings. His parents separated when B was three years old, and after that point he had a series of chaotic and unstable caretaking situations. B's mother had psychiatric problems; she made two suicide attempts during B's childhood, one of which lead to hospitalization. When he was eight, B's mother asked that B and one brother be put up for adoption. For the next two years, B bounced from one foster home to another. He was often kicked out of foster homes for lying, stealing, and acting defiant. He had fewer and fewer contacts with his mother and did not appear to have any close bonds with adults or other children in his life. When B was 10, his mother's parental rights were formally terminated.

In one of his foster care placements, B had an argument with his roommate. After being reprimanded for something he did not think was his fault, B set fire to some papers that were in his roommate's dresser. Shortly thereafter, he reported to the staff that he smelled smoke. The fire department was summoned, and the fire was extinguished without extensive damage. B was placed in a psychiatric hospital for approximately 10 months, during which time a thorough psychiatric evaluation was completed. The clinician concluded that B was "a depressed and angry boy who idealized a relationship between himself and his mother and father. He could not admit that his mother was rejecting him and appeared to have displaced this anger through fire setting and violent episodes" (Kolko & Ammerman, 1988; p. 247).

B made modest improvements with individual therapy and was discharged to a foster home. After four months in this foster home, B was found spreading kerosene around the neighbor's house. He was placed in a temporary emergency shelter, where he tried to ignite a deodorant can to be used as a torch. At this point, he was admitted to yet another psychiatric hospital. At $13\frac{1}{2}$ years old, B continued be defiant, verbally aggressive, and destructive. Another thorough psychological evaluation was conducted at the hospital. The assessment included behavioral observation by B's primary worker on the unit and by the staff, completion of the CBCL and the Firesetting Screen by the primary worker, and B's completion of the Youth Self-Report, Interview for Aggression, Hostility–Guilt Inventory, Matson Evaluation of Social Skills of Youngsters, Children's Action Tendency Scale, Trait Anger Scale, Children's Inventory of Anger, Children's Depression Inventory, Bellevue Index of Depression–Modified, Coopersmith Self-Esteem Inventory, and the Firesetting Inventory. Results from this evaluation showed B to be a sad and angry boy who set fires when he reached a peak of sadness and anger.

Based on the results of this assessment, a comprehensive cognitive-behavioral treatment was completed. B was taught better impulse control techniques, and his feelings of sadness and anger were dealt with directly. Successful in this treatment, B was eventually discharged to a long-term residential treatment facility for emotionally disturbed children. A follow-up assessment conducted after six months showed that B maintained many of his therapeutic gains. For example, although he was still somewhat defiant and oppositional, B had not set any fires even after a particularly troubling visit with his biological mother. This case illustrates how assessments can be used to formulate treatment plans, to evaluate the effectiveness of treatment, and to verify the stability of treatment gains in a follow-up evaluation.

SOURCE: Kolko & Ammerman (1988).

geared toward teachers' perceptions, and the Youth Self-Report (YSR) is meant to be completed by older children and adolescents (Achenbach & Rescorla, 2001). Parents and teachers can complete the measures for children ages 6 to 18, and children ages 11 to 18 can complete the YSR. There are also parent-report measures (CBCL/1$\frac{1}{2}$–5) and caretaker/day care worker measures (C-TRF) for children between the ages of 1$\frac{1}{2}$ and 5 who have not yet begun formal schooling (Achenbach & Rescorla, 2000). Interestingly, this system has also been expanded into young adulthood, with a measure known as the Young Adult Self-Report (YASR), which can be completed by people ages 18 to 30, and a measure known as the Young Adult Behavior Checklist (YABCL), which can be completed by parents of young adults ages 18 to 30 (Achenbach, 1997b). Although all of these measures are dimensional, rather than categorical, they can be used to help inform the clinician about the appropriateness of *DSM* diagnoses (Achenbach & Dumenci, 2001; Achenbach & Rescorla, 2001). These measures are also used extensively in research (see Box 5.2 for an example).

The three primary measures—CBCL, TRF, and YSR—have been studied extensively and are well normed. Thousands of parents, teachers, and nonclinical as well as clinical youth were involved in the original development and revisions of these measures, so they have been extremely well validated. When the measures are scored, a child's profile is related to the normative data in order to establish how that child compares with other children of the same gender and in the same age range. These standardized *T* scores (with a mean of 50 and standard deviation of 10) are calculated in order to provide a standard comparison of the target child with children in the normative sample. Children who receive a *T* score of 70 or above on the broadband factors are considered to be in the clinical range, because their behavior is consistent with those children in the normative sample who were receiving clinical services. A *T* score of 70 is comparable to the 98th percentile, which means that 98% of the children in the normative sample received lower ratings for that factor. Thus, a *T* score of 70 or above is meant to identify only those children whose behavior is well beyond what most children exhibit.

On all three primary measures (CBCL, TRF, YSR), there are three main broadband scores that can be derived for emotional/behavioral problems: total behavior problems, internalizing problems, and externalizing problems. Internalizing problems can be further broken down into three narrowband scales: anxious/depressed, withdrawn/depressed, and somatic complaints. There are three narrowband scales that do not fall under internalizing or

externalizing problems: social problems, thought problems, and attention problems. Externalizing problems consist of two narrowband scales: rule-breaking behavior and aggressive behavior. Table 5.6 provides sample items from the narrowband scales. Note that the wording of the items differ somewhat depending on whether the measure is to be filled out by a parent (CBCL), a teacher (TRF), or an adolescent (YSR). Note also that these measures yield *T* scores related to the child's competence in a number of domains.

A significant strength of these measures is that they allow comparisons across informants. The computerized scoring programs let clinicians assess the cross-informant agreement for the child being assessed. Not only can you see how the child, parent, and teacher rate the child's behavior, but you can also see how those rates of agreement or disagreement compare with the normative sample. This information is helpful if a child is being rated very differently by multiple individuals in his or her life. Overall, the CBCL, TRF, and YSR provide a wealth of valid information that can be used to help children in innumerable ways. Because the norms on measures are updated frequently, interested students may want to check the ASEBA Web site (www.aseba.org) for the latest information.

TABLE 5.6 Sample Items from the CBCL, TRF, and YSR

INTERNALIZING		EXTERNALIZING
Anxious/ Depressed	**Social Problems**	**Rule-Breaking Behavior**
Cries a lot	Too dependent	Lies and cheats
Fears doing bad things	Doesn't get along with others	Steals
Worries	Gets teased	Swears
Withdrawn/ Depressed	**Thought Problems**	**Aggressive Behavior**
Refuses to talk	Hears things	Argues a lot
Secretive	Repeats certain acts	Gets in fights
Withdrawn	Sees things	Teases a lot
Somatic Complaints	**Attention Problems**	
Feels dizzy	Can't concentrate	
Headaches	Daydreams	
Nausea	Poor schoolwork	

Source: Achenbach & Rescorla (2001).

BOX *5.2*

USING BEHAVIOR CHECKLISTS TO EXPLORE GENETIC INFLUENCES

Genetic and environmental influences can be explored with the use of behavior checklists. One research team (Towers et al., 2000) used the CBCL and TRF to examine genetic and environmental influences in a sample of monozygotic twins, dizygotic twins, and nontwin siblings. They found that:

- Shared environment (i.e., aspects of the environment that are similar for siblings) did not influence any behaviors significantly.

- Nonshared environment (i.e., aspects of the environment that are different for siblings) had the highest degree of influence on most behaviors (such as aggression, delinquency, anxious/depressed, and withdrawn), but did not influence attention problems or social problems.

- Genetic influences were found in attention problems, anxious/depressed, withdrawn, and social problems.

Overall, this type of study shows that behavior checklists can be used in analyses of genetic and environmental influences of children's emotional/behavioral problems.

Another strong system of assessment is known as the Behavior Assessment System for Children (BASC; C. R. Reynolds & Kamphaus, 1992). The BASC uses multiple informants (children, parents, and teachers), and the self-reports can be completed by children as young as eight. Additional normative data continue to be gathered, along with additional studies of the psychometric properties (Doyle, Ostrander, Skare, Crosby, & August, 1997; Kamphaus, Huberty, DiStefano, & Petoskey, 1997). The BASC is comparable to the system developed by Achenbach given that the measures are broad and that they assess children in multiple contexts. BASC allows both emotional/behavioral problems and competencies to be assessed. Within the BASC, parents and teachers report on the child's externalizing problems (aggression, hyperactivity, and conduct problems); internalizing problems (anxiety, depression, and somatization); school problems (attention problems are rated by both parents and teachers, whereas learning problems are rated only by teachers); other problems (atypicality and withdrawal); and adaptive skills (adaptability, leadership, social skills, and study skills). In addition, an overall behavioral symptoms index is calculated for both parent and teacher ratings. Children's and adolescents' reports within the BASC yield the following scores: clinical maladjustment (anxiety, atypicality, locus of control, social stress, and somatization); school maladjustment (attitude toward school, attitude toward teacher, and sensation seeking); other problems (depression and sense of inadequacy); and personal adjustment (relations with parents, interpersonal relations, self-esteem, and self-reliance). An overall emotional symptoms index is also calculated for children's and adolescents' self-reports.

Overall, both the BASC and the system involving the CBCL, TRF, and YSR are well established and well vali-

dated in the research literature. Both styles of assessment allow a dimensional approach to understanding children's and adolescents' behavior, given that scores are based on a continuum rather than on dichotomous categorizations. In a comprehensive assessment of a child or adolescent, it behooves the clinician to use one of these systems in order to assess broadly for problems and competencies in the child or adolescent. They are also sometimes appropriate for allowing a clinician to gain a more specific understanding of certain presenting problems that the child or adolescent is experiencing. In these cases, it is wise for the clinician to include measures that are specific to the referral problem. A few of these specific measures are discussed below, but note that there are hundreds of measures that are not discussed in this chapter. In addition, assessments for possible child victimization, such as physical abuse or sexual abuse, are often necessary (Hamby & Finkelhor, 2000), as are specialized assessments when child custody is under dispute (Bow & Quinnell, 2001; Hagan & Castagna, 2001). Well-trained clinicians and clinical researchers often have to do their homework to find the right measures to assess the characteristics of interest. These clinicians and researchers would, of course, be looking for measures that have strong psychometric properties. All of the following measures are well established and have strong psychometric properties (i.e., good reliability and validity).

Measures of Depression and Suicide

One of the most widely used self-report measures is the Children's Depression Inventory (CDI; Kovacs, 1992). Based on a downward extension of the Beck Depression Inventory for adults (Beck, Steer, & Garbin, 1988), the CDI is used to assess children's feelings of depression,

BOX *5.3*

SUBJECTIVE DISTRESS

Imagine that you are referred a 12-year-old girl who continues to get in trouble at school for talking too much and for being a class clown. When you meet with the girl and her single father, the girl seems to be unfazed by her "problems," whereas her father says that he is at his wit's end. The father explains that the girl has been suspended from school multiple times for her antics, which necessitates that he take a day off work (he receives no pay for those missed days). After talking with the father, and later talking with the teachers, you understand that the adults in this girl's life clearly want her behavior changed. It is also clear that the girl does not believe she has a problem. She later confides in you that she likes the attention that children in school give her when she goofs off in class and that she likes her days of suspension because they give her some of the only time that she can spend with her father.

In formal assessments, children and adolescents are usually asked to report on the occurrence of their behavior, but they are often not asked how they feel about their behavior. There are a number of studies that show interesting patterns when you ask adolescents and parents how they feel about the adolescents' behavior (Phares & Compas, 1990; Phares & Danforth, 1994; A. M. Smith & Phares, 1999). In a non-clinical sample of adolescents, adolescents felt significantly more distress over their internalizing problems than over their externalizing problems (Phares & Compas, 1990). In a clinical sample of adolescents with high levels of emotional/behavioral problems, adolescents did not feel different levels of distress over their internalizing versus externalizing behaviors (A. M. Smith & Phares, 1999). Mother, fathers, and teachers all reported that adolescents' externalizing behaviors were significantly more distressing to them than the internalizing behaviors were (Phares & Danforth, 1994; A. M. Smith & Phares, 1999). As would be expected, mothers, fathers, teachers, and adolescents all were motivated to change those internalizing and externalizing problems that they found distressing.

Overall, these studies suggest that adolescents, parents, and teachers should be asked not only about the frequency of behaviors but also about their feelings toward those behaviors. It may be that other forces are at work to reward the behaviors (such as attention from peers, parents, or teachers). It is important for clinicians to know about these rewards for problematic behaviors before trying to change the behaviors.

---

negative mood, interpersonal problems, ineffectiveness, anhedonia, and negative self-esteem. Although there has been some evidence to suggest that the CDI also assesses anxiety (Crowley & Emerson, 1996; J. Lerner et al., 1999) and some externalizing problems (Craighead, Smucker, Craighead, & Ilardi, 1998; Weiss et al., 1992), the measure is most often used to assess depression in children and adolescents ages 7 to 17.

In order to assess the possibility of suicide, a number of measures have been developed that assess suicidal ideation. For example, the Scale for Suicide Ideation (Beck, Kovacs, & Weissman, 1979) assesses an individual's degree of suicidality. Although this scale was originally developed for adults, it has since been validated with children and adolescents (Allan, Kashani, Dahlmeier, Taghizadeh, & Reid, 1997). Another scale, the Suicidal Ideation Questionnaire–Junior (SIQ-Jr.; W. M. Reynolds, 1988b), is a self-report measure for the child or adolescent to report on the type, severity, and frequency of suicidal thoughts. The Reasons for Living Inventory for Adolescents (RFL-A) assesses the potential risk for adolescent suicide (Gutierrez, Osman, Kopper, & Barrios, 2000). Overall, these scales can ascertain the frequency and severity of suicidal ideation in children and adolescents who are willing to share those feelings with a clini-

cian. These types of scales are often used in conjunction with interviewing that is specific to suicidal ideation and behavior (Shaffer & Pfeffer, 2001).

Measures of Anxiety

Two global measures of anxiety are the Revised Children's Manifest Anxiety Scale (R-CMAS; C. R. Reynolds & Richmond, 1997) and the State-Trait Anxiety Inventory for Children (Spielberger, 1973). These measures assess children's self-reports of their overall level of anxiety. Recent research on the R-CMAS suggests that the measure is multidimensional (White & Farrell, 2001). Other measures, such as the Social Anxiety Scale for Children–Revised (La Greca & Stone, 1993) and the Social Phobia and Anxiety Inventory for Children (Beidel, Turner, & Morris, 1995) are used to assess social anxiety specifically.

Measures of Inattention and Hyperactivity

The most widely used measures of inattention and hyperactivity are the Conners' Ratings Scales (Conners, 1990). There is a parent report version, the Conners' Parent Rat-

Reprinted with special permission of King Features Syndicate.

ing Scale, and a teacher report version, the Conners' Teacher Rating Scale. Some researchers have also used a preschool teacher version (Fantuzzo et al., 2001) and an adolescent self-report version (B. H. Smith, Pelham, Gnagy, Molina, & Evans, 2000). Although there are different versions of each measure with different numbers of items, most of the measures assess characteristics such as hyperactivity, inattention, and conduct problems. Overall, the Conners measures are used to assess externalizing problems in children ages 6 to 17 years old. There are also recent norms that can be used for preschoolers (L. S. Miller, Koplewicz, & Klein, 1997).

Measures of Disruptive Behaviors

Parents and teachers can complete the Revised Behavior Problem Scale (RBPC; Quay & Peterson, 1983), which results in scales that include conduct disorder and social-ized aggression. Although the RBPC is often thought of as a global measure, it has been used primarily in the assessment of disruptive behaviors. Two other measures that were developed specifically for children with disruptive behaviors are the Eyberg Child Behavior Inventory (ECBI; Eyberg, 1992) and the Sutter-Eyberg Student Behavior Inventory (SESBI; Eyberg, 1992). The ECBI is completed by parents, and the SESBI is completed by teachers. These measures can be completed for children ages 2 to 16. The unique addition to these measures is that parents and teachers are asked not only about the frequency of the behaviors but also about whether or not they consider the behaviors to be a problem. In this way, the clinician can get a good understanding of the level of behaviors and also the distress that these behaviors are causing in parents and teachers.

Case Study: Jennifer, An Example of Fears and Anxieties

Jennifer is an eight-year-old girl who is terribly frightened by insects and who experiences extreme amounts of worry and somatic complaints. She often avoids locations where she might run across insects (such as the kitchen). Her worries center around her "not being good enough," "making mistakes," "being teased by others," and "being in accidents." The somatic complaints, which have no medical cause, include headaches, stomachaches, sweating, and a racing heart when she sees an insect.

For the assessment, Jennifer was interviewed with the Anxiety Disorders Interview Schedule for Children (ADIS-C), and she completed a number of self-report questionnaires such as the Fear Survey Schedule for Children–Revised (FSSC-R), the Revised Children's Manifest Anxiety Scale (RCMAS), and the State-Trait Anxiety Inventory for Children (STAIC). In addition, Jennifer's mother completed the ADIS-Parent version, the FSSC-R, and the RCMAS to report on Jennifer's fears and anxieties. During the assessment, Jennifer's mother also acknowledged that she was afraid of insects herself and that she had always been a worrier. Based on this evaluation, Jennifer was found to have excessive levels of fear and anxiety.

Jennifer and her mother were invited to participate in a 10-week cognitive-behavioral treatment program that was geared toward the alleviation of fears and anxiety. With the use of fear hierarchies, positive reinforcement, and self-control training, Jennifer was able to conquer her fear of insects. Assessments at the end of treatment, and follow-up assessments at 3, 6, and 12 months after treatment, showed that Jennifer's fears and worries had decreased significantly and had remained low even a year after treatment.

SOURCE: Silverman & Ginsburg (1995).

Measures of Competence and Adaptive Functioning

Competence, self-esteem, and adaptive functioning are all important features to assess in children, even if they are being referred for problem behavior. Although parents and teachers (and often children) tend to focus on the problems that the child is experiencing, it is important for the clinician to assess the strengths and competencies that the child exhibits. Some of the most widely used measures of competence were developed by Dr. Susan Harter and her colleagues. The Self-Perception Profile for Children (Harter, 1985) is used with children in 3rd through 8th grade, and the Self-Perception Profile for Adolescents is used with adolescents in 8th through 12th grade (Harter, 1988). There are also versions for preschool children, college students, and adults. The rationale behind the Harter measures is that perceived competence is domain specific. That is, rather than asking children how they feel about themselves overall, it is more accurate to ask them how they feel about themselves in different topic areas. For that reason, these measures assess children's and adolescents' views of themselves in a number of different domains, including social, scholastic, athletic, physical appearance, and behavioral conduct. Adolescents are also asked about competence within the job and dating domains. In addition to these domains, both children and adolescents are asked for their overall sense of global self-worth, which is comparable to overall ratings of self-esteem.

In order to assess adaptive functioning, the Vineland Adaptive Behavior Scales (Sparrow, Balla, & Cicchetti, 1984) are used. Primarily used in assessments for developmental disabilities, the Vineland assesses such characteristics as daily living skills, communication, socialization, and motor skills. The Vineland is most often administered to the parent, caretaker, or teacher and can be used for individuals from infancy through adulthood.

Factors That Influence Parents' Ratings on Checklists

Parents' psychological distress appears to influence their ratings of children's behavior somewhat (Boyle & Pickles, 1997; Najman et al., 2000; Phares, Compas, & Howell, 1989; Sawyer, Streiner, & Baghurst, 1998; Youngstrom, Loeber, & Stouthamer-Loeber, 2000). Given the connections between parental depression, for example, and behavior problems in children, researchers were concerned that parental psychological symptoms were inappropriately increasing parents' reports of chil-

dren's emotional/behavioral problems. Overall, it appears that parental distress may increase ratings of children's emotional/behavioral problems to a small degree, but parental ratings remain a valid and useful technique for assessing children's and adolescents' emotional/behavioral problems (Boyle & Pickles, 1997; Najman et al., 2000; Sawyer et al., 1998). (See Box 5.3, which discusses how children and adolescents feel about their behavior, and Box 5.4, which raises the question of who is right when different informants give different information.)

PERSONALITY ASSESSMENT

All of the previously discussed measures are based on observable behavior in one way or another. Interviews, behavioral assessment, and checklists all rely on either reports or actual observations of behavior. In contrast, personality assessments often try to look beyond the behavior to find a deeper meaning to the child's or adolescent's functioning. Personality assessments fall roughly into two categories: personality inventories and projective measures.

Personality Inventories

Personality inventories are paper-and-pencil measures that usually ask about the child's functioning without asking about specific behaviors. For example, the answers on a personality inventory would be compared with the profiles of known reference groups (e.g., children who are depressed or children who are out of touch with reality) so that the child's or adolescent's profile could be compared with the profiles of those reference groups. Often the items on the measures do not seem to have anything to do with the child's behavior, but an inference can be drawn between the profile of answers and the behavior of the child. This inference is one of the biggest points that separates behavioral measures from personality measures.

There are two primary personality inventories used with children and adolescents. The Personality Inventory for Children–2 (PIC-2; Lachar & Gruber, 2001) is completed by parents about their children. In addition to scales that highlight different facets of children's functioning—such as delinquency, somatic concerns, social withdrawal, and social skills deficits—there is also a scale on the PIC-2 that assesses family dysfunction. The Minnesota Multiphasic Personality Inventory–Adolescent version (MMPI-A; Butcher et al., 1992) is an offshoot of the well-known MMPI-2 that was developed for adults (Butcher, Dahlstrom, Graham, Tellegen, & Kaemmer,

BOX *5.4*

WHO IS RIGHT?

When divergent information is gathered from different informants, who is right? This is actually a trick question because the answer is that everyone is right. There is no gold standard of a child's or adolescent's behavior, so clinicians can expect multiple informants to offer different perspectives on the child's behavior (Achenbach, McConaughy, & Howell, 1987) A meta-analysis of different informants (Achenbach et al., 1987) showed that informants in similar roles (e.g., parent with parent, teacher with teacher) tend to see the child's behavior in the most comparable manner (with correlations that average .60). Adults in different roles (e.g., parent with teacher) tend to have ratings that correspond to a significant but small amount (with correlations that average .28). Children and the adults in their lives (such as parent with child, teacher with child) tend to correspond to a significant but small degree (with correlations that average .22). Correlations tend to be higher for all informant pairs when externalizing (versus internalizing) problems are rated and when children (versus adolescents) are rated.

Thus, clinicians are often left with the daunting task of trying to make sense out of divergent information. It behooves a clinician to consider all of the informants' perspectives on children's and adolescents' behavior. Rather than searching for the "right" informant, it is worthwhile to consider the different perspectives from all informants in order to gain a better understanding of children's and adolescents' functioning.

Interesting patterns have emerged in studies that have asked clinicians and parents which informant is the best for children's and adolescents' behavior (Loeber, Green, & Lahey, 1990; Phares, 1997a). Of special interest is that different informants might be able to provide better information about specific types of children's behavior. Both clinicians and parents thought that teachers were especially useful for reporting children's problems with inattentiveness and hyperactivity. Clinicians and parents both felt that parents were better at reporting on children's internalizing problems (Loeber et al., 1990; Phares, 1997a). Finally, parents thought that mothers, fathers, and children were better at reporting on family difficulties than were teachers (Phares, 1997a). Overall, these studies suggest the importance of gathering information from different informants in order to gain a thorough understanding of the child's or adolescent's functioning.

1989). Like the MMPI-2, the MMPI-A is a self-report measure. The MMPI-A follows the same strategy as the MMPI-2, by comparing adolescents' responses with known reference groups. Adolescents can be compared with groups who were known to experience such problems as depression, psychopathic deviance, hysteria, and mania. Additional critical items and specialized scales can help identify specific problems such as substance abuse (Gallucci, 1997).

Although there is a wealth of data on the use of personality inventories in adults, there are relatively few studies that use personality inventories with children and adolescents. One widely used personality measure with adults to explore the "big five" personality traits is known as the Neuroticism Extroversion Openness Personality Inventory, Revised (NEO-PI-R; Costa & McCrae, 1992). Although there was some attempt to create a measure that explored the "little five" personality traits in children (John, Caspi, Robins, & Moffitt, 1994), this technique was never developed into a widely used measure. Overall, the majority of research into child and adolescent functioning has relied on more behavioral measures, partly because these measures have been validated more extensively than personality measures with children.

Projective Measures

In **projective measures** clients are presented with an ambiguous stimulus, onto which they are encouraged to project their innermost thoughts and concerns (Weiner & Kuehnle, 1998). There are a number of types of projective measures, many of which are used with both children and adults. Note that there have been controversies related to the psychometric properties and utility of projective measures, especially with children and adolescents. Advocates argue that projectives can be used to gain a better understanding of children and adolescents than is provided by behavioral measures (Weiner, 2001; Weiner & Kuehnle, 1998). Especially when children or adolescents are reluctant to disclose information, the projective technique might allow them to share information without really knowing they are doing so.

Critics worry that the projective technique allows clinicians to infer too far beyond the information that is provided by the child or adolescent (Hunsley & Bailey, 1999). In addition, many studies of the psychometric properties of projectives have found them to be lacking in strong empirical support (Hunsley & Bailey, 2001). Even with these criticisms, there are a large number of clinicians who use projective techniques in assessing children and adolescents. It appears, however, that projectives are being replaced by behavior rating scales to a large extent (Kamphaus, Petoskey, & Rowe, 2000). The wisest course of action may be to use projective techniques in conjunction with more empirically validated measures that can provide a broad overview of the child's or adolescent's functioning.

Probably the most widely known projective measure is the Rorschach inkblot test. Developed in the 1940s (Rorschach, 1942), the inkblots provide an ambiguous stimulus onto which clients report what they see. There are usually 10 different inkblot cards that are presented, and the clinician most often asks the question "What might this be?" The clinician then asks the client to describe what he or she saw. Though many clinicians do not use a formal coding system with this test, several do exist. The one that shows the most promise is the Exner coding system (Exner & Weiner, 1995; Weiner, 2001). Norms have been developed for children ranging from 5 to 16 years of age. Note, however, that the psychometric properties of the Rorschach have been called into question, especially when the test is used with children (Hunsley & Bailey, 2001).

The Children's Apperception Test (CAT; Bellak, 1993) is another projective measure often used with children and young adolescents. Based on the Thematic Apperception Test (TAT; Bellak, 1993) developed for adults, the CAT consists of pictures about which the child or adolescent is asked to tell a story. There is one set of cards with animal figures for children 3 to 10 years old and another set with human figures for older children and adolescents. Children and adolescents are usually presented with 10 cards, one at a time, and they are asked to tell a story about what is happening in the picture. The story should have a beginning, a middle, and an end. The clinician then interprets the stories for themes or inner conflicts that the child is expressing. Unfortunately, there are no standardized methods for interpretation of the CAT, so clinicians are left to interpret the stories as best they see fit. The majority of research on the CAT was completed more than 40 years ago, and there are no norms available for the measure (Weiner & Kuehnle, 1998).

Two drawing techniques are also used in a projective manner. The Draw-A-Person (DAP) task and the House-Tree-Person (HTP) task are meant to allow the child's or adolescent's inner issues to be reflected in a drawing. The DAP task consists of asking the child to draw a person and then asking the child about that person (Koppitz, 1968, 1984). Interpretations are based on characteristics within the drawing. It is thought that children put feelings about themselves into the person they draw (Zalsman et al., 2000). Figure 5.3 shows the DAP of a five-year-old boy whose parents are divorced. The disconnections between the head, body, and arms in the drawing are thought to reflect feelings of insecurity (DiLeo, 1973). Unfortunately, the psychometric properties of DAP techniques have not been well established.

Like the DAP, the HTP is meant to access feelings and inner issues from the child or adolescent (Buck, 1985). In the HTP task, the child is asked to draw a picture of a house, then a tree, then a person. The house is thought to symbolize home life and family relationships, the tree is thought to represent the child's personal feelings about her- or himself, and the person is thought to further symbolize the child's self-perceptions as well as his or her thoughts about the future. Standardized scoring of either of these drawing techniques is almost nonexistent, so the psychometric properties are also nonexistent.

Another projective technique is represented by sentence completion tasks. In these tasks, children and adolescents are asked to complete a sentence, such as "I wish . . ." or "My father . . ." or "I am afraid of . . ." There are formalized systems of interpretation for sentence completion tasks (Hart, Kehle, & Davies, 1983; Rotter,

FIGURE 5.3   A Five-Year-Old Boy's Draw-A-Person
Source: DiLeo (1973).

Lah, & Rafferty, 1992), but most clinicians interpret these sentences with their own clinical judgment. Like so many other projective techniques, the psychometric properties of these tasks are limited, but some clinicians may find these tasks helpful in an overall comprehensive assessment of a child or adolescent.

FAMILY ASSESSMENT

Nearly all of the previously discussed measures have focused on children's and adolescents' functioning. In a comprehensive assessment, it is imperative to assess the family's functioning in order to ascertain whether or not the family is contributing to the child's or adolescent's problems. As mentioned in Chapter 2, family theorists believe that many problems in children and adolescents are merely symbolic of larger problems within the family system. An assessment of the family should be included even if the clinician does not consider her- or himself to be a family clinician (Rey et al., 2000). There is a wealth of research that suggests family factors can create or at least exacerbate problems in children and adolescents. Thus, it is crucial to assess family functioning whenever children or adolescents are experiencing problems.

Note that clinicians must be flexible in their definitions of the word *family*. Sometimes children and adolescents have no genetic connection, and even no legal connection, to those individuals who are raising them and whom they consider family. It is important for clinicians to use the child's terminology rather than imposing traditional family terminology onto the child. For example, if a child raised since birth by an ex-girlfriend of his deceased father refers to this woman as "Ann," then the clinician should use Ann's name rather than referring to her as "mother." Similarly, if a child refers to her stepfather as

---

Case Study: Alan, Maternal Psychological Problems and Neglect

Alan was first referred to a treatment center for maltreated children and their families when he was five years old. His mother, Mary, has had a long history of psychiatric difficulties and had been diagnosed with schizophrenic disorder. Alan's father abandoned his mother one week prior to Alan's birth. Although Mary thought about giving Alan up for adoption, she opted to keep him since she had always wanted a baby. Alan was hospitalized for pneumonia as a neonate and was hospitalized for asthma when he was two years old and again when he was four years old. Mary acknowledged that she had difficulty keeping a job and maintaining her public assistance payments. She often worked part-time cleaning houses and doing laundry, but she reported that these tasks were difficult to manage in her own home. She also reported that the refrigerator would often break in her apartment, so she kept food on the windowsill. If Alan wanted milk or juice, he was told to go to his grandparents' apartment, which was in the same apartment complex.

Mary reported that Alan was accident-prone at home and that he never followed her directions. Alan would often leave the house at night and run around the neighborhood unattended. When Alan was five, the school counselor noticed that he would steal from other children, eat out of the garbage, be late or absent from school, and be dirty and unkempt when he did show up. He rarely completed his homework. When asked about eating out of the garbage, Alan reported, "I'm hungry and there isn't enough food at home." The school counselor made the referral to the treatment center.

In order to begin treatment, the clinicians first completed assessments on Alan and his mother. Alan had average intelligence and appropriate academic achievement, but he also had elevated emotional/behavioral problems. He was diagnosed with attention-deficit/hyperactivity disorder, pica (a disorder that involves eating nonfood substances), and oppositional defiant disorder. After her own evaluation, Mary was diagnosed with schizophrenic disorder. She reported that she heard voices when no one was around, and that she often felt that strangers did not like her and that they talked about her behind her back. She felt that she could not keep a job because the stress had been overwhelming since her first "nervous breakdown."

The clinicians began treatment to help Alan in individual sessions and to help Mary with parenting skills. After a year, treatment was terminated because Mary failed to show up for appointments, both for herself and for Alan. After another year, Mary and Alan re-joined the program. At this time, Alan was assessed again and was found to have deteriorated significantly. His IQ was now in the low-average range, his academic achievement scores were delayed, his adaptive skills were found to be in the low-average range, and his projective tests showed him to be impulse-ridden, anxious, unstable, and confused. His anxiety and impulsiveness were apparently related to inner feelings of emptiness, emotional hunger, and vulnerability.

When Alan was 13, Mary still was not able to care for him adequately and she had difficulty maintaining any therapeutic contacts. As Alan approached adolescence, Mary became less and less able to deal with his behavior. Alan would often run away from home and would rarely show up for school. For these reasons, Alan was placed in a therapeutic residential center where he was given a stable, structured, and nurturing environment that provided appropriate adult role models. Although the original goal was to help Mary provide this type of environment for Alan, it did not appear that she was capable of doing so. Thus, a long-term out-of-home placement was necessary.

SOURCE: Green (1991).

"Dad" because he's the only father she has ever known, then it is important for the clinician to honor that terminology. In my own clinical and supervision work, I have seen amazing definitions of families that children have accommodated into their lives. Similarly, work in other countries has shown the importance of culturally sensitive assessment of families (Rey et al., 2000). As in all other areas, clinicians must not impose their value system onto the family but must instead try to understand the relationships and values within the family who is seeking help.

One of the first tools that many clinicians use to understand a family during an assessment is a **genogram**, which provides a schematic representation of the family (McGoldrick & Gerson, 1985). Figure 5.4 shows a genogram for the family of the novelist Virginia Woolf. Once the major family members have been identified for

the current and recent past generations, the clinician can interview the family about any specific patterns of behavior. For example, a clinician working with a 15-year-old adolescent girl who was abusing alcohol might want to look at the family genogram with an eye toward who else in the family had abused alcohol or other substances. Genograms are usually completed by the clinician while asking the parents and children their recollections. The genogram can be a graphic way of illustrating multigenerational problems that children and adolescents might be experiencing.

Two of the most widely used measures of family functioning are the Family Environment Scale (FES; Moos & Moos, 1981) and the Family Adaptability and Cohesion Scale (FACES; Olson, Portner, & Bell, 1982). Both of these paper-and-pencil measures can be completed by

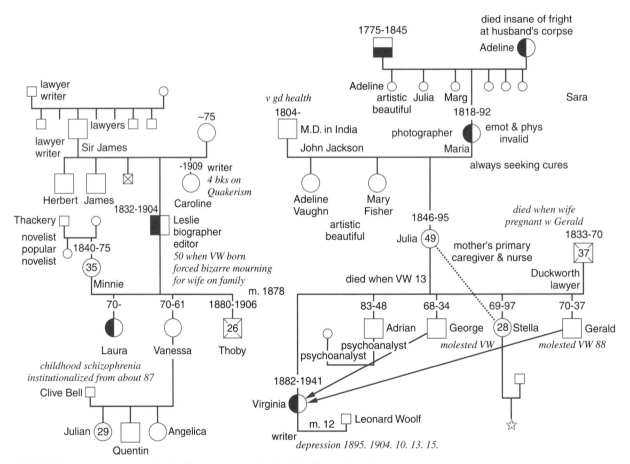

FIGURE 5.4 Example of a Family Genogram for Virginia Woolf, the Novelist

Note: Circles represent females, squares represent males. A circle and square who are connected by a line were married (with date of marriage marked by *m.*), lines coming down from them are their offspring. Dates above circles and squares are the birth and death dates of that person. Highlighted characteristics—such as lawyer, writer—were chosen to show patterns of creativity within this family system.

Source: McGoldrick, Gerson, & Shellenberger (1999).

children as well as parents, and both can be used to compare different responses within the family. The FES yields 10 subscales: cohesion, expressiveness, conflict, independence, achievement orientation, intellectual-cultural orientation, active-recreational orientation, moral-religious emphasis, organization, and control. Norms are provided for families in general, as well as for families of different ethnicities, constellations, and sizes (Moos & Moos, 1981). The FACES yields two factors, each made up of four subscales: cohesion (which consists of disengaged, separated, connected, and enmeshed) and adaptability (which consists of rigid, structured, flexible, and chaotic). Both the FES and the FACES have been well validated and both show excellent psychometric properties.

The Kinetic Family Drawing (KFD; R. C. Burns, 1982) is considered a projective technique, but because it focuses on family functioning it is also considered a measure of family assessment. Similar to other drawing techniques, the KFD asks the child or adolescent to draw a picture that is then interpreted by the clinician. In this case, children and adolescents are asked to draw a picture of their family doing something. After the picture is drawn, the child is asked to explain what is happening in the picture and what will happen in the characters' future. The picture is then interpreted for issues that are relevant to the child and the family. For example, if a child "forgets" to draw one parent, it may be that the parent is absent a lot from the child's life or that the child feels abandoned emotionally by the parent. Clinicians look at the positioning of the family members (e.g., who is standing next to whom, which is thought to represent social alliances) and at the size of the family members (with larger characters having more power in the child's view of the family). Like many projective techniques, there are almost no norms or well-established scoring systems for the KFD technique (Weiner & Kuehnle, 1998). Some clinicians use the KFD as another way of interviewing children about their families. With this measure serving as an impetus for an interview, the technique can be useful as long as the clinician's interpretations are consistent with other, more objective information.

Figure 5.5 shows a KFD drawn by an eight-year-old girl whose father is severely depressed and whose mother is emotionally unavailable (R. C. Burns & Kaufman, 1972). The clinician noted what the girl said in describing the drawing. The fact that the father is in bed and the mother is working on a church project without interacting with the children might suggest that the girl sees her parents as distant. The fact that the five-year-old brother and the cat are all the same size as the eight-year-old girl might suggest that the girl feels inconsequential to her parents and that she also feels connected to her brother and the cat (R. C. Burns & Kaufman, 1972).

Another way of assessing functioning within the family is to assess parenting competence. Although the assessment of parental competence is a relatively new

FIGURE 5.5 Kinetic Family Drawing by an Eight-Year-Old Girl

Source: R. C. Burns & Kaufman (1972).

addition to the assessment of families, it is worthwhile to consider, given that parenting competence can influence children's and adolescents' lives so meaningfully. Scales such as the Parenting Scale can assess strengths and weaknesses within mothers' and fathers' parenting techniques (Arnold, O'Leary, Wolff, & Acker, 1993). A complete clinical assessment to verify at least minimal parenting competence can be completed through a battery of questionnaires and interviews (Budd & Holdsworth, 1996). Parenting efficacy and control can be assessed through standardized measures (Lovejoy, Verda, & Hays, 1997). Even the potential for abusing one's children can be estimated with a scale known as the Child Abuse Potential Inventory, although this measure sometimes identifies parents incorrectly as having the potential to abuse their children (Ammerman & Patz, 1996; Milner, 1986, 1994). These assessment techniques offer new ways to assess and consider competence of parents and caretakers. They also offer another way of looking at the context of the child's problems rather than just assessing the child's problems directly.

The test of a first-rate intelligence is the ability to hold two opposed ideas in the mind at the same time, and still retain the ability to function.

—F. Scott Fitzgerald

ASSESSING INTELLECTUAL FUNCTIONING AND ACADEMIC ACHIEVEMENT

Intellectual functioning and academic functioning are important to assess for a number of different referral problems. The most obvious such problems are school-related ones. In these cases, teachers often suggest that parents have their child assessed for a learning disorder. In cases where a child is having attentional problems, it also makes sense to have the child's intelligence and cognitive functioning tested.

A number of standardized measures of intelligence can be used with youngsters. Beginning in infancy, the Bayley Scales of Infant Development (Bayley, 1969) can be used to assess the intellectual functioning of infants, and the McCarthy Scales of Children's Abilities (McCarthy, 1972) can be used with toddlers. In most cases, intelligence testing in infants and toddlers is completed only when there are concerns about limited intellectual abilities. In addition, intelligence tests in infancy and early childhood do not provide strong predictions for intellectual functioning in later childhood, adolescence,

or adulthood (Kaufman & Lichtenberger, 1998). For this reason, intellectual testing in infancy is completed only in rare cases.

Beginning in preschool and following into adulthood, there are a number of tests that can be given to assess intelligence. A series of tests originally developed by Dr. David Wechsler can be used from preschool to adulthood. The Wechsler Primary and Preschool Intelligence Scale–Revised (WPPSI-R; Wechsler, 1989); the Wechsler Intelligence Scale for Children–Third Edition (WISC-III; Wechsler, 1991); and the Wechsler Adult Intelligence Scale–Third Edition (WAIS-III; Psychological Corporation, 1997) can be used to assess intellectual functioning throughout the life span. Note that the Wechsler Intelligence Scale for Children–Fourth Edition (WISC-IV) is currently under development (Sparrow & Davis, 2000). The Stanford-Binet Intelligence Scale: Fourth Edition (Thorndike, Hagen, & Sattler, 1986) can be used from two years old to adulthood. Although the Stanford-Binet is meaningful from a historical sense, a number of reviewers have questioned the construct validity and normative data on the measure and have suggested that the Stanford-Binet no longer be used (Kaufman & Lichtenberger, 1998). Several other intelligence tests can be used with children (reviewed in Kaufman & Lichtenberger, 1998; Sparrow & Davis, 2000), but this section will highlight the WISC-III because of its widespread use in the United States and around the world (Sparrow & Davis, 2000).

The WISC-III is used with children ages 6 to 16 and can usually be completed in less than two hours. The test is given in a one-on-one situation with a highly trained examiner who knows how to administer the measure and who is fully trained on the psychometric theory behind test development. As shown in Table 5.7, the WISC-III is broken down into subscales that reflect a variety of skills. Each child receives an overall Full Scale Intelligence Quotient (FSIQ) as well as a Verbal IQ (VIQ) and a Performance IQ (PIQ). The Factor Scores are also reported by most clinicians. Note that the FSIQ, VIQ, PIQ, and Factor Scores are all established with a mean of 100 and a standard deviation of 15. Thus, only 2% of the population is expected to score above 130 (which is 2 standard deviations above the mean) and only 2% of the population is expected to score below 70 (which is 2 standard deviations below the mean).

Overall, the WISC-III is well standardized and has been very well validated. The psychometric properties on the measure are excellent, and the utility of the WISC-III has been well established (Kaufman, 1994). However, like most other standardized intelligence measures, the WISC-III has some limitations: (1) heavy cultural load-

TABLE 5.7 Subscales on the Wechsler Intelligence Scale for Children–Third Edition (WISC-III)

Verbal	Performance	Factor Scores
Information	Picture Completion	Verbal Compre-hension Index
Similarities	Picture Arrangement	Perceptual Organi-zation Index
Arithmetic	Block Design	
Vocabulary	Object Assembly	Freedom from Dis-tractibility Index
Comprehension	Coding	Processing Speed Index
Digit Span (optional)	Mazes (optional)	
	Symbol Search (optional)	

Source: Wechsler (1991). Wechsler Intelligence Scale for Children–Third Edition. Copyright 1997 by the Psychological Corpora-tion Assessment Company. Reproduced by permission. All rights reserved. "Wechsler Intelligence Scale for Children" and "WISC" are trademarks of the Psychological Corporation, a Harcourt Assessment Company, registered in the United States of America and/or other jurisdictions.

ings and school-based qualities of many of the subtests, which seem to inadvertently penalize bilingual, minority, and learning-disordered children (G. C. N. Hall & Baron-gan, 2002), and (2) the focus on speed of responses, which seems to penalize methodical, hesitant, and careful children (Kaufman, 1994). These limitations are impor-tant to keep in mind, especially when assessing a child who might not be able to perform at her or his maximum capacity because of the test itself. In addition, criticisms are likely to continue with the WISC-IV (Sparrow & Davis, 2000).

Some of these same criticisms have been mentioned in relation to the most widely used measure of aca-demic achievement, the Woodcock-Johnson Psycho-Educational Battery–Third Edition (WJ-III; Woodcock, McGrew, & Mather, 2000). The WJ-III assesses chil-dren's and adolescents' acquired knowledge within the school setting. Different ages are assessed on different subscales, but the broadband factors at all ages include Broad Reading, Broad Mathematics, and Written Expres-sion. The WJ-III can be used in conjunction with an intel-ligence test to ascertain whether or not the child or adolescent exhibits a learning disorder. In addition, chil-dren and adolescents who are struggling in their academic work can be assessed to identify areas of strength and weakness.

It is noble to teach oneself, but still nobler to teach others— and less trouble.

—Mark Twain

EDUCATIONAL ASSESSMENT

Nearly all of the assessment techniques discussed so far can be completed within the school system. Most should be completed only by school psychologists and clinical psychologists, given the training necessary for conduct-ing an assessment in a competent and ethical manner. There are schoolwide testing programs in which teachers can participate (e.g., group achievement testing and scholastic testing), and these tests can be helpful in adding information to the assessment of an individual child or adolescent. Individual testing, however, is most often completed by a school psychologist who can spend time with the child and her or his family.

It is important for professionals within the school sys-tem to follow their own state's admission, retention, and dismissal (ARD) procedures for students who might be placed in special education (Stetson, 1992). In most states, there is a five-step process that must be completed for children to receive special services within the school system:

• Level I: Screening and initial identification.
• Level II: Diagnosis to establish eligibility.
• Level III: Placement and individualized treatment plan development.
• Level IV: Instructional planning.
• Level V: Evaluation.

It is important for clinicians to know what options for remediation are available within the child's school sys-tem. Table 5.8 lists some of the host of special education classes for children in need. Note that school systems also offer special services and special full-time classrooms for children who are emotionally disturbed, physically dis-abled, and multiply handicapped (Stetson, 1992).

School psychologists, working in conjunction with teachers, have access to a wealth of information about a child's functioning. They are in an enviable position of not only assessing children and adolescents but also mak-ing recommendations that can be instituted in the school setting. Interestingly, evaluations from school psycholo-gists and private clinical psychologists often look similar: Comparable measures are used, similar informants are asked to participate, and similar conclusions are drawn (Kamphaus et al., 2000).

TABLE 5.8 Special Classes Available in Most School Districts and Criteria for Placement

Type of Class	IQ Criterion	Achievement Criterion	Cognitive Learning Deficiences
Reading and Title I	70 and above	Functioning 2 years or more below grade level	No requirement
Pull-out resource	70 and above	Achievement is more than 1 standard deviation below potential as measured on stadardized tests	No requirement
Full-time learning disabled	70 and above	Achievement is more than 1 standard deviation below potential as measured on stadardized tests	Deficiency in one or more areas
Educable mentally retarded	50–70	No requirement	No requirement
Trainable mentally retarded	Below 50	No requirement	No requirement
Academically talented	130 and above	Typically 2 years or more above present grade level	No requirement

SOURCE: Stetson (1992).

Nearly all of the measures mentioned in this chapter can be used within the school system, and many rely on information from teachers and other school personnel (e.g., observations, functional assessments, behavior rating scales). Sometimes school psychologists have a more difficult time than private clinicians gaining family participation in the assessment process, but this difficulty may be due to the fact that with private clinicians parents usually seek out the assessment whereas for school assessments parents most often do not initiate the process. Overall, there is a great deal of overlap between assessments done within the school system and those completed in a community or private setting (Kamphaus et al., 2000; Oakland & Cunningham, 1999). In some ways, this commonality works to the benefit of children, given that most professional settings have comparable standards for assessments. Those interested in more information about assessment procedures within the school setting are encouraged to read *Assessment of At-Risk and Special Needs Children*, second edition (Witt et al., 1998).

NEUROPSYCHOLOGICAL ASSESSMENT

Neuropsychological assessment has become a specialization within the field of clinical psychology (Hartlage & Long, 1997). With the primary purpose of finding brain-related deficits and lesions, neuropsychological assessment can pinpoint functional problems that might be missed by broader measures (Riccio & Reynolds, 1998). Neuropsychological assessment has often been used when there are concerns about the ramifications of a traumatic brain injury or other medically based illnesses, but it has also been used when children show the possibility of such problems as learning disorders, autism, attention-deficit/hyperactivity disorder, conduct disorder, depression, and anxiety disorders (Tramontana & Hooper, 1997). There is an increasing need for neuropsychological assessments within the field of special education (Holmes & Holmes, 1996). Common neuropsychological assessment techniques for children include the Halstead-Reitan Neuropsychological Test Batteries for Children (described by Nussbaum & Bigler, 1997); the Nebraska Neuropsychological Children's Battery (described by Golden, 1997); and the Wide Range Assessment of Memory and Learning (Sheslow & Adams, 1990). In addition to using a standardized intellectual test, a thorough neuropsychological evaluation might include assessment of the following areas (D'Amato, Rothlisberg, & Rhodes, 1997):

- Perceptual/sensory
- Motor functions
- Verbal functions
- Nonverbal functions
- Attention/learning/processing
- Communication/language skills
- Academic achievement
- Personality/behavior
- Educational/classroom environment

In addition to the many areas that are usually assessed in neuropsychological assessments, more complex and comprehensive assessments might also include neuroimaging with magnetic resonance imaging (MRI) or computerized tomography (CT; Bigler, Nilsson, Burr, & Boyer, 1997; Eliez & Reiss, 2000). In a review of 10 years of neuroimaging studies, the authors concluded that neuroimaging "holds great promise" for the assessment of psychological disorders (Hendren, DeBacker, & Pandina, 2000). Results from neuroimaging studies, however, suggest that it is not yet specific enough to serve as a primary diagnostic instrument. In addition, neuroimaging is quite expensive and cannot be performed during every neuropsychological assessment. It can, however, provide another avenue of understanding the brain-related mechanisms that might be influencing a child's behavior or academic functioning.

STRENGTHS AND WEAKNESSES OF STANDARDIZED TESTING

Overall, there are a number of strengths to the assessment procedures mentioned in this chapter (see Table 5.9). Given the variety of well-standardized and well-normed measures, there is rarely a problem in finding an appropriate measure to help quantify a child's or adolescent's problems.

Nearly all of these measures, however, presuppose the willingness and cooperation of the informants who are involved. It is possible that parents might want to present their child in either a much better or a much worse light than is accurate. In these cases, parental interviews and checklists might be distorted and the clinician might be led astray. The inclusion of multiple informants and direct observation can usually circumvent any bias from an individual informant.

A major clinical issue arises, however, when it is the child or adolescent who does not want to be assessed and who might not think that he or she has a problem. It is extraordinarily rare for children or adolescents to refer themselves for an assessment (Srebnik, Cauce, & Baydar, 1996). Although there are some unique cases of children hanging around the guidance counselor's office in order to receive help, it is rare that clinicians in the community or in private settings get a call from children who are reporting distress over their behavior. More likely, teachers and parents are the ones who first become distressed with a child's behavior, and they are usually the ones who initiate the assessment process (either within the school in the case of teachers or in the community in the case of parents).

It is incumbent on all clinicians and school psychologists to keep this issue in mind when assessing children and adolescents. Children may not feel that the referral problem is really a problem, but they may feel that there are other problems that were not mentioned in the intake phone call. One potential drawback in an intake phone

TABLE 5.9 Examples and Overview of Each Type of Assessment Technique

Type of Assessment	Examples
Interviews	Unstructured
	Semistructured (e.g., SCICA)
	Structured (e.g., DISC)
Behavioral assessment	Behavioral observation
	Functional assessment
	Self-monitoring
Checklists	Broad measures (e.g., CBCL, BASC)
	Specific measures (e.g., CDI, R-CMAS)
Personality assessment	Personality inventories (e.g., MMPI-2, PIC)
	Projective measures (e.g., Rorschach, CAT)
Family assessment	Genograms, measures (e.g., FACES, FES)
Intellectual and achievement assessment	WISC-III WJ-III
Educational assessment	Screening, diagnosis, placement, instructional planning, and evaluation
Neuropsychological assessment	Halstead-Reitan Neuropsychological Test Batteries
	Nebraska Neuropsychological Children's Battery

call from a parent is that it may allow the clinician to stay focused on the child's problems rather than looking more broadly at problems within the family, the school, or the community. Unfortunately, assessments of children and adolescents have, historically, focused on the problems within the child or adolescent individually. Clinical psychologists and school psychologists are now taking a broader look at the many factors that can influence emotional/behavioral problems in children and adolescents. Thus, they are conducting comprehensive assessments that often look around and beyond the child to ascertain what is distressing and what can lead to a better outcome.

One final caveat to keep in mind is the potential bias of many psychological assessment techniques (G. C. N. Hall & Barongan, 2002). Although many measures have been developed and normed for use with ethnically and culturally diverse groups of children and adolescents, clinicians must take care to ensure that tests are not being used in ways that will inadvertently harm children and adolescents from ethnic minority groups. Those interested in learning more about assessment are encouraged to read *Assessment of Children: Cognitive Applications,* fourth edition (Sattler, 2001) and *Assessment of Children:* *Behavioral and Clinical Applications*, fourth edition (Sattler, 2002), both of which provide comprehensive and updated summaries of clinical child assessment.

SUMMARY AND KEY CONCEPTS

Assessment is the process of testing and evaluating children and adolescents to ascertain their functioning. **Multimethod assessment** includes many methods of assessment (e.g., interviews, checklists, behavioral observation, and standardized intellectual testing). The use of **multiple informants** is a strategy that includes many different informants on the child's behavior (e.g., the parents, teachers, and the child him- or herself).

Multiaxial Assessment of Children and Adolescents

Multiaxial assessment consists of the evaluation of children and adolescents from multiple perspectives on six axes: parent reports, teacher reports, cognitive functioning, physical assessment, and direct assessment.

Interviews with Children and Their Parents

Most often, the clinical process begins with an **intake phone call**, in which the parents describe the problems their child or family is experiencing. **Unstructured interviews**, the most common form of interviews, allow clinicians to ask questions that seem relevant to the referral problem in whatever order they deem appropriate. **Rapport**, the feeling of connectedness at the foundation of the therapeutic relationship, is one of the first goals of an unstructured interview. In **semistructured interviews** clinicians are provided with a suggested template for an interview format that they can follow or that they can deviate from as they see fit. **Structured interviews**, usually used for diagnostic purposes, must follow a specific sequence with little to no deviation from the format.

Behavioral Assessment

There are three primary types of behavioral assessment, all of which can be done in conjunction with other assessment techniques. **Behavioral observation** is completed when the clinician or other professional observes the child's behavior. A common pattern is for the clinician to look at the **antecedents** (what comes before the behavior) and the **consequences** (what occurs after the behavior). **Functional assessment** occurs when the child is observed actually conducting the behaviors of interest (e.g., the clinician assesses social skills while the child is actually interacting with other children). **Self-monitoring** allows the child him- or herself to keep track of behavior that is in need of changing. In all these behavioral assessment techniques there is some concern about **reactivity**—a child changing behavior in reaction to the assessment.

Checklists and Rating Scales

The most common broad measures of children's behavior are the Achenbach system (comprised of the CBCL, TRF, YSR, and other associated measures) and the BASC (comprised of parent, teacher, and child/adolescent reports). There are also a number of measures that assess specific behaviors and emotions.

Personality Assessment

Personality inventories (such as the MMPI-2 and PIC) are paper-and-pencil measures that are used to assess the underlying constructs of personality functioning. **Projective measures** (such as the Rorschach inkblot test, CAT, drawings, and sentence completion tasks) are meant to provide children with an ambiguous stimulus onto which they can project their innermost thoughts, feelings, and concerns.

Family Assessment

Genograms are used as a schematic representation of the family constellation and the constellation of previous generations. Paper-and-pencil measures and Kinetic Family Drawings can also be used to assess the family environment and other aspects of family functioning.

Assessing Intellectual Functioning and Academic Achievement

A wide range of standardized measures can be used to assess intellectual functioning and academic achievement. These measures are all administered individually to the child, and the child's results are compared with the normative data on the measures to provide standardized scores.

Educational Assessment

Clinical psychologists and school psychologists conduct surprisingly similar assessments for children and adolescents.

Neuropsychological Assessment

Neuropsychological assessment is a specialization within clinical psychology that allows more specific assessments of children's and adolescents' brain-related limitations that influence behavior.

Strengths and Weaknesses of Standardized Testing

The clear strengths of standardized testing involve the strong psychometric properties of most measures. The primary weaknesses have to do with the assumptions that children and their parents are willing to provide accurate and honest information to the clinician.

KEY TERMS

assessment	intake phone call	rapport	functional	neuropsychological
multimethod	unstructured	behavioral	assessment	assessment
assessment	interviews	observation	self-monitoring	
multiple informants	semistructured	antecedents	reactivity	
multiaxial	interviews	consequences	projective measures	
assessment	structured interviews		genogram	

SUGGESTED READINGS

Greenfeld, Josh. *A Child Called Noah*. New York: Pocket Books, 1970. This book is a poignant account of a father who, over time, realizes that his son is autistic. Assessment issues and misdiagnosis are discussed throughout the book.

Pelzer, David. *A Child Called "It"*. Deerfield Beach, FL: Health Communications, Inc., 1995. This powerful autobiography by a severely abused individual is the first in a trilogy. Assessment issues arise regarding what to consider a "normal" reaction to a devastating situation.

SUGGESTED VIEWINGS

Benny and Joon (1993). Jeremiah S. Chechik (director), Barry Berman (writer). VHS/DVD. This wonderful romantic comedy explores what is normal and what is abnormal in adolescents.

Heathers (1989). Michael Lehmann (director), Daniel Waters (writer). VHS/DVD. This macabre comedy looks at teenagers who may or may not be experiencing emotional/behavioral problems.

CHAPTER 6

THERAPEUTIC INTERVENTIONS WITH CHILDREN, ADOLESCENTS, AND FAMILIES

CHAPTER SUMMARY

Identify the problem bring it out
don't kick or punch or even shout
attack the problem and not the fear
listen with your open mind and ear
cause you are you and I am me
but we are us and us are we

Focus on the problem don't leave it behind
treat others with respect and feeling kind
take responsibility for your action
and you'll get a feeling of satisfaction
cause you are you and I am me
but we are us and us are we

—Shamar, age 10 and homeless
(Children's Defense Fund–Minnesota, 1990; p. 2)

Like assessment, therapy with children and adolescents is often limited by the reluctance of youth to seek out these services themselves. In most cases parents and school professionals identify children for therapy services (Poduska, 2000). It is almost unheard of to have a child (especially a young child) ask for professional help for a specific behavioral problem (Logan & King, 2001; Srebnik, Cauce, & Baydar, 1996). Some clinicians have spent an entire career of working with children and families without ever receiving a call from a child or adolescent who wants help. Further, many children brought to therapy by their parents do not understand why their parents have sought services. For example, in one study of children referred for therapy, 63% of the parent–child pairs failed to agree on the specific problems that were in need of treatment (Yeh & Weisz, 2001). Even when problems were grouped into general categories, almost 34% of the parent–child pairs still did not overlap in their identification of behaviors in need of treatment (Yeh & Weisz, 2001). Thus, therapists who work with children, adolescents, and families face interesting challenges that clinicians working with individual adults often do not face.

In addition to helping undergraduate and graduate students who hope to become child clinicians understand these issues, college professors who teach courses on therapeutic interventions need to emphasize the importance of using empirical research to identify effective therapies for emotional/behavioral problems. Too often, students simply find a therapeutic modality they like or one that fits their personality style, and then they seek training in that modality. Unfortunately, this process can mean that clinicians may come to conduct relatively ineffective therapies that provide only limited benefits for children and families. As in so many other areas of psychology, we in developmental psychopathology cannot rely on a "one therapy fits all" approach. It is imperative that therapeutic interventions be subjected to rigorous empirical testing in order to verify their effectiveness for specific problems. Increasingly, insurance companies and health maintenance organizations will cover only those therapies that have been documented as effective (Compas & Gotlib, 2002; G. M. Reed, Levant, Stout, Murphy, & Phelps, 2001). Even with this documentation, however, the large majority of health maintenance organizations and insurance companies within the United States do not cover mental health services for children or adults (Kiesler, 2000).

It is important, too, to acknowledge that therapeutic services for children in developing countries are limited at best (Rahman, Mubbashar, Harrington, & Gater, 2000). Although significant advances have been made with helping children in Western cultures, effective intervention and prevention programs are often not available outside developed nations (Rahman et al., 2000).

A number of therapy-oriented books and special issues of journals organize their discussions around treatment of specific types of developmental psychopathology (e.g., Mash & Barkley, 1998; Rapport, 2001; VanHasselt & Hersen, 1998), whereas other books organize their discussions around specific types of treatment (e.g., Hibbs & Jensen, 1996; LeCroy, 1994; Ollendick, 1998). Although both of these organizational styles have their merits, this chapter uses the latter. So that students understand the differences and similarities between the various therapeutic modalities, the book as a whole discusses each type separately. This chapter reviews a number of different settings for therapy and a number of different therapeutic modalities, including psychodynamic, behavioral, cognitive–behavioral, and family systems therapies, as well as psychopharmacological interventions (i.e., medications).

After discussing these differing modalities, the chapter focuses on studies of their effectiveness. Given the importance of preventing problems rather than waiting for them to occur, the chapter ends with a section on prevention programs that work. Although they are not covered in this textbook, it is important for readers to know that computer software and the Internet are being targeted for many behavioral health care interventions with adults (Budman, 2000; Smith & Senior, 2001; VandenBos & Williams, 2000).

SETTINGS FOR INTERVENTIONS

The case studies presented throughout this book highlight a number of locations and settings of therapy and other interventions. For the most severe examples of developmental psychopathology, **inpatient settings** can provide intensive treatment in a safe environment for the child (e.g., Green et al., 2001). Children usually stay at an inpatient setting 24 hours a day for a prescribed amount of time. Although longer stays (sometimes extending into months or years) used to be commonplace in inpatient settings, shorter stays (usually no more than a few weeks) are more common these days (Pottick, Barber, Hansell, & Coyne, 2001; Pottick, McAlpine, & Andelman, 2000). Inpatient settings include psychiatric hospitals, psychiatric wards of general hospitals, and psychiatric wards of children's hospitals. There are both private and public inpatient settings across the United States and in many other countries. To address children's intense therapeutic needs, inpatient settings usually employ a multidisciplinary team made up of psychiatrists, psychiatric nurses, social workers, psychologists, educators, physical therapists, recreational therapists, and staff workers. **Treatment plans** that identify problematic behaviors, long-term goals, short-term goals, and specific interventions are often used in inpatient settings in order to coordinate treatment among these diverse professionals (see Box 6.1).

Children receiving services in an inpatient setting are usually unable to be stabilized in any less restrictive environment. It is not uncommon to find children on an inpatient unit who are a danger to themselves or others, or who require intensive intervention in a structured setting.

Children who require intensive long-term treatment can also be placed in a **residential treatment facility**. Like inpatient settings, residential treatment facilities are 24-hour facilities in which children live away from home for intensive therapeutic treatment, sometimes for years. Unlike inpatient settings, however, residential treatment

BOX 6.1

TREATMENT PLANS

In any type of therapeutic work with children and adolescents, the therapist should have some goals and plans for treatment. The term *treatment plan* is used to describe a written, formalized plan for the range of therapeutic interventions that will be attempted and to delineate the goals of the treatment. Within the school system, individualized education plans are comparable to treatment plans. A portion of a treatment plan is presented below for a child with low self-esteem who is still living at home and attending the neighborhood school. These are only sample items; actual treatment plans are usually much more extensive. Note that behavioral definitions, long-term goals, short-term objectives, and therapeutic interventions are all described in objective, behavioral terms. Therapists often share treatment plans with children and their parents in order to facilitate common goals in therapy. Treatment plans usually have a suggested time frame for evidence of improvement and also acknowledge that therapeutic progress should be reevaluated at given points to verify the ongoing success of the treatment.

SOURCE: Jongsma, Peterson, & McInnis (1996).

Behavioral Definitions

1. Client seems unable to accept compliments.
2. Client verbalizes self-disparaging remarks, including "I'm stupid" and "I'm ugly."

Long-Term Goals

1. Client will demonstrate willingness to accept compliments and to initiate positive statements about self.
2. Client will make verbalizations that show the acceptance of the core belief he or she is lovable and capable.

Short-Term Objectives

1. Client will identify accomplishments that are consistent with improved self-image.
2. Client will acknowledge and verbalize awareness of self-disparaging statements.

Therapeutic Interventions

1. Therapist will ask the client and the client's parents to keep a daily log with one positive statement about the client each day.
2. Therapist will confront and reframe self-disparaging comments that the client makes.

---

facilities are usually not in a hospital. Some residential treatment facilities are located in the rural outskirts of a city or in a suburb, but others are in the heart of a city. Children placed in residential treatment facilities cannot function in a less restrictive environment and cannot live at home. Residential treatment facilities provide a structured, therapeutic environment and also attend to children's academic and educational needs (e.g., Lyons, Uziel-Miller, Reyes, & Sokol, 2000).

Whereas residential treatment facilities usually house relatively large numbers of children, **group homes** and **therapeutic foster care homes** tend to provide comparable services to smaller numbers of children in a home-like environment. Both group homes and therapeutic foster care homes are often headed by a small staff (sometimes just two adults), whose members try to run the homes in a comfortable but structured manner. Public funding may be available for placing a child in a group or therapeutic foster care home. Children's psychological and educational needs are met off-site (e.g., the child may be taken to therapy appointments with a psychologist and may attend the local neighborhood school). Because children in these settings are still living away

from their own families, group homes and therapeutic foster care homes are still considered restrictive environments. The biggest difference between the two types of homes is that children in the foster care system have been either temporarily or permanently separated from their biological parents through the child protective process. In some cases, parental rights have been terminated (e.g., due to abuse or neglect) and the children are awaiting adoption. Other children in foster care homes might have parents who are working toward reunification (e.g., the parents were found to be abusive but are taking parenting classes or undergoing substance abuse treatment in order to gain back their parental rights). As with so many treatment options for children, the quality of group homes and therapeutic foster care homes varies greatly, from therapeutic to harmful. State agencies monitor and license both types of homes, but many still show a great need for improvement.

Children who are discharged from an inpatient setting or a residential treatment facility but who are still in need of intensive services may attend **day hospitals**. A day hospital can be used for children who are able to live at home with their own family but who require relatively structured therapeutic activities during the day. Most often, day hospital programs are used to help children make the transition from an inpatient setting to an outpatient setting (e.g., Milin, Coupland, Walker, & Fisher-Bloom, 2000).

The most common sites of therapeutic intervention are **outpatient settings** designed for children who live with their own family but need some type of therapeutic intervention. Examples of outpatient settings include community mental health centers, private practice or independent practice offices, and child guidance centers. Children, adolescents, and families most often receive therapy or counseling from psychologists, psychiatrists, counselors, or social workers in an outpatient setting. If a child had been hospitalized for psychiatric reasons, part of the discharge planning would probably include follow-up therapy services in an outpatient setting.

Although both individual and group therapy can be conducted in any setting, group therapy tends to take place in inpatient settings, residential treatment facilities, group homes, and day hospitals. Outpatient settings are more often focused on individual and family therapy (Trull & Phares, 2001). With some disorders (e.g., conduct disorder, substance abuse), group therapy can actually be countertherapeutic. Specifically, trying to conduct group therapy with adolescents who have conduct problems (e.g., stealing or otherwise breaking the law) or who

abuse substances (e.g., alcohol, marijuana, and cocaine) may actually lead to more problem behavior rather than less (Dishion, McCord, & Poulin, 1999). It appears that less-experienced adolescents will learn from more-experienced adolescents about new kinds of illicit activities and strategies for going undetected. Thus, mental health practitioners should make the match between behavior problems and treatment modality carefully.

Increasing numbers of children are also receiving mental health services at school. These **school-based mental health services** are often funded through public monies that have been set aside for the mental health needs of children. School psychologists, clinical psychologists, social workers, and other mental health professionals all conduct therapy and counseling for students who need help for emotional/behavioral difficulties. As noted in Box 6.2, not all children in need of services receive them. The advantage of school-based mental health services is that the services can be administered without relying on the parent (e.g., for transportation) and can be made available to many children in need of services. One study of clinically referred children found that parents were more likely to follow through on recommendations regarding school-based interventions than they were to those regarding professional clinic-based interventions (MacNaughton & Rodrigue, 2001). A disadvantage of school-based mental health services is that,

---

BOX 6.2

WHO RECEIVES SERVICES?

There are a number of children, adolescents, and families who need professional help for psychological problems but who never receive it. One study suggested that at least 17% of children and adolescents who experienced severe psychopathology never received any professional interventions for their problems (Flisher et al., 1997). Many researchers have compared characteristics of children and adolescents who receive services with those youngsters who do not receive services (Costello & Janiszewski, 1990; Flisher et al., 1997; Goodman et al., 1997; Howard & Hodes, 2000). In a national study of nearly 1,300 children and adolescents (Goodman et al., 1997), the researchers found that, compared with those who did not receive services, children who did receive services:

- Experienced higher levels of psychopathology.
- Showed lower levels of competence.

- Were more likely to have more than one disorder (i.e., showed comorbid disorders).
- Were more likely to be non-Hispanic Caucasian Americans.
- Were less likely to be prepubertal girls.
- Tended to have parents who were more educated, more dissatisfied with their family functioning, less involved in monitoring their children's behavior, and more likely to have received mental health treatment themselves.

The fact that children who received services were more disturbed and had more comorbid disorders does suggest that some of the neediest children are receiving services. The race/ethnicity and parental factors, however, suggest that there may be biases in the referral systems for children or, conversely, that mental health professionals need to make themselves more available to those who have not typically accessed their services (Goodman et al., 1997).

"You always get to be the therapist! I never get to be the therapist!"

too often, treatment focuses only on the child rather than including family or environmental factors (Logan & King, 2001).

An increasing number of public mental health dollars are being targeted for school-based mental health services with the goal of reaching as many troubled children as possible (Oakland & Cunningham, 1999). In addition to therapeutic programs, many prevention programs are also being housed within the school setting (Farrell, Meyer, Kung, & Sullivan, 2001; Weissberg, 2000).

There is no one setting that appears more advantageous than any other. For example, a study know as the Fort Bragg Evaluation Project (FBEP) compared a continuum-of-care model for children and adolescents (where services ranged from hospitalization and crisis management to outpatient therapy) and the prevailing model of therapy services (where families identify and arrange their own mental health services). The project hypothesized that the continuum-of-care approach would allow more integrated services and would cost less money than traditional service delivery. At one year (Bickman et al., 1995) and even five years (Bickman, Lambert, Andrade, & Penaloza, 2000) after the project, researchers found no differences in the mental health functioning of groups treated with the two different models. In addition, they found that the continuum-of-care model cost more money than did the traditional service delivery model. Although the FBEP study did not evaluate each treatment setting separately, it appears that there were no differences in outcome based on access to services (Bickman et

al., 2000). Interesting, the FBEP study also showed that there was no "dose effect" related to length of treatment (Andrade, Lambert, & Bickman, 2000). In other words, regardless of the location of services, children who received a short round of treatment did not show differences in behavioral problems when compared with children who received lengthy treatment. The comparability between these two groups was evident at 6-month and 12-month follow-ups (Andrade et al., 2000).

All of the settings described above have been found to be potentially therapeutic for children and adolescents (Kutash & Rivera, 1996). A diverse array of therapeutic interventions can be conducted in any setting. Likewise, it is possible to conduct similar types of therapies in varying settings. In addition, different therapeutic interventions can be used to address the same problem effectively (see Box 6.3 for an example). The different forms of therapeutic intervention—psychodynamic, behavioral, cognitive-behavioral, family systems, and psychopharmacological—are discussed in the following sections of this chapter.

Fortunately [psycho]analysis is not the only way to resolve inner conflicts. Life itself still remains a very effective therapist.
—Karen Horney

PSYCHODYNAMIC THERAPIES

Psychodynamic therapies have received almost no empirical support for their effectiveness (M. C. Roberts, Vernberg, & Jackson, 2000; Russ, 1998b; Target & Fonagy, 1998; Weiss, Catron, & Harris, 2000) and are therefore discussed here for their historical importance rather than for their current usefulness. Long-term psychoanalysis, which provided the foundation of many psychodynamic therapies developed initially by Sigmund Freud, tends not to be used with children and adolescents (Target & Fonagy, 1998). Many play therapies are based on the same principles (e.g., working through transference onto the therapist, dealing with unconscious conflicts and motivations) and are used with some frequency for children and young adolescents (Roberts et al., 2000; Russ, 1998a). In fact, Sigmund Freud's protégée, Melanie Klein (1927), and his daughter, Anna Freud (1927), were among the first professionals to use play therapy with children.

Play therapy is a type of therapy in which the child engages with various toys, dolls, and activities while the therapist observes and interacts with the child. Play therapy is usually conducted with children no younger than 3 and no older than 12 (Dodds, 1985). It is also usually reserved for children who are experiencing internalizing

Although play therapy has not received a great deal of empirical support, therapists can use empirically supported treatments within the context of the playroom setting.

- Drawing materials, such as crayons, pencils, felt-tip pens, paper, chalkboard, and chalk.
- Dollhouses, with dolls of different family constellations (e.g., single-parent households, or households with two mothers) and of different races and ethnicities.
- Hand puppets of people and animals.
- Nerf balls (or other soft balls that will not destroy the therapy room).
- Building blocks, of either wood or Styrofoam.
- Communication facilitators, such as telephones, card games, and punching bags.
- Therapeutic games and books (e.g., games or books that were designed specifically for therapy and that focus on feelings, thoughts, behaviors, and other relevant issues in therapy).

Although play therapy per se has not received a great deal of empirical support (M. C. Roberts et al., 2000), it is possible for play to be incorporated into other, more effective modalities. For example, behavioral therapies, cognitive-behavioral therapies, and even family therapies can integrate play into sessions that continue to focus on behavior change (Knell, 1998). One meta-analysis showed that play therapy was most effective when parents were involved and when there were 30 to 35 sessions (LeBlanc & Ritchie, 1999). In addition, child therapy appears to be most effective when parents have a strong relationship with the therapist (Nevas & Farber, 2001). As noted at the beginning of this section, however, psychodynamic therapies with children have not been shown to be effective by any rigorous or well-controlled study and thus are not a good choice for trying to help children (Roberts et al., 2000).

types of problems such as fears, anxieties, guilt, poor self-image, jealousy, anger, and grief (Dodds, 1985). The primary rationale behind play therapy is that the modality of "playing" allows children to act out their psychological issues and to speak more freely about their concerns with the therapist than they would otherwise do (Dodds, 1985). Therapists might comment on children's playing activities during the therapy session (e.g., "That mommy doll seems sad when the daddy doll yells at her"), or they may notice and interpret children's issues that are evident through play in order to address the issues at a later point.

Although therapists vary in their favorite toys and activities for the modality of play, some of the following items are commonly found in play therapy rooms:

- Tactile materials, such as clay, sand, water, and finger paints.

BEHAVIORAL THERAPIES

Behavioral therapies can be broken down into two broad categories: child-oriented interventions and parent-oriented interventions. In general, most behavioral therapies rely on behavioral principles that have been well established. Behavioral therapies are used extensively with children and are especially helpful for children with limited intellectual functioning (e.g., children with developmental disabilities). Behavioral treatment of children with conduct problems has even been shown to help parental and family functioning (Kazdin & Wassell, 2000). Many behavioral principles have been integrated into cognitive-behavioral therapies and family therapies.

Child-Oriented Interventions

The purest form of behavioral therapy with individual children is known as **applied behavior analysis** (see the Association for Behavior Analysis website at www. wmich.edu/aba). Applied behavior analysis relies primarily on operant conditioning principles to change problematic behavior (Hudson, 1998). There is a great deal of focus on the antecedents (i.e., what comes before) and the consequences (i.e., what comes after) of the child's observable behavior. Within-subject designs (defined in Chapter 4 as studies where a baseline of the maladaptive behavior is established, treatment is administered, and then treatment is removed and again administered) are a common method of exploring treatment effectiveness within applied behavior analysis (Compas & Gotlib, 2002). Table 6.1 lists and defines concepts that are used extensively in applied behavior analysis.

In addition to these basic behavioral techniques, there are other, more complex ones that have been used in behavior therapy. **Token economies** are usually used to increase adaptive behaviors. Children are given a small list of behaviors that are to be accomplished each day (e.g., make your bed in the morning, set the table for dinner, and brush your teeth at night). For each behavior they accomplish, the children receive a token (e.g., a poker chip). In a variation of the token economy, parents keep "star charts" on which a star or other visual indication is placed next to the behavior for that day. Children can then "cash in" their tokens or stars at predetermined intervals (e.g., 10 token equals getting one extra book read at bedtime or five stars equals favorite dessert after dinner). Token economies work best if they are simple enough for the child to understand, if the rewards and consequences to behaviors are clear and consistently followed, and if the rewards are truly desirable to the child.

Systematic desensitization is usually used to decrease anxiety symptoms and specific phobias (Marx & Gross, 1998). First, clients are taught progressive muscle relaxation. Then, with the aid of their therapist, they construct a "fear hierarchy" of anxiety-provoking situations or stimuli. For example, a child who is phobic of dogs might develop the following hierarchy (from least to most anxiety provoking):

BOX *6.3*

HELPING CHILDREN AND ADOLESCENTS WITH THEIR SEXUAL ORIENTATION

Although there is no single therapy designed to help children and adolescents who are struggling with their sexual orientation, there are a number of issues that need to be addressed in this regard (Division 44, 2000; Savin-Williams & Diamond, 1999). Therapists should first note that, whereas homosexuality used to be considered a psychiatric disorder in and of itself (American Psychiatric Association, 1968), it has not been listed as a disorder for more than 25 years. In fact, most professionals now believe that homosexuality is a natural part of human diversity.

Little is known about children and adolescents who are dealing with their sexual orientation. Youngsters who must deal with their sexual orientation, or who have clearly identified themselves as bisexual or homosexual, have different difficulties in adjustment than youngsters who are not dealing with these issues (Lock & Steiner, 1999). Compared with heterosexual youth, gay male and lesbian youth are more at risk for verbal and physical abuse, both at home and at school—and such abuse is associated with greater risk for psychological difficulties (Savin-Williams, 1994). In therapy, children and adolescents who are dealing with their sexual orientation may take any of the following as a central theme:

- Feelings of differentness.
- Disclosure to others of their feelings of differentness.
- Social and cultural ramifications of being different.
- Whether or not to "come out" to individuals in their lives (including parents, friends, and teachers).
- Finding supportive and trusted allies (including parents, friends, and teachers).

It is also possible for therapists to work with a gay male, lesbian, or bisexual youth whose concerns are irrelevant to his or her sexual orientation (Savin-Williams & Diamond, 1999). Thus, therapists should be prepared to deal with issues of sexual orientation with children and adolescents but not to focus solely on those issues. Interested readers are referred to the article entitled "Guidelines for Psychotherapy with Lesbian, Gay, and Bisexual Clients" (Division 44, 2000). Division 44 of the American Psychological Association, known as the Society for the Psychological Study of Lesbian, Gay and Bisexual Issues, promotes research, education, professional development, and public policy related to the diversity of sexual orientations.

- Thinking about a small dog.
- Thinking about a big dog.
- Being in the same building as a small dog who is on a chain.
- Being in the same building as a big dog who is on a chain.
- Being across the room from an unchained small dog.
- Being across the room from an unchained big dog.
- Having a small dog barking loudly and hovering over the child.
- Having a big dog barking loudly and hovering over the child.

Fear hierarchies usually contain 20 to 25 items (Marx & Gross, 1998). After the hierarchy is established, the therapist has the child use his or her relaxation strategies while imagining each step of the hierarchy (beginning with the least anxiety-provoking step). Children would move on to the next item of the hierarchy only after they

mastered relaxation in association with the previous anxiety-provoking item. Eventually, each of the items on the hierarchy are acted out behaviorally while being paired with relaxation. Again, children would move to the next step of their hierarchy only after feeling relaxed with the previous behaviors. Systematic desensitization is quite effective in treating specific phobias and other focused anxieties in childhood and adolescence (Marx & Gross, 1998).

Overall, applied behavior analysis and other child-orientated interventions are very effective for a number of behavioral problems in children and adolescents (Hudson, 1998; Marx & Gross, 1998). One of the clear advantages to child-orientated behavioral therapies is the ease with which these techniques can be used in the school setting as well as in the home setting (Martens, Witt, Daly, & Vollmer, 1999).

TABLE 6.1   Definitions of Basic Behavioral Concepts

Techniques Used to Strengthen or Increase Adaptive Behaviors	Techniques Used to Weaken or Decrease Maladaptive Behaviors
• *Reinforcement:* Reinforcement occurs when a behavior is strengthened or increased after administration of a predetermined object or event (the reinforcer). The term *positive reinforcement* is used to signify the application of a pleasant reward (e.g., a smile, a pat on the back, a token, or a food item). Behaviors must already be in the child's repertoire before they can be reinforced.	• *Differential reinforcement of incompatible, alternative, or other behavior:* Behaviors that are contrary to the maladaptive behavior are reinforced in order to decrease the maladaptive behavior (e.g., in order to decrease a boy's out-of-seat behavior, a teacher might verbally reward boy anytime he is working on his academic activities at his desk).
• *Prompting:* If the desired behavior does not yet exist, prompting can be used to teach the new behavior. Prompting can be in the form of physical prompts (e.g., a parent guides a child's hand with a spoonful of food to the child's mouth); verbal prompts (e.g., a teacher tells a child with a reading problem to sound out the syllables before attempting the word); or visual prompts (e.g., a picture of the dog's food dish is put on the refrigerator to remind the child to feed the dog).	• *Extinction:* Rewards that were maintaining a problematic behavior are withdrawn, leading to the eventual disappearance of the behavior.
• *Shaping:* In shaping, successive approximations to the final desired behavior are reinforced. The idea is to gradually shape the child's behavior.	• *Time-out:* In its truest form, time-out is used to remove the child from any reinforcers that are maintaining the maladaptive behavior (e.g., if the child is getting attention for throwing a tantrum, then time-out would be used to remove the child from that attention).
• *Chaining:* For complex behaviors, each step in the behavior is taught and then linked to the next step of the behavior (a child learning to tie her shoes is first taught to pull the laces tight, then to make a loop out of one of the laces, etc.).	• *Punishment:* Two methods of punishment are common— the removal of a positive reinforcer (which is also known as response cost; e.g., refusing dessert to a child who did not eat his or her vegetables at dinner) and the administration of an aversive stimulus (e.g., spanking or yelling at a child who has exhibited a maladaptive behavior).
• *Modeling:* Desirable behaviors are demonstrated for the child (either by the therapist, by another child, or via videotape) in order to teach the child the desired behavior.	

SOURCE: Hudson (1998).

Token economies, such as star charts, are often effective in helping children increase adaptive behaviors.

Always obey your parents, when they are present.

—Mark Twain

Parent-Oriented Interventions

Many of the behavioral techniques discussed above have been integrated into what is known as **behavioral parent training** (Barkley, 1997d). Behavioral parent training is used primarily for children ages 2 to 11, and the treatment is actually administered to the parents. More recently, behavioral parent training programs have been developed for parents of adolescents (Barkley, Edwards, & Robin, 1999). Quite often, therapists who work with parents on behavioral parent training never even meet the children or adolescents they are helping. Behavioral parent training is often administered in a limited number of sessions (e.g., 10 sessions), which focus on the following concepts (Barkley, 1997d; Barkley et al., 1999; Webster-Stratton & Hooven, 1998):

- Paying attention to and rewarding good behavior. (Sometimes parents who think that their children never show good behavior are instructed to "catch their child being good.")

- Ignoring bad behavior (if feasible and if the behavior does not endanger the child or another person).

- Allow natural consequences to occur when possible and feasible (e.g., playing roughly with the cat may lead to a natural consequence of getting scratched, which may decrease the likelihood of the child playing roughly with the cat in the future).

- Model appropriate behavior (e.g., if parents want their children to stop yelling all the time, they should examine their own way of communicating to make sure that they are not inadvertently modeling maladaptive behavior).

- Provide consistent and known consequences to behavior (with the idea that consistency includes different situations, by different parents and caretakers, at different times of the day, and no matter what "different" mood the parent is experiencing at the time).

- Anticipate problem behavior and plan for how it will be handled (e.g., if parents take children grocery shopping and the children always run wild through the aisles, make contingencies for this behavior that are known to the children before they enter the store).

- Do not make idle threats that cannot be completed; instead, follow through on reasonable established consequences (e.g., not "If you don't buckle your seat belt right now, I will never drive you anywhere again" but rather "You must buckle your seat belt before I can drive you to your friend's house").

- Limit the use of punishments (if any).

Behavioral parent training is extraordinarily effective in reducing externalizing behaviors in children, with especially good results for children diagnosed with oppositional defiant disorder (Sanders, Markie-Dadds, Tully, & Bor, 2000; Webster-Stratton & Hooven, 1998) and attention-deficit/hyperactivity disorder (Barkley, 1997a, 1997d). These interventions have been found to be effec-

Case Study: Behavioral Treatment of Susan's Self-Injurious Behavior

At the age of 19, Susan was placed in an institution for severely and profoundly developmentally delayed adolescents and young adults. She was the 9th of 14 children and grew up in an impoverished rural setting with her parents and siblings. Susan has a very diminutive stature and is African American. Susan's prenatal history, infancy, and childhood were marred with many health-related complications, including spina bifida, hydrocephalus, malnutrition, and pneumonia. Her developmental milestones were met either extraordinarily late or not at all. She continues to have no verbal language abilities and communicates with a series of grunts and moans. With intellectual functioning estimated to be below 20, Susan is classified as experiencing profound mental retardation.

Susan had hit and bit herself throughout her life, but with increasing frequency as she got older. She often had self-inflicted bruises on her face and body. The treatment team at the institution designed a behavioral therapy program in order to decrease this self-injurious behavior. Specifically, hitting (operationally defined for Susan as hitting or slapping her own body with her hand or elbow) and biting (operationally defined as putting any part of her hand or fingers into her mouth) were identified as the target behaviors for intervention. After baseline observation to quantify the occurrence of these behaviors, two patterns were noted. Susan's self-injurious behaviors were evidenced only when she was not involved in any other activity; also, she would hit herself when asked to wake up in the morning—and this behavior was often inadvertently rewarded by staff who let her stay in bed for a longer period of time.

Treatment strategies encompassed two primary techniques. First, differential reinforcement of other behaviors (DRO) was used to reinforce behaviors other than the target behaviors. For the DRO treatment, Susan's behavior was observed every five minutes for a period of five seconds. If Susan did not hit or bite herself during this five second period, she was given a desirable food reward (e.g., raisins, nuts, or M&M's) and was given a social reward (e.g., the staff person would say "Good playing, Susan" or would pat her on the back). The second technique was overcorrection, which includes positive practice (i.e., teaching

an appropriate behavior and reinforcing the desired behavior through many repetitions). Overcorrection for hitting required that staff move Susan's arms down to her side and then above her head when she hit herself, and then have Susan rub lotion on the area she just hit. This process was repeated five times after each instance of Susan hitting herself. Overcorrection for biting was instituted by having a staff member brush Susan's teeth, tongue, and gums lightly for three minutes with a toothbrush soaked in oral antiseptic after each instance of biting.

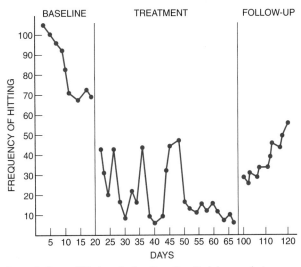

Susan's Rate of Hitting during Baseline, Training, and at Three-Month Follow-up

Note: Each data point is the average of 2 days.

As the figure above shows, Susan's baseline rate of hitting was quite high, but the rate was successfully decreased during active treatment and relatively well maintained at the three-month follow-up. Although not shown in the figure, the treatment of Susan's biting behaviors led to their decrease and eventual disappearance.

SOURCE: Matson & Friedt (1988).

---

tive with many family constellations, including single and divorcing mothers (Martinez & Forgatch, 2001), and mothers in shelter for a battered women (Jouriles et al., 2001).

COGNITIVE-BEHAVIORAL THERAPIES

Cognitive-behavioral therapies are like behavioral therapies in that both emphasize behavior change. They differ, however, in that cognitive-behavioral therapies focus

on cognitions (i.e., private thoughts) in addition to observable behaviors. Table 6.2 highlights the general characteristics that underlie the cognitive-behavioral approach.

The diverse array of specific intervention strategies used within cognitive-behavioral therapies includes the following (Hart & Morgan, 1993):

- *Cognitive modeling,* in which clients are taught to change their cognitions by observing a model who is verbalizing appropriate cognitions and thought processes.

TABLE 6.2 General Characteristics of the Cognitive-Behavioral Approach

1. The cognitive-behavioral approach makes an intentional attempt to combine skills from previously opposing therapies, such as cognitive, behavioral, and semantic therapies.

2. Cognitions (i.e., private thoughts experienced by the client) are important for the therapist to know about and try to alter.

3. Cognitions mediate behavior and learning (i.e., in order to change behavior, the therapist must consider cognitions).

4. Children's and adolescents' behaviors are "reciprocally determined," which means that cognitions and behaviors are related—changing one can change the other.

SOURCE: Hart & Morgan (1993). Published in A. J. Finch Jr., W. Michael Nelson III, & Edith S. Ott, *Cognitive-Behavioral Procedures with Children and Adolescents,* copyright © 1993 by Allyn & Bacon. Reprinted by permission.

- *Self-instruction,* in which clients are trained to alter self-statements before and after a difficult situation by using contingent consequences or modeling.

- *Cognitive restructuring,* in which clients are taught to replace irrational beliefs and faulty thought patterns with adaptive cognitions through logical analyses of the irrational beliefs and thoughts.

- *Cognitive problem-solving,* in which clients are taught to deal with stressors by preparing for these stressors and by using such techniques as self-instruction, self-monitoring, and cognitive rehearsal.

Figure 6.1 shows a cognitive-behavioral therapy that focuses on a number of points of intervention, including the stimulus (e.g., what precedes the cognition or behavior); the organism's internal reaction (e.g., the cognition); the response (e.g., the behavior); and the consequence (e.g., what happens after the behavior; Elliott, Busse, & Shapiro, 1999). This stimulus-organism-response-consequence (S-O-R-C) model highlights a number of places for possible intervention.

Cognitive-behavioral therapies have been used for a wide variety of emotional/behavioral problems, including depression (Carey, 1993; Lewinsohn, Clarke, Rohde, Hops, & Seeley, 1996); anxiety (Grace, Spirito, Finch, & Ott, 1993; Kendall & Treadwell, 1996); impulsivity and hyperactivity (Anastopoulos, Barkley, & Sheldon, 1996; Kendall & Braswell, 1993); aggression (Finch, Nelson, & Moss, 1993; Webster-Stratton, 1994); body image and eating disorders (Robin, Bedway, Siegel, & Gilroy, 1996); and limited social skills (LeCroy, 1994). In general, cognitive-behavioral therapies are quite effective in treating children's and adolescents' emotional/behavioral

Case Study: Cognitive-Behavioral Treatment of Impulsivity

Adam is an 11-year-old boy who was diagnosed with attention-deficit/hyperactivity disorder. Although he was receiving medication to control his behavior, he remained relatively impulsive. In school, he blurted out answers, interrupted others, demanded that he get his own way, and yelled periodically. The impulsivity was especially noticeable in social situations, during which Adam would push other children and inappropriately try to grab the ball during team sports. Partly because of these behaviors, Adam had no friends and was not sought out as a playmate by others in his class.

Eventually, Adam was referred to a psychologist for a cognitive-behavioral treatment known as self-instructional training (Kendall & Braswell, 1993). The treatment began by teaching Adam five self-instructions to be used when facing a difficult or unique situation. The self-instructional statements are as follows (with the concept they represent following in parentheses):

- "Let's see, what am I supposed to do?" (Problem Definition)

- "I have to look at all the possibilities." (Problem Approach)

- "I better concentrate and focus in, and think only of what I'm doing right now." (Focusing of Attention)

- "I think it's this one . . ." (Choosing an Answer)

- Either: "Hey, not bad. I really did a good job" (Self-Reinforcement) or "Oh, I made a mistake. Next time I'll try to go slower and concentrate more, and maybe I'll get the right answer." (Coping Statement)

These five "steps" were first said out loud by Adam and then eventually faded into thoughts that Adam would review in future circumstances. After Adam learned these steps, he practiced and rehearsed them with the therapist on academic tasks and then on social situations. The therapist also modeled self-control in role-play situations in the therapy sessions (e.g., the therapist would play a young child, then be exposed to a stressor such as another child stealing the basketball, then would talk through the steps and make choices accordingly while Adam was watching). This treatment also included behavioral contingencies (both self-reward for a job well done and social rewards from the therapist).

After 20 sessions of treatment, Adam showed significant decreases in his impulsivity and showed greater engagement in friendship networks. By the end of treatment, he was being invited to sleep over at a friend's house, was asked by his classmates to join them on a bicycle trip, and showed significant improvement in his schoolwork.

SOURCE: Kendall & Braswell (1993).

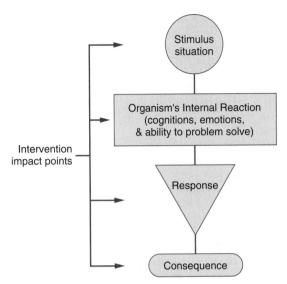

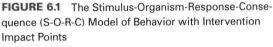

Intervention impact points

FIGURE 6.1 The Stimulus-Organism-Response-Consequence (S-O-R-C) Model of Behavior with Intervention Impact Points

Source: Elliott et al. (1999).

problems (Kendall, Marrs, & Chu, 1998). Characteristics that improve the possibility of effective cognitive-behavioral therapy include a focus on generalizing the newly acquired skills to multiple situations (e.g., trying to generalize the skills to both the home and school environments), integrating naturally occurring reinforcers into the treatment, and finding ways to provide maintenance

of the newly acquired skills (Kendall et al., 1998). A number of cognitive-behavioral therapies also include parents in the treatment so that the parents become another agent of change (e.g., Stark, Swearer, Kurowski, Sommer, & Bowen, 1996). Cognitive-behavioral techniques can also be used with individual child clients or in a group therapy setting with a number of children addressing similar clinical problems (Evans & Sullivan, 1993).

Parentage is a very important profession, but no test of fitness for it is ever imposed in the interest of the children.
—George Bernard Shaw

FAMILY SYSTEMS THERAPIES

Family systems theories, from which **family systems therapies** are derived, suggest that children's emotional/behavioral problems are only a reflection of problems within the family system (Kaslow, 2001). The term **identified problem** (or identified patient) is often used to signify the child whose problem was the impetus for treatment. Most family therapists will work with children only when their family is also willing to be involved in therapy. Given that the problem is thought to be located within the family (and often within the parent–parent dyad), therapy is thought to be most beneficial when all family members are involved. Some effective family therapies focus on the family management skills of the parents (e.g., supervising

Family therapists see the problem as residing in the family system—not just in the child.

BOX *6.4*

ARE FATHERS INCLUDED IN THERAPY FOR CHILD AND ADOLESCENT PROBLEMS?

Like research on family issues, therapy for children's emotional/behavioral problems has a long history of blaming mothers and ignoring fathers (Phares, 1996). One survey of social workers and school psychologists found that fathers were included in only 6.27% of therapy sessions, whereas mothers were included in 38.01% of therapy sessions (Lazar, Sagi, & Fraser, 1991). The remainder of the sessions involved only the individual child. Fathers were more likely to be included if the therapists were male, held more egalitarian beliefs, were newer on the job, had more academic work in family therapy, were employed by an agency that supported parental involvement in treatment, and were able to offer flexible scheduling for appointments (including evening and weekend appointments). This study suggests that sometimes personal characteristics of therapists have more to do with who is included in therapy than the needs of the family. Similar patterns have been found with regard to including children in family-oriented therapy (Johnson & Thomas, 1999).

Overall, there is a need for therapists to at least consider including fathers in therapy for children's emotional/behavioral difficulties. Many suggestions are available about how to include fathers in therapy (Hecker, 1991), but the most important step is to at least invite fathers to participate in therapy. There is evidence that mother-blaming is not completely pervasive, at least among family therapists (McCollum & Russell, 1992). There is, however, a need to remain vigilant about considering the father's role in both the development and treatment of psychopathology in children and adolescents.

---

their children's or adolescents' activities, providing appropriate discipline, and creating opportunities for positive parent–youngster activities) in addition to overall family functioning (Eddy & Chamberlain, 2000).

Because of the complexity of families these days, therapists must use their judgment about whom to involve in therapy: Should the noncustodial father be involved? Should the grandparents who provide more caretaking than the parents be involved? Often these decisions are fluid, with the therapist first requesting to see one portion of the family and then, as therapy progresses, requesting to have additional family members participate in therapy sessions. These issues are relevant not only for family therapists in the United States (Kaslow, 2001) but also for family therapists in a diverse array of countries, including Israel (Halpern, 2001); the Virgin Islands (Dudley-Grant, 2001); and Japan (Kameguchi & Murphy-Shigematsu, 2001).

A number of techniques are used in family therapy that may not be used frequently in therapy with an indi-

---

BOX *6.5*

THE CHANGING FAMILY STRUCTURE IN MICRONESIA

Family therapists must pay attention to culture and family history. As an example of the complexity of this issue, note how family structure has changed over the course of time in Micronesia, which includes Guam, the Northern Mariana Islands, and the Marshall Islands:

Pre–U.S. Contact (Prior to World War II)	1960s–1970s	1980s–1990s

Intergenerational extended families
  Grandparents
  Parents
  Children
  Unmarried
  aunts/uncles
Mutual marital separation
	Intergenerational families
	  Grandparents
	  Parents
	  Children
	
	Legalization of divorce
		Nuclear families
		Parents
		Children
		
		High divorce rate

SOURCE: Untalan & Camacho (1997).

Case Study: Family Therapy for Michael's Aggression

Brian (age 8), Michael (age 9), and Robert (age 10) all lived with their mother (Jane Smith) and stepfather (Jeff Smith). Mr. Smith used to abuse Mrs. Smith physically, and both parents have a history of spanking the boys severely as a method of punishment. Michael was the identified problem (IP) in that he often showed aggression, impulsivity, and explosiveness when his parents told him what to do. Michael's problems emerged at around the same time Mr. Smith joined the family. Michael's behavioral outbursts became so severe that he was admitted to a psychiatric hospital three times in the preceding two years. During each hospitalization, he showed significant improvement in the hospital and then deteriorated rapidly when placed back in the family home.

The therapists hypothesized that Michael's aggression served a function in the family of trying to prevent Mr. Smith from abusing Mrs. Smith (e.g., Mr. and Mrs. Smith allied against Michael and hit him for his transgressions, which may have alleviated Mr. Smith's desire to hit Mrs. Smith). The family therapy noted below was conducted while Michael was still hospitalized. As a therapeutic intervention, a "speaking wand" was used—whoever held the wand could speak and not be interrupted. In the verbatim therapy transcript below, Mr. and Mrs. Smith are referred to as Dad and Mom, respectively.

THERAPIST 1:   All right, while you have the wand, share what you think needs to change for Michael to come home. [*Holding the wand in the direction of the parents.*] Who'll start?

MOM: [*Reaches for the wand.*] I will. Michael needs to take his time-outs. He needs to learn how to deal with his anger without outbursts. [*Hands the wand to Dad.*]

DAD: [*Handing the wand to Robert.*] Boys first. If I share what I think, they won't share their own ideas.

ROBERT: [*Remains silent and appears confused.*]

THERAPIST 1:   Maybe you can tell us what you wish for when Michael comes home.

ROBERT: That he stops his tantrums. [*Hands wand to Brian.*]

BRIAN: [*Pushes the wand away.*]

MOM: You have to take it.

THERAPIST 2:   Good, Jane. You tell the boys what you would like to see happen.

BRIAN: [*Still hesitates and appears anxious and says nothing.*]

Later in this session and in subsequent sessions, the therapists try to help the children gain a "voice" in this family and try to reunify the parents so that the children are not between them. In addition, the parents are referred to couples therapy so that the history of domestic violence could be dealt with separately from the children. Family therapy was continued to ensure that the children were disengaged from their parents' troubled relationship.

SOURCE: Kemenoff, Jachimczyk, & Fussner (1999, pp. 119–120).

---

vidual child (Worden, 1994). For example, family therapists often **reframe** (or relabel) some behavior within the family to make it more conducive to change. For example, rather than being labeled manipulative or rebellious, a teenager might be characterized as still needing his or her parents' involvement. Family therapists also use **structural interventions** to change the organizational patterns within the family (e.g., giving a homework assignment where the parents have to do some type of activity without the children in order to strengthen the parental unit). When conducting therapy, family therapists often use **circular questioning**, which allows the therapist to explore the interconnectedness between family members. A circular question is a question posed to one person about someone else in the family (e.g., "Mr. Johnson, how do you think that Rashida feels about this present conflict?"). Circular questioning elucidates relationships within the family and often enables clients to voice their own thoughts in response to the answer to the original question (e.g., Rashida may then pipe up and share how she actually feels about the conflict). In all of their interactions with a family, therapists must be vigi-

lant about remaining neutral in relation to the family relationships. Often families have different factions or coalitions (some are more overt than others), and often these factions want the therapist to side with them. It is important that therapists acknowledge these relationships but also that they avoid getting pulled into the family's dysfunctional system.

Overall, family therapy is effective with treatment of children's emotional/behavioral problems (Brock & Barnard, 1992; Hazelrigg, Cooper, & Borduin, 1987). Particular success has been found when children's emotional/behavioral problems are related to or are exacerbated by difficulties within the family. It is not uncommon that interparental conflict is dealt with in family therapy, and often children are "excused" from therapy when parental issues are addressed. In fact, family therapy may turn into couples therapy (Gurman, 2001). As is obvious from the connections between interparental conflict and children's emotional/behavioral problems, family therapy or couples therapy that decreases interparental conflict is likely to reduce children's emotional/behavioral problems (Gurman, 2001).

Most family therapists agree about the importance of acknowledging families' cultural orientation (see, e.g., Box 6.5), including issues regarding ethnicity, race, religion, country of origin, level of acculturation, and preferred mode of communication (G. C. N. Hall & Barongan, 2002; McGoldrick, Giordano, & Pearce, 1996). In general, good family therapy with ethnically diverse clients looks very similar to good family therapy with clients from the same cultural background as the therapist (Paniagua, 1998). It is imperative, however, that family therapists, like all other therapists, be alert to issues of culture that may affect the therapeutic process (G. C. N. Hall & Barongan, 2002; Paniagua, 1998).

As our children grow, so must we grow to meet their changing emotional, intellectual, and designer-footwear needs.

—Dave Barry

PSYCHOPHARMACOLOGICAL INTERVENTIONS

In addition to the many psychotherapies and behavioral therapies available for children, adolescents, and their families, there are also a number of **psychopharmacological interventions** (i.e., medications) that can help alleviate problematic symptoms of developmental psychopathology. Although only physicians (such as psychiatrists or developmental pediatricians) can prescribe medications, it is incumbent upon child therapists and researchers to be informed about medications for children's emotional/behavioral problems (Barnett & Neel, 2000; Klusman, 2001). During psychological assessments, it is not uncommon for the assessor to recommend some type of therapy in addition to a medical evaluation for the appropriateness of medication. Table 6.3 lists many of the most common medications used to treat children's emotional/behavioral problems.

As with any type of intervention, medications for children's and adolescents' emotional/behavioral problems have pros and cons. The advantages of medication center on the effectiveness rates and ease of administration (as opposed to more involved therapies). All of the medications listed in Table 6.3 are effective to some degree. However, there is only limited support for the effectiveness of **antidepressants** in treating childhood depression (Brown & Sawyer, 1998; B. J. Burns, Hoagwood, & Mrazek, 1999). Because depression in children has been studied only relatively recently, extensive research on the use of antidepressants is lacking. Of the studies that have been conducted, there is equivocal evidence about the

effectiveness of antidepressant medication in treating child and adolescent depression (Brown & Sawyer, 1998).

Like antidepressants, **anxiolytics** (i.e., antianxiety medications) have not been studied extensively in children and adolescents. There is limited evidence for their effectiveness with some types of anxiety disorders (generalized anxiety disorder, obsessive-compulsive disorder, and separation anxiety disorder), but these studies have been hampered by the lack of good diagnostic definitions (Brown & Sawyer, 1998; Singh & Ellis, 1998).

Antipsychotic medication tends to be the treatment of choice to decrease hallucinations, delusions, and other symptoms of schizophrenia. Although other therapies can help with treatment compliance, family conflict, and social skill deficits that are associated with schizophrenia, antipsychotic medication is the primary means by which hallucinations and delusions are controlled (Singh & Ellis, 1998). In general, children who were older, who had a later onset of schizophrenia, and who had higher intellectual functioning tended to experience better outcomes with antipsychotic medications (Spencer, Kafantaris, Padron-Gayol, Rosenberg, & Campbell, 1992). Because there are a number of potentially severe side effects with many antipsychotic medications (such as **tardive dyskinesia**, a permanent condition in which the child makes repetitive stereotypical movements such as facial grimaces), antipsychotic medication should be used only in the most severe cases of schizophrenia and should be monitored closely (Brown & Sawyer, 1998).

With regard to **psychostimulants**, there is a great deal of evidence that psychostimulants, prescribed primarily for attention-deficit/hyperactivity disorder (ADHD), are effective in enhancing children's and adolescents' concentration, attention, and behavioral control (Brown & Sawyer, 1998; Burns et al., 1999). There is mixed evidence, however, regarding whether psychostimulants can decrease the aggressive behavior that is often associated with ADHD (Brown & Sawyer, 1998). Psychostimulants do not help academic functioning significantly (Brown & Sawyer, 1998). As effective as psychostimulants appear to be, there is evidence that approximately 75% of ADHD children show improved functioning while taking a psychostimulant, whereas 25% show either no improvement or decreased levels of functioning (Barkley, 1997a).

Overall, antipsychotic medications and psychostimulant medications have received the strongest empirical support for use with children and adolescents experiencing schizophrenia and ADHD, respectively (Riddle, Kastelic, & Frosch, 2001). Of all of these medications, psychostimulants continue to receive the most rigorous and careful empirical investigation. Medications of all types are used fairly regularly with children and adolescents with emotional/behavioral problems.

Given this wide usage, it is important to acknowledge that there are a number of potential drawbacks to the use of medication for treating emotional/behavioral problems in children and adolescents (Brown & Sawyer, 1998; Burns et al., 1999; Riddle et al., 2001). The most salient drawback is the possibility of side effects from the medications. All of the medications listed in Table 6.3 have the possibility of side effects, which range from mild irritants to serious and life-threatening problems. Some antidepressants (e.g., Tofranil, Anafranil, and Nardil) are associated with cardiac conditions, coma, and death from hypertensive crisis. Other antidepressants (e.g., Prozac,

Zoloft, and Paxil, all of which are selective serotonin reuptake inhibitors) have not been associated with severe side effects, but can be associated with decreased appetite, agitation, and insomnia. Although most anxiolytics have not been associated with serious side effects, some (e.g., Valium and Ativan) can become a drug of abuse for some children and adolescents. Also, it is relatively common for children and adolescents to experience fatigue and dizziness while using anxiolytics. Antipsychotic medications have already been noted for the possibility of severe side effects such as tardive dyskinesia, but they are also known to create less severe side effects, such as sedation, restlessness, and insomnia. Psychostimulants are associated with a range of adverse effects, including insomnia, dysphoria, and hypertension (Dexedrine);

TABLE 6.3 Common Medications Used to Treat Children's and Adolescents' Emotional/Behavioral Problems

Class of Drug	Generic Name	Trade Name	Indications
Antidepressants			
Tricyclics	Imipramine	Tofranil	Depression, enuresis
	Clomipramine	Anafranil	Depression, obsessive-compulsive disorder
Monoamine inhibitors	Oxidase		
	Phenelzine	Nardil	Atypical depression (often with anxiety)
Selective serotonin reuptake inhibitors	Fluoxetine	Prozac	Depression, obsessive-compulsive disorder
	Sertraline	Zoloft	Depression
	Paroxetine	Paxil	Depression, obsessive-compulsive disorder, panic disorder
Anxiolytics (Antianxiety)			
Benzodiazepines	Diazepam	Valium	Anxiety disorders
			Behavior disorders
			Emotional lability
	Lorazepam	Ativan	Anxiety
Others	Alprazolam	Xanax	Anxiety, panic disorder
	Buspirone	BuSpar	Anxiety
Antipsychotics			
Phenothiazines	Chlorpromazine	Thorazine	Acute psychotic states
	Thioridazine	Mellaril	Autistic disorder, pervasive development disorder
	Trifluoperazine	Stelazine	Tourette's disorder
Others	Haloperidol	Haldol	Psychotic disorder
	Clozapine	Clozaril	Drug-resistant schizophrenia
Psychostimulants			
	Dextro-amphetamine	Dexedrine	Attention-deficit/hyperactivity disorder
	Methylphenidate	Ritalin	Attention-deficit/hyperactivity disorder
	Pemoline	Cylert	Attention-deficit/hyperactivity disorder
	Destro-amphetamine-Sachharate/Sufate	Adderall	Attention-deficit/hyperactivity disorder

SOURCE: Adapted from Brown & Sawyer (1998).

anorexia, weight loss or failure to gain weight, growth retardation, and motor tics (Ritalin); liver dysfunction (Cylert); and palpitations, restlessness, and cardiomyopathy (Adderall).

Given all of these potential side effects, physicians and parents must weigh the benefits of any medication against the potential harm it may do (Kramer, Loney, Ponto, Roberts, & Grossman, 2000; Riddle et al., 2001). In addition, physicians and parents must monitor children's behavior closely in order to identify any adverse effects from the medication as soon as those effects appear.

A somewhat less salient, but equally important, drawback to the use of medication is the message that the medication sends to children about their problems (Hobbs, 1975; Johnston & Leung, 2001; Rappaport & Chubinsky, 2000). If children are told to take a pill in order to control their behavior, they may end up feeling that they have no control over their behavior themselves. An interesting study was conducted to assess children's and parents' attributions of children's behavior in relation to different types of treatment (Borden & Brown, 1989). All of the children in the study received cognitive therapy to deal with externalizing problems, most of which were consistent with a diagnosis of ADHD. In addition to the cognitive therapy that focused on self-control, children were assigned randomly to receive either no medication, active medication (Methylphenidate/Ritalin), or a placebo pill that contained no active medication. Parents and children were later asked to report their attributions of children's abilities to control their behavior and to solve problems.

As shown in Figure 6.2, both parents and children tended to attribute successful behavioral control and problem solving to the child when the child was not receiving any type of pill (whether Ritalin or a placebo). Parents and children attributed success to medication when children were taking a pill, and especially when children were taking a placebo. This study suggests that the act of taking a pill (whether it is an actual medication or a placebo) can change the way in which both parent and child feel about the child's abilities to solve problems and control his or her own behavior (Borden & Brown, 1989). Such external attributions for success may inadvertently work against children's gaining control over their behavior. It may be especially troublesome when children are removed from medication, since children and parents may expect children's behavior to deteriorate without psychopharmacological interventions.

When children and adolescents are prescribed medications, there is also a strong message that the problem is within the individual (Hobbs, 1975). Unfortunately, a rush to medicate children might circumvent the possibility of identifying problems (e.g., interparental conflict, ongoing abuse, learning difficulties) that could be treated more effectively by some other means. A thorough and thoughtful assessment of children and adolescents with emotional/behavioral problems should consider factors outside the child that may be at the root of the child's behavior or that may be exacerbating the child's behavior. If a therapist administers medication without exploring these other factors, then it is unlikely that the child's behavior will be improved over time (Hobbs, 1975). In addition, medications can only suppress the maladaptive behaviors; they cannot teach the child appropriate behaviors.

Overall, medications are useful in childhood and adolescence, especially for problems of ADHD and schizo-

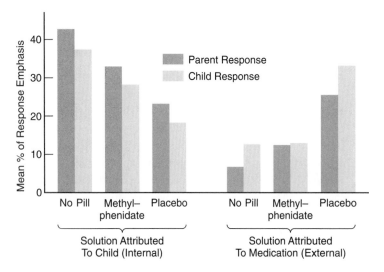

FIGURE 6.2 Similarity of Parent and Child Attributions for the Solution of Child's Presenting Problems

Source: Borden & Brown (1989).

phrenia but they are not without their problems. Given the potential serious adverse effects of medications, parents and physicians alike must consider their use thoughtfully and thoroughly. In addition, medications can be used in conjunction with therapy so that behavioral changes can be instituted that will remain even after the child is removed from the active medication.

I am growing stronger and more serene each day with my therapy and my twelve-step support groups. I do believe I am "over the hill" and am on the downside of all of this. I know that I will carry scars for life, but I am growing in confidence that healing is possible.

—Karen Seal, survivor of incest (Rhodes & Rhodes, 1996, p. 341)

EFFECTIVENESS OF THERAPEUTIC INTERVENTIONS

In a survey of more than 4,000 clients conducted by *Consumer Reports* (1995), the overwhelming majority of therapy clients said that the therapy had been beneficial. Of those who described their emotional state as "very poor" when they began therapy, nearly 90% said that the therapy had helped "somewhat" or "a lot" (Consumer Reports, 1995). Given this overwhelming support for the effectiveness of therapy, why would any further study be required? Although a survey like the one cited above may be important from a consumer standpoint, it tells us little about the effectiveness of different types of therapies. In addition, it does not provide a rigorous test of the effectiveness of therapy. It may be that any type of intervention (from therapy to reading a self-help book to playing with a puppy) could be rated as helpful; therefore, these results tell us little about the actual effectiveness of professional therapy.

The primary method of research on therapy effectiveness is the **outcome study**. In an outcome study, clients with comparable psychological problems are assigned randomly to either a group who receives the therapy of interest or some type of control group. There are many types of control groups (Kendall, Flannery-Schroeder, & Ford, 1999), including:

- No-treatment control groups, in which clients receive no intervention of any kind but are assessed at the same time as clients in the active therapy group.
- Wait-list control groups, in which clients receive no intervention at the beginning of the study but then receive the active treatment at the completion of the study (usually 10–16 weeks later).

- Attention-placebo/nonspecific control groups, in which clients receive attention or some other type of contact from the therapist but do not receive the active treatment.
- Standard treatment/routine care control, in which clients receive the regular treatment or services that would have been provided even if they had not been in the study.

The importance of including a control group in an outcome study is to verify that improvements in clients' behavior are actually due to the target therapy rather than merely the passage of time (as would be assessed in the no-treatment and wait-list control groups) or attention from a therapist (as would occur in attention-placebo/nonspecific control groups). The strength of including a standard treatment/routine care control group is to compare the effectiveness of the new therapy with the effectiveness of the therapy that is already established.

Although outcome studies are the first step to exploring the effectiveness of a therapy, there is growing concern that therapy conducted within an outcome study is not comparable to therapy conducted in the community at large (Henggeler & Randall, 2000; Weisz, Donenberg, Han, & Weiss, 1995). Most therapy outcome studies clarify specific techniques that will be used, and many follow a manual that delineates the specific treatment techniques. In the real world away from the research lab, however, clinicians are often not as structured in their delivery of therapeutic services, nor do they adhere closely to the therapy manual (Huey, Henggeler, Brondino, & Pickrel, 2000; Scaturo, 2001). One important aspect of conducting therapy outcome studies is to find ways to translate the findings into the larger practicing community of therapists (Henggeler & Randall, 2000). The American Psychological Association currently has a task force dedicated to making research findings from outcome studies more accessible to clinicians in the community (Weisz, Hawley, Pilkonis, Woody, & Follette, 2000).

Any one outcome study can inform us about a specific treatment with a specific sample of children, adolescents, or families. A more comprehensive way to investigate the effectiveness of therapy is to conduct a **meta-analysis**, which allows the statistical combination of a number of outcome studies to gain an overall understanding of the effectiveness of that type of therapy. There are a number of steps involved in conducting a meta-analysis (Durlak, 1999):

- Develop and specify the research questions.
- Conduct an adequate search of the research literature.

- Code the studies that are relevant to the research questions.
- Decide what type of effect sizes and other statistics will be used.
- Complete the statistical analyses.
- Summarize conclusions and provide interpretations of the results.

Note that meta-analyses provide the combined results of outcome studies that explored similar types of treatments (e.g., cognitive-behavioral therapy) for similar types of problems (e.g., social phobia). Although meta-analyses provide a powerful tool in establishing the effectiveness of different therapies, they can be misleading if the authors are not careful in explaining their limitations. For example, meta-analyses that use single-subject designs (where a treatment is administered to only one or two clients) would not have the same statistical power as meta-analyses that use larger sample sizes. In addition, if researchers select only published studies for their meta-analysis, they may inadvertently be stacking the deck toward finding differences between the target therapy and the control groups. Known as the **file-drawer problem**, this issue is of concern because studies that find differences (e.g., between a new treatment and a control group or between a new treatment and an established treatment) are somewhat more likely to be published than studies that do not find these differences (Durlak, 1999). Given this potential bias, many researchers who conduct meta-analyses try to include studies from both published and unpublished sources, such as journals and *Dissertation Abstracts*, respectively (Durlak, 1999).

One of the first large-scale meta-analyses conducted for child and adolescent therapy was published in 1985 (Casey & Berman, 1985). As shown in Table 6.4, the authors found that the mean effect size for all therapies was .71, which means that the average child who received therapy was better off than 76% of the children who did not receive therapy (based on a conversion of the effect size to percentages). Overall, the researchers found that most therapies (other than psychodynamic therapy) were more effective than no treatment. Further, they found that characteristics of the therapist (e.g., experience level, educational level, gender) did not show differences in treatment effectiveness rates. They did, however, find differences based on children's problems. Therapies were more effective for problems like hyperactivity, phobias, and somatic complaints than they were for social adjustment problems such as aggression or withdrawal (Casey & Berman, 1985). A comparable follow-up meta-analysis

TABLE 6.4 Effects of Psychotherapy with Children

Treatment	N of Studies[a]	Effect Size	
		M	**SD**
All therapies	64	0.71[b]	0.73
Behavioral therapies	37	0.91[b]	0.77
Behavioral	26	0.96[b]	0.79
Cognitive behavioral	14	0.81[b]	0.84
Nonbehavioral therapies	29	0.40[b]	0.37
Client centered	20	0.49[b]	0.65
Dynamic	5	0.21	0.22

[a] The number of studies does not sum to 64 because some studies examined more than one form of therapy.
[b] The mean effect size differs reliably from zero ($p < .05$).
SOURCE: Casey & Berman (1985).

found that behavioral therapies were somewhat more effective than nonbehavioral therapies, and that therapies were more effective for children than for adolescents (Weisz, Weiss, Alicke, & Klotz, 1987).

Since the time of these meta-analyses, a number of other meta-analyses have been completed for treatment of children's and adolescents' emotional/behavioral problems (Baer & Nietzel, 1991; Weisz & Weiss, 1993; Weisz, Weiss, Han, Granger, & Morton, 1995). Results continue to suggest that children who receive treatment are better off emotionally and behaviorally than 76% to 79% of children who do not receive treatment (reviewed by Kazdin, 1996).

In an effort to synthesize outcome studies and meta-analyses, there has been a recent emphasis on identifying **empirically supported treatments** (Kazdin & Weisz, 1998). A federal task force was developed to help define and identify effective treatments that were supported by empirical research (Chambless et al., 1998; Task Force on Promotion and Dissemination of Psychological Procedures, 1995). Two acceptable categories of empirically supported treatments were identified:

- *Well-established treatments,* which are required to have at least two high-quality between-group studies that show the treatment is either better than another therapy or a placebo, or that the treatment is as effective as a well-established treatment that is already in use. The treatments must have been instituted through the use of a structured manual, and the significant results must have been found by at least two different research groups. Sample characteristics must have been identified clearly.

• *Probably efficacious treatments,* which are required to have at least one or two high-quality between-group studies that show the treatment is better than another therapy or a placebo. The study or studies are allowed to have been conducted by the same research group. Again, the treatment should have been administered with a structured manual and sample characteristics must have been identified clearly.

Throughout the remainder of this textbook, specific effective treatments (both well-established and probably efficacious) will be identified for each disorder or problem. Rather than stating each of those findings here, I will note only that there are a number of effective treatments for a variety of different problems in childhood and adolescence. The overwhelming majority of well-established treatments and probably efficacious treatments can be conceptualized as cognitive-behavioral, behavioral, or cognitive (Weisz & Hawley, 1998). The specific treatments that are most clearly well-established within the area of childhood and adolescence are behavior modification for enuresis, behavioral parent training programs for

children with oppositional problems, and cognitive-behavioral therapy for adolescents with bulimia (Chambless et al., 1998). Note, however, that much more work is needed to establish whether empirically supported treatments are effective for different groups of children, such as ethnic minority children or impoverished children (G. C. N. Hall & Barongan, 2002). For example, one parent training study found that the factors of single parenthood and immigrant status were related to low involvement in treatment, whereas poverty, family disturbance, and parental depressive symptoms were not related to treatment involvement (Cunningham et al., 2000). In contrast, in a study of outpatient treatment for adolescents in Finland, low parental socioeconomic status was the most meaningful predictor of early dropout from therapy (Pelkonen, Marttunen, Laippala, & Loennqvist, 2000). In addition to exploring individual and family characteristics that are related to treatment effectiveness, it is also important to identify which treatment factors are associated with better versus worse outcomes of specific treatment programs (Southam-Gerow, Kendall, & Weersing, 2001). For example, Box 6.6 shows effective treatment strategies for childhood sexual abuse.

The area of attention-deficit/hyperactivity disorder (ADHD) provides a model that illustrates how treatment

BOX *6.6*

TREATING SURVIVORS OF CHILDHOOD SEXUAL ABUSE

Although there are limited studies in this area, the trauma related to childhood sexual abuse can be treated effectively (Litrownik & Castillo-Canez, 2000; Stevenson, 1999). Even though clinicians have used many different therapy orientations, there are usually common themes across these therapies, including enhancement of interpersonal relationships, dealing directly with the trauma of sexual abuse, and processing the traumatic experiences that are most distressing. As shown in Figure 6.4, dealing with these issues is effective in reducing psychological symptoms related to childhood sexual abuse (Litrownik & Castillo-Canez, 2000).

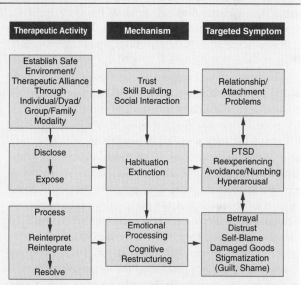

FIGURE 6.4 Schematic Summary of Empirical Findings
Source: Litrownik & Castillo-Canez (2000).

outcome research can be done. In a nationwide assessment of treatment effectiveness, the Multisite Treatment Study of ADHD (MTA) evaluates different modalities of treatment of ADHD in various settings (see S. B. Campbell, 2000; Wells et al., 2000). In addition to evaluating behavioral treatments, effectiveness of medications are also evaluated. The MTA study provides a model for how effective outcome studies can be developed. Although there are promising findings for the treatment of developmental psychopathology (including ADHD), there are also promising findings related to preventing developmental psychopathology before it ever occurs.

PREVENTION PROGRAMS THAT WORK

Throughout this book, effective prevention programs will be highlighted. Prevention programs often try to enhance protective factors in the lives of children—examples include a program designed to create supportive teacher–student relationships to decrease the likelihood of childhood aggression (Hughes, Cavell, & Jackson, 1999); a television series developed to teach positive parenting skills (Sanders, Montgomery, & Brechman-Toussaint, 2000); a program for teaching adolescents and their parents cognitive and interpersonal skills in order to prevent adolescent depression (Shochet et al., 2001); and an extensive program set up to provide services to impoverished families and communities (Knitzer, 2000). Preventive efforts can be located in many settings, including preschools and schools (Farrell, Meyer, Kung, & Sullivan, 2001; Webster-Stratton, Reid, & Hammond, 2001); the child welfare system (Zeanah et al., 2001); hospitals (Ialongo, Kellam, & Poduska, 2000); and the community (Felner, Felner, & Silverman, 2000).

There are three types of prevention programs: **primary prevention programs**, which focus on the entire community; **secondary prevention programs**, which focus on children at risk for emotional/behavioral problems; and **tertiary prevention programs**, which attempt to prevent the recurrence of emotional/behavioral problems that already exist (Albee & Gullotta, 1996; Felner et al., 2000). Primary prevention programs are considered "universal" because they are designed for the entire population. Secondary prevention programs are considered "selected" because they focus on certain individuals who have experiences that put them at risk for developing emotional/behavioral problems. Tertiary prevention programs are considered "indicated" because they target individuals who are already experiencing emotional/behavioral problems (Knitzer, 2000).

As an example, effective programs for the prevention of violent behavior in children have been targeted at many different levels (Group for the Advancement of Psychiatry, 1999):

- Primary prevention: gun control.
- Secondary prevention: gun-free zones around schools in violent areas.
- Tertiary prevention: gun confiscation and conflict resolution training for violent youth.

Prevention programs have been targeted at all of these levels for many different emotional/behavioral problems in children and adolescents (Felner et al., 2000); for preventing sexual victimization (Davis & Gidycz, 2000); and for preventing violent tendencies, such as sexual coercion (Pacifici, Stoolmiller, & Nelson, 2001) and gun violence (Mulvey & Cauffman, 2001).

In keeping with this book's focus on developmental processes, it is important to acknowledge that different prevention programs should be targeted at varying age groups. For example, prenatal services and well-baby health services should be geared to pregnant women and infants up to the age of two, programs that decrease the upheaval at school would be appropriate for elementary school students as they transition to middle school, educational and vocational programs could help young adults who have not yet found their niche, and health and social-service efforts might be most appropriate for elderly individuals (Felner et al., 2000). Prevention programs run the gamut from widely administered programs that are not effective—such as Drug Awareness Resistance Education (DARE), which attempts to prevent substance abuse—to highly effective prevention programs such as Life Skills Training, which decreases substance abuse by teaching social skills and personal problem-solving skills (Dusenbury & Falco, 1997).

Figure 6.3 shows a model of child abuse prevention strategies in which a number of characteristics can be targeted for preventive efforts, including increasing parents' social support and educating parents on child development (Culbertson & Schellenbach, 1992). This type of comprehensive model is usually needed for complex problems like child abuse.

In general, effective prevention programs are thought to be more cost-efficient (i.e., it takes fewer dollars to prevent problems than to deal with long-term treatment of problems that develop) and are designed to prevent continued suffering by children and their families (Albee, 1982; Knitzer, 2000; Spence, 1998). In addition to the effective programs highlighted in this textbook, there are

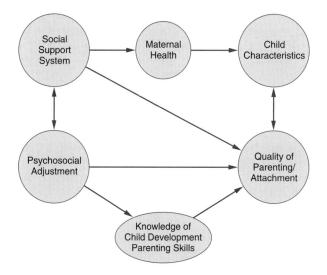

FIGURE 6.3 A Model of Child Abuse Prevention
Source: Culbertson & Schellenbach (1992).

many others throughout the world. These programs show a wide range of modalities and focus on the prevention of a wide array of problems. The following is a brief list of the types of successful prevention programs that are being instituted around the world:

- Preventing emotional/behavioral problems in children of parents with psychopathology in the Netherlands

(Verburg, Janssen, Rikken, Hoefnagels, & vanWillenswaard, 1992).

- Preventing physical illness and mental health problems through social action in Ghana (Sefa-Dedeh, 1992).
- Preventing disruptive behavior through a television series on families in Australia (Sanders, Montgomery, & Brechman-Toussaint, 2000).
- Prevention of violence through school prevention programs in the United States (Farrell, Meyer, & White, 2001; Hampton, Jenkins, & Gullotta, 1996).
- Prevention of mental health problems and intellectual delays through integrated child care services in India (Sonty, 1992).
- Prevention of child abuse through fostering parental competence in Poland (Sek, Bleja, & Sommerfeld, 1992).

Overall, prevention is an integral part of helping children. What better humanistic goal is there than to prevent problems from occurring rather than waiting to treat them after they occur? Given the often devastating consequences of developmental psychopathology for children, families, and society, continued support is warranted for prevention programs and public policy changes that help children (Albee & Gullotta, 1966; Knitzer, 2000; Winett, 1998).

SUMMARY AND KEY CONCEPTS

There are a number of ways in which children and adolescents are helped through therapeutic interventions, including psychodynamic therapy, behavioral therapy, cognitive-behavioral therapy, family systems therapy, and psychopharmacological interventions (i.e., medications).

Settings for Interventions

Therapy can be conducted in a number of different settings, most of which institute a **treatment plan** that identifies problem behaviors, long-term goals, short-term goals, and specific interventions that will be administered in order to help the child. The range of settings varies from **inpatient settings** (which are usually in a hospital setting and require that children stay in the facility 24 hours a day), **residential treatment facilities** (where children reside for a greater length of time and which are usually away from a hospital setting), **group homes** and **therapeutic foster care homes** (which usually serve fewer children than in residential treatment facilities), **day hospitals** (which allow children to receive services during the day but live at home with their family), **outpatient settings** (which allow children to visit with a therapist on usually a weekly basis in the therapist's

office), and **school-based mental health services** (which allow children to receive mental health services at school).

Psychodynamic Therapies

Although traditional **psychodynamic therapies** are rarely conducted with children or adolescents, **play therapy** is an offshoot of psychodynamic therapy that is still used with children.

Behavioral Therapies

Behavioral therapies consist of two broad categories: child-orientated interventions and parent-oriented interventions. The most traditional form of behavioral therapy is called **applied behavior analysis**, which applies behavioral principles to children's emotional/behavioral problems. More complex behavioral therapies are also used extensively with children and adolescents, including **token economies** (giving a token or other symbol for adaptive behaviors and then allowing children to "cash in" their tokens for a desired object or activity) and **systematic desensitization** (pairing relaxation with progressively anxiety-producing situations from a hierarchy of fears). **Behavioral parent training** is the primary behavioral therapy that can be conducted with parents.

Cognitive-Behavioral Therapies

Cognitive-behavioral therapies combine principles from behavioral therapies with principles from cognitive therapies. Therapists work with children and adolescents to alter maladaptive cognitions, enhance coping and problem-solving skills, eliminate maladaptive behavior, and enhance adaptive behavior.

Family Systems Therapies

Based on family systems theories, **family systems therapies** conceptualize children's and adolescents' emotional/behavioral problems as being reflective of a problem within the family system. The child who is experiencing the emotional/behavioral problem is referred to as the **identified problem** (or identified patient). Family therapists use a number of techniques that are relatively unique to family therapy, including using a **reframe** (where a symptom is relabeled in a more positive light), **structural interventions** (which are used to change the organizational patterns within the family), and **circular questioning** (where one family member is asked about another family member's perspective).

Psychopharmacological Interventions

Psychopharmacological interventions involve any of various psychiatric medications that can be prescribed by a physician to treat children's emotional/behavioral problems, including **antidepressants** (to treat depression), **anxiolytics** (to treat anxiety problems), **antipsychotic medications** (to treat schizophrenia or other psychotic disorders), and **psychostimu-**lants (to treat ADHD). Care must be taken (by both physicians and parents) to monitor any adverse side effects (such as **tardive dyskinesia**, which is a permanent neuromuscular disorder that can develop after using antipsychotic medication).

Effectiveness of Therapeutic Interventions

The primary way that therapeutic effectiveness is studied is through an **outcome study** (where clients are assigned randomly to either a treatment group or a control group). In order to summarize the results of outcome studies statistically, a **meta-analysis** can be completed that combines the results of many outcome studies and evaluates the overall effectiveness of the therapies that are of interest. Note that a potential problem with meta-analyses is that many studies are not published when they do not find differences between treatments (a problem that is known as the **file-drawer problem**). Recently, there has been a focus on **empirically supported treatments** that are evaluated for the rigor and strength of research findings.

Prevention Programs That Work

In addition to the therapeutic interventions that are effective in helping children and adolescents with their emotional/behavioral problems, there are also many programs that have been instituted to prevent emotional/behavioral problems from occurring in the first place. Prevention programs can target entire communities (**primary prevention programs**), at-risk children (**secondary prevention programs**), and children who have already experienced problems (**tertiary prevention programs**).

KEY TERMS

inpatient settings	psychodynamic	cognitive-behavioral	antidepressants	empirically
treatment plans	therapies	therapies	anxiolytics	supported
residential treatment	play therapy	family systems	antipsychotic	treatments
facility	behavioral therapies	therapies	medication	primary prevention
group homes	applied behavior	identified problem	tardive dyskinesia	programs
therapeutic foster	analysis	reframe	psychostimulants	secondary
care homes	token economies	structural	outcome study	prevention
day hospitals	systematic	interventions	meta-analysis	programs
outpatient settings	desensitization	circular questioning	file-drawer problem	tertiary prevention
school-based mental	behavioral parent	psychopharmacologi-		programs
health services	training	cal interventions		

SUGGESTED READINGS

Napier, Augustus Y., & Whitaker, Carl A. *The Family Crucible*. New York: Harper Trade, 1978. In this true story that reads like a compelling novel, Drs. Napier and Whitaker work with a troubled family and provide direct examples of family therapy in action.

Manning, Martha. *Undercurrents*. San Francisco: Harper San Francisco, 1994. In this powerful autobiography, Dr. Manning describes her own depression and treatment throughout her work as a therapist.

SUGGESTED VIEWINGS

Girl, Interrupted (1999). James Mangold (director and screenwriter), based on memoir by Susanna Kayson. VHS/DVD. Based on an eloquent autobiography of the same name (Kaysen, 1993), this film illustrates the inpatient treatment of a young woman for depression, suicidal wishes, and problems with adjustment. Both the film and the book also explore the issue of who is "crazy" and who is reacting normally to abnormal situations during older adolescence.

The Sixth Sense (1999). M. Night Shyamalan (director and writer). VHS/DVD. In this intriguing movie, a child therapist is shown conducting unique therapy sessions. Although the main point of the film is not this therapeutic intervention, the therapist shows good examples of rapport building with a hesitant child client.

CHAPTER 7

RISK FACTORS AND ISSUES OF PREVENTION

CHAPTER SUMMARY

We are always too busy for our children; we never give them the time or interest they deserve. We lavish gifts upon them; but the most precious gift—our personal association, which means so much to them—we give grudgingly.

—Mark Twain

As mentioned in Chapter 1, **risk factors** are characteristics, events, or processes that put the individual at risk for the development of psychological problems. The presence of a risk factor in a child's or adolescent's life increases the likelihood that he or she will develop emotional/behavioral problems (Arrington & Wilson, 2000). Risk factors can be conceptualized as falling into three broad categories (Werner, 1995; Werner & Smith, 2001):

1. Individual characteristics of the infant, child, or adolescent (e.g., troubled attachment to the caregiver, difficult temperament).

2. Characteristics within the family (e.g., parental psychopathology, parental death, interparental conflict, child abuse and maltreatment, family dysfunction).

3. Characteristics of the school or community (e.g., overcrowded schools, poverty, violence within the community).

This chapter covers these factors in the order listed above. Note that Chapters 9–16, on individual types of psychopathology, will also address the risk factors specific to the development of each clinical disorder.

Temperament is evident in infants at the time of birth and infants can be categorized as easy babies (like the one in this picture), slow-to-warm-up babies, and difficult babies.

The first cry of a newborn baby in Chicago or Zamoango, in Amsterdam or Rangoon, has the same pitch and key, each saying "I am! I have come through! I belong!"

–Carl Sandburg

TEMPERAMENT AND ATTACHMENT

Both temperament and attachment are studied primarily in the beginning years of life. **Temperament** reflects the infant's personal, individual style regarding the expression of needs and emotions. Temperament is thought to be present at birth and is assumed to be due largely to genetic and constitutional factors, with only some influence from environmental factors. Infants can be classified into three types according to temperament (Thomas & Chess, 1977):

- *Easy babies* tend to be relatively predictable in their sleeping and eating habits, seldom cause a fuss, and react to new or novel situations with pleasure and cheer.
- *Slow-to-warm-up* babies encounter new situations with wariness and trepidation, but they eventually come around to enjoy the new situation.
- *Difficult babies* show no regular patterns of eating or sleeping and tend to be irritable the majority of the time.

The overwhelming majority of babies are easy babies. In general, temperament in infancy is consistent with temperament in later toddlerhood, childhood, and adolescence (Thomas & Chess, 1977).

The difficult temperamental style is considered to be a risk factor for the development of psychopathology in later years. For example, individuals who showed a difficult and highly reactive temperamental style as infants were more likely than others to show problematic levels of anxiety when they were seven years old (Kagan, Snidman, Zentner, & Peterson, 1999). Difficult temperament in infancy and toddlerhood has also been associated with the development of externalizing problems such as aggression in adolescent boys (Mesman & Koot, 2000). Although temperament is thought to be somewhat innate, the match between infant temperament and caretaker tolerance for the infant's behavior may relate to the child's adaptational outcome (Campbell, 1998).

The other primary risk factor within the individual is attachment. As noted in Chapter 2, **attachment** is the relationship that develops between the infant and the caregiver over the first year of life. Most often, this relationship is a deep, enduring, and affectionate bond between the infant and caretaker (usually a parent). There are four primary types of attachment (Karen, 1994):

- *Secure attachment,* in which infants show a desire to be with their parent, use their parent as a secure base from which to explore unfamiliar settings, and show joy when reunited with their parent after a separation.
- *Avoidant anxious insecure attachment,* in which infants ignore or avoid their parent when reunited after a separation.
- *Ambivalent anxious insecure attachment,* in which infants protest when their parent leaves the room but then appear to be angry and rejecting when the parent returns to them after a brief separation.
- *Disorganized anxious insecure attachment,* in which infants provide mixed signals such as crying when

being returned to their parent or reaching out for their parent while looking away.

The majority of infants show secure attachment with their primary caretaker (Cassidy & Mohr, 2001; Karen, 1994). Attachment style is seen as a risk factor when the infant shows any of the anxious insecure attachment styles (avoidant, ambivalent, or disorganized). Children who showed insecure attachment in infancy showed greater problems with compliance in school, more peer isolation,

more emotional/behavioral problems, greater rates of depression, and greater rates of conduct problems in childhood and adolescence (S. B. Campbell, 1998; Cicchetti, Rogosch, & Toth, 1997; Speltz, DeKlyen, & Greenberg, 1999). Note that anxious insecure attachment is not itself a type of psychopathology, nor does it appear to lead directly to any single type of psychopathology. Rather, it appears that anxious insecure attachment leads to additional problems that are linked to the development

---

BOX 7.1

HELPING PARENTS CONNECT WITH THEIR INFANTS

Many young, impoverished parents, especially teenage mothers, have difficulty dealing with the demands of an infant in addition to other life stressors. Many times, these difficulties lead to the infant's being at risk for physical abuse, emotional/behavioral problems, and limited academic and intellectual functioning later in childhood. Some of these problems may be due either to the lack of adequate information for the young parents or to the limited attachment that is formed between an infant and a parent under severe stress (Olds, 1988).

The Prenatal/Early Infancy Program was developed by Olds (1988) and was designed to prevent some of these difficulties. This program targeted parents under 19 who had low socioeconomic status. Although you might think that this type of program would target only teenage mothers, more than 40% of the participants were married and a number of others were living with the baby's father. The program recruited parents before the infant was born so that adequate prenatal care could be encouraged and so that a bond could be developed between the parents and the support staff from the research team. A primary component of this program was that support staff would make home visits to encourage the parents to receive the services. The following were components of the program:

- *Prenatal education,* which included helping expectant mothers with healthy food intake and exercise; helping expectant mothers avoid drugs, alcohol, and cigarettes; teaching parents to identify possible signs of pregnancy complications; educating parents on labor and delivery issues; preparing parents for the demands of early care of their newborn; helping parents learn about appropriate health care options available to them and the newborn; and helping parents with job training or educational pursuits as needed.
- *Infancy education,* which included teaching parents about infants' temperaments, helping parents identify ways in which to promote socioemotional and cognitive

development in their infants, and helping to promote the physical development of the infant.
- *Informal support,* which included helping parents identify appropriate family members and friends who could help with the process of becoming new parents, as well as encouraging them to seek help from the program's support staff.
- *Connecting to formal services,* which included informing parents about the different public resources that were available to them, such as legal aid, child care, medical, and dental services.

These support services were provided from before the child's birth to the time the child was two years old. For the first six weeks of the child's life, the support staff visited the parents weekly. From the time the infant was six weeks old to four months old, the support staff visited the parents every two weeks, then every three weeks from the ages of 4 to 14 months, every month from the ages of 14 to 20 months, and finally every six weeks from the ages of 20 to 24 months.

Positive effects of the program were evidenced at many stages of infants' and children's lives. Babies were less likely to be born prematurely and were less likely to be born at a low birth weight than infants whose parents had not participated in the program. These changes may have been due to the reduction in cigarette, alcohol, and drug use among parents in the program. Infant–parent attachment was significantly stronger and more adaptive than in nonprogram infant–parent dyads. This secure attachment appeared to be connected to a host of other strengths within these families. Notably, there was a 75% reduction of documented cases of child physical abuse at follow-up when compared with children whose parents had not participated in the program. Overall, this intensive prevention program showed that intervening with young parents can prevent a host of problems associated with later development of emotional/behavioral problems in children.

Source: Olds (1988)

of psychopathology (Sroufe, Carlson, Levy, & Egeland, 1999). Box 7.1 describes a program designed to help parents connect with their infants.

It is important to note that attachment can be considered a reciprocal process between infants and caretakers rather than an individual characteristic of the infant. There is evidence that the parent's or caretaker's behavior with the infant can influence attachment style significantly. Parents and caretakers who tend to be abrupt, angry, and intolerant of their infant are likely to have an infant with some type of anxious insecure attachment (S. B. Campbell, 1998). Given that these parental behaviors would most likely continue through the infant's childhood and adolescence, it may be that these parental behaviors serve as a risk factor either separate from or in addition to the attachment style in infancy.

GENETIC PREDISPOSITION

As discussed in Chapter 2, a number of emotional/behavioral problems are associated with a genetic predisposition (Rutter, Silberg, O'Connor, & Simonoff, 1999b). Such problems include depression, anxiety, conduct problems, attention problems, hyperactivity, substance abuse problems, pervasive developmental problems, schizophrenia, learning problems, and intellectual deficits (Rutter et al., 1999b). Surprisingly, even poor achievement and social maladjustment after parental divorce are linked to genetic risk factors (O'Connor, Caspi, DeFries, & Plomin, 2000). Among all of the genetic risk factors, the one that has received the most empirical attention is parental psychopathology.

If there is anything that we wish to change in the child, we should first examine it and see whether it is not something that could better be changed in ourselves.

—Carl Gustav Jung

PARENTAL PSYCHOPATHOLOGY

Researchers have explored the risk factor of parental psychopathology extensively. As mentioned in Chapter 4, the primary research design to study parental psychopathology is called the high-risk design, which presupposes that offspring of a parent who experiences psychopathology are at high risk for development of some type of psychopathology. Beginning with research in the 1950s on parents diagnosed with schizophrenia (reviewed in Rolf, Masten, Cicchetti, Neuchterlein, & Weintraub, 1990), a

great number of researchers have explored the ramifications of having a parent with a clinical disorder. In the early days of this research, parents diagnosed with depression were used as a control group to be compared with parents diagnosed with schizophrenia. Ironically, researchers found that the offspring of parents with schizophrenia and the offspring of parents with depression were at increased risk for the development of emotional/behavioral problems (Rolf et al., 1990). Thus, control groups were later defined as offspring of parents without any type of psychopathology. Since those early studies, nearly every clinical disorder has been explored within the context of parental psychopathology. Unfortunately, the majority of research has explored psychopathology in mothers and has all but ignored psychopathology in fathers (Phares, 1996).

Clinical disorders in *mothers* ranging from depression (Goodman & Gotlib, 1999; Hammen, 1991) to anxiety disorders (Warner, Mufson, & Weissman, 1995) to substance abuse (Luthar, Cushing, Merikangas, & Rounsaville, 1998) to schizophrenia (Erlenmeyer-Kimling et al., 1984) all put children at risk for the development of psychopathology. Clinical disorders in *fathers* ranging from depression (Jacob & Leonard, 1986) to alcohol abuse (Weinberg, Dielman, Mandell, & Shope, 1994) to schizophrenia (Erlenmeyer-Kimling et al., 1984) all put children and adolescents at risk for the development of psychopathology (reviewed in Phares, 1996).

Adding to the complexity of this research area is the tendency for individuals to pair up with other individuals with comparable levels of mental health functioning. The term **assortative mating** is used to describe the fact that clinically disturbed individuals tend to become involved with and have children with other clinically disturbed individuals (Foley et al., 2001; Merikangas, Weissman, Prusoff, & John, 1988). Given this pattern, it is possible that children may be exposed to two parents with clinical disorders. There is also a greater likelihood for parents who experience psychopathology to show higher rates of interparental conflict, higher rates of separation, and a greater likelihood of divorce (if they were married), so children are often exposed to interparental conflict and parental separation in addition to the parental psychopathology (Merikangas et al., 1988). Thus, the study of children at high risk for the development of psychopathology due to parental psychopathology is quite complex.

A central question in the research on parental psychopathology relates to whether the increased risk for the child is based on a genetic predisposition or on disturbed parenting. As discussed in Chapter 2, it is not clear what

Case Study: Louie, Son of an Alcoholic Father

Comedian Louie Anderson (1991) wrote a funny but heart-wrenching book called *Dear Dad: Letters from an Adult Child*. The book is a compilation of letters that Louie wrote to his deceased father, who had experienced severe problems with alcohol abuse during Louie's childhood. The letters illustrate the devastation of parental alcohol abuse. Not only was Louie's father often absent (both physically and emotionally) due to the alcohol abuse, but he was often verbally abusive. The rest of this case contains quotes from the book (the first from a stand-up comedy routine, the rest in letters to his father).

My dad never hit us . . . he carried a gun. Oh, he never shot us . . . he'd just go "Click-click!" (p. xiii)

Secretly, I always wished someone would deck you, just once, but the one time I saw you splayed out frightened me in a way your abuse never did. It was a weekend afternoon and you and I were the only ones home. I was watching TV and heard a horrible crash. You were drunk and had fallen down the basement stairs. You were lying there, unconscious. I raced downstairs and tried to get you up. But I couldn't. So I put a pillow under your head and sat there until Mom got home.
"Why is Dad like this?" I asked Mom.
"He's drunk," she said matter-of-factly.
"Why?"
"He's been drinking."

"But why?"
But why, Dad? I'd still really like to know the answer. It's something I think about when I'm sitting on my balcony on a clear night, gazing at the view of the city. (p. 45)

The following exchange occurred when Louie's father wanted to take Louie into a bar:

"Ah, come on," you urged. "It's only for a minute."
"But, Dad . . . ?" I whined.
"You fucking baby, come on."
What choice did I have? What twelve-year-old boy wants to be called a fucking baby by his father? (p. 72)

At the end of this drinking episode, the father piled Louie and his brother into the car and drove while he was intoxicated enough to fall asleep at a stop sign.

When describing a shelter for abused, neglected, and runaway children where he worked the night shift, Louie presents a realization about himself in relation to his father:

In the sad eyes and weary, bruised faces of the children I was assigned to watch over, I found an aching emptiness that was similar to what I felt in my own heart. I understood their silence, their refusal to cry, and when they did cry or wake from bad dreams, I could honestly tell them, "I understand." (p. 131)

SOURCE: Anderson (1991).

percentage of the variance is accounted for by genetic predisposition and what percentage is accounted for by characteristics within the family and environment. Interestingly, few disorders show direct genetic transmission from parent to child. Studies that show children of depressed mothers and depressed fathers are at increased risk for the development of psychopathology do not show that there is a direct genetic link between parental depression and children's depression. One comprehensive review suggested that parental depression without concomitant interparental conflict was related to internalizing problems in children, such as depression or anxiety, but that parental depression in combination with interparental conflict was associated with externalizing problems in children, such as oppositional defiant disorder and conduct disorder (Downey & Coyne, 1990). This type of review suggests that there is a complex set of characteristics that relate to the genetic and environmental factors that put children and adolescents at risk for the development of psychopathology when their parent or parents experience psychopathology.

PARENTAL LOSS DUE TO DEATH

As with so many other issues within developmental psychopathology, there are no easy answers to the question of how parental death affects children and adolescents. Approximately 3.4% of children and adolescents in the United States have lost one or both parents to death (D. C. Clark, Pynoos, & Goebel, 1994). Two-thirds of those children have lost a father. A number of studies have shown that children and adolescents who have lost a parent to death tend to show grief reactions and heightened levels of emotional/behavioral problems long after the death (reviewed by Dowdney, 2000). However, only 20% or so of bereaved children develop a diagnosable mental disorder (Dowdney, 2000). Thus, many instance of parental death are not always associated with increases in problems (Mireault & Compas, 1996; VanEerdewegth, Bieri, Parrilla, & Clayton, 1982). The risk of problems appears to be influenced by a number of different factors. Specifically, children who lose a parent to death are more likely to develop emotional/behavioral problems if any of the

Case Study: The Parker Family, a Case of Interparental Conflict and Parental Problems

Alex, a 16-year-old, has been suspended from school for eight days for fighting. He has a twin brother, Andrew, and the boys live with their mother, Leslie, and their father, Jerry. Leslie is a full-time homemaker, and Jerry is a salesperson for retirement plans. The oldest daughter, Barbara, is 20 and lives with her boyfriend in another city. The family sought family therapy due to Alex's suspension and due to acting-out problems with Andrew. Alex had thrown a knife at Andrew previously, but the family did not seek help after that incident.

Rather than just focusing on the presenting problems, the family therapist asked questions about who runs the family (i.e., control); who gets upset the most (i.e., affective involvement); and how the parents get along (i.e., interparental conflict). It soon became evident that there were a host of other problems within the family, and the therapist hypothesized that the boys' acting out behavior was serving as a shield for the parents' marital difficulties. The parents' problems included the following:

- The mother felt abandoned by her husband, given that he worked 14-hour days and was not involved in family matters except when she forced his involvement.

- The mother and father argued a lot about how to handle the boys' behavior, about their lack of closeness to each other, and about their different interests (he liked to watch television and she liked to shop).

- The father had experienced a drinking problem for 25 years, but when he finally gave up alcohol 3 years previously, the mother did not even seem to notice. The mother and father had argued a great deal when the father was abusing alcohol. After he quit, they had nothing to talk about, so they became even more distant. When the boys' acting-out behavior began (shortly after their father stopped drinking), the parents found something else about which to argue. The therapist hypothesized that arguing was the only way the parents could communicate and feel close to each other, even if the closeness was negative.

- The father was currently trying to lose weight, but the mother belittled his success. She felt that no good changes would come from improvements within the family.

After approximately 12 sessions (the majority of which involved only the parents and not the children), the family therapist was able to help the parents find productive ways to communicate and to feel close again without arguing.

This case illustrates the connection between interparental conflict and children's acting-out behavior. In addition, it highlights the need for therapists to look at presenting problems within the context of the family system.

SOURCE: Prevatt (1999a).

---

following occur (Clark et al., 1994; Dowdney, 2000; Parkes, 1990):

- There are multiple deaths at one time (e.g., both parents, or a parent and a sibling).

- The parental death was sudden.

- The parental death was due to suicide or homicide.

- The child who loses a parent had psychological difficulties even before the parent died.

- The child had a conflicted relationship with the deceased parent.

- The surviving parent or caretakers are significantly distressed and have limited abilities to deal with the child's needs.

- There is an unstable home environment after the parent's death.

Overall, parental death appears to be a risk factor for the development of emotional/behavioral problems, but not for all children. Children who were well adjusted and who had a good relationship with the parent prior to the parent's death, children who have time to deal with the death (both in preparation and in response to the death),

and children who have a stable and nurturing family environment after the loss of their parent appear to show no greater risk than other children for the development of emotional/behavioral problems or psychopathology.

I remember them arguing a lot. All the time. I mean, I never saw them express any emotional tenderness toward each other.
—Michelle, 14 years old (Royko, 1999, p. 17)

INTERPARENTAL CONFLICT

One of the most consistent findings in the study of developmental psychopathology is the adverse effects of interparental conflict on child and adolescent functioning (Grych, Fincham, Jouriles, & McDonald, 2000; Hetherington, 1999; Hetherington, Bridges, & Insabella, 1998; Kelly, 2000). In fact, these findings are consistent internationally (Liu et al., 2000). Whether or not parents are still together, when parents argue—and especially when parents put their children in the middle of their arguments—children suffer. Interestingly, children and adolescents appear to function better in a nonconflicted divorced family than in a conflicted intact family (Hetherington &

Case Study: Devastated Darryl

In order to gain more "hands on" experience with developmental psychopathology, you are going to be presented with a case and then you will be asked to formulate a treatment plan. In doing so, you will be challenged to apply your learning in an active manner. This process is similar to what practicing clinicians must take part in when ever they begin seeing a new client.

Once you have developed your own ideas, you will be presented with suggestions from The Adolescent Psychotherapy Treatment Planner *(Jongsma, Peterson, & McInnis, 2000a), which is reprinted from a series called* PracticePlanners™ *that provides specific help to practicing clinicians. This case is meant to help you apply and integrate your learning. Hopefully, this exercise will also illustrate some of the actual techniques that are used by practicing clinicians.*

Darryl is a 13-year-old African American boy whose parents divorced more than two years ago. He is currently at risk for being held back in school (due to failure to complete assignments and poor performance on tests). Darryl has missed quite a few days of school in the past year because of illnesses that do not appear to have any medical reason (e.g., stomachaches and headaches). Darryl is intermittently withdrawn and belligerent with his mother. He appears sad quite often, but then appears quite angry at other times. Darryl has gotten into fights with neighborhood teenagers on two occasions recently. Darryl's mother is concerned that he has begun drinking alcohol, though Darryl denies having done so.

Before the divorce, Darryl had a close relationship with both his father and his mother. Although his parents argued a lot before the divorce, Darryl was able to talk with both parents frequently and he seemed to enjoy family dinners together in particular. Darryl and his father used to go running together and they both enjoyed watching professional basketball together. Immediately after Darryl's parents separated, his father withdrew from the family and spent less and less time with Darryl and his twin sister. Darryl has not had any contact with his father in the past year. He wonders if he caused his parents' divorce, since he was beginning to spend more time with his friends right before his parents separated.

Darryl, his mother, and his twin sister took part in the initial interview. Although his father was contacted and invited to be part of the treatment, he declined. During the interview, Darryl appeared sad and upset, especially when talking about his father. He did, however, brighten up when talking about his maternal grandfather, with whom he has a good relationship. Darryl reported that he had some good friends, but that he had begun "hanging out" with other teenagers who tended to get in trouble. Darryl developed good rapport with you, but appeared to want to seem older than his age. For example, when speaking of the possibility of girlfriends, he used phrases that might be spoken by a 17-year-old boy rather than a 13-year-old boy.

Darryl's medical history and developmental milestones were all within the normal range. He and his father had been in a car accident when he was a toddler, but he did not receive any major injuries (largely due to the high-quality car seat that his father had purchased).

Treatment Plan

Based on what you have learned from this textbook so far, try to write a treatment plan that would address Darryl and his family's concerns. Make sure to include behavioral definitions, long-term goals, short-term objectives, and therapeutic interventions. After you have written out your treatment plan, turn to the next section to review what is suggested in *The Adolescent Psychotherapy Treatment Planner* (Jongsma et al., 2000a).

Behavioral Definitions

1. _____
2. _____
3. _____
4. _____
5. _____
6. _____
7. _____
8. _____
9. _____
10. _____

Long-Term Goals

1. _____
2. _____
3. _____
4. _____
5. _____
6. _____
7. _____
8. _____
9. _____
10. _____

Short-Term Objectives

1. _____
2. _____
3. _____
4. _____
5. _____
6. _____
7. _____
8. _____
9. _____
10. _____

Therapeutic Interventions

1. _____
2. _____
3. _____
4. _____
5. _____
6. _____
7. _____
8. _____
9. _____
10. _____

From *The Child Psychotherapy Treatment Planner*—Jongsma, Peterson, and McInnis (2000a)

(continued)

Case Study: Devastated Darryl *(continued)*

DIVORCE REACTION

BEHAVIORAL DEFINITIONS

1. Infrequent contact or loss of contact with a parental figure due to separation or divorce.
2. Loss of contact with a positive support network due to a geographic move.
3. Feelings of guilt accompanied by the unreasonable belief of having behaved in some manner to cause his/her parent's divorce and/or failed to prevent the divorce from occurring.
4. Strong feelings of grief and sadness combined with feelings of low self-worth, lack of confidence, social withdrawal, and loss of interest in activities that normally bring pleasure.
5. Intense emotional outbursts (e.g., crying, yelling, swearing) and sudden shifts in mood due to significant change in the family system.
6. Marked increase in frequency and severity of acting-out, oppositional, and aggressive behaviors since the onset of the parents' marital problems, separation, or divorce.
7. Significant decline in school performance and lack of interest or motivation in school-related activities.
8. Excessive use of alcohol and drugs as a maladaptive coping mechanism to ward off painful emotions surrounding separation or divorce.
9. Pattern of engaging in sexually promiscuous or seductive behaviors to compensate for the loss of security or support within the family system.
10. Pseudomaturity as manifested by denying or suppressing painful emotions about divorce and often assuming parental roles or responsibilities.
11. Numerous psychosomatic complaints in response to anticipated separations, stress, or frustration.

LONG-TERM GOALS

1. Accept the parents' separation or divorce with consequent understanding and control of feelings and behavior.
2. Establish and/or maintain secure, trusting relationships with the parents.
3. Create a strong, supportive social network outside of the immediate family to offset the loss of affection, approval, or support from within the family.
4. Eliminate feelings of guilt and statements that reflect self-blame for the parents' divorce.
5. Elevate and stabilize mood.
6. Refrain from using drugs or alcohol and develop healthy coping mechanisms to effectively deal with changes in the family system.
7. Cease maladaptive pattern of engaging in sexually promiscuous or seductive behaviors to meet needs for affection, affiliation, and acceptance.
8. Parents establish and maintain a consistent, yet flexible, visitation arrangement that meets the client's emotional needs.
9. Parents establish and maintain appropriate parent-child boundaries in discipline and assignment of responsibilities.
10. Parents consistently demonstrate mutual respect for one another, especially in front of the children.

SHORT-TERM OBJECTIVES

1. Identify and express feelings related to the parents' separation or divorce.
2. Tell the story of the parents' separation or divorce.
3. Describe how the parents' separation or divorce has impacted personal and family life.
4. Express thoughts and feelings within the family system regarding parental separation or divorce.
5. Parents demonstrate understanding and empathy for how the divorce has impacted the client's life.
6. Recognize and affirm self as not being responsible for the parents' separation or divorce.
7. Parents verbalize an acceptance of responsibility for the dissolution of the marriage.

THERAPEUTIC INTERVENTIONS

1. Actively build the level of trust with the client in individual sessions through consistent eye contact, active listening, unconditional positive regard, and warm acceptance to improve his/her ability to identify and express feelings connected to the parents' separation or divorce.
2. Explore, encourage, and support the client in verbally expressing and clarifying his/her feelings associated with the separation or divorce.
3. Develop a timeline where the client records significant developments that have positively or negatively impacted his/her personal and family life, both before and after the divorce. Allow the client to verbalize his/her feelings about the divorce and subsequent changes in the family system.

(continued)

Case Study: Devastated Darryl *(continued)*

8. Recognize and verbally acknowledge that the parents will not be reuniting in the future and that he/she cannot bring the parents back together.

9. Identify positive and negative aspects of the parents' separation or divorce.

10. Identify and verbalize unmet needs to the parents.

11. Reduce the frequency and severity of angry, depressed, and anxious moods.

12. Decrease the frequency and intensity of emotional outbursts that occur in response to changes in the family or around periods of transfer from one parent's home to another.

13. Express feelings of anger about the parents' separation or divorce through controlled, respectful verbalizations and healthy physical outlets.

14. Reduce the frequency and severity of acting-out, oppositional, and aggressive behaviors.

15. Parents establish appropriate boundaries and follow through with consequences for acting-out, oppositional, or aggressive behaviors.

16. Parents verbally recognize how their guilt and failure to follow through with limits contributes to client's acting-out or aggressive behaviors.

17. Complete school and homework assignments on a regular basis.

18. Decrease the frequency of somatic complaints.

19. Parents assign an appropriate amount of household responsibilities or tasks to the client and siblings.

20. Noncustodial parent verbally recognizes his/her pattern of overindulgence and begins to set limits on money and/or time spent in leisure or recreational activities.

21. Noncustodial parent begins to assign household responsibilities and/or require the client to complete homework during visits.

22. Reduce the frequency of immature and irresponsible behaviors.

23. Parents cease making unnecessary, hostile, or overly critical remarks about the other parent in the presence of the children.

24. Parents recognize and agree to cease the pattern of soliciting information about and/or sending messages to the other parent through the children.

25. The disengaged or uninvolved parent follows through with recommendations to spend greater quality time with the client.

4. Use the empty chair technique to help the client express mixed emotions he/she feels toward both parents about the separation or divorce.

5. Ask the client to keep a journal where he/she records experiences or situations that evoke strong emotions pertaining to the divorce. Share the journal in therapy sessions.

6. Assist the client in developing a list of questions about the parents' divorce, then finding possible answers for each question.

7. Hold family therapy sessions to allow the client and siblings to express feelings about the separation or divorce in the presence of the parents.

8. Encourage the parents to provide opportunities at home (e.g., family meetings) to allow the client and siblings to express their feelings about the separation or divorce and subsequent changes in the family system.

9. Explore the factors contributing to the client's feelings of guilt and self-blame about the parents' separation or divorce.

10. Assist the client in realizing that his/her negative behaviors did not cause the parents' divorce to occur and that he/she does not have the power or control to bring the parents back together.

11. Conduct a family therapy session where the parents affirm that the client and siblings are not responsible for the separation or divorce.

12. Challenge and confront statements by the parents that place blame or responsibility for the separation or divorce on the client or siblings.

13. Assign the client the homework of listing both positive and negative aspects of the parents' divorce. Process the list in the following session and allow the client to express different emotions.

14. Empower the client by reinforcing his/her ability to cope with the divorce and make healthy adjustments.

15. Provide support for the client in session to allow for expression of sad, depressed, or anxious feelings.

16. Direct the parents to spend 10 to 15 minutes of one-on-one time with the client and siblings on a regular or daily basis.

17. Assist the client in identifying activities (e.g., making popcorn and watching movies, playing a board game) that help the client make the transition from one parent's home to another without exhibiting excessive emotional distress, fighting, or arguing.

18. Assist the client in making a connection between underlying painful emotions about the divorce and angry outbursts or aggressive behaviors.

19. Identify appropriate and inappropriate ways to express anger about the parents' separation or divorce or changes in the family.

BOX *7.2*

CHILDREN OF DIVORCE TELL IT LIKE IT IS

The following are excerpts from Dr. David Royko's (1999) *Voices of the Children of Divorce*:

Sally, 6 *I was two. I don't really remember it, but I feel bad and sad, because you really like your dad and mom. So I usually just cry because I get so sad and mad because my mom and dad are divorced. (p. 196)*

Arnie, 13 *The arguments were hard to listen to in the evening time or morning time. In the daytime they were just skirmishes, nighttime they were full-blown wars. Yell, yell, yell, yell, yell. About bills, financial disagreements, taxes, all that lovely stuff. (p. 14)*

Nicole, 19 *I hated being in the middle. They still say things to me now, seven years after the divorce, about the other parent, and they expect me to laugh at a bad joke about them or to say something bad about them or to agree with something bad that's said about them. That's just a horrible thing to make somebody do, because they both know that I still care a lot about both of them. (p. 49)*

Leroy, 15 *When your mother and father split up, I don't care what age you are, if you love them at all, it hurts. It hurts bad. (p. 29)*

Ted, 12 *My friend's parents are getting a divorce. I told him, "It won't be fun. You won't like it. But after a while you'll get used to it." (p. 189)*

Tom, 12 *When I was little, I thought the divorce was my fault, but it's sort of out of my mind. I don't remember. It's probably just the guilt of it. (p. 48)*

Serena, 11 *If I had three wishes, I'd ask for a thousand more wishes. Then I'd make every single wish be that my mom and dad would get back together and stay together forever—plus one wish for my dog, that he didn't die. (p. 201)*

Al, 16 *My parents get along a lot better now than before Dad moved out and they got divorced. He'll come over for dinner and stuff. (p. 40)*

SOURCE: Royko (1999).

BOX *7.3*

WHY IS THE RESEARCH ASSISTANT YELLING AT DADDY?

Given that children cannot be randomly assigned to experience interparental conflict or not, how can researchers argue that interparental conflict "causes" emotional/behavioral problems in children? Some creative research designs have been developed to help answer this question.

Dr. E. Mark Cummings has headed one research team that explores children's exposure to conflict and anger with an experimental design. Cummings and his colleagues (reviewed in Cummings & Davies, 1994) have run studies that expose children to background anger. A typical design is to bring a child into the research room and have him or her take part in games or activities. After the researcher leaves the room, two people (sometimes the researcher and a stranger, sometimes the researcher and the child's parent, sometimes the child's parent and a stranger) get into a heated argument in the hallway. Sometimes the argument occurs in the room with the child. In other conditions, the two people engage in loud but congenial conversations (to serve as a

control group condition). Members of the research team observe the child's reactions. Overall, children tend to become quite distressed and agitated when exposed to background anger. In many instances, children (especially boys) show signs of aggressiveness after exposure to background anger.

This design allows researchers to take a close look at children's reactions to anger and conflict without exposing children to excessive amounts of interparental conflict in the home. The investigators using this design have also found that some type of reconciliation or rapprochement observed by the child will help negate the effects of background anger. For example, if the research assistant who yelled at the parent later apologizes and explains that he or she is under stress, children's functioning tends to return to what it was before the angry interchange. Children and parents in these studies are debriefed about their participation, and there have been no negative long-term effects.

SOURCE: Cummings & Davies (1994).

SIPRESS

Stanley-Hagan, 1999; Kelly, 2000). If, however, the conflict continues both before and after a divorce, then children in divorced homes tend to fare worse than those in intact families (Amato, 2001; Hetherington & Stanley-Hagan, 1999). Box 7.2 offers some children's perspectives on divorce and interparental conflict.

The issue of interparental conflict (and other psychosocial factors) is integral to the understanding of the connections between family constellation and child functioning. Early research suggested that children from divorced families were more maladjusted and remained more maladjusted than children in two-parent homes (reviewed by Hetherington et al., 1998). More recently, however, studies have found overwhelming evidence that family constellation is not the most crucial variable in children's functioning (Kelly, 2000). There are often greater numbers of problems found in children in single-parent families and in stepfamilies, but when factors such as interparental conflict, family adversity, and poor socioeconomic status are considered, the meaningfulness of family constellation disappears (Clarke-Stewart, Vandell, McCartney, Owen, & Booth, 2000; Nicholson, Fergusson, & Horwood, 1999). Thus, in the exploration of functioning, children's exposure to interparental conflict is more important than whether they live with one or two parents. Box 7.3 describes a study designed to explore how children are affected by exposure to conflict.

Interparental conflict has been linked to a number of problems in children and adolescents, including externalizing problems, internalizing problems, social problems, and interpersonal problems (Cummings, 1997; Kelly, 2000). Evidence also suggests that interparental conflict

puts children more at risk for externalizing problems than for internalizing problems (Kelly, 2000). Although some studies find age differences and gender differences regarding the impact of interparental conflict, most researchers find that interparental conflict negatively affects children of all ages and of both genders (Hetherington & Stanley-Hagan, 1999; Cummings & Davies, 1994).

One of the most damaging types of interparental conflict appears to be **triangulation**, which occurs when the child is put in the middle of the parents' arguments (Margolin, Gordis, & John, 2001). In addition, conflict that remains unresolved or that is resolved away from the child appears to be quite detrimental to children and adolescents (Cummings & Davies, 1994). Parents can help their children deal with conflict by allowing children to understand how the conflict was resolved (e.g., that the parents compromised on their disagreement or that they discussed the issue and then reached a mutually satisfying conclusion). Obviously, not all conflict is meant to be discussed in front of children, but it is important to model good conflict-resolution skills for children so that they understand how to deal with their own anger and conflict in other situations (Cummings & Davies, 1994).

Note that a number of programs have been developed to help prevent the difficulties that are associated with interparental conflict (e.g., Wolchick et al., 2000). In addition, preventive mediation rather than litigation during divorce and child custody resolution appears to be associated with decreased interparental conflict and better outcomes for children 12 years after parental divorce (Emery, Laumann-Billings, Waldron, Sbarra, & Dillon,

2001). Such prevention programs appear to be promising for lowering the risk of children's maladjustment due to interparental conflict and divorce.

My mother was with violent men. A series of them. Some of my earliest memories are of my father beating his mule and the mule running away one day. I think there was something in me that thought, he's going to get mad enough, he's going to do the same thing to me. So when he was whipping me with his razor strap, I must have been absolutely terrified.

—David Ray (Rhodes & Rhodes, 1996, p. 66)

CHILD PHYSICAL ABUSE

Physical abuse of children consists of aversive or inappropriate control strategies, including beatings and consistent inappropriate use of physical coercion. Parents often do not consider the physical aggression they display toward their children to be abusive, even when their behavior is severe enough to be labeled as such by professionals and by state law (Mahoney, Donnelly, Lewis, & Maynard, 2000). In many states, the indicator of physical abuse is a mark left on the child (e.g., from the child's being hit by a hand or a belt, or being burned intentionally).

It is estimated that between 5% and 26% of children and adolescents in the United States and similar countries are victims of physical abuse each year (Emery & Laumann-Billings, 1998; Flisher et al., 1997). This estimate represents a wide range due to the difficulty in identifying child abuse, the secretive nature of this problem, and the difficulty in proving allegations of child abuse. Although both boys and girls are equally at risk for physical abuse, it appears that age and gender interact when epidemiological patterns are considered. Boys under the age of 12 and girls over the age of 12 are the children at highest risk for physical abuse (Azar, Ferraro, & Breton, 1998). Children who witness the abuse of one parent by another (most often, children who see their father physically abusing their mother) are significantly more likely to be physically abused than children who do not witness such abuse (Emery & Laumann-Billings, 1998). Also, children with physical and intellectual disabilities are more likely to be physically abused than nondisabled children (Westcott & Jones, 1999). Children in poorer communities are more at risk for child physical abuse, but this connection appears to be more true for Caucasian American families than for African American families (Korbin, Coulton, Chard, Platt-Houston, & Su, 1998). The number of children who are abused may vary from year to year, but the totals are staggering. Comparable concerns are evident in many other countries, such as India (Hunter, Jain, Sadowski, & Sanhueze, 2000) and countries within Eastern Europe (Sicher et al., 2000).

Child physical abuse is thought to put children at risk for a whole host of emotional/behavioral problems. In general, it is associated with childhood depression, conduct disorder, oppositional defiant disorder, agoraphobia, overanxious disorder, generalized anxiety disorder, poor

When children are abused physically, the wounds can be both physical and psychological.

social competence, and global impairment (Flisher et al., 1997; Shonk & Cicchetti, 2001). Physical abuse is also associated with bullying, victimization, and rejection by peers (Bolger & Patterson, 2001; Shields & Cicchetti, 2001). Approximately one-fourth to one-half or more of children who experience physical abuse go on to experience post-traumatic stress disorder (PTSD; reviewed in Emery & Laumann-Billings, 1998). Severe, long-lasting physical abuse puts children at even greater risk for PTSD (Emery & Laumann-Billings, 1998). The effects of child physical abuse can sometimes continue into adulthood if the problems are not dealt with in childhood (Brown, Cohen, Johnson, & Smailes, 1999; Stevenson, 1999). Approximately one-third of physically abused children go on to abuse their own children (Kaufman & Zigler, 1987). Table 7.1 lists some of the difficulties associated with abusive parents and their abused children.

There are noticeable connections between physical abuse and brain development in children. Specifically, brain development is hampered in physically abused

Case Study: Joe and Erin, Physically Abused Children

Erin was 10 years old and her brother, Joe, was 12. They attended the same school and were well-behaved children. Erin was a bit on the quiet side, and Joe was involved in many activities. Both children showed up to school with bruises and scratches on a regular basis, but the teachers assumed that they were just lively children who received injuries in the course of their activities. Erin and Joe's parents took part in school functions and seemed to be conscientious parents.

Concern was raised, however, when Erin showed up at school with a black eye. She told one of her friends that her father had hit her, but to the teacher, Erin said that she had been hit by a baseball her brother had thrown. During the interview, the therapist noted that Erin had a number of marks on her body that appeared to be cigarette burns. When asked about the marks, Erin stated that they were mosquito bites. When Joe was questioned about Erin's black eye, he reported that she had run into the bedroom door by accident. Neither child reported any difficulties with their parents. Given the conflicting stories, the seriousness of the burns, and the multitude of bruises, the child protective services removed the children from the home. Shortly thereafter, the children were allowed to return to the home if the father moved out. The children also began intensive therapy to deal with the abuse.

Over the course of therapy, the children finally admitted that they had received a great deal of "punishment" from their father. It began when their parents argued over the lack of money in the house. The mother found a job, which required that she work from 3:00 P.M. to midnight. After the mother began working, the father took care of the children when he returned home from work in the afternoon. The father grew more and more angry about having to watch the children. He would scold them if they did not have dinner ready when he got home, and he would yell at them when they did not finish their homework. More recently, he spanked them for what he perceived were their misbehaviors. His anger eventually became more extreme, and he hit Joe and threw Erin against a wall. One day when Erin had not finished her math homework, her father administered a cigarette burn for each math problem that was left unfinished. The black eye that was noticed by the teachers occurred after Erin had dropped something in the kitchen and her father hit her in the eye with his fist.

The children never wanted to report their father's behavior because they did not want to get him in trouble. They both felt that they deserved the "punishment" to some extent because they misbehaved.

When the parents were interviewed by the same therapist, the father finally admitted to the mother that the abuse allegations were true. The mother was shocked and upset. She had assumed that the allegations were false and that there had been a terrible misunderstanding. The father broke down and cried, saying that he did not want to lose his family but that he had been stressed about financial issues and took his stress out on the children. For approximately one month, the mother stated that she would divorce the father because of the abuse. She felt immense anger toward him, and she felt a great deal of guilt for leaving her children with their father in the afternoons and evenings due to her work schedule. Both parents began attending group therapy, which included other abusive parents and their nonabusing partners. The father began making strides in his anger control and in attempting to communicate his concerns appropriately. The mother decided to work on saving the marriage and to work toward allowing her husband back in the home with the children.

The children continued to work with the therapist on issues of betrayal and anger management. Joe had become more and more angry at his father and had begun fighting at school. Over the course of therapy, the children seemed ready to be reunited with their father; at the same time, the father had made significant improvements in group therapy. After the family was reunited, family therapy sessions were continued for six months. Rules were established about how to punish the children's behavior appropriately and how to reward them for good behavior. One year after the case was closed, the child protective services agency did a follow-up to verify that the physical abuse had not reappeared. Both children were well adjusted, and neither reported any abusive incidents. The mother had gone back to college to work on a teaching certificate, and the father had received a promotion in the bank in which he worked.

SOURCE: R. K. Morgan (1999).

TABLE 7.1   **Parent Problem Areas and Child Problem Areas Related to Abuse**

	Parent problem area	Child problem area
Infancy and toddlerhood	Insensitive and noncontingent responsiveness	Attachment problems
	Poor ability to tolerate stresses such as prolonged crying, sleep problems, and feeding difficulties	Health-related difficulties, such as under-nourishment, low birth weight, prematurity, and physical trauma (e.g., shaken baby syndrome)
	Failures to engage in behaviors that foster language, social, and emotional development	Lags in toilet training, motor skills, speech, and language development, and socialization
	Lack of attention to safety issues and health needs/knowledge deficit	Anxiety
	Expectancies that infants and toddlers are able to perspective take, are capable of intentional provoking behavior, and can provide the parent comfort	Inappropriate sexual behavior
	Deficits in skills to comfort/soothe child, utilize distraction, redirection, and environmental management as a means to reduce aversive child behavior and manage child behavior	Nightmares
Early and middle childhood	Inconsistent and indiscriminant use of discipline	High levels of noncompliance
	Overuse of physical strategies to manage behavior	Developmental and academic problems
	Lack of use of optimal socialization strategies (such as explanation)	Social cognitive difficulties (e.g., expression and recognition of affect; perspective-taking; empathy, social problem-solving)
	General lack of interaction	Heightened aggression
	A negative bias in overlabeling child behavior as evidence of misbehavior (even developmentally appropriate behavior)	Poor social skills
	Poor ability to deal with stress of self-regulation problems in children (e.g., noncompliance)	Conduct problems; firesetting
	Unrealistic expectations of children's perspective-taking abilities, self-regulation skill, ability to place parental needs ahead of their own, to engage in self-care, and other household duties	Social withdrawal
		Cognitive delays such as greater distractibility
		Inconsistent school attendance
		Fatigue
		Low self-esteem
		Difficulty trusting others
		Trauma/stress-related symptoms (regressed behavior)
		Poor conflict resolution skills
Adolescence	Failure to use age-appropriate child management strategies	Overrepresented among runaways, delinquents, and truants
	Excessive attempts to control	Poor academic performance
	Decreased ability to tolerate teenagers' moves toward autonomy	Poor stress/anger management skills
	Poor ability to deal with emerging sexuality	Social skill and peer interaction problems
	Unrealistic expectations of taking on adult responsibilities	Conduct problems
		Depression, suicidal, or self-injurious behavior

SOURCE: Azar et al. (1998).

children even when there are not direct head injuries (Glaser, 2000). New technology, such as the use of magnetic resonance imaging (MRI) has helped professionals identify physical abuse in children that previously might have gone undetected (Chabrol, Decarie, & Fortin, 1999).

Frequently, children are exposed to physical abuse in the context of other risk factors, which makes them even more vulnerable to the development of problems. For example, children who were physically abused and who also had a parent diagnosed with schizophrenia were even more likely to show heightened levels of aggression and delinquency than those children exposed to either physical abuse or a schizophrenic parent alone (Walker, Downey, & Bergman, 1989). Children who were physically abused and who were exposed to violence within the community were more at risk for the development of emotional/behavioral problems (Lynch & Cicchetti, 1998).

In a study with direct ramifications for prevention of child physical abuse, physically abusive fathers were found to have lower rates of emotional support when compared with their nonabusing peers (Coohey, 2000). Specifically, abusive fathers were disengaged from their social network and their kin. It may be that friends, in-laws, and other kin discourage fathers' abusive behavior toward children (Coohey, 2000). These findings might help design prevention programs that would engage fathers in healthy social networks. Although there are more treatment programs for the effects of physical abuse than there are prevention programs, some outstanding prevention programs have been implemented both within the United States (Cicchetti, Toth, & Rogosch, 2000; Fisher, Gunnar, Chamberlain, & Reid, 2000) and in other countries (Sicher et al., 2000).

Overall, physical abuse often leads to devastating consequences for children and adolescents. Even sadder is the fact that many children who are physically abused are also at risk for sexual abuse.

CHILD SEXUAL ABUSE

Child sexual abuse has many different and complex definitions, but the majority of definitions focus on sexual exploitation due to the inequality of power between the perpetrator and the child (Haugaard, 2000). Sexual abuse can include anal, oral, genital, or breast contact, and can also include exposing children to sexual behaviors or sexual material that are not appropriate to the age of the child. Although official estimates of the prevalence of childhood sexual abuse average around 2%, retrospective studies of adolescents who report sexual abuse during childhood suggest that approximately 12.8% of girls and 4.3% of boys have been sexually abused (MacMillan et al., 1997). These figures are considered underestimates, given the hesitation that many children and adolescents have about reporting such abuse. Even so, these figures show that girls are at significantly greater risk for sexual abuse than are boys. For sexual abuse in infancy, the ratio of girls to boys is 2:1; in school-aged children, 3:1; and in adolescence, approximately 6:1 (Wekerle & Wolfe, 1996). Children who live with a mother who was physically abused are 12 to 14 times more likely to be sexually abused than children whose mother was not physically abused (Emery & Laumann-Billings, 1998). Girls who live with a stepfather (or other unrelated male) and who live with their substance-abusing mother with a history of sexual abuse are at particularly great risk for being abused sexually (McCloskey & Bailey, 2000). Children with physical or cognitive disabilities are also at greater risk for sexual abuse, and in such cases the majority of children appear to be acquainted with the perpetrator (Keating, 1998). Child sexual abuse appears to occur in all socioeconomic classes and racial/ethnic groups to an equal degree (Azar et al., 1998).

Like child physical abuse, child sexual abuse tends to have devastating consequences for its survivors. The apparent consequences of childhood sexual abuse, however, vary according to a number of personal, familial, and abuse-related factors (Saywitz, Mannarino, Berliner, & Cohen, 2000; also, see Chapter 3 regarding a controversy about sexual abuse research). The risk for psychological maladjustment after the sexual abuse increases when any of the following factors occur (reviewed by Spaccarelli, 1994):

- The abuse is perpetrated by a father or father figure.
- There is a great degree of sexual contact, including intercourse.
- The abuse is perpetrated over a long time.
- Coercion, physical force, and threats are used to perpetrate the abuse.
- Lack of support, disbelief, and victim-blaming follow the child's reporting of the abuse.

The effects of child sexual abuse are variable. While some children never show any adverse effects, the majority show everything from moderate to extreme negative sequelae. Children who have poor coping strategies in relation to the sexual abuse (such as becoming self-destructive or becoming avoidant) are more likely to experience long-term maladjustment into adulthood than

Case Study: Martha, Sexual Abuse Survivor

At the age of 16, Martha was experiencing severe abdominal pain and pain in her genital area. In addition, she experienced severe anxiety. After a thorough medical evaluation that indicated no known cause for the pain, Martha was referred to a psychiatric clinic to determine whether the pain was related to any emotional distress. Martha had a sister who was one year younger and a brother who was two years older.

Martha and her mother readily admitted that Martha had been sexually abused by her father between the ages of 10 and 13. At that time, the father left the house because he did not want to be "bothered" by the family any longer. When the sexual abuse first began, Martha reported it to her mother, who felt helpless to change her husband's behavior and who did not see that there was anything all that harmful about the sexual involvement. Although Martha begged her mother to stop her father from sexually abusing her and her sister, the mother made no attempts do so. After the father moved out the house, Martha did not have any significant contact with him, so she did not appear to be in danger of continued sexual abuse. The father was alco-

holic and, after leaving the family, was arrested a number of times for drunk and disorderly conduct.

Although Martha did not show any overt emotional/behavioral troubles in school, she had never been a stellar student and was failing all her classes by the time she was 16. She had a great many friends, with whom she sometimes got into trouble (e.g., once the police were called when Martha and her sister were having a party when their mother was at work). Martha reported that she began smoking at the age of 14 to "settle her nerves," but she denied any use of alcohol or drugs. Martha's pelvic and abdominal pain periodically became intense, but the symptoms would disappear when she became involved in activities or when she got a phone call from a friend.

After a psychological evaluation, Martha was referred for therapy due to her unresolved issues related to the sexual abuse and due to her severe anger at her father. Although both Martha and her mother appeared receptive to Martha's therapy, they never made an appointment for therapy or any other intervention.

SOURCE: Leon (1990).

---

are children who show adaptive coping techniques (Merrill, Thomsen, Sinclair, Gold, & Milner, 2001). One retrospective study of childhood sexual abuse suggested that history of sexual abuse was more predictive of suicidality in adults than was a current diagnosis of depression (Read, Agar, Barker-Collo, Davies, & Moskowitz, 2001). There is relatively clear evidence that women who report a history of sexual abuse are more likely than nonabused women to experience more relationship problems and more sexual difficulties (Rumstein-McKean & Hunsley, 2001).

There are a number of ways of conceptualizing the negative impact of childhood sexual abuse. The traumagenic dynamics model highlights four primary factors that relate to adverse outcomes in children after sexual abuse (Finkelhor, 1988):

- Exposure to age-inappropriate sexual behaviors and traumatic sexualization.

- Feelings of powerlessness related to the child's inability to prevent the abuse.

- Other individuals stigmatizing the child or otherwise conveying negative feelings about the child because of the sexual abuse.

- Feelings of betrayal when a trusted individual perpetrates abuse, or feelings of betrayal at the lack of being protected from the sexual abuse.

A more recent integrative approach is the transactional model. Figure 7.1 shows a number of complex factors from this model that lead to the possibility of psychological symptoms related to child sexual abuse. As the figure shows, there are bidirectional influences between abuse stress (such as the actual abuse and the response to disclosure of abuse), coping strategies (how the child tries to cope with the sexual abuse), cognitive appraisals (how the child thinks about the sexual abuse), and psychological symptoms. In addition, support resources (such as family or individual supports for the child) and other moderating factors (such as age, gender, and personality variables) can influence both children's coping strategies and cognitive appraisals (Spaccarelli, 1994). This model indicates the complexity of trying to determine the impact of childhood sexual abuse.

Overall, childhood sexual abuse has been linked to PTSD, anxiety, depression, sexual difficulties or sexual acting out, teenage pregnancy, and externalizing problems (Rumstein-McKean & Hunsley, 2001). For the majority of children and their loved ones, childhood sexual abuse is a devastating stressor with which to deal. Effective treatments have been developed for post-traumatic symptoms related to childhood sexual abuse (N. J. King et al., 2000). Given the often significant adverse effects of childhood abuse and maltreatment, a number of prevention programs have also been developed (see Box 7.4).

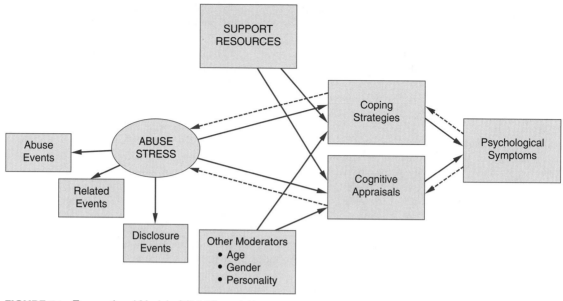

FIGURE 7.1 Transactional Model of Child Sexual Abuse
Source: Spaccarelli (1994).

The wound caused by words is worse than the wound of bodies.

—Proverb of Africa

CHILD PSYCHOLOGICAL MALTREATMENT

Psychological or emotional maltreatment of children has received less attention in the research literature than either physical or sexual abuse. Largely due to the difficulty of defining psychological maltreatment and the difficulty of identifying psychologically maltreated children, this topic has remained unexplored until relatively recently. Psychological abuse can be defined as a pattern of acts or verbalizations that damage the child psychologically with regard to cognitive, affective, behavioral, or physical functioning of the child. The following are examples of psychological abuse (Brassard, Germain, & Hart, 1987):

- Rejection—when children are actively rejected or made scapegoats in the family and when children are given constant negative evaluations about themselves.

- Terrorizing—when children are threatened, inordinately teased, or (depending on age) are intentionally terrified by adults around them.

- Isolating—when children are kept from socializing with others, including being locked in a closet or a basement for long periods of time.

- Degrading—when children are called names and belittled constantly, even when they have accomplished something worthwhile.

- Missocializing—when children are encouraged to break the law, such as stealing for their parents, or when children are encouraged to engage in age-inappropriate behaviors such as drinking, smoking, using drugs, or having sex.

Although some of these comments or behaviors may be evidenced by even the most competent parents, psychological abuse is identified when there is a consistent pattern of these types of comments and behaviors. As with other types of abuse, psychological maltreatment is associated with a range of problems in children, including internalizing problems, externalizing problems, and low self-esteem (Azar et al., 1998). Psychological maltreatment is difficult to identify, given the hidden nature of the trauma and the sometimes ambiguous definitions (Hamarman & Bernet, 2000). Clinicians, teachers, and other caring adults can be on the alert for psychological abuse by listening to how parents talk to their children and by noticing when children make particularly self-disparaging comments that might represent what they have heard from their parents (Azar et al., 1998).

BOX 7.4

PREVENTION OF CHILD SEXUAL ABUSE

Given the devastation of child sexual abuse, there have been efforts across the nation to institute programs to prevent its occurrence. Many of the programs based in preschools and in elementary schools focus on informing children about "good" touch and "bad" touch, empowering children to say no to taking part in activities that make them uncomfortable, and encouraging them to tell a trusted adult about any attempted or actual abuse. These types of programs have been successful with regard to information retention, measured by giving children an informational test before and after the training (Davis & Gidycz, 2000; Finkelhor, Asdigian, & Dziuba-Leatherman, 1995; Kolko, 1988; Liang, Bogat, & McGrath, 1993). The most effective programs are long-term ones that use behavioral skills training (Davis & Gidycz, 2000). In addition, these programs usually train teachers to notice the possible signs of child sexual abuse and inform teachers about how to report occurrences of child sexual abuse (Liang et al., 1993).

Prevention programs, however, are not without their drawbacks. Some people have criticized the nationwide focus on teaching children how to protect themselves while little is done to prevent adults from actually abusing children. The following are a few of their concerns (Conte, Wolf, & Smith, 1989; Melton, 1992; Pelcovitz, Adler, Kaplan, Packman, & Krieger, 1992; Renk, Liljequist, Steinberg, Bosco, & Phares, 2002; Trudell & Whatley, 1988):

- Putting the onus on children, rather than adults, to stop sexual abuse is inappropriate and may send the message that children can just say no to sexual abuse and make it stop.
- Surveys of sexual offenders suggest that even if a child does say no or in some other way is able to prevent his or her own sexual abuse, the offender will just find another target for the abuse.

- Prevention programs tend to focus on people outside the family as abusers, and few programs focus on the fact that the majority of harm (both physical abuse and sexual abuse) comes from within the family or from trusted friends of the family.

Some preventionists have suggested that, in addition to the school-based programs described above, more attention should be paid to actually preventing sexual offenders from wanting to offend. Many suggestions have been proposed, including early sex education to promote responsible sexuality that does not include power and domination (Renk et al., 2002; G. J. R. Williams, 1983) and disentangling the connections at the societal level (as evidenced in the media as well as in homes across the nation) between sex and power (Tutty, 1991). Interestingly, fathers who are highly involved in their child's life during infancy are much less likely to sexually abuse their child than fathers who are relatively uninvolved, so there has been a call to encourage responsible and involved fathering that could prevent the occurrence of sexual abuse within the family (Parker & Parker, 1986). In addition to these prevention strategies, there has also been increased focus on keeping sexual offenders and sexual predators away from children by either mandating further treatment or by reporting the offenders' whereabouts to the neighborhood and to the community (J. E. B. Myers, 1996).

Overall, the prevention of child sexual abuse is extraordinarily complex. There are no easy answers, yet it appears that multifaceted approaches that include many different levels of prevention (e.g., school-based programs with children, working with teachers to identify signs of sexual abuse, helping parents to understand how to recognize signs of abuse, responsible sexuality training at many grade levels, media messages about the inappropriateness of controlling a child through sexual domination) are most appropriate.

FAMILY DYSFUNCTION

In addition to parental functioning and abuse within the family, there are a number of other family factors that can put children and adolescents at risk for the development of psychopathology. Factors within the family that have been associated with the development of problems include high rates of hostility and competitiveness (McHale & Rasmussen, 1998); family-related and parent-related stress (Rudolph & Hammen, 1999); maladaptive family environment (Jacobson & Rowe, 1999); problematic family system (Dadds, 1995); parental negative affect

and negative control (Deater-Deckard, Fulker, & Plomin, 1999); negative expressed emotion (Wamboldt & Wamboldt, 2000); and maladaptive parenting style (Hoge, Andrews, & Leschied, 1996). Sometimes these factors are related to risk factors that have already been discussed (e.g., depressed parents may show more hostility toward their children than nondepressed parents). Thus, children are often exposed to multiple risk factors within the family environment.

Case Study: The D'Niale Family, Psychological and Emotional Abuse

The D'Niale family consists of a mother, father, a two-year-old boy (Sonny Jr.), a five-year-old boy (Joey), and an eight-year-old girl (Francine). The two older children are Mrs. D'Niale's children from previous relationships. The family was known to child protective service agents because of multiple generations of abuse and neglect. The family is Caucasian and lives in poverty.

At the time of the evaluation, Mrs. D'Niale showed signs of severe depression and had also shown inadequate parenting skills. Mr. D'Niale experienced alcohol dependency and often had alcohol-related seizures and periods of violence related to the alcohol dependency. In one violent episode, he pushed the refrigerator off the balcony after he ran out of beer. Luckily, no one was underneath the refrigerator when it hit the ground four stories below. Mr. D'Niale recently had been arrested for breaking and entering, and was awaiting sentencing. Both parents reported a great deal of interparental conflict. All three children show emotional/behavioral problems. The two-year-old, Sonny Jr., is very aggressive with everyone, including his siblings and parents. The five-year-old, Joey (who was physically abused as a child and who had witnessed his mother being beaten and raped when he was younger), was very quiet and withdrawn. The eight-year-old, Francine (who had been neglected for long periods of time when she was an infant and who had been physically abused by her mother), showed signs of conduct disorder. Francine had already been taken away from Mrs. D'Niale's custody and was living with her grandmother.

During the evaluation (for which Mr. D'Niale was noticeably absent), Mrs. D'Niale showed clear signs of psychological abuse toward her children. She constantly belittled her children and called them names. She referred to Joey as a sissy, a baby, and as stupid. She referred to Sonny Jr. (who had a soiled diaper during the entire four-hour interview) as "a stinker" and "my little shit." Mrs. D'Niale also used terrorizing with her children in an attempt to control them. For example, when Sonny Jr. dropped a glass of milk, Mrs. D'Niale replied, "Clean that up or I'll break your fingers." She also threatened to put Joey in a garbage can, to burn the children with her lit cigarette, and to break their bones. She reported that she forbids the children from playing with neighborhood children and she often refuses to let the children attend school.

Overall, this case illustrates clear psychological abuse in addition to patterns of physical abuse, neglect, and parental psychopathology. The children were referred for therapy to deal with the effects of the abuse, and the parents were offered numerous services to deal with their issues. Unfortunately, these types of complicated cases (especially when there are multiple generations of dysfunction) are difficult to treat without immense, multifaceted intervention services, which include individual therapy, family therapy, parent training, educational support, social service help with employment and financial issues, and possible medical interventions when needed.

SOURCE: Brassard, Hart, & Hardy (1991).

I used to like school a lot. Now since they got divorced, it's just okay. Really, I don't like anything that much anymore.

—Dexter, 13 years old (Royko, 1999, p. 197)

INADEQUATE EDUCATIONAL RESOURCES

Turning away from family-related risk factors, it is also important to acknowledge the risk factors related to the educational system and the larger community. There are a number of risk factors in the school system, including difficult transitions from elementary to middle school (Holmbeck & Shapera, 1999), lack of school connectedness (Jacobson & Rowe, 1999), and less than optimal school settings (Luthar, 1999).

In general, higher numbers of school transitions that children have to experience are associated with increased risk for emotional/behavioral problems (Felner, Ginter, & Primavera, 1982). The transition between elementary school and middle school seems to be particularly difficult for a great many adolescents, partly due to the many changes that this transition brings (e.g., having one

teacher in elementary school and having upward of six teachers in middle school; Felner et al., 1982). Higher educational levels tend to be associated with more complex school environments and more complex social systems, so adolescents must deal with a great deal of changes as they move from elementary school to middle school to high school (Holmbeck & Shapera, 1999).

School connectedness occurs when children feel that their teachers care about them, that the school is fair in its policies, that the school is a safe environment, and that they belong at the school. Lack of connectedness is associated with emotional/behavioral problems (Jacobson & Rowe, 1999). The direction of this association is not clear, given that distressed children could perceive low school connectedness because of possible cognitive distortions related to their level of distress. Regardless of the direction of this association, it appears that the less connected and the more marginalized children feel at school, the greater their risk for emotional/behavioral problems (Jacobson & Rowe, 1999).

School environments vary from dismal to optimal. Schools that provide a less-than-optimal environment for

BOX *7.5*

HELPING CHILDREN WITH SCHOOL TRANSITIONS

Because of the problems that often occur when children transition into middle school or high school, a number of prevention programs have been instituted to see if the structure of the school can help children negotiate these transitions more successfully. One such program is called the School Transitional Environment Program (STEP; Felner & Adan, 1988). This program has been applied to children who were at risk not only because of their school transition status but also because they were impoverished and of minority ethnic status, they received little support from their families or community, and they were entering puberty.

Through STEP, teachers and administrators were trained to help children with school transition. In addition, changes in the school environment were made to help children with the transition. Some of these changes included:

- Reorganizing the social system so that children had at least four classes with the same group of classmates.
- Assigning students to a homeroom that served as a solid base from which students could learn about the rest of the school and where the students could be monitored and helped by the homeroom teacher.

- Helping teachers develop teamwork mentalities to help students and to help each other give students the emotional and academic support they needed.

Overall, STEP was very effective. Children who were involved in it showed lower absentee rates, were less likely to drop out of school, and had better academic achievement than children who were not exposed to it.

Note that STEP was administered to children in selected schools based on the overall risk factors for most children. As noted in Chapter 6, this type of prevention program is called secondary prevention. Primary prevention programs would target general populations of children whether or not they are risk for the development of problems, and tertiary prevention programs would select only those children who have already evidenced problems. Overall, STEP is a nice example of a secondary prevention program that can be administered to children to help prevent problems that typically occur due to transition into middle school.

SOURCE: Felner & Adan (1988).

students are associated with a host of risk factors for children's emotional/behavioral problems. For example, greater class size is associated with poorer academic achievement and decreased functioning (Children's Defense Fund, 1999). Poor schools tend to be overcrowded, have a low teacher–student ratio, have few resources for basic educational opportunities as well as enrichment opportunities, and have teachers and administrators with low expectations of academic success for their students (Luthar, 1999). All of these factors are linked to poor academic achievement and high rates of emotional/behavioral problems in children and adolescents (Luthar, 1999). It appears that children and adolescents who are exposed to poor educational environments are often also those who are exposed to poverty, low socioeconomic status, and violence within their communities.

POVERTY AND LOW SOCIOECONOMIC STATUS

In general, low socioeconomic status and poverty have been linked to greater rates of emotional/behavioral rates in children and adolescents (J. G. Johnson, Cohen,

Dohrenwend, Link, & Brook, 1999; Luthar, 1999; Rutter, 1999a; Samaan, 2000). Figure 7.2 indicates that younger children and adolescents at the most severe levels of poverty have higher rates of emotional/behavioral problems than other youth (Urban Institute, 1999b).

Poverty, however, is not a distinct factor as much as it is a constellation of factors that co-occur when there is little money or few other resources within the family. Teenage mothers are more likely than older mothers to live within poverty and to raise their children in poverty (Luthar, 1999). Households headed by single parents, most often single mothers, are overrepresented in low socioeconomic neighborhoods (Luthar, 1999). Homelessness (Buckner, Bassuk, Weinreb, & Brooks, 1999; Embry, VanderStoep, Evens, Ryan, & Pollock, 2000) and family instability (Ackerman, Kogos, Youngstrom, Schoff, & Izard, 1999) are also associated with living in poverty. Children from ethnic and racial minority groups are overrepresented in impoverished neighborhoods (Luthar, 1999).

As mentioned in Chapter 1, the rates of children living in poverty in the United States and other countries are staggering (see Box 7.6). Around 22% of all children under the age of 18 in the United States live at or below

Case Study: Oswald, A Boy From a Disadvantaged Environment

Oswald is an 11-year-old, African American boy living in public housing with his 36-year-old mother and his seven siblings. One other brother died in an accident two years ago. Oswald's father was also killed in this accident. Before this accident, there had been five boys and four girls. Oswald was the fourth oldest child. The family has been receiving public assistance in the form of Aid to Families with Dependent Children (AFDC) for more than five years. The family lived in an apartment that had a total of four rooms (including the living room and kitchen), so the siblings often got in each other's way and would fight to maintain some space for themselves. There were no quiet places to read or do homework in the house.

Oswald's mother, Mrs. Williams, wanted to have Oswald's intelligence tested. Oswald had been in a special education class for children with borderline or retarded intellectual functioning. In addition, Oswald had been showing aggression, usually unprovoked, both at school and at home.

Oswald was born prematurely and suffered from a number of medical problems when he was a baby. His developmental milestones (e.g., crawling, walking, and talking) tended to come a bit later than would be expected. When Oswald first began school, he was referred for intelligence testing because of "partial lack of communication and reading impairment." At that time, his intellectual functioning fell into the mildly retarded range (IQ below 70 with limited adaptive abilities). In second grade, Oswald tested in the IQ range of borderline intellectual functioning (IQ between 70 and 80). Oswald had always been in special education classes at school.

The family had experienced numerous traumas, many of which were related to limited financial resources. The father had been only marginally employed, and the family became even more destitute after his death. In addition, the family was emotionally devastated by the loss of Mr. Williams and one of the boys. Mrs. Williams reported that Mr. Williams had always been the disciplinarian and had always made sure to know the children's whereabouts. Mrs. Williams tried to carry on these behaviors after her husband's death, but she found it difficult to do so. She was especially concerned about the safety of her children, given the dangerous and often violent neighborhood in which they lived. She rarely left the house and rarely let the children leave the house for anything other than school due to her fear of the harm that might come to them. When she did leave the house, Mrs. Williams would phone the children every 15 minutes to make sure that they were all right.

Because of the difficulties with her children, Mrs. Williams started treatment to help with parenting issues and to help make decisions about Oswald's educational future. Oswald also saw a male social worker for counseling in order to work on his anger management and aggression issues. With therapy, Mrs. Williams learned how to set appropriate limits on her children's behavior. She was also encouraged to find enjoyable activities for herself. She became more involved in the church, began dating a man in the same housing project, and began working part-time as a cleaning woman to help with the financial strain on the household. Mrs. Williams reported that she felt very relaxed when she was at work, because she felt that she was helping her children without having to worry about them constantly.

Oswald developed a very therapeutic bond with his social worker, but his behavior became progressively worse. He was suspended a number of times from school. The social worker and teacher set up a token economy through which Oswald could earn tokens for good behavior at school and his mother could reward him at home (e.g., with extra attention or by letting him stay in a room by himself for a certain amount of time without interruption from his brothers and sisters). The token economy appeared to be working well. Unfortunately, Mrs. Williams and Oswald stopped coming to therapy and did not respond to the therapists' repeated invitations to continue their work together.

SOURCE: Leon (1990).

---

the poverty line (Baugher & Lamison-White, 1996). This percentage varies widely depending on the child's ethnic and racial background, with 16.8% of Caucasian American children, 45.9% of African American children, and 40.4% of Hispanic children living in poverty (Baugher & Lamison-White, 1996). Although many people think of inner-city children when they think of poverty, note that poverty exists in many different types of communities, including rural communities (Murry & Brody, 1999).

Rates of childhood psychopathology are higher in impoverished communities than in communities with adequate resources, even after controlling for genetic predispositions (Caspi, Taylor, Moffitt, & Plomin, 2000). Figure 7.3 shows the possible effects of neighborhoods and the community across the life span. Poverty, however, appears to affect African American children to an even larger degree than children from other ethnic and racial backgrounds (Luthar, 1999). In addition, children living in poverty who are also exposed to harsh or inconsistent parenting and severe stressors are even more likely to develop emotional/behavioral problems than are children living in poverty who are not exposed to those factors (Brody et al., 2001; McLoyd, 1998). Low amounts of parental monitoring (e.g., parents who do not keep track of where their children spend their time and who do not set limits on their children's activities) were also associated with greater externalizing problems in a group of impoverished and unsafe neighborhoods (Pettit, Bates, Dodge, & Meece,

Poverty is associated with emotional/behavioral problems in children.

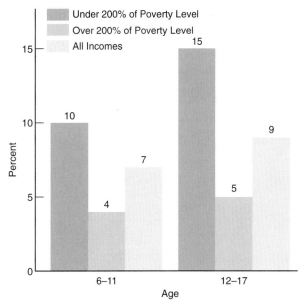

FIGURE 7.2 Children with High Levels of Behavioral and Emotional Problems, by Age and Family Income, 1997
Source: Urban Institute (1999b).

1999). Homelessness was related to internalizing problems but not to externalizing problems when other factors of poverty were controlled (Buckner et al., 1999). Family instability, which was defined as the number of times families moved or changed settings, was directly related to increased emotional/behavioral problems in children as young as seven (Ackerman et al., 1999).

Overall, low socioeconomic status and poverty are associated with increased risk for the development of emotional/behavioral problems in children and adolescents. As with so many other risk factors, the risk factor of low socioeconomic status is compounded by other factors such as neighborhood safety, single-parent homes, stressors within the family, family instability, and lack of resources (McLoyd, 1998). Violence within the community also appears to be confounded with living in impoverished neighborhoods.

BOX *7.6*

WHO ARE POOR CHILDREN IN THE UNITED STATES?

- 71% have a family member who is employed.
- 59% live in families headed by a single female.
- 34% live in families with two parents.
- 31% are African American.
- 35% are Caucasian American.
- 29% are Hispanic.

- 5% are Asian American or Pacific Islander.
- 56% live in areas that are suburban or rural.

Note that although the poverty line for a three-person family in 1997 was drawn at an annual income of $12,802, the average poor family with children in that year survived on an income of approximately $8,688.

SOURCE: Children's Defense Fund (1999).

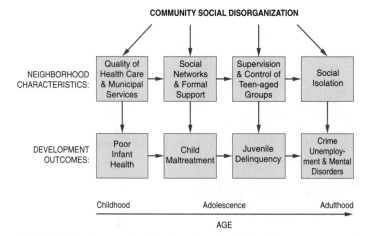

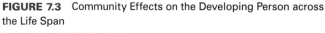

FIGURE 7.3 Community Effects on the Developing Person across the Life Span

Source: Caspi & Moffitt (1995).

Injustice anywhere is a threat to justice everywhere.

—Dr. Martin Luther King Jr.

VIOLENCE WITHIN THE COMMUNITY

Sadly, children living in poverty often witness violence or are themselves the victims of violence. In a survey of first- and second-grade students living in the inner city of Washington, D.C., 90% of the children reported having witnessed at least one arrest and over one-third reported that they have seen a dead body in the community (Richters & Martinez, 1993). In Miami, 87% of inner-city adolescents reported having witnessed a beating or mug-

ging, 38% reported that they were the victim of a beating or mugging, and nearly 42% reported that they had witnessed a murder (Berman, Kurtines, Silverman, & Serafini, 1996). Over 85% of impoverished children in foster care had witnessed an act of violence within their lives, and the large majority had witnessed violence within the six months preceding the study (B. D. Stein et al., 2001).

Witnessing violence in the community has been associated with a wide range of emotional/behavioral problems. Toddlers and young children tend to show greater sleep disturbance, irritability, poor concentration, depression, and anxiety after being exposed to violence in the community (reviewed in Luthar, 1999). Older children and adolescents also show higher rates of depression,

---

BOX 7.7

THE STATE OF AMERICA'S CHILDREN

In the United States, here is what a day in the life of a child looks like:

Every 1 second a student in public school is suspended.

Every 9 seconds a student in high school drops out of school.

Every 16 seconds a child or teenager under the age of 18 is arrested.

Every 40 seconds a baby is born into poverty.

Every 1 minute a baby is born to a mother who is a teenager.

Every 2 minutes a baby is born with low birth weight.

Every 3 minutes a child is arrested on drug abuse charges.

Every 18 minutes a baby dies.

Every 2 hours a child under the age of 20 is killed by a gun.

Every 4 hours a child under the age of 20 commits suicide.

Every 11 hours a youth under the age of 25 dies from HIV infection/AIDS.

SOURCE: Children's Defense Fund (1999).

aggression, and PTSD when exposed to violence (reviewed in Luthar, 1999). It appears that children's reactions to witnessing violence in the community may be related to how their family deals with the violence. For example, young children showed increased emotional/behavioral problems in relation to community violence when their mothers also showed high levels of distress (Linares et al., 2001).

Violence is present in communities well beyond the inner city. In fact, acts of violence, such as physical fighting, are evident to some degree in most schools and in most communities. Exposure to excessive amounts of physical fighting can put children at risk for the development of both internalizing and externalizing problems (Fitzpatrick, 1997).

Violence within the family can also be devastating. Child physical abuse was covered earlier in the chapter, but there is also concern about children who witness physical violence between their parents or other caretakers. Exposure to family violence (also known as domestic violence) is associated with increased emotional/behavioral problems and decreased self-esteem (Grych, Jouriles, Swank, McDonald, & Norwood, 2000; Henning, Leitenberg, Coffey, Bennett, & Jankowski, 1997; Kolbo, 1996). Exposure to domestic violence is also associated with a greater risk for being physical abused (McGuigan, Vuchinich, & Pratt, 2000). Problems are evident in children who witness family violence and who witness parental stress as a result of the family violence (Levendosky & Graham-Bermann, 1998). The risk of developing psychopathology is four times greater for children who witness violence within the family than for children from nonviolent homes (Cummings, Davies, & Campbell, 2000).

Beyond the family and the community, children are often exposed to horrendous examples of violence that are experienced in times of war. In one study of Palestinian children who experienced war trauma, an overwhelming number developed PTSD (Thabet & Vostanis, 1999). The cumulative effects of witnessing greater numbers of war-related traumas were associated with greater numbers of PTSD symptoms.

Overall, the effects of children witnessing violence can be intense and long-standing. These effects, however, are mediated by a number of other factors such as the amount of exposure, how the adults in the child's life handle the exposure to violence, and the number of other risk factors to which the child is exposed in addition to the violence (Luthar, 1999). Preventive efforts have focused on decreasing access to firearms and increasing conflict resolution skills in youth and their families (Group for the Advancement of Psychiatry, 1999).

SUMMARY AND KEY CONCEPTS

Risk factors are characteristics, events, or processes that put a child or adolescent at risk for the development of psychological difficulties.

Temperament and Attachment

Temperament is the infant's personal and individual style regarding the frequency of expression of needs and emotions. Infants differ at birth in their temperamental style. **Attachment** is the relationship that develops between infants and their caretakers (usually their parents), which is usually characterized by a deep, enduring, and affectionate bond between the infant and the caretaker.

Genetic Predisposition

Most emotional/behavioral problems have been linked, to some extent, to genetic risk factors.

Parental Psychopathology

Nearly every type of parental psychopathology, in both mothers and fathers, has been linked to an increased likelihood of emotional/behavioral problems in children and adolescents. The effects of parental psychopathology are exacerbated when both parents show psychopathology, which is not uncommon given the process of **assortative mating** (when someone who has a clinical disorder has children with someone else who has a clinical disorder).

Parental Loss Due to Death

Although losing a parent to death is devastating for most children and adolescents, the risk for emotional/behavioral problems related to the loss increases when certain characteristics are present (e.g., multiple loses at the same time, sudden parental death).

Interparental Conflict

The connections between interparental conflict (i.e., fighting and arguing between parents) and child maladjustment are among the most consistent findings in the study of developmental psychopathology. Interparental conflict is associated with greater risk for emotional/behavioral problems whether or not the parents are living together. One of the most devastating types of interparental conflict is **triangulation**, when parents put the child in the middle of their arguments.

Child Physical Abuse

Not surprisingly, child physical abuse is associated with greater risk for the development of emotional/behavioral problems in childhood and adolescence. Often, child physical abuse is evident in the context of other risk factors (e.g., insecure attachment, parental psychopathology, interparental conflict).

Child Sexual Abuse

Like physical abuse, child sexual abuse is associated with a great number of emotional/behavioral problems for children and adolescents. The effects of child sexual abuse are especially devastating when certain factors are present (e.g., the perpetrator is a father or father figure, when the abuse has occurred over a long period of time).

Child Psychological Maltreatment

Psychological maltreatment of children has not been studied as much as child physical abuse or child sexual abuse, however, it appears to be an important risk factor to consider in the lives of children.

Family Dysfunction

Many types of other family dysfunctions have been linked to increased risk for emotional/behavioral problems, including hostility and competitiveness, stress, maladaptive family environments, troubled family systems, negative parental affect, and maladaptive parenting styles.

Inadequate Educational Resources

The school environment can have an impact on children's emotional well-being as well as their academic and intellectual functioning. Problems can arise when there are difficult transitions (e.g., from elementary school to middle school), when there is a lack of school connectedness, and when there are less-than-optimal school conditions (e.g., overcrowding, limited educational resources).

Poverty and Low Socioeconomic Status

Approximately 22% of children in the United States live at or below the poverty line. Poverty and low socioeconomic status have been associated with greater emotional/behavioral problems in children and adolescents.

Violence within the Community

A surprisingly high number of children and adolescents have been the victims of or have observed violence in their communities. Children who witness violence within their own family (e.g., spousal abuse) show four times more psychopathology than children from nonviolent families.

KEY TERMS

risk factors	temperament	attachment	assortative mating	triangulation

SUGGESTED READINGS

Brady, Katherine. *Father's Day*. New York: Dell Publishing, 1979. This classic autobiography gives a graphic detail of the devastation created by childhood sexual abuse.

Pelzer, David. *The Lost Boy*. Deerfield Beach, FL: Health Communications, Inc., 1997. This book is the second part of a three-part autobiography (which began with *A Child Called "It"*) that describes the ramifications of childhood physical abuse. This volume describes the additional harm that can come from the foster care system when children are removed from their home due to abuse.

SUGGESTED VIEWINGS

Corrina, Corrina (1994). Jessie Nelson (director and writer). VHS/DVD. This beautiful and poignant film shows the struggles and strengths of a girl whose mother has died. In a lighthearted manner, the girl's nanny becomes an incredibly stable force in her life. Issues of racism and prejudice are also interwoven in this story.

Nuts (1987). Martin Ritt (director), Tom Topor, Darryl Ponicsan, and Alvin Sargent (screenwriters), based on play by Tom Topor. VHS/DVD. This powerful film describes the story of the adult ramifications to childhood sexual abuse and abuse of power within the family.

CHAPTER 8

PROTECTIVE FACTORS AND ISSUES OF PREVENTION

CHAPTER SUMMARY

Your children need your presence more than your presents.
                                            —Jesse Jackson

Over the past two decades, there has been increasing emphasis within the field of psychology on the positive side of human beings. Often known as positive psychology, this emphasis has led to a better understanding of human happiness and subjective well-being (Diener, 2000); optimism (Seligman, 1991); and the ordinary strengths within human development (Masten, 2001).

Consistent with these explorations of positive aspects of human behavior, many developmental psychopathologists have been interested in identifying positive factors in children's lives that seem to protect them from adverse circumstances. **Protective factors** are those characteristics within an individual child, family, or community that serve to decrease the likelihood that the child will develop psychopathology in the face of adversity. Although many characteristics serve as healthy factors in children's lives, they are referred to as protective factors only when they are associated with overcoming otherwise adverse circumstances and risk factors (e.g., poverty, abuse, interparental conflict). Studies on protective factors tend to be sensitive to cultural and ethnic issues, but there is still a need for more attention to cultural diversity within the context of research on protective factors (Arrington &

Wilson, 2000). Risk factors were covered in Chapter 7, and the current chapter focuses on protective factors.

A primary research strategy in the study of protective factors has been to examine **resilience** within children (see Luthar, Cicchetti, & Becker, 2000; Masten, 2001; Pedro-Carroll, 2001; and Taylor & Wang, 2000 for excellent reviews). Resilience is the process by which children overcome adverse circumstances and develop into healthy and competent young adults. There were many pioneering efforts into the study of resilience in the 1960s and 1970s (Anthony, 1974; Garmezy, 1974; Rutter, 1979; Werner & Smith, 1982). These studies laid the groundwork for understanding the strengths within children and their environments that protect children from adverse situations. Most often, researchers collect data from a large group of children who are at risk for developing adverse outcomes due to individual or environmental circumstances. When these children are followed over time, some of them will in fact develop adverse outcomes (e.g., psychopathology or criminal behavior), but some of them will develop into well-functioning and psychologically healthy adolescents and young adults. Investigation of these resilient children helps researchers identify the characteristics within the children or within their environment that protect them from the initial adverse circumstances. Box 8.1 highlights the work of Dr. Emmy

BOX *8.1*

DR. EMMY WERNER'S PIONEERING WORK ON THE ISLAND OF KAUAI

A classic series of studies of protective factors and resilience in children was conducted by Dr. Emmy Werner and her colleagues on the Hawaiian island of Kauai (Werner, 1995; Werner & Smith, 1982, 1992, 2001). The research team included pediatricians, psychologists, public health workers, and social workers. Werner and her colleagues collected information on nearly 700 children who were born on Kauai in 1955. The majority of children born onto the island remain on the island during their entire life, so the island provides an ideal opportunity for longitudinal research that follows children throughout their lives.

Data were collected on the participants prenatally, and at the ages of 1, 2, 10, 18, 32, and early 40s (with continued follow-up interviews planned for the future). As children, approximately 30% of the participants were considered to be at high risk for development of psychological problems due to prenatal stress, perinatal stress, chronic poverty, chronic interparental conflict, parental divorce, or parental psychopathology. Two-thirds of the children with four or more risk factors early in life ended up developing serious emotional/behavioral problems or learning problems by the age of 10 or developed mental health problems, criminal problems, or pregnancy by the age of 18. One-third of the children with four or more risk factors developed into well-functioning, psychologically healthy adolescents and young adults. The key to identifying protective factors was to investigate the characteristics of the children who were at risk initially, but who then ended up leading healthy and productive lives in later adolescence and early adulthood.

Over the course of their investigation, Werner and her colleagues (summarized in Werner & Smith, 2001) identified a number of factors within the individual, family, and community that served as protective factors for these resilient children. During infancy and early childhood, resilient children were more likely to be described as active, cuddly, good-natured, affectionate, and "easy to deal with" when compared with children who did not show resilience. During middle childhood and adolescence, resilient children showed good communication skills, good problem-solving skills, interests in special hobbies or activities, internal locus of control and self-efficacy, positive self-concept, and adequate (though not necessarily gifted) intellectual functioning.

Protective factors within the family centered on having at least one competent and emotionally stable person with whom the child could bond (such as a competent grandparent if the parents were unable to provide this type of support). Interestingly, resilient children often sought out these competent role models and, in turn, became role models and caretakers for younger siblings or others who were in need of help. Protective factors within the community focused on the availability of competent role models outside the family (e.g., a teacher, coach, religious leader, or competent friend). There were also notable protective factors within the community that helped high-risk adolescents and young adults rebound from their troubled lives. In particular, adult education programs, religious activities, marriage to a competent partner, affiliation with a supportive friend, and voluntary military service were noted to help some troubled older adolescents and young adults become more competent than their background would have suggested.

Overall, the work by Werner and colleagues has been crucial in the understanding of risk and protective factors within children and adolescents. This unique sample, and the continued efforts to follow these grown children and their offspring, has provided a wealth of information about the lives of children and families. Interested students are encouraged to read *Journeys from Childhood to Midlife: Risk, Resilience, and Recovery* (Werner & Smith, 2001).

Werner, whose research has been groundbreaking in the study of resilient children.

The study of resilient children over the past 25 years has led to some promising findings about what factors serve to protect children from adverse environments. Table 8.1 shows three primary groupings of variables that serve as protective factors: characteristics within the individual, within the family, and within the extrafamilial context.

All of these factors are important in the development of resilient children, so all will be covered to some extent in this chapter. Note that one limitation in this research knowledge, which parallels other limitations in developmental psychopathology, is that the majority of what we know comes from correlational and longitudinal studies. Given that research in this area cannot be completed with an experimental design (e.g., randomly assign some children to an adverse environment without the presence of any protective factors and assign other children to an adverse environment with the presence of protective factors), the causal links in this area of research are still somewhat tenuous. Luckily, relatively consistent results have been found and replicated with children from different ethnic groups within the United States, such as African American and Asian American, as well as within different countries worldwide (Masten & Coatsworth,

TABLE 8.1 Characteristics of Resilient Children and Adolescents

Source	Characteristic
Individual	Good intellectual functioning
	Appealing, sociable, easygoing disposition
	Self-efficacy, self-confidence, high self-esteem
	Talents
	Faith
Family	Close relationship to caring parent figure
	Authoritative parenting: warmth, structure, high expectations
	Socioeconomic advantages
	Connections to extended supportive family networks
Extrafamilial Context	Bonds to prosocial adults outside the family
	Connections to prosocial organizations
	Effective schools

SOURCE: Masten & Coatsworth (1998).

1998; Rutter, 1979; Serafica, 1997; Werner & Smith, 2001). Even with this solid research base, however, findings should be interpreted cautiously until more research with an experimental or a quasi-experimental design can be completed.

INTELLECTUAL FUNCTIONING

Adequate intelligence has been identified consistently as a protective factor from adverse environments (Anthony & Cohler, 1987; Masten & Coatsworth, 1998; Werner & Smith, 2001). Note, however, that these findings are not as simple as just finding that better intelligence is related to better outcome. Rather, it appears that average or above-average intellectual functioning is associated with other characteristics that are related to healthy outcomes. For example, higher verbal abilities (one component of intellectual functioning) in children of depressed mothers were associated with decreased risk for depressive symptoms in the children (Malcarne, Hamilton, Ingram, & Taylor, 2000). In addition, children with at least average intelligence who are raised in adverse environments may have a better chance of doing well in school and in seeking out teachers to help them with their work (Masten & Coatsworth, 1998). Academic achievement can help the child stay more invested in school rather than disengaging from school and other prosocial activities. Adequate intellectual functioning is also associated with information-processing skills, which may in turn help the child negotiate peer relationships and academic involvements. Compared with children of lower intelligence, intelligent children may be more creative and effective in solving problems, so they may negotiate difficulties in a more effective manner (Werner & Smith, 2001). Higher intelligence was found to be a particularly important protective factor against the development of antisocial behavior during adolescence (Masten et al., 1999).

Overall, average intelligence has been identified as a protective factor in nearly every study that has investigated

Case Study: A Neurosurgeon Who Grew Up in the Inner City

Dr. Ben Carson gained international attention for coordinating a team of surgeons who were able to separate conjoined twins (also known as Siamese twins) who were joined at the back of the head. The parents of these seven-month-old infants had all but given up hope for being able to have both twins survive such a surgery. Most of the physicians they contacted either would not do the surgery or would suggest the plan of saving only one twin. Over five months, Carson planned the complex and dangerous surgery with a surgical team of more than 70 professionals. The surgery took more than 22 hours. Both twins survived and are functioning well.

Given this extraordinary story, it is even more extraordinary to learn that Carson grew up in a single-parent home in the inner city of Detroit with few prospects for success. As an African American, he experienced a great deal of racism and preju-

dice when he attended a school in which Caucasian American children were the clear majority. His mother had insisted that he be bused to this school so that he could get an adequate education. His mother also insisted that he study hard, follow her rules (e.g., watching only three television shows a week and reading two entire books a week), and be respectful to his elders. In addition to the academic tenacity he developed, Carson also exhibited great intellect even at a very young age. His mother reported that he had always been very bright, but she needed to help him apply himself to his academic studies. Obviously, this strategy paid off not only for Carson but also for the thousands of children he has helped with his neurosurgical skills. The story of Dr. Ben Carson illustrates a number of protective factors, including intelligence, a stable and determined parent, and strong beliefs in one's ability to persevere.

SOURCE: Carson & Murphey (1990).

Case Study: A Family Coping with Incest

Amy's maternal grandfather, Melvin, had been sexually abusing her for more than 10 years. At the age of 14, Amy reported the abuse to her mother, Belle, but her mother did not believe her. At the age of 15, Amy reported the abuse to a teacher, who reported it to child protective authorities. Although she still did not believe Amy, the mother finally accepted the allegations when Amy's two younger siblings reported that they had also been sexually abused by the grandfather. The child protective agency mandated that the grandfather have no more contact with the children and that Belle take Amy to therapy.

Amy's mother and father have been divorced for many years, and Belle just recently remarried and is expecting a baby within the month. Conflict often arises in the family, in which Amy's mother and stepfather blame Amy for doing something wrong. In arguments, the mother and stepfather frequently side against Amy and her siblings. Given the family distress, Amy expressed interest in going to live with her biological father. Although Amy's father has told Amy that she can live with him, he has informed the child protective agency that Amy cannot live with him.

The following verbatim transcript is from a family therapy session with Amy and Belle. The hearing refers to a legal procedure during which Amy had to testify about the abuse. This portion of the session occurred after Amy asked to speak with her mother about something that made her sad.

BELLE: [*sitting down*] OK.

AMY: [*speaks in a high, childlike voice and shrinks back a bit*] OK, what?

BELLE: You want to speak to me.

AMY: [*still in a childlike voice*] Yeah, I do.

BELLE: [*crosses arms and looks guarded*] About?

AMY: About our relationship.

BELLE: Yeah?

AMY: It's not going too well.

BELLE: [*tensely*] Well, it's not worse than it has been. It's gonna take some time, Amy.

AMY: [*voice gets small*] I know, Mom, but I don't feel like I'm getting any support from you.

BELLE: Like how?

AMY: Just, [*pause*] you weren't here for [pause] the hearing.

BELLE: [*slightly interrupting in a sharp voice*] I know that and we discussed that, and it was agreed by you that it was okay. Neither of us had any clue what that hearing really was about. [*pauses as she continues to look at Amy, whose head is down as if being punished*] We discussed that at length before we ever left. [*pause*] Isn't that right? And what did you say?

AMY: I don't remember.

BELLE: Tsk.

AMY: I don't.

BELLE: You said that it was perfectly all right for H and T [*a couple from church*] to . . .

AMY: I know, but that's . . .

BELLE: [*starts to finish her sentence but stops*]

AMY: . . . because you all planned to go on vacation.

BELLE: [*sharply*] Amy, we were perfectly willing to stay if we needed to.

AMY: But y'all needed to get away.

BELLE: Well, that's true too. [pause] But we still discussed it with you, and you said, "no," that it was fine for them to take you. [*long pause*]

AMY: Just—[*pause*] I feel neglected by you.

BELLE: How?

AMY: [*voice gets smaller and words become hard to understand, mumbles*] You don't show you love me.

BELLE: [*sounds impatient*] Like how am I supposed to?

AMY: [*shoulders hunched, head down, starts to cry*] When I do good in school, you don't tell me I do a good job.

BELLE: [*slightly raises voice*] Amy that is not true.

AMY: Yes, it is.

BELLE: It is not.

AMY: When I come home and tell you I have 95's [*pause*] on papers, I don't hear "Good job."

BELLE: That is not true. I have commented on every single good paper that you have brought. [*Amy shakes her head no and looks at Belle.*]

This case illustrates a number of adverse circumstances that Amy has endured (sexual abuse, and lack of support from her mother, stepfather, and father). Some of the protective factors that had strengthened Amy's ability to deal with these difficulties included a supportive teacher, and good coping skills (e.g., she did not blame herself for the sexual abuse, she sought out a supportive teacher frequently). The therapist worked on ways in which Belle could reconnect with Amy and tried to help Belle become more supportive of Amy. Mother and daughter began having "girl times" together, many of which were initiated by Belle. Amy's difficult behavior decreased, and both mother and daughter reported greater closeness and harmony within the family.

SOURCE: E. C. Lawrence (1999, pp. 176–177).

the connection between intellectual functioning and healthy outcomes (Masten et al., 1999). Although the mechanisms are not completely clear, it appears that higher intelligence is associated with myriad skills that are predictive of competent outcomes. In fact, some researchers have argued that a child's intellectual functioning and the quality of parenting he or she receives are the two most crucial protective factors in the prevention of psychopathology and other adverse outcomes (Masten et al., 1999).

Parents learn a lot from their children about coping with life.
—Muriel Spark

SELF-EFFICACY AND COPING STYLES

Self-efficacy is a term used to describe a cognitive structure in which children have come to expect success and to believe that they can perform successfully in any new challenging situation (Bandura, 1986). In general, self-efficacy is associated with healthy outcomes in children as well as in adults (Bandura, 1986). It appears that individuals who have high self-efficacy will try harder and remain more engaged in challenging tasks—and therefore will more often succeed in those tasks—than individuals with low self-efficacy (Bandura, 1986). More recently, self-efficacy has also been associated with "pleasure in mastery," which occurs when children and adolescents enjoy activities that challenge them to excel (Masten et al., 1999).

High self-efficacy has been identified as a factor that serves to protect children from adverse circumstances (Masten & Coatsworth, 1998; Werner & Smith, 2001). Children with higher rates of self-efficacy stay engaged in tasks longer and succeed at tasks to a greater degree than children with lower rates of self-efficacy (Masten et al., 1999). Given that children from adverse environments often encounter more challenges than children from stable environments, higher rates of self-efficacy appear to help at-risk children in a number of venues, including the home, school, and community. Remember that self-efficacy is a cognitive process rather than an actual process of succeeding. The idea behind the importance of self-efficacy as a protective factor is that at-risk children with high self-efficacy will persevere even in challenging situations because they believe they can succeed in those situations. Children with lower levels of self-efficacy may give up more quickly on a task and will therefore be less able to succeed in that task. Overall, self-efficacy has been iden-

tified consistently as a protective factor associated with resilience in children (Masten & Coatsworth, 1998).

Like self-efficacy, coping style has been identified as an individual characteristic that can serve to protect children from adverse circumstances (Compas, Connor-Smith, Saltzman, Thomsen, & Wadsworth, 2001). In particular, children show resilience when they are able to appraise a potentially stressful situation in a manner that helps their ability to cope with the situation (Werner & Smith, 2001; Wyman, Sandler, Wolchik, & Nelson, 2000). Children with good problem-solving coping skills tend to be more resilient than children without those skills (Dumont & Provost, 1999). In a study of urban children, resilient children showed significantly better problem-solving coping skills than did children who were stress-affected (Cowen et al., 1997). Children who seek the help of others when faced with a challenge that exceeds their ability to cope also show better resilience to adverse environments (Dumont & Provost, 1999). Children who can call on stable adults or peers to help them cope with difficult situations show higher rates of competence and lower rates of emotional/behavioral problems (Werner & Smith, 2001).

Overall, both self-efficacy and coping style have been associated with great resilience against adverse environments. Although both factors are categorized as occurring within the individual, they can be enhanced by adequate support and role models within and outside of the family. In addition, both self-efficacy and coping style have been linked to intellectual functioning and problem-solving skills, so neither factor serves as a protective factor alone (Masten et al., 1999).

Once you bring life into the world, you must protect it. We must protect it by changing the world.
—Elie Wiesel

FAMILY FACTORS

Factors within the family that serve as protective factors include a close relationship with a caretaker or parent; parenting style; and connections to a network of family members such as grandparents, aunts, and uncles.

A close and stable relationship with at least one parent or caretaker has consistently been shown to protect children from adverse circumstances (Masten & Coatsworth, 1998). For brevity, the word *parent* will be used in this section to signify any adult caretaker who has primary responsibility for the child's well-being. Note that there

There are many aspects of families that can serve as protective factors, such as close and stable relationships with well-functioning parents and siblings.

are few differences in the impact of caring and stable parenting, regardless of whether the parenting is coming from a biological mother, biological father, stepmother, stepfather, grandparent, aunt, uncle, older sibling, or non-relative (Black, Dubowitz, & Starr, 1999). The important thing to consider in children's well-being is the type of parenting they receive, not from whom they receive it. In some ways, parents are considered to be the most important agents of socialization in a child's life, so competent and caring parenting is a salient protective factor for children born to adverse circumstances (Scarr & Deater-Deckard, 1997).

The protective nature of caring and consistent parenting begins in infancy, where secure attachment serves as a protective factor for infants who have been exposed to trauma or other adverse circumstances (Sroufe, Carlson, Levy, & Egeland, 1999). Secure attachment is usually associated with parents who provide nurturing and warm interactions with the infant in a stable and consistent manner. These parenting characteristics also serve as protective factors later in the child's life.

As early as three years old, African American children living in urban poverty showed better cognitive and language competence and fewer behavioral problems when their father was nurturant and satisfied with his parenting role (Black et al., 1999). In a study of kindergarten children, parents' positive affect and support were associated with the children's social competence (Isley, O'Neil, Clatfelter, & Parke, 1999) in an ethnically diverse sample. At-risk children ages seven to nine who lived in urban poverty showed better overall functioning when they received competent parenting from a caregiver with stable psychosocial resources (Wyman et al., 1999). Within the African American community, parents who held Afri-

Case Study: A Mother's Love

In an extraordinary book that documents the lives of homeless families, Jonathan Kozol (1988) illustrates the devastation poverty wreaks on children and families. There are also illustrations of resilience in the face of horrific living circumstances. One notable family is Rachel and her four children, ages 11 months to 12 years old. They live in the Northeast, in a public housing project where the living conditions are often deplorable (e.g., there is often little heat during the winter). Rachel noted that she had to sign a statement when she moved into the one-room space that she would not cook anything in her room. She noted that this rule necessitates that children live on inadequate nutrition (such as bologna sandwiches), when she can afford the food.

Even in the face of these horrible life circumstances, Rachel has managed to remain a stable and caring influence in her children's lives. She spends time with them and helps the older ones with their homework. She reads the Bible to her children and speaks to them of the day when they will have a better life. Away from her children, she acknowledges that she is scared and that she does not sleep at night so that she can watch over her children and prevent any harm from coming to them. With her children, however, she presents a confident and stable will that keeps them from worrying when or if they will have a next meal. Rachel has tried her best to allow her children to remain "innocent" and to protect them from the harsh realities of living in extreme poverty.

Source: Kozol (1988).

centric values (especially related to collective work and personal responsibility) had children who were less likely than other children to become involved in illicit drug use (Belgrave, Townsend, Cherry, & Cunningham, 1997). Parental involvement, especially as demonstrated through family mealtime, is associated with a host of positive outcomes for children (Schwarzchild, 2000).

During adolescence, parental support and stress-buffering interactions were associated with less risk for substance use, including tobacco, alcohol, and marijuana (Wills & Cleary, 1996; Yoshikawa, 1994). Parental and family support have even decreased the influence of deviant peers and decreased the likelihood of Hispanic/Latino/Latina adolescents' substance use (Frauenglass, Routh, Pantin, & Mason, 1997). Parental monitoring of young adolescents' behavior (e.g., knowing the whereabouts of their children) was associated with more secure attachment and better adolescent outcomes (Kerns, Aspelmeier, Gentzler, & Grabill, 2001). Positive parental behavior and family functioning was associated with better academic functioning and better adjustment in adolescents (Gorman-Smith, Tolan, Henry, & Florsheim, 2000; Voydanoff & Donnelly, 1999).

Similarly, urban adolescents living in poverty with parents who provided support and protection from daily hassles had low rates of depression and antisocial behavior (Seidman et al., 1999). African American adolescents who received high levels of parental warmth tended to show corresponding emotional/behavioral adjustment (McCabe, Clark, & Barnett, 1999). Both African American and Mexican American adolescents flourished in families with at least one competent parent (Gorman-Smith et al., 2000). Within Asian American and Latin American adolescents in the United States, strong feelings of family obligations and family connection with their parents were associated with good family relationships, strong peer relationships, and high motivations to succeed in school (Fuligni, Tseng, & Lam, 1999). Parental expectations and positive family attention served as protective factors against suicide in a sample of Native American adolescents (Dexheimer, Pharris, Resnick, & Blum, 1997). In a sample from Colombia, South America, family support served a protective role after adolescents witnessed violence against a family member (Kliewer, Murrelle, Mejia, Torres de G., & Angold, 2001).

Overall, there is clear support for the protective nature of stable and nurturing caretaking. In fact, there is evidence that parenting resources play a larger protective role than many other protective factors (Masten et al., 1999). Protective factors within the family have been used as a mechanism to help families in therapy (Rutter, 1999b). Research findings about protective factors within the family are consistent with studies on parenting styles that have identified the **authoritative parenting style** as a protective factor. Authoritative parenting is characterized by warmth, age-appropriate structure, and high expectations (Baumrind, 1971) and is associated with children who are friendly, independent, cooperative, socially responsible, and academically advanced (Baumrind, 1971; Steinberg, Lamborn, Darling, Mounts, & Dornbusch, 1994). Other parenting styles, which include permissive parents (who do not set any limits or provide any structure for their children's behavior) and authoritarian parents (who provide strict limits and structure to their children, while providing little warmth) are associated with adverse outcomes, such as being withdrawn and unhappy (Baumrind, 1971). Note that authoritative parenting is associated with positive outcomes even in children of separated and divorced parents (Hetherington & Clingempeel, 1992; Hetherington & Stanley-Hagan, 1999).

BOX 8.2

OUT OF THE MOUTHS OF BABES

A fascinating book entitled *What Preteens Want Their Parents to Know* was written by Ryan Holladay and Friends (1994) when Ryan was just 12 years old. The book provides a collection of suggestions from young adolescents to their parents. Although some of the suggestions are specific to parents, many could be useful to teachers, coaches, grandparents, and others who care about young adolescents. These suggestions tend to focus on the positive side of the adolescent–parent relationship, which is consistent with how parents (and others) can help develop a strong and stable relationship with adolescents. Here is just a sample of the suggestions:

- Listening is one of the best ways to show me you love me (p. 27).
- Have at least one meal as a family each day (p. 60).
- Your praise means more to me than anyone else's (p. 71).
- Teach me right and wrong (p. 94).
- Look at family photo albums with me and tell me about the relatives (p. 137).

FIGURE 8.1 Drawing by a Nine-Year-Old Girl from Puerto Rico Who Was Asked to Draw a Picture of Her Family
Source: DiLeo (1973).

One specific aspect of authoritative parenting seems to be the use of scaffolding. **Scaffolding** occurs when parents provide structure and support for the child's next level of development (Vygotsky, 1978). An example is when parents take their not-yet-crawling infant and help shape the infant's legs and arms into the crawling position. The infant may be able to crawl a step or two with this help, and then may eventually learn how to move his or her own legs and arms in the necessary position for crawling. Scaffolding can occur at any developmental stage and is helpful primarily when the child is at the cusp of making new advancements. The essence of scaffolding is that parents provide support and structure for the child to move to a more advanced level of functioning, whether in an academic, social, moral, or physical domain. Scaffolding is one of the many mechanisms that helps supportive and nurturing parents enhance their children's functioning and protects their children from adverse circumstances (Masten & Coatsworth, 1998).

Although the research has focused on parents and other direct caretakers, there is also overwhelming evidence members of the extended family can offer protective factors (Masten & Coatsworth, 1998). Figure 8.1 shows a family drawing made by a girl who has a large and close extended family (DiLeo, 1973). Studies on supportive extended family networks tend to show findings similar to those in the parenting literature. Specifically, relatives and others in the family system who treat children with support and nurturance serve as protection against otherwise adverse circumstances (Masten & Coatsworth, 1998). Support and warmth from kin (i.e., relatives and other family members) have been associated with a host of positive outcomes, such as decreases in acting out, shyness, and anxious behavior, even in the face of great stressors in adolescents' lives (McCabe et al., 1999). Box 8.3 discusses how grandparents can play a particularly important role in their grandchildren's lives.

Overall, many factors within the family are associated with the development of resilient children. Sometimes children are put at risk due to factors within the family (e.g., parental psychopathology, interparental conflict, severe poverty, abuse), and there are no available supports

Grandparents and other stable elders can serve an important protective role in children's lives.

THE IMPORTANCE OF GRANDPARENTS AND THEIR WISDOM

Nobody can do for little children what grandparents do. Grandparents sort of sprinkle stardust over the lives of little children.

—Alex Haley

Whether they are full-time caretakers or occasional visitors, grandparents can serve an extraordinarily important role in children's lives. A good grandparent–grandchild relationship has been shown to be a protective factor with at-risk children (Grizenko & Pawliuk, 1994) and with adolescent mothers (M. M. Black & Nitz, 1996). The protective function of grandparents is often due to grandparents' focus on the positive aspects of their grandchildren and their ability to serve as competent role models (Werner, 1995; Werner & Smith, 2001). In addition, grandparents help children learn about themselves within a much larger context, that of an extended family and of generations of family members, in order for children to feel part of something larger than themselves (M. M. Black & Nitz, 1996). Grandparents can serve important roles for their grandchildren, whether or not the grandchildren are at risk for the development of problems.

Novelist Alice Hoffman's (1996) amusing and poignant recollection of advice from her grandmother, Lillie Lulkin, included the following:

- When crossing the street, never trust the judgment of drivers. They may not stop for you.
- Anything served in a fancy restaurant can be equaled in your own kitchen. As a matter of fact, everything can be made out of potatoes—bread, soup, pancakes, cake.
- Between men and women, love is not only blind, but stupid.
- Don't kid yourself—nothing lasts forever.
- Sleep is overrated. Who needs it?
- Don't think that good deeds go unforgotten.
- Bathing on a cold day is worse for your health than a little dirt will ever be.
- Being old is not what you think it is. You feel the same. You are the same. The woman beside you is the girl she once was. Remember that. Remember me.

within the family to help protect them from this adversity. It is heartening to learn that protective factors can exist outside the family as well as within it.

I wish I could help people
cuz they need help right now
cuz other people need
to help other people
so they can get more stuff

They need a lot of stuff
so they can
eat every day

—Dorothy, 11 years old and homeless
(Children's Defense Fund–Minnesota, 1990; p. 34)

ROLE MODELS OUTSIDE THE FAMILY

In addition to the protective factors within the family, there are a number of protective factors outside the family. Of special note is the importance that one or two special individuals can play in a child's life. Even a child from an adverse home environment can be helped significantly by a stable and caring role model outside the fam-

ily (Masten & Coatsworth, 1998). Typical role models are teachers, coaches, and friends, but many others can serve in a similar capacity—religious leaders, neighbors, scout troop leaders, parents of a friend, and so on.

Many adults can look back on their childhood and recall a teacher who took special interest in their well-being. When children do not have many other appropriate role models within their lives, teachers can serve a very important purpose in the child's growth and development. In fact, many preventionists argue that teachers are among

BOX *8.4*

MENTORS FROM ALL WALKS OF LIFE

In her eloquent memoir, *Lanterns: A Memoir of Mentors*, Dr. Marian Wright Edelman (1999) describes the many different mentors that she has had in her life. Born into a large, impoverished African American family living in the segregated South, Edelman went on to become a civil rights attorney and the president of the Children's Defense Fund. She attributes much of her professional and personal success to a number of mentors throughout her life:

- Her parents.
- Community elders.
- Religious leaders.

- Teachers.
- Professors.
- Dr. Martin Luther King Jr. and other civil rights leaders.

While reflecting on her life, Edelman also noted how historical figures (such as Harriet Tubman and Sojourner Truth) can serve as role models and mentors to children who learn about them in school and through reading. As someone who has experienced many cycles of life, Edelman also highlights how children can serve as mentors and role models for adults in a way that will empower both the children and the adults.

the most appropriate individuals to serve in a protective role with children, given that children spend so much time in the school setting (Consortium on the School-based Promotion of Social Competence, 1994). Teachers who provide clear expectations of children's educational and personal success can help children develop great self-efficacy and try hard to achieve their goals (Hawkins, 1997). A positive student–teacher relationship decreased the likelihood of aggression, especially in students with unsupportive parents (Hughes, Cavell, & Jackson, 1999). Teachers can also serve both to empower children to take appropriate control over their own lives and to encourage children's personal responsibility for their own actions (Meyers, 1989). Overall, teachers not only can serve as role models and mentors but also can show care and consideration to children who might not otherwise experience that type of respect.

Similar to the connection with a teacher, children's connections to their schools are also associated with resilient outcomes. Specifically, children and adolescents who feel a sense of community at their school (Battistich & Hom, 1997) and who feel a sense of identification with their school (Honora, 1999) show better emotional/behavioral and academic outcomes than those who feel no sense of community or identity. Strong connections with a teacher or other school personnel can enhance this type of school identification in children and adolescents.

Like teachers, coaches can serve an important role for children who are involved in sports activities. Whether they are volunteers from the local recreation center or professionals in a competitive high school sport, coaches can have an astounding impact on their players' feelings and well-being. Researchers have conducted some fasci-

nating studies on how youngsters are affected by coaches (reviewed in Smith & Smoll, 1997). As you might imagine, coaches who are supportive in their interactions with their child and adolescent players tend to have players who are happier with their performances and who feel better about their athletic abilities (Smith & Smoll, 1997). The best outcomes for child and adolescent athletes are associated with coaches who:

- Show a high degree of positive reinforcement for both desired performance and for effort.

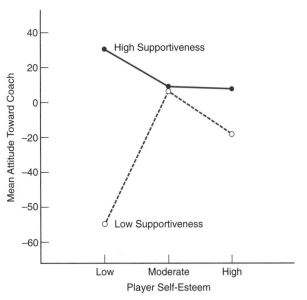

FIGURE 8.2 Mean Evaluations of Coaches by Young Athletes as a Function of Athletes' Self-esteem and Supportiveness of the Coach

Source: Smith & Smoll (1997)

- Deal with player mistakes by providing encouragement and technical instruction.

- De-emphasize the importance of winning and emphasize the importance of enjoying the game and improving one's own performance.

This research also noted that negative, punitive, and hostile actions from coaches can have devastating effects on child and adolescent athletes. Negativity from coaches was associated with low self-esteem and poor attitudes in children (Smith & Smoll, 1997). Interestingly, children with high self-esteem before beginning the sport tended to fare better in the context of low supportiveness from the coach. Figure 8.2 shows that child and adolescent athletes evaluated their coaches more positively if the coach was supportive or if the child had adequate self-esteem even when the coach was not supportive.

Overall, coaches, teachers, and other adults in children's lives can serve to enhance the resilience of children. Friends of children can also serve a protective function. Just as involvement with friends who have deviant behavior can lead to problematic behavior in children (Frauenglass et al., 1997), having competent and caring friends can serve as a protective factor against adverse environments (Werner, 1995; Werner & Smith, 2001). Notably, there is evidence that children and adolescents

are quite active in their choice of friends (Brook, Whiteman, Brook, & Gordon, 1982). This finding suggests that, rather than passively being swayed by the "wrong" group of friends, troubled children and adolescents tend to seek out other troubled youngsters with whom to become friends (Brook et al., 1982).

Based on an extensive meta-analysis, researchers found that children's friendships served to promote social and emotional growth, especially with strong and close friendships (Newcomb & Bagwell, 1995). Childhood friendships also serve as a protective factor against peer victimization in schools, such as being teased or being picked on (E. V. E. Hodges, Boivin, Vitaro, & Bukowski, 1999). Specifically, children with at least one close friend were less likely to be victimized by others and, when they were victimized, they showed fewer emotional/behavioral problems as a result of the victimization than those children who did not have a close friend (E. V. E. Hodges et al., 1999). Children can also serve as peer-tutors and mentors within the school system (Foot, Morgan, & Shute, 1990). Peer-tutoring appears to help both the giver and the recipient, with improvements in self-esteem, academic functioning, and social skills shown by both groups of children (Foot et al., 1990). Thus, children's friendships can serve a strong protective role for children who are at risk for the development of emotional/behavioral problems.

Overall, there are a variety of individuals outside of the family who can serve in a protective function to help increase the resilience of children against adverse environments. As will be discussed in Chapter 17, one of the best ways to help children as a nonprofessional is to become a mentor or role model for an at-risk child. Many programs, such Big Brothers/Big Sisters and the Boys and Girls Clubs, serve an integral role in helping find competent mentors for children who otherwise might not have such positive influences in their lives.

PROSOCIAL ORGANIZATIONS

Children can become involved in any number of prosocial activities associated with resilience: sports, religious activities, after-school clubs, creative and artistic endeavors, and volunteer activities. It appears that such activities can help children build feelings of competence and achievement; find appropriate role models; develop a friendship network; and take advantage of educational, academic, and creative opportunities (Masten & Coatsworth, 1998). Note that none of these activities serve directly as a protective factor. Rather, the quality of

Close friendships serve a protective role in the lives of children and adolescents (even when the friends are within the family).

Case Study: A Competent Friend Serving as a Role Model

Eva is a sophomore in high school in an impoverished urban area. She was born in Trinidad but came to the United States to live with her aunt and uncle. She recently moved in with her mother, who came to the United States from Trinidad a few years ago. In addition to living in impoverished circumstances, Eva has a very conflicted relationship with her mother and a somewhat conflicted relationship with her father. Eva had experienced great difficulties in school, but recently her school performance and self-esteem have improved. When an interviewer asked her if there was anyone in her life she looked up to, Eva replied:

> *That I look up to? Yeah, my best friend, Tamara. I've always looked up to her and then, there's like I'm inter-*

ested in poetry. I write a lot of poetry. And I like a lot of black poets, like Langston Hughes. Like in my freshman year, I used to be like an average student—a "C" student. And then I felt good about myself. I don't know, I think I got it from my friend Tamara. She encouraged me. And like this year I'm doing real good. And getting honors and stuff. I don't know, I think it was really her . . . [Tamara] would always compete with me like, you know, "Oh, I bet you can't do it." It wasn't in the negative stuff. Like she used to be like, "I bet you can't get the honor roll before I do." (p. 238)

SOURCE: Way (1998).

---

the activities themselves and of the adults who serve as mentors within them must be considered when evaluating their protective role in a child's life.

As mentioned earlier with regard to coaches, sports activities can help protect children from the harsh ramifications of an otherwise adverse environment. Not only can sports activities expose children and adolescents to appropriate role models in coaches and trainers, but involvement in sports can also help children obtain a healthy and active lifestyle (Bar-Or, 1996). Sports activities are helpful for children experiencing cancer (Elkin, Tye, Hudson, & Crom, 1998) as well as many other childhood difficulties such as diabetes, low self-esteem, and poor academic performance (Bar-Or, 1996). Team sports (also known as refereed sports) such as basketball and soccer seem to serve more of a protective function than individual sports (also known as judged sports) such as gymnastics and competitive dance (Zucker, Womble, Williamson, & Perrin, 1999). Specifically, judged sports such as gymnastics were associated with eating disorders, body image problems and other emotional/behavioral problems more often than were refereed sports such as basketball (Zucker et al., 1999).

Involvement in religious and spiritual activities may also serve as a protective factor for children at risk for the development of emotional/behavioral problems (Mahoney, Pargament, Tarakeshwar, & Swank, 2001; Winfield, 1995). Attendance at a place of worship has been associated with decreased risk for substance abuse in both African American and Caucasian American adolescents (S. L. Albrecht, Amey, & Miller, 1996) and with decreased risk for suicide in Inuit youth (Kirmayer, Boothroyd, & Hodgins, 1998). Spirituality, regardless of attendance at a place of worship, has also been found to

serve in a protective role among children and adolescents at risk for the development of emotional/behavioral problems (Haight, 1998) and substance abuse (L. Miller, Davies, & Greenwald, 2000). Parents' spirituality is associated with more positive parenting, which is in turn associated with better child outcomes (Mahoney et al., 2001). In a sample of older adolescents, religious faith was associated with optimism and better coping skills (Plante, Yancey, Sherman, & Guertin, 2000). Involvement in spiritual activities exposes children to social support and a larger community of role models (Samaan, 2000). Overall, some type of faith or commonly held belief system that is shared either within or outside the family serves a protective function for at-risk children and adolescents (Masten & Coatsworth, 1998).

Involvement in extracurricular activities also serves a protective function in children's lives. Involvement in after-school clubs and other enrichment activities predicted better academic achievement in elementary school students (Kurtz-Costes, Meece, & Floryan, 1999). Structured extracurricular activities also predicted emotional adjustment more than two years later in elementary school students (Posner & Vandell, 1999). Unstructured activities, such as watching television and hanging out, were found to predict maladjustment in children (Posner & Vandell, 1999). Overall, structured extracurricular activities such as after-school clubs, library activities, and crafts activities were associated with resilience in children and adolescents.

Involvement in the arts is also associated with enhanced emotional/behavioral functioning in children and adolescents. Although research on the specific type of involvement in the arts (e.g., the visual arts versus the musical arts) is limited, artistic and creative activities in

BOX *8.5*

PREVENTION WORKS

The Houston Parent–Child Development Center (D. L. Johnson, 1988) is one of many prevention programs that attempts to enhance the amount of protective factors in children's lives in order to prevent the development of emotional/behavioral problems. This program was targeted at young Mexican American families who lived in an impoverished community. Families were invited into the program when their infant was one year old, and the program followed these infants for two years. Home visits were conducted and enrichment day care facilities were offered for those interested in such services. Services were provided in both English and in Spanish, depending on the family's choice of language. Among the strategies that were implemented to try to prevent emotional/behavioral problems were:

- Parent education in order to increase parental warmth, support, and structure.

- Enhanced enriching activities for the infants and toddlers to increase motor, intellectual, and social-emotional development.
- Staff members who helped parents increase their social support network and their involvement with other supportive individuals.
- Medical care and education about how to access additional medical resources for the family.
- Financial resources and education about how to deal with financial stressors that might arise in the family.

At the end of the project, as well as at follow-up after five and eight years, children who participated in the prevention program showed higher intellectual functioning, better academic performance, and lower emotional/behavior problems than children who did not participate. This program illustrates that knowledge about protective factors can be applied to prevention programs in order to enhance protective factors for at-risk children.

---

general serve a protective function for at-risk children (Werner, 1995; Werner & Smith, 2001). The use of popular hip-hop or rap music in prevention programs is associated with decreased risk for transmission of HIV in African American adolescents (Stephens, Braithwaite, & Taylor, 1998). Artistic involvement is associated with increased self-esteem and decreased rates of substance abuse, and is used in prevention programs within low-income urban families (Emshoff, Avery, Raduka, & Anderson, 1996). It may be that, like other protective factors, involvement in the arts can help expose at-risk children and adolescents to other opportunities and lifestyles in addition to helping children and adolescents develop feelings of competence and pride in their own skills.

Involvement in volunteer activities has not received a great deal of empirical attention, but it appears that such activities can serve as a protective factor in at-risk children (Werner, 1995; Werner & Smith, 2001). Interestingly, there has been a wealth of research on elderly individuals' involvement in volunteer activities. In elderly populations, volunteerism has been associated with better physical health, better mental health, and longer life span (Oman, Thoresen, McMahon, 1999). Volunteerism was an even stronger protective factor than social support or involvement in religious organizations (Oman et al., 1999). Although this research was conducted with an eld-

erly population (ages 55 to 85), these findings have relevance for children's and adolescents' involvement in volunteer activities. Volunteerism can help an individual feel pride in helping others, can expose the individual to other appropriate role models and mentors, and can create feelings of personal competence and personal accomplishment in the individual (Oman et al., 1999). These factors appear to be just as relevant for children and adolescents as they are for older adults.

Although the focus has been on resilience against the development of emotional/behavioral problems, most of the protective factors associated with prosocial activities also serve to decrease the likelihood of other adverse outcomes such as poor physical health (Jessor, Turbin, & Costa, 1998) and poor academic performance (McDonald & Sayger, 1998). These protective factors are associated with resilience in children and adolescents from a diverse array of ethnic and racial backgrounds, including African American and Caucasian American (Jessor et al., 1998), Hispanic/Latino/Latina Americans (Alva, 1995), Pacific Islanders (Werner & Smith, 2001), Native Americans (McCubbin, Thompson, Thompson, & Fromer, 1998), Asian Americans (Fuligni et al., 1999), and children and adolescents from across the globe (Albee, Bond, & Monsey, 1992; Fuligni, 1998). Box 8.5 discusses a prevention program designed to increase the protective characteristics in a child's environment in order to decrease the likelihood of emotional/behavioral problems.

Overall, studies of protective factors, resilience, and prevention programs are well established in the research literature. A number of recent articles (Masten, 2001; Pedro-Carroll, 2001) and books (Cicchetti, Rappaport, Sandler, & Weissberg, 2000) are available with comprehensive updates for interested students.

SUMMARY AND KEY CONCEPTS

Protective factors are characteristics in children's lives that are associated with competent outcomes even in adverse circumstances. Children from adverse environments who overcome these obstacles due to protective factors in their lives are thought to show **resilience**.

Intellectual Functioning

Children with at least average intelligence are thought to be more resilient to adverse environments than are children with lower levels of intellectual functioning.

Self-Efficacy and Coping Styles

Self-efficacy is shown when children expect success and when they believe that they can perform successfully in any new or challenging situation. Good coping skills and problem-solving skills have also been found to serve as protective factors against adverse circumstances.

Family Factors

A number of factors within the family seem to serve as protective factors, including a close relationship with a stable parent or primary caretaker, authoritative parenting, and kinship networks with stable and caring relatives such as grandparents. Parents with an **authoritative parenting style**—which is characterized by warmth, age-appropriate structure, and high expectations—tend to have children who show resilience even in the face of adverse circumstances. **Scaffolding** (providing support and structure for the child's next level of development) is one of the many appropriate behaviors that these parents tend to show.

Role Models Outside the Family

Just like individuals within the family, individuals outside the family can also serve a protective function. Of particular note is that teachers, coaches, and competent friends have been shown to serve in protective functions for at-risk children.

Prosocial Organizations

Children can get involved in various prosocial activities that help to serve a protective function in their lives. Involvement in sports and other athletic activities, religious or spiritual activities, after-school clubs, creative and artistic endeavors, and volunteer activities can help to increase resilience in children and adolescents.

KEY TERMS

protective factors	resilience	self-efficacy	authoritative parenting style	scaffolding

SUGGESTED READINGS

McBride, James. *The Color of Water: A Black Man's Tribute to His White Mother*. New York: Riverhead Books, 1996. In this eloquent memoir, McBride describes a number of risk factors that he encounters throughout his life (e.g., racism, poverty, broken family, unstable environment) and shows how protective factors (especially a strong and caring mother) helped him triumph over adverse circumstances.

Walker, Lou Ann. *A Loss for Words: The Story of Deafness in a Family*. New York: Harper and Row Publishers, 1986. In this poignant memoir, Walker illustrates the many protective factors that were evident in her life as a hearing child of deaf parents.

SUGGESTED VIEWINGS

The Cure (1995). Peter Horton (director), Robert Kuhn (writer). VHS. This alternately amusing and painful film tells the story of two young boys, one who is HIV-positive and one who is not. Their childhood antics and wild adventures illustrate the protective nature of stable friendships.

Kramer vs. Kramer (1979). Robert Benton (director and screenwriter), based on novel by Avery Corman. VHS/DVD. In this classic film, the protective nature of a competent and stable father is shown to overcome the adverse effects of interparental conflict, divorce, and an absent mother.

CHAPTER 9

MOOD DISORDERS, DEPRESSIVE SYNDROMES, AND DEPRESSIVE MOODS

CHAPTER SUMMARY

Night
to sit under a tree
by the light of the moon
listening to the sounds of the night
thinking about the good and bad things that happened in your
    life
and while you are thinking you think about your favorite
but saddest song and cry in a sad way.
        —Billy, 10 years old and homeless
(Children's Defense Fund–Minnesota, 1990; p. 22).

Nearly everyone has felt sad or depressed at some point. Therefore, it would seem that depression does not need to be defined because it is so well known. There were, however, many misconceptions historically about depression in infancy, childhood, and adolescence. These misconceptions included the belief that children could not be depressed, the belief in anaclitic depression, and the idea of masked depression.

From the 1930s to the 1960s, the predominant belief among psychoanalytic theorists was that children could not be depressed (Bemporad, 1994). Serious clinical depression was thought possible only when an individual had a fully developed and internalized superego, which theorists believed occurred in late adolescence or young adulthood (Bemporad, 1994). Ironically, some psychodynamic theorists and attachment theorists were identifying depression in infants at approximately the same time that others were questioning the existence of depression in anyone without a fully developed superego.

ANACLITIC DEPRESSION AND FAILURE TO THRIVE IN INFANCY

In the mid-1940s, the term **anaclitic depression** was used to refer to infants who had lost their primary caregiver or whose primary caregiver was physically or emotionally abusive or distant. These infants showed signs of whining, withdrawal, weight loss, impaired social interactions, immobile facial expressions, and slowed or stunted growth (Spitz, 1946). Somewhat later, John Bowlby (1973) became interested in infants who were institutionalized and who received little or no individual care and attention. These infants would often show **failure to thrive**, which is a condition marked by apathy, slow motor development, lack of interest in surroundings, and sometimes lack of interest in food or liquids (Achenbach, 1982). The related concepts of anaclitic depression and failure to thrive represent early understandings of depression in infants.

More recently, the *Diagnostic Classification: 0–3* system conceptualized depression in infants and toddlers with two primary diagnoses (Zero to Three/National Center for Clinical Infant Programs, 1994). **Mood disorder: prolonged bereavement/grief reaction** occurs when an infant loses a primary caretaker and shows signs of crying, withdrawal, disrupted eating and sleeping, regression to previous earlier functioning, detachment, and extreme sensitivity. **Mood disorder: depression of infancy and early childhood** is diagnosed when an infant or toddler shows at least two weeks of depressed or irritable mood, decreased interest in activities that were enjoyable previously, decreased capacity to protest, excessive whining, possibilities of disturbances in sleeping and eating, and limited social interactions. These problems are often associated with disrupted attachment patterns for infants, although other etiologies have been found that are comparable to depression in older children (Schwartz, Gladstone, & Kaslow, 1998; Zero to Three/National Center for Clinical Infant Programs, 1994).

Happiness is an imaginary condition, formerly often attributed by the living to the dead, now usually attributed by adults to children and by children to adults.

—Thomas Szasz

MASKED DEPRESSION

Among the other popular conceptualizations of depression in childhood and adolescence in the late 1960s and early 1970s was **masked depression** (Cytryn & McKnew, 1972; K. Glaser, 1968), a term used when children showed aggressive, hyperactive, or other acting out behaviors in order "to ward off the unbearable feelings of

Children who experience depression are often isolated from their peers.

despair" (Cytryn & McKnew, 1979, p. 327). The idea was that children who showed certain externalizing types of problems were, in reality, depressed. Given the highly inferential nature of the term *masked depression*, and the lack of established validity, the concept has been dropped from more recent conceptualizations of depression in childhood and adolescence (Achenbach, 1982). Note, however, that high rates of comorbidity between depression and some externalizing disorders do exist. As will be noted later in this chapter, in the section on comorbidity, the coexistence of depression and an externalizing disorder is very different from the idea that the externalizing disorder is "masking," or hiding, the true depression. We will now turn to the current conceptualizations of depression in childhood and adolescence.

MAJOR DEPRESSIVE DISORDER

As shown in Table 9.1, **major depressive disorder (MDD)** is defined clearly in the *Diagnostic and Statistical Manual of Mental Disorders, Fourth Edition (DSM-IV)*. By looking at the diagnostic criteria, you can see that MDD is a serious disorder and is more than just temporarily feeling down or sad. The disorder is diagnosed only when there are clear indications of a composite of symptoms in addition to clinical distress or impairment in social, occupational, or educational functioning.

Major depressive disorder can be diagnosed as a single episode or as recurrent. MDD would not be diagnosed if the symptoms were better accounted for by other disorders (such as schizoaffective disorder, schizophrenia, or other similar disorders). MDD is listed on Axis I when it is diagnosed.

Case Study: Jacob, The Withdrawn Boy

Jacob Samuels was seven years old when his second-grade teacher first became concerned about him. For the first two months of school, Jacob just sat at his desk. He did not stand for the Pledge of Allegiance, he did not go to the chalkboard when asked, and he did not walk around the room when allowed. He followed the other children to and from the cafeteria, but he usually sat by himself and he rarely ate anything for lunch.

The teacher arranged a meeting with Jacob's parents, but they did not show up. The teacher then referred Jacob to the school psychologist, who again arranged a meeting with Mr. and Mrs. Samuels. The parents did not show up for that meeting, but they did finally attend a meeting that was scheduled personally by the principal. Jacob's father worked for a plumbing company, and Jacob's mother was a full-time homemaker. Mr. and Mrs. Samuels reported that Jacob was not a discipline problem and they were surprised that the school officials were concerned about him. They acknowledged that he did not have any friends, but they stated that he preferred playing with his younger sister and brother.

When interviewed later by the school psychologist, Jacob sat passively in the office and did not make eye contact with the psychologist. Jacob reported that he had a lot of chores, such as making his bed each morning, changing his sheets once a week, taking out the garbage each night, and taking care of the dog. He stated that sometimes he wished he was the youngest in the family so he would not have so many chores. Jacob also reported that he used to love reading, but that lately he did not enjoy it, so he quit reading except for homework. He also reported that he often could not fall asleep, given his "bad" thoughts. With much probing, the psychologist was able to find out that Jacob some-

times thought about pushing his younger brother off the swing and fantasized about not doing his chores. He cried when he acknowledged that his mother loved him very much, but he thought she was too bossy and he complained that she would not leave him alone to relax and read.

The school psychologist had Jacob complete a Children's Depression Inventory. Jacob scored in the moderately depressed category, with high scores on eating problems, social isolation, feeling sad, sleeping problems, and loss of pleasure in everyday activities.

After diagnosing Jacob with major depressive disorder, the school psychologist developed a treatment plan for Jacob that included cognitive-behavioral therapy with Jacob and family sessions with Jacob's parents. Jacob responded well to the sessions, and his parents' sessions revealed a number of issues that had been troubling to them. Mrs. Jacobs, for example, felt both trapped by her responsibilities as a homemaker and often overwhelmed with life. She had wanted to attend college, but Mr. Jacobs had not been supportive. Through the parents' therapy sessions, Mr. and Mrs. Jacobs developed a plan for Mrs. Jacobs to begin taking classes at the local community college, with the children's grandmother caring for the children while their mother was at school. Mr. Jacobs began to encourage his wife in her educational pursuits. After three months of treatment, both Jacob and his parents were well-functioning and much happier.

Two years later, the therapist checked up on Jacob and his family. In the time since therapy, Jacob had not had any recurrence of depression and his parents were functioning very well. Mrs. Jacobs continued to attend classes at the local college and had decided to become a nurse.

SOURCE: R. K. Morgan (1999).

These diagnostic criteria apply to both adults and children. There has never been a specific diagnosis of childhood depression in any version of *DSM*. When diagnosing a child or adolescent with *DSM-IV*, there are two notes that apply. First, children and adolescents might show irritable mood rather than depressed mood. Second, children might fail to make expected weight gains rather than losing or gaining significant amounts of weight. Although these acknowledgments of developmental differences are appropriate, they ignore the many other differences between depressive symptoms in children versus adults (the section headed "Course of the Disorder" later in this chapter provides further information).

If children or adolescents experience one or more of these symptoms in reaction to an identifiable stressor, but if they do not meet criteria for MDD, they might meet criteria for **adjustment disorder with depressed mood**. This disorder would be diagnosed when a child or adolescent experiences depressed mood, tearfulness, or feelings of hopelessness in reaction to an identifiable stressor that occurred within three months of the psychological symptoms (American Psychiatric Association, 2000). Given

that MDD is considered the more severe disorder, more attention has been paid to it than to adjustment disorder with depressed mood.

Prevalence Rates

As mentioned Chapter 1, the word *prevalence* refers to the number of cases of a particular disorder at any one time. Also discussed in that chapter was the difficulty in establishing accurate prevalence rates that are reflective of children and adolescents of any age, race/ethnicity, gender, and socioeconomic status. Prevalence rates presented in this section refer to the diagnosis of MDD, which represents the categorical approach to defining abnormal child behavior. Based on results from the Methods for the Epidemiology of Child and Adolescent Mental Disorders (MECA) study, rates of MDD range from 0.7% to 7.1% in children and adolescents (Shaffer et al., 1996). This range reflects differences in informants (i.e., youth, parent, or youth and parent combined) and reflects differences in severity of symptoms. Notably, parents tended to report greater rates of depression in adolescents

---

TABLE 9.1 *DSM-IV* Diagnostic Criteria for Major Depressive Episode

A. Five (or more) of the following symptoms have been present during the same 2-week period and represent a change from previous functioning; at least one of the symptoms is either (1) depressed mood or (2) loss of interest or pleasure.

Note: Do not include symptoms that are clearly due to a general medical condition, or mood-incongruent delusions or hallucinations.

(1) depressed mood most of the day, nearly every day, as indicated by either subjective report (e.g., feels sad or empty) or observation made by others (e.g., appears tearful). Note: In children and adolescents, can be irritable mood.

(2) markedly diminished interest or pleasure in all, or almost all, activities most of the day, nearly every day (as indicated by either subjective account or observation made by others).

(3) significant weight loss when not dieting or weight gain (e.g., a change of more than 5% of body weight in a month), or decrease or increase in appetite nearly every day. Note: In children, consider failure to make expected weight gains.

(4) insomnia or hypersomnia nearly every day.

(5) psychomotor agitation or retardation nearly every day (observable by others, not merely subjective feelings of restlessness or being slowed down).

(6) fatigue or loss of energy nearly every day.

(7) feelings of worthlessness or excessive or inappropriate guilt (which may be delusional) nearly every day (not merely self-reproach or guilt about being sick).

(8) diminished ability to think or concentrate, or indecisiveness, nearly every day (either by subjective account or as observed by others).

(9) recurrent thoughts of death (not just fear of dying), recurrent suicidal ideation without a specific plan, or a suicide attempt or a specific plan for committing suicide.

B. The symptoms do not meet criteria for a Mixed Episode of both highs and lows (related to Bipolar Disorder).

C. The symptoms cause clinically significant distress or impairment in social, occupational, or other important areas of functioning.

D. The symptoms are not due to the direct physiological effects of a substance (e.g., a drug of abuse, a medication) or a general medical condition (e.g., hypothyroidism).

E. The symptoms are not better accounted for by Bereavement, i.e., after the loss of a loved one, the symptoms persist for longer than 2 months or are characterized by marked functional impairment, morbid preoccupation with worthlessness, suicidal ideation, psychotic symptoms, or psychomotor retardation.

SOURCE: American Psychiatric Association (2000). Reprinted with permission from the *Diagnostic and Statistical Manual of Mental Disorders, Fourth Edition, Text Revision.* Copyright 2000 American Psychiatric Association.

"Son, it's important to remember that it's O.K. to be depressed."

than reported by the adolescents themselves (King et al., 1997).

Before the MECA study, the most commonly reported prevalence rates for depression suggested that between 2% and 5% of children and adolescents in the community experience MDD at any one time (Garrison et al., 1997; Schwartz et al., 1998). Between 10% and 50% of children and adolescents in outpatient and inpatient psychiatric facilities experience MDD (Fleming & Offord, 1990; Schwartz et al., 1998). Although these prevalence rates reflect the number of children and adolescents who meet criteria for MDD, it is important to note that groups of depressed children are very heterogeneous (i.e., they have a lot of variability of symptoms; Harrington, Rutter, & Fombonne, 1996).

As might be expected, rates of depression increase with age. Depression in preschoolers is relatively rare, with most estimates suggesting that less than 1% of pre-school children in nonclinical facilities show clinical depression (Kashani, Holcomb, & Orvaschel, 1986). In school-age children, prevalence rates range from 2% to 4% (Angold & Rutter, 1992). By the time of adolescence, prevalence rates in nonclinical facilities rise to 7% and higher (Petersen et al., 1993; W. M. Reynolds, 1995). These rates are all significantly higher when clinical samples are studied, such as when children are receiving mental health services on an outpatient or inpatient basis or when they are receiving help from a school psychologist (Kovacs, 1989). One review estimated that at least one out

of every six adolescents receiving inpatient mental health services had a primary diagnosis related to a mood disorder (W. M. Reynolds, 1995).

When considering prevalence rates based on gender, there is an interaction between age and gender. That is, comments cannot be made on prevalence rates based on gender without also commenting on the age of the children under consideration. Before puberty, there is relatively consistent evidence that boys and girls show approximately equal rates of depression (Stark, Bronik, Wong, Wells, & Ostrander, 2000). After puberty, there is consistent evidence that girls show much higher rates of depression than boys, usually estimated at a 2:1 ratio (Hankin & Abramson, 2001; Stark et al., 2000). This gender ratio continues into adulthood, with women showing at least two or three times higher rates of depression than men (Nolen-Hoeksema, 2001). Although there are many theories about why this gender difference occurs in adolescence, the most compelling reasons have to do with psychosocial and cognitive factors. It appears that girls are more oriented toward sociality and cooperation, and are more likely to show ruminative coping styles (where they dwell on their problems rather than trying either to distract themselves or take action against the problems; Nolen-Hoeksema & Girgus, 1994). In addition, girls' maladaptive cognitions appear to be more salient than boys' maladaptive cognitions (Hankin & Abramson, 2001). These factors may put girls at greater risk for depression in adolescence when they are faced with greater personal and social challenges that are brought about by both biological and social stressors.

Prevalence rates based on socioeconomic status (SES) are more difficult to interpret. A number of studies have found that rates of major depression do not differ by SES (Costello et al., 1988; Whitaker et al., 1990). If depression is viewed as a continuous variable, however, higher rates of depressive symptoms have been associated with lower levels of SES (Gore, Aseltine, & Colton, 1993).

There has been very little research into prevalence rates of depression regarding ethnicity and race (Evans & Lee, 1998). A few studies have found no differences in depression rates between African American and Caucasian American youth (Costello et al., 1988; Kandel & Davies, 1982). There is, however, some indication that African American youth, especially boys, may show slightly higher rates of depression than Caucasian American boys (Garrison, Jackson, Marsteller, McKeown, & Addy, 1990). In a comprehensive review of race/ethnicity and adolescent depression, the only firm pattern was that Mexican American adolescents had higher rates of depression than youth in other ethnic groups (Roberts,

TABLE 9.2 Overview of Prevalence Information for Major Depressive Disorder

Prevalence	2–5%
Age	Adolescents > Children
Gender	Before puberty, equal rates; after puberty, Girls > Boys (2:1)
Socioeconomic status	No clear-cut patterns
Race/Ethnicity	Possibility of higher rates in African American boys

2000). These higher rates of depression appear to be due to acculturation, feelings of fatalism, and a lack of control (Roberts, 2000). Depression has been identified in children and adolescents in nearly every region and country, including Asia, Central America, Russia, and Mexico (Evans & Lee, 1998; Johnson-Powell & Yamamoto, 1997).

Overall, the most compelling difference in rates of major depression are found for age (with older children and adolescents showing more depression than younger children) and for gender (with postpubertal girls showing higher rates than any other group of youngsters). Table 9.2 gives an overview of prevalence information of MDD.

Comorbidity

As mentioned in Chapter 1, comorbidity is the co-occurrence of two different disorders in one individual. For many disorders, including depression, comorbidity is the rule rather than the exception. Depression is often found in children and adolescents who are also showing other clinical disorders (Hammen & Compas, 1994; D. Schwartz et al., 1998). In fact, children who are depressed are more likely to be comorbid with another disorder than are adults who are depressed (Cantwell, 1992). The highest rates of comorbidity are between MDD and an anxiety disorder (Angold, Costello, & Erkanli, 1999), with one study finding 75% comorbidity of anxiety disorders in a community sample of depressed adolescents (Kashani et al., 1987). The high rates of comorbidity between depression and anxiety are especially noticeable in girls as opposed to boys (Joiner, Blalock, & Wagner, 1999). Comorbidity between depression and anxiety is so high that the two syndromes often cannot be distinguished as separate problems (Chorpita, Plummer, & Moffitt, 2000; Eley & Stevenson, 1999; Hinden, Compas, Howell, & Achenbach, 1997).

Relatively high rates of comorbidity have been found between depression and a number of other clinical disor-

ders, including conduct disorder, oppositional defiant disorder, attention-deficit/hyperactivity disorder, substance use disorders, and eating disorders (Stark et al., 2000). One study found that 97% of adolescents who were in treatment for depression met criteria for at least one other clinical disorder, such as separation anxiety disorder, conduct disorder, oppositional defiant disorder, and social phobia (Tamplin, Goodyer, & Herbert, 1998). Comorbidity between depression and a substance use disorder is especially high in later adolescence (Rao, Daley, & Hammen, 2000). Overall, the overwhelming evidence shows that MDD is comorbid with a great many other disorders. Thus, high rates of comorbidity are expected for children and adolescents who are diagnosed with MDD, especially if they are seeking treatment for their depression.

Depression is also linked to the onset of other disorders, which are sometimes comorbid with depression and sometimes develop later. Later substance use is more strongly associated with conduct problems than with depressive problems (Miller-Johnson, Lochman, Coie, Terry, & Hyman, 1998). MDD and disruptive disorders, however, are associated with earlier onset of substance use and abuse and higher rates of substance use and abuse in both male and female adolescents (Costello, Erkanli, Federman, & Angold, 1999; Rao et al., 1999). Depression is notable for the disruption in current functioning as well as the link to disturbed functioning in later years.

Course of the Disorder

Symptoms of depression are likely to differ somewhat based on the age of the child. Preschoolers and younger children are more apt to show irritability and somatic complaints rather than reporting dysphoric mood or hopelessness (D. Schwartz et al., 1998). Disturbed sleep patterns are less likely to be seen in preschoolers and children than in adolescents and adults (Emslie, Weinberg, Kennard, & Kowatch, 1994). Adolescents are also more likely to report depressed mood, feelings of hopelessness, and low self-esteem than are younger children (B. Weiss et al., 1992). Self-esteem is inversely related to age in clinical samples (Orvaschel, Beeferman, & Kabacoff, 1997); in other words, the older the child or adolescent, the lower the self-esteem. Poor self-esteem is linked strongly to depression in adolescents (Tram & Cole, 2000).

The average length of a depressive episode varies somewhat, depending on the characteristics of the sample under investigation. Overall, the average length of a depressive episode in children and adolescents ranges from 16 to 36 weeks, with longer episodes found for out-

Case Study: Carly, The Distressed Adolescent

Carly Prochaski, a 15-year-old high school sophomore, had always earned A's in her honors courses. In the last grading period, however, she failed all of her courses. The school counselor became alarmed and recommended that Carly and her parents seek help of a therapist.

During the first interview with the therapist, Carly stated that she did not have any problems and that her parents were overreacting. She realized that her grades had dropped, but she felt sure that she knew the class material. Carly denied feeling sad but did acknowledge that she did not enjoy activities (such as soccer and going to the mall) as much as she did previously. She reported that she had many friends, but when pushed she admitted that she had not done anything with her friends for at least two months. Carly reported that she had gained 10 pounds recently, which concerned her greatly since she had always been thin and trim.

When asked about drug use, Carly denied any use of illicit drugs. She did say that she had tried beer at a party once, but she decided not to drink anymore because she had heard that Native Americans were at greater risk than other people for alcoholism. Carly, a Native American, had been adopted by the Prochaskis as an infant. Although her biological parents were in high school when she was born, she said she often wished that they had not given her up for adoption because she sometimes felt uncomfortable around so many Caucasian Americans.

Mr. and Mrs. Prochaski reported that Carly had always been a happy and healthy child. She achieved excellence in schoolwork and on the soccer field. She had lots of friends and was always appreciated by those around her. When asked about allowing Carly more access to her Native American culture, her parents stated that they had purchased books for her about Native American customs and they always had her take the part of the Indian in school plays. When asked if they had taken Carly to any areas, such as the local reservation, where Carly could meet more Native Americans, Carly's parents said that they had not done so because they did not want her to see "how lazy those people were."

With written permission from the parents and Carly, the psychologist was also able to meet with the school counselor. The school counselor was greatly concerned about Carly, as her behavior had changed rapidly in recent months. Carly, who had never previously missed soccer practices or games even when she was sick, had failed to show up at several practices and one game without notifying the coach. She began withdrawing from others at school and seemed to walk the halls in a daze. The school counselor was also terribly worried about a poem that Carly had written in her English class. The poem described the world as a cold, wintry place without love or warmth. The poem concluded with the protagonist's lying down in the snow to await death.

Before being able to meet with Carly for psychological testing, the psychologist received a call from Carly's parents. The previous afternoon, Carly had taken an entire bottle of aspirin. When her parents could not wake her for dinner, Carly was rushed to the hospital to have her stomach pumped. Although the amount of aspirin was not life-threatening, it was clearly an act to be taken seriously. At the hospital, Carly denied that she tried to kill herself, stating that she had simply lost count of how many aspirin she had taken to alleviate her menstrual cramps.

Carly was put on antidepressant medication and was sent home with her parents. A meeting was scheduled with the psychologist, but the parents canceled the appointment because Carly had been in an excellent mood and had even played several games of Scrabble with them. In addition, Carly had planned a dinner party for a number of her friends that night.

The following week, Carly's father called the psychologist to report that Carly had killed herself the previous night. Late at night, she had filled the bathtub with water, took all of her medication, and slit her wrists. Her parents found her dead in the morning. Carly's parents declined the offer for therapy to deal with their grief about Carly's death. They divorced six months later.

Carly's apparent improvement after being released from the hospital might have served as a warning sign—it is not uncommon that an individual's mood will lighten when he or she makes the final decision to commit suicide. It may have been that Carly was trying to have a good time with her family and friends as a way of saying goodbye to them. This case illustrates the importance of taking a suicide attempt seriously.

SOURCE: R. K. Morgan (1999).

---

patient and inpatient samples of children and shorter ones found for community samples of children (Kovacs, 1996; McCauley et al., 1993).

Children who have been depressed in the past are more likely to experience depression in the future (DelMedico, Weller, & Weller, 1996). For example, one study found that 25% of children and adolescents receiving mental health services for depression experienced another episode of major depression within one year and a total of 54% showed a recurrence of major depression within three years (McCauley et al., 1993). Another study found that the recurrence rate within two years was as high as 69% (Emslie et al., 1997). This greater likelihood of depression also follows children into adulthood, with evidence that at least 60% of depressed children will experience at least one episode of major depression in adulthood. Depressed children are also at greater risk for other clinical disorders in adulthood (Harrington, Fudge, Rutter, Pickles, & Hill, 1990). Overall, depression is a pervasive disorder that is apt to recur for the children and adolescents throughout their lives. The seriousness of this clinical disorder leads to the important question of etiology.

There is no sadder sight than a young pessimist.

—Mark Twain

Etiology

There are a number of theories that try to explain why depression develops in children and adolescents, but there is no overarching theory that has been well established as the definitive explanation. Genetic factors appear to put children at risk, given that children of depressed parents are more likely to develop depression even if the children are raised by nondepressed adoptive parents (Hammen, 1991). In addition, monozygotic twins, even when reared apart, have higher concordance for major depression (i.e., are more similar in their rates of depression) than dizy-

Depression in childhood is associated with depression in adolescence and adulthood.

gotic twins or siblings (Hammen, 1991). There is even a high concordance rate between nontwin siblings who show symptoms of depression and anxiety (Kelvin, Goodyer, & Altham, 1996). Further evidence of a strong genetic influence is provided by the following studies:

- Genetic analyses were found for twins in symptoms of both depression and anxiety (Eley & Stevenson, 1999).

- One twin study found that genetic influences accounted for over 60% of the variance in depression and anxiety (Hudziak, Rudiger, Neale, Heath, & Todd, 2000).

- Common genetic liabilities put children at risk for depression as well as antisocial behavior (O'Connor, McGuire, Reiss, Hetherington, & Plomin, 1998).

- Children with both a depressed parent and a depressed grandparent had significantly high rates of psychopathology, including depression, anxiety disorders, and disruptive disorders (Warner, Weissman, Mufson, & Wickramaratne, 1999; Wickramaratne, Greenwald, & Weissman, 2000).

- Heritability estimates were stronger from severe levels of depression than for depressive symptoms that did not meet criteria for MDD (Eley, 1997).

Overall, there is compelling evidence of a genetic component in the development of depression in children and adolescents. One comprehensive review suggested that approximately 50% of the variance accounting for the development of depression is due to genetic influences (Rutter, Silberg, O'Connor, & Simonoff, 1999b). There is also some evidence of other biological factors in childhood depression.

With regard to biological factors, there are less consistent results for children and adolescents than there are for adults. Factors that look promising for further study include growth hormone abnormalities; elevated serum thyrotropic; and a number of the neurotransmitter systems such as acetylcholine, norepinephrine, serotonin, and neuropeptides (Emslie et al., 1994; Rutter et al., 1999a). Cerebral laterality (e.g., asymmetry between portions of the right and left hemispheres in the brain) has also been implicated in the etiology of childhood depression (Pine et al., 2000). Although these biological factors are beyond the scope of this textbook, suffice it to say that additional investigation into biological factors is warranted (Rutter et al., 1999a).

There is strong evidence that a cognitive-behavioral conceptualization of depression is helpful in understanding the development and maintenance of depression in children and adolescents. Like their adult counterparts, children and adolescents who are depressed tend to show maladaptive cognitions about themselves, their lives, and the future (Gencoz, Voelz, Gencoz, Pettit, & Joiner, 2001; Kaslow, Brown, & Mee, 1994). Their attributional style for negative events shows that all of their internal, stable, and global attributions for bad things that happen to them are associated with depression in adults (Kaslow et al., 1994). Children's cognitive distortions are related to their own ratings of depressive symptoms as well as to their parents' ratings of children's depressive symptoms (Epkins, 1998). In particular, self-critical cognitions and interpersonal concerns were linked to depressive symptomatology in a group of inpatient adolescents (S. J. Frank, Poorman, VanEgeren, & Field, 1997). Interestingly, depressed children may be relatively accurate in some of their negative views of their own social status, but they appear to exaggerate those views (Rudolph & Clark, 2001). There is mixed evidence as to whether or not depressed children actually engage in fewer pleasant events than nondepressed children (Kaslow et al., 1994).

One type of cognitive-behavioral theory that has received a lot of support is the interpersonal theory of depression. Originally developed by James Coyne (1976) to explain depression in adults, the interpersonal theory of depression is now used to explain the development of depression in children and adolescents. A central component of the interpersonal theory of depression is that individuals who seek excessive amounts of reassurance (e.g., by asking people how they look or by looking to others for constant reassurance) tend to be rejected by others, which is then linked to greater feelings of depression. One study found that young adolescents with excessive reassurance-seeking behavior and high levels of depression received greater amounts of interpersonal rejection than adolescents who showed less reassurance-seeking behavior (Joiner, 1999). A strong cognitive component is consistent with the interpersonal theory of depression. Young

adolescents who were depressed tended not only to show negative interpersonal representations about themselves, their family, and their peers but also to be rejected by peers (Rudolph, Hammen, & Burge, 1997). This theory holds promise for explaining the complex cognitive, behavioral, and interpersonal factors that are related to the development of depression in children and adolescents.

Family environment and family functioning also are related to the development and maintenance of depression in children and adolescents. Figure 9.1 shows a kinetic family drawing done by a 13-year-old boy diagnosed with depression (Burns & Kaufman, 1972). In this drawing, the boy shows himself in bed, with his mother's back to him and his father in the distance. Although any interpretation would have to be validated with a more psychometrically sound measure, this drawing could be interpreted to show the boy's disengagement from his family as well as his lethargy and depression (Burns & Kaufman, 1972).

Family dysfunction and conflict are much more prevalent in families with a depressed youngster than in those with nondistressed youngsters (Merikangas, Swendsen, Preisig, & Chazan, 1998; Tamplin et al., 1998), although this type of increased dysfunction is not always found (Olsson, Nordstrom, Arinell, & vonKnorrin, 1999; Pavlidis & McCauley, 2001). When compared with the families of nondepressed adolescents, the families of depressed adolescents showed less supportiveness and more conflict (Sheeber & Sorensen, 1998) as well as poorer parental bonding (D. Stein et al., 2000). Parents of depressed children showed significantly higher levels of critical expressed emotion than did parents of children diagnosed with attention-deficit/hyperactivity disorder and parents of children in a nonclinical group (Asarnow, Tompson, Woo, & Cantwell, 2001). Adolescents' negative perceptions of their families were associated with increased risk for depression and antisocial behavior (Garnefski, 2000). Other family risk factors include loss

FIGURE 9.1 Kinetic Family Drawing by a 13-Year-Old Boy Diagnosed with Depression
Source: Burns & Kaufman (1972).

and separation, parental rejection, and aggression toward the child (Dadds, 1995).

Although genetic factors have been implicated with regard to the connection between parental depression and child depression, there is compelling evidence that this connection may be influenced by psychosocial factors within the family. Specifically, a comprehensive review of the research on children of depressed parents suggests that the presence or absence of interparental conflict influences children's outcome (Downey & Coyne, 1990). When there were high levels of interparental conflict in families with a depressed parent, children and adolescents experienced externalizing disorders, such as conduct disorder and oppositional defiant disorder. When there were low levels of interparental conflict, children and adolescents showed internalizing problems, such as depression and anxiety disorders (Downey & Coyne, 1990). Overall, family dysfunction appears to be related to the onset and maintenance of depression in children and adolescents.

As discussed later, in Box 9.3, parental depression is associated with emotional/behavioral problems in children. Specifically, both maternal and paternal depressive symptoms are associated with increased emotional/behavioral problems in children (Downey & Coyne, 1990; Hammen, 1991; S. L. Johnson & Jacob, 2000). Interestingly, these associations are found in a diversity of families, including Caucasian American and Chinese American families (S. L. Johnson & Jacob, 2000; Kim & Ge, 2000).

The developmental psychopathology framework can help synthesize the many factors that are related to the development of depression in children and adolescents (Cicchetti, Rogosch, & Toth, 1997). As will be discussed later in the chapter, there are a number of risk factors, such as social/interpersonal factors, familial factors, and peer relationships, that are associated with the development of depression (D. Schwartz et al., 1998). Within the

developmental psychopathology framework, researchers view the development of depression from an ecological transactional framework, where biological, psychological, and social systems interact to affect the child's functioning (Cicchetti & Toth, 1998).

As with most other clinical disorders of childhood and adolescence, there is no clear-cut understanding of why depression develops in children or adolescents. The most likely explanation encompasses multiple factors that put the child at risk for the development of depression. For example, one study found that depressed adolescents of depressed mothers showed higher levels of cognitive distortions and poorer interpersonal behaviors than did depressed adolescents without a history of maternal depression (Hammen & Brennan, 2001). Figure 9.2 provides a multifactorial, transactional model of child and adolescent depression that attempts to integrate many etiological factors into one comprehensive model (Hammen & Rudolph, 1996). This type of integrative model provides a framework that should help further research into the etiology of depression in children and adolescents.

Noble deeds and hot baths are the best cures for depression.

—Dodie Smith

Treatment

Given the sometimes devastating outcome of child and adolescent depression, it is heartening to find that there are effective treatments. Sometimes, however, it is difficult for depressed children to be identified for services. One large national study found that children reported a greater need to be treated for depressive symptoms, whereas parents reported a greater need for their children to be treated for disruptive behavior (Wu et al., 1999). Once depressed children are identified for services, there is no standard treatment that stands out as the only effec-

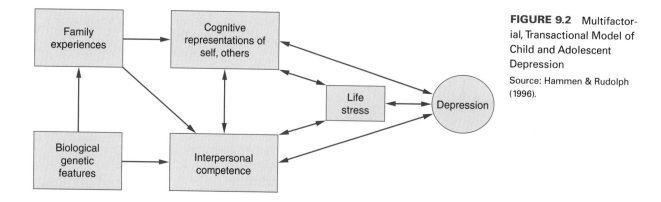

FIGURE 9.2 Multifactorial, Transactional Model of Child and Adolescent Depression

Source: Hammen & Rudolph (1996).

tive therapy. There are a number of intervention strategies that appear to help alleviate depression within children and adolescents.

Although there is compelling evidence of the effectiveness of antidepressant medication for adults, findings are more equivocal for children and adolescents. A number of studies have failed to show that tricyclic antidepressants or specific serotonin reuptake inhibitors are any more effective than placebos in the treatment of depressed children and adolescents (R. T. Brown & Sawyer, 1998; Kazdin & Marciano, 1998). Electroconvulsive therapy (ECT) has also been used for treatment of depression in children, but the results are mixed and the procedures are very controversial (P. Knapp, 2001; Rudnick, 2001).

A number of psychosocial treatments are effective with both children and adolescents. Many of these interventions have been administered in the school setting, with promising results (Kazdin & Marciano, 1998). Treatments tend to focus on cognitive-behavioral aspects of therapy, such as cognitive restructuring, self-control issues, behavior problem-solving, and affective regulation (Kaslow, Croft, & Hatcher, 1999; Wilkes, Belsher, Rush, & Frank, 1994). One meta-analysis found that cognitive-behavioral treatments that focused on improving self-esteem in depressed youngsters showed significantly greater improvements than treatments that focused only on behavior change or social skills (Haney & Durlak, 1998). Many effective therapies include a family component as well (Kaslow et al., 1999), and family therapy has proved to be effective in treating children who are depressed (Kaslow & Racusin, 1994). Interestingly, cognitive-behavioral therapy appears to be effective at decreasing maladaptive cognitions, whereas family therapy appears to be effective at reducing family conflict and problems within the parent–child relationship (Kolko, Brent, Baugher, Bridge, & Birmaher, 2000). There is evidence that treatment of depression is more difficult when adolescents are also diagnosed with substance abuse or dependence (Rohde, Clarke, Lewinsohn, Seeley, & Kaufman, 2001).

Box 9.1 highlights the types of treatment components that have been explored in outcome studies to evaluate the effectiveness of treatment for depression. Overall, these cognitive-behavioral therapies decrease depressive symptoms in children and adolescents.

BOX *9.1*

TREATMENT OF MAJOR DEPRESSIVE DISORDER IN ADOLESCENTS

A typical way of testing the effectiveness of treatment for a psychological disorder is to conduct an outcome study that compares one treatment with another (e.g., Brent, Kolko, Birmaher, Baugher, & Bridge, 1999). An integral part of conducting an outcome study is to assign clients randomly to different therapeutic interventions, rather than just reviewing how clients fared in different treatments. Random assignment helps the researcher trust the results, with the idea that if clients in one type of therapy experience better outcomes, then the better outcomes are due to the superiority of that treatment and not to some other factor.

After a number of outcome studies are conducted, other researchers can synthesize the results and conduct a meta-analysis that provides a better overview of treatment effectiveness. One such meta-analysis of psychosocial treatments for adolescent depression found that 63% of clients showed improvement at the end of treatment, with an overall effect size of 1.27 (Lewinsohn & Clarke, 1999). The following treatment strategies are particularly effective:

Cognitive techniques
    Constructive thinking (rational emotive therapy, cognitive therapy)

    Positive self-talk
    Self-coaching skills
    Coping skills
    Self-change skills (self-monitoring, goal setting, self-reinforcement)
Family context techniques
    Conflict resolution
    Communication skills
    Parenting skills
Behavioral techniques
    Problem-solving skills
    Increasing pleasant activities
    Social skills (assertiveness, making friendships, role modeling)
Affective education and management techniques
    Relaxation
    Anger management

SOURCE: Lewinsohn & Clarke (1999).

Case Study: Henry, The Adolescent Dealing with Parental Alcoholism

Henry, who is 16 years old, was identified as possibly depressed in a schoolwide screening to identify children at risk for depression. Based on both the screening questionnaire and subsequent questionnaires and interviews, Henry reported a great deal of depressive symptomatology. At about the same time, Henry's teacher recommended that he see the school psychologist because of his declining school performance, lethargy, and constant appearance of being sad.

After receiving permission from his parents, Henry was allowed to begin therapy at school for his depression. Upon meeting the therapist, Henry appeared sad and slow moving, and his speech was slow and monotone. Henry reported that he lived with his mother, who was alcoholic, and that he had a paper route to help support the family. Henry stated that he had few friends and rarely engaged in any social activities. He said that he had been feeling quite sad and down for at least two or three months. He also mentioned that he had accidentally hit a hitchhiker while he was driving the family car three weeks ago. The hitchhiker was in a coma. Henry described this event as yet another example of the hopelessness of life. Although Henry thought a lot about dying, he did not have any active plans to harm himself, nor had he ever tried to harm himself previously.

Given the vast number of depressive symptoms that Henry exhibited (anhedonia, feelings of worthlessness, helplessness,

sadness, low mood, loss of pleasure in previously enjoyable events, thoughts of death), therapy began immediately. The treatment plan called for cognitive-behavioral therapy, which was administered in two 50-minute sessions a week for five weeks. The goals of therapy included helping Henry build self-help skills and social problem-solving skills that he could apply to real-life situations. Other goals were to teach Henry self-control skills, self-monitoring techniques, self-evaluation skills, and self-reinforcement skills. In addition, a major emphasis in therapy was to modify Henry's cognitive distortions and help him develop better cognitive strategies. Henry's treatment was administered in group format, with three other adolescents who were depressed. The group format allows adolescents to work on the development of social skills and to realize that they are not alone in many of their concerns.

After completion of treatment, Henry did not show signs of depression, and he stated that he was feeling optimistic about the future. At five-week and at one-year follow-ups, Henry continued to show no symptoms of depression. Although the cognitive-behavioral treatment was effective for Henry, some type of intervention for his mother's alcoholism might also help Henry in the long run.

SOURCE: W. M. Reynolds (1988a).

When considering empirically supported treatments, however, only two treatments meet the criteria as probably efficacious and no treatments have met the criteria for well-established treatments (Kaslow & Thompson, 1998). The two that were found to be probably efficacious were psychosocial and cognitive-behavioral treatments (Lewinsohn, Clarke, Rohde, Hops, & Seeley, 1996; Stark, Rouse, & Livingston, 1991). Although most of the other treatments were found to be effective, they did not meet the rigorous criteria for being defined as probably efficacious or well-established treatments. Overall, there are effective treatments for child and adolescent depression, most of which are cognitive-behavioral.

Prevention

There have been a number of tertiary and secondary prevention programs related to childhood depression. Tertiary programs involve children who show elevated symptoms of depression but who do not yet meet the criteria for MDD. Tertiary programs using social problem-solving and cognitive interventions are effective in decreasing depressive symptomatology in children and adolescents (Clarke et al., 1995; Jaycox, Reivich, Gillham, & Seligman, 1994).

Secondary prevention programs focus on children who are at risk for the development of depression because of their parents' depression. Therapists often use cognitive psychoeducational programs to help children of depressed parents, with components aimed at both children and their parents. These types of programs improve parenting skills, and children's coping skills, both of which decrease the children's risk of developing depression themselves (Beardslee et al., 1993). Although many of these prevention programs have been instituted with middle-class families, there are promising results that show comparable preventive intervention programs to be effective for culturally diverse urban families (Podorefsky, McDonald-Dowdell, & Beardslee, 2001). Other types of secondary prevention programs are aimed at children who have experienced some type of medical crisis, such as a bone fracture (Lewinsohn, Seeley, Hibbard, Rohde, & Sack, 1996), or at pregnant teen mothers (O'Hara, 1995). Given the devastation to children, adolescents, and families when depression develops in youngsters, preventive efforts seem to be a promising way to decrease or even prevent distress in children's lives.

Unfortunately, there are no widespread primary prevention programs that specifically target depression

(Cummings, Davies, & Campbell, 2000; Petersen et al., 1993). Although some primary prevention programs target other aspects of functioning, it is possible that some of these programs may also help alleviate the development of depression in children and adolescents. For example, primary prevention programs that teach problem-solving skills and help participants develop social competence may also help prevent the onset of depression in children and adolescents (Weissberg, Caplan, & Harwood, 1991). Much more work is needed in the area of primary prevention of depression in children and adolescents.

CHILD AND ADOLESCENT SUICIDE

The actual number of adolescents who kill themselves is relatively small—approximately 2,000 to 2,500 adolescents per year in the United States—but these numbers may be an underestimate, given that some deaths due to accidents (such as a car accident or a drug overdose) may have been intentional. Still, suicide is the third leading cause of death for adolescents between the ages of 15 and 24 (Spirito & Donaldson, 1998), and the devastation of a completed suicide is immeasurable. In addition, between 6% and 10% of adolescents report that they have tried to kill themselves at some point, but did not succeed (G. L. Ackerman, 1993; Centers for Disease Control, 1995). At least 60% of adolescents report that they know another

adolescent who tried to commit suicide (G. L. Ackerman, 1993). Gay, lesbian, bisexual, and transgendered youth appear to be at increased risk for suicide attempts (Savin-Williams, 2001). Further, adolescent suicide is an international concern, with the highest rates of adolescent suicide occurring in Sri Lanka, Finland, Switzerland, Austria, and Canada (Spirito & Donaldson, 1998).

Instead of thinking of suicide as an all-or-none event, therapists must recognize that there are gradations of suicidality in children and adolescents. Table 9.3 shows the Pfeffer Spectrum of Suicidal Behavior, which is very useful in conceptualizing suicidality in children and adolescents.

Suicide is connected with the experience of major depressive disorder (Flisher, 1999). In a review of children and adolescents who made fatal suicide attempts, between 30% and 76% experienced some type of mood disorder (Flisher, 1999). Even more striking was that between 79% and 96% of children and adolescents who completed a suicide met criteria for some type of clinical disorder (Flisher, 1999). Thus, suicides are most often completed with children and adolescents who are significantly distressed in some way.

Suicide can be conceptualized as having primarily two components: thoughts and actions. It is not uncommon for individuals of any age to have fleeting thoughts of death or suicide when significantly distressed. Adolescents who attempt suicide, however, are likely to report

Case Study: George, The Adolescent with Many Problems

George was 16 years old when he was admitted to a juvenile detention center. Upon admission, George was withdrawn. Later that afternoon, George wrapped his neck with his shoelaces and tape, which resulted in severe breathing difficulty. He was semiconscious when the detention center staff found him. After George was taken to the hospital, he continued to be withdrawn, but he did say that he would continue to try to kill himself and that no one could stop him. He admitted that he had been depressed recently—and that he had difficulty sleeping, limited appetite, feelings of guilt, and chronic suicidal ideation.

When asked about his history, George's parents reported that George had experienced a normal childhood until he was 13 years old. They reported that, around that time, he began using drugs (LSD, marijuana, and sedatives), started doing poorly in school, ran away from home, and attempted suicide by taking an overdose of aspirin. At the age of 14, George had an argument with the principal and was expelled from school. After a thorough psychological evaluation, George was placed in a group home so that he could work on self-control and so that his rela-

tionship with his parents could be dealt with therapeutically. During his time in the group home, George's behavior improved immensely and his relationship with his parents also improved due to family counseling. He attended school regularly and held an after-school job. In addition, he did not appear to be involved in any illegal activities or drug use.

About six months prior to admission to the detention center, George became involved in drugs again and began additional illegal activities (including 10 episodes of breaking and entering). George can recall feeling depressed around this time. Due to the illegal activity, he was sent to the juvenile detention center. He improved immensely in the detention center, so he was released to live with his parents again. Approximately three weeks before readmission to the detention center, George left with some friends to try to drive to Texas in a stolen car. After he was caught, he was readmitted to the detention center. George became terribly depressed, feeling immense guilt over his illegal activities and how he had let down his parents. These feelings of guilt seemed to lead to his suicide attempt.

SOURCE: Spitzer et al. (1994).

very high levels of **suicidal ideation** (thoughts about killing oneself; Spirito, Overholser, & Vinnick, 1995). One study found that self-esteem was the biggest difference between adolescents who thought about killing themselves and those who actually tried to commit suicide, with lower self-esteem shown in the latter group (Milling, Campbell, Bush, & Laughlin, 1996). A significant portion of adolescents (31%) expect their suicide attempt to cause their own death, and the majority of those who survive an attempt (57%) are sorry or ambivalent about having survived (Spirito & Donaldson, 1998). Approximately one-third of adolescent attempts are planned and two-thirds are carried out on impulse (L. Brown, Overholser, Spirito, & Fritz, 1991). Adolescents who plan their suicide seem to be more depressed, more hopeless, and ideational than those whose attempt was not planned (L. Brown et al., 1991). In addition, suicidal adolescents tend to demand more perfection from themselves, which they then feel they cannot live up to, which is associated with hopelessness and eventual suicidal ideation (P. L. Hewitt, Newton, Flett, & Callander, 1997).

In all age groups, including adults, females are more likely than males to attempt suicide, but males are more likely than females to complete suicides (Lewinsohn, Rohde, Seeley, & Baldwin, 2001; Spirito & Donaldson, 1998). This pattern is likely due to the method of suicide attempt, with boys using more lethal methods, such as firearms and hanging, and girls trying to overdose on drugs (Spirito & Donaldson, 1998). There are no well-established patterns of suicide attempts or completions based on race, ethnicity, or socioeconomic status (Spirito & Donaldson, 1998), and the only clear-cut patterns with regard to race, ethnicity, and culture are that Native American and Aboriginal Canadian youth show higher rates of suicide than their peers (Evans & Lee, 1998). Suicide, however, is evident in every group, including Hispanic/Latina females, who were thought previously to be at low risk (Zayas, Kaplan, Turner, Romano & Gonzalez-Ramos, 2000). Box 9.2 further discusses race/ethnicity and suicide.

The ratio of suicide attempts to completed suicides is approximately 10 to 1 (Kerr & Milliones, 1995). Most completed suicides by adolescents in the United States (65%) are carried out with the use of a gun (Holinger, 1990). When suicidal adolescents have access to firearms in their home, they are 75 times more likely to kill themselves than suicidal adolescents who do not have access to firearms (Brent et al., 1991). Guns are twice as likely to be in the homes of adolescents who complete a suicide than adolescents with a failed suicide attempt or adolescents with a psychiatric problem (Brent et al., 1991). Interestingly, preventive efforts have been targeted to get parents to remove guns from the homes of suicidal adolescents, but one study found that only 26.9% of the families removed guns from the home of their suicidal adolescent (Brent, Baugher, Birmaher, Kolko, & Bridge, 2000). The second most common method of completed suicides is hanging (Spirito & Donaldson, 1998). The most common way that adolescents attempt but do not complete suicide is through drug overdose (Spirito & Donaldson, 1998).

One study explored the idea that exposure to violence in the community would be associated with greater risk for depression and suicide in young inner-city adolescents (Mazza & Reynolds, 1999). Interestingly, this study found that there was not a direct link between exposure to violence and depression or suicide when post-traumatic stress disorder (PTSD) was taken into account. In other words, adolescents who were exposed to high levels of violence in the community were likely to develop PTSD. Adolescents who developed PTSD were also at risk for developing depression and for feeling suicidal (Mazza & Reynolds, 1999). This study shows the complexity of factors that are related to the development of suicidal ideation and intention.

For adolescents of all racial and ethnic backgrounds, there are a number of well-established risk factors for suicide (Garland & Zigler, 1993; Goldston et al., 2001; Joiner, Rudd, Rouleau, & Wagner, 2000; Kerr & Milliones, 1995; R. A. King et al., 2001), including:

- Clinical disorders, such as depression, drug abuse, and alcohol abuse.

TABLE 9.3 Pfeffer Spectrum of Suicidal Behavior

Level	Behavior Pattern
1. Nonsuicidal	No evidence of self-destructive thoughts or actions
2. Suicidal ideation	Thoughts or verbalizations of suicidal intention
3. Suicidal threat	Verbalization of impending suicidal action and/or precursor action that, if carried out, would lead to harm
4. Mild attempt	Actual self-destructive act that realistically would not have endangered life and did not necessitate intensive care unit
5. Serious attempt	Actual self-destructive action that realistically could have led to the child's death and may have necessitated intensive care unit

Source: Pfeffer (1986).

Handguns and other firearms are extremely lethal methods for attempting suicide.

- Personality and interpersonal factors, such as hopelessness, impulsivity, cognitive distortions, poor coping skills, and poor social skills.
- Prior suicide attempt.
- Family factors, such as parental clinical disorder, sexual abuse, physical abuse.
- Stressful life events and high levels of daily hassles.
- Exposure to suicide (e.g., by a classmate, friend, or family member).
- Access to lethal methods, such as access to guns.
- Primary medical factors, such as chronic illness, concerns about pregnancy, sexually transmitted disease.
- Specific suicidal plan (with concrete, realistic, accessible, and lethal plans holding the greatest concern).

Overall, adolescent suicide is a far-reaching problem. Children and adolescents who make suicidal statements or who make suicidal gestures should be taken very seriously. Quite often, the precipitating event is a stressor related to parents, school, friends, or dating relationships (Hawton & Fagg, 1992; Kerr & Milliones, 1995). Even if an outsider might consider the precipitating event to be minor, such events are of great concern to adolescents themselves. Thus, it is imperative that therapists, teachers, parents, friends, and family members not ignore or downplay a child's or adolescent's stated wish to die. One study did find that both fathers and mothers take adolescents' suicide attempts quite seriously (Wagner, Aiken, Mullaley, & Tobin, 2000). Based on reports about the day before the suicide attempt, the time of discovery of the attempt, and the day after the attempt, parents reported greater caring feelings, sadness, and anxiety after the suicide attempt. In addition, parents were more likely to make supportive rather than hostile comments after discovering the suicide attempt (Wagner et al., 2000).

Beyond traditional therapies for suicidal adolescents (such as cognitive-behavioral therapy), there is growing interest in prevention. Suicide hotlines are often set up in communities with the idea that distressed adolescents would call the hotline rather than trying to take their own life. The rates of suicide in such communities are lower than in those without suicide hotlines (Shaffer, Garland, Fisher, Bacon, & Vieland, 1990). The greatest users of suicide hotlines are Caucasian females (Shaffer et al., 1990), which suggests that, although suicide hotlines are effective in helping some adolescents, they are not effective with all groups of suicidal adolescents.

Curriculum-based prevention programs have been established in a number of school systems to try to reach large groups of adolescents (Garland & Zigler, 1993). These programs are considered primary prevention programs because they are administered to all adolescents in a particular school system regardless of whether or not the adolescents are at risk for suicide. Parents, teachers, and school administrators often participate in such programs along with adolescents. These school-based programs usually have the following goals:

- To raise awareness of adolescent suicide and associated problems.
- To train participants to notice and identify adolescents who might be at risk for suicide.

BOX 9.2

RACE/ETHNICITY AND SUICIDE

As with many other topics, research into suicide of children and adolescents has all but ignored racial and ethnic background. Studies that have been conducted show a number of similarities between suicidal youth of all races and ethnicities. For example, African American adolescents who attempted suicide had less supportive social networks, reported more stressful life events, showed more impaired interpersonal problem-solving skills, experienced more maladaptive thought patterns, and were able to generate fewer adaptive alternatives to resolve stressful problems than nonsuicidal adolescents (C. A. King, Raskin, Gdowski, Butkus, & Opipari, 1990; Trautman, Rotheram-Borus, Dopkins, & Lewin, 1991). These results tend to mirror the results of studies with adolescents from other racial and ethnic groups.

A unique challenge in working with suicidal African American adolescents from impoverished urban areas is that traditional methods of intervention (such as individual psychotherapy) are neither feasible nor effective at addressing the root of adolescents' problems (Summerville, Kaslow, & Doepke, 1996). A case example to illustrate this point was provided for a 16-year-old African American female whose mother was addicted to crack cocaine. The girl, named Tee, became pregnant at the age of 14 and, during the pregnancy, was raped. She had her second child at the age of 16, but the

child died of sudden infant death syndrome at five months old. Tee had wanted to go back to school, but after the death of her second child, and the overwhelming lack of support from her family or the social service system, she tried to kill herself with an overdose of Tylenol. Tee survived the suicide attempt, but it was obvious that traditional therapy would not address the essence of Tee's problems, nor would her severe life stressors be resolved through psychotherapy (Summerville et al., 1996).

The clinical researchers who worked with Tee developed a comprehensive treatment program for suicidal adolescents in impoverished settings (Summerville et al., 1996). In addition to traditional work on cognitive-behavioral factors and interpersonal problem-solving skills with these adolescents, there is also a focus on outreach programs that get the adolescent's parent or caretaker involved in the treatment. The interventions are based in the community rather than in a location that is difficult for the adolescent to reach, and there is an attempt to provide continuity of care between the emergency room that intervened in the suicide attempt and the community-based outpatient care facility. These strategies attempt to make treatment more accessible and more comprehensive for adolescents who already have a great many challenges in their lives.

- To educate participants about community resources and referral processes for adolescents who are suicidal.

Overall, there have been mixed results on these types of prevention programs. Although some programs are helpful in imparting information to adolescents, many are ineffective and even disturbing to adolescents (Shaffer, Garland, Vieland, Underwood, & Busner, 1991). Most of these programs were not developed with the integration of empirically based knowledge and may therefore inadver-

tently work against the goals of the program. One study reported that suicidal students found the program upsetting and distressing rather than reassuring and helpful (Shaffer et al., 1991).

Given the conflicting evidence about the effectiveness of suicide prevention programs, there is a great need to develop ones that are more comprehensive and more effective. Suggestions for comprehensive prevention programs include targeting the reduction of risk factors in the lives of adolescents, increasing family support and

Case Study: Alexa, Survivor of Childhood Abuse

Alexa had been both physically and verbally abused by her mother throughout her childhood. Apparently, Alexa's father did not intervene to help her. She states:

I tried to kill myself one day—it was a halfhearted attempt at best. I didn't even break the skin. That's when I left home and stayed with friends of mine. I had just

graduated from high school . . . My father was eating lamb chops at the table when the police were there. Picture my father eating lamb chops while the police came—this is about as passive as you get. Please don't disturb my dinner, I'm eating now. Everything chaos around him.

SOURCE: Rhodes & Rhodes (1996, p. 202).

family functioning, increasing community-based programs and community support, and decreasing the availability of guns (Brent et al., 2000; Christoffel, 2000; Shaffer & Pfeffer, 2001). Overall, a concerted effort is needed to reduce the prevalence of suicidal ideation and suicide attempts in adolescents. Because many of the risk factors for suicide are comparable to the risk factors for other problems (such as depression, substance abuse, delinquency, teenage pregnancy), suicide prevention programs could help prevent many other problems in adolescents' lives.

DYSTHYMIC DISORDER

In contrast to major depressive disorder, which can be short-lived but intense, **dysthymic disorder** is a longer-term, somewhat less intense experience of depression. The term *dysthymic* refers to the inability to experience joy and other pleasant emotions over an extended period of time. As defined in Table 9.4, dysthymic disorder is diagnosed when a child experiences at least one year of depressed mood, during which time the child does not meet criteria for MDD. There is far less research into children's and adolescents' experience of dysthymia than there is for MDD. This point is illustrated by the fact that prevalence rates for dysthymia were not reported in the overall results of the MECA study (Shaffer et al., 1996). In fact, the MECA research group noted that dysthymic disorder is in need of further research (Schwab-Stone et al., 1996). When research has been conducted, it appears that dysthymic disorder is present in 2% to 4% of children and adolescents in community samples (Garrison et al., 1997; Kovacs, 1997).

The limited information that is available indicates that dysthymic disorder is a very distressing disorder. The average length of dysthymia is 3.9 years (Kovacs, Obrosky, Gatsonis, & Richards, 1997), but it is not unusual for children and adolescents to experience dysthymic disorder for 5 years or longer (Kovacs, Feinberg, Crouse-Novak, Paulauskas, & Finkelstein, 1984). One study found that two years after onset of dysthymic disorder, only 7% of the children had recovered from it (Kovacs et al., 1997). This low rate of recovery is in contrast to an 86% recovery rate from MDD after two years (Kovacs et al., 1997).

Like MDD, dysthymic disorder is highly comorbid with other disorders, such as anxiety disorders, conduct disorder, and other affective disorders (Kovacs, 1997; Kovacs, Akiskal, Gatsonis, & Parrone, 1994; Markowitz, 1995a). When dysthymic disorder is comorbid with

---

TABLE 9.4 *DSM-IV* **Diagnostic Criteria for Dysthymic Disorder**

A. Depressed mood for most of the day, for more days than not, as indicated either by subjective account or observation by others, for at least 2 years. Note: In children and adolescents, mood can be irritable and duration must be at least 1 year.

B. Presence, while depressed, of two (or more) of the following:

   (1) poor appetite or overeating

   (2) insomnia or hypersomnia

   (3) low energy or fatigue

   (4) low self-esteem

   (5) poor concentration or difficulty making decisions

   (6) feelings of hopelessness

C. During the 2-year period (1 year for children or adolescents) of the disturbance, the person has never been without the symptoms in Criteria A and B for more than 2 months at a time.

D. No Major Depressive Episode has been present during the first 2 years of the disturbance (1 year for children and adolescents); i.e., the disturbance is not better accounted for by chronic Major Depressive Disorder, or Major Depressive Disorder, In Partial Remission.

E. There has never been a Manic Episode, a Mixed Episode, or a Hypomanic Episode, and criteria have never been met for Cyclothymic Disorder.

F. The disturbance does not occur exclusively during the course of a chronic Psychotic Disorder, such as Schizophrenia or Delusional Disorder.

G. The symptoms are not due to the direct physiological effects of a substance (e.g., a drug of abuse, a medication) or a general medical condition (e.g., hypothyroidism).

H. The symptoms cause clinically significant distress or impairment in social, occupational, or other important areas of functioning.

Specify if:

   Early Onset: if onset is before age 21 years

   Late Onset: if onset is age 21 years or older

Source: American Psychiatric Association (2000). Reprinted with permission from the *Diagnostic and Statistical Manual of Mental Disorders, Fourth Edition, Text Revision.* Copyright 2000 American Psychiatric Association.

---

externalizing disorders (such as oppositional defiant disorder, conduct disorder, or attention-deficit/hyperactivity disorder), the length of duration of the disorder is almost 2.5 years longer than when the disorder is not comorbid with an externalizing disorder (Kovacs et al., 1997). Children who have experienced both MDD and dysthymic disorder during their lifetime show even greater

Case Study: Jenny, the Girl Who Was Sad for a Very Long Time

Jenny is a nine-year-old who attends third grade and lives with her mother and her 12-year-old brother. She visits her father in a nearby town about twice a month. Her parents divorced when Jenny was seven. Within the next two years, Jenny's mother began working full-time, the family moved to an apartment in another school district, Jenny had to change schools in the middle of the year, and Jenny's mother began dating a man seriously. Two months after announcing her engagement, Jenny's mother brought Jenny in for therapy.

Jenny's mother told the therapist that Jenny had been getting more and more unhappy over the past 18 months. Jenny was lethargic, she did not seem to enjoy activities that she used to enjoy, and she no longer attempted to make any friends. Jenny had been involved in Brownies and gymnastics at her old school, but she did not want to join these activities at her new school. In addition, Jenny stated that she did not like any of the kids at her new school, so she spent her afternoons watching television and waiting for her mother to come home from work. Jenny later acknowledged to the therapist that she feared her mother would leave her when she married the new boyfriend. Jenny already felt abandoned since her mother spent all of her extra time with the boyfriend. Jenny's schoolwork also began to falter, with Jenny often not turning in homework and not doing well on tests. At her old school, Jenny was an above-average student, but at her new school, Jenny was barely passing her classes. In addition, although Jenny used to enjoy visiting her father twice a month, she now dreaded those visits. She reported that she felt uncomfortable because her father spent much of their time together berating her mother.

A full assessment showed that Jenny experienced elevated levels of sadness, but not enough to be diagnosed with major depressive disorder. Jenny had experienced feelings of sadness for a great length of time (at least 18 months), thus a diagnosis of dysthymic disorder was given.

Jenny and her mother began therapy with the following behavioral techniques in the treatment plan:

- Increase the number of pleasant activities in which Jenny engaged.
- Conduct parent training with Jenny's mother to help her learn to reward Jenny's positive interactions and other desirable behaviors.
- Institute a positive reinforcement program (token economy) for Jenny's improved school performance.
- Help Jenny learn new social skills to allow the development of friendships in the new school.

Both Jenny and her mother were very receptive to the therapeutic interventions. Jenny's mother began showing much more attention to Jenny's positive behaviors and Jenny, in turn, began getting involved in many school and social activities. Within a month of beginning therapy, Jenny's grades started to improve and she began showing a happier disposition. At the end of the 10-week treatment, Jenny's behavior and feelings fell within the normal range of standardized assessment measures. At both six-month and one-year follow-ups, Jenny continued to show no signs of dysthymia. She had shown some sadness when her mother got married, but she soon became adjusted to her stepfather's presence in the house. Additionally, she remained actively involved in Brownies, gymnastics, and other school activities. Jenny reported that she was busy with her new friends.

SOURCE: Frame, Johnstone, & Giblin (1988).

---

impairment than those who have experienced just one of those disorders (Goodman, Schwab-Stone, Lahey, Shaffer, & Jensen, 2000).

Treatment for dysthymic disorder tends to be comparable to treatment for MDD. Antidepressant medication has been found to be somewhat helpful for some children (Harrison & Stewart, 1995); however, cognitive-behavioral treatments are also quite effective (Markowitz, 1995b). The combination of medication and psychotherapy may prove to be the most effective treatment strategy. Given that dysthymic disorder is more difficult to treat than MDD, greater efforts are needed to find effective treatments (Markowitz, 1995b).

Overall, dysthymic disorder is a long-term, distressing disorder for children and adolescents. Much more research is needed into the specific course of the disorder and the etiological factors that lead to its development. Many research projects have lumped together MDD and dysthymic disorder, which has lead to a dearth of information about dysthymic disorder specifically. Interestingly, one study found that children diagnosed with MDD and children diagnosed with dysthymic disorder did not differ in any aspect other than current level of symptoms (Goodman et al., 2000). More research on dysthymic disorder is warranted.

BIPOLAR DISORDER AND CYCLOTHYMIC DISORDER

Bipolar disorder is known more commonly as manic depression. It is characterized by extreme highs (which are referred to as manic episodes) and extreme lows (which are referred to as major depressive episodes). There are two primary conceptualizations of bipolar disorder. Bipolar I disorder is characterized by one or more manic or mixed episodes and one or more major depressive episodes. Bipolar II disorder is characterized by one or more major depressive episodes along with at least one hypomanic episode. If the child or adolescent experiences at least one manic or mixed episode, then he or she would not be diagnosed with bipolar II disorder.

Overall, bipolar disorder is considered relatively rare in children and adolescents. It is almost nonexistent in young children, and the prevalence rates in older adolescents are thought to range from 0.4% to 1.2% (Lewinsohn, Klein, & Seeley, 1995). Although the diagnosis of bipolar disorder is somewhat controversial in prepubertal children, there is clear evidence that the disorder exists and that it can be diagnosed effectively (Nottelmann et al., 2001). The recovery rate for an episode of bipolar disorder is relatively quick, with an average recovery rate of six months in adolescents (G. A. Carlson, 1994). The likelihood of recurrence, however, is quite high (G. A. Carlson, 1994). Like other mood disorders, bipolar disorder is highly comorbid with other disorders, such as generalized anxiety disorder, attention-deficit/hyperactivity disorder, and conduct disorder (Kutcher, Robertson, & Bird, 1998).

Bipolar disorder is thought to be highly genetically related, given that a large majority of adolescents diagnosed with bipolar disorder have a close relative with the disorder. One study found that 63% of adolescents diagnosed with bipolar disorder had a first-degree relative, most often a parent, who had also been diagnosed with it (Kafantaris, Coletti, Dicker, Padula, & Pollack, 1998). Other studies have found high concordance rates between parents and adolescents with bipolar disorder (Todd, Reich, Petti, & Joshi, 1996). In particular, children of fathers with bipolar disorder are more at risk than children of mothers with bipolar disorder (Kornberg et al., 2000). In both adolescents and adults, bipolar disorder can be treated effectively with lithium (Geller et al., 1998a, 1998b).

One interesting issue in the study of mania in children and adolescents relates to the specificity of manic symptoms. A number of studies have suggested that when children and adolescents experience symptoms of mania, the symptoms may be related to problems other than bipolar disorder, such as attention-deficit/hyperactivity disorder (G. A. Carlson, 1998; G. A. Carlson & Kelly, 1998). Conversely, it may be that symptoms of mania in adolescents are sometimes misdiagnosed with another type of disorder, such as schizophrenia (W. M. Reynolds, 1995).

Interestingly, bipolar disorder has been linked to great creativity in a number of artists, writers, performers, and musicians (Jamison, 1995). Creative individuals such as Samuel Clemens (Mark Twain), Virginia Woolf, Georgia O'Keeffe, Cole Porter, Charles Mingus, and Vincent van Gogh were all thought to experience bipolar disorder.

Although it is not clear whether the symptoms of bipolar disorder were evident in childhood or adolescence, a number of these individuals did show symptoms by the time of early adulthood (Jamison, 1995). Alongside the great bursts of energy that occurred during their periods of mania, there were also devastating consequences for most of these artists due to despair. Suffice it to say that the diagnosis of bipolar disorder in children and adolescents is still in need of additional research.

Cyclothymic disorder—which shows a longer-term, less intense pattern—is even more rare and less understood in children and adolescents than is bipolar disorder. An analogy might help make this disorder clear: major depressive disorder is to dysthymic disorder just as bipolar disorder is to cyclothymic disorder. In children and adolescents, cyclothymia would be diagnosed when there is evidence of numerous hypomanic symptoms and numerous depressive symptoms over the course of at least one year (American Psychiatric Association, 2000). If the symptoms are severe enough in that year to diagnose a major depressive episode, manic episode, or mixed episode, then cyclothymia would not be diagnosed.

Cyclothymic disorder is not highly prevalent in children and adolescents. One study of children of parents with bipolar disorder found cyclothymic disorder to be more prevalent in children of disordered parents than in children of parents in a nonclinical control group (D. N. Klein, Depue, & Slater, 1985). The average age of onset was 12 years old, with a range from 7 to 15 years old. This study suggested that cyclothymic disorder does exist in children and adolescents, albeit at low rates in the general community. Given the rarity of cyclothymic disorder and the lack of research on the topic, an in-depth discussion is not warranted here. It is important to keep in mind, however, that one of the biggest challenges in diagnosing cyclothymic disorder is distinguishing it from the normal highs and lows that adolescents often experience.

It is not difficult to fill a child's hand.

—Proverb of Africa

DEPRESSION CONCEPTUALIZED IN A DIMENSIONAL MANNER

The bulk of this chapter has focused on categorical conceptualizations of mood disturbances. Although there is a great deal of research on major depressive disorder, and to a lesser extent dysthymic disorder, bipolar disorder, and cyclothymic disorder in children and adolescents, there is also a great deal of concern about subclinical levels of depression. Given the pervasiveness of feelings of sadness at some point in everyone's life, it is important to understand that feelings of depression exist on a continuum from none to severe. The importance of sad feelings is illustrated in the normative data from the Child Behavior Checklist (Achenbach & Rescorla, 2001). Based on a review of 120 parent-reported items of children's behavior in the huge normative sample, the item that most distinguished children who received clinical services from children who did not receive clinical services was the item "unhappy, sad, or depressed." This fact suggests that parents and professionals consider sadness and depression to be a crucial symptom for which children should receive treatment.

Depression has been conceptualized in three primary ways (Petersen et al., 1993):

- Clinical depression.
- Depressive syndrome.
- Depressed mood.

Clinical depression has already been covered in the section on major depressive disorder. Depressive syndromes and depressed mood are thought to be somewhat less severe than clinical depression, but they are no less important to understand and alleviate.

A **depressive syndrome** is less severe than major depressive disorder but more severe than depressed mood. Depressive syndromes are most often identified through empirically validated assessment measures that identify a constellation of emotions and behaviors that co-occur with depression. Feelings and behaviors such as feeling lonely, crying, striving for perfection, feeling unloved, feeling guilty, feeling sad, and worrying are all part of the depressive syndrome. Interestingly, most depressive syndromes have been linked to symptoms of anxiety, with an anxious-depressed syndrome (Achenbach & Rescorla, 2001; Hinden et al., 1997). In fact, depression and anxiety often cannot be distinguished as two separate syndromes through statistical analyses (Achenbach & Rescorla, 2001; Hinden et al., 1997). It is estimated that, at any one time, approximately 5% of nonclinical children and adolescents experience the depressive syndrome (Petersen et al., 1993).

Depressed mood is reflected when the child or adolescent experiences sadness and unhappiness (Petersen et al., 1993). Most often, depressed mood is assessed through a single item on the Child Behavior Checklist (Achenbach & Rescorla, 2001). Depressed mood is less intense and less pervasive than clinical depression or depressive syndrome. When parents of nonclinical children reported on their children's depressed mood, 10% to 20% of boys and 15% to 20% of girls were reported to have experienced depressed mood within the past six months (Achenbach & Rescorla, 2001). When adolescents' self-reports are considered, 20% to 35% of boys and 25% to 40% of girls reported that they had experienced depressed mood within the past six months (Achenbach & Rescorla, 2001). Based on a review of the literature, it is estimated that, at any one time, 35% of children and adolescents experience depressed mood (Petersen et al., 1993).

Interestingly, gender differences in the depressive syndrome and depressed mood parallel gender differences found in youth with major depressive disorder. Although gender differences are even more prevalent in youth receiving clinical services than those who do not, the depressive syndrome and depressed mood are found in adolescent girls to a much greater extent than in adolescent boys (Compas et al., 1997). These findings suggest that there are more commonalities than differences between clinical depression and subclinical levels of depression. In some ways, these comparable findings support the conceptualization of depression on a dimensional basis rather than a categorical basis. Other than severity, there is little that is distinctly different between clinical depression and subclinical depression. An integral part of understanding depression from a dimensional perspective is to understand the risk and protective factors that are related to the development of depressed mood and depressive syndrome.

Risk Factors

A number of risk factors are linked to the development of increased depressive symptoms in children and adolescents. There are few risk factors, however, that have been linked to the development of depressive symptoms only. In other words, many of the risk factors for depressive symptoms also put children at risk for other types of problems. For example, negative body image leads to depressive symptoms and also leads to eating disorders (Attie & Brooks-Gunn, 1992). Low self-esteem and anxiety also are precursors to the development of depressive symptoms (Kovacs, 1990; Reinherz, Giaconia, Hauf, Wasserman, & Paradis, 2000).

Comparable cognitive, peer, and familial risk factors that are associated with the onset of major depressive disorder are also associated with the development of less severe levels of depressive symptoms (Petersen et al., 1993). With regard to cognitive factors, dysphoric children tend to interpret events in a less supportive and less

CHILDREN OF DEPRESSED PARENTS

Parental depression, and specifically maternal depression, is one of the most studied areas in parental psychopathology (Goodman & Gotlib, 2002). A number of studies have investigated parental depression, especially maternal depression, including Tiffany Field's (1984, 2000) work with infants and Marian Radke-Yarrow's (1998) work across the life span. Although children of depressed parents are at risk for the development of depression themselves, they are also at risk for a number of other problems. Children of depressed parents are eight times more likely to develop depression, five times more likely to develop conduct disorder, and three times more likely to develop an anxiety disorder (Wickramaratne & Weissman, 1998).

In an intriguing book entitled *Depression Runs in Families,* Dr. Connie Hammen (1991) outlined the different risk and resilience factors related to children of depressed mothers. Based on extensive work with children of depressed mothers, children of chronically ill mothers, and children of nondistressed mothers, Dr. Hammen and her colleagues have found that children of depressed mothers are influenced by many of the same risk and resilience factors as in many other

adverse circumstances. Risk factors, such as genetic loading, difficult temperament, and parental distress were linked to poorer outcomes for children. Resilience or protective factors such as coping skills, social competence, average or above-average intelligence, lower life stress, and good problem-solving skills were linked to better outcomes for children, even in the face of parental depression. As Figure 9.3 shows, higher numbers of protective factors were associated with lower affective diagnosis ratings.

Even though Dr. Hammen and her colleagues have explored maternal depression primarily, it is important to note that similar findings have been established with regard to paternal depression (reviewed in S. L. Johnson & Jacob, 2000; Phares, 1996; Phares & Compas, 1992; Phares, Duhig, & Watkins, 2002). Whether it is the father or the mother who is depressed, there are comparable risk and protective factors regarding the well-being of the children of depressed parents. When parents are comorbid for disorders (such as depression and alcohol abuse), there is an even greater likelihood for children to experience detrimental outcomes (Warner et al., 1995).

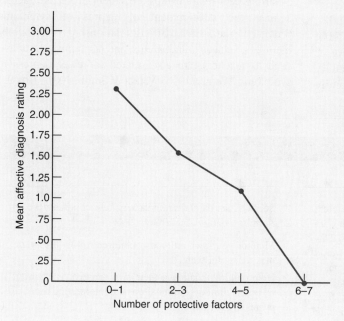

FIGURE 9.3 Lifetime Affective Disorder Ratings by Number of Protective Factors (high-risk random sample; excluded children of normal mothers)

Source: Hammen (1991). Reprinted with permission from Hammen, *Depression Runs in Families.* Copyright 1991, Springer-Verlag New York, Inc.

helpful manner than nondysphoric children (Shirk, Van-Horn, & Leber, 1997). Sad and dysphoric youngsters also tend to have negative interpersonal schemata, which leads them to interpret events in a more negative and hopeless manner (Shirk, Boergers, Eason, & VanHorn, 1998). With regard to peer risk factors, children who were neglected by their peers or who were rejected by their peers tended to show higher rates of depression and **anhedonia**—a state marked by a lack of joy and happiness—than did other children (Hecht, Inderbitzn, & Bukowski, 1998; Reinherz et al., 2000). Notably, children's perceptions of peer acceptance had a stronger link to depressive symptoms than did actual peer acceptance (Kistner, Balthazor, Risi, & Burton, 1999). Homeless and runaway adolescents show heightened levels of depressive symptoms, which seem to be exacerbated by their peer- and non-peer-related experiences when they are on the streets (Whitbeck, Hoyt, & Bao, 2000). Regarding risk factors within the family, parental depression has been identified as a salient risk factor for the development of depressive symptomatology in children and adolescents (see Box 9.3).

Other family factors that have been identified as risk factors for the development of depressive symptoms are interparental conflict (Cummings & Davies, 1994; Kerig, 1998); parental emotional unavailability (Lee & Gotlib, 1991); poor parental bonding (Ingram & Ritter, 2000; Stein et al., 2000); parental negativity (Donenberg & Weisz, 1997); avoidant coping styles within the family (Steele, Forehand, & Armistead, 1997); stressful family events related to parental physical illness (Grant & Compas, 1995); and low family cohesion and expression (Reinherz, Stewart-Berghauer, Pakiz, Frost, & Moeykens, 1989). Physical abuse within the family is linked to depressive symptoms, even when other risk factors are controlled statistically (Kaplan et al., 1998). Overall, there are a number of well-established risk factors associated with the development of depressive symptoms in youngsters.

> My grandma love me
> Even when I'm sad
> I have someone to care for me
> When I'm lonely
> She's there
> My grandma
> Is the one for me.
>
> —Lisa, six years old and homeless
> (Children's Defense Fund–Minnesota, 1990, p. 24)

Protective Factors

As with risk factors, there are few protective factors specifically associated with the prevention of depressive symptoms only. Good parent–child relationships as well as strong peer relationships are salient protective factors against the development of depressive symptoms (Petersen et al., 1993). Strong relationships with family members, such as grandparents, and nonfamily members, such as teachers, are also related to fewer depressive symptoms (Werner, 1995; Werner & Smith, 2001). Box 9.4

BOX 9.4

THE OPTIMISTIC CHILD

Dr. Martin Seligman and colleagues (Seligman, Reivich, Jaycox, & Gillham, 1995) have studied children who are optimistic. The essence of optimism is the way in which children think about causes of events. An optimistic child would not only engage in positive thinking but also see the causes of events in a positive manner, or at a minimum, not see the causes of events in a negative manner. In particular, negative events would not be interpreted as permanent, pervasive, or personal. This explanatory style is the mirror image of what is found in children who are depressed. Optimistic children tend to show extraordinarily low levels of depression and distress, given that their outlook on events helps to buffer against negative events in their lives.

So, how can parents and teachers help children develop an optimistic outlook on life?

- Monitor your own attitudes—children follow the examples we set for them.
- Help children challenge their own negative attributions by brainstorming additional ways of interpreting negative events in their lives.
- Help children learn problem-solving skills.
- Model good social skills, and help children with their social skills.
- Build positive events and interpretations of events into children's everyday lives.

SOURCE: Seligman et al. (1995).

discusses how optimism can serve as a protective factor against the development of depressive symptoms.

Other factors that are thought to protect against the development of depressive symptoms include social support, appropriate family involvement, peer acceptance, and appropriate peer values and involvement (Seidman et al., 1999). Higher self-esteem in African American male adolescents was related to decreased levels of depression in adulthood (Mizell, 1999). Peer warmth was associated with decreased risk for depressive symptoms in samples from both Los Angeles, California, and Tianjin, China (Greenberger, Chen, Tally, & Dong, 2000). Overall, protective factors against the development of depression are comparable to factors that protect against the development of other disorders. These risk and protective factors are important to keep in mind when trying to prevent and treat children's and adolescents' depressive symptoms.

SUMMARY AND KEY CONCEPTS

Anaclitic Depression and Failure to Thrive in Infancy

Anaclitic depression is an old term that refers to infants who lost their primary caregiver and also seemed to have lost their will to live. **Failure to thrive** is a newer term that refers to infants who show apathy, slow motor development, no interest in their surroundings, and little interest in food or liquids. More recently, the *Diagnostic Classification: 0–3* system has identified two types of depression in infants: **mood disorder: prolonged bereavement/grief reaction** and **mood disorder: depression of infancy and early childhood**.

Masked Depression

Masked depression is an old concept that refers to children who seem to show externalizing types of behavior problems but who really are depressed.

Major Depressive Disorder

According to *DSM-IV*, **major depressive disorder (MDD)** is a clinical disorder in which individuals experience at least two weeks of depressed mood, loss of interest, disturbed eating patterns, disturbed sleeping patterns, disturbed activity levels, feelings of worthlessness, diminished concentration, and possible thoughts of death and suicide. A less severe disorder, **adjustment disorder with depressed mood** is also classified in *DSM-IV*, with the primary mood disturbance in reaction to an identifiable event. In terms of treatment, cognitive-behavioral treatments have been found to be superior to other types of treatment in reducing depressive symptomatology. These treatments are considered empirically supported treatments because they were developed and perfected with a research base in mind.

Child and Adolescent Suicide

Between 6% and 10% of adolescents report that they have tried to commit suicide. Thoughts and feelings of wanting to kill oneself are referred to as **suicidal ideation**.

Dysthymic Disorder

According to *DSM-IV*, **dysthymic disorder** is a longer-term but somewhat less intense experience of depression than MDD.

Bipolar Disorder and Cyclothymic Disorder

Bipolar disorder is more commonly known as manic depression, a disorder in which very high highs and very low lows are experienced. Bipolar disorder is almost nonexistent in children and is rare in adolescents. **Cyclothymic disorder** is considered a longer-lasting but less intense disorder than bipolar disorder.

Depression Conceptualized in a Dimensional Manner

Instead of conceptualizing depression in a categorical manner, a growing number of researchers and clinicians feel that it is important to conceptualize depression on a continuum. Approximately 5% of nonclinical children and adolescents experience a **depressive syndrome**, which is a constellation of depressive feelings and behaviors that are considered less severe than major depressive disorder. In addition, approximately 35% of nonclinical children and adolescents experience **depressed mood**, which is characterized by feelings of sadness, being down, and feeling depressed. One type of depressive feeling is termed **anhedonia**, which is the lack of feeling or experiencing joy and happiness.

KEY TERMS

anaclitic depression	mood disorder:	major depressive	suicidal ideation	depressive syndrome
failure to thrive	depression of	disorder (MDD)	dysthymic disorder	depressed mood
mood disorder:	infancy and early	adjustment disorder	bipolar disorder	anhedonia
prolonged	childhood	with depressed	cyclothymic	
bereavement/	masked depression	mood	disorder	
grief reaction				

SUGGESTED READINGS

McCourt, Frank. *Angela's Ashes*. New York: Scribner, 1996. This autobiography illustrates a number of risk factors, including parental depression and parental alcohol abuse.

Craig, Eleanor. *P.S. Your Not Listening*. New York: Signet, 1972. This book, written by a special education teacher, describes a roomful of special needs children, including some children with depressive symptoms.

SUGGESTED VIEWINGS

Dead Poets Society (1989). Peter Weir (director), Tom Schulman (writer). VHS/DVD. An intense look at boys within a prep school setting, with inspirational academic speeches and devastating connections between achievement and suicidality.

Harold and Maude (1971). Hal Ashby (director), Colin Higgins (writer). VHS/DVD. A classic film that follows the intertwined lives of a suicidal adolescent boy and an older woman who survived the Holocaust.

CHAPTER 10

ANXIETY DISORDERS AND PROBLEMS WITH ANXIETY

CHAPTER SUMMARY

Ever since August we been livin' here. The room is either very hot or freezin' cold. When it be hot outside it's hot in here. When it be cold outside we have no heat. We used to live with my aunt but then it got too crowded there so we moved out. We went to welfare and they sent us to the shelter. Then they shipped us to Manhattan. I'm scared of the elevators. 'Fraid they be stuck. I take the stairs.

—Angie, a 12-year-old, African American girl who lives in a homeless shelter (Kozol, 1988, p. 62)

When considering fear and anxiety, it is crucial to acknowledge that many fears are legitimate. Before diagnosing Angie, whose words are quoted above, for a specific phobia of elevators, it would be important to know that the elevator in the shelter where she lives often breaks down between floors. Even when it is working, children in the elevator are at risk for abuse by pedophiles in the building or are pressured to purchase drugs by dealers who frequent the shelter. The issue of whether a child's fears are reasonable is imperative when considering the diagnosis of an anxiety disorder.

When children experience fear and anxiety to more extreme degrees than expected, therapists may suspect some type of anxiety disorder. There are a number of anxiety disorders, including separation anxiety disorder, specific phobia, social phobia, obsessive-compulsive disorder, generalized anxiety disorder, post-traumatic stress disorder, and selective mutism. The main component that links these disorders together is the experience of anxiety, fear, or worrying (Weems, Silverman, & LaGreca, 2000). Note that separation anxiety disorder and selective mutism are located in the section of *DSM-IV* entitled "Disorders Usually First Diagnosed in Infancy, Child-

hood, or Adolescence." The other disorders can be diagnosed in individuals of any age. This chapter describes each of these disorders separately, along with prevalence information. Following these descriptions, the chapter then turns to issues related to comorbidity, course of the disorders, etiology, treatment, and prevention.

Note that there are a few anxiety disorders that will not be covered in this chapter, including panic disorders, acute stress disorder, anxiety disorder due to a general medical condition, and substance-induced anxiety disorder. These disorders tend to be relatively rare in childhood (American Psychiatric Association, 2000) and have not received a great deal of attention from researchers in developmental psychopathology. Students interested in these and other anxiety disorders should consider reading *Anxiety Disorders in Children and Adolescents* (March, 1995) or the June 2000 special issue of *Clinical Psychology Review*.

A crust eaten in peace is better than a banquet partaken in anxiety.

—Aesop

SEPARATION ANXIETY DISORDER

Separation anxiety disorder is characterized by extreme, developmentally inappropriate anxiety when separated from a primary caretaker, such as a parent. The definition in Table 10.1 notes that the distress can occur when the child is separated from the caretaker or even when the child is just thinking about being separated. Children diagnosed with separation anxiety disorder

---

Case Study: Tiny Tina

Tina was 10 years old when she first was referred to a psychiatrist because she hated going to school. She was small in stature and had a sweet personality. The previous year, Tina had hidden in the family's basement to avoid the first day of school. She agreed to go only when her mother agreed to stay with her at school and have lunch with her. Since that time, Tina often showed somatic complaints (e.g., stomachaches and headaches). Recently, her parents had had to physically pick her up out of bed, dress her, feed her, and transport her in order to get Tina to attend school. Tina was usually willing to participate in other activities, such as Girl Scout meetings and sleepovers at a friend's house, but her sister usually accompanied her on these outings. Although Tina missed a great deal of school, she continued to do well in her studies.

During the psychiatrist's interview with Tina, it became obvious that Tina's main concern was not about school but

rather about leaving her family. Tina's mother hypothesized that these concerns began around the time of Tina's grandmother's death. Tina admitted that she worried something awful would happen to her family while she was at school. She seemed not to have these concerns when she took part in other activities, partly because her sister was with her. Because her main concern was about separating from her family, Tina was given a provisional diagnosis of separation anxiety disorder. The word *provisional* here means that the diagnosis is not final until further information is collected. Note that this case illustrates the need to differentiate between separation anxiety disorder and a specific phobia due to fear of the school setting (which is discussed later in this chapter).

SOURCE: Spitzer, Gibbon, Skodol, Williams, & First (1994).

often have nightmares about being separated from their parents and they fear that something awful will happen to their parents when they are not together. Somatic complaints (such as headaches and stomachaches) are common in children with separation anxiety disorder, especially when they are about to be separated from their primary caretaker (Albano, Chorpita, & Barlow, 1996).

Although it is important to know the developmental appropriateness of behavior for any disorder, this issue is especially important with separation anxiety disorder. Normal separation anxiety usually occurs between the ages of 10 and 18 months, with a significant decrease in separation anxiety by the age of two years (American Academy of Pediatrics, 1998). Infants and toddlers who experience normal separation anxiety tend to cling to their caretaker more often and become distressed when separated from their caretaker, even when the caretaker just leaves the room momentarily. The development of

separation anxiety is considered to be positive, because it means that the infant or toddler has developed a good attachment to his or her caretaker. Separation anxiety is considered abnormal only when it occurs well after the normal developmental period or when it is in excess of what would be expected for children of that age.

It is not uncommon for separation anxiety disorder to occur after some type of major life stress, such as the

Separation anxiety is developmentally appropriate in infants and toddlers, but can be problematic in older children and adolescents.

TABLE 10.1 *DSM-IV* Diagnostic Criteria for Separation Anxiety Disorder

A. Developmentally inappropriate and excessive anxiety concerning separation from home or from those to whom the individual is attached, as evidenced by three (or more) of the following:

  (1) recurrent excessive distress when separation from home or major attachment figures occurs or is anticipated

  (2) persistent and excessive worry about losing, or about possible harm befalling, major attachment figures

  (3) persistent and excessive worry that an untoward event will lead to separation from a major attachment figure (e.g., getting lost or being kidnapped)

  (4) persistent reluctance or refusal to go to school or elsewhere because of fear of separation

  (5) persistently and excessively fearful or reluctant to be alone or without major attachment figures at home or without significant adults in other settings

  (6) persistent reluctance or refusal to go to sleep without being near a major attachment figure or to sleep away from home

  (7) repeated nightmares involving the theme of separation

  (8) repeated complaints of physical symptoms (such as headaches, stomachaches, nausea, or vomiting) when separation from major attachment figures occurs or is anticipated

B. The duration of the disturbance is at least 4 weeks.

C. The onset is before age 18 years.

D. The disturbance causes clinically significant distress or impairment in social, academic (occupational), or other important areas of functioning.

E. The disturbance does not occur exclusively during the course of a Pervasive Developmental Disorder, Schizophrenia, or other Psychotic Disorder and, in adolescents and adults, is not better accounted for by Panic Disorder with Agoraphobia.

Specify if:

  Early Onset: if onset occurs before age 6 years

TABLE 10.2 Overview of Prevalence Information for Separation Anxiety Disorder

Prevalence	4%
Age	Children > Adolescents
Gender	Girls > Boys
Socioeconomic status	Lower > Higher
Race/ethnicity	No differences

death of a loved one or a severe car accident within the family (Rapoport & Ismond, 1996). Many children diagnosed with separation anxiety disorder reside in caring, loving, and well-functioning families, although it is not uncommon to find that parents of children with separation anxiety disorder have themselves had some type of anxiety or mood disorder (Rapoport & Ismond, 1996). Most children with separation anxiety disorder come to the attention of clinicians because of their refusal to separate from their parents and go to school (Silverman & Ginsburg, 1998). Approximately three-fourths of children diagnosed with separation anxiety disorder show reluctance to attend school due to the separation from their parents (B. Black, 1995; N. J. King & Bernstein, 2001).

The course of separation anxiety disorder is quite variable, with some youngsters showing **spontaneous remission** (i.e., the disappearance of symptoms without any therapeutic intervention) and others showing many years of difficulty with separating from their parents (B. Black, 1995). A chronic course of separation anxiety disorder is associated with later onset, psychopathology within the family, and comorbidity with other psychiatric disorders (B. Black, 1995).

It is interesting to note that a number of studies have explored separation anxiety in parents. For example, mothers and fathers reported similar levels of separation anxiety when dropping off their children (ages 1–5) at a child care center (Deater-Deckard, Scarr, McCartney, & Eisenberg, 1994). On the other end of the developmental spectrum, mothers and fathers of college students reported somewhat high degrees of separation anxiety (Hock, Eberly, Bartle-Haring, Ellwanger, & Widaman, 2001). Higher degrees of separation anxiety were associated with poorer parent–student attachment for both mothers and fathers.

Prevalence Rates

Table 10.2 provides an overview of prevalence information for separation anxiety disorder. Separation anxiety disorder is relatively common when compared with other psychological disorders. Prevalence rates range from 1% to 13% (Silverman & Ginsburg, 1998), and a prevalence rate of 4% is noted in *DSM-IV* (American Psychiatric Association, 2000). The 4% prevalence rate is consistent with what was found in the Methods for the Epidemiology of Child and Adolescent Mental Disorders (MECA) study when parents' reports and children's reports were combined (Shaffer et al., 1996). The peak age of onset is between seven and nine years (B. Black, 1995). Girls are more likely than boys to experience separation anxiety disorder (Hartung & Widiger, 1998). There is some indication that children from lower socioeconomic status (SES) groups and children whose parents have limited educations are more likely to experience separation anxi-

---

Case Study: Yoshino, The Girl Who Was Afraid of Everything

Yoshino's fears began very early in life. Within the first six months of her life, she showed startle responses to loud noises, cried when there was too much or unexpected sensory stimulation, and flailed her arms and legs as though she was terrified that she would be dropped. Between the ages of six and nine months, Yoshino seemed to be afraid of strangers and of novel stimuli, such as heights and Halloween masks. After she turned one year old, Yoshino showed intense fear of being separated from her parents, of being injured, and of falling into the toilet. By the age of two, Yoshino was terrified of monsters and imaginary creatures, as well as fearing her own death and being robbed. When she was three, Yoshino showed a strong fear of dogs and other large animals, and she also showed extreme distress when she was left alone. By the time she was four, Yoshino was terrified of the dark. Between the ages of six and twelve, Yoshino was fearful of school, of being injured, of natural events

(such as thunderstorms and earthquakes), and of being rejected in social situations. In her later adolescence between the ages of 13 and 18, Yoshino continued to show a great deal of fear about being injured and about being alienated in social settings.

You might be ready to diagnose Yoshino with a number of anxiety disorders given her lifelong series of fears. What you need to know, however, is that Yoshino is perfectly normal. Each of the fears listed at each age are developmentally appropriate and are experienced by the majority of children during that developmental phase. Professionals must know about these normal fears before trying to diagnose an anxiety disorder such as specific phobia. If Yoshino's fears had been excessive and debilitating, then a diagnosis might be warranted. In most cases, however, these fears are part of the normal developmental process and should not be labeled as pathological.

SOURCE: Adapted from Reed, Carter, and Miller (1992).

ety disorder (B. Black, 1995). Almost no research has investigated patterns of prevalence regarding race and ethnicity, but the limited research suggests that there are no racial or ethnic differences in the prevalence rates of separation anxiety disorder (Silverman & Ginsburg, 1998).

First of all, let me assert my firm belief that the only thing we have to fear is fear itself.

— Franklin D. Roosevelt

SPECIFIC PHOBIAS

Formerly known as simple phobias, **specific phobias** are represented by extreme fears of objects or situations (see Table 10.3). As illustrated by Yoshino, many fears are very common and normal during childhood. In addition, there are objects and situations (e.g., having a gun pointed at you or finding yourself face-to-face with a hungry tiger) that would rightly cause concern for any individual. In any given culture, a fear becomes a phobia when it is excessive or unreasonable for individuals in that culture (American Psychiatric Association, 2000). The content of fears appears to be related to cultural experiences (American Psychiatric Association, 2000). For example, fear of magic or spirits is common in many cultures and would

not be diagnosed as a specific phobia unless the fear exceeded the normal experience for most other individuals in that culture. Normal and common fears are discussed in more detail later in this chapter.

It is important to note the aspects of the diagnostic criteria that are unique to children and adolescents rather than adults. Anxiety related to the feared object is often represented by crying, tantrums, freezing, or clinging in children. Children often do not realize that their fear is unreasonable, whereas adults by definition must know that their fear is excessive or unreasonable. Because so many fears are transitory in children, the fear and clinical impairment or distress must be present for at least six months to meet criteria for a specific phobia (American Psychiatric Association, 2000).

The onset of a specific phobia is often associated with a traumatic event (e.g., developing a specific phobia, animal type, after being bit by a dog or after seeing a friend bit by a dog) or is associated with repeated warnings about a certain danger (e.g., being warned repeatedly by one's parents that dogs are dangerous and they should be avoided at all costs). It is not uncommon for children to experience the same types of specific phobias as their first-degree relatives experience. That is, children with a specific phobia, animal type, are likely to have a close relative with a specific phobia, animal type, but the feared animals are often different between family members

---

TABLE 10.3 *DSM-IV* Diagnostic Criteria for Specific Phobia

A. Marked and persistent fear that is excessive or unreasonable, cued by the presence or anticipation of a specific object or situation (e.g., flying, heights, animals, receiving an injection, seeing blood).

B. Exposure to the phobic stimulus almost invariably provokes an immediate anxiety response, which may take the form of a situationally bound or situationally predisposed Panic Attack. *Note:* In children, the anxiety may be expressed by crying, tantrum, freezing, or clinging.

C. The person recognizes that the fear is excessive or unreasonable. *Note:* In children, this feature may be absent.

D. The phobic situation(s) is avoided or else is endured with intense anxiety or distress.

E. The avoidance, anxious anticipation, or distress in the feared situation(s) interferes significantly with the person's normal routine, occupational (or academic) functioning, or social activities or relationships, or there is marked distress about having the phobia.

F. In individuals under age 18 years, the duration is at least 6 months.

G. The anxiety, Panic Attacks, or phobic avoidance associated with the specific object or situation are not better accounted for by another mental disorder, such as Obsessive-Compulsive Disorder (e.g., fear of dirt in someone with an obsession about contamination), Posttraumatic Stress Disorder (e.g., avoidance of stimuli associated with a severe stressor), Separation Anxiety Disorder (e.g., avoidance of school), Social Phobia (e.g., avoidance of social situations because of fear of embarrassment), Panic Disorder with Agoraphobia, or Agoraphobia without History of Panic Disorder.

Specify type:

Animal Type

Natural Environment Type (e.g., heights, storms, water)

Blood-Injection-Injury Type

Situational Type (e.g., airplanes, elevators, enclosed places)

Other Type (e.g., phobic avoidance of situations that may lead to choking, vomiting, or contracting an illness; in children, avoidance of loud sounds or costumed characters)

Even gentle, friendly dogs can cause extreme distress in children and adolescents with a specific phobia of dogs.

(American Psychiatric Association, 2000).

As discussed in Box 10.1, **school refusal** (i.e., refusing to go to school) or **school phobia** (i.e., being fearful of going to school) can be related to a number of different problems. The families of school refusers tend to be less cohesive (i.e., less close) and less adaptable (i.e., less flexible) than the families of nonclinical children (Bernstein, Warren, Massie, & Thuras, 1999). Note that school refusal is not always associated with being absent from school. For example, the child may refuse to go to school, but the parent makes her or him attend school anyway. In a sample of anxiety-based school refusers, there were more days of absenteeism with older versus younger children, children with low levels of fear, and children with less active versus more active families (Hansen, Sanders, Massaro, & Last, 1998).

Surprisingly little research has been completed with specific phobias in children and adolescents. Most children with a specific phobia tend to show all three aspects of anxiety: cognitive, behavioral, and physiological (Albano et al., 1996). Children's cognitions about the feared stimulus tend to be catastrophic (e.g., "If the dog bites me, I will get sick and die"). The behavioral aspect is usually represented by avoidance of the feared object (e.g., children may scream and cry in order to convince their parents that they should not go to school, in the case of school phobia). Physiological characteristics are often represented by rapid heart rate, hyperventilation, shakiness, sweating, and an upset stomach when being confronted with the feared stimulus (Lichtenstein & Annas, 2000). Although specific phobias are intensely distressing to children as well as their parents, specific phobias often remit somewhat quickly during childhood (Silverman & Ginsburg, 1995). Phobic adults, however, often identify the onset of their phobia as occurring during their childhood (Albano et al., 1996).

Prevalence Rates

Table 10.4 gives an overview of prevalence information for specific phobia. Specific phobias are relatively common within childhood and adolescence. Between 2.4% and 3.3% of children and adolescents are thought to meet

---

BOX *10.1*

"DADDY, PLEASE DON'T MAKE ME GO TO SCHOOL"

If you were a clinician and a father reported that every morning his nine-year-old daughter said, "Daddy, please don't make me go to school," what diagnoses (if any) would you consider? School refusal (i.e., refusing to go to school) is relatively common in children (and even some college students). The term *school phobia* is used frequently, but there is no formal diagnosis of school phobia or school refusal. Rather, the symptom of refusing to go to school could be an indication of a number of different problems:

- There is a math test and the child is not prepared.
- Specific phobia—the child is fearful of going to school, and it is not within the first month of the school year.
- Separation anxiety disorder—the child does not want to leave her parents, and it happens that school is the place she is supposed to go.

- Social phobia—the child is terrified of having to interact with his peers and he is afraid that he will do something embarrassing and be ridiculed by his classmates.

Thus, the actual symptom of refusing to go to school or being afraid to go to school can mean very different things for different children. The process of differential diagnosis should help to clarify which disorder, if any, is appropriate for the child. This clarification is especially important for helping to treat children who refuse to go to school (Kearney & Hugelshofer, 2000; Bernstein, Hektner, Borchardt, & McMillan, 2001).

SOURCE: Silverman & Ginsburg (1995); N. J. King & Bernstein (2001).

Case Study: Shy Sylvia

Just like in Chapter 7 in the case of Devastated Darryl, you are going to be asked to formulate a treatment plan. Creating a treatment plan is an integral part of how clinicians help child clients.

Once you have written down your own thoughts, please refer to the suggestions re-printed from The Child Psychotherapy Treatment Planner *(Jongsma, Peterson, & McInnis, 2000b). There are few right or wrong answers to the exercise, rather you are being challenged to think creatively and to apply your knowledge to a realistic case.*

Sylvia is a 7-year-old Hispanic/Latina girl, and she is painfully shy. Although she interacts well with her mother, father, and two older brothers, she avoids contact with other children and adults. Her teachers and after-school caretakers have noted that Sylvia keeps to herself around other children and that she seems to become very nervous when forced to play with other children. She rarely makes eye contact with adults or children and tends to look at the floor whenever she is around others. Sylvia's parents report that she takes part in solitary activities frequently, such as reading and drawing. They have also noted that she needs a great deal of reassurance from them and that she tends to be very sensitive to even the slightest criticism. Her mother reported an example in which Sylvia stayed in her room, crying, for over two hours last week when Sylvia's mother suggested that she should brush her hair because it had become messy.

Sylvia's parents noted that these problems have been evident for as long as they can remember. They recall that she was a particularly clingy and sensitive child, but they assumed that she would grow out of it. Sylvia's father acknowledges that he is a bit uncomfortable around strangers, but that he manages to have good relationships with friends and co-workers. The parents appear to be very concerned about Sylvia's shyness and seem motivated to engage in treatment for these problems.

During your initial interview with Sylvia, she did not make direct eye contact with you except once when you mentioned a children's book that is one of her favorites. She smiled once when her oldest brother tried to tickle her. She sat on the couch in your office as though she were trying to disappear into the cushions. She kept her hands folded during the entire interview and although she answered questions when asked, she did not provide much more than one- or two-word answers. She seemed to be especially anxious (e.g., rigid muscles, arms folded across her chest) when you asked her questions directly.

Sylvia's medical history and developmental milestones are all reported to be normal, with the exception of her difficulties in social relationships. Her academic work is not problematic. No major traumas were reported.

Treatment Plan

Imagine that you are the clinician who has been contacted by Sylvia's parents. One of your first tasks is to develop a treatment plan that will guide your assessment and treatment of Sylvia and

her family. Using what you know about shyness/anxiety and therapeutic interventions, write out a treatment plan for Sylvia and her family. As you can see below, you are expected to delineate a series of behavioral definitions (e.g., the observable symptoms that are problematic), long-term goals, short-term objectives, and therapeutic interventions. Note that short-term objectives and therapeutic interventions are usually linked together so that the clinician can target specific behaviors with specific interventions. Once you have completed this section, turn to the next section to see what professional clinicians suggest for this type of case in *The Child Psychotherapy Treatment Planner* (Jongsma et al., 2000b). Make sure to compare your answers with the professionals' suggestions in order to identify ideas or concepts that you may not have considered.

Behavioral Definitions

1. _____
2. _____
3. _____
4. _____
5. _____
6. _____
7. _____
8. _____
9. _____
10. _____

Long-Term Goals

1. _____
2. _____
3. _____
4. _____
5. _____
6. _____
7. _____
8. _____
9. _____
10. _____

Short-Term Objectives	*Therapeutic Interventions*
1. _____	1. _____
2. _____	2. _____
3. _____	3. _____
4. _____	4. _____
5. _____	5. _____
6. _____	6. _____
7. _____	7. _____
8. _____	8. _____
9. _____	9. _____
10. _____	10. _____

From *The Child Psychotherapy Treatment Planner*—Jongsma, Peterson, and McInnis (2000b)

(continued)

SOCIAL PHOBIA/SHYNESS

BEHAVIORAL DEFINITIONS

1. Hiding, limited or no eye contact, a refusal or reticence to respond verbally to overtures from others, and isolation in most social situations.
2. Excessive shrinking or avoidance of eye contact with unfamiliar people for an extended period of time (i.e., six months or longer).
3. Social isolation and/or excessive involvement in isolated activities (e.g., reading, listening to music in his/her room, playing video games).
4. Extremely limited or no close friendships outside the immediate family members.
5. Hypersensitivity to criticism, disapproval, or perceived signs of rejection from other.
6. Excessive need for reassurance of being liked by others before demonstrating a willingness to get involved with them.
7. Marked reluctance to engage in new activities or take personal risks because of the potential for embarrassment or humiliation.
8. Negative self-image as evidenced by frequent self-disparaging remarks, unfavorable comparisons to others, and a perception of self as being socially unattractive.
9. Lack of assertiveness because of a fear of being met with criticism, disapproval, or rejection.
10. Heightened physiological distress in social setting manifested by increased heart rate, profuse sweating, dry mouth, muscular tension, and trembling.

LONG-TERM GOALS

1. Eliminate anxiety, shyness, and timidity in most social settings.
2. Establish and maintain long-term (i.e., six months) interpersonal or peer friendships outside of the immediate family.
3. Initiate social contacts regularly with unfamiliar people or when placed in new social settings.
4. Interact socially with peers or friends on a regular, consistent basis without excessive fear or anxiety.
5. Achieve a healthy balance between time spent in solitary activity and social interaction with others.
6. Develop the essential social skills that will enhance the quality of interpersonal relationships.
7. Resolve the core conflicts contributing to the emergence of social anxiety and shyness.
8. Elevate self-esteem and feelings of security in interpersonal peer and adult relationships.

SHORT-TERM OBJECTIVES

1. Complete psychological testing.
2. Complete psychoeducational testing.
3. Complete a speech/language evaluation.
4. Comply with the behavioral and cognitive strategies and gradually increase the frequency and duration of social contacts.
5. Agree to initiate one social contact per day.
6. Increase positive self-statements in social interactions.
7. Verbally acknowledge compliments without excessive timidity or withdrawal.
8. Increase positive statements about peer interaction and social experiences.
9. Increase participation in interpersonal or peer group activities.
10. Identify strengths and interests that can be used to initiate social contacts and develop peer friendships.
11. Increase participation in school-related activities.
12. Decrease the frequency of self-disparaging remarks in the presence of peers.
13. Increase assertive behaviors to deal more effectively and directly with stress, conflict, or intimidating peers.

THERAPEUTIC INTERVENTIONS

1. Arrange for psychological testing to assess the severity of the client's anxiety and gain greater insight into the dynamics contributing to the symptoms.
2. Arrange for psychoeducational testing of the client to rule out the presence of a learning disability that may contribute to social withdrawal in school setting.
3. Refer the client for a comprehensive speech/language evaluation to rule out possible impairment that may contribute to social withdrawal.
4. Give feedback to the client and his/her family regarding psychological, psychoeducational, and speech/language testing.
5. Actively build the level of trust with the client through consistent eye contact, active listening, unconditional positive regard, and warm acceptance to help increase his/her ability to identify and express feelings.
6. Design and implement a systematic desensitization program in which the client gradually increases the frequency and duration of social contacts to help decrease his/her social anxiety.

(continued)

Case Study: Shy Sylvia *(continued)*

14. Verbalize how current social anxiety and insecurities are associated with past rejection experiences and criticism from significant others.

15. Enmeshed or overly protective parents identify how they reinforce social anxiety and overly dependent behaviors.

16. Parents reinforce the client's positive social behaviors and set limits on overly dependent behaviors.

17. Verbally recognize the secondary gain that results from social anxiety, self-disparaging remarks, and overdependence on parents.

18. Overly critical parents verbally recognize how their negative remarks contribute to the client's social anxiety, timidity, and low self-esteem.

19. Parents set realistic and age-appropriate goals for the client.

20. Parents comply with recommendations regarding therapy and/or medication evaluations.

21. Express fears and anxiety in individual play-therapy sessions or through mutual storytelling.

22. Identify and express feelings in art.

23. Express feelings and actively participate in group therapy.

24. Take medication as directed by the prescribing physician.

7. Develop reward system or contingency contract to reinforce client for initiating social contacts and/or engaging in play or recreational activities with peers.

8. Train the client to reduce anxiety by using guided imagery in a relaxed state, with the client visualizing himself/herself dealing with various social situations in a confident manner.

9. Assist the client in developing positive self-talk as a means of managing his/her social anxiety or fears.

10. Assign the task of initiating one social contact per day.

11. Use behavioral rehearsal, modeling, and role play to reduce anxiety, develop social skills, and learn to initiate conversation.

12. Praise and reinforce any emerging positive social behaviors.

13. Ask the client to list how he/she is like his/her peers.

14. Encourage participation in extracurricular or positive peer group activities.

15. Instruct client to invite a friend for an overnight visit and/or set up an overnight visit at a friend's home; process any fears and anxiety that arise.

16. Ask the client to make a list or keep a journal of both positive and negative social experiences; process this with the therapist.

17. Explore social situations in which client interacts with others without excessive fear or anxiety. Process these successful experiences and reinforce any strengths or positive social skills that client uses to decrease fear or anxiety.

18. Consult with school officials about ways to increase the client's socialization (e.g., raising flag with group of peers, tutoring a more popular peer, pairing the client with another popular peer on classroom assignments).

19. Provide feedback on any negative social behaviors that interfere with the ability to establish and maintain friendships.

20. Teach assertiveness skills to help communicate thoughts, feelings, and needs more openly and directly.

---

criteria for a specific phobia (Silverman & Ginsburg, 1995), with the MECA study finding a prevalence rate of 2.6% when parents' and children's reports were combined (Shaffer et al., 1996). Higher prevalence rates have been reported in some other countries such as Sweden (Lichtenstein & Annas, 2000). The average age of onset of specific phobias is between 7 and 8 years old, and specific phobias tend to peak between the ages of 10 and 13 (Silverman & Ginsburg, 1998). Girls are more likely than boys to experience a specific phobia (Hartung & Widiger, 1998), although this gender difference is not always found (Albano et al., 1996). It may be that gender role orientation is more important than gender per se in the prevalence rates of specific phobias. One study found that higher levels of masculinity (regardless of whether the

TABLE 10.4 Overview of Prevalence Information for Specific Phobia

Prevalence	2–3%
Age	Children and young adolescents > Older adolescents
Gender	Girls > Boys
Socioeconomic status	Unknown patterns
Race/Ethnicity	Unknown patterns

child was a boy or a girl) were associated with lower levels of fears (Ginsburg & Silverman, 2000). Thus, the gender pattern may have more to do with gender role orientation rather than gender itself. Almost no research has been done to investigate differential prevalence rates regarding socioeconomic status or race and ethnicity (Barrios & O'Dell, 1998; Silverman & Ginsburg, 1998).

SOCIAL PHOBIA

The primary characteristics of **social phobia** revolve around fear in social situations in which the child might embarrass her or himself. According to the definition in Table 10.5, children must have the capacity for social relationships, but they become terrified at having to interact with peers in social or performance situations. This disorder must be differentiated from normal shyness or reticence in social situations, which can be quite common in children (Rapoport & Ismond, 1996). Because symptoms of shyness are transient in children, a diagnosis of social phobia requires at least a six-month duration of symptoms. Note, however, that nonclinical levels of shyness are somewhat traitlike and tend to endure for long periods of time (Rapoport & Ismond, 1996).

The majority of children diagnosed with social phobia

fall into the specific type of generalized social phobia (Albano et al., 1996). That is, most children who meet criteria for social phobia experience the phobia in nearly all social situations. The school setting, however, tends to result in a great deal of distress because of both unstructured and structured encounters with large groups of peers (Beidel & Morris, 1995). Quite often, social phobia develops after a traumatic event, such as falling down a flight of stairs when other children are watching (Beidel & Morris, 1995). Social phobia is also associated with severe concerns about public speaking, such as having to read in front of the class (Beidel & Morris, 1995).

Social anxiety is associated with poor peer interactions and poor social skills (Ginsburg, LaGreca, & Silverman, 1998; Spence, Donovan, & Brechman-Toussaint, 1999). Children and adolescents with social phobia tend to be "loners" and often do not have any friends (Albano et al., 1996). Parents of socially phobic adolescents often lament that their teens do not tie up the phone lines constantly and that their lives are not a blur of teens coming and going from the house (Albano et al., 1996). Children with social anxiety perceive their parents as socially isolating and less socially active than children with low levels of social anxiety (Caster, Inderbitzen, & Hope, 1999). Overall, it appears that children and adolescents diagnosed with social phobia are extremely afraid of being

TABLE 10.5 *DSM-IV* Diagnostic Criteria for Social Phobia

A. A marked and persistent fear of one or more social or performance situations in which the person is exposed to unfamiliar people or to possible scrutiny by others. The individual fears that he or she will act in a way (or show anxiety symptoms) that will be humiliating or embarrassing. *Note:* In children, there must be evidence of the capacity for age-appropriate social relationships with familiar people and the anxiety must occur in peer settings, not just in interactions with adults.

B. Exposure to the feared social situation almost invariably provokes anxiety, which may take the form of a situationally bound or situationally predisposed Panic Attack. *Note:* In children, the anxiety may be expressed by crying, tantrums, freezing, or shrinking from social situations with unfamiliar people.

C. The person recognizes that the fear is excessive or unreasonable. *Note:* In children, this feature may be absent.

D. The feared social or performance situations are avoided or else are endured with intense anxiety or distress.

E. The avoidance, anxious anticipation, or distress in the feared social or performance situation(s) interferes signifi-

cantly with the person's normal routine, occupational (academic) functioning, or social activities or relationships, or there is marked distress about having the phobia.

F. In individuals under age 18 years, the duration is at least 6 months.

G. The fear or avoidance is not due to the direct physiological effects of a substance (e.g., a drug of abuse, a medication) or a general medical condition and is not better accounted for by another mental disorder (e.g., Panic Disorder with or without Agoraphobia, Separation Anxiety Disorder, Body Dysmorphic Disorder, a Pervasive Developmental Disorder, or Schizoid Personality Disorder).

H. If a general medical condition or another mental disorder is present, the fear in Criterion A is unrelated to it, e.g., the fear is not of Stuttering, trembling in Parkinson's disease, or exhibiting abnormal eating behavior in Anorexia Nervosa or Bulimia Nervosa.

Specify if:

Generalized: if the fears include most social situations (also consider the additional diagnosis of Avoidant Personality Disorder)

SOURCE: American Psychiatric Association (2000). Reprinted with permission from the *Diagnostic and Statistical Manual of Mental Disorders, Fourth Edition, Text Revision.* Copyright 2000 American Psychiatric Association.

Case Study: Emily Has No Friends

Since kindergarten, Emily has shown extreme withdrawal and anxiety around peers at school and in the neighborhood. Now that she is seven years old and in the second grade, her teacher recommended that her mother seek professional help for Emily. Emily stands alone in the corner of the playground during recess and does not interact with other children. Even when another child approaches to try to play with her, she withdraws from that child. Emily appears to be afraid of being embarrassed or humiliated by her peers. Emily's mother has often taken her by the hand to play with other children in the neighborhood, but Emily just cries and runs away from the children. Emily does not have any friends at school or in the neighborhood. She has never been invited to another child's birthday party.

Unlike her behavior with peers at school and in the neighborhood, Emily is very socially engaged with her family. At home, she is outgoing and warm and she appears to enjoy the social connections with her family.

Based on these characteristics, a diagnosis of social phobia appears to be warranted. Emily obviously has the capacity for appropriate social interactions (as evidenced by her interactions with her family), but she appears to be afraid of social interactions with her peers in almost any situation.

SOURCE: Spitzer et al. (1994).

TABLE 10.6 Overview of Prevalence Information for Social Phobia

Prevalence	1–3%
Age	Adolescents > Children
Gender	Girls > Boys
Socioeconomic status	Unknown patterns
Race/Ethnicity	Unknown patterns

embarrassed, rejected, or evaluated negatively by their peers (Albano et al., 1996).

Prevalence Rates

Table 10.6 gives an overview of prevalence information for social phobia. Prevalence rates of social phobia in childhood and adolescence range from 1% to 3%, with very low rates in childhood and higher rates in adolescence (Beidel & Morris, 1995; Silverman & Ginsburg, 1998). Social phobia rarely occurs before the age of 10 (Albano et al., 1996). The average age of onset occurs between 11 and 12 years, with more adolescents diagnosed than younger children (Albano et al., 1996; Silverman & Ginsburg, 1998). In clinical samples, girls outnumber boys for treatment of social phobia (Beidel & Morris, 1995; Hartung & Widiger, 1998), although this gender difference is not found in every study (Beidel & Morris, 1995). Data on socioeconomic status, race, and ethnicity remain unclear (Beidel & Morris, 1995).

OBSESSIVE-COMPULSIVE DISORDER

The case study entitled Lady Macbeth provides an eloquent description of a client's experience with **obsessive-compulsive disorder (OCD)**. In a popular book entitled *The Boy Who Couldn't Stop Washing* (Rapoport, 1989), the lay public also became much more familiar with this disorder. OCD is a disorder that occurs when a child or adolescent has disordered thoughts, ideas, or images (called **obsessions**) or disordered, repetitive behaviors (called **compulsions**). As with all disorders, normal levels of obsessiveness and compulsiveness need to be distinguished from abnormal levels of obsessiveness and compulsiveness (Albano et al., 1996; March, Leonard, & Swedo, 1995). It is not unusual for children and adolescents to have certain thoughts that could be considered obsessions (e.g., a child who thinks constantly about her beloved kitten or an adolescent who cannot get a certain friend off his mind) and to show behaviors that might be considered compulsive (e.g., a young child who wants to say "Goodnight, I love you" to each person in the house at his bedtime or an adolescent who insists that her clothes be in a certain order in her closet). These normal idiosyncrasies should not be mistaken for OCD (Zohar & Felz, 2001).

When OCD is present, children and adolescents often have both obsessions and compulsions, but the diagnosis of OCD requires only that either obsessions or compulsions be present. The obsessions or compulsions must cause significant distress, must be time-consuming (occurring for more than one hour per day), or must impact negatively on the child's or adolescent's life. According to the definition in Table 10.7, the diagnostic criteria in *DSM-IV* also note a difference between OCD in children and OCD in adults. Whereas adults have to realize that the symptoms are excessive or unreasonable, children and adolescents do not.

OCD is a very distressing disorder. It appears that compulsions (behavioral excesses) are often completed in order to reduce the anxiety of obsessions (recurrent cog-

Case Study: Lady Macbeth, The Adolescent Who Had to Wash Her Hands

Below is the transcript of an interview session with a girl who meets criteria for obsessive-compulsive disorder. Note that she exhibits both disordered behavior (compulsions) and disordered thoughts (obsessions).

INTERVIEWER: What were the things that you were doing?

CLIENT: In the morning when I got dressed, I was real afraid that there'd be germs all over my clothes and things, so I'd stand there and I'd shake them for half an hour. I'd wash before I did anything—like if I was gonna wash my face, I'd wash my hands first; and if I was gonna get dressed, I'd wash my hands first; and then it got even beyond that point. Washing my hands wasn't enough, and I started to use rubbing alcohol. It was wintertime and cold weather, and this really made my hands bleed. Even if I just held them under water, they'd bleed all over the place, and they looked terrible, and everyone thought I had a disease or something.

INTERVIEWER: And when you were doing that much washing, how much time every day did that take, if you added up all the different parts of it?

CLIENT: It took about six hours a day . . .

INTERVIEWER: You also told me about other things in addition to the washing and worrying about dirt: that you would have plans about how you would do other things.

CLIENT: Okay, well they were like set plans in my mind that if I heard the word, like, something that had to do with germs or disease, it would be considered something bad and so I had things that would go through my mind that were sort of like "cross that out and it'll make it okay" to hear that word.

INTERVIEWER: What sort of things?

CLIENT: Like numbers or words that seemed to be sort of like a protector.

INTERVIEWER: What numbers and what words were they?

CLIENT: It started out to be the number 3 and multiples of 3 and then words like "soap and water," something like that; and then the multiples of 3 got really high, they'd end up to be 123 or something like that. It got real bad then.

INTERVIEWER: At any time did you really believe that something bad would happen if you didn't do these things? Was it just a feeling, or were you really scared?

CLIENT: No! I was petrified that something would really happen . . .

INTERVIEWER: Who were the people you'd worry most would get hurt?

CLIENT: My family, basically my family . . .

SOURCE: Spitzer et al. (1994; pp. 344–46). Reprinted with permission from the *DSM-IV Casebook*. Copyright 1994 American Psychiatric Association.

Robert, why is it necessary for you to walk up and down every aisle three times whenever you go to the pencil sharpener?

SIPRESS

TABLE 10.7 *DSM-IV* Diagnostic Criteria for Obsessive-Compulsive Disorder

A. Either obsessions or compulsions:

Obsessions as defined by (1), (2), (3), and (4):

(1) recurrent and persistent thoughts, impulses, or images that are experienced, at some time during the disturbance, as intrusive and inappropriate and that cause marked anxiety or distress

(2) the thoughts, impulses, or images are not simply excessive worries about real-life problems

(3) the person attempts to ignore or suppress such thoughts, impulses, or images, or to neutralize them with some other thought or action

(4) the person recognizes that the obsessional thoughts, impulses, or images are a product of his or her own mind (not imposed from without as in thought insertion)

Compulsions as defined by (1) and (2):

(1) repetitive behaviors (e.g., hand washing, ordering, checking) or mental acts (e.g., praying, counting, repeating words silently) that the person feels driven to perform in response to an obsession, or according to rules that must be applied rigidly

(2) the behaviors or mental acts are aimed at preventing or reducing distress or preventing some dreaded event or situation; however, these behaviors or mental acts either are not connected in a realistic way with what they are designed to neutralize or prevent or are clearly excessive

B. At some point during the course of the disorder, the person has recognized that the obsessions or compulsions are excessive or unreasonable. *Note:* This does not apply to children.

C. The obsessions or compulsions cause marked distress, are time consuming (take more than 1 hour a day), or significantly interfere with the person's normal routine, occupational (or academic) functioning, or usual social activities or relationships.

D. If another Axis I disorder is present, the content of the obsessions or compulsions is not restricted to it (e.g., preoccupation with food in the presence of an Eating Disorder; hair pulling in the presence of Trichotillomania; concern with appearance in the presence of Body Dysmorphic Disorder; preoccupation with drugs in the presence of a Substance Use Disorder; preoccupation with having a serious illness in the presence of Hypochondriasis; preoccupation with sexual urges or fantasies in the presence of a Paraphilia; or guilty ruminations in the presence of Major Depressive Disorder).

E. The disturbance is not due to the direct physiological effects of a substance (e.g., a drug of abuse, a medication) or a general medical condition.

Specify if:

With Poor Insight: if, for most of the time during the current episode, the person does not recognize that the obsessions and compulsions are excessive or unreasonable

SOURCE: American Psychiatric Association (2000). Reprinted with permission from the *Diagnostic and Statistical Manual of Mental Disorders, Fourth Edition, Text Revision.* Copyright 2000 American Psychiatric Association.

nitions). Imagine a little boy who sometimes has thoughts about hurting his father and who then kneels down and prays in order to "undo" his bad thoughts. Each time he imagines his father being hurt, he kneels down and does a series of prayers. The prayers seem to reduce his anxiety about his thoughts, which inadvertently reinforce the likelihood that he will pray the next time he has a troubling thought about his father. In many cases of OCD, compulsions can take over the child's or adolescent's life, leaving him or her little time to do anything else other than the compulsive behaviors. OCD is often a debilitating problem, and at least 50% of adolescents diagnosed with OCD continue to have the problem into adulthood (Rapoport & Ismond, 1996).

Washing rituals (e.g., hand washing, washing the desk at school); repeating rituals (e.g., saying a certain phrase over and over); and checking behaviors (e.g., repeatedly making sure that their house key is in their backpack) are the most common compulsions in children and adolescents (Albano et al., 1996). The most common obsessions include fear of contamination (e.g., getting germs from dirt, contracting AIDS or another life-threatening illness) and concerns about hurting oneself or a family member (Albano et al., 1996).

Prevalence Rates

Table 10.8 gives an overview of prevalence information for obsessive-compulsive disorder. OCD is thought to be relatively rare, with a lifetime prevalence rate of 1% noted in a study of adolescents (Geffken, Pincus, & Zelikovsky, 1999), and less than 1% in children under the age of 10 (March & Mulle, 1998). Because of the hidden nature of the disorder (i.e., children and adolescents often try to keep their symptoms a secret), many youth experience OCD but never receive help for their problems (March & Mulle, 1998). Thus, these prevalence rates may be an underestimate of the actual occurrence of OCD in childhood and adolescence (Geffken et al., 1999).

OCD most often occurs first in adolescence or early

TABLE 10.8 Overview of Prevalence Information for Obsessive-Compulsive Disorder

Prevalence	1% of adolescents
Age	Adolescents > Children
Gender	No differences
Socioeconomic status	Unknown patterns
Race/ethnicity	No differences (in epidemiological studies)

adulthood (Rapoport & Ismond, 1996). It is rare for a young child to develop OCD. Prevalence rates regarding gender show approximately similar numbers of boys and girls diagnosed with OCD (March & Mulle, 1998). An interesting pattern emerges when age and gender are explored. Boys are more likely to receive a diagnosis of OCD before puberty, whereas girls are more likely to receive a diagnosis of OCD after puberty (March & Mulle, 1998). There has been little research on the prevalence rates of OCD regarding socioeconomic status (Albano et al., 1996). Within community-based epidemiological studies, there does not appear to be any difference in the prevalence of OCD with regard to race and ethnicity (March & Mulle, 1998). Interestingly, proportionally more Caucasian American children than African American children receive treatment for OCD, which suggests that the former might be referred for treatment of OCD more readily than are the latter (March & Mulle, 1998).

GENERALIZED ANXIETY DISORDER

Formerly known as overanxious disorder, **generalized anxiety disorder (GAD)** occurs when children or adolescents experience a pervasive and chronic level of anxiety and worry (see Table 10.9). Most often, the anxiety and worry are somewhat diffuse (e.g., a child who worries about nearly everything), but sometimes the anxiety and worry are focused on a few specific events or activities (e.g., worrying about doing well in reading and feeling anxious about the dog's health and feeling distressed about a friend's parent's marriage). The anxieties and worries are considered to be unrealistic and excessive (Albano et al., 1996). Children often worry about future events (e.g., whether they will make the varsity soccer team in high school even though they are still in grade school) and sometimes worry about adult concerns (e.g., the family finances).

Children diagnosed with GAD tend to be very self-conscious (Silverman & Ginsburg, 1995). They tend to assume that bad things will happen to those around them, and they tend to assume that the negative consequences to events will be a lot worse than most others expect (Albano et al., 1996). Although even nonclinical children have worries about low-frequency events (such as nuclear war), children diagnosed with GAD do not realize that these events are infrequent and unlikely (Albano et al., 1996).

Case Study: Frank, The Worrier

When he was three years old, Frank began to worry that he would die in his sleep. From that time on, he was a light sleeper and he would awaken often during the night. Frank's father had a history of panic disorder and major depression, and Frank's mother had a history of major depression.

By the time he was eight years old, Frank worried about everything. For the past three months, he had been hearing things as he was falling asleep. He often thought that he heard "something that seemed like something mumbling" and he reported that he thought he heard someone breathing in his room. On a number of occasions at night, he thought he saw "flashes of light" and he began experiencing panic attacks (e.g., shortness of breath, tachycardia, tingling in his hands, and extreme fearfulness). The panic attacks lasted approximately 15 to 20 minutes and frightened Frank so much that he no longer would sleep in his own room. With his parents' permission, Frank would go to sleep on the couch in the living room and then, once Frank was sound asleep, his father would carry him to bed.

During the clinical interview, Frank appeared to take pride in his knowledge of his clinical symptomatology. He was able to report each symptom and gave immense details on his troubling experiences. He acknowledged that he worried all the time. Even though he was still in elementary school, he worried that his dropping grades would prevent him from gaining admission to a "good college." Based on interviews with Frank and his parents, Frank received the following multiaxial diagnosis:

Axis I:	Generalized anxiety disorder
	Panic disorder without agoraphobia
Axis II:	No diagnosis (i.e., no personality disorders or developmental disabilities)
Axis III:	None (i.e., no physical illnesses)
Axis IV:	Problems with primary support group; both parents have chronic major depressive disorder, in partial remission
Axis V:	Global Assessment of functioning = 60 (current)

SOURCE: Rapoport & Ismond (1996).

Children with generalized anxiety disorder are often worried and anxious for no apparent reason.

Prevalence Rates

Table 10.10 gives an overview of prevalence information for generalized anxiety disorder. Epidemiological data suggest that GAD is present in 2% to 19% of children and adolescents, with most conservative studies suggesting that GAD is present in 2% to 4% of children and adolescents (Silverman & Ginsburg, 1995). GAD is more prevalent in adolescents than in children (Albano et al., 1996). During adolescence and into adulthood, GAD is more common in females than in males (Silverman & Ginsburg, 1995). Children from middle and higher socioeconomic status families are found more frequently in clinical facilities than are children from lower SES families (Silverman & Ginsburg, 1995). There has been almost no research into the different prevalence rates of GAD within different racial and ethnic groups (Silverman & Ginsburg, 1995).

TABLE 10.9 *DSM-IV* **Diagnostic Criteria for Generalized Anxiety Disorder**

A. Excessive anxiety and worry (apprehensive expectation), occurring more days than not for at least 6 months, about a number of events or activities (such as work or school performance).

B. The person finds it difficult to control the worry.

C. The anxiety and worry are associated with three (or more) of the following six symptoms (with at least some symptoms present for more days than not for the past 6 months). *Note:* Only one item is required in children.

  (1) restlessness or feeling keyed up or on edge

  (2) being easily fatigued

  (3) difficulty concentrating or mind going blank

  (4) irritability

  (5) muscle tension

  (6) sleep disturbance (difficult falling or staying asleep, or restless unsatisfying sleep)

D. The focus of the anxiety and worry is not confined to features of an Axis I disorder, e.g., the anxiety or worry is not about having a Panic Attack (as in Panic Disorder), being embarrassed in public (as in Social Phobia), being contaminated (as in Obsessive-Compulsive Disorder), being away from home or close relatives (as in Separation Anxiety Disorder), gaining weight (as in Anorexia Nervosa), having multiple physical complaints (as in Somatization Disorder), or having a serious illness (as in Hypochondriasis), and the anxiety and worry do not occur exclusively during Post-traumatic Stress Disorder.

E. The anxiety, worry, or physical symptoms cause clinically significant distress or impairment in social, occupational, or other important areas of functioning.

F. The disturbance is not due to the direct physiological effects of a substance (e.g., drug of abuse, a medication) or a general medical condition (e.g., hyperthyroidism) and does not occur exclusively during a Mood Disorder, a Psychotic Disorder, or a Pervasive Developmental Disorder.

SOURCE: American Psychiatric Association (2000). Reprinted with permission from the *Diagnostic and Statistical Manual of Mental Disorders, Fourth Edition, Text Revision.* Copyright 2000 American Psychiatric Association.

TABLE 10.10 **Overview of Prevalence Information for Generalized Anxiety Disorder**

Prevalence	2–4%
Age	Adolescents > Children
Gender	Females > Males
Socioeconomic status	Middle and higher > Lower
Race/Ethnicity	Unknown patterns

Oh, it's scary 'cause all this violence going on now. And I— and I just wonder if it's gonna get worse or if it's gonna be better.

—Marie, a Dominican American teenager who lives in an impoverished urban area (Way, 1998, p. 169)

POST-TRAUMATIC STRESS DISORDER

Post-traumatic stress disorder (PTSD) occurs when children or adolescents experience some type of traumatic event (such as a sexual assault, a terrorist attack, an earthquake, or a car accident) and have even more problems related to the event than would otherwise be expected (see Table 10.11). It can also occur in reaction to the death of a parent (Stoppelbein & Greening, 2000). Symptoms of PTSD in children include depression, anxiety, emotional disturbance, somatic complaints, aggression, and acting out (Foa, Johnson, Feeny, & Treadwell, 2001).

Historically, PTSD was the focus of research on adult veterans of war. Within the past 15 years, however, a great deal of interest has focused on children's and adolescents' experience of PTSD, especially as it relates to the trauma of physical abuse, sexual abuse, and community violence (Lipschitz, Rasmusson, Anyan, Cromwell, & Southwick, 2000; McCloskey & Walker, 2000; Nishith, Mechanic, & Resick, 2000). In addition to the trauma of abuse, PTSD has been investigated with children who have experienced kidnapping, school shootings, fires, domestic violence, floods, hurricanes, war, and other disasters (Amaya-Jackson & March, 1995; Udwin, Boyle, Yule, Bolton, & O'Ryan, 2000).

Events related to the trauma can influence children's PTSD symptoms. For example, watching the explosion of the *Challenger* space shuttle was more distressing to children on the East Coast, who knew more about the teacher on board, than to children on the West Coast (Terr et al., 1999). In general, a greater degree of exposure to the traumatic event is associated with more PTSD symptoms (March, Amaya-Jackson, Terry, & Costanzo, 1997). According to Table 10.11, the criteria in *DSM-IV* highlight the extreme and maladaptive nature with which the individual reacts to the trauma.

Prevalence Rates

Table 10.12 gives an overview an overview of prevalence information for PTSD. Although there are no good epidemiological estimates of PTSD in children and adoles-

---

Case Study: Nina, A Girl Who Fears the Nighttime Visitor

At the age of eight, Nina presented as a sad, very quiet child who almost never smiled. She spent most of her time in her bedroom watching television and was concerned that no one at school liked her. Nina had trouble sleeping and often had nightmares about her father molesting her. She was afraid that her father (who was in jail) would come into her room and hurt her. She herself was afraid of being sent to jail for doing something wrong. Nina felt that her mother picked on her and favored her siblings. Nina's siblings, 9-year-old Sara and 11-year-old Don, often fought with Nina. When at home, Nina was often irritable and sad. When at school, Nina was often aggressive and disruptive.

Based on this clinical picture, you might be inclined to diagnose Nina with some type of anxiety disorder. Nina's history of sexual abuse by her father, however, would lead clinicians to a diagnosis of post-traumatic stress disorder.

The sexual abuse was discovered when Nina was admitted to a hospital for vaginal bleeding and a vaginal discharge. Nina was diagnosed with vaginal warts and gonorrhea. After this diagnosis, Nina confided to a social worker that her father had been sexually abusing her and (to a lesser extent) her sister, Sara, for the past two years. Nina's father would enter the girls' room at night and have vaginal intercourse with Nina. He threatened both girls with severe beatings if they ever told anyone. After witnessing the molestation, Nina's brother, Don, reported the abuse to their mother, who did not believe him. Nina's mother told Nina's father, who then beat Don severely (which occurred frequently even before the abuse disclosure). Nina and Sara told their mother that Don had not been lying, but she just told them to stop "making up stories."

When the social worker finally interviewed Nina's mother about the sexual abuse, she acknowledged that she suspected that her husband was sexually abusing her daughters, but she reported that she would have feared for her life if she had confronted him about the abuse. In the past 12 years of marriage, Nina's father had beaten Nina's mother severely on several occasions. Nina's mother felt that she could not leave her husband because their religion did not allow divorce.

After the sexual abuse was confirmed, the children were put into foster care, the father was sent to jail, and the mother's parental rights were taken away temporarily due to her failure to protect her children from her husband. The children were then allowed to stay with their maternal grandmother while the case was under investigation. Nina and her siblings were finally returned to their mother after she became involved in psychological assessment and treatment for herself and her children.

This case illustrates that sexual abuse can serve as the trauma that leads to post-traumatic stress disorder. In addition, the mother's initial disbelief in the children's allegations of abuse probably exacerbated the trauma for Nina and her sister.

SOURCE: Spitzer et al. (1994).

TABLE 10.11 *DSM-IV* Diagnostic Criteria for Posttraumatic Stress Disorder

A. The person has been exposed to a traumatic event in which both of the following were present:

(1) the person experienced, witnessed, or was confronted with an event or events that involved actual or threatened death or serious injury, or a threat to the physical integrity of self or others

(2) the person's response involved intense fear, helplessness, or horror. *Note:* In children, this may be expressed instead by disorganized or agitated behavior.

B. The traumatic event is persistently reexperienced in one (or more) of the following ways:

(1) recurrent and intrusive distressing recollections of the event, including images, thoughts, or perceptions. *Note:* In young children, repetitive play may occur in which themes or aspects of the trauma are expressed.

(2) recurrent distressing dreams of the event. *Note:* In children, there may be frightening dreams without recognizable content.

(3) acting or feeling as if the traumatic event were recurring (includes a sense of reliving the experience, illusions, hallucinations, and dissociative flashback episodes, including those that occur on awakening or when intoxicated). *Note:* In young children, trauma-specific reenactment may occur.

(4) intense psychological distress at exposure to internal or external cues that symbolize or resemble an aspect of the traumatic event

(5) physiological reactivity on exposure to internal or external cues that symbolize or resemble an aspect of the traumatic event

C. Persistent avoidance of stimuli associated with the trauma and numbing of general responsiveness (not present before the trauma), as indicated by three (or more) of the following:

(1) efforts to avoid thoughts, feelings, or conversations associated with the trauma

(2) efforts to avoid activities, places, or people that arouse recollections of the trauma

(3) inability to recall an important aspect of the trauma

(4) markedly diminished interest or participation in significant activities

(5) feeling of detachment or estrangement from others

(6) restricted range of affect (e.g., unable to have loving feelings)

(7) sense of a foreshortened future (e.g., does not expect to have a career, marriage, children, or a normal life span)

D. Persistent symptoms of increased arousal (not present before the trauma), as indicated by two (or more) of the following:

(1) difficulty falling or staying asleep

(2) irritability or outbursts of anger

(3) difficulty concentrating

(4) hypervigilance

(5) exaggerated startle response

E. Duration of the disturbance (symptoms in Criteria B, C, and D) is more than 1 month.

F. The disturbance causes clinically significant distress or impairment in social, occupational, or other important areas of functioning.

Specify if:

Acute: if duration of symptoms is less than 3 months

Chronic: if duration of symptoms is 3 months or more

Specify if:

With Delayed Onset: if onset of symptoms is at least 6 months after the stressor

SOURCE: American Psychiatric Association (2000). Reprinted with permission from the *Diagnostic and Statistical Manual of Mental Disorders, Fourth Edition, Text Revision.* Copyright 2000 American Psychiatric Association.

cents, it appears that PTSD is relatively common in childhood when compared with other psychological disorders. One review of epidemiological data suggested that 36% of all children and adolescents could meet criteria for PTSD (K. E. Fletcher, 1996). This number is the combination of interesting age trends, where 39% of preschoolers, 33% of elementary school children, and 27% of adolescents met criteria for PTSD (K. E. Fletcher, 1996). Thus, it appears that PTSD is more common in younger children when compared with adolescents. Other studies have suggested lower prevalence rates that are closer to 5% (K. E. Fletcher, 1996). In either case, PTSD is highly prevalent in children and adolescents. It appears that girls are more at risk for the development of PTSD than are boys (K. E. Fletcher, 1996). Little is known about the differential prevalence rates related to socioeconomic status, and there are no known differences when racial and ethnic groups are compared (K. E. Fletcher, 1996). There is surprisingly little research on PTSD in children, other than in reaction to physical and sexual abuse. (Box 10.2, though, highlights a study on children exposed to war.) More research is needed to confirm the scant knowledge that is available currently. This type of research may be enhanced when better assessment measures are developed for the disorder (March, 1999).

TABLE 10.12   Overview of Prevalence Information for Post-traumatic Stress Disorder

Prevalence	5–39%
Age	Younger > Older
Gender	Boys > Girls
Socioeconomic status	Unknown pattern
Race/ethnicity	No differences

SELECTIVE MUTISM

Formerly known as elective mutism, **selective mutism** is diagnosed when children fail to speak in one or more situations when it is obvious that they can speak in other situations (see Table 10.13). The most typical case of selective mutism is when a child speaks well at home but does not speak at school or in other situations away from home (Leonard & Dow, 1995). Current thinking suggests that these children do not speak due to high levels of anxiety rather than to oppositional tendencies (Anstendig, 1999; Dow, Sonies, Scheib, & Moss, 1996).

Children diagnosed with selective mutism tend to be very shy, withdrawn, negative, and isolated especially in the situations where they do not speak (American Psychiatric Association, 2000; Rapoport & Ismond, 1996). After children develop selective mutism, they are often scapegoated and teased by other children (American Psychiatric Association, 2000). The disorder often lasts only a

TABLE 10.13   *DSM-IV* Diagnostic Criteria for Selective Mutism

1. Consistent failure to speak in specific social situations (in which there is an expectation for speaking, e.g., at school) despite speaking in other situations.
2. The disturbance interferes with educational or occupational achievement or with social communication.
3. The duration of the disturbance is at least 1 month (not limited to the first month of school).
4. The failure to speak is not due to a lack of knowledge of, or comfort with, the spoken language required in the social situation.
5. The disturbance is not better accounted for by a Communication Disorder (e.g., Stuttering) and does not occur exclusively during the course of a Pervasive Developmental Disorder, Schizophrenia, or other Psychotic Disorder.

Source: American Psychiatric Association (2000). Reprinted with permission from the *Diagnostic and Statistical Manual of Mental Disorders, Fourth Edition, Text Revision.* Copyright 2000 American Psychiatric Association.

few months, although it can last several years when left untreated (American Psychiatric Association, 2000).

Prevalence Rates

Table 10.14 gives an overview of prevalence information for selective mutism. Selective mutism is quite rare, with far fewer than 1% of children in mental health clinics experiencing the disorder (American Psychiatric Associ-

---

BOX *10.2*

WAR IS NOT HEALTHY FOR CHILDREN AND OTHER LIVING THINGS

The title of this box, a saying from the late 1960s and early 1970s in the United States, remains true currently throughout the world. There are many studies of children who have survived war atrocities (for example, see the special section of *Child Development* 67, no. 1, 1996). Although only one study will be highlighted here, its findings are comparable to those of other studies of children from diverse nations who have been exposed to war.

Palestinian children living in the Gaza Strip (between Israel and Egypt) have been exposed to war and violence for much of their lives. One study of children ages 6 to 11 found that they had been exposed to a large number of traumatic events related to war (Thabet & Vostanis, 1999):

- 56.1% had inhaled tear gas at least once.
- 49.0% had witnessed day raids.

- 41.8% had witnessed night raids.
- 34.3% had seen a friend being beaten.
- 24.7% had seen a friend being shot.
- 4.6% witnessed a close relative being killed.
- 1.2% had experienced broken limbs due to war-related violence.

A total of 72.8% of children in this study experienced mild PTSD reactions at some point during their lives, and 41.0% experienced moderate/severe PTSD reactions during their lives. Higher numbers of war-related traumatic events were associated with more severe PTSD reactions (Thabet & Vostanis, 1999). Overall, this study illustrates the psychological consequences of war on the youngest victims.

Case Study: Quiet Kevin

Kevin is a sweet, energetic, friendly six-year-old who speaks only to members of his immediate family. Since the age of two, Kevin has not spoken to anyone else other than his immediate family. This holds true even when he engages in activities outside of the family (e.g., playing games at school, going to parties, singing in the grocery store, playing piano).

During the clinical interview, Kevin whispered answers to his mother but would not speak to the interviewer directly. Kevin acknowledged that his lack of speaking was a problem that he would like to resolve. He was not, however, able to identify any reason why he did not speak in social situations.

This case represents a relatively clear-cut example of selective mutism. Although many cases of selective mutism do not appear until the child enters school, Kevin's case shows a particularly lengthy course of the disorder. After treatment with behavior therapy and antidepressants, Kevin began to speak periodically in school and he began to speak to his grandparents on the phone. By the end of the second grade, Kevin was talking to nearly everyone (except for his former kindergarten teacher) and he appeared to be a happy, exuberant child. Kevin was even voted class president for the following year.

SOURCE: Spitzer et al. (1994).

TABLE 10.14 Overview of Prevalence Information for Selective Mutism

Prevalence	< 1%
Age	Younger > Older
Gender	Girls > Boys
Socioeconomic status	Unknown patterns
Race/Ethnicity	Unknown patterns

ation, 2000). Exact prevalence rates are thought to be between 0.08% and 0.7% (Leonard & Dow, 1995). Selective mutism is much more common with younger children than with older children or adolescents (American Psychiatric Association, 2000). Symptoms most often occur before the age of five, but referrals for diagnosis and treatment usually occur once the child reaches school age. Selective mutism is more common in girls than in boys (American Psychiatric Association, 2000; Hartung & Widiger, 1998). Almost no epidemiological research has addressed the prevalence rates of selective mutism according to socioeconomic status or race and ethnicity (Leonard & Dow, 1995).

I think the thing I'm most frightened of is the world ending.
—14-year-old Carleen, from England

ALL ANXIETY DISORDERS OF CHILDHOOD AND ADOLESCENCE

Although the different anxiety disorders are each unique, many studies combine children with all of these anxiety disorders together in one sample (Rapoport & Ismond, 1996). Thus, this section will discuss comorbidity, courses of the disorders, etiology, treatment, and preven-

tion broadly for anxiety disorders in childhood and adolescence. Where possible, specific comments will be made about specific disorders.

Comorbidity

Comorbidity is quite common with anxiety disorders in childhood and adolescence (Angold et al., 1999; Kendall, Brady, & Verduin, 2001). The highest rates of comorbidity are between different anxiety disorders themselves (e.g., separation anxiety disorder and generalized anxiety disorder) and between anxiety disorders and mood disorders (e.g., separation anxiety disorder and major depressive disorder; Angold et al., 1999; Seligman & Ollendick, 1998). For example, within an anxiety disorders clinic, one-third of the children with an anxiety disorder met criteria for both separation anxiety disorder and generalized anxiety disorder (Rapoport & Ismond, 1996). Between 30% and 50% of children diagnosed with separation anxiety disorder also meet criteria for major depressive disorder (Rapoport & Ismond, 1996), and a sizable portion also meet criteria for social phobia (Compton, Nelson, & March, 2000). At least one-half of youth diagnosed with obsessive-compulsive disorder (OCD) meet criteria for at least one other disorder (Albano et al., 1998). OCD is also associated with having a tic, but it appears that tics in childhood and early adolescence precede OCD in later adolescence (B. S. Peterson, Pine, Cohen, & Brook, 2001).

These patterns also persist into adulthood. For example, separation anxiety disorder in childhood is often associated with some type of anxiety disorder diagnosis later in adulthood (Rapoport & Ismond, 1996). Overall, comorbidity is the rule rather than the exception with anxiety disorders in childhood and adolescence, as well as in adulthood (Angold et al., 1999).

Course of the Disorder

Different anxiety disorders have different courses within childhood and adolescence. The course of separation anxiety disorder is variable, with some youngsters only having brief problems with the disorder and other youngsters having chronic problems into adolescence (B. Black, 1995). Specific phobias are often associated with a trauma and are relatively quick to remit (Silverman & Ginsburg, 1995). Social phobia disorder is often a chronic problem throughout childhood and adolescence (Albano et al., 1996). Obsessive-compulsive disorder is also a long-term problem, with 50% of OCD cases continuing into adulthood (Rapoport & Ismond, 1996). Generalized anxiety disorder also tends to be a chronic, long-term problem for children and adolescents (Silverman & Ginsburg, 1995). Post-traumatic stress disorder is, by definition, associated with a trauma and has a variable course, with some cases remitting quickly and other cases lasting years (K. E. Fletcher, 1996). Selective mutism tends to remit on its own within a few months of onset (Leonard & Dow, 1995).

> *The basic anxiety, the anxiety of a finite being about the threat of non-being, cannot be eliminated. It belongs to existence itself.*
>
> —Paul Johannes Tillich

Etiology

There are three primary theoretical models that are used currently to help explain the development of anxiety disorders in children and adolescents: biological, behavioral, and cognitive (Kearney & Wadiak, 1999). Biological models (including genetic and neurological models) have received a great deal of attention recently (Pine & Grun, 1999). Much of the support for biological models has come from family studies that have shown strong connections between anxiety disorders in children and anxiety disorders in their parents (Silverman & Ginsburg, 1998). Specifically, children of parents who have an anxiety disorder are more likely than children of nondisordered parents to develop an anxiety disorder (McClure, Brennan, Hammen, & LeBrocque, 2001). Similarly, children diagnosed with an anxiety disorder are more likely to have parents with an anxiety disorder or with high levels of anxiety when compared with parents of nondisordered children (McClure et al., 2001). Both fathers' and mothers' heightened anxiety levels are associated with children's anxiety (Krain & Kendall, 2000) and symptoms of OCD (Lougee, Perlmutter, Nicolson, Garvey, & Swedo, 2000). These family studies do not address whether the connection is based on genetic transmission or environmental influences. Other twin studies, however, have provided clear evidence of at least some genetic influence in the development of anxiety disorders in childhood (Lichtenstein & Annas, 2000; Silverman & Ginsburg, 1998).

There has also been a great deal of interest in the neurobiology of anxiety itself. Unfortunately, the majority of the research in this area has been completed with animals and with adult humans (Sallee & Greenawald, 1995). When children and adolescents are included in studies, there is evidence of structural brain differences between children with and without an anxiety disorder (Sallee & Greenawald, 1995). In addition, OCD appears to be triggered by streptococcal infections in some children. Known collectively as pediatric autoimmune neuropsychiatric disorders associated with streptococcal infection (PANDAS), OCD as well as some tic disorders appear to be triggered by infections in some children (Lougee et al., 2000).

Taken together, these studies suggest that it is likely that both genetic and environmental factors influence the development of anxiety disorders in children and adolescents (Silverman & Ginsburg, 1998). As noted in Box 10.3, there is also evidence that neurobiological factors such as temperament and **behavioral inhibition** (i.e., irritability, shyness, and fearfulness) are related to the onset of anxiety disorders in children and adolescents (Biederman, Rosenbaum, Chaloff, & Kagan, 1995).

Behavioral models gained a lot of attention after the founder of behaviorism, J. B. Watson, showed that phobias could be learned through classical conditioning (Watson & Rayner, 1920). Watson and his colleagues devised a study in which Little Albert, an 11-month-old boy, was shown a white rat. At first Little Albert showed no fear toward the rat and even seemed interested in playing with it. Then the rat was paired with a loud bang that scared the child. After five pairings, Little Albert showed intense fear of the rat. This classic, albeit cruel, study showed that fears could be developed through behavioral principles. Since that time, researchers have explored both classical and operant conditioning models of anxiety disorders as well as social learning models. Operant models suggest that fears are developed from an association between a stimulus (e.g., a dog) and a negative consequence (e.g., a loud and scary bark from the dog). Classical conditioning models suggest that fears are developed from repeated pairings of a stimulus (e.g., an elevator) and an aversive experience (e.g., being trapped in an elevator).

Neither operant models nor classical conditioning models fully explain the development of phobias (Kearney

BOX

BEHAVIORAL INHIBITION: COULD IT BE THE COMMON FACTOR OF ANXIETY DISORDERS?

Anyone who has been around a number of newborns and young infants knows that babies enter the world with different temperamental styles (i.e., ways in which they deal with their environment). As noted in Chapter 7, some babies are mellow (known as easy babies), some require a high degree of maintenance (known as difficult babies), and some are wary of new situations but then seem to enjoy the new situation eventually (known as slow-to-warm-up babies). The study of temperamental style suggests that temperament early in life is related to psychological functioning later in life. Easy babies tend to develop into easy children. Difficult babies tend to develop into difficult children. Slow-to-warm-up babies tend to be wary of new situations throughout their lives. One example of this pattern was shown in a study that followed children for more than seven years. Seven-year-olds who had been classified as highly reactive infants (i.e., with difficult temperament) showed higher rates of anxiety than infants with low reactivity levels (Kagan, Snidman, Zentner, & Peterson, 1999).

One interesting slant on temperament research is the exploration of behavioral inhibition. Behavioral inhibition is a traitlike characteristic in which youngsters show hesitation and inhibition in new situations (Biederman et al., 1995). Specifically, babies who show behavioral inhibition tend to be irritable early in life; shy during toddlerhood, and quiet, introverted, and cautious by the time they reach elementary school (Kagan, Reznick, & Snidman, 1988). Because of the obvious similarities between inhibition and anxiety, a number of researchers have investigated the connections between behavioral inhibition and anxiety disorders in childhood and adolescence (Prior, Smart, Sanson, & Oberklaid, 2000). As can be seen in the figure below, behaviorally inhibited children are much more likely than noninhibited children to experience an anxiety disorder (Biederman et al., 1995).

Overall, there is compelling evidence that children who show behavioral inhibition very early in life are more at risk for the development of an anxiety disorder in childhood. Because behavioral inhibition is considered to be related primarily to biological and genetic factors, the research on behavioral inhibition provides strong evidence of at least some biological and genetic influences in the development of anxiety disorders in childhood and adolescence.

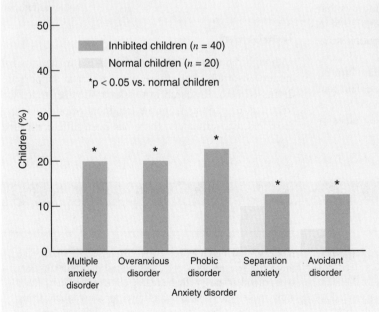

Anxiety Disorders in Inhibited and Normal Children

(Note that overanxious disorder is now considered to be comparable to generalized anxiety disorder.)

Source: Biederman et al. (1995).

& Wadiak, 1999). In order to address this limitation, the **two-factor theory** (reformulated more recently into the avoidance-conditioning model) combined elements from both operant and classical conditioning (Mowrer, 1960). The phobia is initially developed through classical conditioning (i.e., a previously neutral stimulus is paired with an aversive stimulus) and then maintained through operant conditioning (i.e., avoidance of the feared stimulus is associated with reduced distress, which reinforces the avoidance of the feared object).

Social learning, another variant of the behavioral model, suggests that children learn to be fearful from observing others' fear. Much of the research on social learning and anxiety has focused on family influences. For example, family connections in anxiety disorders are thought to be due to children's observations of their anxious parents (Dadds & Barrett, 1996). Although some fears and anxieties in childhood seem to be developed through behavioral principles, many fears and anxieties are not explained well by the behavioral model (Kearney & Wadiak, 1999). (Box 10.4 describes a study on observational learning and monkeys.)

Cognitive models suggest that faulty cognitions and inappropriate focus on anxiety-producing events are at the core of anxiety disorders (Bogels & Zigterman, 2000). The cognitive theory is supported by findings that children with anxiety disorders tend to ruminate about fearful stimuli and tend to misinterpret ambiguous stimuli in an anxiety-provoking manner (Shortt, Barrett, Dadds, & Fox, 2001). There is no question that children with anxiety disorders have faulty cognitions. The real question is whether or not these faulty cognitions lead to the development of anxiety disorders in the first place or whether they are a consequence of anxiety disorders that developed through other mechanisms (Kearney & Wadiak, 1999).

One interesting twist on the cognitive theory is that children who experience limited control early in their lives tend to develop cognitive styles (e.g., interpreting events as out of one's control) that are conducive to the development of anxiety disorders (Chorpita & Barlow, 1998). This theory allows the possibility that the cognitive style puts the child at risk for the development of an anxiety disorder but does not necessarily lead to an anxiety disorder.

Overall, there is some support for all three models of the development of anxiety disorders (biological, behavioral, and cognitive). It is likely that different anxiety disorders may be influenced to different degrees by all three of these causal mechanisms. Many children are probably genetically predetermined to be at risk for the development of an anxiety disorder, and then environmental influences, behavioral factors, and cognitive functioning influence whether or not they actually develop such a disorder (Silverman & Ginsburg, 1998).

To conquer fear is the beginning of wisdom, in the pursuit of truth as in the endeavor after a worthy manner of life.

—Bertrand Russell

Treatment

Although there are a number of possible treatments for anxiety disorders, only those with empirical support are discussed here. Research in this area often separates the treatment of phobias from the treatment of other anxiety disorders. Unfortunately, there has been little controlled

---

BOX 10.4

CAN A MONKEY LEARN TO FEAR A FLOWER?

Imagine seeing a rhesus monkey become terrified when shown a flower. As unusual as it sounds, a team of researchers headed by Dr. Sue Mineka (Cook & Mineka, 1989; Mineka, Davidson, Cook, & Keir, 1984) wanted to explore whether fears could be developed through observational learning. One study found that adolescent monkeys who observed their parents respond fearfully to a snake also responded fearfully to a snake (Mineka et al., 1984). Another study used edited videotapes to explore the biological preparedness of monkeys to fear snakes or other stimuli (Cook & Mineka, 1989). The researchers made a videotape of a monkey showing an extreme fear response to a snake. The monkey's fear response was then edited into four different types of videotapes, with the feared object edited in as either a toy snake, a toy crocodile, a flower, or a toy rabbit. Other monkeys then viewed these videotapes and only those monkeys who observed the videotape with the toy snake and the toy crocodile acquired a fear. This study suggests that certain stimuli (such as snakes and crocodiles for monkeys) are more conducive to phobia development than other stimuli (Cook & Mineka, 1989).

research to assess the effectiveness of treatment for PTSD in children and adolescents (Ruggiero, Morris, & Scotti, 2001). Based on a thorough literature review (Ollendick & King, 1998), two treatments have been found to be well established and effective for specific phobias:

- *Participant modeling,* in which the child observes others dealing appropriately with the feared stimulus and then actively participates in dealing with the feared stimulus.
- *Reinforced practice,* in which the child interacts with the feared stimulus and is given positive reinforcement for dealing with it.

A number of other treatments have been found to be probably efficacious with specific phobias:

- *Imaginal desensitization,* using systematic desensitization with the fear hierarchy imagined, though not acted out, by the client.
- *In vivo desensitization,* using systematic desensitization with the fear hierarchy actually experienced by the client, as discussed in Chapter 6.
- *Filmed modeling,* in which the client watches videotaped actors who are shown dealing appropriately with the feared stimulus.
- *Live modeling,* in which the client observes a person who deals appropriately with the feared stimulus.
- *Cognitive-behavioral interventions,* in which clients learn to challenge faulty cognitions and to replace them with more realistic cognitions.

I'm afraid of lions and tigers, bears, bombs, fires, and very scary monsters.

—seven-year-old Yamikani, from Zimbabwe

With regard to the treatment of other anxiety disorders, cognitive-behavioral procedures (with or without family anxiety management training) were the only treatments that were probably efficacious in the treatment of other anxiety disorders (Ollendick & King, 1998). There are four primary components to cognitive-behavioral interventions for anxiety disorders (Kendall et al., 1992):

1. Children learn to recognize feelings of anxiety and somatic complaints in response to anxiety.

2. Children learn to question and clarify unrealistic and negative cognitions when exposed to an anxiety-producing scenario.

3. Children are taught to make a plan for how to cope with the anxiety-provoking situation in the future.

4. Children are taught to evaluate their success at dealing with an anxiety-provoking situation and to reward themselves for coping well with the situation.

This cognitive-behavioral treatment program can be either used with children alone (Kendall et al., 1992) or enhanced with **family anxiety management training** (Barrett, Duffy, Dadds, & Rapee, 2001). Family anxiety management training involves trying to empower parents and children to become experts in coping with anxiety. Specifically, parents are taught basic behavioral techniques so that they can respond appropriately to their child's anxiety (Barrett et al., 2001). Therapists have helped parents identify their own concerns and anxieties as well as learn problem-solving techniques for dealing with these concerns. Parents and children are also taught communication skills. Overall, cognitive-behavioral procedures with or without family anxiety management training were found to be probably efficacious treatments for anxiety disorders (Ollendick & King, 1998). These treatments are effective with children regardless of whether or not their anxiety disorder is comorbid with another disorder (Kendall et al., 2001; Shortt, Barrett, & Fox, 2001).

Medication for anxiety disorders should be mentioned briefly. Although there is support for use of **anxiolytic agents** (anti-anxiety medications) with adults, there is limited evidence for their effectiveness with children (R. T. Brown & Sawyer, 1998). Even when medications are paired with therapeutic interventions, only modest effectiveness rates are found (Kearney & Silverman, 1998). Specifically, the following effectiveness rates (i.e., what percentage of children were helped by the interventions) were found in a study of children with anxiety disorders (Kearney & Silverman, 1998):

- 42.8%: medication only.
- 27.7%: medication plus general or supportive psychotherapy.
- 65.3%: medication plus behavior therapy.

This study suggests that not all children with an anxiety disorder can be helped by medication, even when it is combined with a therapeutic intervention (Kearney & Silverman, 1998).

With regard to the evaluation of medications by themselves, a number of studies showed that anxiolytic agents were no more effective than placebo pills with the treatment of a number of anxiety disorders in childhood and adolescence (R. T. Brown & Sawyer, 1998). Ironically, antidepressants have been used extensively to treat anxiety disorders (Kearney & Wadiak, 1999). In general,

BOX 10.5

WHAT DO CHILDREN AND THEIR PARENTS WORRY ABOUT?

Although the specific contents of worries and fears are not usually relevant to the treatment or prevention of anxiety disorders, it is interesting to note what types of worries and fears children and their parents experience. Certain fears (e.g., fear of animals) are consistent across age groups, but other fears, worries, and nightmares change developmentally. For example, the frequency of fears and nightmares related to imaginary creatures lessened with age, whereas the frequency of fears and nightmares related to test performance increased with age (Muris, Merckelbach, Gadet, & Moulaert, 2000). Other findings from this study include the following:

- The number one fear listed for children ages 4–6, 7–9, and 10–12 was a fear of animals.

- Children ages 4–6 and 7–9 listed imaginary creatures as their second fear and their most frequent nightmare.

- Children ages 10–12 listed social threats as their second most common fear and being kidnapped as their most common nightmare.

When parents are asked what they worry about with regard to their children, they tend to report concerns over car accidents, bicycle accidents, abduction, head injuries, exposure to environmental toxins, discipline, values, affection, too much television, proper nutrition, and finances (Stickler, 1996). This study also found that parents' fears tended to be influenced by media coverage. Specifically, parents often had exaggerated or unfounded fears based on extensive media coverage on a low-frequency event, such as abduction by a stranger (Stickler, 1996).

---

there is limited empirical support for the use of antidepressants with children who are experiencing an anxiety disorder. With regard to OCD, however, there is support for using antidepressants (Geller et al., 2001; Kearney & Wadiak,1999).

Overall, behavioral and cognitive-behavioral therapies have received the most empirical support for the treatment of anxiety disorders with children and adolescents. Further research is needed in order to establish which treatments work best for which anxiety disorders (Ollendick & King, 1998). In addition, a great deal more research is needed on the effectiveness of anti-anxiety medications (R. T. Brown & Sawyer, 1998).

Courage is resistance to fear, mastery of fear, not absence of fear.

—Mark Twain

Prevention

Although there are not many prevention programs in the area of anxiety disorders, one cognitive-behavioral program in Australia illustrates a nice combination of secondary and tertiary prevention efforts (Dadds, Spence, Holland, Barrett, & Laurens, 1997). The researchers who developed this program wanted to help children who were at risk for developing anxiety disorders as well as those children who had already developed mild anxiety disorders. The prevention and early intervention efforts were completed in an urban area, with a diverse sample of chil-

dren ages 7 to 14. As is consistent with prevention programs, the researchers had a series of screenings to identify children who were appropriate for the program:

- Nearly 2,000 children completed a self-report measure of anxiety (the Revised Children's Manifest Anxiety Scale; C. R. Reynolds & Richmond, 1978).

- Teachers were asked to nominate up to three children in their classroom who showed the highest levels of anxiety (as illustrated by shyness, nervousness, fearfulness, and inhibition) in order to possibly include these students in the program.

- Teachers were asked to nominate up to three children in their classroom who showed the highest levels of disruptive behavior (as illustrated by aggression, impulsivity, and noncompliance) in order to possibly exclude these students from the program.

- Children identified as appropriate in the previous steps were included in a list that was sent back to teachers to ensure that all of the students were actually appropriate for the program (e.g., the students and their parents spoke English, the students were not developmentally delayed, the students did not have a severe learning disability).

- The parents of children who remained viable program participants were contacted to have the program explained to them. Parents were then asked to complete diagnostic interviews and behavior ratings for their children.

These screening procedures identified a total of 128 children as either at risk for the development of an anxiety disorder or already meeting criteria for an anxiety disorder and having parents who were interested in the program. One-half of the children received the preventive intervention program, and the other half was put into the monitoring control condition (i.e., the children's progress was monitored, but they did not receive any active preventive interventions). The preventive intervention program focused on a plan known by the acronym *FEAR*:

- *F*eel good by learning to relax.
- *E*xpect good things to happen by using positive self-talk.
- *A*ctions are important, so make a plan about how to deal with anxiety-provoking stimuli.
- *R*eward yourself for trying to overcome your fears.

The program lasted for 10 weeks, with sessions of one to two hours each. Parents took part in three sessions that focused on helping them deal with their own anxiety and on helping their children cope with anxiety. Children's functioning was evaluated at the end of the intervention/monitoring period and then again at a six-month follow-up. As Figure 10.1 shows, significant improvements emerged for the children in the prevention program, both in terms of reductions in anxiety disorders and in the prevention of onset of new anxiety disorders. Overall, this study shows that prevention and early intervention programs can be effective and are an important resource in the prevention of anxiety disorders.

ANXIETY CONCEPTUALIZED IN A DIMENSIONAL MANNER

The topic of anxiety has been studied extensively from a dimensional perspective. (See, for example, the discussion of children's and parents' worries in Box 10.5 and fears internationally in Box 10.6.) Much of the focus of this dimensional research has examined the interconnections between anxiety and depression (e.g., Chorpita, Plummer, & Moffitt, 2000; Grant & Compas, 1995; Hinden, Compas, Howell, & Achenbach, 1997). The combination of anxiety and depression has been referred to as **negative affect** (e.g., Joiner, Catanzaro, & Laurent, 1996; Lerner et al., 1999). It appears that the experience of negative affect is common to both anxiety and depression, but children who experience anxiety also show physiological hyperarousal (e.g., breathing difficulties, nausea, sweaty palms), whereas children who experi-

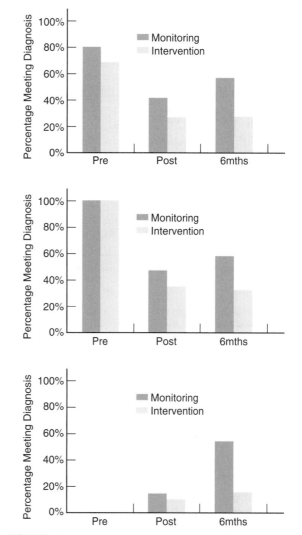

FIGURE 10.1 Results of a Study on a Prevention Program for Anxiety Disorders. (The figure shows diagnostic changes in children in the intervention and monitoring groups at postintervention [post] and six-month follow-up [6 mths] for all children [top panel], children who met *Diagnostic and Statistical Manual of Mental Disorders [4th ed.]* criteria for an anxiety disorder at preintervention [pre; middle panel], and children who were diagnosis-free at preintervention [bottom panel].)

Source: Dadds et al. (1997).

ence depression also experience anhedonia (i.e., not feeling joy or happiness; Joiner et al., 1996). In addition, studies of the discriminant validity of anxiety measures and of depression measures have shown that distinct factors of anxiety and depression can be found separately (Ruggiero, Morris, Beidel, Scotti, & McLeer, 1999). Thus, there is evidence to suggest that children's feelings of anxiety are distinguishable from their feelings of depression.

One of the ways of understanding anxiety from a dimensional perspective is to consider two different types of anxiety: **state anxiety** (i.e., temporary anxiety based on the situation) and **trait anxiety** (i.e., chronic anxiety that is stable across situations). This distinction was popularized by the use of the State–Trait Anxiety Inventory for Children (STAIC; Spielberger, Edwards, & Lushene, 1973), which assesses both situational and chronic levels of anxiety. Other self-report measures that are used to assess anxiety from a dimensional perspective include the Revised Children's Manifest Anxiety Scale (RCMAS; Reynolds & Richmond, 1978) and the Fear Survey Schedule for Children–Revised (FSSC-R; Ollendick, 1983). These measures assess global levels of anxiety and fear rather than making the distinction between state and trait anxiety.

Risk Factors

A number of risk factors have been associated with the development of high levels of anxiety (Donovan & Spence, 2000). In addition to the causative risk factors discussed in the etiology section above (e.g., behavioral inhibition, genetic predisposition), there are a number of other factors that seem to put children at risk for problems with anxiety. One study explored recent achievements and adversities in school-age children (Goodyer, Wright, & Altham, 1990). The researchers found that children who had not had any recent social achievements (e.g., making new friends, being voted into a desirable position at school) and who also had poor friendships appeared to be at greater risk for the development of anxiety problems as well as problems with depression (Goodyer et al., 1990).

Interestingly, certain factors are related to risk for some anxiety problems but not for others. Histories of a single-parent household, family problems, low parental education, poverty, and parental antisocial problems were associated with risk for separation anxiety disorder but not for generalized anxiety disorder (Costello & Angold, 1995). School failure, stressful life events, and parental psychological symptoms were associated with risk for generalized anxiety disorder but not for separation anxiety disorder in children (Costello & Angold, 1995). Anxiety problems in adolescence were associated with earlier stressful life events, continuing adversity, and parental psychopathology (Costello & Angold, 1995). Living in a violent inner-city community was associated with heightened levels of anxiety, especially in relation to exposure to gun violence (D. F. Duncan, 1996). Overall, there are a number of risk factors associated with the development of anxiety problems.

Protective Factors

There are also a number of factors associated with protecting children from the development of anxiety problems. Family support was found to protect against the development of anxiety problems and worries in a sample of urban children exposed to community violence (White, Bruce, Farrell, & Kliewer, 1998). Similarly, in a study of African American sixth-graders who were exposed to family stressors, it was found that parental warmth and kin support (e.g., support from grandparents, aunts, and uncles) were associated with decreased anxiety and shyness (McCabe, Clark, & Barnett, 1999). Thus, parental warmth and kinship social support served as protective factors from the development of anxiety even in children from highly stressed family environments.

BOX *10.6*

FEARS ACROSS THE GLOBE

What children fear depends somewhat on the country in which they live and their socioeconomic (SES) circumstances.

- Chinese children are more likely than children from Western cultures to fear social-evaluative situations (e.g., getting poor grades, performing poorly in a play).

- Children from Caribbean nations are more likely than children from Western cultures to fear things related to nature (e.g., animals, darkness).

- Children from impoverished settings tend to fear rats and cockroaches, whereas children from middle and upper SES settings tend to fear poisonous insects.

- Children from lower SES families tend to experience fear related to the necessities of life (e.g., having something to eat, safety), whereas children from middle and higher SES families tend not to have intense fears about the basic necessities.

SOURCE: Barrios & O'Dell (1998).

On the individual level, personal feelings of perceived competence and positive self-views were associated with decreased risk for anxiety problems in an urban sample of African American and Caucasian American children (Magnus, Cowen, Wyman, Fagen, & Work, 1999). Over-all, a number of protective factors have been found to decrease the likelihood of anxiety problems in childhood. More research is needed in this area to ascertain whether there are other protective factors that could be used to inform prevention programs (Donovan & Spence, 2000).

SUMMARY AND KEY CONCEPTS

Separation Anxiety Disorder

Separation anxiety disorder occurs when a child experiences extreme levels of distress upon separating from his or her primary caretakers. Often, separation anxiety disorder shows **spontaneous remission**, whereby the disorder remits without therapeutic intervention.

Specific Phobias

Specific phobias are extreme and unrealistic fears of objects or situations. **School refusal** (refusing to go to school) and **school phobia** (fearing to go to school) are sometimes associated with a specific phobia but are often associated with other anxiety disorders.

Social Phobia

Social phobia occurs when children fear social situations due to concerns about being embarrassed or humiliated. The social situations must include dealing with peers and not just adults.

Obsessive-Compulsive Disorder

Obsessive-compulsive disorder (OCD) occurs when children experience **obsessions** (recurrent, disordered thoughts) or **compulsions** (repetitive, disordered behaviors). Often, the compulsions are acted out in order to reduce anxiety related to the obsessions.

Generalized Anxiety Disorder

Generalized anxiety disorder (GAD) occurs when children experience pervasive and chronic levels of anxiety. By definition, the anxiety is not focused on one object or situation (as with specific phobia), nor is it associated with social interactions (as with social phobia).

Post-traumatic Stress Disorder

Post-traumatic stress disorder (PTSD) occurs when children deal with a trauma in an even more negative manner than would be expected. Traumas include sexual abuse, physical abuse, a severe car accident, or war. Children often experience psychological symptoms, nightmares, and flashbacks related to the trauma.

Selective Mutism

Selective mutism occurs when children speak in one setting (e.g., home) but not in another (e.g., school). This disorder is now thought to be related to anxiety rather than oppositional behavior.

All Anxiety Disorders of Childhood and Adolescence

There are high rates of comorbidity for anxiety disorders in childhood and adolescence. The courses of anxiety disorders vary. Specific phobias and selective mutism are usually the least chronic, whereas OCD and GAD tend to last for long periods of time and often into adulthood.

The primary etiological explanations of anxiety disorders are biological, behavioral, and cognitive. Family studies, twin studies, and work on **behavioral inhibition** (a temperamental style in which infants are irritable, shy, and fearful) all support a biological explanation of many anxiety disorders of childhood. Behavioral models include classical conditioning and operant conditioning. The **two-factor theory** combines classical conditioning and operant conditioning in explaining the development and maintenance of anxiety disorders. Cognitive theories focus on maladaptive cognitions in the development of anxiety disorders. The most likely explanation encompasses some combination of all three theoretical models.

The primary treatments for anxiety disorders in childhood and adolescence focus on behavioral and cognitive-behavioral interventions. Some cognitive-behavioral interventions also include parents in the treatment, with a **family anxiety management training** component to the treatment. Medications, such as **anxiolytic agents** (which are anti-anxiety medications) and antidepressants have been used to treat anxiety disorders in children and adolescents. In addition to these treatments, a number of prevention programs have been found to be effective in preventing the onset and recurrence of anxiety disorders.

Anxiety Conceptualized in a Dimensional Manner

A great deal of work has explored anxiety from a dimensional perspective. Much of this work has explored the overlap between anxiety and depression, a concept known as **negative affect**. Anxiety has also been conceptualized in a dimensional manner by exploring **state anxiety** (i.e., temporary, situational anxiety) and **trait anxiety** (i.e., chronic, stable anxiety). There are a number of risk factors for the development of anxiety problems. Absence of social achievements, poor friendships, family adversity, school difficulties, and parental psychological problems have all been linked to the development of at least one type of anxiety disorder. Protective factors have also been identified that decrease the likelihood of developing an anxiety disorder. Family support, parental warmth, perceived competence, and positive self-views have all been identified as factors that protect against the development of anxiety problems.

KEY TERMS

separation anxiety
   disorder
spontaneous
   remission
specific phobias
school refusal

school phobia
social phobia
obsessive-
   compulsive
   disorder (OCD)
obsessions

compulsions
generalized anxiety
   disorder (GAD)
post-traumatic stress
   disorder (PTSD)
selective mutism

behavioral inhibition
two-factor theory
family anxiety
   management
   training
anxiolytic agents

negative affect
state anxiety
trait anxiety

SUGGESTED READINGS

Hayden, Torey L. *Murphy's Boy*. New York: Avon, 1983. In this book, a 15-year-old boy is afraid of everything and has not spoken in the past 8 years. After his dedicated special education teacher encourages the boy to break his silence, the boy reveals traumas from his past.

Angelou, Maya. *I Know Why the Caged Bird Sings*. New York: Bantam Doubleday/Dell Publishing, 1983. In this powerful autobiography, writer, poet, political activist, and filmmaker Maya Angelou (1969) describes her traumatic youth filled with legitimate fear and self-imposed silence. In addition to personal trauma, Dr. Angelou writes about racism, injustice, and overcoming the odds.

SUGGESTED VIEWINGS

My Girl (1991). Howard Zieff (director), Laurice Elehwany (writer). VHS/DVD. This film follows the lives of two children, one dealing with the loss of her mother and the other dealing with excessive fears and concerns about his health and his life in general.

School Ties (1992). Robert Mandel (director), Dick Wolf and Darryl Ponicsan (writers). VHS/DVD. In addition to dealing with high levels of anxiety in a student, this film also deals with prejudice and discrimination in an elite boys' school.

ATTENTION-DEFICIT/HYPERACTIVITY DISORDER AND RELATED PROBLEMS

CHAPTER SUMMARY

Delay does not spoil things; it makes them better.

—Proverb of Africa

ATTENTION-DEFICIT/ HYPERACTIVITY DISORDER

You have seen them in the grocery store. You have heard them in the movie theater. You have seen them run up and down the aisle of the airplane as you are waiting for take-off. You probably even remember them from your own years in elementary school. They are children with an excessive amount of energy and a high level of activity. But are they children who meet criteria for the diagnosis of attention-deficit/hyperactivity disorder (ADHD)?

Probably no other childhood disorder has created more controversy and more public debate than ADHD (Anastopoulos, 1999; Milich, Balentine, & Lynam, 2001). Some professionals feel that ADHD is extremely prevalent among children and that medication is effective

in reducing the symptoms (e.g., Barkley, 1998; Rapport & Chung, 2000). Other professionals feel that ADHD is significantly overdiagnosed and that medicating active children is merely an attempt to make them docile (e.g., Breggin & Breggin, 1995). Both ends of this continuum will be discussed in this chapter. First, the chapter presents the current definitions of ADHD within the mainstream professional community. Later, it discusses criticisms of these definitions, along with alternative conceptualizations of high levels of activity.

What we now know as attention-deficit/hyperactivity disorder has a long and variable history (reviewed by Conners, 2000; Rapport & Chung, 2000). As early as 1902, professionals wrote about children who showed severe levels of inattention and lack of impulse control. From that time until the mid-1960s, various terms that focused on brain damage were used to describe these children, such as minimal brain damage syndrome and minimal brain dysfunction.

Case Study: Eddie, The Boy Who Was into Everything

At the age of nine, Eddie was referred to a psychiatrist because of his behavior at school. In the past year, Eddie had been suspended twice for hyperactive and impulsive behavior. Most recently, he had climbed onto the overhead lights of the classroom and caused an uproar when he could not get himself down. His teachers complain that other children cannot concentrate when Eddie is in the room because he walks around constantly. Even when he is seated, his rapid foot and hand movements are disruptive to the other children. Eddie has almost no friends and does not play games with his classmates due to his impulsivity and overly active behavior. After school, he likes to play with his dog or ride his bike alone.

Eddie's mother reports that he has been excessively active since he was a toddler. At the age of three, Eddie would awaken at 4:30 A.M. each day and go downstairs without any supervision. Sometimes he would "demolish" the kitchen or living room, and at other times he would leave the house by himself.

Once when he was four years old, he was found walking alone on a busy street in the early morning. Luckily, a passerby rescued him before he got into traffic.

After being rejected by a preschool because of his hyperactivity and impulsivity, Eddie attended a kindergarten and had a very difficult year. For first and second grade, he attended a special behavioral program. For third grade, he was allowed to attend a regular education class, with pull-out services for help with his behavior.

A psychological assessment of Eddie revealed that he has average intellectual functioning, with academic achievement that is slightly below average. According to the psychologist, Eddie's attention span is "virtually nonexistent." Eddie shows symptoms of hyperactivity, impulsivity, and inattention. After the evaluation, Eddie received stimulant medication (methylphenidate) and appeared to be more in control of his behavior when he took the medication.

SOURCE: Spitzer, Gibbon, Skodol, Williams, & First (1994).

In the first edition of *DSM*, there were no specific diagnoses for what we now know as ADHD (American Psychiatric Association, 1952). The manual did list a number of acute brain disorders that could have been used to encompass minimal brain dysfunctions, but there were no specific diagnoses that related to the constellation of hyperactivity, impulsivity, and inattention. In 1968, *DSM-II* presented the diagnostic category of **hyperkinetic reaction of childhood or adolescence** (American Psychiatric Association, 1968). The entire definition is as follows:

> *This disorder is characterized by overactivity, restlessness, distractibility, and short attention span, especially in young children; the behavior usually diminishes in adolescence. If this behavior is caused by brain damage, it should be diagnosed under the appropriate non-psychotic organic brain syndrome. (p. 50)**

Although this definition is somewhat similar to the current definition of ADHD, it was not until the publication of *DSM-III* that the term *attention-deficit disorder (ADD)* was publicized widely and that the constellation of hyperactivity, impulsivity, and inattention was conceptualized (American Psychiatric Association, 1980). The primary relevant diagnoses in *DSM-III* were (1) attention deficit disorder with hyperactivity (ADD with H) and (2) attention deficit disorder without hyperactivity (ADD without

H). Note that ADD without H was acknowledged as having limited empirical evidence, with unknown prevalence rates and etiological information (American Psychiatric Association, 1980). For this reason, the diagnosis of ADD without H was dropped from the new diagnostic criteria in *DSM-III-R* (Barkley, 1998). The diagnosis of undifferentiated attention-deficit disorder was added to the end of the section titled "Disorders Usually First Evident in Infancy, Childhood, or Adolescence" (American Psychiatric Association, 1987). This disorder was described as follows:

> *This is a residual category for disturbance in which the predominant feature is the persistence of developmentally inappropriate and marked inattention that is not a symptom of another disorder, such as Mental Retardation or Attention-Deficit Hyperactivity Disorder, or of a disorganized and chaotic environment. Some of the disturbances that in* DSM-III *would have been categorized as Attention Deficit Disorder without Hyperactivity would be included in this category. Research is necessary to determine if this is a valid diagnostic category and, if so, how it should be defined. (p. 95)†*

By the time of the publication of *DSM-IV* (American Psychiatric Association, 1994) and *DSM-IV-TR* (American Psychiatric Association, 2000), a form of ADD without H was back in the limelight. According to the

---

*Reprinted with permission from the *Diagnostic and Statistical Manual of Mental Disorders, Second Edition*. Copyright © 1968 American Psychiatric Association.

†Reprinted with permission from the *Diagnostic and Statistical Manual of Mental Disorders, Third Edition, Revised*. Copyright © 1987 American Psychiatric Association.

definition in Table 11.1, the three subtypes of attention-deficit/hyperactivity disorder include combined type (with both hyperactivity-impulsivity and inattention), predominantly inattentive type (which is comparable to ADD without H in *DSM-III*), and predominantly hyper-active-impulsive type (which is comparable to ADHD from *DSM-III-R*). This history shows the changes that can occur in diagnostic definitions. Although some of these decisions were based on empirical evidence, some of these decisions were influenced by the research agendas of the professionals involved in these decisions (Conners, 2000).

The most important thing to remember when reviewing the criteria in Table 11.1 is that the behavior should be above and beyond what is expected for a child of a given age and gender. As with all other diagnoses, children meet criteria only if their behavior is beyond what would be considered developmentally appropriate. Note that there are three primary components to diagnosing ADHD: inattention, hyperactivity, and impulsivity. It is important to highlight the distinctions between these symptoms. *DSM-III* provided one of the great improvements in conceptualizing and diagnosing ADHD by separating inattention from hyperactivity and impulsivity. Like the criteria in

TABLE 11.1 *DSM-IV* Diagnostic Criteria for Attention-Deficit/Hyperactivity Disorder (ADHD)

A. Either (1) or (2):

  (1) six (or more) of the following symptoms of *inattention* have persisted for at least 6 months to a degree that is maladaptive and inconsistent with developmental level:

Inattention

    (1) often fails to give close attention to details or makes careless mistakes in school work, work, or other activities

    (2) often has difficulty sustaining attention in tasks or play activities

    (3) often does not seem to listen when spoken to directly

    (4) often does not follow through on instructions and fails to finish schoolwork, chores, or duties in the workplace (not due to oppositional behavior or failure to understand instructions)

    (5) often has difficulty organizing tasks and activities

    (6) often avoids, dislikes, or is reluctant to engage in tasks that require sustained mental effort (such as schoolwork or home work)

    (7) often loses things necessary for tasks or activities (e.g., toys, school assignments, pencils, books, or tools)

    (8) is often easily distracted by extraneous stimuli

    (9) is often forgetful in daily activities

  (2) six (or more) of the following symptoms of *hyperactivity-impulsivity* have persisted for at least 6 months to a degree that is maladaptive and inconsistent with developmental level:

Hyperactivity

    (1) often fidgets with hands or feet or squirms in seat

    (2) often leaves seat in classroom or in other situations in which remaining seated is expected

    (3) often runs about or climbs excessively in situations in which it is inappropriate (in adolescents or adults, may be limited to subjective feelings of restlessness)

    (4) often has difficulty playing or engaging in leisure activities quietly

    (5) is often "on the go" or often acts as if "driven by a motor"

    (6) often talks excessively

Impulsivity

    (1) often blurts out answers before questions have been completed

    (2) often has difficulty awaiting turn

    (3) often interrupts or intrudes on others (e.g., butts into conversations or games)

B. Some hyperactive-impulsive or inattentive symptoms that caused impairment were present before age 7 years.

C. Some impairment from the symptoms is present in two or more settings (e.g., at school [or work] and at home).

D. There must be clear evidence of clinically significant impairment in social, academic, or occupational functioning.

E. The symptoms do not occur exclusively during the course of a Pervasive Developmental Disorder, Schizophrenia, or other Psychotic Disorder and are not better accounted for by another mental disorder (e.g., Mood Disorder, Anxiety Disorder, Dissociative Disorder, or a Personality Disorder).

Code based on type:

Attention-Deficit/Hyperactivity Disorder, Combined Type:

  if both Criteria A1 and A2 are met for the past 6 months

Attention-Deficit/Hyperactivity Disorder, Predominantly Inattentive Type:

  if Criterion A1 is met but Criterion A2 is not met for the past 6 months

Attention-Deficit/Hyperactivity Disorder, Predominantly Hyperactive-Impulsive Type:

  if Criterion A2 is met but Criterion A1 is not met for the past 6 months

SOURCE: American Psychiatric Association (2000). Reprinted with permission from the *Diagnostic and Statistical Manual of Mental Disorders, Fourth Edition, Text Revision.* © 2000 American Psychiatric Association.

Children can only be diagnosed with ADHD if they show impairment related to the symptoms in two or more environments (such as at school and at home).

DSM-III, the current criteria focus on the distinctiveness of inattention, hyperactivity, and impulsivity.

After considering these symptoms in the diagnosis of ADHD, it is also crucial to acknowledge criteria B (age), C (settings), and D (impairment). Criterion B notes that at least some of the symptoms that cause impairment must have been present before the age of seven. This criterion is important because it shows the chronicity of ADHD. It is especially important in considering the diagnosis of ADHD in adolescents and adults. If there is no evidence that the maladaptive symptoms of hyperactivity, impulsivity, or inattention were present before the age of seven, then the diagnosis of ADHD would not be appropriate. This issue distinguishes between the chronic problem of ADHD (symptoms of which would have been present before the age of seven) and a more situational problem that appeared only at a later age.

Criterion C is of equal, if not more, importance in distinguishing between ADHD and other situational problems. Specifically, criterion C notes that impairment from the symptoms must be present in at least two settings. There are actually two important components to this criterion: Symptoms must be present in two or more settings, and symptoms must cause impairment in two or more settings. For children and adolescents, criterion C is especially important to consider when evaluating behavior in school and at home. Some children appear to be very hyperactive, impulsive, and inattentive at school, but they show few or no signs of disturbance at home. Alternately, other children show significant impairment at home but do not show any symptoms at school. When

children show significant symptoms that cause impairment in one setting but not the other, then a diagnosis of ADHD is not warranted. This issue is of great concern when assessing the symptoms of ADHD.

Finally, criterion D states that individuals must show clinically significant impairment in either the social, academic, or occupational domains. It is important to acknowledge this criterion because a child or adolescent may have high levels of activity, impulsivity, or inattention but still can function well in a diverse array of settings. Often, children can use compensatory strategies for dealing with these difficulties so that they do not experience impairment in social, academic, or occupational settings. For example, a child may compensate for inattention by studying harder and using memory aids. The child may also compensate for her inattentiveness in other settings. In this case, she would not meet criteria for ADHD. Similarly, a child might be extremely overactive compared to his peers, but if he can channel this high energy level into appropriate activities, he would not meet criteria for ADHD.

Criteria B (age), C (settings), and D (impairment) are important to consider because they often disallow a diagnosis of ADHD that would have otherwise been made. Note that one criterion is absent from the formal *DSM-IV* diagnosis of ADHD—there is no formal requirement that children diagnosed with ADHD must experience limitations in their schoolwork. Although academic deficits are quite common in children diagnosed with ADHD (Faraone et al., 1993), these deficits are not necessary for the diagnosis. Thus, it is possible that a child would show

BOX 11.1

ASSESSMENT OF ADHD

Given the importance of a valid diagnosis of ADHD for proper treatment, it seems worthwhile to consider what should be done in a thorough assessment for the presence or absence of ADHD. There are too many examples of children being prescribed a stimulant, such as Ritalin, just because their parents reported that they are too active. A comprehensive assessment should help establish whether or not a child's behavior is out of the range of normal for his or her age and gender. There are a great number of assessment tools used to assess the symptoms of ADHD. As discussed in the text, it is crucial that behaviors in at least two settings are assessed. Because ADHD is highly comorbid with other disorders, the clinician should conduct a thorough and comprehensive assessment. A number of the more established measures are listed below with a brief explanation.

- *Direct observation:* As noted in Chapter 5, direct observations can be done through either standardized mechanisms (e.g., the Direct Observation Form; Achenbach, 1991a) or an unstandardized observational process (e.g., watching a child's behavior and paying attention to its antecedents and consequences). At a minimum, school-age children (especially children in elementary school) should be observed in their classrooms in a number of different tasks (some structured, such as doing math, and some unstructured, such as recess) as well as at least one other setting (e.g., the home, the day care, the assessor's office, a laboratory).

- *Interviews:* Semistructured or structured interviews are appropriate to ascertain whether the symptoms of ADHD are present. One notable structured interview, which can be used for children's self-report as well as parents' report, is the Diagnostic Interview Schedule for Children (DISC; Shaffer, 1996). The DISC results in a comprehensive assessment of a number of diagnoses, including ADHD.

- *Behavior checklists:* There are a number of excellent behavior checklists that can be used with different informants, including parents, teachers, and sometimes children themselves (depending on the age of the child). The Child Behavior Checklist (CBCL) and related measures (Achenbach & Rescorla, 2001) provide a comprehensive overview of children's and adolescents' behavior. These measures include subscales for attention problems, delinquent behavior, and aggressive behavior, but do not include a specific subscale for hyperactivity and impulsivity. The measures in the Behavior Assessment System for Children (BASC; C. R. Reynolds & Kamphaus, 1992) include subscales for hyperactivity and attention problems in addition to a number of other internalizing and externalizing problems. Both the CBCL and the BASC systems of assessment provide broad measures of children's and adolescents' behavior. Other, more specific measures for ADHD include the Conners' Parent Rating Scale and the Conners' Teacher Rating Scale (Conners, 1990). These measures focus on hyperactivity, inattention, and conduct problems. Many assessors use all or some combination of these behavior checklists (Crystal, Ostrander, Chen, & August, 2001).

In addition to these measures, other assessment tools can be used in a comprehensive assessment of ADHD. An intelligence test, for example, can be of great help in evaluating the strengths and weaknesses of a child's intellectual functioning. Similarly, achievement tests can be invaluable in assessing children for ADHD, given that academic problems are often associated the disorder. It is also prudent to assess for children's strengths and competencies, since these factors may be helpful in treating any deficits that are found. As mentioned in Chapter 5, it is also important to consider factors outside of the child that might relate to his or her functioning. Thus, an assessment of the school environment and the home environment would be warranted in trying to gain a thorough understanding of the child's functioning.

SOURCE: Barkley (1997b); DuPaul & Stoner (1994).

---

impairment in social functioning, for example, but would have adequate or even excellent schoolwork.

As mentioned previously, according to the American Psychiatric Association's (2000) *Diagnostic and Statistical Manual of Mental Disorders, Fourth Edition*, there are currently three types of attention-deficit/hyperactivity disorder (ADHD). **ADHD, combined type** is thought to have three primary characteristics: hyperactivity, impulsivity, and inattention. As noted in Table 11.1, children must meet criteria for both hyperactivity-impulsivity and inattention in order to meet criteria for ADHD, combined type. Children who meet criteria for this disorder not only show heightened levels of inappropriate behavior but also have difficulty with sustained attention and concentration.

The second type, known as **ADHD, predominantly inattentive type**, is the diagnosis given to children who have problems with inattention but do not show inappropriate levels of hyperactivity or impulsivity. This diagnosis is comparable to the diagnosis in *DSM-III* known as attention-deficit disorder without hyperactivity (American Psychiatric Association, 1980). Children who meet criteria for this diagnosis often find it difficult to pay attention and to concentrate, but they do not exhibit high levels of energetic behavior or impulsivity. Within many school systems, these children are often still referred to as ADD. The third type, **ADHD, predominantly hyperactive-impulsive type**, is the diagnoses given to children who have problems with hyperactivity and impulsivity but do not appear to have problems with attention or concentration. This diagnosis is comparable to the one in *DSM-III* that was called attention-deficit disorder with hyperactivity. These subtypes have been validated in a number of studies (C. L. Carlson, Shin, & Booth, 1999; Gaub & Carlson, 1997a; Maedgen & Carlson, 2000; Marks, Himelstein, Newcorn, & Halperin, 1999). Some researchers, however, suggest that the subtypes are actu-

ally distinctly different disorders rather than subtypes of one disorder (Milich et al., 2001).

Even with the specificity of criteria for subtypes of ADHD, it is important to acknowledge that ADHD is a diverse and heterogeneous disorder (Whalen & Henker, 1998). Two children diagnosed with any specific type of ADHD could be quite different from each other. It is for this reason that further studies into the specific characteristics of this disorder are needed.

The current diagnostic criteria appear to be well accepted within the mainstream professional community. Both psychologists and psychiatrists, however, continue to try to refine the diagnostic criteria in order to clarify this disorder. For example, after a review of comorbidity within ADHD children, one group of researchers suggested that two subtypes of ADHD exist: ADHD, aggressive subtype, and ADHD, anxious subtype (Jensen, Martin, & Cantwell, 1997a).

Case Study: Beth, The Little Girl Who Did Not Follow Rules

Beth was five and a half years old when her parents brought her to the local child guidance center for an evaluation. Her parents reported that Beth was difficult to discipline at home, and her kindergarten teacher reported that Beth was a discipline problem at school, where she showed inattentiveness, hyperactivity, and distractibility.

Beth lived with her parents, a younger sister, and a younger brother in a lower-middle-class neighborhood. The prenatal period for Beth seemed unproblematic, but there were problems during labor and delivery. After her mother had been in labor for 20 hours, Beth had to be delivered with forceps, at which time it was discovered that the umbilical cord was wrapped around her neck and Beth was blue due to anoxia (lack of oxygen). Although Beth had to stay in the neonatal intensive care unit, she appeared to recover well from the birth trauma.

Beth experienced not only somewhat slowed developmental milestones but also a series of unfortunate accidents. In the year after she turned two, Beth experienced four head injuries, all of which were due to her falling on her head. One incident occurred when Beth fell from a shopping cart, and the others occurred when Beth fell down the stairs or off a chair at home. Beth never lost consciousness during these incidents and did not appear to suffer any immediate consequences. After these accidents, Beth continued to have somewhat delayed development (e.g., she was not toilet trained until the age of 3).

Beth's parents appeared to focus a great deal of their attention on their youngest son, much to the exclusion of Beth and her sister. Beth seemed to react to being ignored by throwing temper tantrums, becoming demanding, and chronically running around the house. Although she would engage in appropri-

ate play, she would lose interest rapidly and then move on to another activity without picking up the toys with which she had just finished playing. Beth's mother reported that nearly all of her interactions with Beth were negative.

Beth showed the same heightened energy levels at school. Her kindergarten teacher reported that Beth was constantly on the go and that she could not stay focused on one task for very long. Beth seemed distracted by any extraneous noise, and it was difficult to redirect her to class work. In addition, Beth seemed to have a great deal of perceptual-motor problems, evidenced in tasks such as drawing and cutting out paper figures.

The psychological evaluation revealed that Beth had very low intellectual functioning, with significant visual-motor deficits. Beth reported low levels of self-esteem. A neurological evaluation revealed that Beth had difficulty with fine motor coordination but there were no overt brain dysfunctions. Behavioral observations revealed that Beth's parents interacted with her primarily when she was misbehaving (e.g., being loud, refusing to do something). Notably, her parents did not interact with her to show her how to complete tasks but rather would just point out when she was doing something wrong. Behavioral observation also confirmed Beth's heightened levels of activity, impulsivity, and inattention.

Overall, Beth met criteria for ADHD, combined type. She exhibited a common problem, in which parents' and teachers' high expectations are not realistic due to the child's limited functioning. It appeared that Beth became frustrated when she did not understand directions and acted out when she became frustrated. Therapy for the parents as well as Beth was recommended.

SOURCE: Leon (1990).

Overall, ADHD commands a great deal of attention within the professional community. In 1999 alone, 27.8% (i.e., more than one-fourth) of the regular research articles in the *Journal of Abnormal Child Psychology* were devoted to ADHD and problems of impulsivity, hyperactivity, and inattention. The remainder of the articles in the journal that year focused on a wide variety of other topics (e.g., depression, conduct disorder, anxiety disorders, externalizing problems, behavior problems, homesickness, and child abuse). In addition, the entire December 2000 issue of *Journal of Abnormal Child Psychology* (vol. 28, no. 6) was devoted to the treatment of ADHD (S. B. Campbell, 2000). There is clearly a great deal of interest and concern over symptoms related to ADHD. One possible reason for the interest in this disorder relates to its high prevalence rates.

How poor are they that have not patience!
What wound did ever heal but by degrees?

—William Shakespeare

Prevalence Rates

Table 11.2 gives an overview of prevalence information for ADHD. As with so many other disorders, prevalence rates of ADHD vary widely depending on what sample is used in the study. When clinical or special education samples are used, between 50% and 60% of children meet criteria for ADHD (Whalen & Henker, 1998). Larger epidemiological studies in the community suggest that between 2% and 10% of children meet criteria for ADHD (reviewed in Barkley, 1998). A commonly cited figure suggests that between 3% and 7% of school-age children meet criteria for ADHD (American Psychiatric Association, 2000). Overall, ADHD is one of the most prevalent disorders in childhood (Halfon & Newacheck, 1999).

With regard to age patterns, symptoms of ADHD tend to appear first in the preschool years (ages three and four), but children tend to be referred for help between the ages of seven and nine (Barkley, 1997a, 1998; Whalen & Henker, 1998). Within clinical samples, it appears that approximately 50% to 80% of children diagnosed with ADHD will continue to meet criteria for ADHD when they are adolescents (Barkley, 1998). Unfortunately, good prevalence data are lacking for adolescent and adult populations (American Psychiatric Association, 2000). In general, however, ADHD is thought to be much more prevalent in children than in adolescents or adults (Barkley, 1998).

Consistent differences in prevalence rates for the genders are found in nearly every country that has been studied (Barkley, 1998; Pineda et al., 1999). Boys outnumber girls with the diagnosis of ADHD at least 2:1, with reports going as high as 9:1 (Hartung & Widiger, 1998; Whalen & Henker, 1998). Higher ratios of boys tend to be found in clinical samples when compared with community samples, which suggests that boys with ADHD might be referred for help even more than girls with ADHD (Costello & Janiszewski, 1990). Boys diagnosed with ADHD are more likely to be comorbid with conduct disorder than are girls (Jensen et al., 1997a). An overwhelming number of studies of ADHD have intentionally included only boys in the sample, given the low numbers of girls who meet criteria for the diagnosis.

When boys and girls with ADHD are compared, interesting patterns emerge. A comprehensive meta-analysis identified both differences and similarities between boys and girls diagnosed with ADHD (Gaub & Carlson, 1997b). When compared with boys, girls diagnosed with ADHD showed lower intellectual functioning, lower levels of hyperactivity, and fewer comorbid externalizing problems. There were no gender differences, however, with regard to fine motor skills, social functioning, academic performance, or impulsivity. In addition, there were no gender differences on family-related variables such as parental depression and parental education (Gaub & Carlson, 1997b). This meta-analysis was not able to ascertain whether or not the gender differences were due to some type of referral bias (e.g., brighter girls with higher levels of activity tend not to be referred for services because teachers do not perceive them to be as much of a problem as girls with lower levels of intellectual functioning).

There is limited research into the prevalence patterns of ADHD with regard to socioeconomic status (SES). The studies that have been conducted suggest that all three subtypes of ADHD are somewhat more prevalent in lower SES communities (Barkley, 1998; Pineda et al., 1999). It appears, however, that this pattern is due to factors other than SES per se. Specifically, when comorbid disorders

TABLE 11.2   Overview of Prevalence Information for Attention-Deficit/Hyperactivity Disorder

Prevalence	3–7% of school-age children
Age	Childhood > Adolescence
Gender	Boys > Girls
Socioeconomic status	No differences when comorbidity is controlled statistically
Race/Ethnicity	Possibly African American > Caucasian American

are controlled statistically, then the differences in SES groups vanish (Barkley, 1998). Thus, it appears that when other comorbid disorders, especially conduct disorder, are controlled statistically, there are no differences in ADHD across the social classes (Barkley, 1998).

There is a marked void of research into the issue of race/ethnicity and ADHD. One review found that out of the thousands of research articles on ADHD, only 16 focused on ADHD in African American children and adolescents (Samuel et al., 1997). When ratings are compared for African American children and Caucasian American children, teachers tend to rate African American children higher on symptoms of ADHD (Epstein, March, Conners, & Jackson, 1998). It is unclear, however, whether these ratings are based on perceptual biases or actual differences in behaviors. In addition, when aggression and defiance are controlled statistically, cultural differences disappear (B. Evans & Lee, 1998). Within the Asian American community, prevalence rates of ADHD are lower than in other racial and ethnic groups (Serafica, 1997). Overall, there has been little research on possible differential prevalence rates based on race/ethnicity.

Researchers have, however, explored prevalence rates across cultures (Whalen & Henker, 1998). ADHD has been found and diagnosed in nearly every culture that has been studied, including Australia, Germany, England, Japan, Ukraine, Uganda, China, and Ethiopia (Barkley, 1998; Gadow et al., 2000; Whalen & Henker, 1998). Although there is evidence of higher rates of ADHD within the United States, this pattern may be due to the diagnostic criteria used in the study. For example, much lower prevalence rates are found in England, but this discrepancy is apparently due to the diagnostic criteria used in England. Diagnostic criteria for **hyperkinetic disorder** from the *International Classification of Diseases–10 (ICD-10)* are now used within Great Britain. Hyperkinetic disorder is comparable to ADHD except that the former is much more severe and neurological deficits must be present (Whalen & Henker, 1998). Fewer children are diagnosed with these more stringent criteria.

In addition to different definitions of ADHD across cultures, there is also a possibility that behaviors may be interpreted differently in different cultures (Yamamoto, Silva, Ferrari, & Nukariya, 1997). For example, children in Puerto Rico tend to show more exaggerated body movements and to interrupt each other more than Caucasian American children (B. Evans & Lee, 1998). Chinese children in Hong Kong were reported to show more hyperactivity than comparison groups in the United States and in the United Kingdom, but this pattern may have been due to less tolerance for activity with these children

Is this boy in Barcelona, Spain showing hyperactivity or acceptable amounts of activity?

(B. Evans & Lee, 1998). Overall, care should be taken to ensure that children are assessed in a manner that is respectful of differences across cultures and nations (Yamamoto et al., 1997).

Genius is nothing but a greater aptitude for patience.

—Georges Louis Leclerc de Buffon

Comorbidity

As with so many disorders in childhood and adolescence, comorbidity is the rule rather than the exception for ADHD (Johnston & Ohan, 1999; Whalen & Henker, 1998). Comorbidity estimates are higher between ADHD and conduct disorder than between ADHD and anxiety disorders (Angold, Costello, & Erkanli, 1999; Biederman, Mick, Faraone, & Burback, 2001; Peterson, Pine, Cohen, & Brook, 2001). Overall, estimates of comorbidity between ADHD and externalizing disorders range from 42% to 93%, whereas comorbidity between ADHD and internalizing disorders are estimated from 13% to 51% (Jensen et al., 1997a). Boys diagnosed with ADHD who show high levels of aggression also reported higher rates of depressive symptoms than did ADHD boys without aggression and boys in a control group (Treuting & Hinshaw, 2001). When compared with boys in a control

BOX *11.2*

ADHD IN THE SCHOOLS

ADHD is one of the most prevalent and challenging behavioral disorders that teachers have to deal with in the classroom (Dowdy, Patton, Smith, & Polloway, 1998; DuPaul & Stoner, 1994). Luckily, there are good strategies teachers can use and good behavioral techniques school psychologists can use to help children with ADHD learn and behave appropriately in the classroom (Dowdy et al., 1998; DuPaul & Stoner, 1994).

Regarding assessment, referral for testing due to possible ADHD is one of the most common requests for school psychologists (DuPaul & Stoner, 1994). Luckily, there are standard assessment batteries and clear diagnostic criteria. In comparison to previous diagnostic systems, it appears that *DSM-IV* is beneficial to school psychologists because the diagnostic criteria are more objective than in previous editions and are based on firm empirical findings (McBurnett, 1996).

For children who are highly active and inattentive, teachers can design special curricula to enhance the students' mastery of the material. For example, breaking assignments into small parts and providing frequent positive reinforcement for

attention and concentration can help keep students with ADHD focused and motivated (Dowdy et al., 1998).

One salient issue regarding ADHD in the schools centers on teachers' expectations and feelings about children with high levels of activity. Rather than diagnosing ADHD in a particular child, a clinician may look at the goodness of fit between student and teacher (Greene, 1995, 1996). One teacher may deal best with children who sit still and do not talk very much, whereas another teacher may deal best with inquisitive children who are very active and interactive. A child with high levels of activity would probably not fare well with the first teacher but may flourish with the second. The goodness-of-fit model argues that we should look at the fit between student and teacher rather than just identifying problems within the child (Greene, 1995, 1996).

Overall, most teachers and school psychologists have to deal with ADHD on a relatively frequent basis. When teachers, parents, and school professionals can work as a team to address ADHD children's academic and psychological needs, the children tend to have more success than when these collaborative efforts are not in place (Dowdy et al., 1998).

group, boys diagnosed with ADHD showed higher levels of sadness, anger, and guilt (Braaten & Rosen, 2000). For both externalizing and internalizing disorders, comorbidity with ADHD is associated with higher levels of impairment, greater use of mental health services, and a poorer prognosis (Whalen & Henker, 1998). These same patterns of comorbidity have been found in other countries, such as Sweden (Kadesjoe & Gillberg, 2001).

In addition to the high rates of comorbidity between ADHD and conduct disorder, there are also high rates of comorbidity between ADHD and learning disorders, with estimates ranging from 10% to 92% (Jensen et al., 1997a). See Box 11.2 for a discussion of ADHD in the school system. ADHD, combined type, tends to be more comorbid with learning disorders than are other subtypes of ADHD (Carlson, Tamm, & Gaub, 1997). As shown in Table 11.3, children and adolescents ages 6 to 17 diagnosed with ADHD were found to have significant academic difficulties in one community-based study (Faraone et al., 1993).

The high comorbidity between ADHD and at least one learning disorder (LD) has lead to speculation that these two problems may be permanently intertwined (Rabiner, Coie, & Conduct Problems Prevention Research Group, 2000; Riccio, Gonzalez, & Hynd, 1994). Specifically,

problems with attention, cognitive functioning, and emotional/behavioral functioning may be common to both ADHD and LD, so it is difficult to disentangle the two disorders in any one child. For example, children who were inattentive in kindergarten showed significant reading problems up to five years later, even when controlling for earlier reading problems (Rabiner et al., 2000). In addition, boys diagnosed with ADHD showed less task persistence (i.e., they gave up sooner) on academic tasks

TABLE 11.3 Percentage of ADHD Children and Adolescents with School Difficulties

Problem	ADHD (*N* = 140)	Control (*N* = 120)
Needed academic tutoring*	56%	25%
Repeated a grade*	30%	13%
Were placed in special class*	35%	2%
Had a reading disorder*	18%	4%
Had an arithmetic disorder*	21%	8%

*Differed significantly between ADHD group and nonclinical control group.

Source: Adapted from Faraone et al. (1993).

than did boys in a control group (Hoza, Pelham, Waschbusch, Kipp, & Owens, 2001). It is also possible that children are inattentive because they are frustrated by the difficult academic material. More research on specific subtypes of ADHD and LD may help clarify these issues, especially if the research samples are more homogeneous in symptom presentation (Riccio et al., 1994).

This issue relates to **differential diagnosis** (i.e., trying to establish which disorder, if any, is appropriate for a particular child). Differential diagnosis is a challenge with ADHD and a number of other disorders. Distinguishing between bipolar disorder/mania and symptoms of ADHD is especially difficult (Carlson, 1998; Geller & Luby, 1997). One study found that inpatient children who experienced symptoms of mania also experienced more severe levels of ADHD than did inpatient children who did not experience mania (Carlson & Kelly, 1998). This issue is of great concern because stimulant medication is countertherapeutic to children with symptoms of mania (R. T. Brown & Sawyer, 1998).

Another difficult differential diagnosis can occur when sexually abused children show symptoms of hyperactivity but also show symptoms of post-traumatic stress disorder (PTSD). There is a great deal of overlap between the symptoms of hyperactivity and PTSD, and in children who have been sexually abused there is a great deal of difficulty in distinguishing between these two disorders (Weinstein, Staffelbach, & Biaggio, 2000). For this reason, it is imperative that clinicians get a full history and conduct a comprehensive assessment in children who show signs of hyperactivity.

Other factors that are associated with inattention, hyperactivity, and impulsivity include troubled social interactions and poor peer relationships (Whalen & Henker, 1998). It is not surprising to find that many children who are inattentive, hyperactive, and impulsive would have trouble making and maintaining friendships. Many of these children are actively disliked by their peers, given their difficulty with sustaining conversations and waiting their turn. There is speculation that some of the same processes that create the difficulties with attention, activity level, and impulsivity also serve to make social relationships difficult (Whalen & Henker, 1998). Children and adolescents diagnosed with ADHD often also have

Case Study: Jonas, A Case of Comorbidity in Action

Jonas was 16 years old when he was brought in for treatment. When he was in elementary school, from grades 1 through 4, he received methylphenidate to treat symptoms of ADHD, predominantly inattentive type. After that time, his symptoms were manageable without medication. Jonas's parents, however, were still concerned that he was attaining only a C average and that he did not show a great deal of interest in academic activities. Jonas was often inattentive in school, and when he did do homework he could not focus on his studies. Both parents were highly educated professionals who wanted Jonas to excel in school.

Over the past six months, Jonas's behavior had deteriorated tremendously. He used to play soccer, but after missing a number of practices, he was finally kicked off the team. He had also been truant from school on a number of occasions. Jonas's parents reported that he was usually already asleep by the time they got home from work on weekdays and he usually stayed over with his friends for entire weekends. He refused to take part in family activities, and when he was at home, he would only watch television or play video games without interacting with the rest of the family. Jonas's parents were terribly concerned that he was depressed and withdrawn.

When Jonas's parents brought him in for a psychological evaluation, he appeared irritated and cynical. He denied that he was depressed, but he did acknowledge that he was often bored and tired. After a lengthy interview, during which strong rapport was established, Jonas finally admitted that he had been drink-

ing heavily for the past year. He would usually skip school and hang out with teenagers from the neighborhood, drinking beer, playing video games, watching television, listening to music, and driving around. Because his parents had given him a car, Jonas was often the one who could drive his friends to get beer and take them around the neighborhood. During the assessment interview, Jonas was most concerned that his parents would forbid him to use the car if they found out that he had been drinking. Apparently, his parents had no idea about his drinking behavior or about the friends with whom he hung out.

This case provides an example of the comorbidity between alcohol abuse and ADHD. Approximately 20% of adolescents who abuse substances also meet criteria for ADHD. Below is the five-axis diagnosis for Jonas.

Axis I:	Attention-deficit/hyperactivity disorder, predominantly inattentive type
	Alcohol abuse
Axis II:	No diagnosis on Axis II
Axis III:	None
Axis IV:	Problems with primary support group: parent–child communication problem
Axis V:	Global assessment of functioning (GAF)=65 (current)

SOURCE: Rapoport & Ismond (1996).

difficult and conflicted relationships with their parents (Edwards, Barkley, Laneri, Fletcher, & Metevia, 2001).

Overall, comorbidity is an especially difficult challenge in the diagnosis and study of ADHD. Some researchers have argued that the high rates of comorbidity between ADHD and other disorders suggest a problem in the diagnostic criteria (Achenbach, 1990/1991; Caron & Rutter, 1991). Other researchers have argued that the high rates are further evidence of the high levels of impairment that children with ADHD experience (Angold et al., 1999; Jensen et al., 1997a). Both of these explanations would suggest that further research is needed into the diagnostic specificity and accuracy of criteria for ADHD.

Course of the Disorder

The majority of ADHD diagnoses are first given to children between the ages of seven and nine (Whalen & Henker, 1998). By diagnostic definition, symptoms must have been present before the age of seven, but many children are not referred for an evaluation of ADHD symptoms until they reach school age. Children who develop the disorder earlier in life (i.e., before the age of six) tend to show greater problems with cognitive functioning, higher rates of comorbidity, more family disadvantage, and a greater likelihood of having the disorder into adolescence (McGee, Williams, & Feehan, 1992). Children who have a later onset of ADHD (i.e., after the age of six) tend to experience the symptoms after developing a reading disorder and tend to have a better prognosis than children with an earlier onset of ADHD (McGee et al., 1992).

Between 50% and 80% of children diagnosed with ADHD continue to meet criteria for the disorder in midadolescence (Barkley, 1998). Thus, there is a high degree of stability in ADHD symptoms (Biederman, Monuteaux, et al., 2001). Adolescents with ADHD show greater risk for car accidents and traffic violations compared to other adolescents (Woodward, Fergusson, & Horwood, 2000). A significant proportion of ADHD children also experience ADHD in adulthood. The continuation of ADHD symptoms from childhood to adolescence to adulthood is more likely for children who show extremely high levels of hyperactivity and impulsivity, who experience aggression and other conduct problems, and who come from distressed families (Barkley, 1998).

ADHD in childhood is also predictive of other emotional/behavioral problems in adolescence and adulthood (E. A. Taylor, 1999). Often, ADHD symptoms are identified long before conduct disorder symptoms (Patterson, DeGarmo, & Knutson, 2000). Notably, children who show impulsivity, hyperactivity, and attentional problems in addition to showing conduct problems are more likely to become chronic criminal offenders than are children with conduct problems who do not experience impulsivity, hyperactivity, and attentional problems (Lynam, 1996). In fact, children with the combination of impulsivity, hyperactivity, inattention, and conduct problems have been referred to as **fledgling psychopaths** because they appear to be destined for a troubled life if no prevention or intervention efforts are instituted (Gresham, Lane, & Lambros, 2000).

A unique feature of ADHD is that it shows **heterotypic continuity**, which means that the specific symptoms change over time but the behavior is still dysfunctional. For example, younger children tend to show gross motor movements in their overactivity whereas older children tend to show restlessness and fidgetiness (DuPaul, McGoey, Eckert, & VanBrakle, 2001; Whalen & Henker, 1998). Both types of behaviors are consistent with the diagnostic criteria and are usually dysfunctional, but the symptoms themselves change over the developmental course. Box 11.3 discusses ADHD in adulthood.

Etiology

There is no clearly established theory of the development of ADHD that has been accepted by all ADHD researchers (Nigg, 2001). There are, however, a number of plausible etiological theories that have empirical support. The majority of plausible explanations for the development of ADHD center on genetic, biological, and neurological factors. There is evidence, for example, that **family-genetic risk factors** play a role in the development and maintenance of ADHD. A series of studies showed that between 25% and 30% of first-degree relatives of children with ADHD also met criteria for ADHD (Whalen & Henker, 1998). In fact, there is evidence that parents with ADHD show significant difficulties in their parenting role, which may exacerbate their children's risk for ADHD (Smalley et al., 2000; Sprich, Biederman, Crawford, Mundy, & Faraone, 2000; M. Weiss, Hechtman, & Weiss, 2000). Consistent with the family-genetic risk factor theory, there is also evidence from twin and adoption studies that ADHD has at least a partial genetic component (Whalen & Henker, 1998). Although the results of twin and adoption studies regarding ADHD have come under attack recently (Joseph, 2000), there appears to be clear evidence of some type of genetic component in the etiology of ADHD (Faraone & Biederman, 2000; Sprich et al., 2000).

Another line of inquiry into the etiology of ADHD includes the investigation of neurobiological patterns,

BOX 11.3

ADHD IN ADULTHOOD

The diagnosis of ADHD in adulthood used to be controversial and suspect. The most salient features of ADHD, such as physical restlessness and behavioral overactivity, are not as present in adulthood as in childhood (Barkley, 1998). Thus, many clinicians and researchers assumed that children outgrew their ADHD by the time they reached adulthood.

There is growing evidence, however, that some adults experience ADHD without having been diagnosed in childhood. Diagnosis of ADHD for the first time in adulthood is difficult because the diagnostic criteria require the existence of symptoms before the age of seven. Most assessments of adults rely on the adult's memory rather than on other data (such as school records or behavioral observations) that could confirm the existence of the symptoms at an early age. In addition, assessments of adults most often rely on the adult client as the sole informant rather than parents and teachers. The problem is further compounded by a lack of reliable and valid tools for assessing symptoms of ADHD in adults. When family members are used for retrospective reports of adults, however, reliable patterns of symptoms can be collected in a valid manner (Faraone, Biederman, Feighner, & Monuteaux, 2000).

Figure 11.1 outlines the decision-making rules that can lead to a diagnosis of ADHD in adults. Because some symptoms of ADHD, especially inattention, are related to other psychological problems (such as anxiety and depression), it is imperative that the clinician conduct a careful differential diagnosis to verify that the problems are related to ADHD rather than to some other disorder. Additionally, because adults with ADHD have even higher rates of comorbidity than do children with ADHD, it is important to assess for disorders in addition to ADHD.

SOURCES: Barkley (1998), Faraone (2000), Nadeau (1995), G. Weiss & Hechtman (1993).

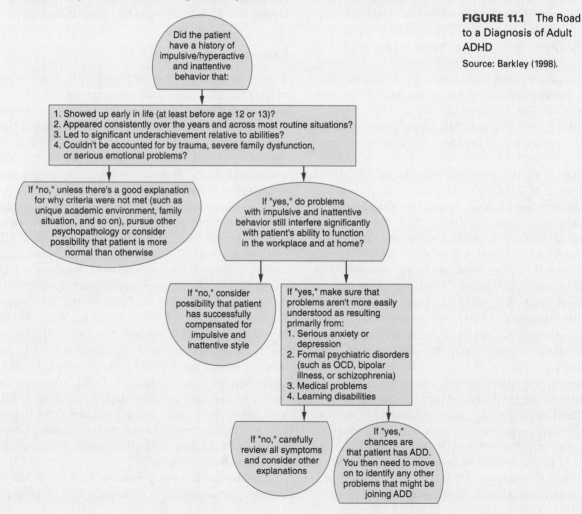

FIGURE 11.1 The Road to a Diagnosis of Adult ADHD

Source: Barkley (1998).

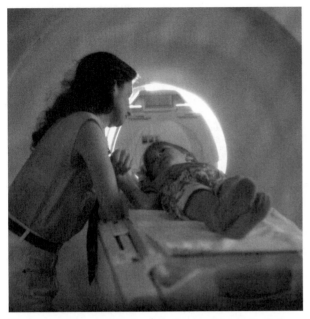

Magnetic resonance imaging is being used increasingly in research on brain structure and brain functioning in children diagnosed with ADHD.

including the study of dopamine and norepinephrine, which are neurotransmitters in the brain that influence behavior (Whalen & Henker, 1998). There has also been a great deal of research into the brain structures and brain functioning of children and adolescents diagnosed with ADHD. A thorough review of this literature suggests that ADHD may be due to abnormalities in the frontal-striatal regions of the brain (Barkley, 1998). These regions are illustrated in Figure 11.2. Overall, there is overwhelming

evidence that ADHD is at least partially due to genetic and biological factors (Rutter, Silberg, O'Connor, & Simonoff, 1999b).

A promising etiological theory of the development and maintenance of ADHD relates to limitations in self-control, which is consistent with the evidence of abnormalities in the frontal-striatal regions of the brain. In a book entitled *ADHD and the Nature of Self-Control*, Dr. Russell Barkley (1997b) outlined his theory that lack of self-control and behavioral inhibitions are the primary characteristics of ADHD. Further, he argued that attentional difficulties are only secondary to difficulties with self-control. As can be seen in Figure 11.3, there are four primary neuropsychological aspects that are required for effective functioning in behavioral inhibition:

- Working memory.
- Self-regulation of affect, motivation, and arousal.
- Internalization of speech.
- Reconstitution (i.e., behavioral analysis and synthesis).

Overall, a number of researchers (Barkley, 1997b, 1997c; Barkley, Edwards, Laneri, Fletcher, & Metevia, 2001; Cepeda, Cepeda, & Kramer, 2000; Nigg, 1999; Quay, 1997) have found that these aspects tend to be limited in children diagnosed with ADHD. Other researchers have found that deficits in behavioral inhibition (Schachar, Mota, Logan, Tannock, & Klim, 2000) and executive functioning (Klorman et al., 1999) can even distinguish children diagnosed with ADHD from children diagnosed with conduct disorder, children comorbid for conduct disorder and ADHD, and nonclinical children. Thus, there

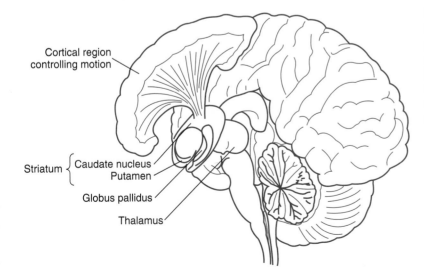

FIGURE 11.2 Diagram of the human brain showing the right hemisphere, and particularly the location of the striatum, globus pallidus, and thalamus. Most of the left hemisphere has been cut away up to the prefrontal lobes to reveal the striatum and other midbrain structures.

Source: Barkley (1998).

Cortical region controlling motion

Striatum { Caudate nucleus
Putamen

Globus pallidus

Thalamus

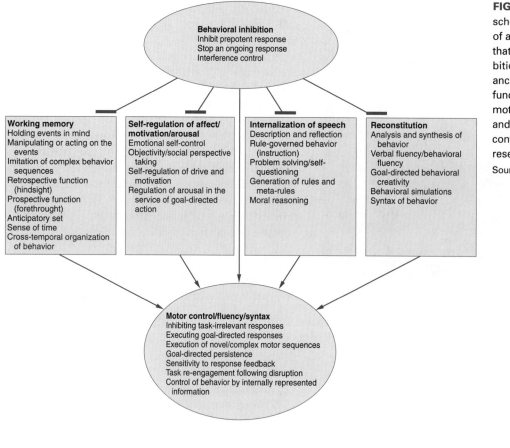

FIGURE 11.3   A schematic configuration of a conceptual model that links behavioral inhibition with the performance of the four executive functions that bring motor control, fluency, and syntax under the control of internally represented information.

Source: Barkley (1997c).

A MOTHER'S EXPERIENCE IN HER OWN WORDS

Yesterday we had a doctor's appointment. This was a nine o'clock appointment with a pediatric specialist in town. We were there at five minutes to nine. I had to take Jeremy out of school to be there. He was there for ADHD . . . and we waited and waited and waited. It got to be 9:15 and the next patient came in and said, "I'm here to see Dr. So-and-So; my appointment is for 9:15." Two minutes later the doctor came out and took him in, and there we were, still sitting, waiting . . .

Jeremy is not the most cooperative child in the world, and in the next 5 to 10 minutes he was sitting there screaming, "My turn, my turn, my turn." . . .

After we'd had 15 or 20 minutes of extra waiting, the doctor came back out and called Jeremy. We'd been there almost an hour. We had the first appointment of the day and we were there almost an hour before we even saw the doctor. I went

in and said, "Before we get started, I have to talk to you about something. We were here for a nine o'clock appointment, and we were here on time. I have a child that I took out of school to be here. I made a nine o'clock appointment so we wouldn't have to wait and we waited anyway . . . This is a child we are talking about, a child who is here for ADHD. He does not do well in a waiting room." He said, "Well, I made the mistake. I was running slow and I didn't read who was first."

This guy is a pediatric specialist. Why can't he be sensitive to these issues? My son was there for hyperactivity. We were there because he can't sit still and cooperate. It just sometimes makes me feel like I'm banging my head against a wall.

Source: Marsh (1995, pp. 16–18).

is relatively good evidence that deficits in self-control and behavioral inhibition are a central part of the difficulties that children with ADHD face. See Box 11.4 for a case illustration of these difficulties.

There is equivocal evidence about the impact of psychosocial family factors on the development and maintenance of ADHD. A number of externalizing behavior problems are associated with a number of adverse family factors, such as interparental conflict, dissimilar parenting styles of mothers and fathers, parental psychopathology, a troubled parent–child relationship, and aversive parental control behaviors (Harvey, 2000; Whalen & Henker, 1998). Most of these factors, however, are associated with conduct problems or with the combination of ADHD and conduct problems rather than the experience of ADHD alone. Other psychosocial and environmental factors have received some empirical support regarding the identification and maintenance of ADHD. For example, a poor goodness of fit between students' behavior and teachers' tolerance for activity and inattention may be related to labeling behaviors as problematic that might not be viewed as problematic in another setting (Greene, 1995, 1996).

In addition to knowing about etiological formulations that have empirical support, it is also important to know about theories that have consistently received no empirical support. During the 1970s, dietary habits, food additives, and sugar consumption were all implicated in the development and maintenance of what we now know as ADHD. Well-controlled studies, however, have shown none of these factors to be related to ADHD (Whalen & Henker, 1998). In other words, the widely held belief that

sugar and/or food additives (such as preservatives) cause hyperactivity have not been found to be true when studied carefully. Although some children have idiosyncratic responses to some foods, the majority of children who meet ADHD criteria would act similarly whether they ingested sugar or a placebo with an inert nonsugar substance in it (Whalen & Henker, 1998).

There is also no consistent evidence that environmental toxins, such as lead, are related to the development and maintenance of ADHD. Although environmental toxins can cause other neurological and cognitive problems, there is no consistent evidence that they are in any way related to ADHD (Whalen & Henker, 1998).

Despite the focus on the problems associated with ADHD, some researchers have acknowledged that ADHD symptoms may be beneficial in some circumstances. Specifically, there is speculation that, from an evolutionary perspective, some characteristics of ADHD were adaptive given the demands of survival at different times throughout history (Jensen, Mrazek et al., 1997; Shelley-Tremblay & Rosen, 1996). For example, the hunter theory would argue that impulsivity, distractibility, and aggression were adaptive for someone who was hunting given the need to have rapid responses and the need to experience flexible thinking in order to survive (Shelley-Tremblay & Rosen, 1996). Although evolutionary theories are speculative, there is some evidence that certain characteristics of ADHD may be adaptive in some settings.

Given that there is such diversity in the experience of ADHD, there may be different etiologies for different children diagnosed with the disorder. Clearly, further research is needed to ascertain whether there are different

Case Study: Mark, The Daydreamer

His mother thinks he is depressed. His father thinks he is lazy and unfocused. Both parents agree that he was a demanding baby who rarely slept and who cried a lot.

Mark is 11 years old and he seems to have chronic problems with paying attention. He is absent-minded and often seems to be lost in a fog. Mark has difficulty following conversations at the dinner table or following jokes with his classmates. In addition to having a limited attention span, Mark has almost no friends and appears to be rigid in his social interactions (e.g., he wants to do certain things over and over again).

Until recently, Mark had been performing adequately in school. He maintained a solid B average for most of his subjects. In the seventh grade, however, Mark's grades began to slip. Although he tried to keep up with the schoolwork, his homework became disorganized and he appeared to daydream a lot

when he was supposed to be studying. Overall, Mark's father reported being disappointed and irritated with him, whereas his mother reported that she felt protective and worried about him.

An evaluation showed that Mark experienced heightened levels of inattention, poor concentration, and poor memory for details. Based on the evaluation, and on information collected from Mark's teachers and parents, Mark was diagnosed with attention-deficit/hyperactivity disorder, predominantly inattentive type. Before he began the eighth grade, Mark was prescribed methylphenidate. During the eighth grade, Mark's grades improved dramatically, as did his behavior. He no longer seemed as inattentive or unable to concentrate as he had in the previous year. In addition, his relationship with his parents improved, and he made two new friends in a basketball program. Mark did not experience any adverse effects of the medication.

Source: Spitzer et al. (1994).

By permission of Mike Luckovich and Creators Syndicate, Inc.

theories that explain the development and maintenance of different subtypes of ADHD or whether there is an overarching theory that helps explain the majority of ADHD cases.

Treatment

Although a number of therapies have been attempted with ADHD, only a selection of effective treatments will be reviewed here: medication, behavioral therapies within the family, and behavioral techniques within the school system. Although other therapies—such as cognitive therapy, family therapy, play therapy, and interpersonal counseling—have been attempted with children diagnosed with ADHD, the primary methods of treatment center on psychopharmacological interventions (i.e., medication) and behavioral therapies. There has been a significant amount of research on cognitive therapies, but they have not been found to be well established as empirically supported treatments (Pelham, Wheeler, & Chronis, 1998). There is a need to disseminate information about effective treatments to mental health practitioners in the community and to the public at large (Rapport, 2001).

When most people think of treatment for ADHD, they probably think immediately of medication. The primary medications that are used to treat ADHD are stimulants, such as methylphenidate (Ritalin), Dexedrine, Cylert, and Adderall (Barkley, 1998). In general, effectiveness rates of stimulant medications range from 50% to 95% (Barkley, 1998), with most researchers concluding that

effectiveness rates hover between 70% and 80% (Pelham et al., 1998). Thus, it is reasonable to assume that between 70% and 80% of ADHD children who are treated with a stimulant medication will show behavioral improvements. When compared directly, both Ritalin and Adderall appeared to be equally effective (Pliszka, Browne, Olvera, & Wynne, 2000). Even those who are skeptical of medication should be impressed by these rates of effectiveness. It is also important to acknowledge, however, that 20% to 30% of ADHD children who are treated with stimulant medications show either no improvement or adverse effects (Pelham et al., 1998).

Even the children who do experience positive effects from stimulant medication do not show improvement in all areas of functioning. Stimulant medications have been found to be very effective in helping to increase attention, concentration, and compliance, and to decrease disruptive behavior, impulsive behavior, and aggression (Brodeur & Pond, 2001; R. T. Brown & Sawyer, 1998). There is some evidence that stimulant medications are effective in helping improve peer relationships, but these positive effects are not found in all studies (R. T. Brown & Sawyer, 1998; Pelham et al., 1998). Unfortunately, stimulant medication has not been found effective in improving academic achievement or self-esteem (R. T. Brown & Sawyer, 1998; Bussing, Zima, & Perwien, 2000). In addition, the strongest behavioral effects of stimulant medications tend to disappear after the medication is withdrawn (R. T. Brown & Sawyer, 1998).

Overall, stimulant medication is well accepted within

the field. Although psychologists cannot prescribe medications, they often refer children to psychiatrists for an evaluation of the appropriateness of medication for symptoms of ADHD. In addition, many psychologists work in conjunction with a psychiatrist or behavioral pediatrician to provide comprehensive treatment services for children diagnosed with ADHD (Barkley, 1998).

As discussed in Box 11.5, however, the use of psychostimulants for the treatment of ADHD is a controversial topic. Approximately 90% of visits to a physician with complaints of hyperactivity result in prescribing a medication, usually methylphenidate (Whalen & Henker, 1998). Over the past decade, use of psychostimulants in the treatment of ADHD has risen dramatically while therapy services have decreased dramatically (Hoagwood, Kelleher, Feil, & Comer, 2000). The prevalence of treating symptoms of ADHD with stimulants is staggering. Within the United States, there has been an eightfold increase in the use of psychostimulants over the past 10 years (Diller, 1999). This pattern is not typical of other countries. In fact, 90% of the prescriptions for methylphenidate worldwide are written in the United States (Diller, 1999). Interestingly, girls and adolescents are less likely to receive psychostimulant medication for symptoms of ADHD than are boys and younger children (Angold, Erkanli, Egger, & Costello, 2000).

The question also arises as to who is prescribing psychostimulants. Compared with pediatricians and child psychiatrists, family practitioners who prescribe psychostimulants for high levels of activity are less likely to conduct formal assessment procedures, are less likely to provide or recommend therapy services, and are less likely to suggest follow-up care for the medication (Hoagwood et al., 2000). At least 50% of children diagnosed with ADHD are treated in a way that is not consistent with the recommendations provided by the American Academy of Child and Adolescent Psychiatry (Hoagwood et al., 2000). Regardless of the effectiveness of psychostimulants for the treatment of ADHD symptoms, these trends are of great concern. Both the American Academy of

---

BOX 11.5

A DIFFERENT VIEW OF ADHD AND MEDICATION

Imagine an eight-year-old named James. James's mother complains that he is constantly underfoot and that he does not pay attention when she gives him lists of chores to complete. James's father complains that James chatters all the time, gets into too many things around the house, and will not sit still and play by himself. James's teacher complains that James is fidgety in class and that he will sit still and listen to her only when they are talking one-on-one. You might already have diagnosed James with ADHD. You might, however, want to consider an alternative explanation.

Dr. Peter Breggin and Ginger Ross Breggin (1995) would argue that James is suffering from a lack of adult attention and that there is a mismatch between James's needs and what those in his environment wish to give him. Rather than treating highly active and inattentive children with methylphenidate or another stimulant medication, the Breggins argue that we should explore environmental changes that might help meet the child's basic needs. We should look at the family system, the school system, and the community system in order to identify how the child's environment can be modified to help the child feel more secure and happy. To make their point, the Breggins identified a new "disorder" called Dad Attention Deficit Disorder (DADD), in which children do not receive enough attention from their fathers and thus act out in an attempt to gain that attention (Breggin & Breggin, 1995). Children with this disorder are "treated" effectively with loving and appropriate attention from their father.

These concepts are obviously quite a departure from mainstream psychology and psychiatry. Interestingly, Peter Breggin is himself a psychiatrist. In his book *Talking Back to Ritalin: What Doctors Aren't Telling You about Stimulants for Children,* Peter Breggin (1998) illustrates the biochemical hazards of medications such as Ritalin and suggests alternatives to treating active children. In another book called *The War against Children: How the Drugs, Programs, and Theories of the Psychiatric Establishment Are Threatening America's Children with a Medical "Cure" for Violence,* Peter and Ginger Ross Breggin (1994) argue that medications are used to force children into docility and submission and that such medications can be considered chemical restraints. In fact, Peter Breggin (1998) says, it is as if we are trying to medicate childhood out of children.

The use of stimulant medication or any other type of medication is potentially controversial. As described in Chapter 6, there are side effects to stimulant medication, such as stunted growth (R. T. Brown & Sawyer, 1998). In addition, Ritalin has become highly controversial since many adolescents have started selling their own Ritalin to other children as an illicit drug. Apparently, some non-ADHD children find that Ritalin can give them an enjoyable buzz.

Child and Adolescent Psychiatry as well as the American Academy of Pediatrics (American Academy of Pediatrics, 2000) have established firm guidelines for the assessment and treatment of ADHD. Physicians should follow these guidelines to make sure that children are not being overmedicated or otherwise improperly medicated.

There are also other concerns regarding the use of stimulant medication. Given that there are relatively high rates of comorbidity between ADHD and substance abuse disorders (Barkley, 1998), a question often arises as to whether stimulant medication is associated with later substance abuse in adolescence and adulthood. The available research does not indicate that stimulant medication is associated with a greater likelihood of substance abuse later in life (Barkley, 1998). Although more longitudinal studies are needed, there is no cause for parents' concerns about stimulant medications leading to substance abuse problems.

Overall, the use of stimulant medications is well accepted within the field but remains quite controversial for some professionals and parents (Barkley, 1998). As discussed in Chapter 6, the attributions of children on medication can sometimes be counterproductive to long-term behavior change. Researchers continue to investigate the strengths and weaknesses of the use of medications in treating ADHD. Many professionals advocate a combination of medication and behavioral therapy because improvements from behavioral therapy tend to remain even after the treatment is terminated (Barkley, 1998; MTA Cooperative Group, 1999).

There are some remedies worse than the disease.

—Publilius Syrus

In addition to medications that are used for treatment of ADHD, there have been a number of therapies that have been tried with ADHD children. **Behavioral parent training** and behavioral interventions in classrooms are well established as empirically supported treatments for ADHD (Pelham et al., 1998). Interestingly, children and adolescents often request the types of parental behaviors that are taught in this therapy (see Box 11.6). The basic premise of behavioral parent training is to help parents execute good behavioral techniques, which facilitate their children's behavioral control (Barkley, 1997d). In a 10-session treatment package, the following topics would be addressed each week (Barkley, 1997d):

1. Teaching parents, through psychoeducational processes, why children misbehave.

2. Helping parents pay attention to their children's behavior (especially teaching parents to "catch" their children behaving well so that they can provide positive reinforcement).

3. Helping parents increase their children's compliance and enhance their children's ability for independent play.

4. Teaching parents about token economies, such as using poker chips, points, or a star chart to reward appropriate behavior.

5. Teaching parents about the appropriate use of time out and other disciplinary actions.

6. Helping parents enhance many of their children's behaviors in addition to the behaviors that were part of the original referral concern.

7. Teaching parents how to anticipate and prevent troubled behavior in their children.

8. Empowering parents to work with teachers to improve their children's behavior at school.

9. Helping parents prepare for the future with regard to challenges that their children will face in maintaining behavioral control.

10. Processing the children's behavioral progress with parents to review what strategies have worked and what strategies should be used in the future.

Behavioral parent training is effective for a number of externalizing problems in children, including ADHD (Pelham et al., 1998). Most often, behavioral parent training is recommended only for children ages 2 to 11 (Barkley, 1997d), although there are now behavioral parent training programs for parents of adolescents as well (Barkley, Edwards, & Robin, 1999). Behavioral parent training has sometimes been combined with problem-solving communication training for families with an adolescent diagnosed with ADHD (Barkley, Edwards, Laneri, Fletcher, & Metevia, 2001). Both treatments (problem-solving communication training alone and behavioral parent training combined with problem-solving communication) have been found to be effective (Barkley et al., 2001).

Some behavioral therapy and parent-training techniques have been presented in books for parents to read themselves. Within the popular press, a book called *Ritalin Is Not the Answer: A Drug-Free, Practical Program for Children Diagnosed with ADD or ADHD* (D. B. Stein, 1999) has received a great deal of attention by providing specific behavioral suggestions that parents can use in conjunction with a trained clinician. Two other books targeted at parents—*Your Defiant Child: Eight*

Steps to Better Behavior (Barkley & Benton, 1998) and *Taking Charge of ADHD: The Complete Authoritative Guide for Parents* (Barkley, 1995)—also include behavioral parent-training strategies. Overall, behavioral parent training has been found to be quite effective in addressing the symptoms of ADHD (Pelham et al., 1998). Although, according to teachers' ratings, the immediate behavioral improvements are not as notable as with medication, the improvements from behavioral parent training tend to remain long after treatment is completed, which is often not the case with stimulant medication (Pelham et al., 1998). The use of both stimulants and behavioral techniques provide a multimodal treatment of ADHD that leads to the best long-term results (Sloan, Jensen, & Kettle, 1999).

Notably, the combination of medication and behavioral treatment has been highlighted as the most effective treatment strategy for children with ADHD. In a huge Multisite Treatment study of ADHD (known as MTA), the combination of medication and behavioral treatment was superior to community care as usual (MTA Cooperative Group, 1999; Pelham et al., 2000) and to medication management alone (Conners et al., 2001). These findings were particularly true for children who were comorbid for both ADHD and at least two other disorders such as an anxiety disorder and conduct disorder (Jensen et al., 2001).

In addition to behavioral parent training programs, a number of behavioral programs have been instituted in the school system. Most of the school-based behavioral programs can be described as **contingency management strategies**, which include token economies, time out, and response-cost procedures (Pelham et al., 1998). Most of these procedures fall within the domain of applied behav-

ior analysis (Baldwin, 1999). These procedures are discussed in greater detail in Chapter 6. Suffice it to say that these procedures all rely on behavioral principles to help children gain control of their behavior. **Token economies** are instituted so that children receive some type of reward after successfully completing specific behaviors. For example, children with ADHD, predominantly hyperactive-impulsive type, might receive a token for every 15 minutes that they sit in their seat during quiet time in class. After receiving five tokens, they might be able to cash them in for a prize (e.g., a fancy pencil or 10 extra minutes to play a computer game). **Time out** is used to try to decrease maladaptive behavior by removing the reinforcements for that behavior. Most often, there is a time-out chair or a time-out section of the room where the child is sent after exhibiting the maladaptive behavior. Most programs that use time out limit the amount of time to one minute per year of the child's age. Thus, a seven-year-old would be put in time out for no more than seven minutes per infraction. **Response-cost procedures** occur when a child has to forfeit something desirable if he or she exhibits a specific maladaptive behavior. The easiest example to imagine in your own life is the fine for returning a rented video or DVD later than the deadline (i.e., the cost of your late response is the loss of your precious money). Within the school system, children might lose a specific amount of time at recess if they speak out of turn during the morning lecture.

Overall, contingency management strategies are well-established, empirically supported treatments (Pelham et al., 1998). A number of other academic interventions are effective as well. Specifically, peer tutoring and task modifications help ADHD children with both their attentional difficulties and their academic performance (DuPaul &

BOX *11.6*

WHAT PRETEENS ARE ASKING FOR

Although there are a number of important lessons to be learned from behavioral parent training (Barkley, 1997d), sometimes these suggestions are surprisingly consistent with what children want from their parents. The book *What Preteens Want Their Parents to Know* (Holladay & Friends, 1994) presents a number of such suggestions. Out of the mouths of babes (or preteens, in this case):

- Encourage me when I do a good job (p. 9).
- Give me reasons for your demands (p. 15).

- Nagging doesn't work in the long run (p. 53).
- Set a good example for me (p. 64).
- Don't make any promises you might not be able to keep (p. 85).
- Don't spend all your time on the child who's acting up. Acknowledge the good as well as the bad (p. 92).
- When telling me about your rules, make sure I understand the consequences (p. 104).

SOURCE: Holladay & Friends (1994).

Eckert, 1998). In fact, a meta-analysis of school-based interventions found that contingency management strategies, as well as academic interventions, were significantly more effective than were cognitive-behavioral treatments with ADHD children (DuPaul & Eckert, 1997).

Even with the support of empirical evidence for these specific treatments, it is important to ascertain which treatment is best for which child (DuPaul, Eckert, & McGoey, 1997). Specifically, the individual strengths and weaknesses of each child should be identified through functional assessment in order to determine the treatment that would be most likely to help alleviate the symptoms of ADHD (DuPaul et al., 1997). In addition, the goodness of fit between teacher and student should be considered, and treatment interventions may need to be addressed with the teacher (or the school system) rather than the student (Greene, 1996). There is a significant need for clinicians to coordinate services with school professionals in order to provide the most comprehensive treatment to children with ADHD (NIH Consensus Development Panel, 2000).

Outside the school system, parent support groups can also be helpful for families dealing with ADHD. The largest ADHD organization for families within the United States is called Children and Adults with Attention-deficit/hyperactivity disorder (CHADD). This organization provides information, referrals, and support services for families dealing with ADHD. Many communities across the United States have local parent support groups that are affiliated with CHADD. Both the national organization and local chapters can be identified through CHADD's Web site (www.chadd.org). The primary criti-

---

Case Study: ADHD within a Family System

Although ADHD is a diagnosis for an individual child, adolescent, or adult, family systems therapists explore the entire family system for etiology, maintenance, and ramifications regarding children with high levels of activity and impulsivity. In the Johnson family, the single mother, Sonya, has two sons, nine-year-old Jim and seven-year-old Jack. Jim was referred to a residential facility because of severe hyperactivity, aggression, cruelty to animals, and oppositional behavior.

Sonya often had her mother (the boys' grandmother) care for them. In observations of their interactions, it became obvious that Sonya did not have any control within the family and that her mother was the one who tried to run things. The family therapists wanted to help change the structure of the family so that Sonya could parent effectively without any interference from her mother. For this reason, the grandmother was excluded from therapy sessions with Sonya and the boys. Below is a verbatim excerpt from a session where the therapists are actively trying to bolster the mother's legitimate right to parent her children. After the mother's power is restored within the family system, the therapists can help the mother with more appropriate parenting strategies that would be consistent with behavioral parent training. The transcript begins when the mother is trying to contain Jim in his chair after he has threatened to leave the session and after he has threatened to hit the therapists.

MOM to JIM: [*while putting her arm across him so he remains in the chair*] Do not move! [*to therapists*] He does things to really get on my nerves. [*to Jim*] You know something. I am taking this radio away! You know that.

JIM: [*pleadingly to Mom*] No!

MOM: You ain't keeping that because you can't listen.

Sonya then proceeds to tell of several incidents in which Jim hits his younger brother, Jack, with the last incident having resulted in Jack's crying.

JIM: No! I told you that Jack started it.

MOM: No! You did. I—

JIM: [*interrupting Mom*] I did not!

THERAPIST 2 to MOM: Let me ask you something. Do you mind that Jim is interrupting you when you are talking with other adults?

MOM: See, he thinks that because I'm talking with someone else I'm not going to do anything about what he's doing.

THERAPIST 2:   Okay. So what are you going to do about it right now? [*Jim, at this point, attempts to get out of his chair.*]

MOM: [*again places her arm across Jim's chair so that he can't get up*] No! You sit here when I am talking. I've come a long way to be here. You are going to sit here and you are going to listen. Because if you don't, you won't be coming home next week. I'll take everything back that I brought for you. Do you think that I can't take back everything that is here? I'm going to prove my point! [*reaches for the items on the table*]

JIM: [*grabbing for the items*] No, no, no. Why? Why?

Sonya, in turn, proceeds to tell the therapists of more incidents in which Jim hits his younger brother.

THERAPIST 1 to MOM: So, what you are saying—[*Jim interrupts*]—I'm not going to listen to your son right now because you are an adult and I am talking to you. So, what you are saying is that Jim's hitting is a big problem. Do you think that he understands that this is a big problem?

SOURCE: Kemenoff, Jachimczyk, & Fussner (1999; p. 138).

cism of organizations such as CHADD is that a specific social or political agenda might exist for the organization. Much of the funding for CHADD comes from pharmaceutical companies, with a majority of the funding coming from CibaGeneva Pharmaceuticals, the manufacturer of Ritalin (Breggin, 1998). The organization has been criticized for promoting the use of psychostimulants, especially Ritalin, while ignoring other therapeutic interventions (Breggin, 1998). For this reason, support organizations such as CHADD should be viewed with caution. Although some may be helped by the information and support provided by CHADD, it is important that families learn about all of their options regarding the identification of and treatment for high levels of activity and inattention in their children.

Patience is the best remedy for every trouble.

—Titus Maccius Plautus

Prevention

Given the implications of a strong neurological etiology in the development of ADHD (Barkley, 1998), little work has been done in the area of prevention. Notably, major collections of writings on prevention programs in general (e.g., Cicchetti, Rappaport, Sandler, & Weissberg, 2000; Price, Cowan, Lorion, & Ramos-McKay, 1988) do not address the prevention of ADHD. Although some of the

work on behavioral parent training could be considered tertiary prevention (i.e., the prevention of further problems related to the symptoms of ADHD), almost no attention has been given to date to preventing the onset of ADHD. This oversight within the professional community may be due to the assumption that ADHD cannot be prevented.

The professional writings that come closest to discussing preventive efforts for ADHD specifically address the goodness of fit between student and teacher (Greene, 1995, 1996). These writings suggest that ADHD primarily manifests itself when there is a poor fit between students' behavior and teachers' expectations; thus, preventive efforts could be directed at making teachers more accepting of students' diverse array of behaviors. Overall, more work is needed to be done to explore whether there are aspects of ADHD that can be prevented or minimized in children before the disorder reaches its full-blown state.

ATTENTION-DEFICIT/HYPERACTIVITY DISORDER CONCEPTUALIZED IN A DIMENSIONAL MANNER

More than any other disorder described in this book, ADHD is lacking in dimensional conceptualizations. ADHD is studied thoroughly within the framework of

---

BOX 11.7

WAITING FOR THE MARSHMALLOW

In an intriguing series of studies, Dr. Walter Mischel and his colleagues identified delay of gratification as a central component to functioning well (Mischel & Ebbesen, 1970; Mischel, Shoda, & Peake, 1988; Rodriguez, Mischel, & Shoda, 1989). In some ways, delay of gratification can be seen as being the polar opposite of impulsivity. In fact, there is evidence to suggest that attentional processes can help delay gratification, which is related to better behavioral outcomes even a decade later (Mischel et al., 1988).

How did these researchers explore this important issue? One of their research paradigms put preschool children (ages four and five) in a situation where they could choose between receiving a less desirable reward immediately or waiting for a more desirable reward (in many cases, a marshmallow). The dependent variable in these studies was how long the children waited for the desirable reward before giving in to the less desirable reward (Mischel & Ebbesen, 1970). They

found that children who waited longer (i.e., who delayed gratification longer) tended to use distraction strategies for themselves (i.e., they did not think about the marshmallow for which they were waiting anxiously). Not only was delay of gratification related to current intellectual and attentional functioning in the preschoolers (Rodriguez et al., 1989), but delay of gratification was also related to such functioning nearly a decade later (Mischel et al., 1988). Specifically, the study showed that children who had delayed gratification longer in preschool were more socially competent, academically competent, and better at coping during adolescence (Mischel et al., 1988). These studies suggest that children's skills in preschool are related to their functioning in adolescence. The studies further suggest that teaching children strategies to delay gratification in early childhood might help improve children's functioning in adolescence and beyond.

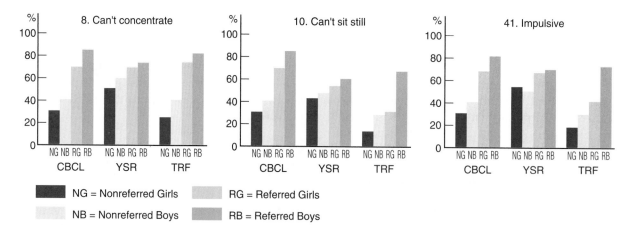

FIGURE 11.4 Percentage of Children for Whom Each Problem Was Endorsed
Source: Achenbach & Rescorla (2001).

diagnostic criteria, but there is extraordinarily little research that conceptualizes attention and activity levels dimensionally. Notably, entire volumes of professional writings that explore dimensional conceptualizations of children's behavior do not include any discussion of ADHD (e.g., Haggerty, Sherrod, Garmezy, & Rutter, 1994; Lenzenweger & Haugaard, 1996; Luthar, Burack, Cicchetti, & Weisz, 1997). One collection of writings from a dimensional perspective includes a chapter on attention, but none on activity levels that might be associated with ADHD (E. Taylor, 1995). There are, however, writings in other areas of psychology that address some of the dimensional issues related to attention, hyperactivity, and impulsivity. As discussed in Box 11.7, even social psychology and personality psychology can help inform researchers interested in impulsivity as it relates to conceptualizing ADHD in a dimensional manner.

Information from standardized measures can help inform us about the prevalence of behaviors related to ADHD from a dimensional perspective. Based on the normative data that were used to standardize the Child Behavior Checklist and related measures (Achenbach & Rescorla, 2001), it appears that the occurrence of inattention, overactivity, and impulsivity are quite common in children of all ages. As can be seen in Figure 11.4, inattention ("can't concentrate"), overactivity ("can't sit still"), and impulsivity ("acts without thinking") are all relatively common for clinical and nonclinical boys and girls across the age span according to parents, youth, and teachers. Children who are referred for clinical services continue to show much higher levels of inattention, overactivity, and impulsivity than children in the nonclinical

group, but children in the nonclinical group also show relatively high levels of these behaviors.

Risk Factors

Given the lack of research into symptoms of ADHD from a dimensional perspective, it is not surprising that there is very little research into the risk factors for symptoms of inattention, overactivity, and impulsivity. Many of the risk factors that are common to other disorders, such as parental psychopathology or low socioeconomic status, are not risk factors for the development of ADHD (Barkley, 1998). Overall, there are no well-established risk factors for the development of ADHD other than the factors that have been implicated in the etiology of ADHD, such as family history and genetic predisposition (Barkley, 1998; Samudra & Cantwell, 1999).

Protective Factors

Like the lack of research into risk factors, there is also a lack of research into factors that would protect children from the development of ADHD. Because stable home and school environments, with consistent and fair rules and consequences, are helpful in decreasing overactivity and impulsivity (Barkley, 1997d), it is not unreasonable to assume that these factors might protect children from the development or maintenance of overactivity and impulsivity. More research is needed to establish whether there are any factors that can protect children from the development of ADHD.

Case Study: Neil, The Boy Who Was Impulsive and Aggressive

Since the age of three, Neil had been hyperactive, inattentive, aggressive, and intrusive into others' personal space. Now, at the age of seven, Neil was admitted to a psychiatric hospital for the fourth time due to his hyperactivity and impulsivity. His impulsivity was especially focused on bothering little girls and pulling up their skirts. He had no friends, tended to get into fights both at school and in the community, and had been suspended from school on a number of occasions.

Neil lived with his biological mother, his older brother, and periodically with his mother's boyfriend. When Neil was three years old, his biological father died suddenly of a heart attack and his mother became depressed and developed a substance abuse problem. Many of Neil's problems seemed to develop after the death of his father. At the age of four, Neil was kicked out of his preschool and subsequently admitted to a psychiatric inpatient unit. He was diagnosed with ADHD and additional conduct problems, and he was put on medication to control the ADHD. Although the medication worked temporarily, his behavior soon began to deteriorate no matter which medication was given. Two more admissions to the psychiatric hospital were attempted when Neil's behavior worsened. No medication seemed to relieve the symptoms of hyperactivity, impulsivity, belligerence, and aggression.

During the most recent admission, the question of sexual abuse arose. Given that Neil's acting-out behavior was of a sexual nature (e.g., pulling up girls' skirts, pinching girls on the butt), the treatment team decided to explore whether there had been any incidents of sexual abuse. At first, Neil denied that anyone had touched him inappropriately or that he had been sexually abused. After a sexual abuse expert was called in, however, Neil acknowledged that his mother's boyfriend had initiated anal intercourse with him when his mother had left Neil and the boyfriend in the same bed together. Specifically, Neil reported: "He bopped me up the butt."

A report was made to child protective services, and an investigation was initiated. During the investigation, the mother's boyfriend was not allowed to have contact with Neil. Unfortunately, no one in Neil's family believed Neil's accusations and his mother was especially hesitant to believe the allegations. Neil's mother repeatedly questioned Neil about the allegations and apparently tried to get him to change his story. Neil eventually reported that it was his deceased father, and not the mother's boyfriend, who had sexually abused him. After further investigation, the child protective services team could not determine clearly who had sexually abused Neil. Although there was clear physical evidence that Neil had been sexually abused, there was no clear evidence that identified the perpetrator. For that reason, the case had to be closed as "unfounded" regarding the mother's boyfriend, and the family was no longer followed by child protective services.

At a one-year follow-up, Neil still exhibited some heightened levels of hyperactivity and aggression, but he was now functioning well in school. Neil no longer showed any acting-out behavior of a sexual nature. Neil's mother showed improved functioning and had secured a full-time job. Her health and psychological functioning had improved significantly. Neil's relationship with his mother's boyfriend was described as positive.

This case illustrates the importance of looking beyond the presenting problems of hyperactivity and impulsivity. It took four admissions to a psychiatric hospital for the professional staff to realize that Neil had been sexually abused. Although he received some treatment related to the abuse, the family refused further treatment once the child protective agency dropped the investigation. The therapy services that were received seemed to have helped Neil and his family to some degree, but more treatment is needed so the entire family can deal with the remaining issues of sexual abuse and family functioning.

Source: Kolko & Stauffer (1991).

SUMMARY AND KEY CONCEPTS

Attention-Deficit/Hyperactivity Disorder

Attention-deficit/hyperactivity disorder (ADHD) is characterized by three primary symptoms: hyperactivity, impulsivity, and inattention. ADHD used to be called **hyperkinetic reaction of childhood or adolescence**. Currently, there are three types of ADHD: **ADHD, combined type** (which consists of hyperactivity, impulsivity, and inattention); **ADHD, predominantly inattentive type** (which consists of inattention, but not hyperactivity and impulsivity); and **ADHD, predominantly hyperactive-impulsive type** (which consists of hyperactivity and impulsivity, but not inattention). In the *ICD-10*, the term **hyperkinetic disorder** is used to diagnose children who are hyperactive, impulsive, inattentive, and who have neurological deficits.

ADHD has high prevalence rates and high comorbidity rates. **Differential diagnosis**, the process of establishing which disorder or disorders are relevant for a particular child, is especially difficult given the high comorbidity rates. Children who exhibit the combination of hyperactivity, impulsivity, inattention, and conduct problems have been referred to as **fledgling psychopaths** because this constellation of behaviors has been associated with antisocial behavior in adulthood. ADHD is unique in showing **heterotypic continuity**, which means that its specific symptoms change over time but the behavior is still dysfunctional.

Family-genetic risk factors are often implicated in the development of ADHD. The frontal-striatal region of the brain has been strongly implicated in the development of ADHD.

Treatments for ADHD center on stimulant medication (such as methylphenidate, known under the brand name Ritalin), **behavioral parent training**, and **contingency management strategies** (such as **token economies**, **time out**, and **response-cost procedures**).

Attention-Deficit/Hyperactivity Disorder Conceptualized in a Dimensional Manner

Unfortunately, there has been very little research into hyperactivity, impulsivity, and inattention from a dimensional perspective.

KEY TERMS

hyperkinetic reaction of childhood or adolescence	ADHD, predominantly inattentive type	hyperkinetic disorder	heterotypic continuity	contingency management strategies
ADHD, combined type	ADHD, predominantly hyperactive-impulsive type	differential diagnosis	family-genetic risk factors	token economies
		fledgling psychopaths	behavioral parent training	time out
				response-cost procedures

SUGGESTED READINGS

Marsh, D. B. *From the Heart: On Being the Mother of a Child with Special Needs*. Bethesda, MD: Woodbine House, 1995. Jayne D. B. Marsh collected interviews, writings, poems, and other poignant communications from mothers of special needs children. Some mothers wrote about their children with ADHD, while other wrote about their children with developmental disabilities, medical illnesses, and psychological problems.

Neuville, Maureen, B. *Sometimes I Get All Scribbly: Living with Attention-Deficit/Hyperactivity Disorder*. New York: RR Stoneworks, 1991. In this memoir, Neuville writes about her son, Brian, who was diagnosed with ADHD. The book includes discussions of Brian's symptoms, as well as the family's struggle to deal with ADHD. An excerpt from the book can also be found in *Attention-Deficit/Hyperactivity Disorder in the Classroom* (Dowdy et al., 1998).

SUGGESTED VIEWINGS

Home Alone (1990). Chris Columbus (director), John Hughes (writer). VHS/DVD. Although he would not meet criteria for attention-deficit/hyperactivity disorder, the young boy in this film certainly shows some heightened levels of energy and impulsivity. In this case, his heightened activity levels actually work to his advantage in many circumstances.

Kids (1995). Larry Clark (director), Harmony Korine (writer). VHS/DVD. This film illustrates a number of problems associated with adolescence, including impulsivity, hyperactivity, and poor decision-making skills. It is a sobering film that explores some of the more difficult aspects of being an adolescent.

CHAPTER 12

DISRUPTIVE DISORDERS, OPPOSITIONAL PROBLEMS, AND CONDUCT PROBLEMS

CHAPTER SUMMARY

. . . When I was thirteen, while robbing a man I turned my head and was hit in the face. The man tried to run, but was tripped by [my friend], who then held him for me. I stomped him for twenty minutes before leaving him unconscious in an alley. Later that night, I learned that the man had lapsed into a coma and was disfigured from my stomping. The police told bystanders that the person responsible for this was a "monster." The name stuck, and I took that as a moniker over my birth name.

—Sanyika Shakur (1993, p. 13), formerly Monster Kody Scott, a gang member in Los Angeles

Aggressive and violent children and adolescents are a concern to everyone. Their presence is salient in the school system as well as in society at large (Doll, 1996; Loeber, Burke, Lahey, Winters, & Zera, 2000; Stahl & Clarizio, 1999). The two primary disruptive disorders that receive attention in developmental psychopathology are oppositional defiant disorder (ODD) and conduct disorder (CD). Both disorders disrupt the lives of children and adolescents as well as those of people around them. Both ODD and CD are considered externalizing disorders. This chapter will describe ODD and CD separately, along with prevalence information for each. Because of the common

Case Study: Jeremy, The Boy Who Swore at the Teacher

Jeremy's mother brought him in for an evaluation when he was 9 years old. He had been a difficult child since nursery school, but his misbehavior had escalated over the past few months. In general, he was disobedient, deceitful, and difficult to manage both at school and at home. Recently, he had sworn at his teacher, which resulted in a three-day suspension. He was reprimanded by a police officer for riding his bicycle in the street. The next day, he again rode his bicycle in the street, failed to use his brakes, and crashed through a storefront window.

Looking back on his development, Jeremy's mother acknowledged that Jeremy behaved well as long as he was supervised and received attention. When he received good attention, he was sweet, charming, and a joy to be around. When he did not receive adequate attention, however, he created prob-

lems. He seemed to annoy other children intentionally, often teasing, tripping, and kicking them. Jeremy also had chronic difficulties with his teachers. He often talked back to them and did not obey them. He showed oppositional behavior to nearly all adults at his school. Despite these difficulties, his grades remained adequate.

Overall, Jeremy's is a relatively classic case of oppositional defiant disorder. Although Jeremy has had police involvement (which would be expected with the more severe diagnosis of conduct disorder), this involvement has been relatively minor. The chronic nature of his negativism and defiant behavior are the hallmark signs of ODD.

SOURCE: Spitzer, Gibbon, Skodol, Williams, & First (1994).

---

characteristics of the disorders, the discussion of comorbidity, courses of the disorders, etiology, treatment, and prevention will be combined to include the disorders together. For students interested in reading more about these disorders, there are two particularly good, recent books that cover ODD, CD, and related problems: *Conduct Disorders and Severe Antisocial Behavior* (Frick, 1998b) and *Handbook of Disruptive Behavior Disorders* (Quay & Hogan, 1999).

The more things are forbidden, the more popular they become.
—Mark Twain

OPPOSITIONAL DEFIANT DISORDER

Oppositional defiant disorder (ODD) occurs when a child shows defiant, oppositional, hostile, and negative behavior for at least six months. Nearly all children show defiance at some point in their lives; ODD is diagnosed only if the defiance, negativism, and hostility are beyond what would be expected for a child of a given age and gender. Children with ODD are often irritating to those around them. They defy the instructions of their parents and teachers, intentionally annoy adults and children, and are angry or spiteful. The diagnostic criteria for ODD, shown in Table 12.1, are meant to distinguish this disorder from normal behavior at different developmental levels.

As with nearly all of the disorders in *DSM-IV,* ODD must cause clinically significant impairment in social, academic, or occupational functioning (criterion B). It is

Although not a formal aspect of the diagnostic criteria, children with oppositional defiant disorder often fight with other children.

TABLE 12.1 *DSM-IV* **Diagnostic Criteria for Oppositional Defiant Disorder**

A. A pattern of negativistic, hostile, and defiant behavior lasting at least 6 months, during which four (or more) of the following are present:

(1) often loses temper

(2) often argues with adults

(3) often actively defies or refuses to comply with adults' requests or rules

(4) often deliberately annoys people

(5) often blames others for his or her mistakes or misbehavior

(6) is often touchy or easily annoyed by others

(7) is often angry and resentful

(8) is often spiteful or vindictive

Note: Consider a criterion met only if the behavior occurs more frequently than is typically observed in individuals of comparable age and developmental level.

B. The disturbance in behavior causes clinically significant impairment in social, academic, or occupational functioning.

C. The behaviors do not occur exclusively during the course of a Psychotic or Mood Disorder.

D. Criteria are not met for Conduct Disorder, and, if the individual is age 18 years or older, criteria are not met for Antisocial Personality Disorder.

SOURCE: American Psychiatric Association (2000). Reprinted with permission from the *Diagnostic and Statistical Manual of Mental Disorders, Fourth Edition, Text Revision.* Copyright 2000 American Psychiatric Association.

possible to imagine a child who exhibits many of the symptoms of ODD but does not show any significant impairment in these areas. The impairment criterion, for example, might not be met for children in highly accommodating environments.

The final criterion (criterion D) is important to keep in mind when considering children with severe symptoms of aggression. Many children show the less severe symptoms that are consistent with both ODD and the more severe symptoms that are consistent with CD, but these children would be diagnosed only with CD. In other words, the diagnosis of CD takes precedence over ODD.

As illustrated in the case study of Jose, oppositional behaviors can be quite normal at different developmental stages. Figure 12.1 shows that oppositional behaviors tend to be relatively frequent in nonreferred young boys and tend to decrease over time (Loeber, Lahey, & Thomas, 1991). These data highlight the importance of knowing developmental trends in children's behaviors before identifying oppositional behavior as deviant. This caveat, however, is not meant to suggest that young children can never exhibit diagnosable disruptive behavior disorders. In one clinical sample of children ages two through five (many of whom were comorbid with ADHD), 41.8% met criteria for CD and 25.3% met criteria for ODD (Keenan & Wakschlag, 2000). The researchers in this study even titled their article "More Than the Terrible Twos" to highlight the fact that even toddlers can show severe behavior problems that are above and beyond what would be expected developmentally (Keenan & Wakschlag, 2000). In addition, violent fantasies evident in early play are associated with later oppositional difficulty (Dunn & Hughes, 2001).

When children meet criteria for ODD, they are often found to have other problems as well. ODD is associated with hyperactivity, academic difficulties, and poor peer relationships (Hinshaw & Anderson, 1996; Loeber, Green, Lahey, Frick, & McBurnett, 2000; Loeber, Burke, et al., 2000).

Case Study: Jose, The Boy Who Only Said No

Jose exhibits a very negativistic pattern of behavior. He says no to nearly every request that is made of him. In addition to saying no, Jose whines to his parents about their requests. He often cries, is irritable, is sullen, and withdraws from those around him. When he is really upset, he throws severe temper tantrums (e.g., throwing himself on the floor, screaming, crying, and begging to get his way).

Jose is also very demanding of his parents' attention. His parents have noticed that his older sister is not nearly as demanding of their attention. Of particular concern to Jose's parents is that Jose seems to act up only around them. They are concerned that they have reinforced his oppositional behaviors. His parents are most concerned about his breath-holding episodes. Sometimes

Jose gets so upset when his parents forbid him from doing something that he holds his breath and gets red in the face. He has not yet fainted from these episodes, but his parents are very worried that he could incur brain damage from holding his breath for so long.

Given Jose's oppositional and negativistic behavior, you might be ready to diagnose him with oppositional defiant disorder. When you find out that he is two years old, however, you should be wary of giving such a diagnosis. All of the behaviors described for Jose are very common among two-year-olds. Although they are sometimes not pleasant for parents or toddlers, the "terrible twos" are not a diagnosis in *DSM-IV*.

SOURCE: Adapted from American Academy of Pediatrics (1998).

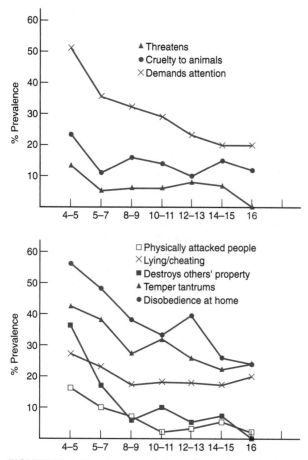

FIGURE 12.1 Prevalence of Selected Disruptive Behaviors by Age in Nonreferred Boys

Source: Loeber et al. (1991); data are from Edelbrock (1989).

TABLE 12.2 Overview of Prevalence Information for Oppositional Defiant Disorder

Prevalence	2–16%
Age	Younger > Older
Gender	Boys > Girls (before puberty); equivalent after puberty
Socioeconomic status	Lower SES > Higher SES
Race/Ethnicity	No consistent patterns

2000; Hartung & Widiger, 1998). This age and gender interaction is probably due to the fact that adolescents with severe cases of ODD, who are mostly boys, tend to be diagnosed with conduct disorder rather than ODD. Thus, the prevalence for girls appears to be the same both before and after puberty, whereas the prevalence for boys decreases after puberty because so many adolescents boys meet criteria for conduct disorder. Children from families with low socioeconomic status (SES) tend to be more at risk for a diagnosis of ODD than are children from families with high SES (Lahey, Miller, Gordon, & Riley, 1999). Although there are mixed findings in some studies, it does not appear that there are any consistent prevalence patterns of ODD based on race and ethnicity (Lahey, Miller, et al., 1999).

Attitudes are caught, not taught.

—Old Quaker saying

CONDUCT DISORDER

Conduct disorder (CD) is a much more serious disorder than oppositional defiant disorder. The primary characteristics of CD include violating the basic rights of others and breaking the societal norms associated with a given developmental level. The definition in Table 12.3 shows that the categories of criteria include aggression toward people and animals, destruction of property, deceitfulness or theft, and serious violations of rules. Symptoms need to have been present within the past year, with at least one symptom present within the past six months.

Because many children and adolescents live in settings where undesirable behavior is actually necessary for survival, it is imperative that the clinician take into consideration the child's or adolescent's living situation before making a diagnosis. Adolescents who are impoverished and living in a high-crime area may have to engage in

A lie can give more pain than a spear.

—Proverb of Africa

Prevalence Rates

Table 12.2 gives an overview of prevalence information of ODD. It is estimated that between 2% and 16% of children meet criteria for ODD (American Psychiatric Association, 2000). A higher percentage (20%) of adoptive children met criteria, especially those with pre-adoption abuse and neglect (Simmel, Brooks, Barth, & Hinshaw, 2001). The disorder is diagnosed more frequently in children than in adolescents. ODD is more prevalent in boys than in girls before puberty, but there are approximately equal numbers of boys and girls who meet criteria for ODD after puberty (American Psychiatric Association,

Case Study: Saigon Pete from Grosse Pointe

Pete, whose mother was Vietnamese and whose father was an American serviceman, lived in Vietnam for his first two years of life. His biological mother put him up for adoption, and he was adopted by a family in the United States. However, his adoptive family abused him—beating and intentionally burning him—so Pete was moved to foster care by the age of two and a half. He was then adopted by a family who lived in Grosse Point, a wealthy suburb of Detroit, Michigan, where he grew up with three other adopted siblings.

Pete adjusted to his new family initially, but he remained somewhat shy and uncommunicative in the early years. He had a large number of friends, but he developed a stormy and difficult relationship with his parents. When he was in junior high school, he began befriending a group of young adolescents who drank beer, smoked marijuana, tortured animals, and skipped school. Pete's academic work plummeted, and he got in trouble for fighting with the popular teenagers at school, vandalizing the neighbors' mailboxes, and shooting at squirrels.

At the age of 14, Pete's acting-out behaviors increased. For example, he and his friends stole a neighbor's car to go joyriding. Around this time, his parents separated and he decided to live with his father rather than move to another state with his mother and siblings. At the age of 15, Pete skipped school more days than not and his drug use escalated. He and his friends were

now heavily involved with using LSD, mescaline, marijuana, and glue. Pete's parents tried to gain some control over him by sending him to a military school, but he was quickly expelled for chronic truancy.

On the day before his 16th birthday, Pete slashed his wrists with a butcher knife, which resulted in severed tendons and nerves. He fell unconscious, but when he regained consciousness, he called one of his friends' mothers, who then had him rushed to the hospital. While at the psychiatric hospital, Pete explained that he had not intended to kill himself. Instead, he stated that he had been dropping acid, thought he heard police sirens outside, and figured that it would be better to slash his wrists than to be arrested. When asked directly, Pete stated that he was not depressed. He did, however, say that his life was worthless and that it would not make a difference whether he lived or died.

The intake team at the psychiatric hospital diagnosed Pete with conduct disorder, adolescent onset type (moderate), due to Pete's illicit activities (e.g., grand theft auto, fighting). They also diagnosed Pete with hallucinogen abuse, cannabis abuse, and adjustment disorder, with depressed mood. They felt that there was not enough evidence for a diagnosis of major depressive disorder or dysthymia, although one of these disorders was probably present.

SOURCE: Spitzer et al. (1994).

fighting to protect themselves, and youngsters from war-ravaged countries may have to be aggressive in order to survive. In these cases, a diagnosis of conduct disorder would not be appropriate (American Psychiatric Association, 2000).

CD can be diagnosed at any age. If the individual meets criteria for both ODD and CD, then the diagnosis of CD would prevail. If the individual is older than 18 and also meets criteria for antisocial personality disorder, then the diagnosis of antisocial personality disorder would supercede that of CD.

There are two primary types of CD: childhood-onset type and adolescent-onset type. Childhood-onset type is considered the more serious of the two because it is associated with chronic problems into adulthood (Frick, 1998b). In fact, some researchers argue that the development of CD is distinctly different for individuals with the childhood-onset type and those with the adolescent-onset type (Moffitt, 1993; Patterson, Reid, & Dishion, 1992). Both types of the disorder are based partially on reciprocal processes between the child and his or her environment. Childhood-onset CD, however, begins with very early difficulties in infant or child temperament and the parent–child relationship, whereas adolescent-onset CD

is associated with exposure to troubled peers in later childhood and adolescence (Loeber, Burke, et al., 2000; McCabe, Hough, Wood, & Yeh, 2001; Moffitt, 1993). Based on *DSM-IV* criteria, the severity of CD can be noted as mild, moderate, or severe.

There is growing evidence that another distinction between types of CD is warranted. In addition to considering childhood-onset and adolescent-onset types of CD, there is also evidence to suggest that children and adolescents with CD also fall along a continuum of **callous–unemotional traits** (Frick & Ellis, 1999). Callous traits are characterized by a lack of empathy and the use of others for one's own gain. Unemotional traits are characterized by lack of guilt and remorse, and limited affect and feelings. This concept is consistent with the idea of psychopathy in adults (Frick & Ellis, 1999). Children and adolescents diagnosed with CD who show high levels of callous–unemotional traits tend to become adults with the most severe forms of antisocial behavior (Frick & Ellis, 1999).

Previous categorizations of CD focused on whether youth were involved in these activities with a group or alone. In *DSM-III-R* (American Psychiatric Association, 1987), CD was broken down into a group type (also

TABLE 12.3 *DSM-IV* Diagnostic Criteria for Conduct Disorder

A. A repetitive and persistent pattern of behavior in which the basic rights of others or major age-appropriate societal norms or rules are violated, as manifested by the presence of three (or more) of the following criteria in the past 12 months, with at least one criterion present in the past 6 months:

Aggression to people and animals

(1) often bullies, threatens, or intimidates others

(2) often initiates physical fights

(3) has used a weapon that can cause serious physical harm to others (e.g., a bat, brick, broken bottle, knife, gun)

(4) has been physically cruel to people

(5) has been physically cruel to animals

(6) has stolen while confronting a victim (e.g., mugging, purse snatching, extortion, armed robbery)

(7) has forced someone into sexual activity

Destruction of property

(8) has deliberately engaged in fire setting with the intention of causing serious damage

(9) has deliberately destroyed others' property (other than by fire setting)

Deceitfulness or theft

(10) has broken into someone else's house, building, or car

(11) often lies to obtain goods or favors or to avoid obligations (i.e., "cons" others)

(12) has stolen items of nontrivial value without confronting a victim (e.g., shoplifting, but without breaking and entering; forgery)

Serious violations of rules

(13) often stays out at night despite parental prohibitions, beginning before age 13 years

(14) has run away from home overnight at least twice while living in parental or parental surrogate home (or once without returning for a lengthy period)

(15) is often truant from school, beginning before age 13 years

B. The disturbance in behavior causes clinically significant impairment in social, academic, or occupational functioning.

C. If the individual is age 18 years or older, criteria are not met for Antisocial Personality Disorder.

Specify type based on age at onset:

Childhood-Onset Type: onset of at least one criterion characteristic of Conduct Disorder prior to age 10 years

Adolescent-Onset Type: absence of any criteria characteristic of Conduct Disorder prior to age 10 years

Specify severity:

Mild: few if any conduct problems in excess of those required to make the diagnosis *and* conduct problems cause only minor harm to others

Moderate: number of conduct problems and effect on others intermediate between "mild" and "severe"

Severe: many conduct problems in excess of those required to make the diagnosis *or* conduct problems cause considerable harm to others

SOURCE: American Psychiatric Association (2000). Reprinted with permission from the *Diagnostic and Statistical Manual of Mental Disorders, Fourth Edition, Text Revision.* Copyright © 2000 American Psychiatric Association.

Case Study: Reginald, The "Handful"

Reginald has always been a "handful." He repeated both first and second grades. Due to his disruption in the classroom, Reginald usually spent more time in the principal's office than in his regular classroom. He was suspended from school recently for setting up a blockade to demand money from younger children on their way home from school.

When he was not at school, Reginald's behavior was also problematic. Reginald's mother found items in his room that she believed were stolen, he damaged the neighbor's property on more than one occasion, he lied constantly, and he often left the house late at night and would not say where he was going.

By the age of 11, Reginald's teacher asked his mother to take him for psychological help because he was bullying and fighting with other children at school. Reginald's mother is a single-mother, who works two part-time jobs to try to support the family. Reginald and his three siblings are often left unsupervised at home.

Reginald met criteria for conduct disorder, childhood-onset type. The evaluation also showed that Reginald had limited intellectual functioning (Full Scale IQ = 66; Verbal IQ = 57; Performance IQ = 78). Below is the multiaxial diagnosis:

Axis I: Conduct Disorder, Childhood-Onset Type (Moderate)

Axis II: Mild Mental Retardation

Axis III: None (No known physical problems)

Axis IV: Problems with primary support group: family disruption

Educational problems: academic problems

Axis V: Global Assessment of Functioning = 45 (current)

SOURCE: Rapoport & Ismond (1996).

known as a socialized type) and a solitary, aggressive type. Although these distinctions continue to be meaningful, the age-of-onset typing and callous–unemotional conceptualizations appear to be the most useful (Frick, 1998b; Hinshaw & Anderson, 1996).

The most severe behaviors related to CD, such as armed robbery or sexual assault, are rare at any age. Other behaviors related to CD, however, are evident even in nonclinical samples. Specifically, truancy, alcohol use, and use of marijuana are all relatively infrequent in younger childhood but are much more prevalent in adolescence (Loeber et al., 1991). In general, the less severe symptoms related to CD increase over time in nonclinical samples. Property and status offenses are more common in adolescence than in childhood (Lahey et al., 2000).

When children or adolescents meet criteria for CD, they usually have a number of other problems as well (Loeber, Burke, et al., 2000; Kazdin, 1997). CD is associated with oppositional attitudes toward parents, teachers, and other authority figures (Kazdin, 1997). Youth diagnosed with CD tend to have academic difficulties, such as failing classes, scoring poorly on academic achievement tests, and dropping out of school before graduation (Kazdin, 1995). CD is also associated with peer difficulties, such as being disliked or rejected by nondeviant peers and being socially ineffective (Kazdin, 1997). Children and adolescents diagnosed with CD also tend to show high levels of hyperactivity (Hinshaw & Anderson, 1996). Substance use and early, risky sexual behavior are associated with CD as well (Dishion, French, & Patterson, 1995).

Prevalence Rates

Table 12.4 gives an overview of prevalence information for conduct disorder. Overall, approximately 1% to 10% of adolescents experience CD (American Psychiatric

TABLE 12.4 Overview of Prevalence Information for Conduct Disorder

Prevalence	1–10% overall; 6% to 16% for boys; 2% to 9% for girls
Age	Adolescents > Children
Gender	Boys > Girls
Socioeconomic status	Lower > Higher
Race/Ethnicity	No consistent patterns

Association, 2000). The prevalence rates of CD vary by gender. Between 6% and 16% of boys, and between 2% and 9% of girls, meet criteria for CD (American Psychiatric Association, 1994). More adolescents than children are diagnosed with CD. As is obvious from the prevalence rates, more boys than girls are diagnosed with CD (Eme & Kavanaugh, 1995; Lahey et al., 2000). Interestingly, symptoms also vary between boys and girls (American Psychiatric Association, 2000; Cote, Zoccolillo, Tremblay, Nagin, & Vitaro, 2001; Hartung & Widiger, 1998; Loeber, Burke, et al., 2000; Loeber & Stouthamer-Loeber, 1998). Boys with CD tend to exhibit confrontational and aggressive behaviors, such as stealing, vandalizing property, fighting, and acting out at school. Girls with CD tend to exhibit more nonconfrontational behaviors, such as running away, skipping school, abusing substances, and prostituting themselves. There is consistent evidence that CD is more prevalent in youth from families with low socioeconomic status (SES) than youth from families with middle and high SES (Lahey, Miller, et al., 1999). Notably, violent activities associated with CD seem to be more biologically based in adolescents from high-SES neighborhoods, whereas violence is more associated with contextual factors such as poor parent–adolescent relationships in adolescents from low-SES neighborhoods (Beyers, Loeber, Wikstrom, & Stouthamer-Loeber, 2001).

Case Study: Shaniqua, The "Born Liar"

Shaniqua was 16 years old when she was admitted to a psychiatric hospital for her behavioral problems. The admission was preceded by many years of conduct problems. By the age of 12, Shaniqua was already known to the authorities because of truancy and petty theft. Over the past four years, she had continued to steal from local stores, set fires in vacant lots, and lie chronically. Shaniqua was still in junior high school because of academic difficulties. Recently, however, she had been expelled after she and her friends were caught smoking marijuana in the gym.

Shaniqua's parents reported that they had lost all control of her. When they tried to reprimand her, she would leave the house and stay out all night. They stated that she was a "born liar."

During her stay in the psychiatric hospital, Shaniqua became demanding and disruptive. She befriended a number of other troubled girls and demanded that she be the center of attention. When the staff would not bow to her every request, Shaniqua would storm out of group therapy meetings and cause a scene. Although she presented a tough exterior, the staff at the hospital thought that Shaniqua felt insecure and dependent underneath. Shaniqua met criteria for CD.

SOURCE: Spitzer et al. (1994).

Although the research is sometimes equivocal, there is no consistent evidence of different prevalence patterns of CD regarding race or ethnicity (Lahey, Miller, et al., 1999).

Antisocial Personality Disorder (APD)

A brief discussion of **antisocial personality disorder (APD)** is warranted. As indicated in Table 12.5, APD can be diagnosed only in individuals over the age of 18. Considered a personality disorder, APD is noted on Axis II of a *DSM-IV* multiaxial assessment. The basic characteristics of APD are a chronic pattern of violating others' rights and a long-term disregard for others' well-being. For a diagnosis of APD, there must be evidence of these behaviors from the age of 15, and evidence of CD before the age of 15. Retrospective reports are often necessary to ascertain whether the adult showed symptoms of CD in childhood or adolescence. In general, retrospective reports by adults diagnosed with APD tend to be more accurate when the adult's current behavior is consistent with his or her past behavior (Rueter, Chao, & Conger, 2000).

The term **psychopath** is often used to describe individuals with APD, especially those individuals who show callousness and lack of emotion (Frick, 1998b). Note that adolescents diagnosed with CD who later meet criteria for APD are also highly comorbid for substance abuse disorders (Kratzer & Hodgins, 1997). There is evidence that children with the combination of hyperactivity, impulsivity, attention problems, and conduct problems can be considered **fledgling psychopaths** (Lynam, 1996). That is, children with this constellation of problems are very likely to develop severe problems with APD. Given that 50% to 60% of the known crimes are committed by 5% to 6% of known juvenile and adult offenders, these severe cases of APD are important to identify and treat (Lynam, 1996).

It is so remarkably easy just to tell the truth in this world, that I often marvel that there are so many madly foolish, so wretchedly stupid, that they hide truth.

—Jack London

TABLE 12.5 *DSM-IV* Diagnostic Criteria for Antisocial Personality Disorder

A. There is a pervasive pattern of disregard for and violation of the rights of others occurring since age 15 years, as indicated by three (or more) of the following:

   (1) failure to conform to social norms with respect to lawful behaviors as indicated by repeatedly performing acts that are grounds for arrest

   (2) deceitfulness, as indicated by repeated lying, use of aliases, or conning others for personal profit or pleasure

   (3) impulsivity or failure to plan ahead

   (4) irritability and aggressiveness, as indicated by repeated physical fights or assaults

   (5) reckless disregard for safety of self or others

   (6) consistent irresponsibility, as indicated by repeated failure to sustain consistent work behavior or honor financial obligations

   (7) lack of remorse, as indicated by being indifferent to or rationalizing having hurt, mistreated, or stolen from another

B. The individual is at least age 18 years.

C. There is evidence of Conduct Disorder . . . with onset before age 15 years.

D. The occurrence of antisocial behavior is not exclusively during the course of Schizophrenia or a Manic Episode.

SOURCE: American Psychiatric Association (2000). Reprinted with permission from the *Diagnostic and Statistical Manual of Mental Disorders, Fourth Edition, Text Revision.* Copyright 2000 American Psychiatric Association.

OPPOSITIONAL DEFIANT DISORDER AND CONDUCT DISORDER

A great deal of research has been completed on ODD and CD. In much of this work, the diagnoses of ODD and CD are combined and investigated together. This pattern of combining children diagnosed with ODD and those diagnosed with CD is partly due to the similarity in symptoms between the two disorders. As Figure 12.2 shows, there are two primary dimensions onto which symptoms of ODD and CD fall: **covert/overt** and **destructive/nondestructive** (Frick, 1998a).

The covert/overt dimension shows that some behaviors are more secretive (covert), such as stealing, setting fires, running away, and skipping school, whereas others are more obvious (overt), such as fighting, being cruel, arguing, and defying adults. The destructive/nondestructive dimension suggests that some behaviors are more destructive, such as vandalism and being cruel to animals, whereas others are nondestructive, such as using substances and annoying others. Overall, this template helps clarify the organization of symptoms of both ODD and CD.

Because of the overlap of symptoms in both ODD and CD, many researchers have tried to establish commonalities and distinctions between these two disorders. A number of researchers have argued that ODD and CD are

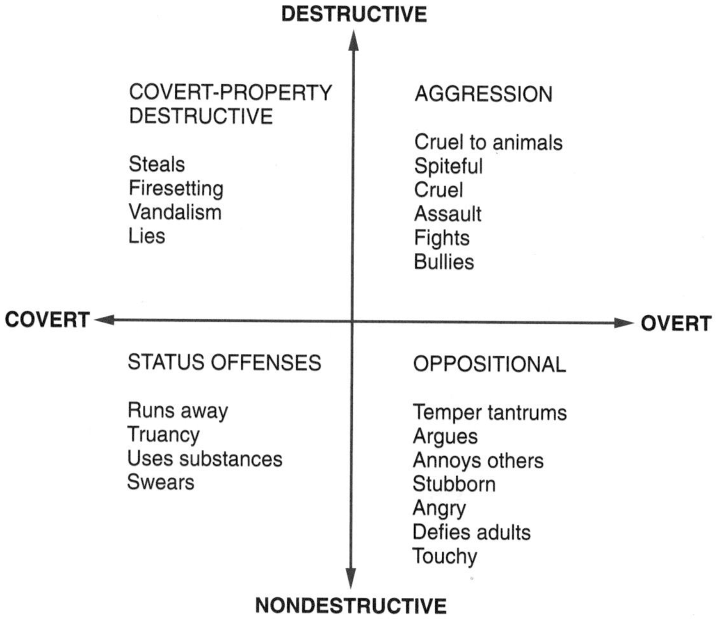

DESTRUCTIVE

COVERT-PROPERTY
DESTRUCTIVE

Steals
Firesetting
Vandalism
Lies

AGGRESSION

Cruel to animals
Spiteful
Cruel
Assault
Fights
Bullies

COVERT ← → **OVERT**

STATUS OFFENSES

Runs away
Truancy
Uses substances
Swears

OPPOSITIONAL

Temper tantrums
Argues
Annoys others
Stubborn
Angry
Defies adults
Touchy

NONDESTRUCTIVE

FIGURE 12.2 These clusters of behaviors are based on the meta-analysis of 60 factor analyses conducted by Frick et al. (1993). The clusters are formed from the intersection of two dimensions of behavior covariation. The horizontal dimension captures a bipolar dimension ranging from overt to covert patterns of behavior, and the vertical dimension captures a dimension ranging from destructive to nondestructive types of behavior.

Source: Frick (1998a).

actually just different ends of the spectrum for the same disorder (reviewed by Borduin, Henggeler, & Manley, 1995). Other researchers, however, have tried to distinguish between the symptoms of the two disorders. In support of the distinctness of the two disorders is the fact that symptoms of ODD tend to have a much earlier onset than the symptoms of CD (Loeber et al., 1991). In addition, nearly all youth diagnosed with CD have a history of

ODD, but not all children with ODD go on to develop CD (Loeber et al., 1991).

Although current mainstream thinking suggests that ODD and CD are distinctly different disorders, the discussion of characteristics of ODD and CD remain intertwined in many professional publications (e.g., Quay & Hogan, 1999). For this reason, the remaining topics of comorbidity, courses of the disorders, etiology, treatment,

Case Study: Stuart, Comorbidity in Action

When he was eight years old, Stuart was referred for psychological evaluation and treatment due to many years of oppositional behavior, overactivity, social problems, and school problems. His mother reported that he had always been overly active and difficult to manage. When he first started school, his teachers found him to be hyperactive, aggressive, and unable to learn. He was known as a class "pest" because he would bother other children when they were working quietly and he would talk back to the teacher. Although he attended school regularly, he could not read or do math. He did, however, know the alphabet.

During the current year of school, Stuart remained aggressive, socially isolated, and impulsive. He soiled his pants frequently. At home, he refused to follow his mother's requests and he threw temper tantrums. Stuart's father was involved minimally with discipline of Stuart because the father had been battling a terminal illness for the past two years. Within the past six months, Stuart's father had been in and out of the hospital. Overall, the family system was very stressed. Following is the diagnostic formulation for Stuart:

Axis I:	Oppositional defiant disorder
	Attention-deficit/hyperactivity disorder, combined type
	Encopresis, without constipation and overflow incontinence
	Reading disorder
	Mathematics disorder
Axis II:	No diagnosis on Axis II
Axis III:	None
Axis IV:	Problems with primary support group: illness in parent
	Educational problems: learning difficulties
Axis V:	Global assessment of functioning (GAF) = 45 (current)
	Global assessment of functioning (GAF) = 50 (highest level past year)

SOURCE: Rapoport & Ismond (1996).

prevention, risk factors, and protective factors are discussed for ODD and CD together. Where possible, specific patterns are mentioned for ODD and CD separately.

Comorbidity

By definition, ODD and CD cannot be diagnosed in the same child at the same time. There are, however, a number of disorders that are highly comorbid with both ODD and CD. In general, higher rates of comorbidity are found in clinical samples than in nonclinical samples (Lahey, Miller, et al., 1999). ODD co-occurs significantly with ADHD (Lahey, Miller, et al., 1999). In addition, ODD is sometimes comorbid with mood disorders, anxiety disorders, and language processing disorders (Greene & Doyle, 1999).

Conduct disorder is very highly comorbid with ADHD (Angold et al., 1999). In samples of CD youth, between 65% and 90% also meet criteria for ADHD (Frick, 1998a). CD is also commonly comorbid with depression and anxiety (Angold et al., 1999; Frick, 1998a). Comorbidity with internalizing disorders is especially salient for girls who are diagnosed with CD (Keenan, Loeber, & Green, 1999). CD and substance use disorders tend to co-occur as well (Borduin et al., 1995). As with so many other disorders, comorbidity with disruptive disorders is the rule rather than the exception.

Courses of the Disorders

Given the characteristic symptoms of ODD and CD, it is important to know that aggression and antisocial behavior are among the most stable behaviors in humans. For example, aggression in kindergarten was predictive of aggression, poor peer relationships, and dysfunctional teacher–child interactions many years later (Ladd & Burgess, 1999). Correlations between earlier and later aggression range from .63 to .92, which suggests that aggression early in childhood is a strong predictor of aggression later in adolescence (Loeber & Stouthamer-Loeber, 1998). These stability estimates are comparable to the stability of intellectual functioning, which is also considered to be among the most stable of human characteristics.

As for the developmental course, ODD tends to develop gradually, with symptoms usually first showing up at home and then generalizing to the school setting (American Psychiatric Association, 2000). With CD, less severe symptoms such as lying and shoplifting tend to show up first and the more severe symptoms, such as burglary and sexual assault, tend to show up later (American Psychiatric Association, 2000). Aggression in either ODD or CD is associated with unemployment in early and middle adulthood (Kokko & Pulkkinen, 2000).

Of great importance are the characteristics that are associated with the progression from ODD to CD to APD. Although not all ODD children develop CD and not all CD adolescents go on to develop APD in adulthood, there is a fair amount of continuity between these disorders (Loeber & Hay, 1997; Maughan & Rutter, 1998). An extensive review of the research literature (Frick & Loney, 1999) reveals that the stability and continuity of these disorders is associated with:

- Parental history of APD or criminal involvement.
- Problematic family environments (e.g., limited parental supervision).
- Low socioeconomic status and economic disadvantage.
- Early onset of severe conduct problems (before the age of 11).
- Severe aggression.

BOX *12.1*

LIKE FATHER, LIKE SON

Whether it is due to genetic transmission, environmental factors, or more likely a combination of the two, there is a strong connection between antisocial behavior in fathers and antisocial behavior in sons (Frick, 1998b; Phares, 1996; 1997b). The fathers of CD boys show much greater rates of APD and aggression than the fathers of nonclinical boys (Goetting, 1994; Reeves, Werry, Elkind, & Zametkin, 1987). Similar results are evident when comparing groups of boys with different diagnoses. Specifically, fathers of CD boys were significantly more likely than fathers of ADHD boys, depressed boys, and anxiety-disordered boys to show APD and aggression (Frick, Lahey, Christ, Loeber, & Green, 1991; Reeves et al., 1987). Overall, there is a clear connection between fathers' and sons' levels of oppositional difficulties, conduct problems, and aggression (Frick, 1998b; Phares, 1996, 1997b).

Shoplifting is a common behavior in adolescents diagnosed with conduct disorder.

- High numbers and large variability of types of conduct problems.
- Comorbidity with ADHD.
- Low intellectual functioning.

As discussed in Box 12.1, there are strong ties between criminality in parents and children, especially between fathers and sons (Frick, 1998b). It is not surprising to learn that the progression from ODD to CD to APD is associated with parental criminality and a history of parental APD. Problematic family environments are also associated with the chronicity of these disorders. For example, parents who do not monitor their children's behavior and parents who are not involved in their children's lives tend to have children who move from ODD to CD to APD (Bird et al., 2001; Dishion et al., 1995). Interparental conflict is also characteristic of the problematic

family environments that are associated with children moving from ODD to CD to APD (Dishion et al., 1995). In general, low socioeconomic status and economic disadvantage are considered risk factors for the development of ODD and CD, but impoverishment is also associated with the chronicity of these disruptive behavior disorders (Luthar, 1999).

As discussed already, earlier onset of severe symptoms is associated with greater chronicity of ODD, CD, and APD (Frick, 1998b). Specifically, early onset of CD is associated with greater likelihood of developing APD in adulthood (American Psychiatric Association, 2000). This pattern makes a great deal of sense when you consider a young child who is already violating the rights of others before he or she even goes through puberty. Severe levels of aggression are also associated with the move from ODD, CD, to APD (McMahon & Wells, 1998). Again, this finding makes a great deal of sense given that ODD children who are aggressive are already showing more severe problems than ODD children who are not violent in their oppositional behavior. Children are also more likely to move from ODD to CD to APD when they show high levels of conduct problems and a great variety in their conduct problems (McMahon & Wells, 1998; G. R. Patterson, 1996). When children have already diversified and become engaged in a number of types of antisocial behaviors, they seem to be more entrenched in this antisocial lifestyle.

Regarding the co-occurrence of other disorders, comorbidity with ADHD is associated with a more severe and chronic outcome (Offord & Bennett, 1996). Interestingly, comorbidity with anxiety is associated with less severe disturbance, and comorbidity with depression is not associated with any patterns related to the course of ODD or CD (Frick, 1998a). Lower intellectual functioning is also associated with the chronic pattern from ODD to CD to APD (McMahon & Wells, 1998). It may be that children with low IQs do not have the intellectual resources to find alternative outlets for their behavior and so remain involved in antisocial activities. Overall, these characteristics are well established from years of research into the chronic patterns of ODD, CD, and APD.

Etiology

One of the ways in which etiological factors for any disorder are studied is to compare and contrast the different correlates of different disorders. As Table 12.6 shows, the correlates of CD and ADHD are different. Thus, although there is a great deal of comorbidity between CD

BOX *12.2*

IS THERE MALICIOUS INTENT?

You are driving the speed limit (like every other law-abiding driver) and someone pulls up on your bumper and starts honking and waving his arms. What do you assume is going on? Do you interpret his actions as hostile, get angry at him, and consider what type of road rage you will exhibit? Do you feel differently when you realize that the man is trying to warn you that your backpack is still on the roof of your car?

Consider another scenario. You leave an acquaintance in your room for a few minutes and when you return you find that your cell phone is broken. What do you assume happened? Was the cell phone already broken before you left the room? Did the acquaintance accidentally break the cell phone? Did she break it on purpose?

These ambiguous vignettes are presented with the idea of showing how attributions can influence reactions. In both scenarios, if your first thought was that the person was trying to do you harm, you would probably respond much more negatively than if you assumed that there was no malicious intent.

Research on attributions (with age-appropriate scenarios, such as losing a ball or breaking a radio) has helped researchers and mental health practitioners identify dysfunctional attributions in aggressive children and adolescents. Specifically, some aggressive children and adolescents interpret ambiguous situations as hostile (Coy, Speltz, DeKlyen, & Jones, 2001; Crick & Dodge, 1994; Dodge & Frame, 1982; Shahinfar, Kupersmidt, & Matza, 2001). Children who exhibit hostile attributional bias often react aggressively when they interpret their peers' behavior in a hostile manner (Dodge & Frame, 1982). This bias tends to be part of a vicious cycle, whereby children's aggressive reactions are met with peer rejection, which is then associated with more aggressive behaviors and the seeking out of deviant peers (C. Johnston & Ohan, 1999).

The connections between attributions and behaviors have indicated two types of aggression: reactive aggression and proactive aggression. Reactive aggression occurs when children interpret an action as threatening and then react to it defensively (Dodge & Coie, 1987). Proactive aggression occurs without any perceived provocation, with the intent of gaining something from the aggressive behavior, such as stealing a basketball (Dodge & Coie, 1987). Reactive aggression is more prevalent in children with a history of physical abuse, poor peer relationships, and social-cognitive processing deficits (Dodge, Lochman, Harnish, Bates, & Pettit, 1997; D. Schwartz et al., 1998). Proactive aggression is associated with children who show callous–unemotional traits (Frick, 1998b).

Overall, this research on social-cognitive factors related to aggression has identified important subtypes of aggressive children and adolescents. This work has helped researchers identify prevention strategies that can challenge children's hostile attributional biases (Coie & Jacobs, 1993).

---

and ADHD, there appears to be specific and different etiological correlates to each of the two disorders.

A number of compelling etiological theories attempt to explain the development of ODD and CD; these include genetic and biological influences, familial psychosocial factors, and environmental influences. Compared to ADHD, there is more support for environmental influences than for genetic or biological influences in the development of ODD and CD (Frick, 1998a). For example, poor parenting during infancy is associated with risk for the development of externalizing disorders in later adolescence (S. L. Olson, Bates, Sandy, & Lanthier, 2000; Shaw, Owens, Giovannelli, & Winslow, 2001). Also see Box 12.2 for a cognitive explanation of aggression.

Support for genetic and biological influences in the development of ODD and CD comes from the connections between parental psychopathology (especially APD) and CD, as well as findings from studies of twins (Altepeter & Korger, 1999; Lytton, 2000; Simonoff, Pickles, Meyer, Silberg, & Maes, 1998; Taylor, Iacono, & McGue, 2000). For example, identical twins tend to have higher concordance rates for CD than do fraternal twins, which suggests a genetic component in the development of CD (Altepeter & Korger, 1999). One twin study of CD in Australia found that a high percentage of the variance

TABLE 12.6 Summary of the Differential Correlates to Conduct Disorder and ADHD

Conduct Disorder	ADHD
Parental criminality/antisocial behavior	Parental ADHD
Parental substance abuse	Poor academic achievement
Ineffective parenting practices	Poor performance on neuro-psychological tests of frontal lobe functioning
Parental divorce/marital conflict	Poor response inhibition
Socioeconomic disadvantage	

SOURCE: Frick (1998b).

was accounted for by genetic influences (Slutske et al., 1997). In addition, there is evidence that temperamental style, which is thought to be partially genetically determined, is associated with the possible development of CD. Specifically, having a difficult temperament in infancy is associated with aggression in later childhood (Altepeter & Korger, 1999).

There has also been evidence to suggest that the brain functioning of ODD and CD children differs from that of nonclinical children. Specifically, studies of EEG recordings suggest that children with disruptive disorders show different brain functioning in the frontal lobe when compared with nonclinical children (Baving, Laucht, & Schmidt, 2000). The frontal lobe has also been implicated in a number of other disorders, including ADHD (Barkley, 1998; Baving et al., 2000). The actual mechanisms of transmission, however, are not well established at this point.

In addition to the possibility of genetic predispositions to CD, a number of familial psychosocial factors have been implicated in the development of ODD and CD (C. L. Carlson, Tamm, & Hogan, 1999; Kilgore, Snyder, & Lentz, 2000). Many of these factors focus on less than optimal parenting practices. These parenting practices are found in both mothers and fathers, and remain significant even after controlling for genetic effects (J. M. Meyer et al., 2000). The following is a partial list of parenting characteristics that have been associated with the development of ODD and CD (Frick, 1998b):

- Inadequate monitoring of the child's behavior.
- Limited involvement in the child's life.

JIMMY, SIXTH-GENERATION PAIN IN THE ASS

- Inconsistent, harsh, and potentially abusive discipline practices.
- Limited warmth and positive reinforcement of the child's accomplishments.
- Inadequate problem-solving skills.
- High levels of interparental conflict, especially in front of the child.
- Chronic coercive and negative interactions with the child.

All of these factors have been studied extensively, and all have received support for playing a causative role in the development of ODD and CD (G. R. Patterson, 1996). In a seminal book entitled *Coercive Family Process*, Dr. Gerald R. Patterson (1982) described the **coercion theory** of families with an oppositional and conduct disordered child: Parents exhibit inadequate and harsh parenting practices, children react by acting out, which in turn leads to more harsh parenting. It is important to acknowledge the reciprocal nature of interactions within families: The family is a system and parents influence children, but children also influence parents. Note that these patterns are evident in both the mother–child and father–child relationship (Denham et al., 2000).

In addition to genetic, biological, and familial influences, there is also support for environmental influences in the development of ODD and CD. The primary environmental influence associated with the onset of ODD and CD is living in poverty (McGee & Williams, 1999). Socioeconomic disadvantage has been found consistently to be linked to the development of ODD and CD. The specific mechanisms are not well known, given that many children who grow up in poverty do not develop any emotional/behavioral problems (McGee & Williams, 1999). It may be that socioeconomic disadvantage is tied to a number of other risk factors, such as exposure to violence, inadequate housing and nutrition, stress, and deviant peers (Luthar, 1999; Perez-Smith, Albus, & Weist, 2001). See Box 12.3 for a discussion of race/ethnicity disadvantage and aggression.

Deviant peers, in particular, have been linked to conduct problems. In the process known as **deviancy training**, adolescents with conduct problems tend to exacerbate problem behaviors in other adolescents (Dishion, McCord, & Poulin, 1999; Dishion, Spracklen, Andrews, & Patterson, 1996; Poulin, Dishion, and Haas, 1999). Unfortunately, higher percentages of deviant peers are evident in impoverished neighborhoods and environments (Luthar, 1999).

Figure 12.3 is an illustration of the many environmental influences that çan be involved in the development of ODD and CD (Dishion et al., 1995). As the figure shows, children and adolescents are influenced by interpersonal factors, relationship processes, behavior settings, and community contexts. All of these factors are important to consider in the development of oppositional behavior and conduct problems (Dishion et al., 1995).

Overall, there is support for a number of etiological explanations of the development of ODD and CD, but there is no one theory that has gained support exclusively. Rather, it is probable that ODD and CD are developed due to a number of factors, including a genetic predisposition combined with inadequate parenting and less than optimal environmental factors (Lahey, Waldman, & McBurnett, 1999; Quay & Hogan, 1999).

Note, however, that because of the potentially causative role that family factors play in the development of ODD and CD, clinicians should assess characteristics of the family as well as the child referred for an evaluation (McMahon & Estes, 1997). Thus, in addition to conducting a thorough evaluation of the child, clinicians should evaluate parental functioning (e.g., psychopathology); parenting practices (e.g., level of monitoring); interparental conflict; and relevant environmental characteristics of the family (McMahon & Estes, 1997). This type of thorough assessment will not only help delineate the nature of the problems in the child's life but will also help in the treatment of oppositional behavior and conduct problems.

Greatness is not secured by violence.

—Proverb of Africa

Treatment

A comprehensive review of treatments for ODD and CD identified two treatments as well established and empirically supported (Brestan & Eyberg, 1998). Both are variants of **behavioral parent training**, which focuses on teaching parents appropriate and effective parenting strategies. One treatment is administered via videotape and allows parents to observe other parents modeling appropriate parenting skills (Webster-Stratton, 1990, 1994). Clinicians usually show groups of parents the videotape and then lead discussions on how to implement the strategies in the parents' own families. The other treatment is usually administered with groups of parents and follows a manual called *Living with Children: New Methods for Parents and Teachers* (G. R. Patterson & Gullion, 1968). Both methods include teaching parents to:

- Monitor their children's behavior and activities (e.g., knowing their children's friends, discussing where the child goes after school and when out with friends).

- Pay attention to good behavior (even if parents have to "catch" their child being good) and reward it.

- Identify and provide consequences for inappropriate behavior (e.g., providing consistent negative conse-

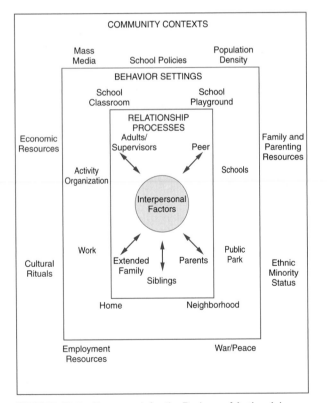

FIGURE 12.3 Framework for the Ecology of Antisocial Behavior

Source: Dishion et al. (1995).

PROMOTING PARENTS' PROBLEM-SOLVING AND EFFECTIVE COPING STRATEGIES

Source: Webster-Stratton & Herbert (1994).

BOX *12.3*

RACE, ETHNICITY, AND RESEARCH METHODOLOGY

No clear racial or ethnic patterns are evident regarding prevalence rates of ODD or CD. Some studies find more Caucasian American youth evidencing CD, others find more African American youth evidencing CD, and still others find more Latino/Hispanic youth evidencing CD (Lahey, Waldman, et al., 1999). Thus, there are no clear patterns of CD regarding race and ethnicity.

Why, then, is there evidence of higher rates of aggression and antisocial behavior in ethnic minorities when compared to Caucasian Americans? A number of studies have documented that African Americans as a group display higher rates of aggressive and delinquent behavior than Caucasian Americans as a group (Hinshaw & Park, 1999). Other studies have shown that African American adolescent boys who do not have a job are at increased risk for externalizing problems, such as juvenile delinquency (Luthar, 1999). When compared with Caucasian American youth, African American youth in impoverished urban neighborhoods appear to become involved in criminal activities to a greater extent and to be less cautious about others' continuing involvement in crime (Luthar, 1999). Overall, the line of research that explores aggression and criminal activity has found consistent racial and ethnic differences, especially when African Americans are compared with Caucasian Americans.

The findings from these two lines of research appear contradictory. That is, they do so until you look closely at the research methods used in the studies. Most of the studies that explore delinquency in youth use samples of adjudicated and incarcerated youth (Yung & Hammond, 1997). Thus, when racial and ethnic differences are found in adolescents in juvenile detention facilities, a number of factors other than actual behavior could be involved. Of foremost concern are the possibly discriminatory practices regarding arrest, detention, and sentencing (Yung & Hammond, 1997). It may be that African Americans are more at risk for arrest, detention, and incarceration (rather than probation) than are Caucasian Americans (Yung & Hammond, 1997).

Given that there are no clear differences in CD for different racial and ethnic groups when large-scale epidemiological studies are completed, it is likely that factors other than behavior are related to the racial and ethnic differences that are found in studies of incarcerated youth (Hinshaw & Park, 1999). In addition, when socioeconomic status is controlled for in these studies, racial and ethnic differences disappear (Hinshaw & Park, 1999). In other words, aggressive and criminal behaviors found in samples of adjudicated youth appear to be strongly associated with poverty rather than race and ethnicity per se. These issues highlight the importance of understanding the design of a study in relation to its results.

---

quences for maladaptive behavior or, when appropriate, ignoring bad behavior).

- Remain calm and consistent when implementing consequences to maladaptive behavior.

- Instigate warm and caring interactions with children.

These principles from behavioral parent training have been found to be effective in decreasing maladaptive behavior in oppositional and conduct-disordered children (Brestan & Eyberg, 1998), as well as in hyperactive and inattentive children (Pelham, Wheeler, & Chronis, 1998).

Ten other treatments for ODD and CD have been found to be probably efficacious (Brestan & Eyberg, 1998):

1. Anger control training.
2. Anger coping therapy.
3. Assertiveness training.
4. Delinquency prevention program.
5. Multisystemic therapy.
6. Parent–child interaction therapy.
7. Parent training program.
8. Problem-solving skills training.
9. Rational-emotive therapy.
10. Time-out plus signal seat treatment.

The details of these treatments are beyond the scope of this book, but note that nearly all of the treatments are behavioral or cognitive-behavioral. Most of them are considered probably efficacious rather than well supported because further research is needed to replicate the initial positive findings (Brestan & Eyberg, 1998; Sheldrick, Kendall, & Heimberg, 2001). Other variations on behavioral parent training also look promising. For example, in a success-based, noncoercive treatment program that is similar to behavioral parent training, mothers of young children from violent homes were able to learn appropriate parenting skills, which were associated with decreased child behavior problems (Ducharme, Atkinson, & Poulton, 2000).

Case Study: Partying Patricia

Just like in Chapter 7 (Devastated Darryl) and Chapter 10 (Shy Sylvia), you get to create a treatment plan for a complex case. Clinicians often use treatment plans to help guide their therapeutic strategies and to evaluate whether or not those strategies have been successful.

After jotting down your own treatment plan for this case, take a look at the suggestions reprinted from The Family Therapy Treatment Planner *(Dattilio & Jongsma, 2000) and compare your treatment plan with one that a professional might have developed.*

Patricia is a 16-year-old Caucasian girl who lives with her biological mother, stepfather, and three younger brothers (one of whom is a biological brother and two of whom are her half-brothers, ages 13, 6, and 4, respectively). Patricia and her mother argue almost constantly about nearly every aspect of Patricia's life (e.g., school, friends, dating, caring for her younger siblings, style of clothes, and curfew). For example, Patricia has begun wearing clothes that are "like a prostitute," according to her mother. Although Patricia's stepfather tries to stay out of the arguments, he has recently found it necessary to step in and try to gain control of Patricia's behavior (which has lead to even more conflict in the family). Patricia's mother appreciates her husband's attempt to control Patricia but feels that he is taking away her authority with her daughter. Patricia's mother and stepfather find themselves arguing about Patricia with increasing frequency, and even her younger brothers seem distressed by the situation.

Patricia feels that both her mother and her stepfather are painfully out-of-date in their ideas about teenagers. For example, she reports that none of her friends have a curfew and so she feels justified in coming home at 4:00 A.M. on weekends. Most often, Patricia attends parties at the local college where her boyfriend lives in a fraternity house. Although her parents have set a curfew of midnight, they are usually unable to stay up that late to see if Patricia makes it home on time. Patricia has skipped from school frequently to spend time with her boyfriend. She plans to get an apartment with him when she is 18 so that she can escape from her parents' rules.

Patricia's parents report that she used to be a warm, friendly child who was always compliant with adults. Her biological parents divorced when she was very young, and she has limited contact with her biological father. Patricia's mother and stepfather married when Patricia was 6 and her biological brother was 3. Her youngest brothers were born when she was 10 and 12. Her parents report that she used to like helping with the babies, but that for the past few years she has withdrawn significantly from helping around the house. Although she continues to be affectionate with her younger siblings, she no longer is willing to take care of them when asked. During the past few years, the arguments between Patricia and her mother have increased. The most recent argument had to do with how Patricia wants to spend spring break. According to Patricia, "All of my friends are going to stay in a hotel on the beach for the whole week and my stupid parents won't let me go." Unbeknownst to her parents, Patricia plans to go away with her boyfriend for spring break.

During the initial interview with Patricia, her parents, and her younger brothers, it appeared obvious where the lines have been drawn. For example, Patricia sat on a chair by herself separate from the rest of the family, while her brothers and parents crowded cozily onto a large couch. Patricia was jovial with her brothers but seemed to disagree with nearly every statement made by her parents. She sighed loudly when her mother talked and said "Ugh" when her mother began to cry. When asked directly about her experiences, Patricia reported that she just wanted her parents to get off her back so that she could be an adult. She frequently cited how "uptight" her parents were and wished aloud that they were more like her friends' parents who allegedly do not set limits on their teenagers' behavior.

Patricia's medical history was significant for asthma, which has since been managed effectively. Her developmental history was notable in that she achieved major milestones (e.g., crawling, walking, talking, toilet training, reading, and writing) significantly earlier than expected.

Treatment Plan

Please create a treatment plan for Patricia and her family. You should include behavioral definitions, long-term goals, short-term objectives, and therapeutic interventions. It may be most helpful to consider this case from a family systems perspective. After you have developed your own treatment plan, please compare it with the treatment plan from *The Family Therapy Treatment Planner* (Dattilio & Jongsma, 2000).

Behavioral Definitions

1. _____
2. _____
3. _____
4. _____
5. _____
6. _____
7. _____
8. _____
9. _____
10. _____

Long-Term Goals

1. _____
2. _____
3. _____
4. _____
5. _____
6. _____
7. _____
8. _____
9. _____
10. _____

(continued)

Case Study: Partying Patricia   *(continued)*

Short-Term Objectives	Therapeutic Interventions
1. _____	1. _____
2. _____	2. _____
3. _____	3. _____
4. _____	4. _____
5. _____	5. _____
6. _____	6. _____
7. _____	7. _____
8. _____	8. _____
9. _____	9. _____
10. _____	10. _____

From *The Family Therapy Treatment Planner*—Dattilio and Jongsma (2000)

ADOLESCENT/PARENT CONFLICTS

BEHAVIORAL DEFINITIONS

1. Parents experience conflicts with adolescent child that begin to interfere with the family's overall functioning.
2. Parents argue with each other over how to respond to the adolescent's disruptive nonconforming behaviors.
3. Family members resent the adolescent-centered conflict, increasing tension in the home.
4. Parents feel a loss of control and the adolescent feels empowered by parent's dilemma, making his/her own rules and resisting parental intervention.
5. Adolescent acts out in areas of substance abuse, sexuality, school performance, and/or delinquency.

LONG-TERM GOALS

1. Parents arrive at some level of agreement regarding how to respond to the adolescent.
2. Parents reduce the effects of the adolescent's misbehavior on other family members.
3. Parents learn new methods for working together to achieve harmony and balance in the family.
4. Parents devise and enforce a set of rules and standards that promote peace and harmony in the family.
5. Parents feel empowered to take control of the family and react firmly to adolescent acting out.

SHORT-TERM OBJECTIVES

1. Define the specifics about what needs to change in the adolescent's behavior.
2. Parents clarify philosophy on parenting expectations for the adolescent.
3. Parents and adolescent cooperate with psychological testing to identify specific areas of parent/child conflict.
4. Identify family, school, or marital factors that may be contributing to the adolescent's undesirable behavior.
5. Parents identify their strengths and weaknesses in parenting style.
6. Parents read books and watch videotapes on parenting adolescents.
7. Parents develop and implement a monitoring system for the adolescent's whereabouts, and indicate any deficiencies in the monitoring system.
8. Parents identify and record the occurrence of a specific desirable behavior of the adolescent's that they would like to see increase in frequency.
9. Implement a behavioral contract to increase the frequency of the adolescent's target behavior.
10. Increase the frequency of positive social- or activity- oriented interactions between parents and the adolescent.

THERAPEUTIC INTERVENTIONS

1. Open up the forum for family members to share their perception of the adolescent's behavior and discuss feelings about the adolescent's behavior.
2. Assess whether the adolescent's acting-out behavior is transient or is a more stable pattern.
3. Have parents share their philosophy on parenting and what expectations they have for their son or daughter.
4. Explore familial interaction patterns or dynamics that may be exacerbating the conflict between adolescent and parents (underlying conflicts, family-of-origin issues, unrealistic expectations, marital problems, etc.).
5. Explore familial interaction patterns or dynamics that may be exacerbating the conflict between adolescent and parents (underlying conflicts, family-of-origin issues, unrealistic expectations, marital problems, etc.).
6. Explore environmental stressors that may be exacerbating the adolescent's acting out (e.g., family transitions, inconsistent rules, school or social difficulties, peer relationships, or peer pressure).
7. Role-play a parent/adolescent conflict to assess how parents solve the problem; give parents feedback regarding the strengths and weaknesses of their approach.

(continued)

Case Study: Partying Patricia *(continued)*

11. Establish and implement consequences for negative adolescent behavior (e.g., the use of response cost).

12. Parents identify and make an effort to terminate any undesirable behaviors that they may be modeling for the adolescent.

13. Parents confer with each other frequently to increase mutual support in parenting.

14. Parents use structured dialogue techniques to ensure good parental communication for problem solving.

15. Parents minimize criticism of the other's parenting efforts.

16. Parents discuss disagreements only at times when discussion is likely to be constructive, and not in the presence of the children.

17. Parents identify and replace distorted cognitive beliefs that relate to parenting their teenager.

18. Family members hold family meetings regularly and conform to the rules of interaction.

19. Family members demonstrate empathy and respect for other individual's points of view by paraphrasing or reflecting speaker's position before responding.

20. Parents list alternatives to their current parenting methods.

21. Parents enact alternative parenting styles and evaluate their effectiveness.

22. Identify and challenge unreasonable beliefs and expectations regarding adolescent behaviors.

23. Parents establish consistent house rules and regulations.

24. Family establishes a regular dinner hour and sets rules regarding how often members will be present.

25. Parents go out alone at least one night per week for socialization and/or recreation.

8. Teach how the adolescent's strengths can be augmented and his/her weaknesses diminished.

9. Ask parents to develop monitoring for their adolescent, knowing *where* he/she is, *who* he/she is with, *what* he/she is doing, and *when* he/she will be home.

10. Assign parents to record their joint monitoring efforts with the adolescent as a homework assignment.

11. Ask parents to discuss their successes at monitoring and to identify events or situations in which monitoring requires improvement.

12. Ask parents to select a behavior of the adolescent's that they would like to see decrease or diminish. Ask them to record its occurrence every day for a week, and notice the behaviors or situations that precede it (antecedents) and follow it (consequences).

13. Have parents decide on an appropriate reward system (e.g., verbal praise, use of the car, allowance) to reinforce the positive target behavior of the adolescent; seek agreement between parents and adolescent for this behavioral contract.

14. Recommend that each parent increase the number of parent-initiated, casual, positive conversations with the adolescent.

15. Develop with parents a response cost/procedure to use in conjunction with the adolescent's targeted negative behavior; assign implementation and review success.

16. If parents are modeling for the adolescent the behavior they would like to extinguish (e.g., yelling or becoming sarcastic), have parents become aware and contract to change their own behavior before trying to change the same behavior in the adolescent.

17. Teach parents techniques of anger control to better mediate conflict.

18. Ask parents to role-play support for each other regarding their reaction to the adolescent's misbehavior; have the supportive parent ask (in a supportive, non-threatening manner) how the other parent deals with the misbehavior and whether the supportive parent can do anything in the future to help.

19. Have parents contract to support the other's parenting by not interfering during the other's parent/adolescent interactions or with the other's decisions (i.e., avoid splitting their parental unity.

20. Help each parent identify when they are engaging in criticizing the other parent in a nonconstructive manner.

21. Help parents establish a practice of meeting in private so they can discuss parenting decisions and come to a mutual agreement before presenting it to the adolescent.

One of these treatments, **multisystemic therapy**, provides insight into a comprehensive treatment for oppositional and conduct-disordered youth (Henggeler, Schoenwald, Borduin, Rowland, & Cunningham, 1998). The idea behind multisystemic therapy is that children and adolescents with conduct problems have difficulties at a number of different levels (personal, social/peers, familial, societal) and experience difficulties in a number of different settings (home, school, neighborhood, larger community). The therapy is designed to intervene at whatever level and in whatever context necessary. Thus, for any given adolescent, the therapist may engage in individual therapy, family therapy, school consultation, peer interventions, or couples therapy with the adolescent's parents (Henggeler et al., 1998). Therapeutic interventions are equally as diverse. Although many of the interventions are behavioral or cognitive-behavioral, therapists use the therapeutic orientation that seems most appropriate for that adolescent and that family. At the core of multisystemic therapy is that children and adolescents are part of systems that must be treated (Henggeler et al., 1998), which is consistent with the rationale for family therapy with delinquent adolescents (Robbins, Alexander, & Turner, 2000).

Multisystemic therapy has been found to be very effective, even with chronic juvenile offenders (Henggeler et al., 1998). The strongest improvements have been found when therapists closely follow the multisystemic therapy guidelines (Huey, Henggeler, Brondino, & Pickrel, 2000). Adolescents who received the treatment showed fewer behavioral problems and were less likely to be re-arrested than were adolescents who received "usual services." Note, however, that like other treatments for conduct problems, multisystemic therapy does not work for everyone. One follow-up study found that 71% of adolescents who received "usual services" had been re-arrested within four years, whereas 26% of adolescents who received multisystemic therapy had been re-arrested in that same time period (McMahon & Wells, 1998). This difference in re-arrest rate shows that multisystemic therapy can be successful, but the 26% figure (i.e., more than one-fourth of the adolescents who received multisystemic therapy were still re-arrested) also shows the difficulty of treating these adolescents.

Multisystemic therapy has also been used with adolescents who abuse substances and with adolescent sex offenders (Henggeler et al., 1998). The treatment was most effective when therapists were well trained and well supervised. Overall, multisystemic therapy is a promising therapy for children and adolescents who may have no other therapeutic alternatives (McMahon & Wells, 1998).

For all of these treatments, it appears that treatments are less effective when conduct-disordered clients and their families perceive barriers to the treatment (Kazdin & Wassell, 1999). Barriers to treatment include stressors (such as disagreements about taking part in therapy), treatment demands (such as perceiving that treatment is too demanding or costly), relevance of treatment (such as feeling that the treatment is relevant to the child's problems), and relationship with the therapist (such as feeling supported by the therapist). Higher levels of perceived

barriers to treatment were associated with less therapeutic improvement in conduct-disordered children (Kazdin & Wassell, 1999). Overall, clients' perceptions of barriers to therapy should be considered when working with conduct-disordered youth and their families.

In addition to the therapeutic interventions just reviewed, medications have also been used to treat ODD and CD. Due to the high levels of comorbidity with ADHD, many ODD and CD children are treated with stimulants such as Ritalin (methylphenidate), Dexedrine (dextroamphetamine), and Cylert (pemoline; Altepeter & Korger, 1999; R. T. Brown & Sawyer, 1998). In general, these medications tend to be most effective for children who are comorbid with ADHD, but there is some evidence that stimulants may reduce aggressive behaviors in some ODD and CD children and adolescents who are not comorbid with ADHD (Altepeter & Korger, 1999). Clonidine, which was established originally to treat hypertension, can be used to treat hyperactivity, low frustration tolerance, aggressive behaviors, and oppositional behaviors. There are, however, potentially serious side effects to Clonidine, such as extreme hypertension if the medication is withdrawn suddenly (Altepeter & Korger, 1999). Also note that Clonidine has not been studied in clinical trials for the treatment of aggression and low frustration tolerance (McMahon & Wells, 1998). Thus, its use should be studied further before widely prescribing it for conduct problems.

Other medications tend to be used for symptoms that are associated with oppositional behaviors and conduct problems. For example, lithium has been used to decrease aggression when there are also high levels of mania. Antipsychotic medications have also been used to decrease aggression (R. T. Brown & Sawyer, 1998). Antidepressant medications and antianxiety medications are used with ODD and CD children who are comorbid for depression and anxiety, respectively. One antianxiety medication, Buspar (buspirone) has received recent attention for its effectiveness in reducing aggression and assaultive behavior in children diagnosed with ODD or CD (Altepeter & Korger, 1999).

Overall, there are a number of promising treatments for ODD and CD, but the disorders continue to be difficult to treat. Because of the intense parental involvement that is required in the most effective therapies, treatment effectiveness relies on parents' abilities to a large extent. For this reason, a number of treatments have been tried in the school system (Hoff & DuPaul, 1998). One year-long psychoeducational treatment program for youngsters was not effective in reducing disruptive behavior at two-year follow-up (Shelton et al., 2000). Conversely, one after-school treatment program for early-career juvenile offenders was effective at reducing the likelihood of future criminal offenses (W. C. Myers et al., 2000).

Given the functional impairments that are present in the parents of many ODD and CD children (e.g., parental psychopathology, interparental conflict, disengaged parenting styles), it is not surprising to find that many ODD and CD children cannot be helped effectively by the treatments that are known to work, especially those without a parental treatment component. Some children with severe conduct problems are placed in residential facilities or therapeutic foster care settings (Chamberlain, 1996). Many of these facilities use a variety of the treatments just described. The most effective residential facilities use multiple therapies that focus on many different aspects of adolescents, their family, their peer group, and their environment (Chamberlain, 1996).

Unfortunately, a number of interventions through the juvenile justice system are not effective. Boot camps, for example, are associated with either no therapeutic gains or even higher rates of re-arrest than are services as usual (M. Jones, 1997). Thus, effective programs for the treatment of CD and criminal behavior require multimodal involvement from youth, families, schools, and the community (Henggeler et al., 1998). When children and adolescents receive effective treatments for conduct problems, there are often improvements not only in the child or adolescent but also in the parents and in the family system (Kazdin & Wassell, 2000). Thus, the search for effective treatments for conduct problems continues, with the hope of finding ways to improve the lives of children, adolescents, their families, and members of their social network.

Prevention

Because of the personal and societal costs of ODD and CD, a number of prevention programs have attempted to prevent these disorders from ever developing (August, Realmuto, Hektner, & Bloomquist, 2001; Farrell, Meyer, & White, 2001; Koretz & Lazar, 1992; Reid, 1993; Stoolmiller, Eddy, & Reid, 2000; T. K. Taylor, Eddy, & Biglan, 1999; Tremblay, LeMarquand, & Vitaro, 1999). Box 12.4 presents a discussion of television violence, which also has ramifications for prevention programs. Prevention programs have included work with:

- Social skills and interpersonal skills training.
- Academic skills training.
- Parenting skills training (including individuals who were expecting their first child).
- Peer training.

BOX *12.4*

DOES TELEVISION CAUSE VIOLENCE?

Nearly every time there is a school shooting or other horrific act of violence perpetrated by a youngster, a discussion of television violence will undoubtedly take place. There is no question that violence is pervasive in the media and that children watch a great deal of television. A total of 71.2% of television programs shown in prime time have some violent content, with an average of 5.3 violent scenes per hour (Huston & Wright, 1998). On Saturday mornings, 92.0% of programs were found to contain violence, with 23.0 violent scenes per hour (Huston & Wright, 1998). Preschoolers, on average, watch 27 hours of television per week (Centerwall, 2000). Overall, reviews of the scholarly literature and meta-analyses conclude consistently that television violence is associated with higher levels of aggression (Huston & Wright, 1998). But why do some television watchers become more violent than others?

One possible explanation is the context of the violence (Kunkel et al., 1995). Violence that is perceived as real is associated with higher levels of aggression than fictional violence, such as violence in cartoons (Huston & Wright, 1998). Violence that encourages viewers to identify with the aggressor is also associated with higher levels of aggression (Donnerstein, Slaby, & Eron, 1994).

There are also familial characteristics that must be considered when investigating the effects of television violence. For example, children of parents who communicate with them and show high levels of warmth toward them tend to view fewer acts of violence on television than do other children (Huston & Wright, 1998). Given that ODD and CD are associated with harsh parenting, it would not be surprising to find that aggressive children seek out violent programming (Huston & Wright, 1998).

Overall, the connections between television violence and children's aggression are complex. Although there is no question about the connection between viewing violence and exhibiting aggression, the causal links have yet to be established.

- Day care worker training.
- Teacher training.
- School-based preventive interventions.

In addition to programs that are targeted at preventing oppositional problems and conduct problems specifically, there are a host of other prevention programs that could indirectly reduce the likelihood of ODD and CD. For example, programs that attempt to prevent violence within the family, such as child physical abuse, may indirectly help prevent ODD and CD since physical abuse is a risk factor for the development of these disorders (Jouriles et al., 2001; Murray, Guerra, & Williams, 1997).

One representative prevention program that targets CD specifically is a delinquency prevention program (Tremblay, Pagani-Kurtz, Masse, Vitaro, & Phil, 1995) for preschoolers at risk for the development of ODD and CD. The researchers who developed this program taught the basic principles of behavioral parent training to parents of preschool children who were identified as at risk for the development of ODD and CD. In order to reach out to these parents, the researchers visited the families' homes, rather than expecting the families to attend meetings at the research center. This type of outreach was found to be an effective way to engage families in preventive interventions. Overall, this prevention program reduced the incidence of ODD and CD, even when children were followed up six years later (Tremblay et al., 1999).

Another far-reaching prevention program is the Families and Schools Together (FAST) program (Conduct Problems Prevention Research Group, 1992), which targets first-graders at risk for conduct problems and provides enrichment services for the child, family, and school. Specifically, first-grade teachers provide a 57-session program to promote social competence, program staff provide academic tutoring and social skills training, and a family coordinator provides parent training and home visits (Conduct Problems Prevention Research Group, 1999a, 1999b; Orrell-Valente, Pinderhughes, Valente, & Laird, 1999). Overall, the FAST program is very effective at lowering the risk of aggression, hyperactivity, and disruptive behaviors and is effective at increasing children's social competence, academic functioning, and emotional well-being (Conduct Problems Prevention Research Group, 1999a, 1999b; Orrell-Valente et al., 1999). Interestingly, matching family coordinators on race/ethnicity and socioeconomic status with the families increases the family members' engagement with the program (Orrell-Valente et al., 1999). Overall, the FAST program is a very useful program for the prevention of ODD and CD.

The most effective prevention programs tend to provide multiple levels of preventive interventions, such as working with children, parents, and teachers (T. K. Taylor et al., 1999). A television series on families and the Positive Parenting Program together suggest that the mass media can be effective in the prevention of defiant behaviors (Sanders, Montgomery, & Brechman-Toussaint, 2000). The home-school partnership is especially important for comprehensive prevention programs (Webster-Stratton, 1993b). Decreasing associations with deviant peers is also very important for the long-term prevention

---

Case Study: Eddie, Wally, and Deana Try to Make Sense Out of "Being Bad"

The following is a verbatim transcript of a discussion between a teacher and her kindergarten students. Apparently, the concepts of good and bad depend on the adult's response.

EDDIE: Sometimes I hate myself.

TEACHER: When?

EDDIE: When I'm naughty.

TEACHER: What do you do that's naughty?

EDDIE: You know, naughty words. Like "shit." That one.

TEACHER: That makes you hate yourself?

EDDIE: Yeah, when my dad washes my mouth with soap.

TEACHER: What if he doesn't hear you?

EDDIE: Then I get away with it. Then I don't hate myself.

WALLY: If I'm bad, like take the food when it's not time to eat yet and my mom makes me leave the kitchen, then I hate myself because I want to stay with her in the kitchen.

EDDIE: And here's another reason when I don't like myself. This is a good reason. Sometimes I try to get the cookies on top of the refrigerator.

TEACHER: What's the reason you don't like yourself?

EDDIE: Because my mom counts to ten fast and I get a spanking and my grandma gets mad at her.

DEANA: Here's when I *like* myself: when I'm coloring and my mommy says, "Stop coloring. We have to go out." And I tell her I'm coloring and she says "Okay, I'll give you ten more minutes."

TEACHER: What if you have to stop what you're doing?

DEANA: When she's in a big hurry. That's when she yells at me. Then I don't like myself.

SOURCE: Paley (1981, pp. 54–55). Reprinted by permission of the publisher from *Wally's Stories* by Vivian G. Paley, Cambridge, Mass.: Harvard University Press, Copyright © 1981 by the President and Fellows of Harvard College.

of CD (Vitaro, Brendgen, Pagani, Tremblay, & McDuff, 1999; Vitaro, Brendgen, & Tremblay, 2000). More work is needed, however, to establish and institute effective prevention programs (Tremblay et al., 1999).

It is better to spend the night in irritation at an offense than in repentance for taking revenge.

—Proverb of Africa

OPPOSITIONAL PROBLEMS AND CONDUCT PROBLEMS CONCEPTUALIZED IN A DIMENSIONAL MANNER

Unlike ADHD, oppositional problems and conduct problems have often been conceptualized is a dimensional

manner (Lahey, Miller, et al., 1999). As the case study of Jose illustrated earlier in the chapter, the "terrible twos" can look surprisingly similar to serious oppositional problems. One study found that 40% of preschoolers exhibited at least one antisocial behavior each day, such as pushing or shoving other children, or doing something sneaky (Willoughby, Kupersmidt, & Bryant, 2001). Both oppositional behaviors and mild conduct problems occur frequently throughout childhood in most children. Even within nonclinical samples, oppositional behaviors tend to decrease over time whereas conduct-related problems tend to increase over time (Loeber et al., 1991).

One example of conceptualizing oppositional and conduct problems in a dimensional manner is illustrated with the use of the Child Behavior Checklist (Achenbach & Rescorla, 2001). Figure 12.4 shows a behavior profile completed by the father of a 15-year-old boy with aggres-

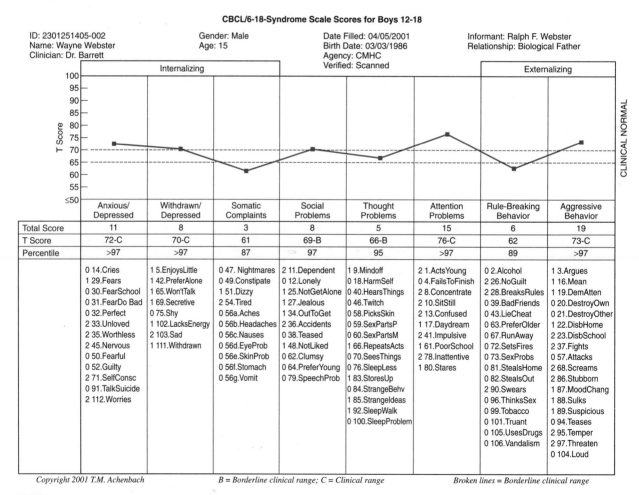

FIGURE 12.4   Computer-Scored Syndrome Profile from CBCL Completed for Wayne Webster by His Father

Source: Achenbach & Rescorla (2001).

sive problems. This profile represents a pattern of both externalizing problems (i.e., aggressive problems) and internalizing problems (i.e., anxious/depressed, withdrawn/depressed) as well as other problems (i.e., social problems, attention problems).

Overall, dimensional conceptualizations of oppositional and conduct problems are useful. Some researchers have even argued that ODD and CD should be conceptualized as a continuum of disruptive behaviors rather than two separate disorders (reviewed by Borduin et al., 1995). In either case, a number of risk factors are associated with the development of oppositional and conduct problems. Many of these risk factors have been targeted for prevention efforts in order to decrease the likelihood that children would develop oppositional and conduct problems (McMahon & Wells, 1998).

Risk Factors

Regarding oppositional problems, children who have at least one parent with a history of mood disorder, ODD, CD, ADHD, APD, or a substance-related disorder are more at risk for the development of oppositional problems than are other children (American Psychiatric Association, 2000). When there is a great deal of upheaval in the child care procedures (e.g., changes in day care, different primary caretakers in the home), children seem to be more likely to develop oppositional problems than when there is consistency in child care procedures (American Psychiatric Association, 2000). In addition, children who experience harsh, inconsistent, or neglectful parenting are more at risk for the development of oppositional problems than are children who receive consistent, warm, and nurturing parenting (American Psychiatric Association, 2000; K. Klein, Forehand, & Family Health Project Research Group, 2000; Stormshak, Bierman, McMahon, Lengua, & Conduct Problems Prevention Research Group, 2000). See also Box 12.5 for a discussion of corporal punishment and children's aggression.

Regarding conduct problems and antisocial behavior, risk factors include prenatal and perinatal difficulties, difficult infant temperament, neuropsychological deficits, inconsistent parenting, harsh discipline, parental rejection, lack of parental supervision, father absence, having a delinquent sibling, inconsistent caregiving procedures, early placement in an institution, large family size,

---

BOX 12.5

SPARE THE ROD, SPOIL THE CHILD?

Corporal punishment is defined as "the use of physical force with the intention of causing a child to experience pain, but not injury, for the purpose of correction or control of the child's behavior " (Straus, 1994, p. 4). The issue of corporal punishment in general, and spanking in particular, is of great importance when working with families of oppositional and aggressive children. Given the connections between aggression in parents and aggression in children (Frick, 1998b), it is worthwhile to consider the amount and effects of corporal punishment with children. As discussed in Chapter 7, there is sometimes a fine line between corporal punishment and physical abuse.

One major review of corporal punishment in the United States suggested that it is quite prevalent (Straus & Stewart, 1999). The following patterns were found:

- Nearly 60% of infants, 90% of 4-year-olds, 75% of 8-year-olds, and 60% of 10-year-olds are hit by their parents.
- More parents in the low socioeconomic status (SES) group than in the high SES group hit their children.
- Even when controlling for SES, more African American parents hit their children than do parents of other

ethnic/racial heritages, including Caucasian American parents.

- More boys are hit by their parents than are girls.
- More mothers than fathers hit their children.
- More parents in the South hit their children than in the Northeast or West.

The high prevalence of corporal punishment is surprising, given that corporal punishment is not an effective method of behavior control (Straus & Stewart, 1999). Specifically, corporal punishment is associated with higher levels of misbehavior even after controlling for initial levels of misbehavior (Mahoney, Donnelly, Lewis, & Maynard, 2000). Corporal punishment is associated with aggression and fear of the parent. Although it may teach children about inappropriate behavior, corporal punishment does not teach them about appropriate behavior (Straus & Stewart, 1999). Given the extensive research on the negative effects of corporal punishment, many scholars (Mahoney et al. 2000; Straus & Stewart, 1999) as well as the American Academy of Pediatrics (1998) argue that little or no corporal punishment should be perpetrated on children.

Family conflict and inconsistent parenting in early childhood can serve as risk factors for the development of conduct problems in later childhood.

neglect, physical abuse, sexual abuse, befriending delinquent peers, and attending a substandard school (American Psychiatric Association, 2000; Henry, Tolan, & Gorman-Smith, 2001; Kazdin, 1997; Loeber, Burke et al., 2000; Pfiffner, McBurnett, & Rathouz, 2001; Wolfe, Scott, Wekerle, & Pittman, 2001). Physical fighting at an early age also has a strong association with physical violence at a later age (Loeber, Green, Lahey, & Kalb, 2000). A history of parental psychopathology or criminality— such as parental APD, alcohol dependence, mood disorders, schizophrenia, ADHD, or CD—is also associated with the development of conduct problems in youth (American Psychiatric Association, 2000; Kazdin, 1997; Wakschlag & Keenan, 2001). Chronic school failure and involvement in special education services is associated with the development of CD and delinquency (Fink, 1990). Witnessing violence within the community is also associated with increased risk for developing antisocial behaviors (Halliday-Boykins & Graham, 2001; Miller, Wasserman, Neugebauer, Gorman-Smith, & Kamboukos, 1999; Weist, Acosta, & Youngstrom, 2001). Witnessed community violence served to be a risk factor, even when there was low conflict within the family (Miller et al., 1999).

One study of severe delinquents illustrates the known risk factors for disruptive behaviors (Chamberlain, 1996). This was a sample of severely delinquent adolescent boys, with a mean age of 14.54 years. On average, their juvenile justice records began before the age of 12, and they had already been arrested nearly 11 times. The following risk factors were evident for a number of the boys (percent-

ages of prevalence are noted in parentheses):

- Family violence (66%).
- Single-parent home (57%).
- Severe poverty (53%).
- Victim of physical abuse (51%).
- Three or more siblings (28%).
- Siblings institutionalized (21%).
- Father convicted (15%).
- Victim of sexual abuse (11%).
- Mother hospitalized (9%).

On average, the boys experienced 6.96 risk factors. This sample highlights the prevalence of risk factors in groups of adolescents with conduct problems and also shows that multiple risk factors are often present in the lives of these adolescents (Chamberlain, 1996).

It is quite common that children with oppositional and conduct problems have multiple risk factors that are associated with the development of these problems (McGee & Williams, 1999). Risk factors are often referred to as "coming in packages" because many risk factors co-occur together, such as poverty, large family size, poor housing, overcrowding, poor parental supervision, parental criminality, and interparental conflict (Kazdin, 1997). The neighborhood in which children and adolescents live is also thought to encompass many risk factors, such as community violence, inadequate schools, and deviant peers (Leventhal & Brooks-Gunn, 2000). Higher numbers of risk factors, also known as cumulative risk factors, are associated with a greater likelihood of experiencing oppositional and conduct problems (Forehand, Biggar, & Kotchick, 1998; McGee & Williams, 1999).

Protective Factors

Protective factors have not been studied to the same extent that risk factors have been studied in relation to oppositional and conduct problems (Kazdin, 1995). There are, however, a number of factors that seem to protect children from developing oppositional and conduct problems, even in the context of adverse environments (Kazdin, 1997; Koretz & Lazar, 1992; McCabe, Clark, & Barnett, 1999; Schoppe, Mangelsdorf, & Frosch, 2001; Seidman et al., 1999; Yoshikawa, 1994):

- Good relationship with consistent caregiver (either a parent or a nonparent).
- Warm, consistent, caring, and involved parents.
- Connections to stable adult outside the family.
- Above-average intelligence.
- Competence in multiple skill areas.
- Good social skills.

- Connections to nondeviant friends.
- Being firstborn.
- Easy temperament.
- Internal locus of control.
- Adequate school achievement.
- Social support from relatives.

High IQ and involved parents were the two most important protective factors regarding antisocial behavior (A. S. Masten et al., 1999). However, all of the factors listed above have been associated with decreasing the likelihood of developing CD (A. S. Masten et al., 1999). Thus, even a child born into poverty and living in a violent community might avoid developing oppositional and conduct problems if these protective factors are present. Note that many of the protective factors interact with each other. For example, a child's good social skills may make it easier for a parent to engage in warm and caring interactions (Kazdin, 1997).

Interestingly, many of these protective factors are not specific to preventing oppositional and conduct problems. As discussed in Chapter 8, most of these protective factors are associated with decreased likelihood of many emotional/behavioral problems.

Case Study: One Teacher's Story of Why She Teaches

Michael was seven years old and had never attended school on a regular basis. When he did show up for school, he showed defiance, threw tantrums, and talked back to teachers. He often ran away from school. Truant officers already knew Michael and his family quite well. Michael lived with his grandmother, aunts, and many cousins in a small apartment. His mother's whereabouts were "unknown," and his father did not have contact with him.

When Michael joined this teacher's special education classroom, the first thing she noticed was his smell and his appearance. Michael apparently had not taken a bath in years, and his clothes were unwashed adult's clothes that hung on him like he was a hanger. His fingernails were filled with grimy black dirt, and his hair was greasy and filthy.

Although Michael could not read or write, the first thing the teacher chose to tackle was his cleanliness and his appearance. She had new clothes donated from a local store and allowed Michael to choose a new item each day he attended school. She taught him how to use soap and water, including how to wash under his fingernails and how to wash his hair. Within weeks,

Michael was showing up to school consistently in clean clothes and with good hygiene.

Next, the teacher wanted to help Michael improve his academic work. She knew he could not read, so she never pressured him to read out loud with the other children. Rather, she allowed him to follow along with the reading group. Sometimes the teacher would offer Michael the chance to do "echo reading," during which she would read a short passage and then Michael would repeat what she said.

One day in reading group, Michael raised his hand to read out loud. Although he struggled a bit with the passage, he lifted his head and showed a beaming smile when he was finished. During the rest of the year, Michael showed up to school every day, even when he was sick. Many years later, he continues to do well in school and to behave appropriately. As the teacher said, "He now knows he is worthy of someone's care and attention; he had only needed some encouragement, love, and guidance. Don't we all?" (Clarkson, 1999, p. 180).

SUMMARY AND KEY CONCEPTS

Oppositional Defiant Disorder (ODD)
Oppositional defiant disorder (ODD) is a disruptive disorder characterized by oppositional, hostile, defiant, and negative interactions.

Conduct Disorder (CD)
Conduct disorder (CD) is a disruptive disorder that is characterized by the violation of basic rights of others and by breaking social norms. CD is much more severe than ODD. **Callous–unemotional traits** are characterized by a lack of empathy and a lack of feelings. A subset of youth diagnosed with CD show callous–unemotional traits.

Antisocial personality disorder (APD) is diagnosed only in adults (over the age of 18) and is characterized by disregard for and the violation of rights of others. The term **psychopath** is often used when describing individuals diagnosed with APD. The term **fledgling psychopaths** is used to describe children and adolescents who show a combination of hyperactivity, impulsivity, attention problems, and conduct problems.

Oppositional Defiant Disorder and Conduct Disorder
Symptoms of both ODD and CD appear to fall onto two primary dimensions: **covert/overt** and **destructive/nondestructive**. There are high rates of comorbidity for both ODD and CD. Regarding the courses of the disorders, there are a number of characteristics that are associated with the progression from ODD to CD to APD. There is no single theory that explains the development of ODD or CD. **Coercion theory** suggests that coercive family processes can put a child at risk for the development of oppositional and conduct disordered behaviors. Through a process known as **deviancy training**, troubled adolescents tend to develop more problems when they associate with other troubled adolescents.

A number of effective treatments have been identified for ODD and CD, most of which are behavioral or cognitive-behavioral. **Behavioral parent training** teaches parents effective parenting skills. **Multisystemic therapy** is a comprehensive treatment program that includes work with the adolescent, the family, the school system, peers, and any other important systems in the adolescent's life. A number of prevention programs have been instituted, but further research is needed in this area.

Oppositional Problems and Conduct Problems Conceptualized in a Dimensional Manner
There has been a good deal of research that explores oppositional and conduct problems from a dimensional perspective. A number of risk factors have been identified that are related to the onset of oppositional and conduct problems. Although there is less work on protective factors, a number of protective factors have been identified that decrease the risk for the onset of oppositional and conduct problems.

KEY TERMS

oppositional defiant disorder (ODD)	callous–unemotional traits	psychopath fledgling psychopaths	destructive/ nondestructive	behavioral parent training
conduct disorder (CD)	antisocial personality disorder (APD)	covert/overt	coercion theory deviancy training	multisystemic therapy

SUGGESTED READINGS

Meyer, Peter. *Death of Innocence.* New York: Berkley Books, 1985. Two young girls are raped, tortured, and left to die. The perpetrators are not hardened criminals, but rather 15- and 16-year-old boys. The violence took place not in a tough inner city, but rather in tranquil Essex Junction, Vermont. This book reconstructs what happened to the two girls and how the two boys developed into rapists and murderers.

McCall, Nathan. *Makes Me Wanna Holler: A Young Black Man In America.* New York: Vintage Books, 1994. In this powerful autobiography, McCall describes his difficult childhood and turbulent adolescence. By the time he was 15, he was carrying a gun and participating in numerous criminal activities (including rape and armed robbery). After serving a sentence for armed robbery, McCall was able to turn his life around and eventually become a journalist for the *Washington Post.*

SUGGESTED VIEWINGS

Boyz N the Hood (1991). John Singleton (director and writer). VHS/DVD. This powerful film shows the impact of inner-city gang activity on adolescents, even when they are trying to stay out of the gang.

Gone in 60 Seconds (2000). Dominic Sena (director), Scott Rosenberg (writer). VHS/DVD. In this film about grand theft auto, a number of adolescents are shown getting involved in criminal activities early in their lives.

CHAPTER 13

ALCOHOL AND SUBSTANCE USE AND ABUSE

CHAPTER SUMMARY

Anytime is hard to be a kid.

—Pindi, 13 years old, United States

Compared with other types of developmental psycho-pathology in childhood and adolescence, only limited amounts of research have been completed in the areas of substance abuse and dependence (Gilvarry, 2000; Luthar, Cushing, & McMahon, 1997). This dearth of research is ironic given that substance use (including alcohol use) is common among adolescents and even some children. Most children and adolescents who drink alcohol and use other substances do not go on to develop substance-related disorders (Waldron, 1998). Experimentation with substances is so common during youth that some researchers have argued that it is developmentally appropriate, especially in that it serves to help the processes of

becoming independent from parental controls and bonding more strongly with peers (Allison, Leone, & Spero, 1990). Other researchers, however, have noted that substance use is always illegal for minors in the United States and that this illegal activity is often associated with other problems, such as delinquency, shoplifting, truancy, and breaking curfew (reviewed in Waldron, 1998).

This chapter explores both ends of the spectrum. First, substance-related disorders will be discussed to show the problems associated with substance use gone awry; then substance use will be discussed from a dimensional perspective to explore the functioning of children and adolescents who do not develop clinical disorders but who use illicit substances. The chapter concludes with a section on nicotine use in children and adolescents.

ALCOHOL ABUSE, ALCOHOL DEPENDENCE, SUBSTANCE ABUSE, AND SUBSTANCE DEPENDENCE

There are more than 114 substance-related diagnoses in *DSM-IV* (American Psychiatric Association, 2000). These disorders can be diagnosed in adults as well as in children and adolescents. The substance-related disorders that are most prevalent, and of primary concern for children and adolescents, are substance abuse and substance dependence. According to the definition in Table 13.1, **substance abuse** requires use of a substance that harms the child or adolescent in some way by causing clinically significant impairment or distress, but without signs of tolerance or withdrawal. Table 13.2 shows that **substance dependence** requires use of a substance that not only harms the child or adolescent but also shows signs of tolerance or withdrawal. By definition, substance dependence is considered more severe than substance abuse; thus, the diagnosis of the former takes precedence over that of the latter. The following classes of substances can be diagnosed for both substance abuse and substance dependence:

- Alcohol.
- Amphetamine (e.g., speed, diet pills, Ritalin).
- Cannabis (marijuana).
- Cocaine (including cocaine powder and crack).
- Hallucinogen (e.g., LSD, mescaline).
- Inhalant (e.g., paint thinner, glue, spray paint, Liquid Paper).
- Opioid (e.g., morphine, heroin, codeine, methadone).

TABLE 13.1 *DSM-IV* Diagnostic Criteria for Substance Abuse

A. A maladaptive pattern of substance use leading to clinically significant impairment or distress, as manifested by one (or more) of the following, occurring within a 12-month period:

(1) recurrent substance use resulting in a failure to fulfill major role obligations at work, school, or home (e.g., repeated absences or poor work performance related to substance use; substance-related absences, suspensions, or expulsions from school; neglect of children or household)

(2) recurrent substance use in situations in which it is physically hazardous (e.g., driving an automobile or operating a machine when impaired by substance use)

(3) recurrent substance-related legal problems (e.g., arrests for substance-related disorderly conduct)

(4) continued substance use despite having persistent or recurrent social or interpersonal problems caused or exacerbated by the effects of the substance (e.g., arguments with spouse about consequences of intoxication, physical fights)

B. The symptoms have never met the criteria for Substance Dependence for this class of substance.

TABLE 13.2 *DSM-IV* Diagnostic Criteria for Substance Dependence

A maladaptive pattern of substance use, leading to clinically significant impairment or distress, as manifested by three (or more) of the following, occurring at any time in the same 12-month period:

(1) tolerance, as defined by either of the following:

(a) a need for markedly increased amounts of the substance to achieve intoxication or desired effect

(b) markedly diminished effect with continued use of the same amount of the substance

(2) withdrawal, as manifested by either of the following:

(a) the characteristic withdrawal syndrome for the substance . . .

(b) the same (or a closely related) substance is taken to relieve or avoid withdrawal symptoms

(3) the substance is often taken in larger amounts or over a longer period than was intended

(4) there is a persistent desire or unsuccessful efforts to cut down or control substance use

(5) a great deal of time is spent in activities necessary to obtain the substance (e.g., visiting multiple doctors or driving long distances), use the substance (e.g., chain-smoking), or recover from its effects

(6) important social, occupational, or recreational activities are given up or reduced because of substance use

(7) the substance use is continued despite knowledge of having a persistent or recurrent physical or psychological problem that is likely to have been caused or exacerbated by the substance (e.g., current cocaine use despite recognition of cocaine-induced depression, or continued drinking despite recognition that an ulcer was made worse by alcohol consumption)

Specify if:

With Physiological Dependence: evidence of tolerance or withdrawal (i.e., either Item 1 or 2 is present)

Without Physiological Dependence: no evidence of tolerance or withdrawal (i.e., neither Item 1 nor 2 is present)

- Phencyclidine (PCP).

- Sedative, hypnotic, or anxiolytic (e.g., sleeping pills, barbiturates, antianxiety medications).

- Other or unknown substances (e.g., anabolic steroids, nitrite inhalants such as "poppers," nitrous oxide).

The following substances can be diagnosed for substance dependence only, and not for substance abuse:

- Nicotine dependence (e.g., cigarettes, chewing tobacco).

- Polysubstance (i.e., many substances together).

The only other substance covered in *DSM-IV* that has not yet been mentioned is caffeine. In addition to caffeine, all of the substances mentioned above (except nicotine and polysubstances) can be used to diagnose intoxication.

Caffeine intoxication is represented by excessive ingestion of caffeine (e.g., two to three cups of brewed coffee in rapid succession) followed by symptoms such as nervousness, restlessness, muscle twitching, and psychomotor agitation. For intoxication to be diagnosed, clinically significant distress or impairment in social, occupational, or other areas of functioning must be present. Note that there are different symptoms of intoxication for specific substances.

Note also that the criteria given in Tables 13.1 and 13.2 are used for alcohol as well as for other substances. The research literature on substance abuse and dependence in children and adolescents is usually combined. This combination of disorders is often referred to as **substance use disorders** (Weinberg & Glantz, 1999). As noted above, this section discusses both alcohol abuse/dependence and

Case Study: Chelsea, The Party Girl

Chelsea began drinking alcohol at school parties when she was 12 years old. At first, she did not like the taste of beer; but she felt that all of her friends were drinking, so she went along with them. She later learned that she preferred vodka-spiked punch, because it had a sweeter taste than beer. When Chelsea was 14, she and her friends began attending parties at a local fraternity house. Not only could they drink as much alcohol as they wanted, but the fraternity members would often give them bottles of beer to take home so they could get drunk during the week. On more than one occasion, Chelsea and her friends got drunk at school on beer they brought in plastic containers.

When she was 15 and a sophomore in high school, Chelsea and a friend went to a fraternity party, as they did almost every weekend. The two girls became quite drunk, and Chelsea's friend was raped while she was unconscious. Chelsea felt that the incident was her fault for not protecting her friend. She tried to stop drinking but succeeded for only two days before she was drinking again with her friends at school. Three months later Chelsea was picked up by campus police at 3 A.M. while she was stumbling around the local college campus and mumbling incoherently. She was admitted to a hospital with a blood alcohol level of 0.20, which is over twice the legal limit for driving in most states. When Chelsea was in the hospital, it became apparent that she met criteria for alcohol dependence, with physiological dependence. Chelsea reported that she had been drinking every day for quite some time and that many days she drank just to keep from getting headaches.

When contacted, Chelsea's parents reported that they had no idea that she was drinking alcohol (although Chelsea's mother reported having had some suspicions). They did not realize that Chelsea had been truant from school on numerous occasions, and they had not noticed that Chelsea had been hiding her report cards, which showed her failing grades and unexcused absences. When Chelsea's parents were able to visit her at the hospital, her father said, "Chelsea, my mother died from alcoholism, and there is no way I'm going to let this get you too. We are all going to fight this together."

Chelsea and her parents began attending therapy together, and Chelsea joined an Alcoholics Anonymous group that consisted of adolescents and young adults at the university. Chelsea stayed away from alcohol for three months. Then, at a graduation party with her friends, she began drinking again but called her father after she had finished three drinks. At that point, she decided not to attend any more parties with her friends.

Chelsea got a job at a local stable where she developed a great interest in showing and caring for horses. She befriended a number of other adolescents who worked with horses, and the owner of the stable provided her with many healthy outlets for her interest.

Meanwhile, the family therapy was uncovering years of trouble within the family that had never been addressed. Chelsea and her mother had become more and more confrontational with each other, but Chelsea's father had had no idea about these problems. Chelsea's mother had not wanted to bother Chelsea's father about her suspicions regarding their daughter's abuse of alcohol. Chelsea's parents also reported great concern over letting Chelsea become independent from them, although ironically they had not monitored her behavior closely before the hospitalization. The family therapist worked to help Chelsea become more independent in an age-appropriate manner rather than by using alcohol. The therapist also worked with the family to facilitate communication and to help the parents bond as a unit.

Chelsea was able to maintain A and B grades. In addition to working at the stable, she also volunteered at a local rape crisis center. She remained sober through her high school graduation and went on to attend a college out of state.

Source: R. K. Morgan (1999).

other substance abuse/dependence. Where possible, however, specific information will be given for alcohol and other substances separately and for abuse and dependence separately.

Substance abuse by children and adolescents has potentially serious negative ramifications. Within the family environment, adolescents who abuse substances often experience poor parent–child communication, poor parental supervision and discipline, and interpersonal conflict with their parents and siblings (Gilvarry, 2000). Within the school environment, adolescent substance abusers often show inadequate academic performance and increased levels of emotional/behavioral problems (Bukstein & VanHasselt, 1995). Within the peer network, adolescent substance abusers often are involved with a deviant peer group and are engaged in conflict with their peers (Dishion, McCord, & Poulin, 1999). Within the larger community, adolescent substance abusers are often

involved in delinquent behaviors and illegal activities (Gilvarry, 2000).

In addition to these areas of concern are the problems due to physiological effects of substances. Alcohol, sedatives, hypnotics, and opiates such as heroin all serve to depress the central nervous system, whereas substances such as cocaine, amphetamines, and phencyclidine stimulate the central nervous system. Substances such as LSD and mescaline can cause hallucinations (Gilvarry, 2000). In addition to these physiological effects, most substances serve to alter decision making and judgment and can negatively influence fine motor and gross motor skills (Bukstein & VanHasselt, 1995). In the case of overdose, substances can lead to permanent impairment or death.

I drank when I was happy and I drank when I was anxious and I drank when I was bored and I drank when I was depressed, which was often.

—Caroline Knapp (1996, p. 1)

Prevalence Rates

Table 13.3 gives an overview of prevalence information for substance use disorders. A number of epidemiological studies have been conducted to assess the prevalence of substance use disorders in children and adolescents. In the Methods for the Epidemiology of Child and Adolescent Mental Disorders (MECA) study, 2.0% of adolescents met criteria for a substance use disorder (Kandel et al., 1997). In a study of rural youth from the Southeast, 6.0% of the sample met criteria for a substance use disorder (Costello, Erkanli, Federman, & Angold, 1999). Other epidemiological studies have found higher rates of substance use disorders in children and adolescents (Gilvarry, 2000).

In studies of adolescents in treatment, the highest prevalence rates of substance use disorders (82.6%) were found in treatment facilities that specialized in alcohol and drug treatment, with high rates of substance use disorders also found in adolescents within the juvenile jus-

Adolescents who abuse substances often befriend other adolescents who abuse substances.

TABLE 13.3 Overview of Prevalence Information for Substance Use Disorders

Prevalence	2.0%
Age	Adolescents > Children
Gender	No consistent pattern
Socioeconomic status	Lower > Higher
Race/ethnicity	African Americans > Caucasian Americans and Hispanic/Latino/Latina Americans

tice system (62.1%), the community mental health system (40.8%), special education classes for severely emotionally disturbed adolescents within the school system (23.6%), and the child welfare system (19.2%; Aarons, Brown, Hough, Garland, & Wood, 2001). Thus, clinicians working within treatment settings are likely to have adolescent clients with substance use disorders.

Rates of alcohol abuse, alcohol dependence, substance abuse, and substance dependence increase with age, ranging from 1.4% at 14 years old to 8.7% at 17 years old (Kandel et al., 1997). This finding parallels the growing use of substances from early adolescence to later adolescence (Waldron, 1998). Childhood prevalence rates appear to reach their peak between the ages of 15 and 19 (Gilvarry, 2000).

Findings from studies on gender effects are complicated. Many studies have found comparable rates of substance use disorders for boys and girls when substances are combined (Costello et al., 1999; Duncan, Strycker, & Duncan, 1999; Kandel et al., 1997). Specific substances, however, often show gender differences in use. For example, boys were more likely than girls to smoke marijuana

and to use crack cocaine, but it is unclear whether these usage patterns were related to patterns of abuse and dependence (Costello et al., 1999). More family dysfunctions, such as more conflict and less cohesion, were found in substance-abusing girls when compared with substance-abusing boys (Dakof, 2000). In general, girls who show substance abuse and dependence tend to be more debilitated than are boys who show similar problems (V. Johnson & Pandina, 2000). Both girls and boys, however, show similar patterns of risk factors for the development of substance abuse (Costello et al., 1999).

Children and adolescents from the lower socioeconomic bracket tend to show higher rates of substance use disorders (Kandel et al., 1997).

Regarding race and ethnicity, Hispanic/Latino/Latina children and adolescents showed the lowest rates of substance use disorders, whereas African American children and adolescents showed the highest rates (Kandel et al., 1997). Prevalence rates for Caucasian American children and adolescents fell between these two groups. High rates of alcohol abuse and dependence are found within samples of Native American youth (Sattler, 1998).

BOX *13.1*

ALCOHOL AND THE FAMILY

Research on parents who abuse alcohol has focused almost exclusively on fathers, while neglecting mothers (Leonard et al., 2000; Phares, 1996, 1997b). This pattern is unusual, given that nearly all other types of psychopathology have been investigated in mothers more than in fathers. This pattern is probably due to the higher prevalence of alcohol abuse and dependence in men versus women (American Psychiatric Association, 2000).

Overall, there is strong evidence that parents (especially fathers) who abuse substances are more likely to have children (especially boys) who abuse substances (Chassin, Curran, Hussong, & Colder, 1996; Chassin, Pitts, DeLucia, & Todd, 1999; Leonard et al., 2000; Loukas, Fitzgerald, Zucker, & vonEye, 2001; Windle & Davies, 1999; Windle & Tubman, 1999). Children of alcoholic parents are four to nine times more likely to experience alcohol abuse or dependence at some point in their lives than are children of nonalcoholic parents (Windle & Tubman, 1999). This risk appears to remain to some degree even after fathers stop drinking (DeLucia, Belz, & Chassin, 2001). Note, however, that the majority of children of alcoholic parents do not go on to abuse alcohol. Thus, although there is a statistical connection between alcohol misuse in parents and children, the children of alcoholic parents do not inevitably abuse alcohol in their own lives (Windle & Tubman, 1999).

The higher rates of alcohol abuse and dependence in children of alcoholics are related to genetic predisposition in the children, physiological vulnerabilities in the children, and parenting behaviors that create a less than optimal environment for the child (Vik, Brown, & Myers, 1997). The genetic predisposition seems stronger for boys than for girls (Windle & Tubman, 1999). Physiological vulnerabilities are apparent in children of alcoholics in that they seem to need more alcohol to achieve the same effects as their peers, a factor known as sensitivity (Vik et al., 1997). Thus, children of alcoholics often drink more alcohol to achieve the same state as their peers, which in turn is related to problematic drinking.

Even when children of alcoholic parents show problems, they do not always show problems with alcohol. Parental alcoholism was associated with heightened drinking in adolescents when the adolescents also showed high levels of externalizing problems but not when the adolescents showed high levels of internalizing problems (Hussong, Curran, & Chassin, 1998). In the discussion of etiologies later in this chapter, note that Figure 13.3 suggests multiple factors that are related to adolescents' heightened risk for problems when they have a parent with alcohol dependence.

Note that there has also been concern about higher rates of substance abuse disorders among gay, lesbian, bisexual, transgender, and questioning adolescents (Jordan, 2000). Children and adolescents within a sexual minority seem to be at risk for developing substance use disorders, so efforts have been made to highlight the need for preventive programs for these youth (Jordan, 2000).

There are also higher rates of substance abuse and dependence in adolescents who have run away from home and those who are homeless (Whitbeck & Hoyt, 1999). Although the direction of causality is not clear (i.e., Did they become homeless and then start abusing substances or did they start abusing substances and then become homeless?), there are significant negative ramifications for adolescents' substance abuse in this vulnerable population (Whitbeck & Hoyt 1999).

A few hours ago I was at the bank, and a nice woman came up to me and said, "Oh, you're the comedian who doesn't use the F-word."

"I use it all the time," I said. "'Family.' It's the dirtiest word I know."

She laughed and said, "No, not that one. The other F-word."

"You couldn't mean me," I smiled, "because I use that one all the time, too."

"You do?"

"Sure." I nodded. "'Father.' It's right up there with 'family.' Almost interchangeable."

—Louie Anderson (1991, p. 21),
a comedian whose father was alcoholic

Comorbidity

Rates of comorbidity for substance use disorders (including alcohol abuse and dependence) are quite high. Comorbidity is common between substance use disorders and conduct disorder, with suggestions that nearly half of substance-abusing adolescents also meet criteria for conduct disorder (Frick, 1998b; Kandel et al., 1999; Kazdin, 1995; Waldron, 1998; Weinberg & Glantz, 1999). Although there appears to be a connection between substance use disorders and attention-deficit/hyperactivity disorder (ADHD), this connection disappears when conduct problems are controlled statistically (Disney, Elkins, McGue, & Iacono, 1999; Weinberg & Glantz, 1999). In other words, there is not a strong connection between ADHD and substance abuse or dependence (Disney et al., 1999). A connection between depression and substance abuse in late adolescence is found in many studies (Costello et al., 1999; Kandel et al., 1999; Rao, Daley, & Hammen, 2000), but not in all (Weinberg & Glantz, 1999). Alcohol dependence, however, is related to suici-

dal behavior (Hufford, 2001). There is a strong relationship between binge eating disorders (such as bulimia) and substance use disorders (Ross & Ivis, 1999). Most anxiety disorders do not appear to be well established as comorbid features of substance use disorders (Weinberg & Glantz, 1999), but there is evidence of comorbidity between substance use disorders and post-traumatic stress disorder in adolescents (Giaconia et al., 2000).

Comorbidity has ramifications for future functioning. One longitudinal study that followed African American youth from 6th grade to 10th grade (Miller-Johnson, Lochman, Coie, Terry, & Hyman, 1998) found that the combination of depression and conduct disorder in 6th grade was highly related to alcohol and marijuana use in 10th grade. Conduct disorder alone was also related to higher levels of substance use later in adolescence, but depression alone was not related to later substance use (Miller-Johnson et al., 1998). Overall, comorbidity is associated with lower levels of functioning and greater rates of impairment (Windle & Davies, 1999; Zeitlin, 1999).

Course of the Disorder

As noted earlier, most adolescents use substances but do not develop substance use disorders. Adolescents who do not develop problems with substances tend not to make the substances part of their everyday life and do not commit to the use of substances as part of their own identity (Waldron, 1998). In general, earlier use of substances is associated with higher rates of substance abuse and dependence (Hawkins, Catalano, & Miller, 1992). Adolescents who go on to abuse substances tend to follow a relatively common progression, from using alcohol and cigarettes, to smoking marijuana, to using hard drugs such as cocaine or heroine (Waldron, 1998). This process has been referred to as the **gateway phenomenon**, with the idea that earlier drug use (e.g., use of marijuana) provides a gateway to using harder substances. It is important to note, however, that a great many adolescents use marijuana without developing more severe substance abuse or dependence problems (Waldron, 1998). The section on risk factors that appears later in this chapter is helpful in identifying who is at risk for developing substance abuse and who is less likely to develop substance abuse.

In general, there are a number of stages that children and adolescents might pass through before developing a substance use disorder (Sattler, 1998):

• *Experimental stage*—where adolescents' use of substances is due to curiosity, interest in risk taking, and sometimes peer pressure.

Case Study: David, Whose Father Abused Alcohol

David's mother devoted nearly all of her time to trying to take care of David's father, who was an alcoholic. Although David and his mother had once been close, he felt ignored by her now that his father's alcoholism had worsened. David was very concerned about his parents, and he was motivated to keep them together.

However, around the age of 15, David began smoking marijuana. His grades began dropping and he began causing problems at school. His teachers and other school personnel noticed extreme changes in his behavior. After his substance use was discovered, he was admitted to an inpatient unit for treatment of substance abuse and dependence. After he was discharged from the inpatient facility, David resumed drinking alcohol and smoking marijuana. His guidance counselor suggested that he get involved in therapy and that his parents take an active role in the therapy.

The therapist helped the family see that David might be using his self-destructive behavior and substance use to gain attention from his mother. The therapist also helped the parents see that David's behavior was tied closely to his parents' functioning. David's father finally became motivated to address his own alcoholism. After individual treatment and involvement in Alcoholics Anonymous, David's father stopped drinking.

David had one more relapse with excessive drinking and smoking marijuana but then remained sober at a three-year follow-up. His parents' marriage improved significantly after David's father's treatment for alcoholism. David's mother also found that not having to deal with her husband's alcoholism allowed her to spend more time with David.

SOURCE: Sweet (1991).

- *Social stage*—where adolescents use substances only with friends who are also experimenting with the substances.
- *Instrumental stage*—where adolescents use substances to alter their feelings and behavior, such as to feel more calm in response to stress or to feel more loose in a situation that causes them anxiety.
- *Habitual stage*—where adolescents develop the habit of using substances and ignore other facets of their life.
- *Compulsive stage*—where adolescents become focused on gaining access to their substance of choice and neglect nearly all other aspects of their life.

These stages are illustrated in Figure 13.1. Although not all adolescents progress through these stages, it is typical that adolescents who abuse substances have passed through the earlier stages of less severe substance use (Sattler, 1998). Substance dependence is usually evident at the habitual stage and the compulsive stage, but interventions are appropriate at a much earlier stage whenever possible (Sattler, 1998).

In addition to these stages, there are other factors associated with the course of substance abuse and dependence. The majority of comorbid disorders seem to appear well before the onset of substance use disorders. For example, conduct disorder and depression were found to occur many years before the onset of substance use and

Intravenous drug use is often associated with adolescents at the habitual and compulsive stages in the development of substance use disorders.

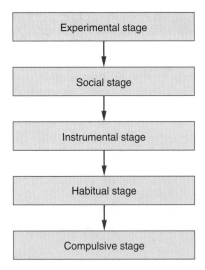

FIGURE 13.1   Stages in Becoming a Substance Abuser
Source: Sattler (1998).

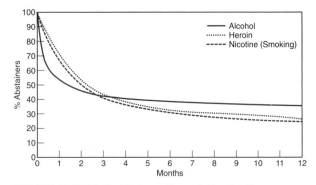

FIGURE 13.2   Typical Relapse Rates Following Treatment for Problematic Patterns of Substance Use
Source: Pagliaro & Pagliaro (1996).

abuse (Costello et al., 1999). Earlier generalized anxiety disorder was associated with increased risk for alcohol abuse, but earlier separation anxiety disorder was associated with a decreased risk for alcohol abuse (Kaplow, Curran, Angold, & Costello, 2001). Persistent delinquency in early childhood predicted substance use in early adolescence as well as later adolescence (Loeber, Stouthamer-Loeber, & White, 1999). Social impairment (e.g., lacking social skills, difficulty in maintaining friendships) was predictive of alcohol abuse and drug abuse in a four-year follow-up of young adolescents (Greene et al., 1999). Boys whose fathers abused substances were at greater risk for oppositional defiant disorder, conduct disorder, anxiety disorders, and mood disorders, which in turn were related to increased risk for developing a substance use disorder (D. B. Clark, Parker, & Lynch, 1999). Overall, there are a number of precursors to the development of substance abuse and dependence.

It is important to note that substance use disorders have ramifications for the physical health of children and adolescents. Adolescents who use substances and who show risk-taking behavior are likely to report physical injuries related to the substance use (Spirito, Jelalian, Rasile, Rohrbeck, & Vinnick, 2000). Another study found that substance-abusing adolescents engaged in more behaviors that put them at risk for contracting the human immunodeficiency virus (HIV) than did adolescents diagnosed with another psychiatric disorder and adolescents in a nonclinical control group (Deas-Nesmith, Brady, White, & Campbell, 1999).

Unfortunately, even with treatment, substance abuse tends to reoccur. Figure 13.2 shows that relapse after treatment (i.e., going back to abusing a substance) is common, with the number of abstainers dropping sharply within the first three months after intensive therapeutic services (Pagliaro & Pagliaro, 1996). Ways to prevent relapse are discussed later in the treatment section of this chapter. If treatment and relapse prevention are not effective, adolescents with alcohol abuse problems are at risk for substance use disorders, major depression, borderline personality disorder, and antisocial personality disorder in early adulthood (Rohde, Lewinsohn, Kahler, Seeley, & Brown, 2001).

Etiology

As with so many other disorders, it is likely that multiple etiological factors lead to the development of substance abuse and dependence (Cicchetti & Rogosch, 1999b). A number of factors have been implicated in the development of substance abuse and dependence, including biological, familial, interpersonal (cognitive), cultural, and societal factors (Waldron, 1998).

Biological theories have gained support from family studies and twin studies (Vik et al., 1997). In general, there are high concordance rates between parents' and adolescents' substance abuse (Vik et al., 1997). Biological theories, however, rarely account for a huge portion of the variance that explains the development of substance abuse and dependence (Waldron, 1998). One review of behavioral genetics research concluded that genetic factors provide a moderate amount of influence in the development of alcohol abuse in boys but only a modest amount of influence in girls (Vik et al., 1997). Similarly, both environmental and biological factors play roles in the development of substance abuse problems.

Case Study: T. S., Who Likes Drag Racing and Cocaine

T. S., a 19-year-old inner-city youth, was picked up by an ambulance that his friend called after T. S. had snorted a great deal of cocaine. T. S. was belligerent and argumentative, and he showed signs of cocaine intoxication (e.g., his eyes were dilated, his breathing was irregular, and his pulse was rapid and irregular). After he was stabilized, T. S. acknowledged that he had been using many different drugs since the age of 13. He began using alcohol and marijuana around that time, then added speed and cocaine, and by the age of 17 had settled on cocaine as his drug of choice.

He would often steal money from his mother or steal car stereos in order to purchase cocaine. His mother, who herself had a drinking problem, seemed unaware of her son's problems. He told her that he received good grades and that he played on the high school basketball team, neither of which were true.

T. S.'s mother, however, did not question these accomplishments even though she had no evidence in support of T. S.'s claims. In fact, T.S. had already dropped out of high school and was spending his days and nights getting high and drag racing with his friends into the early-morning hours.

When he was admitted to the emergency room, T. S. was asked if he could control his drug use. He replied angrily, "Of course I could. No problem. I just don't see any damn good reason to stop." The hospital staff diagnosed T. S. with cocaine abuse. If they could have gathered more information, they might have diagnosed T. S. with cocaine dependence. Given the history of conduct problems and current antisocial behavior, T. S. also received a provisional diagnosis of antisocial personality disorder.

SOURCE: Spitzer, Gibbons, Skodol, Williams, & First (1994).

. . . [The] delivery of my premature son was unlikely to have been a joyous occasion. Most fetal alcohol babies emerge not in a tide, the facsimile of saline, primordial, life-granting sea, but instead enter this world tainted with stale wine. Their amniotic fluid literally reeks of Thunderbird or Ripple . . .

—Michael Dorris (1989, p. 261) about his adopted son, Adam, who was diagnosed with fetal alcohol syndrome

Children of alcoholics provide an interesting test of behavioral genetics theories. As discussed in Box 13.1, higher alcohol use in children of alcoholics appears to be related to genetic predisposition, physiological differences, and environmental factors, such as limited parental control (Leonard et al., 2000; Vik et al., 1997). Children of parents who abuse other substances may be subjected to even more pernicious physiological effects (Mayes & Bornstein, 1997). For example, children born to mothers who use cocaine during pregnancy experience neurological deficits that are related to abnormal brain development while in utero (Mayes & Bornstein, 1997). These children begin life at a disadvantage and are often exposed to less than optimal environments that can further limit their potential for good functioning.

Regarding familial factors, the connections between parents' and adolescents' substance abuse and dependence may be due to a number of different factors. Parents' drug use can influence adolescents directly through a genetic predisposition and through modeling the behavior, but it can also influence adolescents indirectly through impaired parenting and limited control when the parent is under the influence of the substance (Waldron, 1998). Parents' attitudes toward alcohol use, and especially fathers' attitudes toward alcohol use, are associated closely with young children's attitudes toward alcohol use (Brody, Ge, Katz, & Arias, 2000).

Note that authoritative parenting (i.e., warm, nurturing interactions combined with age-appropriate structure and limits) is associated with decreased likelihood of substance use disorders in adolescents (Fletcher & Jefferies, 1999). Conversely, parental rejection is associated with adolescents' favorable attitudes toward both substance use and intent to use substances (Teichman & Kefir, 2000). Adolescents who feel rejected by their fathers are at even greater risk for substance use and abuse than adolescents who feel rejected by their mothers (Teichman & Kefir, 2000).

One theory that has tied these factors together is the **dynamic diathesis-stress model** of developmental psychopathology (Windle & Tubman, 1999). This model suggests that individuals are vulnerable to psychopathology due to personal characteristics (such as biological risk or maladaptive coping skills), but do not develop psychopathology unless they are challenged with significant stressors. Figure 13.3 shows that a family history of alcoholism can be related to many factors (such as biological risk, temperament/cognitive factors, family environment, and extrafamilial environment) that can influence stressors and be related to a diverse array of adverse outcomes (e.g., externalizing problems, internalizing problems, and health problems; Windle & Tubman, 1999). Thus, parental alcohol abuse and dependence can be related to a number of problems within children's lives.

When connections are found between parental alcohol consumption and children's behavior, it is important to remember the reciprocity of interactions between parents

Broader Multifaceted Sociocultural and Historical Contextual Factors

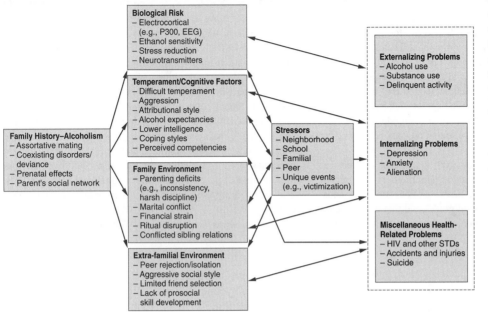

FIGURE 13.3: Dynamic Diathesis-Stress Model of Developmental Psychopathology: An Application to Children of Alcoholics (COAs)

Source: Windle & Tubman (1999). Originally published in Wendy K. Silverman & Thomas H. Ollendick, *Developmental Issues in the Clinical Treatment of Children,* Copyright ©1999 by Allyn & Bacon. Reprinted by permission.

and children. Rather than assuming that high parental alcohol intake "causes" emotional/behavioral problems in children, mental health practitioners must keep in mind that difficult behaviors in children may lead parents to ingest more alcohol. As discussed in Chapter 12, a series of studies have suggested that children who show externalizing behavior problems can lead the adults with whom they interact to drink more alcohol (Pelham et al., 1997).

Cognitive theoretical models of substance abuse and dependence focus on adolescents' perceptions of benefits of using substances (e.g., peer acceptance) and costs to using substances (e.g., harmful effects, parental disapproval; Waldron, 1998). As discussed in Box 13.2, expectancies of the effects of alcohol and drug use have also been implicated in the development of substance abuse and dependence patterns.

Behavioral models of substance abuse and dependence have focused on the antecedents and consequences of using and abusing substances. For example, if using a substance decreases anxiety in a stressful situation, then use of that substance is reinforced by the pleasant effects from the substance (Waldron, 1998). Some researchers have argued that using substances to cope with stress initially helps the adolescent feel better but then leads to more problems (Wills & Filer, 1996).

There are a number of etiological factors that show which children and adolescents are at risk for developing

alcohol dependence in adulthood. Specifically, many of these studies have followed children and adolescents who abuse substances into adulthood to find which children and adolescents develop substance dependence (reviewed in Zucker, Fitzgerald, & Moses, 1995). Children and adolescents are most likely to develop alcohol dependence in adulthood when the following characteristics are present (Zucker et al., 1995):

- Childhood antisocial behavior and aggression.
- Childhood problems with academic achievement.
- Poor social and interpersonal connections in childhood.
- High levels of activity in childhood.
- Poor or inadequate parenting and low levels of parent–child contact.
- Parental psychopathology and inadequate parental role modeling.

Foolishness often precedes wisdom.

—Proverb of Africa

Treatment

Compared with research on treatment for other types of developmental psychopathology, the research is limited regarding empirically supported treatments for children and adolescents with substance use disorders (Winters,

Case Study: Doug, The "Booze Brother"

Doug's childhood was relatively normal. His father sold insurance and his mother was a full-time homemaker. Doug played basketball in grade school and was quite popular. He never spent very much time on schoolwork and tended to earn C's in most of his subjects.

Doug's family appeared normal from the outside, but Doug felt that there were many problems below the surface. His father was away from home a great deal and drank a fair amount when he was home. Also, the father was a dominant person who, when he was drunk or had a bad day, verbally abused Doug. Doug's mother was anxious and stressed much of the time. She smoked cigarettes incessantly and was prescribed tranquilizers to help with her anxiety.

Doug attended a different middle school than most of his friends. He tried to gain the popularity he had had in grade school by playing basketball, but he did not make the school team. Not only was Doug ridiculed at school for not making the team, but his father was very vocal about his disappointment in Doug's failure. Doug spent less and less time with his old friends in the neighborhood and began spending more time with kids at school who showed no interest in their academic work. Doug became more and more rebellious. He stole a carton of his mother's cigarettes and gave them to his new friends at school. He began smoking at that point and continues smoking to this day.

Doug's problem behavior continued through middle school and into early high school. He talked back to teachers and refused to follow his parents' commands. His father became even more domineering in reaction to Doug's rebelliousness, which escalated the situation further.

Around the beginning of high school, Doug got a job in a local garage. He continued to socialize with other disenfranchised youth and would often party with them. Doug became known as a "Booze Brother" because of his frequent alcohol use. He was suspended from school twice for being drunk and once for having marijuana in his locker. He was then expelled when he was found to be selling marijuana to other students. Afterward, Doug was put in a drug and alcohol rehabilitation facility. Doug stated that he "served his time" in this facility but that it did not change his mind about any of his behaviors.

Once he was discharged, he continued to party and to sell drugs. He had found that the job at the garage did not provide enough money for his growing drug habit, nor was it exciting enough for him. He enjoyed being the supplier at parties and felt that he was popular again. Doug's parents, and especially his father, continued to berate him for his poor schoolwork. Doug dealt with the difficulties at home by partying with his friends.

One night at a friend's party, Doug had made a lot of money selling drugs to other teenagers. He decided to splurge on himself, so he bought some high-quality bourbon, marijuana, and a number of pills. After finishing a fifth of bourbon, smoking marijuana, and taking a number of pills, Doug began to walk down the stairs, slipped, and fell through a plate glass window. He broke his arm, fractured his leg, and received gashes that led to permanent scars all over his face and body. The paramedics were amazed that he survived the drug overdose as well as the fall.

After being stabilized medically, Doug was admitted into another inpatient unit that specialized in drug and alcohol treatment. He did well in the hospital and was allowed to live at home during his senior year of high school. Unfortunately, Doug's parents neither supervised his activities closely nor spent much time with him, and he returned to his old friends. Within two months of his discharge from the hospital, Doug was once again caught selling drugs at school and sent to a drug rehabilitation center. He did well in the treatment center and was doing well upon discharge, but it remains to be seen if his improvements will last over the long term.

SOURCE: R. G. Meyer (1989).

1999). In general, adolescents are difficult to treat for substance abuse and dependence because they often lack motivation to change their behaviors (Waldron, 1998). Overall, the average rate of abstaining from substances after treatment is 38% at six-month follow-up and 32% at one-year follow-up (Williams & Chang, 2000). These numbers show the difficulty in treating adolescent substance abuse and dependence effectively.

Although a number of treatments are used for adolescent substance abuse, little empirical work has been completed to establish the most effective ones. Most treatments are better than no treatments in reducing substance abuse and in reducing other emotional/behavioral problems (Waldron, Slesnick, Brody, Turner, & Peterson, 2001; R. J. Williams & Chang, 2000). There are a diverse array of treatments, including psychosocial treatments (which range from needle exchange to outpatient therapy to inpatient therapeutic communities); traditional and 12-step models (which include Alcoholics Anonymous and other abstinence-focused treatments); cognitive-behavioral models (which focus on cognitions as well as behaviors as the point of intervention); family therapy models (which focus on the family as a unit, rather than focusing on the individual substance abuser); and psychopharmacological treatments (Waldron, 1998; Waldron et al., 2001).

In general, there has been little research into the differential effectiveness of these treatments to test which are more effective than others (R. J. Williams & Chang, 2000). Most of the outcome research in this area has

BOX *13.2*

IS WHAT YOU BELIEVE WHAT YOU GET?

If you thought that alcohol would make your face look ugly every time you had some, would you drink? Probably not. If, in contrast, you thought that alcohol would make you attractive and funny every time you had some, then you might be more inclined to drink on a regular basis. These questions point to the premise of the research on expectancies.

In the context of this research, *expectancies* can be defined as what an individual expects or anticipates from ingesting a substance (Vik et al., 1997). Expectancies relate to the expected reinforcing qualities of the substance and to the outcomes anticipated from its use. Most individuals' expectancies are developed through observational learning (e.g., watching parents, peers, or characters in the media using the substance) and through direct experience (Vik et al., 1997).

Expectancies can be measured meaningfully in children even before they begin drinking (M. E. Dunn & Goldman, 1996, 1998; P. M. Miller, Smith, & Goldman, 1990). A sample question is: How often do adults feel HAPPY when they drink alcohol? The possible answers are: Never, Sometimes, Usually, and Always (M. E. Dunn & Goldman, 1998). Expectancies are correlated with drinking from very early elementary school into adulthood (Deas, Riggs, Langenbucher, Goldman, & Brown, 2000; M. E. Dunn & Goldman, 1998).

In children from 3rd through 12th grades, expectancies are represented by two dimensions: Arousal–sedation and positive–negative. As can be seen in Figure 13.4, these dimensions are characterized by feelings and experiences

that children and adolescents expect to occur when someone drinks alcohol (M. E. Dunn & Goldman, 1998).

In general, younger children expect more negative and sedating effects, but as they age, they begin to expect more positive and arousing effects. This change appears to be related to greater exposure to peer and adult drinking (Cumsille, Sayer, & Graham, 2000). Children and adolescents who expect more positive effects and who expect more arousing effects are more likely to drink alcohol than those children and adolescents who expect negative and sedating effects (M. E. Dunn & Goldman, 1998). This pattern is evident at all ages and becomes especially salient in adolescence and young adulthood. Of great importance is that alcohol expectancies are better at predicting problem drinking than are demographic and background variables (Christiansen & Goldman, 1983).

Research on alcohol expectancies has great relevance to preventive interventions. Because children's expectancies can influence their likelihood of drinking alcohol, providing early preventive interventions that challenge expectancies for positive and arousing effects of alcohol could help prevent alcohol use and abuse in childhood, adolescence, and early adulthood (Cumsille et al., 2000; M. S. Goldman, 1999). This type of expectancy challenge prevention program has been effective with older adolescent college students (Darkes & Goldman, 1998; M. E. Dunn, Lau, & Cruz, 2000) and is being explored for middle and high school children (M. S. Goldman, 1999).

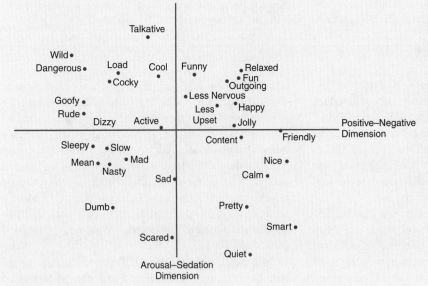

FIGURE 13.4 Individual-differences scaling stimulus configuration for alcohol expectancy words representing modes of meaning within a hypothetical expectancy memory network for children in grades 3–12. The horizontal dimension represents evaluation (positive–negative), and the vertical dimension represents arousal–sedation.

Source: M. E. Dunn & Goldman (1998).

focused on family-based interventions and cognitive-behavioral interventions (M. G. Myers, Brown, & Vik, 1998; Waldron et al., 2001). Family therapies that involve multiple systems in the adolescent's life (such as peers, the family, and school personnel) are more effective than individual treatments with adolescents (Cormack & Carr, 2000). One such treatment has involved intensive engagement of families of substance abusing Hispanic/Latino adolescents (Szapocznik et al., 1988). This research suggests that families and other systems (e.g., peer networks and the educational system) need to receive attention when treating adolescents who abuse substances (M. G. Myers et al., 1998).

Cognitive-behavioral interventions tend to focus on adolescents' cognitions in relation to their behaviors of engaging in substance use and abuse. Typical cognitive-behavioral interventions might include (M. G. Myers et al., 1998):

- Motivational enhancement.
- Introduction of functional analysis (such as using a behavioral chain worksheet).
- Cognitive-behavioral skills training modules.
- Assertiveness training.
- Training on giving and receiving criticism and expressing feelings.
- Dealing with conflict, anger, and frustration.
- Managing negative emotions.
- **Relapse prevention** (i.e., trying to prevent the reoccurrence of substance abuse after treatment).

One cognitive-behavioral strategy is to focus on the antecedents and consequences of substance use and abuse. A sample behavioral chain worksheet is shown in

Figure 13.5 to illustrate how adolescents can gain awareness of what comes before and after their substance use. The behavioral chain worksheet is used to help adolescents identify a triggering event; their thoughts, feelings, behavior; and positive as well as negative consequences to any alcohol or drug use (M. G. Myers et al., 1998).

Note that relapse prevention is of great importance in the treatment of substance abuse and dependence (Marlatt & Gordon, 1985). Many adolescents are treated effectively when they are away from home (e.g., in a residential facility) but then begin to abuse substances once they return. Relapse prevention helps adolescents identify their own high-risk situations (e.g., the graduation party where they know all of their friends will be drinking), cope with these high-risk situations, learn effective refusal skills for when they are offered substances, and develop alternative interests that would put them in fewer high-risk situations (M. G. Myers et al., 1998). Many relapse prevention interventions focus on the need to develop a new peer network that is not engaged in substance use and abuse.

Maintenance of therapeutic gains can be difficult. Having siblings who abuse substances can decrease the likelihood of maintaining therapeutic gains after treatment (Latimer, Winters, Stinchfield, & Traver, 2000). Poorer therapeutic outcome is also associated with a long history of substance abuse, low family support, low self-esteem, and more delinquent behavior (M. G. Myers et al., 1998). Treatments tend to work best with adolescents who have at least one protective factor in their favor, who receive peer and parental support, who had low rates of substance use before treatment, who receive sufficiently long treatment, who complete treatment, and who participate in aftercare (Latimer, Newcomb, Winters, & Stinchfield, 2000; R. J. Williams & Chang, 2000). Overall, the most

Trigger ———	Thought ———	Feeling ———	Behavior ———	Consequences	
				Positive	Negative
1. Gathering with friends, offered drugs	I'll feel left out if I don't use They'll think I'm lame if I say no	Anxious, uncomfortable	Use drugs	Feel comfortable with peers, have a good time, enjoy high	Guilt, feel like failure Hangover Spent money Punishment, loss of privileges Parents upset
2. Argument with parents	They don't listen or understand I'm sick of being blamed for everything	Angry, frustrated	Use drugs	Forget about argument, feel relaxed, feel less angry	Parents more angry Problems not addressed

FIGURE 13.5 Sample Behavior Chain Worksheet

Source: M. G. Myers et al. (1998).

effective treatments of substance abuse and dependence in adolescents focus on a wide variety of facets of adolescents' lives, including individual characteristics (e.g., cognitions and motivations); familial characteristics (e.g., parental monitoring); issues related to the peer network (e.g., the need to find friends who do not abuse substances); and aftercare or relapse maintenance issues (M. G. Myers et al., 1998).

One reason why I don't drink is because I wish to know when I am having a good time.

—Nancy Astor

Prevention

There are a number of effective prevention programs that help decrease the likelihood that children and adolescents will abuse substances (e.g., Spoth, Redmond, & Shin, 2001; Spoth, Reyes, Redmond, & Shin, 1999). These programs can be administered in schools, in communities, and via mass media (Schinke, Botvin, & Orlandi, 1991). School-based prevention programs, often disseminated throughout an entire school system, can also involve parents (Spoth et al., 2001). Typical substance use prevention programs in schools include the following aspects (Botvin & Dusenbury, 1989; Dusen-

bury & Falco, 1997; Meyers & Nastasi, 1999; Schinke et al., 1991):

- Teaching children factual information about the harmful effects of alcohol and illicit drugs.
- Teaching children drug refusal skills (e.g., how to say no when offered a substance and still feel good about yourself).
- Enhancing children's and adolescents' feelings of personal and social competence.
- Training teachers, aides, and parents how to talk with children about substance use, as well as teaching them the warning signs of substance use.
- Maintaining follow-up on the prevention program, often with booster sessions that are implemented on a recurrent basis.
- Helping to create a substance-intolerant social climate within the school system.

Many of these programs have been found to be effective in decreasing use of substances, especially nonalcohol substances (Schinke et al., 1991). A program called Life Skills Training, which teaches personal and social skills, has been especially effective at preventing substance use (Dusenbury & Falco, 1997). Note, however, that informa-

---

Case Study: Family Therapy and Treatment for Drug and Alcohol Dependence

Bob and Mary have four children, ages eight, six, four, and two. Bob was recently released from prison and has a lengthy drug and alcohol abuse history. Bob and Mary had been separated for four months, and just reunited two weeks ago. Within the last two weeks, Bob has had two setbacks, in which he began drinking again and using drugs. This family therapy session includes Bob, Mary, and their two oldest children, eight-year-old Susie and six-year-old Alicia. The therapist is using a brief, solution-focused family therapy. Bob is in individual treatment for his drug and alcohol problems. The current therapy is meant to deal with the harm that has been caused within the family. In this session, the therapist has just noted that the children look bored (as a way of engaging them in the therapy session), when the following interactions took place:

BOB: [*nodding toward Susie*] She's probably a lot more interested in it. It affects her a lot more than it does the younger ones.

THERAPIST: Is that right?

BOB: Yes.

THERAPIST: How does it affect her?

BOB: She mentioned to me—actually, she has, too [*pointing to Alicia*]—that they don't like me drinking. They've seen what it's done.

THERAPIST: Let me ask you, Susie, how is your dad different when he doesn't drink?

SUSIE: He's nicer. He takes us places.

THERAPIST: You like that, going places with your dad.

SUSIE: Yesterday we went to the beach.

THERAPIST: You went to the beach.

SUSIE: My dad is always nice, but I don't like when he drinks. I can tell. My mom always tells me when he drinks, but I can tell sometimes by myself because I can tell when he gets home in the morning . . .

THERAPIST: And you went to the beach yesterday. How was it?

SUSIE: Fun.

THERAPIST: [*to Bob*] How did you manage to take the kids to the beach yesterday? How did that happen?

SUSIE: We went jet skiing, but I took a friend to the beach. It was just my dad and me and my friend. He went jet skiing with my uncle.

THERAPIST: So you and Dad and your friend went to the beach. I'll bet that was very special for you . . .

SOURCE: Klar & Berg (1999, pp. 255–56).

tion-based programs and fear-inducing tactics alone are not effective in reducing substance use (Botvin & Dusenbury, 1989). The Drug Abuse Resistance Education (DARE) program is an example of a widespread but ineffective program for prevention of substance use (Dusenbury & Falco, 1997). The DARE program, which is often provided by law enforcement agencies, is very popular but shows few positive effects. A number of long-term follow-up studies have found no differences in use of drugs, attitudes toward drugs, or self-esteem between youth who did and youth who did not participate in the DARE program (Lynam et al., 1999; Rosenbaum & Hanson, 1998). There are efforts under way to improve the effectiveness of the DARE program, but to date the program has been unsuccessful at preventing substance use and abuse (Lynam et al., 1999; Rosenbaum & Hanson 1998). Interactive programs in schools, where the staff can interact with students, are more effective than noninteractive programs. Noninteractive prevention programs reduced substance abuse rates by 4%, whereas interactive prevention programs reduced substance abuse rates by 21% (Tobler, 2000).

Community-based primary prevention programs have often been instituted with groups of parents, especially parents of adolescents (Schinke et al., 1991). Prevention programs often work with parents to prevent drinking and drug use in their own children. Trying to make the prevention program specific to families' needs is associated with more effective preventive efforts (Hogue & Liddle, 1999). In addition to working with parents regarding their own children, many of these programs also help parents to become more involved in community efforts that prevent the misuse of substances. One of the most well known prevention groups is Mothers Against Drunk Driving (MADD).

Another version of a community-based program, which is not really meant as a prevention strategy, has to do with the cost of substances. A number of communities have shown that when prices of alcohol and cigarettes are raised, usage rates among adolescents decrease significantly (Hawkins et al., 1992). Although raising prices has rarely been intended for preventive reasons, the decrease in adolescent substance use after raised prices is a welcome benefit.

Mass-media prevention programs have been used extensively; however, there are inconsistent results on their effectiveness (Schinke et al., 1991). Most of these prevention campaigns have used public service announcements to caution children and adolescents about using alcohol and illicit drugs. The inconsistent results may be due to the lack of controlled studies in this area. There is a need to dismantle prevention programs that are administered through the mass media in order to identify which components work (Schinke et al., 1991).

Overall, some prevention programs have been found to be effective, but many others appear to miss those most in need of the services. For example, many prevention programs have helped decrease the onset of substance use among nonabusers but have not decreased the likelihood for intensified substance use among children and adolescents who are already abusing the substance (Shinke et al., 1991). Given that the United States spends

---

BOX 13.3

SUBSTANCE USE AND ABUSE AROUND THE GLOBE

Substance use and abuse is problematic for adolescents throughout the world. The following are some brief highlights of research findings with adolescents from a diverse array of cultures:

- A review of research on Arab adolescents in Israel, Jordan, and the Palestinian authority found that drug abuse was more prevalent in Israeli Arab adolescents than in Israeli Jewish adolescents and that Jordanian adolescents who were dependent on substances showed higher levels of education than did Palestinian adolescents who were dependent on substances (S. Weiss, Sawa, Abdeen, & Yanai, 1999).

- A total of 11% of adolescents in Taiwan reported having a substance use disorder. The highest rates of substance

use disorders were found for boys, adolescents living in rural communities, and adolescents from academically impoverished backgrounds (Chong, Chan, & Cheng, 1999).

- Chinese youth who live in Hong Kong and Chinese youth who live in mainland China show similarly moderate rates of drinking alcohol (Lo & Globetti, 2000).

- Within the United States, African American adolescents from low-income urban areas who received high levels of parental monitoring were less likely to engage in substance use, selling drugs, sexual behavior, school truancy, and violence than were adolescents who received low levels of monitoring (Li, Feigelman, & Stanton, 2000).

more than $2.45 billion on drug abuse prevention and research programs each year, it is surprising that more effective prevention programs have not been identified and implemented (Arthur & Blitz, 2000). More efforts are needed to tie together research findings with prevention programs that are instituted nationwide in order to try to reduce the number of adolescents who use and abuse substances (Stoil, Hill, Jansen, Sambrano, & Winn, 2000). Box 13.3 lists a sampling of research findings from around the globe.

ALCOHOL AND SUBSTANCE USE AND ABUSE CONCEPTUALIZED IN A DIMENSIONAL MANNER

In contrast to most of the disorders discussed in this book, the use and abuse of alcohol and other substances have been studied extensively from a dimensional perspective. It should come as no surprise that substance use is relatively prevalent among children and especially adolescents. In the Methods for the Epidemiology of Child and Adolescent Mental Disorders (MECA) study of children ages 9 to 18, 47.8% reported having had an alcoholic beverage, 5.0% reported having smoked marijuana, and 0.5% reported having used cocaine at some point in their lives (Kandel et al.,1997). The MECA study tended to find somewhat lower rates of substance use than other studies, which was probably due to the style of data collection (i.e., interviews). Specifically, studies with confidential self-report questionnaires tend to find higher rates of substance use than do studies that use interviews (Kandel et al., 1997). In an interview-based study of rural children from the southeast, 54.1% of girls and 50.2% of boys reported using alcohol by the age of 16 (Costello et al., 1999). This same study found that 10.5% of girls and 14.9% of boys had tried marijuana by the age of 16. Higher rates of usage are often found in anonymous surveys. In a national anonymous survey, 80.7% of high school seniors reported having drunk alcohol sometime within their lives and 48.4% reported having used some type of illicit drug (L. D. Johnston, O'Malley, & Bachman, 1995).

As with patterns of substance abuse, patterns of substance use suggest that substance use increases with age (Sattler, 1998). There are interesting developmental differences when adolescents are compared with adults. In contrast to adults, adolescents who use substances (especially alcohol) tend to use less frequently and tend to have lower overall intake, but tend to ingest more of the substance at one time (Deas et al., 2000; Sattler, 1998).

Specifically, *binge drinking,* defined as having five or more alcoholic drinks on one occasion, has been associated with psychosocial problems as well as physical health problems (Waldron, 1998). Approximately 30% of high school students report binge drinking, with many more boys than girls reporting that they are likely to binge drink (Dryfoos, 1997).

Substance use varies with gender, but the patterns are complex. For example, younger adolescent boys (12–13 years old) and older adolescent boys (16–18 years old) drink more alcohol than their same-aged female peers, but middle school adolescent boys and girls (14–15 years old) show similar levels of drinking alcohol (Farrell, Kung, White, & Valois, 2000; Vik et al., 1997).

Substance use is often more prevalent in communities of low socioeconomic status, but the types of substances may vary. For example, the use of cocaine powder appears to be more prevalent among middle-class and wealthy adolescents, whereas crack cocaine is more prevalent in adolescents from impoverished backgrounds (Luthar, 1999).

With regard to substance use patterns and race/ethnicity, different patterns are evident when use rather than abuse is explored. Although abuse patterns tend to show the highest rates in African Americans, usage patterns tend to show the highest rates in Caucasian Americans and Native Americans (Sattler, 1998; Vik et al., 1997). African American high school seniors report significantly lower levels of alcohol use than Caucasian Americans and Hispanic/Latino/Latina Americans (Nettles & Pleck, 1994; Vik et al., 1997). Caucasian American high school students report higher usage of hallucinogens, amphetamines, inhalants, barbiturates, and tranquilizers than do African American and Hispanic/Latino/Latina youth (Vik et al., 1997).

Even subclinical levels of substance use are associated with difficulties in functioning. Adolescents who use substances show poorer academic achievement, more negative affect, and poorer psychosocial functioning than adolescents who do not use substances (Vik et al., 1997).

Risk Factors

Theories of adolescent substance use have focused on the risk factors associated with the onset of clinical substance use. These theories often focus on three types of influence: social, attitudinal, and intrapersonal (Petraitis, Flay, & Miller, 1995).

A great deal of research has investigated risk factors for alcohol and substance use and abuse. The following

---

Case Study: Drinking and Driving

In her own words, Errica Erikson describes her experience as an adolescent in a small northwestern town:

We drank one beer, then a few more, soon I was stumbling around looking for Jessica.

"What time is it?" I asked her when I saw her getting warm by the fire.

"Eleven-fifty, why?" she said in a slurred voice.

"We have to be home by twelve!" I cried with wide eyes.

The two of us then stumbled toward her car and drove away from the music and noise.

"Be careful, but try to hurry!" I said.

The road had a lot of turns and corners on it. As soon as it became straight, the car began to pick up

speed. I closed my eyes because everything was becoming blurry and hard to see.

All of a sudden I felt myself flying through the air. Jessica screamed and my eyes shot open. We were in the air, then the car rolled, stopping only because it hit a fence post. Our heads hit the windshield so hard, we were knocked out.

I sat there in the dark, blood running down my face. I reached over and shook Jessica.

"Jessica wake up!" I cried. "Wake up! Please, Jessica!" I shook her so hard, yet she made no response. "Jessica!" I cried again in desperation. Moments passed, then she groaned.

SOURCE: Shandler (1999; pp. 38–39).

---

are some of the primary risk factors that have been identified (Allison et al., 1999; Goldman, 1999; Griffin, Botvin, Scheier, Diaz, & Miller, 2000; Hawkins et al., 1992; Hoffmann, Cerbone, & Su, 2000; Leonard et al., 2000; Sullivan & Farrell,1999):

- High levels of externalizing problems or delinquent behavior.
- Spending time with peers after school, with no adult supervision.
- Peer pressure to use drugs.
- Peers who engaged in drinking and using drugs.
- Peer approval of substance use.
- Family approval of substance use.
- Poor parenting practices, with little monitoring of children's behavior.
- Low self-esteem.
- History of sexual activity.
- High rates of stressful life events.
- High emotional distress.
- High sensation-seeking needs.
- Positive expectancies about the effects of substances.
- Low academic achievement.
- School norms for drug use.
- Drug and alcohol availability.
- Extreme poverty.
- Disorganized and disenfranchised neighborhood.

For girls, early menarche (i.e., onset of menstruation) is associated with drinking alcohol at an earlier age and

with drinking a higher quantity of alcohol (Dick, Rose, Viken, & Kaprio, 2000). Note that many of these risk factors can be considered individual or interpersonal, such as high sensation-seeking needs and low self-esteem, whereas other risk factors can be considered contextual, such as extreme poverty and living in a disorganized neighborhood (Hawkins et al., 1992).

In a comprehensive study of risk factors for substance use in an urban African American population, five primary factors were identified: intentions to use substances, having a history of sexual intercourse, showing externalizing and delinquent behaviors, feeling peer pressure to use substances, and having peers who used substances (Sullivan & Farrell,1999). It appears that the more risk factors that were present (from 0 to 5), the more substance use reported. See Box 13.4 for a more in-depth discussion of peer pressure.

Different risk factors are sometimes related to increased risk of use or abuse of specific substances. In a national sample, adolescents who had a history of familial alcohol problems, who had been physically or sexually assaulted, or who had witnessed violence were at an increased risk for alcohol abuse/dependence (Kilpatrick et al., 2000). Adolescents who had a history of familial drug problems, had been physically assaulted, had witnessed violence, or had experienced post-traumatic stress disorder were more at risk than other adolescents for marijuana abuse/dependence (Kilpatrick et al., 2000). Similar risk factors were found for adolescents who were at risk for abuse and dependence on harder drugs than marijuana, with the additions of a history of familial alcohol problems and having experienced a sexual assault (Kilpatrick et al., 2000).

Note that many of these risk factors, especially lack of parental monitoring and high rates of family conflict, are associated with a number of emotional/behavioral problems in children and adolescents (Ary et al., 1999). These risk factors seem to be especially salient for the development of externalizing problems (Ary et al., 1999). The risk factors that are most strongly connected to substance use disorders (and not other internalizing disorders) are: larger family size, lower socioeconomic status, hyperactivity, attention problems, and aggression (Reinherz, Giaconia, Hauf, Wasserman, & Paradis, 2000). Also see Box 13.5, which discusses the connections between substance use and adolescent pregnancy.

Protective Factors

In addition to the wealth of knowledge about risk factors, there is also a great deal of information available on factors that seem to protect children and adolescents from developing alcohol and substance abuse problems. The following is a list of some of the major protective factors that have been identified (Elder, Leaver-Dunn, Wang, Nagy, & Green, 2000; L. Miller, Davies, & Greenwald, 2000; Sullivan & Farrell, 1999; Wills, Sandy, Yaeger, & Shinar, 2001):

- Feeling committed to school.
- Being involved in extracurricular activities (such as sports and activity clubs).
- Attending a place of worship (such as church, synagogue, or mosque).
- Communicating with parents when distressed.
- Getting involved in demanding activities when distressed.
- Showing positive emotions.

BOX 13.4

PEER PRESSURE

A common concern is that peers will pressure children and adolescents into using and abusing substances. Evidence shows, however, that children and adolescents choose friends who are consistent with their own attitudes toward substance use and abuse (Engels, Knibbe, DeVries, Drop, & VanBreukelen, 1999). In this process, known as *selective association,* adolescents actively select a social network that is consistent with their attitudes about substance use rather than being influenced by the peers who happen to be in their social network (Engels et al., 1999). Selective association was also discussed in Chapter 2.

There is no question, however, that patterns of substance use and abuse are remarkably similar within peer groups. In fact, there is more similarity among friends regarding substance use than there is for academic orientation and ethnic identity, especially for Caucasian American and Asian American adolescents (Hamm, 2000). Part of this connection may be due to the effects of peers' sensation-seeking behavior. Pairs of friends who had a high degree of sensation seeking tended to influence each other to use alcohol and marijuana more so than when pairs of friends who did not have a high level of sensation seeking (Donohew et al., 1999).

Overall, substance-using and substance-abusing adolescents tend to socialize with others who exhibit the same behaviors (Kandel, 1978; Kandel, Kessler, & Margulies, 1978). This socializing can lead to additional "deviancy training," whereby troubled adolescents engage in even more troubling behavior (such as substance use and abuse) due to peer influences (Dishion et al., 1999).

The issue of differential influences of peers versus parents is important. One study found that peer and sibling substance use and abuse were more strongly related to adolescents' substance use and abuse than were parents' patterns of substance use and abuse (Windle, 2000). The parent–child relationship can help prevent adolescents from using and abusing substances, but parental influences are strongest when adolescents are not involved with a substance-using peer group (Gerrard, Gibbons, Zhao, Russell, & Reis-Bergan, 1999). Further, parental social support seems to protect girls more so than boys from the deleterious effects of deviant peers (Marshal & Chassin, 2000).

How children and adolescents spend their time is also related to substance use and abuse. In a study of 6th and 7th graders, adolescents who spent time after school with peers reported higher rates of substance use than did adolescents who spent time after school alone at home, with their parents, or in organized after-school activities (Flannery, Williams, & Vazsonyi, 1999). This pattern was also true for increased levels of delinquency and aggression.

Note that in addition to pressure from peers to use or not use substances, the norms for substance use in the particular school are related to adolescents' substance use (Allison et al., 1999). Specifically, school norms for drug use accounted for variance above and beyond peer influences and parental influences in predicting adolescents' substance use (Allison et al., 1999). Thus, the norms for use or nonuse of substances that are present in the adolescent's school are important to assess.

- Expecting success in one's future endeavors.

- Not having any close adult role models who use substances inappropriately.

- Feeling intolerant of deviant behaviors in others.

- Having a supportive family.

- Experiencing a positive parent–child relationship.

- Having parents who expect positive academic achievement.

- Having peers who expect positive academic achievement.

- Living with two parents (one of whom may be a stepparent).

- Showing good school attendance.

These protective factors have been identified as helpful for a diverse array of populations. In a study of urban African American youth, a number of protective factors were found to decrease the likelihood of alcohol and drug use (Sullivan & Farrell, 1999). Notably, protective factors that kept adolescents involved in school and community activities served to prevent the use and abuse of alcohol and other substances. In addition, family commitment to abstaining from alcohol and drugs served as a protective factor for African American and Hispanic/Latino/Latina adolescents (P. B. Johnson & Johnson, 1999). Family sanctions against any use of substances (including nicotine) were also found to prevent the use of substances in both rural and urban adolescents (Scheer, Borden, & Donnermeyer, 2000).

BOX 13.5

SEX, DRUGS, AND BABIES

By 12th grade, 66% of girls and 70% of boys in the United States report that they have had sexual intercourse (Dryfoos, 1997). Having multiple sexual partners is related to a higher risk for pregnancy in adolescence (Valois, Oeltmann, Waller, & Hussey, 1999). Although both the rates of sexual intercourse among adolescents and the teen birth rate decreased somewhat during the 1990s, figures from the end of the decade showed that 44 babies out of every 1,000 were born to an adolescent mother (Children's Defense Fund, 1999). Younger siblings of pregnant adolescents are at increased risk for becoming pregnant (East & Jacobson, 2001). Poor parental supervision and monitoring, a distant parent–child relationship, prior sexual abuse, low socioeconomic status, and living in a dangerous neighborhood are also risk factors for pregnancy during adolescence (B. C. Miller, Benson, & Galbraith, 2001).

The teen birth rate is much higher in the United States than in most other industrialized countries—it is twice that of Great Britain, 4 times that of Spain and Sweden, 7 times that of the Netherlands and Denmark, and 15 times higher than in Japan (Coley & Chase-Lansdale, 1998). Overall, a great many infants are born to adolescent mothers and fathers. Parenthetically, fathers of babies born to adolescent mothers are on average two to three years older than the mothers (Coley & Chase-Lansdale, 1998). Thus, the fathers are not always still in adolescence but may have already reached adulthood.

Alcohol and drug use and abuse are related to adolescent pregnancy (Coley & Chase-Lansdale, 1998; Kellogg, Hoffman, & Taylor, 1999). Although the directionality is not well established, it appears that alcohol and drugs can limit ado-

lescents' judgment and decision-making processes and may allow them to be less concerned than they would be otherwise about having unprotected sex.

Unfortunately, alcohol and drug use do not always cease when adolescents realize that they are pregnant. One study, which found significant alcohol usage among pregnant teenagers, also found that the amount of alcohol ingested during pregnancy was related directly to lower functioning and growth in the babies born to these mothers (Cornelius, Goldshmidt, Taylor, & Day, 1999). In addition, the timing of alcohol use during pregnancy can have differential negative effects on the fetus (Cornelius et al., 1999). Any amount of alcohol use during pregnancy can be harmful to the fetus, and extreme levels of alcohol use during pregnancy are related to fetal alcohol syndrome and (Dorris, 1989). Smoking (Albrecht et al., 1999) and drug abuse (Farrow, Watts, Krohn, & Olson, 1999) are also quite prevalent among pregnant adolescents.

Overall, there is a disturbing connection between substance use and pregnancy in adolescence. Prevention efforts have been focused at many levels of this problem, including prevention of unprotected sexual activities, prevention of pregnancy, and programs for parenting teenagers once the baby is born (Coley & Chase-Lansdale, 1998). Prevention efforts are particularly important because of the connections between teen pregnancy and child maltreatment (Kaufman & Zigler, 1992). Teen pregnancy is linked to child maltreatment, especially for adolescents who live in poverty. For these reasons, programs targeted at preventing substance use and unprotected sex may also help prevent some cases of child abuse.

Source: Kaufman & Zigler (1992).

Many of these protective factors also serve to protect children and adolescents from other problematic behaviors. For example, factors that protect children and adolescents from developing alcohol and substance use problems also seem to protect children and adolescents from delinquency and sexual involvement (Lerner & Galambos, 1998).

Never let me smoke.

—Advice from a preteen to parents
(Holladay & Friends, 1994, p. 133)

NICOTINE

Teen smoking has received a great deal of attention recently, largely due to the settlements from lawsuits that have been brought against tobacco companies. Although prevalence of smoking has decreased with adults, it has not decreased among adolescents (Anda et al., 1999). Studies vary somewhat in prevalence, but it is estimated that 43% of high-school-age adolescents have used tobacco, 14% to 15% of adolescents smoke cigarettes on a regular basis, and 4% have chewed smokeless tobacco (Costello et al., 1999; Dryfoos, 1997; Moolchan, Ernst, & Henningfield, 2000). Caucasian American youth are significantly more likely to smoke cigarettes, with African American youth reporting the lowest rates of smoking cigarettes (Dryfoos, 1997). The prevalence rates of smoking among Hispanic/Latino/Latina youth fall in the middle of these two groups. Whereas the rates of smoking in Caucasian adolescents tend to decrease as they reach

adulthood, rates of smoking appear to increase into young adulthood for African American youth (L. A. Robinson & Klesges, 1997). In other words, Caucasian adolescents appear to begin smoking at an earlier age than African American adolescents, but smoking rates in African Americans reach and surpass the smoking rates of Caucasians as they reach older adolescence and early adulthood. Across all racial and ethnic groups, it is estimated that 75% of adolescent smokers will continue to smoke as adults (Moolchan et al., 2000).

There are a number of risk factors associated with use of tobacco products. In a study of more than 9,000 individuals, smoking in adolescence was associated with adverse childhood experiences, such as sexual abuse, physical abuse, emotional abuse, domestic violence, parental divorce, having a substance-abusing household member, having a household member with psychiatric problems, or having an incarcerated household member (Anda et al., 1999).

Comorbidity of psychiatric disorders also appears to be a risk factor for smoking cigarettes. Depressive symptoms and emotional distress, in particular, are associated with smoking in adolescence (Orlando, Ellickson, & Jinnett, 2001; Windle & Windle, 2001). In a longitudinal study that followed African American youth from 6th grade to 10th grade, the researchers found that comorbidity between depression and conduct disorder in early adolescence was related strongly to tobacco use in later adolescence (Miller-Johnson et al., 1998). Another study found that depression and anxiety predicted smoking in 14- and 15-year-old adolescents and also made them vulnerable to peers' pro-smoking influences (Patton et al., 1998).

There are a number of prevention programs that try to discourage children and adolescents from starting to smoke and that try to help children and adolescents discontinue smoking if they have already started.

The majority of research on adolescents and nicotine has focused on use of nicotine rather than on nicotine dependence. One study, however, did explore adolescents who met criteria for nicotine dependence (Riggs, Mikulich, Whitmore, & Crowley, 1999). Referring back to Table 13.2, recall that nicotine dependence would be evidenced by adolescents who showed a maladaptive pattern of nicotine use (e.g., smoking) in which they show either tolerance (e.g., needing to smoke more to be as satisfied as before) or signs of withdrawal (e.g., irritability, anger, insomnia, depressed mood, restlessness, difficulty concentrating, decreased heart rate, and increased appetite when not smoking for long periods of time; American Psychiatric Association, 2000). Results from the study on nicotine dependence showed that adolescents who met criteria for nicotine dependence also were highly comorbid for other disorders, such as conduct disorder, attention-deficit/hyperactivity disorder, major depression, and other substance use disorders (Riggs et al., 1999).

Relatively little research has been done on smoking cessation in children and adolescents. One review suggested that nicotine replacement therapy (such as using a nicotine patch) was potentially problematic and had limited effectiveness with adolescents (Patten, 2000). A number of effective treatment programs have been identified for adults who wish to quit smoking, but very little work has been done to treat children and adolescents who smoke. Studies with adults have suggested that following up smoking cessation programs with direct mailings to the clients can help them abstain from using tobacco (Brandon, Collins, Juliano, & Lazev, 2000). These types of studies could be fruitful with treatments of child and adolescent smokers.

When compared with treatment, prevention of smoking in children and adolescents has received more attention from researchers. Attitudes toward smoking and tobacco use are important to understand before instituting prevention programs. One study used videotapes of a child actor to assess attitudes of middle school students toward the use of tobacco (Kury, Rodrigue, & Perri, 1998). Students were shown a video and told that this student would be joining the school. The video showed the child either smoking, using smokeless (chewing) tobacco, or not using any tobacco product. Students were then asked to complete measures that assessed their attitudes toward the peer. This study found that the nonsmoking peer was rated most favorably, followed by the peer who was using smokeless tobacco. The results of this study suggest that, at least in middle school, attitudes toward smokers tend toward be less favorable than toward nonsmokers (Kury et al., 1998).

Other factors have been effective in reducing the prevalence of smoking by children and adolescents. For example, enforcement of youth access laws to cigarettes has been associated with significant decreases in the rates of youth smoking (Jason, Berk, Schnopp-Wyatt, & Talbot, 1999). Nationwide, the minimum legal age for purchasing cigarettes is 18. Most communities, however, inadvertently allow children and adolescents access to tobacco products. One study found that 70% of stores allowed the sale of tobacco products to minors (Jason et al., 1999). In communities that enforce the laws that limit youth access to cigarettes, youth smoking decreases dramatically. One community that enforced youth access laws was able to show a reduction in smoking by seventh and eighth graders from 16% to 5% (Jason et al., 1999). Overall, communities that show regular enforcement of youth access laws show underage smoking rates that average 8.1%, whereas approximately 15.5% of youth smoke in communities that do not regularly enforce youth access laws (Jason et al., 1999). These findings have important implications for the prevention of smoking.

Words are, of course, the most powerful drug used by [human]kind.

—Rudyard Kipling

SUMMARY AND KEY CONCEPTS

Alcohol Abuse, Alcohol Dependence, Substance Abuse, and Substance Dependence

Substance abuse is diagnosed when children or adolescents use a substance (such as alcohol, marijuana, or cocaine) to such an extent that it impairs their functioning in some way. **Substance dependence** is diagnosed when children or adolescents not only abuse a substance but also show either tolerance or withdrawal symptoms. Substance abuse and substance dependence are often referred to collectively as **substance use disor-**ders. Substance use disorders are relatively common in adolescence and are highly comorbid with other disorders.

Substance use disorders usually begin with relatively mild substances (such as alcohol or marijuana) and move on to harder substances (such as cocaine or heroin). This process is known as the **gateway phenomenon**. Substance use disorders are thought to have multiple etiologies, with the **dynamic diathesis-stress model** providing an integrative theory of substance use disorders.

A number of treatments have been attempted with substance use disorders in adolescents. Family-based interventions and cognitive-behavioral interventions show the most promise in the treatment of adolescent substance abuse and dependence. Even after effective treatment of a substance use disorder, it is important to try to prevent the reoccurrence of the problem with **relapse prevention** programs. Many primary prevention programs have been instituted to prevent the onset of substance use and abuse.

Alcohol and Substance Use and Abuse Conceptualized in a Dimensional Manner

Unlike many other disorders, substance problems have received extensive attention from a dimensional perspective. There are a number of risk factors related to the development of substance problems. There are also many protective factors that decrease the likelihood of developing substance use problems.

Nicotine.

A significant percentage of children and adolescents have tried cigarettes or smokeless chewing tobacco. Although treatment programs for smoking cessation are rare for children and adolescents, there are a number of programs to prevent the onset of smoking early in life.

KEY TERMS

substance abuse	substance use	gateway	dynamic diathesis-	relapse prevention
substance dependence	disorders	phenomenon	stress model	

SUGGESTED READINGS

Hamill, Pete. *A Drinking Life*. Boston: Little, Brown, and Company, 1994. In this powerful memoir, Hamill discusses how he learned at an early age that drinking alcohol was part of what helped a boy become a man. After a long-term battle with alcoholism and 20 years of sobriety, Hamill recalls the influences from childhood and adolescence that were related to his difficulty with alcohol.

Knapp, Caroline. *Drinking: A Love Story*. New York: Bantam Doubleday, Dell Publishing Group, 1997. In her poignant and painful memoir, Knapp describes her first drink as a 14-year-old and her subsequent battle with alcohol. She finally gave up alcohol when, inadvertently, she almost caused serious injury to two children.

SUGGESTED VIEWINGS

Trainspotting (1996). Danny Boyle (director), John Hodge (screenwriter), based on novel by Irvine Welsh. VHS/DVD. This film portrays the underbelly of substance dependence, including vivid scenes to illustrate the negative effects of substance use.

Go (1999). Doug Liman (director), John August (writer). VHS/DVD. This film illustrates casual substance use as well as severe substance dependence in a group of adolescents.

CHAPTER *14*

SEVERE AND PERSISTENT DISORDERS: PERVASIVE DEVELOPMENTAL DISORDERS, DEVELOPMENTAL DISABILITIES, AND SCHIZOPHRENIA IN CHILDHOOD AND ADOLESCENCE

CHAPTER SUMMARY

Children have but little charity for one another's defects.

—Mark Twain

This chapter combines three primary areas of concern—pervasive developmental disorders, developmental disabilities, and schizophrenia—all of which are considered severe problems. Although all three areas have common issues of severity and limited prognoses for independent living, they are distinctly separate syndromes that should not be confused with one another. In the 1950s and 1960s there was a great deal of confusion about whether autistic disorder and schizophrenia in childhood were the same disorder or distinctly different disorders (McClellan & Werry, 1999), but it is now clearly understood that these two disorders are distinctly different, with different treatments and prognoses. Thus, it is important to identify the specific symptoms and characterizations of each.

Clinicians are often faced with the challenge of having to use differential diagnosis to tease apart these difficult disorders. Psychiatrists, clinical psychologists, and school psychologists must understand them, given that both mental health professionals and professionals within the school system are likely to encounter children who exhibit them (Kalat & Wurm, 1999). In addition, pediatricians are often the first professionals to identify problems in these children. For this reason, new clinical practice guidelines have been developed so that pediatricians and mental health professionals can work cooperatively with children who might be experiencing autism, pervasive developmental disorders, intellectual deficits, or other difficulties (Interdisciplinary Council on Developmental and Learning Disorders, 2000).

PERVASIVE DEVELOPMENTAL DISORDERS

Pervasive developmental disorders are all characterized by long-standing and overarching deficits in functioning. Four primary pervasive developmental disorders will be covered in this section: autistic disorder, Asperger's disorder, Rett's disorder, and childhood disintegrative disorder. Of these four, autistic disorder is probably the best known.

Autistic Disorder

First identified by Leo Kanner in 1943 as early infantile autism (Kanner, 1943), **autistic disorder** is characterized by impairments in social interaction, communication, and stereotyped or atypical behavior (American Psychiatric Association, 2000). As noted in Table 14.1, autistic disorder is a severe disorder that is evident from very early in a child's life.

Prevalence Rates. Although a great deal of attention in the media and in research has been given to autistic disorder, it is interesting to note that the disorder is quite rare. The prevalence rate is usually estimated at 5 cases per 10,000, which is the equivalent of 0.05% of the population (American Psychiatric Association, 2000). Although many parents do not begin to suspect problems until children reach the age of three or four, it is thought that children are born with autistic disorder and that subtle signs of autism can be identified even in infancy (Schreibman & Charlop-Christy, 1998). Autism is much more common in boys than in girls, with most estimates

Case Study: Jimmy, A Young Boy Who Was Diagnosed with Autistic Disorder

When Jimmy was five years old, his parents took him to an inpatient psychiatric facility in order to have him evaluated. Jimmy lived with his parents, Mr. and Mrs. Peterson, and his 15-year-old sister. There was no history of psychiatric or psychological problems within the family.

Although Jimmy was five, he could use only a few words and tended to scream or gesture to get what he wanted. In addition, his parents described him as "impossible to manage," given his high activity level. So far, he had failed to become toilet trained. Jimmy's parents kept thinking that he would outgrow these difficulties, but they finally realized that some type of formal evaluation might help identify Jimmy's problems.

The mother's pregnancy, Jimmy's birth, and Jimmy's early years were all considered normal. Jimmy had not experienced any major medical illness or injuries. Mr. and Mrs. Peterson did note, however, that Jimmy had not liked to be held when he was an infant. When anyone tried to hold him, Jimmy would often arch his back and scream until he was put down again. He did not make eye contact as an infant and almost never smiled. By the age of three, Jimmy still seemed to prefer the company of objects rather than that of people.

Currently, Jimmy did little else other than run around the house, spin a toy, bang objects together, or rock back and forth in a chair—all for hours at a time. He had only about 20 words

in his vocabulary, and he continued to communicate by making shrill crying noises when he wanted something.

The three-week evaluation on the inpatient unit confirmed a diagnosis of autistic disorder. Given his impairment in social interactions, impairment in communication skills, and stereotypical patterns of behavior, this diagnosis appeared to be appropriate.

Jimmy was admitted to the treatment facility for three months, with a goal of improving his social interactions, compliance with commands, and behavioral control. Jimmy's parents were also taught behavioral management skills that could help them with Jimmy's behavior once he returned home. A special education school near Jimmy's home was identified as an appropriate educational placement for him, and the special education teacher coordinated with the staff of the treatment facility in order to maintain the behavioral system that they had instituted.

Based on a one-year follow-up, there was evidence that Jimmy had improved somewhat in his communication skills and in his social interactions. These improvements, however, did not negate a continued diagnosis of autistic disorder. Jimmy continued to have severe impairments in communication and social interactions. His intensive treatment through the special education school and through his parents' interventions at home were maintained.

SOURCE: Leon (1990).

TABLE 14.1 *DSM-IV* Diagnostic Criteria for Autistic Disorder

A. A total of six (or more) items from (1), (2), and (3), with at least two from (1), and one each from (2) and (3):

(1) qualitative impairment in social interaction, as manifested by at least two of the following:

a) marked impairment in the use of multiple nonverbal behaviors such as eye-to-eye gaze, facial expression, body postures, and gestures to regulate social interaction

b) failure to develop peer relationships appropriate to developmental level

c) a lack of spontaneous seeking to share enjoyment, interests, or achievements with other people (e.g., by a lack of showing, bringing, or pointing out objects of interest)

d) lack of social or emotional reciprocity

(2) qualitative impairments in communication as manifested by at least one of the following:

a) delay in, or total lack of, the development of spoken language (not accompanied by an attempt to compensate through alternative modes of communication such as gesture or mime)

b) in individuals with adequate speech, marked impairment in the ability to initiate or sustain a conversation with others

c) stereotyped and repetitive use of language or idiosyncratic language

d) lack of varied, spontaneous make-believe play or social imitative play appropriate to developmental level

(3) restricted repetitive and stereotyped patterns of behavior, interests, and activities, as manifested by at least one of the following:

a) encompassing preoccupation with one or more stereotyped and restricted patterns of interest that is abnormal either in intensity or focus

b) apparently inflexible adherence to specific, nonfunctional routines or rituals

c) stereotyped and repetitive motor mannerisms (e.g., hand or finger flapping or twisting, or complex whole-body movements)

d) persistent preoccupation with parts of objects

B. Delays or abnormal functioning in at least one of the following areas, with onset prior to age 3 years: (1) social interaction, (2) language as used in social communication, or (3) symbolic or imaginative play.

C. The disturbance is not better accounted for by Rett's Disorder or Childhood Disintegrative Disorder.

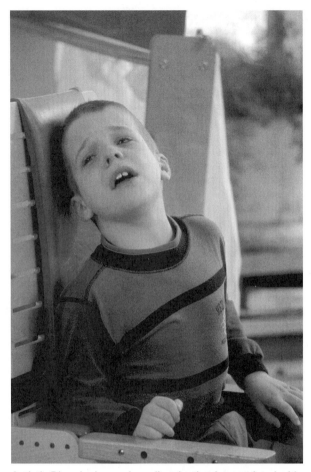

Autistic Disorder is a serious disorder that is associated with severe impairments in many, but not all, diagnosed children and adolescents.

TABLE 14.2 Overview of Prevalence Information for Autistic Disorder

Prevalence	<1% (5 cases per 10,000, or 0.05%)
Age	Usually identified in early toddlerhood or in preschool
Gender	Males > Females (4:1)
Socioeconomic status	No known patterns
Race/ethnicity	No known patterns

suggesting a 4:1 ratio (Ciaranello & Ciaranello, 1995). Girls with autistic disorder, however, are thought to show more severe impairments in intellectual functioning than boys with the disorder (Newsom, 1998; Schreibman & Charlop-Christy, 1998). There are no known patterns of autistic disorder with regard to socioeconomic status or race/ethnicity. In fact, autism has been identified in every socioeconomic status group and in nearly every racial/ethnic group (Schreibman & Charlop-Christy, 1998). Cross-cultural studies have also shown that both symptoms and prevalence rates of autism are consistent across Western and Eastern cultures (Evans & Lee, 1998).

A great deal of media attention has been given to a unique aspect of autistic disorder in which a child diagnosed with the disorder shows one skill or a set of skills often beyond imagination. Such a child is referred to as an autistic savant (Klin & Volkmar, 1997). Known as **splinter skills**, these unique abilities are often not present even in the most intellectually gifted nonautistic individuals. Such skills include the ability to perform complex mathematical problems quickly and with perfect accuracy, being able to identify the day of the week that a particular date landed on within the past 200 years, being able to rapidly count objects within a short time, or being able to recreate a musical composition after hearing it only once (Klin & Volkmar, 1997). Though fascinating, splinter skills are not well understood, especially given that many autistic savants test within the mentally retarded range on traditional intelligence tests. Note, however, that despite the media attention, autistic savants represent only about 5% of all individuals diagnosed with autistic disorder (Klin & Volkmar, 1997). Thus, the overwhelming majority of individuals with autistic disorder do not show evidence of any extraordinary skills.

Comorbidity. The most common disorder comorbid with autistic disorder is mental retardation. Although it is difficult to accurately measure the IQ of children with autism, the majority of autistic individuals (with estimates as high as 75%) also meet criteria for mental retardation (American Psychiatric Association, 2000). Their IQs usually fall in the moderate range of retardation, with a common range of 35–50. Note that nearly half of children diagnosed with autistic disorder are nonverbal (i.e., mute) and the remaining children show either language deficits such as echolalia (i.e., repeating what is said to them) or severely limited language abilities (Schreibman & Charlop-Christy, 1998). There are other features associated with autistic disorder—such as hyperactivity, aggression, self-injurious behavior, mood problems, and compulsive type behaviors—but these are thought to be part of the sequelae to the disorder rather than distinctly different comorbid disorders (American Psychiatric Association, 2000).

To take care of Noah for twenty minutes is to know how radically ill he is.

—Josh Greenfeld, about his son who is autistic

Course of the Disorder. It is commonly thought that children are born with autism rather than developing it over time. Both longitudinal studies and careful studies at different developmental levels have identified characteristics of autism throughout the life span. Although some of these symptoms can be decreased or alleviated by intensive behavioral therapy, the typical developmental course of autism is as follows (Capps, Losh, & Thurber, 2000; Mitchell & Burkhardt, 1996):

- Infants with autism appear to be limited in their social responsiveness (e.g., avoiding eye-to-eye contact and not seeking out social interactions with caregivers); tend to focus on idiosyncratic pieces of objects (e.g., only looking at the hand of a teddy bear and never exploring the rest); and often show extreme distress when any routines are changed.

- Toddlers with autism show significant delays and deficits in verbal language. These delays, often the first signs that something is wrong, typically motivate parents to seek a formal evaluation of their child.

- Children with autism continue to show significant deficits in social interactions and may also appear to display poor coordination and gross motor movements. It is not uncommon for children with autism to show nonfunctioning routines and rituals (e.g., touching all of the shiny objects within one room) and stereotyped movements (e.g., hand flapping, rocking, and spinning). If redirected or forbidden from engaging in these behaviors, children with autism often become very distressed and frustrated.

- Puberty may be somewhat delayed for individuals with autism. Other features (e.g., social deficits, limited language abilities, stereotyped behaviors) usually continue through adolescence and into adulthood. Autistic individuals who are somewhat verbal tend to focus their language on concrete objects rather than abstract conceptualizations (e.g., reporting what others ate at lunch rather than joining in on a discussion about a television show).

Unless intensive therapeutic interventions are completed, most of the deficits associated with autistic disorder continue into adulthood. Adults with autism are rarely able to live independently; most live with family members, in group homes, or in other structured and protected environments (Mitchell & Burkhardt, 1996). Some longitudinal studies have found that most children with autism (90%) grow up to be adults who continue to have significant deficits in language and intellectual functioning, which necessitate some type of sheltered living arrangement (Werry, 1996). Although better outcomes are expected for individuals with an IQ above 50 and with language skills developed by the age of five, the overwhelming majority of children with autism will continue to show signs of the disorder throughout their lives (American Psychiatric Association, 2000; Werry, 1996).

Etiology. The early theoretical work on autism is replete with blaming parents, especially mothers, for the development of autism. Some were labeled as "refrigerator parents" and told that their emotional distance and coldness toward their child led to the development of his or her autism (Kanner, 1943). However, these parent-blaming theories have never been supported by empirical evidence and are handily dismissed in current discussions of the etiology of autism (Schreibman & Charlop-Christy, 1998). More recently, there has been interest in the **theory of mind**, which suggests that children with autism do not develop appropriate cognitive functioning and cannot conceptualize mental representations of individuals in a way that allows them to predict others' behavior (Schreibman & Charlop-Christy, 1998). Although this hypothesis is intriguing, there has been limited evidence to support it (Schreibman & Charlop-Christy, 1998; Wellman, Cross, & Watson, 2001).

Case Study: The Mother of a Child Diagnosed with Autism, in Her Own Words

Asher was seen twice before my husband and I got the diagnosis. It took every ounce of courage I could muster to go that day. The therapist delivered the original diagnosis of "pervasive developmental disorder with autistic tendencies." The first words out of his mouth are forever etched in my psyche: "I want you to know that *nothing* you could possibly have done could cause your son to do the things he does." I will always be grateful to him for these words. Here we were, hearing one of the most difficult diagnoses, and both my husband and I remember our most prominent emotion on that day was *relief*. We were *not* crazy. We had not irreparably damaged our son. There was a professional who understood his behavior and was willing to support our family through the harrowing days ahead. Our thanks go out to him.

SOURCE: Marsh (1995, p. 31).

BOX *14.1*

INTENSIVE BEHAVIORAL THERAPY FOR AUTISM

One of the most promising findings to come out of research on the treatment of autistic disorder is the work of Ivar Lovaas and his colleagues at the University of California, Los Angeles (UCLA; Lovaas, 1987; McEachlin, Smith, & Lovaas, 1993). Over 30 years, Dr. Lovaas and his research group have established an intensive treatment program that uses behavioral strategies to treat the symptoms of autism. Although there are slight variations in the treatment strategies, some of the common characteristics are:

- Intensive one-on-one behavioral therapy lasting more than 40 hours per week for over two years.
- Therapeutic interventions are most often delivered by college students, though parents are also trained in the behavioral methods.
- Operant teaching techniques (e.g., rewarding successive approximations toward the goal of making eye contact with the therapist) are used.
- Some punishment techniques are used to decrease severe aversive behaviors (e.g., bitter lemon juice is squirted in the mouth of a child who bites his hand).
- Behaviors that are targeted include social skills/social interactions, language skills, cognitive functioning, and self-care skills.
- Treatment is usually completed in the child's home, in order to maximize generalizability of the effects of treatment. As treatment gains are made, treatment is then moved to other settings (such as the preschool or school setting) in order to further address generalizability issues.

Many studies have assessed the effectiveness of these treatment strategies (reviewed in Rogers, 1998). Overall, approximately half of the children who received intensive treatment in the UCLA studies showed significant gains, whereas children in control groups showed almost no significant gains. For example, children who received treatment had an average increase in IQ of 25 to 30 points compared to children in the control groups (Lovaas, 1987). Nearly half of the children who received treatment were able to attend regular education classrooms all the way through high school, whereas none of the children in the control groups was able to attend a regular education classroom (McEachlin et al., 1993). As Figure 14.1 shows, vast improvements occurred over a number of years, especially for those children identified as showing the best outcomes.

The remarkable results for some of these children continued into adulthood. At follow-up in young adulthood, many of the successfully treated young adults cannot be distin-

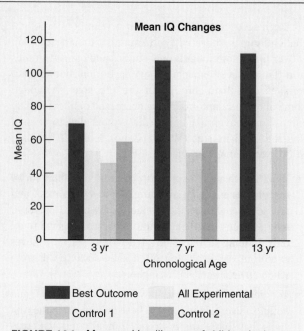

FIGURE 14.1 Measured intelligence of children in the Experimental and Control Groups in the UCLA early intervention studies. The light blue bars represent all Experimental Group children combined; the dark blue bars represent the subset of the Experimental Group with the best outcomes. The two types of medium blue bars represent the Control Groups. Control Group 2 was lost to follow-up after the assessment of seven-year-olds.

Source: Newsom (1998). The data are from Lovaas (1987) and McEachlin, Smith, and Lovaas (1993).

guished from other young adults who did not have a history of autism. Using the same treatment methods, other research groups have found comparable results (Newsom, 1998). Overall, this treatment modality appears to be very promising for at least a subset of children diagnosed with autistic disorder. Better results were found for children who received treatment earlier and who had somewhat higher functioning before beginning treatment (Rogers, 1998). Further research is needed to establish why some children respond so remarkably to the treatment and why some do not. In addition, the practicality of the treatments (e.g., with regard to both time and effort) must be considered in relation to the effects of the treatment. Overall, however, these behavioral treatment methods are the most promising treatments for autistic disorder that have been identified to date.

The most overwhelming evidence currently suggests that autism is due to some type of organic deficit (Durand & Mapstone, 1999; Kalat & Wurm, 1999; Rutter, 2000; Schreibman & Charlop-Christy, 1998; Treffert, 1999). The exact nature of the deficit, however, remains unclear. There is evidence of a genetic component in autism, given that there are extremely high concordance rates for monozygotic twins who have autism (Treffert, 1999). There is also evidence of some underlying problems in neurochemical, neuroanatomical, and other central nervous system functions (Hendren, DeBacker, & Pandina, 2000; Kalat & Wurm, 1999; Schreibman & Charlop-Christy, 1998; Treffert, 1999). These deficits most often seem to occur during the prenatal period (Gillberg, 1999). To date, there is still a great deal of confusion about what actually causes autism. Although research on etiology appears to point to organic deficits, more research is needed before identifying what specific organic deficits put children at risk for autistic disorder.

For the purposes of treatment, however, a clearly established etiology may not be crucial. Even without a clear understanding of etiology, it appears possible to treat the symptoms of autism. In order to use behavioral therapies, the focus should be on the antecedents and consequences to specific behaviors rather than on trying to find the overall etiology of the disorder (Lovaas & Smith, 1989).

Treatment. Nearly all of the effective treatments for the symptoms of autism have been behavioral. Behavioral interventions have been used to increase the use of appropriate language, increase social skills, increase social connections, increase attention, decrease aggression, decrease self-injurious behavior, and decrease hyperactivity (Durand & Mapstone, 1999; Schreibman & Charlop-Christy, 1998). The Treatment and Education of Autistic and Related Communication Handicapped Children (TEACCH) program is a well-known and effective behavioral teaching system for autistic children (Mesibov, 1997). As discussed in Box 14.1, behavioral therapies for autistic disorder are extremely complex and time-intensive. Based on years of research, these behavior therapies can help alleviate a great many deficits in children with autism (Wahlberg & Ratotori, 1996).

Regarding other treatment strategies, antipsychotic medication (such as haloperidol) has been used to control severe aggressive behavior in children with autism (M. Campbell, Gonzalez, Ernst, Silva, & Werry, 1993; Tanguay, 2000). Recently, selective serotonin reuptake inhibitor (SSRI) medication, which is a type of antidepressant, has been found to be effective in decreasing aggression and hyperactivity in children diagnosed with autism (Tanguay, 2000). There is some evidence that the combination of behavioral treatments and antipsychotic medication is far superior to the use of medication alone in controlling severe aggression in children with autism (R. T. Brown & Sawyer, 1998). There have been no effective medications, however, for increasing social interactions or language abilities in children with autism (Wahlberg & Ratotori, 1996). Overall, the most promising treatments for autism are the intensive behavioral therapies that have shown effective results with a subset of children who have the disorder.

As noted in Chapter 4, the concept of facilitated communication (in which a facilitator was thought to help autistic children convey their inner thoughts and feelings through typing on a keyboard) has been shown to be completely inappropriate (Durand & Mapstone, 1999). In a review of the empirical research on facilitated communication, the overwhelming conclusion was that facilitators, and not autistic individuals, were conveying the messages (Rimland, 1994). Despite initial hopes that facilitated communication was a way to unlock the mysteries of autism, the method has been shown to be completely useless.

Prevention. Given that so little is understood about the actual etiology of autistic disorder, it has been virtually impossible to identify prevention strategies. The best hope for prevention of the devastating effects of autism is in the combination of early identification and early intensive treatment (Lovaas, 1987). Until the mechanisms of the disorder are better understood, true prevention programs will probably be impossible to develop. Early identification and early intensive intervention, however, provide hope for preventing the severe complications and limited prognosis for children with autism (Lovaas, 1987).

Human kind cannot bear very much reality.

—T. S. Eliot

Asperger's Disorder

Considered a pervasive developmental disorder, **Asperger's disorder** is comparable to autistic disorder, but without the severe language deficits. Identified in the 1940s by Austrian psychiatrist Hans Asperger, it appeared as a formal diagnosis for the first time in *DSM-IV* (American Psychiatric Association, 1994). The definition in Table 14.3 indicates that Asperger's disorder is a chronic disorder that impacts on many facets of a child's life.

The early descriptions of children with Asperger's disorder were very comparable to descriptions of children with autistic disorder (reviewed in Treffert, 1999). Later, Asperger's cases were reviewed with more current cases that did not fully meet criteria for autistic disorder, and the following differences were noted (Wing, 1981):

- Intellectual functioning appears to be average or above average in children with Asperger's disorder, whereas children with autistic disorder tend to show significantly impaired intellectual functioning.

- Language development tends not to be delayed in children with Asperger's disorder, but use of language can still be somewhat idiosyncratic or unusual. For example, children with Asperger's disorder may be able to carry on a conversation, but they might not make adjustments for the social context of these conversations (e.g., they might talk to a two-year-old the same way they talk with an adult).

- The physical gait and motor skills of children with Asperger's disorder tend to be limited and can be described as clumsy, whereas the physical abilities of children with autistic disorder tend not to be problematic.

- Social interactions of children with Asperger's disorder tend to be limited (e.g., these children may be seen as peculiar or naive in their social interactions) but not as severely limited as children diagnosed with autistic disorder. Many children with Asperger's disorder seem to desire social interactions but lack the skills with which to engage in them smoothly.

Some researchers have questioned whether Asperger's disorder and autistic disorder are really two separate and distinct disorders. Many consider Asperger's disorder to be a less severe form of autistic disorder—that is, merely a reflection of children with autistic disorder who are high functioning. In addition, the criterion that no significant delay in language be present has been criticized (Fitzgerald, 1999). A few researchers have even questioned whether Asperger's disorder actually exists (Mayes, Calhoun, & Crites, 2001).

Because Asperger's disorder first appeared as a formal diagnosis only in 1994 with the publication of *DSM-IV* (American Psychiatric Association, 1994), no extensive research has been done on it. Although Asperger's disorder is thought to be rare (affecting less than 1% of the population), it appears to be more prevalent than autistic disorder. Specifically, Asperger's disorder is thought to be present in approximately 3 children per 1,000, which suggests that it is three to five times as common as autistic disorder (Treffert, 1999). Like autistic disorder, Asperger's disorder is much more common in boys than in girls (Wing, 1981).

TABLE 14.3 *DSM-IV* Diagnostic Criteria for Asperger's Disorder

A. Qualitative impairment in social interaction, as manifested by at least two of the following:

  (1) marked impairment in the use of multiple nonverbal behaviors such as eye-to-eye gaze, facial expression, body postures, and gestures to regulate social interaction

  (2) failure to develop peer relationships appropriate to developmental level

  (3) a lack of spontaneous seeking to share enjoyment, interests, or achievements with other people (e.g., by a lack of showing, bringing, or pointing out objects of interest to other people)

  (4) lack of social or emotional reciprocity

B. Restricted repetitive and stereotyped patterns of behavior, interests, and activities, as manifested by at least one of the following:

  (1) encompassing preoccupation with one or more stereotyped and restricted patterns of interest that is abnormal either in intensity or focus

  (2) apparently inflexible adherence to specific, nonfunctional routines or rituals

  (3) stereotyped and repetitive motor mannerisms (e.g., hand or finger flapping or twisting, or complex whole-body movements)

  (4) persistent preoccupation with parts of objects

C. The disturbance causes clinically significant impairment in social, occupational, or other important areas of functioning.

D. There is no clinically significant general delay in language (e.g., single words used by age 2 years, communicative phrases used by age 3 years).

E. There is no clinically significant delay in cognitive development or in the development of age-appropriate self-help skills, adaptive behavior (other than in social interaction), and curiosity about the environment in childhood.

F. Criteria are not met for another specific Pervasive Developmental Disorder or Schizophrenia.

Source: American Psychiatric Association (2000). Reprinted with permission from the *Diagnostic and Statistical Manual of Mental Disorders, Fourth Edition, Text Revision.* Copyright © 2000 American Psychiatric Association.

Comorbidity rates have not been established for Asperger's disorder. It is rare to see Asperger's disorder comorbid with mental retardation, as is seen with autistic disorder, but it is not clear whether children with Asperger's disorder are also at risk for other psychiatric disorders. There is some evidence that symptoms of Asperger's disorder are consistent with symptoms of nonverbal learning disorders (Rourke & Tsatsanis, 2000).

Impaired social interactions are a cornerstone of Asperger's disorder.

Like autistic disorder, Asperger's disorder is thought to be a pervasive, lifelong problem. Given that Asperger's disorder is less severe than autistic disorder, however, its prognosis is less bleak. Although individuals with Asperger's disorder often continue to show deficits in social interactions and other functioning throughout their lives, they can live independently and productively (Werry, 1996).

The etiology of Asperger's disorder continues to remain a mystery. As with autistic disorder, there is evidence that Asperger's disorder is due to some type of organic pathology (Treffert, 1999). The exact nature of the etiology of Asperger's disorder, however, has not been well established. Treatment and prevention of Asperger's disorder also remain understudied. The best hypotheses suggest that effective treatments for autistic disorder would be effective for Asperger's disorder. Specifically, behavioral therapy and social skills training in a group therapy format have been suggested as effective treatments for the symptoms of Asperger's disorder (Treffert, 1999). In addition, medications (such as selective serotonin reuptake inhibitor antidepressants and antipsychotics) may be helpful in treating any aggression and behavioral difficulties associated with Asperger's disorder (Tanguay, 2000).

Overall, there is still very limited information about children diagnosed with Asperger's disorder. As noted above, the diagnosis itself remains a bit controversial (Treffert, 1999). Now that Asperger's disorder is a formal diagnosis in the *DSM*, it is possible that increased research into the disorder will clarify these complex issues regarding diagnostic definitions, etiology, treatment, and prevention.

Other Pervasive Developmental Disorders

Two other primary pervasive developmental disorders are listed in *DSM-IV*. Both **Rett's disorder** and **childhood disintegrative disorder** are new entries, not included in previous versions of the *DSM*. As Tables 14.4 and 14.5 indicate, both Rett's disorder and childhood disintegrative disorder are similar in that the infant's neonatal and early infancy months appear to be normal. In Rett's disorder, there are usually significant deficits that appear somewhere before the age of 4 years old; in childhood disintegrative disorder, significant deficits appear somewhere before the age of 10.

Rett's disorder is very rare and continues to be poorly understood. To date, only girls have been diagnosed with it (American Psychiatric Association, 2000). There is some indication that the etiology for Rett's disorder is related to neurological complications (Naidu, 1997; Werry, 1996). Given that the disorder has been identified only in girls, an early hypothesis was that the disorder was somehow linked to the X chromosome (Kalat & Wurm, 1999). This hypothesis, however, has not been supported by further research (Kalat & Wurm, 1999). In the few cases of Rett's disorder that have been followed into adulthood, the prognosis appears to be even more poor than in autistic disorder (Naidu, 1997; Werry, 1996). Individuals with Rett's disorder can usually function only within a very structured and sheltered environment, and their psychomotor problems often continue to worsen over time (Werry, 1996). With more attention to this debilitating disorder now that it is included in *DSM-IV,* more research may lead to a better understanding of it. The same can be said for childhood disintegrative disorder.

Also known as Heller's disease, childhood disintegrative disorder is extraordinarily rare (Hendry, 2000). Worldwide, there have been fewer than 100 documented cases (Werry, 1996). In these cases, the average age of onset was between 3.3 and 4 years, with approximately four times as many boys than girls with the disorder (Volkmar, 1992). There is so little research on this disorder that its course of development, etiological factors, treatment, and prevention are not well understood. The symptoms of childhood disintegrative disorder often appear to be very similar to autistic disorder, but the age of onset and the loss of previously normal functioning set the former apart from latter (Hendry, 2000). There is some evidence that childhood disintegrative disorder is a neurological disorder and that there is no formal recovery from it (Werry, 1996). With the inclusion of this troubling and perplexing disorder in *DSM-IV*, it is hoped that more research attention will be given to it.

TABLE 14.4 *DSM-IV* Diagnostic Criteria for Rett's Disorder

A. All of the following:

   (1) apparently normal prenatal and perinatal development

   (2) apparently normal psychomotor development through the first 5 months after birth

   (3) normal head circumference at birth

B. Onset of all of the following after the period of normal development:

   (1) deceleration of head growth between ages 5 and 48 months

   (2) loss of previously acquired purposeful hand skills between ages 5 and 30 months with the subsequent development of stereotyped hand movements (e.g., hand-wringing or hand washing)

   (3) loss of social engagement early in the course (although often social interaction develops later)

   (4) appearance of poorly coordinated gait or trunk movements

   (5) severely impaired expressive and receptive language development with severe psychomotor retardation

SOURCE: American Psychiatric Association (2000). Reprinted with permission from the *Diagnostic and Statistical Manual of Mental Disorders, Fourth Edition, Text Revision*. Copyright © 2000 American Psychiatric Association.

PERVASIVE DEVELOPMENTAL DISORDERS CONCEPTUALIZED IN A DIMENSIONAL MANNER

In some ways, the mere existence of the diagnoses of Asperger's disorder and autistic disorder is helpful in conceptualizing pervasive developmental disorders in a dimensional manner (Klin & Volkmar, 1997). Given that Asperger's disorder can be considered less severe than autistic disorder, these two disorders are clearly on the same continuum of pervasive developmental disorders. As noted earlier, some researchers question whether Asperger's disorder is distinct from autistic disorder (Mayes et al., 2001), considering it instead a mild version of autism (Rutter & Schopler, 1992).

TABLE 14.5 *DSM-IV* Diagnostic Criteria for Childhood Disintegrative Disorder

A. Apparently normal development for at least the first 2 years after birth as manifested by the presence of age-appropriate verbal and nonverbal communication, social relationships, play, and adaptive behavior.

B. Clinically significant loss of previously acquired skills (before age 10 years) in at least two of the following areas:

   (1) expressive or receptive language

   (2) social skills or adaptive behavior

   (3) bowel or bladder control

   (4) play

   (5) motor skills

C. Abnormalities of functioning in at least two of the following areas:

   (1) qualitative impairment in social interaction (e.g., impairment in nonverbal behaviors, failure to develop peer relationships, lack of social or emotional reciprocity)

   (2) qualitative impairments in communication (e.g., delay or lack of spoken language, inability to initiate or sustain a conversation, stereotyped and repetitive use of language, lack of varied make-believe play)

   (3) restricted, repetitive, and stereotyped patterns of behavior, interests, and activities, including motor stereotypes and mannerisms

D. The disturbance is not better accounted for by another specific Pervasive Developmental Disorder or by Schizophrenia.

SOURCE: American Psychiatric Association (2000). Reprinted with permission from the *Diagnostic and Statistical Manual of Mental Disorders, Fourth Edition, Text Revision*. Copyright © 2000 American Psychiatric Association.

Pervasive developmental disorders can also be conceptualized in a dimensional manner because of their common deficits. Shared attention (i.e., paying attention to two different tasks at once such as looking at a ball and sharing the ball with someone), for example, is a common limitation among children with autistic disorder and Asperger's disorder (Sigman, 1996). Deficits in social responses and social interactions are also common among most of the pervasive developmental disorders (Sigman, 1996). Deficits in cognitive functioning and executive functioning may underlie the deficits in social understanding (Sigman, 1996). These types of deficits can be seen in children at different developmental stages, so any deficits must be severe before one of the pervasive developmental disorder diagnoses can be applied (Klin & Volkmar, 1997).

Risk Factors

Unlike many other psychological problems, it is difficult to identify risk factors for pervasive developmental disorders, other than those associated with etiology. Organic factors (e.g., central nervous system abnormalities, neuroanatomical abnormalities, neurological deficits) have been associated with autism, for example, but few other risk factors have been identified (Schreibman & Charlop-Christy, 1998).

Protective Factors

As with risk factors, there is little information on protective factors in relation to the pervasive developmental disorders. Other than intensive early intervention, there are no known factors that can help prevent the severe sequelae associated with these disorders. Early intervention programs tend to focus on extremely structured and intensive training programs, so it may be that structured environments serve a protective function (Lovaas, 1987). It is clear, however, that even the most structured environment cannot protect children from the onset of pervasive developmental disorders, nor can it assure a better prognosis.

A coconut shell full of water is a sea to an ant.

—Proverb of Africa

DEVELOPMENTAL DISABILITIES

Developmental disability is synonymous with the disorder that is also known as **mental retardation**. Although the formal diagnostic criteria continue to use the term *mental retardation,* many advocates working within the field prefer the term *developmental disability* because it is less stigmatizing and has less of a negative history (Sattler, 1992; V. G. Weisz, 1995). In addition, the term *developmental disability* emphasizes the developmental nature that characterizes this disorder. In essence, though, the terms *developmental disability* and *mental retardation* can be used interchangeably. Table 14.6 provides the diagnostic criteria for mental retardation that are found in *DSM-IV* (American Psychiatric Association, 2000).

Note that the primary characteristics of mental retardation include low intellectual functioning and limited adaptive functioning. This combination of symptoms is crucial in diagnosing mental retardation correctly. Individuals who have an IQ below 70 but who are otherwise able to show adequate adaptive functioning would not be diagnosed with mental retardation. Note also that the diagnostic criteria present various categories of mental retardation, distinguished by the severity of the intellectual deficits. Within the educational system, the following terms are used to signify severity level (Sattler, 1992; Singh, Oswald, & Ellis, 1998):

TABLE 14.6 *DSM-IV* Diagnostic Criteria for Mental Retardation

A. Significantly subaverage intellectual functioning: an IQ of approximately 70 or below on an individually administered IQ test (for infants, a clinical judgment of significantly subaverage intellectual functioning).

B. Concurrent deficits or impairments in present adaptive functioning (i.e., the person's effectiveness in meeting the standards expected for his or her age by his or her cultural group) in at least two of the following areas: communication, self-care, home living, social/interpersonal skills, use of community resources, self-direction, functional academic skills, work, leisure, health, and safety.

C. The onset is before age 18 years.

Degree of severity reflecting level of intellectual impairment:

Mild mental retardation:	IQ level 50–55 to approximately 70
Moderate mental retardation:	IQ level 35–40 to 50–55
Severe mental retardation:	IQ level 20–25 to 35–40
Profound mental retardation:	IQ level below 20 or 25
Mental Retardation:	Severity unspecified

Source: American Psychiatric Association (2000). Reprinted with permission from the *Diagnostic and Statistical Manual of Mental Disorders, Fourth Edition, Text Revision.* Copyright © 2000 American Psychiatric Association.

Case Study: Natasha, A Girl Diagnosed with Mild Mental Retardation

Natasha was referred for an evaluation when she was nine years old. Although she had been slow in her preschool, kindergarten, first-grade, and second-grade activities, no formal evaluations had been recommended until she reached the third grade.

Natasha lived with her parents and three older siblings. Her parents were both employed full-time and none of her siblings had any academic or intellectual difficulties. The pregnancy with Natasha had been uneventful, and in her early years she was characterized as a happy and healthy child. Natasha's parents did, however, note that she had been delayed in some of her developmental milestones. For example, Natasha was approximately one year behind in her language abilities, play activities, toilet training, and self-help skills (such as tying her shoes and dressing herself).

Natasha attended preschool for three years, partly because the preschool teacher did not think she was ready for kindergarten. Once she began kindergarten, she lagged behind other children in her academic and physical abilities. In first grade, she fell even further behind her classmates in reading, and by the second grade she still could not read even though she was tutored daily. By third grade, Natasha could read only at the first-grade level, whereas her classmates were reading third- and fourth-grade material. At this time, Natasha was also beginning to be teased by her classmates. Although she had always been friendly and social, Natasha seemed especially vulnerable to the cruel comments of her classmates.

The formal evaluation by the school psychologist revealed that Natasha had a full-scale IQ of 65, that she was in the sixth percentile of achievement in reading, and that she was in the fourth percentile of achievement in mathematics. Based on an assessment of her adaptive functioning, Natasha scored within the normal range on activities related to social interactions, but scored nearly two years below her chronological age in physical skills and adaptive skills. Based on these assessment results, Natasha was diagnosed with mental retardation, mild.

Natasha remained in regular education classes for the majority of the day but was pulled out for special education services in reading and math. The special education teacher also coordinated with Natasha's regular education teachers over the years in order to provide appropriate in-class assignments. This arrangement was continued until Natasha reached the end of the 12th grade. In addition, Natasha's parents enrolled her in a special resource program on Saturday mornings that taught adaptive skills to children and adolescents with developmental disabilities. Children were taught to make simple purchases (e.g., buying gifts for their parents), to cook simple meals (e.g., macaroni and cheese), to read a schedule for public transportation, to balance a checkbook, and to vote. Natasha seemed very receptive to learning these new skills and she thrived in these classes.

After 12th grade, Natasha was given a special diploma that acknowledged her 12 years of attendance at school and her involvement in special education services but that clarified her inability to receive a regular high school diploma. She got a job in a factory after high school, where she worked for two years. She then married, had children, and became a stay-at-home mother.

SOURCE: R. K. Morgan (1999).

- A person with mild mental retardation is referred to as **educable**. Children with this severity of mental retardation can develop social and communication skills, and can often achieve academic skills up to the sixth-grade level. Higher academic functioning is often limited, even with intensive special education services in the higher grades. With proper support, individuals identified as educable can develop vocational skills and may be able to live somewhat independently as adults.

- A person with moderate mental retardation is referred to as **trainable**. Individuals with this level of severity can develop communication and social skills, and can often achieve academic work that is consistent with the fourth grade if special education services are provided. With some support, these individuals can be employed in unskilled and semiskilled jobs as adults. Independent living is rare for individuals with moderate mental retardation, but structured group settings are not uncommon for individuals with this level of impairment.

- An individual with severe mental retardation is referred to as **severely/profoundly handicapped**. Individuals with this level of severity often have limited language abilities, poor motor skills, severely limited self-help skills, and little hope for academic achievement. In older adolescence and early adulthood, individuals with severe mental retardation may be able to work within a sheltered workshop setting, but their work and caretaking habits would need to be supervised closely.

- An individual with mental retardation beyond the severe/profound level is referred to as **custodial**. Individuals with this level of severity most often do not show any self-care skills, verbal abilities, or motor skills. Care and supervision by others is almost always necessary. Many individuals identified as custodial never develop basic skills that would be expected of young children (e.g., bowel and bladder control, the ability to feed oneself, the ability to clothe oneself).

Although the diagnostic criteria in *DSM-IV* (American Psychiatric Association, 2000) have been widely accepted, it should be noted that the American Association on mental retardation (AAMR) provides a slightly different definition of mental retardation (Matson & Smiroldo, 1999). Specifically, the AAMR sets the IQ cutoff at 75 rather than 70 (which increases the prevalence rates of mental retardation) but does not use categories of mental retardation based on the severity of intellectual deficits (American Association on Mental Retardation, 1992). The AAMR requires that the child's environment be considered before diagnosing mental retardation. The criteria for deficits in adaptive functioning are comparable between *DSM-IV* and the AAMR.

Although there is still professional interest in developmental disabilities, note that other disorders (such as autistic disorder) have gained much more attention in recent years. As Figure 14.2 indicates, the amount of research on mental retardation has remained relatively constant, while the amount of research on autistic disorder has continued to rise steadily (Newsom, 1998).

Prevalence Rates

Table 14.7 gives an overview of prevalence information for mental retardation. The overall prevalence rates of mental retardation average around 1% of the population (American Psychiatric Association, 2000). These rates, however, vary depending on the severity of the disorder.

The overwhelming majority of individuals with mental retardation (85%) fall into the mild category, which represents an IQ ranging from 50 or 55 to 70 (Singh et al., 1998). The next most prevalent group falls within the moderate range, with approximately 10% of individuals diagnosed with mental retardation showing an IQ between 35–40 and 50–55 (Singh et al., 1998). The other categories of mental retardation—severe (3–4% of individuals with mental retardation) and profound (1–2% of individuals with mental retardation)—are far more rare.

Given that mental retardation is in most cases thought to be evident from birth, there are no known patterns that show differences in prevalence across age. In other words, although mental retardation (especially mild mental retardation) may not be identified until childhood, it is thought that the rates of mental retardation remain constant throughout the life span (Biasini, Grupe, Huffman, & Bray, 1999).

As with many of the other disorders discussed in this chapter, boys are much more likely than girls to be diagnosed with mental retardation. The ratio of boys to girls is approximately 1.6:1 (Singh et al., 1998). The prevalence rates based on socioeconomic status (SES) and race/ethnicity depend somewhat on what type of etiology is responsible for the development of the mental retardation. Higher rates of mild mental retardation, which are thought to be due to environmental influences, tend to be found in children from low-SES families and children from ethnic minority populations who are living in poverty (Sattler, 1992). These same patterns, however, are

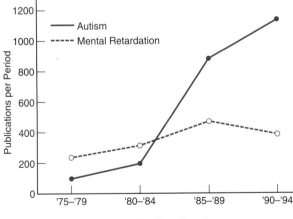

FIGURE 14.2 Number of references in the PsycINFO database for autism (filled circles) and mental retardation (open circles) for consecutive five-year periods

Source: Newsom (1998).

TABLE 14.7 Overview of Prevalence Information for Mental Retardation (MR)

Prevalence	1.0% overall
Mild	2.7% of population (85% of individuals with MR)
Moderate	0.2% of population (10% of individuals with MR)
Severe	0.1% of population (3–4% of individuals with MR)
Profound	0.05% of population (1–2% of individuals with MR)
Age	Usually evident from birth, except in mild category
Gender	Boys > Girls (approximately 1.6:1 ratio)
Socioeconomic status	Mixed pattern based on hypothesized etiology
Race/ethnicity	Mixed pattern based on hypothesized etiology

not evident in genetically related and organically related causes of mental retardation (Sattler, 1992).

Comorbidity

Although there are some psychological disorders that co-occur with mental retardation, the highest levels of comorbidity are with other neurological problems. Epilepsy is quite commonly found in individuals with mental retardation, and the rates of epilepsy appear to be higher for individuals with more severe levels (Singh et al., 1998). Cerebral palsy, motor impairments, visual impairments (e.g., blindness), and hearing impairments (e.g., deafness) are also much more common in individuals diagnosed with mental retardation than in individuals of normal intelligence (Biasini et al., 1999).

With regard to other types of psychopathology, estimates range from 10% to 40% of disorders comorbid with mental retardation (Reiss, 1990). This range occurs due to different studies and different methods of identifying psychological disorders that are comorbid with mental retardation. Specifically, studies that use case files of children and adolescents with mental retardation find that approximately 10% are diagnosed with both mental retardation and another psychological disorder (Reiss, 1990). When studies use psychopathology rating scales of children and adolescents in institutional settings or clinical settings, then estimates of the prevalence rates of comorbidity tend to fall closer to 40% (Reiss, 1990). In either case, it is clear that a substantial number of children and adolescents are diagnosed with mental retardation in addition to another type of psychopathology. Types of comorbid psychopathologies include attention-deficit/hyperactivity disorder and major depressive disorder (Handen, 1998). The term **dual diagnosis** is often used to refer to individuals who are diagnosed with both mental retardation and another type of psychopathology (Hodapp & Dykens, 1996). When dimensional conceptualizations of emotional/behavioral problems are explored, a high percentage of children and adolescents (between 38% and 65%) continue to show emotional/behavioral problems (J. W. Jacobson, 1982) and social problems (Bellanti, Bierman, & Conduct Problems Prevention Research Group, 2000). Overall, it is not uncommon that other psychological, behavioral, and social problems co-occur with mental retardation.

I often hear people comment on how happy kids with Down syndrome are and how loving . . . That image of "dumb and happy" is so unfair. Joel is a typical child; sometimes he's happy and loving and sometimes he's downright miserable . . . Sounds like a typical six-year-old, doesn't it?

—Mother of a child with Down's syndrome
(Marsh, 1995, pp. 10–11)

Course of the Disorder

Overall, children and adolescents with developmental disabilities will continue to show delays throughout their lives. Interestingly, individuals with mental retardation show even more consistency across time in their intellectual functioning (based on standardized IQ tests) than do individuals with normal or above-average intelligence (Sattler, 1992). Children and adolescents with mental retardation can continue to learn new skills and challenge themselves for greater accomplishments throughout their lives, but they usually will continue to show developmental delays when compared to same-aged peers (Sattler, 1992).

Etiology

There are many possible etiologies that lead to mental retardation, but between 30% and 40% of the cases have no known risk factor or genetic marker (Singh et al., 1998). It is likely that different types of mental retardation have different etiologies (Dykens & Hodapp, 2001). Table 14.8 presents possible known etiologies of mental retardation; these include hereditary disorders based on parental genotype, early alterations of embryonic development, problems in later pregnancy and perinatal problems, acquired childhood diseases or accidents, and environmental influences. Although prenatal testing (e.g., amniocentesis and chorionic villus sampling) can be used to detect some chromosomal abnormalities before birth, the majority of etiologies of mental retardation cannot be detected prenatally.

Treatment

Consistent with federal statutes (e.g., PL 94-142 and the Individuals with Disabilities Education Act) that support education and treatment in the least restrictive environment, there is a fair amount of consensus that children and adolescents with developmental disabilities should be included in public educational systems whenever possible. Although many countries, including the United States, have had a history of relegating children and ado-

TABLE 14.8 Etiological Factors Associated with Mental Retardation

Predisposing Factor	Approximate % of Population with MR	Examples of Specific Disorder or Condition
Hereditary disorders	5%	Inborn errors of metabolism (e.g., Tay-Sachs disease, phenylketonuria); other single-gene abnormalities (e.g., neurofibromatosis); chromosomal aberrations (e.g., fragile X syndrome)
Early alterations of embryonic development	30%	Chromosomal abnormalities (e.g., Down's syndrome related to trisomy 21); prenatal exposure to toxins (e.g., maternal alcohol consumption or substance abuse, intrauterine infections)
Later pregnancy and perinatal problems	10%	Fetal malnutrition, placental insufficiency, prematurity, hypoxia, trauma, low birth weight, intracranial hemorrhage
Acquired childhood diseases/accidents	5%	Infections (e.g., meningitis, encephalitis); demyelinating or degenerative disorders (e.g., leukodystrophies); malnutrition; head trauma (e.g., car or household accidents, child abuse); poisoning (e.g., lead, mercury); environmental deprivation (e.g., psychosocial disadvantage, neglect, or deprivation)
Environmental influences and other mental disorders	15–20%	Deprivation, child abuse, severe mental disorders
Unknown	30–40%	

Source: Singh et al. (1998).

lescents with mental retardation to the back wards of state hospitals and residential facilities, there has been a concerted effort over the past 30 years to bring children and adolescents with mental retardation into the mainstream (Handen, 1998; Singh et al., 1998). Children who have been mainstreamed show greater educational and behavioral improvements than those who receive full-time special education services (Kavale & Forness, 1999).

The majority of educational interventions for children and adolescents with mental retardation occur within public school systems (Biasini et al., 1999). Many higher-functioning children with mental retardation can be mainstreamed in regular education classrooms, whereas low-functioning children are often provided educational services in special education classrooms (Biasini et al., 1999).

With regard to psychological and behavioral issues, treatments for mental retardation vary according to the level of severity of the child's or adolescent's functioning and what specific symptoms are being addressed in the treatment. The majority of effective treatments are behavioral (e.g., operant behavioral techniques and other skills-training techniques to teach self-help skills, communication skills, vocational techniques, and social skills; Handen, 1998; Matson & Smiroldo, 1999). Applied behavior analysis techniques (i.e., the operant conditioning principles discussed in Chapter 6) have been especially useful with teaching basic skills to children with severe limitations in their behavioral repertoire (Handen, 1998). Treatments can also include family interventions to help families deal with the challenges of having a child or adolescent with a developmental disability (Biasini et al., 1999).

Antipsychotic medication has been used with some developmentally delayed children who show severe signs of aggression. The evidence is unclear as to whether antipsychotic medication is helpful in maintaining behavioral control over children with mental retardation (R. T. Brown & Sawyer, 1998). Other medications—such as antidepressants, anti-anxiety, and psychostimulant medications—have been used with developmentally delayed children and adolescents, but there is little empirical evidence to support their continued use (Branford, Bhaumik, & Naik, 1998; Handen, 1998; Singh et al., 1998). In fact, one study found that there were no positive benefits to the use of antidepressants in 40% of cases and an actual deterioration of behavior in an additional 25% of cases (Branford et al., 1998). Because of past overreliance on medications in residential facilities for children with developmental disabilities, there are now strict guidelines that must be followed before placing children in such facilities on psychotropic or other medications (R. T. Brown & Sawyer, 1998).

Prevention

Given the varied etiologies for different types of mental retardation, there are a number of possible avenues for prevention. Mental retardation due to hereditary disorders (e.g., Tay-Sachs) might be prevented by early genetic counseling with parents who are carriers of the disorder (Handen, 1998). Prenatal testing can identify some types

Like most children, children with Down's syndrome can have many assets and strengths in addition to their limitations.

of abnormal embryonic development (e.g., Down's syndrome) so that decisions can be made regarding the continuation of the pregnancy. Other problems related to abnormal embryonic development can be prevented by educating pregnant women about the harmful effects of substance use and by allowing pregnant women access to treatment for alcohol and drug problems (Handen, 1998). Many problems in later pregnancy and perinatal problems (e.g., fetal malnutrition, low birth weight) can be prevented by good prenatal care. Some childhood diseases related to the development of mental retardation (e.g., meningitis) can be prevented or at least controlled through public health interventions (Handen, 1998). Many childhood accidents (e.g., head injuries from car

accidents, poisoning) can be prevented by creating a child-safe environment (e.g., having children always use a car seat or seat belt, storing household cleaners and other poisons well out of the reach of children). Finally, environmental influences (e.g., child abuse, deprivation) can be prevented by communitywide primary prevention programs and secondary prevention programs that target parents who are at risk for maltreatment of their children (Handen, 1998). Although not all causes of mental retardation can be eliminated, the prevention strategies outlined above can reduce its incidence (Handen, 1998).

Case Study: The Mother of a Child Diagnosed with Down's Syndrome, in Her Own Words

My first real acknowledgment that something was different came when one of our doctors arrived to examine our son, Joel . . . It was Easter morning, and unfortunately my husband had returned home to gather our other two children and to share the good news of the birth of his new son with our closest friends. So I was alone when our pediatrician came in for the initial exam. At first I thought nothing of his questions about Joel's appearance being different from that of our other two children, and even joked about the fact that we had finally gotten a child with a small nose. When he finally shared his suspicions with me that Joel had Down's syndrome, he was holding the baby.

The warm memories of his caring and concern helped carry me through many of the difficult times ahead . . . I was imme-

diately moved into a private room, and for me that was very important. I had only needed to listen to my roommate make one phone call to be convinced that I simply could not bear to listen to another person share their joy right now. My world had just fallen apart. I had been on top of the world with my wonderful Easter gift one moment, and suddenly crashed to the depths the next . . .

The days I spent in the hospital were a time when rules were bent a bit and the staff was sensitive to what I needed. There was one afternoon when I think there were about 15 people in my room . . . I realize that it's often difficult to know what to say, but I appreciated those people who took the risk and didn't avoid me.

SOURCE: Marsh (1995, pp. 45–47).

DEVELOPMENTAL DISABILITIES CONCEPTUALIZED IN A DIMENSIONAL MANNER

Intellectual functioning clearly exists on a continuum. Although the diagnostic criteria for mental retardation are important for research and classification purposes, there is growing awareness of the importance of considering developmental disabilities from a dimensional perspective. In fact, there are signs of progress in trying to humanize the conceptualizations of intellectual functioning. A number of current themes are of special importance in considering the dimensional conceptualization of developmental disabilities (from Robinson, Zigler, & Gallagher, 2000; Sattler, 1992):

- Focusing on the commonalities between individuals of low intelligence and those of high intelligence, rather than focusing on the differences between these two groups.

- Highlighting the fact that children and adolescents with limited intellectual abilities can still make improvements in their lives and can strive to meet high expectations if they are given the proper guidance and support.

- Questioning the concept of mental retardation, given the dimensional nature of intellectual functioning and given the importance of so many human characteristics other than intelligence.

BOX *14.2*

A CLASSIC STUDY THAT HIGHLIGHTS "CHANGES" IN INTELLECTUAL FUNCTIONING

Although intellectual functioning is thought to be relatively stable throughout life, a number of studies have shown that enrichment programs can help raise intellectual functioning in children and adolescents (Hodapp & Zigler, 1995). In an interesting study with an experimental design, it was also established that teachers' expectations about children's intellectual functioning can alter children's scores on standardized intelligence tests (Rosenthal & Jacobson, 1966). For this study, students in grades 1 through 6 were given an intelligence test at the beginning of the school year and again at the end of the school year. Teachers were told that the test would identify children who were "blooming" and "spurting," and thus would be expected to show significant increasing in their intellectual functioning over the course of the academic year. In actuality, the test was an IQ test and did not have any predictive validity about intellectual growth spurts.

After the IQ testing at the beginning of the year, teachers were given a list of the top 10 students in their class who were expected to "bloom" that year. The researchers had, however, assigned children to this list randomly (i.e., there were no IQ differences between the children on the list and children not placed on the list). The design of the study was intended to see if teachers' expectations about children's performance could actually change IQ functioning in the children during the course of the year. Note that such deception would probably not be allowed under the current regulations for ethical treatment of human subjects; in 1966, however, this type of study was thought not only to be harmless but also to provide exceedingly important information about teachers' expectations.

Figure 14.3 shows that children in the experimental group (who had been randomly assigned to be "bloomers") did in

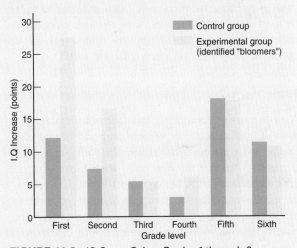

FIGURE 14.3 IQ Score Gains: Grades 1 through 6

Source: *Forty Studies That Changed Psychology* (3rd ed.) By Hock, copyright © 1999. Reprinted by permission of Prentice-Hall, Inc., Upper Saddle River, NJ.

fact show significant increases in IQ by the end of the year. This pattern was especially notable for first- and second-grade children. The study's results suggested that teachers' expectations for intellectual growth can actually lead to greater intellectual growth, especially in younger children. It may have been that teachers saw younger children's intelligence as more malleable and less set than older children's intelligence, and thus the impact of expectations had a larger effect in the earlier grades.

SOURCE: Hock (1999); Rosenthal & Jacobson (1966).

- De-emphasizing and even abandoning the use of labeling, given that individuals' functioning is better conceptualized by their strengths and weaknesses rather than by a formal diagnostic label.

- Increasing the acceptance of individual differences and the tolerance for deviance from societal norms.

- Highlighting the need for continued protection and expansion of the legal rights of children and adolescents with limited intellectual abilities.

- Highlighting the importance of prevention of intellectual limitations, especially due to the environmental influences that are associated with some etiologies of mental retardation.

- Emphasizing the coordination and planned implementation of educational and psychological services for children and adolescents with limited intellectual functioning and adaptive skills.

These themes are present in a number of professional settings (e.g., school systems, training programs in psychology, medical facilities) and should continue to be the focus of attention in this area. More research is needed on exploring developmental disabilities from a truly developmental perspective (Hodapp & Zigler, 1995).

Risk Factors

As with autistic disorder, the risk factors for the development of limited intellectual functioning and limited adaptive behavior are confounded with the etiologies that are thought to lead to these deficits. Risk factors include genetic abnormalities, biological predispositions, maternal alcohol and drug use during pregnancy, poor prenatal health care, childhood accidents, child abuse, deprivation, poverty, malnutrition, and the existence of other severe forms of psychopathology (Singh et al., 1998). As noted above, in the section on prevention, many but not all of these risk factors can be decreased or even eliminated. See also Box 14.2 for a study that explored teachers' expectations and intelligence.

Protective Factors

Depending on the etiology of developmental disabilities, there are some protective factors that can lead to better outcomes for children who have limited intellectual and adaptive abilities. The section on prevention, above, mentioned a number of strategies that might lead to a decrease in the incidence of limited intellectual and adaptive functioning (e.g., genetic counseling, better prenatal care, pre-

vention of poverty). In addition, enriched environments can help children of nearly any intellectual ability to perform at higher levels (Hodapp & Zigler, 1995). Prevention programs such as Head Start are based on the idea of overcoming environmental deprivations by providing intensive, enriched environments for children who might not otherwise receive educationally and intellectually enriching activities in the home (Hodapp & Zigler, 1995). Because the etiology of many cases of mental retardation has not been identified, it is difficult to clarify specific protective factors. In general, however, providing enriched and stable environments for children of all intellectual and adaptive levels should only serve to help them in their continued growth.

Be it life or death, we crave only reality.

—Henry David Thoreau

SCHIZOPHRENIA

Although the term **schizophrenia** was originally meant to signify a "split mind," the diagnosis of this disorder has nothing to do with split or multiple personalities (unless you consider the "split" from reality). According to the definition in Table 14.9, schizophrenia is a severe disorder that encompasses being out of touch with reality (e.g., having beliefs that are not true, hearing voices that no one else can hear, or seeing things that others cannot see) and having significant deficits in social, occupational, or academic functioning due to the limited contact with reality. Note that **delusions** are beliefs that are inaccurate (such as a 16-year-old boy believing that he is Denzel Washington) whereas **hallucinations** are sensory/perceptual occurrences that are inaccurate (e.g., hearing voices, seeing visions, or smelling odors that do not exist).

Prevalence Rates

Table 14.10 gives an overview of prevalence for schizophrenia in childhood and adolescents. Given the devastating effects the disorder, it is heartening to find that early-onset schizophrenia in children and adolescents is quite rare. Prevalence rates suggest that fewer than 1% of children under the age of 19 experience schizophrenia, with most estimates as low as 0.25% (McClellan et al., 2001; Nicolson & Rapoport, 1999; Werry, 1996). Schizophrenia has almost never been documented in children under the age of 5, and it is very rare before the age of 15 (McClellan & Werry, 1999). For boys, the first psychotic break of early-onset schizophrenia is often between the

TABLE 14.9 *DSM-IV* Diagnostic Criteria for Schizophrenia

A. *Characteristic symptoms:* Two (or more) of the following, each present for a significant portion of time during a 1-month period (or less if successfully treated):

   (1) delusions

   (2) hallucinations

   (3) disorganized speech (e.g., frequent derailment or incoherence)

   (4) grossly disorganized or catatonic behavior

   (5) negative symptoms, i.e., affective flattening, alogia, or avolition

   Note: Only one Criterion A symptom is required if delusions are bizarre or hallucinations consist of a voice keeping up a running commentary on the person's behavior or thoughts, or two or more voices conversing with each other.

B. *Social/occupational dysfunction:* For a significant portion of the time since the onset of the disturbance, one or more major areas of functioning such as work, interpersonal relations, or self-care are markedly below the level achieved prior to the onset (or when the onset is in childhood or adolescence, failure to achieve expected level of interpersonal, academic, or occupational achievement).

C. *Duration:* Continuous signs of the disturbance persist for at least 6 months. This 6-month period must include at least 1 month of symptoms (or less if successfully treated) that meet Criterion A (i.e., active-phase symptoms).

Types:

   Paranoid Type

   Disorganized Type

   Catatonic Type

   Undifferentiated Type

   Residual Type

SOURCE: American Psychiatric Association (2000). Reprinted with permission from the *Diagnostic and Statistical Manual of Mental Disorders, Fourth Edition, Text Revision.* Copyright ©2000 American Psychiatric Association.

TABLE 14.10 Overview of Prevalence Information for Schizophrenia in Childhood and Adolescence

Prevalence	<1% (approximately 0.25%)
Age	Adolescence and older (very rare in children)
Gender	Boys > Girls (2:1 ratio)
Socioeconomic status	No known patterns
Race/ethnicity	No known patterns

ages of 15 and 24, whereas females often experience their first psychotic break between the ages of 20 and 29 (Harrop & Trower, 2001; Werry, 1996). As with so many of the other disorders described in this chapter, early-onset schizophrenia is much more common in boys than in girls, with most estimates suggesting a 2:1 ratio (McClellan & Werry, 1999; Werry, 1996). This gender distribution, however, tends to equal out after adolescence—prevalence rates of schizophrenia in older adolescents and adults show no gender differences (Yee & Sigman, 1998). Within childhood and adolescence, there are no strong patterns of prevalence related to socioeconomic status or race/ethnicity (Yee & Sigman, 1998). Within adults, however, schizophrenia appears to be inappropriately overdiagnosed in African American communities (Carter & Neufeld, 1998). The prevalence rates of schizophrenia are relatively consistent worldwide, in both developed and developing countries (Carter & Neufeld, 1998).

Comorbidity

Schizophrenia in childhood and adolescence commonly co-occurs with other psychiatric disorders. One study found that 69% of children with schizophrenia also met criteria for another psychiatric disorder (Russell, Bott, & Sammons, 1989). The most common comorbid disorders were conduct disorder and depression. Within samples of adolescents diagnosed with schizophrenia, over half (54%) were found to have comorbid substance abuse diagnoses (Werry, McClellan, Andrews, & Ham, 1994). Although lower IQ scores are found in children and adolescents diagnosed with schizophrenia, the IQ scores are rarely in the range that would justify a diagnosis of mental retardation and tend to be higher than those found with children and adolescents diagnosed with autistic disorder (Dawson & Castelloe, 1992). Overall, comorbidity is the rule rather than the exception in children and adolescents diagnosed with schizophrenia.

Course of the Disorder

Schizophrenia that first appears in childhood or adolescence is a severe and often lifelong disorder. Although schizophrenia rarely is identified in young children, there is some evidence that there are early signs, albeit subtle, in children who develop schizophrenia in later childhood or adolescence. Delayed developmental milestones (e.g., walking later than usual or developing language later than usual), poor early academic work, high levels of impulsivity, and high levels of social withdrawal are often identified retrospectively in children who develop schizophrenia in later childhood or adolescence (Yee & Sigman, 1998).

Most often, the first psychotic break in later childhood or adolescence is followed by multiple other breaks throughout the child's life (McClellan & Werry, 1999). After schizophrenia develops, many other noticeable complications often arise, such as social isolation, academic deficits, and economic impairment (Andreasen & Carpenter, 1993; McClellan et al., 2001). The long-term prognosis for children and adolescents who are diagnosed with schizophrenia is not especially promising (Werry, 1996). In general, the earlier the onset, the poorer the prognosis—but these results have not always been found (Dawson & Castelloe, 1992; Werry, 1996). Childhood-onset schizophrenia shows a fair amount of continuity into adulthood (Nicolson & Rapoport, 2000; Poulton et al., 2000). Overall, there is rarely a full recovery from schizophrenia. The best hope that many individuals with schizophrenia have is for remission from active symptoms through intensive therapeutic and psychopharmacological interventions (McClellan & Werry, 1999).

Etiology

Although research on schizophrenia has been more limited in children and adolescents than in adults, certain patterns of etiology have been found. There is strong evidence of a genetic component to the development of schizophrenia (Hendren et al., 2000; Nicolson & Rapoport, 2000). Based on behavioral genetics research, the more genetic comparability between individuals, the higher the concordance for schizophrenia. Concordance rates for schizophrenia are approximately 9% for nontwin siblings, 13% when one biological parent is diagnosed with schizophrenia, 17% in dizygotic (nonidentical) twins, 46% when both biological parents are diagnosed with schizophrenia, and 48% in monozygotic (identical) twins (Gottesman, 1991). Children of schizophrenic mothers were at greater risk for the onset of the disorder, as well as for other disorders, regardless of whether they were reared by the schizophrenic mother or by psychologically healthy adoptive parents (Higgins et al., 1997). Higher paternal age is also associated with greater risk for schizophrenia (Raschka, 2000).

There is also strong evidence of prenatal and other biological factors that lead to the development of schizophrenia (Susser, Brown, & Matte, 2000). Specifically, disruptions in brain development during the prenatal period are associated with increased risk for schizophrenia in childhood and adulthood (Susser et al., 2000). Significantly more complications during pregnancy were found for children and adolescents who later developed schizophrenia than for the prenatal period of children and adolescents in a control group (Nicolson & Rapoport, 2000). Studies using magnetic resonance imaging (MRI) and positron-emission tomography (PET) suggest that brain abnormalities are evident in children and adolescents with schizophrenia (Hendren et al., 2000; Nicolson & Rapoport, 2000; Yeo et al., 1997). A decrease in cortical gray matter in the frontal and temporal regions is evident in children with schizophrenia (Rapoport et al., 1999). Thus, there is compelling evidence of a strong genetic and biological link toward the predisposition the disorder.

Note, however, that genetic and biological factors do not explain all of the variance accounted for in the development of schizophrenia in children and adolescents. Other biological markers and neurodevelopmental markers have been studied, but to date there is no strong evidence of other clear etiologies of schizophrenia in these areas (Yee & Sigman, 1998). There has been some promising work in the area of communication deviance and expressed emotion within families. **Communication deviance** is characterized by a confusing and unclear communication style within the family, and **expressed emotion** is characterized by hostile, critical, and overinvolved levels of emotional communication within the family (Yee & Sigman, 1998). Both communication deviance and expressed emotion are found at higher levels in families with offspring who are schizophrenic than in families without schizophrenic offspring (Yee & Sigman, 1998). Although it is not thought that communication deviance or expressed emotion could be the sole etiological factor that would lead to the development of schizophrenia, these factors may exacerbate the likelihood that a child or adolescent with a genetic predisposition toward schizophrenia could end up developing the disorder (Yee & Sigman, 1998).

Treatment

Treatment for schizophrenia in children and adolescents tends to take a multimodal approach. That is, children and adolescents diagnosed with schizophrenia tend to be involved in a number of different interventions, including medication, behavior therapy, social skills training, special educational services, and family therapy (McClellan et al., 2001). The primary treatment of choice for schizophrenia at any age is the use of antipsychotic medications. Antipsychotic medications (such as haloperidol and clozapine) are more effective than placebo pills and psychotherapy for alleviating the active symptoms of schizo-

Case Study: Cathy, A 14-Year-Old with Psychotic Symptoms

Cathy, age 14, was found by a classmate in the restroom at school. Cathy had slit her wrists and was taken to an inpatient psychiatric ward for evaluation. Upon her initial interview, Cathy reported that the "troops" were taking over the school and that they were trying to get to her. She reported that most of the children at school had already been invaded by the troops and that their brains had been taken out and replaced by washing machines. Although no one else could hear the noise, Cathy reported that the constant noise of helicopters outside of the hospital was proof of the invasion of the troops. Cathy reported that she did not really want to die, but that death was better than invasion by the troops. Cathy was diagnosed with schizophrenia, paranoid type.

Cathy's parents reported that she had become more reclusive in the past year. Although she had one friend in the past, this friendship had apparently been cut off about one year ago. Cathy's father (who showed up to the interview wearing military fatigues) reported that Cathy just needed a "good swat on the butt" to stop her nonsense and attention-seeking behavior. He also stated that he would be leaving the country shortly for paramilitary training in South America to prepare for militia duties when war was declared on the U.S. government.

Regarding her developmental history, Cathy's mother reported that Cathy had been a sickly baby and that she had been slow to achieve some developmental milestones. Of note, Cathy's father thought that Cathy was jealous of her younger sister, who often met developmental milestones before Cathy. Cathy's sister, Shelly, was 13 years old, and their younger brother was 4 years old.

During the family interviews, it became obvious that certain alliances existed within the family. Neither parent seemed especially close to Cathy. Cathy's father was very attentive and complementary about Cathy's sister, whereas Cathy's mother was very close to Cathy's little brother. It became obvious that there were some boundary issues and possible sexual abuse issues within the family when Cathy's sister complained that her father helped her dry herself off after showers, slept in the same bed with her, and touched her breasts occasionally. Cathy's mother reported that she was not concerned about her husband's behavior as long as he did not touch her (the mother). Cathy's mother went on to report that she allowed her four-year-old son to sleep with her and to breastfeed frequently, but that she had not allowed her husband to sleep with her since their son was born.

Treatment was planned from a three-pronged approach. First, antipsychotic medication was given to Cathy in order to decrease her symptoms of schizophrenia (e.g., delusions, hallucinations, illogical thinking, and paranoia). Second, Cathy became involved in individual therapy sessions to deal with her personal concerns and lack of friends. Finally, family therapy was conducted with the entire family. The medication and individual sessions with Cathy appeared to be successful. Her symptoms of schizophrenia decreased significantly and she became more social with peers. The family therapy sessions, however, became problematic. After the report that Cathy's father touched the girls' breasts, a report had to be made with child protective services. Cathy's sister and her mother denied any problems when child protective services investigated the report, so the case could not be pursued. The family discontinued family therapy after the abuse report was made, which was also around the same time that Cathy's father left for militia training in South America. Cathy's mother stated that the father was not sure if or when he would return to the family.

After six months, Cathy had to be hospitalized again with active symptoms of schizophrenia. She was later discharged to a group home that specialized in the treatment of adolescents with severe psychological problems. At a two-year follow-up, Cathy was still living in the group home and had not experienced any active symptoms of schizophrenia in the previous two years.

SOURCE: R. K. Morgan (1999).

---

phrenia, such as hallucinations, delusions, and illogical thinking (R. T. Brown & Sawyer, 1998; McClellan et al., 2001). More research is needed, however, to investigate the optimal medications for children and adolescents with schizophrenia and to explore the long-term effects of using antipsychotic medication with youngsters (Werry, 1996). One step in the direction of more careful medication management of children and adolescents diagnosed with schizophrenia was the development of treatment guidelines and practice parameters developed by the American Academy of Child and Adolescent Psychiatry (McClellan & Werry, 1994).

Other types of therapy in combination with medications are also helpful for children with schizophrenia (Yee & Sigman, 1998). Behavior therapy can be used to help

youngsters with schizophrenia modify their behavior (such as increasing self-help skills and compliance with medication regimens; Dawson & Castelloe, 1992). Social skills training can be used to improve the social connections that children with schizophrenia might not otherwise develop (Dawson & Castelloe, 1992). Special educational services can help children and adolescents gain more academic skills (Yee & Sigman, 1998). When there are a large number of family problems, such as high levels of negative expressed emotion and communication deviance, family therapy is highly effective in addition to medication (Ducommun-Nagy, 1999).

Overall, multimodal treatments (especially in conjunction with antipsychotic medications) have been found to help manage some of the symptoms of schizophrenia in childhood and adolescence, but no actual "cures" for schizophrenia have been found to date (Yee & Sigman, 1998). Even with intensive treatment, children and adolescents need to be monitored closely and supervised in order to ensure that their symptoms of schizophrenia do not become exacerbated.

Prevention

Given the high genetic loading for a predisposition toward schizophrenia, it is worthwhile to consider targeting prevention efforts at children who are at risk of developing the disorder due to their parents' own diagnosis of schizophrenia (Dawson & Castelloe, 1992). Only limited attention has been given to preventive efforts with children of schizophrenic parents, but this work often centers on increasing the structure in the child's environment, providing the child with adult role models outside the family, and decreasing adverse communication styles within the family (Yee & Sigman, 1998). Efforts to prevent the development of schizophrenia are sorely in need of attention, given the devastating effects of this disorder once it develops.

Don't part with your illusions. When they are gone, you may still exist, but you have ceased to live.

—Mark Twain

SCHIZOPHRENIA CONCEPTUALIZED IN A DIMENSIONAL MANNER

Unfortunately, little attention has been given to conceptualizing schizophrenia from a dimensional standpoint. Partly because the disorder is so severe, it is rare that children or adolescents show different levels of gradation of schizophrenic symptoms. It may be worthwhile, however, for researchers to try to conceptualize schizophrenia dimensionally. Doing so may help elucidate the meaning and experience of children's and adolescents' symptoms.

Risk Factors

Like so many of the other problems discussed in this chapter, the risk factors linked to the development of schizophrenia are closely tied to the hypothesized etiologies for the disorder. Children and adolescents of parents with schizophrenia are at an increased risk for the development of schizophrenia as well as other psychological disorders. Specifically, children who have at least one

biological parent (and especially children who have two biological parents) diagnosed with schizophrenia are at increased risk for the development of schizophrenia (Yee & Sigman, 1998). These findings are connected to both a genetic risk (i.e., having a genetic predisposition toward the development of schizophrenia) and an environmental risk (i.e., being raised by a parent who is disordered; Yee & Sigman, 1998). Children from families where there are high levels of communication deviance and expressed emotion are also at high risk for the development of schizophrenia, especially in the context of a genetic predisposition (Yee & Sigman, 1998).

Another possible marker for the development of schizophrenia is having an attentional problem (Cornblatt, Dworkin, Wolf, & Erlenmeyer-Kimling, 1996). Although attentional problems are common among many developmental psychopathologies (e.g., attention-deficit/hyperactivity disorder, major depressive disorder), the attentional difficulties related to schizophrenia tend to be more fundamental and may be related to additional sensory stimulation (e.g., hallucinations or delusions) that are not found commonly in other disorders (Cornblatt et al., 1996). This area is clearly in need of more research, since promising findings have been identified when looking for attentional difficulties as a risk factor for the development of schizophrenia in childhood and adolescence (Cornblatt et al., 1996). Few other risk factors have been identified that put children and adolescents at risk for the development of symptoms related to schizophrenia.

Protective Factors

Unfortunately, there has been little research into factors that might protect children from developing schizophrenia when they are exposed to the risk factors just discussed. There is some evidence that providing a stable home environment, offering access to stable mentors and role models outside the family, and increasing appropriate communication skills within the family will help protect at-risk children from developing symptoms of schizophrenia (Yee & Sigman, 1998).

SUMMARY AND KEY CONCEPTS

Pervasive Developmental Disorders

The first pervasive developmental disorder covered in this chapter is **autistic disorder**, which is a disorder characterized by severe limitations in social interaction, communication, and stereotyped or atypical behavior. A small subset of children (5%) diagnosed with autistic disorder are referred to as **autistic savant** because they show special abilities known as **splinter skills** in addition to their symptoms of autism. There are no clearly known etiologies for autism, but one theory that has received attention recently (with only limited support) was the **theory of mind**, which suggests that children with autism have significant limitations in cognitive functioning and mental representation that limit their ability to predict others' behavior.

The second pervasive developmental disorder covered in this chapter is known as **Asperger's disorder**, which some considered to be a mild form of autistic disorder. Children with Asperger's disorder show adequate language abilities but deficits in social interactions and stereotyped behavior. **Rett's disorder** and **childhood disintegrative disorder**, both of which are very rare, are also included in the discussion of pervasive developmental disorders. Rett's disorder is characterized by adequate development through the first five months of life but deterioration before the age of 48 months (four years old). Childhood disintegrative disorder is characterized by normal development for the first two years of life, with decompensation in language, social behavior, bowel or bladder control, play skills, or motor skills before the age of 10.

Pervasive Developmental Disorders Conceptualized in a Dimensional Manner

There has been some argument that the distinction between Asperger's disorder and autistic disorder is one of severity rather than distinct differences. Thus, Asperger's disorder may be seen as falling lower on the continuum of severity than autistic disorder.

Developmental Disabilities

Currently, the term **developmental disability** is used interchangeably with **mental retardation**. According to the diagnostic criteria, mental retardation is diagnosed when children show significant impairments in intellectual functioning (i.e., an IQ lower than 70) and show limitations in their adaptive functioning. Within the field of education, those with mild mental retardation are known as **educable**; those with moderate mental retardation are known as **trainable**; those with severe mental retardation are known as **severely/profoundly handicapped**; and those with mental retardation beyond the severe level are known as **custodial**. Comorbidity is common in children diagnosed with mental retardation, and the term **dual diagnosis** is often used to refer to comorbidity within this group.

Developmental Disabilities Conceptualized in a Dimensional Manner

Intellectual functioning occurs on a continuum, so it is not uncommon to consider the range of intellectual functioning in children rather than focusing on whether or not they meet criteria for mental retardation.

Schizophrenia

Schizophrenia is characterized by being out of touch with reality—believing things that are not true (known as **delusions**); hearing voices or seeing things that are not there (known as **hallucinations**); and showing significant deficits in academic, occupational, or social functioning due to these symptoms. Most etiological factors focus on organic deficits, but there is also evidence that **communication deviance** (maladaptive, confusing, and unclear communication within the family) and **expressed emotion** (hostile, critical, and overinvolved emotions within the family) can increase the risk for the development of schizophrenia in children and adolescents.

Schizophrenia Conceptualized in a Dimensional Manner

Because of the severity of the symptoms of schizophrenia, it is rare to find children or adolescents with only low levels of symptoms of schizophrenia.

KEY TERMS

autistic disorder	Rett's disorder	developmental	severely/profoundly	delusions
autistic savant	childhood	disability	handicapped	hallucinations
splinter skills	disintegrative	mental retardation	custodial	communication
theory of mind	disorder	educable	dual diagnosis	deviance
Asperger's disorder		trainable	schizophrenia	expressed emotion

SUGGESTED READINGS

Grandin, Temple. *Thinking in Pictures and Other Reports from My Life With Autism*. New York: Vintage Books, 1995. Although diagnosed with autism from early childhood, Dr. Grandin went on to earn a doctorate and to work as an animal scientist. In this insightful memoir, Dr. Grandin shares a unique experience of the inner workings of autism and shows how her unique differences allowed her to excel in a career where social isolation from humans can be considered a strength.

Schiller, Lori, & Bennett, Amanda. *The Quiet Room: A Journey Out of the Torment of Madness*. New York: Warner Books, 1995. Lori Schiller's autobiography includes graphic depictions of her descent into schizophrenia, which began in adolescence. In addition to Schiller's own recollections, her parents, brothers, roommate, and therapist also add their perspectives on Schiller's problems and her ultimate recovery and stabilization.

SUGGESTED VIEWINGS

Rainman (1988). Barry Levinson (director), Ronald Bass and Barry Morrow (writers). VHS/DVD. This powerful film illustrates autism and brotherly love in a poignant and charming manner. In addition to autism, splinter skills of autistic savants are also illustrated.

What's Eating Gilbert Grape (1993). Lasse Hallstrome (director), Peter Hedges (screenwriter), based on novel by Peter Hedges. VHS/DVD. The young brother in this film shows developmental disabilities and limited intellectual abilities in a way that is rarely captured in film. His strengths that overcome these limitations, as well as a strong family unit, are also illustrated.

CHAPTER 15

LEARNING DISORDERS AND PROBLEMS IN LEARNING

CHAPTER SUMMARY

Learning is not attained by chance, it must be sought for with ardor and attended to with diligence.

—Abigail Adams

Imagine that you are nine years old and you have to read the following passage out loud to your class. Your classmates and your teacher would all expect you to be able to pronounce the words clearly, without pausing too much between them. Go ahead and try it:

> Many words look funny when they are reversed. You may find that you have to inspect words letter-by-letter. Then, you run into letters that are especially difficult because they seem reversible, like a and s, or h and n, or b and d. There are words that look reversible too, like on-no, was-saw, and dog-god. It is especially embarrassing if you finally figure out a word, Words like "and," "the," and "but" are likely to be difficult each time they are encountered.

You probably found that passage to be a bit of a challenge. Even if you could identify words, you may have found it hard to maintain your train of thought—that is, toward the end of the sentence you may have forgotten what the beginning of the sentence said. You may have also found that reading the passage aloud required a great deal of concentration.

Now try reading the same passage in a slightly different format:

> *Many words look funny when they are reversed. You may find that you have to inspect words letter-by-letter. Then, you run into letters that are especially difficult because they seem reversible, like a and s, or h and n, or b and d. There are words that look reversible too, like on-no, was-saw, and dog-god. It is especially embarrassing if you finally figure out a word, just to see it again without recognizing the word. Words like "and," "the," and "but" are likely to be difficult each time they are encountered.*

This time, the passage probably was not a significant challenge to read and comprehend. Unless you have learning difficulties, or unless you have begun studying a foreign language recently, you probably take your reading abilities for granted. The point of this exercise is not only to remind you how difficult it is to learn to read but also to suggest what it might be like to have a problem with reading. Please note, however, that the mirror-image passage is *not* meant to imply that children with learning disorders see everything in reverse—they do not. Some children do reverse numbers and letters occasionally, but it is almost unheard of to have everything reversed in mirror-image (Sattler, 1998). Also note that not only might reading present a problem for the individual but many school exercises (e.g., asking students to read aloud) make it a social problem as well, especially with regard to possible teasing from classmates or feelings of personal embarrassment.

Oh, what a tangled web do parents weave
When they think that their children are naive.

—Ogden Nash

LEARNING DISORDERS

Formerly known as academic skills disorders, **learning disorders (LD)** are identified when children or adolescents are unable to perform academically up to the level that would be expected based on their intellectual potential. There are three primary types of LD listed in *DSM-IV*: reading disorder, mathematics disorder, and disorder of written expression (American Psychiatric Association, 2000). There is also a diagnosis known as learning disorder, not otherwise specified, which could be diagnosed when a child is having extraordinary difficulties with learning but does not meet criteria for any of the other three diagnoses of learning disorders.

As Table 15.1 indicates, the three primary diagnoses for LD all focus on a significant discrepancy between a child's academic achievement and intellectual functioning (with academic achievement falling well below what would be expected for that level of intellectual functioning). Note that these discrepancies must be documented through individual standardized testing rather than through measures administered to large groups. The discrepancy must also interfere significantly with academic functioning or with other daily activities that require skills related to that functioning. Note that if a sensory deficit is present (e.g., visual impairment, hearing impairment), the academic limitations must be in excess of what would be expected for an individual with that deficit.

Based on these diagnostic criteria, children with learning difficulties must be assessed individually to ascertain their level of intellectual functioning and their level of academic achievement in the specific areas of difficulties. An example of an individual intelligence test is the Wechsler Intelligence Schedule for Children–Third Edition (WISC-III) and an example of an individual achievement test is the Woodcock-Johnson-III: Tests of Achievement (WJ-III). Note that, although these diagnoses are listed in the section of *DSM-IV* entitled "Disorders Usually First Diagnosed in Infancy, Childhood, or Adolescence," the learning disorders diagnoses can be applied to adults as

Reading aloud in front of the classroom can be terrifying for children with a reading disorder.

TABLE 15.1 *DSM-IV* **Diagnostic Criteria for Three Types of Learning Disorders**

DIAGNOSTIC CRITERIA FOR READING DISORDER

A. Reading achievement, as measured by individually administered standardized tests of reading accuracy or comprehension, is substantially below that expected given the person's chronological age, measured intelligence, and age-appropriate education.

B. The disturbance in Criterion A significantly interferes with academic achievement or activities of daily living that require reading skills.

C. If a sensory deficit is present, the reading difficulties are in excess of those usually associated with it.

DIAGNOSTIC CRITERIA FOR MATHEMATICS DISORDER

A. Mathematical ability, as measured by individually administered standardized tests, is substantially below that expected given the person's chronological age, measured intelligence, and age-appropriate education.

B. The disturbance in Criterion A significantly interferes with academic achievement or activities of daily living that require mathematical ability.

C. If a sensory deficit is present, the difficulties in mathematical ability are in excess of those usually associated with it.

DIAGNOSTIC CRITERIA FOR DISORDER OF WRITTEN EXPRESSION

A. Writing skills, as measured by individually administered standardized tests (or functional assessments of writing skills), are substantially below those expected given the person's chronological age, measured intelligence, and age-appropriate education.

B. The disturbance in Criterion A significantly interferes with academic achievement or activities of daily living that require the composition of written texts (e.g., writing grammatically correct sentences and organized paragraphs).

C. If a sensory deficit is present, the difficulties in writing skills are in excess of those usually associated with it.

SOURCE: American Psychiatric Association (2000). Reprinted with permission from the *Diagnostic and Statistical Manual of Mental Disorders, Fourth Edition, Text Revision.* Copyright ©2000 American Psychiatric Association.

well. In fact, a number of young adults first request testing for learning disorders when they find it difficult to master college-level material (Sattler, 2002).

Terms that are consistent with the *DSM-IV* criteria for LD are used throughout this chapter. Note, however, that some researchers use other terminology to describe the same disorders. Reading disorder is often referred to as **dyslexia**, mathematics disorder is often referred to as **dyscalculia**, and disorder of written expression is often referred to as **dysgraphia** (Culbertson, 1998; Shaywitz,

1998). Although there are slight variations in meaning— and professionals might purposely use different terms for different reasons—these terms are generally comparable. This point is especially important to keep in mind regarding dyslexia. Nonprofessionals may think of dyslexia exclusively as a reading problem in which a child reverses letters. Professionals, however, currently believe dyslexia to be consistent with the overarching diagnosis of reading disorder (Culbertson, 1998).

A number of researchers have identified a fourth type of LD, although this disorder is not formally reflected in *DSM-IV*. **Social-emotional learning disorders**, also known as nonverbal learning disorders, are experienced by children who show problems with social perception, spatial skills, time orientation, and directionality (Little, 1999; Rourke & Tsatsanis, 2000). Children with nonverbal learning disorders also show deficits in spatial and emotional aspects of language, such as understanding the content of stories and being able to identify the main character's feelings in a story (Worling, Humphries, & Tannock, 1999). Overall, these children show significant deficits in nonverbal abilities.

If these symptoms sound familiar to you, try re-reading the diagnostic symptoms for Asperger's disorder listed in Chapter 14. A number of researchers and clinicians have argued that nonverbal learning disabilities and Asperger's disorder are either highly related or even the same disorder (Rourke & Tsatsanis, 2000; Volkmar & Klin, 1998). It is not completely clear whether social-emotional learning disorders are a distinct disorder or whether they are a learning disorder that is combined with social skills deficits (Culbertson, 1998). In either case, there has been a great deal of empirical research into the ramifications of social-emotional learning disorders, with a focus on trying to understand this troubling problem.

A child who asks questions isn't stupid.

—Proverb of Africa

Prevalence Rates

Table 15.2 gives an overview of prevalence information for learning disorders. According to *DSM-IV*, the prevalence of LD ranges from 2% to 10%, with approximately 5% of children and adolescents in public schools meeting criteria for a learning disorder (American Psychiatric Association, 2000). It is estimated that 4% of children and adolescents in public schools meet criteria for a reading disorder. Another 1% of school-age children meet criteria for mathematics disorders, without a comorbid reading disorder. Although there are no strong studies to estimate

Case Study: Janet, Who Is a "Slow Learner"

Janet is 13 years old and attends the sixth grade in a regular classroom (not a special education classroom). Her current teacher describes her as a "slow learner with a poor memory." The teacher goes further to say that Janet learns almost nothing in group settings and that she must be attended to on an individual basis in order for her to grasp any new concepts. Janet is currently failing reading and is almost failing English, arithmetic, and spelling. Her academic strengths appear to be in art and sports.

Janet did not show any significant problems in her developmental history. She had her tonsils out when she was five years old and she had a number of ear infections (chronic otitis) when she was young. Her other developmental milestones, such as crawling, walking, and talking, all appeared to be on time.

Janet, however, has had school problems almost from the very beginning of school. She failed the first grade and noted that her teacher was "mean." She was placed into a special education classroom in first grade but then removed due to chronic fighting with her classmates.

Now that Janet is in sixth grade, she continues to have some interpersonal problems at school in addition to her academic difficulties. Although she seems to be a friendly child, she is quite sensitive about her academic difficulties. She feels that she gets "bossed around" at school, but she does report having a great many friends in her neighborhood.

An evaluation for a learning disorder revealed that Janet has intelligence in the average range but significant deficits in her reading achievement scores. She currently reads at the fourth-grade level. Her other academic achievement scores, such as spelling and arithmetic, were somewhat delayed but did not show significant deficits.

Janet meets criteria for a reading disorder. Her other academic achievements were not significantly delayed, so no other learning disorder diagnoses were appropriate. Janet's behavioral difficulties were thought to be associated with her reading disorder, so no other emotional/behavioral disorders were appropriate.

SOURCE: Spitzer, Gibbons, Skodol, Williams, & First (1994).

---

the prevalence rates, it is thought that disorders of written expression (without comorbid reading disorders) are relatively rare, with an estimated prevalence of less than 1% of school-age children (American Psychiatric Association, 2000).

Reading disorders encompass the overwhelming majority of learning disorders, with four out of five learning disorders being diagnosed as a reading disorder or a reading disorder in combination with a mathematics disorder or a disorder of written expression. Note that mathematics disorders and disorders of written expression are

TABLE 15.2 Overview of Prevalence Information for Learning Disorders

Prevalence	
Overall LD	2–10%
Reading	4%
Mathematics	1%
Written expression	<1%
Age	
Reading	Onset by age 7
Mathematics	Onset by age 8
Written expression	Onset by age 7
Gender	Boys (although there is equivocal evidence)
Socioeconomic status	Unknown
Race/ethnicity	Unknown

usually diagnosed in addition to reading disorders (American Psychiatric Association, 2000). In other words, it is rare to find a child with a mathematics disorder or a disorder of written expression who does not also meet criteria for a reading disorder. Figure 15.1 provides a writing sample of an eight-year-old girl who ultimately was diagnosed with both a reading disorder and a disorder of written expression.

Age patterns are difficult to synthesize because learning problems often become evident as academic tasks become more difficult. Although learning disorders can be diagnosed at any age, it is rare that they are identified before children enter kindergarten (Elbert, 1999). A common age for the first referral for a reading disorder is seven, given that reading tasks become formalized around this age (Culbertson, 1998). Mathematics disorders are usually first identified around the age of eight, when arithmetic assignments become more rigorous (Culbertson, 1998). Disorders of written expression are less well documented, but there is some evidence that first referrals can occur around the age of seven (Culbertson, 1998). Overall, the older children are when they are first referred for an LD evaluation, the less severe their impairments tend to be (Elbert, 1999). In other words, children with less severe learning problems can usually show adequate, albeit limited, academic achievement in the early grades but may begin to show significant deficits in the middle school years.

With regard to gender, most clinical studies find that

FIGURE 15.1 Writing Sample of Eight-Year-Old Girl With a Reading Disorder and a Disorder of Written Expression
Source: Mather & Jaffe (1992).

learning disorders of all types are more common in boys than in girls. These studies find that between 60% and 80% of children referred for help with reading disorders are boys (American Psychiatric Association, 2000). Note, however, that in epidemiological studies, the gender differences tend to be less evident (American Psychiatric Association, 2000; Elbert, 1999). This difference may be due to the fact that compared to girls, boys are referred more quickly for services or are more disruptive and thus are identified for services earlier (Shaywitz, Shaywitz, Fletcher, & Escobar, 1990). In addition, it may be that teachers confuse learning disorders with limited aptitude and thus refer boys for services more often than girls (Shaywitz et al., 1990). Overall, there is evidence that boys are somewhat more susceptible to learning disorders than are girls, but the gender difference in prevalence rates is not as strong as originally thought (Elbert, 1999).

With regard to epidemiological patterns in socioeconomic status (SES) and race/ethnicity, surprisingly little research has addressed these issues for LD. Although children from lower SES homes and children from ethnic minority groups are disproportionately represented in special education classes, it is not clear whether these patterns are due to actual epidemiological rates or due to biases within the referral and identification process (Halfon & Newacheck, 1999; Sattler, 2002). Note that there is almost no research on ethnic and racial groups other than African American and Latino/Latina/Hispanic (Serafica, 1997). For example, since 1984 the U.S. Department of Education has not reported rates of special education use by Asian Americans (Serafica, 1997).

Comorbidity

As with so many other disorders, comorbidity with a learning disorder is the rule rather than the exception. It is not

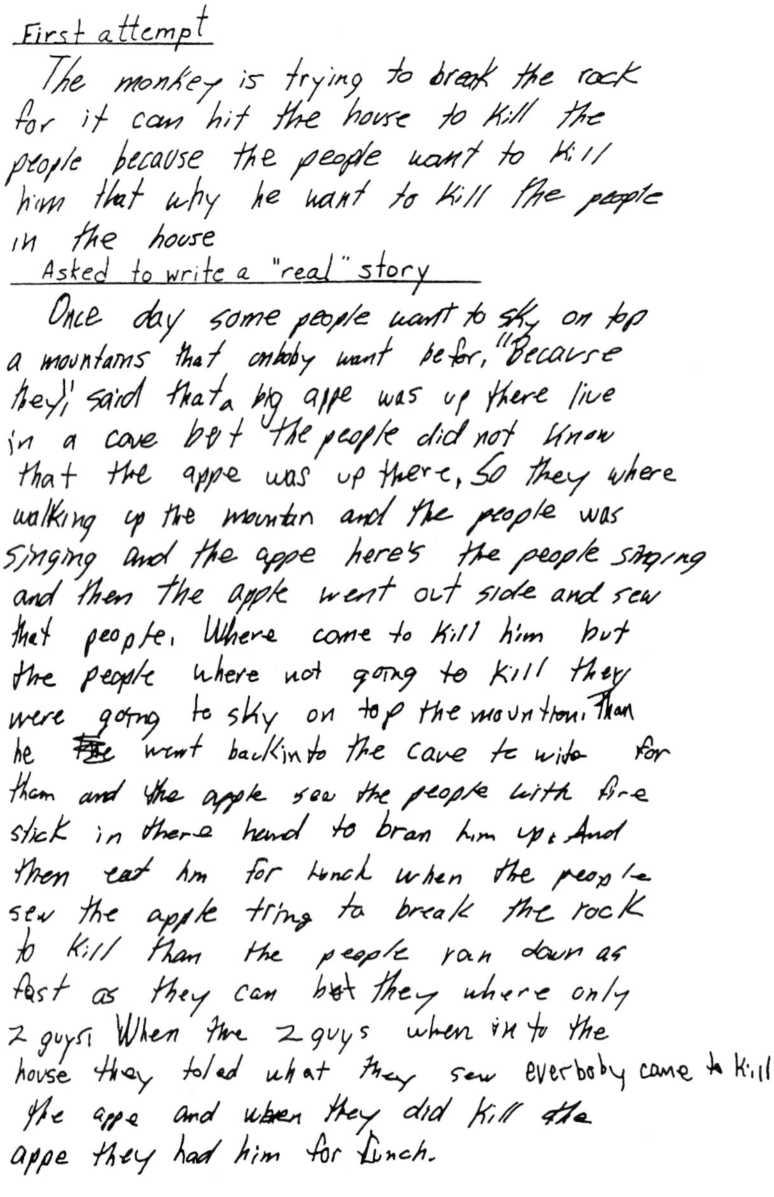

First attempt

The monkey is trying to break the rock for it can hit the house to kill the people because the people want to kill him that why he want to kill the people in the house

Asked to write a "real" story

Once day some people want to sky on top a mountains that onboby want befor, "Because they," said that a big appe was up there live in a cave but the people did not know that the appe was up there, So they where walking up the mountan and the people was singing and the appe here's the people singing and then the appe went out side and sew that people, Where come to kill him but the people where not going to kill they were going to sky on top the mountion. Than he went back into the cave te wide for them and the appe sew the people with fire stick in there hend to bran him up, And then eat hm for lunch when the people sew the appe tring to break the rock to kill than the people ran down as fast as they can but they where only 2 guys, When the 2 guys when in to the house they toled what they sew everboby came to kill the appe and when they did kill the appe they had him for Lunch.

FIGURE 15.2 Flavio's Writing Sample Illustrating Good Story Grammar but Poor Language and Visual Recall Skills (Note also the aggressive themes in the writing sample)

Source: Mather & Jaffe (1992).

uncommon for children, adolescents, and even adults who experience a learning disorder to also experience one or more other psychiatric disorders (Curran & Hollins, 1996; Willcutt & Pennington, 2000). Although estimated comorbidity with LD has varied from 10% to 92%, it now appears that a realistic range is from 19% to 26% (Barkley, 1990; Culbertson, 1998). Reading disorders are associated with greater risk for both internalizing and externalizing disorders (Willcutt & Pennington, 2000). Disorders that co-occur commonly with LD are language disorders and ADHD (Culbertson, 1998). Children diagnosed with LD are also prone to have social deficits and interpersonal problems (Sprouse, Hall, Webster, & Bolen, 1998).

The high comorbidity rates between LD and language disorders have received a lot of empirical attention. Language disorders and communication disorders appear to be highly related to learning disorders, especially reading disorders (Weindrich, Jennen-Steinmetz, Laucht, Esser, & Schmidt, 2000). Given that language and communication skills are central to the ability to read, it is not surprising that language disorders, communication disorders, and learning disorders co-occur quite often (Lewis, Freebairn, & Taylor, 2000a). Language and communication disorders also show high comorbidity rates with other psychological disorders (Richman & Wood, 1999; Toppelberg & Shapiro, 2000). It is likely that the high comorbidity rates between language disorders, communication disorders, and reading disorders are due to the common mechanisms involved in the development of all of these disorders (Richman & Wood, 1999; Toppelberg & Shapiro, 2000).

Comorbidity between LD and ADHD has also received a great deal of attention given its frequency (Maynard, Tyler, & Arnold, 1999; Willcutt, Pennington, & DeFries, 2000). In general, children who are comorbid for both LD and ADHD tend to have significant impairments in both learning and attention/behavioral control. For example, children in grades 2 through 4 who met criteria for both LD and ADHD showed more significant impairment in their learning problems than did children without the comorbid diagnosis of ADHD (Bussing, Zima, Belin, & Forness, 1998). Even children diagnosed with LD who did not meet criteria for ADHD were shown to have deficits in attention comparable to those of children diagnosed with ADHD (Mayes, Calhoun, & Crowell, 1998). With regard to social functioning, teachers rated elementary school children with comorbid LD and ADHD as less socially perceptive than children without any disorder (Sprouse et al., 1998). As illustrated in Figure 15.2, children with LD sometimes also have high levels of aggression, which can be reflected in their writing samples (Mather & Jaffe, 1992). Flavio's biological mother abused drugs and drank alcohol while pregnant. He has never had any contact with his biological father. Flavio is currently 12 years old and has had numerous placements in the foster care system over the past 10 years.

High comorbidity rates, especially between LD and ADHD, have been discussed critically in the professional literature. Some critics have called the current diagnostic system a "Balkanization process," meaning that it tends to create new and independent diagnostic categories when using currently existing categories might be more appropriate (Kavale & Forness, 1998). Specifically, researchers have suggested identifying co-occurring problems across many different disorders, such as problems in social skills or attention, rather than developing new and more complex disorders (Kavale & Forness, 1998).

Help me with my homework when I need you to.

—Advice from preteens to their parents
(Holladay & Friends, 1994, p. 119)

Course of the Disorder

As noted in the prevalence section, above, learning disorders are usually not identified until first or second grade for most children, with reading disorders and disorders of written expression usually being identified earlier than mathematics disorders (American Psychiatric Association, 2000). Children with higher intelligence and children with less severe learning disorders tend not to be

---

Case Study: Matt's Mother Advocates for Him, in Her Own Words

My son Matt is going to middle school next year, so I started to activate the process to change schools, to transition him. I was told by our learning strategist and everybody else that we had to make an appointment with the principal. So I called the office and asked to make the appointment with the principal, and I was told they don't do that. They said that I had to go through the guidance office, so they switched me to the guidance office. I told them that my son would be coming there next year and I wanted to make an appointment with the principal. The guidance office told me they couldn't do that until I talked with a guidance counselor, so a little later a woman called me and asked why on earth would I want to talk to the principal and what was the problem. I tried to explain to her that my son would be coming there next year and that he was a rather unique child, that he has attention-deficit hyperactivity disorder (ADHD), learning disorder (LD), and is gifted . . .

I tried to explain to this guidance counselor how difficult things are for him and that he needs a computer in the classroom. Her response was that the transition team would decide that. She asked if this was in his Individualized Education Program (IEP) and I said, "Yes, it is, that he needs a computer in the classroom.

He is totally mainstreamed with a computer. He has attention deficit and it is very difficult for him to make transitions of any kind." She said, "Well, we do a wonderful job of transitioning all the students, this is what we do, and I'm sure he will be just fine. Why do you really think you want to talk to the principal?" " I want to talk to him about the type of student he is getting next year," I said. She said, "Well, I really don't think that's necessary." "Well then," I said, "I'd like to at least come in and observe the classrooms." She answered, "Well, I don't know if I can arrange it. We'll see if I can arrange it. Call me back in March." . . .

So I started over. I called the school again and I said, "I want to speak to the principal." I got the principal and I said, "I would like to have a meeting with you." So I go in this Friday. It's just an example of how we are handled. The guidance counselor just wasn't listening at all to anything I was saying: the fact that what my son has is debilitating enough to make him non-functional in the regular classroom, that he has to see psychiatrists, talk to counselors, work as a team; and this is her way of trying to help him prepare? So I decided what he needed and just did it without her.

Source: Marsh (1995, pp. 13–16).

Teachers can be an integral part of helping identify children with learning problems and in helping to remedy those problems.

identified as having a learning disorder until later in their academic schooling (Elbert, 1999). Continuity of learning disorders is not always evident. One study found that only 28% of first-graders with significant learning problems were identified as having problems in third grade (Shaywitz, Escobar, Shaywitz, Fletcher, & Makuch, 1992).

There are, however, long-term ramifications to learning disorders. Nearly 40% of children or adolescents diagnosed with LD drop out of school before high school graduation (American Psychiatric Association, 1994). This rate is more than 1.5 times higher than the dropout rate of non LD children. Even in adulthood, a large number of those diagnosed with LD experience difficulty in their occupational pursuits and social interactions (American Psychiatric Association, 2000).

Early identification and early intervention, however, are thought to prevent a lifetime of difficulties (American Psychiatric Association, 2000). Without some type of educational intervention (e.g., tutoring, special educa-

tional services, intensive educational strategies), it is rare that a severe learning disorder will dissipate over time (Culbertson, 1998). Given that later learning in most academic subjects relies on earlier fundamental information, once children fall significantly behind in a school subject it is difficult for them to catch up without intensive intervention strategies. With educational enhancement strategies in place, however, children and adolescents with LD can expect to continue their education into college and even graduate school if they so desire (Elbert, 1999).

Etiology

There is no single etiological factor that has been identified in the development of LD (Shaywitz, 1998). Three factors have been identified most often as leading to a greater risk for the development of a learning disorder (Sattler, 1998):

BOX *15.1*

HOW AMERICA STANDS

Among industrialized countries, the United States ranks:

1st	in military technology
1st	in gross domestic product
1st	in the number of millionaires and billionaires
1st	in defense expenditures

10th   in eighth-grade science scores
21st   in eighth-grade math scores

Source: Children's Defense Fund (1999).

- Genetic factors.
- Biological factors.
- Ineffective learning strategies.

Studies in behavioral genetics suggest that learning disorders may be genetic. Notably, there is often a strong family history of LD in children with a documented learning disorder (Lyon, 1996). Studies of monozygotic twins and dizygotic twins have shown higher concordance rates for LD in monozygotic twins, which suggests a genetic component to the disorder (Kranzler, 1999). In addition, children with LD are more likely to have experienced prenatal and perinatal complications and to show electrophysiological abnormalities (Lyon, 1996). These studies, however, are far from conclusive. For example, the family history of LD may put a child at greater risk for develop-

ing a learning disorder due to genetic factors, but it also may put a child at greater risk due to environmental factors (e.g., a parent who cannot help with homework or who is ambivalent about the need for academic excellence or who does not expect academic success in the child).

Biological factors, such as problems in perceptual systems, perceptual-motor functioning, neurological organization, and oculomotor functioning, may be related to the development of a learning disorder (Culbertson, 1998; Sattler, 1998). It is not uncommon for children with LD to show a number of these difficulties. Although no clear-cut basis for these problems has been identified, there is speculation that children with LD may have experienced some type of minor birth trauma or may have experienced chronic middle ear infection before the age of four (Sattler, 1998). It may be that these biological factors lead to

---

Case Study: Nigel, The Boy Who Showed Problems in Reading

Nigel is 13 years old but still in the fifth grade. He was held back for two different academic years because of his difficulties with mastering academic work. He shows particular difficulty with reading and spelling, but also shows problems in math. Nigel did not show any major developmental problems or academic problems until he reached the third grade. Behaviorally, Nigel appears to be somewhat anxious and withdrawn, but he does not show any conduct problems at school or at home.

Nigel lives with his four brothers and sisters as well as his parents. He receives special educational services once a week. He is also involved in speech therapy, which began when he was three years old. His parents monitor his homework each night and try to help in any way they can. Both of Nigel's parents, all of his aunts and uncles, and nearly all of his siblings have had significant learning problems.

On request from his teachers and parents, Nigel was evaluated for LD by a school psychologist. The comprehensive assessment included tests of intellectual functioning, academic achievement functioning, and behavior. Nigel's intelligent quotient (IQ) was in the average range, but there was a significant discrepancy between his verbal IQ and performance IQ. Specifically, Nigel's verbal IQ fell into the borderline range (which is below the low average category), whereas his performance IQ fell into the superior range. Nigel had difficulty with verbal tasks, especially vocabulary, and he had strengths in putting blocks and puzzles together. His academic achievement tests showed that he was performing at or below the third-grade level in nearly all areas, including reading, spelling, arithmetic, word recognition, comprehension, and listening skills. Behaviorally, Nigel was quiet and shy. During the classroom observation, Nigel tended to work by himself or ask other children for help; he rarely asked the teacher for help.

Based on the results of this evaluation, Nigel was diagnosed with a reading disorder. Although he showed significant deficits

in mathematics as well, he did not meet criteria for mathematics disorder. A treatment and educational plan was developed that first addressed Nigel's difficulties in reading and spelling, and then focused on Nigel's difficulties in mathematics. Nigel received 30 weeks of intensive intervention from his reading teacher, who was trained in special education. Interventions included developing better skills in sight reading, focusing on words that were frequently misspelled, overcorrecting reading and spelling errors, and finding reading materials that were of interest to Nigel in order to enhance his motivation to learn to read better. After the intervention, Nigel improved significantly in his reading and spelling abilities. The reading teacher planned to continue to provide additional help to Nigel in the classroom setting, but it was determined that he no longer required this intensive one-on-one intervention. Nigel's mathematics difficulties were to be addressed in the following school year.

At six-month follow-up, Nigel was reading at about six months behind his classmates, a significant improvement on his previous two-year delay in reading. Behaviorally, he showed more self-confidence in the classroom and began to interact socially with more of his peers. His parents had also taken a much more active role with Nigel and his siblings in order to ensure that reading and other homework assignments were completed each evening.

This case illustrates a classic example of a reading disorder. Although his reading problems were not identified until third grade, Nigel probably had been having difficulties before then. In addition to interventions regarding the reading disorder, it is important to consider the social-emotional functioning of children and adolescents with learning disorders. The social ramifications of being a 13-year-old in a class with mostly 10-year-olds should be addressed in addition to intervening with the learning disorder.

SOURCE: Singh, Beale, & Snell (1988).

abnormalities in cognitive processing. Limitations in visual perception, attention, memory, and linguistic processes—all of which have the common element of cognitive processing—appear to be pervasive among children and adolescents diagnosed with a learning disorder (American Psychiatric Association, 2000). Most notably, children who develop reading disorders tend to have deficits in word recognition, which seem to be related to deficits in phonological awareness (i.e., these children seem to have limited abilities in being able to "notice, think about, or manipulate sounds in words"; Lyon & Cutting, 1998, p. 481).

Note that these phonological deficits and language disorders are thought to be a key feature of reading disorders (Lovett, Steinbach, & Frijters, 2000; Swank, 1999). Specifically, children with language deficits and phonological deficits are highly likely to develop reading disorders (Lewis, Freebairn, & Taylor, 2000b; McArthur, Hogben, Edwards, Heath, & Mengler, 2000). Although phonological deficits are also common in other disorders (such as autism), it appears that phonological deficits are a key factor in the development of reading disorders (Frith & Happe, 1998).

Using an ineffective learning strategy has also been identified as a factor that may lead to a learning disorder (Sattler, 1998). Children may not learn the most effective ways of solving academic problems and thus may fall behind in their academic achievement. Specifically, they may not learn how to analyze problems effectively, how to relate a current problem with problems that were solved in the past, how to implement a strategy for conceptualizing a problem that is to be solved, or how to evaluate their own performance and adjust their performance accordingly (Sattler, 1998).

Overall, there are no clear etiological factors that are known to lead consistently to the development of a learning disorder. Like so many other disorders, learning disorders are likely to be developed from a complex combination of factors that result in children's and adolescents' inability to learn in the way that other youth learn.

Treatment

Interventions for LD usually involve some combination of educational and psychological interventions, so the classic conceptualization of "treatment" does not always apply. For example, although psychostimulant medication (such as Ritalin) is effective in reducing aversive behavior in children diagnosed with ADHD, it has little effectiveness in raising achievement scores in children diagnosed with both LD and ADHD (R. T. Brown, Lee, & Donegan, 1999).

Overall, the school system is probably the most salient site for interventions with LD. As noted in Box 15.2, over half of the children receiving special education services

---

BOX 15.2

SPECIAL EDUCATIONAL SERVICES IN SCHOOLS

Who receives services through the Individuals with Disabilities Education Act (IDEA)?

- 51.1% had specific learning disorders.
- 21.1% had speech and language impairments.
- 11.6% were diagnosed with mental retardation.
- 8.6% experienced severe emotional disturbances.
- 7.6% fell into other categories, such as multiple disabilities, hearing impairments, heath problems, orthopedic disabilities, autism, or traumatic brain injury.

Where did these children receive special education services?

- 39.8% were in a regular classroom, and most of these children received brief "pullout" services for their special education needs, which totaled no more than 21% of the school day.

- 31.7% were in a resource room, which means that they received special services in a resource room for between 21% and 60% of the school day.
- 23.5% were in a separate class, which means that they received special education services for 60% or more of the day, usually in a self-contained special education classroom.
- 3.7% were in a separate day school, designed in most cases to serve the needs of children and adolescents with either learning, physical, or severe emotional difficulties.
- 0.8% were in a residential facility, including full-time facilities.
- 0.5% were homebound or in a hospital environment, usually because they could not function in a school setting or because they required additional mental health services.

SOURCE: Sattler (1998).

through the Individuals with Disabilities Education Act (IDEA) were receiving services for LD (Sattler, 1998). The majority of these children either received services with special pullout programs from their regular education classroom or received part-time services within an educational resource room. Because of mainstreaming, there has been a strong push to keep special education children in regular education classrooms rather than in special education classrooms (Kavale & Forness, 1999).

Although empirical studies in this area are limited, there is some evidence that special education services can help children and adolescents overcome LD (Elliott, Busse, & Shapiro, 1999). Most special educational services try to incorporate some of the following (Elliott et al., 1999):

- Instructional interventions (e.g., using special education teaching methods that maximize children's ability to learn new material).

- School–home notes (e.g., regarding what work needs to be done and how parents and teachers can work together to help children).

- Performance feedback (e.g., providing children with direct feedback about their academic performance).

- Self-management (e.g., helping children learn how to manage their own time and behavior within the academic setting).

- Contingency management interventions (e.g., teachers providing reinforcement to increase on-task behaviors, work completion, and accuracy).

- Cognitive-based interventions (e.g., self-instructional training to help increase on-task behavior and self-control in academic activities).

- Peer tutoring (e.g., having peers help peers on academic tasks).

- Group contingencies (e.g., rewarding the entire class for maximal efforts by most children).

- Cooperative learning (e.g., having students work together in small groups or in teams in order to maximize the learning of all students in the group).

In addition, there are examples of unique and innovative intervention programs such as one called "I Don't Like to Write but I Love to Get Published," which helps motivate reluctant writers to improve their writing skills by working for a classroom newspaper (Alber, 1999). These techniques are somewhat effective in intervening with children who have a learning disorder. The majority of these techniques can be instituted in either regular or special education classrooms. There is a small but significant advantage for children to be mainstreamed (Kavale & Forness, 1999).

A great deal of attention has also been paid to the effectiveness of phonological training for children with reading disorders. Phonological training uses techniques like word identification training to help children gain mastery over reading and writing (Lovett et al., 2000). Given the connection between language deficits and reading disorders, it is not surprising to find that programs like phonological training are effective (Lovett et al., 2000;

Reynolds, Elksnin, & Brown, 1996). There is evidence that longer periods of phonological training are associated with the greatest benefits, especially for children with severe reading difficulties (Gillon & Dodd, 1997).

Note, however, that not all summaries of special educational efforts have been promising. Based on a thorough meta-analysis of five types of special education interventions for LD, few of the interventions were found to have a strong impact on educational functioning (Kavale & Forness, 1999). As Table 15.3 shows, only one of the interventions—applied behavior analysis—achieved a large mean effect size (.80 and above) and the majority showed medium to small mean effect sizes. Overall, this research suggests that some special educational strategies, such as applied behavior analysis, early intervention, and psycholinguistic training, are more promising than others, such as modality instruction or perceptual-motor training (Kavale & Forness, 1999).

Given that most special education interventions are conducted in the school system, it is important to look at the match between children's needs and the services they receive within the school system. There are concerns about what types of children are placed in special education classrooms meant for children diagnosed with LD. One study of children in grades 2 through 4 found that a majority of those diagnosed with ADHD or other serious emotional/behavioral disorders were placed in special education services for LD, even though they did not need primary services for LD (M F. Lopez, Forness, MacMillan, & Bocian, 1996). In general, it appeared that child study teams (who place children in special educational services) were hesitant about placing children in classrooms for severely emotionally disturbed (SED) children and instead placed these children in services for LD. This placement pattern can work against the best interests of both behaviorally troubled children and children diagnosed with LD. In LD classrooms, children with severe behavioral problems may be helped by the extra attention on learning problems, but there will be little intervention for their behavioral problems. Conversely, children diagnosed with LD but without behavior disorders will experience a more troubling classroom environment because of the inclusion of children who might be better served in an SED classroom (M. F. Lopez et al., 1996). Overall, additional attention must be given to appropriate services for both LD and non-LD children within the special education system.

In addition to attention to services within the school setting, there has been increasing interest in helping teachers and school psychologists increase usage of the home environment. The thought is that teachers, special educators, and school psychologists have access to children for only a limited portion of the day (usually about six or seven hours), while parents and other caretakers have access to children for the remainder of the day and all day on weekends (Christenson & Buerkle, 1999). There has been growing interest in trying to engage parents in the educational system in such a way as to enhance their children's learning and educational attainments. Judging from the drawing in Figure 15.3, you might imagine that the child's best interests would be served if the teacher could work with the foster parents to provide a more stable and enriching home environment.

TABLE 15.3 Summary of Meta-Analyses in Special Education Services for LD

Interventions	Number of Studies	Mean Effect Size	Standard Deviation Of Effect Size
Perceptual-motor training	180	.08	.27
Psycholinguistic training	34	.39	.54
Modality instruction	39	.15	.28
Early intervention	74	.40	.62
Applied behavior analysis	41	.93*	1.16

*Large effect size.

SOURCE: Kavale & Forness (1999).

FIGURE 15.3 Picture Drawn by a Boy (Age 12 years, 10 months) Who Was a Foster Child in a Deplorable Home

Source: DiLeo (1973).

Historically, parents were contacted by school personnel only if something was wrong (e.g., the child was failing a course or was truant). Often, the relationship between parents and school personnel was strained because of a lack of common goals and an adversarial atmosphere (Christenson & Buerkle, 1999). More recently, many school personnel have made a concerted effort to connect with families in a cooperative manner that works to benefit children and adolescents who are struggling with their academic functioning. In keeping with this new emphasis, the following suggestions have been made to help school psychologists become educational partners with families in order to enhance children's school success (Christenson & Buerkle, 1999):

- Disseminate information to parents about the school curriculum and the ideal home curriculum.

- Establish parent–educator problem solving in order to create a partnership between parents and educators so that the home environment can become more conducive to educational activities.

- Engage in solution-oriented family–school meetings so that parents feel that their time in school meetings is productive and works toward the best interests of their child.

- Engage in conjoint behavioral consultation that allows the school psychologist to serve as a consultant between parents and teachers in order to develop mutually agreed-upon solutions for the child's academic difficulties.

- Develop family–school teams so that parents can become more involved in setting policies and can help within the school system.

Overall, this new focus on families as educational partners has been effective (Christenson & Buerkle, 1999). When teachers, special educators, school psychologists, and parents work together to enhance children's school success, the best interests of the child are facilitated. One study of parents and students involved in collaborative teaching models that included a parent–teacher partnership showed that parents and students were highly satisfied with this model and reported that students' self-esteem and academic understanding increased because of the collaborative methods (Gerber & Popp, 1999). More research is needed in this area to ascertain the specific mechanisms of change, but the empirical work so far has been promising (Christenson & Buerkle, 1999).

The love of learning, the sequestered nooks, and all the sweet serenity of books.

—Henry Wadsworth Longfellow

Prevention

Because there has been only limited success with educational interventions to treat LD, there has been a renewed focus on prevention. The majority of empirical work that explores the prevention of LD has focused on the prevention of reading disorders (Lyon & Cutting, 1998).

Educationally enriching environments, such as those in Head Start programs, can be beneficial for children when the programs are maintained for an extended amount of time.

Because reading disorders are thought to be due to difficulties with word recognition, which are brought about by difficulties with phonological awareness, most preventive interventions seek to train students in phonological awareness at an early age (Lyon & Cutting, 1998). Many prevention programs work with children in kindergarten to enhance their phonological awareness (Torgesen, Wagner, Rashotte, & Conway, 1997). These early intervention and prevention programs have been found to be effective in reducing the risk for development of a reading disorder (Blachman, 1997). Phonological awareness prevention programs tend to present the information in a gamelike format so that children can learn how to analyze words and synthesize or blend parts of words into the entire word (Lyon & Cutting, 1998). Overall, there are a number of early intervention programs that are effective in preventing the onset of diagnosable reading disorders (Lyon & Cutting, 1998). Studies on the prevention of mathematics disorders and disorders of written expression are still needed.

LEARNING DISORDERS AND LEARNING PROBLEMS CONCEPTUALIZED IN A DIMENSIONAL MANNER

Even in *DSM-IV*, there is an acknowledgment that learning problems might not be due to a learning disorder within the individual. In order to diagnose LD, the clinician must first rule out other characteristics such as normal variations in academic attainment, lack of educational opportunity, poor teaching methods, and cultural factors (American Psychiatric Association, 2000).

In terms of conceptualizing learning problems in a dimensional manner, it is important to acknowledge that lots of children have problems in learning at different times in their academic endeavors. A total of 7% of Caucasian American children, 13% of African American children, and 38% of Hispanic/Latino/Latina children never finish high school, but only a small subset of these children have documented learning disorders (Children's Defense Fund, 1999). Thus, there are many problems that children experience with learning that are not encompassed by the diagnostic criteria of LD. Although categorical conceptualizations of LD are used in most Western countries, there is growing interest in conceptualizing learning problems in a dimensional manner in order to serve children's needs more directly (Ghesquiere & Ruijssenaars, 1998).

Rather than focusing on specific learning disorders, it may be more meaningful to explore learning problems and difficulties that are associated with learning problems. For example, assessing functional skills (e.g., orientation, attention, basic sensory functions, modality-specific learning, cross-modal sensory integration, higher-level linguistic and phonological skills, and higher-order cognitive abilities) may be more appropriate than assessing specific academic areas (Culbertson, 1998). In other words, there might be cognitive impairments and deficits in processing that are more relevant to learning problems and are more amenable to interventions than the overarching diagnoses of learning disorders.

Although most school systems require formal diagnoses in order to classify children as in need of special

---

BOX 15.3

GETTING A HEAD START ON EDUCATION (AND LIFE)

One of the most well known prevention programs is Head Start. Although begun initially to enhance social competence in preschool children from impoverished backgrounds (Zigler, 1979), Head Start quickly became a prevention program that addressed many needs of children from economically disadvantaged circumstances and children from ethnic minority groups.

In its original conceptualization, Head Start involved a brief summer school experience for preschoolers before they began kindergarten. The initial program focused on development of social competence and social skills to help children get along with one another. The program soon developed into a longer and more intensive program that addressed social-emotional needs, academic needs, and family enhancement needs (Murray, Guerra, & Williams, 1997). Short-term gains were noted in children's social-emotional, intellectual, and academic functioning (Darlington, Royce, Snipper, Murray, & Lazar, 1980). Research on Head Start suggests that the longer the intervention is offered, the more positive the effects for children and families involved in it (Darlington et al., 1980).

Unfortunately, the gains based on short-term Head Start programs with no follow-up or sustained enrichment activities tend to be short lived (V. E. Lee, Brooks-Gunn, Schnur, & Liaw, 1990). There is consistent evidence that enrichment activities should be given on a longer term basis for maximal preventive effects for academic, intellectual, and social-emotional functioning (V. E. Lee et al., 1990).

education services, comparable educational interventions might be appropriate whether or not children meet formal diagnostic criteria for learning disorders (Adelman & Taylor, 1993). For example, a treatment plan for a child diagnosed with a learning disorder would look very similar to a treatment plan for a child who was showing underachievement in the school setting (Jongsma, Peterson, & McInnis, 1996).

Overall, the diagnoses of LD are similar to other diagnoses discussed in this book. Although there are advantages to using formal diagnostic criteria, there are also disadvantages to these criteria. It is important to maintain a broad view of learning and educational problems in order to prevent focusing solely on diagnostic definitions of LD. Too often, children struggle with their academic work and yet cannot receive special services because they do not meet criteria for a learning disorder. If they do not find some type of additional remedial educational services (e.g., a dedicated teacher, a parent who helps each night with homework, or a tutor who can provide additional academic enrichment activities) they may continue to struggle and then eventually quit school. Overall, children's learning difficulties are no less tolerable just because they do not meet formal diagnostic criteria for a learning disorder.

Risk Factors

There are a number of factors that appear to put children at risk for educational and learning deficits. Within the individual child, children who believe that intellectual functioning and academic achievement are fixed and stable tend to do more poorly in school than children who believe that functioning is related to effort (Stipek & Gralinski, 1996). Attentional problems and problems in self-regulation are consistently identified as risk factors for the development of learning problems (reviewed in Masten & Coatsworth, 1998). Emotional/behavioral problems are also evident in a large number of children with learning problems, but it is not clear if emotional/behavioral problems put children at risk for learning problems or vice versa (Sattler, 2002). Children and adolescents who have emotional/behavioral problems are significantly more likely to drop out before high school graduation than their counterparts without emotional/behavioral problems, even after controlling for rates of educational achievement (Masten & Coatsworth, 1998).

Many environmental conditions, such as poverty, large family size, and limited parental education are associated with greater learning problems and limited educational attainment (Sattler, 2002). Attending schools that are ineffective and overcrowded can serve as a risk factor for limited educational achievement (Children's Defense

---

Case Study: Darryl, The Boy Who Showed Problems with Reading

Darryl was a fifth grader who had already had three different teachers since school began for the year. Further, before this year, Darryl had never attended any school for longer than a few months. His current school was in an impoverished area within San Francisco. Like many of his impoverished classmates, Darryl always seemed to wear wrinkled, dirty clothes that were either too big or too little for him.

At school, his desk was located near the teacher's desk because he had a habit of reaching out and touching or hitting other children who were seated near him. He also refused to participate in classroom activities and was especially adamant about not participating in oral reading activities. His handwriting was atrocious, and he never seemed to be able to stay within the lines on the paper.

Athletically, Darryl did not fare much better. He could not seem to kick the ball straight in kickball, nor could he hit a baseball. He tended to be ignored or teased by other children. Even the loners in his class seemed to stay away from him.

From all of these accounts, it might have made sense to refer Darryl to a school psychologist for an evaluation for a learning disorder. One day, however, a new teacher noticed that Darryl put his book up to his face (nearly touching his nose) while trying to look at pictures. The teacher referred Darryl for an eye exam with the school nurse the very next day, and the nurse, in turn, referred Darryl to an optometrist who provided eyeglasses to low-income children. Although Darryl's mother could not drive, she was able to take Darryl to the optometrist's office on public transportation.

When Darryl showed up at school with his "Coke bottle" glasses, his entire outlook on life appeared to be different. He was able to read in class. In a game of kickball, he kicked the ball on his first try and made it to first base. He stopped hitting and grabbing children because he could see them now. He began reading everything in sight, including multiple books from the school library. His writing improved significantly because he could see the lines on the paper.

This case illustrates the need to look at basic functioning and sensory issues before diagnosing a learning disorder. Given his poor eyesight, Darryl had missed, and could have continued to miss, valuable educational experiences had his new teacher not been perceptive enough to notice his difficulties with sight. This case also illustrates how a small intervention (i.e., helping a child get affordable reading glasses) can tremendously change the child's outlook on reading and on the educational experience.

SOURCE: E. Wright (1999).

Fund, 1999). Box 15.4 discusses proposed changes to the educational system.

Overall, there are a number of personal, familial, and environmental risk factors associated with the development of learning problems. Many of these risk factors also put the child at risk for the development of other emotional/behavioral problems (Masten & Coatsworth, 1998). Prevention programs such as Head Start target these overarching risk factors in an effort to prevent the myriad problems that might develop in children and adolescents, rather than solely focusing on the prevention of learning difficulties.

What one knows is, in youth, of little moment; they know enough who know how to learn.

—Henry Brooks Adams

Protective Factors

There are a number of factors that appear to protect children from the development of a learning disorder. On the individual level of the student, children who attribute their academic success to their own hard work and who attribute academic failures to lack of effort tend to show better academic functioning and fewer academic problems (reviewed in Masten & Coatsworth, 1998). In relation to the school environment, school success and academic attainment appear to be enhanced by the following characteristics (Stipek, 1997):

- Access to success experiences by students early in their educational experiences.

- Teachers who have high expectations of success for their students.

- Students who have been encouraged to develop self-confidence in their ability to learn new material.

- Students with high expectations and firm goals for themselves within the educational setting.

- Teachers who communicate individual and personal regard for students, especially teachers who express unconditional positive regard for their students.

In addition to these school-related protective factors, there are also familial factors that appear to protect children from the development of learning disorders. Authoritative parenting—in which parents provide age-appropriate structure with warmth, concern, and high expectations for their children—has been associated with good academic functioning (Dornbusch, Ritter, Leiderman, Roberts, & Fraleigh, 1987). Parental involvement in the educational process has also been linked to better academic outcomes and fewer learning disorders for children (Ryan, Adams, Gullotta, Weissberg, & Hampton, 1995). One interesting prevention study suggested that increasing parental involvement in the school system had direct effects on increasing children's academic functioning (Steinberg, Lamborn, Dornbusch, & Darling, 1992). Overall, there are a number of protective factors within the school system, within the family, and within children themselves that serve to protect children from developing learning problems.

BOX 15.4

AN EDUCATIONAL SYSTEM THAT NEEDS AN OVERHAUL

Given the difficulty that exists in remediation and prevention of learning problems, a number of scholars have proposed sweeping changes to the educational system in order to reduce institutional barriers to learning. Some suggestions from Dr. Howard Adelman and his colleagues include:

- Looking beyond the diagnosis of LD to explore the many learning problems that children encounter (Adelman, 1992).

- Focusing on institutional barriers to learning that are inherent in the structure of the current educational system (Adelman, 1992).

- Expanding the concept of intervention beyond teaching (Adelman, 1992).

- When teaching is the intervention of choice, personalizing instruction for children in order to enhance their individual motivational and educational needs (L. Taylor & Adelman, 1999).

- Tying together social policy issues and practice issues in order to form school–home–community partnerships that will reduce barriers to learning within the school system (Adelman & Taylor, 1997; Adelman, Taylor, & Schnieder, 1999).

- Reconceptualizing learning disorders from being within the individual child to a more accurate reflection of the problems that are inherent in the educational, social, and political systems (Adelman & Taylor, 1993).

BOX *15.5*

EFFECTIVE SCHOOLS AS A PROTECTIVE FACTOR

There is growing evidence that children who attend effective schools are better off on a number of academic and behavioral indices than children who attend less effective schools. In particular, attendance at an effective school appears to serve as a protective factor against the development of learning disorders. The characteristics of effective schools that are consistent across a number of countries include:

- Leadership in the school that is strong and positive.
- A focus and emphasis on academic learning.
- High expectations for the success of students.

- Consistent expectations for students, with the use of collegial and joint planning for students' academic activities.
- Active involvement of students in the daily functioning of the school and in the overall life of the school.
- Active involvement of parents in the overall functioning and life of the school.
- Consistent monitoring of students' academic progress.
- Incentives and rewards for academic excellence and for high levels of effort.

SOURCE: Mortimore (1995).

SUMMARY AND KEY CONCEPTS

Learning Disorders

Learning disorders are diagnosed when children's academic achievement is significantly lower than what would be expected based on their intellectual functioning. There are three primary types of learning disorders: reading disorder (also known as **dyslexia**), mathematics disorder (also known as **dyscalculia**), and disorder of written expression (also known as **dysgraphia**). For each of these disorders, there must be a significant discrepancy between intellectual functioning and academic achievement (both of which were assessed by individually administered standardized tests), the deficits in achievement must impact negatively on academic functioning or daily activities, and the deficits must be in excess of any problems that might be expected for any sensory deficit that is present. A newer category of learning disorder that has not yet been included in *DSM-IV* are the **social-emotional learning disorders**. Children with a social-emotional learning disorder show significant deficits in nonverbal abilities, social perception, spatial skills, time orientation, and directionality. Learning disorders are often comorbid with other disorders, especially language disorders and ADHD.

Although no clear-cut etiologies lead to LD, there is evidence that some combination of genetic factors, biological factors (including cognitive processing problems), and ineffective learning strategies put children at risk for the development of a learning disorder.

Learning Disorders and Learning Problems Conceptualized in a Dimensional Manner

Many children experience significant problems with learning but do not meet criteria for a formal diagnosis of LD. Certain features that are consistent across learning problems (e.g., attentional abilities, phonological skills, and higher-order cognitive abilities) may be more useful to identify and remediate than learning disorders per se.

KEY TERMS

learning disorders   dyslexia   dyscalculia   dysgraphia   social-emotional learning disorder

SUGGESTED READINGS

Pelzer, David. *A Man Called "Dave"*. New York: Penguin, 1999. In this follow-up to *A Child Called "It"* (1995) and *The Lost Boy* (1997), Pelzer continues his autobiography that recounts parental abuse and his subsequent difficulties within the social service system. In this book, Pelzer also highlights the learning difficulties that were brought about largely by the upheavals in his personal life and tells how he overcame these difficulties.

Cher, & Coplon, Jeff. *The First Time*. New York: Pocket Books, 1998. In addition to describing the interesting and difficult childhood history of the singer/actress named Cher, this book also highlights the learning difficulties that Cher endured and eventually overcame.

SUGGESTED VIEWINGS

Stanley and Iris (1990). Martin Ritt (director), Harriet Frank, Jr., and Irving Ravetch (screenwriters), based on novel by Pat Barker. VHS. This touching film illustrates an adult's reading disorder, revealing both its personal and occupational ramifications.

Dangerous Minds (1995). John N. Smith (director), Ronald Bass (screenwriter), based on memoir by Lou Anne Johnson. VHS/DVD. Based on a true story, this film highlights one teacher's struggle with and triumph over learning problems in adolescents who would otherwise have been forgotten by the educational system.

CHAPTER 16

PEDIATRIC PSYCHOLOGY AND HEALTH PSYCHOLOGY FOR CHILDREN AND ADOLESCENTS

CHAPTER SUMMARY

I have cerebral palsy. For me, it's a lot easier to make friends on the computer than it is to make friends on Earth. But I don't want to meet my e-mail friends. It's nice to have the mystery.

—Tamara, 14, South Africa

PEDIATRIC PSYCHOLOGY

Pediatric psychology is where the field of psychology meets the field of medicine. Also known as child health psychology, pediatric psychology encompasses several aspects of child functioning in relation to physical health and well-being (Tarnowski & Brown, 2000). The focus of pediatric psychology includes research, consultation, assessment, and treatment (Drotar, 2000; Hamlett & Stabler, 1995; La Greca & Schuman, 1999). Prevention programs, such as health promotion, are an integral part of pediatric psychology (Durlak, 2000). Table 16.1 presents a diverse array of topics covered within the field.

Some psychological disorders (e.g., eating disorders, elimination disorders) tend to be discussed within pediatric psychology because of their connections with health-involved behaviors. Other psychological or physical disorders (e.g., somatoform disorders, factitious disorders, and genetic chromosomal disorders) are almost always tied to the discussion of pediatric psychology or health psychology because of their direct relevance to physical health and symptoms. Within the field of pediatric psychology, however, there is also a great deal of attention to issues that are not specific to psychological disorders. For example, pediatric psychology focuses on how chronic ill-

nesses in children (e.g., diabetes, sickle-cell anemia, cancer, and AIDS) and in parents (e.g., cancer, AIDS) influence children's emotional/behavioral functioning. There is an emphasis on treatment and prevention of problems within the area of pediatric psychology (Briggs-Gowan, Horwitz, Schwab-Stone, Leventhal, & Leaf, 2000). In particular, there is a strong focus on maintaining health and on promoting positive health behaviors (Durlak, 2000). Thus, pediatric psychology is the application of developmental psychopathology to the physical well-being of children, adolescents, and families.

Pediatric psychology is a relatively new area of study in relation to other fields. Whereas the *Journal of Pediatric Psychology* was first published in 1976, the *Journal of Abnormal Psychology* was first published in 1906. As can be seen in Table 16.2, a wide variety of physical, health, and emotional issues are covered in the *Journal of Pediatric Psychology*. Another indication of the breadth, and newly established status of pediatric psychology is that the Society of Pediatric Psychology was recognized formally as a division of the American Psychological Association (APA; Division 54) in 1999. Obviously, work in pediatric psychology had taken place before these two events. Publishing a journal and establishing a division within the APA, however, were symbolic of the formal existence of pediatric psychology as an area of specialty. Most often, pediatric psychologists are trained first as clinical child psychologists and researchers, and then they specialize in pediatric issues throughout their training.

TABLE 16.1   Selected Topics Covered in the *Handbook of Pediatric Psychology, 2nd ed.*

Issues That Cut across the Field

Pediatric psychology consultation

Adherence to prescribed medical regimens

Family systems in pediatric research and practice

Management of pain and distress

Psychosocial adjustment of children with chronic physical conditions

Anticipatory grief and bereavement

Prevention of emotional and behavioral distress in children's chronic illness

Prevention of injuries and disease

Health promotion

Physical Conditions

Pediatric asthma

Cystic fibrosis

Insulin-dependent diabetes mellitus in childhood

Sickle cell disease and hemophilia

Leukemia and other childhood cancers

Sexual behaviors and problems of adolescents

Neuropsychological aspects of pediatric infectious diseases

Neurobehavioral effects of brain injury in children

Juvenile rheumatoid arthritis

Cardiovascular disease

Renal and liver disease

Pediatric burns

Prematurity and the neonatal intensive care unit

Pediatric abdominal disorders

Developmental, Behavioral, and Emotional Problems

Pediatric feeding problems

Failure to thrive

Elimination disorders (enuresis and encopresis)

Habit disorders (bruxism, trichotillomania, and tics)

Sleep disturbances of children

Physical abuse, sexual abuse, and neglect

Behavioral compliance in a pediatric context

Attention-deficit/hyperactivity disorder

Autism and mental retardation

Anorexia nervosa, bulimia nervosa, and obesity

Special Issues

Pediatric medical rehabilitation

Adolescent health issues

Pediatric pharmacology and psychopharmacology

Psychoneuroimmunology

Environmental toxins

Source: M. C. Roberts (1995).

TABLE 16.2   Content of Empirical Papers Published in the *Journal of Pediatric Psychology*

Topic	% of studies
Chronic pediatric conditions	30.0%
High-risk infants/toddlers	11.0
Developmental issues/problems	9.6
Acute medical conditions	8.7
Pediatric AIDS/HIV	8.3
Pediatric injury	6.4
Central nervous system conditions	4.1
Physical disabilities	3.7
Other	9.2

Source: La Greca (1997).

my hand holds the taco
against the will of my anorexic mind.
but most days I'm strong
the self i know as my Flesh
is the winner.
it fights my other self,
the irrational self that is my Thoughts,
that tells me not to consume,
that tells me that food is evil.

–E.G.K.Z., 17, Northeastern United States (Shandler, 1999, p. 16)

EATING DISORDERS

Anorexia nervosa and bulimia nervosa are the two primary eating disorders that occur in childhood or adolescence. Both problems are associated with a severe pattern of maladaptive eating. In cases of **anorexia nervosa**, the pattern of maladaptive eating is characterized by extremely limited intake of food, whereas **bulimia nervosa** is characterized by the intake and then purging of excessive amounts of food. Both disorders are extremely serious and are potentially life-threatening (American Psychiatric Association, 2000).

Anorexia Nervosa

As Table 16.3 indicates, anorexia nervosa is characterized by being underweight, being terrified of gaining more weight, experiencing body image disturbance, and experiencing amenorrhea (the cessation of menstruation in a previously menstruating female, usually diagnosed after three consecutive menstrual cycles). There are two types of anorexia nervosa: restricting type, in which individuals solely restrict their diet and do not engage in any bingeing or purging behavior, and binge-eating/purging type, in which individuals regularly engage in binge-eating or purging in order to maintain their low weight. Note that the primary distinction between anorexia nervosa, binge-eating/purging type, and bulimia nervosa is that individuals with anorexia nervosa remain significantly underweight whereas individuals with bulimia nervosa remain at a normal or heavier-than-normal weight.

Prevalence Rates. Table 16.4 gives an overview of prevalence information for anorexia nervosa. Although anorexia nervosa has received a lot of media attention, the

Gymnast Christy Henrich died of complications related to anorexia nervosa.

TABLE 16.3 *DSM-IV* Diagnostic Criteria for Anorexia Nervosa

1. Refusal to maintain body weight at or above a minimally normal weight for age and height (e.g., weight loss leading to maintenance of body weight less than 85% of that expected; or failure to make expected weight gain during period of growth, leading to body weight less than 85% of that expected).

2. Intense fear of gaining weight or becoming fat, even though underweight.

3. Disturbance in the way in which one's body weight or shape is experienced, undue influence of body weight or shape on self-evaluation, or denial of the seriousness of the current low body weight.

4. In postmenarcheal females, amenorrhea, i.e., the absence of at least three consecutive menstrual cycles. (A woman is considered to have amenorrhea if her periods occur only following hormone, e.g., estrogen, administration.)

Specify type:

Restricting Type: during the current episode of Anorexia Nervosa, the person has not regularly engaged in binge-eating or purging behavior (i.e., self-induced vomiting or the misuse of laxatives, diuretics, or enemas)

Binge-Eating/Purging Type: during the current episode of Anorexia Nervosa, the person has regularly engaged in binge-eating or purging behavior (i.e., self-induced vomiting or the misuse of laxatives, diuretics, or enemas)

SOURCE: American Psychiatric Association (2000). Reprinted with permission from the *Diagnostic and Statistical Manual of Mental Disorders, Fourth Edition, Text Revision.* Copyright ©2000 American Psychiatric Association.

prevalence of the full-blown disorder is actually quite low. Approximately 0.5% of adolescent females and young adult women experience anorexia nervosa (American Psychiatric Association, 2000). As will be discussed later in this chapter, in the section on dimensional conceptualizations of eating disorders, the experience of body image problems and some level of food restrictions is much higher than the prevalence rate of anorexia nervosa.

The overwhelming majority of individuals who experience anorexia nervosa are female. Most estimates suggest that 90% of diagnosed cases of anorexia nervosa are girls and women (American Psychiatric Association, 2000). Note, however, that anorexia nervosa does occur in boys and men and is often overlooked because of the focus on girls and women with this disorder. For males diagnosed with anorexia nervosa, it is not unusual to see extreme exercise as the primary modality of weight control (D. A. Williamson, Bentz, & Rabalais, 1998).

TABLE 16.4 Overview of Prevalence Information for Anorexia Nervosa

Prevalence	0.5% of adolescent females and young adult females
Age	Adolescence and young adulthood > Childhood or adulthood
Gender	Females > males
Socioeconomic status	Middle and higher SES > Lower SES
Race/ethnicity	Caucasian American > Other races/ethnicities

Anorexia nervosa tends to be associated with individuals from middle and higher socioeconomic status (Attie & Brooks-Gunn, 1995). Race and ethnicity have not been studied thoroughly, but the majority of cases tend to be within the Caucasian American community (Garner & Myerholtz, 1998). Interestingly, anorexia nervosa is much more prevalent in industrialized countries, where there is an abundance of food and an emphasis on being thin, than in developing countries (American Psychiatric Association, 2000). Worldwide, the highest prevalence rates for anorexia nervosa occur in the United States, Canada, the European countries, Australia, Japan, New Zealand, and South Africa (American Psychiatric Association, 2000).

Bulimia Nervosa

In contrast to the severe restrictive eating patterns that occur with anorexia nervosa, bulimia nervosa is characterized by frequent episodes of bingeing and purging. As Table 16.5 indicates, binge eating occurs when individuals consume large quantities of food within short amounts of time and when individuals have a subjective sense of being out of control regarding their food intake. In conjunction with the binge eating, individuals also partake in inappropriate compensatory activities, such as intentional vomiting, use of laxatives, fasting, or excessive exercise. Although nearly all people have binged or purged at some

---

Case Study: "I Just Want to Lose a Few More Pounds"

When Janet was 12 years old, she began dieting because her friends and family had teased her about being "pudgy." At the start of her dieting, Janet weighed 110 pounds and measured over five feet tall. At the age of 14, Janet was admitted to a psychiatric hospital weighing only 62 pounds (with a height of five feet, two inches). She had long since stopped menstruating. At that time, Janet lived with her parents, an older sister, and a younger brother. Janet's father was a very successful engineer who worked long hours and frequently brought work home in the evenings and on weekends. Janet considered her family to be very high in achievement motivation, with a lot of pressure to excel at every aspect of their lives. Expression of strong feelings was not supported within the family; in fact, Janet's parents felt that talking about feelings was a sign of immaturity. Sexual issues and sex education were also taboo subjects within the family.

Growing up, Janet had appeared to be well-adjusted and healthy. She had a number of friends and maintained a straight-A average in school. Janet reported that she studied extensively to earn her high grades, and that she was happy with her academic achievements. As Janet became more concerned about her weight loss between the ages of 12 and 14, she seemed to withdraw from her friends but still maintained her straight-A grades.

At the time of admission to the psychiatric hospital, Janet was distressed about her appearance and felt that her weight loss had become too severe. She reported, however, that she could no longer control her dieting and admitted to consuming only 400 calories or less per day while undertaking excessive amounts of exercise. Psychological assessment revealed that Janet did not show any severe signs of psychopathology but that she had ambivalence about separating from the family and growing up.

A behavioral program was established in the hospital so that Janet would be encouraged to gain weight. Janet was given meals in her room alone and she was weighed each morning. If she lost weight from one day to the next, she was not allowed to leave her hospital room for the entire day. If she maintained or gained weight, then she was allowed to interact with other clients at the hospital and to get involved with enjoyable activities for the rest of that day. During the 10-week hospitalization, Janet failed to maintain or gain weight on only five separate occasions. Janet was involved in individual therapy to address her concerns about weight, her developing autonomy from her parents, and her social involvement with friends. Janet's family was involved in family therapy to help the family members express their feelings and develop their own standards of achievement. By the end of the hospitalization, Janet weighed 93 pounds and reported that she felt happier and more self-confident than before the treatment.

Upon discharge, Janet went back to school and reestablished a number of friendships. She began dating and reported a great deal of satisfaction in attending dances and going out with friends. Although there were a few times when her eating behavior became too restrictive, Janet was able to maintain appropriate food intake with the help of her therapist and her parents. At the 18-month follow-up, Janet had achieved a normal weight and had continued to participate in social activities as well as maintaining good academic progress.

SOURCE: Leon (1990).

TABLE 16.5 *DSM-IV* Diagnostic Criteria for Bulimia Nervosa

A. Recurrent episodes of binge eating. An episode of binge eating is characterized by both of the following:

　1) eating, in a discrete period of time (e.g., within any 2-hour period), an amount of food that is definitely larger than most people would eat during a similar period of time and under similar circumstances

　2) a sense of lack of control over eating during the episode (e.g., a feeling that one cannot stop eating or control what or how much one is eating)

B. Recurrent inappropriate compensatory behavior in order to prevent weight gain, such as self-induced vomiting; misuse of laxatives, diuretics, enemas, or other medications; fasting; or excessive exercise.

C. The binge eating and inappropriate compensatory behaviors both occur, on average, at least twice a week for 3 months.

D. Self-evaluation is unduly influenced by body shape and weight.

E. The disturbance does not occur exclusively during episodes of Anorexia Nervosa.

Specify type:

　Purging Type: during the current episode of Bulimia Nervosa, the person has regularly engaged in self-induced vomiting or the misuse of laxatives, diuretics, or enemas

　Nonpurging Type: during the current episode of Bulimia Nervosa, the person has used other inappropriate compensatory behaviors, such as fasting or excessive exercise, but has not regularly engaged in self-induced vomiting or the misuse of laxatives, diuretics, or enemas

SOURCE: American Psychiatric Association (2000). Reprinted with permission from the *Diagnostic and Statistical Manual of Mental Disorders, Fourth Edition, Text Revision.* Copyright © 2000 American Psychiatric Association.

TABLE 16.6 Overview of Prevalence Information for Bulimia Nervosa

Prevalence	1%–3% of adolescent females and young adult females
Age	Adolescence and young adulthood > childhood and adulthood
Gender	Females > males
Socioeconomic status	Middle and higher SES > Lower SES
Race/ethnicity	Caucasian American > Other races/ethnicities

point in their lives, the diagnosis of bulimia nervosa is appropriate only when the binge-purge cycle occurs at least twice a week for at least three months and when there is significant negative body image. The two types of bulimia nervosa include purging type, in which individuals use self-induced vomiting or laxatives as their compensatory strategy, and nonpurging type, in which individuals use other compensatory strategies, such as fasting or excessive exercise.

　　Prevalence Rates. Table 16.6 gives an overview of prevalence rates for bulimia nervosa. Although bulimia nervosa is slightly more prevalent than anorexia nervosa, it is still relatively infrequent compared to other types of developmental psychopathology. Bulimia nervosa is thought to occur in approximately 1%–3% of adolescent and young adult females (American Psychiatric Association, 2000). Bulimia nervosa is much more likely to occur

in adolescence and young adulthood. Over 90% of individuals diagnosed with bulimia nervosa are female; thus, it is quite rare to diagnose bulimia nervosa in boys and men. When boys and men are diagnosed with bulimia nervosa, they appear to be more likely than girls and women to have had premorbid obesity (American Psychiatric Association, 2000). Little is known about patterns of bulimia nervosa based on socioeconomic status (SES), however, bulimia nervosa appears to be more prevalent in individuals from middle and higher SES families (Attie & Brooks-Gunn, 1995; D. A. Williamson et al., 1998). Within the United States, bulimia nervosa has a much higher prevalence in Caucasian American girls and women than in girls and women from other ethnic and racial groups (American Psychiatric Association, 2000). Worldwide, bulimia nervosa tends to be most prevalent in industrialized countries, such as the United States, Canada, the European countries, Australia, Japan, New Zealand, and South Africa (American Psychiatric Association, 2000).

　　For the remainder of issues regarding eating disorders (comorbidity, course of the disorder, etiology, treatment, prevention, and dimensional conceptualizations), both anorexia nervosa and bulimia nervosa will be combined in the discussion. Although there are patterns that will be highlighted for each disorder separately, a number of the issues that deserve attention are comparable for both.

Comorbidity of Eating Disorders

Anorexia nervosa is often associated with higher rates of depressive symptoms and specific symptoms of major depressive disorder such as difficulty sleeping, irritability, and social withdrawal. These symptoms, however, are also present in non-anorexic individuals who are experiencing starvation, so it is not clear whether these depressive symptoms are related to the anorexic behavior or to the physical starvation (American Psychiatric Association, 2000). For this reason, depressive symptoms must be assessed carefully in individuals with anorexia nervosa. Even with this caveat, however, there is evidence of higher rates of depression and anxiety in older adolescents and young adults diagnosed with anorexia nervosa (Garner & Myerholtz, 1998; Lewinsohn, Striegel-Moore, & Seeley, 2000). For example, between 50% and 70% of clients diagnosed with an eating disorder also meet criteria for either major depressive disorder or dysthymia (Attie & Brooks-Gunn, 1995; Linscheid & Fleming, 1995). Symptoms of obsessive-compulsive disorder (OCD) are also fairly common in individuals diagnosed with anorexia nervosa, especially when these behaviors are related to food (American Psychiatric Association, 2000).

Bulimia nervosa is associated with higher rates of depression and anxiety (Lewinsohn et al., 2000). Substance abuse and dependence (especially alcohol and stimulant abuse and dependence) are comorbid in approximately one-third of individuals with bulimia nervosa (American Psychiatric Association, 2000). Personality disorders, such as borderline personality disorder, are relatively common in individuals diagnosed with bulimia nervosa as well as anorexia nervosa (Garner & Myerholtz, 1998).

Course of the Disorders

Both anorexia nervosa and bulimia nervosa are likely to first appear during adolescence or young adulthood. The average age of onset of anorexia nervosa is between 14 and 18 (American Psychiatric Association, 2000; Linscheid & Fleming, 1995). Anorexia nervosa rarely occurs before puberty or after the age of 40. Anorexia nervosa often first develops after a traumatic or stressful event, such as leaving home to go to college.

Bulimia nervosa usually has an onset in late adolescence or early adulthood. Like anorexia nervosa, bulimia nervosa is rarely first diagnosed in young children or older adults (American Psychiatric Association, 2000). The first occurrence of bulimia nervosa is often linked to the end of a period of dieting or restricted eating. Bulimia nervosa may come and go throughout an individual's life. Most often, individuals seek treatment for bulimia nervosa only after years of maladaptive eating patterns (American Psychiatric Association, 2000).

Etiology of Eating Disorders

There have been a number of theories proposed to help explain the development and maintenance of eating disorders. Genetic theories have found support in the higher rates of eating disorders among monozygotic twins when compared with dizygotic twins or other relatives (Garner & Myerholtz, 1998). Specifically, monozygotic twins tend to have a concordance rate of 50% for eating disorders, whereas dizygotic twins tend to have a concordance rate of only 10%. These data suggest a genetic link in the development of eating disorders (Garner & Myerholtz, 1998). Behavioral genetics studies have implicated both genetic and environmental characteristics in the development of eating disorders (Klump, McGue, & Iacono, 2000). Biological theories have also suggested a link in the development of eating disorders. Some biological mechanisms that have been implicated in the development of eating disorders are disturbances in neurotransmitters and disturbances in hormone regulation (Mizes & Miller, 2000; D. A. Williamson et al., 1998). Although biological theories can help explain a part of the development of eating disorders, they do not represent full explanations.

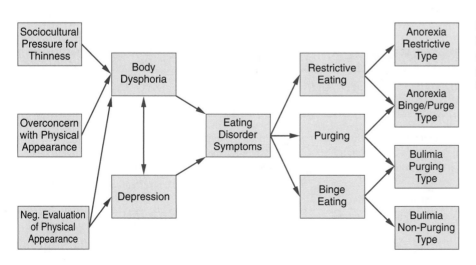

FIGURE 16.1 Psychosocial Risk Factor Model for Anorexia and Bulimia Nervosa

Source: D. A. Williamson et al. (1998).

Recent theories regarding the development of eating disorders have focused on psychosocial etiologies for the disorders. Included in these theories are societal pressures for thinness, cognitive internalizations of unrealistic images that are portrayed in the media, and familial factors related to appearance and achievement (J. K. Thompson & Stice, 2001; D. A. Williamson et al., 1998). The father–daughter relationship appears to be particularly salient in the development of body dissatisfaction and eating disorders (Berg, Crosby, Wonderlich, & Hawley, 2000; Huon & Walton, 2000; Vincent & McCabe, 2000). Figure 16.1 illustrates how a number of factors can lead to the development of anorexia nervosa and bulimia nervosa.

Overall, there is no one theory that helps explain the development and maintenance of eating disorders. Many of the risk factors illustrated in Figure 16.1 seem to add to the vulnerability of girls and women to eating disorders. The best explanation of the actual etiology of both anorexia nervosa and bulimia nervosa is likely to be a combination of many of these theories, including genetic vulnerability, biological disturbances, and psychosocial risk factors.

Treatment of Eating Disorders

A number of treatments for eating disorders have been established, including nutritional counseling, individual therapy, group therapy, family therapy, pharmacotherapy, 12-step approaches (such as Overeaters Anonymous), and behavioral contracts (Eisler et al., 2000; Gore, Vander-Wal, & Thelen, 2001; Mizes & Miller, 2000; Nye & Johnson, 1999). The most consistent effective results have come from cognitive-behavioral therapies that focus on both individuals' behavior and their cognitions (Mizes & Miller, 2000; Wegner & Wegner, 2001; Weltzin & Bolton,

1998; D. A. Williamson, Duchmann, Barker, & Bruno, 1998). As discussed in Box 16.1, a number of cognitive distortions may be present in individuals with eating disorders and body image problems. Cognitive-behavioral therapies can address these cognitive distortions in order to replace the troubled thinking with more realistic thoughts and beliefs.

One particularly effective treatment for bulimia nervosa is known as exposure plus response prevention (Rosen & Leitenberg, 1985). The idea behind this treatment is that clients are exposed to "forbidden foods" (e.g., highly caloric foods) that distress them, asked to ingest a certain amount of the foods, and then prevented from purging the food while they address their maladaptive cognitions with the therapist's help. This treatment has been found to be effective whether it is delivered in individual therapy or group therapy (Rosen & Leitenberg, 1985).

Overall, eating disorders are highly treatable, but distressed individuals must first try to access treatment (or have their parents access treatment for them). Like any other problem, clients must want to change their lives or at least to reduce the distress related to their problems before they can be helped by treatment.

Prevention of Eating Disorders

Given the distress and the sometimes life-threatening ramifications of eating disorders, it is disheartening to find that there are not more programs specifically designed to prevent them (Linscheid & Fleming, 1995). Although treatment programs often include a tertiary prevention component, designed to prevent the reoccurrence of the disorder, there are few formal programs for the prevention of eating disorders in children and adolescents (Levine & Smolak, 2001; Thompson, Heinberg, Altabe,

---

BOX 16.1

COMMON COGNITIVE DISTORTIONS AMONG INDIVIDUALS WITH EATING DISORDERS AND BODY IMAGE PROBLEMS

- "I just can't control myself. Last night when I had dinner in a restaurant, I ate everything I was served, although I had decided ahead of time that I was going to be very careful. I am so weak."
- "I've gained 2 pounds, so I can't wear shorts anymore."
- "If I gain one pound, I'll go on and gain a hundred pounds."

- "Two people laughed and whispered something to each other when I walked by. They were probably saying that I looked unattractive. I *have* gained 3 pounds . . . "
- "If I eat a sweet, it will be converted instantly into stomach fat."

SOURCE: Garner & Bemis (1982).

& Tantleff-Dunn, 1999). Interestingly, there has been a great deal of attention to promoting healthy eating behaviors as a way of preventing illness and obesity (Perry, Story, & Lytle, 1997). These programs may help some children and adolescents learn how to eat in a healthy manner, but the focus on healthy eating does not address the issue of body image dissatisfaction in girls who are already of average weight.

Dimensional Conceptualizations of Body Image Problems

More than any other disorders in this textbook, eating disorders have been evaluated extensively from a dimensional conceptualization. In particular, attention has been given to the development of body image problems and body dissatisfaction. Even without meeting criteria for an eating disorder, body image problems and body dissatisfaction can be very distressing and disturbing.

Approximately 60% to 70% of average-weight adolescent girls have tried dieting (Gross & Rosen, 1988). The majority of these girls began dieting before the age of 15. Given this high prevalence of dieting, it is not surprising to learn that the overwhelming majority of adolescent girls report feeling dissatisfied with their body. This phenomenon has been referred to as "normative discontent," given the high prevalence of body image dissatisfaction within groups of adolescent girls (Rodin, Silberstein, Striegel-Moore, 1985). High levels of body image dissatisfaction have also been found in samples of children (J. K. Thompson & Smolak, 2001) and younger preadolescent girls (Wood, Becker, & Thompson, 1996).

It appears that higher levels of internalization of cultural norms of thinness are associated with higher levels of body image dissatisfaction (J. K. Thompson & Stice, 2001). Weight concerns are associated with higher rates of psychological distress and lower rates of well-being, even when actual weight is controlled statistically (McHale, Corneal, Crouter, & Birch, 2001). It appears, however, that body image concerns may occur prior to the development of depressive symptoms rather than the other way around. Specifically, a four-year longitudinal study found that body image concerns and eating disturbances during early adolescence were associated with higher rates of depression four years later (Stice, Hayward, Cameron, Killen, & Taylor, 2000).

There are a number of risk factors associated with poor body image and with the development of full-blown eating disorders. These risk factors include being female, coming from a middle or high socioeconomic status family, engaging in competitive appearance-related sports (such as dance or gymnastics), and having a close relative (such as a mother) who experienced an eating disorder or other body image problems (Neumaerker, Bettle, Neumaerker, & Bettle, 2000; J. K. Thompson & Smolak, 2001; D. A. Williamson et al., 1998).

Given the high prevalence of body image dissatisfaction, it is unfortunate that there are few factors known to protect adolescent girls from developing poor body image. Interestingly, some researchers have suggested that populations with low amounts of body image dissatisfaction (such as African American girls and women in the United States, or girls and women in some non-industrialized countries) should be explored in order to identify protective factors (Attie & Brooks-Gunn, 1995; Mulholland & Mintz, 2001). This type of work has suggested that the cultural values placed on thinness and weight restriction serve to put adolescent girls at risk for body image dissatisfaction, so preventive efforts are needed to change the sociocultural values regarding weight and beauty (Attie & Brooks-Gunn, 1995; J. K. Thompson & Stice, 2001).

Overall, eating disorders and body image dissatisfaction appear to be related to genetic, biological, psychosocial, and sociocultural factors. Prevention and treatment of eating disorders and body image disturbances are of great importance, given the often devastating effects of these problems. Interested students are encouraged to read *Body Image, Eating Disorders, and Obesity in Youth: Assessment, Prevention, and Treatment* (J. K. Thompson & Smolak, 2001), which provides a comprehensive discussion of these issues.

ELIMINATION DISORDERS

Enuresis and encopresis are the two main types of elimination disorders. **Enuresis** occurs when children cannot or will not control their urinary functioning (e.g., wetting the bed or wetting themselves at school). **Encopresis** occurs when children cannot or will not control their bowel functioning. Both of these disorders are diagnosed only if there are no medical causes for the behavior and if the child is older than five (in the case of enuresis) or four (in the case of encopresis).

Enuresis

As indicated in Table 16.7, the diagnostic criteria for enuresis are very clear about the behavioral manifestations of the disorder. That is, the voiding of urine has to be repeated (e.g., at least twice a week for at least three

TABLE 16.7 *DSM-IV* Diagnostic Criteria for Enuresis

A. Repeated voiding of urine into bed or clothes (whether involuntary or intentional).

B. The behavior is clinically significant as manifested by either a frequency of twice a week for at least 3 consecutive months or the presence of clinically significant distress or impairment in social, academic (occupational), or other important areas of functioning.

C. Chronological age is at least 5 years (or equivalent developmental level).

D. The behavior is not due exclusively to the direct physiological effect of a substance (e.g., a diuretic) or a general medical condition (e.g., diabetes, spina bifida, a seizure disorder).

Specify type:

Nocturnal Only

Diurnal Only

Nocturnal and Diurnal

SOURCE: American Psychiatric Association (2000). Reprinted with permission from the *Diagnostic and Statistical Manual of Mental Disorders, Fourth Edition, Text Revision.* Copyright © 2000 American Psychiatric Association.

TABLE 16.8 Overview of Prevalence Information for Enuresis

Prevalence	15%–20% of 5-year-olds
Age	Younger > Older
Gender	Boys > Girls
Socioeconomic status	Lower SES > Middle or higher SES
Race/ethnicity	Unknown patterns

consecutive months) or there has to be clear distress or impairment related to the lack of urinary control (American Psychiatric Association, 2000). Given that many urinary accidents are due to physiological causes, it is imperative that clinicians first verify that children have had a thorough medical exam before diagnosing and treating enuresis from a psychological or behavioral standpoint. There are three types of enuresis: nocturnal only, diurnal only, and both nocturnal and diurnal. Although not noted in *DSM-IV*, most researchers consider that there are two additional categorizations in the understanding of enuresis: primary and secondary. Primary enuresis occurs when children have never gained urinary control, and secondary enuresis occurs when children had previously gained control over their urinary functioning but subsequently lost it (C. E. Walker, 1998). Secondary enuresis usually appears between the ages of 5 and 8 (C. E. Walker, 1995). Nearly 80% of cases of enuresis are considered primary (C. E. Walker, 1995).

Prevalence Rates. Table 16.8 gives an overview of prevalence information for enuresis. Nocturnal enuresis is much more common than diurnal enuresis. *DSM-IV* cites prevalence rates for enuresis at 5%–10% for children at the age of 5, 3%–5% for 10-year-olds, and 1% for adolescents older than 14 (American Psychiatric Association, 2000). More often, prevalence rates are estimated to be 15%–20% for five-year-olds and 1%–2% for adolescents (C. E. Walker, 1998). Understandably, rates of enuresis

tend to decrease with age. It is estimated that rates of enuresis in young adult populations average approximately 1% (C. E. Walker, 1998). Boys tend to be diagnosed with enuresis more so than girls, with the ratio of boys to girls in clinical treatment settings for enuresis averaging 2:1 (C. E. Walker, 1998). Children from families in the lower socioeconomic brackets tend to show more enuresis than do children from middle and higher socioeconomic brackets (C. E. Walker, 1998). To date, there are no clear data on differential patterns of enuresis based on race or ethnicity. Internationally, however, there is evidence that children in China gain urinary control at an earlier age than American children and that there is a lower prevalence of enuresis in China than in the United States (Liu, Sun, Uchiyama, Li, & Okawa, 2000).

Other Characteristics of Enuresis. Enuresis is not linked with other disorders for most children. Although there were early conceptualizations of a triad of enuresis, fire setting, and cruelty to animals, this hypothesis has not been supported by empirical investigations (C. E. Walker, 1995). In terms of etiology, primary nocturnal enuresis is highly heritable. When both parents have a history of enuresis, 77% of their children meet criteria for enuresis, and when one parent has a history of enuresis, 42% of their children can be diagnosed with enuresis (Luxem & Christophersen, 1999).

There are a number of treatments for enuresis, especially for the nocturnal type. Interventions include support and encouragement, periodic waking, retention control and sphincter exercises, psychotherapy, family therapy, hypnosis, pharmacological treatments, cognitive interventions, and behavioral treatments (Calkins, C. E. Walker, & Howe, 1994; C. E. Walker, 1998). Behavioral treatments such as the urine alarm system (formerly known as the bell-and-pad; C. E. Walker, 1998) are the most successful types of treatment for nocturnal enuresis, which is consistent with an applied behavior analysis perspective. This method is illustrated in the case study of Sophie. Psychopharmacological treatments, especially in conjunction with behavioral techniques, have also been found to be effective (Shaffer & Waslick,

Case Study: Sophie, The Nine-Year-Old Who Still Wet the Bed

Although Sophie was referred originally for learning problems, her problems with nocturnal enuresis soon became apparent during the initial assessment. Sophie lived with her father, mother, and two older siblings. She had achieved appropriate diurnal bladder and bowel control by the age of two but had never mastered nocturnal bladder control and had wet the bed almost every night of her life. A recent medical evaluation indicated that there were no medical or physical problems that were contributing to Sophie's enuresis. A family history showed that Sophie's mother had wet the bed until she was 14 years old, at which time she stopped with no outside intervention.

Sophie's parents had tried a number of interventions to help her remain dry at night, including restricting liquid intake late at night, waking her up periodically during the night to use the toilet, and giving her rewards for remaining dry all night. To date, none of these strategies had worked. Sophie expressed a strong desire to remain dry during the night because her bedwetting problems limited her from spending the night with friends and going camping. Other than the enuresis and school difficulties, Sophie was a well-adjusted girl with lots of friends and a good relationship with her parents and siblings. Formal evaluation revealed that Sophie had average intelligence and average academic functioning.

Evaluation of the enuresis began with collecting baseline data. For two weeks, Sophie and her parents were asked to keep track of how many nights she wet the bed. For those two weeks, Sophie wet the bed every night.

A behavioral treatment, sometimes known as the bell-and-pad, was chosen because of its effectiveness. The rationale

behind this treatment is to wake children as soon as they urinate even a little at night. This feedback is meant to help children develop their own internal "alarms" when they have the urge to urinate at night. A device is placed in the child's bed that sounds an alarm when any moisture is placed on it. After being awoken by the alarm, children are to go to the toilet to complete their urination and they also are told to remove and replace the wet bed sheets and to reset the alarm before going back to sleep. In addition, the first week of treatment includes scheduled appointments when the child is woken up and told to try to use the toilet. It should be noted that the bell-and-pad system is developed in such a way that children cannot get shocked by the device's electrical wires.

As Figure 16.2 shows, Sophie's treatment progressed in a typical manner. During the first week, while Sophie was still getting used to the equipment, she wet the bed six of the seven nights. During the second week, she had four wet nights. During the third week, she had no wet nights. During the following 10 weeks, she did not wet the bed once. Follow-up conducted at 3, 6, and 12 months showed that Sophie had not wet the bed once after successful completion of treatment.

This case represents a typical treatment program for nocturnal enuresis. Sophie and her family were very motivated toward treatment and they showed a great deal of compliance with the treatment regimen. When other issues are present in the family (e.g., inconsistency in parental compliance with treatment), treatment can be more difficult to institute.

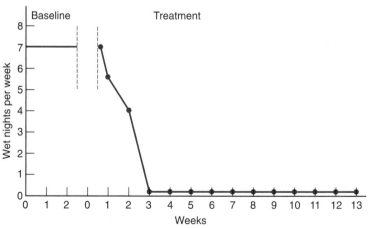

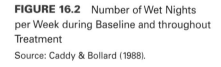

FIGURE 16.2 Number of Wet Nights per Week during Baseline and throughout Treatment

Source: Caddy & Bollard (1988).

1996). Overall, enuresis is very treatable, assuming that there are no other significant factors that affect the child's or family's functioning.

Prevention efforts have been aimed at helping parents learn better ways of toilet training their children, without traumatizing themselves or their children in the process (Christophersen & Rapoff, 1992; Ondersma & Walker, 1998). Overall, there are many ways to help children learn control over their urinary functioning before enuresis occurs, and there are many effective treatments of enuresis once it does occur.

Encopresis

As noted in Table 16.9, encopresis occurs when children do not control their bowel functioning either unintentionally or intentionally over a period of at least three months (American Psychiatric Association, 2000). Children must be at least four years old (or the equivalent developmentally) before the diagnosis would be appropriate. As with enuresis, a full physical exam should be completed before diagnosing encopresis in order to verify that the lack of bowel control is not due to a medical problem.

Most often, children with encopresis show signs of fecal retention and constipation (i.e., not being able to defecate; Christophersen & Rapoff, 1992). As the children retain their feces, the feces become hard and compacted in the colon, and thus painful to expel. As the colon becomes fuller and fuller, the child has less and less control over when the feces will be expelled. Thus, the passage of feces can occur without the child's intentional control (Christophersen & Rapoff, 1992). Although not formally categorized in *DSM-IV*, there appear to be three primary types of encopresis: soiling done in a manipulative and intentional manner, diarrhea and loose stools

due to excessive stress, and constipation due to the unintentional retention of feces (C. E. Walker, 1998). The overwhelming majority of children with encopresis (80%–90%) show this latter pattern (C. E. Walker, 1998).

Prevalence Rates. Table 16.10 gives an overview of prevalence information for encopresis. Approximately 1%–2% of children experience encopresis (American Psychiatric Association, 2000; Luxem & Christophersen, 1999). Within pediatric populations of children, the prevalence is about 3% (Luxem & Christophersen, 1999). Studies of age patterns have not been conducted in a thorough manner, but it appears that younger children are more likely than older children to experience encopresis (Luxem & Christophersen, 1999). Most cases of encopresis do not last into adolescence, and the disorder is extremely rare in adulthood (C. E. Walker, 1995). Boys are more likely than girls to experience encopresis, with estimates of the ratio as high as a 6:1 (Luxem & Christophersen, 1999). There are no clearly established patterns of encopresis based on socioeconomic status, race, or ethnicity (Ondersma & Walker, 1998).

Other Characteristics of Encopresis. Although encopresis is not known to be comorbid with other psychiatric disorders, approximately 30% of children with encopresis also are diagnosed with enuresis (C. E. Walker, 1995). Children with encopresis show a slightly higher level of emotional problems, but it is not clear whether these problems are comorbid disorders or whether these emotional problems are related to the distress over the encopresis itself (C. E. Walker, 1995).

Regarding the course of the disorder, encopresis tends to be more prevalent in children than in adolescents. Most cases of encopresis remit by the time of adolescence (Ondersma & C. E. Walker, 1998), even without treatment.

Unlike enuresis, encopresis shows no link between children and parents. That is, parents of encopretic children are no more likely to have experienced encopresis than parents of non-encopretic children (C. E. Walker, 1995). There are, however, other etiological factors that appear to be associated with the development of encopresis (Christophersen & Rapoff, 1992), including:

TABLE 16.9 *DSM-IV* Diagnostic Criteria for Encopresis

A. Repeated passage of feces into inappropriate places (e.g., clothing or floor) whether involuntary or intentional.

B. At least one such event a month for at least 3 months.

C. Chronological age is at least 4 years (or equivalent developmental level).

D. The behavior is not due exclusively to the direct physiological effects of a substance (e.g., laxatives) or a general medical condition except through a mechanism involving constipation.

SOURCE: American Psychiatric Association (2000). Reprinted with permission from the *Diagnostic and Statistical Manual of Mental Disorders, Fourth Edition, Text Revision.* Copyright © 2000 American Psychiatric Association.

TABLE 16.10 Overview of Prevalence Information for Encopresis

Prevalence	1%–2%
Age	Younger children >Adolescents
Gender	Boys > Girls
Socioeconomic status	No patterns
Race/ethnicity	No patterns

- Not enough roughage in the diet.
- A diet with too many dairy products.
- Not enough intake of fluids.
- Intentional fecal retention by the child (to avoid painful stools).
- Medications that may lead to constipation.
- Troubling emotional factors in the child.

Treatment depends somewhat on the type of encopresis the child is experiencing. Children who show manipulative soiling would be most appropriate for some type of psychological, behavioral, or family therapy that deals with children's manipulations and children's need to control the environment (Ondersma & Walker, 1998). Children who show encopresis through diarrhea or who show the more common type of encopresis through constipation tend to be appropriate for somewhat similar types of treatment. Treatments include medical interventions, changes of diet, biofeedback, and behavioral treatments (C. E. Walker, 1995). Medical interventions and behavioral treatments have been found to be most effective in treating for encopresis (Ondersma & Walker, 1998). All of these treatments seek to reduce the retention of feces and to increase the likelihood of defecating in the toilet when appropriate. Overall, encopresis is a very treatable disorder.

Prevention of encopresis has focused primarily on appropriate toilet training and appropriate eating habits. Because the cycle of encopresis often begins with a poor diet (e.g., not enough roughage, too many dairy products, too little intake of liquids), prevention efforts have focused on increasing appropriate eating habits and subsequent toileting habits with children (Christophersen & Rapoff, 1992).

Dimensional Conceptualizations of Elimination Disorders

In most Western cultures, toilet training is accomplished between the ages of 18 and 30 months (C. E. Walker, 1998). Of course, "accidents" can occur after that time. It has been estimated that 40% of 3-year-olds, 22% of 5-year-olds, 10% of 10-year-olds, and 3% of 15-year-olds have some type of elimination accident (Luxem & Christophersen, 1999). Although these accidents do not qualify for the diagnosis of enuresis or encopresis, they can be quite distressing to the child and the parents. When asked about their primary concerns, parents of young children cite toileting as second only to negative behaviors (Mesibov, Schroeder, & Wesson, 1993). It appears that parents have higher expectations about toilet training than do professionals. In a survey of parents and pediatricians, parents reported that their children should be able to remain dry throughout the night consistently by the age of three whereas pediatricians did not expect dry nights consistently until children were over five (Luxem & Christophersen, 1999). Although parents have a large number of concerns about their children's development of appropriate toileting practices, it is relatively rare that these minor problems develop into formally diagnosable disorders such enuresis and encopresis.

SOMATOFORM DISORDERS AND FACTITIOUS DISORDERS

Both somatoform and factitious disorders provide intense challenges for pediatricians and pediatric psychologists. In the simplest terms, **somatoform disorders** are characterized by the existence of medically unexplained physical symptoms that seem to persist and to get worse over time. Physical symptoms that are expressed through somatoform disorders are thought to be exaggerated, but not intentionally made up (Garber, 1998). That is, symptoms do not appear to be under the voluntary control of the client (American Psychiatric Association, 2000). **Factitious disorders**, in contrast, are thought to be physical symptoms intentionally falsified to meet some psychological need of the client. Such symptoms are often manufactured by the client, such as with the ingestion of foreign substances or injections of chemicals (Libow, 1998). The biggest challenge with both somatoform and factitious disorders is establishing that there really is no legitimate medical explanation for the symptoms that are being presented.

Within the category of somatoform disorders, there are actually a number of separate diagnoses in the *DSM-IV*, including somatization disorder, pain disorder, hypochondriasis, and body dysmorphic disorder. **Somatization disorder** is a combination of pain, gastrointestinal, sexual, and pseudoneurological symptoms that persist over long periods of time but have no known medical cause (American Psychiatric Association, 2000). **Pain disorder** is present when the primary complaints are related to pain and when psychological symptoms seem to be enhancing the development, maintenance, or exacerbation of the experience of pain (American Psychiatric Association, 2000). **Hypochondriasis** occurs when individuals believe or fear that they have a serious medical disorder based on their misinterpretation of physical symptoms or bodily sensations (American Psychiatric Association, 2000).

Body dysmorphic disorder is present when individuals are preoccupied or even obsessed with negative aspects of their body, such as a large nose or short fingers (American Psychiatric Association, 2000). All of these somatoform disorders also require either that there be clinically significant distress related to the physical symptoms or that the symptoms impair social, academic, occupational, or other important areas of functioning.

There are no clear-cut prevalence rates for somatoform disorders in children and adolescents. Estimates suggest that between 1% and 10% of children and adolescents have met criteria for a somatoform disorder at some point in their lives (Edwards & Finney, 1994; Garber, 1998). The rates of comorbidity between somatoform disorders and other psychiatric disorders are quite high. Depending on the sample, between 50% and 100% of children and adolescents diagnosed with one of the somatoform disorders also meet criteria for another psychiatric disorder (Garber, 1998). These estimates, however, are based on small samples of children and have not been well established through extensive research protocols. Although physical symptoms without known medical causes are actually quite common in children, there is still limited research on the formal diagnosis of any of the somatoform disorders within child and adolescent populations.

One strategy that has been used in both the assessment and the eventual treatment of somatoform disorders is to have children and adolescents self-monitor their symptoms. Figure 16.3 provides an example of a self-monitoring protocol that could be used to assess recurrent stomach pain in relation to eating and other daily activities. Treatments of somatoform disorders tend to focus on behavioral treatments, cognitive-behavioral treatments, relaxation, and biofeedback (Campo & Reich, 1999; Edwards & Finney, 1994). Many of these treatments are effective with children and adolescents experiencing some type of somatoform disorder (Garber, 1998). Usually, a pediatric psychologist would work in conjunction with a pediatrician to institute these treatments.

In contrast to somatoform disorders, factitious disorders occur when physical symptoms are intentionally manufactured or created by children and adolescents (American Psychiatric Association, 2000). The child or adolescent presumably creates the symptoms in order to remain in the "sick role," for which they receive attention and caring behaviors. If symptoms are produced or feigned intentionally and if there are external incentives (e.g., receiving financial gains, avoiding legal responsibility for one's actions), then the diagnosis would be **malingering** (which is a V-code) rather than factitious disorder.

Factitious disorders are very rare in children and adolescents and have been investigated primarily through case studies (Libow, 1998; Pankratz, 1999). For this reason, little is known about their presentation, epidemiology, assessment, and treatment. It is crucial, however, to provide a thorough medical evaluation of a client's physical symptoms before concluding that he or she is showing factitious disorder (Libow, 1998).

Factitious disorder by proxy, also known as Munchausen by proxy, occurs when physical symptoms are created in children or adolescents by another person, usually a parent (Pankratz, 1999). Factitious disorder by proxy is included in Appendix B of *DSM-IV*, which provides diagnoses for further study (American Psychiatric

Code# _____	Daily Monitoring Form		Date: _____
Time	Stomach Pain Rating (0–4)	Check how long your stomachache lasted	What were you doing when you had your stomachache?
Breakfast		— about a few minutes — about 1/2 hour — about 1 hour — about 2 hours or more	
Lunch		— about a few minutes — about 1/2 hour — about 1 hour — about 2 hours or more	
Dinner		— about a few minutes — about 1/2 hour — about 1 hour — about 2 hours or more	
Bedtime		— about a few minutes — about 1/2 hour — about 1 hour — about 2 hours or more	

FIGURE 16.3 Example of a Self-Monitoring Diary for Children

Source: Edwards and Finney (1994). Published in Roberta A. Olson et al., *The Sourcebook of Pediatric Psychology,* Copyright © 1994 by Allyn & Bacon. Reprinted by permission.

Association, 2000). Factitious disorder by proxy is similar to factitious disorder in that symptoms are created intentionally. The primary difference between the two is that in factitious disorder by proxy, the parents or other caregivers are the ones who serve in the sick role by proxy. The disorder would thus be diagnosed in the parent or caretaker, rather than in the child or adolescent. Most often, parents or other caregivers use some type of drug or substance to induce symptoms in the child. On average, it takes between one and two years to identify factitious disorder by proxy correctly, given that numerous medical tests and treatments are usually given before realizing that it is the parent or caretaker who is causing the symptoms intentionally (Pankratz, 1999).

Although factitious disorder by proxy is relatively rare, fictional stories about it have gained a great deal of attention in the media. Characters illustrating factitious disorder by proxy have shown up in venues as diverse as the movie *The Sixth Sense* and the detective novel *Devil's Waltz*, by Jonathan Kellerman (1993). Such media attention has caused some researchers to fear that this rare disorder will be overdiagnosed and real physical illnesses in children will thus be overlooked (Pankratz, 1999).

To repeat, both somatoform disorders and factitious disorders are quite rare in children and adolescents. When these disorders are present, however, they provide a unique challenge for physicians and pediatric psychologists given the difficulty in accurate diagnosis and the care that needs to be taken in treating ostensibly medical illnesses with psychological and behavioral techniques (Libow, 1998).

Dimensional Conceptualizations of Somatoform and Factitious Disorder

Somatoform disorders are not well documented within child and adolescent populations, but physical symptoms without any known medical cause are actually quite common among children and adolescents. Nearly half of all children and adolescents complain of some physical symptom within any two-week time period, and approximately 15% report four or more symptoms within a two-week time period (Campo & Reich, 1999). Age patterns of symptom complaints vary according to the symptoms. Complaints of recurrent abdominal pain tend to be most prevalent with younger children, complaints of headaches tend to be more prevalent among older children, and complaints of many physical symptoms at one time tend to increase with age (Campo & Reich, 1999). Regarding gender, girls tend to request more medical care for their physical symptoms than do boys, but many complaints (e.g., recurrent pain) occur equally between boys and girls (Campo & Reich, 1999). There have been equivocal findings regarding physical symptom complaints, socioeconomic status, and race/ethnicity (Campo & Reich, 1999). Children's somatic complaints appear to show comparable rates across most industrialized nations (Garralda & Rangel, 1999; Rollman, 1998). There appears to be a fair amount of continuity in complaints of physical symptoms across the lifespan (Garralda & Rangel, 1999).

Factitious disorders and factitious disorder by proxy have been less well investigated in terms of the dimensional conceptualizations of these problems (Libow, 1998). Although feigning physical symptoms is commonplace during childhood and adolescence, such behavior is not thought to be related to factitious disorders (Kager, Arndt, & Kenny, 1992). Overall, much more research is needed to understand the diagnostic conceptualizations as well as the dimensional conceptualizations of factitious disorders and factitious disorder by proxy.

GENETIC CHROMOSOMAL DISORDERS

There are a number of genetic chromosomal disorders that should be mentioned briefly to provide examples of the breadth of problems with which pediatric psychologists work. **Turner's syndrome** is a rare, sex-linked chromosomal abnormality that occurs in girls. The prevalence rate is approximately 1 in 5,000 girls (Money, 1993). Girls with Turner's syndrome are short in stature; tend to lack secondary sexual characteristics (e.g., breast development, pubic-hair growth); and are prone to kidney and heart defects (J. L. Orten, 1990). In addition to these consistent problems, girls with Turner's syndrome occasionally show spatial skill deficits, mathematical skill deficits, social isolation, impulsivity, and hyperactivity (McCauley, Ito, & Kay, 1986; J. L. Orten, 1990; J. K. Williams, 1994). Girls with Turner's syndrome are also at greater risk for being teased by their peers (especially teasing about body appearance), and this teasing is associated with depression and self-image problems (Rickert, Hassed, Hendon, & Cunniff, 1996). Although girls with Turner's syndrome face numerous difficulties, many (e.g., educational achievement, occupational status, and personal well-being) resolve themselves by adulthood (J. D. Orten & Orten, 1992).

Another disorder of interest to pediatric psychologists is **Klinefelter's syndrome**, a sex-linked disorder that occurs in males who have an XXY chromosomal structure (Cody & Hynd, 1999). Other variations of Klinefelter's syndrome show two or more X chromosomes and one or more Y chromosomes in males (Mandoki, Sumner, Hoffman, & Riconda, 1991). The prevalence of Klinefelter's syndrome is approximately 1 in 900 newborn boys (Money, 1993). Boys with this syndrome used to be thought to show higher rates of criminality and psychiatric problems than boys without the syndrome, but well-controlled studies have shown this pattern to be incorrect (Cody & Hynd, 1999; Mandoki et al., 1991). Boys with Klinefelter's syndrome do, however, show language deficits, academic problems, emotional/behavioral problems, and neuromaturational lags more than other boys (Mandoki et al., 1991; Rovert, Netley, Keenan, Bailey, & Stewart, 1996).

Turner's syndrome and Klinefelter's syndrome are just two of the many genetic and chromosomal problems that occur in children. Although these types of syndromes are rare, pediatric psychologists often work with children who exhibit them, given these children's need for intensive medical and psychological services.

OTHER DISORDERS

There are a number of other disorders that are of concern to pediatric psychologists. Two important disorders in pediatric psychology are sleep disorders and tic disorders.

Sleep Disorders

Sleep disorders include narcolepsy (unintentionally falling asleep), insomnia (not being able to fall asleep), and hypersomnia (sleeping too much; Sadeh & Gruber, 1998). Approximately 25% of children experience some type of sleep disturbance during childhood, but not all of these disturbances qualify as sleep disorders (Carlson & Cordova, 1999). In fact, formal sleep disorders like narcolepsy, insomnia, and hypersomnia are quite rare in childhood (Carlson & Cordova, 1999). One study of sleep disorders in adolescents reported a prevalence rate of 4% for insomnia, but much lower rates for other sleep disorders (Ohayon, Roberts, Zulley, Smirme, & Priest, 2000). Other difficulties, such as not sleeping through the night, not wanting to take naps, and experiencing nightmares are much more common in infancy and early childhood (Field & Liepack, 1999; Owens, Spirito, McGuinn, & Nobile, 2000). Sleep difficulties in infancy (especially difficulties in self-soothing at night) are associated with sleep difficulties in toddlerhood (Gaylor, Goodlin-Jones, & Anders, 2001).

Many sleep difficulties can be treated through behavioral methods. One particularly good book on helping parents with their children's sleep difficulties is Dr. Richard Ferber's (1985) *Solve Your Child's Sleep Problems*. Dealing with sleep problems has the added benefit of improving children's daytime behavior (Aronen, Paavonen, Fjaellberg, Soininen, & Toerroenen, 2000; Wiggs & Stores, 1999).

Tic Disorders

Tic disorders are also of concern to pediatric psychologists. Tics are a stereotyped, sudden, unintentional, recurrent movement or vocalization. Tic disorders are often comorbid with other psychiatric disorders, such as mood disorders (Coffey et al., 2000a); anxiety disorders (Coffey et al., 2000b); and attention-deficit/hyperactivity disorder (T. Spencer et al., 1999). One prospective longitudinal study suggested that tics in childhood were predictive of obsessive-compulsive disorder in late adolescence and early adulthood (B. S. Peterson, Pine, Cohen, & Brook, 2001). Overall, there were many associations between tics, attention-deficit/hyperactivity disorder, and obsessive compulsive disorder (B. S. Peterson et al., 2001).

Although rare in childhood, Tourette's disorder is probably the best known tic disorder due to its severity (D. W. Evans, King, & Leckman, 1996; Sallee & Spratt, 1998). Children with Tourette's disorder show both motor and verbal tics, and often make vocalizations that are considered quite inappropriate (e.g., unintentionally saying a curse word in the middle of a conversation; American Psychiatric Association, 2000). Tourette's disorder and other tic and movement disorders appear to have significant genetic and biological etiologies (Giedd, Rapoport, Garvey, Perlmutter, & Swedo, 2000; Sallee & Spratt, 1998).

CHRONIC ILLNESS IN CHILDREN AND CHILDREN'S WELL-BEING

Although all of the problems discussed thus far in this chapter are relevant to pediatric psychology, the overwhelming majority of work in pediatric psychology focuses on the connections between physical illness and children's well-being. A meta-analysis indicated that children with chronic physical illnesses show significantly more internalizing and externalizing emotional/ behavioral problems than their physically healthy peers (Lavigne & Faier-Routman, 1992). In general, poorer psychological outcome is associated with physical illnesses that (Sattler, 1998):

- Are unpredictable or recurrent (e.g., sickle-cell anemia, asthma, epilepsy).

- Are severe and chronic (e.g., sickle-cell anemia, cystic fibrosis).

- Require frequent monitoring and self- or parent-administered medical treatments as well as frequent medical visits or rehabilitation (e.g., diabetes, cystic fibrosis).

- Lead to multiple hospitalizations or that require constant bed rest (e.g., cancer).

- Are life-threatening (e.g., some types of cancer or renal disease).

- Are obvious to others (e.g., illnesses or treatments that lead to scars or hair loss).

- Are related to some type of social stigma (e.g., AIDS, some physical differences).

- Require numerous painful treatments (e.g., cancer).

There are too many chronic illnesses to cover in this chapter, but a few selected topics will be reviewed. Interested readers are referred to a number of excellent books on pediatric psychology, including *The Handbook of Pediatric and Adolescent Health Psychology* (Goreczny & Hersen, 1999); *The Handbook of Pediatric Psychology* (M. C. Roberts, 1995); *The Sourcebook of Pediatric Psychology* (Olson, Mullins, Gillman, & Chaney, 1994); *Handbook of Research in Pediatric and Clinical Child Psychology* (Drotar, 2000); *Cognitive Aspects of Chronic Illness in Children* (R. T. Brown, 1999); *Readings in Pediatric Psychology* (M. C. Roberts, Koocher, Routh, & Willis, 1993); and *Casebook of Child and Pediatric Psychology* (M. C. Roberts & Walker, 1989). In addition, review of the *Journal of Pediatric Psychology* is likely to increase students' interest in this fascinating area. Box 16.2 also provides parents' experiences with their children with chronic problems.

For the purposes of this chapter, the chronic illnesses of childhood diabetes, sickle-cell anemia, cancer, and HIV/AIDS will be covered. These illnesses provide some

---

BOX 16.2

PARENTS OF CHILDREN WITH CHRONIC PHYSICAL PROBLEMS, IN THEIR OWN WORDS

One of the most difficult aspects of parenting a child with special needs is the feeling of isolation that many of us experience. Many times, family and friends, not knowing what to say or do, will avoid conversation regarding the child, or even avoid the parents altogether. (p. 118)

What you said didn't help, you know; your snappy, "Look, Kathy, you've just got to learn to accept this" stunned me. Accept it? I wanted to scream, accept it? I'll never accept this, never ever accept that my baby has cerebral palsy, is "developmentally delayed" . . . or might never walk or talk. It's just not acceptable to me that she will have pain, be "different" . . . and may have a reduced life span. (pp. 2–3)

Being heard is the single most important idea . . . Jeremy has cancer and no one would listen to me saying that this kid was sick. I went here, I went there, we took him to the hospital, we were told, "There's nothing to worry about." . . . A biopsy was all I wanted! If the pediatrician hadn't listened to me, things would not have happened the way they did. The cancer wouldn't have been found in time, the chemotherapy wouldn't have worked, and Jeremy

wouldn't be here. What it boils down to is an instinct. (pp. 3–4)

It is always music to my ears when I hear a health professional or a teacher acknowledge the different aspects of my daughter that are positive. It acknowledges her wholeness, rather than her brokenness. (p. 68)

One evening after eight, our pediatrician stopped in to say hello after doing rounds visiting his patients. We had been admitted by the pediatric oncologist, so we were not officially considered our pediatrician's patients. He looked tired to me. Unexpectedly, he came over and asked me if he could hold Jeremy and sit and rock him for a few minutes—and he did . . . It was the most striking act of kindness by a physician I have ever seen. (pp. 35–36)

I am a very private person. I am not one to share my tears easily with others. But I am finding that I need to share my sadness and anger with others, those who understand feelings about parenting a child with special needs. (p. 129)

SOURCE: Marsh (1995)

indication of the type of work in which pediatric psychologists get involved and also highlight the need for multidisciplinary teams of pediatricians, specialist physicians, nurses, psychiatrists, educators, physical therapists, nutritionists, and pediatric psychologists to work together in order to help children cope with these difficult illnesses.

Juvenile Onset Diabetes

Formally known as insulin-dependent diabetes or Type I diabetes, juvenile onset diabetes is a lifelong disease for which there is no complete cure. Diabetes that first appears in adulthood is known as either non-insulin-dependent diabetes or Type II diabetes. Common symptoms associated with the diagnosis of diabetes in childhood are frequent need to urinate, excessive thirst, eating large quantities of food and still feeling hungry, and rapid weight loss. These symptoms, in addition to a medical evaluation that shows ketonuria (ketones in the urine) and blood glucose level greater than 200 mg/dl, suggest that the child has insulin-dependent diabetes.

Approximately 1 out of 600 children will develop diabetes in childhood (S. B. Johnson, 1998). This figure is relatively consistent within the United States and non-Scandinavian European countries, but rates are higher in the Scandinavian countries and lower in the Asian countries. Within the United States, girls and boys are at equal risk for juvenile onset diabetes, and Caucasian Americans are 1.5 times more likely to develop the disease than are African Americans. Although there are no formal age

stipulations when diagnosing the disease, most cases of diabetes are diagnosed around puberty (S. B. Johnson, 1998).

Medical treatment of diabetes is complicated, and many issues arise related to compliance with the treatment regimen. Management of diabetes includes monitoring blood glucose levels at least twice a day (which means drawing blood twice a day); receiving shots of insulin once or more per day, following strict dietary rules (e.g., eating at regular times during the day and limiting or deleting sugar and saturated fats from the diet); and routine exercise (Silverstein, 1994). Depending on the age of the diagnosed child, either parents or children themselves are responsible for completing these daily management techniques. Normal developmental processes, such as gaining independence and autonomy, can sometimes be hampered by parents' attempts to control adolescents' eating behavior in order to control symptoms of diabetes (Maharaj, Rodin, Connolly, Olmsted, & Daneman, 2001).

Among the severe complications that can occur when there is chronic noncompliance with treatment (and even sometimes when there is complete compliance with treatment) are cognitive deficits, blindness, renal failure, nerve disease, amputation of a limb due to associated vascular disease, heart disease, coma, and death (S. B. Johnson, 1998; Rovert & Fernandes, 1999; Silverstein, 1994). Given the severity of complications related to juvenile onset diabetes, compliance with treatment is considered crucial for the well-being of the child. Treatment compli-

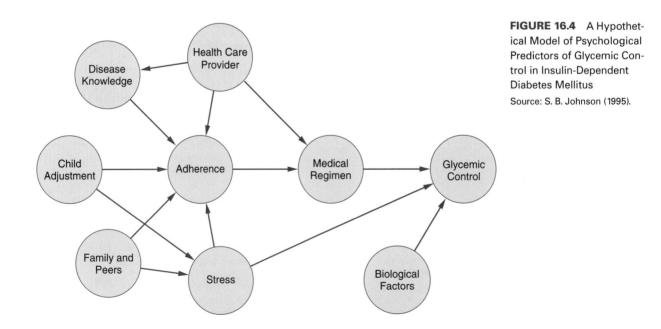

FIGURE 16.4 A Hypothetical Model of Psychological Predictors of Glycemic Control in Insulin-Dependent Diabetes Mellitus

Source: S. B. Johnson (1995).

ance decreases with more complex medical regimens, when children and families must make lifestyle changes, and as children grow older (S. B. Johnson, 1995). As Figure 16.4 shows, adherence to the medical management of diabetes in children is conceptualized as a central component in the control of the disease (S. B. Johnson, 1995).

Often when significant patterns of noncompliance or nonadherence with treatment are evident, children and their families are referred to a pediatric psychologist.

Pediatric psychologists can engage in a variety of psychological treatments (S. B. Johnson, 1995, 1998), but the most common are:

- Education.
- Behavioral or social-learning interventions.
- Relaxation and biofeedback training.
- Family therapy.

Case Study: The Family of a Child with Diabetes

Alli was eight years old when she was diagnosed with insulin-dependent diabetes mellitus. She lives with her biological mother (Patty), father (Jeff), and 14-year-old brother. Alli was described as an average student with a strong will and excellent skills as a soccer player. She had been quite healthy until one week when she began feeling ill. After being diagnosed with diabetes by her pediatrician, Alli was admitted to the hospital in order to be stabilized.

While in the hospital, the psychologist who worked on the diabetes team worked with the family from a psychoeducational model in order to help the family cope with the demands of the disease. First, the psychologist made initial contact with the family (a process known as engagement), and assessed the family for potential problems with adherence to the medical regimen. The psychologist was especially interested in the family's level of knowledge about diabetes, their willingness to learn about the disease, their willingness to develop problem-solving strategies related to the chronic care of diabetes, and their ability to work cooperatively on shared tasks. The psychologist also assessed the family for any underlying issues that would create resistance to the effective treatment of the diabetes. From a psychoeducational standpoint, the psychologist helped share information with the family in a way that the family could understand and also tried to develop additional skills within the family. The psychologist also emphasized the need to prevent problems before they occurred. The following transcript was from an early session with the family. As it shows, the family is relatively healthy in dealing with each other and with the adjustment to Alli's diagnosis.

THERAPIST: At this point, you may be feeling overwhelmed with all the information you have been getting.

PATTY: Yes—how are we going to do all of this? The consequences for not keeping her diabetes in control are devastating. And she is already so strong willed, how will we be able to make sure that she will do what she is supposed to? Maybe I should quit work.

ALLI: I don't want to give shots.

JEFF: Maybe we should cancel our spring vacation and stay at home.

THERAPIST: Yes, you do sound like this has been overwhelming. We'll take one point at a time. First, you should

know that how you are feeling is very typical. It takes a while to sort through all the information and figure out how the new routines will work in your family. That's why the care team is here, to answer questions and offer advice. And you will be able to do all of this, including giving yourself shots when you are ready. What usually happens is that at first, families stick to the routine precisely. Then, as you get more familiar with the routine, it may slip a little. Then what usually happens is that you develop a routine that works for your family and in different situations. While you have to change routines to care for the diabetes, you want to hold off on making other major changes for awhile.

PATTY: But if the routine slips, won't that have major consequences down the road?

THERAPIST: There is a little room for tolerance in the routine. We'll make sure you have time to talk with Dr. Smith regarding the short-term and long-term consequences. Would that be helpful?

PATTY: Yes, thanks.

THERAPIST: Are there any areas that you feel might be a problem?

ALLI: Shots!

THERAPIST: Wow, that really seems to be worrying you. What are you doing for your care right now?

ALLI: I am doing finger sticks. I did two today.

PATTY: Yes, she did, and she read the meter as well.

THERAPIST: How do you do a finger stick? Can you show me?

ALLI: Sure. [*demonstrates*]

PATTY: And she only had to be shown this once.

THERAPIST: Really. You sure are a fast learner.

JEFF: Yes, she can be.

THERAPIST: What else have you been learning?

ALLI: About diet. The diet lady brought by fake food for us to see.

THERAPIST: There is a lot to learn about that too.

ALLI: Yep.

SOURCE: Fournier & Rae (1999, p. 320).

Treatment for medical nonadherence and noncompliance can be very effective and helpful for children and families (S. B. Johnson, 1998). As illustrated in the case study of Alli, the higher functioning the family unit, the less likelihood there is of medical nonadherence.

Sickle-Cell Disease

Sickle-cell disease is a genetic disorder that occurs in approximately 1 out of every 400 African Americans within the United States (Lemanek, Buckloh, Woods, & Butler, 1995). The disease can also occur in individuals descended from Italy, Greece, Asia Minor, and other countries around the Mediterranean Sea and the Caribbean Sea. Sickle-cell anemia is the most severe form of sickle-cell disease. The disease is usually not identified until after the age of six months. After that age, symptoms begin to occur such as severe episodes of pain, severe infections, strokes, and anemia. In later childhood, retarded growth and delays in sexual maturity are present (Lemanek et al., 1995). Medical interventions related to sickle-cell disease have included newborn screening, pain management, transfusion therapy, surgery, and comprehensive care (Lemanek et al., 1995).

Pediatric psychologists often get involved in helping children with sickle-cell disease because of its emotional/behavioral sequelae. Children with sickle-cell disease often exhibit poorer self-esteem, poorer peer relationships, delayed academic competence, more internalizing problems, and more externalizing behavior problems than their physically healthy peers (Frank, Allison,

& Cant, 1999; Lemanek et al., 1995). In addition to pediatric psychologists working to intervene with these emotional/behavioral problems, they can also get involved in trying to help the family cope with this devastating illness. Family conflict and distress is associated with increases in emotional/behavioral problems in children with sickle-cell disease (Kell, Kliewer, Erickson, & Ohene-Frempong, 1998; R. J. Thompson et al., 1999). Thus, working to find effective coping mechanisms within the family would help to reduce the maladaptive functioning of children with sickle-cell disease (Ievers, Brown, Lambert, Hsu, & Eckman, 1998; R. J. Thompson, Gil, Burbach, Keith, & Kinney, 1993).

Overall, sickle-cell disease is a severe illness that influences not only children but the entire family as well. Pediatric psychologists have been actively involved in trying to help children and families cope with this lifelong disease.

Healing is a matter of time, but it is sometimes also a matter of opportunity.

—Hippocrates

Childhood Cancer

Cancer occurs in approximately 1 out of 600 children before the age of 15 (Cecalupo, 1994). Close to 40% of childhood cancer is diagnosed between the ages of birth and four years old. Boys are more at risk for cancer than are girls, and Caucasian American children have slightly higher rates of cancer than do African American children (Cecalupo, 1994).

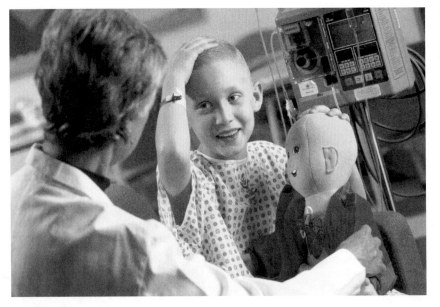

Physicians and psychologists often try to help pediatric cancer patients cope with the effects of treatment, such as hair loss.

Among the different types of cancer that occur in childhood are acute leukemia, brain tumors, lymphoma, neuroblastoma, soft tissue sarcomas, and bone tumors. Although many cancers that occur in adults are associated with lifestyle choices (e.g., smoking) and environmental toxins (e.g., exposure to radioactive materials), cancers in childhood tend to be associated with genetic predispositions, chromosomal abnormalities, immune deficiencies, or other developmental abnormalities (Cecalupo, 1994). Medical interventions are geared toward treating the cancer directly, but pediatric psychologists often become involved with helping the child and family cope with the medical treatments and the diagnosis of cancer itself (Friedman, Latham, & Dahlquist, 1998). There have been many interventions developed to help children deal with the aversive and sometimes extremely painful treatment regimens that are necessary to battle cancer. Most of these interventions use behavioral and cognitive behavioral techniques to help the child deal with these stressful and painful procedures (Friedman et al., 1998). School psychologists and other educational professionals also can become involved in helping children diagnosed with

Case Study: A Teenager Who Is Battling Cancer

Penny is 15 years old and lives with her parents and older brother. After being diagnosed with leukemia when she was 10 years old, she endured three years of chemotherapy, which led to a two-year remission. Penny then relapsed and underwent a bone marrow transplant, with the donor marrow coming from her 18-year-old brother.

Penny's parents had both been successful attorneys in a small town when Penny was first diagnosed with leukemia. After the diagnosis, the family moved to a larger city in order to be closer to a cancer treatment center. In addition, Penny's mother quit her job in order to be able to focus on Penny's doctor's appointments and prolonged treatment. During the relapse, Penny, her mother, and her father all reported no psychological difficulties. Penny had been a good student, and even with homeschooling (which was necessitated by the medical treatments and their side effects) she had continued to excel in her academic work. Both Penny and her mother reported exceedingly good mental health, and Penny's father reported only mild levels of psychological distress. The psychologists on staff at the oncology unit, however, hypothesized that Penny, her mother, and, to a lesser extent, her father were still in denial about the seriousness of Penny's medical condition. For example, Penny denied any concerns about her own mortality and refused to be part of any discussions with the medical staff. In addition, both parents reported significant dissatisfaction with their marriage.

After the bone marrow transplant, Penny and her parents began to show more signs of distress. Penny's usual style of coping with medical procedures deteriorated, and she began clinging to her mother during her hospital stay. Penny's mother seemed to deal with her own distress by trying to control the medical procedures, so much so that the medical staff often refused to care for Penny because of their aversive interactions with Penny's mother. During the six-month hospital stay, Penny and her mother were inseparable—in fact, Penny refused to go anywhere (even down the hall for a walk) without her mother. Once treatment was completed, Penny was discharged with directions not to see anyone outside of the family because of concerns about her weakened immune system. After four months passed, Penny's mother called the psychological staff to request help in transitioning Penny back to school.

Penny's mother reported that Penny had concerns about her appearance, though Penny correctly noted that she had an expensive blond wig that looked real and that hid her limited hair growth. Penny did, however, express a great deal of concern about leaving her mother and going to school alone. She had not seen any peers for over a year, and she had not been actively involved with friends for a number of years. She expressed a great desire to become more actively involved with peers and with learning to drive by herself, but she also expressed extreme anxiety about separation from her mother.

Penny began cognitive-behavioral therapy, with a focus on short-term anxiety management. The therapists developed an anxiety hierarchy began with Penny riding the elevator with a staff person (but without her mother) in the hospital for a medical appointment and ended with Penny driving alone to a fast-food restaurant during daylight hours by herself. Penny was taught progressive muscle relaxation and cognitive reframing in order to deal with her anxious thoughts.

After two months of therapy, Penny had conquered her fears and was able to function independently from her parents at an age-appropriate level. She also developed a number of friendships at school, which also increased her feelings of autonomy. Penny's parents were offered marital and individual therapy, but neither parent reported any interest. Penny's mother and father seemed to remain somewhat in denial of their own distress, and both appeared to have resigned themselves to an unhappy and unsupportive marriage.

This case study illustrates how life-saving medical treatments can have a negative impact on normal developmental milestones. Developmentally, it would have been important to encourage Penny to become more involved with friends before, during, and after medical treatment. Medically, however, Penny would have been at risk for further medical problems had she begun socializing extensively. In many cases within the realm of pediatric psychology, medical treatments must (by necessity) take precedence over psychological treatments.

SOURCE: Friedman et al. (1998).

cancer given that some types of cancer and treatment for cancer are associated with academic deficits and neuropsychological deficits (Powers, Vannatta, Noll, Cool, & Stehbens, 1995).

Not surprisingly, childhood cancer is associated with emotional/behavioral problems in children and distress in their parents (Challinor et al., 1999). Survey studies suggest that the most stressful time for families in the process of childhood cancer is at the time of diagnosis (Friedman et al., 1998), although there are also increased rates of parental distress during painful medical procedures (Manne et al., 2001). Children and adolescents do surprisingly well during cancer treatment, but there are some factors specifically associated with good emotional/behavioral functioning related to childhood cancer. Families that were well functioning before the diagnosis of cancer and families in which there is a strong and nonconflicted parental relationship tend to fare better throughout the treatment process (Friedman et al., 1998). A strong and nonconflicted parent–child relationship (especially the mother–child relationship) is associated with less distress among adolescents with cancer (Manne & Miller, 1998). Better emotional/behavioral outcomes are also associated with the way in which medical staff members deal with the family. Specifically, parents report better outcomes when they are provided clear and direct information about the cancer and cancer treatment, when they are provided support from a liaison who serves to facilitate the relationship between the family and the medical staff, and when they receive help with utilizing and maximizing their own coping resources (Friedman et al., 1998).

In terms of parental distress, parents' rates of trait anxiety before the diagnosis of cancer in their child were associated with greater rates of distress after cancer treatment (Hoekstra-Weebers, Jasper, Kamps, & Klip, 1999). Parents whose children have functional limitations due to the illness (e.g., not being able to play with friends, limited self-care skills) experienced more psychological distress than parents whose children did not show functional limitations (Silver, Westbrook, & Stein, 1998).

Given that one-third of children with cancer do not survive, continued involvement by pediatric psychologists is important through the dying process of the child and through the grieving process for the family. Although the research is limited in how best to help parents cope with losing a child to cancer, pediatric psychologists are often involved in helping support the family during the grieving process and to help serve as a liaison between the family and the medical staff after losing a child.

Although there have been significant advances in the treatment of childhood cancer, the impact of this disease is still overwhelming for many families. This topic has been and continues to be of central focus for pediatric psychologists due to the severity of the disease and the impact that it has on the child and family.

My main message is that I want these kids to learn from my mistake, so that what happened to me doesn't happen to them.

—Earvin "Magic" Johnson (1992, p. 356) regarding his
HIV-positive status due to unprotected sex

HIV and AIDS in Children and Adolescents

Worldwide, more than 1 million children and adolescents are infected with the human immunodeficiency virus (HIV; L. K. Brown, Lourie, & Pao, 2000), which causes the disease know as acquired immunodeficiency syndrome (AIDS). Although this number is devastating, it should be noted that the percentage of children infected with HIV is still very small compared to the large number of adults infected with HIV. Of all the cases of AIDS documented within the United States, only 2% of the individuals are children under the age of 18 (Wolters, Brouwers, & Perez, 1999). Within the United States, nearly 80% of children and adolescents infected with HIV or who have AIDS are either African American or Hispanic/Latino/Latina (Wolters et al., 1999).

HIV targets the immune system and destroys T4 cells (also known as helper T cells). Once HIV is in the immune system, it may not manifest into symptoms for 8 years or more (Zeichner & Read, 1999). Ultimately, however, HIV leaves the host's immune system weakened and unable to defend itself against opportunistic infections and other problems. One prevalent infection is pneumocystis carinii pneumonia, which is one of the markers that allows the formal diagnosis of AIDS (Zeichner & Read, 1999).

There are a number of ways in which children and adolescents can become infected with HIV. In the early days of the AIDS epidemic, some children became infected through transfusions of tainted blood. Children with hemophilia and other illnesses that required a large amount of blood infusions were particularly at risk for receiving blood that was HIV-positive. Since the advent of stringent testing protocols for donated blood in 1985, it is thought that the blood supply within the United States has been relatively free from tainted blood (Wolters et al., 1999). More recently, there have been two primary ways in which children and adolescents are at risk for HIV infection. First, infants born to HIV-positive mothers or mothers who have been diagnosed with AIDS are at increased risk of infection. Second, children and adolescents who exchange bodily fluids with an infected individual, usually through unprotected sexual contact, are at risk of infection. Although there have been some rare cases of young children becoming infected through sexual abuse (Armistead, Forehand, Steele, & Kotchick, 1998), the majority of cases in children and adolescents involve adolescents who have engaged in consensual unprotected sex with an infected partner (Wolters et al., 1999). Because the two primary mechanisms of transmission are so different from each other, children who are infected through maternal transmission will be discussed separately from adolescents who are infected through unprotected sexual contact.

The overwhelming majority of children under the age of 13 infected with HIV (91%) were infected from their HIV-positive mother (Wolters et al., 1999). This form of transmission (from mother to infant) is known as **vertical transmission**. Most of the mothers were infected via intravenous drug use or unprotected sex with an infected partner (who may or may not be the father of the infected infant). The infections of infants usually occurs either in utero (as HIV passes through the placenta), through maternal secretions at the time of birth, or through breast feeding (Wolters et al., 1999). It is estimated that between 12.9% and 39% of infants of infected mothers also are infected (Hutto, 1994). Medical treatment of mothers who are pregnant, such as the use of azidothymidine (AZT), decreases the risk of transmission to the infant to between 8%–10% (Wolters et al., 1999).

Infants who are infected through vertical transmission seem to fall into two categories—rapid versus slow disease progression. Infants who are diagnosed early as HIV-positive and who show early symptoms within the first year of life tend to experience a more aggressive form of HIV and subsequent development of AIDS (Wolters et al., 1999). These children show many more medical problems (e.g., opportunistic infections, growth retardation, hepatitis, fever, anemia, and diarrhea) and have a much shorter life span than children who show a later onset of symptoms. It remains unclear why some infants show rapid and others show slower disease progression, but it may be that there are different strains of HIV or that there are other genetic or biological factors at work (Wolters et al., 1999). Regardless of the age of onset of AIDS-related symptoms, children infected with HIV often experience central nervous system difficulties and cognitive deficits in addition to the severe physical problems associated

with AIDS (L. K. Brown et al., 2000). Shortened life span is characteristic of children diagnosed with AIDS. Approximately 20% of children diagnosed with AIDS die by the age of three (Armistead et al., 1998) and 35% will die by the age of five (L. K. Brown et al., 2000).

> *No one ever told me that, as a 15-year-old kid, I could end up . . . having someone for a partner who was [HIV]-infected.*
>
> —Kerri, who died of AIDS-related complications before reaching adulthood (J. D. Fisher & Fisher, 1994)

The other primary mode of transmission of HIV is unprotected sex during adolescence. Within the United States, approximately 20% of individuals who are HIV-positive, but who have not yet developed AIDS are in the age range of 13 to 24 (Samples, Goodman, & Woods, 1998). The overwhelming majority of girls who became infected with HIV during adolescence do so through unprotected heterosexual sex (Samples et al., 1998). Boys infected during adolescence are more likely to do so by having sex with other boys or men, but they are also at risk for HIV transmission through sex with girls or women (Samples et al., 1998).

AIDS has become a leading cause of death in adolescents and young adults (L. K. Brown et al., 2000). Complications related to HIV and AIDS are the third most common cause of death for African American adolescent girls (behind homicide and accidents); the fifth most common cause of death for African American adolescent boys (behind homicide, accidents, suicide, and heart disease); and the seventh most common cause of death among Caucasian American adolescent girls and boys (behind accidents, suicide, homicide, malignancies, heart disease, and congenital anomalies; Becker, Rankin, & Rickel, 1998). There is no doubt that HIV and AIDS are serious problems with the adolescent age group. Also more and more children who were infected with HIV through vertical transmission or through early blood transfusions with tainted blood, have now reached adolescence and are sexually active (Samples et al., 1998). This group provides another complexity in the mission to prevent transmission of HIV. There is evidence to suggest that HIV-positive adolescents whose parents discuss sexual issues with them are more likely to disclose their HIV status to their sexual partners than those adolescents whose parents do not discuss sexual issues with them (Parsons et al., 1998).

Pediatric psychologists have gotten involved in child and adolescent HIV and AIDS cases primarily through research, assessment, and therapeutic treatments. Because of the cognitive and psychological ramifications of AIDS, psychologists often conduct psychosocial assessments and family assessments to determine how children and their families might be helped most (Armistead et al., 1998; Sattler, 1998). Adolescents with psychological problems (especially those with conduct problems) are at an increased risk for HIV infection due to increased risky sexual behavior (Donenberg, Emerson, Bryant, Wilson, & Weber-Shifrin, 2001). For adolescents with or without preexisting psychological problems, treatments include individual therapy with children and family therapy. Therapy can focus on many issues, including anxiety, depression, medical compliance, and bereavement in families who lose a child to AIDS (Armistead et al., 1998).

Within pediatric psychology and social psychology, a great deal of attention has been given to prevention of HIV and AIDS transmission, especially with the prevention of transmission through adolescents' unprotected sex. Unfortunately, simple education programs (e.g., teaching adolescents about the dangers of unprotected sex) are not effective in getting them to adopt abstinence or safer sex practices (R. A. Olson, Huszti, & Youll, 1995). One successful prevention program targeted mothers of adolescents and helped them to talk with their children about sexuality and AIDS-related issues (Lefkowitz, Sigman, & Au, 2000). This program was successful in reducing risk of HIV transmission in adolescents. Overall, effective prevention programs to reduce adolescents' risk of HIV transmission need to be multidimensional and thorough (J. D. Fisher & Fisher, 1992), including topics such as:

- Perceiving yourself as a sexual being.
- Learning the behaviors that are necessary for protecting yourself from HIV transmission (e.g., abstinence, use of a latex condom with antispermicidal agents such as Nonoxynol-9 that are associated with killing HIV, outercourse rather than intercourse sexual activities).
- Learning to negotiate the use of safer sex methods with a potential sexual partner.
- Finding the strength to not begin a relationship or to leave a relationship with someone who is not willing to use safer sex methods.
- Buying latex condoms or finding public health facilities where latex condoms are available at no cost.
- Seeking out and receiving HIV testing, if appropriate.
- Sticking with risk-reduction practices, even when remaining with the same partner for a long time.
- Self-reinforcement for good risk-reduction practices in order to prevent relapse into riskier behaviors.

These behaviors can be conceptualized within an **information-motivation-behavioral (IMB) skills model** of AIDS risk behavior change (J. D. Fisher, Fisher, Misovich, Kimble, & Malloy, 1996). AIDS risk reduction has been advanced with prevention programs that include all of these elements (J. D. Fisher et al., 1996). More programs are needed in this area, given the risk in which sexually active adolescents find themselves these days (R. A. Olson et al., 1995).

In fifty years, I think there will be a cure for AIDS. Many people in Zimbabwe are dying because of that dangerous disease and there is no cure yet. AIDS does not choose—elderly, young, poor, it will kill. When I grow up, I can invent that medicine. I can study a lot and then I can cure the people and they will live a long life.

—Trust, 13, Zimbabwe

CHRONIC ILLNESS IN PARENTS AND CHILDREN'S WELL-BEING

Just as researchers that have investigated children of psychologically distressed parents, there is also a long line of research into the functioning of children of medically ill parents. In fact, children of medically ill parents have sometimes been used as a control group to compare and contrast functioning with children of psychologically distressed parents (Hammen, 1991). Some of this work has also been extended to evaluate the process of parental illness and parental death, as in the case of research on parental AIDS (Armistead et al., 1998) and parental cancer (Mireault & Compas, 1996). Although the research literature is too large to summarize for the purposes of this chapter, a few studies are highlighted in order to provide examples of research in this area.

Parental AIDS

There are growing numbers of "AIDS orphans" who have lost parents to the disease (Finney & Miller, 1999; Rotheram-Borus, Stein, & Lin, 2001). In some countries, especially in many African nations, entire generations of adults have been wiped out by the AIDS pandemic and huge numbers of infants and children have become orphans because of this disease (Walders & Drotar, 2000). Also, children whose parents are currently battling AIDS may be inadvertently abandoned emotionally given the devastating medical complications related to the disease. Parents who experience AIDS often find it difficult to maintain a strong parent–child bond, to provide appropri-

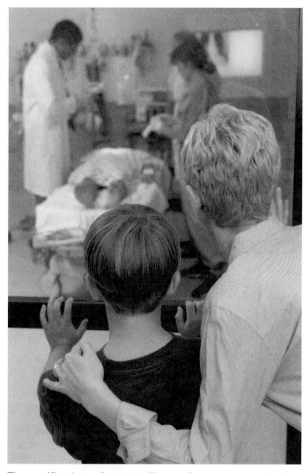

The ramifications of parental illness often vary according to the protective resources that children have in their lives (such as a strong and stable caretaker who is not ill).

ate nurturing for their children, and to protect their children from the stigma associated with AIDS (Finney & Miller, 1999). It is not unusual to find higher rates of depression and anxiety in parents with AIDS as well as in their children, regardless of whether or not the children are infected with HIV (Rotheram-Borus et al., 2001). Because many parents with AIDS were infected through intravenous drug use, parental substance abuse and dependence add to the difficulties that might influence the parent–child relationship. These familial issues are further complicated by the social and economic isolation that often occurs as a result of the AIDS diagnosis in parents (Finney & Miller, 1999). Unfortunately, because of economic and social barriers that prevent access to mental health services, children whose parents are diagnosed with AIDS are not likely to receive psychological help even when they need it. More work is needed to under-

stand the influence of parental AIDS and to allow easier access to therapeutic interventions for children who are in need of help (Rotheram-Borus et al., 2001).

Parental Cancer

In addition to parental AIDS, parental cancer has received a great deal of attention. Interestingly, there is evidence that adolescents who lose a parent to cancer are no more psychologically distressed than adolescents whose parents continue to survive with cancer (Mireault & Compas, 1996). When comparing anxiety, depression, and stress-related symptoms of adolescents with either a mother or a father diagnosed with cancer, the most significant effects emerged for adolescent girls who were dealing with maternal cancer (Compas et al., 1994). Specifically, adolescent girls whose mothers were battling cancer showed the highest level of distress when compared with younger or older girls, boys of all ages, and children of all ages who were dealing with their fathers' cancer. These studies highlight the need to look at gender differences, developmental differences, and family functioning differences within the broad spectrum of parental cancer.

Although mechanisms of effects may differ depending on the parental medical illness that is studied, certain themes provide clues as to how parental medical illness may relate to children's functioning. The primary pathways of influence appear to be social learning and modeling, changes in the parent–child relationship, family functioning, interparental conflict, appraisals of illness-related stressors, and coping styles (Compas, Worsham, Ey, & Howell, 1996; Finney & Miller, 1999). There continues to be a great need for further research into the influences of parental medical illness, especially with attention to helping children cope with parental illness.

TREATMENT ISSUES IN PEDIATRIC PSYCHOLOGY

Treatment and intervention issues have been discussed throughout the chapter, but a few overarching points are necessary to understand the context of therapeutic treatment in pediatric psychology. Because there is a correspondence between high health care use and higher rates of psychological distress in children, it is important for physicians and other medical personnel to be aware of the need to refer their pediatric patients for psychological help when necessary (Kinsman, Wildman, & Smucker, 1999).

Case Study: A Family Dealing with AIDS

Rochelle is seven years old and is living with AIDS. Both her mother and her father were diagnosed with AIDS. Rochelle's father was a chronic intravenous drug user who apparently became infected through the use of tainted needles. Rochelle's father apparently infected her mother long before Rochelle's birth and unbeknownst to either parent. Rochelle has a younger sister, Alicia, who is not HIV-positive. At the age of two, Rochelle was diagnosed as HIV-positive; her mother received the same diagnosis around the same time. When Rochelle was five years old, her mother was diagnosed with AIDS. When Rochelle was six years old, her father (with whom she had only limited contact) was shot to death outside of his home.

As a single parent, Rochelle's mother, Maggie, relies primarily on her family of origin for social and financial support. Rochelle's maternal grandmother learned of Maggie's and Rochelle's initial HIV infection after an argument with Rochelle's father. Maggie's brother (Rochelle's uncle) still has not been informed about the family's HIV and AIDS status, but rather has been told that Maggie is battling cancer. Maggie has become increasingly ill, and her medical condition is getting more difficult to hide.

When she first learned of her daughter's and her own diagnosis, Maggie became so depressed that she could not care for her children. At that time, Maggie's mother (Rochelle's grandmother) cared for the two girls. After approximately one year, Maggie was able to care for her children again. For the next two years, the family functioned without any major crises. Maggie was able to care for the girls and was able to maintain her own health in a relatively stable manner. Rochelle had still not been informed of her own HIV status, nor had she been told about why her mother was so sick periodically. Although the medical and psychological staff had encouraged her to tell Rochelle the truth about her mother's and her own illness, Maggie chose not to do so.

When Rochell was five, she and her younger sister were enrolled in a Head Start program. Rochelle's health began to deteriorate somewhat (with frequent ear infections and sinusitis), but Rochelle reported that she loved going to Head Start even though she had to miss many days because of feeling bad. In particular, Rochelle and her sister seemed to show a strong and supportive bond. When Rochelle was six, the school district recommended that she move on to a kindergarten class, but her mother, pediatrician, and social worker all felt that Rochelle would be traumatized by being separated from her sister. Although Rochelle was academically ready to be advanced to the next grade, socially, emotionally, and physically, she was still quite vulnerable. In addition, because Rochelle was not expected to survive to adulthood, her academic pursuits were thought to be less important than her current emotional well-being. Thus, Rochelle was allowed to stay in the Head Start program with her sister.

Rochelle's health and her mother's health have since deteriorated significantly. Now seven, Rochelle is no longer able to attend Head Start because she has to receive multiple daily infusion treatments and is fed through a tube. Maggie is also severely limited because of her health problems and can no longer care for her children. Presently, Maggie's mother is taking care of the girls as well as Maggie. Maggie is expected to live no longer than one or two months, and Rochelle is expected to live no longer than one year. Although Rochelle's grandmother is willing to take care of both girls for now, she is willing to take permanent custody of Rochelle's younger sister only and not Rochelle. Maggie wants the girls to remain together, but after her death, the girls may be separated due to the grandmother's desire to care only for Rochelle's sister. If this situation occurs, Rochelle would have to be placed in a special medical foster home away from her sister and other relatives.

SOURCE: Armistead et al. (1998).

There are a variety of effective treatments in the area of pediatric psychology. Empirically supported treatments have been identified for many specific illnesses within the realm of pediatric psychology. Most of the treatments that have been well established are within the cognitive-behavioral and behavioral orientations (McQuaid & Nassau, 1999). In addition to these more traditional treatments, there have been a number of innovative treatments that add to the multidisciplinary approach taken within the field of pediatric psychology. Pediatric summer camps (Briery & Rabian, 1999), parent-to-parent support groups (Ainbinder et al., 1998), and family-centered treatments (G. King, King, Rosenbaum, & Goffin, 1999) have all been associated with reductions in psychological symptoms of children and their families who are dealing with medical illnesses. Overall, there is a great deal of concern within the field of pediatric psychology to lessen children's and families' psychological distress when dealing with medical illness.

PREVENTION ISSUES IN PEDIATRIC PSYCHOLOGY

In addition to the treatment of psychological distress related to medical illnesses, pediatric psychologists place a great deal of emphasis on the prevention of psychological distress. Primary prevention programs often attempt to prevent the occurrence of medical illnesses before they occur (e.g., prevention of HIV transmission, promotion of healthy lifestyles in order to prevent obesity, heart disease, and some types of cancer later in life; Wurtele, 1995). Primary prevention programs in pediatric psychology, often referred to as health promotion programs (Wurtele, 1995), are geared toward the entire population of children and adolescents rather than just children and adolescents who are at risk for the development of psychological problems. Health promotion programs for children and adolescents often focus on:

- Increasing physical activity and fitness.
- Improving nutrition.
- Reducing the use of tobacco.
- Reducing the use of alcohol and other drugs.
- Enhancing health-related programs in schools and in the community.

In addition, many AIDS risk reduction programs have been instituted that not only target the reduction of HIV transmission, but also target transmission of other sexually transmitted diseases and the prevention of teenage pregnancy (J. D. Fisher et al., 1996; Lefkowitz et al., 2000; Sagrestano & Paikoff, 1997). A number of effective primary prevention programs related to pediatric psychology have been instituted within the United States and worldwide (Wurtele, 1995).

In contrast to primary prevention programs within the area of pediatric psychology, secondary prevention programs attempt to prevent the occurrence of psychological distress in relation to physical illnesses that have already occurred (D. L. Anderson, Brown, & Williams, 1999). Remember that secondary prevention programs tend to focus on groups of children and adolescents who are at risk for the development of emotional/behavioral problems. In the area of pediatric psychology, children and adolescents are considered at risk due to their medical illness or their parents' medical illness. Secondary prevention programs can also focus on early intervention and early identification of children and adolescents who are likely to develop psychological problems (D. L. Anderson et al., 1999). The majority of secondary prevention efforts within the field of pediatric psychology have focused on preventing distress related to hospitalization and aversive medical procedures such as injections, chemotherapy, lumbar punctures, and surgery (Harbeck-Weber & McKee, 1995; Varni, Blount, Waldron, & Smith, 1995). Many of these prevention strategies use cognitive-behavioral techniques (e.g., guided imagery, visualization, progressive relaxation, cognitive restructuring, modeling, and stress inoculation) and the development of other coping strategies to help children deal with aversive medical procedures (Harbeck-Weber & McKee, 1995; Rudolph, Dennig, & Weisz, 1995). Other strategies, such as anticipatory guidance, social support, and support for the family have also been used. Overall, there are a number of effective secondary prevention techniques that are used routinely with children who are experiencing either acute or chronic medical illnesses and are undergoing aversive medical procedures.

The area of pediatric psychology has been involved in prevention efforts to a greater extent than many other areas in developmental psychopathology. The focus on health promotion and on prevention of psychological distress could be used as a model for professionals within other areas in developmental psychopathology.

SUMMARY AND KEY CONCEPTS

Pediatric Psychology
Pediatric psychology is the application of psychological methods to health issues and behaviors.

Eating Disorders
There are two primary types of eating disorders. **Anorexia nervosa** occurs when an individual is significantly underweight due to restrictive eating methods and when there is great fear of gaining more weight. **Bulimia nervosa** occurs when an individual eats large quantities of food (i.e., binges) and then tries to eliminate the food intake through artificial methods such as use of laxatives or self-induced vomiting (i.e., purging).

Elimination Disorders
There are two primary types of elimination disorders. **Enuresis** occurs when individuals over the age of five cannot or will not control their urinary functioning for at least three consecutive months. **Encopresis** occurs when individuals over the age of four cannot or will not control their bowel functioning for at least three months.

Somatoform Disorders and Factitious Disorders
Somatoform disorders occur when there are medically unexplained physical or medical symptoms that seem to get worse over time. Within the category of somatoform disorders, there are a number of specific disorders, including **somatization disorder** (the combination of pain, gastrointestinal, sexual, and pseudoneurological symptoms); **pain disorder** (the existence of pain that seems to be heightened by psychological distress); **hypochondriasis** (the belief in or fear of a serious medical disorder based on misinterpretation of physical symptoms); and **body dysmorphic disorder** (the preoccupation or obsession with negative aspects of one's body). Although symptoms within somatoform disorders are thought to be exaggerated, they are not falsified intentionally. In contrast, physical symptoms in

factitious disorders are thought to be falsified intentionally with the end goal of serving in the "sick role." If physical symptoms are feigned for external incentives (such as money), then the diagnosis would be **malingering**, which is a V-code. If parents or other caretakers create symptoms in their children, in order to receive sympathy or to serve in the sick role through their child, then the parents or caretakers would be diagnosed with **factitious disorder by proxy**.

Genetic Chromosomal Disorders

There are a number of genetic chromosomal disorders of concern to pediatric psychologists. **Turner's syndrome** occurs in girls and creates short stature, limited secondary sexual characteristics, and potentially life-threatening medical problems such as heart and kidney problems. **Klinefelter's syndrome** occurs in boys who are born with an XXY chromosomal structure (or some other chromosomal structure with two or more X chromosomes and one or more Y chromosomes). Boys with Klinefelter's syndrome tend to show deficits in language, academic functioning, emotional/behavioral functioning, and neuromaturational functioning.

Other Disorders

Sleep disorders and **tic disorders** are additional problems that are of concern to pediatric psychologists.

Chronic Illness in Children and Children's Well-Being

Children and adolescents with chronic illnesses (e.g., diabetes, sickle-cell disease, cancer, and HIV/AIDS) tend to experience heightened emotional/behavioral problems. Within the area of HIV/AIDS, infants can become infected from their HIV-positive mother through **vertical transmission**, or children and adolescents can become infected through sexual contact with an infected individual. One model for the prevention of HIV and AIDS, the **information-motivation-behavioral (IMB) skills model**, suggests that adolescents must receive comprehensive prevention programs to reduce their risk for transmission of HIV and AIDS.

Chronic Illness in Parents and Children's Well-Being

Just like children of parents with psychological problems, children of parents with chronic medical illnesses (e.g., HIV/AIDS, cancer) are at risk for heightened emotional/behavioral problems.

Treatment Issues in Pediatric Psychology

A number of empirically supported treatments have been documented within the field of pediatric psychology. The majority of the treatments are within the behavioral and cognitive-behavioral orientation.

Prevention Issues in Pediatric Psychology

More than any other area within the study of developmental psychopathology, pediatric psychology has been dedicated to prevention efforts. Primary prevention efforts have focused on health promotion.

KEY TERMS

pediatric psychology	somatoform	hypochondriasis	Turner's syndrome	information-
anorexia nervosa	disorders	body dysmorphic	Klinefelter's	motivation-
bulimia nervosa	factitious disorders	disorder	syndrome	behavioral (IMB)
enuresis	somatization	malingering	sleep disorders	skills model
encopresis	disorder	factitious disorder	tic disorders	
	pain disorder	by proxy	vertical transmission	

SUGGESTED READINGS

Hornbacher, Marya. *Wasted: A Memoir of Anorexia and Bulimia.* New York: Harper Perennial, 1998. This memoir provides an intimate portrait of issues related to body image, anorexia, and bulimia. Hornbacher describes what it was like to be bulimic at the age of 9 and to be anorexic at the age of 15. She also describes the painful and difficult process of trying to gain control over her eating habits and her life.

Grealy, Lucy. *Autobiography of a Face.* New York: Harper Trade, 1995. Written while Grealy was a young adult, this book describes what it was like to be diagnosed with cancer at the age of nine and to lose one-third of her jaw to prevent the recurrence of the disease. She describes the literal pain of the medical illness and the psychological pain of looking different due to the life-saving surgery.

SUGGESTED VIEWINGS

Lorenzo's Oil (1992). George Miller (director), George Miller and Nick Enright (writers). VHS. Based on a true story, this film portrays two parents' desperate fight to save their son from a mysterious illness. The film illustrates the horror of seeing a child succumb to an illness and shows the inner strength in parents that can serve to protect children from the psychological ramifications of a medical illness.

Mask (1985). Peter Bogdanovich (director), Anna Hamilton Phelan (writer). VHS/DVD. Based on a true story, this film follows the life and premature death of an adolescent with severe cranio-facial deformities. The mother's role of advocating for a disabled but talented son is illustrated in all of its complexity.

CHAPTER 17

WAYS TO HELP CHILDREN

CHAPTER SUMMARY

Youth are looking for something; it's up to adults to show them what is worth emulating.

—Jesse Jackson

One of the most compelling reasons to understand abnormal child behavior is to find ways to help children in need. In every level of society and every level of educational pursuit, there are many ways to prevent problems from developing in children and additional ways to help children and families once problems appear. To repeat the African proverb that Hillary Clinton (1996) used for the title of her book: It takes a village to help children grow up to be healthy, strong, well-functioning, and self-fulfilled members of society.

HOW NONPROFESSIONALS AND PARAPROFESSIONALS CAN HELP CHILDREN

Even untrained, but caring, college students and other individuals can find a number of ways to help children. As discussed in Chapter 8, one of the most salient protective factors against the development of problem behavior in children is one or more strong and stable role models. A recent public broadcasting campaign was aimed at helping adults see that helping children can be easily integrated into their own lives. In an ad directed toward parents, the commentator suggested that parents include another child when going on outings or participating in activities with their own children. The idea behind this ad was to help expand the network of caring adults in children's lives. Likewise, as a caring individual you can take a special interest in children in your neighborhood, in your apartment complex, or at your place of worship. You can have a strong positive impact on the lives of infants, toddlers, and children, for example, by babysitting or by volunteering at a day care. Children often thrive on positive attention from competent, caring adults—and you can easily be one of those important adults in a child's life.

There are a number of national programs (e.g., Big Brothers/Big Sisters and Boys and Girls Clubs of America) as well as local programs through police departments, recreation centers, and local schools that provide opportunities to mentor children who might otherwise find it difficult to have stable role models in their lives. Most communities also have other programs that allow volunteers to have a positive impact on the lives of children. For example, most communities have some type of protected living environment (often called a shelter) for children and their parents who have been exposed to domestic violence. Similarly, nearly every community has some type of protected living environment for children who themselves have been abused or neglected by their parents. Often individuals from the community are encouraged to volunteer in these settings (after a rigorous background check) to provide the children with positive influences and experiences. There is also a nationwide organization that allows individuals to advocate for abused and neglected children in the court system. These court-appointed special advocates are referred to as guardians ad litem. Although many states require that a court-appointed guardian or special advocate be an attorney, many other states allow for trained volunteers to become guardians ad litem. As an attorney who has been involved in child advocacy across the nation, Virginia Weisz (1995) describes in detail ways in which children can be helped through volunteer activities and through the legal system. Figure 17.1 shows the process by which allegations of child abuse are processed (Azar, 1992). Even nonprofessionals (e.g., a concerned neighbor or a clerk in a store) can make a formal report of child abuse to the local child protective agency and the report will be processed appropriately.

Many inpatient and residential facilities for distressed children also fill positions with either volunteer or paid workers. Different states have different credentialing and licensing requirements for psychiatric technicians, residential aides, or houseparents. A few phone calls to local facilities should help interested students understand the requirements for such positions in their local area.

Case Study: Community Elders as Co-Parents and Mentors

In her eloquent memoir, Dr. Marion Wright Edelman (1999), president of the Children's Defense Fund, writes about the co-parents and elders that were central to the community in which she grew up. In describing two particularly wonderful role models, she stated, "They had no children of their own but mothered many children as if we belonged to them" (p. 10).

From taking special interest in the neighborhood children, to always having food to give to those who were hungry, to providing care and supervision when the children's parents were unable to watch them, these community elders provided the structure and warmth that are necessary to allow children to thrive. There are many such examples in many communities across the world.

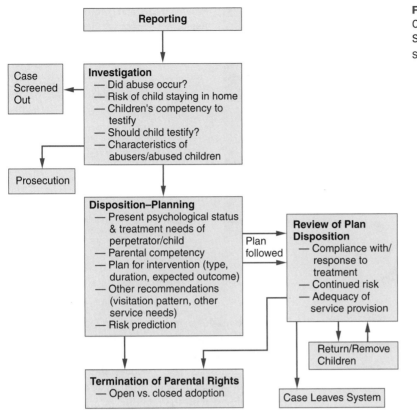

FIGURE 17.1 Movement of Child Abuse Cases through Social Service and Legal Systems
Source: Azar (1992).

As mentioned in Chapter 8, coaches of various sports can have a positive influence on children's well-being. Competent, caring, and supportive coaches can have numerous beneficial effects for both the quality of athletic development and for the psychological well-being of children involved in sports (Smith & Smoll, 1997).

There are also a number of nonprofit social and political organizations that are involved in advocating for children's mental health needs. The New York Society for Prevention of Cruelty to Children was originally an off-shoot of the Society for the Prevention of Cruelty to Animals. As noted in Chapter 1, the first legal case of child abuse was prosecuted in 1874 under the domain of protection of animals because there was no society for the protection of children. Since that time, various national and local organizations have become active in protecting the rights of abused children and in attempting to prevent child abuse internationally. Within the United States, the Children's Defense Fund is a nonprofit organization that serves as a watchdog for the rights and well-being of children. Through Stand for Children and other national and international campaigns, the Children's Defense Fund

tracks and publicizes the plight of children and families. The organization often publishes voting records of politicians regarding child-oriented legislation and publishes state-by-state lists regarding child poverty, educational opportunities, and other relevant issues for children and families.

In addition to helping children and families, volunteers often find that their experience enriches their own lives. Working as a volunteer or paid paraprofessional can help individuals learn more about their profession of interest. A colleague of mine who is now a developmental psychologist studying language development tells the story of how she knew she wanted to work with children when she was an undergraduate student. She wisely tested out this interest by volunteering as a student teacher at a local elementary school. She found that she was fascinated by the children but had no interest in full-time teaching. Her career goals might have been quite different had she not had the volunteer experience. Volunteer work can help students not only identify their professional interests but also become more desirable candidates for relevant jobs or graduate training programs.

Providing care and comfort to children in need can be accomplished with or without advanced training.

Respect depends on reciprocity.

—Proverb of Africa

Transitioning from a Paraprofessional to a Professional

Students, nonprofessionals, and paraprofessionals interested in helping children can move on to any of numerous careers. Although most of these careers require a graduate degree, there are often paid positions in the community for those who have completed a bachelor's degree and adequate relevant experience. These positions are too various to mention, but doing some homework in your community should help you identify some opportunities. In addition, while doing volunteer work (e.g., in a mental health facility or in a shelter for abused children), students often learn about paid positions that are available before and after completing their bachelor's degree.

It is likely that a number of students choose to major in psychology or education because they want to enter professions in which they can dedicate their lives to helping children in need. Specifically, within most of these professions there is the ability to become a direct service provider such as a clinician or therapist, a consultant or supervisor who works with direct service providers, or a researcher.

It is also important to note that there are many different career paths to reach the same goal. For example, if you wish to become a therapist in order to help children through direct services, you could become a psychologist (either at the master's or doctoral level), a social worker (either at the master's or doctoral level), or a psychiatrist (after going to medical school and completing a residency in psychiatry and a fellowship in child psychiatry). Some school psychologists also conduct therapy, especially group therapy within the school setting. Conversely, all of these disciplines, with the addition of criminology, provide opportunities for conducting research that is meaningful for children, adolescents, and families. Box 17.1 lists some resources for those interested in applying to graduate school in psychology and related fields.

HOW HAVING A CAREER IN PSYCHOLOGY CAN HELP CHILDREN

Within the field of psychology, there are many ways to help children. A common mistake that undergraduates make when first identifying their interests is to say that they want to be a "child psychologist." Most students making this statement mean that they want to work clinically with children (e.g., doing therapy and testing). The statement, however, actually would translate to a graduate program in developmental psychology where students learn about research with children but do not learn about therapy or assessment of children. Thus, if you are interested in becoming a psychologist who works therapeutically with children, chances are that you should be exploring clinical psychology and counseling psychology programs.

Many years ago, a doctoral degree (e.g., a Ph.D. or Psy.D.) was required of those who wished to conduct

BOX *17.1*

USEFUL RESOURCES FOR APPLYING TO GRADUATE SCHOOL AND IDENTIFYING APPROPRIATE GRADUATE PROGRAMS

If you are interested in attending graduate school, there are a number of resources that might be helpful in identifying appropriate graduate programs and in elucidating the application process. Most universities have career counseling centers, advising offices, and resource centers where additional information might be available. In addition, professors and current graduate students who serve as teaching assistants can speak to your individual interests and needs for graduate training. It takes some homework on the part of the student, but informed applicants to graduate programs usually receive much better outcomes than uninformed and ill-prepared applicants. The following are some of the nationally available resources that you might find helpful:

* *Getting In: A Step-by-Step Plan for Gaining Admission to Graduate School in Psychology* (American Psychological Association, 1993)
* *Graduate Study in Psychology* (American Psychological Association, 2000a)
* *Preparing for Graduate Study in Psychology: 101 Questions and Answers* (Buskist & Sherburne, 1996)
* *Directory of Graduate Programs in Clinical Child and Pediatric Psychology* (Tarnowski & Simonian, 1997)
* *Insider's Guide to Graduate Programs in Clinical and Counseling Psychology: 2000/2001 Edition* (Mayne, Norcross, & Sayette, 2000)
* *Doctoral Programs in Family Psychology* (American Psychological Association, 1997a)
* *Directory of School Psychology Graduate Programs* (Thomas, 1998)
* *Graduate Study in Educational and Psychological Measurement, Quantitative Psychology and Related Fields* (Collins, 2000)
* *Credentialing Requirements for School Psychologists* (Curtis, Hunley, & Prus, 1998)
* *Graduate Training in Behavior Therapy and Experimental-Clinical Psychology* (Association for the Advancement of Behavior Therapy, 1997)
* *Summary Information on Master of Social Work Programs* (Council on Social Work Education, 1999)
* *Selecting a Doctoral Research Education Program in Communication Sciences and Disorders* (American Speech-Language-Hearing Association, 2000)

* *Applying Psychology* (Quinn, 1995)
* *The Handbook of Psychology* (Appleby, 1997)
* *Career Paths in Psychology: Where Your Degree Can Take You* (Sternberg, 1997)
* *The Psychologist's Guide to an Academic Career* (Rheingold, 1994)
* *Psychology/Careers for the 21st Century* (American Psychological Association, 2000b)
* *Negotiating Graduate School: A Guide for Graduate Students* (Rossman, 1995)
* *Succeeding in Graduate School: The Career Guide for Psychology Students* (Walfish & Hess, 2001)

There are also a number of Web sites that are helpful in learning about career opportunities and graduate education in the field:

Organization	Website
American Psychological Association	www.apa.org
American Psychological Society	www.psychologcalscience.org
Society for a Science of Clinical Psychology (APA, Division 12)	http://pantheon.yale.edu/~tat22
Society for Research in Child Development	www.scrd.org
Society of Clinical Child and Adolescent Psychology (APA, Division 53)	www.clinicalchildpsychology.org
National Association of School Psychologists	www.nasponline.org
Association for Advancement of Behavior Therapy	www.aabt.org
Association for Behavior Analysis	www.wmich.edu/~aba
Council on Social Work Education	www.cswe.org
American Psychiatric Association	www.psych.org
American Art Therapy Association	www.arttherapy.org
Society for Neuroscience	www.sfn.org

SUPPORTING AND ADVOCATING FOR PARENTS

Source: Webster-Stratton & Herbert (1994).

therapy with children, adolescents, and families . Because of the changing health care system, among many other factors, it is now possible to plan a career as a therapist with a master's degree in clinical or counseling psychology (Hays-Thomas, 2000; Levant, Moldawsky, & Stigall, 2000). Although the salaries of master's-level therapists remain lower on average than those of doctoral-level therapists, master's-level therapists have many opportunities for working with children, adolescents, and families. In fact, many health maintenance organizations (HMOs) and other institutions prefer hiring master's-level therapists because they can reimburse for therapy at a lower rate than doctoral-level therapists can. Note, however, that in most states master's-level clinicians cannot be licensed as independent psychologists. Rather, they can be licensed at a lower level of certification (e.g., licensed mental health counselor, marriage and family counselor). Box 17.2 gives more details on the licensure process for different graduate degrees, and Box 17.3 lists and describes the degrees that are discussed in the following sections.

An increasing number of doctoral-level therapists have begun supervising master's-level (and sometimes bachelors-level) therapists without conducting direct therapy themselves. The pros and cons of this trend are beyond the scope of this textbook, but there are a number of other resources for students who are interested in further understanding the ramifications of master's-level therapists and health maintenance organizations (Deal, Shiono, & Behrman, 1998; Hays-Thomas, 2000; Trull & Phares, 2001).

In general, the options for graduate work within psychology include receiving an M.A., Ph.D., or Psy.D. in clinical psychology or receiving an M.A., Ph.D., or

Ed.D. in counseling psychology (Mayne et al., 2000; Norcross, Sayette, Mayne, Karg, & Turkson, 1998). Unfortunately, the degrees and programs offered at different universities differ widely. For example, clinical psychology programs tend to be housed in departments of psychology, whereas counseling psychology programs tend to be housed in departments of education. Interested students should try to use the resources listed in Box 17.1 to identify the location and availability of programs that match their interests. Note also that, historically, clinical psychology has focused on more severe problems than does counseling psychology. Some of these distinctions have been blurred over the years, but counseling psychology programs generally tend to focus a bit more on clients with less severe psychopathology who are seeking services through schools or mental health clinics, whereas clinical psychology programs focus on the wide range of psychopathology that is presented in many different settings (e.g., inpatient facilities, Veteran's Administration hospitals, children's hospitals, outpatient settings, and schools).

Ph.D. or Master's in Clinical Psychology

The doctoral degree in clinical psychology is meant to be a **scientist-practitioner** degree. The training model that encompasses scientist-practitioner training suggests that students must learn to be both scientists (i.e., trained in research techniques) and practitioners (i.e., trained in clinical therapy and assessment techniques). Some doctoral programs focus on the research side, and others focus on the practice side, but most attempt to train students in both research and clinical skills. For accreditation by the American Psychological Association (APA), graduate programs must now define their specific goals (e.g., as primarily research programs, primarily therapy or assessment programs, or as hybrid programs that focus equally on research and practice) and then the programs are evaluated on the success with which these goals are reached. For students interested in doctoral programs in clinical psychology, it is highly advantageous to attend a graduate program that is accredited by the APA. Many internships, which are completed after graduate coursework but before the Ph.D. is conferred, require that students come from an APA-accredited graduate program. There are also other accreditation entities, such as the Academy of Psychological Clinical Science (which is affiliated with the American Psychological Association, with an emphasis on clinical science rather than clinical

<table>
<tr><td>**BOX 17.2**</td></tr>
</table>

A WORD ABOUT LICENSURE AND CERTIFICATION

Because there are no national or international licensure or certification boards, specific information about licensure and certification varies from state to state and country to country. The following information can be used as a general guideline, but interested students should contact their state's licensing board to identify the specific requirements and options within that state. These governing bodies are often located in the same city as the state capitol and are often housed within a department of professional regulation.

License or Certification	Training Requirements and Practice Options
Licensed psychologist	Ph.D. or Psy.D. in clinical or counseling psychology required in nearly all states. Postdoctoral supervised hours required. Can practice independently, and can use the term *psychologist* to describe professional status.
Licensed mental health counselor (or comparable term)	Usually minimum of master's degree required. Degree can be in clinical or counseling psychology, guidance counseling, rehabilitation counseling, or related area. Postmaster's supervised hours required. Can practice usually within a group practice, though some independent practice is allowed.
Marriage and family counselor	Usually minimum of master's degree required, with specialization in children, marriage, and families.
Licensed clinical social worker	Master's degree (or higher) in social work required. Postgraduate supervised hours required. Can usually practice independently, but often work is within group practice or organization.
Licensed school psychologist	Ph.D. or Ed.D. in school psychology or educational psychology required. Postgraduate supervised hours required. Most often, practice is within school system.
Certified educational specialist	Master's degree (or higher) in school psychology or educational psychology required. Postgraduate supervised hours required. Most often, practice is within school system.
Psychiatrist	M.D. from medical school plus four-year residency in psychiatry are required. Specialization as a child psychiatrist requires another one-year fellowship in child psychiatry. Practices can be independent, in group settings, or in hospital settings.

practice) as well as regional and state accreditation entities, but the APA remains the most visible and potent accrediting entity in clinical psychology at this time.

The idea behind scientist-practitioner programs (which are also referred to as **Boulder model programs**, after a conference in Boulder, Colorado) is that research knowledge is needed to treat and assess clients effectively and clinical knowledge is needed to conduct relevant research (Baker & Benjamin, 2000). This textbook is written from a scientist-practitioner model, with emphasis on the importance of both research knowledge and clinical knowledge. For a more thorough discussion of the scientist-practitioner model, as well as other models of training within clinical psychology, see *Introduction to Clinical Psychology: Science and Practice* (Compas & Gotlib, 2002).

Doctoral scientist-practitioner programs usually include courses in theory; psychometrics; psychopathology; assessment; therapy; ethics; core issues within psychology (e.g., biological aspects of behavior, cognitive and affective aspects of behavior, social aspects of behavior, history and systems of psychology, human development, individual differences in behavior); research methods, and statistics. Most programs require the completion of an empirical master's thesis and an empirical dissertation. Most programs also require between one and four years of supervised clinical practicum work in addition to a one-year full-time clinical internship. Within most clinical psychology programs, students can gravitate toward work with children, adolescents, and families along with learning about adult functioning. Some programs (e.g., those at the University of Miami and West Virginia University) have specific programs in clinical child psychology that do not require a great deal of training in adult functioning. Many other programs allow students to focus their clinical work and research on children, adolescents, and families along with learning about adult functioning. Box 17.4 discusses the pros and cons of choosing a program that focuses primarily on children.

Clinical psychologists are trained to help children by using empirically supported treatments.

The Ph.D. in clinical psychology allows students to pursue careers in research; academia; independent practice; practice within an organization (e.g., a community mental health center, health maintenance organization, or hospital); and consultation. Successful applicants for research jobs and academic jobs must have a great deal of research experience and scholarly publication experience (Ilardi, Rodriguez-Hanley, Roberts, & Seigel, 2000). Note that there is a desperate need for researchers who represent ethnic minority backgrounds and who study issues related to ethnic minority psychology (Hall & Maramba, 2001). Practice-oriented careers require many hours of supervised clinical experience in a particular area of expertise (e.g., working clinically with children diagnosed with attention-deficit/hyperactivity disorder). Careers within consultation require supervised experience within the consultant's area of expertise (e.g., consulting on the burn unit of a children's hospital). In general, the Ph.D. in clinical

psychology affords more career options than does the master's in clinical psychology.

Note, however, that admission into a doctoral program in clinical psychology is extremely competitive. Many doctoral programs receive 300 or 400 applications for every 6 or 7 openings. Thus, having a strong grade point average (usually 3.5 or better), strong Graduate Record Exam scores (usually well above 1200 or 1300 when verbal and quantitative scores are combined), stellar letters of recommendation, and a strong record of research (with conference presentations and publications) are highly desirable when applying to these programs. Although students can gain admission with lower credentials, most APA-accredited doctoral programs in clinical psychology are looking for students with this type of profile. Parenthetically, note that Graduate Record Exam (GRE) scores and undergraduate grade point average (GPA) are associated with success in graduate school. Specifically, higher GREs and GPAs were associated with higher GPAs in graduate school, comprehensive examination scores, ratings by faculty, and numbers of publications (Kuncel, Hezlett, & Ones, 2001). The subject test of the GRE (also known as the advanced test) was even more predictive of success in graduate school than were the verbal and quantitative scores on the general GRE (Kuncel et al., 2001).

Master's programs in clinical psychology mirror doctoral programs in their emphasis, but they tend to be two-year rather than five-year programs, and they tend to have less stringent requirements for admission. Master's programs often offer similar types of coursework, but the empirical requirements end with the master's thesis rather than continuing on for the doctoral dissertation. Graduate programs that offer a master's degree only are referred to as **terminal master's programs**. Doctoral programs award the master's degree on the way to the doctoral degree and not as a final degree.

The focus of different master's programs within clinical psychology varies greatly. Some programs are practice oriented, some are research oriented, and some are consistent with a scientist-practitioner model. Students should try to match their interests with the focus of the program. The APA does not accredit master's-level programs, nor does it accredit programs (e.g., developmental, industrial/organizational, or behavioral neuroscience) outside of the realm of clinical, counseling, or school psychology.

If students are interested in the doctoral degree, it is in their best interest to gain admission to a doctoral program from the start, if possible. In general, it is difficult to transfer from a terminal master's program straight into a doctoral program without first going through the admissions

Case Study: Coping with Divorce

Being a therapist can help children immensely. Here are some examples, from the work of Royko (1999), of the many ways in which adults and therapists can help children cope with parental divorce:

- A 12-year-old boy said, "We had to go see a counselor after my parents got their separation but not because of that. It was because my brother and I started fighting really bad, and they thought I had hurt him" (p. 191).

- A 19-year-old woman stated, "I think my brother took the pain inside himself. He'd go off and hang out with his friends a lot, but I know that he didn't talk with them about it. He was dealing with it on his own without anybody else, and I think that's just the way some people have to deal with it. I think he wouldn't have known what to do if somebody had come to him and said, 'Hey, let's sit down and talk about this.' If it were, say, my mom's best friend, I think he would have felt like he was going against my dad, being a traitor. So I think

you have to figure out what type of a person they are and then help them out accordingly" (p. 184).

- A 12-year-old boy wrote, "The therapist I see, I tell him whatever happened, and then at the end he'll scribble something in his notebook, really short, and say, 'Okay, that's it for today.' I like him. It's just the helpfulness that I get from him that feels good" (p. 184).

- A 19-year-old woman reflected, "I guess it was good that I had a lot of adult influences. My mom's best friend's a pastor. I talked to her a lot . . . My fifth grade teacher is still my favorite teacher I ever had, and he was the one I had when I was going through the separation. He was somebody else that I could go and talk to, and I had a really close best friend at the time. I'd hang out with her a lot and try to get out of the house. It helped" (p. 192).

SOURCE: Royko (1999).

---

process for the doctoral program. If students are interested in the doctoral degree but cannot gain admission into a doctoral program, then using the master's degree as a stepping-stone into a doctoral program is a viable option. These students, however, would probably find that only a small portion of their coursework and clinical work from their master's program would transfer to a doctoral program once they gained admission. Many of the references in Box 17.1 detail the pros and cons of gaining admission into a doctoral versus a master's program.

Psy.D. in Clinical Psychology

A number of professional schools of psychology offer a **doctor of psychology (Psy.D.)** degree in clinical psychology. These programs focus almost exclusively on the practice side of psychology (e.g., therapy, assessment, consultation). The first Psy.D. program was developed in 1968 (D. R. Peterson, 1971), and there are Psy.D. programs found in nearly every state in the union. Some Psy.D. programs are housed within academic universities (e.g., Rutgers and Baylor Universities), but the majority are found at self-sustained professional schools that are not affiliated directly with any university (e.g., the California Schools of Professional Psychology, Argosy University, and the Illinois Schools of Professional Psychology). Although some Psy.D. and professional school programs in clinical psychology have obtained accreditation from the APA, the majority have not obtained this accreditation (Norcross et al., 1998; Trull & Phares, 2001).

Coursework in Psy.D. programs tends to focus more on theory and clinical applications than on research methodology and statistics. In addition, a great deal of time is focused on direct clinical experience (e.g., clinical practica in assessment and therapy). Graduation from a professional school and the degree of Psy.D. should enable most students to seek licensure as a psychologist in most states. Some states, however, are moving to the requirement that the graduate training must have taken place in an APA-accredited program, so students must be cognizant of the accreditation of these professional schools and of the licensure requirements in their state.

Ph.D. in Experimental Psychopathology

On the other end of the spectrum, programs in **experimental psychopathology** focus solely on research rather than on clinical training. Although programs in experimental psychopathology are somewhat rare, some universities (e.g., Stanford) have extraordinary training programs in research on issues related to psychopathology. The idea behind programs in experimental psychopathology is that empirical research can be conducted on clinical issues without spending time learning clinical skills such as therapy or assessment techniques. Overall, a program in experimental psychopathology would be excellent for students who wish to conduct research in the field of developmental psychopathology but who do not wish to spend time learning clinical skills. Applying

BOX *17.3*

ACADEMIC DEGREES AT A GLANCE

In order to familiarize students with various academic degrees, this box lists selected degrees that are relevant to helping children. Note that the time frames given here are approximate. Programs nearly always require a certain set of classes, minimum credit hours, or specific activities (e.g., completing an internship, writing a thesis or dissertation) rather than requiring a certain number of years of schooling.

- *Associate of arts (A.A.):* The A.A. degree is earned after two years of college, which are usually completed at a community college.

- *Bachelor of arts (B.A.), bachelor of science (B.S.),* or *bachelor of social work (B.S.W.):* Bachelor's degrees are earned after four years of undergraduate work (either with an A.A. and two additional years, or four years at a college or university). The B.A. is usually awarded for disciplines in liberal arts and the social sciences (e.g., psychology, criminology, education); the B.S. is usually awarded for disciplines in the hard sciences (e.g., biology, chemistry); and the B.S.W. is solely for a bachelor's degree completed in social work. Note that some universities offer both the B.A. and the B.S. within the same discipline, depending on the content of the coursework (e.g., a general psychology major may lead to a B.A., but a psychology major with heavy emphasis in biology and physiology may lead to a B.S.). Schooling after the bachelor's degree is considered to be graduate work. Nearly all master's and doctoral programs require entrants to have a bachelor's degree.

- *Master's of arts (M.A.)* or *master's of science (M.S.):* Master's degrees are usually two-year graduate degrees that are completed after the bachelor's degree. As with the B.A. and B.S., the M.A. is usually awarded in most liberal arts and social science disciplines whereas the M.S. is awarded when the hard sciences are represented in the discipline. A thesis is usually required for both the M.A. and the M.S. degrees.

- *Master of social work (M.S.W.):* The M.S.W. is usually a two-year graduate degree in social work. In addition to course requirements, there are usually a fair amount of clinical practicum requirements.

- *Educational specialist (Ed.S.):* The Ed.S. is usually a two-year graduate program that is comparable to the M.A. in education, but without the thesis requirement.

Many students can work toward both the Ed.S. and the M.A. in education at the same time. Some jobs within the school system require the Ed.S., even if applicants already have their M.A. in education.

- *Doctor of education (Ed.D.):* The Ed.D. degree is a doctoral graduate degree that usually requires four to five years of graduate work in education (either an M.A. in education plus two to three years of additional graduate work or four to five years of graduate training in a doctoral program). A dissertation is usually required.

- *Doctor of philosophy (Ph.D.):* The Ph.D. is a doctoral graduate degree that usually requires five to six years of graduate work. Ph.D. degrees are offered in most social science disciplines (e.g., psychology, criminology, women's studies) and hard science disciplines (e.g., biology and chemistry). The requirements for the Ph.D. in psychology vary depending on the area of specialization, with primarily research requirements in developmental psychology and both research and clinical practicum requirements (including a one-year, full-time clinical internship) in clinical psychology. A dissertation is usually required.

- *Doctor of psychology (Psy.D.):* The Psy.D. is a doctoral graduate degree that usually requires five years of graduate work. Course requirements focus on the practice of psychology, and there are heavy clinical practicum requirements (including a one-year clinical internship). Although a master's and a dissertation are often required, these projects tend to be literature reviews rather than original empirical research.

- *Doctor of social work (D.S.W.):* The D.S.W. is a five-year graduate degree in social work (or an M.S.W. with three additional years of graduate work). Within the field of social work, the M.S.W. is considered the practice-oriented degree, whereas the D.S.W. is primarily for those who want to conduct research and teach in the discipline of social work.

- *Medical doctor (M.D.):* The M.D. is completed after four years of medical school. After medical school, students complete a residency in their area of specialization. Residencies vary in length depending on the area of specialization, with psychiatry residencies lasting four years. Specialization as a child psychiatrist requires an additional one-year fellowship in child psychiatry.

developmental and clinical science to real-world issues can be a very powerful mechanism through which to improve the lives of children (Lerner, Fisher, & Weinberg, 2000; McCall & Groark, 2000).

Ph.D., Ed.D. or Master's in Counseling Psychology

As mentioned previously, programs in counseling psychology tend to focus on less severe types of problems than do clinical psychology programs. There are exceptions to this rule, but counseling psychology programs generally train students to work within school settings, outpatient mental health settings, and university counseling center settings. Because many counseling psychology programs are housed within departments of education, much of the training tends to focus on the educational side of emotional/behavioral problems. Within many counseling psychology programs at the doctoral and master's levels, there is a focus on scientist-practitioner models of training.

Ph.D. or Master's in Developmental Psychology

As noted earlier, when students say that they want to specialize in "child psychology," they are (usually unknowingly) referring to the field of developmental psychology. This scholarly discipline, however, is not well suited for students who wish to work clinically and therapeutically with children, adolescents, and families. Both the Ph.D. and the master's in developmental psychology are academic, research-oriented degrees. Programs in developmental psychology tend to be housed within departments of psychology and tend to focus on research on very specific issues related to development (e.g., language development, social development). Although developmental programs focused on children under the age of 18 in the past, there has been increasing focus on life-span development that addresses developmental processes from conception until death.

The Ph.D. or master's degree in developmental psychology would allow successful students to conduct research in areas related to developmental psychology. Many researchers within the field of developmental psychopathology have degrees in developmental psychology, with an emphasis on developmental psychopathology. Still other researchers within the field of developmental psychopathology have doctoral degrees in clinical psychology or have medical degrees with specialization in child psychiatry. Overall, the field of developmental psychology is an important one for students interested in conducting research with children, adolescents, and families.

HOW HAVING A CAREER IN SOCIAL WORK CAN HELP CHILDREN

Historically, the field of social work has dealt with children through social and administrative institutions (e.g., child protection agencies, adoption agencies). Although the emphasis in training continues to focus on administrative mechanisms of helping, social work is now a diverse field that allows career opportunities in many different settings. Like psychologists, social workers can be found helping children in hospitals, schools, community mental health centers, and private outpatient clinics as well as in governmental agencies such as child protective agencies and adoption agencies. Different graduate programs focus on different aspects of the field (e.g., direct clinical services versus work within a child protective agency), so students should try to match their career interests with the focus of the graduate program.

Bachelor of Social Work

As noted in Box 17.3, there are three degrees possible within social work—the B.S.W., the M.S.W., and the D.S.W. The B.S.W. is completed at the undergraduate level and often affords students the opportunity to work at entry-level positions within governmental agencies (e.g., child protective services). Although the B.S.W. is not required for admission into an M.S.W. program, the B.S.W. gives extensive training in the field of social work and often requires direct practicum experience for the completion of the degree.

Master of Social Work

The M.S.W. is the most prevalent degree within the field of social work. Whether their bachelor's degree is in social work, psychology, education, or another related area, applicants to M.S.W. programs are expected to have an extensive amount of practicum or work experience in the field. The M.S.W. allows students to work toward licensure after graduation. Most states require additional supervised hours in order to be licensed as a clinical social worker. Licensed clinical social workers can conduct therapy, complete social history and functional assessments, work as child advocates, provide counseling services in schools, and serve as consultants in hospitals. The M.S.W. degree does not usually require any research training, so it is considered more of a practice degree than a research degree.

Doctor of Social Work

The D.S.W. is considered a research degree. The D.S.W. degree is most often sought by individuals who wish to become a professor and conduct research.

Overall, the lines between social work and psychology have blurred over the years. In general, social workers are trained to consider child and adolescent functioning within a broader context (e.g., the community, the school, the family) than are psychologists. These distinctions, however, have blurred as more and more social workers conduct individual therapy and more and more psychologists work within different contexts related to children, adolescents, and families.

HOW HAVING A CAREER IN EDUCATION CAN HELP CHILDREN

There are a variety of ways to help children through the educational system. From general education teachers, to special education teachers, to guidance counselors, to school psychologists, there are a number of different professionals within the school system who have an impact on children daily.

Teachers

Teachers in regular education classrooms have a phenomenal impact on children. They are not expected to have training in special education, but they are often called on to deal with behavioral difficulties. Teachers may be the first individuals to identify children who might be in need of help, and they can play an important role in helping children gain access to appropriate specialists (e.g., school psychologists, speech therapists). Teachers can help intervene with one child or hundreds of children, depending on their interests and activities (Gruwell, 1999). Although requirements vary by state or country, most teachers can be certified after completion of a bachelor's degree with approximately one year of additional certification courses (if the bachelor's degree was not in education) and a series of practicum experiences as a student teacher.

Special Education Teachers

Special education teachers are trained not only in educational teaching methods but also in helping children with special needs. Special education teachers often specialize in one type of special education service (e.g., children with severe physical disabilities, children with emotional difficulties, or children with limited intellectual functioning). Depending on their specialty, special education teachers could work in a resource room and provide pull-out services for children for a limited amount of time per week or they could have their own classroom to which a group of children is assigned full-time. Although requirements vary by state or country (as they do for other teachers) special education teachers are expected to have completed their bachelor's degree, specialized credentialing coursework in special education, and student teaching experiences in special education classes. Although it is not usually required, some special education teachers also have obtained a master's degree in special education.

Case Study: In Praise of Teachers

Esther Wright (1999) collected stories from teachers about why they chose the profession:

- A special education teacher wrote, "These extraordinary children arrived filled with invisible gifts in hand, just for me. They challenged me to emerge from my cocoon of complacency and ignorance" (p. 150).

- A current teacher wrote about her own drama teacher from high school, "Mr. Emmelhainz made the finest contribution a teacher can make; he helped his students help themselves. He believed in them, in their ability and in their worthiness of respect" (p. 154).

- A teacher on the verge of retiring after a long and successful career stated, "Each day I witness the competence of my fellow teachers who are dedicated and excellent role models. They are like candles that light others while consuming themselves" (p. 91).

- Speaking of her student, a sixth-grade teacher noted, "Formally, I was Andrew's mentor. Informally, he was mine" (p. 7).

Special education teachers have advanced training in effective teaching techniques for children with special needs.

Guidance Counselors

Guidance counselors can also have a meaningful impact on many children. They often provide a wealth of services for children and adolescents, ranging from scheduling academic classes, to teaching anger management classes, to helping with college applications, to talking with troubled children and their parents. The types of activities in which guidance counselors engage depend on the needs of the school and the students in that school system. Guidance counselors most often have a master's in counseling education.

School Psychologists and Educational Specialists

School psychologists and educational specialists can help children who, for the most part, are having emotional/behavioral difficulties. Many school psychologists also do a great deal of testing and evaluation (e.g., to determine if a child has a learning disorder). They can therefore serve in roles to help evaluate or treat children. Although evaluations for specific learning disorders or emotional/behavioral problems are almost always done in a one-on-one situation with children, many school psychologists and educational specialists conduct group

---

Case Study: The Girl Who Wouldn't Talk

Jadie was nearly eight years old when she entered the classroom for severely emotionally disturbed children that was run by Torey Hayden (1991). She had the diagnosis of what is now known as selective mutism. Jadie spoke at home but had never uttered a word or whisper at school. Upon meeting Jadie, her teacher noticed that she walked in a manner that suggested she was carrying a very heavy load of books (i.e., she remained hunched over constantly, whether walking or sitting).

After a somewhat brief time in this classroom, Jadie began speaking with her teacher. Although previous professionals had tried hard to get Jadie to speak, Hayden worked with her in a nonconfrontational manner and allowed her to begin communicating on her own terms. After Jadie was speaking for a while, Hayden asked her to try to stand up straight. Jadie had already been evaluated by the school nurse and by her pediatrician, who both ascertained that she did not have a medical problem that

was causing her to bend over constantly. When Hayden was trying gently to coax Jadie to stand up straight, Jadie replied that she had to keep bent over "To keep my insides from falling out" (p. 34).

Long and intensive work by this caring teacher revealed that Jadie had experienced severe abuse. Hayden was able to uncover Jadie's troubling experiences and to help her deal with these issues. Eventually, Jadie was placed into a foster care setting and grew up to be a competent, yet still somewhat withdrawn, young woman. She was able to attend high school without any additional special educational help and she went on to attend college and study English literature. This case illustrates the impact of a caring and competent special education teacher who had the patience and determination that were necessary to reach into the world of a troubled young girl.

SOURCE: Hayden (1991).

interventions (e.g., prevention programs, group therapy, behavioral management classes) in order to help children change their behavior. For example, school psychologists are increasingly being asked to provide school-based programs to prevent youth violence (Evans & Rey, 2001). School psychologists and educational specialists also can serve as consultants to teachers who need help with behavioral issues in their classrooms. In general, educational specialists would have earned either an Ed.S. or master's degree in school psychology. School psychologists, in contrast, often have earned a Ph.D. or an Ed.D. in school psychology or educational psychology. There is a great deal of overlap in the training of school psychologists and clinical child psychologists, but school psychologists usually receive more intensive training in educational and school-system issues than do clinical child psychologists (Mattison, 2000; Tryon, 2000).

Other Professionals

In addition to the training that occurs in departments of education, it should be noted that many other professionals can help children within the school system. Mental health counselors (with a master's in clinical or counseling psychology), clinical psychologists (with a Ph.D. or Psy.D. in clinical psychology), and social workers (with an M.S.W.) often work within the school system in order to help children through counseling or, in the case of clinical psychologists, through therapy and assessments. An increasing amount of government funding for mental health services is expected to be targeted for school systems across the United States (Oakland & Cunningham, 1999). There may be even greater opportunities for professionals to help children through work within the school system in the future.

HOW HAVING A CAREER IN MEDICINE CAN HELP CHILDREN

The field of medicine includes many avenues through which to help children with psychological problems. In addition to trained medical professionals, a number of other professionals work in medical settings to help children who are medically and emotionally challenged.

Psychiatric Nurses

Within the nursing profession, there is a specialization of psychiatric nursing through which training is gained in mental health issues. Psychiatric nurses often work within psychiatric hospitals or inpatient units where children and adolescents receive intensive treatment for psychological problems. Psychiatric nurses can deal with the medical side of mental health (e.g., administering medications that have been prescribed) as well as the psychological side of mental health (e.g., conducting a mental health history assessment, providing therapeutic interventions).

BOX 17.4

SPECIFICITY VERSUS BREADTH IN TRAINING

One choice that students must make when considering options in graduate training is the extent to which they wish to specialize in their early graduate training. Students who know they wish to work only with children might seek graduate training that specializes in children (e.g., a clinical child psychology Ph.D. program rather than a more general clinical psychology Ph.D. program or graduate training in early education, special education, or school psychology rather than a more general education program). Students who want broader training might seek a more general program that allows some specialization with children (e.g., a clinical psychology M.A., Ph.D., or Psy.D. program that teaches skills related to both children and adults). Within the field of psychiatry, general medical skills are taught in medical school before students can specialize in psychiatry while on residency (which usually focuses on all age groups), and then further specialization is required in a child fellowship. Thus, students interested in psychiatry are mandated to gain general medical and psychiatric skills before specializing in child psychiatry.

When considering the specificity versus breadth issue, there are pros and cons to both types of programs. Ultimately, students must consider their own interests before choosing a program. It should be noted, however, that working with children often means working with adults (i.e., parents). In order to feel completely competent in working with children and adolescents, it behooves students to gain some type of training and research knowledge in work with adults and families.

Psychiatrists

Probably the best-known medical professionals who help children with emotional/behavioral difficulties are child psychiatrists. As mentioned earlier, child psychiatrists have completed a bachelor's degree (usually in biology or another pre-med major); medical school (which allows rotations through all of the various specialties including psychiatry); a four-year psychiatric residency; and, most often, another one-year child fellowship. Given their training, psychiatrists can prescribe medications and can conduct therapy. Although it is relatively rare, some psychiatrists also are involved actively in research with children, adolescents, and families. Note that one of the biggest differences between clinical psychologists and psychiatrists surrounds the use of medications, the completion of research, and the ability to conduct psychological testing. Psychiatrists (and not clinical psychologists) can prescribe medication for psychological difficulties. As discussed in Box 17.5, however, this difference is under review.

Clinical psychologists from Ph.D. programs (and not psychiatrists or most clinical psychologists from Psy.D. programs) are trained in research methods and can conduct empirical research with children, adolescents, and families. Clinical psychologists (both from Ph.D. and Psy.D. programs) are usually trained in conducting psychological assessments and evaluations. Although psychiatrists are trained in the use of some assessment techniques (e.g., interviews, mental status exams), they are not usually trained in how to administer or interpret standardized psychological tests such as intelligence testing, achievement testing, or emotional/behavioral measures. Both clinical psychologists and psychiatrists are trained in therapy and various interventions.

Developmental Pediatricians

Another, somewhat lesser known specialization within the medical field is developmental pediatrics. Developmental pediatricians usually specialize in pediatrics for

---

BOX 17.5

PRESCRIPTION PRIVILEGES FOR CLINICAL PSYCHOLOGISTS?

Historically, one of the primary differences between clinical psychologists and psychiatrists was the prescription privilege—the ability to prescribe medication. Psychiatrists have the medical training that allows them to prescribe medication, whereas clinical psychologists are not allowed to prescribe medication even if they have completed coursework in psychopharmacology (the study of drugs and behavior). Recently, however, some clinical psychologists have argued that prescription privileges should be available to psychologists who complete enough training in psychopharmacology (reviewed in Gutierrez & Silk, 1998). In fact, the American Psychological Association's Council of Representatives is in favor of prescription privileges for practicing psychologists, and a number of states have introduced legislation that would allow psychologists to prescribe medication after sufficient training (Hanson et al., 1999). One study, known as the Psychopharmacology Demonstration Project, showed that clinical psychologists with appropriate training can prescribe medications in an effective and ethical manner (Newman, Phelps, Sammons, Dunivin, & Cullen, 2000). At the time of this writing, the state of New Mexico now allows clinical psychologists with appropriate training to prescribe medication.

There are strongly held beliefs on both sides of this issue (Klusman, 2001; Plante, Boccaccini, & Andersen, 1998; Sammons, Gorny, Zinner, & Allen, 2000). On the one hand,

clinical psychologists generally have a thorough understanding of behavior, usually have a good understanding of their clients' problems, and could help clients with both psychotherapy and medication when needed (Gutierrez & Silk, 1998). In addition, allowing clinical psychologists to prescribe medications would enable more clients to have access to services (Sammons et al., 2000). These points help support the option of prescription privileges for clinical psychologists. On the other hand, there are a number of questions that have been raised about prescription privileges for clinical psychologists. Clinical psychologists who have no formal medical training beyond some coursework in psychopharmacology may put clients in danger due to their lack of thorough medical knowledge (Gutierrez & Silk, 1998). In addition, clinical psychologists would be furthering their involvement in the medical model rather than exploring environmental and behavioral interventions that could help alleviate suffering (Albee, 1998). As the saying goes, give people a hammer and all they see are nails. There is concern that prescription privileges will hamper clinical psychologists' therapeutic interventions and dissuade them from exploring preventive strategies for psychological problems.

Overall, there is no easy answer to this issue. Those in the psychological and medical communities have strongly held beliefs on both sides (Barnett & Neel, 2000; Plante et al., 1998; Sammons et al., 2000). Where do you stand?

their three-year residency (after medical school), then complete a fellowship in developmental pediatrics. Like child psychiatrists, developmental pediatricians can prescribe medications and can conduct therapy. Their special knowledge of pediatrics and developmental processes allows them to focus on the normative side of development as well as on the abnormal side.

Other Professionals

A number of other professionals can work within medical settings. The psychological management of health and disease is a growing area for clinical psychologists (Janicke & Finney, 2001; Levant et al., 2001). The area of health promotion is very active for pediatric psychologists who focus on prevention programs to help enhance healthy outcomes for children (Durlak, 2000). Clinical psychologists (especially pediatric psychologists) and social workers often work within pediatric settings (e.g., an oncology unit for children) or children's hospitals in order to help children who are experiencing medical difficulties. Any type of inpatient setting for children must somehow address the educational needs of the children on the unit, so special educators and school psychologists often work within inpatient settings to help disturbed children with their educational needs. Overall, there are a number of diverse disciplines through which children can be helped in medical settings. Hospitals and other medical settings often use multidisciplinary teams (consisting of professionals from multiple and diverse disciplines) in order to help children, adolescents, and families. Many professionals deal with families, as discussed in Box 17.6.

Anybody who is in a position to discipline others should first learn to accept discipline himself [or herself].

—Malcolm X

HOW HAVING A CAREER IN THE JUDICIAL JUSTICE SYSTEM CAN HELP CHILDREN

There are a number of ways in which to help children through a career in the judicial justice system. Some professionals who start out in law enforcement find that they can serve children in many ways.

School Resource Officers

Resource officers in elementary, middle, and high schools often play a vital role in the well-being of children and adolescents. Although their training is usually within law enforcement (many have trained to be a police officer or a sheriff), resource officers tend to also deal with emotional/behavioral issues that arise for troubled children and adolescents. Many resource officers serve in a preventive role, getting to know students well enough to know when they are at risk for showing problematic behavior. In addition, resource officers can serve as role models for children and adolescents who might not have contact with stable adults other than their teachers. Individuals trained in law enforcement also often have the opportunity to work with adjudicated youth (e.g., youngsters who are serving time in a juvenile detention center, who are living at a therapeutic "boot camp," or who are in a diversionary program to help prevent future criminal activities). These opportunities tend to arise for law enforcement officers who receive additional training regarding children and adolescents and those who show a special proclivity toward helping children, adolescents, and families.

Criminologists

The field of criminology offers interested students excellent training and opportunities. Although graduate work in criminology does not allow professionals to conduct therapy or assessments, criminologists can conduct research on criminal behavior or other legal issues related to children and adolescents. **Criminologists** usually earn a master's or doctoral degree in criminology. Criminologists might study patterns of violence within schools or within the community and might serve as consultants to prevention programs to decrease this violence. Criminologists can also get involved in studying issues related to juvenile crime and the etiologies of such criminal behavior. The juvenile justice system often employs criminologists in many different capacities.

Forensic Psychologists

Within the field of psychology, there is specialized training in forensic psychology that is most consistent with work done in the criminal justice system. **Forensic psychologists**, who usually earn a Ph.D. in clinical psychology with a specialization in forensic psychology, can engage in a wide variety of activities related to children's mental health. They can conduct assessments such as custody evaluations or evaluations to ascertain competency to stand trial. They can conduct therapy with troubled youngsters either individually, in groups, or with their families. Forensic psychologists often serve as expert witnesses in court cases that have both psychological and legal ramifications. They also can get involved in consulting on legal cases, such as consulting with attorneys on mental health issues regarding children or with providing information about a child's ability to understand the charges against him or her. Overall, a doctoral degree in clinical psychology with a specialization in forensic psychology can open the door to many opportunities in helping children. There are also a few select graduate programs (e.g., at the University of Virginia and the University of Nebraska) that offer joint programs in clinical psychology and the law. Graduates of these programs have training both as clinical psychologists and as attorneys, so they have extraordinary professional credentials.

Attorneys and Judges

Attorneys and judges are also in a position to help children through the judicial system. Attorneys are needed to represent children in custody disputes, child protective litigation, juvenile criminal charges, and other legal issues. Organized programs, such as guardian ad litem programs and child protective services, usually have a staff of attor-

neys (paid and volunteer) who try to ensure that the best interests of the child are represented in legal proceedings. Likewise, judges in family court, dependency court, and juvenile criminal court also make the decisions that have direct ramifications for children. Judges who understand the needs of children and families (and who understand that sometimes the needs of children are different from those of their parents) are likely to help children immensely through the legal decisions they make.

It is easier to build strong children than to repair broken men [and women].

—Frederick Douglass

HOW HAVING A CAREER IN PREVENTION CAN HELP CHILDREN

Any book on developmental psychopathology would be incomplete without a discussion of helping children through preventive efforts. There is no one field or discipline that

---

BOX 17.6

WORKING WITH FAMILIES

As noted throughout this chapter, there are many ways to achieve the same goal. Working with families is a perfect example. Many professionals, such as clinical psychologists, social workers, psychiatrists, pediatricians, and school psychologists, and even many nonprofessionals can work to help families function better. Table 17.1 delineates strategies to help deal with family systems issues. These strategies can be used by any professional who has training and competence in this area. Overall, professionals' specific discipline is often not as meaningful as their area of expertise.

TABLE 17.1 Parent Education Strategies for Different Family Dynamics

Family System Issues	Parent Education Approaches
Family communication	Active listening
Dysfunctional communication patterns	Confrontation and problem-solving skills
	Examination of irrational beliefs
Emotional distance between family members	Analysis of children's mistaken goals
Enmeshed families (too little distance) messages	Use of logical consequences
Disengaged families (too much distance)	Confrontation skills
	Communication skills
	Family meetings
Family role structuring	Assertive discipline
Inverted hierarchy (lack of parental authority)	Behavior modification
Split parental team	Use of logical consequences
	Parental communication and negotiation

SOURCE: Gunn & Fisher (1999).

trains preventionists. Historically, programs with the word *community* in them (e.g., community psychology or community psychiatry) were more involved in prevention efforts than other programs (Rappaport & Seidman, 2000). More recently, however, prevention has been integrated into a diverse array of fields and training activities. Within clinical psychology, graduate students can even focus on preventive interventions during their clinical internship (Humphreys, 2000). Most training in prevention also integrates training on multicultural issues (Hall & Barongan, 2002).

Professionals who are dedicated to the prevention of developmental psychopathology can be trained in a variety of other disciplines, including behavioral medicine, social work, education, medicine, criminology, and law. Other disciplines—such as public health, communication, and sociology—can also become involved in prevention efforts by studying issues related to prevention and by consulting on prevention programs. Applying research findings from prevention programs can be one way of improving the lives of children through communitywide efforts that focus on public policy and social justice (R. M. Lerner et al., 2000; McCall & Groark, 2000). Overall, there are many avenues to the goal of helping children through prevention efforts.

SUMMARY AND KEY CONCEPTS

How Nonprofessionals and Paraprofessionals Can Help Children

Volunteering in local organizations, serving as a mentor for a child, and coaching a sports team are just a few of the ways in which nonprofessionals can become an important part of children's lives. Serving as a role model can help add to the protective features found in a child's otherwise troubled life.

How Having a Career in Psychology Can Help Children

Within the field of psychology, the primary specialization through which graduate students learn therapy, assessment, and research skills is clinical psychology. Programs that focus on both clinical skills (e.g., therapy and assessment skills) and research skills (e.g., developing, conducting, and disseminating empirical research) are called **scientist-practitioner** programs. Also known as **Boulder model programs** (after a conference held in Boulder, Colorado), these programs have the philosophy that good clinical practice is informed by research knowledge and good research practice is informed by clinical practice. If students wish to obtain a master's degree without proceeding to the doctoral degree, then they should seek a **terminal master's program**. In contrast to scientist-practitioner programs, **doctor of psychology (Psy.D.)** programs focus solely on clinical practice without much or any focus on the development of research skills. On the other end of the spectrum, programs in **experimental psychopathology** focus on the development of empirical research skills with little to no training in clinical skills. Other training programs within the field of psychology include counseling psychology (which historically has focused on less severe mental health problems than clinical psychology) and developmental psychology (which focuses on the empirical study of children and normative developmental processes without any training in clinical skills).

How Having a Career in Social Work Can Help Children

Within the field of social work, students can seek the bachelor's degree (B.S.W.), the master's degree (M.S.W.), or the doctoral degree (D.S.W.). Social workers often work within governmental agencies (e.g., child protective agencies), but they can also work in their own independent practices, or in schools, hospitals, or mental health clinics.

How Having a Career in Education Can Help Children

The field of education is replete with opportunities to help children. Teachers in general education classrooms, special education teachers, guidance counselors, school psychologists, and educational specialists all have training within the field of education and can have a significant impact on the lives of many children.

How Having a Career in Medicine Can Help Children

The medical field also affords many opportunities through which to help children. Psychiatric nurses, psychiatrists, and developmental pediatricians all receive specialized training to help individuals with mental health and psychiatric problems.

How Having a Career in the Judicial Justice System Can Help Children

Although many individuals may think of the judicial justice system as a system that punishes children and adolescents for criminal transgressions, there are actually a number of career opportunities that allow professionals in the judicial system to help children when they need it most. School resource officers, **criminologists**, **forensic psychologists**, attorneys, and judges can have a significant impact on children's lives when children are involved in criminal, family, or dependency court proceedings.

How Having a Career in Prevention Can Help Children

Although there is not one specific discipline that trains professionals to work on prevention projects regarding children, there are a number of fields that can lead to work in prevention. Many disciplines, including psychology, social work, education, medicine, criminology, law, public health, communication, and sociology can lead to careers in prevention programs and the empirical study of prevention of psychopathology.

KEY TERMS

scientist-practitioner	terminal master's	doctor of	experimental	forensic
Boulder model	program	psychology	psychopathology	psychologists
programs		(Psy.D.)	criminologists	

SUGGESTED READINGS

Wright, Esther. *Why I Teach*. Rocklin, CA: Prima Publishing, 1999. In this collection of vignettes from teachers, a number of inspirational stories arise that show how teachers can make a difference in children's lives.

Hayden, Torey, L. *Ghost Girl*. New York: Avon Books, 1991. This powerful story of a troubled girl with a horrific past illustrates the impact that a caring and extraordinary teacher can have.

SUGGESTED VIEWINGS

Simon Birch (1998). Mark Steven Johnson (director and screenwriter), based on novel by John Irving. VHS/DVD. Although this film focuses on family issues and loss, it also illustrates the protective role that a caring person (in this case, the mother of a friend) can play in a child's life.

To Sir, With Love (1966). James Clavel (director and screenwriter), based on novel by E. R. Braithwaite. VHS/DVD. In this classic film, a teacher in the inner city becomes a role model and mentor to a number of troubled adolescents.

REFERENCES

Aarons, G. A., Brown, S. A., Hough, R. L., Garland, A. F., & Wood, P. A. (2001). Prevalence of adolescent substance use disorders across five sectors of care. *Journal of the American Academy of Child and Adolescent Psychiatry, 40*, 419–426.

Achenbach, T. M. (1974). *Developmental psychopathology.* New York: Wiley.

Achenbach, T. M. (1982). *Developmental psychopathology* (2nd ed.). New York: Wiley.

Achenbach, T. M. (1990/1991). "Comorbidity" in child and adolescent psychiatry: Categorical and quantitative perspectives. *Journal of Child and Adolescent Psychopharmacology, 1*, 271–278.

Achenbach, T. M. (1991a). *Integrative guide for the 1991 CBCL/4–18, YSR, and TRF Profiles.* Burlington, VT: University of Vermont Department of Psychiatry.

Achenbach, T. M. (1991b). *Manual for the Child Behavior Checklist/4–18 and 1991 Profile.* Burlington, VT: University of Vermont Department of Psychiatry.

Achenbach, T. M. (1991c). *Manual for the Teacher's Report Form and 1991 Profile.* Burlington, VT: University of Vermont Department of Psychiatry.

Achenbach, T. M. (1992). *Manual for the Child Behavior Checklist/2–3 and 1992 Profile.* Burlington, VT: University of Vermont Department of Psychiatry.

Achenbach, T. M. (1997). *Manual for the Young Adult Behavior Checklist and Young Adult Self-Report.* Burlington, VT: University of Vermont Department of Psychiatry.

Achenbach, T. M. (1998). Diagnosis, assessment, taxonomy, and case formulations. In T. H. Ollendick & M. Hersen (Eds.), *Handbook of child psychopathology* (3rd ed., pp. 63–87). New York: Plenum.

Achenbach, T. M., & Dumenci, L. (2001). Advances in empirically based assessment: Revised cross-informant syndromes and new DSM-oriented scales for the CBCL, YSR, and TRF: Comment on Lengua, Sadowksi, Friedrich, and Fisher (2001). *Journal of Consulting and Clinical Psychology, 69*, 699–702.

Achenbach, T. M., & Edelbrock, C. (1983). *Manual for the Child Behavior Checklist and Revised Child Behavior Profile.* Burlington, VT: University of Vermont Department of Psychiatry.

Achenbach, T. M., Howell, C. T., McConaughy, S. H., & Stanger, C. (1995a). Six-year predictors of problems in a national sample of children and youth: I. Cross-informant syndromes. *Journal of the American Academy of Child and Adolescent Psychiatry, 34*, 336–347.

Achenbach, T. M., Howell, C. T., McConaughy, S. H., & Stanger, C. (1995b). Six-year predictors of problems in a national sample of children and youth: II. Signs of disturbance. *Journal of the American Academy of Child and Adolescent Psychiatry, 34*, 488–498.

Achenbach, T. M., Howell, C. T., McConaughy, S. H., & Stanger, C. (1995c). Six-year predictors of problems in a national sample of children and youth: III. Transitions to young adult syndromes. *Journal of the American Academy of Child and Adolescent Psychiatry, 34*, 658–669.

Achenbach, T. M., Howell, C. T., Quay, H. C., & Conners, C. K. (1991). National survey of problems and competencies among four- to six-teen-year-olds. *Monographs of the Society for Research in Child Development, 56* (3, Serial No. 225).

Achenbach, T. M., & McConaughy, S. H. (1997). *Empirically based assessment of child and adolescent psychopathology: Practical applications* (2nd ed.). Thousand Oaks, CA: Sage.

Achenbach, T. M., McConaughy, S. H., & Howell, C. T. (1987). Child/adolescent behavioral and emotional problems: Implications of cross-informant correlations for situational specificity. *Psychological Bulletin, 101*, 213–232.

Achenbach, T. M., & Rescorla, L. A. (2000). *Manual for the Achenbach System of Empirically Based Assessment (ASEBA) Preschool Forms and Profiles.* Burlington, VT: University of Vermont, Research Center for Children, Youth, and Families.

Achenbach, T. M., & Rescorla, L. A. (2001). *Manual for the Achenbach System of Empirically Based Assessment (ASEBA) School-Age Forms and Profiles.* Burlington, VT: University of Vermont, Research Center for Children, Youth, and Families.

Ackerman, B. P., Kogos, J., Youngstrom, E., Schoff, K., & Izard, C. (1999). Family instability and the problem behaviors of children from economically disadvantaged families. *Developmental Psychology, 35*, 258–268.

Ackerman, G. L. (1993). A congressional view of youth suicide. *American Psychologist, 48*, 183–184.

Ackerman, N. W. (1958). *The psychodynamics of family life.* New York: Basic Books.

Adelman, H. S. (1992). LD: The next 25 years. *Journal of Learning Disabilities, 25*, 17–22.

Adelman, H. S. (1995). Clinical psychology: Beyond psychopathology and clinical interventions. *Clinical Psychology: Science and Practice, 2*, 28–44.

Adelman, H. S., & Taylor, L. (1993). *Learning problems and learning disabilities: Moving forward.* Pacific Grove, CA: Brooks/Cole.

Adelman, H. S., & Taylor, L. (1997). Addressing barriers to learning: Beyond school-linked services and full-service schools. *American Journal of Orthopsychiatry, 67*, 408–421.

Adelman, H. S., Taylor, L., & Schnieder, M. V. (1999). A school-wide component to address barriers to learning. *Reading and Writing Quarterly: Overcoming Learning Difficulties, 15*, 277–302.

Ainbinder, J. G., Blanchard, L. W., Singer, G. H. S., Sullivan, M. E., Powers, L. K., Marquis, J. G., Santelli, B., & the Consortium to Evaluate Parent to Parent. (1998). A qualitative study of parent to parent support for parents of children with special needs. *Journal of Pediatric Psychology, 23*, 99–109.

Ainsworth, M. D. S., Blehar, M. C., Waters, E., & Wall, S. (1978). *Patterns of attachment: A psychological study of the strange situation.* Hillsdale, NJ: Erlbaum.

Albano, A. M., Chorpita, B. F., & Barlow, D. H. (1996). Childhood anxiety disorders. In E. J. Mash, & B. A. Barkley (Eds.), *Child psychopathology* (pp. 196–241). New York: Guilford.

Albee, G. W. (1982). Preventing psychopathology and promoting human potential. *American Psychologist, 37*, 1043–1050.

Albee, G. W. (1998). Fifty years of clinical psychology: Selling our soul to the devil. *Applied and Preventive Psychology, 7*, 189–194.

Albee, G. W., Bond, L. A., & Monsey, T. V. C. (Eds.). (1992). *Improving children's lives: Global perspectives on prevention*. Newbury Park, CA: Sage.

Albee, G. W. & Gullotta, T. P. (Eds.). (1996). *Primary prevention works*. Thousand Oaks, CA: Sage.

Alber, S. R. (1999). "I don't like to write but I love to get published": Using a classroom newspaper to motivate reluctant writers. *Reading and Writing Quarterly: Overcoming Learning Difficulties, 15*, 355–360.

Albrecht, S. A., Cornelius, M. D., Braxter, B., Reynolds, M. D., Stone, C., & Cassidy, B. (1999). An assessment of nicotine dependence among pregnant adolescents. *Journal of Substance Abuse Treatment, 16*, 337–344.

Albrecht, S. L., Amey, C., & Miller, M. K. (1996). Patterns of substance abuse among rural black adolescents. *Journal of Drug Issues, 26*, 751–781.

Allan, W. D., Kashani, J. H., Dahlmeier, J., Taghizadeh, P., & Reid, J. C. (1997). Psychometric properties and clinical utility of the scale for suicide ideation with inpatient children. *Journal of Abnormal Child Psychology, 25*, 465–473.

Allison, K. W., Crawford, I., Leone, P. E., Trickett, E., Perez-Febles, A., Burton, L. M., & LeBlanc, R. (1999). Adolescent substance use: Preliminary examinations of school and neighborhood context. *American Journal of Community Psychology, 27*, 111–141.

Allison, K. W., Leone, P. E., & Spero, E. R. (1990). Drug and alcohol use among adolescents: Social context and competence. In P. E. Leone (Ed.), *Understanding troubled and troubling youth* (pp. 173–193). Newbury Park, CA: Sage.

Altepeter, T. S., & Korger, J. N. (1999). Disruptive behavior: Oppositional defiant disorder and conduct disorder. In S. D. Netherton, D. Holmes, & C. E. Walker (Eds.), *Child and adolescent psychological disorders: A comprehensive textbook* (pp. 118–138). New York: Oxford University Press.

Alva, S. A. (1995). Academic invulnerability among Mexican American students: The importance of protective resources and appraisals. In A. M. Padilla (Ed.), *Hispanic psychology: Critical issues in theory and research* (pp. 288–302). Thousand Oaks, CA: Sage.

Amato, P. R. (2001). Children of divorce in the 1990s: An update of the Amato and Keith (1991) meta-analysis. *Journal of Family Psychology, 15*, 355–370.

Amaya-Jackson, L., & March, J. S. (1995). Posttraumatic stress disorder. In J. S. March (Ed.), *Anxiety disorders in children and adolescents* (pp. 276–300). New York: Guilford.

Ambrosini, P., & Dixon, J. F. (1996). *Schedule for Affective Disorders & Schizophrenia for School-Age Children (K-SADS-IVR)*. Philadelphia: Allegheny University of the Health Sciences.

American Academy of Pediatrics (1998). *Caring for your baby and young child: Birth to age 5*. New York: Bantam Books.

American Academy of Pediatrics (2000). Diagnosis and evaluation of the child with Attention-Deficit/Hyperactivity Disorder. *Pediatrics, 105*, 1158–1170.

American Association on Mental Retardation (1992). *Mental retardation: Definition, classification, and systems of support*. Washington, D.C.: Author.

American Psychiatric Association (1952). *Diagnostic and statistical manual of mental disorders*. Washington, D.C.: Author.

American Psychiatric Association (1968). *Diagnostic and statistical manual of mental disorders* (2nd ed.). Washington, D.C.: Author.

American Psychiatric Association (1980). *Diagnostic and statistical manual of mental disorders* (3rd ed.). Washington, D.C.: Author.

American Psychiatric Association (1987). *Diagnostic and statistical manual of mental disorders* (3rd ed. rev.). Washington, D.C.: Author.

American Psychiatric Association (1994). *Diagnostic and statistical manual of mental disorders* (4th ed.). Washington, D.C.: Author.

American Psychiatric Association (1998). *DSM-IV Sourcebook* (Vol 4). Washington, D.C.: Author.

American Psychiatric Association (2000). *Diagnostic and statistical manual of mental disorders* (4th ed, text revision). Washington, D.C.: Author.

American Psychological Association (1987). *Casebook on ethical principles of psychologists*. Washington, DC: Author.

American Psychological Association (1992). Ethical principles of psychologists and code of conduct. *American Psychologist, 47*, 1597–1611.

American Psychological Association (1993). *Getting in: A step-by-step plan for gaining admission to graduate school in psychology*. Washington, DC: Author.

American Psychological Association (1994). Guidelines for child custody evaluations in divorce proceedings. *American Psychologist, 49*, 677–680.

American Psychological Association (1995). Guidelines for providers of psychological services to ethnic, linguistic, and culturally diverse populations. In D. N. Bersoff (Ed.), *Ethical conflicts in psychology* (pp. 348–351). Washington, D.C.: American Psychological Association.

American Psychological Association (1997a). *Doctoral programs in family psychology*. Washington, DC: Author.

American Psychological Association (1997b). *Journals in psychology: A resource for authors* (5th ed.). Washington, DC: Author.

American Psychological Association (2000a). *Graduate study in psychology*. Washington, DC: Author.

American Psychological Association (2000b). *Psychology/careers for the 21st century*. Washington, DC: Author.

American Psychological Association (2001). *Publication manual of the American Psychological Association* (5th ed.). Washington, DC: Author.

American Speech-Language-Hearing Association (2000). *Selecting a doctoral research education program in communication sciences and disorders*. Rockville, MD: Fulfillment Operations.

Ammerman, R. T., & Patz, R. J. (1996). Determinants of child abuse potential: Contribution of parent and child factors. *Journal of Clinical Child Psychology, 25*, 300–307.

Anastopoulos, A. D. (1999). Attention-Deficit/Hyperactivity Disorder. In S. D. Netherton, D. Holmes, & C. E. Walker (Eds.), *Child and adolescent psychological disorders: A comprehensive textbook* (pp. 98–117). New York: Oxford University Press.

Anastopoulos, A. D., Barkley, R. A., & Sheldon, T. L. (1996). Family based treatment: Psychosocial intervention for children and adolescents with Attention Deficit Hyperactivity Disorder. In E. D. Hibbs & P. S. Jensen (Eds.), *Psychosocial treatments for child and adolescent disorders: Empirically based strategies for clinical practice* (pp. 267–284). Washington, DC: American Psychological Association.

Anda, R. F., Croft, J. B., Felitti, V. J., Nordenberg, D., Giles, W. H., Williamson, D. F., & Giovino, G. A. (1999). Adverse childhood experiences and smoking during adolescence and adulthood. *Journal of the American Medical Association, 282*, 1652–1658.

Anderson, D. L., Brown, R. T., & Williams, L. (1999). Summaries, training, ethics, and direction. In R. T. Brown (Ed.), *Cognitive aspects of chronic illness in children* (pp. 386–406). New York: Guilford.

Anderson, E. R., & Greene, S. M. (1999). Children of stepparents and blended families. In W. K. Silverman & T. H. Ollendick (Eds.), *Developmental issues in the clinical treatment of children* (pp. 342–357). Boston: Allyn & Bacon.

Anderson, L. (1991). *Dear Dad: Letters from an adult child*. New York: Penguin.

Andrade, A. R., Lambert, E. W., & Bickman, L. (2000). Dose effect in psychotherapy: Outcomes associated with negligible treatment. *Journal of the American Academy of Child and Adolescent Psychiatry, 39*, 161–168.

Andreasen, N. C., & Carpenter, W. T. (1993). Diagnosis and classification of schizophrenia. *Schizophrenia Bulletin, 19*, 199–214.

Angelou, M. (1969). *I know why the caged bird sings*. New York: Random House.

Angold, A., Costello, E. J., & Erkanli, A. (1999). Comorbidity. *Journal of Child Psychology and Psychiatry, 40*, 57–87.

Angold, A., Erkanli, A., Egger, H. L., & Costello, E. J. (2000). Stimulant treatment for children: A community perspective. *Journal of the American Academy of Child and Adolescent Psychiatry, 39*, 975–984.

Angold, A., & Rutter, M. (1992). Effects of age and pubertal status in a large clinical sample. *Development and Psychopathology, 4*, 5–28.

Anstendig, K. D. (1999). Is selective mutism an anxiety disorder? Rethinking its *DSM-IV* classification. *Journal of Anxiety Disorders, 13*, 417–434.

Anthony, E. J. (1974). The syndrome of the psychologically invulnerable child. In E. J. Anthony & C. Koupernik (Eds.), *The child in his family: Children at psychiatric risk* (pp. 529–545). New York: Wiley.

Anthony, E. J., & Cohler, B. J. (Eds.) (1987). *The invulnerable child*. New York: Guilford.

Appleby, D. (1997). *The handbook of psychology*. New York: Longman.

Armistead, L., Forehand, R., Steele, R., & Kotchick, B. (1998). Pediatric AIDS. In T. H. Ollendick & M. Hersen (Eds.), *Handbook of child psychopathology* (3rd ed., pp. 463–481). New York: Plenum.

Armstrong, F. D., & Drotar, D. (2000). Multi-institutional and multidisciplinary research collaboration: Strategies and lessons from cooperative trials. In D. Drotar (Ed.), *Handbook of research in pediatric and clinical child psychology* (pp. 281–303). New York: Plenum.

Arnett, J. J. (2000). Emerging adulthood: A theory of development from the late teens through the twenties. *American Psychologist, 55*, 469–480.

Arnold, D. S., O'Leary, S. G., Wolff, L. S., & Acker, M. M. (1993). The Parenting Scale: A measure of dysfunctional parenting in discipline situations. *Psychological Assessment, 5*, 137–144.

Aronen, E. T., Paavonen, E. J., Fjaellberg, M., Soininen, M. & Toerroenen, J. (2000). Sleep and psychiatric symptoms in school-age children. *Journal of the American Academy of Child and Adolescent Psychiatry, 39*, 502–508.

Arrington, E. G., & Wilson, M. N. (2000). A re-examination of risk and resilience during adolescence: Incorporating culture and diversity. *Journal of Child and Family Studies, 9*, 221–230.

Arseneault, L., Moffitt, T. E., Caspi, A., Taylor, P. J., & Silva, P. A. (2000). Mental disorders and violence in a total birth cohort: Results from the Dunedin Study. *Archives of General Psychiatry, 57*, 979–986.

Arthur, M. W., & Blitz, C. (2000). Bridging the gap between science and practice in drug abuse prevention through needs assessment and strategic community planning. *Journal of Community Psychology, 28*, 241–255.

Ary, D. V., Duncan, T. E., Biglan, A., Metzler, C. W., Noell, J. W., & Smolkowski, K. (1999). Development of adolescent problem behavior. *Journal of Abnormal Child Psychology, 27*, 141–150.

Ary, D. V., Duncan, T. E., Duncan, S. C., & Hops, H. (1999). Adolescent problem behavior: The influence of parents and peers. *Behaviour Research and Therapy, 37*, 217–230.

Asarnow, J. R., Tompson, M., Woo, S., & Cantwell, D. P. (2001). Is expressed emotion a specific risk factor for depression or a nonspecific correlate of psychopathology? *Journal of Abnormal Child Psychology, 29*, 573–583.

Associated Press (2001, November 23). Deaths of Gaza children inflame Mideast. *USA Today*, pp. 1–3.

Association for the Advancement of Behavior Therapy. (1997). *Graduate training in behavior therapy and experimental-clinical psychology*. New York: Author.

Attie, I., & Brooks-Gunn, J. (1992). Development issues in the study of eating problems and disorders. In J. H. Crowther, S. E. Hobfoll, M. A. P. Stephens, & D. L. Tennenbaum (Eds.), *The etiology of bulimia: The individual and familial context* (pp. 35–50). Washington, D.C.: Hemisphere.

Attie, I., & Brooks-Gunn, J. (1995). The development of eating regulation across the life span. In D. Cicchetti & D. J. Cohen (Eds.), *Developmental psychopathology: Vol. 2, Risk, disorder, and adaptation* (pp. 332–368). New York: Wiley.

August, G. J., Realmuto, G. M., Hektner, J. M., & Bloomquist, M. L. (2001). An integrated components preventive intervention for aggressive elementary school children: The early risers program. *Journal of Consulting and Clinical Psychology, 69*, 614–626.

Azar, S. T. (1992). Legal issues in the assessment of family violence involving children. In R. T. Ammerman & M. Hersen (Eds.), *Assessment of family violence: A clinical and legal sourcebook* (pp. 47–70). New York: Wiley.

Azar, S. T., Ferraro, M. H., & Breton, S. J. (1998). Intrafamilial child maltreatment. In T. H. Ollendick & M. Hersen (Eds.), *Handbook of child psychopathology* (3rd ed., pp. 483–504).

Baer, R. A., & Nietzel, M. T. (1991). Cognitive and behavioral treatment of impulsivity in children: A meta-analytic review of the outcome literature. *Journal of Clinical Child Psychology, 20*, 400–412.

Baker, D. B., & Benjamin, L. T. (2000). The affirmation of the scientist-practitioner: A look back at Boulder. *American Psychologist, 55*, 241–247.

Baldwin, S. (1999). Applied behavior analysis in the treatment of ADHD: A review and rapprochement. *Ethical Human Sciences and Services, 1*, 35–59.

Bandura, A. (1986). *Social foundations of thought and action: A social cognitive theory*. Englewood Cliffs, NJ: Prentice-Hall.

Bandura, A., Ross, D., & Ross, S. A. (1961). Transmission of aggression through imitation of aggressive models. *Journal of Abnormal and Social Psychology, 63*, 575–582.

Barbarin, O. A., Whitten, C. F., Bond, S., & Conner-Warren, R. (1999). The social and cultural context of coping with sickle cell disease: II. The role of financial hardship in adjustment to sickle cell disease. *Journal of Black Psychology, 25*, 294–315.

Barkley, R. A. (1990). *Attention-deficit hyperactivity disorder: A handbook for diagnosis and treatment*. New York: Guilford.

Barkley, R. A. (1995). *Taking charge of ADHD: The complete authoritative guide for parents*. New York: Guilford.

Barkley, R. A. (1997a). Attention-Deficit/Hyperactivity Disorder. In E. J. Mash & L. G. Terdal (Eds.), *Assessment of childhood disorders* (3rd ed., pp. 71–129). New York: Guilford.

Barkley, R. A. (1997b). *ADHD and the nature of self-control*. New York: Guilford.

Barkley, R. A. (1997c). Behavioral inhibition, sustained attention, and executive functions: Constructing a unifying theory of ADHD. *Psychological Bulletin, 121*, 65–94.

Barkley, R. A. (1997d). *Defiant children: A clinician's manual for assessment and parent training* (2nd ed.). New York: Guilford.

Barkley, R. A. (1998). *Attention-Deficit Hyperactivity Disorder: A handbook for diagnosis and treatment* (2nd ed.). New York: Guilford.

Barkley, R. A., & Benton, C. M. (1998). *Your defiant child: Eight steps to better behavior*. New York: Guilford.

Barkley, R. A., Conners, C. K., Barclay, A., Gadow, K., Gittelman, R., Sprague, R. L., & Swanson, J. (1990). Task force report: The appropriate role of clinical child psychologists in the prescribing of psychoactive medication for children. *Journal of Clinical Child Psychology, 19 (Suppl.),* 1–38.

Barkley, R. A., Edwards, G. H., Laneri, M., Fletcher, K., & Metevia, L. (2001). The efficacy of problem-solving communication training alone, behavior management training alone, and combination for parent-adolescent conflict in teenagers with ADHD and ODD. *Journal of Consulting and Clinical Psychology, 69,* 926–941.

Barkley, R. A., Edwards, G. H., Laneri, M., Fletcher, K., & Metevia, L. (2001). Executive functioning, temporal discounting, and sense of time in adolescents with attention deficit hyperactivity disorder (ADHD) and oppositional defiant disorder (ODD). *Journal of Abnormal Child Psychology, 29,* 541–556.

Barkley, R. A., Edwards, G. H., & Robin, A. L. (1999). *Defiant teens: A clinician's manual for assessment and family intervention.* New York: Guilford.

Barnett, J. E., & Neel, M. L. (2000). Must all psychologists study psychopharmacology? *Professional Psychology: Research and Practice, 31,* 619–627.

Bar-Or, O. (Ed.). (1996). *The child and adolescent athlete.* New York: Blackwell Science.

Barrett, P. M., Duffy, A. L., Dadds, M. R., & Rapee, R. M. (2001). Cognitive-behavioral treatment of anxiety disorders in children: Long-term (6–year) follow-up. *Journal of Consulting and Clinical Psychology, 69,* 135–141.

Barrios, B. A., & O'Dell, S. L. (1998). Fears and anxieties. In E. J. Mash & R. A. Barkley (Eds.), *Treatment of childhood disorders* (2nd ed., pp. 249–298). New York: Guilford.

Bateson, G., Jackson, D. D., Haley, J., & Weakland, J. (1956). Towards a theory of schizophrenia. *Behavioral Science, 1,* 251–264.

Battistich, V. A., Elias, M. J., & Branden-Muller, L. R. (1992). Two school-based approaches to promoting children's social competence. In G. W. Albee, L. A. Bond, & T. V. C. Monsey (Eds.), *Improving children's lives: Global perspectives on prevention* (pp. 217–234). Newbury Park, CA: Sage.

Battistich, V. A., & Hom, A. (1997). The relationship between students' sense of their school as a community and their involvement in problem behaviors. *American Journal of Public Health, 87,* 1997–2001.

Baugher, E., & Lamison-White, L. (1996). *U.S. Bureau of the Census, Current Population Reports, Series P60–194, Poverty in the United States: 1995.* Washington, D.C.: Government Printing Office.

Baumrind, D. (1971). Current patterns of parental authority. *Developmental Psychology Monographs, 4 (1, part 2).*

Baving, L., Laucht, M., & Schmidt, M. H. (2000). Oppositional children differ from healthy children in frontal brain activation. *Journal of Abnormal Child Psychology, 28,* 267–275.

Bayley, N. (1969). *Bayley Scales of Infant Development: Birth to two years.* San Antonio: The Psychological Corporation.

Beardslee, W. R., Salt, P., Poterield, K., Rothberg, P. S., van de Velde, P., Swatling, S., Hoke, L., Moilanen, D. L., & Wheelock, I. (1993). Comparison of preventive interventions for families with parental affective disorder. *Journal of the American Academy of Child and Adolescent Psychiatry, 32,* 254–263.

Beck, A. T. (1976). *Cognitive therapy and emotional disorders.* New York: International Universities Press.

Beck, A. T., Kovacs, M., & Weissman, A. (1979). Assessment of suicidal intention: The Scale for Suicide Ideation. *Journal of Consulting and Clinical Psychology, 47,* 343–352.

Beck, A. T., Steer, R. A., & Garbin, M. G. (1988). Psychometric properties of the Beck Depression Inventory: Twenty-five years of evaluation. *Clinical Psychology Review, 8,* 77–100.

Becker, E., Rankin, E., & Rickel, A. U. (1998). *High-risk sexual behavior: Interventions with vulnerable populations.* New York: Plenum.

Beidel, D. C., & Morris, T. L. (1995). Social phobia. In J. S. March (Ed.), *Anxiety disorders in children and adolescents* (pp. 181–211). New York: Guilford.

Beidel, D. C., Turner, S. M., & Morris, T. L. (1995). A new inventory to assess childhood social anxiety and phobia: The Social Phobia and Anxiety Inventory for Children. *Psychological Assessment, 7,* 73–79.

Belgrave, F. Z., Townsend, T. G., Cherry, V. R., & Cunningham, D. M. (1997). The influence of an Africentric worldview and demographic variables on drug knowledge, attitudes, and use among African American youth. *Journal of Community Psychology, 25,* 421–433.

Bellak, L. (1993). *The T.A.T., C.A.T., and S.A.T. in clinical use* (5th ed). Boston: Allyn & Bacon.

Bellanti, C. J., Bierman, K. L., & Conduct Problems Prevention Research Group. (2000). Disentangling the impact of low cognitive ability and inattention on social behavior and peer relationships. *Journal of Clinical Child Psychology, 29,* 66–75.

Bemporad, J. R. (1994). Dynamic and interpersonal theories of depression. In W. M. Reynolds & H. F. Johnston (Eds.), *Handbook of depression in children and adolescents* (pp. 81–95). New York: Plenum.

Berg, M. L., Crosby, R. D., Wonderlich, S. A., & Hawley, D. (2000). Relationship of temperament and perceptions of nonshared environment in bulimia nervosa. *International Journal of Eating Disorders, 28,* 148–154.

Berman, S. L., Kurtines, W. M., Silverman, W. K., & Serafini, L. T. (1996). The impact of exposure to crime and violence on urban youth. *American Journal of Orthopsychiatry, 66,* 329–336.

Bernstein, D. P., Cohen, P., Velez, C. N., Schwab-Stone, M., Siever, L. J., & Shinsato, L. (1993). Prevalence and stability of the *DSM-III-R* Personality Disorders in a community-based survey of adolescents. *American Journal of Psychiatry, 150,* 1237–1243.

Bernstein, G. A., Hektner, J. M., Borchardt, C. M., & McMillan, M. H. (2001). Treatment of school refusal: One-year follow-up. *Journal of the American Academy of Child and Adolescent Psychiatry, 40,* 206–213.

Bernstein, G. A., Warren, S. L., Massie, E. D., & Thuras, P. D. (1999). Family dimensions in anxious-depressed school refusers. *Journal of Anxiety Disorders, 13,* 513–528.

Bersoff, D. M., & Bersoff, D. N. (1999). Ethical perspectives in clinical research. In P. C. Kendall, J. N. Butcher, & G. N. Holmbeck (Eds.), *Handbook of research methods in clinical psychology* (2nd ed., pp. 31–53). New York: Wiley.

Besharov, D. J. (1990). *Recognizing child abuse: A guide for the concerned.* New York: Free Press.

Beutler, L. E., & Moleiro, C. (2001). Clinical versus reliable and significant change. *Clinical Psychology: Science and Practice, 8,* 441–445.

Beyers, J. M., Loeber, R., Wikstrom, P. H., & Stouthamer-Loeber, M. (2001). What predicts adolescent violence in better-off neighborhoods? *Journal of Abnormal Child Psychology, 29,* 369–381.

Biasini, F. J., Grupe, L., Huffman, L., & Bray, N. W. (1999). Mental retardation: A symptom and a syndrome. In S. D. Netherton, D. Holmes, & C. E. Walker (Eds.), *Child and adolescent psychological disorders: A comprehensive textbook* (pp. 6–23). New York: Oxford University Press.

Bickman, L., Guthrie, P. R., Foster, E. M., Lambert, E. W., Summerfelt, W. T., Breda, C. S., & Heflinger, C. A. (1995). *Evaluating managed mental health services: The Fort Bragg experiment.* New York: Plenum.

Bickman, L., Lambert, E. W., Andrade, A. R., & Penaloza, R. V. (2000). The Fort Bragg continuum of care for children and adolescents: Mental health outcomes over 5 years. *Journal of Consulting and Clinical Psychology, 68,* 710–716.

Biederman, J., Mick, E., Faraone, S. V., & Burback, M. (2001). Patterns of remission and symptom decline in conduct disorder: A four-year prospective study of an ADHD sample. *Journal of the American Academy of Child and Adolescent Psychiatry, 40,* 290–298.

Biederman, J., Monuteaux, M. C., Greene, R. W., Braaten, E., Doyle, A. E., & Faraone, S. V. (2001). Long-term stability of the Child Behavior Checklist in a clinical sample of youth with attention deficit hyperactivity disorder. *Journal of Clinical Child Psychology, 30,* 492–502.

Biederman, J., Rosenbaum, J. F., Chaloff, J., & Kagan, J. (1995). Behavioral inhibition as a risk factor. In. J. S. March (Ed.), *Anxiety disorders in children and adolescents* (pp. 61–81). New York: Guilford.

Biklen, D. (1990). Communication unbound: Autism and praxis. *Harvard Educational Review, 60,* 291–314.

Biklen, D., & Cardinal, D. N. (1997). *Contested words, contested science: Unraveling the facilitated communication controversy.* New York: Teachers College Press.

Biklen, D., Morton, M. W., Saha, S. N., & Duncan, J. (1991). I AMN NOT A UTISTIVC ON THJE TYP" ("I'm not autistic on the typewriter"). *Disability, Handicap and Society, 6,* 161–180.

Bigler, E. D., Nilsson, D. E., Burr, R. B., & Boyer, R. S. (1997). Neuroimaging in pediatric neuropsychology. In C. R. Reynolds & E. Fletcher-Janzen (Eds.), *Handbook of clinical child neuropsychology* (2nd ed., pp. 342–355). New York: Plenum.

Birbaumer, N. & Flor, H. (1998). Psychobiology. In C. E. Walker (Ed.), *Comprehensive clinical psychology* (Vol 1, pp. 115–172). Oxford, England: Elsevier Science.

Bird, H. R. (1996). Epidemiology of childhood disorders in a cross-cultural context. *Journal of Child Psychology and Psychiatry, 37,* 35–49.

Bird, H. R., Canino, G. J., Davies, M., Zhang, H., Ramirez, R., & Lahey, B. B. (2001). Prevalence and correlates of antisocial behaviors among three ethnic groups. *Journal of Abnormal Child Psychology, 29,* 465–478.

Blachman, B. (Ed.). (1997). *Foundations of reading acquisition and dyslexia: Implications for early intervention.* Mahwah, NJ: Lawrence Erlbaum.

Black, B. (1995). Separation anxiety disorder and panic disorder. In J. S. March (Ed.), *Anxiety disorders in children and adolescents* (pp. 212–234). New York: Guilford.

Black, M. M., Dubowitz, H., & Starr, R. H. (1999). African American fathers in low income, urban families: Development, behavior, and home environment of their three-year-old children. *Child Development, 70,* 967–978.

Black, M. M., & Nitz, K. (1996). Grandmother co-residence, parenting, and child development among low income, urban teen mothers. *Journal of Adolescent Health, 18,* 218–226.

Bogels, S. M., & Zigterman, D. (2000). Dysfunctional cognitions in children with social phobia, separation anxiety disorder, and generalized anxiety disorder. *Journal of Abnormal Child Psychology, 28,* 205–211.

Bolger, K. E., & Patterson, C. J. (2001). Developmental pathways from child maltreatment to peer rejection. *Child Development, 72,* 549–568.

Borden, K. A., & Brown, R. T. (1989). Attributional outcomes: The subtle messages of treatment for attention deficit disorder. *Cognitive Therapy and Research, 13,* 147–160.

Bordens, K. S., & Abbott, B. B. (1988). *Research design and methods: A process approach.* Mountain View, CA: Mayfield.

Borduin, C. M., Henggeler, S. W., & Manley, C. M. (1995). Conduct and oppositional disorders. In V. B. VanHasselt & M. Hersen (Eds.), *Handbook of adolescent psychopathology* (pp. 349–383). New York: Lexington Books.

Borduin, C. M., Schaeffer, C. M., & Heiblum, N. (1999). Relational problems: The social context of child and adolescent disorders. In S. D. Netherton, D. Holmes, & C. E. Walker (Eds.), *Child and adolescent psychological disorders: A comprehensive textbook* (pp. 498–519). New York: Oxford University Press.

Bostic, J. Q., & Pataki, C. (2000). All the world's a stage. *Journal of the American Academy of Child and Adolescent Psychiatry, 39,* 1565–1567.

Botvin, G. J., & Dusenbury, L. (1989). Substance abuse prevention and the promotion of competence. In L. A. Bond & B. E. Compas (Eds.), *Primary prevention and promotion in the schools* (pp. 146–178). Newbury Park, CA: Sage.

Bow, J. N., & Quinnell, F. A. (2001). Psychologists' current practices and procedures in child custody evaluations: Five years after American Psychological Association guidelines. *Professional Psychology: Research and Practice, 32,* 261–268.

Bowen, M. (1978). *Family therapy in clinical practice.* Northvale, NY: Jason Aronson.

Bowlby, J. (1969). *Attachment.* New York: Basic Books.

Bowlby, J. (1973). *Attachment and loss: Vol. 2. Separation anxiety and anger.* New York: Basic Books.

Boyce, W. T., Frank, E., Jensen, P. S., Kessler, R. C., Nelson, C. A., Steinberg, L., & The MacArthur Foundation Research Network on Psychopathology and Development (1998). Social context in developmental psychopathology: Recommendations for future research from the MacArthur Network on Psychopathology and Development. *Development and Psychopathology, 10,* 143–164.

Boyle, M. H., & Pickles, A. R. (1997). Influence of maternal depressive symptoms on ratings of childhood behavior. *Journal of Abnormal Child Psychology, 25,* 399–412.

Braaten, E. B., & Rosen, L. A. (2000). Self-regulation of affect in attention deficit-hyperactivity disorder (ADHD) and non-ADHD boys: Differences in empathic responding. *Journal of Consulting and Clinical Psychology, 68,* 313–321.

Brandenburg, N. A., Friedman, R. M., & Silver, S. E. (1990). The epidemiology of childhood psychiatric disorders: Prevalence findings from recent studies. *Journal of the American Academy of Child and Adolescent Psychiatry, 29,* 76–83.

Brandon, T. H., Collins, B. N., Juliano, L. M., & Lazev, A. B. (2000). Preventing relapse among former smokers: A comparison of minimal interventions through telephone and mail. *Journal of Consulting and Clinical Psychology, 68,* 103–113.

Branford, D., Bhaumik, S., & Naik, B. (1998). Selective serotonin reuptake inhibitors for the treatment of perseverative and maladaptive behaviours of people with intellectual disability. *Journal of Intellectual Disability Research, 42,* 301–396.

Brassard, M. R., Germain, R., & Hart, S. N. (1987). *Psychological maltreatment of children and youth.* Elmsford, NY: Pergamon.

Brassard, M. R., Hart, S. N., & Hardy, D. B. (1991). Psychological and emotional abuse of children. In R. T. Ammerman & M. Hersen (Eds.), *Case studies in family violence* (pp. 255–270). New York: Plenum.

Braswell, L., August, G. J., Bloomquist, M. L., Realmuto, G. M., Skare, S. S., & Crosby, R. D. (1997). School-based secondary prevention for children with disruptive behavior: Initial outcomes. *Journal of Abnormal Child Psychology, 25,* 197–208.

Breggin, P. R. (1998). *Talking back to Ritalin: What doctors aren't telling you about stimulants for children.* Monroe, ME: Common Courage Press.

Breggin, P. R., & Breggin, G. R. (1994). *The war against children: How the drugs, programs, and theories of the psychiatric establishment are threatening America's children with a medical "cure" for violence.* New York: St. Martin's Press.

Breggin, P. R., & Breggin, G. R. (1995). The hazards of treating "Attention-Deficit/Hyperactivity Disorder" with Methylphenidate (Ritalin). *Journal of College Student Psychotherapy, 10,* 55–72.

Brent, D. A., Baugher, M., Birmaher, B., Kolko, D. J., & Bridge, J. (2000). Compliance with recommendations to remove firearms in families participating in a clinical trial for adolescent depression. *Journal of the American Academy of Child and Adolescent Psychiatry, 39,* 1220–1226.

Brent, D. A., Kolko, D. J., Birmaher, B., Baugher, M., & Bridge, J. (1999). A clinical trial for adolescent depression: Predictors of additional treatment in the acute and follow-up phases of the trial. *Journal of the American Academy of Child and Adolescent Psychiatry, 38,* 263–270.

Brestan, E. V., & Eyberg, S. M. (1998). Effective psychosocial treatments of conduct-disordered children and adolescents: 29 years, 82 studies, and 5,272 kids. *Journal of Clinical Child Psychology, 27,* 180–189.

Briery, B. G., & Rabian, B. (1999). Psychosocial changes associated with participation in a pediatric summer camp. *Journal of Pediatric Psychology, 24,* 183–190.

Briggs-Gowan, M. J., Horwitz, S. M., Schwab-Stone, M. E., Leventhal, J. M., & Leaf, P. J. (2000). Mental health in pediatric settings: Distribution of disorders and factors related to service use. *Journal of the American Academy of Child and Adolescent Psychiatry, 39,* 841–849.

Brock, G. W., & Barnard, C. P. (1992). *Procedures in marriage and family therapy* (2nd ed.). Boston: Allyn & Bacon.

Brodeur, D. A., & Pond, M. (2001). The development of selective attention in children with attention deficit hyperactivity disorder. *Journal of Abnormal Child Psychology, 29,* 229–239.

Brody, G. H., Ge, X., Conger, R., Gibbons, F. X., Murry, V. M., Gerrard, M., & Simons, R. L. (2001). The influence of neighborhood disadvantage, collective socialization, and parenting on African American children's affiliation with deviant peers. *Child Development, 72,* 1231–1246.

Brody, G. H., Ge, X., Katz, J., & Arias, I. (2000). A longitudinal analysis of internalization of parental alcohol-use norms and adolescent alcohol use. *Applied Developmental Science, 4,* 71–79.

Bronfenbrenner, U. (1979). *The ecology of human development: Experiments by nature and design.* Cambridge, MA: Harvard University Press.

Brook, J. S., Whiteman, M., Brook, D. W., & Gordon, A. S. (1982). Paternal and peer characteristics: Interactions and association with male college students' marijuana use. *Psychological Reports, 51,* 1319–1330.

Brown, J., Cohen, P., Johnson, J. G., & Smailes, E. M. (1999). Childhood abuse and neglect: Specificity and effects on adolescent and young adult depression and suicidality. *Journal of the American Academy of Child and Adolescent Psychiatry, 38,* 1490–1496.

Brown, L., Overholser, J., Spirito, A., & Fritz, G. (1991). The correlates of planning in adolescent suicide attempts. *Journal of the American Academy of Child and Adolescent Psychiatry, 30,* 95–99.

Brown, L. K., Lourie, K. J., & Pao, M. (2000). Children and adolescents living with HIV and AIDS: A review. *Journal of Child Psychology and Psychiatry, 41,* 81–96.

Brown, R. T. (1999). *Cognitive aspects of chronic illness in children.* New York: Guilford.

Brown, R. T., Lee, D., & Donegan, J. E. (1999). Psychopharmacotherapy with school-aged children. In C. R. Reynolds & T. B. Gutkin (Eds.), *The handbook of school psychology* (3rd ed., pp. 822–862). New York: Wiley.

Brown, R. T., & Sawyer, M. G. (1998). *Medications for school-age children: Effects on learning and behavior.* New York: Guilford.

Buck, J. N. (1985). *The House-Tree-Person technique: Revised manual.* Los Angeles: Western Psychological Services.

Buckner, J. C., Bassuk, E. L., Weinreb, L. F., & Brooks, M. G. (1999). Homelessness and its relation to the mental health and behavior of low-income school-age children. *Developmental Psychology, 35,* 246–257.

Budd, K. S., & Holdsworth, M. J. (1996). Issues in clinical assessment of minimal parenting competence. *Journal of Clinical Child Psychology, 25,* 2–14.

Budman, S. H. (2000). Behavioral health care dot-com and beyond: Computer-mediated communications in mental health and substance abuse treatment. *American Psychologist, 55,* 1290–1300.

Bukstein, O. G., & VanHasselt, V. B. (1995). Substance use disorders. In V. B. VanHasselt & M. Hersen (Eds.), *Handbook of adolescent psychopathology: A guide to diagnosis and treatment* (pp. 384–406). New York: Lexington Books.

Burns, B. J., Hoagwood, K., & Mrazek, P. J. (1999). Effective treatment for mental disorders in children and adolescents. *Clinical Child and Family Psychology Review, 2,* 199–254.

Burns, R. C. (1982). *Self-growth in families: Kinetic Family Drawings (K-F-D) research and application.* New York: Brunner/Mazel.

Burns, R. C., & Kaufman, S. H. (1972). *Actions, styles and symbols in kinetic family drawings (KFD-D): An interpretative manual.* New York: Brunner/Mazel.

Bushman, B. J., & Anderson, C. A. (2001). Media violence and the American public: Scientific facts versus media misinformation. *American Psychologist, 56,* 477–489.

Buskist, W., & Sherburne, T. R. (1996). *Preparing for graduate study in psychology: 101 questions and answers.* Needham Heights, MA: Allyn & Bacon.

Bussing, R., Zima, B. T., Belin, T. R., & Forness, S. R. (1998). Children who qualify for LD and SED programs: Do they differ in level of ADHD symptoms and comorbid psychiatric conditions? *Behavioral Disorders, 23,* 85–97.

Bussing, R., Zima, B. T., & Perwien, A. R. (2000). Self-esteem in special education children with ADHD: Relationship to disorder characteristics and medication use. *Journal of the American Academy of Child and Adolescent Psychiatry, 39,* 1260–1269.

Butcher, J. N., Dahlstrom, W. G., Graham, J. R., Tellegen, A., & Kaemmer, B. (1989). *Minnesota Multiphasic Personality Inventory-2 (MMPI-2): Manual for administration and scoring.* Minneapolis, MN: University of Minnesota Press.

Butcher, J. N., Williams, C. L., Graham, J. R., Archer, R. P., Tellegen, A., Ben-Porath, Y. S., & Kaemmer, B. (1992). *Minnesota Multiphasic Personality Inventory (MMPI-A): Manual for administration, scoring, and interpretation.* Minneapolis: University of Minnesota Press.

Cacioppo, J. T., Berntson, G. G., Sheridan, J. F., & McClintock, M. K. (2000). Multilevel integrative analyses of human behavior: Social neuroscience and the complementing nature of social and biological approaches. *Psychological Bulletin, 126,* 829–843.

Caddy, G. R., & Bollard, J. (1988). Enuresis. In M. Hersen & C. G. Last (Eds.), *Child behavior therapy casebook* (pp. 347–357). New York: Plenum.

Calkins, D. L., Walker, C. E., & Howe, A. C. (1994). Elimination disorders: Psychological issues. In R. A. Olson, L. L. Mullins, J. B. Gillman, & J. M. Chaney (Eds.), *The sourcebook of pediatric psychology* (pp. 46–54). Boston: Allyn & Bacon.

Campbell, M., Gonzalez, N. M., Ernst, M., Silva, R. R., & Werry, J. S. (1993). Antipsychotics (neuroleptics). In J. S. Werry & M. G. Aman (Eds.), *Practitioner's guide to psychoactive drugs for children and adolescents* (pp. 269–296). New York: Plenum.

Campbell, S. B. (1998). Developmental perspectives. In T. H. Ollendick & M. Hersen (Eds.), *Handbook of child psychopathology* (3rd ed., pp. 3–35). New York: Plenum.

Campbell, S. B. (2000). Editor's note. *Journal of Abnormal Child Psychology, 28*, 481.

Campo, J. V., & Reich, M. D. (1999). Somatoform disorders. In S. D. Netherton, D. Holmes, & C. E. Walker (Eds.), *Child and adolescent psychological disorders: A comprehensive textbook* (pp. 320–343). New York: Oxford University Press.

Canino, G., Bird, H. R., & Canino, I. A. (1997). Methodological challenges in cross-cultural research of childhood psychopathology: Risk and protective factors. In C. T. Nixon & D. A. Northrup (Eds.), *Evaluating mental health services: How do programs for children "work" in the real world? Children's mental health services* (Vol. 3, pp. 259–276). Thousand Oaks, CA: Sage.

Canter, M. B., Bennett, B. E., Jones, S. E., & Nagy, T. F. (1994). *Ethics for psychologists: A commentary on the APA ethics code*. Washington, D.C.: American Psychological Association.

Cantwell, D. P. (1992). Clinical phenomenology and nosology. *Child and Adolescent Psychiatric Clinics of North America, 1*, 1–11.

Cantwell, D. P., Lewinsohn, P. M., Rohde, P., & Seeley, J. R. (1997). Correspondence between adolescent report and parent report of psychiatric diagnostic data. *Journal of the American Academy of Child and Adolescent Psychiatry, 36*, 610–619.

Caplan, P. J. (1995). *They say you're crazy: How the world's most powerful psychiatrists decide who's normal*. Reading, MA: Addison-Wesley.

Caplan, P. J., & Hall-McCorquodale, I. (1985). Mother-blaming in major clinical journals. *American Journal of Orthopsychiatry, 55*, 345–353.

Capps, L., Losh, M., & Thurber, C. (2000). "The frog ate the bug and made his mouth sad": Narrative competence in children with autism. *Journal of Abnormal Child Psychology, 28*, 193–204.

Carey, M. P. (1993). Child and adolescent depression: Cognitive-behavioral strategies and interventions. In A. J. Finch, W. M. Nelson, & E. S. Ott (Eds.), *Cognitive-behavioral procedures with children and adolescents: A practical guide* (pp. 289–314). Boston: Allyn & Bacon.

Carlson, C. L., Shin, M., & Booth, J. (1999). The case for *DSM-IV* subtypes in ADHD. *Mental Retardation and Developmental Disabilities Research Reviews, 5*, 199–206.

Carlson, C. L., Tamm, L., & Gaub, M. (1997). Gender differences in children with ADHD, ODD, and co-occurring ADHD/ODD identified in a school population. *Journal of the American Academy of Child and Adolescent Psychiatry, 36*, 1706–1714.

Carlson, C. L., Tamm, L., & Hogan, A. E. (1999). The child with oppositional defiant disorder and conduct disorder in the family. In H. C. Quay & A. E. Hogan (Eds.), *Handbook of disruptive behavior disorders* (pp. 337–352). New York: Kluwer Academic/Plenum.

Carlson, C. R., & Cordova, M. J. (1999). Sleep disorders in childhood and adolescence. In S. D. Netherton, D. Holmes, & C. E. Walker (Eds.), *Child and adolescent psychological disorders: A comprehensive textbook* (pp. 415–438). New York: Oxford University Press.

Carlson, G. A. (1994). Adolescent bipolar disorder: Phenomenology and treatment implications. In W. M. Reynolds & H. F. Johnston (Eds.), *Handbook of depression in children and adolescents* (pp. 41–60). New York: Plenum.

Carlson, G. A. (1998). Mania and ADHD: Comorbidity or confusion. *Journal of Affective Disorders, 51*, 177–187.

Carlson, G. A., & Kelly, K. L. (1998). Manic symptoms in psychiatrically hospitalized children—what do they mean? *Journal of Affective Disorders, 51*, 123–135.

Caron, C., & Rutter, M. (1991). Comorbidity in child psychopathology: Concepts, issues and research strategies. *Journal of Child Psychology and Psychiatry, 32*, 1063–1080.

Carson, B., & Murphey, C. (1990). *Gifted hands: The Ben Carson story*. Grand Rapids, MI: Zondervan.

Carter, J. R., & Neufeld, R. W. J. (1998). Cultural aspects of understanding people with schizophrenic disorders. In S. S. Kazarian & D. R. Evans (Eds.), *Cultural clinical psychology: Theory, research, and practice* (pp. 246–266). New York: Oxford University Press.

Casey, R. J., & Berman, J. S. (1985). The outcome of psychotherapy with children. *Psychological Bulletin, 98*, 388–400.

Caspi, A. (2000). The child is father of the man: Personality continuities from childhood to adulthood. *Journal of Personality and Social Psychology, 78*, 158–172.

Caspi, A., & Moffitt, T. E. (1995). The continuity of maladaptive behavior: From description to understanding in the study of antisocial behavior. In D. Cicchetti & D. J. Cohen (Eds.), *Developmental psychopathology: Vol 2. Risk, disorder, and adaptation* (pp. 472–511). New York: Wiley.

Caspi, A., Taylor, A., Moffitt, T. E., & Plomin, R. (2000). Neighborhood deprivation affects children's mental health: Environmental risks identified in a genetic design. *Psychological Science, 11*, 338–342.

Cassidy, J., & Mohr, J. J. (2001). Unsolvable fear, trauma, and psychopathology: Theory, research, and clinical considerations related to disorganized attachment across the life span. *Clinical Psychology: Science and Practice, 8*, 275–298.

Cassidy, J., & Shaver, P. R. (Eds.). (1999). *Handbook of attachment: Theory, research, and clinical applications*. New York: Guilford.

Caster, J. B., Inderbitzen, H. M., & Hope, D. (1999). Relationship between youth and parent perceptions of family environment and social anxiety. *Journal of Anxiety Disorders, 13*, 237–251.

CDF Reports (1999). Gun violence: Nearly thirteen children die from gunfire every day in America. *CDF Reports, 20*, 1–2, 12–13.

Cecalupo, A. (1994). Childhood cancers: Medical issues. In R. A. Olson, L. L. Mullins, J. B. Gillman, & J. M. Chaney (Eds.), *The sourcebook of pediatric psychology* (pp. 90–97). Boston: Allyn & Bacon.

Centers for Disease Control (1995). Suicide among children, adolescents, and young adults—United States, 1980–1992. *Morbidity and Mortality Weekly Report, 44*, 289–291.

Centerwall, B. S. (2000). Television and violent crime. In D. S. Del-Campo & R. L. DelCampo (Eds.), *Taking sides: Clashing views on controversial issues in childhood and society* (3rd ed., pp. 148–155). Guilford, CT: Dushkin/McGraw-Hill.

Cepeda, N. J., Cepeda, M. L., & Kramer, A. F. (2000). Task switching and attention deficit hyperactivity disorder. *Journal of Abnormal Child Psychology, 28*, 213–226.

Chabrol, B., Decarie, J. C., & Fortin, G. (1999). The role of cranial MRI in identifying patients suffering from child abuse and presenting with unexplained neurological findings. *Child Abuse and Neglect, 23*, 217–228.

Challinor, J. M., Miaskowski, C. A., Franck, L. S., Slaughter, R. E., Matthay, K. K., Kramer, R. F., Veatch, J. J., Paul, S. M., Amylon,

M. D., & Moore, I. M. (1999). Somatization, anxiety and depression as measures of health-related quality of life of children/adolescents with cancer. *International Journal of Cancer, Supplement, 12*, 52–57.

Chamberlain, P. (1996). Community-based residential treatment for adolescents with conduct disorder. In T. H. Ollendick & R. J. Prinz (Eds.), *Advances in clinical child psychology* (Vol. 18, pp. 63–90). New York: Plenum.

Chambless, D. L., Baker, M. J., Baucom, D. H., Beutler, L. E., Calhoun, K. S., Crits-Christoph, P., Daiuto, A., DeRubeis, R., Detweiler, J., Haaga, D. A. F., Johnson, S. B., McCurry, S., Mueser, K. T., Pope, K. S., Sanderson, W. C., Shoham, V., Stickle, T., Williams, D. A., & Woody, S. (1998). Update on empirically validated therapies, II. *The Clinical Psychologist, 51*, 3–16.

Chassin, L., Curran, P. J., Hussong, A. M., & Colder, C. R. (1996). The relation of parent alcoholism to adolescent substance use: A longitudinal follow-up study. *Journal of Abnormal Psychology, 105*, 70–80.

Chassin, L., Pitts, S. C., DeLucia, C., & Todd, M. (1999). A longitudinal study of children of alcoholics: Predicting young adult substance use disorders, anxiety, and depression. *Journal of Abnormal Psychology, 108*, 106–119.

Cher, & Coplon, J. (1998). *The first time.* New York: Simon and Schuster.

Children's Defense Fund. (1999). *The state of America's children yearbook.* Washington, D.C.: Author.

Children's Defense Fund–Minnesota (1990). *157,000 children: Facts and feelings about being on welfare in Minnesota.* St. Paul, MN: Author.

Chong, M. Y., Chan, K. W., & Cheng, A. T. A. (1999). Substance use disorders among adolescents in Taiwan: Prevalence, sociodemographic correlates and psychiatric comorbidity. *Psychological Medicine, 29*, 1387–1396.

Chorpita, B. F., & Barlow, D. H. (1998). The development of anxiety: The role of control in the early environment. *Psychological Bulletin, 124*, 3–21.

Chorpita, B. F., Plummer, C. M., & Moffitt, C. E. (2000). Relations of tripartite dimensions of emotion to childhood anxiety and mood disorders. *Journal of Abnormal Child Psychology, 28*, 299–310.

Christiansen, B. A., & Goldman, M. S. (1983). Alcohol-related expectancies versus demographic/background variables in the prediction of adolescent drinking. *Journal of Consulting and Clinical Psychology, 51*, 249–257.

Christenson, S. L., & Buerkle, K. (1999). Families as educational partners for children's school success: Suggestions for school psychologists. In C. R. Reynolds & T. B. Gutkin (Eds.), *The handbook of school psychology* (3rd ed., pp. 707–744). New York: Wiley.

Christoffel, K. K., (2000). Commentary: When counseling parents on guns doesn't work: Why don't they get it? *Journal of the American Academy of Child and Adolescent Psychiatry, 39*, 1226–1228.

Christophersen, E. R., & Rapoff, M. A. (1992). Toileting problems in children. In C. E. Walker & M. C. Roberts (Eds.), *Handbook of clinical child psychology* (2nd ed., pp. 399–411). New York: Wiley.

Ciaranello, A. L., & Ciaranello, R. D. (1995). The neurobiology of infantile autism. *Annual Review of Neuroscience, 18*, 101–128.

Cicchetti, D. (1990). A historical perspective on the discipline of developmental psychopathology. In J. Rolf, A. Masten, D. Cicchetti, K. Nuechterlein, & S. Weintraub (Eds.), *Risk and protective factors in the development of psychopathology* (pp. 2–28). New York: Cambridge University Press.

Cicchetti, D., Rappaport, J., Sandler, I., & Weissberg, R. P. (Eds.). (2000). *The promotion of wellness in children and adolescents.* Washington, D.C.: CWLA Press.

Cicchetti, D., & Rogosch, F. A. (1999a). Conceptual and methodological issues in developmental psychopathology research. In P. C. Kendall, J. N. Butcher, & G. N. Holmbeck (Eds.), *Handbook of research methods in clinical psychology* (2nd ed., pp. 433–465). New York: Wiley.

Cicchetti, D., & Rogosch, F. A. (1999b). Psychopathology as risk for adolescent substance use disorders: A developmental psychopathology perspective. *Journal of Clinical Child Psychology, 28*, 355–365.

Cicchetti, D., Rogosch, F. A., & Toth, S. L. (1997). Ontogenesis, depressotypic organization, and the depressive spectrum. In S. S. Luthar, J. A. Burack, D. Cicchetti, & J. R. Weisz (Eds.), *Developmental psychopathology: Perspectives on adjustment, risk, and disorder* (pp. 273–313). New York: Cambridge University Press.

Cicchetti, D., & Toth, S. L. (1995). Developmental psychopathology and disorders of affect. In D. Cicchetti & D. J. Cohen (Eds.), *Developmental psychopathology: Vol 2. Risk, disorder, and adaptation* (pp. 369–420). New York: Wiley.

Cicchetti, D., & Toth, S. L. (1997). Transactional ecological systems in developmental psychopathology. In S. S. Luthar, J. A. Burack, D. Cicchetti, & J. R. Weisz (Eds.), *Developmental psychopathology: Perspectives on adjustment, risk, and disorder* (pp. 317–349). New York: Cambridge University Press.

Cicchetti, D., & Toth, S. L. (1998).The development of depression in children and adolescents. *American Psychologist, 53*, 221–241.

Cicchetti, D., Toth, S. L., & Rogosch, F. A. (2000). The development of psychological wellness in maltreated children. In D. Cicchetti, J. Rappaport, I. Sandler, & R. P. Weissberg (Eds.), *The promotion of wellness in children and adolescents* (pp. 395–426). Washington, D.C.: CWLA Press.

Clark, D. B., Parker, A. M., & Lynch, K. G. (1999). Psychopathology and substance-related problems during early adolescence: A survival analysis. *Journal of Clinical Child Psychology, 28*, 333–341.

Clark, D. C., Pynoos, R. S., & Goebel, A. E. (1994). Mechanisms and processes of adolescent bereavement. In R. J. Haggerty, L. R. Sherrod, N. Garmezy, & M. Rutter (Eds.), *Stress, risk, and resilience in children and adolescents: Processes, mechanisms, and interventions* (pp. 100–146). New York: Cambridge University Press.

Clark, L. A., Watson, D., & Reynolds, S. (1995). Diagnosis and classification of psychopathology: Challenges to the current system and future directions. *Annual Review of Psychology, 46*, 121–153.

Clarke, G. N., Hawkins, W., Murphy, M., Sheeber, L. B., Lewinsohn, P. M., & Seeley, J. R. (1995). Targeted prevention of unipolar depressive disorder in an at-risk sample of high school adolescents: A randomized trial of a group cognitive intervention. *Journal of the American Academy of Child and Adolescent Psychiatry, 34*, 312–321.

Clarke-Stewart, K. A., Vandell, D. L., McCartney, K., Owen, M. T., & Booth, C. (2000). Effects of parental separation and divorce on very young children. *Journal of Family Psychology, 14*, 304–326.

Clarkson, S. (1999) Beyond street smarts. In E. Wright (Ed.), *Why I teach* (pp. 177–180). Rocklin, CA: Prima.

Clinton, H. R. (1996). *It takes a village and other lessons children teach us.* New York: Simon and Schuster.

Cody, H., & Hynd, G. (1999). Klinefelter syndrome. In S. Goldstein, C. Reynolds (Eds.), *Handbook of neurodevelopmental and genetic disorders in children.* New York: Guilford.

Coffey, B. J., Biederman, J., Geller, D. A., Spencer, T. J., Kim, G. S., Bellordre, C. A., Frazier, J. A., Cradock, K., & Magovcevic, M. (2000a). Distinguishing illness severity from tic severity in children and adolescents with Tourette's disorder. *Journal of the American Academy of Child and Adolescent Psychiatry, 39*, 556–561.

Coffey, B. J., Biederman, J., Smoller, J. W., Geller, D. A., Sarin, P., Schwartz, S., & Kim, G. S. (2000b). Anxiety disorders and tic severity in juveniles with Tourette's disorder. *Journal of the American Academy of Child and Adolescent Psychiatry, 39*, 562–568.

Coie, J. D., Dodge, K. A., Terry, R., & Wright, V. (1991). The role of aggression in peer relations: An analysis of aggression episodes in boys' play groups. *Child Development, 62*, 812–826.

Coie, J. D., & Jacobs, M. R. (1993). The role of social context in the prevention of conduct disorder. *Development and Psychopathology, 5*, 263–275.

Coley, R. L., & Chase-Lansdale, P. L. (1998). Adolescent pregnancy and parenthood: Recent evidence and future directions. *American Psychologist, 53*, 152–166.

Collins, L. (2000). *Graduate study in educational and psychological measurement, quantitative psychology, and related fields.* Pennsylvania State University, University Park, PA: Author.

Collins, W. A., Maccoby, E. E., Steinberg, L., Hetherington, E. M., & Bornstein, M. H. (2000). Contemporary research on parenting: The case for nature and nurture. *American Psychologist, 55*, 218–232.

Comings, D. E. (1997). Genetic aspects of childhood behavioral disorders. *Child Psychiatry and Human Development, 27*, 139–150.

Compas, B. E., Connor-Smith, J. K., Saltzman, H., Thomsen, A. H., & Wadsworth, M. E. (2001). Coping with stress during childhood and adolescence: Problems, progress, and potential in theory and research. *Psychological Bulletin, 127*, 87–127.

Compas, B. E., & Gotlib, I. H. (2002). *Introduction to Clinical Psychology: Science and Practice.* Boston: McGraw-Hill.

Compas, B. E., Hinden, B. R., & Gerhardt, C. A. (1995). Adolescent development: Pathways and processes of risk and resilience. *Annual Review of Psychology, 46*, 265–293.

Compas, B. E., Oppedisano, G., Connor, J. K., Gerhardt, C. A., Hinden, B. R., Achenbach, T. M., & Hammen, C. (1997). Gender differences in depressive symptoms in adolescence: Comparison of national samples of clinically referred and nonreferred youths. *Journal of Consulting and Clinical Psychology, 65*, 617–626.

Compas, B. E., Worsham, N. L., Epping-Jordan, J. E., Grant, K. E., Mireault, G., Howell, D. C., & Malcarne, V. L. (1994). When Mom or Dad has cancer: Markers of psychological distress in cancer patients, spouses, and children. *Health Psychology, 13*, 507–515.

Compas, B. E., Worsham, N. L., Ey, S., & Howell, D. C. (1996). When Mom or Dad has cancer II: Coping, cognitive appraisals, and psychological distress in children of cancer patients. *Health Psychology, 15*, 167–175.

Compton, S. N., Nelson, A. H., & March, J. S. (2000). Social phobia and separation anxiety symptoms in community and clinical samples of children and adolescents. *Journal of the American Academy of Child and Adolescent Psychiatry, 39*, 1040–1046.

Conduct Problems Prevention Research Group (1992). A developmental and clinical model for the prevention of conduct disorder: The FAST Track Program. *Development and Psychopathology, 4*, 509–527.

Conduct Problems Prevention Research Group (1999a). Initial impact of the fast track prevention trial for conduct problems: I. The high-risk sample. *Journal of Consulting and Clinical Psychology, 67*, 631–647.

Conduct Problems Prevention Research Group (1999b). Initial impact of the fast track prevention trial for conduct problems: II. Classroom effects. *Journal of Consulting and Clinical Psychology, 67*, 648–657.

Conners, C. K. (1990). *Conners' Teacher Rating Scales/Conners' Parent Rating Scales Manual.* North Tonawanda, NY: Multi-Health Systems, Inc.

Conners, C. K. (2000). Attention-Deficit/Hyperactivity Disorder: Historical development and overview. *Journal of Attention Disorders, 3*, 173–191.

Conners, C. K., Epstein, J. N., March, J. S., Angold, A., Wells, K. C., Klaric, J., Swanson, J. M., Arnold, L. E., Abikoff, H. B., Elliott, G. R.,

Greenhill, L. L., Hechtman, L., Hinshaw, S. P., Hoza, B., Jensen, P. S., Kraemer, H. C., Newcorn, J. H., Pelham, W. E., Severe, J. B., Vitiello, B. & Wigal, T. (2001). Multimodal treatment of ADHD in the MTA: An alternative outcome analysis. *Journal of the American Academy of Child and Adolescent Psychiatry, 40*, 159–167.

Consortium on the School-Based Promotion of Social Competence. (1994). The school-based promotion of social competence: Theory, research, practice, and policy. In R. J. Haggerty, L. R. Sherrod, N. Garmezy, & M. Rutter (Eds.), *Stress, risk, and resilience in children and adolescents: Processes, mechanisms, and interventions* (pp. 268–316). New York: Cambridge University Press.

Consumer Reports. (1995). Mental health: Does therapy help? *Consumer Reports,* November, 734–739.

Conte, J. R., Wolf, S., & Smith, T. (1989). What sexual offenders tell us about prevention strategies. *Child Abuse and Neglect, 13*, 293–301.

Coohey, C. (2000). The role of friends, in-laws, and other kin in father-perpetrated child physical abuse. *Child Welfare, 79*, 373–402.

Cook, M., & Mineka, S. (1989). Observational conditioning of fear to fear-relevant versus fear-irrelevant stimuli in rhesus monkeys. *Journal of Abnormal Psychology, 98*, 448–459.

Corey, G., Corey, M. S., & Callanan, P. (1988). *Issues and ethics in the helping professions* (3rd ed.). Pacific Grove, CA: Brooks/Cole.

Cormack, C., & Carr, A. (2000). Drug abuse. In A. Carr (Ed.), *What works with children and adolescents?: A critical review of psychological interventions with children, adolescents and their families* (pp. 155–177). New York: Routledge.

Cornblatt, B. A., Dworkin, R. H., Wolf, L. E., & Erlenmeyer-Kimling, L. (1996). Markers, developmental processes, and schizophrenia. In M. F. Lenzenweger & J. J. Haugaard (Eds.), *Frontiers of developmental psychopathology* (pp. 125–147). New York: Oxford University Press.

Cornelius, M. D., Goldshmidt, L., Taylor, P. M., & Day, N. L. (1999). Prenatal alcohol use among teenagers: Effects on neonatal outcomes. *Alcoholism: Clinical and Experimental Research, 23*, 1238–1244.

Costa, P. T., Jr., & McCrae, R. (1992). *Revised NEO Personality Inventory: NEO-PI and NEO Five-Factor Inventory (NEO-FFI: Professional Manual).* Odessa, FL: Psychological Assessment Resources.

Costello, E. J., & Angold, A. (1995). Epidemiology. In J. S. March (Ed.), *Anxiety disorders in children and adolescents* (pp. 109–124). New York: Guilford.

Costello, E. J., & Angold, A. (1996). Developmental psychopathology. In R. B. Cairns, G. H. Elder, & E. J. Costello (Eds.), *Developmental science* (pp. 168–189). New York: Cambridge University Press.

Costello, E. J., Burns, B. J., Angold, A., & Leaf, P. J. (1993). How can epidemiology improve mental health services for children and adolescents? *Journal of the American Academy of Child and Adolescent Psychiatry, 32*, 1106–1117.

Costello, E. J., Costello, A. J., Edelbrock, C., Burns, B. J., Dulcan, M. K., Brent, D., & Janiszewski, S. (1988). Psychiatric disorders in pediatric primary care. *Archives of General Psychiatry, 45*, 1107–1116.

Costello, E. J., Erkanli, A., Federman, E., & Angold, A. (1999). Development of psychiatric comorbidity with substance abuse in adolescents: Effects of timing and sex. *Journal of Clinical Child Psychology, 28*, 298–311.

Costello, E. J., & Janiszewski, S. (1990). Who gets treated? Factors associated with referral in children with psychiatric disorders. *Acta Psychiatrica Scandinavica, 81*, 523–529.

Cote, S., Zoccolillo, M., Tremblay, R. E., Nagin, D., & Vitaro, F. (2001). Predicting girls' conduct disorder in adolescence from childhood trajectories of disruptive behaviors. *Journal of the American Academy of Child and Adolescent Psychiatry, 40*, 678–684.

Council on Social Work Education (1999). *Summary information on master of social work programs*. Alexandria, VA: Author.

Cowen, E. L., Work, W. C., & Wyman, P. A. (1997). The Rochester Child Resilience Project (RCRP): Facts found, lessons learned, future directions divined. In S. S. Luthar, J. A. Burack, D. Cicchetti, & J. R. Weisz (Eds.), *Developmental psychopathology: Perspectives on adjustment, risk, and disorder* (pp. 527–547). New York: Cambridge University Press.

Cowen, E. L., Wyman, P. A., Work, W. C., Kim, J. Y., Fagen, D. B., & Magnus, K. B. (1997). Follow-up study of young stress-affected and stress-resilient urban children. *Development and Psychopathology, 9*, 565–577.

Cox, M. J., & Paley, B. (1997). Families as systems. *Annual Review of Psychology, 48*, 243–267.

Coy, K., Speltz, M. L., DeKlyen, M., & Jones, K. (2001). Social-cognitive processes in preschool boys with and without oppositional defiant disorder. *Journal of Abnormal Child Psychology, 29*, 107–119.

Coyne, J. C. (1976). Toward an interactional description of depression. *Psychiatry, 39*, 28–40.

Craighead, W. E., Smucker, M. R., Craighead, L. W., & Ilardi, S. S. (1998). Factor analysis of the Children's Depression Inventory in a community sample. *Psychological Assessment, 10*, 156–165.

Crawford, I., McLeod, A., Zamboni, B. D., & Jordan, M. B. (1999). Psychologists' attitudes toward gay and lesbian parenting. *Professional Psychology: Research and Practice, 30*, 394–401.

Crick, N. R., & Dodge, K. A. (1994). A review and reformulation of social information processing mechanisms in children's social adjustment. *Psychological Bulletin, 15*, 74–101.

Crowley, S. L., & Emerson, E. N. (1996). Discriminant validity of self-reported anxiety and depression in children: Negative affectivity or independent constructs? *Journal of Clinical Child Psychology, 25*, 139–146.

Crystal, D. S., Ostrander, R., Chen, R. S., & August, G. J. (2001). Multimethod assessment of psychopathology among DSM-IV subtypes of children with attention-deficit/hyperactivity disorder: Self-, parent-, and teacher reports. *Journal of Abnormal Child Psychology, 29*, 189–205.

Culbertson, J. L. (1998). Learning disabilities. In T. H. Ollendick & M. Hersen (Eds.), *Handbook of child psychopathology* (3rd ed., pp. 117–156). New York: Plenum.

Culbertson, J. L., & Schellenbach, C. J. (1992). Prevention of maltreatment in infants and young children. In D. J. Willis, E. W. Holden, & M. Rosenberg (Eds.), *Prevention of child maltreatment: Developmental and ecological perspectives* (pp. 47–77). New York: Wiley.

Cummings, E. M. (1997). Marital conflict, abuse, and adversity in the family and child adjustment: A developmental psychopathology perspective. In D. A. Wolfe & R. J. McMahon (Eds.), *Child abuse: New directions in prevention and treatment across the lifespan* (pp. 3–26). Thousand Oaks, CA: Sage.

Cummings, E. M., & Davies, P. (1994). *Children and marital conflict: The impact of family dispute and resolution*. New York: Guilford.

Cummings, E. M., Davies, P., & Campbell, S. B. (2000). *Developmental psychopathology and family process: Theory, research, and clinical implications*. New York: Guilford.

Cumsille, P. E., Sayer, A. G., & Graham, J. W. (2000). Perceived exposure to peer and adult drinking as predictors of growth in positive alcohol expectancies during adolescence. *Journal of Consulting and Clinical Psychology, 68*, 531–536.

Cunningham, C. E., Boyle, M., Offord, D., Racine, Y., Hundert, J., Scord, M., & McDonald, J. (2000). Tri-ministry study: Correlates of school-based parenting course utilization. *Journal of Consulting and Clinical Psychology, 68*, 928–933.

Curran, J., & Hollins, S. (1996). The prevention of mental illness in people with learning disability. In T. Kendrick & A. Tyler (Eds.), *The prevention of mental illness in primary care* (pp. 113–129). Cambridge, England: Cambridge University Press.

Curtis, M. J., Hunley, S. A., & Prus, J. R. (1998). *Credentialing requirements for school psychologists*. Bethesda, MD: National Association of School Psychologists Publications.

Cytryn, L., & McKnew, D. H. (1972). Proposed classification of childhood depression. *American Journal of Psychiatry, 129*, 149–155.

Cytryn, L., & McKnew, D. H. (1979). Affective disorders. In J. Noshpitz (Ed.), *Basic handbook of child psychiatry* (Vol. 2, pp. 300–340). New York: Basic Books.

Dadds, M. R. (1995). *Families, children, and the development of dysfunction*. Thousand Oaks, CA: Sage.

Dadds, M. R., & Barrett, P. M. (1996). Family processes in child and adolescent anxiety and depression. *Behaviour Change, 13*, 231–239.

Dadds, M. R., Spence, S. H., Holland, D. E., Barrett, P. M., & Laurens, K. R. (1997). Prevention and early intervention for anxiety disorders: A controlled trial. *Journal of Consulting and Clinical Psychology, 65*, 627–635.

Dakof, G. A. (2000). Understanding gender differences in adolescent drug abuse: Issues of comorbidity and family functioning. *Journal of Psychoactive Drugs, 32*, 25–32.

Dallam, S. J., Gleaves, D. H., Cepeda-Benito, A., Silberg, J. L., Kraemer, H. C., & Spiegel, D. (2001). The effects of child sexual abuse: Comment on Rind, Tromovitch, and Bauserman (1998). *Psychological Bulletin, 127*, 715–733.

D'Amato, R. C., Rothlisberg, B. A., & Rhodes, R. L. (1997). Utilizing a neuropsychological paradigm for understanding common educational and psychological tests. In C. R. Reynolds & E. Fletcher-Janzen (Eds.), *Handbook of clinical child neuropsychology* (2nd ed., pp. 270–295). New York: Plenum.

Danish, S. J., & Donohue, T. R. (1996). Understanding the media's influence on the development of antisocial and prosocial behavior. In R. L. Hampton, P. Jenkins, & T. P. Gullotta (Eds.), *Preventing violence in America* (pp. 133–155). Thousand Oaks, CA: Sage.

Darkes, J., & Goldman, M. S. (1998). Expectancy challenge and drinking reduction: Process and structure in the alcohol expectancy network. *Experimental and Clinical Psychopharmacology, 6*, 64–76.

Darlington, R. B., Royce, J. M., Snipper, A. S., Murray, H. W., & Lazar, I. (1980). Preschool programs and later school competence of children from low-income families. *Science, 208*, 202–204.

Dattilio, F. M., & Jongsma, A. E. (2000). *The family therapy treatment planner*. New York: Wiley.

Davis, M. K., & Gidycz, C. A. (2000). Child sexual abuse prevention programs: A meta-analysis. *Journal of Clinical Child Psychology, 29*, 257–265.

Dawson, G., & Castelloe, P. (1992). Autism. In C. E. Walker & M. C. Roberts (Eds.), *Handbook of clinical child psychology* (2nd ed., pp. 375–397). New York: Wiley.

Deal, L. W., Shiono, P. H., & Behrman, R. E. (1998). Children and managed health care: Analysis and recommendations. *The Future of Children, 8*, 4–24.

Deas, D., Riggs, P., Langenbucher, J., Goldman, M., & Brown, S. (2000). Adolescents are not adults: Developmental considerations in alcohol users. *Alcoholism: Clinical and Experimental Research, 24*, 232–237.

Deas-Nesmith, D., Brady, K. T., White, R., & Campbell, S. (1999). HIV-risk behaviors in adolescent substance abusers. *Journal of Substance Abuse Treatment, 16*, 169–172.

Deater-Deckard, K. (2000). Parenting and child behavioral adjustment in early childhood: A quantitative genetic approach to studying family processes. *Child Development, 72,* 468–484.

Deater-Deckard, K., Fulker, D. W., & Plomin, R. (1999). A genetic study of the family environment in the transition to early adolescence. *Journal of Child Psychology and Psychiatry, 40,* 769–775.

Deater-Deckard, K., Scarr, S., McCartney, K., & Eisenberg, M. (1994). Paternal separation anxiety: Relationships with parenting stress, child-rearing attitudes, and maternal anxieties. *Psychological Science, 5,* 341–346.

DelMedico, V., Weller, E., & Weller, R. (1996). Childhood depression. In L. Hechtman (Ed.), *Do they grow out of it? Long-term outcomes of childhood disorders* (pp. 101–119). Washington, D.C.: American Psychiatric Press.

DeLucia, C., Belz, A., & Chassin, L. (2001). Do adolescent symptomatology and family environment vary over time with fluctuations in paternal alcohol impairment? *Developmental Psychology, 37,* 207–216.

Denham, S. A., Workman, E., Cole, P. M., Weissbrod, C., Kendziora, K. T., & Zahn-Waxler, C. (2000). Prediction of externalizing behavior problems from early to middle childhood: The role of parental socialization and emotion expression. *Development and Psychopathology, 12,* 23–45.

Depue, R. A., Collins, P. F., & Luciana, M. (1996). A model of neurobiology-environment interaction in developmental psychopathology. In M. F. Lenzenweger & J. J. Haugaard (Eds.), *Frontiers of developmental psychopathology* (pp. 44–77). New York: Oxford University Press.

Dexheimer Pharris, M., Resnick, M. D., & Blum, R. W. (1997). Protecting against hopelessness and suicidality in sexually abused American Indian adolescents. *Journal of Adolescent Health, 21,* 400–406.

Dick, D. M., Rose, R. J., Viken, R. J., & Kaprio, J. (2000). Pubertal timing and substance use: Associations between and within families across late adolescence. *Developmental Psychology, 36,* 180–189.

Diener, E. (2000). Subjective well-being: The science of happiness and a proposal for a national index. *American Psychologist, 55,* 34–43.

Dierker, L. C., Merikangas, K. R., & Szatmari, P. (1999). Influence of parental concordance for psychiatric disorders on psychopathology in offspring. *Journal of the American Academy of Child and Adolescent Psychiatry, 38,* 280–288.

Dietz, T. L. (1998). An examination of violence and gender role portrayals in video games: Implications for gender socialization and aggressive behavior. *Sex Roles, 38,* 425–442.

DiLeo, J. H. (1973). *Children's drawings as diagnostic aids.* New York: Brunner/Mazel.

Diller, L. H. (1999). Attention-Deficit/Hyperactivity Disorder. *New England Journal of Medicine, 340,* 1766.

Dishion, T. J., French, D. C., & Patterson, G. R. (1995). The development and ecology of antisocial behavior. In D. Cicchetti & D. J. Cohen (Eds.), *Developmental psychology: Vol 2. Risk, disorder, and adaptation* (pp. 421–471). New York: Wiley.

Dishion, T. J., McCord, J., & Poulin, F. (1999). When interventions harm: Peer groups and problem behavior. *American Psychologist, 54,* 755–764.

Dishion, T. J., Spracklen, K. M., Andrews, D. W., & Patterson, G. R. (1996). Deviancy training in male adolescents friendships. *Behavior Therapy, 27,* 373–390.

Disney, E. R., Elkins, I. J., McGue, M., & Iacono, W. G. (1999). Effects of ADHD, conduct disorder, and gender on substance use and abuse in adolescence. *American Journal of Psychiatry, 156,* 1515–1521.

Division 44 (2000). Guidelines for psychotherapy with lesbian, gay, and bisexual clients. *American Psychologist, 55,* 1440–1451.

Dodds, J. B. (1985). *A child psychotherapy primer: Suggestions for the beginning therapist.* New York: Human Sciences Press.

Dodge, K. A., & Coie, J. D. (1987). Social information-processing factors in reactive and proactive aggression in children's peer groups. *Journal of Personality and Social Psychology, 53,* 389–409.

Dodge, K. A., & Frame, C. L. (1982). Social cognitive biases and deficits in aggressive boys. *Child Development, 53,* 620–635.

Dodge, K. A., Lochman, J. E., Harnish, J. D., Bates, J. E., & Pettit, G. S. (1997). Reactive and proactive aggression in school children and psychiatrically impaired chronically assaultive youth. *Journal of Abnormal Psychology, 106,* 37–51.

Doll, B. (1996). Prevalence of psychiatric disorders in children and youth: An agenda for advocacy by school psychology. *School Psychology Quarterly, 11,* 20–46.

Donenberg, G. R., Emerson, E., Bryant, F. B., Wilson, H., & Weber-Shifrin, E. (2001). Understanding AIDS-risk behavior among adolescents in psychiatric care: Links to psychopathology and peer relationships. *Journal of the American Academy of Child and Adolescent Psychiatry, 40,* 642–653.

Donenberg, G. R., & Weisz, J. R. (1997). Experimental task and speaker effects on parent-child interactions of aggressive and depressed/anxious children. *Journal of Abnormal Child Psychology, 25,* 367–387.

Donnerstein, E., Slaby, R. G., & Eron, L. D. (1994). The mass media and youth aggression. In L. D. Eron, J. H. Gentry, & P. Schlegel (Eds.), *Reason to hope: A psychosocial perspective on violence and youth* (pp. 219–250). Washington, DC: American Psychological Association.

Donohew, R. L., Hoyle, R. H., Clayton, R. R., Skinner, W. F., Colon, S. E., & Rice, R. E. (1999). Sensation seeking and drug use by adolescents and their friends: Models for marijuana and alcohol. *Journal of Studies on Alcohol, 60,* 622–631.

Donohue, B., Hersen, M., & Ammerman, R. T. (1995). Historical overview. In M. Hersen & R. T. Ammerman (Eds.), *Advanced abnormal child psychology* (pp. 3–19). Hillsdale, NJ: Lawrence Erlbaum.

Donohue, B., Hersen, M., & Ammerman, R. T. (2000). Historical overview. In M. Hersen & R. T. Ammerman (Eds.), *Advanced abnormal child psychology* (2nd ed., pp. 3–14). Hillsdale, NJ: Lawrence Erlbaum.

Donovan, C. L., & Spence, S. H. (2000). Prevention of childhood anxiety disorders. *Clinical Psychology Review, 20,* 509–531.

Dornbusch, S. M., Ritter, P. L., Leiderman, P. H., Roberts, D. F., & Fraleigh, M. J. (1987). The relation of parenting style to adolescent school performance. *Child Development, 58,* 1244–1257.

Dorris, M. (1989). *The broken cord.* New York: Harper Perennial.

Dow, S. P., Sonies, B. C., Scheib, D., & Moss, S. E. (1996). Practical guidelines for the assessment and treatment of selective mutism. *Annual Progress in Child Psychiatry and Child Development,* 452–472.

Dowdney, L., (2000). Childhood bereavement following parental death. *Journal of Child Psychology and Psychiatry and Allied Disciplines, 41,* 819–830.

Dowdy, C. A., Patton, J. R., Smith, T. E. C., & Polloway, E. A. (1998). *Attention-deficit/hyperactivity disorder in the classroom.* Austin, TX: Pro-Ed, Inc.

Downey, G., & Coyne, J. C. (1990). Children of depressed parents: An integrative review. *Psychological Bulletin, 108,* 50–76.

Doyle, A., Ostrander, R., Skare, S., Crosby, R. D., & August, G. J. (1997). Convergent and criterion-related validity of the Behavior

Assessment system for Children-Parent Rating Scale. *Journal of Clinical Child Psychology, 26*, 276–284.

Drew, C. J., Hardman, M. L., & Hart, A. W. (1996). *Designing and conducting research: Inquiry in education and social science* (2nd ed.). Boston: Allyn & Bacon.

Drotar, D. (Ed.). (2000). *Handbook of research in pediatric and clinical child psychology: Practical strategies and methods*. New York: Plenum.

Drotar, D., Timmons-Mitchell, J., Williams, L. L., Palermo, T. M., Levi, R., Robinson, J. R., Riekert, K. A., & Walders, N. (2000). Conducting research with children and adolescents in clinical and applied settings: Practical lessons from the field. In D. Drotar (Ed.), *Handbook of research in pediatric and clinical child psychology* (pp. 261–280). New York: Plenum.

Dryfoos, J. G. (1997). The prevalence of problem behaviors: Implications for programs. In R. P. Weissberg, T. P. Gullotta, R. L. Hampton, B. A. Ryan, & G. R. Adams (Eds.), *Healthy children 2010: Enhancing children's wellness* (pp. 17–46). Thousand Oaks, CA: Sage.

Ducharme, J. M., Atkinson, L., & Poulton, L. (2000). Success-based, noncoercive treatment of oppositional behavior in children from violent homes. *Journal of the American Academy of Child and Adolescent Psychiatry, 39*, 995–1004.

Ducommun-Nagy, C. (1999). Contextual therapy. In D. M. Lawson & F. F. Prevatt (Eds.), *Casebook in family therapy* (pp. 1–26). Belmont, CA: Brooks/Cole.

Dudley-Grant, G. R. (2001). Eastern Caribbean family psychology with conduct-disordered adolescents from the Virgin Islands. *American Psychologist, 56*, 47–57.

Dumont, M., & Provost, M. A. (1999). Resilience in adolescents: Protective role of social support, coping strategies, self-esteem, and social activities on experience of stress and depression. *Journal of Youth and Adolescence, 28*, 343–363.

Duncan, D. F. (1996). Growing up under the gun: Children and adolescents coping with violent neighborhoods. *Journal of Primary Prevention, 16*, 343–356.

Duncan, S. C., Strycker, L. A., & Duncan, T. E. (1999). Exploring associations in developmental trends of adolescent substance use and risky sexual behavior in a high-risk population. *Journal of Behavioral Medicine, 22*, 21–34.

Dunn, J., & Hughes, C. (2001). "I got some swords and you're dead!": Violent fantasy, antisocial behavior, friendship, and moral sensibility in young children. *Child Development, 72*, 491–505.

Dunn, J., & Plomin, R. (1990). *Separate lives: Why siblings are so different*. New York: Basic Books.

Dunn, M. E., & Goldman, M. S. (1996). Empirical modeling of an alcohol expectancy memory network in elementary school children as a function of grade. *Experimental and Clinical Psychopharmacology, 4*, 209–217.

Dunn, M. E., & Goldman, M. S. (1998). Age and drinking-related differences in the memory organization of alcohol expectancies in 3rd-, 6th-, 9th-, and 12th-grade children. *Journal of Consulting and Clinical Psychology, 66*, 579–585.

Dunn, M. E., Lau, H. C., & Cruz, I. Y. (2000). Changes in activation of alcohol expectancies in memory in relation to changes in alcohol use after participation in an expectancy challenge program. *Experimental and Clinical Psychopharmacology, 8*, 566–575.

DuPaul, G. J., & Eckert, T. L. (1997). The effects of school-based interventions for attention deficit hyperactivity disorder: A meta-analysis. *School Psychology Review, 26*, 5–27.

DuPaul, G. J., & Eckert, T. L. (1998). Academic interventions for students with Attention Deficit Hyperactivity Disorder: A review of the literature. *Reading and Writing Quarterly: Overcoming Learning Difficulties, 14*, 59–82.

DuPaul, G. J., Eckert, T. L., & McGoey, K. E. (1997). Interventions for students with attention deficit hyperactivity disorder: One size does not fit all. *School Psychology Review, 26*, 369–381.

DuPaul, G. J., McGoey, K. E., Eckert, T. L., & VanBrakle, J. (2001). Preschool children with attention-deficit/hyperactivity disorder: Impairments in behavioral, social, and school functioning. *Journal of the American Academy of Child and Adolescent Psychiatry, 40*, 508–515.

DuPaul, G. J., & Stoner, G. (1994). *ADHD in the schools: Assessment and intervention strategies*. New York: Guilford.

Durand, V. M., & Mapstone, E. (1999). Pervasive developmental disorders. In W. K. Silverman & T. H. Ollendick (Eds.), *Developmental issues in the clinical treatment of children* (pp. 307–317). Boston: Allyn & Bacon.

Durlak, J. A. (1999). Meta-analytic research methods. In P. C. Kendall, J. N. Butcher, & G. N. Holmbeck (Eds.), *Handbook of research methods in clinical psychology* (2nd ed., pp. 419–429). New York: Wiley.

Durlak, J. A. (2000). Health promotion as a strategy in primary prevention. In D. Cicchetti, J. Rappaport, I. Sandler, & R. P. Weissberg (Eds.), *The promotion of wellness in children and adolescents* (pp. 221–241). Washington, D.C.: CWLA Press.

Dusenbury, L., & Falco, M. (1997). School-based drug abuse prevention strategies: From research to policy and practice. In R. P. Weissberg, T. P. Gullotta, R. L. Hampton, B. A. Ryan, & G. R. Adams (Eds.), *Healthy children 2010: Enhancing children's wellness* (pp. 47–75). Thousand Oaks, CA: Sage.

Dykens, E. M., & Hodapp, R. M. (2001). Research in mental retardation: Toward an etiologic approach. *Journal of Child Psychology and Psychiatry and Allied Disciplines, 42*, 49–71.

East, P. L., & Jacobson, L. J. (2001). The younger siblings of teenage mothers: A follow-up of their pregnancy risk. *Developmental Psychology, 37*, 254–264.

Eaves, L. J., Silberg, J. L., Meyer, J. M., Maes, H. H., Simonoff, E., Pickles, A., Rutter, M. Neale, M. C., Reynolds, C. A., Erikson, M. T., Heath, A. C., Loeber, R., Truett, K. R., & Hewitt, J. K. (1997). Genetics and developmental psychopathology: 2. The main effects of genes and environment on behavioral problems in the Virginia twin study of adolescent behavioral development. *Journal of Child Psychology and Psychiatry, 38*, 965–980.

Eddy, J. M., & Chamberlain, P. (2000). Family management and deviant peer association as mediators of the impact of treatment condition on youth antisocial behavior. *Journal of Consulting and Clinical Psychology, 68*, 857–863.

Edelbrock, C. (1989). [Prevalence of externalizing behaviors]. Unpublished data, Department of Psychiatry, University of Massachusetts Medical Center, Worcester. Reported in Loeber, Lahey, & Thomas (1991).

Edelman, M. W. (1999). *Lanterns: A memoir of mentors*. Boston: Beacon Press.

Edwards, G. H., Barkley, R. A., Laneri, M., Fletcher, K., & Metevia, L. (2001). Parent-adolescent conflict in teenagers with ADHD and ODD. *Journal of Abnormal Child Psychology, 29*, 557–572.

Edwards, M. C., & Finney, J. W. (1994). Somatoform disorders: Psychological issues. In R. A. Olson, L. L. Mullins, J. B. Gillman, & J. M. Chaney (Eds.), *The sourcebook of pediatric psychology* (pp. 380–391). Boston: Allyn & Bacon.

Eisenberg, N., Spinrad, T. L., & Cumberland, A. (1998). The socialization of emotion: Reply to commentaries. *Psychological Inquiry, 9*, 317–333.

Eisler, I., Dare, C., Hodes, M., Russell, G., Dodge, E., & LeGrange, D. (2000). Family therapy for adolescent anorexia nervosa: The results of a controlled comparison of two family interventions. *Journal of Child Psychology and Psychiatry and Allied Disciplines, 41*, 727–736.

Elbert, J. C. (1999). Learning and motor skills disorders. In S. D. Netherton, D. Holmes, & C. E. Walker (Eds.), *Child and adolescent psychological disorders: A comprehensive textbook* (pp. 24–50). New York: Oxford University Press.

Elder, C., Leaver-Dunn, D., Wang, M. Q., Nagy, S., & Green, L. (2000). Organized group activity as a protective factor against adolescent substance use. *American Journal of Health Behavior, 24*, 108–113.

Eley, T. C. (1997). Depressive symptoms in children and adolescents: Etiological links between normality and abnormality: A research note. *Journal of Child Psychology and Psychiatry, 38*, 861–865.

Eley, T. C., & Stevenson, J. (1999). Exploring the covariation between anxiety and depression symptoms: A genetic analysis of the effects of age and sex. *Journal of Child Psychology and Psychiatry, 40*, 1273–1282.

Elias, M. J., & Clabby, J. F. (1989). *Social decision making skills: A curriculum guide for the elementary grades*. Rockville, MD: Aspen.

Elias, M. J., & Clabby, J. F. (1991). *School-based enhancement of children and adolescents' social problem solving skills*. San Francisco: Jossey-Bass.

Eliez, S., & Reiss, A. L. (2000). MRI neuroimaging of childhood psychiatric disorders: A selective review. *Journal of Child Psychology and Psychiatry and Allied Disciplines, 41*, 679–694.

Elkin, T. D., Tye, V. L., Hudson, M., & Crom, D. (1998). Participation in sports by long-term survivors of childhood cancer. *Journal of Psychosocial Oncology, 16*, 63–73.

Elliott, S. N., Busse, R. T., & Shapiro, E. S. (1999). Intervention techniques for academic performance problems. In C. R. Reynolds & T. B. Gutkin (Eds.), *The handbook of school psychology* (3rd ed., pp. 664–685). New York: Wiley.

Embry, L. E., VanderStoep, A., Evens, C., Ryan, K. D., & Pollock, A. (2000). Risk factors for homelessness in adolescents released from psychiatric residential treatment. *Journal of the American Academy of Child and Adolescent Psychiatry, 39*, 1293–1299.

Eme, R. (1979). Sex differences in childhood psychopathology: A review. *Psychological Bulletin, 86*, 574–595.

Eme, R. F., & Kavanaugh, L. (1995). Sex differences in conduct disorder. *Journal of Clinical Child Psychology, 24*, 406–426.

Emery, R. E., & Laumann-Billings, L. (1998). An overview of the nature, causes, and consequences of abusive family relationships: Toward differentiating maltreatment and violence. *American Psychologist, 53*, 121–135.

Emery, R. E., Laumann-Billings, L., Waldron, M. C., Sbarra, D. A., & Dillon, P. (2001). Child custody mediation and litigation: Custody, contact, and coparenting 12 years after initial dispute resolution. *Journal of Consulting and Clinical Psychology, 69*, 323–332.

Emshoff, J., Avery, E., Raduka, G., & Anderson, D. J. (1996). Findings from Super Stars: A health promotion program for families to enhance multiple protective factors. *Journal of Adolescent Research, 11*, 68–96.

Emslie, G. J., Rush, A. J., Weinberg, W. A., Gullion, C. M., Rintelmann, J., & Hughes, C. W. (1997). Recurrence of major depressive disorder in hospitalized children and adolescents. *Journal of the American Academy of Child and Adolescent Psychiatry, 36*, 785–792.

Emslie, G. J., Weinberg, W. A., Kennard, B. D., & Kowatch, R. A. (1994). Neurobiological aspects of depression in children and adolescents. In W. M. Reynolds & H. F. Johnston (Eds.), *Handbook of depression in children and adolescents* (pp. 143–165). New York: Plenum.

Engels, R. C. M. E., Knibbe, R. A., DeVries, H., Drop, M. J., & Van-Breukelen, G. J. P. (1999). Influences of parental and best friends' smoking and drinking on adolescent use: A longitudinal study. *Journal of Applied Social Psychology, 29*, 337–361.

Epkins, C. C. (1998). Mother- and father-rated competence, child-perceived competence, and cognitive distortions: Unique relations with children's depressive symptoms. *Journal of Clinical Child Psychology, 27*, 442–451.

Epstein, J. N., March, J. S., Conners, C. K., & Jackson, D. L. (1998). Racial differences on the Conners Teacher Rating Scale. *Journal of Abnormal Child Psychology, 26*, 109–118.

Erlenmeyer-Kimling, L., Marcuse, Y., Cornblatt, B., Friedman, D., Rainer, J. D., & Rutschmann, J. (1984). The New York High-Risk Project. In N. F. Watt, E. J. Anthony, L. C. Wynne, & J. E. Rolf (Eds.), *Children at risk for schizophrenia: A longitudinal perspective* (pp. 169–189). New York: Cambridge University Press.

Evans, B., & Lee, B. K. (1998). Culture and child psychopathology. In S. S. Kazarian & D. R. Evans (Eds.), *Cultural clinical psychology: Theory, research, and practice* (pp. 289–315). New York: Oxford University Press.

Evans, D. W., King, R. A., & Leckman, J. F. (1996). Tic disorders. In E. J. Mash & R. A. Barkley (Eds.), *Child psychopathology* (pp. 436–454). New York: Guilford.

Evans, G. D., & Rey, J. (2001). In the echoes of gunfire: Practicing psychologists' responses to school violence. *Professional Psychology: Research and Practice, 32*, 157–164.

Evans, H. L., & Sullivan, M. A. (1993). Children and the use of self-monitoring, self-evaluation, and self-reinforcement. In A. J. Finch, W. M. Nelson, & E. S. Ott (Eds.), *Cognitive-behavioral procedures with children and adolescents: A practical guide* (pp. 67–89). Boston: Allyn & Bacon.

Exner, J. E., Jr., & Weiner, I. B. (1995). *The Rorschach: A comprehensive system: Vol. 3. Assessment of children and adolescents* (2nd ed.). New York: Wiley.

Eyberg, S. M. (1992). Parent and teacher behavior inventories for the assessment of conduct problem behaviors in children. In L. Vande-Creek, S. Knapp, & T. L. Jackson (Eds.), *Innovations in clinical practice: A source book* (Vol. 11, pp. 261–270). Sarasota, FL: Professional Resource Exchange.

Fantuzzo, J., Grim, S., Mordell, M., McDermott, P., Miller, L., & Coolahan, K. (2001). A multivariate analysis of the Revised Conners' Teacher Rating Scale with low-income, urban preschool children. *Journal of Abnormal Child Psychology, 29*, 141–152.

Faraone, S. V. (2000). Attention deficit hyperactivity disorder in adults: Implications for theories of diagnosis. *Current Directions in Psychological Science, 9*, 33–36.

Faraone, S. V., & Biederman, J. (2000). Nature, nurture, and attention deficit hyperactivity disorder. *Developmental Review, 20*, 568–581.

Faraone, S. V., Biederman, J., Feighner, J. A., & Monuteaux, M. C. (2000). Assessing symptoms of attention deficit hyperactivity disorder in children and adults: Which is more valid? *Journal of Consulting and Clinical Psychology, 68*, 830–842.

Faraone, S. V., Biederman, J., Lehman, B. K., Spencer, T., Norman, D., Seidman, L. J., Kraus, H., Perrin, J., Chen, W. J., & Tsuang, M. T. (1993). Intellectual performance and school failure in children with attention deficit hyperactivity disorder and in their siblings. *Journal of Abnormal Psychology, 102*, 616–623.

Farrell, A. D., Kung, E. M., White, K. S., & Valois, R. F. (2000). The structure of self-reported aggression, drug use, and delinquent behaviors during early adolescence. *Journal of Clinical Child Psychology, 29,* 282–292.

Farrell, A. D., Meyer, A. L., Kung, E. M., & Sullivan, T. N. (2001). Development and evaluation of school-based violence prevention programs. *Journal of Clinical Child Psychology, 30,* 207–220.

Farrell, A. D., Meyer, A. L., & White, K. S. (2001). Evaluation of responding in peaceful and positive ways (RIPP): A school-based prevention program for reducing violence among urban adolescents. *Journal of Clinical Child Psychology, 30,* 451–463.

Farrow, J. A., Watts, D. H., Krohn, M. A., & Olson, H. C. (1999). Pregnant adolescents in chemical dependency treatment: Description and outcomes. *Journal of Substance Abuse Treatment, 16,* 157–161.

Feinberg, M. E., & Hetherington, E. M. (2000). Sibling differentiation in adolescence: Implications for behavioral genetic theory. *Child Development, 71,* 1512–1524.

Feinberg, M. E., Neiderhiser, J. M., Simmens, S., Reiss, D., & Hetherington, E. M. (2000). Sibling comparison of differential parental treatment in adolescence: Gender, self-esteem, and emotionality as mediators of the parenting-adjustment association. *Child Development, 71,* 1611–1628.

Felner, R. D., & Adan, A. M. (1988). The school transitional environment project: An ecological intervention and evaluation. In R. H. Price, E. L. Cowen, R. P. Lorion, & J. Ramos-McKay (Eds.), *14 ounces of prevention: A casebook for practitioners* (pp. 111–122). Washington, D. C.: American Psychological Association.

Felner, R. D., Felner, T. Y., & Silverman, M. M. (2000). Prevention in mental health and social intervention: Conceptual and methodological issues in the evolution of the science and practice of prevention. In J. Rappaport, J. & E. Seidman (Eds.), *Handbook of community psychology* (pp. 9–42). New York: Kluwer Academic/Plenum.

Felner, R. D., Ginter, M., & Primavera, J. (1982). Primary prevention during school transitions: Social support and environmental structure. *American Journal of Community Psychology, 10,* 277–290.

Ferber, R. (1985). *Solve your child's sleep problems.* New York: Simon and Schuster.

Fergusson, D. M., Horwood, L. J., & Lynskey, M. T. (1993). Prevalence and comorbidity of *DSM-III-R* diagnoses in a birth cohort of 15-year-olds. *Journal of the American Academy of Child and Adolescent Psychiatry, 32,* 1127–1134.

Field, T. M. (1984). Early interactions between infants and their postpartum depressed mothers. *Infant Behavior and Development, 7,* 517–522.

Field, T. M. (2000). Infants of depressed mothers. In S. L. Johnson & A. M. Hayes (Eds.), *Stress, coping, and depression* (pp. 3–22). Mahwah, NJ: Lawrence Erlbaum.

Field, T. M., & Liepack, S. (1999). Infancy. In W. K. Silverman & T. H. Ollendick (Eds.), *Developmental issues in the clinical treatment of children* (pp. 77–87). Boston: Allyn & Bacon.

Filipek, P. A. (1999). Neuroimaging in the developmental disorders: The state of the science. *Journal of Child Psychology and Psychiatry, 40,* 113–128.

Finch, A. J., Nelson, W. M., & Moss, J. H. (1993). Childhood aggression: Cognitive-behavioral therapy strategies and interventions. In A. J. Finch, W. M. Nelson, & E. S. Ott (Eds.), *Cognitive-behavioral procedures with children and adolescents: A practical guide* (pp. 148–205). Boston: Allyn & Bacon.

Fink, C. M. (1990). Special education students at risk: A comparative study of delinquency. In P. E. Leone (Ed.), *Understanding troubled and troubling youth* (pp. 61–81). Newbury Park, CA: Sage.

Finkelhor, D. (1988). The trauma of sexual abuse: Two models. In G. E. Wyatt & G. J. Powell (Eds.), *Lasting effects of child sexual abuse* (pp. 61–82). Newbury Park, CA: Sage.

Finkelhor, D., Asdigian, N., & Dziuba-Leatherman, J. (1995). The effectiveness of victimization prevention instruction: An evaluation of children's responses to actual threats and assaults. *Child Abuse and Neglect, 19,* 141–153.

Finney, J. W., & Miller, K. M. (1999). Children of parents with medical illness. In W. K. Silverman & T. H. Ollendick (Eds.), *Developmental issues in the clinical treatment of children* (pp. 433–442). Boston: Allyn & Bacon.

Fisher, C. B., Hatashita-Wong, M., & Greene, L. I. (1999). Ethical and legal issues. In W. K. Silverman & T. H. Ollendick (Eds.), *Developmental issues in the clinical treatment of children* (pp. 470–486). Boston: Allyn & Bacon.

Fisher, J. D., & Fisher, W. A. (1992). Changing AIDS-risk behavior. *Psychological Bulletin, 111,* 455–474.

Fisher, J. D., & Fisher, W. A. (1994). *People like us—Revised* (video). The AIDS Risk Reduction Projects at the University of Connecticut and the University of Western Ontario. Original copyright 1992, Storrs, CT: University of Connecticut.

Fisher, J. D., Fisher, W. A., Misovich, S. J., Kimble, D. L., & Malloy, T. E. (1996). Changing AIDS risk behavior: Effects of an intervention emphasizing AIDS risk reduction information, motivation, and behavioral skills in a college student population. *Health Psychology, 15,* 114–123.

Fisher, P. A., Gunnar, M. R., Chamberlain, P., & Reid, J. B. (2000). Preventive intervention for maltreated preschool children: Impact on children's behavior, neuroendocrine activity, and foster parent functioning. *Journal of the American Academy of Child and Adolescent Psychiatry, 39,* 1356–1364.

Fitzgerald, M. (1999). Criteria for Asperger's disorder. *Journal of the American Academy of Child and Adolescent Psychiatry, 38,* 1071.

Fitzpatrick, K. M. (1997). Fighting among America's youth: A risk and protective factors approach. *Journal of Health and Social Behavior, 38,* 131–148.

Flannery, D. J., Williams, L. L., & Vazsonyi, A. T. (1999). Who are they with and what are they doing? Delinquent behavior, substance use, and early adolescents' after-school time. *American Journal of Orthopsychiatry, 69,* 247–253.

Fleming, J. E., & Offord, D. R. (1990). Epidemiology of childhood depressive disorders: A critical review. *Journal of the American Academy of Child and Adolescent Psychiatry, 29,* 571–580.

Fletcher, A. C., & Jefferies, B. C. (1999). Parental mediators of associations between perceived authoritative parenting and early adolescent substance use. *Journal of Early Adolescence, 19,* 465–487.

Fletcher, K. E. (1996). Childhood posttraumatic stress disorder. In E. J. Mash, & B. A. Barkley (Eds.), *Child psychopathology* (pp. 242–276). New York: Guilford.

Flisher, A. J. (1999). Annotation: Mood disorder in suicidal children and adolescents: Recent developments. *Journal of Child Psychology and Psychiatry, 40,* 315–324.

Flisher, A. J., Kramer, R. A., Grosser, R. C., Alegria, M., Bird, H. R., Bourdon, K. H., Goodman, S. H., Greenwald, S., Horwitz, S. M., Moore, R. E., Narrow, W. E., & Hoven, C. W. (1997). Correlates of unmet need for mental health services by children and adolescents. *Psychological Medicine, 27,* 1145–1154.

Flisher, A. J., Kramer, R. A., Hoven, C. W., Greenwald, S., Alegria, M., Bird, H. R., Canino, G., Connell, R., & Moore, R. E. (1997). Psychosocial characteristics of physically abused children and adolescents. *Journal of the American Academy of Child and Adolescent Psychiatry, 36,* 123–131.

Foa, E. B., Johnson, K. M., Feeny, N. C., & Treadwell, K. R. H. (2001). The child PTSD symptom scale: A preliminary examination of its psychometric properties. *Journal of Clinical Child Psychology, 30,* 376–384.

Foley, D. L., Pickles, A., Simonoff, E., Maes, H. H., Silberg, J. L., Hewitt, J. K. & Eaves, L. J. (2001). Parental concordance and comorbidity for psychiatric disorder and associate risks for current psychiatric symptoms and disorders in a community sample of juvenile twins. *Journal of Child Psychology and Psychiatry and Allied Disciplines, 42,* 381–394.

Fonagy, P. (1998). Psychodynamic theory. In C. E. Walker (Ed.), *Comprehensive clinical psychology* (Vol. 1, pp. 423–447). Oxford, England: Elsevier Science.

Foot, H. C., Morgan, M. J., & Shute, R. H. (1990). *Children helping children.* New York: Wiley.

Forehand, R., Biggar, H., & Kotchick, B. A. (1998). Cumulative risk across family stressors: Short- and long-term effects for adolescents. *Journal of Abnormal Child Psychology, 26,* 119–128.

Fournier, C. J., & Rae, W. A. (1999). Psychoeducational family therapy. In D. M. Lawson & F. F. Prevatt (Eds.), *Casebook in family therapy* (pp. 310–326). Belmont, CA: Wadsworth.

Frame, C. L., Johnstone, B., & Giblin, M. S. (1988). Dysthymia. In M. Hersen & C. G. Last (Eds.), *Child behavior therapy casebook* (pp. 71–83). New York: Plenum.

Frank, N. C., Allison, S. M., & Cant, M. E. C. (1999). Sickle cell disease. In R. T. Brown (Ed.), *Cognitive aspects of chronic illness in children* (pp. 172–189). New York: Guilford.

Frank, S. J., Poorman, M. O., VanEgeren, L. A., & Field, D. T. (1997). Perceived relationships with parents among adolescent inpatients with depressive preoccupations and depressed mood. *Journal of Clinical Child Psychology, 26,* 205–215.

Frauenglass, S., Routh, D. K., Pantin, H. M., & Mason, C. A. (1997). Family support decreases influence of deviant peers on Hispanic adolescents' substance use. *Journal of Clinical Child Psychology, 26,* 15–23.

Freud, A. (1927). Four lectures on child analysis. In *The Writings of Anna Freud* (Vol. 1, pp. 3–69). New York: International Universities Press.

Freud, S. (1894/1962). *Standard edition of the complete psychological works of Sigmund Freud (Vol. 3).* London: Hogarth.

Frick, P. J. (1998a). Conduct disorders. In T. H. Ollendick & M. Hersen (Eds.), *Handbook of child psychopathology* (3rd ed., pp. 213–237). New York: Plenum.

Frick, P. J. (1998b). *Conduct disorders and severe antisocial behavior.* New York: Plenum.

Frick, P. J. (2000). Laboratory and performance-based measures of childhood disorders: Introduction to the special section. *Journal of Clinical Child Psychology, 29,* 475–478.

Frick, P. J., & Ellis, M. (1999). Callous-unemotional traits and subtypes of conduct disorder. *Clinical Child and Family Psychology Review, 2,* 149–168.

Frick, P. J., Lahey, B. B., Christ, M. A. G., Loeber, R., & Green, S. (1991). History of childhood behavior problems in biological relatives of boys with attention-deficit hyperactivity disorder and conduct disorder. *Journal of Clinical Child Psychology, 20,* 445–451.

Frick, P. J., Lahey, B. B., Loeber, R., Tannenbaum, I. E., VanHorn, Y., Christ, M. A. G., Hart, E. L., & Hanson, K. (1993). Oppositional defiant disorder and conduct disorder: A meta-analytic review of factor analyses and cross-validation in a clinic sample. *Clinical Psychology Review, 13,* 319–340.

Frick, P. J., & Loney, B. R. (1999). Outcomes of children and adolescents with oppositional defiant disorder and conduct disorder. In H. C. Quay & A. E. Hogan (Eds.), *Handbook of disruptive behavior disorders* (pp. 507–524). New York: Kluwer Academic/Plenum.

Frick, P. J., & Loney, B. R. (2000). The use of laboratory and performance-based measures in the assessment of children and adolescents with conduct disorders. *Journal of Clinical Child Psychology, 29,* 540–554.

Friedman, A. G., Latham, S. A., & Dahlquist, L. M. (1998). Childhood cancer. In T. H. Ollendick & M. Hersen (Eds.), *Handbook of child psychopathology* (3rd ed., pp. 435–461). New York: Plenum.

Frith, U., & Happe, F. (1998). Why specific developmental disorders are not specific: On-line and developmental effects in autism and dyslexia. *Developmental Science, 1,* 267–272.

Fromm-Reichmann, F. (1948). Notes on the development of treatment of schizophrenics by psychoanalytic psychotherapy. *Psychiatry, 11,* 263–273.

Fuligni, A. J. (1998). The adjustment of children from immigrant families. *Current Directions in Psychological Science, 7,* 99–103.

Fuligni, A. J., Tseng, V., & Lam, M. (1999). Attitudes toward family obligations among American adolescents with Asian, Latin American, and European backgrounds. *Child Development, 70,* 1030–1044.

Gadow, K. D., Nolan, E. E., Litcher, L., Carlson, G. A., Panina, N., Golovakha, E., Sprafkin, J., & Bromet, E. J. (2000). Comparison of attention-deficit/hyperactivity disorder symptoms subtypes in Ukrainian school children. *Journal of the American Academy of Child and Adolescent Psychiatry, 39,* 1520–1527.

Gallucci, N. T. (1997). On the identification of patterns of substance abuse with the MMPI-A. *Psychological Assessment, 9,* 224–232.

Garber, J. (1998). Somatoform disorders in childhood and adolescence. In T. Ollendick (Ed.), *Comprehensive clinical psychology* (Vol. 5, pp. 655–681). Oxford, England: Elsevier Science.

Garber, J., & Kaminski, K. M. (2000). Laboratory and performance-based measures of depression in children and adolescents. *Journal of Clinical Child Psychology, 29,* 509–525.

Garland, A. F., & Zigler, E. (1993). Adolescent suicide prevention: Current research and social policy implications. *American Psychologist, 48,* 169–182.

Garmezy, N. (1974). The study of competence in children at risk for severe psychopathology. In E. J. Anthony & C. Koupernik (Eds.), *The child in his family: Children at psychiatric risk* (pp. 77–97). New York: Wiley.

Garnefski, N. (2000). Age differences in depressive symptoms, antisocial behavior, and negative perceptions of family, school, and peers among adolescents. *Journal of the American Academy of Child and Adolescent Psychiatry, 39,* 1175–1181.

Garner, D. M., & Bemis, K. M. (1982). A cognitive-behavioral approach to anorexia nervosa. *Cognitive Therapy and Research, 6,* 123–150.

Garner, D. M., & Myerholtz, L. E. (1998). Eating disorders. In T. Ollendick (Ed.), *Comprehensive clinical psychology* (Vol. 5, pp. 591–628). Oxford, England: Elsevier Science.

Garralda, M. E., & Rangel, L. A. D. (1999). Somatoform disorders and chronic physical illness. In H. C. Steinhausen & F. C. Verhulst (Eds.), *Risks and outcomes in developmental psychopathology* (pp. 231–249). New York: Oxford University Press.

Garrison, C. Z., Jackson, K. L., Marsteller, F., McKeown, R., & Addy, C. (1990). A longitudinal study of depressive symptomatology in young adolescents. *Journal of the American Academy of Child and Adolescent Psychiatry, 29,* 581–585.

Garrison, C. Z., Waller, J. L., Cuffe, S. P., McKeon, R. E., Addy, C. L., & Jackson, K. L. (1997). Incidence of major depressive disorder and dysthymia in young adolescents. *Journal of the American Academy of Child and Adolescent Psychiatry, 36,* 458–465.

Gaub, M., & Carlson, C. L. (1997a). Behavioral characteristics of *DSM-IV* ADHD subtypes in a school-based population. *Journal of Abnormal Child Psychology, 25,* 103–111.

Gaub, M., & Carlson, C. L. (1997b). Gender differences in ADHD: A meta-analysis and critical review. *Journal of the American Academy of Child and Adolescent Psychiatry, 36*, 1036–1045.

Gaylor, E. E., Goodlin-Jones, B. L., & Anders, T. F. (2001). Classification of young children's sleep problems: A pilot study. *Journal of the American Academy of Child and Adolescent Psychiatry, 40*, 61–67.

Geffken, G. R., Pincus, D. B., & Zelikovsky, N. (1999). Obsessive compulsive disorder in children and adolescents: Review of background, assessment, and treatment. *Journal of Psychological Practice, 5*, 15–31.

Geisinger, K. F. (2000). Psychological testing at the end of the millennium: A brief historical review. *Professional Psychology: Research and Practice, 31*, 117–118.

Geller, B., Cooper, T. B., Sun, K., Zimerman, B., Frazier, J., Williams, M., & Heath, J. (1998). Double-blind and placebo-controlled study of lithium for adolescent bipolar disorders with secondary substance dependency. *Journal of the American Academy of Child and Adolescent Psychiatry, 37*, 171–178.

Geller, B., Cooper, T. B., Zimerman, B., Frazier, J., Williams, M., Heath, J., & Warner, K. (1998). Lithium for prepubertal depressed children with family history predictors of future bipolarity: A double-blind, placebo-controlled study. *Journal of Affective Disorders, 51*, 165–175.

Geller, B., & Luby, J. (1997). Child and adolescent bipolar disorder: A review of the past 10 years. *Journal of the American Academy of Child and Adolescent Psychiatry, 36*, 1168–1176.

Geller, D. A., Hoog, S. L., Heiligenstein, J. H., Ricardi, R. K., Tamura, R., Kluszynski, S., & Jacobson, J. G. (2001). Fluoxetine treatment for obsessive-compulsive disorder in children and adolescents: A placebo-controlled clinical trial. *Journal of the American Academy of Child and Adolescent Psychiatry, 40*, 773–779.

Gencoz, T., Voelz, Z. R., Gencoz, F., Pettit, J. W., & Joiner, T. E. (2001). Specificity of information processing styles to depressive symptoms in youth psychiatric inpatients. *Journal of Abnormal Child Psychology, 29*, 255–262.

Gerber, P. J., & Popp, P. A. (1999). Consumer perspectives on the collaborative teaching model: Views of students with and without LD and their parents. *Remedial and Special Education, 20*, 288–296.

Gerrard, M., Gibbons, F. X., Zhao, L., Russell, D. W., & Reis-Bergan, M. (1999). The effect of peers' alcohol consumption on parental influence: A cognitive mediational model. *Journal of Studies on Alcohol, Supplement 13*, 32–44.

Ghesquiere, P., & Ruijssenaars, A. J. J. M. (1998). Does categorical special education make sense? The Flemish special education system in the international debate. *British Journal of Developmental Disabilities, 44*, 53–63.

Giaconia, R. M., Reinherz, H. Z., Hauf, A. C., Paradis, A. D., Wasserman, M. S., & Langhammer, D. M. (2000). Comorbidity of substance use and post-traumatic stress disorders in a community sample of adolescents. *American Journal of Orthopsychiatry, 70*, 253–262.

Giedd, J. N., Rapoport, J. L., Garvey, M. A., Perlmutter, S., & Swedo, S. E. (2000). MRI assessment of children with obsessive-compulsive disorder or tics associated with streptococcal infection. *American Journal of Psychiatry, 15*, 281–283.

Gillberg, C. (1999). Neurodevelopmental processes and psychological functioning in autism. *Development and Psychopathology, 11*, 567–587.

Gilligan, C. (1993). *In a different voice: Psychological theory and women's development.* Cambridge, MA: Harvard University Press.

Gillon, G., & Dodd, B. (1997). Enhancing the phonological processing skills of children with specific reading disability. *European Journal of Disorders of Communication, 32*, 67–90.

Gilvarry, E. (2000). Substance abuse in young people. *Journal of Child Psychology and Psychiatry, 41*, 55–80.

Ginsburg, G. S., & Silverman, W. K. (2000). Gender role orientation and fearfulness in children with anxiety disorders. *Journal of Anxiety Disorders, 14*, 57–67.

Ginsburg, G. S., La Greca, A. M., & Silverman, W. K. (1998). Social anxiety in children with anxiety disorders: Relation with social and emotional functioning. *Journal of Abnormal Child Psychology, 26*, 175–185.

Gladwell, M. (1998). Do parents matter? *The New Yorker*, August 17, 54–65.

Glaser, D. (2000). Child abuse and neglect and the brain—a review. *Journal of Child Psychology and Psychiatry, 41*, 97–116.

Glaser, K. (1968). Masked depression in children and adolescents. In S. Chess and A. Thomas (Eds.), *Annual progress in child psychiatry and child development* (Vol. 1, pp. 345–355). New York: Brunner/Mazel.

Gliner, J. A., Morgan, G. A., & Harmon, R. J. (2000). Single-subject designs. *Journal of the American Academy of Child and Adolescent Psychiatry, 39*, 1327–1329.

Goetting, A. (1994). The parenting-crime connection. *Journal of Primary Prevention, 14*, 169–186.

Golden, C. J. (1997). The Nebraska Neuropsychological Children's Battery. In C. R. Reynolds & E. Fletcher-Janzen (Eds.), *Handbook of clinical child neuropsychology* (2nd ed., pp. 237–251). New York: Plenum.

Goldman, M. S. (1999). Risk for substance abuse: Memory as a common etiological pathway. *Psychological Science, 10*, 196–198.

Goldsmith, H. H., & Gottesman, I. I. (1996). Heritable variability and variable heritability in developmental psychopathology. In M. F. Lenzenweger & J. J. Haugaard (Eds.), *Frontiers of developmental psychopathology* (pp. 5–43). New York: Oxford University Press.

Goldston, D. B., Daniel, S. S., Reboussin, B. A., Reboussin, D. M., Frazier, P. H., & Harris, A. E. (2001). Cognitive risk factors and suicide attempts among formerly hospitalized adolescents: A prospective naturalistic study. *Journal of the American Academy of Child and Adolescent Psychiatry, 40*, 91–99.

Goodman, S. H., & Gotlib, I. H. (1999). Risk for psychopathology in the children of depressed mothers: A developmental model for understanding mechanisms of transmission. *Psychological Review, 106*, 458–490.

Goodman, S. H., & Gotlib, I. H. (Eds.) (2002). *Children of depressed parents: Mechanisms of risk and implications for treatment.* Washington, D.C.: American Psychological Association.

Goodman, S. H., Hoven, C. W., Narrow, W. E., Cohen, P., Fielding, B., Alegria, M., Leaf, P. J., Kandel, D., Horwitz, S. M., Bravo, M., Moore, R., & Dulcan, M. K. (1998). Measurement of risk for mental disorders and competence in a psychiatric epidemiologic community survey: The National Institute of Mental Health Methods for the Epidemiology of Child and Adolescent Mental Disorders (MECA) study. *Social Psychiatry, 33*, 162–173.

Goodman, S. H., Lahey, B. B., Fielding, B., Dulcan, M., Narrow, W., & Regier, D. (1997). Representativeness of clinical samples of youths with mental disorders: A preliminary population-based study. *Journal of Abnormal Psychology, 106*, 3–14.

Goodman, S. H., Schwab-Stone, M., Lahey, B. B., Shaffer, D., & Jensen, P. S. (2000). Major depression and dysthymia in children and adolescents: Discriminant validity and differential consequences in a community sample. *Journal of the American Academy of Child and Adolescent Psychiatry, 39,* 761–770.

Goodwin, B. J. (1997). Multicultural competence in family practice. In D. T. Marsh & R. D. Magee (Eds.), *Ethical and legal issues in professional practice with families* (pp. 75–93). New York: Wiley.

Goodyer, I. M., Wright, C., & Altham, P. (1990). Recent achievements and adversities in anxious and depressed school age children. *Journal of Child Psychology and Psychiatry and Allied Disciplines, 31,* 1063–1077.

Gore, S., Aseltine, R. H., & Colton, M. E. (1993). Gender, social-relational involvement, and depression. *Journal of Research on Adolescence, 3,* 101–125.

Gore, S. A., VanderWal, J. S., & Thelen, M. H. (2001). Treatment of eating disorders in children and adolescents. In J. K. Thompson, & L. Smolak (Eds.), *Body image, eating disorders, and obesity in youth: Assessment, prevention, and treatment* (pp. 293–311). Washington, DC: American Psychological Association.

Goreczny, A., J., & Hersen, M. (1999). *Handbook of pediatric and adolescent health psychology.* Boston: Allyn & Bacon.

Gorman-Smith, D., Tolan, P. H., Henry, D. B., & Florsheim, P. (2000). Patterns of family functioning and adolescent outcomes among urban African American and Mexican American families. *Journal of Family Psychology, 14,* 436–457.

Gothelf, D., Apter, A., Brand-Gothelf, A., Offer, N., Ofek, H., Tano, S., & Pfeffer, C. R. (1998). Death concepts in suicidal adolescents. *Journal of the American Academy of Child and Adolescent Psychiatry, 37,* 1279–1286.

Gottesman, I. I. (1991). *Schizophrenia genesis: The origins of madness.* New York: Freeman.

Grace, N., Spirito, A., Finch, A. J., & Ott, E. S. (1993). Coping skills for anxiety control in children. In A. J. Finch, W. M. Nelson, & E. S. Ott (Eds.), *Cognitive-behavioral procedures with children and adolescents: A practical guide* (pp. 257–288). Boston: Allyn & Bacon.

Graham, S. (1992). "Most of the subjects were white and middle class": Trends in published research on African Americans in selected APA journals, 1979–1989. *American Psychologist, 47,* 629–639.

Grandin, T. (1995). *Thinking in pictures and other reports from my life with autism.* New York: Random House.

Grant, K. E., & Compas, B. E. (1995). Stress and anxious-depressed symptoms among adolescents: Searching for mechanisms of risk. *Journal of Consulting and Clinical Psychology, 63,* 1015–1021.

Grealy, L. (1994). *Autobiography of a face.* New York: HarperCollins.

Green, A. H. (1991). Child neglect. In R. T. Ammerman & M. Hersen (Eds.), *Case studies in family violence* (pp. 135–152). New York: Plenum.

Green, J., Kroll, L., Imrie, D., Frances, F. M., Begum, K., Harrison, L., & Anson, R. (2001). Health gain and outcome predictors during inpatient and related day treatment in child and adolescent psychiatry. *Journal of the American Academy of Child and Adolescent Psychiatry, 40,* 325–332.

Greenberg, M. T., DeKlyen, M., Speltz, M. L., & Endriga, M. C. (1997). The role of attachment processes in externalizing psychopathology in young children. In L. Atkinson & K. J. Zucker (Eds.), *Attachment and psychopathology* (pp. 196–222). New York: Guilford.

Greenberger, E., Chen, C., Tally, S. R., & Dong, Q. (2000). Family, peer, and individual correlates of depressive symptomatology among U.S. and Chinese adolescents. *Journal of Consulting and Clinical Psychology, 68,* 209–219.

Greene, R. W. (1995). Students with ADHD in school classrooms: Teacher factors related to compatibility, assessment, and intervention. *School Psychology Review, 24,* 81–93.

Greene, R. W. (1996). Students with Attention-Deficit Hyperactivity Disorder and their teachers: Implications of a goodness-of-fit perspective. In T. H. Ollendick & R. J. Prinz (Eds.), *Advances in clinical child psychology (Vol. 18)* (pp. 205–230). New York: Plenum.

Greene, R. W., Biederman, J., Faraone, S. V., Wilens, T. E., Mick, E., & Blier, H. K. (1999). Further validation of social impairment as a predictor of substance use disorders: Findings from a sample of siblings of boys with and without ADHD. *Journal of Clinical Child Psychology, 28,* 349–354.

Greene, R. W., & Doyle, A. E. (1999). Toward a transactional conceptualization of oppositional defiant disorder: Implications for assessment and treatment. *Clinical Child and Family Psychology Review, 2,* 129–148.

Gresham, F. M., Lane, K. L., & Lambros, K. M. (2000). Comorbidity of conduct problems and ADHD: Identification of "fledgling psychopaths." *Journal of Emotional and Behavioral Disorders, 8,* 83–93.

Griffin, K. W., Botvin, G. J., Scheier, L. M., Diaz, T., & Miller, N. L. (2000). Parenting practices as predictors of substance use, delinquency, and aggression among urban minority youth: Moderating effects of family structure and gender. *Psychology of Addictive Behaviors, 14,* 174–184.

Grizenko, N., & Pawliuk, N. (1994). Risk and protective factors for disruptive behavior disorders in children. *American Journal of Orthopsychiatry, 64,* 534–544.

Gross, J., & Rosen, J. C. (1988). Bulimia in adolescents: Prevalence and psychosocial correlates. *International Journal of Eating Disorders, 7,* 51–61.

Group for the Advancement of Psychiatry (1999). Violent behavior in children and youth: Preventive intervention from a psychiatric perspective. *Journal of the American Academy of Child and Adolescent Psychiatry, 38,* 235–241.

Gruwell, E. (1999). *The freedom writers diary.* New York: Random House.

Grych, J. H., Fincham, F. D., Jouriles, E. N., & McDonald, R. (2000). Interparental conflict and child adjustment: Testing the mediational role of appraisals in the cognitive-contextual framework. *Child Development, 71,* 1648–1661.

Grych, J. H., Jouriles, E. N., Swank, P. R., McDonald, R., & Norwood, W. D. (2000). Patterns of adjustment among children of battered women. *Journal of Consulting and Clinical Psychology, 68,* 84–94.

Gunn, W. B., & Fisher, B. L. (1999). Systemic approaches–Family therapy. In *Counseling and psychotherapy with children and adolescents: Theory and practice for school and clinical settings* (3rd ed., pp. 351–375). New York: Wiley.

Gurman, A. S. (2001). Brief therapy and family/couple therapy: An essential redundancy. *Clinical Psychology: Science and Practice, 8,* 51–65.

Guthrie, R. V. (1998). *Even the rat was White: A historical view of psychology* (2nd ed.). Boston: Allyn & Bacon.

Gutierrez, P. M., Osman, A., Kopper, B. A., & Barrios, F. X. (2000). Why young people do not kill themselves: The reasons for living inventory for adolescents. *Journal of Clinical Child Psychology, 29,* 177–187.

Gutierrez, P. M., & Silk, K. R. (1998). Prescription privileges for psychologists: A review of the psychological literature. *Professional Psychology: Research and Practice, 29,* 213–222.

Haas, L. J., Malouf, J. L., & Mayerson, N. H. (1995). Ethical dilemmas in psychological practice: Results of a national survey. In D. N. Bersoff (Ed.), *Ethical conflicts in psychology* (pp. 90–98). Washington, D.C.: American Psychological Association.

Hagan, M. A., & Castagna, N. (2001). The real numbers: Psychological testing in custody evaluations. *Professional Psychology: Research and Practice, 32,* 269–271.

Haggerty, R. J., Sherrod, L. R., Garmezy, N., & Rutter, M. (Eds.) (1994). *Stress, risk, and resilience in children and adolescents: Processes, mechanisms, and interventions.* New York: Cambridge University Press.

Haight, W. L. (1998). "Gathering the spirit" at First Baptist Church: Spirituality as a protective factor in the lives of African American children. *Social Work, 43,* 213–221.

Haley, J. (1976). *Problem-solving therapy.* San Francisco: Jossey-Bass.

Halfon, N., & Newacheck, P. W. (1999). Prevalence and impact of parent-reported disabling mental health conditions among U.S. children. *Journal of the American Academy of Child and Adolescent Psychiatry, 38,* 600–609.

Hall, G. C. N., & Barongan, C. (2002). *Multicultural psychology.* Upper Saddle River, NJ: Prentice Hall.

Hall, G. C. N., & Maramba, G. G. (2001). In search of cultural diversity: Recent literature in cross-cultural and ethnic minority psychology. *Cultural Diversity and Ethnic Minority Psychology, 7,* 12–26.

Hall, G. S. (1904). *Adolescence.* New York: Appleton.

Halliday-Boykins, C. A., & Graham, S. (2001). At both ends of the gun: Testing the relationship between community violence exposure and youth violent behavior. *Journal of Abnormal Child Psychology, 29,* 383–402.

Halpern, E. (2001). Family psychology from an Israeli perspective. *American Psychologist, 56,* 58–64.

Hamarman, S., & Bernet, W. (2000). Evaluating and reporting emotional abuse in children: Parent-based, action-based focus aids in clinical decision-making. *Journal of the American Academy of Child and Adolescent Psychiatry, 39,* 928–930.

Hamby, S. L., & Finkelhor, D. (2000). The victimization of children: Recommendations for assessment and instrument development. *Journal of the American Academy of Child and Adolescent Psychiatry, 39,* 829–840.

Hamill, P. (1994). *A drinking life.* Boston: Little, Brown.

Hamilton, C. E. (2000). Continuity and discontinuity of attachment from infancy through adolescence. *Child Development, 71,* 690–694.

Hamlett, K. W., & Stabler, B. (1995). The developmental progress of pediatric psychology consultation. In M. C. Roberts (Ed.), *Handbook of pediatric psychology* (pp. 39–54). New York: Guilford.

Hamm, J. V. (2000). Do birds of a feather flock together? The variable bases for African American, Asian American, and European American adolescents' selection of similar friends. *Developmental Psychology, 36,* 209–219.

Hammen, C. (1991). *Depression runs in families: The social context of risk and resilience in children of depressed mothers.* New York: Springer-Verlag.

Hammen, C., & Brennan, P. A. (2001). Depressed adolescents of depressed and nondepressed mothers: Tests of an interpersonal impairment hypothesis. *Journal of Consulting and Clinical Psychology, 69,* 284–294.

Hammen, C., & Compas, B. E. (1994). Unmasking unmasked depression in children and adolescents: The problem of comorbidity. *Clinical Psychology Review, 14,* 585–603.

Hammen, C., & Rudolph, K. D. (1996). Childhood depression. In E. J. Mash & R. A. Barkley (Eds.), *Child psychopathology* (pp. 153–195). New York: Guilford.

Hampton, B. R., & Gottlieb, M. C. (1997). Ethical concerns regarding gender in family practice. In D. T. Marsh & R. D. Magee (Eds.), *Ethical and legal issues in professional practice with families* (pp. 50–74). New York: Wiley.

Hampton, R. L., Jenkins, P., & Gullotta, T. P. (1996). *Preventing violence in America.* Thousand Oaks, CA: Sage.

Handen, B. L. (1998). Mental retardation. In E. J. Mash & R. A. Barkley (Eds.), *Treatment of childhood disorders* (2nd ed., pp. 369–415). New York: Guilford.

Haney, P., & Durlak, J. A. (1998). Changing self-esteem in children and adolescents: A meta-analytic review. *Journal of Clinical Child Psychology, 27,* 423–433.

Hankin, B. L., & Abramson, L. Y. (2001). Development of gender differences in depression: An elaborated cognitive vulnerability-transactional stress theory. *Psychological Bulletin, 127,* 773–796.

Hansen, C., Sanders, S. L., Massaro, S., & Last, C. G. (1998). Predictors of severity of absenteeism in children with anxiety-based school refusal. *Journal of Clinical Child Psychology, 27,* 246–254.

Hanson, K. M., Louie, C. E., VanMale, L. M., Pugh, A. O., Karl, C., Muhlenbrook, L., Lilly, R. L., & Hagglund, K. J. (1999). Involving the future: The need to consider the views of psychologists-in-training regarding prescription privileges for psychologists. *Professional Psychology: Research and Practice, 30,* 203–208.

Harbeck-Weber, C., & McKee, D. H. (1995). Prevention of emotional and behavioral distress in children experiencing hospitalization and chronic illness. In M. C. Roberts (Ed.), *Handbook of pediatric psychology* (pp. 167–184). New York: Guilford.

Harrington, R., Fudge, H., Rutter, M., Pickles, A., & Hill, J. (1990). Adult outcomes of childhood and adolescent depression: Psychiatric status. *Archives of General Psychiatry, 47,* 465–473.

Harrington, R., Rutter, M., & Fombonne, E. (1996). Developmental pathways in depression: Multiple meanings, antecedents, and endpoints. *Development and Psychopathology, 8,* 601–616.

Harris, J. R. (1995). Where is the child's environment? A group socialization theory of development. *Psychological Review, 102,* 458–489.

Harris, J. R. (1998a). *The nurture assumption: Why children turn out the way they do.* New York: Free Press.

Harris, J. R. (1998b). The trouble with assumptions. *Psychological Inquiry, 9,* 294–297.

Harrison, W. M., & Stewart, J. W. (1995). Pharmacotherapy of dysthymic disorder. In J. H. Kocsis & D. N. Klein (Eds.), *Diagnosis and treatment of chronic depression* (pp. 124–145). New York: Guilford.

Harrop, C., & Trower, P. (2001). Why does schizophrenia develop at late adolescence? *Clinical Psychology Review, 21,* 241–266.

Hart, D. H., Kehle, T. J., & Davies, M. V. (1983). Effectiveness of sentence completion techniques: A review of the Hart Sentence Completion Test. *School Psychology Review, 12,* 428–434.

Hart, K. J., & Morgan, J. R. (1993). Cognitive-behavioral procedures with children: Historical context and current status. In A. J. Finch, W. M. Nelson, & E. S. Ott (Eds.), *Cognitive-behavioral procedures with children and adolescents: A practical guide* (pp. 1–24). Boston: Allyn & Bacon.

Harter, S. (1985). *Manual for the Self-Perception Profile for Children.* Denver: University of Denver.

Harter, S. (1988). *Manual for the Self-Perception Profile for Adolescents.* Denver: University of Denver.

Hartlage, L. C., & Long, C. J. (1997). Development of neuropsychology as a professional psychological specialty: History, training, and credentialing. In C. R. Reynolds & E. Fletcher-Janzen (Eds.), *Handbook of clinical child neuropsychology* (2nd ed., pp. 3–16). New York: Plenum.

Hartung, C. M., & Widiger, T. A. (1998). Gender differences in the diagnosis of mental disorders: Conclusions and controversies of the *DSM-IV. Psychological Bulletin, 123,* 260–278.

Hartup, W. W. (1999). Constraints on peer socialization: Let me count the ways. *Merrill-Palmer Quarterly, 45,* 172–183.

Harvey, E. A. (2000). Parenting similarity and children with attention-deficit/hyperactivity disorder. *Child and Family Behavior Therapy, 22,* 39–54.

Haugaard, J. J. (2000). The challenge of defining child sexual abuse. *American Psychologist, 55,* 1036–1039.

Hawker, D. S. J., & Boulton, M. J. (2000). Twenty years' research on peer victimization and psychosocial maladjustment: A meta-analytic review of cross-sectional studies. *Journal of Child Psychology and Psychiatry, 41,* 441–455.

Hawkins, J. D. (1997). Academic performance and school success: Sources and consequences. In R. P. Weissberg, T. P. Gullotta, R. L. Hampton, B. A. Ryan, & G. R. Adams (Eds.), *Healthy children 2010: Enhancing children's wellness* (pp. 278–305). Thousand Oaks, CA: Sage.

Hawkins, J. D., Catalano, R. F., & Miller, J. Y. (1992). Risk and protective factors for alcohol and other drug problems in adolescence and early adulthood: Implications for substance abuse prevention. *Psychological Bulletin, 112,* 64–105.

Hawton, K., & Fagg, J. (1992). Deliberate self-poisoning and self-injury in adolescents: A study of characteristics and trends in Oxford, 1976–1989. *British Journal of Psychiatry, 161,* 816–823.

Hayden, T. L. (1983). *Murphy's boy.* New York: Avon Books.

Hayden, T. L. (1991). *Ghost girl.* New York: Avon Books.

Hays-Thomas, R. L. (2000). The silent conversation: Talking about the master's degree. *Professional Psychology: Research and Practice, 31,* 339–345.

Hazelrigg, M. D., Cooper, H. M., & Borduin, C. M. (1987). Evaluating the effectiveness of family therapies: An integrative review and analysis. *Psychological Bulletin, 101,* 428–442.

Hecht, D. B., Inderbitzen, H. M., & Bukowski, A. L. (1998). The relationship between peer status and depressive symptoms in children and adolescents. *Journal of Abnormal Child Psychology, 26,* 153–160.

Hecker, L. L. (1991). Where is Dad?: 21 ways to involve fathers in family therapy. *Journal of Family Psychotherapy, 2,* 31–45.

Hendren, R. L., DeBacker, I., & Pandina, G. J. (2000). Review of neuroimaging studies of child and adolescent psychiatric disorders from the past 10 years. *Journal of the American Academy of Child and Adolescent Psychiatry, 39,* 815–828.

Hendry, C. N. (2000). Childhood disintegrative disorder: Should it be considered a distinct diagnosis? *Clinical Psychology Review, 20,* 77–90.

Henggeler, S. W., & Randall, J. (2000). Conducting randomized treatment studies in real-world settings. In D. Drotar (Ed.), *Handbook of research in pediatric and clinical child psychology* (pp. 447–461). New York: Plenum.

Henggeler, S. W., Schoenwald, S. K., Borduin, C. M., Rowland, M. D., & Cunningham, P. B. (1998). *Multisystemic treatment of antisocial behavior in children and adolescents.* New York: Guilford.

Henning, K., Leitenberg, H., Coffey, P., Bennett, T., & Jankowski, M. K. (1997). Long-term psychological adjustment to witnessing interparental physical conflict during childhood. *Child Abuse and Neglect, 21,* 501–515.

Henry, B., Caspi, A., Moffitt, T. E., Harrington, H. L., & Silva, P. A. (1999). Staying in school protects boys with poor self-regulation in childhood from later crime: A longitudinal study. *International Journal of Behavioral Development, 23,* 1049–1073.

Henry, D. B., Tolan, P. H., & Gorman-Smith, D. (2001). Longitudinal family and peer group effects on violence and nonviolent delinquency. *Journal of Clinical Child Psychology, 30,* 172–186.

Hetherington, E. M. (Ed.). (1999). *Coping with divorce, single parenting, and remarriage: A risk and resiliency perspective.* Hillsdale, NJ: Lawrence Erlbaum.

Hetherington, E. M., Bridges, M., & Insabella, G. M. (1998). What matters? What does not? Five perspectives on the association between marital transitions and children's adjustment. *American Psychologist, 53,* 167–184.

Hetherington, E. M., & Clingempeel, W. G. (1992). Coping with marital transitions. *Monographs of the Society for Research in Child Development, 57,* 2–3 (Serial No. 227).

Hetherington, E. M., & Stanley-Hagan, M. (1999). The adjustment of children with divorced parents: A risk and resiliency perspective. *Journal of Child Psychology and Psychiatry, 40,* 129–140.

Heubeck, B. G. (2000). Cross-cultural generalizability of CBCL syndromes across three continents: From the USA and Holland to Australia. *Journal of Abnormal Child Psychology, 28,* 439–450.

Hewitt, P. L., Newton, J., Flett, G. L., & Callander, L. (1997). Perfectionism and suicide ideation in adolescent psychiatric patients. *Journal of Abnormal Child Psychology, 25,* 95–101.

Hewitt, J. K., Silberg, J. L., Rutter, M., Simonoff, E., Meyer, J. M., Maes, H., Pickles, A., Neale, M. C., Loeber, R., Erickson, M. T., Kendler, K. S., Heath, A. C., Truett, K. R., Reynolds, C. A., & Eaves, L. J. (1997). Genetics and developmental psychopathology: 1. Phenotypic assessment in the Virginia twin study of adolescent behavioral development. *Journal of Child Psychology and Psychiatry, 38,* 943–963.

Hibbs, E. D., & Jensen, P. S. (Eds.). (1996). *Psychosocial treatments for child and adolescent disorders: Empirically based strategies for clinical practice.* Washington, D.C.: American Psychological Association.

Higgins, J., Gore, R., Gutkind, D., Mednick, S. A., Parnas, J., Schulsinger, F., & Cannon, T. D. (1997). Effects of child-rearing by schizophrenic mothers: A 25-year follow-up. *Acta Psychiatrica Scandinavica, 96,* 402–404.

Hinden, B. R., Compas, B. E., Howell, D. C., & Achenbach, T. M. (1997). Covariation of the anxious-depressed syndrome during adolescence: Separating fact from artifact. *Journal of Consulting and Clinical Psychology, 65,* 6–14.

Hinshaw, S. P., & Anderson, C. A. (1996). Conduct and oppositional defiant disorders. In E. J. Mash & R. A. Barkley (Eds.), *Child psychopathology* (pp. 113–149). New York: Guilford.

Hinshaw, S. P., & Park, T. (1999). Research problems and issues: Toward a more definitive science of disruptive behavior disorders. In H. C. Quay & A. E. Hogan (Eds.), *Handbook of disruptive behavior disorders* (pp. 593–620). New York: Kluwer Academic/Plenum.

Hintze, J. M., & Shapiro, E. S. (1999). School. In W. K. Silverman & T. H. Ollendick (Eds.), *Developmental issues in the clinical treatment of children* (pp. 156–170). Boston: Allyn & Bacon.

Hoagwood, K., Kelleher, K. J., Feil, M., & Comer, D. M. (2000). Treatment services for children with ADHD: A national perspective. *Journal of the American Academy of Child and Adolescent Psychiatry, 39,* 198–206.

Hobbs, N. (1975). *The futures of children: Categories, labels, and their consequences.* San Francisco: Jossey-Bass.

Hock, E., Eberly, M., Bartle-Haring, S., Ellwanger, P., & Widaman, K. F. (2001). Separation anxiety in parents of adolescents: Theoretical significance and scale development. *Child Development, 72,* 284–298.

Hock, R. R. (1999). *Forty studies that changed psychology: Explorations into the history of psychological research* (3rd ed.). Upper Saddle River, NJ: Prentice Hall.

Hodapp, R. M. (1997). Developmental approaches to children with disabilities: New perspectives, populations, prospects. In S. S. Luthar, J. A. Burack, D. Cicchetti, & J. R. Weisz (Eds.), *Developmental psychopathology: Perspectives on adjustment, risk, and disorder* (pp. 189–207). New York: Cambridge University Press.

Hodapp, R. M., & Dykens, E. M. (1996). Mental retardation. In E. J. Mash & R. A. Barkley (Eds.), *Child psychopathology* (pp. 362–389). New York: Guilford.

Hodapp, R. M., & Zigler, E. (1995). Past, present, and future issues in the developmental approach to mental retardation and developmental disabilities. In D. Cicchetti & D. J. Cohen (Eds.), *Developmental psychopathology: Vol. 2. Risk, disorder, and adaptation* (pp. 299–331). New York: Wiley.

Hodges, E. V. E., Boivin, M., Vitaro, F., & Bukowski, W. M. (1999). The power of friendship: Protection against an escalating cycle of peer victimization. *Developmental Psychology, 35*, 94–101.

Hodges, K. (1997). *Child Adolescent Schedule (CAS)*. Ypsilanti: Eastern Michigan University.

Hoekstra-Weebers, J. E. H. M., Jasper, J. P. C., Kamps, W. A., & Klip, E. C. (1999). Risk factors for psychological maladjustment of parents of children with cancer. *Journal of the American Academy of Child and Adolescent Psychiatry, 38*, 1526–1535.

Hoff, K. E., & DuPaul, G. J. (1998). Reducing disruptive behavior in general education classrooms: The use of self-management strategies. *School Psychology Review, 27*, 290–303.

Hoffman, A. (1996). Advice from my grandmother. In S. S. Fiffer & S. Fiffer (Eds.), *Family: American writers remember their own* (pp. 3–9). New York: Pantheon.

Hoffman, B. (1972). *Albert Einstein: Creator and rebel*. New York: Viking.

Hoffmann, J. P., Cerbone, F. G., & Su, S. S. (2000). A growth curve analysis of stress and adolescent drug use. *Substance Use and Misuse, 35*, 687–716.

Hofstra, M. B., VanderEnde, J., & Verhulst, F. C. (2000). Continuity and change of psychopathology from childhood into adulthood: A 14–year follow-up study. *Journal of the American Academy of Child and Adolescent Psychiatry, 39*, 850–858.

Hoge, R. D., Andrews, D. A., & Leschied, A. W. (1996). An investigation of risk and protective factors in a sample of youthful offenders. *Journal of Child Psychology and Psychiatry and Allied Disciplines, 37*, 419–424.

Hogue, A., & Liddle, H. A. (1999). Family-based preventive intervention: An approach to preventing substance use and antisocial behavior. *American Journal of Orthopsychiatry, 69*, 278–293.

Holinger, P. C. (1990). The causes, impact, and preventability of childhood injuries in the United States. *American Journal of Diseases of Children, 144*, 670–676.

Holladay, R., & Friends (1994). *What preteens want their parents to know*. New York: McCracken.

Hollon, S. D., & Beck, A. T. (1994). Cognitive and cognitive-behavioral therapies. In A. E. Bergin & S. L. Garfield (Eds.), *Handbook of psychotherapy and behavior change* (4th ed., pp. 428–466). New York: Wiley.

Holmbeck, G. N., & Shapera, W. E. (1999). Research methods with adolescents. In P. C. Kendall, J. N. Butcher, & G. N. Holmbeck (Eds.), *Handbook of research methods in clinical psychology* (2nd ed., pp. 634–661). New York: Wiley.

Holmes, C. B., & Holmes, D. A. (1996). Neuropsychological assessment in special education. In A. F. Rotatori, J. O. Schwenn, & S. Burkhardt (Eds.), *Advances in special education: Assessment and psychopathology issues in special education* (pp. 157–175). Greenwich, CT: JAI Press.

Honora, D. (1999, August). *African American adolescents and the psychosocial process of school identification*. Paper presented at the American Psychological Association, Boston, MA.

Hornbacher, M. (1998). *Wasted: A memoir of anorexia and bulimia*. New York: Harper Perennial.

Howard, M., & Hodes, M. (2000). Psychopathology, adversity, and service utilization of young refugees. *Journal of the American Academy of Child and Adolescent Psychiatry, 39*, 368–377.

Hoza, B., Pelham, W. E., Waschbusch, D. A., Kipp, H., & Owens, J. S. (2001). Academic task persistence of normally achieving ADHD and control boys: Performance, self-evaluations, and attributions. *Journal of Consulting and Clinical Psychology, 69*, 271–283.

Hudson, A. (1998). Applied behavior analysis. In T. Ollendick (Ed.), *Comprehensive clinical psychology* (Vol. 5, pp. 107–130). Oxford, England: Elsevier Science.

Hudson, A., Melita, B., & Arnold, N. (1993). Brief report: A case study assessing the validity of facilitated communication. *Journal of Autism and Developmental Disorders, 23*, 165–173.

Hudziak, J. J., Rudiger, L. P., Neale, M. C., Heath, A. C., & Todd, R. D. (2000). A twin study of inattentive, aggressive, and anxious/depressed behaviors. *Journal of American Academy of Child and Adolescent Psychiatry, 39*, 469–476.

Huey, S. J., Henggeler, S. W., Brondino, M. J., & Pickrel, S. G. (2000). Mechanisms of change in multisystemic therapy: Reducing delinquent behavior through therapist adherence and improved family and peer functioning. *Journal of Consulting and Clinical Psychology, 68*, 451–467.

Hufford, M. R. (2001). Alcohol and suicidal behavior. *Clinical Psychology Review, 21*, 797–811.

Hughes, J. N., Cavell, T. A., & Jackson, T. (1999). Influence of the teacher–student relationship on childhood conduct problems: A prospective study. *Journal of Clinical Child Psychology, 28*, 173–184.

Humphreys, K. (2000). Beyond the mental health clinic: New settings and activities for clinical psychology internships. *Professional Psychology: Research and Practice, 31*, 300–304.

Hunsley, J., & Bailey, J. M. (1999). The clinical utility of the Rorschach: Unfulfilled promises and an uncertain future. *Psychological Assessment, 11*, 266–277.

Hunsley, J., & Bailey, J. M. (2001). Whither the Rorschach? An analysis of the evidence. *Psychological Assessment, 13*, 472–485.

Hunter, W. M., Jain, D., Sadowski, L. S., & Sanhueza, A. I. (2000). Risk factors for severe child discipline practices in rural India. *Journal of Pediatric Psychology, 25*, 435–447.

Huon, G. F., & Walton, C. J. (2000). Initiation of dieting among adolescent females. *International Journal of Eating Disorders, 28*, 226–230.

Hussong, A. M., Curran, P. J., & Chassin, L. (1998). Pathways of risk for accelerated heavy alcohol use among adolescent children of alcoholic parents. *Journal of Abnormal Child Psychology, 26*, 453–466.

Huston, A. C., Donnerstein, E., Fairchild, H., Feshbach, N. D., Katz, P. A., Murray, J. P., Rubinstein, E. A., Wilcox, B. L., & Zuckerman, D. (1992). *Big world, small screen: The role of television in American society*. Lincoln: University of Nebraska Press.

Huston, A. C., & Wright, J. C. (1998). Mass media and children's development. In I. E. Sigel & K. A. Renninger (Eds.), *Handbook of child psychology: Vol. 4. Child psychology in practice* (5th ed., pp. 999–1058). New York: Wiley.

Hutto, S. C. (1994). Pediatric HIV infection and AIDS: Medical issues. In R. A. Olson, L. L. Mullins, J. B. Gillman, & J. M. Chaney (Eds.), *The sourcebook of pediatric psychology* (pp. 218–224). Boston: Allyn & Bacon.

Ialongo, N. S., Kellam, S. G., & Poduska, J. (2000). A developmental epidemiological framework for clinical child and pediatric psychology research. In D. Drotar (Ed.), *Handbook of research in pediatric and clinical child psychology* (pp. 3–19). New York: Plenum.

Ievers, C. E., Brown, R. T., Lambert, R. G., Hsu, L., & Eckman, J. R. (1998). Family functioning and social support in the adaptation of caregivers of children with sickle cell syndromes. *Journal of Pediatric Psychology, 23,* 377–388.

Ilardi, S. S., Rodriguez-Hanley, A., Roberts, M. C., & Seigel, J. (2000). On the origins of clinical psychology faculty: Who is training the trainers? *Clinical Psychology: Science and Practice, 7,* 346–354.

Ingram, R. E., Hayes, A., & Scott, W. (2000). Empirically supported treatments: A critical analysis. In C. R. Snyder, & R. E. Ingram (Eds.), *Handbook of psychological change: Psychotherapy processes and practices for the 21st century* (pp. 40–60). New York: Wiley.

Ingram, R. E., & Ritter, J. (2000). Vulnerability to depression: Cognitive reactivity and parental bonding in high-risk individuals. *Journal of Abnormal Psychology, 109,* 588–596.

Interdisciplinary Council on Developmental and Learning Disorders (2000). *Clinical practice guidelines.* Bethesda, MD: Author.

Isley, S. L., O'Neil, R., Clatfelter, D., & Parke, R. D. (1999). Parent and child expressed affect and children's social competence: Modeling direct and indirect pathways. *Developmental Psychology, 35,* 547–560.

Jackson, H., & Nuttall, R. L. (2001). A relationship between childhood sexual abuse and professional sexual misconduct. *Professional Psychology: Research and Practice, 32,* 200–204.

Jacob, T., & Leonard, K. (1986). Psychosocial functioning in children of alcoholic fathers, depressed fathers and control fathers. *Journal of Studies on Alcohol, 47,* 373–380.

Jacobson, J. W. (1982). Problem behavior and psychiatric impairment within a developmentally disabled population: I. Behavior frequency. *Applied Research in Mental Retardation, 3,* 121–139.

Jacobson, K. C. & Rowe, D.C. (1999). Genetic and environmental influences on the relationships between family connectedness, school connectedness, and adolescent depressed mood: Sex differences. *Developmental Psychology, 35,* 926–939.

Jamison, K. R. (1995). Manic-depressive illness and creativity. *Scientific American, Feb,* 62–67.

Janicke, D. M., & Finney, J. W. (2001). Children's primary health care services: A social-cognitive model of sustained high use. *Clinical Psychology: Science and Practice, 8,* 228–241.

Jason, L. A., Berk, M., Schnopp-Wyatt, D. L., & Talbot, B. (1999). Effects of enforcement of youth access laws on smoking prevalence. *American Journal of Community Psychology, 27,* 143–160.

Jasper, K. (1993). Monitoring and responding to media messages. *Eating Disorders, 1,* 109–114.

Jaycox, L. H., Reivich, K. J., Gillham, J., & Seligman, M. E. P. (1994). Prevention of depressive symptoms in school children. *Behavioral Research and Therapy, 32,* 801–816.

Jensen, P. S. (2001). Clinical equivalence: A step, a misstep, or just a misnomer? *Clinical Psychology: Science and Practice, 8,* 436–440.

Jensen, P. S., Hinshaw, S. P., Kraemer, H. C., Lenora, N., Newcorn, J. H., Abikoff, H. B., March, J. S., Arnold, L. E., Cantwell, D. P., Conners, C. K., Elliott, G. R., Greenhill, L. L., Hechtman, L., Hoza, B., Pelham, W. E., Severe, J. B., Swanson, J. M., Wells, K. C., Wigal, T., & Vitiello, B. (2001). ADHD comorbidity findings from the MTA study: Comparing comorbid subgroups. *Journal of the American Academy of Child and Adolescent Psychiatry, 40,* 147–158.

Jensen, P. S., Martin, D., & Cantwell, D. P. (1997). Comorbidity in ADHD: Implications for research, practice, and *DSM-V. Journal of the American Academy of Child and Adolescent Psychiatry, 36,* 1065–1079.

Jensen, P. S., Mrazek, D., Knapp, P. K., Steinberg, L., Pfeffer, C., Schowalter, J., & Shapiro, T. (1997). Evolution and revolution in child psychiatry: ADHD as a disorder of adaptation. *Journal of the American Academy of Child and Adolescent Psychiatry, 36,* 1672–1679.

Jensen, P. S., Rubio-Stipec, M., Canino, G., Bird, H. R., Dulcan, M. K., Schwab-Stone, M. E., & Lahey, B. B. (1999). Parent and child contributions to diagnosis of mental disorder: Are both informants always necessary? *Journal of the American Academy of Child and Adolescent Psychiatry, 38,* 1569–1579.

Jensen, P. S., & Watanabe, H. (1999). Sherlock Holmes and child psychopathology assessment approaches: The case of the false-positive. *Journal of the American Academy of Child and Adolescent Psychiatry, 38,* 138–146.

Jessor, R., Turbin, M. S., & Costa, F. M. (1998). Protective factors in adolescent health behavior. *Journal of Personality and Social Psychology, 75,* 788–800.

John, O. P., Caspi, A., Robins, R. W., & Moffitt, T. E. (1994). The "little five": Exploring the nomological network of the five-factor model of personality in adolescent boys. *Child Development, 65,* 160–178.

Johnson, D. L. (1988). Primary prevention of behavior problems in young children: The Houston parent–child development center. In R. H. Price, E. L. Cowen, R. P. Lorion, & J. Ramos-McKay (Eds.), *14 ounces of prevention: A casebook for practitioners* (pp. 44–52). Washington, D.C.: American Psychological Association.

Johnson, E. M. (1992). *My life.* New York: Fawcett Crest.

Johnson, J. G., Cohen, P., Dohrenwend, B. P., Link, B. G., & Brook, J. S. (1999). A longitudinal investigation of social causation and social selection processes involved in the association between socioeconomic status and psychiatric disorders. *Journal of Abnormal Psychology, 108,* 490–499.

Johnson, L., & Thomas, V. (1999). Influences on the inclusion of children in family therapy. *Journal of Marital and Family Therapy, 25,* 117–123.

Johnson, P. B., & Johnson, H. L. (1999). Cultural and familial influences that maintain the negative meaning of alcohol. *Journal of Studies on Alcohol, Supplement 13,* 79–83.

Johnson, S. B. (1995). Insulin-dependent diabetes mellitus in childhood. In M. C. Roberts (Ed.), *Handbook of pediatric psychology* (pp. 263–285). New York: Guilford.

Johnson, S. B. (1998). Juvenile diabetes. In T. H. Ollendick & M. Hersen (Eds.), *Handbook of child psychopathology* (3rd ed., pp. 417–434). New York: Plenum.

Johnson, S. L., & Jacob, T. (2000). Moderators of child outcome in families with depressed mothers and fathers. In S. L. Johnson & A. M. Hayes (Eds.), *Stress, coping, and depression* (pp. 51–67). Mahwah, NJ: Lawrence Erlbaum.

Johnson, V., & Pandina, R. J. (2000). Alcohol problems among a community sample: Longitudinal influences of stress, coping, and gender. *Substance Use and Misuse, 35,* 669–686.

Johnson-Powell, G., & Yamamoto, J. (Eds.). (1997). *Transcultural child development: Psychological assessment and treatment.* New York: Wiley.

Johnston, C. & Leung, D. W. (2001). Effects of medication, behavioral, and combined treatments on parents' and children's attributions for the behavior of children with attention-deficit hyperactivity disorder. *Journal of Consulting and Clinical Psychology, 69,* 67–76.

Johnston, C., & Ohan, J. L. (1999). Externalizing disorders. In W. K. Silverman & T. H. Ollendick (Eds.), *Developmental issues in the clinical treatment of children* (pp. 279–294). Boston: Allyn & Bacon.

Johnston, L. D., O'Malley, P. M., & Bachman, J. G. (1995). *National survey results on drug use from Monitoring the Future Study, 1975–1994: Vol. 1. Secondary school students.* Rockville, MD: U.S. Department of Health and Human Services.

Joiner, T. E. (1999). A test of interpersonal theory of depression in youth psychiatric inpatients. *Journal of Abnormal Child Psychology, 27,* 77–85.

Joiner, T. E., Blalock, J. A., & Wagner, K. D. (1999). Preliminary examination of sex differences in depressive symptoms among adolescent psychiatric inpatients: The role of anxious symptoms and generalized negative affect. *Journal of Clinical Child Psychology, 28,* 211–219.

Joiner, T. E., Catanzaro, S. J., & Laurent, J. (1996). Tripartite structure of positive and negative affect, depression, and anxiety in child and adolescent psychiatric inpatients. *Journal of Abnormal Psychology, 105,* 401–409.

Joiner, T. E., & Lonigan, C. J. (2000). Tripartite model of depression and anxiety in youth psychiatric inpatients: Relations with diagnostic status and future symptoms. *Journal of Clinical Child Psychology, 29,* 372–382.

Joiner, T. E., Rudd, M. D., Rouleau, M. R., & Wagner, K. D. (2000). Parameters of suicide crises vary as a function of previous suicide attempts in youth inpatients. *Journal of the American Academy of Child and Adolescent Psychiatry, 39,* 876–880.

Jones, C. (2001, October 19). An agonizing road for kids of Sept. 11. *USA Today,* pp. 1–8.

Jones, M. (1997). Is less better? Boot camp, regular probation and rearrest in North Carolina. *American Journal of Criminal Justice, 21,* 147–161.

Jones, S. E. (2001). Ethics code draft published for comment. *Monitor on Psychology, 32,* 1–3.

Jongsma, A. E., Peterson, L. M., & McInnis, W. P. (1996). *The child and adolescent psychotherapy treatment planner.* New York: Wiley.

Jongsma, A. E., Peterson, L. M., & McInnis, W. P. (2000a). *The adolescent psychotherapy treatment planner.* New York: Wiley.

Jongsma, A. E., Peterson, L. M., & McInnis, W. P. (2000b). *The child psychotherapy treatment planner.* New York: Wiley.

Jordan, K. M. (2000). Substance abuse among gay, lesbian, bisexual, transgender, and questioning adolescents. *School Psychology Review, 29,* 201–206.

Joseph, J. (2000). Not in their genes: A critical view of the genetics of attention-deficit hyperactivity disorder. *Developmental Review, 20,* 539–567.

Jouriles, E. N., McDonald, R., Spiller, L., Norwood, W. D., Swank, P. R., Stephens, N. Ware, H., & Buzy, W. M. (2001). Reducing conduct problems among children of battered women. *Journal of Consulting and Clinical Psychology, 69,* 774–785.

Kadesjoe, B., & Gillberg, C. (2001). The comorbidity of ADHD in the general population of Swedish school-age children. *Journal of Child Psychology and Psychiatry and Allied Disciplines, 42,* 487–492.

Kafantaris, V., Coletti, D. J., Dicker, R., Padula, G., & Pollack, S. (1998). Are childhood psychiatric histories of bipolar adolescents associated with family history, psychosis, and response to lithium treatment? *Journal of Affective Disorders, 51,* 153–164.

Kagan, J., Reznick, J. S., & Snidman, N. (1988). Biological bases of childhood shyness. *Science, 240,* 167–171.

Kagan, J., Snidman, N., Zentner, M., & Peterson, E. (1999). Infant temperament and anxious symptoms in school-age children. *Development and Psychopathology, 11,* 209–224.

Kager, V. A., Arndt, E. K., & Kenny, T. J. (1992). Psychosomatic problems of children. In C. E. Walker & M. C. Roberts (Eds.), *Handbook of clinical child psychology* (2nd ed., pp. 303–317). New York: Wiley.

Kalat, J. W., & Wurm, T. (1999). Implications of recent research in biological psychology for school psychology. In C. R. Reynolds & T. B. Gutkin (Eds.), *The handbook of school psychology* (3rd ed., pp. 271–290). New York: Wiley.

Kalichman, S. C. (1993). *Mandated reporting of suspected child abuse: Ethics, law, and policy.* Washington, D.C.: American Psychological Association.

Kameguchi, K., & Murphy-Shigematsu, S. (2001). Family psychology and family therapy in Japan. *American Psychologist, 56,* 65–70.

Kamphaus, R. W., Huberty, C. J., DiStefano, C., & Petoskey, M. D. (1997). A typology of teacher-rated child behavior for a national U.S. sample. *Journal of Abnormal Child Psychology, 25,* 453–463.

Kamphaus, R. W., Petoskey, M. D., & Rowe, E. W. (2000). Current trends in psychological testing of children. *Professional Psychology: Research and Practice, 31,* 155–164.

Kandel, D. B. (1978). Homophily, selection, and socialization in adolescent friendships. *American Journal of Sociology, 84,* 427–436.

Kandel, D. B., & Davies, M. (1982). Epidemiology of depressive mood in adolescents. *Archives of General Psychiatry, 39,* 1205–1212.

Kandel, D. B., Johnson, J. G., Bird, H. R., Canino, G., Goodman, S. H., Lahey, B. B., Regier, D. A., & Schwab-Stone, M. (1997). Psychiatric disorders associated with substance use among children and adolescents: Findings from the Methods for the Epidemiology of Child and Adolescent Mental Disorders (MECA) Study. *Journal of Abnormal Child Psychology, 25,* 121–132.

Kandel, D. B., Johnson, J. G., Bird, H. R., Weissman, M. M., Goodman, S. H., Lahey, B. B., Regier, D. A., & Schwab-Stone, M. (1999). Psychiatric comorbidity among adolescents with substance use disorders: Findings from the MECA study. *Journal of the American Academy of Child and Adolescent Psychiatry, 38,* 693–699.

Kandel, D. B., Kessler, R. C., & Margulies, R. Z. (1978). Antecedents of adolescent initiation into stages of drug use: A developmental analysis. *Journal of Youth and Adolescence, 7,* 13–40.

Kanner, L. (1943). Autistic disturbances of affective contact. *Nervous Child, 2,* 217–250.

Kaplan, S. J., Pelcovitz, D., Salzinger, S., Weiner, M., Mandel, F. S., Lesser, M. L., & Labruna, V. E. (1998). Adolescent physical abuse: Risk for adolescent psychiatric disorders. *American Journal of Psychiatry, 155,* 954–959.

Kaplow, J. B., Curran, P. J., Angold, A., & Costello, E. J. (2001). The prospective relation between dimensions of anxiety and the initiation of adolescent alcohol use. *Journal of Clinical Child Psychology, 30,* 316–326.

Karen, R. (1994). *Becoming attached.* New York: Warner Books.

Kashani, J. H., Carlson, G. A., Beck, N. C., Hoeper, E. W., Corcoran, C. M., McAllister, J. A., Fallahi, C., Rosenberg, T. K., & Reid, J. C. (1987). Depression, depressive symptoms, and depressed mood among a community sample of adolescents. *American Journal of Psychiatry, 144,* 931–934.

Kashani, J. H., Holcomb, W. R., & Orvaschel, H. (1986). Depression and depressive symptoms in preschool children from the general population. *American Journal of Psychiatry, 143,* 1138–1143.

Kaslow, F. W. (2001). Families and family psychology at the millennium: Intersecting crossroads. *American Psychologist, 56,* 37–46.

Kaslow, N. J., Brown, R. T., & Mee, L. L. (1994). Cognitive and behavioral correlates of childhood depression: A developmental perspective. In W. M. Reynolds & H. F. Johnston (Eds.), *Handbook of depression in children and adolescents* (pp. 97–121). New York: Plenum.

Kaslow, N. J., Croft, S. S., & Hatcher, C. A. (1999). Depression and bipolar disorder in children and adolescents. In S. D. Netherton, D. Holmes, & C. E. Walker (Eds.), *Child and adolescent psychological disorders: A comprehensive textbook* (pp. 264–281). New York: Oxford University Press.

Kaslow, N. J., Deering, C. G., & Racusin, G. R. (1994). Depressed children and their families. *Clinical Psychology Review, 14,* 39–59.

Kaslow, N. J., & Racusin, G. R. (1994). Family therapy for depression in young people. In W. M. Reynolds & H. F. Johnston (Eds.), *Handbook of depression in children and adolescents* (pp. 345–363). New York: Plenum.

Kaslow, N. J., & Thompson, M. P. (1998). Applying the criteria for empirically supported treatments to studies of psychosocial interventions for child and adolescent depression. *Journal of Clinical Child Psychology, 27*, 146–155.

Kaufman, A. S. (1994). *Intelligence testing with the WISC-III*. New York: Wiley.

Kaufman, A. S., & Lichtenberger, E. O. (1998). Intellectual assessment. In C. R. Reynolds (Ed.), *Comprehensive clinical psychology: Assessment* (Vol. 4, pp. 187–238). Oxford, England: Elsevier Science.

Kaufman, J., & Zigler, E. (1987). Do abused children become abusive parents? *American Journal of Orthopsychiatry, 57*, 186–192.

Kaufman, J., & Zigler, E. (1992). The prevention of child maltreatment: Programming, research, and policy. In D. J. Willis, E. W. Holden, & M. Rosenberg (Eds.), *Prevention of child maltreatment: Developmental and ecological perspectives* (pp. 269–295). New York: Wiley.

Kavale, K. A., & Forness, S. R. (1998). Covariance in learning disability and behavior disorder: An examination of classification and placement issues. In T. E. Scruggs & M. A. Mastropieri (Eds.), *Advances in learning and behavioral disabilities* (Vol. 12, pp. 1–42). Greenwich, CT: JAI Press.

Kavale, K. A., & Forness, S. R. (1999). Effectiveness of special education. In C. R. Reynolds & T. B. Gutkin (Eds.), *The handbook of school psychology* (3rd ed., pp. 984–1024). New York: Wiley.

Kaysen, S. (1993). *Girl, interrupted*. New York: Turtle Bay Books.

Kazarian, S. S., & Evans, D. R. (Eds.). (1998). *Cultural clinical psychology: Theory, research, and practice*. New York: Oxford University Press.

Kazdin, A. E. (1989). Developmental psychopathology: Current research, issues, and directions. *American Psychologist, 44*, 180–187.

Kazdin, A. E. (1995). *Conduct disorders in childhood and adolescence* (2nd ed.). Thousand Oaks, CA: Sage.

Kazdin, A. E. (1996). Developing effective treatments for children and adolescents. In E. D. Hibbs & P. S. Jensen (Eds.), *Psychosocial treatments for child and adolescent disorders: Empirically based strategies for clinical practice* (pp. 9–18). Washington, DC: American Psychological Association.

Kazdin, A. E. (1997). Conduct disorder across the life-span. In S. S. Luthar, J. A. Burack, D. Cicchetti, & J. R. Weisz (Eds.), *Developmental psychopathology: Perspectives on adjustment, risk, and disorder* (pp. 248–272). New York: Cambridge University Press.

Kazdin, A. E. (2001). Almost clinically significant ($p < .01$): Current measures may only approach clinical significance. *Clinical Psychology: Science and Practice, 8*, 455–462.

Kazdin, A. E., & Marciano, P. L. (1998). Childhood and adolescent depression. In E. J. Mash & R. A. Barkley (Eds.), *Treatment of childhood disorders* (2nd ed., pp. 211–248). New York: Guilford.

Kazdin, A. E., & Wassell, G. (1999). Barriers to treatment participation and therapeutic change among children referred for conduct disorder. *Journal of Clinical Child Psychology, 28*, 160–172.

Kazdin, A. E., & Wassell, G. (2000). Therapeutic changes in children, parents, and families resulting from treatment of children with conduct problems. *Journal of the American Academy of Child and Adolescent Psychiatry, 39*, 414–420.

Kazdin, A. E., & Weisz, J. R. (1998). Identifying and developing empirically supported child and adolescent treatments. *Journal of Consulting and Clinical Psychology, 66*, 19–36.

Kearney, C. A., & Hugelshofer, D. S. (2000). Systemic and clinical strategies for preventing school refusal behavior in youth. *Journal of Cognitive Psychotherapy, 14*, 51–65.

Kearney, C. A., & Silverman, W. K. (1998). A critical review of pharmacotherapy for youth with anxiety disorders: Things are not as they seem. *Journal of Anxiety Disorders, 12*, 83–102.

Kearney, C. A., & Wadiak, D. (1999). Anxiety disorders. In S. D. Netherton, D. Holmes, & C. E. Walker (Eds.), *Child and adolescent psychological disorders: A comprehensive textbook* (pp. 282–303). New York: Oxford University Press.

Keating, K. A. (1998). Sexual abuse of persons with disabilities. *Advances in Special Education, 11*, 279–289.

Keenan, K., Loeber, R., & Green, S. (1999). Conduct disorder in girls: A review of the literature. *Clinical Child and Family Psychology Review, 2*, 3–19.

Keenan, K., & Wakschlag, L. S. (2000). More than the terrible twos: The nature and severity of behavior problems in clinic-referred preschool children. *Journal of Abnormal Child Psychology, 28*, 33–46.

Keiley, M. K., Bates, J. E., Dodge, K. A., & Pettit, G. S. (2000). A cross-domain growth analysis: Externalizing and internalizing behaviors during 8 years of childhood. *Journal of Abnormal Child Psychology, 28*, 161–179.

Kell, R. S., Kliewer, W., Erickson, M. T., & Ohene-Frempong, K. (1998). Psychological adjustment of adolescents with sickle cell disease: Relations with demographic, medical, and family competence variables. *Journal of Pediatric Psychology, 23*, 301–312.

Kellerman, J. (1993). *Devil's waltz*. New York: Bantam.

Kellogg, N. D., Hoffman, T. J., & Taylor, E. R. (1999). Early sexual experiences among pregnant and parenting adolescents. *Adolescence, 34*, 293–303.

Kelly, J. B. (2000). Children's adjustment in conflicted marriage and divorce: A decade review of research. *Journal of the American Academy of Child and Adolescent Psychiatry, 39*, 963–973.

Keltner, D., Caps, L., Kring, A. M., Young, R. C., & Heerey, E. A. (2001). Just teasing: A conceptual analysis and empirical review. *Psychological Bulletin, 127*, 229–248.

Kelvin, R. G., Goodyer, I. M., & Altham, P. M. E. (1996). Temperament and psychopathology amongst siblings of probands with depressive and anxiety disorders. *Journal of Child Psychology and Psychiatry and Allied Disciplines, 37*, 543–550.

Kemenoff, S., Jachimczyk, J., & Fussner, A. (1998). Structural family therapy. In D. M. Lawson & F. F. Prevatt (Eds.), *Casebook in family therapy* (pp. 111–145). Belmont, CA: Brooks/Cole.

Kendall, P. C., Brady, E. U., & Verduin, T. L. (2001). Comorbidity in childhood anxiety disorders and treatment outcome. *Journal of the American Academy of Child and Adolescent Psychiatry, 40*, 787–794.

Kendall, P. C., & Braswell, L. (1993). *Cognitive-behavioral therapy for impulsive children* (2nd ed.). New York: Guilford.

Kendall, P. C., Chansky, T. E., Kane, M. T., Kim, R. S., Kortlander, E., Ronan, K. R., Sessa, F. M., & Siqueland, L. (1992). *Anxiety disorders in youth: Cognitive-behavioral interventions*. Needham Heights, MA: Allyn & Bacon.

Kendall, P. C., Flannery-Schroeder, E. C., & Ford, J. D. (1999). Therapy outcome research methods. In P. C. Kendall, J. N. Butcher, & G. N. Holmbeck (Eds.), *Handbook of research methods in clinical psychology* (2nd ed., pp. 330–363). New York: Wiley.

Kendall, P. C., Marrs, A. L., & Chu, B. C. (1998). Cognitive-behavioral therapy. In T. Ollendick (Ed.), *Comprehensive clinical psychology* (Vol. 5, pp. 131–148). Oxford, England: Elsevier Science.

Kendall, P. C., & Treadwell, K. R. H. (1996). Cognitive-behavioral treatment for childhood anxiety disorders. In E. D. Hibbs & P. S. Jensen

(Eds.), *Psychosocial treatments for child and adolescent disorders: Empirically based strategies for clinical practice* (pp. 23–41). Washington, DC: American Psychological Association.

Kerig, P. K. (1998). Moderators and mediators of the effects of interparental conflict on children's adjustment. *Journal of Abnormal Child Psychology, 26*, 199–212.

Kerns, K. A., Aspelmeier, J. E., Gentzler, A. L., & Grabill, C. M. (2001). Parent–child attachment and monitoring in middle childhood. *Journal of Family Psychology, 15*, 69–81.

Kerr, M. M., & Milliones, J. (1995). Suicide and suicidal behavior. In V. B. VanHasselt & M. Hersen (Eds.), *Handbook of adolescent psychopathology: A guide to diagnosis and treatment* (pp. 653–664). New York: Lexington Books.

Kiesler, C. A. (2000). The next wave of change for psychology and mental health services in the health care revolution. *American Psychologist, 55*, 481–487.

Kilgore, K., Snyder, J., & Lentz, C. (2000). The contribution of parental discipline, parental monitoring, and school risk to early-onset conduct problems in African American boys and girls. *Developmental Psychology, 36*, 835–845.

Kilpatrick, D. G., Acierno, R., Saunders, B., Resnick, H. S., Best, C. L., & Schnurr, P. P. (2000). Risk factors for adolescent substance abuse and dependence: Data from a national sample. *Journal of Consulting and Clinical Psychology, 68*, 19–30.

Kim, S. Y., & Ge, X. (2000). Parenting practices and adolescent depressive symptoms in Chinese American families. *Journal of Family Psychology, 14*, 420–435.

Kim, W. J., Kim, L. I., & Rue, D. S. (1997). Korean American Children. In G. Johnson-Powell & J. Yamamoto (Eds.), *Transcultural child development: Psychological assessment and treatment* (pp. 183–207). New York: Wiley.

King, C. A., Katz, S. H., Ghaziuddin, N., Brand, E., Hill, E., & McGovern, L. (1997). Diagnosis and assessment of depression and suicidality using the NIMH Diagnostic Interview Schedule for children (DISC-2.3). *Journal of Abnormal Child Psychology, 25*, 173–181.

King, C. A., Raskin, A., Gdowski, C. L., Butkus, M., & Opipari, L. (1990). Psychological factors associated with urban adolescent female suicide attempts. *Journal of the American Academy of Child and Adolescent Psychiatry, 29*, 221–235.

King, G., King, S., Rosenbaum, P., & Goffin, R. (1999). Family-centered caregiving and well-being of parents of children with disabilities: Linking process with outcome. *Journal of Pediatric Psychology, 24*, 41–53.

King, N. J., & Bernstein, G. A. (2001). School refusal in children and adolescents: A review of the past 10 years. *Journal of the Academy of Child and Adolescent Psychiatry, 40*, 197–205.

King, N. J., Tonge, B. J., Mullen, P., Myerson, N., Heyne, D., Rollings, S., Martin, R., & Ollendick, T. H. (2000). Treating sexually abused children with posttraumatic stress symptoms: A randomized clinical trial. *Journal of the American Academy of Child and Adolescent Psychiatry, 39*, 1347–1355.

King, R. A., Schwab-Stone, M., Flisher, A. J., Greenwald, S., Kramer, R. A., Goodman, S. H., Lahey, B. B., Shaffer, D., & Gould, M. S. (2001). Psychosocial and risk behavior correlates of youth suicide attempts and suicidal ideation. *Journal of the American Academy of Child and Adolescent Psychiatry, 40*, 837–846.

Kinsman, A. M., Wildman, B. G., & Smucker, W. D. (1999). Brief report: Parent report about health care use: Relationship to child's and parent's psychosocial problems. *Journal of Pediatric Psychology, 24*, 435–439.

Kirkland, K., & Kirkland, K. L. (2001). Frequency of child custody evaluation complaints and related disciplinary action: A survey of the

Association of State and Provincial Psychology Boards. *Professional Psychology: Research and Practice, 32*, 171–174.

Kirmayer, L. J., Boothroyd, L. J., & Hodgins, S. (1998). Attempted suicide among Inuit youth: Psychosocial correlates and implications for prevention. *Canadian Journal of Psychiatry, 43*, 816–822.

Kistner, J., Balthazor, M., Risi, S., & Burton, C. (1999). Predicting dysphoria in adolescence from actual and perceived peer acceptance in childhood. *Journal of Clinical Child Psychology, 28*, 94–104.

Klar, H., & Berg, I. K. (1999). Solution-focused brief therapy. In D. M. Lawson & F. F. Prevatt (Eds.), *Casebook in family therapy* (pp. 232–258). Belmont, CA: Brooks/Cole.

Klein, D. N., Depue, R. A., & Slater, J. F. (1985). Cyclothymia in the adolescent offspring of parents with bipolar disorder. *Journal of Abnormal Psychology, 94*, 115–127.

Klein, K., Forehand, R., & Family Health Project Research Group. (2000). Family processes as resources for African American children exposed to a constellation of sociodemographic risk factors. *Journal of Clinical Child Psychology, 29*, 53–65.

Klein, M. (1927). Symposium on child analysis. *International Journal of Psychoanalysis, 8*, 339–370.

Klein, M. (1957). *Envy and gratitude*. New York: Basic Books.

Kliewer, W., Murrelle, L., Mejia, R., Torres de G., Y., & Angold, A. (2001). Exposure to violence against a family member and internalizing symptoms in Colombian adolescents: The protective effects of family support. *Journal of Consulting and Clinical Psychology, 69*, 971–982.

Klin, A., & Volkmar, F. R. (1997). The pervasive developmental disorders: Nosology and profiles of development. In S. S. Luthar, J. A. Burack, D. Cicchetti, & J. R. Weisz (Eds.), *Developmental psychopathology: Perspectives on adjustment, risk, and disorder* (pp. 208–226). New York: Cambridge University Press.

Klorman, R. (1995). Psychophysiological determinants. In M. Hersen & R. T. Ammerman (Eds.), *Advanced abnormal child psychology* (pp. 59–85). Hillsdale, NJ: Lawrence Erlbaum.

Klorman, R., Hazel-Fernandez, L. A., Shaywitz, S. E., Fletcher, J. M., Marchione, K. E., Holahan, J. M., Stuebing, K. K., & Shaywitz, B. A. (1999). Executive functioning deficits in attention-deficit/hyperactivity disorder are independent of oppositional defiant or reading disorder. *Journal of the American Academy of Child and Adolescent Psychiatry, 38*, 1148–1155.

Klump, K. L., McGue, M., & Iacono, W. G. (2000). Age differences in genetic and environmental influences on eating attitudes and behaviors in preadolescent and adolescent female twins. *Journal of Abnormal Psychology, 109*, 239–251.

Klusman, L. E. (2001). Prescribing psychologists and patients' medical needs: Lessons from clinical psychiatry. *Professional Psychology: Research and Practice, 32*, 496–500.

Knapp, C. (1996). *Drinking: A love story*. New York: Delta/Dell.

Knapp, P. (2001). Ethics of ECT for children: Reply. *Journal of the Academy of Child and Adolescent Psychiatry, 40*, 387–388.

Knapp, S., & VandeCreek, L. (1990). Application of the duty to protect HIV-positive patients. *Professional Psychology: Research and Practice, 21*, 161–166.

Knell, S. M. (1998). Cognitive-behavioral play therapy. *Journal of Clinical Child Psychology, 27*, 28–33.

Knitzer, J. (2000). Helping troubled children and families: A paradigm of public responsibility. In J. Rappaport & E. Seidman (Eds.), *Handbook of community psychology* (pp. 541–563). New York: Kluwer Academic/Plenum.

Kokko, K., & Pulkkinen, L. (2000). Aggression in childhood and long-term unemployment in adulthood: A cycle of maladaptation and some protective factors. *Developmental Psychology, 36*, 463–472.

Kolbo, J. R. (1996). Risk and resilience among children exposed to family violence. *Violence and Victims, 11,* 113–128.

Kolko, D. J. (1988). Educational programs to promote awareness and prevention of child sexual victimization: A review and methodological critique. *Clinical Psychology Review, 8,* 195–209.

Kolko, D. J., & Ammerman, R. T. (1988). Firesetting. In M. Hersen & C. G. Last (Eds.), *Child behavior therapy casebook* (pp. 243–262). New York: Plenum.

Kolko, D. J., Brent, D. A., Baugher, M., Bridge, J., & Birmaher, B. (2000). Cognitive and family therapies for adolescent depression: Treatment specificity, mediation, and moderation. *Journal of Consulting and Clinical Psychology, 68,* 603–614.

Kolko, D. J., & Stauffer, J. (1991). Child sexual abuse. In R. T. Ammerman & M. Hersen (Eds.), *Case studies in family violence* (pp. 153–170). New York: Plenum.

Koocher, G. P., & Keith-Spiegel, P. (1990). *Children, ethics, and the law: Professional issues and cases.* Lincoln: University of Nebraska Press.

Koocher, G. P., & Keith-Spiegel, P. (1998). *Ethics in psychology: Professional standards and cases* (2nd ed.). New York: Oxford University Press.

Koppitz, E. M. (1968). *Psychological evaluation of children's human figure drawings.* New York: Grune & Stratton.

Koppitz, E. M. (1984). *Psychological evaluation of human figure drawings by middle school pupils.* New York: Grune & Stratton.

Korbin, J. E., Coulton, C. J., Chard, S., Platt-Houston, C., Su, M. (1998). Impoverishment and child maltreatment in African American and European American neighborhoods. *Development and Psychopathology, 10,* 215–233.

Korchin, S. J. (1976). *Modern clinical psychology.* New York: Basic Books.

Koretz, D. S., & Lazar, J. B. (1992). New directions in research in the prevention of conduct disorder. In G. W. Albee, L. A. Bond, & T. V. C. Monsey (Eds.), *Improving children's lives* (pp. 296–307). Newbury Park, CA: Sage.

Kornberg, J. R., Brown, J. L., Sadovnick, A. D., Remick, R. A., Keck, P. E., McElroy, S. L., Rapaport, M. H., Thompson, P. M., Kaul, J. B., Vrabel, C. M., Schommer, S. C., Wilson, T., Pizzuco, D., Jameson, S., Schibuk, L., & Kelsoe, J. R. (2000). Evaluating the parent-of-origin effect in bipolar affective disorder. Is a more penetrant subtype transmitted paternally? *Journal of Affective Disorders, 59,* 183–192.

Kovacs, M. (1985). Children's Depression Inventory (CDI). *Psychopharmacology Bulletin, 21,* 995–998.

Kovacs, M. (1989). Affective disorder in children and adolescents. *American Psychologist, 44,* 209–215.

Kovacs, M. (1990). Comorbid anxiety disorders in childhood-onset depressions. In J. D. Maser & C. R. Cloninger (Eds.), *Comorbidity of mood and anxiety disorders* (pp. 272–281). Washington, D. C.: American Psychiatric Press.

Kovacs, M. (1992). *Children's Depression Inventory Manual.* North Tonawanda, NY: Multi-Health Systems, Inc.

Kovacs, M. (1996). Presentation and course of major depressive disorder during childhood and later years of the life span. *Journal of the American Academy of Child and Adolescent Psychiatry, 35,* 705–715.

Kovacs, M. (1997). Chronic depression in childhood. In H. S. Akiskal & G. B. Cassano (Eds.), *Dysthymia and the spectrum of chronic depressions* (pp. 208–219). New York: Guilford.

Kovacs, M., Akiskal, H. S., Gatsonis, C., & Parrone, P. L. (1994). Childhood-onset dysthymic disorder: Clinical features and prospective naturalistic outcome. *Archives of General Psychiatry, 51,* 365–374.

Kovacs, M., Feinberg, T. L., Crouse-Novak, M., Paulauskas, S. L., & Finkelstein, R. (1984). Depressive disorders in childhood: I. A longitudinal prospective study of characteristics and recovery. *Archives of General Psychiatry, 41,* 229–237.

Kovacs, M., Obrosky, S., Gatsonis, C., & Richards, C. (1997). First-episode major depressive and dysthymic disorder in childhood: Clinical and sociodemographic factors in recovery. *Journal of the American Academy of Child and Adolescent Psychiatry, 36,* 777–784.

Kozol, J. (1988). *Rachel and her children: Homeless families in America.* New York: Fawcett Columbine.

Krahn, G. L., & Eisert, D. (2000). Qualitative methods in clinical psychology. In D. Drotar (Ed.), *Handbook of research in pediatric and clinical child psychology* (pp. 145–164). New York: Plenum.

Krain, A. L., & Kendall, P. C. (2000). The role of parental emotional distress in parent report of child anxiety. *Journal of Clinical Child Psychology, 29,* 328–335.

Kramer, J. R., Loney, J., Ponto, L. B., Roberts, M. A., & Grossman, S. (2000). Predictors of adult height and weight in boys treated with methylphenidate for childhood behavior problems. *Journal of the American Academy of Child and Adolescent Psychiatry, 39,* 517–524.

Kranzler, J. H. (1999). Current contributions of the psychology of individual differences to school psychology. In C. R. Reynolds & T. B. Gutkin (Eds.), *The handbook of school psychology* (3rd ed., pp. 223–246). New York: Wiley.

Kratochwill, T. R., Sheridan, S. M., Carlson, J., & Lasecki, K. L. (1999). Advances in behavioral assessment. In C. R. Reynolds & T. B. Gutkin (Eds.), *The handbook of school psychology* (3rd ed., pp. 350–382). New York: Wiley.

Kratzer, L., & Hodgins, S. (1997). Adult outcomes of child conduct problems: A cohort study. *Journal of Abnormal Child Psychology, 25,* 65–81.

Kuncel, N. R., Hezlett, S. A., & Ones, D. S. (2001). A comprehensive meta-analysis of the predictive validity of the Graduate Record Examinations: Implications for graduate student selection and performance. *Psychological Bulletin, 127,* 162–181.

Kunkel, D., Wilson, B., Donnerstein, E., Linz, D., Smith, S., Gray, T., Blumenthal, E., & Potter, W. J. (1995). Measuring television violence: The importance of context. *Journal of Broadcasting and Electronic Media, 39,* 284–291.

Kunkel, D., Wilson, B. J., Linz, D., Potter, J., Donnerstein, E., Smith, S. L., Blumenthal, E., & Gray, T. (1996). *The national television violence study.* Studio City, CA: Mediascope.

Kurtz-Costes, B. E., Meece, J. L., & Floryan, J. A. (1999, August). *Children's out-of-school activities and academic achievement: A longitudinal study.* Poster presented at the American Psychological Association, Boston, MA.

Kury, S. P., Rodrigue, J. R., & Perri, M. G. (1998). Smokeless tobacco and cigarettes: Differential attitudes and behavioral intentions of young adolescents toward a hypothetical new peer. *Journal of Clinical Child Psychology, 27,* 415–422.

Kutash, K., & Rivera, V. R. (1996). *What works in children's mental health services?* Baltimore: Paul H. Brookes.

Kutcher, S., Robertson, H. A., & Bird, D. (1998). Premorbid functioning in adolescent onset bipolar I disorder: A preliminary report from an ongoing study. *Journal of Affective Disorders, 51,* 137–144.

Kutchins, H., & Kirk, S. A. (1997). *Making us crazy: DSM: The psychiatric bible and the creation of mental disorders.* New York: Free Press.

L'Abate, L. (Ed.). (1994). *Handbook of developmental family psychology and psychopathology.* New York: Wiley.

L'Abate, L. (Ed.). (1998). *Family psychopathology: The relational roots of dysfunctional behavior*. New York: Guilford.

Lachar, D., & Gruber, C. P. (2001). *Personality Inventory for Children—Second Edition (PIC-2)*. Los Angeles: Western Psychological Services.

Ladd, G. W., & Burgess, K. B. (1999). Charting the relationship trajectories of aggressive, withdrawn, and aggressive/withdrawn children during early grade school. *Child Development, 70*, 910–929.

La Greca, A. M. (1990). *Through the eyes of the child: Obtaining self-reports from children and adolescents*. Boston: Allyn & Bacon.

La Greca, A. M. (1997). Reflections and perspectives on pediatric psychology: Editor's vale dictum. *Journal of Pediatric Psychology, 22*, 759–770.

La Greca, A. M., & Schuman, W. B. (1999). Research methods in pediatric psychology. In P. C. Kendall, J. N. Butcher, & G. N. Holmbeck (Eds.), *Handbook of research methods in clinical psychology* (2nd ed., pp. 537–561). New York: Wiley.

La Greca, A. M., & Stone, W. L. (1993). The Social Anxiety Scale for Children-Revised. Factor structure and concurrent validity. *Journal of Clinical Child Psychology, 22*, 17–27.

Lahey, B. B., Flagg, E. W., Bird, H. R., Schwab-Stone, M. E., Canino, G., Dulcan, M. K., Leaf, P. J., Davies, M., Brogan, D., Bourdon, K., Horwitz, S. M., Rubio-Stipec, M., Freeman, D. H., Lichtman, J. H., Shaffer, D., Goodman, S. H., Narrow, W. E., Weissman, M. M., Kandel, D. B., Jensen, P. S., Richters, J. E., & Regier, D. A. (1996). The NIMH Methods for the Epidemiology of Child and Adolescent Mental Disorders (MECA) Study: Background and methodology. *Journal of the American Academy of Child and Adolescent Psychiatry, 35*, 855–864.

Lahey, B. B. Miller, T. L., Gordon, R. A., & Riley, A. W. (1999). Developmental epidemiology of the disruptive behavior disorders. In H. C. Quay & A. E. Hogan (Eds.), *Handbook of disruptive behavior disorders* (pp. 23–48). New York: Kluwer Academic/Plenum.

Lahey, B. B., Schwab-Stone, M., Goodman, S. H., Waldman, I. D., Canino, G., Rathouz, P. J., Miller, T. L., Dennis, K. D., Bird, H., & Jensen, P. S. (2000). Age and gender differences in oppositional behavior and conduct problems: A cross-sectional household study of middle childhood and adolescence. *Journal of Abnormal Psychology, 109*, 488–503.

Lahey, B. B., Waldman, I. D., & McBurnett, K. (1999). The development of antisocial behavior: An integrative causal model. *Journal of Child Psychology and Psychiatry, 40*, 669–682.

Laing, R. D., & Esterson, A. (1965). *Sanity, madness and the family*. London: Tavistock.

Lande, R. G. (1993). The video violence debate. *Hospital and Community Psychiatry, 44*, 347–351.

Latimer, W. W., Newcomb, M., Winters, K. C., & Stinchfield, R. D. (2000). Adolescent substance abuse treatment outcome: The role of substance abuse problem severity, psychosocial, and treatment factors. *Journal of Consulting and Clinical Psychology, 68*, 684–696.

Latimer, W. W., Winters, K. C., Stinchfield, R., & Traver, R. E. (2000). Demographic, individual, and interpersonal predictors of adolescent alcohol and marijuana use following treatment. *Psychology of Addictive Behaviors, 14*, 162–173.

Lavigne, J. V., & Faier-Routman, J. (1992). Psychological adjustment to pediatric physical disorders: A meta-analytic review. *Journal of Pediatric Psychology, 17*, 133–158.

Lawrence, C. M., & Thelen, M. H. (1995). Body image, dieting, and self-concept: Their relation in African-American and Caucasian children. *Journal of Clinical Child Psychology, 24*, 41–48.

Lawrence, E. C. (1999). The humanistic approach of Virginia Satir. In D. M. Lawson & F. F. Prevatt (Eds.), *Casebook in family therapy* (pp. 169–187). Belmont, CA: Wadsworth.

Lazar, A., Sagi, A., & Fraser, M. W. (1991). Involving fathers in social services. *Children and Youth Services Review, 13*, 287–300.

Leaf, P. J., Alegia, M., Cohen, P., Goodman, S. H., Horwitz, S. M., Hoven, C. W., Narrow, W. E., Vaden-Kiernan, M., & Regier, D. A. (1996). Mental health service use in the community and schools: Results from the four-community MECA Study. *Journal of the American Academy of Child and Adolescent Psychiatry, 35*, 889–897.

LeBlanc, M., & Ritchie, M. (1999). Predictors of play therapy outcomes. *International Journal of Play Therapy, 8*, 19–34.

Lebow, J. L., & Gurman, A. S. (1998). Family systems and family psychology. In C. E. Walker (Ed.), *Comprehensive clinical psychology* (Vol. 1, pp. 473–496). Oxford, England: Elsevier Science.

Leckman, J. F., & Mayes, L. C. (1998). Understanding developmental psychopathology: How useful are evolutionary accounts? *Journal of the American Academy of Child and Adolescent Psychiatry, 37*, 1011–1021.

LeCroy, C. W. (1994). *Handbook of child and adolescent treatment manuals*. New York: Lexington Books.

Lee, C. M., & Gotlib, I. H. (1991). Family disruption, parental availability and child adjustment. In R. Prinz (Ed.), *Advances in behavioral assessment of children and families* (Vol. 5, pp. 173–202). New York: Kingsley.

Lee, V. E., Brooks-Gunn, J., Schnur, E., & Liaw, F. (1990). Are Head Start effects sustained? A longitudinal follow-up comparison of disadvantaged children attending Head Start, no preschool, and other preschool programs. *Child Development, 61*, 495–507.

Lefkowitz, E. S., Sigman, M., & Au, T. K. (2000). Helping mothers discuss sexuality and AIDS with adolescents. *Child Development, 71*, 1383–1394.

Leitenberg, H., Yost, L. W., & Carroll-Wilson, M. (1986). Negative cognitive errors in children: Questionnaire development, normative data, and comparisons between children with and without self-reported symptoms of depression, low self-esteem, and evaluation anxiety. *Journal of Consulting and Clinical Psychology, 54*, 528–536.

Lemanek, K. L., Buckloh, L. M., Woods, G., & Butler, R. (1995). Diseases of the circulatory system: Sickle cell disease and hemophilia. In M. C. Roberts (Ed.), *Handbook of pediatric psychology* (pp. 286–309). New York: Guilford.

Lenzenweger, M. F., & Haugaard, J. J. (Eds.). (1996). *Frontiers of developmental psychopathology*. New York: Oxford University Press.

Leon, G. R. (1990). *Case histories of psychopathology* (4th ed.). Boston: Allyn & Bacon.

Leonard, H., & Dow, S. (1995). Selective mutism. In J. S. March (Ed.), *Anxiety disorders in children and adolescents* (pp. 235–250). New York: Guilford.

Leonard, K. E., Elden, R. D., Wong, M. M., Zucker, R. A., Puttler, L. I., Fitzgerald, H. E., Hussong, A., Chassin, L., & Mudar, P. (2000). Developmental perspectives on risk and vulnerability in alcoholic families. *Alcoholism: Clinical and Experimental Research, 24*, 238–240.

Lerner, J., Safren, S. A., Henin, A., Warman, M., Heimberg, R. G., & Kendall, P. C. (1999). Differentiating anxious and depressive self-statements in youth: Factor structure of the Negative Affect Self-Statement Questionnaire among youth referred to an anxiety disorders clinic. *Journal of Clinical Child Psychology, 28*, 82–93.

Lerner, R. M., Fisher, C. B., & Weinberg, R. A. (2000). Toward a science for and of the people: Promoting civil society through the application of developmental science. *Child Development, 71*, 11–20.

Maharaj, S., Rodin, G., Connolly, J., Olmsted, M., & Daneman, D. (2001). Eating problems and the observed quality of mother–daughter interactions among girls with Type 1 diabetes. *Journal of Consulting and Clinical Psychology, 69,* 950–958.

Mahler, M. (1968). *On human symbiosis and the vicissitudes of individuation.* New York: International Universities Press.

Mahoney, A., Donnelly, W. O., Lewis, T., & Maynard, C. (2000). Mother and father self-reports of corporal punishment and severe physical aggression toward clinic-referred youth. *Journal of Clinical Child Psychology, 29,* 266–281.

Mahoney, A., Pargament, K. I., Tarakeshwar, N., & Swank, A. B. (2001). Religion in the home in the 1980s and 1990s: A meta-analytic review and conceptual analysis of links between religion, marriage, and parenting. *Journal of Family Psychology, 15,* 559–596.

Malcarne, V. L., Hamilton, N. A., Ingram, R. E., & Taylor, L. (2000). Correlates of distress in children at risk for affective disorder: Exploring predictors in the offspring of depressed and nondepressed mothers. *Journal of Affective Disorders, 59,* 243–251.

Mandoki, M. W., Sumner, G. S., Hoffman, R. P., & Riconda, D. L. (1991). A review of Klinefelter's syndrome in children and adolescents. *Journal of the American Academy of Child and Adolescent Psychiatry, 30,* 167–172.

Manne, S., & Miller, D. (1998). Social support, social conflict, and adjustment among adolescents with cancer. *Journal of Pediatric Psychology, 23,* 121–130.

Manne, S., Nereo, N., DuHamel, K., Ostroff, J., Parsons, S., Martini, R., Williams, S., Mee, L., Sexson, S., Lewis, J., Vickberg, S. J., & Redd, W. H. (2001). Anxiety and depression in mothers of children undergoing bone marrow transplant: Symptom prevalence and use of the Beck Depression and Beck Anxiety Inventories as screening instruments. *Journal of Consulting and Clinical Psychology, 69,* 1037–1047.

Manning, M. (1994). *Undercurrents: A therapist's reckoning with her own depression.* New York: HarperCollins.

March, J. S. (Ed.). (1995). *Anxiety disorders in children and adolescents.* New York: Guilford.

March, J. S. (1999). Assessment of pediatric posttraumatic stress disorder. In P. A. Saigh & J. D. Bremner (Eds.), *Posttraumatic stress disorder: A comprehensive text* (pp. 199–218). Boston: Allyn & Bacon.

March, J. S., Amaya-Jackson, L., Terry, R., & Costanzo, P. (1997). Posttraumatic symptomatology in children and adolescents afer an industrial fire. *Journal of the American Academy of Child and Adolescent Psychiatry, 36,* 1080–1088.

March, J. S., Leonard, H. L., & Swedo, S. (1995). Obsessive-compulsive disorder In J. S. March (Ed.), *Anxiety disorders in children and adolescents* (pp. 251–275). New York: Guilford.

March, J. S., & Mulle, K. (1998). *OCD in children and adolescents: A cognitive-behavioral treatment manual.* New York: Guilford.

Margolin, G., Gordis, E. B., & John, R. S. (2001). Coparenting: A link between marital conflict and parenting in two-parent families. *Journal of Family Psychology, 15,* 3–21.

Markowitz, J. C. (1995a). Comorbidity of dysthymic disorder. In J. H. Kocsis & D. N. Klein (Eds.), *Diagnosis and treatment of chronic depression* (pp. 41– 57). New York: Guilford.

Markowitz, J. C. (1995b). Psychotherapy of dysthymic disorder. In J. H. Kocsis & D. N. Klein (Eds.), *Diagnosis and treatment of chronic depression* (pp. 146–168). New York: Guilford.

Marks, D. J., Himelstein, J., Newcorn, J. H., & Halperin, J. M. (1999). Identification of AD/HD subtypes using laboratory-based measures: A cluster analysis. *Journal of Abnormal Child Psychology, 27,* 167–175.

Marlatt, G. A., & Gordon, J. R. (1985). *Relapse prevention: Maintenance strategies in the treatment of addictive behaviors.* New York: Guilford.

Marsh, J. D. B. (1995). *From the heart: On being the mother of a child with special needs.* Bethesda, MD: Woodbine House.

Marshal, M. P., & Chassin, L. (2000). Peer influence on adolescent alcohol use: The moderating role of parental support and discipline. *Applied Developmental Science, 4,* 80–88.

Martens, B. K., Witt, J. C., Daly, E. J., & Vollmer, T. R. (1999). Behavior analysis: Theory and practice in educational settings. In C. R. Reynolds & T. B. Gutkin (Eds.), *The handbook of school psychology* (3rd ed., pp. 638–663). New York: Wiley.

Martinez, C. R., & Forgatch, M. S. (2001). Preventing problems with boys' noncompliance: Effects of a parent training intervention for divorcing mothers. *Journal of Consulting and Clinical Psychology, 69,* 416–428.

Marx, B. P., & Gross, A. M. (1998). Behavioral treatment. In T. H. Ollendick & M. Hersen (Eds.), *Handbook of child psychopathology* (pp. 581–602). New York: Plenum.

Mash, E. J., & Barkley, R. A. (Eds.). (1998). *Treatment of childhood disorders* (2nd ed.). New York: Guilford.

Mash, E. J., & Dozois, D. J. A. (1996). Child psychopathology: A developmental-systems perspective. In E. J. Mash & R. A. Barkley (Eds.), *Child psychopathology* (pp. 3–60). New York: Guildford Press.

Masten, A. S. (2001). Ordinary magic: Resilience processes in development. *American Psychologist, 56,* 227–238.

Masten, A. S., & Coatsworth, J. D. (1998). The development of competence in favorable and unfavorable environments: Lessons from research on successful children. *American Psychologist, 53,* 205–220.

Masten, A. S., Hubbard, J. J., Gest, S. D., Tellegen, A., Garmezy, N., & Ramirez, M. (1999). Competence in the context of adversity: Pathways to resilience and maladaptation from childhood to late adolescence. *Development and Psychopathology, 11,* 143–169.

Masten, A. S., Miliotis, D., Graham-Bermann, S. A., Ramirez, M., & Neemann, J. (1993). Children in homeless families: Risks to mental health and development. *Journal of Consulting and Clinical Psychology, 61,* 335–343.

Masten, W. G., Stacks, J. R., Caldwell-Colbert, A. T., & Jackson, J. S. (1996). Behavioral treatment of a selective mute Mexican-American boy. *Psychology in the Schools, 33,* 56–60.

Mather, N., & Jaffe, L. E. (1992). *Woodcock-Johnson Psycho-educational Battery-Revised: Recommendations and reports.* New York: Wiley.

Matson, J. L., & Friedt, L. R. (1988). Severe and profound mental retardation. In M. Hersen & C. G. Last (Eds.), *Child behavior therapy casebook* (pp. 113– 127). New York: Plenum.

Matson, J. L., & Smiroldo, B. B. (1999). Intellectual disorders. In W. K. Silverman & T. H. Ollendick (Eds.), *Developmental issues in the clinical treatment of children* (pp. 295–306). Boston: Allyn & Bacon.

Mattison, R. E. (2000). School consultation: A review of research on issues unique to the school environment. *Journal of the American Academy of Child and Adolescent Psychiatry, 39,* 402–413.

Maughan, B., & Rutter, M. (1998). Continuities and discontinuities in antisocial behavior from childhood to adult life. In T. H. Ollendick & R. J. Prinz (Eds.), *Advances in Clinical Child Psychology* (Vol. 20, pp. 1–47). New York: Plenum.

Mayes, L. C., & Bornstein, M. H. (1997). The development of children exposed to cocaine. In S. S. Luthar, J. A. Burack, D. Cicchetti, & J. R. Weisz (Eds.), *Developmental psychopathology: Perspectives on adjustment, risk, and disorder* (pp. 166–188). New York: Cambridge University Press.

Mayes, S. D., Calhoun, S. L., & Crites, D. L. (2001). Does *DSM-IV* Asperger's disorder exist? *Journal of Abnormal Child Psychology*, *29*, 263–271.

Mayes, S. D., Calhoun, S. L., & Crowell, E. W. (1998). WISC-III profiles for children with and without learning disabilities. *Psychology in the Schools*, *35*, 309–316.

Maynard, J., Tyler, J. L., & Arnold, M. (1999). Co-occurrence of attention-deficit disorder and learning disability: An overview of research. *Journal of Instructional Psychology*, *26*, 183–187.

Mayne, T. J., Norcross, J. C., & Sayette, M. A. (2000). *Insider's guide to graduate programs in clinical and counseling psychology: 2000/2001 Edition.* New York: Guilford.

Mazza, J. J., & Reynolds, W. M. (1999). Exposure to violence in young inner-city adolescents: Relationships with suicidal ideation, depression, and PTSD symptomatology. *Journal of Abnormal Child Psychology*, *27*, 203–213.

McArthur, G. M., Hogben, J. H., Edwards, V. T., Heath, S. M., & Mengler, E. D. (2000). On the "specifics" of specific reading disability and specific language impairment. *Journal of Child Psychology and Psychiatry and Allied Disciplines*, *41*, 869–874.

McBride, J. (1996). *The color of water: A black man's tribute to his white mother.* New York: Riverhead Books.

McBurnett, K. (1996). Development of the *DSM-IV*: Validity and relevance for school psychologists. *School Psychology Review*, *25*, 259–273.

McCabe, K. M., Clark, R., & Barnett, D. (1999). Family protective factors among urban African American youth. *Journal of Clinical Child Psychology*, *28*, 137–150.

McCabe, K. M., Hough, R., Wood, P. A., & Yeh, M. (2001). Childhood and adolescent onset conduct disorder: A test of the developmental taxonomy. *Journal of Abnormal Child Psychology*, *29*, 305–316.

McCall, N. (1994). *Makes me wanna holler: A young black man in America.* New York: Random House.

McCall, R. B., & Groark, C. J. (2000). The future of applied child development research and public policy. *Child Development*, *71*, 197–204.

McCarthy, D. A. (1972). *Manual for the McCarthy Scales of Children's Abilities.* San Antonio: Psychological Corporation.

McCaskill, P. A., Toro, P. A., & Wolfe, S. M. (1998). Homeless and matched housed adolescents: A comparative study of psychopathology. *Journal of Clinical Child Psychology*, *27*, 306–319.

McCauley, E., Ito, J., & Kay, T. (1986). Psychosocial functioning in girls with Turner's syndrome and short stature: Social skills, behavior problems, and self-concept. *Journal of the American Academy of Child Psychiatry*, *25*, 105–112.

McCauley, E., Myers, K., Mitchell, J., Calderon, R., Schloredt, K., & Treder, R. (1993). Depression young people: Initial presentation and clinical course. *Journal of the American Academy of Child and Adolescent Psychiatry*, *32*, 714–722.

McClellan, J., & Werry, J. (1994). Practice parameters for the assessment and treatment of children and adolescents with schizophrenia. *Journal of the American Academy of Child and Adolescent Psychiatry*, *33*, 616–635.

McClellan, J. M., & Werry, J. S. (1999). Schizophrenic psychosis. In H. C. Steinhausen & F. C. Verhulst (Eds.), *Risks and outcomes in developmental psychopathology* (pp. 267–282). New York: Oxford University Press.

McClellan, J., Werry, J., Bernet, W., Arnold, V., Beitchman, J., Benson, S., Bukstein, O., Kinlan, J., Rue, D., & Shaw, J. (2001). Practice parameter for the assessment and treatment of children and adolescents with schizophrenia. *Journal of the American Academy of Child and Adolescent Psychiatry*, *40 (Supplement 7)*, 4S-23S.

McCloskey, L. A., & Bailey, J. A. (2000). The intergenerational transmission of risk for child sexual abuse. *Journal of Interpersonal Violence*, *15*, 1019–1035.

McCloskey, L. A., & Walker, M. (2000). Posttraumatic stress in children exposed to family violence and singe-event trauma. *Journal of the American Academy of Child and Adolescent Psychiatry*, *39*, 108–115.

McClure, E. B., Brennan, P. A., Hammen, C., & LeBrocque, R. M. (2001). Parental anxiety disorders, child anxiety disorders, and the perceived parent–child relationship in an Australian high-risk sample. *Journal of Abnormal Child Psychology*, *29*, 1–10.

McCollum, E. E., & Russell, C. S. (1992). Mother-blaming in family therapy: An empirical investigation. *American Journal of Family Therapy*, *20*, 71–76.

McConaughy, S. H. (2000). Self-report: Child clinical interviews. In E. S. Shapiro & T. R. Kratochwill (Eds.), *Conducting school-based assessments of child and adolescent behavior* (pp. 170–202). New York: Guilford.

McConaughy, S. H., & Achenbach, T. M. (2001). *Manual for the Semistructured Clinical Interview for Children and Adolescents* (2nd ed.). Burlington: University of Vermont, Center for Children, Youth, and Families.

McCubbin, H. I., Thompson, E. A., Thompson, A. I., & Fromer, J. E. (1998). *Resiliency in Native American and immigrant families.*

McDermott, P. A., & Weiss, R. V. (1995). A normative typology of healthy, subclinical, and clinical behavior styles among American children and adolescents. *Psychological Assessment*, *7*, 162–170.

McDonald, L., & Sayger, T. V. (1998). Impact of a family and school based prevention program on protective factors for high risk youth. *Drugs and Society*, *12*, 61–85.

McEachlin, J. J., Smith, T., & Lovaas, O. I. (1993). Long-term outcome for children with autism who received early intensive behavioral treatment. *American Journal Mental Retardation*, *97*, 359–372.

McGee, R., & Williams, S. (1999). Environmental risk factors in oppositional-defiant disorder and conduct disorder. In H. C. Quay & A. E. Hogan (Eds.), *Handbook of disruptive behavior disorders* (pp. 419–440). New York: Kluwer Academic/Plenum.

McGee, R., Williams, S., & Feehan, M. (1992). Attention deficit disorder and age of onset of problem behaviors. *Journal of Abnormal Child Psychology*, *20*, 487–502.

McGoldrick, M., & Gerson, R. (1985). *Genograms in family assessment.* New York: Norton.

McGoldrick, M., Gerson, R., & Shellenberger, S. (1999). *Genograms: Assessment and intervention* (2nd ed.). New York: Norton.

McGoldrick, M., & Giordano, J., (1996). Overview: Ethnicity and family therapy. In M. McGoldrick, J. Giordano, & J. K. Pearce (Eds.), *Ethnicity and family therapy* (2nd ed., pp. 1–27). New York: Guilford.

McGoldrick, M., Giordano, J., & Pearce, J. K. (Eds.). (1996). *Ethnicity and family therapy* (2nd ed). New York: Guilford.

McGuigan, W. M., Vuchinich, S., & Pratt, C. C. (2000). Domestic violence, parents' view of their infant, and risk for child abuse. *Journal of Family Psychology*, *14*, 613–624.

McGuire, J., Nieri, D., Abbott, D., & Sheridan, K. (1995). Do Tarasoff principles apply in AIDS-related psychotherapy? Ethical decision making and the role of therapist homophobia and perceived client dangerousness. *Professional Psychology: Research and Practice*, *26*, 608–611.

McHale, J. P., & Rasmussen, J. L. (1998). Coparental and family group-level dynamics during infancy: Early family precursors of child and family functioning during preschool. *Development and Psychopathology*, *10*, 39–59.

McHale, S. M., Corneal, D. A., Crouter, A. C., & Birch, L. L. (2001). Gender and weight concerns in early and middle adolescence: Links with well-being and family characteristics. *Journal of Clinical Child Psychology, 30,* 338–348.

McLoyd, V. C. (1998). Socioeconomic disadvantage and child development. *American Psychologist, 53,* 185–204.

McLoyd, V. C., & Steinberg, L. (Eds.). (1998). *Studying minority adolescents: Conceptual, methodological, and theoretical issues.* Mahwah, NJ: Lawrence Erlbaum.

McMahon, R. J., & Estes, A. M. (1997). Conduct problems. In E. J. Mash & L. G. Terdal (Eds.), *Assessment of childhood disorders* (3rd ed., pp. 130–193). New York: Guilford.

McMahon, R. J., & Wells, K. C. (1998). Conduct problems. In *Treatment of childhood disorders* (2nd ed., pp. 111–207). New York: Guilford.

McQuaid, E. L., & Nassau, J. H. (1999). Empirically supported treatments of disease-related symptoms in pediatric psychology: Asthma, diabetes, and cancer. *Journal of Pediatric Psychology, 24,* 305–328.

Meehl, P. E. (2001). Comorbidity and taxometrics. *Clinical Psychology: Science and Practice, 8,* 507–519.

Melton, G. B. (1992). The improbability of prevention of sexual abuse. In D. J. Willis, E. W. Holden, & M. Rosenberg (Eds.), *Prevention of child maltreatment: Developmental and ecological perspectives.* New York: Wiley.

Melton, G. B., & Ehrenreich, N. S. (1992). Ethical and legal issues in mental health services for children. In C. E. Walker & M. C. Roberts (Eds.), *Handbook of clinical child psychology* (2nd ed., pp. 1035–1055). New York: Wiley.

Merikangas, K. R., Dierker, L. C., & Szatmari, P. (1998). Psychopathology among offspring of parents with substance abuse and/or anxiety disorders: A high-risk study. *Journal of Child Psychology and Psychiatry, 39,* 711–720.

Merikangas, K. R., Swendsen, J. D., Preisig, M. A., & Chazan, R. Z. (1998). Psychopathology and temperament in parents and offspring: Results of a family study. *Journal of Affective Disorders, 51,* 63–74.

Merikangas, K., Weissman, M., Prusoff, B. A., & Johns, K. (1988). Assortative mating and affective disorders: Psychopathology in offspring. *Psychiatry, 51,* 48–57.

Merrens, M. R., & Brannigan, G. G., eds. (1996). *The developmental psychologists: Research adventures across the life span.* New York: McGraw-Hill.

Merrill, L. L., Thomsen, C. J., Sinclair, B. B., Gold, S. R., & Milner, J. S. (2001). Predicting the impact of child sexual abuse on women: The role of severity, parental support, and coping strategies. *Journal of Consulting and Clinical Psychology, 69,* 992–1006.

Mesibov, G. B. (1997). Formal and informal measures on the effectiveness of the TEACCH programme. *Autism, 1,* 25–35.

Mesibov, G. B., Schroeder, C. S., & Wesson, L. (1993). Parental concerns about their children. In M. C. Roberts, G. P. Koocher, D. K. Routh, & D. J. Willis (Eds.), *Readings in pediatric psychology* (pp. 307–316). New York: Plenum.

Mesman, J., & Koot, H. M. (2000). Common and specific correlates of preadolescent internalizing and externalizing psychopathology. *Journal of Abnormal Psychology, 109,* 428–437.

Meyer, G. J., Finn, S. E., Eyde, L. D., Kay, G. G., Moreland, K. L., Dies, R. R., Eisman, E. J., Kubiszyn, T. W., & Reed, G. M. (2001). Psychological testing and psychological assessment: A review of evidence and issues. *American Psychologist, 55,* 128–165.

Meyer, J. M., Rutter, M., Silberg, J. L., Maes, H. H., Simonoff, E., Shillady, L. L., Pickles, A., Hewitt, J. K., & Eaves, L. J. (2000). Familial aggregation for conduct disorder symptomatology: The role of genes, marital discord and family adaptability. *Psychological Medicine, 30,* 759–774.

Meyer, P. (1985). *Death of innocence.* New York: Berkley Books.

Meyer, R. G. (1989). *Cases in developmental psychology and psychopathology.* Boston: Allyn & Bacon.

Meyers, J. (1989). The practice of psychology in the schools for the primary prevention of learning and adjustment problems in children: A perspective from the field of education. In L. A. Bond & B. E. Compas (Eds.), *Primary prevention and promotion in the schools* (pp. 391–422). Newbury Park, CA: Sage.

Meyers, J., & Nastasi, B. K. (1999). Primary prevention in school settings. In C. R. Reynolds & T. B. Gutkin (Eds.), *The handbook of school psychology* (3rd ed., pp. 764–799). New York: Wiley.

Milich, R., Balentine, A. C., & Lynam, D. R. (2001). ADHD combined type and ADHD predominantly inattentive type are distinct and unrelated disorders. *Clinical Psychology: Science and Practice, 8,* 463–488.

Milin, R., Coupland, K., Walker, S., & Fisher-Bloom, E. (2000). Outcome and follow-up study of an adolescent psychiatric day treatment school program. *Journal of the American Academy of Child and Adolescent Psychiatry, 39,* 320–328.

Miller, B. C., Benson, B., & Galbraith, K. A. (2001). Family relationships and adolescent pregnancy risk: A research synthesis. *Developmental Review, 21,* 1–38.

Miller, B. C., Fan, X., Christensen, M., Grotevant, H. D., & vanDulmen, M. (2000). Comparisons of adopted and nonadopted adolescents in a large, nationally representative sample. *Child Development, 71,* 1458–1473.

Miller, B. C., Fan, X., Grotevant, H. D., Christensen, M., Coyl, D., & vanDulmen, M. (2000). Adopted adolescents' overrepresentation in mental health counseling: Adoptees' problems or parents' lower threshold for referral? *Journal of the American Academy of Child and Adolescent Psychiatry, 39,* 1504–1511.

Miller, L., Davies, M., & Greenwald, S. (2000). Religiosity and substance use and abuse among adolescents in the National Comorbidity Survey. *Journal of the American Academy of Child and Adolescent Psychiatry, 39,* 1190–1197.

Miller, L. S., Koplewicz, H. S., & Klein, R. G. (1997). Teacher ratings of hyperactivity, inattention, and conduct problems in preschoolers. *Journal of Abnormal Child Psychology, 25,* 113–119.

Miller, L. S., Wasserman, G. A., Neugebauer, R., Gorman-Smith, D., & Kamboukos, D. (1999). Witnessed community violence and antisocial behavior in high-risk, urban boys. *Journal of Clinical Child Psychology, 28,* 2–11.

Miller, P. M., Smith, G. T., & Goldman, M. S. (1990). Emergence of alcohol expectancies in childhood: A possible critical period. *Journal of Studies on Alcohol, 51,* 343–349.

Miller-Johnson, S., Lochman, J. E., Coie, J. D., Terry, R. & Hyman, C. (1998). Comorbidity of conduct and depressive problems at sixth grade: Substance use outcomes across adolescence. *Journal of Abnormal Child Psychology, 26,* 221–232.

Milling, L, Campbell, N. B., Bush, E., & Laughlin, A. (1996). Affective and behavioral correlates of suicidality among hospitalized preadolescent children. *Journal of Clinical Child Psychology, 25,* 454–462.

Milner, J. S. (1986). *The Child Abuse Potential Inventory* (2nd ed.). Webster, NC: Psytec.

Milner, J. S. (1994). Assessing physical child abuse risk: The Child Abuse Potential Inventory. *Clinical Psychology Review, 14,* 547–583.

Mineka, S., Davidson, M., Cook, M., & Keir, R. (1984). Observational conditioning of snake fear in rhesus monkeys. *Journal of Abnormal Psychology, 93,* 355–372.

Minuchin, S. (1974). *Families and family therapy.* Cambridge, MA: Harvard University Press.

Minuchin, S., Montalvo, B., Guerney, B., Rosman, B., & Schumer, F. (1967). *Families of the slums.* New York: Basic Books.

Mireault, G. C., & Compas, B. E. (1996). A prospective study of coping and adjustment before and after a parent's death from cancer. *Journal of Psychosocial Oncology, 14,* 1–18.

Mischel, W., & Ebbesen, E. B. (1970). Attention in delay of gratification. *Journal of Personality and Social Psychology, 16,* 329–337.

Mischel, W., Shoda, Y., & Peake, P. K. (1988). The nature of adolescent competencies predicted by preschool delay of gratification. *Journal of Personality and Social Psychology, 54,* 687–696.

Mitchell, K., & Burkhardt, S. A. (1996). The developmental course of autistic disorder in males. In A. F. Rotatori, J. O. Schwenn, & S. Burkhardt (Eds.), *Advances in special education: Assessment and psychopathology issues in special education* (pp. 97–107). Greenwich, CT: JAI Press.

Mizell, C. A. (1999). Life course influences on African American men's depression: Adolescent parental composition, self-concept, and adult earnings. *Journal of Black Studies, 29,* 467–490.

Mizes, J. S., & Miller, K. J. (2000). Eating disorders. In M. Hersen & R. T. Ammerman (Eds.), *Advanced abnormal child psychology* (pp. 441–465). Mahwah, NJ: Lawrence Erlbaum.

Moffitt, T. E. (1993). Adolescence-limited and life-course persistent antisocial behavior: A developmental taxonomy. *Psychological Review, 100,* 674–701.

Money, J. (1993). Specific neurocognitional impairments associated with Turner (45,X) and Klinefelter (47,XXY) syndromes: A review. *Social Biology, 40,* 147–151.

Moolchan, E. T., Ernst, M., & Henningfield, J. E. (2000). A review of tobacco smoking in adolescents: Treatment implications. *Journal of the American Academy of Child and Adolescent Psychiatry, 39,* 682–693.

Moore, S., Donovan, B., Hudson, A., & Dykstra, J. (1993). Evaluation of eight case studies of facilitated communication. *Journal of Autism and Developmental Disorders, 23,* 531–539.

Moos, R. H., & Moos, B. S. (1981). *Family Environment Scale Manual.* Palo Alto, CA: Consulting Psychologists Press.

Morgan, D. L., & Morgan, R. K. (2001). Single-participant research design: Bringing science to managed care. *American Psychologist, 55,* 119–127.

Morgan, G. A., Gliner, J. A., & Harmon, R. J. (2000). Quasi-experimental designs. *Journal of the American Academy of Child and Adolescent Psychiatry, 39,* 794–796.

Morgan, M. (1995). *How to interview sexual abuse victims.* Thousand Oaks, CA: Sage.

Morgan, R. K. (1999). *Case studies in child and adolescent psychopathology.* Upper Saddle River, NJ: Prentice Hall.

Mortimore, P. (1995). The positive effects of schooling. In M. Rutter (Ed.), *Psychosocial disturbances in young people: Challenges for prevention* (pp. 333–363). Cambridge, UK: Cambridge University Press.

Mowrer, O. H. (1960). *Learning theory and behavior.* New York: Wiley.

MTA Cooperative Group (1999). A 14–month randomized clinical trial of treatment strategies for attention-deficit/hyperactivity disorder. *Archives of General Psychiatry, 56,* 1073–1086.

Mulholland, A. M., & Mintz, L. B. (2001). Prevalence of eating disorders among African American women. *Journal of Counseling Psychology, 48,* 111–116.

Mulvey, E. P., & Cauffman, E. (2001). The inherent limits of predicting school violence. *American Psychologist, 55,* 797–802.

Muris, P., Merckelbach, H., Gadet, B., & Moulaert, V. (2000). Fears, worries, and scary dreams in 4- to 12-year-old children: Their content, developmental pattern, and origins. *Journal of Clinical Child Psychology, 29,* 43–52.

Murray, M. E., Guerra, N. G., & Williams, K. R. (1997). Violence prevention for the 21st century. In R. P. Weissberg, T. P. Gullotta, R. L. Hampton, B. A. Ryan, & G. R. Adams (Eds.), *Healthy children 2010: Enhancing children's wellness* (pp. 105–128). Thousand Oaks, CA: Sage.

Murray, V. M., & Brody, G. H. (1999). Self-regulation and self-worth of Black children reared in economically stressed, rural, single mother-headed families: The contribution of risk and protective factors. *Journal of Family Issues, 20,* 458–484.

Myers, J. E. B. (1996). Societal self-defense: New laws to protect children from sexual abuse. *Child Abuse and Neglect, 20,* 255–258.

Myers, M. G., Brown, S. A., & Vik, P. W. (1998). Adolescent substance use problems. In E. J. Mash & R. A. Barkley (Eds.), *Treatment of childhood disorders* (2nd ed., pp. 692–729). New York: Guilford.

Myers, W. C., Burton, P. R. S., Sanders, P. D., Donat, K. M., Cheney, J., Fitzpatrick, T. M., & Monaco, L. (2000). Project Back-on-Track at 1 year: A delinquency treatment program for early-career juvenile offenders. *Journal of the American Academy of Child and Adolescent Psychiatry, 39,* 1127–1134.

Myles, B. S., & Simpson, R. L. (1994). Facilitated communication with children diagnosed as autistic in public school settings. *Psychology in the Schools, 31,* 208–220.

Nadeau, K. G. (Ed.). (1995). *A comprehensive guide to Attention Deficit Disorder in adults: Research, diagnosis, and treatment.* New York: Brunner/Mazel.

Naidu, S. B. (1997). Rett syndrome. *Indian Journal of Pediatrics, 64,* 651–659.

Najman, J. M., Williams, G. M., Nikles, J., Spence, S., Bor, W., O'Callaghan, M., LeBrocque, R., & Andersen, M. J. (2000). Mothers' mental illness and child behavior problems: Cause–effect association or observation bias? *Journal of the American Academy of Child and Adolescent Psychiatry, 39,* 592–602.

Napier, A. Y., & Whitaker, C. A. (1978). *The family crucible.* New York: Bantam Books.

Nathan, P. E. (1997). In the final analysis, it's the data that count. *Clinical Psychology: Science and Practice, 4,* 281–284.

Nathan, P. E., & Langenbucher, J. W. (1999). Psychopathology: Description and classification. *Annual Review of Psychology, 50,* 79–107.

Nettles, S. M., & Pleck, J. H. (1994). Risk, resilience, and development: The multiple ecologies of black adolescents in the United States. In R. J. Haggerty, L. R. Sherrod, N. Garmezy, & M. Rutter (Eds.), *Stress, risk, and resilience in children and adolescents: Processes, mechanisms, and interventions* (pp. 147–181). New York: Cambridge University Press.

Neugebauer, R. (1979). Medieval and early modern theories of mental illness. *Archives of General Psychiatry, 36,* 477–483.

Neugeboren, J. (1997). *Imagining Robert: My brother, madness, and survival.* New York: Holt and Company.

Neumaerker, K. J., Bettle, N., Neumaerker, U., & Bettle, O. (2000). Age- and gender-related psychological characteristics of adolescent ballet dancers. *Psychopathology, 33,* 137–142.

Neuville, M. B. (1995). *Sometimes I get all scribbly: Living with Attention-Deficit/Hyperactivity Disorder.* Austin, TX: Pro-Ed.

Nevas, D. B., & Farber, B. A. (2001). Parents' attitudes toward their child's therapist and therapy. *Professional Psychology: Research and Practice, 32,* 165–170.

New York Times (1874). Mr. Bergh enlarging his sphere of usefulness: Inhuman treatment of a little waif—her treatment—a mystery to be cleared up. Page 8.

Newcomb, A. F., & Bagwell, C. L. (1995). Children's friendship relations: A meta-analytic review. *Psychological Bulletin, 117*, 306–347.

Newman, R., Phelps, R., Sammons, M. T., Dunivin, D. L., & Cullen, E. A. (2000). Evaluation of the psychopharmacology demonstration project: A retrospective analysis. *Professional Psychology: Research and Practice, 31*, 598–603.

Newsom, C. (1998). Autistic disorder. In E. J. Mash & R. A. Barkley (Eds.), *Treatment of childhood disorders* (2nd ed., pp. 416–467). New York: Guilford.

Nicholson, J. M., Fergusson, D. M., Horwood, L. J. (1999). Effects on later adjustment of living in a stepfamily during childhood and adolescence. *Journal of Child Psychology and psychiatry, 40*, 405–416.

Nicolson, R., & Rapoport, J. L. (1999). Childhood-onset schizophrenia: Rare but worth studying. *Biological Psychiatry, 46*, 1418–1428.

Nicolson, R., & Rapoport, J. L. (2000). Childhood-onset schizophrenia: What can it teach us? In J. L. Rapoport (Ed.), *Childhood onset of "adult" psychopathology: Clinical and research advances* (pp. 167–192). Washington, D.C.: American Psychiatric Press.

Nigg, J. T. (1999). The ADHD response-inhibition deficit as measured by the stop task: Replication with *DSM-IV* combined type, extension, and qualification. *Journal of Abnormal Child Psychology, 27*, 393–402.

Nigg, N. T. (2001). Is ADHD a disinhibitory disorder? *Psychological Bulletin, 127*, 571–598.

NIH Consensus Development Panel (2000). National Institutes of Health Consensus Development Conference statement: Diagnosis and treatment of attention-deficit/hyperactivity disorder (ADHD). *Journal of the American Academy of Child and Adolescent Psychiatry, 39*, 182–193.

Nishith, P., Mechanic, M. B., & Resick, P. A. (2000). Prior interpersonal trauma: The contribution to current PTSD symptoms in female rape victims. *Journal of Abnormal Psychology, 109*, 20–25.

Nolen-Hoeksema, S. (2001). Gender differences in depression. *Current Directions in Psychological Science, 10*, 173–180.

Nolen-Hoeksema, S., & Girgus, J. S. (1994). The emergence of gender differences in depression during adolescence. *Psychological Bulletin, 114*, 424–443.

Noll, R. B., McKellop, J. M., Vannatta, K., & Kalinyak, K. (1998). Child-rearing practices of primary caregivers of children with sickle cell disease: The perspective of professionals and caregivers. *Journal of Pediatric Psychology, 23*, 131–140.

Norcross, J. C., Sayette, M. A., Mayne, T. J., Karg, R. S., & Turkson, M. A. (1998). Selecting a doctoral program in professional psychology: Some comparisons among Ph.D. counseling, Ph.D. clinical, and Psy.D. clinical psychology programs. *Professional Psychology: Research and Practice, 29*, 609–614.

Nottelmann, E., Biederman, J., Birmaher, B., Carlson, G. A., Chang, K. D., Fenton, W. S., Geller, B., Hoagwood, K. E., Hyman, S. E., Kendler, K. S., Koretz, D. S., Kowatch, R. A., Kupfer, D. J., Leibenluft, E., Nakmura, R. K., Nottelmann, E. D., Stover, E., Vitiello, B., Weiblinger, G., & Weller, E. (2001). National Institute of mental Health research roundtable on prepubertal bipolar disorder. *Journal of the American Academy of Child and Adolescent Psychiatry, 40*, 871–878.

Nussbaum, N. L., & Bigler, E. D. (1997). Halstead-Reitan Neuropsychological Test Batteries for Children. In C. R. Reynolds & E. Fletcher-Janzen (Eds.), *Handbook of clinical child neuropsychology* (2nd ed., pp. 219–236). New York: Plenum.

Nye, S. S., & Johnson, C. L. (1999). Eating disorders. In S. D. Netherton, D. Holmes, & C. E. Walker (Eds.), *Child and adolescent psychological disorders: A comprehensive textbook* (pp. 397–414). New York: Oxford University Press.

Oakland, T., & Cunningham, J. (1999). The futures of school psychology: Conceptual models for its development and examples of their applications. In C. R. Reynolds & T. B. Gutkin (Eds.), *The handbook of school psychology* (3rd ed., pp. 34–53). New York: Wiley.

O'Connor, T. G., Caspi, A., DeFries, J. C., & Plomin, R. (2000). Are associations between parental divorce and children's adjustment genetically mediated? An adoption study. *Developmental Psychology, 36*, 429–437.

O'Connor, T. G., McGuire, S., Reiss, D., Hetherington, E. M., & Plomin, R. (1998). Co-occurrence of depressive symptoms and antisocial behavior in adolescence: A common genetic liability. *Journal of Abnormal Psychology, 107*, 27–37.

Oesterheld, J. R., Fogas, B., & Rutten, S. (1998). Ethical standards for research on children. *Journal of the American Academy of Child and Adolescent Psychiatry, 37*, 684–685.

Offord, D. R., & Bennett, K. J. (1996). Conduct disorder. In L. Hechtman (Ed.), *Do they grow out of it? Long-term outcomes of childhood disorders* (pp. 77–99). Washington, D.C.: American Psychiatric Press.

Offord, D. R., Boyle, M. H., & Racine, Y. (1989). Ontario child health study: Correlates of disorder. *Journal of the American Academy of Child and Adolescent Psychiatry, 28*, 856–860.

O'Hara, M. W. (1995). *Postpartum depression: Causes and consequences.* New York: Springer-Verlag.

Ohayon, M. M., Roberts, R. E., Zulley, J., Smirne, S., & Priest, R. G. (2000). Prevalence and patterns of problematic sleep among older adolescents. *Journal of the American Academy of Child and Adolescent Psychiatry, 39*, 1549–1556.

Olds, D. L. (1988). The prenatal/early infancy project. In R. H. Price, E. L. Cowen, R. P. Lorion, & J. Ramos-McKay (Eds.), *14 ounces of prevention: A casebook for practitioners* (pp. 9–23). Washington, DC: American Psychological Association.

Ollendick, T. H. (1983). Reliability and validity of the Revised Fear Survey Schedule for Children (FSSC-R). *Behaviour Research and Therapy, 21*, 685– 692.

Ollendick, T. H. (Ed.). (1998). *Comprehensive clinical psychology* (Vol. 5). Oxford, England: Elsevier Science.

Ollendick, T. H., & King, N. J. (1998). Empirically supported treatments for children with phobic and anxiety disorders: Current status. *Journal of Clinical Child Psychology, 27*, 156–167.

Olson, D. H., Portner, J., & Bell, R. (1982). *Faces II: Family Adaptability and Cohesion Evaluation Scales.* St. Paul: University of Minnesota, Family Social Science.

Olson, R. A., Mullins, L. L., Gillman, J. B., & Chaney, J. M. (Eds.). (1994). *The sourcebook of pediatric psychology.* Boston: Allyn & Bacon.

Olson, R. A., Huszti, H., & Youll, L. K. (1995). Sexual behaviors and problems of adolescents. In M. C. Roberts (Ed.), *Handbook of pediatric psychology* (pp. 327–341). New York: Guilford.

Olson, S. L., Bates, J. E., Sandy, J. M., & Lanthier, R. (2000). Early developmental precursors of externalizing behavior in middle childhood and adolescence. *Journal of Abnormal Child Psychology, 28*, 119–133.

Olsson, G. I., Nordstrom, M. L., Arinell, H., & vonKnorring, A. L. (1999). Adolescent depression: Social network and family climate: A case-control study. *Journal of Child Psychology and Psychiatry, 40*, 227–237.

Oman, D., Thoresen, C. E., & McMahon, K. (1999). Volunteerism and mortality among the community-dwelling elderly. *Journal of Health Psychology, 4*, 301–316.

Ondersma, S. J., Chaffin, M., Berliner, L., Cordon, I., Goodman, G. S., & Barnett, D. (2001). Sex with children is abuse: Comment on Rind, Tromovitch, and Bauserman (1998). *Psychological Bulletin, 127*, 707–714.

Ondersma, S. J., & Walker, C. E. (1998). Elimination disorders. In T. H. Ollendick & M. Hersen (Eds.), *Handbook of child psychopathology* (3rd ed., pp. 355–378). New York: Plenum.

Orlando, M., Ellickson, P. L., & Jinnett, K. (2001). The temporal relationship between emotional distress and cigarette smoking during adolescence and young adulthood. *Journal of Consulting and Clinical Psychology, 69*, 959–970.

Orrell-Valente, J. K., Pinderhughes, E. E., Valente, E., & Laird, R. D. (1999). If it's offered, will they come? Influences on parents' participation in a community-based conduct problems prevention program. *American Journal of Community Psychology, 27*, 753–783.

Orten, J. D., & Orten, J. L. (1992). Achievement among women with Turner's syndrome. *Families in Society, 73*, 424–431.

Orten, J. L. (1990). Coming up short: The physical, cognitive, and social effects of Turner's syndrome. *Health and Social Work, 15*, 100–106.

Orvaschel, H., Beeferman, D., & Kabacoff, R. (1997). Depression, self-esteem, sex, and age in a child and adolescent clinical sample. *Journal of Clinical Child Psychology, 26*, 285–289.

Owens, J. A., Spirito, A., McGuinn, M., & Nobile, C. (2000). Sleep habits and sleep disturbance in elementary school-aged children. *Journal of Developmental and Behavioral Pediatrics, 21*, 27–36.

Pacifici, C., Stoolmiller, M., & Nelson, C., (2001). Evaluating a prevention program for teenagers on sexual coercion: A differential effectiveness approach. *Journal of Consulting and Clinical Psychology, 69*, 552–559.

Pagliaro, A. M., & Pagliaro, L. A. (1996). *Substance use among children and adolescents: Its nature, extent, and effects from conception to adulthood*. New York: Wiley.

Paley, V. G. (1981). *Wally's stories*. Cambridge, MA: Harvard University Press.

Palfreman, J. (Writer, Producer, Director). (1993, October 19). *Prisoners of silence*. [Frontline Documentry]. Corporation for Public Broadcasting.

Paniagua, F. A. (1998). *Assessing and treating culturally diverse clients: A practical guide* (2nd ed.). Thousand Oaks, CA: Sage.

Pankratz, L. (1999). Factitious disorders and factitious disorders by proxy. In S. D. Netherton, D. Holmes, & C. E. Walker (Eds.), *Child and adolescent psychological disorders: A comprehensive textbook* (pp. 304–319). New York: Oxford University Press.

Parke, R. D. (1996). Fathers, play, and emotion: A research odyssey. In M. R. Merrens & G. G. Brannigan (Eds.), *The developmental psychologists: Research adventures across the life span* (pp. 136–150). New York: McGraw-Hill.

Parke, R. D. (2000). Beyond white and middle class: Cultural variations in families—Assessments, processes, and policies. *Journal of Family Psychology, 14*, 331–333.

Parker, H., & Parker, S. (1986). Father–daughter sexual abuse: An emerging perspective. *American Journal of Orthopsychiatry, 56*, 531–549.

Parkes, C. M. (1990). Risk factors in bereavement: Implications for the prevention and treatment of pathologic grief. *Psychiatric Annals, 20*, 308–313.

Parsons, J. T., Butler, R., Kocik, S., Norman, L., Nuss, R., & the Adolescent Hemophilia Behavioral Intervention Evaluation Projects (HBIEP) Study Group. (1998). *Journal of Pediatric Psychology, 23*, 57–65.

Patten, C. A. (2000). A critical evaluation of nicotine replacement therapy for teenage smokers. *Journal of Child and Adolescent Substance Abuse, 9*, 51–75.

Patterson, G. R. (1982). *Coercive family process*. Eugene, OR: Castalia.

Patterson, G. R. (1996). Some characteristics of a developmental theory for early-onset delinquency. In M. F. Lenzenweger & J. J. Haugaard (Eds.), *Frontiers of developmental psychopathology* (pp. 81–124). New York: Oxford University Press.

Patterson, G. R., DeGarmo, D. S., & Knutson, N. (2000). Hyperactive and antisocial behaviors: Comorbid or two points in the same process? *Development and Psychopathology, 12*, 91–106.

Patterson, G. R., & Gullion, M. E. (1968). *Living with children: New methods for parents and teachers*. Champaign, IL: Research Press.

Patterson, G. R., Reid, J. B., & Dishion, T. J. (1992). *Antisocial boys*. Eugene, OR: Castalia.

Patterson, T. E., & Lusterman, D. (1996). The relational reimbursement dilemma. In F. W. Kaslow (Ed.), *Handbook of relational diagnosis and dysfunctional family patterns* (pp. 46–58). New York: Wiley.

Patton, G. C., Carlin, J. B., Coffey, C., Wolfe, R., Hibbert, M., & Bowes, G. (1998). Depression, anxiety, and smoking initiation: A prospective study over 3 years. *American Journal of Public Health, 88*, 1518–1522.

Paul, J. L. (Ed.). (1997). *Ethics and decision making in local schools: Inclusion, policy, and reform*. Baltimore: P. H. Brookes.

Pavlidis, K., & McCauley, E. (2001). Autonomy and relatedness in family interactions with depressed adolescents. *Journal of Abnormal Child Psychology, 29*, 11–21.

Pedro-Carroll, J. (2001). The promotion of wellness in children and families: Challenges and opportunities. *American Psychologist, 56*, 993–1004.

Pelcovitz, D., Adler, N. A., Kaplan, S., Packman, L., & Krieger, R. (1992). The failure of a school-based child sexual abuse prevention program. *Journal of the American Academy of Child and Adolescent Psychiatry, 31*, 887–892.

Pelham, W. E., Gnagy, E. M., Greiner, A. R., Hoza, B., Hinshaw, S. P., Swanson, J. M., Simpson, S., Shapiro, C., Bukstein, O., Baron-Myak, C., & McBurnett, K. (2000). Behavioral versus behavioral and pharmacological treatment in ADHD children attending a summer treatment program. *Journal of Abnormal Child Psychology, 28*, 507–525.

Pelham, W. E., Lang, A. R., Atkeson, B., Murphy, D. A., Gnagy, E. M., Greiner, A. R., Vodde-Hamilton, M., & Greenslade, K. E. (1997). Effects of deviant child behavior on parental distress and alcohol consumption in laboratory interactions. *Journal of Abnormal Child Psychology, 25*, 413–424.

Pelham, W. E., Wheeler, T., & Chronis, A. (1998). Empirically supported psychosocial treatments for Attention Deficit Hyperactivity Disorder. *Journal of Clinical Child Psychology, 27*, 190–205.

Pelkonen, M., Marttunen, M., Laippala, P., & Loennqvist, J. (2000). Factors associated with early dropout from adolescent psychiatric outpatient treatment. *Journal of the American Academy of Child and Adolescent Psychiatry, 39*, 329–336.

Pelzer, D. (1995). *A child called "It."* Deerfield Beach, FL: Health Communications.

Pelzer, D. (1997). *The lost boy: A foster child's search for the love of a family*. Deerfield Beach, FL: Health Communications.

Pelzer, D. (1999). *A man named Dave*. Deerfield Beach, FL: Health Communications.

Penfold, P. S. (1985). Parent's perceived responsibility for children's problems. *Canadian Journal of Psychiatry, 30*, 255–258.

Perez-Smith, A. M., Albus, K. E., & Weist, M. D. (2001). Exposure to violence and neighborhood affiliation among inner-city youth. *Journal of Clinical Child Psychology, 30*, 464–472.

Perry, C. L., Story, M., & Lytle, L. A. (1997). Promoting healthy dietary behaviors. In R. P. Weissberg, T. P. Gullotta, R. L. Hampton, B. A. Ryan, & G. R. Adams (Eds.), *Healthy children 2010: Enhancing children's wellness* (pp. 214–249). Thousand Oaks, CA: Sage.

Petersen, A. C., Compas, B. E., Brooks-Gunn, J., Stemmler, M., Ey, S., & Grant, K. E. (1993). Depression in adolescence. *American Psychologist, 48*, 155–168.

Peterson, B. S., Pine, D. S., Cohen, P., & Brook, J. S. (2001). Prospective, longitudinal study of tic, obsessive-compulsive, and attention-deficit/hyperactivity disorders in an epidemiological sample. *Journal of the Academy of Child and Adolescent Psychiatry, 40*, 685–695.

Peterson, D. R. (1971). Status of the doctor of psychology program. *Professional Psychology, 2*, 271–275.

Peterson, J. L., & Newman, R. (2000). Helping to curb youth violence: The APA-MTV "Warning Signs" initiative. *Professional Psychology: Research and Practice, 31*, 509–514.

Peterson, L., & Tremblay, G. (1999). Importance of developmental theory and investigation to research in clinical child psychology. *Journal of Clinical Child Psychology, 28*, 448–456.

Petraitis, J., Flay, B. R., & Miller, T. Q. (1995). Reviewing theories of adolescent substance use: Organizing pieces in the puzzle. *Psychological Bulletin, 117*, 67–86.

Pettit, G. S., Bates, J. E., Dodge, K. A., & Meece, D. W. (1999). The impact of after-school peer contact of early adolescent externalizing problems is moderated by parental monitoring, perceived neighborhood safety, and prior adjustment. *Child Development, 70*, 768–778.

Pfeffer, C. R. (1986). *The suicidal child*. New York: Guilford.

Pfiffner, L. J., McBurnett, K., & Rathouz, P. J. (2001). Father absence and familial antisocial characteristics. *Journal of Abnormal Child Psychology, 29*, 357–367.

Phares, V. (1992). Where's Poppa?: The relative lack of attention to the role of fathers in child and adolescent psychopathology. *American Psychologist, 47*, 656–664.

Phares, V. (1996). *Fathers and developmental psychopathology*. New York: Wiley.

Phares, V. (1997a). Accuracy of informants: Do parents think that mother knows best? *Journal of Abnormal Child Psychology, 25*, 165–171.

Phares, V. (1997b). Psychological adjustment, maladjustment, and father-child relationships. In M. E. Lamb (Ed.), *The role of the father in child development* (3rd ed., pp. 261–283). New York: Wiley.

Phares, V. (1999). *Poppa psychology: The role of fathers in children's mental well-being*. Westport, CT: Praeger.

Phares, V., & Compas, B. E. (1990). Adolescents' subjective distress over their emotional/behavioral problems. *Journal of Consulting and Clinical Psychology, 58*, 596–603.

Phares, V., & Compas, B. E. (1992). The role of fathers in child and adolescent psychopathology: Make room for Daddy. Psychological Bulletin, *111*, 387–412.

Phares, V., Compas, B. E., & Howell, D. C. (1989). Perspectives on child behavior problems: Comparisons of children's self-reports with parent and teacher reports. *Psychological Assessment, 1*, 68–71.

Phares, V., & Danforth, J. S. (1994). Adolescents', parents', and teachers' distress over adolescents' behavior. *Journal of Abnormal Child Psychology, 22*, 721–732.

Phares, V., Duhig, A. M., & Watkins, M. M. (2002). Family context: Fathers and other supports. In S. H. Goodman, & I. H. Gotlib (Eds.), *Children of depressed parents: Mechanisms of risk and implications for treatment* (pp. 203–225). Washington, D.C.: American Psychological Association.

Phares, V., & Lum, J. J. (1996). Family demographics of clinically referred children: What we know and what we need to know. *Journal of Abnormal Child Psychology, 24*, 787–801.

Phillips, B. N. (1999). Strengthening the links between science and practice: Reading, evaluating, and applying research in school psychology. In C. R. Reynolds & T. B. Gutkin (Eds.), *The handbook of school psychology* (3rd ed., pp. 56–77). New York: Wiley.

Pilgrim, C., Luo, Q., Urberg, K. A., & Fang, X. (1999). Influence of peers, parents, and individual characteristics on adolescent drug use in two cultures. *Merrill-Palmer Quarterly, 45*, 85–107.

Pine, D. S., & Grun, J. (1999). Childhood anxiety: Integrating developmental psychopathology and affective neuroscience. *Journal of Child and Adolescent Psychopharmacology, 9*, 1–12.

Pine, D. S., Kentgen, L. M., Bruder, G. E., Leite, P., Bearman, K., Ma, Y., Klein, R. G. (2000). Cerebral laterality in adolescent major depression. *Psychiatry Research, 93*, 135–144.

Pineda, D., Ardila, A., Rosselli, M., Arias, B. E., Henao, G. C., Gomez, L. F., Mejia, S. E., & Miranda, M. L. (1999). Prevalence of attention-deficit/hyperactivity disorder symptoms in 4- to 17-year-old children in the general population. *Journal of Abnormal Child Psychology, 27*, 455–462.

Plante, T. G., Boccaccini, M., & Andersen, E. (1998). Attitudes concerning professional issues impacting psychotherapy practice among members of the American Board of Professional Psychology. *Psychotherapy, 35*, 34–42.

Plante, T. G., Yancey, S., Sherman, A., & Guertin, M. (2000). The association between strength of religious faith and psychological functioning. *Pastoral Psychology, 48*, 405–412.

Pliszka, S. R., Browne, R. G., Olvera, R. L., & Wynne, S. K. (2000). A double-blind, placebo-controlled study of Adderall and methylphenidate in the treatment of attention-deficit/hyperactivity disorder. *Journal of the American Academy of Child and Adolescent Psychiatry, 39*, 619–626.

Plomin, R., & Crabbe, J. (2000). DNA. *Psychological Bulletin, 126*, 806–828.

Podorefsky, D. L., McDonald-Dowdell, M., & Beardslee, W. R. (2001). Adaptation of preventive interventions for a low-income, culturally diverse community. *Journal of the American Academy of Child and Adolescent Psychiatry, 40*, 879–886.

Poduska, J. M. (2000). Parents' perceptions of their first graders' need for mental health and educational services. *Journal of the American Academy of Child and Adolescent Psychiatry, 39*, 584–591.

Posner, J. K., & Vandell, D. L. (1999). After-school activities and the development of low-income urban children: A longitudinal study. *Developmental Psychology, 35*, 868–879.

Pottick, K. J., Barber, C. C., Hansell, S., & Coyne, L. (2001). Changing patterns of inpatient care for children and adolescents at the Menninger Clinic, 1988–1994. *Journal of Consulting and Clinical Psychology, 69*, 573–577.

Pottick, K. J., McAlpine, D. D., & Andelman, R. B. (2000). Changing patterns of psychiatric inpatient care for children and adolescents in general hospitals, 1988–1995. *American Journal of Psychiatry, 157*, 1267–1273.

Poulin, F., Dishion, T. J., & Haas, E. (1999). The peer influence paradox: Friendship quality and deviancy training within male adolescent friendships. *Merrill-Palmer Quarterly, 45*, 42–61.

Poulton, R., Caspi, A., Moffitt, T. E., Cannon, M., Murray, R., & Harrington, H. L. (2000). Children's self-reported psychotic symptoms and adult schizophreniform disorder: A 15-year longitudinal study. *Archives of General Psychiatry, 57*, 1053–1058.

Power, T. J., Costigan, T. E., Leff, S. S., Eiraldi, R. B., & Landau, S. (2001). Assessing ADHD across settings: Contributions of behavioral assessment to categorical decision making. *Journal of Clinical Child Psychology*, *30*, 399–412.

Powers, S. W., Vannatta, K., Noll, R. B., Cool, V. A., & Stehbens, J. A. (1995). Leukemia and other childhood cancers. In M. C. Roberts (Ed.), *Handbook of pediatric psychology* (pp. 310–326). New York: Guilford.

Prevatt, F. F. (1999a). Milan systemic therapy. In D. M. Lawson & F. F. Prevatt (Eds.), *Casebook in family therapy* (pp. 188–209). Belmont, CA: Wadsworth.

Prevatt, F. F. (1999b). Personality assessment in the schools. In C. R. Reynolds & T. B. Gutkin (Eds.), *The handbook of school psychology* (3rd ed., pp. 434–451). New York: Wiley.

Price, R. H., Cowen, E. L., Lorion, R. P., & Ramos-McKay, J. (Eds.). (1988). *14 ounces of prevention: A casebook for practitioners.* Washington, DC: American Psychological Association.

Prior, M., & Cummins, R. (1992). Questions about facilitated communication and autism. *Journal of Autism and Developmental Disorders*, *22*, 331–338.

Prior, M., Smart, D., Sanson, A., & Oberklaid, F. (2000). Does shy-inhibited temperament in childhood lead to anxiety problems in adolescence? *Journal of the American Academy of Child and Adolescent Psychiatry*, *39*, 461–468.

Proctor, R. W., & Capaldi, E. J. (2001). Empirical evaluation and justification of methodologies in psychological science. *Psychological Bulletin*, *127*, 759–772.

Pryzwansky, W. B., & Wendt, R. N. (1999). *Professional and ethical issues in psychology: Foundations of practice.* New York: W. W. Norton and Company.

Psychological Corporation (1997). *Wechsler Adult Intelligence Scale-Third edition (WAIS-III).* San Antonio, TX: Author.

Quay, H. C. (1997). Inhibition and attention deficit hyperactivity disorder. *Journal of Abnormal Child Psychology*, *25*, 7–13.

Quay, H. C., & Hogan, A. E. (Eds.). (1999). *Handbook of disruptive behavior disorders.* New York: Kluwer Academic/Plenum.

Quay, H. C., & Peterson, D. R. (1983). *Interim manual for the Revised Behavior Problem Checklist.* Coral Gables, FL: University of Miami.

Quinn, V. N. (1995). *Applying psychology* (3rd ed.). New York: McGraw-Hill.

Quittner, A. L. (2000). Improving assessment in child clinical and pediatric psychology: Establishing links to process and functional outcomes. In D. Drotar (Ed.), *Handbook of research in pediatric and clinical child psychology* (pp. 119–143). New York: Plenum.

Rabiner, D., Coie, J. E., & Conduct Problems Prevention Research Group (2000). Early attention problems and children's reading achievement: A longitudinal investigation. *Journal of the American Academy of Child and Adolescent Psychiatry*, *39*, 859–867.

Radecki, T. E. (1990). Cartoon monitoring. *National Coalition on Television Violence News.* April–June, p. 9.

Radke-Yarrow, M. (1998). *Children of depressed mothers: From early childhood to maturity.* New York: Cambridge University Press.

Rahman, A., Mubbashar, M., Harrington, R., & Gater, R. (2000). Annotation: Developing child mental health services in developing countries. *Journal of Child Psychology and Psychiatry*, *41*, 539–546.

Rao, U., Daley, S. E., & Hammen, C. (2000). Relationship between depression and substance use disorders in adolescent women during the transition to adulthood. *Journal of the American Academy of Child and Adolescent Psychiatry*, *39*, 215–222.

Rao, U., Ryan, N. D., Dahl, R. E., Birmaher, B., Rao, R., Williamson, D. E., & Perel, J. M. (1999). Factors associated with the development of

substance use disorder in depressed adolescents. *Journal of the American Academy of Child and Adolescent Psychiatry*, *38*, 1109–1117.

Rapoport, J. L. (1989). *The boy who couldn't stop washing.* Washington, DC: American Psychiatric Press.

Rapoport, J. L., Giedd, J. N., Blumenthal, J., Hamburger, S., Jeffries, N., Fernandez, T., Nicolson, R., Bredwell, J., Lenane, M., Zijdenbos, A., Paus, T., & Evans, A. (1999). Progressive cortical change during adolescence in childhood-onset schizophrenia: A longitudinal magnetic resonance imaging study. *Archives of General Psychiatry*, *56*, 649–654.

Rapoport, J. L., & Ismond, D. R. (1996). *DSM-IV training guide for diagnosis of childhood disorders.* New York: Brunner/Mazel.

Rappaport, J., & Seidman, E. (Eds.). (2000). *Handbook of community psychology.* New York: Kluwer Academic/Plenum.

Rappaport, N., & Chubinsky, P. (2000). The meaning of psychotropic medications for children, adolescents, and their families. *Journal of the American Academy of Child and Adolescent Psychiatry*, *39*, 1198–1200.

Rapport, M. D. (2001). Bridging theory and practice: Conceptual understanding of treatments for children with attention deficit hyperactivity disorder (ADHD), obsessive-compulsive disorder (OCD), autism, and depression. *Journal of Clinical Child Psychology*, *30*, 3–7.

Rapport, M. D., & Chung, K. M. (2000). Attention deficit hyperactivity disorder. In M. Hersen & R. T. Ammerman (Eds.), *Advanced abnormal child psychology* (pp. 413–440). Mahwah, NJ: Lawrence Erlbaum.

Rapport, M. D., Chung, K., Shore, G., Denney, C. B., & Isaacs, P. (2000). Upgrading the science and technology of assessment and diagnosis: Laboratory and clinic-based assessment of children with ADHD. *Journal of Clinical Child Psychology*, *29*, 555–568.

Raschka, L. B. (2000). Paternal age and schizophrenia in dizygotic twins. *British Journal of Psychiatry*, *176*, 400–401.

Read, J., Agar, K., Barker-Collo, S., Davies, E., & Moskowitz, A. (2001). Assessing suicidality in adults: Integrating childhood trauma as a major risk factor. *Professional Psychology: Research and Practice*, *32*, 367–372.

Reagan, T. (2000). *Non-Western educational traditions: Alternative approaches to educational thought and practice* (2nd ed.). Mahwah, NJ: Lawrence Erlbaum.

Reaves, R. P., & Ogloff, J. R. P. (1996). Laws that affect the practice of psychology. In L. J. Bass, S. T. DeMers, J. R. P. Ogloff, C. Peterson, J. L. Pettifor, R. P. Reaves, T. Retfalvi, N. P. Simon, C. Sinclair, & R. M. Tipton (Eds.), *Professional conduct and discipline in psychology* (pp. 109–116). Washington, DC: American Psychological Association.

Reed, G. M., Levant, R. F., Stout, C. E., Murphy, M. J., & Phelps, R. (2001). Psychology in the current mental health marketplace. *Professional Psychology: Research and Practice*, *32*, 65–70.

Reed, L. J., Carter, B. D., & Miller, L. C. (1992). Fear and anxiety in children. In E. E. Walker & M. C. Roberts (Eds.), *Handbook of clinical child psychology* (2nd ed., pp. 237–260). New York: Wiley.

Reeves, J. C., Werry, J. S., Elkind, G. S., & Zametkin, A. (1987). Attention deficit, conduct, oppositional, and anxiety disorders in children: II. Clinical characteristics. *Journal of the American Academy of Child and Adolescent Psychiatry*, *26*, 144–155.

Reich, W. (Ed.). (1996). *Diagnostic Interview for Children and Adolescents–Revised (DICA-R) 8.0.* St. Louis: Washington University.

Reid, J. B. (1993). Prevention of conduct disorder before and after school entry: Relating interventions to developmental findings. *Development and Psychopathology*, *5*, 243–262.

Reinherz, H. Z., Giaconia, R. M., Hauf, A. M. C., Wasserman, M. S., & Paradis, A. D. (2000). General and specific childhood risk factors for depression and drug disorders by early adulthood. *Journal of the American Academy of Child and Adolescent Psychiatry, 39,* 223–231.

Reinherz, H. Z., Stewart-Berghauer, G., Pakiz, B., Frost, A. K., & Moeykens, B. A. (1989). The relationship of early risk and current mediators to depressive symptomatology in adolescence. *Journal of the American Academy of Child and Adolescent Psychiatry, 28,* 942–947.

Reiss, S. (1990). Prevalence of dual diagnosis in community-based programs in the Chicago metropolitan area. *American Journal on Mental Retardation, 94,* 578–584.

Renk, K., Liljequist, L., Steinberg, A., Bosco, G., & Phares, V. (2002). Prevention of child sexual abuse: Are we doing enough? *Trauma, Violence, and Abuse, 3,* 68–84.

Reppucci, N. D., & Aber, M. S. (1992). Child maltreatment prevention and the legal system. In D. J. Willis, E. W. Holden, & M. Rosenberg (Eds.), *Prevention of child maltreatment: Developmental and ecological perspectives* (pp. 249–266). New York: Wiley.

Reschly, D. J., & Bersoff, D. N. (1999). Law and school psychology. In C. R. Reynolds & T. B. Gutkin (Eds.), *The handbook of school psychology* (3rd ed., pp. 1077–1112). New York: Wiley.

Rey, J. M., Peng, R., Morales-Blanquez, C., Widyawati, I., Peralta, V., & Walter, G. (2000). Rating the quality of the family environment in different cultures. *Journal of the American Academy of Child and Adolescent Psychiatry, 39,* 1168–1174.

Reynolds, A. M., Elksnin, N., & Brown, F. R., (1996). Specific reading disabilities: Early identification and long-term outcome. *Mental Retardation and Developmental Disabilities Research Reviews, 2,* 21–27.

Reynolds, C. R., & Kamphaus, R. W. (1992). *Behavior Assessment System for Children Manual.* Circle Pines, MN: American Guidance Service.

Reynolds, C. R., & Richmond, B. O. (1978). What I think and feel: A revised measure of children's manifest anxiety. *Journal of Abnormal Child Psychology, 6,* 271–280.

Reynolds, C. R., & Richmond, B. O. (1997). What I think and feel: A revised measure of children's manifest anxiety. *Journal of Abnormal Child Psychology, 25,* 15–20.

Reynolds, W. M. (1988a). Major depression. In M. Hersen & C. G. Last (Eds.), *Child behavior therapy casebook* (pp. 85–100). New York: Plenum.

Reynolds, W. M. (1988b). *Suicidal Ideation Questionnaire: Professional manual.* Odessa, FL: Psychological Assessment Resources.

Reynolds, W. M. (1995). Depression. In V. B. VanHasselt & M. Hersen (Eds.), *Handbook of adolescent psychopathology: A guide to diagnosis and treatment* (pp. 297–348). New York: Lexington Books.

Rheingold, H. L. (1994). *The psychologist's guide to an academic career.* Washington, DC: American Psychological Association.

Rhodes, G., & Rhodes, R. (1996). *Trying to get some dignity: Stories of triumph over childhood abuse.* New York: William Morrow.

Riccio, C. A., Gonzalez, J. J., & Hynd, G. W. (1994). Attention-deficit hyperactivity disorder (ADHD) and learning disabilities. *Learning Disability Quarterly, 17,* 311–322.

Riccio, C. A., & Reynolds, C. R. (1998). Neuropsychological assessment of children. In C. R. Reynolds (Ed.), *Comprehensive clinical psychology: Assessment* (Vol. 4, pp. 267–301). Oxford, England: Elsevier Science.

Richman, L. C., & Wood, K. M. (1999). Psychological assessment and treatment of communication disorders: Childhood language subtypes. In S. D. Netherton, D. Holmes, & C. E. Walker (Eds.), *Child and adolescent psychological disorders: A comprehensive textbook* (pp. 51–75). New York: Oxford University Press.

Richters, J. E., & Martinez, P. E. (1993). Violent communities, family choices, and children's chances: An algorithm for improving the odds. *Development and Psychopathology, 5,* 609–627.

Rickert, V. I., Hassed, S. J., Hendon, A. E., & Cunniff, C. (1996). The effects of peer ridicule on depression and self-image among adolescent females with Turner syndrome. *Journal of Adolescent Health, 19,* 34–38.

Riddle, M. A., Kastelic, E. A., & Frosch, E. (2001). Pediatric psychopharmacology. *Journal of Child Psychology and Psychiatry, 42,* 73–90.

Rie, H. E. (1971). Historical perspective of concepts of child psychopathology. In H. E. Rie (Ed.), *Perspectives in child psychopathology* (pp. 3–50). Chicago: Aldine-Atherton.

Riggs, P. D., Mikulich, S. K., Whitmore, E. A., & Crowley, T. J. (1999). Relationship of ADHD, depression and non-tobacco substance use disorders to nicotine dependence in substance-dependent delinquents. *Drug and Alcohol Dependence, 54,* 195–205.

Rimland, B. (1994). Facilitated communication update. *Autism Research Review International, 8,* 6.

Rind, B., Tromovitch, P., & Bauserman, R. (1998). A meta-analytic examination of assumed properties of child sexual abuse using college samples. *Psychological Bulletin, 124,* 22–53.

Robbins, M. S., Alexander, J. F., & Turner, C. W. (2000). Disrupting defensive family interactions in family therapy with delinquent adolescents. *Journal of Family Psychology, 14,* 688–701.

Roberts, M. C. (Ed.). (1995). *Handbook of pediatric psychology* (2nd ed.). New York: Guilford.

Roberts, M. C., Koocher, G. P., Routh, D. K., & Willis, D. J. (Eds.). (1993). *Readings in pediatric psychology.* New York: Plenum.

Roberts, M. C., Vernberg, E. M., & Jackson, Y. (2000). Psychotherapy with children and families. In C. R. Snyder, & R. E. Ingram (Eds.), *Handbook of psychological change: Psychotherapy processes and practices for the 21st century* (pp. 500–519). New York: Wiley.

Roberts, M. C., & Walker, C. E. (Eds.). (1989). *Casebook of child and pediatric psychology.* New York: Guilford.

Roberts, R. E. (2000). Depression and suicide behaviors among adolescents: The role of ethnicity. In I. Cuellar & F. A. Paniagua (Eds.), *Handbook of multicultural mental health: Assessment and treatment of diverse populations* (pp. 359–388). San Diego: Academic Press.

Robin, A. L., Bedway, M., Siegel, P. T., & Gilroy, M. (1996). Therapy for adolescent anorexia nervosa: Addressing cognitions, feelings, and the family's role. In E. D. Hibbs & P. S. Jensen (Eds.), *Psychosocial treatments for child and adolescent disorders: Empirically based strategies for clinical practice* (pp. 239–259). Washington, DC: American Psychological Association.

Robins, L. N., & Regier, D. A. (1991). *Psychiatric disorders in America.* New York: Free Press.

Robinson, L. A., & Klesges, R. C. (1997). Ethnic and gender differences in risk factors for smoking onset. *Health Psychology, 16,* 499–505.

Robinson, N. M., Zigler, E., & Gallagher, J. J. (2000). Two tails of the normal curve: Similarities and differences in the study of mental retardation and giftedness. *American Psychologist, 55,* 1413–1424.

Rodin, J., Silberstein, L. R., & Striegel-Moore, R. H. (1985). Woman and weight: A normative discontent. In T. B. Sonderegger (Ed.), *Psychology and gender: Nebraska symposium on motivation* (pp. 267–307). Lincoln: University of Nebraska Press.

Rodriguez, M. L., Mischel, W., & Shoda, Y. (1989). Cognitive person variables in the delay of gratification of older children at risk. *Journal of Personality and Social Psychology, 57,* 358–367.

Rogers, S. J. (1998). Empirically supported comprehensive treatments for young children with autism. *Journal of Clinical Child Psychology, 27,* 168–179.

Rohde, P., Clarke, G. N., Lewinsohn, P. M., Seeley, J. R., & Kaufman, N. K. (2001). Impact of comorbidity on a cognitive-behavioral group treatment for adolescent depression. *Journal of the American Academy of Child and Adolescent Psychiatry*, *40*, 795–802.

Rohde, P., Lewinsohn, P. M., Kahler, C. W., Seeley, J. R., & Brown, R. A. (2001). Natural course of alcohol use disorders from adolescence to young adulthood. *Journal of the American Academy of Child and Adolescent Psychiatry*, *40*, 83–90.

Rolf, J., Masten, A. S., Cicchetti, D., Neuchterlein, K. H., & Weintraub, S. (Eds.). (1990). *Risk and protective factors in the development of psychopathology*. New York: Cambridge University Press.

Rollman, G. B. (1998). Culture and pain. In S. S. Kazarian & D. R. Evans (Eds.), *Cultural clinical psychology: Theory, research, and practice* (pp. 267–286). New York: Oxford University Press.

Rorschach, H. (1942). *Psychodiagnostics*. Bern, Switzerland: Hans Huber (Original work published in 1921).

Rosen, J. C., & Leitenberg, H. (1985). Exposure plus response prevention treatment of bulimia. In D. M. Garner & P. E. Garfinkel (Eds.), *Handbook of psychotherapy for anorexia nervosa and bulimia* (pp. 193–209). New York: Guilford.

Rosenbaum, D. P., & Hanson, G. S. (1998). Assessing the effects of school-based drug education: A six-year multilevel analysis of Project D.A.R.E. *Journal of Research in Crime and Delinquency*, *35*, 381–412.

Rosenthal, R. & Jacobson, L. (1966). Teachers' expectancies: Determinants of pupils' IQ gains. *Psychological Reports*, *19*, 115–18.

Ross, H. E., & Ivis, F. (1999). Binge eating and substance use among male and female adolescents. *International Journal of Eating Disorders*, *26*, 245–260.

Rossman, M. H. (1995). *Negotiating graduate school: A guide for graduate students*. Thousand Oaks, CA: Sage.

Rothbaum, F., Morelli, G., Pott, M., & Liu-Constant, Y. (2000). Immigrant-Chinese and Euro-American parents' physical closeness with young children: Themes of family relatedness. *Journal of Family Psychology*, *14*, 334–348.

Rothbaum, F., Weisz, J., Pott, M., Miyake, K., & Morelli, G. (2000). Attachment and culture: Security in the United States and Japan. *American Psychologist*, *55*, 1093–1104.

Rotheram-Borus, M. J., & Stein, J. A. (1999). Problem behavior of adolescents whose parents are living with AIDS. *American Journal of Orthopsychiatry*, *69*, 228–239.

Rotheram-Borus, M. J., Stein, J. A., & Lin, Y. Y. (2001). Impact of parent death and an intervention on the adjustment of adolescents whose parents have HIV/AIDS. *Journal of Consulting and Clinical Psychology*, *69*, 763–773.

Rotter, J. B., Lah, M. I., & Rafferty, J. E. (1992). *Manual: Rotter Incomplete Sentences Blank* (2nd ed.). Orlando, FL: Psychological Corporation.

Rourke, B. P., & Tsatsanis, K. D. (2000). Nonverbal learning disabilities and Asperger syndrome. In A. Klin & F. R. Volkmar (Ed.), *Asperger syndrome* (pp. 231–253). New York: Guilford.

Rovert, J., & Fernandes, C. (1999). Insulin-dependent diabetes mellitus. In R. T. Brown (Ed.), *Cognitive aspects of chronic illness in children* (pp. 142–171). New York: Guilford.

Rovert, J., Netley, C., Keenan, M., Bailey, J., & Stewart, D. (1996). The psychoeducational profile of boys with Klinefelter syndrome. *Journal of Learning Disabilities*, *29*, 180–196.

Royko, D. (1999). *Voices of children of divorce*. New York: Golden Books.

Rudnick, A. (2001). Ethics of ECT for children. *Journal of the Academy of Child and Adolescent Psychiatry*, *40*, 387.

Rudolph, K. D., & Clark, A. G. (2001). Conceptions of relationships in children with depressive and aggressive symptoms: Social-cognitive distortion or reality? *Journal of Abnormal Child Psychology*, *29*, 41–56.

Rudolph, K. D., Dennig, M. D., & Weisz, J. R. (1995). Determinants and consequences of children's coping in the medical setting: Conceptualization, review, and critique. *Psychological Bulletin*, *118*, 328–357.

Rudolph, K. D., & Hammen, C. (1999). Age and gender as determinants of stress exposure, generation, and reactions in youngsters: A transactional perspective. *Child Development*, *70*, 660–677.

Rudolph, K. D., Hammen, C., & Burge, D. (1997). A cognitive-interpersonal approach to depressive symptoms in preadolescent children. *Journal of Abnormal Child Psychology*, *25*, 33–45.

Rueter, M. A., Chao, W., & Conger, R. D. (2000). The effect of systematic variation in retrospective conduct disorder reports on antisocial personality disorder diagnoses. *Journal of Consulting and Clinical Psychology*, *68*, 307–312.

Ruggiero, K. J., Morris, T. L., Beidel, D. C., Scotti, J. R., & McLeer, S. V. (1999). Discriminant validity of self-reported anxiety and depression in children: Generalizability to clinic-referred and ethnically diverse populations. *Assessment*, *6*, 259–267.

Ruggiero, K. J., Morris, T. L., & Scotti, J. R. (2001). Treatment for children with posttraumatic stress disorder: Current status and future directions. *Clinical Psychology: Science and Practice*, *8*, 210–227.

Rumstein-McKean, O., & Hunsley, J. (2001). Interpersonal and family functioning of female survivors of childhood sexual abuse. *Clinical Psychology Review*, *21*, 471–490.

Russ, S. W. (1998a). Play therapy. In T. Ollendick (Ed.), *Comprehensive clinical psychology* (Vol. 5, pp. 221–244). Oxford, England: Elsevier Science.

Russ, S. W. (1998b). Psychodynamically based therapies. In T. H. Ollendick & M. Hersen (Eds.), *Handbook of child psychopathology* (pp. 537–556). New York: Plenum.

Russell, A. T., Bott, L., & Sammons, C. (1989). The phenomenology of schizophrenia occurring in childhood. *Journal of the American Academy of Child and Adolescent Psychiatry*, *28*, 399–407.

Rutter, M. (1979). Protective factors in children's responses to stress and disadvantage. In M. W. Kent & J. E. Rolf (Eds.), *Primary prevention of psychopathology: Vol. 3. Social competence in children* (pp. 49–74). Hanover, NH: University Press of New England.

Rutter, M. (1996). Developmental psychopathology: Concepts and prospects. In M. F. Lenzeneger & J. J. Haugaard (Eds.), *Frontiers of developmental psychopathology* (pp. 209–237). New York: Oxford University Press.

Rutter, M. (1999). Psychosocial adversity and child psychopathology. *British Journal of Psychiatry*, *174*, 480–493.

Rutter, M. (2000). Genetic studies of autism: From the 1970s into the millennium. *Journal of Abnormal Child Psychology*, *28*, 3–14.

Rutter, M., & Schopler, E. (1992). Classification of pervasive developmental disorders: Some concepts and practical considerations. *Journal of Autism and Developmental Disorders*, *22*, 459–482.

Rutter, M., Silberg, J., O'Connor, T., & Simonoff, E. (1999a). Genetics and child psychiatry: I. Advances in quantitative and molecular genetics. *Journal of Child Psychology and Psychiatry*, *40*, 3–18.

Rutter, M., Silberg, J., O'Connor, T., & Simonoff, E. (1999b). Genetics and child psychiatry: II Empirical research findings. *Journal of Child Psychology and Psychiatry*, *40*, 19–55.

Ryan, B. A., Adams, G. R., Gullotta, T. P., Weissberg, R. P., & Hampton, R. L. (1995). *The family-school connection: Theory, research and practice*. Thousand Oaks, CA: Sage.

Sadeh, A., & Gruber, R. (1998). Sleep disorders. In T. Ollendick (Ed.), *Comprehensive clinical psychology* (Vol. 5, pp. 629–653). Oxford, England: Elsevier Science.

Sagrestano, L. M., & Paikoff, R. L. (1997). Preventing high-risk sexual behavior, sexually transmitted diseases, and pregnancy among adolescents. In R. P. Weissberg, T. P. Gullotta, R. L. Hampton, B. A. Ryan, & G. R. Adams (Eds.), *Healthy children 2010: Enhancing children's wellness* (pp. 76–104). Thousand Oaks, CA: Sage.

Sales, B. D., Krauss, D. A., Sacken, D. M., & Overcast, T. D. (1999). The legal rights of students. In C. R. Reynolds & T. B. Gutkin (Eds.), *The handbook of school psychology* (3rd ed., pp. 1113–1144). New York: Wiley.

Sallee, F. R., & Spratt, E. G. (1998). Tics and Tourette's disorder. In T. H. Ollendick & M. Hersen (Eds.), *Handbook of child psychopathology* (3rd ed., pp. 337–353). New York: Plenum.

Sallee, R., & Greenawald, J. (1995). Neurobiology. In J. S. March (Ed.), *Anxiety disorders in children and adolescents* (pp. 3–34). New York: Guilford.

Samaan, R. A. (2000). The influences of race, ethnicity, and poverty on the mental health of children. *Journal of Health Care for the Poor and Underserved, 11*, 100–110.

Sammons, M. T., Gorny, S. W., Zinner, E. S., & Allen, R. P. (2000). Prescriptive authority for psychologists: A consensus of support. *Professional Psychology: Research and Practice, 31*, 604–609.

Samples, C. L., Goodman, E., & Woods, E. R. (1998). Epidemiology and medical management of adolescents. In P. A. Pizzo & C. M. Wilfert (Eds.), *Pediatric AIDS: The challenge of HIV infection in infants, children, and adolescents* (3rd ed., pp. 615–643). Baltimore: Williams and Wilkins.

Samudra, K., & Cantwell, D. P. (1999). Risk factors for attention-deficit/hyperactivity disorder. In H. C. Quay & A. E. Hogan (Eds.), *Handbook of disruptive behavior disorders* (pp. 199–220). New York: Kluwer Academic.

Samuel, V. J., Curtis, S., Thornell, A., George, P., Taylor, A., Brome, D. R., Biederman, J., & Faraone, S. V. (1997). The unexplored void of ADHD and African-American research: A review of the literature. *Journal of Attention Disorders, 1*, 197–207.

Sanders, M. R., Markie-Dadds, C., Tully, L. A., & Bor, W. (2000). The triple-P Positive Parenting Program: A comparison of enhanced, standard, and self-directed behavioral family intervention for parents of children with early onset conduct problems. *Journal of Consulting and Clinical Psychology, 68*, 624–640.

Sanders, M. R., Montgomery, D. T., & Brechman-Toussaint, M. L. (2000). The mass media and the prevention of child behavior problems: The evaluation of a television series to promote positive outcomes for parents and their children. *Journal of Child Psychology and Psychiatry, 41*, 939–948.

Sanger, J., Wilson, J., Davies, B., & Whitakker, R. (1997). *Young children, videos and computer games: Issues for teachers and parents.* Washington, DC: Falmer.

Satcher, D. (2000). Mental health: A report of the Surgeon General—Executive summary. *Professional Psychology: Research and Practice, 31*, 5–13.

Satcher, D. (2001). *Surgeon General releases a national action agenda on children's mental health.* Bethesda, MD: US Department of Health and Human Services.

Satir, V. (1983). *Conjoint family therapy.* Palo Alto, CA: Science and Behavior Books.

Sattler, J. M. (1992). *Assessment of children* (3rd ed. rev.). San Diego: Jerome M. Sattler.

Sattler, J. M. (1998). *Clinical and forensic interviewing of children and families.* San Diego, CA: Jerome M. Sattler.

Sattler, J. M. (2001). *Assessment of children: Cognitive applications* (4th ed.). San Diego: Jerome M. Sattler.

Sattler, J. M. (2002). *Assessment of children: Behavioral and clinical applications* (4th ed.). San Diego: Jerome M. Sattler.

Savin-Williams, R. C. (1990). *Gay and lesbian youth: Expressions of identity.* New York: Hemisphere.

Savin-Williams, R. C. (1994). Verbal and physical abuse as stressors in the lives of lesbian, gay male, and bisexual youths: Associations with school problems, running away, substance abuse, prostitution, and suicide. *Journal of Consulting and Clinical Psychology, 62*, 261–269.

Savin-Williams, R. C. (2001). Suicide attempts among sexual-minority youths: Population and measurement issues. *Journal of Consulting and Clinical Psychology, 69*, 983–991.

Savin-Williams, R. C., & Diamond, L. M. (1999). Sexual orientation. In W. K. Silverman & T. H. Ollendick (Eds.), *Developmental issues in the clinical treatment of children* (pp. 241–258). Boston: Allyn & Bacon.

Sawyer, M. G., Streiner, D. L., & Baghurst, P. (1998). The influence of distress on mothers' and fathers' reports of childhood emotional and behavioral problems. *Journal of Abnormal Child Psychology, 26*, 407–414.

Saywitz, K. J., Mannarino, A. P., Berliner, L., & Cohen, J. A. (2000). Treatment for sexually abused children and adolescents. *American Psychologist, 55*, 1040–1049.

Scarr, S., & Deater-Deckard, K. (1997). Family effects on individual differences in development. In S. S. Luthar, J. A. Burack, D. Cicchetti, & J. R. Weisz (Eds.), *Developmental psychopathology: Perspectives on adjustment, risk, and disorder* (pp. 115–136). New York: Cambridge University Press.

Scaturo, D. J. (2001). The evolution of psychotherapy and the concept of manualization: An integrative perspective. *Professional Psychology: Research and Practice, 32*, 522–530.

Schachar, R., Mota, V. L., Logan, G. D., Tannock, R., & Klim, P. (2000). Confirmation of an inhibitory control deficit in attention-deficit/hyperactivity disorder. *Journal of Abnormal Child Psychology, 28*, 227–235.

Scheer, S. D., Borden, L. M., & Donnermeyer, J. F. (2000). The relationship between family factors and adolescent substance use in rural, suburban, and urban settings. *Journal of Child and Family Studies, 9*, 105–115.

Schiller, L., & Bennett, A. (1994). *The quiet room: A journey out of the torment of madness.* New York: Warner Books.

Schinke, S. P., Botvin, G. J., & Orlandi, M. A. (1991). *Substance abuse in children and adolescents: Evaluation and intervention.* Newbury Park, CA: Sage.

Scholle, S. H., & Kelleher, K. J. (1998). Managed care: Opportunities and threats for children with serious emotional disturbance and their families. In M. H. Epstein & K. Kutash (Eds.), *Outcomes for children and youth with emotional and behavioral disorders and their families: Programs and evaluation best practices* (pp. 659–684). Austin, TX: Pro-Ed.

Schoppe, S. J., Mangelsdorf, S. C., & Frosch, C. A. (2001). Coparenting, family process, and family structure: Implications for preschoolers' externalizing behavior problems. *Journal of Family Psychology, 15*, 526–545.

Schreibman, L., & Charlop-Christy, M. H. (1998). Autistic disorder. In T. H. Ollendick & M. Hersen (Eds.), *Handbook of child psychopathology* (3rd ed., pp. 157–179). New York: Plenum.

Schwab-Stone, M. E., Shaffer, D., Dulcan, M. K., Jensen, P. S., Fisher, P., Bird, H. R., Goodman, S. H., Lahey, B. B., Lichtman, J. H., Canino, G., Rubio-Stipec, M. & Rae, D. S. (1996). Criterion validity of the NIMH Diagnostic Interview Schedule for Children Version 2.3

(DISC-2.3). *Journal of the American Academy of Child and Adolescent Psychiatry, 35,* 878–888.

Schwartz, D., Dodge, K. A., Coie, J. D., Hubbard, J. A., Cillessen, A. H. N., Lemerise, E. A., & Bateman, H. (1998). Social-cognitive and behavioral correlates of aggression and victimization in boys' play groups. *Journal of Abnormal Child Psychology, 26,* 431–440.

Schwartz, J. A. J., Gladstone, T. R. G., & Kaslow, N. J. (1998). Depressive disorders. In T. H. Ollendick & M. Hersen (Eds.), *Handbook of child psychopathology* (3rd ed., pp. 269–289). New York: Plenum.

Schwartz, S. (1992). *Cases in abnormal psychology.* New York: Wiley.

Schwarzchild, M. (2000). Alienated youth. Help from families and schools. *Professional Psychology: Research and Practice, 31,* 95–96.

Sefa-Dedeh, A. (1992). Improving children's lives: The case for primary prevention in Ghana. In G. W. Albee, L. A. Bond, & T. V. C. Monsey (Eds.), *Improving children's lives: Global perspectives on prevention* (pp. 63–72). Newbury Park, CA: Sage.

Seidman, E., Chesir-Teran, D., Friedman, J. L., Yoshikawa, H., Allen, L., Roberts, A., & Aber, J. L. (1999). The risk and protective functions of perceived family and peer microsystems among urban adolescents in poverty. *American Journal of Community Psychology, 27,* 211–237.

Sek, H., Bleja, A., & Sommerfeld, A. (1992). Fostering parental competence in Poland. In G. W. Albee, L. A. Bond, & T. V. C. Monsey (Eds.), *Improving children's lives: Global perspectives on prevention* (pp. 253–260). Newbury Park, CA: Sage.

Seligman, L. D., & Ollendick, T. H. (1998). Comorbidity of anxiety and depression in children and adolescents: An integrative review. *Clinical Child and Family Psychology Review, 1,* 125–144.

Seligman, M. E. P. (1991). *Learned optimism.* New York: Knopf.

Seligman, M. E. P., Reivich, K., Jaycox, L., & Gillham, J. (1995). *The optimistic child.* Boston: Houghton Mifflin.

Selvini-Palazzoli, M., Boscolo, L., Cecchin, G., & Prata, G. (1978). *Paradox and counterparadox.* New York: Jason Aronson.

Serafica, F. C. (1997). Psychopathology and resilience in Asian American children and adolescents. *Applied Developmental Science, 1,* 145–155.

Shaffer, D. (1996). *Diagnostic Interview Schedule for Children (DISC-IV).* New York: New York State Psychiatric Institute.

Shaffer, D., Fisher, P., Dulcan, M. K., Davies, M., Piacentini, J., Schwab-Stone, M. E., Lahey, B. B., Bourdon, K., Jensen, P. S., Bird, H. R., Canino, G., & Regier, D. A. (1996). The NIMH Diagnostic Interview Schedule for Children Version 2.3 (DISC-2.3): Description, acceptability, prevalence rates, and performance in the MECA Study. *Journal of the American Academy of Child and Adolescent Psychiatry, 35,* 865–877.

Shaffer, D., Fisher, P., Lucas, C. P., Dulcan, M. K., & Schwab-Stone, M. E. (2000). NIMH Diagnostic Interview Schedule for Children Version IV (NIMH DISC-IV): Description, differences from previous versions, and reliability of some common diagnoses. *Journal of the American Academy of Child and Adolescent Psychiatry, 39,* 28–38.

Shaffer, D., Garland, A., Fisher, P., Bacon, K., & Vieland, V. (1990). Suicide crisis centers: A critical reappraisal with special reference to the prevention of youth suicide. In F. E. Goldston, C. M. Heinicke, R. S. Pynoos, & J. Yager (Eds.), *Prevention of mental health disturbance in childhood* (pp. 135–166). Washington, D. C.: American Psychiatric Association Press.

Shaffer, D., Garland, A., Vieland, V., Underwood, M., & Busner, C. (1991). The impact of curriculum-based suicide prevention programs for teenagers. *Journal of the American Academy of Child and Adolescent Psychiatry, 30,* 588–596.

Shaffer, D., & Pfeffer, C. R. (2001). Practice parameter for the assessment and treatment of children and adolescents with suicidal behav-

ior. *Journal of the American Academy of Child and Adolescent Psychiatry, 40 (Supplement 7),* 24S-51S.

Shaffer, D., & Waslick, B. D. (1996). Elimination and sleep disorders. In J. M. Wiener (Ed.), *Diagnosis and psychopharmacology of childhood and adolescent disorders* (2nd ed.). New York: Wiley.

Shahinfar, A., Kupersmidt, J. B., & Matza, L. S. (2001). The relation between exposure to violence and social information processing among incarcerated adolescents. *Journal of Abnormal Psychology, 110,* 136–141.

Shakur, S. (1993). *Monster: The autobiography of an L.A. gang member.* New York: Penguin Books.

Shandler, S. (1999). *Ophelia speaks.* New York: Harper Perennial.

Shaw, D. S., Owens, E. B., Giovannelli, J., & Winslow, E. B. (2001). Infant and toddler pathways leading to early externalizing disorders. *Journal of the American Academy of Child and Adolescent Psychiatry, 40,* 36–43.

Shaywitz, S. E. (1998). Current concepts: Dyslexia. *New England Journal of Medicine, 338,* 307–312.

Shaywitz, S. E., Escobar, M. D., Shaywitz, B. A., Fletcher, J. M., & Makuch, R. (1992). Evidence that dyslexia may represent the lower tail of a normal distribution of reading ability. *New England Journal of Medicine, 326,* 145–150.

Shaywitz, S. E., Shaywitz, B. A., Fletcher, J. M., & Escobar, M. D. (1990). Prevalence of reading disability in boys and girls. *Journal of the American Medical Association, 264,* 998–1002.

Sheeber, L., & Sorensen, E. (1998). Family relationships of depressed adolescents: A multimethod assessment. *Journal of Clinical Child Psychology, 27,* 268–277.

Sheehan, W., & Garfinkel, B. D. (1988). Adolescent autoerotic deaths. *Journal of the American Academy of Child and Adolescent Psychiatry, 27,* 367–370.

Sheldrick, R. C., Kendall, P. C., Heimberg, R. G. (2001). The clinical significance of treatments: A comparison of three treatments for conduct disordered children. *Clinical Psychology: Science and Practice, 8,* 418–430.

Shelley-Tremblay, J. F., & Rosen, L. A. (1996). Attention deficit hyperactivity disorder: An evolutionary perspective. *Journal of Genetic Psychology, 157,* 443–453.

Shelton, T. L., Barkley, R. A., Crosswait, C., Moorehouse, M., Fletcher, K., Barrett, S., Jenkins, L., & Metevia, L. (2000). Multimethod psychoeducational intervention for preschool children with disruptive behavior: Two-year post-treatment follow-up. *Journal of Abnormal Child Psychology, 28,* 253–266.

Shepherd, M., Oppenheim, B., & Mitchell, S. (1971). *Childhood behavior and mental health.* New York: Grune and Stratton.

Sheslow, D., & Adams, W. (1990). *Wide Range Assessment of Memory and Learning.* Wilmington, DE: Jastak Associates.

Shields, A., & Cicchetti, D. (2001). Parental maltreatment and emotion dysregulation as risk factors for bullying and victimization in middle childhood. *Journal of Clinical Child Psychology, 30,* 349–363.

Shirk, S. R., Boergers, J., Eason, A., & VanHorn, M. (1998). Dysphoric interpersonal schemata and preadolescents' sensitization to negative events. *Journal of Clinical Child Psychology, 27,* 54–68.

Shirk, S. R., VanHorn, M., & Leber, D. (1997). Dysphoria and children's processing of supportive interactions. *Journal of Abnormal Child Psychology, 25,* 239–249.

Shochet, I. M., Dadds, M. R., Holland, D., Whitefield, K., Harnett, P. H., & Osgarby, S. M. (2001). The efficacy of a universal school-based program to prevent adolescent depression. *Journal of Clinical Child Psychology, 30,* 303–315.

Shonk, S. M., & Cicchetti, D. (2001). Maltreatment, competency deficits, and risk for academic and behavioral maladjustment. *Developmental Psychology*, *37*, 3–17.

Shortt, A. L., Barrett, P. M., Dadds, M. R., & Fox, T. L. (2001). The influence of family and experimental context on cognition in anxious children. *Journal of Abnormal Child Psychology*, *29*, 585–596.

Shortt, A. L., Barrett, P. M., & Fox, T. L. (2001). Evaluating the FRIENDS Program: A cognitive-behavioral group treatment for anxious children and their parents. *Journal of Clinical Child Psychology*, *30*, 525–535.

Sicher, P., Lewis, O., Sargent, J., Chaffin, M., Friedrich, W. N., Cunningham, N., Thomas, R., Thomas, P., & Villani, V. S. (2000). Developing child abuse prevention, identification, and treatment systems in Eastern Europe. *Journal of the American Academy of Child and Adolescent Psychiatry*, *39*, 660–667.

Sigman, M. (1996). Behavioral research in childhood autism. In M. F. Lenzenweger & J. J. Haugaard (Eds.), *Frontiers of developmental psychopathology* (pp. 190–206). New York: Oxford University Press.

Silver, E. J., Westbrook, L. E., & Stein, R. E. K. (1998). Relationship of parental psychological distress to consequences of chronic health conditions in children. *Journal of Pediatric Psychology*, *23*, 5–15.

Silverman, W. K., & Ginsburg, G. S. (1995). Specific phobia and generalized anxiety disorder. In J. S. March (Ed.), *Anxiety disorders in children and adolescents* (pp. 151–180). New York: Guilford.

Silverman, W. K., & Ginsburg, G. S. (1998). Anxiety disorders. In T. H. Ollendick & M. Hersen (Eds.), *Handbook of child psychopathology* (3rd ed., pp. 239–268). New York: Plenum.

Silverman, W. K., & Nelles, W. B. (1988). The Anxiety Disorders Interview Schedule for Children. *Journal of the American Academy of Child and Adolescent Psychiatry*, *27*, 772–778.

Silverman, W. K., & Ollendick, T. H. (Eds.), *Developmental issues in the clinical treatment of children*. Boston: Allyn & Bacon.

Silverstein, J. (1994). Diabetes: Medical issues. In R. A. Olson, L. L. Mullins, J. B. Gillman, & J. M. Chaney (Eds.), *The sourcebook of pediatric psychology* (pp. 111–117). Boston: Allyn & Bacon.

Silverstein, L. B., & Phares, V. (1996). Expanding the parenting paradigm: An examination of dissertation research 1986–1994. *Psychology of Women Quarterly*, *20*, 39–53.

Simeonsson, R. J., & Rosenthal, S. L. (1992). Developmental models and clinical practice. In C. E. Walker & M. C. Roberts (Eds.), *Handbook of clinical child psychology* (2nd ed., pp. 19–31). New York: Wiley.

Simmel, C., Brooks, D., Barth, R. P., & Hinshaw, S. P. (2001). Externalizing symptomatology among adoptive youth: Prevalence and preadoption risk factors. *Journal of Abnormal Child Psychology*, *29*, 57–69.

Simola, S. K., Parker, K. C. H., & Froese, A. P. (1999). Relational V-code conditions in a child and adolescent population do warrant treatment. *Journal of Marriage and Family Counseling*, *25*, 225–236.

Simonoff, E. (2000). Extracting meaning from comorbidity: Genetic analyses that make sense. *Journal of Child Psychology and Psychiatry*, *41*, 667–674.

Simonoff, E., Pickles, A., Meyer, J., Silberg, J., & Maes, H. (1998). Genetic and environmental influences on subtypes of conduct disorder behavior in boys. *Journal of Abnormal Child Psychology*, *26*, 495–509.

Singh, N. N., Beale, I. L., & Snell, D. L. (1988). Learning disorders. In M. Hersen & C. G. Last (Eds.), *Child behavior therapy casebook* (pp. 193–206). New York: Plenum.

Singh, N. N., & Ellis, C. R. (1998). Pharmacological therapies. In T. Ollendick (Ed.), *Comprehensive clinical psychology* (Vol. 5, pp. 267–294). Oxford, England: Elsevier Science.

Singh, N. N., Oswald, D. P., & Ellis, C. R. (1998). Mental retardation. In T. H. Ollendick & M. Hersen (Eds.), *Handbook of child psychopathology* (3rd ed., pp. 91–116). New York: Plenum.

Skuse, D. H. (2000). Behavioural neuroscience and child psychopathology: Insights from model systems. *Journal of Child Psychology and Psychiatry*, *41*, 3–31.

Sloan, M. T., Jensen, P. S., & Kettle, L. (1999). Assessing the services for children with ADHD: Gaps and opportunities. *Journal of Attention Disorders*, *3*, 13–29.

Slomkowski, C., Rende, R., Congen, K. J., Simons, R. L., & Conger, R. D. (2001). Sisters, brothers, and delinquency: Evaluating social influences during early and middle adolescence. *Child Development*, *72*, 271-283.

Slutske, W. S., Heath, A. C., Dinwidde, S. H., Madden, P. A. F., Bucholz, K. K., Dunne, M. P., Statham, D. J., & Martin, N. G. (1997). Modeling genetic and environmental influences in the etiology of conduct disorder: A study of 2,682 adult twin pairs. *Journal of Abnormal Psychology*, *106*, 266–279.

Smalley, S. L., McGough, J. J., Del Homme, M., NewDelman, J., Gordon, E., Kim, T., Liu, A., & McCracken, J. T. (2000). Familial clustering of symptoms and disruptive behaviors in multiplex families with attention-deficit/hyperactivity disorder. *Journal of the American Academy of Child and Adolescent Psychiatry*, *39*, 1135–1143.

Smith, A. M., & Phares, V. (1999). Adolescents' subjective distress over their emotional/behavioral problems and the self-system model: Competence, control, and motivation to change. Manuscript under review.

Smith, B. H., Pelham, W. E., Gnagy, E., Molina, B., & Evans, S. (2000). The reliability, validity, and unique contributions of self-report by adolescents receiving treatment for attention-deficit/hyperactivity disorder. *Journal of Consulting and Clinical Psychology*, *68*, 489–499.

Smith, M. A., & Senior, C. (2001). The Internet and clinical psychology: A general review of the implications. *Clinical Psychology Review*, *21*, 129–136.

Smith, R. E., & Smoll, F. L. (1997). Coaching the coaches: Youth sports as a scientific and applied behavioral setting. *Current Directions in Psychological Science*, *6*, 16–21.

Snow, D. L., Grady, K., & Goyette-Ewing, M. (2000). A perspective on ethical issues in community psychology. In J. Rappaport & E. Seidman (Eds.), *Handbook of community psychology* (pp. 897–917). New York: Kluwer Academic/Plenum.

Solomon, J., & George, C. (Eds.). (1999). *Attachment disorganization*. New York: Guilford.

Sonne, J. L. (1994). Multiple relationships: Does the new ethics code answer the right questions? *Professional Psychology: Research and Practice*, *25*, 336–343.

Sonty, N. (1992). A multimodal approach to prevention: A review of India's integrated child development scheme. In G. W. Albee, L. A. Bond, & T. V. C. Monsey (Eds.), *Improving children's lives: Global perspectives on prevention* (pp. 191–199). Newbury Park: Sage.

Sonuga-Barke, E. J. S. (1998). Categorical models of childhood disorder: A conceptual and empirical analysis. *Journal of Child Psychology and Psychiatry*, *39*, 115–133.

Southam-Gerow, M. A., Kendall, P. C., & Weersing, V. R. (2001). Examining outcome variability: Correlates of treatment response in a child and adolescent anxiety clinic. *Journal of Clinical Child Psychology*, *30*, 422– 436.

Spaccarelli, S. (1994). Stress, appraisal, and coping in child sexual abuse: A theoretical and empirical review. *Psychological Bulletin*, *116*, 340–362.

Sparrow, S. S., Balla, D. A., & Cicchetti, D. V. (1984). *Vineland Adaptive Behavior Scales*. Circle Pines, MN: American Guidance Service.

Sparrow, S. S., Carter, A. S., Racusin, G., & Morris, R. (1995). Comprehensive psychological assessment through the life span: A developmental approach. In D. Cicchetti & D. J. Cohen (Eds.), *Developmental psychopathology* (Vol. 1, pp. 81–105). New York: Wiley.

Sparrow, S. S., & Davis, S. M. (2000). Recent advances in the assessment of intelligence and cognition. *Journal of Child Psychology and Psychiatry, 41*, 117–131.

Speltz, M. L., DeKlyen, M., & Greenberg, M. T. (1999). Attachment in boys with early onset conduct problems. *Development and Psychopathology, 11*, 269–285.

Spence, S. H. (1998). Preventive interventions. In T. Ollendick (Ed.), *Comprehensive clinical psychology* (Vol. 5, pp. 295–315). Oxford, England: Elsevier Science.

Spence, S. H., Donovan, C., & Brechman-Toussaint, M. (1999). Social skills, social outcomes, and cognitive features of childhood social phobia. *Journal of Abnormal Psychology, 108*, 211–221.

Spencer, E. K., Kafantaris, V., Padron-Gayol, M., Rosenberg, C. R., & Campbell, M. (1992). Haloperidol in schizophrenic children: Early findings from a study in progress. *Psychopharmacology Bulletin, 28*, 183–186.

Spencer, T., Biederman, J., Coffey, B., Geller, D., Wilens, T., & Faraone, S. (1999). The 4-year course of tic disorders in boys with attention-deficit/hyperactivity disorder. *Archives of General Psychiatry, 56*, 842–847.

Spielberger, C. D., Edwards, D. C., & Luschehe, R. E. (1973). *Manual for the State-Trait Anxiety Inventory for Children*. Palo Alto, CA: Consulting Psychologists Press.

Spirito, A., & Donaldson, D. (1998). Suicide and suicide attempts during adolescence. In T. Ollendick (Ed.), *Comprehensive clinical psychology* (Vol. 5, pp. 463–485). Oxford, England: Elsevier Science.

Spirito, A., Jelalian, E., Rasile, D., Rohrbeck, C., & Vinnick, L. (2000). Adolescent risk taking and self-reported injuries associated with substance use. *American Journal of Drug and Alcohol Abuse, 26*, 113–123.

Spirito, A., Overholser, J., & Vinnick, L. (1995). Adolescent suicide attempters in general hospitals: Psychological evaluation and disposition handling. In J. L. Wallander & L. J. Siegel (Eds.), *Adolescent health problems: Behavioral perspectives* (pp. 97–116). New York: Guilford.

Spitz, R. A. (1946). Anaclitic depression: An inquiry into the genesis of psychiatric conditions in early childhood, II. *Psychoanalytic Study of the Child, 2*, 313–342.

Spitzer, R. L., Gibbon, M., Skodol, A. E., Williams, J. B. W., & First, M. B. (1994). *DSM-IV casebook*. Washington, DC: American Psychiatric Press.

Spoth, R. L., Redmond, C., & Shin, C. (2001). Randomized trial of brief family interventions for general populations: Adolescent substance use outcomes 4 years following baseline. *Journal of Consulting and Clinical Psychology, 69*, 627–642.

Spoth, R., Reyes, M. L., Redmond, C., & Shin, C. (1999). Assessing a public health approach to delay onset and progression of adolescent substance use: Latent transition and log-linear analyses of longitudinal family preventive intervention outcomes. *Journal of Consulting and Clinical Psychology, 67*, 619–630.

Sprich, S., Biederman, J., Crawford, M. H., Mundy, E., & Faraone, S. V. (2000). Adoptive and biological families of children and adolescents with ADHD. *Journal of the American Academy of Child and Adolescent Psychiatry, 39*, 1432–1437.

Sprouse, C. A., Hall, C. W., Webster, R. E., & Bolen, L. M. (1998). Social perception in students with learning disabilities and attention-deficit/hyperactivity disorder. *Journal of Nonverbal Behavior, 22*, 125–134.

Srebnik, D., Cauce, A. M., & Baydar, N. (1996). Help-seeking pathways for children and adolescents. *Journal of Emotional and Behavioral Disorders, 4*, 210–220.

Sroufe, L. A. (1989). Pathways to adaptation and maladaptation: Psychopathology as developmental deviation. In D. Cicchetti (Ed.), *The emergence of a discipline: Rochester symposium on developmental psychopathology* (Vol. 1, pp. 13–40). Hillsdale, NJ: Lawrence Erlbaum.

Sroufe, L. A. (1997). Psychopathology as an outcome of development. *Development and Psychopathology, 9*, 251–268.

Sroufe, L. A., Carlson, E. A., Levy, A. K., & Egeland, B. (1999). Implications of attachment theory for developmental psychopathology. *Development and Psychopathology, 11*, 1–13.

Stahl, N. D., & Clarizio, H. F. (1999). Conduct disorder and comorbidity. *Psychology in the Schools, 36*, 41–50.

Stanard, R., & Hazler, R. (1995). Legal and ethical implications of HIV and duty to warn for counselors: When does Tarasoff apply? *Journal of Counseling and Development, 73*, 397–400.

Stark, K. D. (1990). *Childhood depression: School-based intervention*. New York: Guilford.

Stark, K. D., Bronik, M. D., Wong, S., Wells, G., & Ostrander, R. (2000). Depressive disorders. In M. Hersen & R. T. Ammerman (Eds.), *Advanced abnormal child psychology* (pp. 291–326). Mahwah, NJ: Lawrence Erlbaum.

Stark, K. D., Rouse, L., & Livingston, R. (1991). Treatment of depression during childhood and adolescence: Cognitive-behavioral procedures for the individual and family. In P. Kendall (Ed.), *Child and adolescent therapy* (pp. 165–206). New York: Guilford.

Stark, K. D., Swearer, S., Kurowski, C., Sommer, D., & Bowen, B. (1993). Targeting the child and the family: A holistic approach to treating child and adolescent depressive disorders. In E. D. Hibbs & P. S. Jensen (Eds.), *Psychosocial treatments for child and adolescent disorders: Empirically based strategies for clinical practice* (pp. 207–238). Washington, DC: American Psychological Association.

State, M. W., Lombroso, P. J., Pauls, D. L., & Leckman, J. F. (2000). The genetics of childhood psychiatric disorders: A decade of progress. *Journal of the American Academy of Child and Adolescent Psychiatry, 39*, 946–962.

Steele, R. G., Forehand, R., & Armistead, L. (1997). The role of family processes and coping strategies in the relationship between parental chronic illness and childhood internalizing problems. *Journal of Abnormal Child Psychology, 25*, 83–94.

Stein, B. D., Zima, B. T., Elliott, M. N., Burnam, M. A., Shahinfar, A., Fox, N. A., & Leavitt, L. A. (2001). Violence exposure among school-age children in foster care: Relationship to distress symptoms. *Journal of the American Academy of Child and Adolescent Psychiatry, 40*, 588–594.

Stein, D., Williamson, D. E., Birmaher, B., Brent, D. A., Kaufman, J., Dahl, R. E., Perel, J. M., & Ryan, N. D. (2000). Parent–child bonding and family functioning in depressed children and children at high risk and low risk for future depression. *Journal of the American Academy of Child and Adolescent Psychiatry, 39*, 1387–1395.

Stein, D. B. (1999). *Ritalin is not the answer: A drug-free, practical program for children diagnosed with ADD or ADHD*. San Francisco: Jossey-Bass.

Steinberg, L., & Avenevoli, S. (2000). The role of context in the development of psychopathology: A conceptual framework and some speculative propositions. *Child Development, 71*, 66–74.

Steinberg, L., Lamborn, S. D., Darling, N., Mounts, N. S., & Dornbusch, S. M. (1994). Over-time changes in adjustment and competence among adolescents from authoritative, authoritarian, indulgent, and neglectful families. *Child Development, 65,* 754–770.

Steinberg, L., Lamborn, S. D., Dornbusch, S. M., & Darling, N. (1992). Impact of parenting practices on adolescent achievement: Authoritative parenting, school involvement, and encouragement to succeed. *Child Development, 63,* 1266–1281.

Stephens, T., Braithwaite, R. L., & Taylor, S. E. (1998). Model for using hip-hop music for small group HIV/AIDS prevention counseling with African American adolescents and young adults. *Patient Education and Counseling, 35,* 127–137.

Sternberg, R. J. (1997). *Career paths in psychology: Where your degree can take you.* Washington, DC: American Psychological Association.

Sternberg, R. J., & Grigorenko, E. (2000). *Our labeled children: What every parent and teacher needs to know about learning disabilities.* New York: Perseus Books Group.

Stetson, E. G. (1992). Clinical child psychology and educational assessment. In C. E. Walker & M. C. Roberts (Eds.), *Handbook of clinical child psychology* (2nd ed., pp. 101–131). New York: Wiley.

Stevenson, J. (1999). The treatment of the long-term sequelae of child abuse. *Journal of Child Psychology and Psychiatry, 40,* 89–111.

Stice, E., Hayward, C., Cameron, R. P., Killen, J. D., & Taylor, C. B. (2000). Body-image and eating disturbances predict onset of depression among female adolescents: A longitudinal study. *Journal of Abnormal Psychology, 109,* 438–444.

Stickler, G. B. (1996). Worries of parents and their children. *Clinical Pediatrics, 35,* 84–90.

Stipek, D. (1997). Success in school—for a head start in life. In S. S. Luthar, J. A. Burack, D. Cicchetti, & J. R. Weisz (Eds.), *Developmental psychopathology: Perspectives on adjustment, risk, and disorder* (pp. 75–92). New York: Cambridge University Press.

Stipek, D., & Gralinski, J. H. (1996). Children's beliefs about intelligence and school performance. *Journal of Educational Psychology, 88,* 397–407.

Stoil, M. J., Hill, G. A., Jansen, M. A., Sambrano, S., & Winn, F. J. (2000). Benefits of community-based demonstration efforts: Knowledge gained in substance abuse prevention. *Journal of Community Psychology, 28,* 375–389.

Stoolmiller, M., Eddy, J. M., & Reid, J. B. (2000). Detecting and describing preventive intervention effects in a universal school-based randomized trial targeting delinquent and violent behavior. *Journal of Consulting and Clinical Psychology, 68,* 296–306.

Stoppelbein, L., & Greening, L. (2000). Posttraumatic stress symptoms in parentally bereaved children and adolescents. *Journal of the American Academy of Child and Adolescent Psychiatry, 39,* 1112–1119.

Stormshak, E. A., Bierman, K. L., McMahon, R. J., Lengua, L. J., & Conduct Problems Prevention Research Group. (2000). Parenting practices and child disruptive behavior problems in early elementary school. *Journal of Clinical Child Psychology, 29,* 17–29.

Straus, M. A. (1994). *Beating the devil out of them: Corporal punishment in American families.* San Francisco: Jossey-Bass/Lexington Books.

Straus, M. A., & Stewart, J. H. (1999). Corporal punishment by American Parents: National data on prevalence, chronicity, severity, and duration, in relation to child and family characteristics. *Clinical Child and Family Psychology Review, 2,* 55–70.

Sue, S., Kurasaki, K. S., & Srinivasan, S. (1999). Ethnicity, gender, and cross-cultural issues in clinical research. In P. C. Kendall, J. N. Butcher, & G. N. Holmbeck (Eds.), *Handbook of research methods in clinical psychology* (2nd ed., pp. 54–71). New York: Wiley.

Sullivan, T. N., & Farrell, A. D. (1999). Identification and impact of risk and protective factors for drug use among urban African American adolescents. *Journal of Clinical Child Psychology, 28,* 122–136.

Summerville, M. B., Kaslow, N. J., & Doepke, K. J. (1996). Psychopathology and cognitive and family functioning in suicidal African-American adolescents. *Current Directions I Psychological Science, 5,* 7–11.

Susser, E., Brown, A., & Matte, T. (2000). Prenatal antecedents of neuropsychiatric disorder over the life course: Collaborative studies of United States birth cohorts. In J. L. Rapoport (Ed.), *Childhood onset of "adult" psychopathology: Clinical and research advances* (pp. 121–146). Washington, DC: American Psychiatric Press.

Swan, K., Meskill, C. & DeMaio, S. (Eds.). (1998). *Social learning from broadcast television.* Cresskill, NJ: Hampton Press.

Swank, L. K. (1999). Specific developmental disorders: The language-learning continuum. *Child and Adolescent Psychiatric Clinics of North America, 8,* 89–112.

Sweet, E. S. (1991). What do adolescents want? What do adolescents need? Treating the chronic relapser. *Journal of Adolescent Chemical Dependency, 1,* 1–8.

Swendsen, J. D., & Merikangas, K. R. (2000). The comorbidity of depression and substance use disorders. *Clinical Psychology Review, 20,* 173–189.

Szapocznik, J., Perez-Vidal, A., Brickman, A. L., Foote, F., Santisteban, D., Hervis, O., & Kurtines, W. A. (1988). Engaging adolescent drug abusers and their families in treatment: A strategic structural systems approach. *Journal of Consulting and Clinical Psychology, 56,* 552–557.

Tamplin, A., Goodyer, I. M., & Herbert, J. (1998). Family functioning and parent general health in families of adolescents with major depressive disorder. *Journal of Affective Disorders, 48,* 1–13.

Tanguay, P. E. (2000). Pervasive developmental disorders: A 10-year review. *Journal of the American Academy of Child and Adolescent Psychiatry, 39,* 1079–1095.

Target, M., & Fonagy, P. (1998). Psychodynamic therapy. In T. Ollendick (Ed.), *Comprehensive clinical psychology* (Vol. 5, pp. 245–266). Oxford, England: Elsevier Science.

Tarnowski, K. J., & Brown, R. T. (2000). Psychological aspects of pediatric disorders. In M. Hersen & R. T. Ammerman (Eds.), *Advanced abnormal child psychology* (pp. 131–150). Mahwah, NJ: Lawrence Erlbaum.

Tarnowski, K. J., & Simonian, S. (1997). *Directory of graduate programs in clinical child and pediatric psychology.* Hillsdale, NJ: Lawrence Erlbaum.

Task Force on Promotion and Dissemination of Psychological Procedures. (1995). Training in and dissemination of empirically-validated psychological treatments: Report and recommendations. *The Clinical Psychologist 8,* 3–24.

Taylor, E. (1995). Dysfunctions of attention. In D. Cicchetti & D. J. Cohen (Eds.), *Developmental psychopathology: Vol. 2. Risk, disorder, and adaptation* (pp. 243–273). New York: Wiley.

Taylor, E. A. (1999). Hyperkinetic disorders. In H. C. Steinhausen & F. C. Verhulst (Eds.), *Risks and outcomes in developmental psychopathology* (pp. 151–164). New York: Oxford University Press.

Taylor, J., Iacono, W. G., & McGue, M. (2000). Evidence for a genetic etiology of early-onset delinquency. *Journal of Abnormal Psychology, 109,* 634–643.

Taylor, L., & Adelman, H. S. (1999). Keeping reading and writing problems in broad perspective. *Reading and Writing Quarterly: Overcoming Learning Difficulties, 15,* 351–353.

Taylor, L., Adelman, H. S., & Kaser-Boyd, N. (1985). Exploring minors' reluctance and dissatisfaction with psychotherapy. *Professional Psychology: Research and Practice, 16*, 418–425.

Taylor, R. D., & Wang, M. C. (2000). *Resilience across contexts: Family, work, culture, and community.* Mahwah, NJ: Lawrence Erlbaum.

Taylor, R. L. (1997). *Assessment of exceptional students: Educational and psychological procedures* (4th ed.). Boston: Allyn & Bacon.

Taylor, T. K., Eddy, J. M., & Biglan, A. (1999). Interpersonal skills training to reduce aggressive and delinquent behavior: Limited evidence and the need for an evidence-based system of care. *Clinical Child and Family Psychology Review, 2*, 169–182.

Teichman, M., & Kefir, E. (2000). The effects of perceived parental behaviors, attitudes, and substance use on adolescent attitudes toward and intent to use psychoactive substances. *Journal of Drug Education, 30*, 193–204.

Terr, L. C., Bloch, D. A., Michel, B. A., Shi, H., Reinhardt, J. A., & Metayer, S. (1999). Children's symptoms in the wake of Challenger: A field study of distant-traumatic effects and an outline of related conditions. *American Journal of Psychiatry, 156*, 1536–1544.

Thabet, A. A. M., & Vostanis, P. (1999). Post-traumatic stress reactions in children of war. *Journal of Child Psychology and Psychiatry, 40*, 385–391.

Thomas, A. (1998). *Directory of school psychology graduate programs.* Bethesda, MD: National Association of School Psychologists Publications.

Thomas, A., & Chess, S. (1977). *Temperament and development.* New York: Brunner/Mazel.

Thompson, J. K., Heinberg, L. J., Altabe, M., & Tantleff-Dunn, S. (1999). *Exacting beauty: Theory, assessment, and treatment of body image.* Washington, DC: American Psychological Association.

Thompson, J. K., & Smolak, L. (Eds.). (2001). *Body image, eating disorders, and obesity in youth: Assessment, prevention, and treatment.* Washington, DC: American Psychological Association.

Thompson, J. K., & Stice, E. (2001). Thin-ideal internalizing: Mounting evidence for a new risk factor for body-image disturbance and eating pathology. *Current Directions in Psychological Science, 10*, 181–183.

Thompson, M. P., Kaslow, N. J., Kingree, J. B., King, M., Bryant, L., & Rey, M. (1998). Psychological symptomatology following parental death in a predominantly minority sample of children and adolescents. *Journal of Clinical Child Psychology, 27*, 434–441.

Thompson, R. J., Armstrong, F. D., Kronenberger, W. G., Scott, D., McCabe, M. A., Smith, B., Radcliffe, J., Colangelo, L., Gallagher, D., Islam, S., & Wright, E. (1999). Family functioning, neurocognitive functioning, and behavior problems in children with sickle cell disease. *Journal of Pediatric Psychology, 24*, 491–498.

Thompson, R. J., Gil, K. M., Burbach, D. J., Keith, B. R., & Kinney, T. R. (1993). Psychological adjustment of mothers of children and adolescents with sickle cell disease: The role of stress, coping methods, and family functioning. *Journal of Pediatric Psychology, 18*, 549–559.

Thompson, R. J., Gustafson, K. E., Gil, K. M., Godfrey, J., & Murphy, L. M. B. (1998). Illness specific patterns of psychological adjustment and cognitive adaptational processes in children with cystic fibrosis and sickle cell disease. *Journal of Clinical Psychology, 54*, 121–128.

Thorndike, R. L., Hagen, E. P., & Sattler, J. M. (1986). *Stanford-Binet Intelligence Scale: Fourth Edition.* Chicago: Riverside.

Tobler, N. S. (2000). Lessons learned. *Journal of Primary Prevention, 20*, 261–274.

Todd, R. D., Reich, W., Petti, T., & Joshi, P. (1996). Psychiatric diagnoses in the child and adolescent members of extended families identified through adult bipolar affective disorder probands. *Journal of the American Academy of Child and Adolescent Psychiatry, 35*, 664–671.

Toppelberg, C. O., & Shapiro, T. (2000). Language disorders: A 10-year research update review. *Journal of the American Academy of Child and Adolescent Psychiatry, 39*, 143–152.

Torgesen, J. K., Wagner, R. K., Rashotte, C. A., & Conway, T. (1997). Preventative and remedial interventions for children with severe reading disabilities. *Learning Disabilities: A Multidisciplinary Journal, 8*, 51–62.

Totten, G., Lamb, D. H., & Reeder, G. D. (1990). Tarasoff and confidentiality in AIDS-related psychotherapy. *Professional Psychology: Research and Practice, 21*, 155–160.

Towers, H., Spotts, E., Neiderhiser, J. M., Hetherington, E. M., Plomin, R., & Reiss, D. (2000). Genetic and environmental influences on teacher ratings of the Child Behavior Checklist. *International Journal of Behavioral Development, 24*, 373–381.

Tram, J. M., & Cole, D. A. (2000). Self-perceived competence and the relation between life events and depressive symptoms in adolescence: Mediator or moderator? *Journal of Abnormal Psychology, 109*, 753–760.

Tramontana, M. G., & Hooper, S. R. (1997). Neuropsychology of child psychopathology. In C. R. Reynolds & E. Fletcher-Janzen (Eds.), *Handbook of clinical child neuropsychology* (2nd ed., pp. 120–139). New York: Plenum.

Trautman, P. D., Rotheram-Borus, M. J., Dopkins, S. A., & Lewin, N. (1991). Psychiatric diagnoses in minority female adolescent suicide attempters. *Journal of the American Academy of Child and Adolescent Psychiatry, 30*, 617–622.

Treffert, D. A. (1999). Pervasive developmental disorders. In S. D. Netherton, D. Holmes, & C. E. Walker (Eds.), *Child and adolescent psychological disorders: A comprehensive textbook* (pp. 76–97). New York: Oxford University Press.

Tremblay, R. E., LeMarquand, D., & Vitaro, F. (1999). The prevention of oppositional defiant disorder and conduct disorder. In H. C. Quay & A. E. Hogan (Eds.), *Handbook of disruptive behavior disorders* (pp. 525–555). New York: Kluwer Academic/Plenum.

Tremblay, R. E., Pagani-Kurtz, L., Masse, L. C., Vitaro, F., & Phil, R. (1995). A bimodal preventive intervention for disruptive kindergarten boys: Its impact through mid-adolescence. *Journal of Consulting and Clinical Psychology, 63*, 560–568.

Treuting, J. J., & Hinshaw, S. P. (2001). Depression and self-esteem in boys with attention-deficit/hyperactivity disorder: Associations with comorbid aggression and explanatory attributional mechanisms. *Journal of Abnormal Child Psychology, 29*, 23–39.

Trudell, B., & Whatley, M. H. (1988). School sexual abuse prevention: Unintended consequences and dilemmas. *Child Abuse and Neglect, 12*, 103–113.

Trull, T., & Phares, E. J. (2001). *Clinical psychology: Concepts, methods, and profession* (6th ed.). Belmont, CA: Wadsworth.

Tryon, G. S. (2000). Doctoral training issues in school and clinical child psychology. *Professional Psychology: Research and Practice, 31*, 85–87.

Turner, S. L., Hamilton, H., Jacobs, M., Angood, L. M., & Dwyer, D. H. (1997). The influence of fashion magazines on the body image satisfaction of college women: An exploratory analysis. *Adolescence, 32*, 603–614.

Turner, S. M., DeMers, S. T., Fox, H. R., & Reed, G. M. (2001). APA guidelines for test user qualifications: An executive summary. *American Psychologist, 56*, 1099–1113.

Tutty, L. M. (1991). Child sexual abuse: A range of prevention options. *Journal of Child and Youth Care, Fall*, 23–41.

Udwin, O., Boyle, S., Yule, W., Bolton, D., & O'Ryan, D. (2000). Risk factors for long-term psychological effects of a disaster experienced in adolescence: Predictors of post traumatic stress disorder. *Journal of Child Psychology and Psychiatry and Allied Disciplines*, *41*, 969–979.

Untalan, F. F., & Camacho, J. M. (1997). Children of Micronesia. In G. Johnson-Powell & J. Yamamoto (Eds.), *Transcultural child development: Psychological assessment and treatment* (pp. 305–327). New York: Wiley.

Updegraff, K. A., McHale, S. M., & Crouter, A. C. (2000). Adolescents' sex-typed friendship experiences: Does having a sister versus a brother matter? *Child Development*, *71*, 1597–1610.

Urban Institute (1999a). Adults' environment and behavior: Mental health and parents. *Snapshots of America's Families*, January, 1999. Washington, DC: Author.

Urban Institute (1999b). Children's environment and behavior: Behavioral and emotional problems in children. *Snapshots of America's Families*, January, 1999. Washington, DC: Author.

Valois, R. F., Oeltmann, J. E., Waller, J., & Hussey, J. R. (1999). Relationship between number of sexual intercourse partners and selected health risk behaviors among public high school adolescents. *Journal of Adolescent Health*, *25*, 328–335.

VandenBos, G. R., & Williams, S. (2000). The Internet versus the telephone: What is telehealth anyway? *Professional Psychology: Research and Practice*, *31*, 490–492.

Van Eerdewegh, M. M., Bieri, M. D., Parrilla, R. H., & Clayton, P. J. (1982). The bereaved child. *British Journal of Psychiatry*, *140*, 23–29.

Van Evra, J. (1998). *Television and child development* (2nd ed.). Mahwah, NJ: Lawrence Erlbaum.

VanHasselt, V. B., & Hersen, M. (Eds.). (1998). *Handbook of psychological treatment protocols for children and adolescents*. Mahwah, NJ: Lawrence Erlbaum.

Varni, J. W., Blount, R. L., Waldron, S. A., & Smith, A. J. (1995). Management of pain and distress. In M. C. Roberts (Ed.), *Handbook of pediatric psychology* (pp. 105–123). New York: Guilford.

Vasey, M. W., Lonigan, C. J. (2000). Consider the clinical utility of performance-based measures of childhood anxiety. *Journal of Clinical Child Psychology*, *29*, 493–508.

Verburg, H., Janssen, H., Rikken, M., Hoefnagels, C., & vanWillenswaard, E. M. (1992). The Dutch way of prevention. In G. W. Albee, L. A. Bond, & T. V. C. Monsey (Eds.), *Improving children's lives: Global perspectives on prevention* (pp. 177–190). Newbury Park: Sage.

Vik, P. W., Brown, S. A., & Myers, M. G. (1997). Adolescent substance use problems. In E. J. Mash & L. G. Terdal (Eds.), *Assessment of childhood disorders* (3rd ed., pp. 717–748). New York: Guilford.

Villani, S. (2001). Impact of media on children and adolescents: A 10-year review of the research. *Journal of the Academy of Child and Adolescent Psychiatry*, *40*, 392–401.

Vincent, M. A., & McCabe, M. P. (2000). Gender differences among adolescents in family, and peer influences on body dissatisfaction, weight loss, and binge eating behaviors. *Journal of Youth and Adolescence*, *29*, 205–221.

Vitaro, F., Brendgen, M., Pagani, L., Tremblay, R. E., & McDuff, P. (1999). Disruptive behavior, peer association, and conduct disorder: Testing the developmental links through early intervention. *Development and Psychopathology*, *11*, 287–304.

Vitaro, F., Brendgen, M., & Tremblay, R. E. (2000). Influence of deviant friends on delinquency: Searching for moderator variables. *Journal of Abnormal Child Psychology*, *28*, 313–325.

Volkmar, F. R. (1992). Childhood disintegrative disorder: Issues for *DSM-IV*. *Journal of Autism and Developmental Disorders*, *22*, 625–642.

Volkmar, F. R., & Klin, A. (1998). Asperger syndrome and nonverbal learning disabilities. In E. Schopler & G. B. Mesibov (Eds.), *Asperger syndrome or high functioning autism? Current issues in autism* (pp. 107–121). New York: Plenum.

Voydanoff, P., & Donnelly, B. W. (1999). Risk and protective factors for psychological adjustment and grades among adolescents. *Journal of Family Issues*, *20*, 328–349.

Vygotsky, L. S. (1978). *Mind in society: The development of higher psychological processes*. Cambridge, MA: Harvard University Press.

Wagner, B. M., Aiken, C., Mullaley, P. M., & Tobin, J. J. (2000). Parents' reactions to adolescents' suicide attempts. *Journal of the American Academy of Child and Adolescent Psychiatry*, *39*, 429–436.

Wahlberg, T. (1998). Cognitive-behavioral modification of children and young adolescents with special problems. In A. F. Rotatori, J. O. Schwenn, & S. Burkhardt (Eds.), *Advances in special education* (Vol. 11, pp. 223–253). Greenwich, CT: JAI Press.

Wahlberg, T., & Ratotori, A. (1996). Various treatment modalities for autistic individuals. In A. F. Rotatori, J. O. Schwenn, & S. Burkhardt (Eds.), *Advances in special education: Assessment and psychopathology issues in special education* (pp. 109–131). Greenwich, CT: JAI Press.

Wakschlag, L. S., & Keenan, K. (2001). Clinical significance and correlates of disruptive behavior in environmentally at-risk preschoolers. *Journal of Clinical Child Psychology*, *30*, 262–275.

Walders, N., & Drotar, D. (2000). Understanding cultural and ethnic influences in research with child clinical and pediatric psychology populations. In D. Drotar (Ed.), *Handbook of research in pediatric and clinical child psychology* (pp. 165–188). New York: Kluwer Academic/Plenum.

Waldman, I. D., & Lilienfeld, S. O. (2001). Applications of taxometric methods to problems of comorbidity: Perspectives and challenges. *Clinical Psychology: Science and Practice*, *8*, 520–527.

Waldron, H. B. (1998). Substance abuse disorders. In T. Ollendick (Ed.), *Comprehensive clinical psychology* (Vol. 5, pp. 539–563). Oxford, England: Elsevier Science.

Waldron, H. B., Slesnick, N., Brody, J. L., Turner, C. W., & Peterson, T. R. (2001). Treatment outcomes for adolescent substance abuse at 4- and 7-month assessment. *Journal of Consulting and Clinical Psychology*, *69*, 802–813.

Walfish, S., & Hess, A. K. (Eds.). (2001). *Succeeding in graduate school: The career guide for psychology students*. Mahwah, NJ: Lawrence Erlbaum.

Walker, C. E. (1995). Elimination disorders: Enuresis and encopresis. In M. C. Roberts (Ed.), *Handbook of pediatric psychology* (pp. 537–557). New York: Guilford.

Walker, C. E. (1998). Elimination disorders. In T. Ollendick (Ed.), *Comprehensive clinical psychology* (Vol. 5, pp. 565–589). Oxford, England: Elsevier Science.

Walker, E., Downey, G., & Bergman, A. (1989). The effects of parental psychopathology and maltreatment on child behavior: A test of the diathesis-stress model. *Child Development*, *60*, 15–24.

Walker, L. A. (1986). *A loss for words: The story of deafness in a family*. New York: Harper & Row.

Wamboldt, M. Z., & Wamboldt, F. S. (2000). Role of the family in the onset and outcome of childhood disorders: Selected research findings. *Journal of the Academy of Child and Adolescent Psychiatry*, *39*, 1212–1219.

Warner, V., Mufson, L., & Weissman, M. M. (1995). Offspring at high and low risk for depression and anxiety: Mechanisms of psychiatric disorder. *Journal of the American Academy of Child and Adolescent Psychiatry, 34*, 786–797.

Warner, V., Weissman, M. M., Mufson, L., & Wickramaratne, P. J. (1999). Grandparents, parents, and grandchildren at high risk for depression: A three-generation study. *Journal of American Academy of Child and Adolescent Psychiatry, 38*, 289–296.

Waters, E., Hamilton, C. E., & Weinfield, N. S. (2000). The stability of attachment security from infancy to adolescence and early adulthood: General introduction. *Child Development, 71*, 678–683.

Waters, E., Merrick, S., Treboux, D., Crowell, J., & Albersheim, L. (2000). Attachment security in infancy and early adulthood: A twenty-year longitudinal study. *Child Development, 71*, 684–689.

Watson, J. (1986). Parental attributions of emotional disturbance and their relation to the outcome of therapy: Preliminary findings. *Australian Psychologist, 21*, 271–282.

Watson, J. B. (1913). Psychology as the behaviourist views it. *Psychological Review, 20*, 158–177.

Watson, J. B., & Rayner, R. (1920). Conditioned emotional reactions. *Journal of Experimental Psychology, 3*, 1–14.

Way, N. (1998). *Everyday courage: The lives and stories of urban teenagers.* New York: New York University Press.

Webster-Stratton, C. (1990). Enhancing the effectiveness of self-administered videotape parent training for families with conduct-problem children. *Journal of Abnormal Child Psychology, 18*, 479–492.

Webster-Stratton, C. (1993). Strategies for helping early school-aged children with oppositional defiant and conduct disorders: The importance of home-school partnerships. *School Psychology Review, 22*, 437–457.

Webster-Stratton, C. (1994). Advancing videotape parent training: A comparison study. *Journal of Consulting and Clinical Psychology, 62*, 583–593.

Webster-Stratton, C., & Herbert, M. (1994). *Troubled families/Problem children.* New York: Wiley.

Webster-Stratton, C., & Hooven, C. (1998). Parent training for child conduct problems. In T. Ollendick (Ed.), *Comprehensive clinical psychology* (Vol. 5, pp. 185–219). Oxford, England: Elsevier Science.

Webster-Stratton, C., Reid, M. J., & Hammond, M. (2001). Preventing conduct problems, promoting social competence: A parent and teacher training partnership in Head Start. *Journal of Clinical Child Psychology, 30*, 283–302.

Wechsler, D. (1989). *Manual for the Wechsler Preschool and Primary Scale of Intelligence–Revised (WPPSI-R).* San Antonio, TX: Psychological Corporation.

Wechsler, D. (1991). *Manual for the Wechsler Intelligence Scale for Children–Third Edition (WISC-III).* San Antonio, TX: Psychological Corporation.

Weems, C. F., Silverman, W. K., & LaGreca, A. M. (2000). What do youth referred for anxiety problems worry about? Worry and its relation to anxiety and anxiety disorders in children and adolescents. *Journal of Abnormal Child Psychology, 28*, 63–72.

Wegner, J. T., & Wegner, A. Z. (2001). Cognitive-behavioral therapy and other short-term approaches in the treatment of eating disorders. In B. P. Kinoy (Ed.), *Eating disorders: New directions in treatment and recovery* (2nd ed., pp. 112–126). New York: Columbia University Press.

Weinberg, N. Z., Dielman, T. E., Mandell, W., & Shope, J. T. (1994). Parental drinking and gender factors in the prediction of early adolescent alcohol use. *International Journal of the Addictions, 29*, 89–104.

Weinberg, N. Z., & Glantz, M. D. (1999). Child psychopathology risk factors for drug abuse: Overview. *Journal of Clinical Child Psychology, 28*, 290–297.

Weindrich, D., Jennen-Steinmetz, C., Laucht, M., Esser, G., & Schmidt, M. H. (2000). Epidemiology and prognosis of specific disorders of language and scholastic skills. *European Child and Adolescent Psychiatry, 9*, 186–194.

Weiner, I. B. (2001). Advancing the science of psychological assessment: The Rorschach inkblot method as exemplar. *Psychological Assessment, 13*, 423–432.

Weiner, I. B., & Kuehnle, K. (1998). Projective assessment of children and adolescents. In C. R. Reynolds (Ed.), *Comprehensive clinical psychology: Assessment* (Vol. 4, pp. 431–458). Oxford, England: Elsevier Science.

Weinstein, D., Staffelbach, D., & Biaggio, M. (2000). Attention-deficit hyperactivity disorder and post-traumatic stress disorder: Differential diagnosis in childhood sexual abuse. *Clinical Psychology Review, 20*, 359–378.

Weiss, B., Catron, T., & Harris, V. (2000). A 2-year follow-up of the effectiveness of traditional child psychotherapy. *Journal of Consulting and Clinical Psychology, 68*, 1094–1101.

Weiss, B., Weisz, J. R., Politano, M., Carey, M., Nelson, W. M., & Finch, A. J. (1992). Relations among self-reported depressive symptoms in clinic-referred children versus adolescents. *Journal of Abnormal Psychology, 101*, 391–397.

Weiss, G., & Hechtman, L. T. (1993). *Hyperactive children grown up: ADHD in children, adolescents, and adults* (2nd ed.). New York: Guilford.

Weiss, M., Hechtman, L., & Weiss, G. (2000). ADHD in parents. *Journal of the American Academy of Child and Adolescent Psychiatry, 39*, 1059–1061.

Weiss, S., Sawa, G. H., Abdeen, Z., & Yanai, J. (1999). Substance abuse studies and prevention efforts among Arabs in the 1990s in Israel, Jordan and the Palestinian authority: A literature review. *Addiction, 94*, 177–198.

Weissberg, R. P. (2000). Improving the lives of millions of school children. *American Psychologist, 55*, 1360–1373.

Weissberg, R. P., Caplan, M. Z., & Harwood, R. L. (1991). Promoting competent young people in competence-enhancing environments: A systems-based perspective on primary prevention. *Journal of Consulting and Clinical Psychology, 59*, 830–841.

Weist, M. D., Acosta, O. M., & Youngstrom, E. A. (2001). Predictors of violence exposure among inner-city youth. *Journal of Clinical Child Psychology, 30*, 187–198.

Weisz, J. R., Donenberg, G. R., Han, S. S., & Weiss, B. (1995). Bridging the gap between laboratory and clinic in child and adolescent psychotherapy. *Journal of Consulting and Clinical Psychology, 63*, 688–701.

Weisz, J. R., & Hawley, K. M. (1998). Finding, evaluating, refining, and applying empirically supported treatments for children and adolescents. *Journal of Clinical Child Psychology, 27*, 206–216.

Weisz, J. R., Hawley, K. M., Pilkonis, P. A., Woody, S. R., & Follette, W. C. (2000). Stressing the (other) three Rs in the search for empirically supported treatments: Review procedures, research quality, relevance to practice and the public interest. *Clinical Psychology: Science and Practice, 7*, 243–258.

Weisz, J. R., McCarty, C. A., Eastman, K. L., Chaiyasit, W., & Suwanlert, S. (1997). Developmental psychopathology and culture: Ten lessons from Thailand. In S. S. Luthar, J. A. Burack, D. Cicchetti, & J. R. Weisz (Eds.), *Developmental psychopathology: Perspectives on adjustment, risk, and disorder* (pp. 568–592). New York: Cambridge University Press.

Weisz, J. R., Suwanlert, S., Chaiyasit, W., Weiss, B., Achenbach, T. M., & Trevathan, D. (1988). Epidemiology of behavioral and emotional problems among Thai and American Children: Teacher reports of ages 6–11. *Journal of Child Psychology and Psychiatry, 30*, 471–484.

Weisz, J. R., Suwanlert, S., Chaiyasit, W., Weiss, B., Walter, B., & Anderson, W. (1988). Thai and American perspectives on over- and undercontrolled child behavior problems: Exploring the threshold model among parents, teachers, and psychologists. *Journal of Consulting and Clinical Psychology, 56*, 601–609.

Weisz, J. R., & Weiss, B. (1991). Studying the referability of child clinical problems. *Journal of Consulting and Clinical Psychology, 59*, 266–273.

Weisz, J. R., & Weiss, B. (1993). *Effects of psychotherapy with children and adolescents.* Newbury Park, CA: Sage.

Weisz, J. R., Weiss, B., Alicke, M. D., & Klotz, M. L. (1987). Effectiveness of psychotherapy with children and adolescents: A meta-analysis for clinicians. *Journal of Consulting and Clinical Psychology, 55*, 542–549.

Weisz, J. R., Weiss, B., Han, S. S., Granger, D. A., & Morton, T. (1995). Effects of psychotherapy with children and adolescents revisited: A meta-analysis of treatment outcome studies. *Psychological Bulletin, 117*, 450–468.

Weisz, V. G. (1995). *Children and adolescents in need: A legal primer for the helping professional.* Thousand Oaks, CA: Sage.

Wekerle, C., & Wolfe, D. A. (1996). Child maltreatment. In E. J. Mash & R. A. Barkley (Eds.), *Child psychopathology* (pp. 492–537). New York: Guilford.

Wellman, H. M., Cross, D., & Watson, J. (2001). Meta-analysis of theory-of-mind development: The truth about false belief. *Child Development, 72*, 655–684.

Wells, K. C., Pelham, W. E., Kotkin, R. A., Hoza, B., Abikoff, H. B., Abramowitz, A., Arnold, L. E., Cantwell, D. P., Conners, C. K., Del Carmen, R., Elliott, G., Greenhill, L. L., Hechtman, L., Hibbs, E., Hinshaw, S. P., Jensen, P. S., March, J. S., Swanson, J. M., & Schiller, E. (2000). Psychosocial treatment strategies in the MTA Study: Rationale, methods, and critical issues in design and implementation. *Journal of Abnormal Child Psychology, 28*, 483–505.

Weltzin, T. E., & Bolton, B. G. (1998). Bulimia nervosa. In V. B. Van-Hasselt & M. Hersen (Eds.), *Handbook of psychological treatment protocols for children and adolescents* (pp. 435–465). Mahwah, NJ: Lawrence Erlbaum.

Werner, E. E. (1995). Resilience in development. *Current Directions in Psychological Science, 4*, 81–85.

Werner, E. E., & Smith, R. S. (1982). *Vulnerable but invincible: A study of resilient children.* New York: McGraw-Hill.

Werner, E. E., & Smith, R. S. (1992). *Overcoming the odds: High risk children from birth to adulthood.* Ithaca, NY: Cornell University Press.

Werner, E. E., & Smith, R. S. (2001). *Journeys from childhood to midlife: Risk, resilience, and recovery.* Ithaca, NY: Cornell University Press.

Werry, J. S. (1996). Pervasive developmental, psychotic, and allied disorders. In L. Hechtman (Ed.), *Do they grow out of it? Long-term outcomes of childhood disorders* (pp. 195–223). Washington, DC: American Psychiatric Press.

Werry, J. S., McClellan, J. M., Andrews, L. K., & Ham, M. (1994). Clinical features and outcome of child and adolescent schizophrenia. *Schizophrenia Bulletin, 20*, 619–630.

Westcott, H. L., & Jones, D. P. H. (1999). Annotation: The abuse of disabled children. *Journal of Child Psychology and Psychiatry, 40*, 497–506.

Whalen, C. K., & Henker, B. (1998). Attention-deficit/hyperactivity disorder. In T. H. Ollendick & M. Hersen (Eds.), *Handbook of child psychopathology* (3rd ed., pp. 181–211). New York: Plenum.

Whitaker, A., Johnson, J., Saffer, D., Rapoport, J. L., Kalikow, K., Walsh, B. T., Davies, M., Braiman, S., & Dolinsky, A. (1990). Uncommon troubles in young people: Prevalence estimates of selected psychiatric disorders in a nonreferred adolescent population. *Archives of General Psychiatry, 47*, 487–496.

Whitbeck, L. B., & Hoyt, D. R. (1999). *Nowhere to grow: Homeless and runaway adolescents and their families.* New York: Aldine de Gruyter.

Whitbeck, L. B., Hoyt, D. R., & Bao, W. N. (2000). Depressive symptoms and cooccurring depressive symptoms, substance abuse, and conduct problems among runaway and homeless adolescents. *Child Development, 71*, 721–732.

White, K. S., Bruce, S. E., & Farrell, A. D., & Kliewer, W. (1998). Impact of exposure to community violence on anxiety: A longitudinal study of family social support as a protective factor for urban children. *Journal of Child and Family Studies, 7*, 187–203.

White, K. S., & Farrell, A. D. (2001). Structure of anxiety symptoms in urban children: Competing factor models of the Revised Children's Manifest Anxiety Scale. *Journal of Consulting and Clinical Psychology, 69*, 333–337.

Wickramaratne, P. J., Greenwald, S., & Weissman, M. M. (2000). Psychiatric disorders in the relatives of probands with prepubertal-onset or adolescent-onset major depression. *Journal of the American Academy of Child and Adolescent Psychiatry, 39*, 1396–1405.

Wickramaratne, P. J., & Weissman, M. M. (1998). Onset of psychopathology in offspring by developmental phase and parental depression. *Journal of the Academy of Child and Adolescent Psychiatry, 37*, 933–942.

Widiger, T. A., & Clark, L. A. (2000). Toward *DSM-V* and the classification of psychopathology. *Psychological Bulletin, 126*, 946–963.

Wiener, J. M. (1999). Violence and mental illness in adolescence. In R. L. Hendren (Ed.), *Disruptive behavior disorders in children and adolescents* (Vol. 18, pp. 175–189). Washington, DC: American Psychiatric Press.

Wiggs, L., & Stores, G. (1999). Behavioural treatment for sleep problems in children with severe learning disabilities and challenging daytime behaviour: Effect on daytime behaviour. *Journal of Child Psychology and Psychiatry and Allied Disciplines, 40*, 627–635.

Wilkes, T. C. R., Belsher, G., Rush, A. J., & Frank, E. (1994). *Cognitive therapy for depressed adolescents.* New York: Guilford.

Willcutt, E. G., & Pennington, B. F. (2000). Psychiatric comorbidity in children and adolescents with reading disability. *Journal of Child Psychology and Psychiatry and Allied Disciplines, 41*, 1039–1048.

Willcutt, E. G., Pennington, B. F., & DeFries, J. C. (2000). Etiology of inattention and hyperactivity/impulsivity in a community sample of twins with learning difficulties. *Journal of Abnormal Child Psychology, 28*, 149–159.

Williams, G. J. R. (1983). Responsible sexuality and the primary prevention of child abuse. In G. W. Albee, S. Gordon, & H. Leitenberg (Eds.), *Promoting sexual responsibility and preventing sexual problems* (pp. 251–272). Hanover, NH: University Press of New England.

Williams, J. K. (1994). Behavioral characteristics of children with turner syndrome and children with learning disabilities. *Western Journal of Nursing Research, 16*, 26–35.

Williams, R. J., & Chang, S. Y. (2000). A comprehensive and comparative review of adolescent substance abuse treatment outcome. *Clinical Psychology: Science and Practice, 7*, 138–166.

Williamson, D. A., Bentz, B. G., & Rabalais, J. Y. (1998). Eating disorders. In T. H. Ollendick & M. Hersen (Eds.), *Handbook of child psychopathology* (3rd ed., pp. 291–305). New York: Plenum.

Williamson, D. A., Duchmann, E. G., Barker, S. E., & Bruno, R. M. (1998). Anorexia nervosa. In V. B. VanHasselt & M. Hersen (Eds.), *Handbook of psychological treatment protocols for children and adolescents* (pp. 413–434). Mahwah, NJ: Lawrence Erlbaum.

Willoughby, M., Kupersmidt, J., & Bryant, D. (2001). Overt and covert dimensions of antisocial behavior in early childhood. *Journal of Abnormal Child Psychology, 29*, 177–187.

Wills, T. A., & Cleary, S. D. (1996). How are social support effects mediated? A test with parental support and adolescent substance use. *Journal of Personality and Social Psychology, 71*, 937–952.

Wills, T. A., & Cleary, S. D. (2000). Testing theoretical models and frameworks in child health research. In D. Drotar (Ed.), *Handbook of research in pediatric and clinical child psychology* (pp. 21–49). New York: Plenum.

Wills, T. A., & Filer, M. (1996). Stress-coping model of adolescent substance use. In T. H. Ollendick & R. J. Prinz (Eds.), *Advances in clinical child psychology* (Vol. 18, pp. 91–132). New York: Plenum.

Wills, T. A., Sandy, J. M., Yaeger, A., & Shinar, O. (2001). Family risk factors and adolescent substance use: Moderation effects for temperament dimensions. *Developmental Psychology, 37*, 283–297.

Windle, M. (2000). Parental, sibling, and peer influences on adolescent substance use and alcohol problems. *Applied Developmental Science, 4*, 98–110.

Windle, M., & Davies, P. T. (1999). Depression and heavy alcohol use among adolescents: Concurrent and prospective relations. *Development and Psychopathology, 11*, 823–844.

Windle, M., & Tubman, J. G. (1999). Children of alcoholics. In W. K. Silverman & T. H. Ollendick (Eds.), *Developmental issues in the clinical treatment of children* (pp. 393–414). Boston: Allyn & Bacon.

Windle, M., & Windle, R. C. (2001). Depressive symptoms and cigarette smoking among middle adolescents: Prospective associations and intrapersonal and interpersonal influences. *Journal of Consulting and Clinical Psychology, 69*, 215–226.

Winett, R. A. (1998). Prevention: A proactive-developmental-ecological perspective. In T. H. Ollendick & M. Hersen (Eds.), *Handbook of child psychopathology* (pp. 637–671). New York: Plenum.

Winfield, L. F. (1995). The knowledge base on resilience in African-American adolescents. In L. J. Crockett & A. C. Crouter (Eds.), *Pathways through adolescence: Individual development in relation to social contexts* (pp. 87–118). Mahwah, NJ: Lawrence Erlbaum.

Wing, L. (1981). Asperger's Syndrome: A clinical account. *Psychological Medicine, 11*, 115.

Winters, K. C. (1999). Treating adolescents with substance use disorders: An overview of practice issues and treatment outcome. *Substance Abuse, 20*, 203–225.

Witt, J. C., Elliott, S. N., Daly, E. J., Gresham, F. M., & Kramer, J. J. (1998). *Assessment of at-risk and special needs children* (2nd ed.). New York: McGraw-Hill.

Wolchik, S. A., West, S. G., Sandler, I. N., Tein, J. Y., Coatsworth, D., Lengua, L., Weiss, L., Anderson, E. R., Greene, S. M., & Griffin, W. A. (2000). An experimental evaluation of theory-based mother and mother–child programs for children of divorce. *Journal of Consulting and Clinical Psychology, 68*, 843–856.

Wolfe, D. A. (1999). *Child abuse: Implication for child development and psychopathology.* Thousand Oaks, CA: Sage.

Wolfe, D. A., Scott, K., Wekerle, C., & Pittman, A. L. (2001). Child maltreatment: Risk for adjustment problems and dating violence in adolescence. *Journal of the American Academy of Child and Adolescent Psychiatry, 40*, 282–289.

Wolters, P. L., Brouwers, P., & Perez, L. A. (1999). Pediatric HIV infection. In R. T. Brown (Ed.), *Cognitive aspects of chronic illness in children* (pp. 105–141). New York: Guilford.

Wood, K. C., Becker, J. A., & Thompson, J. K. (1996). Body image dissatisfaction in preadolescent children. *Journal of Applied Developmental Psychology, 17*, 85–100.

Woodcock, R. W., McGrew, K. S., & Mather, N. (2000). *Woodcock-Johnson psycho-educational battery-III.* Itasca, IL: Riverside.

Woodward, L. J., & Fergusson, D. M. (1999). Childhood peer relationship problems and psychosocial adjustment in late adolescence. *Journal of Abnormal Child Psychology, 27*, 87–104.

Woodward, L. J., Fergusson, D. M., & Horwood, L. J. (2000). Driving outcomes of young people with attentional difficulties in adolescence. *Journal of the American Academy of Child and Adolescent Psychiatry, 39*, 627–634.

Worden, M. (1994). *Family therapy basics.* Pacific Grove, CA: Brooks/Cole.

World Health Organization. (1992). *The ICD-10 classification of mental and behavioural disorders: Clinical descriptions and diagnostic guidelines.* Geneva, Switzerland: Author.

Worling, D. E., Humphries, T., & Tannock, R. (1999). Spatial and emotional aspects of language inferencing in nonverbal learning disabilities. *Brain and Language, 70*, 220–239.

Wright, E. (1999). *Why I teach.* Rocklin, CA: Prima.

Wright, J. C., Zakriski, A. L., & Drinkwater, M. (1999). Developmental psychopathology and the reciprocal patterning of behavior and environment: Distinctive situational and behavioral signatures of internalizing, externalizing, and mixed-syndrome children. *Journal of Consulting and Clinical Psychology, 67*, 95–107.

Wright, J. C., & Zakriski, A. L. (2001). A contextual analysis of externalizing and mixed syndrome boys: When syndromal similarity obscures functional dissimilarity. *Journal of Consulting and Clinical Psychology, 69*, 457–470.

Wu, P., Hoven, C. W., Bird, H. R., Moore, R. E., Cohen, P., Alegria, M., Dulcan, M. K., Goodman, S. H., Horwitz, S. M., Lichtman, J. H., Narrow, W. E., Rae, D. S., Regier, D. A., & Roper, M. T. (1999). Depressive and disruptive disorders and mental health service utilization in children and adolescents. *Journal of the American Academy of Child and Adolescent Psychiatry, 38*, 1081–1090.

Wurtele, S. K. (1995). Health promotion. In M. C. Roberts (Ed.), *Handbook of pediatric psychology* (pp. 200–216). New York: Guilford.

Wyman, P. A., Cowen, E. L., Work, W. C., Hoyt-Meyers, L., Magnus, K. B., & Fagen, D. B. (1999). Caregiving and developmental factors differentiating young at-risk urban children showing resilient versus stress-affected outcomes: A replication and extension. *Child Development, 70*, 645–659.

Wyman, P. A., Sandler, I., Wolchik, S., & Nelson, K. (2000). Resilience as cumulative competence promotion and stress protection: Theory and intervention. In D. Cicchetti, J. Rappaport, I. Sandler, & R. P. Weissberg (Eds.), *The promotion of wellness in children and adolescents* (pp. 133–184). Washington, DC: CWLA Press.

Yamamoto, J., Silva, J. A., Ferrari, M., & Nukariya, K. (1997). Culture and psychopathology. In G. Johnson-Powell & J. Yamamoto (Eds.), *Transcultural child development: Psychological assessment and treatment* (pp. 34–57). New York: Wiley.

Yanagida, E. H. (1998). Ethical dilemmas in the clinical practice of child psychology. In R. M. Anderson, T. I. Needels, & H. V. Hall (Eds.),

Avoiding ethical misconduct in psychology specialty areas. Springfield, IL: Charles C. Thomas.

Yee, C. M., & Sigman, M. D. (1998). Schizophrenia in children and adolescents. In T. Ollendick (Ed.), *Comprehensive clinical psychology* (Vol. 5, pp. 703–723). Oxford, England: Elsevier Science.

Yeh, M., & Weisz, J. R. (2001). Why are we here at the clinic? Parent–child (dis)agreement on referral problems at outpatient treatment entry. *Journal of Consulting and Clinical Psychology, 69,* 1018–1025.

Yeo, R. A., Hodde-Vargas, J., Hendren, R. L., Vargas, L. A., Brooks, W. M., Ford, C. C., Gangestad, S. W., & Hart, B. L. (1997). Brain abnormalities in schizophrenia-spectrum children: Implications for a neurodevelopmental perspective. *Psychiatry Research: Neuroimaging, 76,* 1–13.

Yoshikawa, H. (1994). Prevention as cumulative protection: Effects of early family support and education on chronic delinquency and its risks. *Psychological Bulletin, 115,* 28–54.

Youngstrom, E., Loeber, R., & Stouthamer-Loeber, M. (2000). Patterns and correlates of agreement between parent, teacher, and male adolescent ratings of externalizing and internalizing problems. *Journal of Consulting and Clinical Psychology, 68,* 1038–1050.

Yung, B. R., & Hammond, W. R. (1997). Antisocial behavior in minority groups: Epidemiological and cultural perspectives. In D. M. Stoff, J. Breiling, & J. D. Maser (Eds.), *Handbook of antisocial behavior* (pp. 474–495). New York: Wiley.

Zahn-Waxler, C., Schmitz, S., Fulker, D., Robinson, J., & Emde, R. (1996). Behavior problems in 5-year-old monozygotic and dizygotic twins: Genetic and environmental influences, patterns of regulation, and internalization of control. *Development and Psychopathology, 8,* 103–122.

Zalsman, G., Netanel, R., Fischel, T., Freudenstein, O., Landau, E., Orbach, I., Weizman, A., Pfeffer, C. R., & Apter, A. (2000). Human figure drawings in the evaluation of severe adolescent suicidal behavior. *Journal of the American Academy of Child and Adolescent Psychiatry, 39,* 1024–1031.

Zayas, L. H., Kaplan, C., Turner, S., Romano, K., & Gonzalez-Ramos, G. (2000). Understanding suicide attempts by adolescent Hispanic females. *Social Work, 45,* 53–63.

Zeanah, C. H. (Ed.). (1999). *Handbook of infant mental health* (2nd ed.). New York: Guilford.

Zeanah, C. H., Larrieu, J. A., Heller, S. S., Valliere, J., Hinshaw-Fuselier, S., Aoki, Y., & Drilling, M. (2001). Evaluation of a preventive intervention for maltreated infants and toddlers in foster care. *Journal of the American Academy of Child and Adolescent Psychiatry, 40,* 214–221.

Zeichner, S. L., & Read, J. S. (Eds.). (1999). *Handbook of pediatric HIV care.* Philadelphia: Lippincott, Williams, and Wilkins.

Zeitlin, H. (1999). Psychiatric comorbidity with substance misuse in children and teenagers. *Drug and Alcohol Dependence, 55,* 225–234.

Zero to Three/National Center for Clinical Infant Programs. (1994). *Diagnostic classification of mental health and developmental disorders of infancy and early childhood (Diagnostic classification: 0–3).* Washington, DC: Author.

Zigler, E. (1979). Project Head Start: Success or failure? In E. Zigler & J. Valentine (Eds.), *Project Head Start: A legacy of the War on Poverty* (pp. 495–507). New York: Free Press.

Zigler, E., & Phillips, L. (1961). Psychiatric diagnosis: A critique. *Journal of Abnormal and Social Psychology, 63,* 607–618.

Zohar, A. H., & Felz, L. (2001). Ritualistic behavior in young children. *Journal of Abnormal Child Psychology, 29,* 121–128.

Zucker, N. L., Womble, L. G., Williamson, D. A., & Perrin, L. A. (1999). Protective factors for eating disorders in female college athletes. *Eating Disorders: The Journal of Treatment and Prevention, 7,* 207–218.

Zucker, R. A., Fitzgerald, H. E., & Moses, H. D. (1995). Emergence of alcohol problems and the several alcoholisms: A developmental perspective on etiologic theory and life course trajectory. In D. Cicchetti & D. J. Cohen (Eds.), *Developmental psychopathology: Vol 2. Risk, disorder, and adaptation* (pp. 677–711). New York: Wiley.

PHOTO CREDITS

INDEX